Financial Aid for Veterans, Military Personnel, and Their Families 2021 - 2023

Fourteenth Edition

Gail A. Schlachter
R. David Weber

A Listing of Scholarships, Fellowships, Grants-in-Aid, and Other Sources of Free Money Available Primarily or Exclusively to Veterans, Military Personnel, and Their Family Members, Plus a Set of Six Indexes (Program Title, Sponsoring Organization, Residency, Tenability, Subject, and Deadline Date)

AdmitHub
Boston, Massachusetts

© 2020 AdmitHub

All rights reserved. No part of this publication may be reproduced, stored in a retrieval system, or transmitted, in any form or by any means, electronic, mechanical, photocopying, recording, or otherwise, except for the inclusion of brief quotations in a review, without the prior permission in writing from the publisher. AdmitHub vigorously defends its copyrighted material.

AdmitHub
Harvard Innovation Launch Lab
114 Western Ave.
Boston, MA 02134
    (617) 575-9369
        E-mail: rsp@admithub.com
Visit our web site: www.admithub.com

Manufactured in the United States of America

Contents

Foreword 5

Introduction 7
   Why This Directory Is Needed 7
   What's Unique about the Directory 7
   What's Excluded 8
   What's Updated 9
   How the Directory Is Organized 10
   How to Use the Directory 11
   Plans to Update the Directory 12
   Acknowledgements 12
   Sample Entry 13

About the Authors 14

Financial Aid Programs 15
   Scholarships 17
      Veterans 19
      Military Personnel 79
      Family Members 170
   Fellowships **329**
      Veterans 331
      Military Personnel 360
      Family Members 397

Indexes **433**
   Program Title Index 435
   Sponsoring Organization Index 463
   Residency Index 471
   Tenability Index 477
   Subject Index 483
   Calendar Index 493

Foreword

About Dr. Gail Schlachter and Reference Service Press

Dr. Gail Ann Schlachter (1943-2015), original founder of Reference Service Press, was working as a librarian in the mid-1970s when she recognized that women applying for college faced significant obstacles finding information about financial aid resources designed to help them. This challenge inspired her to publish her ground-breaking book, Directory of Financial Aids for Women, in 1977. The book's success prompted additional financial aid directories for other underserved communities, including the present volume for Native Americans.

By 1985, the business had become so successful that she left her job as a publishing company executive to run her company, Reference Service Press, full-time. Over the years, the company's offerings expanded to over two dozen financial aid titles covering many different types of students—law students, business students, students studying abroad, and many more. The company's success was driven by its database of tens of thousands of financial aid programs, laboriously hand-built over the decades and kept current to exacting specifications. In 1995, Reference Service Press once again broke new ground by launching one of the first-ever searchable electronic databases of financial aid resources (initially through America Online). For more background about the founding and success of Reference Service Press, see Katina Strauch's 1997 "Against the Grain" interview with Dr. Schlachter, available at http://docs.lib.purdue.edu/cgi/viewcontent.cgi?article=2216&context=atg.

Dr. Schlachter was also a major figure in the library community for nearly five decades. She served: as reference book review editor for RQ (now Reference and User Services Quarterly) for 10 years; as president of the American Library Association's Reference and User Services Association; as editor of the Reference and User Services Association Quarterly; seven terms on the American Library Association's governing council; and as a member of the association's Executive Board at the time of her death. She was posthumously inducted into the California Library Association Hall of Fame. The University of Wisconsin School of Library and Information Studies named Dr. Schlachter an "Alumna of the Year," and she was recognized with both the Isadore Gilbert Mudge Citation and the Louis Shores/Oryx Press Award.

Dr. Schlachter will be remembered for how her financial aid directories helped thousands of students achieve their educational and professional dreams. She also will be remembered for her countless contributions to the library profession. And, as an American Library Association Executive Board resolution from June 2015 says, she will be remembered, "most importantly, for her mentorship, friendship, and infectious smile." Yet, despite her impressive lifetime of professional accomplishments, Dr. Schlachter always was most proud of her family, including her husband Stuart Hauser, her daughter Dr. Sandy Hirsh (and Jay Hirsh) and son Eric Goldman (and Lisa Goldman), and her grandchildren Hayley, Leah, Jacob, and Dina.

Introduction

WHY THIS DIRECTORY IS NEEDED

More than one third of America's population today has either direct or indirect ties to the armed services. This includes more than 25 million veterans, 3 million active-duty military personnel, and millions of their family members (spouses, parents, children, grandchildren, and other descendants).

Over the years, a number of organizations have attempted to reward the members of these groups in a variety of ways. In 1944, Congress established the Veterans Administration (now called the Department of Veterans Affairs) to develop programs for the benefit of the men and women who served in previous wars. Today, the DVA provides a wide variety of funding opportunities to veterans and their families. Many state governments have also established or expanded programs that complement federal benefits. In addition, voluntary and other private organizations (most notably the American Legion) have raised millions of dollars to provide financial aid to their members, other veterans or military personnel, or their family members. Similarly, to recruit, retain, and reward their personnel (especially since the advent of the all-volunteer military), the armed services have developed wide-ranging benefits for members and those who are related to them. In all, billions of dollars a year are now set aside in the form of publicly- and privately-funded scholarships, fellowships, grants-in-aid, and other sources of financial aid for veterans, military personnel, and their family members.

While numerous print and online listings have been prepared to identify and describe general financial aid opportunities (those open to all segments of society), none of those resources have ever covered more than a small portion of the programs available primarily or exclusively for veterans, military personnel, or their family members. That's why AdmitHub has issued *Financial Aid for Veterans, Military Personnel, and Their Families,* which identifies billions of dollars set aside for individuals with ties to the military to support study, research, creative activities, career development, and much more.

WHAT'S UNIQUE ABOUT THE DIRECTORY?

Financial Aid for Veterans, Military Personnel, and Their Families is the first and only publication to provide comprehensive information on the more than 1,400 programs aimed specifically at those with ties to the military. The listings in the 2021-2023 edition of this book cover every major field of study, are sponsored by more than 550 different private and public agencies and organizations, and are open to all levels of applicants—from high school students, to college students, to professionals and others. By using this directory, the one out of three Americans eligible for military-related benefits (and the counselors, advisers, and librarians who are there to serve them) can easily identify the vast array of available funding programs. And, not only does *Financial Aid for Veterans, Military Personnel, and Their Families* provide the most comprehensive coverage of available funding, it also displays the most informative program descriptions (on the average, more than twice the detail found in any other listing).

In addition to this extensive and focused coverage, the directory offers several other unique features. First of all, hundreds of funding opportunities listed here have never been covered in any other source. So, even if you have checked elsewhere, you will want to look at *Financial Aid for Veterans, Military Personnel, and Their Families* for additional leads. Further, all the funding described here is substantial; every program offers at least $1,000, and many award $20,000 or more or pay all college expenses. And, here's another plus: all of the funding programs in this edition of the directory offer "free" money; not one of the programs will ever require you to pay anything back (provided, of course, that you meet the program requirements).

Unlike other funding directories, which generally follow a straight alphabetical arrangement, *Financial Aid for Veterans, Military Personnel, and Their Families* groups entries by both types of program (scholarships and fellowships) and recipient groups (veterans, military personnel, and their family members)—thus making it easy to pinpoint appropriate programs. The same convenience is offered in the indexes, where the entries are also subdivided by program type and recipient group. With this arrangement, users with one set of characteristics (e.g., veterans) will be able to find all programs set aside specifically for them—and not be distracted or have to waste time sorting through descriptions of programs intended for members of the other groups.

In fact, everything about the directory has been designed to make your search for funding as easy as possible. You can identify programs not only by recipient group, but by program title, sponsoring organizations, where you live, where you want to spend the money, specific subject areas, and even deadline date (so fundseekers working within specific time constraints can locate programs that are still open). Plus, you'll find all the information you need to decide if a program is a match for you: purpose, eligibility requirements, financial data, duration, special features, limitations, number awarded, and application deadline. You even get fax numbers, toll-free numbers, e-mail addresses, and web site locations (when available), along with complete contact information, to make your requests for applications proceed smoothly.

The unique value of *Financial Aid for Veterans, Military Personnel, and Their Families* has been consistently praised by the reviewers. *Reference Book Review* wrote, "This is the most comprehensive guide available on the subject of financial aid for those with ties to the military." The directory was "enthusiastically reviewed" by *American Reference Books Annual* (which judged it to be "exceptionally useful"), was called "comprehensive" and "authoritative" by *Midwest Book Review,* and was pronounced "easy to use" by *College & Research Library News.* In the view of *Booklist,* "This book fills a noteworthy gap" and libraries across the country "should make this well-conceived and useful information source a part of their reference collection." Perhaps Military.com summed it up best: "the definitive source."

WHAT'S EXCLUDED?

While this book is intended to be the most comprehensive source of information on funding available to veterans, military personnel, and their family members, there are some programs we've specifically excluded from the directory:

- *Awards open equally to other segments of the population.* Only funding opportunities set aside specifically for those with ties to the military are covered here. Many organizations, such as law firms, identify veterans as an underrepresented group and combine them with others such as ethnic minorities and people with disabilities; those programs are no longer included in this directory.

- *Programs administered by individual academic institutions solely for their own students.* The directory identifies "portable" programs—ones that can be used at any number of schools. Financial aid administered by individual schools specifically for their own students is not covered. Write directly to the schools you are considering to get information on their offerings.

- *Service or nonmonetary programs for veterans, military personnel, and their family members.* To obtain information about service programs benefits (e.g., job counseling, medical and dental care, treatment for alcohol or drug dependency) or nonmonetary benefits (such as burial flags, presidential certificates, or complimentary licenses for hunting and fishing), check with your state veteran's agency, your local DVA office, or the most recent annual edition of the DVA's *Federal Benefits for Veterans and Dependents.*

- *Indirect aid programs,* where funds go to military-related agencies rather than directly to veterans, military personnel, or their family members. To obtain that information, check with your state veteran's agency or your local DVA office.

- *Money for study or research outside the United States.* Since there are comprehensive and up-to-date directories that describe the funding available for study and research abroad, only programs that support study, research, or other activities in the United States are covered here. Similarly, service for military organizations other than to the armed forces of the United States (as by immigrants who served in the military of their home country before coming to the United States or by service members of the Confederacy) is excluded.

- *Restrictive geographic coverage.* In general, programs are excluded if they are open only to residents of a narrow geographic area (anything below the state level). Many military facilities have spouses' clubs that raise funds for scholarships for personnel with a tie to the base. Those clubs perform a valuable service for service members and their families who live on the base or in the area. However, their focus is on a single specific military facility so they have been excluded from this directory.

- *Programs limited to personnel who have served on a single Navy ship.* Some of the ships may have a large contingent of current and former personnel, but their emphasis is too narrow for this directory to include.

- *Programs offering limited financial support.* Comprehensive coverage is provided in this directory only for programs that can substantively impact the financial situation of veterans, military personnel, and their family members. Scholarships, fellowships, and grants-in-aid must pay at least $1,000 a year or they are not included here. Also excluded are programs that offer military personnel the opportunity to pursue college training but do not provide any financial support beyond their current salary.

- *Money that must be repaid.* Only "free money" is identified here. If a program requires repayment or charges interest, it's not listed. Now you can find out about billions of dollars in aid and know (if you meet the program requirements) that not one dollar of that will ever need to be repaid. Similarly, loan repayment programs, while a valuable benefit to former students who are veterans or military personnel, had to be excluded to limit this directory to a manageable size.

WHAT'S UPDATED?

The preparation of each new edition of *Financial Aid for Veterans, Military Personnel, and Their Families* involves extensive updating and revision. To insure that the information included in the directory is both reliable and current, the editors at AdmitHub 1) reviewed and updated all relevant programs covered in the previous edition of the directory, 2) collected information on all programs open to veterans, military personnel, and their families that were added to the AdmitHub funding database since the last edition of the directory, and then 3) searched extensively for new program leads in a variety of sources, including printed directories, news reports, journals, newsletters, house organs, annual reports, and sites on the Internet. We only include program descriptions that are written directly from information supplied by the sponsoring organization in print or online (no information is ever taken from secondary sources).

The 2021-2023 edition of the directory completely revises and updates the earlier edition. Programs that have ceased operations have been dropped. Profiles of continuing programs have been rewritten to reflect operations in 2021-2023; nearly 80% of these programs reported substantive changes in their locations, requirements (particularly application deadline), or benefits since 2014. In addition, more than 450 new entries have been added to the program section of the directory. The resulting listing presents the 1,400+ biggest and best sources of free money available to those with ties to the military, including scholarships and fellowships.

INTRODUCTION

HOW THE DIRECTORY IS ORGANIZED

Financial Aid for Veterans, Military Personnel, and Their Families is divided into two separate sections: 1) a descriptive list of financial aid programs designed primarily or exclusively for veterans, military personnel, and their family members; and 2) a set of six indexes to help you find the funding you need.

Funding Available to Veterans, Military Personnel, and Their Families. The first section of the directory describes 1,430 financial aid programs set aside primarily or exclusively for those with ties to the military. Entries in this section are grouped into the following two categories to guide readers in their search for a specific kind of financial assistance:

- **Scholarships:** Programs that support studies at the undergraduate level in the United States. Money is available to entering or continuing students in any type of public or private postsecondary institution, ranging from technical schools and community colleges to major universities in the United States.

- **Fellowships:** Programs that support study, research, projects, or other activities for entering or continuing graduate students as well as professionals and postdoctorates in the United States.

Each of these two categories is further divided into three recipient groupings: veterans, military personnel, and their family members (children, spouses, parents, grandchildren, other relatives, etc.). Within these subdivisions, entries are arranged by program title. Programs that supply more than one type of assistance or assistance to more than one specific group are listed in all relevant subsections. For example, both undergraduate *and* graduate veterans may apply for the Lucille Parish Ward Veteran's Award, so that program is described in the "Veterans" section of both the Scholarship *and* Fellowship chapters.

Each program entry in the directory has been designed to provide a concise profile that includes information (when available) on program title, organization address, telephone numbers (including toll-free and fax numbers), e-mail addresses and web site, purpose, eligibility, money awarded, duration, special features, limitations, number of awards, and application deadline (see the sample entry on page 7).

The information reported for each of the programs in this section was gathered from research conducted through the first half of 2020. While the listing is intended to cover as comprehensively as possible the biggest and best sources of free money available to veterans, military personnel, and their families, some sponsoring organizations did not post information online or respond to our research inquiries and, consequently, are not included in this edition of the directory.

Indexes. To help you find the aid you need, we have constructed six indexes; these will let you access the listings by program title, sponsoring organization, residency, tenability, subject focus, and deadline date. These indexes use a word-by-word alphabetical arrangement. Note: numbers in the index refer to entry numbers, not to page numbers in the book.

Program Title Index. If you know the name of a particular funding program and want to find out where it is covered in the directory, use the Program Title Index. To assist you in your search, every program is listed by all its known names, former names, and abbreviations. Since one program can be listed in more than one subsection (e.g., a program providing assistance to veterans at both the undergraduate and graduate levels is listed in two subsections), each entry number in the index has been coded to indicate program type (e.g., S = Scholarships) and the intended recipient group (e.g., V = Veterans). By using this coding system, readers can turn directly to the programs that match their financial needs and eligibility characteristics.

Sponsoring Organization Index. This index provides an alphabetical listing of the 550 agencies that offer funding to veterans, military personnel, and their families. As in the Program Title Index, entry numbers have been coded to indicate both program type and recipient group.

Residency Index. Some programs listed in this book are restricted to veterans, military personnel, or their families in a particular state or region. Others are open to those with ties to the military wherever they live. This index helps you identify programs available only to residents in your area as well as programs that have no residency requirements. Further, to assist you in your search, we've also indicated the program types and recipient groups eligible for the funding offered to residents in each of the areas listed in the index.

Tenability Index. This index identifies the geographic locations where the funding described in the directory may be used. Index entries (city, county, state, region) are arranged alphabetically and subdivided by program type and recipient group. Use this index when you or your family members are looking for money to support research, study, or other activities in a particular geographic area.

Subject Index. This index allows the reader to use more than 250 subject headings to identify the subject focus of each of the financial aid opportunities designed primarily or exclusively for veterans, military personnel, and their families listed in the first section of the directory. Extensive "see" and "see also" references are provided to aid in the search for appropriate funding.

Calendar Index. Since most financial aid programs have specific deadline dates, some may have closed by the time you begin to look for funding. You can use the Calendar Index to determine which programs are still open. This index is arranged by recipient group and divided by program type (e.g., scholarships, grants-in-aid) and month during which the deadline falls. Filing dates can and quite often do vary from year to year; consequently, this index should be used only as a guide for deadlines beyond 2014.

HOW TO USE THE DIRECTORY

Here are some tips to help you get the most out of the funding opportunities listed in this edition of *Financial Aid for Veterans, Military Personnel, and Their Families.*

To Locate Programs Offering a Particular Type of Assistance. If you are looking for programs offering a particular type of funding (e.g., a scholarship for undergraduate courses, a fellowship for graduate study), turn to the appropriate category in the first section (scholarships or fellowships) and read through all the entries in the subsection that applies (i.e., veterans, military personnel, or family members). Since programs with multiple purposes are listed in every appropriate location, each of the three target population subsections functions as a self-contained entity. In fact, you can browse through any of the sections or subsections in the directory without first consulting an index.

To Find Information on a Particular Financial Aid Program. If you know the name of a particular financial aid program, the type of assistance offered by the program (e.g., fellowship, grant-in-aid) and the intended recipients (veterans, military personnel, or family members), then go directly to the appropriate category in the first section of the directory, where you will find the program profiles arranged alphabetically by title. But be careful: program titles can be misleading. The Air Force Health Professions Scholarship Program is available only to graduate students and therefore is listed under Fellowships not Scholarships. Consequently, if you are looking for a specific program and do not find it in the subsection you have checked, be sure to refer to the Program Title Index to see if it is covered elsewhere in the directory. To save time, always check the Program Title Index first if you know the name of a specific award but are not sure under which subsection it would be listed.

To Locate Programs Sponsored by a Particular Organization. The Sponsoring Organization Index makes it easy to determine groups that provide financial assistance to veterans, military personnel, and their families, or to identify specific financial aid programs offered by a particular organization. Each entry number in the index is coded to identify program type and recipient group, so that you can quickly target appropriate entries.

To Browse Quickly Through the Listings. Turn to the type of funding and recipient sections that interest you and read the "Summary" paragraph in each entry. In seconds, you'll know if this is an opportunity that might apply to you. If it is, read the rest of the information in the entry to make sure you meet all of the program requirements before writing or going online for an application form. Please, save your time and energy. Don't apply if you don't qualify!

To Locate Programs Open to Residents of or Tenable in a Particular Area. The Residency Index identifies financial aid programs open to veterans, military personnel, or their family members who reside in a particular state, region, or country. The Tenability Index shows where the money can be spent. In both indexes, "see" and "see also" references are used liberally, to help you find the funding that's right for you, and index entries for a particular geographic area are divided by both program type and recipient group. When using these indexes, always check the listings under the term "United States," since the programs indexed there have no geographic restrictions and can be used in any area.

To Locate Financial Aid Programs for Veterans, Military Personnel, and Their Families in a Particular Subject Area. Turn to the Subject Index first if you are interested in identifying financial aid programs for veterans, military personnel, or their family members that focus on a particular subject area. To help you structure your search, the type of funding indexed (scholarships, fellowships, grants-in-aid) and the recipient group (veterans, military personnel, family members) are clearly identified. Extensive cross-references are provided.

To Locate Financial Aid Programs for Veterans, Military Personnel, or Their Families by Deadline Date. If you are working with specific time constraints and want to weed out the financial aid programs whose filing dates you won't be able to meet, turn first to the Calendar Index and check the program references listed under the recipient group, program type, and month. Note: not all sponsoring organizations supplied deadline information; those programs are listed under the "Deadline not specified" entries in the index. To identify every relevant financial aid program, regardless of filing dates, read through all the entries in each of the program categories (scholarships, fellowships. grants-in-aid) and recipient subsections (veterans, military personnel, family members) that apply.

To Locate Financial Aid Programs Open to All Segments of the Population. Only programs available to individuals with ties to the military are listed in this publication. However, there are thousands of other programs that are open equally to all segments of the population. To identify these programs, talk to your local librarian, check with your financial aid office on campus, look at the list of RSP print resources on the page opposite the title page in this directory, or see if your library subscribes to Reference Service Press' interactive online funding database; for more information on that resource, go online to: www.rspfunding.com/esubscriptions.html.

PLANS TO UPDATE THE DIRECTORY

This volume, covering 2021-2023, is the fourteenth edition of *Financial Aid for Veterans, Military Personnel, and Their Families.* The next edition will cover the years 2024-2026 and will be released in the first half of 2023.

ACKNOWLEDGEMENTS

A debt of gratitude is owed all the organizations that contributed information to this edition of *Financial Aid for Veterans, Military Personnel, and Their Families.* Their generous cooperation has helped to make this publication a current and comprehensive survey of awards.

INTRODUCTION

SAMPLE ENTRY

(1) **[43]**

(2) **ANNE GANNETT VETERANS AWARD**

(3) National Federation of Music Clubs
1646 West Smith Valley Road
Greenwood, IN 46142
(317) 882-4003
Fax: (317) 882-4019
E-mail: info@nfmc-music.org
Web: www.nfmc-music.org/competitionscategory/senior-division

(4) **Summary** To provide financial assistance for undergraduate education to music students whose careers have been delayed or interrupted as a result of their service in the U.S. armed forces.

(5) **Eligibility** This program is open to veterans who are former music students but interrupted their education to serve in the U.S. Armed Forces and wish to resume music undergraduate or graduate study in pursuit of a career in music. Applicants must be U.S. citizens, but membership in the National Federation of Music Clubs (NFMC) is not required. Along with their application, they must submit a 30-minute recording of a musical performance or audition. Selection is based on worthiness, character, background, musical talent, potential ability, and financial need.

(6) **Financial data** The stipend is $2,000.

(7) **Duration** 1 year.

(8) **Additional information** The application fee is $20.

(9) **Number awarded** 1 each odd-numbered year.

(10) **Deadline** April of each odd-numbered year.

DEFINITION

(1) **Entry number:** Consecutive number that is given to each entry and used to identify the entry in the index.

(2) **Program title:** Title of scholarship, fellowship, grant-in-aid, or other source of free money described in the directory.

(3) **Sponsoring organization:** Name, address, telephone number, toll-free number, fax number, e-mail address, and/or web site (when information was supplied) for the organization sponsoring the program.

(4) **Summary:** Identifies the major program requirements; read the rest of the entry for additional detail.

(5) **Eligibility:** Describes qualifications required of applicants, application procedures, and selection process.

(6) **Financial data:** Financial details of the program, including fixed sum, average amount, or range of funds offered, expenses for which funds may and may not be applied, and cash-related benefits supplied (e.g., room and board).

(7) **Duration:** Period for which support is provided; renewal prospects.

(8) **Additional information:** Any unusual (generally nonmonetary) benefits, restrictions, or requirements associated with the program.

(9) **Number awarded:** Total number of recipients each year or other specified period.

(10) **Deadline:** The month by which applications must be submitted.

ABOUT THE AUTHORS

Dr. Gail Ann Schlachter (1943-2015) worked for more than three decades as a library manager, a library educator, and an administrator of library-related publishing companies. Among the reference books to her credit are the biennially-issued *Directory of Financial Aids for Women* and two award-winning bibliographic guides: *Minorities and Women: A Guide to Reference Literature in the Social Sciences* (which was chosen as an "outstanding reference book of the year" by *Choice*) and *Reference Sources in Library and Information Services* (which won the first Knowledge Industry Publications "Award for Library Literature"). She was the reference book review editor for *RQ* (now *Reference and User Services Quarterly*) for 10 years, was a past president of the American Library Association's Reference and User Services Association, was the editor-in-chief of the *Reference and User Services Association Quarterly,* and was serving her sixth term on the American Library Association's governing council at the time of her death. In recognition of her outstanding contributions to reference service, Dr. Schlachter was named the University of Wisconsin School of Library and Information Studies "Alumna of the Year" and was awarded both the Isadore Gilbert Mudge Citation and the Louis Shores/Oryx Press Award.

Dr. R. David Weber taught history and economics at Los Angeles Harbor College (in Wilmington, California) for many years and continues to teach history as an emeritus professor. During his years of full-time teaching there, and at East Los Angeles College, he directed the Honors Program and was frequently chosen the "Teacher of the Year." He has written a number of critically-acclaimed reference works, including *Dissertations in Urban History* and the three-volume *Energy Information Guide.* With Gail Schlachter, he is the author of Reference Service Press' *Financial Aid for Persons with Disabilities and Their Families,* which was selected by *Library Journal* as one of the "best reference books of the year," and a number of other award-winning financial aid titles, including the *College Student's Guide to Merit and Other No-Need Funding,* which was chosen as one of the "outstanding reference books of the year" by *Choice.*

About the Foreword Author

Professor Eric Goldman, who served as a consultant in the research process and wrote the foreword for this edition of *Directory of Financial Aids for Women,* teaches intellectual property and cyberlaw at Santa Clara University Law School, where he is also the co-director of the High Tech Law Institute. Previously, he was general counsel for Epinions.com and an attorney at the Silicon Valley law firm of Cooley Godward. Professor Goldman knows first-hand the value of financial aid. Thanks in part to the scholarships he received, he was able to graduate from law school debt free!

Financial Aid Programs for Veterans, Military Personnel and Their Families

Scholarships •

Fellowships •

Scholarships

Veterans •

Military Personnel •

Family Members •

Described here are 1092 funding programs available to veterans, military personnel, and their family members who are or will be entering or continuing students in public or private postsecondary institutions, ranging from technical schools and community colleges to major universities in the United States. All of this is "free" money. Not one dollar will need to be repaid (provided, of course, that recipients meet all program requirements). Of these listings, 221 are available to veterans, 296 to military personnel, and 575 to their family members (spouses, children, grandchildren, parents, and other relatives). If you are looking for a particular program and don't find it in this section, be sure to check the Program Title Index to see if it is covered elsewhere in the directory.

Veterans

[1]
10TH MOUNTAIN DIVISION (LIGHT INFANTRY) SCHOLARSHIPS

Northern New York Community Foundation, Inc.
131 Washington Street
Watertown, NY 13601
(315) 782-7110   Fax: (315) 782-0047
E-mail: info@nnycf.org
Web: www.nnycf.org/scholarships/scholarships-available

Summary To provide financial assistance for college to current and former members of the 10th Mountain Division and their dependents.

Eligibility This program is open to current and former members of the 10th Mountain Division and their dependents (children and spouses). Applicants must be high school seniors applying for the freshmen year or traditional or non-traditional students enrolled as full-time undergraduates in any year of college or technical school. They must also be members of the 10th Mountain Division Association. Along with their application, they must submit a 150-word essay on the character traits that have contributed the most to their success, how they have contributed to their success, and how each will contribute to their success in life. High school juniors who will graduate early because they are in an advanced placement program may also apply. Interviews are required. Selection is based on academic achievement, personal data, and financial need.

Financial data The stipend is $5,000 per year.

Duration 1 year; recipients may reapply.

Number awarded Varies each year; recently, 8 were awarded.

Deadline March of each year.

[2]
37TH DIVISION VETERANS SCHOLARSHIP GRANT

37th Division Veterans Association
c/o Mandy Oberyszyn, Executive Director
312 Ridge Side Drive
Powell, OH 43065
(614) 228-3788   Fax: (614) 228-3793
E-mail: mandy@37thdva.org
Web: www.37thdva.org/grants

Summary To provide financial assistance for college to members of the 37th Division Veterans Association and their descendants.

Eligibility This program is open to veterans and descendants of veterans who served honorably with a unit of the 37th Infantry Division until its deactivation in 1968. The veteran must be an active or life member of the association or, if deceased, must have been a member at the time of his death. Applicants may be seniors in high school or already enrolled in a college program. They must have a GPA of 2.25 or higher. Along with their application, they must submit transcripts that include ACT and/or SAT scores, a statement of future educational and career goals, and a 2-page essay on why they should be selected to receive this grant. Financial need is not considered in the selection process.

Financial data The stipend is $1,000.

Duration 1 year.

Number awarded Varies each year.

Deadline April of each year.

[3]
3M "HIRE OUR HEROES" SCHOLARSHIPS AND TOOL GRANTS

Collision Repair Education Foundation
Attn: Administrative Coordinator
5125 Trillium Boulevard
Hoffman Estates, IL 60192
(847) 463-5283   Toll Free: (888) 722-3787
Fax: (847) 463-5483
E-mail: Janet.Marczyk@ed-foundation.org
Web: www.collisioneducationfoundation.org

Summary To provide financial assistance, in the form of scholarships and tool grants, to veterans and their families preparing for a career in automotive collision repair.

Eligibility This program is open to collision repair students who are currently serving or have recently served in the military, as well as their immediate family. Applicants must have completed at least 1 semester at a school that offers an auto collision/auto body repair program. Selection is based on past academic achievement, future plans, and financial need.

Financial data Recently, the program offered stipends of $2,000 to veterans and military personnel, $2,500 to family members, and tool grants to veterans.

Duration 1 year.

Additional information This program is sponsored by 3M Company.

Number awarded Varies each year; recently, the program awarded 12 scholarships to veterans and military personnel, 7 scholarships to family members, and 40 tool kit grants to veterans.

Deadline February of each year.

[4]
43D INFANTRY DIVISION VETERANS ASSOCIATION SCHOLARSHIPS

43d Infantry Division Veterans Association
c/o David Thiede, Secretary/Treasurer
P.O. Box 7281
Berlin, CT 06037
E-mail: 43rdvets@gmail.com
Web: www.43rd-infantry-division.org

Summary To provide financial assistance for college to members of the 43d Infantry Division Veterans Association and their families.

Eligibility This program is open to members of the association; the wives, children, grandchildren, and great-grandchildren of members; and the widows, children, grandchildren, and great-grandchildren of deceased members who were in good standing at the time of their death. Descendants of members of the 43d Infantry Division who died on active duty with the division during World War II are also eligible. Financial need is considered in the selection process.

Financial data The stipend is $1,000.

Duration 1 year.

Number awarded 4 each year.

Deadline May of each year.

[5]
506TH AIRBORNE INFANTRY REGIMENT ASSOCIATION SCHOLARSHIP

506th Airborne Infantry Regiment Association
c/o Alfred May, Scholarship Committee
30 Sweetman Lane
West Milford, NJ 07480-2933
(973) 728-1458   E-mail: alfredmay@aol.com
Web: www.506infantry.org

Summary To provide financial assistance for college or graduate school to former members of the 506th Airborne Infantry Regiment and their families.
Eligibility This program is open to veterans who served with the 506th Airborne Infantry Regiment and their children, grandchildren, spouses, and siblings. Applicants must be entering or attending an undergraduate or graduate program at a college or university in the United States. They must submit a statement describing their personal achievements and career objectives. Selection is based on academic excellence, quality of the institution the applicant has chosen to attend, and financial need.
Financial data The stipend is $1,500 or $1,000.
Duration 1 year; nonrenewable.
Additional information This program includes the Currahee Scholarship Award, the Marcia and John Lally Scholarship Award, the Eugene and Marilyn Overton Scholarship Award, the SPC Edwin Roodhouse Memorial Scholarship Award, the NAVILLUS Award, and the CPT Luke Wullenwaber Memorial Scholarship Award.
Number awarded 3 at $1,500 and 3 at $1,000 each year.
Deadline April of each year.

[6]
82ND AIRBORNE DIVISION ASSOCIATION AWARDS

82nd Airborne Division Association
Attn: Educational Fund Treasurer
P.O. Box 87482
Fayetteville, NC 28304-7482
(281) 814-2377   E-mail: patrickcopening@gmail.com
Web: www.82ndairborneassociation.org

Summary To provide financial assistance for college to members of the 82d Airborne Division Association and their dependent children.
Eligibility Eligible to apply for this award are 1) dependent children of 82nd Airborne Division Association voting members; 2) dependent children of 82nd Airborne servicemen killed in combat; 3) dependent children of deceased Life or All American members of the 82nd Airborne Division Association; and 4) former active-duty 82nd Airborne Division troopers who are association members, are within 2 years of honorable discharge, and served no more than 2 enlistments. Applicants must be enrolled full time in an accredited university or college. Selection is based on academic achievement and financial need. In years when a suitable candidate applies, 1 of these awards for dependent children is designated the General Mathew B. Ridgeway Scholarship and 1 for former troopers as the Past President Herb Altman Memorial Scholarship.
Financial data The stipend is $2,000 per year. Recipients of the Ridgeway and Alman scholarships, if awarded, receive an additional $1,500. Funds are paid to the recipient's college or university.
Duration 1 semester (the second in a school year); recipients may reapply for up to 3 additional annual awards.
Additional information Membership in the association is open to anyone who ever served in the 82nd Airborne Division, anyone who is currently serving on active duty in jump status, and anyone who has ever served in any of the uniformed services on either jump or glider status and was honorably discharged.
Number awarded Varies each year; recently, 36 were awarded. In the past 15 years, this program has awarded $2,143,800 in scholarships.
Deadline October of each year.

[7]
AAPA VETERANS CAUCUS SCHOLARSHIPS

American Academy of Physician Assistants-Veterans Caucus
Attn: Scholarship Program
P.O. Box 362
Ossining, NY 10562
(803) 328-1864   Fax: (704) 838-8494
E-mail: rmunsee@veteranscaucus.org
Web: www.veteranscaucus.org/scholarships

Summary To provide financial assistance to veterans of any of the uniformed services who are studying to become physician assistants.
Eligibility This program is open to U.S. citizens who are currently enrolled in a physician assistant program. Applicants must be honorably discharged members of 1 of the 7 uniformed services of the United States. Along with their application, they must submit a personal statement about what led them to attend PA school; their background, present, and future intentions; and why they deserve to receive a scholarship. Selection is based on military honors and awards received, civic and college honors and awards received, professional memberships and activities, potential for future achievement, and GPA.
Financial data The stipend is $2,000.
Duration 1 year.
Additional information This program includes the following named scholarships: the Albert T. Kissel Memorial Scholarship, the Donna Jones Moritsugu Memorial Scholarship, the SSGT Craig Ivory Memorial Scholarships, the Lt. Col. David Gwinn Memorial Scholarship, the Jesse Edwards Memorial Scholarship, and the Vicki Lianne Moritsugu Memorial Scholarship.
Number awarded Varies each year.
Deadline February of each year.

[8]
ADRIENNE ALIX SCHOLARSHIP

American Legion Auxiliary
Department of New Hampshire
Attn: Department Auxiliary Secretary
121 South Fruit Street, Suite 103
Concord, NH 03301-2412
(603) 856-8942   E-mail: nhalasec@legionnh.org
Web: www.legionnh.org

Summary To provide financial assistance to New Hampshire residents, including those recently discharged from the military, who wish to refresh or upgrade their skills at a school in any state.

Eligibility This program is open to New Hampshire residents and to members of a unit of the American Legion Auxiliary, Department of New Hampshire, who have been members for at least 3 consecutive years. Applicants must be 1) reentering the workforce or upgrading skills; 2) displaced from the workforce; or 3) recently discharged honorably from the military. They must be interested in taking a refresher course or advancing their knowledge or techniques needed in today's workforce at a school in any state. Along with their application, they must submit a 500-word essay explaining their career goals and objectives.
Financial data The stipend is $1,000.
Duration 1 year.
Number awarded 1 each year.
Deadline March of each year.

[9]
AFCEA WAR VETERANS SCHOLARSHIPS
Armed Forces Communications and Electronics
  Association
Attn: AFCEA Educational Foundation
4114 Legato Road, Suite 1000
Fairfax, VA 22033-3342
(703) 631-6147   Toll Free: (800) 336-4583, ext. 6147
Fax: (703) 631-4693   E-mail: edfoundation@afcea.org
Web: www.afcea.org

Summary To provide financial assistance to veterans and military personnel who served in designated Overseas Contingency Operations and are working on an undergraduate degree in fields related to the support of U.S. intelligence enterprises.
Eligibility This program is open to active-duty and honorably discharged U.S. military members (including Reservists and National Guard personnel) who served in Operation Enduring Freedom, Operation Iraqi Freedom, Operation New Dawn, Operation Inherent Resolve, or Operation Freedom's Sentinel. Applicants must be enrolled as full- or part-time sophomores or juniors at a 4-year institution in the United States and working on an undergraduate degree in biometrics, computer forensics science, computer programming, computer science, cyber security, engineering (computer, electrical, electronics, network, robotics, telecommunications), geospatial science, information technology, information resources management, mathematics, network security, operations research, physics, robotics, statistics, or strategic intelligence at a school in any state. They must have a GPA of 3.0 or higher. Selection is based on merit.
Financial data The stipend is $2,500.
Duration 1 year.
Additional information This program began in 2005 as the Afghanistan and Iraq War Veterans Scholarships with funding from the Northern Virginia Chapter of AFCEA.
Number awarded Up to 12 each year: 6 for the fall semester and 6 for the spring semester.
Deadline April of each year for fall semester; November of each year for spring semester.

[10]
AHIMA VETERANS SCHOLARSHIP
American Health Information Management Association
Attn: AHIMA Foundation
233 North Michigan Avenue, 21st Floor
Chicago, IL 60601-5809
(312) 233-1131   Fax: (312) 233-1537
E-mail: info@ahimafoundation.org
Web: www.ahimafoundation.org

Summary To provide financial assistance to veterans and spouses of veterans and active-duty service personnel who are interested in working on an undergraduate or graduate degree in health information management (HIM) or health information technology (HIT).
Eligibility This program is open to 1) veterans of the armed forces, including Army, Navy, Air Force, Marine Corps, Coast Guard, Reserves, and National Guard; and 2) spouses and surviving spouses of servicemembers, including active-duty military, retirees, veterans, and wounded warriors. Applicants must be working full time on a degree in HIM or HIT at the associate, bachelor's, post-baccalaureate, master's, or doctoral level. They must have at least 6 credit hours remaining after the date of the award. Along with their application, they must submit an essay of 250 to 400 words on their educational and career ambitions, record of military service, record of personal achievement, community service, desire to serve others and make a positive community impact, and leadership potential. In the selection process, preference is given to 1) physically wounded or disabled veterans; 2) surviving spouses; and 3) those who served in a combat tour of duty.
Financial data Stipends are $1,000 for associate degree students, $1,500 for bachelor's degree or post-baccalaureate certificate students, $2,000 for master's degree students, or $2,500 for doctoral degree students.
Duration 1 year.
Additional information Effective in 2018, this program includes the John Kloss Memorial Veteran Scholarship and other scholarships supported by Nuance Communications and the Walter Reed Society.
Number awarded 4 each year.
Deadline September of each year.

[11]
ALASKA NATIONAL GUARD STATE TUITION REIMBURSEMENT PROGRAM
Alaska National Guard
Attn: Education Services Office
Army Guard Road, Building 49000
P.O. Box 5800
Joint Base Elmendorf-Richardson, AK 99505-5800
(907) 428-6477   Fax: (907) 428-6929
E-mail: maria.j.alvarez10.mil@mail.mil
Web: www.dmva.alaska.gov/FamilyServices/Education

Summary To provide financial assistance to current and former members of the Alaska National Guard who wish to attend a college or university in the state.
Eligibility This program is open to members of the Alaska National Guard (Air and Army) and Naval Militia who have a rating of E-1 through O-5, including warrant officers, and are attending a university program in Alaska. Eligibility extends to members who 1) have satisfactorily completed their service contract and who served honorably in federal active service

or federally-funded state active service after September 11, 2001; or 2) have been separated or discharged from the Guard because of a service-connected injury, disease, or disability. First priority is given to undergraduates; if funding is available, students working on a second bachelor's degree or a master's degree may be supported. Non-prior servicemembers must complete Initial Active Duty for Training (IADT); prior servicemembers are eligible immediately.
Financial data Recipients are entitled to reimbursement equivalent to 100% of the cost of tuition and fees at the University of Alaska, to a maximum of $4,500 per fiscal year.
Duration 1 semester; may be renewed for a total of 144 semester credits.
Number awarded Varies each year.
Deadline Applications may be submitted at any time, but they must be received at least 90 days after the last official day of the class or term.

[12]
ALBERT M. BECKER MEMORIAL MILITARY SCHOLARSHIP
New York American Legion Press Association
Attn: Scholarship Chair
P.O. Box 424
Sanborn, NY 14132
E-mail: jackbutton@hotmail.com
Web: nyalpa.webs.com/pubslinksannualevents.htm

Summary To provide financial assistance to veterans and specified military personnel from New York who are interested in careers in communications.
Eligibility This program is open to New York residents who are 1) veterans with an honorable discharge; or 2) currently-serving members of the National Guard or military Reserve. Membership in the American Legion family is not required, but extra credit is given for membership. Applicants must be enrolled or planning to enroll full time at an accredited college, university, or trade school in any school to work on a degree in communications (including public relations, journalism, reprographics, newspaper design or management, web page design, video design, social media communications, photojournalism, American history, political science, public communications, or other field of study related to the goals of the sponsor or the American Legion family). Along with their application, they must submit a 500-word essay on their field of study, the reasons for choosing their field of study, and their goals upon completion of study. Financial need and class standing are not considered. U.S. citizenship is required.
Financial data The stipend is $1,000.
Duration 1 year.
Number awarded 1 each year.
Deadline April of each year.

[13]
ALLIED.COM MILITARY SCHOLARSHIP
Allied Van Lines
One Parkview Plaza
Oakbrook Terrace, IL 60180
Toll Free: (800) 689-8684
Web: www.allied.com/military-scholarship

Summary To provide financial assistance to current and former military personnel and their families who are interested in attending college to study fields related to logistics.
Eligibility This program is open to current and honorably discharged members of the military, their spouses, and their children under 21 years of age or (if currently attending college) under 23 years of age. Applicants must be enrolled or planning to enroll full time at a 4-year college or university and major in military logistics, supply chain management, or operational management. They must be U.S. citizens or permanent residents. Along with their application, they must submit an essay of 400 to 800 words on why a career in logistics/supply chain management is their college major of choice. Financial need is not considered in the selection process.
Financial data The stipend is $1,000.
Duration 1 year.
Additional information This program began in 2015.
Number awarded 2 each year.
Deadline September of each year.

[14]
AMERICAN AIRLINES VETERAN'S INITIATIVE SCHOLARSHIP
Women in Aviation International
Attn: Scholarships
Morningstar Airport
3647 State Route 503 South
West Alexandria, OH 45381-9354
(937) 839-4647   Fax: (937) 839-4645
E-mail: scholarships@wai.org
Web: www.wai.org/education/scholarships

Summary To provide financial assistance to members of Women in Aviation International (WAI) who are also veterans and interested in earning a degree or certificate in a field related to aviation maintenance.
Eligibility This program is open to WAI members who served honorably in the U.S. armed services and are interested in aviation or aeronautical education or training. Applicants must be enrolled or planning to enroll in an accredited flight school, institution, or college. Along with their application, they must submit a 500-word essay and professional resume that include their aviation history and goals, what they have done for themselves to achieve their goals, where they see themselves in 5 and 10 years, involvement in aviation activities, how the scholarship will help them achieve their objectives, and their present financial need. Selection is based on achievements, teamwork, leadership skills, motivation, and community service involvement.
Financial data The stipend is $5,000.
Duration Funds must be used within 1 year.
Additional information WAI is a nonprofit professional organization dedicated to encouraging women to consider an aviation career and to providing educational outreach activities and networking resources to women active in the industry. This program was established in 2012 by American Airlines.
Number awarded 2 each year.
Deadline November of each year.

SCHOLARSHIPS: VETERANS

[15]
AMERICAN LEGION AUXILIARY SCHOLARSHIP FOR NON-TRADITIONAL STUDENTS

American Legion Auxiliary
3450 Founders Road
Indianapolis, IN 46268
(317) 569-4500 Fax: (317) 569-4502
E-mail: alahq@alaforveterans.org
Web: www.alaforveterans.org

Summary To provide financial assistance for college to nontraditional students affiliated with the American Legion.
Eligibility This program is open to members of the American Legion, American Legion Auxiliary, or Sons of the American Legion who have paid dues for the 2 preceding years and the calendar year in which application is being made. Applicants must be nontraditional students who are either 1) returning to school after some period of time during which their formal education was interrupted; or 2) just beginning their education at a later point in life. Each department (state) of the American Legion Auxiliary may nominate 1 student for this scholarship. Selection is based on academic achievement (25%), character and leadership (25%), initiative and goals (25%), and financial need (25%).
Financial data The stipend is $2,000, paid directly to the school.
Duration 1 year.
Additional information Applications are available from the president of the candidate's own unit or from the secretary or education chair of the department.
Number awarded 5 each year: 1 in each division of the American Legion Auxiliary.
Deadline Applications must be submitted to the unit president by February of each year.

[16]
AMVETS GENERATION T SCHOLARSHIPS

AMVETS National Headquarters
Attn: National Programs Director
4647 Forbes Boulevard
Lanham, MD 20706-3807
(301) 459-9600 Toll Free: (877) 7-AMVETS, ext. 4027
Fax: (301) 459-7924 E-mail: klathroum@amvets.org
Web: www.amvets.org/amvets-generation-t-scholarships

Summary To provide financial assistance for trade school to veterans and their spouses.
Eligibility This program is open to veterans and their spouses who are U.S. citizens; children are not eligible. Applicants must have completed high school or a GED program and be enrolled in an eligible construction trade program.
Financial data Stipends range up to $5,000.
Duration 1 year.
Additional information This program is supported by the Generation T program of Lowe's.
Number awarded Approximately 75 each year.
Deadline April or July of each year.

[17]
AMVETS NATIONAL SCHOLARSHIPS FOR VETERANS

AMVETS National Headquarters
Attn: National Programs Director
4647 Forbes Boulevard
Lanham, MD 20706-3807
(301) 459-9600 Toll Free: (877) 7-AMVETS, ext. 4027
Fax: (301) 459-7924 E-mail: klathroum@amvets.org
Web: www.amvets.org/scholarships

Summary To provide financial assistance for college or graduate school to veterans.
Eligibility This program is open to veterans who are U.S. citizens. Applicants must be interested in working full or part time on an undergraduate degree, graduate degree, or certification from an accredited trade/technical school. They must have exhausted all other government aid. Selection is based on financial need, academic promise, military duty and awards, volunteer activities, community services, jobs held during the past 4 years, and an essay of 50 to 100 words on "What a Higher Education Means to Me."
Financial data The stipend is $1,000 per year.
Duration Up to 4 years.
Number awarded 3 each year.
Deadline April of each year.

[18]
ANGEA SCHOLARSHIP

Alaska National Guard Enlisted Association
Attn: Scholarship Program
P.O. Box 5302
Joint Base Elmendorf-Richardson, AK 99505-5302
E-mail: akenlisted@angea.org
Web: www.angea.org

Summary To provide financial assistance to members of the Alaska National Guard Enlisted Association (ANGEA) and their families who are interested in attending college in any state.
Eligibility This program is open to current and retired members of the Alaska Air and Army National Guard who are current members of ANGEA and their dependents. Applicants must be enrolled or planning to enroll at an accredited college, university, or vocational/technical school in any state. Along with their application, they must submit a letter that includes their educational and career goals; a list of awards, honors, extracurricular activities, and organizational involvement; information on their civic involvement, moral leadership, or other constructive characteristics demonstrating commitment to community, state, and/or country; and a statement on their financial need.
Financial data A stipend is awarded (amount not specified).
Duration 1 year.
Number awarded 1 or more each year.
Deadline March of each year.

[19]
ANNE GANNETT VETERANS AWARD

National Federation of Music Clubs
1646 West Smith Valley Road
Greenwood, IN 46142
(317) 882-4003   Fax: (317) 882-4019
E-mail: info@nfmc-music.org
Web: www.nfmc-music.org

Summary To provide financial assistance for undergraduate education to music students whose careers have been delayed or interrupted as a result of their service in the U.S. armed forces.

Eligibility This program is open to veterans who are former music students but interrupted their education to serve in the U.S. Armed Forces and wish to resume music undergraduate or graduate study in pursuit of a career in music. Applicants must be U.S. citizens, but membership in the National Federation of Music Clubs (NFMC) is not required. Along with their application, they must submit a 30-minute recording of a musical performance or audition. Selection is based on worthiness, character, background, musical talent, potential ability, and financial need.

Financial data The stipend is $2,000.

Duration 1 year.

Additional information The application fee is $20.

Number awarded 1 each odd-numbered year.

Deadline April of each odd-numbered year.

[20]
APPLICATIONS INTERNATIONAL CORPORATION IMPACT SCHOLARSHIPS

American Society of Safety Professionals
Attn: ASSP Foundation
Scholarship Award Program
520 North Northwest Highway
Park Ridge, IL 60068-2538
(847) 699-2929   Fax: (847) 296-3769
E-mail: asspfoundation@assp.org
Web: foundation.assp.org/scholarships-and-grants

Summary To provide financial assistance to students working on a degree related to occupational safety, especially those who have served in the military.

Eligibility This program is open to students, including international students, who are working full or part time on an undergraduate or graduate degree in occupational safety, health, environment, or a closely-related field. Priority is given to students who have served in the military. Associate degree students must have completed at least 24 semester hours and bachelor's degree students at least 60 semester hours. Membership in the American Society of Safety Professionals (ASSP) is not required, but members receive priority. Applicants must have a GPA of 3.0 or higher as an undergraduate or 3.5 or higher as a graduate student. Along with their application, they must submit 5 short essays of up to 500 words each on the following topics: 1) what drew them to the field of safety and how their education has affected their views of the field; 2) their goals and plans for reaching those; 3) their leadership and volunteer positions within the safety community; 4) the greatest takeaway from their current year in school; and 5) what makes them stand out as an applicant. Selection is based on academic performance, leadership activity in ASSP and the broader safety community, motivations for entering the field, and letters of recommendation.

Financial data The stipend is $15,000 or $10,000 per year.

Duration 1 year; recipients may reapply.

Additional information This program is sponsored by Applications International Corporation.

Number awarded 5 each year: 1 at $15,000 and 4 at $10,000.

Deadline November of each year.

[21]
ARMY AVIATION ASSOCIATION OF AMERICA SCHOLARSHIPS

Army Aviation Association of America Scholarship
  Foundation
Attn: AAAA Scholarship Foundation
593 Main Street
Monroe, CT 06468-2806
(203) 268-2450   Fax: (203) 268-5870
E-mail: scholarship@quad-a.org
Web: www.quad-a.org/Scholarship/Scholarship/about.aspx

Summary To provide financial aid for undergraduate or graduate study to members of the Army Aviation Association of America (AAAA) and their relatives.

Eligibility This program is open to current AAAA members and the spouses, children, grandchildren, and unmarried siblings of current or deceased members. Applicants must be enrolled or accepted for enrollment as an undergraduate or graduate student at an accredited college or university. They must include a 300-word essay on their life experiences, work history, and aspirations. Some scholarships are specifically reserved for enlisted, warrant officer, company grade, and Department of the Army civilian members. Selection is based on academic merit and personal achievement.

Financial data Stipends range from $1,000 to $5,000 per year.

Duration Scholarships may be for 1 year, 2 years, or 4 years.

Number awarded Varies each year; recently, $516,000 in scholarships was awarded to 304 students. Since the program began in 1963, the foundation has awarded more than $4 million to more than 4,100 qualified applicants.

Deadline Interested students must submit a pre-qualifying form by March of each year. The final application is due in April.

[22]
ARMY NURSE CORPS ASSOCIATION SCHOLARSHIPS

Army Nurse Corps Association
Attn: Scholarship Program
8000 IH-10 West, Suite 600
San Antonio, TX 78230-3887
(210) 650-3534   Toll Free: (888) 742-9910
E-mail: education@e-anca.org
Web: www.e-anca.org/Scholarships

Summary To provide financial assistance to students who have a connection to the Army and are interested in working on an undergraduate or graduate degree in nursing.

Eligibility This program is open to U.S. citizens attending colleges or universities that have accredited programs offering undergraduate or graduate degrees in nursing. Applicants must be 1) students currently enrolled in an accredited baccalaureate or advanced nursing or nurse anesthesia program who are serving or have served (and received an honorable discharge) in any branch and at any rank of a component of the Active Army, Army National Guard, or Army Reserve; or 2) nursing or anesthesia students whose parent(s), spouse, or child(ren) are serving or have served in a component of the Active Army, Army National Guard, or Army Reserve. Along with their application, they must submit a personal statement on their professional career objectives, reasons for applying for this scholarship, financial need, special considerations, personal and academic interests, and why they are preparing for a nursing career. Students who are receiving any support from any branch of the military, including ROTC scholarships, are not eligible.

Financial data The stipend is $3,000. Funds are sent directly to the recipient's school.

Duration 1 year.

Additional information Although the sponsoring organization is made up of current, retired, and honorably discharged officers of the Army Nurse Corps, it does not have an official affiliation with the Army. Therefore, students who receive these scholarships do not incur any military service obligation.

Number awarded Varies each year.

Deadline March of each year.

[23]
ARMY WOMEN'S FOUNDATION LEGACY SCHOLARSHIPS

Army Women's Foundation
Attn: Scholarship Committee
P.O. Box 5030
Fort Lee, VA 23801-0030
(804) 734-3078   E-mail: info@awfdn.org
Web: www.awfdn.org/scholarships/general-information

Summary To provide financial assistance for college or graduate school to women who are serving or have served in the Army and their children.

Eligibility This program is open to 1) women who have served or are serving honorably in the U.S. Army, U.S. Army Reserve, or Army National Guard; and 2) children of those women. Applicants must be 1) high school graduates or GED recipients enrolled at a community college or technical certificate program who have a GPA of 2.5 or higher; 2) sophomores or higher at an accredited college or university who have a GPA of 3.0 or higher; or 3) students enrolled in or accepted to a graduate program who have a GPA of 3.0 or higher. Along with their application, they must submit a 2-page essay on why they should be considered for this scholarship; their future plans as related to their program of study; their community service, activities, and work experience; and how the Army has impacted their life and/or goals. Selection is based on merit, academic potential, community service, and financial need.

Financial data The stipend is $2,500 for college and graduate students or $1,000 for community college and certificate students.

Duration 1 year; recipients may reapply.

Number awarded Varies each year; recently, 21 soldiers and 10 children received these scholarships.

Deadline January of each year.

[24]
ASSOCIATION OF AVIATION ORDNANCEMEN EDUCATIONAL FOUNDATION SCHOLARSHIPS

Association of Aviation Ordnancemen
Attn: Robert L. Crow Scholarship Foundation
c/o Rick Garza, Committee Chair
10213 Rolling Green Way
Fort Washington, MD 20744
Web: www.aaoweb.org/AAO/Scholar

Summary To provide financial assistance to members of the Association of Aviation Ordnancemen, their families, and dependents of deceased aviation ordnancemen of the Navy or Marine Corps.

Eligibility This program is open to 1) regular and associate members of the Association of Aviation Ordnancemen; 2) dependents and immediate relatives (siblings, grandchildren) of regular and associate members; and 3) dependents of deceased aviation ordnancemen of the U.S. Navy or Marine Corps. Applicants must be enrolled or planning to enroll at a college, university, trade/technical school, or postsecondary specialty school in any state. Selection is based on academic record, goals, eligibility for and award of other scholarships and educational grants, and financial need.

Financial data Stipends recently ranged from $2,000 to $4,000 per year.

Duration 1 year; recipients may reapply.

Additional information This program began in 1979. It currently consists of scholarships designated as Robert L. Crow Awards and others named after current donors.

Number awarded Varies each year; recently, 5 were awarded: 1 each at $4,000, $3,000, and $2,500 (the Robert L. Crow Awards) and 2 at $2,000 (the Ed Scott Memorial Scholarship and the award In Memory of James E. Thompson).

Deadline June of each year.

[25]
AT&T VETERANS SCHOLARSHIPS

AT&T Veterans
Attn: Scholarships
208 South Akard Street
Dallas, TX 75202
E-mail: ATTVetsScholarship@att.com
Web: www.attveterans.com/scholarships

Summary To provide financial assistance for college to veterans who submit outstanding essays on their military service.

Eligibility This program is open to veterans who are enrolled in at least 1 class at an accredited college or university or a technical training institute. Applicants must submit an essay, between 1,000 and 1,500 words in length, on the most impactful life lesson that they took from their military service and how that lesson will be applied in their personal and professional life. Selection is based on originality of thought and structure; quality of grammar and composition; and creativity and depth of thought.

Financial data The stipend is usually $1,000.

Duration 1 year.

Number awarded 1 or more each year.
Deadline July of each year.

[26]
AT&T WAR MEMORIAL SCHOLARSHIP
Arkansas Community Foundation
5 Allied Drive, Suite 51110
Building 5, llth Floor
Little Rock, AR 72201
(501) 372-1116   Toll Free: (800) 220-ARCF
Fax: (501) 372-1166   E-mail: arcf@arcf.org
Web: www.arcf.org/about/funds

Summary To provide financial assistance to veterans in Arkansas who plan to attend college in the state.
Eligibility This program is open to residents of Arkansas who are veterans of any branch of the armed services. Applicants must be attending or planning to attend an accredited 2- or 4-year college in Arkansas as an undergraduate or graduate student. Selection is based on financial need, community leadership, and potential to succeed in college.
Financial data The stipend is $2,500.
Duration 1 year.
Additional information This program is sponsored by AT&T.
Number awarded 1 each year.
Deadline March of each year.

[27]
BOSTON POST SAME SCHOLARSHIPS
Society of American Military Engineers-Boston Post
c/o Lisa Branson, Scholarship Committee Chair
CDM Smith
75 State Street, Suite 701
Boston, MA 02109
(617) 901-8281   Fax: (617) 345-3901
E-mail: brandonlo@cdmsmith.com
Web: www.same.org

Summary To provide financial assistance to residents of New England majoring in a program related to construction at a college in any state.
Eligibility This program is open to residents of New England who are currently enrolled in an accepted engineering or architecture program, preferably in civil engineering, environmental engineering, architecture, or other construction-related program, at a college or university in any state. Applicants must have completed at least 1 academic year and have at least 1 year remaining. They must be nominated by their institution. Along with their application, they must submit a resume describing their academic and career objectives, extracurricular and community activities, work experience, and special interests or hobbies; transcripts; documentation of financial need; and a personal letter describing their qualifications and needs. An interview is required. Selection is based on academic achievement, financial need, extracurricular and community activities, the letter, and the interview. Preference is given to applicants who are enrolled in ROTC (preferably not a recipient of an ROTC scholarship), have current or prior service in the U.S. armed forces, are interested in the U.S. Public Health Service, and/or are interested in other public service with federal, state, or local government. U.S. citizenship is required.

Financial data The stipend averages approximately $4,000 per year.
Duration 1 year.
Number awarded Approximately 25 each year.
Deadline February of each year.

[28]
BRAXTON BRAGG CHAPTER AUSA SCHOLARSHIPS
Association of the United States Army-Braxton Bragg Chapter
Attn: Vice President for Scholarship Programs
P.O. Box 70036
Fort Bragg, NC 28307
(910) 396-3755   E-mail: hbraxtonbraggc@nc.rr.com
Web: www.ausa.org/chapters/braxton-bragg-chapter

Summary To provide financial assistance to members of the Braxton Bragg Chapter of the Association of the United States Army (AUSA) in North Carolina and their dependents who are interested in attending college or graduate school in any state.
Eligibility This program is open to chapter members and their families in North Carolina who are working on or planning to work on an undergraduate, graduate, or technical degree at a college or technical school in any state. Applicants must submit a 500-word essay on a topic that changes annually (recently, students were asked to explain how a person makes a difference in our world); letters of recommendation; a list of personal accomplishments; and a transcript that includes their ACT or SAT score. Selection is based on academic achievement (50%), participation in extracurricular activities at school (25%), and participation in community service activities (25%).
Financial data The stipend is $1,000.
Duration 1 year; recipients may reapply.
Additional information Membership in the Braxton Bragg Chapter is open to all Army active, National Guard, and Reserve members in North Carolina, along with Department of the Army civilians, retirees, concerned citizens, and family members.
Number awarded Varies each year; recently, 15 were awarded.
Deadline April of each year.

[29]
CAESAR VIGLIENZONE MEMORIAL SCHOLARSHIP
Marines' Memorial Association
c/o Marines Memorial Club and Hotel
609 Sutter Street
San Francisco, CA 94102
(415) 673-6672, ext. 293   Toll Free: (800) 5-MARINE
Fax: (415) 441-3649
E-mail: scholarship@marineclub.com
Web: www.marinesmemorial.org

Summary To provide financial assistance to veterans who are interested in attending college to major in any field.
Eligibility This program is open to veterans who have served in any branch of the U.S. armed forces and received an honorable discharge. Applicants must be enrolled as full-time sophomores, juniors, or seniors working on a degree in any field. They must have a GPA of 3.0 or higher. Membership in the sponsoring organization is not required. Along with

their application, they must submit an essay of up to 500 words on why they chose their specific path of study, what they hope to accomplish after graduation with their degree, and how their efforts will benefit others in their community. Selection is based on the essay, academic merit, references, and financial need.
Financial data The stipend is $5,000 per year.
Duration 1 year; recipients may reapply for up to 3 additional years.
Number awarded 1 each year.
Deadline April of each year.

[30]
CALIFORNIA FEE WAIVER PROGRAM FOR RECIPIENTS OF THE MEDAL OF HONOR AND THEIR CHILDREN
California Department of Veterans Affairs
Attn: Division of Veterans Services
1227 O Street, Room 101
P.O. Box 942895
Sacramento, CA 94295
(916) 653-2573   Toll Free: (800) 952-5626
Fax: (916) 653-2563   TDD: (800) 324-5966
Web: www.calvet.ca.gov

Summary To provide financial assistance for college to veterans in California who received the Medal of Honor and their children.
Eligibility This program is open to recipients of the Medal of Honor and their children younger than 27 years of age who are residents of California. Applicants must be attending or planning to attend a community college, branch of the California State University system, or campus of the University of California.
Financial data Full-time college students receive a waiver of tuition and registration fees at any publicly-supported community or state college or university in California.
Duration 1 year; may be renewed.
Number awarded Varies each year.
Deadline Deadline not specified.

[31]
CALIFORNIA LEGION AUXILIARY PAST PRESIDENTS' PARLEY NURSING SCHOLARSHIPS
American Legion Auxiliary
Department of California
401 Van Ness Avenue, Suite 319
San Francisco, CA 94102-4570
(415) 861-5092   Fax: (415) 861-8365
E-mail: calegionaux@calegionaux.org
Web: www.calegionaux.org/scholarships.htm

Summary To provide financial assistance to California residents who are veterans or members of their families and interested in studying nursing at a school in the state.
Eligibility This program is open to California residents who are veterans with wartime service or the spouse, widow(er), or child of such a veteran. Applicants must be entering or currently enrolled in an accredited nursing school in California and working on a licensed vocational nurse, registered nurse, or other recognized nursing degree. Selection is based on the application (25%), scholarship (25%), character and leadership (25%), and financial need (25%).
Financial data The stipend is $2,000.
Duration 1 year.
Number awarded 1 each year.
Deadline March of each year.

[32]
CALIFORNIA LEGION AUXILIARY SCHOLARSHIPS FOR CONTINUING AND/OR REENTRY STUDENTS
American Legion Auxiliary
Department of California
401 Van Ness Avenue, Suite 319
San Francisco, CA 94102-4570
(415) 861-5092   Fax: (415) 861-8365
E-mail: calegionaux@calegionaux.org
Web: www.calegionaux.org/scholarships.htm

Summary To provide financial assistance to California residents who are active-duty military personnel, veterans, or children of veterans and require assistance to continue their education.
Eligibility This program is open to California residents who are 1) active-duty military personnel; 2) veterans of World War I, World War II, Korea, Vietnam, Grenada/Lebanon, Panama, or Desert Shield/Desert Storm; and 3) children of veterans who served during those periods of war. Applicants must be continuing or reentry students at a college, university, or business/trade school in California. Selection is based on the application (25%), scholarship (25%), character and leadership (25%), and financial need (25%).
Financial data The stipend is $1,000 or $500.
Duration 1 year.
Additional information This program includes 1 scholarship designated as the Mel Foronda Memorial Scholarship.
Number awarded 5 each year: 3 at $1,000 and 2 at $500.
Deadline March of each year.

[33]
CALIFORNIA NON-RESIDENT COLLEGE FEE WAIVER PROGRAM FOR MILITARY PERSONNEL AND DEPENDENTS
California Department of Veterans Affairs
Attn: Division of Veterans Services
1227 O Street, Room 101
P.O. Box 942895
Sacramento, CA 94295
(916) 653-2573   Toll Free: (800) 952-5626
Fax: (916) 653-2563   TDD: (800) 324-5966
Web: www.calvet.ca.gov

Summary To waive non-resident fees at public institutions in California for undergraduate or graduate students from other states who are active-duty military personnel, recently-discharged veterans, or dependents of active-duty military personnel.
Eligibility This program is open to residents of states outside California who are 1) veterans of the U.S. armed forces who spent more than 1 year on active duty in California immediately prior to being discharged; 2) members of the U.S. armed forces stationed in California on active duty; or 3) the natural or adopted child, stepchild, or spouse of a member of the U.S. armed forces stationed in California on active duty. Applicants must be attending or planning to attend a community college, branch of the California State University system, or campus of the University of California as an undergraduate or graduate student.

Financial data This program waives non-resident fees of qualifying military personnel, veterans, and families who attend publicly-supported community or state colleges or universities in California.
Duration 1 year; may be renewed until completion of an undergraduate degree or for 1 additional year for military personnel working on a graduate degree; nonrenewable for graduate students who are children or spouses.
Number awarded Varies each year.
Deadline Deadline not specified.

[34]
CAPITOL AREA CHAPTER MOAA COLLEGE SCHOLARSHIP PROGRAM

Military Officers Association of America-Capitol Area Chapter
c/o Major DeLee M. Dankenbring, Treasurer
992 Pennine Ridge Way
Grand Ledge, MI 48837-9809
(517) 614-6090
Web: www.cacmoaa.org/Scholarships.aspx

Summary To provide financial assistance for college or graduate school in any state to residents of Michigan who are disabled veterans, members of the Military Officers Association of America (MOAA) or their children or grandchildren, or children of deceased or disabled servicemembers.
Eligibility This program is open to 1) disabled military servicemembers who entered service after September 11, 2001 and whose home of record is Michigan; 2) members of the national and Capitol Area Chapter of the MOAA and their children and grandchildren; and 3) children of servicemembers who entered the armed forces from Michigan and died or were disabled in the line of duty. Applicants must be enrolled or planning to enroll in a program of college or university study, job training, or graduate school. They must have a GPA of 2.0 or higher. Along with their application they must submit transcripts (that include SAT/ACT scores for high school seniors), a list of honors and awards that includes any ROTC or military training, a 200-word essay on their career goals, and a brief explanation of their financial need.
Financial data The stipend ranges from $1,000 to $1,250 per year.
Duration 1 year; recipients may reapply.
Number awarded Varies each year.
Deadline March of each year.

[35]
CAPTAIN FREDERICK C. BRACE III MEMORIAL SCHOLARSHIP

American Academy of Physician Assistants-Veterans Caucus
Attn: Scholarship Program
P.O. Box 362
Ossining, NY 10562
(803) 328-1864   Fax: (704) 838-8494
E-mail: rmunsee@veteranscaucus.org
Web: www.veteranscaucus.org/scholarships

Summary To provide financial assistance to Air Force veterans and their dependents who are studying to become physician assistants.
Eligibility This program is open to U.S. citizens who are currently enrolled in a physician assistant program. Applicants must be honorably discharged members of the United States Air Force or the dependent of an Air Force veteran. Along with their application, they must submit a personal statement about what led them to attend PA school; their background, present, and future intentions; and why they deserve to receive a scholarship. Selection is based on military honors and awards received, civic and college honors and awards received, professional memberships and activities, potential for future achievement, and GPA.
Financial data The stipend is $2,000.
Duration 1 year.
Number awarded 1 each year.
Deadline February of each year.

[36]
CAPTAIN SEAN P. GRIMES PHYSICIAN ASSISTANT EDUCATIONAL SCHOLARSHIP AWARD

Society of Army Physician Assistants
Attn: Scholarship Committee
P.O. Box 623
Monmouth, IL 61462
(309) 734-5446   Fax: (309) 734-4489
E-mail: orpotter@aol.com
Web: www.sapa.org/scholarships

Summary To provide financial assistance to current and former Army personnel interested in attending a college or university to become a physician assistant.
Eligibility This program is open to Army personnel who are currently on active duty, in the Reserves or National Guard, or veterans with any MOS and in pay grades E-5 through O-4. Applicants must be interested in attending an accredited college or university in order to either 1) gain initial training as a physician assistant; or 2) if already a physician assistant, work on a bachelor's, master's, or doctoral degree. They must have a GPA of 2.5 or higher and be able to demonstrate financial need. Selection is based on academic record, community and professional activities, future goals as a physician assistant, and financial need.
Financial data The stipend is $6,000.
Duration 1 year.
Additional information This program began in 2006.
Number awarded 1 each year.
Deadline January of each year.

[37]
CARROLL H. PAYNE MEMORIAL SCHOLARSHIP ENDOWMENT

First Command Educational Foundation
Attn: Scholarship Programs Manager
1 FirstComm Plaza
Fort Worth, TX 76109-4999
(817) 569-2940   Toll Free: (877) 872-8289
Fax: (817) 569-2970   E-mail: scholarships@fcef.com
Web: www.fcef.com/scholarships

Summary To provide financial assistance to college students who have ties to the military.
Eligibility This program is open to college-bound high school students, current college students, and adults seeking advanced education. Applicants must have a tie to the military. They must apply through a local military organization that supports military families, such as a DoD school, officers' spouses' club, National Guard organization, or veteran orga-

nization. Individuals who have received military academy appointments or ROTC scholarships are also eligible. The organization must normally agree to provide half the cost of the scholarship and apply to this sponsor for the balance. Partner organizations select the recipients.

Financial data Each partner organization may apply for up to $2,000 in matching funds from this sponsor. Individual scholarships range from $1,000 to $4,000 but may be greater if the partner organization agrees to pay all the additional cost.

Duration 1 year; recipients may reapply.

Additional information This sponsor was established in 1983 as the nonprofit affiliate of First Command Financial Services, Inc.

Number awarded Varies each year; recently, this sponsor partnered with 50 community organizations to award $81,030 in scholarships to 61 students.

Deadline Each partner organization sets its own deadline.

[38]
COL CARL F. BASWELL COMBAT WOUNDED ENGINEER SCHOLARSHIP

Army Engineer Association
Attn: Director Washington DC Operations
P.O. Box 30260
Alexandria, VA 22310-8260
(703) 428-7084   Fax: (703) 428-6043
E-mail: xd@armyengineer.com
Web: www.armyengineer.com/scholarships

Summary To provide financial assistance for college to U.S. Army Engineers who were wounded in combat in Iraq or Afghanistan.

Eligibility This program is open to U.S. Army Engineers who were wounded in combat and received a Purple Heart during Operation Iraqi Freedom or Operation Enduring Freedom. Applicants must be working on or planning to work on an associate, bachelor's, or master's degree at an accredited college or university. Along with their application, they must submit a 1-page essay outlining why they should be selected for an award, including a paragraph on their financial need and their evaluation of their potential for success.

Financial data The stipend is $2,500.

Duration 1 year.

Additional information This program began in 2010.

Number awarded 1 each year.

Deadline June of each year.

[39]
COLD WAR VETERANS ENGINEERING AND SCIENCE SCHOLARSHIPS

Marines' Memorial Association
c/o Marines Memorial Club and Hotel
609 Sutter Street
San Francisco, CA 94102
(415) 673-6672, ext. 293   Toll Free: (800) 5-MARINE
Fax: (415) 441-3649
E-mail: scholarship@marineclub.com
Web: www.marinesmemorial.org

Summary To provide financial assistance to members of the Marines' Memorial Association from all branches of the armed forces and their descendants who are interested in studying a field of STEM in college.

Eligibility This program is open to active members of the association and their children and grandchildren. Applicants must be high school seniors or students currently enrolled full time in an undergraduate degree program in a field of STEM. Along with their application, they must submit an essay of up to 500 words on why they chose their specific path of study, what they hope to accomplish after graduation with their degree, and how their efforts will benefit others in their community. Graduating high school seniors must submit a high school transcript and SAT or ACT scores; continuing college students must submit a college transcript. Selection is based on the essay, academic merit, references, and financial need.

Financial data The stipend is $2,500 per year.

Duration 1 year; recipients may reapply for up to 3 additional years.

Additional information Membership in the association is open to veterans of the Marines, Army, Navy, Air Force, or Coast Guard and to personnel currently serving in a branch of the armed forces. This program began in 2014.

Number awarded 3 each year.

Deadline April of each year.

[40]
COLONEL RICHARD HALLOCK SCHOLARSHIPS

Marines' Memorial Association
c/o Marines Memorial Club and Hotel
609 Sutter Street
San Francisco, CA 94102
(415) 673-6672, ext. 293   Toll Free: (800) 5-MARINE
Fax: (415) 441-3649
E-mail: scholarship@marineclub.com
Web: www.marinesmemorial.org

Summary To provide financial assistance for college to members of the Marines' Memorial Association from all branches of the armed forces and their descendants.

Eligibility This program is open to active members of the association and their children and grandchildren. Applicants must be high school seniors or students currently enrolled full time in an undergraduate degree program in any field at a college or university. Along with their application, they must submit an essay of up to 500 words on why they chose their specific path of study, what they hope to accomplish after graduation with their degree, and how their efforts will benefit others in their community. Graduating high school seniors must submit a high school transcript and SAT or ACT scores; continuing college students must submit a college transcript. Selection is based on the essay, academic merit, references, and financial need.

Financial data The stipend is $2,500 per year.

Duration 1 year; recipients may reapply for up to 3 additional years.

Additional information Membership in the association is open to veterans of the Marines, Army, Navy, Air Force, or Coast Guard and to personnel currently serving in a branch of the armed forces.

Number awarded 2 each year.

Deadline April of each year.

[41]
COLORADO LEGION AUXILIARY DEPARTMENT SCHOLARSHIP FOR NON-TRADITIONAL STUDENTS

American Legion Auxiliary
Department of Colorado
7465 East First Avenue, Suite D
Denver, CO 80230
(303) 367-5388   Fax: (303) 367-5388
E-mail: dept-sec@alacolorado.com
Web: www.alacolorado.com/scholarships.html

Summary To provide financial assistance to nontraditional students who are members of American Legion organizations in Colorado and interested in attending college in the state.

Eligibility This program is open to members of the American Legion, American Legion Auxiliary, or Sons of the American Legion in Colorado who have been members for the past 2 years and the current year. Applicants must be 1) nontraditional students returning to the classroom after some period of time in which their formal education was interrupted; or 2) nontraditional students who are just beginning their education at a later point in life or continuing to work on a degree. Selection is based on character and leadership (25%), an essay and the application (25%), scholarship and grades (25%), and financial need (25%).

Financial data The stipend is $2,000.

Duration 1 year; nonrenewable.

Number awarded 1 each year.

Deadline Applications must be submitted to the unit president by February of each year.

[42]
COLORADO LEGION AUXILIARY PAST PRESIDENT'S PARLEY HEALTH PROFESSIONAL SCHOLARSHIP

American Legion Auxiliary
Department of Colorado
7465 East First Avenue, Suite D
Denver, CO 80230
(303) 367-5388   Fax: (303) 367-5388
E-mail: dept-sec@alacolorado.com
Web: www.alacolorado.com/scholarships.html

Summary To provide financial assistance to wartime veterans and their descendants in Colorado who are interested in attending school in the state to prepare for a career in nursing.

Eligibility This program is open to 1) daughters, sons, spouses, granddaughters, and great-granddaughters of veterans; and 2) veterans who served in the armed forces during eligibility dates for membership in the American Legion. Applicants must be Colorado residents who are seeking training in any field of health at a school in the state. Along with their application, they must submit a 500-word essay on the topic, "Americanism." Selection is based on that essay (25%), scholastic ability (25%), financial need (25%), references (13%), and dedication to medical field (12%).

Financial data Stipends range from $500 to $1,000.

Duration 1 year; nonrenewable.

Number awarded Varies each year, depending on the availability of funds.

Deadline April of each year.

[43]
CONNECTICUT TUITION WAIVER FOR VETERANS

Connecticut State Universities and Colleges
61 Woodland Street
Hartford, CT 06105
(860) 723-0013   E-mail: fitzgeralde@ct.edu
Web: www.ct.edu/admission/veterans

Summary To provide financial assistance for college to certain Connecticut veterans and military personnel and their dependents.

Eligibility This program is open to 1) honorably-discharged Connecticut veterans who served at least 90 days during specified periods of wartime; 2) active members of the Connecticut Army or Air National Guard; 3) Connecticut residents who are a dependent child or surviving spouse of a member of the armed forces killed in action on or after September 11, 2001 who was also a Connecticut resident; and 4) Connecticut residents who are a dependent child or surviving spouse of a person officially declared missing in action or a prisoner of war while serving in the armed forces after January 1, 1960. Applicants must be attending or planning to attend a public college or university in the state.

Financial data The program provides a waiver of 100% of tuition for general fund courses at the 4 campuses of Connecticut State University, 50% of tuition for extension and summer courses at campuses of Connecticut State University, 100% of tuition at the 12 Connecticut community colleges, and 50% of fees at Charter Oak State College.

Duration Up to 4 years.

Additional information This is an entitlement program; applications are available at the respective college financial aid offices.

Number awarded Varies each year.

Deadline Deadline not specified.

[44]
COUNCIL OF COLLEGE AND MILITARY EDUCATORS VETERANS SCHOLARSHIPS

Council of College and Military Educators
c/o Jim Yeonopolus, Scholarship Committee Chair
Central Texas College
P.O. Box 1800
Killeen, TX 76540-1800
(254) 526-1781   Fax: (254) 526-1750
E-mail: jim.yeonopolus@ctcd.edu
Web: www.ccmeonline.org/scholarships

Summary To provide financial assistance to veterans of the armed services who are interested in working on an undergraduate or master's degree.

Eligibility This program is open to veterans of the uniformed services who are currently enrolled full time at an accredited institution that is a member of the Council of College and Military Educators (CCME) and working on an associate, bachelor's, or master's degree. Undergraduates must have a GPA of 2.5 or higher and graduate students must have a GPA of 3.0 or higher. Along with their application, they must submit an essay of 400 to 750 words on how they would describe military leadership. Financial need is not considered in the selection process.

Financial data The stipend is $1,000. Funds are paid directly to the student.

Duration 1 year; nonrenewable.

SCHOLARSHIPS: VETERANS

Number awarded 5 each year.
Deadline October of each year.

[45]
CSM LEONARD MAGLIONE MEMORIAL SCHOLARSHIPS

Association of the United States Army-Rhode Island Chapter
c/o LTC Robert A. Galvanin, President
31 Canoe River Drive
Mansfield, MA 02048
(508) 339-5301   E-mail: bpje5310@verizon.net
Web: www.riroa.org/ausari/scholarship.htm

Summary To provide financial assistance to members of the Rhode Island Chapter of the Association of the United States Army (AUSA) and their families who are interested in attending college or graduate school in any state.

Eligibility This program is open to members of the AUSA Rhode Island Chapter and their family members (spouses, children, and grandchildren). Applicants must be high school seniors or graduates accepted at an accredited college, university, or vocational/technical school in any state or current undergraduate or graduate students. Along with their application, they must submit a 250-word essay on why they feel their achievements should qualify them for this award. Selection is based on academic and individual achievements; financial need is not considered. Special consideration is given to students or graduates of LaSalle Academy in Providence (the alma mater of this program's namesake), especially those preparing for a career in the arts or engineering or enrolled or planning to enroll in Army ROTC.

Financial data The stipend is $1,000.
Duration 1 year.
Additional information Membership in the AUSA is open to everyone who supports a strong national defense, with special concern for the Army. That includes Regular Army, National Guard, Army Reserve, government civilians, retired soldiers, Wounded Warriors, veterans, concerned citizens and family members.
Number awarded Several each year.
Deadline April of each year.

[46]
DALE SPENCER SCHOLARSHIP FUND

Arizona Community Foundation
Attn: Director of Scholarships
2201 East Camelback Road, Suite 405B
Phoenix, AZ 85016
(602) 381-1400   Toll Free: (800) 222-8221
Fax: (602) 381-1575
E-mail: scholarship@azfoundation.org
Web: www.azfoundation.academicworks.com

Summary To provide financial assistance to residents of Arizona who are veterans or current military personnel and interested in attending college in the state.

Eligibility This program is open to veterans and current active duty members of the U.S. armed forces in Arizona. Applicants must be able to demonstrate significant financial need. Preference is given to those who are current or former participants in the foster care system.

Financial data The stipend is $1,000.
Duration 1 year; nonrenewable.

Number awarded Varies each year.
Deadline May of each year.

[47]
DANIEL DREVNICK MEMORIAL FUND SCHOLARSHIPS

Daniel Drevnick Memorial Fund
P.O. Box 251566
Woodbury, MN 55125-6566
(651) 324-2122   Fax: (651) 730-7467
E-mail: Ken@HeroAtHome.org
Web: www.heroathome.org/apply-for-a-scholarship

Summary To provide financial assistance to veterans in Iowa, Minnesota, and Wisconsin who are studying law enforcement at a technical college or university in the state.

Eligibility This program is open to residents of Iowa, Minnesota, and Wisconsin who served in the military any time after September 11, 2001. Applicants must have completed Basic and Advanced Individual Training and have been honorably discharged. They must be enrolled in a law enforcement program at a technical college or university in their state. Current and widowed spouses and children of veterans from Iowa, Minnesota, or Wisconsin are also eligible. Along with their application, they must submit an essay on why they feel they should be considered for a scholarship.

Financial data The stipend is $1,000.
Duration 1 year.
Additional information This program began in 2012.
Number awarded 10 each year.
Deadline Deadline not specified.

[48]
DARLENE HOOLEY SCHOLARSHIP FOR OREGON VETERANS

Oregon Community Foundation
Attn: Administrative Assistant for Scholarships
1221 S.W. Yamhill Street, Suite 100
Portland, OR 97205-2108
(503) 227-6846   Fax: (503) 274-7771
E-mail: opearsall@oregoncf.org
Web: www.oregoncf.org/grants-scholarships/scholarships

Summary To provide financial assistance to veterans in Oregon who served recently and are interested in working on an undergraduate or graduate degree at a college in the state.

Eligibility This program is open to Oregon National Guard members and Reservists who served after September 11, 2001; there is no minimum length of service requirement. Applicants must be enrolled or planning to enroll either full or part time as an undergraduate or graduate student at a college or university in Oregon. Along with their application, they must submit 150-word essays on the following topics: 1) their specific educational plans and career goals and what inspires them to achieve those; 2) a significant change or experience that has occurred in their life; 3) a personal accomplishment and the strengths and skills they used to achieve it; 4) what they have done for their family or community that they care about the most and why; and 5) their military service and the impact it had on their life.

Financial data Stipends of scholarships offered by this foundation range from $200 to $10,000 and average approximately $2,700.

Duration 1 year; may be renewed up to 5 additional years.
Number awarded Varies each year.
Deadline March of each year.

[49]
DAVID AND REBECCA BARTEL VETERAN'S SCHOLARSHIP

Society of Exploration Geophysicists
Attn: SEG Foundation
8801 South Yale, Suite 500
P.O. Box 702740
Tulsa, OK 74170-2740
(918) 497-5500   Fax: (918) 497-5557
E-mail: scholarships@seg.org
Web: www.seg.org/scholarships

Summary To provide financial assistance to veterans who are interested in working on an undergraduate or graduate degree in applied geophysics or a related field.
Eligibility This program is open to retired or honorably discharged veterans of the armed forces (Army, Marine Corps, Navy, or Air Force), the National Guard (Army or Air), the U.S. Coast Guard, or the U.S. Merchant Marine. Preference is given to veterans who are medically disabled. Applicants must intend to work on an undergraduate or graduate degree directed toward a career in applied geophysics or a closely-related field (e.g., earth or environmental sciences, geology, geoscience, or physics). Along with their application, they must submit a 250-word essay on their interest in geophysics. Financial need is not considered in the selection process.
Financial data Stipends provided by this sponsor range from $500 to $10,000; recently, undergraduate stipends averaged more than $3,100 per year and graduate stipends averaged more than $4,500 per year.
Duration 1 academic year; may be renewable, based on scholastic standing, availability of funds, and continuance of a course of study leading to a career in applied geophysics.
Number awarded 1 each year.
Deadline February of each year.

[50]
DEPARTMENT OF NEBRASKA VFW STATE SCHOLARSHIPS

Veterans of Foreign Wars of the United States-
  Department of Nebraska
Attn: Scholarship Chair
2431 North 48th Street
Lincoln, NE 68504
(402) 464-0674   Fax: (402) 464-0675
E-mail: Johnl@vfwne.org
Web: vfwne.com/di/vfw/v2/default.asp?pid=6204

Summary To provide financial assistance to members of the Veterans of Foreign Wars (VFW), the VFW Auxiliary, and their families in Nebraska who wish to attend college in the state.
Eligibility This program is open to members of the Nebraska chapter of the VFW, the VFW Auxiliary, and their spouses, children, stepchildren, and grandchildren. Applicants must have completed at least 1 year of full-time study at a college or university in Nebraska. They must be able to demonstrate financial need.
Financial data A stipend is awarded (amount not specified).
Duration 1 year.
Additional information This program includes named awards designated as the Past State Commanders Scholarship, the Darrell Thibault VFW State Memorial Scholarship, the Nathan Grossman VFW State Memorial Scholarship, the Phillips Scholarship, and the Connie Liebsack Memorial Scholarship.
Number awarded At least 5 each year.
Deadline March of each year.

[51]
DIANE LAM MINORITY WOMAN VETERAN SCHOLARSHIP

Washington State Business and Professional Women's
  Foundation
Attn: Scholarship Committee
860 S.W. 143rd Street
Seattle, WA 98166
(206) 439-8282   Fax: (206) 439-8296
Web: www.bpwwafoundation.org/apply-for-a-scholarship

Summary To provide financial assistance to female veterans who are members of minority groups and interested in returning to college.
Eligibility This program is open to women who can document their status as a minority and a veteran. Applicants must be interested in returning to school to gain skills or get back to the job market. They must be able to demonstrate scholastic ability and financial need. Along with their application, they must submit a 100-word statement on their career goal and how their education will help them accomplish that goal. U.S. citizenship is required.
Financial data The stipend is $1,000.
Duration 1 year.
Number awarded 1 each year.
Deadline June of each year.

[52]
DKF VETERANS ASSISTANCE FOUNDATION SCHOLARSHIPS

DKF Veterans Assistance Foundation
P.O. Box 7166
San Carlos, CA 94070
(650) 595-3896   E-mail: admin@dkfveterans.com
Web: www.dkfveterans.com/apply.html

Summary To provide financial assistance for college in any state to California residents who are veterans of Operation Enduring Freedom (OEF) in Afghanistan or Operation Iraqi Freedom (OIF) or the dependents of deceased or disabled veterans of those actions.
Eligibility This program is open to 1) veterans of the U.S. armed forces (including the Coast Guard) who served in support of OEF or OIF within the central command area of responsibility; and 2) dependents of those veterans who were killed in action or incurred disabilities rated as 75% or more. Applicants must be residents of California enrolled or planning to enroll full time at a college, university, community college, or trade institution in any state. Along with their application, they must submit a cover letter introducing themselves and their educational goals.
Financial data The stipend is $5,000 per year for students at universities and state colleges or $1,500 per year for students at community colleges and trade institutions.

SCHOLARSHIPS: VETERANS

Duration 1 year; may be renewed up to 3 additional years, provided the recipient maintains a GPA of 3.0 or higher.
Additional information This foundation was established in 2005.
Number awarded A limited number of these scholarships are awarded each year.
Deadline Deadline not specified.

[53]
DONALDSON D. FRIZZELL MEMORIAL SCHOLARSHIPS

First Command Educational Foundation
Attn: Scholarship Programs Manager
1 FirstComm Plaza
Fort Worth, TX 76109-4999
(817) 569-2940　　　Toll Free: (877) 872-8289
Fax: (817) 569-2970　　E-mail: scholarships@fcef.com
Web: www.fcef.com/scholarships

Summary To provide financial assistance to students, especially those with ties to the military, entering or attending college or graduate school.
Eligibility This program is open to 1) members of a U.S. uniformed service (active, Guard, Reserve, retired, or non-retired veteran) and their spouses and dependents; 2) clients of First Command Financial Services and their family members; 3) dependent family members of First Command Advisors or field office staff members; or 4) non-contractual ROTC students. Applicants may be traditional students (high school seniors and students already enrolled at a college, university, or accredited trade school) or nontraditional students (those defined by their institution as nontraditional and adult students planning to return to a college, university, or accredited trade school). They must have a GPA of 3.0 or higher and be working on a trade school certification or associate, undergraduate, or graduate degree. Applicants must submit 1-page essays on 1) their active involvement in community service programs; 2) the impact of financial literacy on their future; and 3) why they need this scholarship. Selection is based primarily on the essays, academic merit, and financial need.
Financial data The stipend is $3,000. Funds are disbursed directly to the recipient's college, university, or trade school.
Duration 1 year.
Additional information The sponsoring organization was formerly known as the USPA & IRA Educational Foundation, founded in 1983 to provide scholarships to the children of active, retired, or deceased military personnel.
Number awarded Varies each year; recently, 10 were awarded.
Deadline The online application process begins in February of each year and continues until April or until 2,500 applications have been received.

[54]
DR. AURELIO M. CACCCOMO FAMILY FOUNDATION MEMORIAL SCHOLARSHIP

AMVETS National Headquarters
Attn: National Programs Director
4647 Forbes Boulevard
Lanham, MD 20706-3807
(301) 459-9600　　　Toll Free: (877) 7-AMVETS, ext. 4027
Fax: (301) 459-7924　　E-mail: klathroum@amvets.org
Web: www.amvets.org/scholarships

Summary To provide financial assistance for college to veterans, National Guard members, and Reservists.
Eligibility This program is open to U.S. citizens who are veterans or members of the National Guard or Reserves. Applicants must be interested in working full or part time on an undergraduate degree or certification from an accredited trade/technical school. They must have exhausted all other government aid. Selection is based on financial need, academic promise, military duty and awards, volunteer activities, community services, jobs held during the past 4 years, and an essay of 50 to 100 words on "This award will help me achieve my career/vocational goal, which is..."
Financial data The stipend is $3,000.
Duration 1 year; nonrenewable.
Number awarded 2 each year.
Deadline April of each year.

[55]
DR. NANCY M. SCHONHER SCHOLARSHIP

Marines' Memorial Association
c/o Marines Memorial Club and Hotel
609 Sutter Street
San Francisco, CA 94102
(415) 673-6672, ext. 293　　Toll Free: (800) 5-MARINE
Fax: (415) 441-3649
E-mail: scholarship@marineclub.com
Web: www.marinesmemorial.org

Summary To provide financial assistance to women who have a tie to the military and are interested in working on a degree in a health-related field.
Eligibility This program is open to women who 1) are active-duty service members or reservists in the U.S. armed forces; 2) have separated honorably from the U.S. armed forces within the past 6 years; 3) are a current or former corpsman or medic in any branch of the U.S. armed forces; or 4) are the child or grandchild of an active member of the Marines' Memorial Association. Applicants must be planning to enroll in 1) an advanced medical program with the goal of becoming a nurse, nurse practitioner, physician's assistant, or medical doctor (M.D. or O.D.) from an accredited American college or university; or 2) an accredited paramedic program (must have completed the EMT Basic training program, have taken the National Registry EMT Examination, hold an EMT Certificate, and have at least 6 months' work experience). Membership in the sponsoring organization is not required. Along with their application, they must submit an essay of up to 500 words on why they chose their specific path of study, what they hope to accomplish after graduation with their degree, and how their efforts will benefit others in their community. Selection is based on the essay, academic merit, references, and financial need. Preference is given to Navy Corpsmen.

Financial data The stipend is $5,000.
Duration 1 year.
Additional information Membership in the association is open to veterans of the Marines, Army, Navy, Air Force, or Coast Guard and to personnel currently serving in a branch of the armed forces. This program began in 2017.
Number awarded 1 each year.
Deadline April of each year.

[56] EDMUND K. GROSS EDUCATION SCHOLARSHIP

Marines' Memorial Association
c/o Marines Memorial Club and Hotel
609 Sutter Street
San Francisco, CA 94102
(415) 673-6672, ext. 293   Toll Free: (800) 5-MARINE
Fax: (415) 441-3649
E-mail: scholarship@marineclub.com
Web: www.marinesmemorial.org

Summary To provide financial assistance to members of the Marines' Memorial Association from all branches of the armed forces and their descendants who are interested in studying education in college.
Eligibility This program is open to active members of the association and their children and grandchildren. Applicants must be enrolled or planning to enroll full time in an undergraduate degree program in education at a college or university. Along with their application, they must submit an essay of up to 500 words on why they chose their specific path of study, what they hope to accomplish after graduation with their degree, and how their efforts will benefit others in their community. Graduating high school seniors must submit a high school transcript and SAT or ACT scores; continuing college students must submit a college transcript. Selection is based on the essay, academic merit, references, and financial need.
Financial data The stipend is $2,500 per year.
Duration 1 year; recipients may reapply for up to 3 additional years.
Additional information Membership in the association is open to veterans of the Marines, Army, Navy, Air Force, or Coast Guard and to personnel currently serving in a branch of the armed forces.
Number awarded 1 each year.
Deadline April of each year.

[57] EDUCATION FOUNDATION FOR THE COLORADO NATIONAL GUARD GRANTS

National Guard Association of Colorado
Attn: Education Foundation, Inc.
P.O. Box 440889
Aurora, CO 80044-0889
(303) 909-6369   Fax: (720) 535-5925
E-mail: BernieRogoff@comcast.net
Web: www.efcong.org

Summary To provide financial assistance to members of the Colorado National Guard and their families who are interested in attending college or graduate school in any state.
Eligibility This program is open to current and retired members of the Colorado National Guard and their dependent unmarried children and spouses. Applicants must be enrolled or planning to enroll full or part time at a college, university, trade school, business school, or graduate school in any state. Along with their application, they must submit an essay, up to 2 pages in length, on their desire to continue their education, what motivates them, their financial need, their commitment to academic excellence, and their current situation. Selection is based on academic achievement, community involvement, and financial need.
Financial data Stipends are generally at least $1,000 per year.
Duration 1 year; may be renewed.
Number awarded Normally, 15 to 25 of these grants are awarded each semester.
Deadline July of each year for fall semester; January of each year for spring semester.

[58] ELARY GROMOFF, JR. MILITARY VETERAN SCHOLARSHIP

The Aleut Corporation
Attn: Aleut Foundation
703 West Tudor Road, Suite 102
Anchorage, AK 99503-6650
(907) 646-1929   Toll Free: (800) 232-4882
Fax: (907) 646-1949   E-mail: taf@thealeutfoundation.org
Web: www.thealeutfoundation.org

Summary To provide financial assistance to Native Alaskans who are veterans and shareholders of The Aleut Corporation or their descendants working on a degree in any field at a school in any state.
Eligibility This program is open to Native Alaskans who are original enrollees or descendants of original enrollees of The Aleut Corporation (TAC). Applicants must have completed at least 1 year of a bachelor's, 2- or 4-year vocational, master's, or Ph.D. degree in any field at a school in any state. They must have served in the military, be enrolled full time and have a GPA of 3.0 or higher. Along with their application, they must include a letter of intent, up to 500 words in length, that describes their educational goals and objectives and their expected graduation date.
Financial data A stipend is awarded (amount not specified).
Duration 1 year.
Additional information The Aleut Corporation is 1 of 13 Alaska Native Regional Corporations created under the Alaska Native Claims Settlement Act of 1971.
Number awarded 1 each year.
Deadline June of each year.

[59] ENLISTED ASSOCIATION OF THE NATIONAL GUARD OF IOWA AUXILIARY SCHOLARSHIP PROGRAM

Enlisted Association of the National Guard of Iowa
  Auxiliary
c/o Lori Waters, President
1005 Second Street S.W.
Altoona, IA 50009
(515) 490-3202   E-mail: bullriderfan@msn.com
Web: www.eangi.org/auxiliary-scholarship

Summary To provide financial assistance to members of the Enlisted Association of the National Guard of Iowa

SCHOLARSHIPS: VETERANS

(EANIG) Auxiliary and their families who are interested in attending college in any state.

Eligibility This program is open to EANGI Auxiliary members and their spouses, dependents, and grandchildren. Applicants must be enrolled, accepted for enrollment, or in the process of applying to a college or vocational/technical school as a full-time undergraduate or graduate student. Along with their application, they must submit a letter describing specific fats about their desire to continue their education and why they need financial assistance. Selection is based on character, leadership, and need.

Financial data The stipend is $1,000.

Duration 1 year; recipients may reapply.

Number awarded 2 each year.

Deadline February of each year.

[60]
EPG VETERANS SCHOLARSHIPS

Energy Polymer Group
c/o David Nuss, Scholarship Committee Member
Akron Rubber Development Laboratory, Inc.
2887 Gilchrist Road
Akron, OH 44305
(330) 794-6600   Toll Free: (866) 778-ARDL
Fax: (330_ 794-6610   E-mail: david_nuss@ardl.com
Web: www.energypolymergroup.org

Summary To provide financial assistance to veterans in fields of interest to the Energy Polymer Group (EPG).

Eligibility This program is open to veterans who are working full time on a bachelor's or master's degree at an accredited 4-year college or university. Both members and nonmembers of the EPG are eligible. Selection is based on GPA, participation in activities, awards and honors received, work experience, and a statement of career objectives.

Financial data The stipend is $3,000 per year.

Duration 1 year; recipients may reapply.

Number awarded Varies each year; recently, 3 were awarded.

Deadline February of each year.

[61]
EVELYN B. HAMILTON HEALTH CARE SCHOLARSHIP

Marines' Memorial Association
c/o Marines Memorial Club and Hotel
609 Sutter Street
San Francisco, CA 94102
(415) 673-6672, ext. 293   Toll Free: (800) 5-MARINE
Fax: (415) 441-3649
E-mail: scholarship@marineclub.com
Web: www.marinesmemorial.org

Summary To provide financial assistance to members of the Marines' Memorial Association from all branches of the armed forces and their descendants who are interested in studying health care in college.

Eligibility This program is open to active members of the association and their children and grandchildren. Applicants must be high school seniors or students currently enrolled in an undergraduate degree program in a discipline within the field of health care. Along with their application, they must submit an essay of up to 500 words on why they chose their specific path of study, what they hope to accomplish after graduation with their degree, and how their efforts will benefit others in their community. Graduating high school seniors must submit a high school transcript and SAT or ACT scores; continuing college students must submit a college transcript. Selection is based on the essay, academic merit, references, and financial need.

Financial data The stipend is $2,500 per year.

Duration 1 year; recipients may reapply for up to 3 additional years.

Additional information Membership in the association is open to veterans of the Marines, Army, Navy, Air Force, or Coast Guard and to personnel currently serving in a branch of the armed forces.

Number awarded 1 each year.

Deadline April of each year.

[62]
FLEET RESERVE ASSOCIATION MEMBER SCHOLARSHIPS

Fleet Reserve Association
Attn: FRA Education Foundation
125 North West Street
Alexandria, VA 22314-2754
(703) 683-1400   Toll Free: (800) FRA-1924
Fax: (703) 549-6610   E-mail: scholars@fra.org
Web: www.fra.org

Summary To provide financial assistance for college or graduate school to members of the Fleet Reserve Association (FRA) and their families.

Eligibility This program is open to members of the FRA and the children, grandchildren, great-grandchildren, and spouses of living or deceased members. Applicants must be enrolled or planning to enroll as full-time undergraduate or graduate students. Along with their application, they must submit transcripts that include (for high school students and college freshmen) SAT and/or ACT scores; a list of school and community activities; at least 2 letters of recommendation; and an essay on why they want to go to college and what they intend to accomplish with their degree. Selection is based on academic record, financial need, extracurricular activities, leadership skills, and participation in community activities. U.S. citizenship is required.

Financial data Stipends range from $1,000 to $5,000.

Duration 1 year; may be renewed.

Additional information Membership in the FRA is open to current and former enlisted members of the Navy, Marine Corps, and Coast Guard. This program includes awards designated as the MCPO Ken E. Blair Scholarship, the Robert M. Treadwell Annual Scholarship, the Donald Bruce Pringle Family Scholarship, the Tom and Karen Snee Scholarship, the Angelo and Mildred Nunez Scholarships, the Express Scripts Scholarships, the US Family Health Scholarship, and the Navy Department Branch 181 Scholarship.

Number awarded Varies each year; recently, 10 were awarded: 6 at $5,000, 2 at $4,000, 1 at $3,000, and 1 at $2,000.

Deadline April of each year.

[63]
FLEET RESERVE ASSOCIATION NON-MEMBER SCHOLARSHIPS

Fleet Reserve Association
Attn: FRA Education Foundation
125 North West Street
Alexandria, VA 22314-2754
(703) 683-1400   Toll Free: (800) FRA-1924
Fax: (703) 549-6610   E-mail: scholars@fra.org
Web: www.fra.org

Summary To provide financial assistance for college or graduate school to sea service personnel and their families.

Eligibility This program is open to 1) active-duty, Reserve, honorably-discharged veterans, and retired members of the U.S. Navy, Marine Corps, and Coast Guard; and 2) their spouses, children, grandchildren, and great-grandchildren. Applicants must be enrolled or planning to enroll as full-time undergraduate or graduate students, but neither they nor their family member are required to be members of the sponsoring organization. Along with their application, they must submit transcripts that include (for high school students and college freshmen) SAT and/or ACT scores; a list of school and community activities; at least 2 letters of recommendation; and an essay on why they want to go to college and what they intend to accomplish with their degree. Selection is based on academic record, financial need, extracurricular activities, leadership skills, and participation in community activities. U.S. citizenship is required.

Financial data Stipends range up to $5,000 per year.
Duration 1 year; may be renewed.
Additional information This program includes the GEICO Scholarship and the Rosemary Posekany Memorial Scholarship.
Number awarded Varies each year; recently, 6 were awarded: 5 at $5,000 and 1 at $1,000.
Deadline April of each year.

[64]
FLORIDA NAVY NURSE CORPS ASSOCIATION SCHOLARSHIPS

Florida Navy Nurse Corps Association
c/o Margaret Holder, Scholarship Committee
1033 Inverness Drive
St. Augustine, FL 32092
E-mail: maholder@me.com
Web: www.nnca.org/join-nnca-2/local-chapters/fnnca

Summary To provide financial assistance to undergraduate and graduate nursing students, especially residents of Florida with ties to the military.

Eligibility This program is open to students, including registered nursing continuing their studies, who are working on a baccalaureate or graduate degree in nursing. Applicants must have completed at least 1 clinical nursing course and have a GPA of 3.0 or higher. They may be full- or part-time students. Along with their application, they must submit an essay, up to 500 words in length, on the reasons they are qualified for the scholarship, how it will benefit them, career goals, and potential for contribution to the profession. Preference is given in order to current active-duty and Reserve service members, veterans of military service, family members of current or former military service personnel, civil service employees, and residents of Florida. Financial need is considered in the selection process.

Financial data The stipend is $1,500. Funds are paid directly to the student.
Duration 1 year.
Number awarded 2 each year.
Deadline October of each year.

[65]
FOOTWEAR WARRIORS HIGHER EDUCATION SCHOLARSHIPS

Two Ten Footwear Foundation
Attn: Scholarship Director
1466 Main Street
Waltham, MA 02451
(781) 736-1512   Toll Free: (800) FIND-210, ext. 1512
Fax: (781) 736-1555   E-mail: scholarship@twoten.org
Web: www.twoten.org

Summary To provide financial assistance for higher education to veterans who are employed in or returning to work in the footwear industry.

Eligibility This program is open to veterans who are enrolled to planning to enroll at a college or university in any state. Either they or their parents must have been employed in the footwear industry for at least 2 years. U.S. citizenship or permanent resident status is required. Selection is based on academic performance, personal character, and financial need.

Financial data Stipends range up to $4,000 per year, depending on the need of the recipient.
Duration 1 year; may be renewed up to 3 additional years, provided the recipient maintains a GPA of 2.5 or higher.
Additional information This program, which began in 2013, is currently managed by Scholarship Management Services, a division of Scholarship America.
Number awarded 1 each year.
Deadline March of each year.

[66]
FORCE RECON ASSOCIATION SCHOLARSHIPS

Force Recon Association
c/o Al Sniadecki, Scholarship Committee Chair
2928 Cambridgeshire Drive
Carrollton, TX 75007
E-mail: commchief@forcerecon.com
Web: www.forcerecon.com/join.htm

Summary To provide financial assistance for college to members of the Force Recon Association and their dependents.

Eligibility This program is open to members of the Force Recon Association and family members of a relative who served both in the U.S. Marine Corps and was or is assigned to a Force Reconnaissance Company. The relative must be either an active or deceased member of the Force Recon Association. Family members include wives and widows, sons and daughters (including adopted and stepchildren), grandchildren, and great-grandchildren. Applicants may be pursuing scholastic, vocational, or technical education. Along with their application, they must submit a personal statement on why they desire this scholarship, their proposed course of study, their progress in their current course of study, and their long-range career goals. Selection is based on academic

achievement, letters of recommendation, demonstrated character, and the written statements.
Financial data A stipend is awarded (amount not specified).
Duration 1 year; may be renewed.
Number awarded 1 or more each year.
Deadline June of each year.

[67]
FORT WORTH POST SAME SCHOLARSHIP

Society of American Military Engineers-Fort Worth Post
c/o J.B. West, Scholarship Chair
Halff Associates
4000 Fossil Creek Boulevard
Fort Worth, TX 76137
(817) 205-7981   E-mail: warwagon16@gmail.com
Web: www.samefortworth.org/scholarship-application

Summary To provide financial assistance to engineering, architecture, and science college and graduate students, especially those at colleges and universities in Texas.
Eligibility This program is open to U.S. citizens who are currently enrolled in college or graduate school; preference is given to students at colleges and universities in Texas. Applicants must be working full time on a degree in an engineering, architecture, or science-related field. Along with their application, they must submit a 500-word essay that covers why they are preparing for a career in engineering, architecture, or a related science, their understanding of the Society of American Military Engineers (SAME) and how involvement with the organization will help them to achieve their academic and professional aspirations and objectives, and what distinguishes them from other candidates. Selection is based on academic achievement, character, personal merit, and commitment to the field of engineering. Special consideration is given to veterans and students enrolled in ROTC.
Financial data The stipend for the highest-ranked student enrolled in engineering and ROTC is $2,000. Other stipend amounts vary.
Duration 1 year.
Number awarded Varies each year.
Deadline April of each year.

[68]
FRANK N. BROWN VETERAN TO TEACHER SCHOLARSHIPS

Veterans of Foreign Wars of the United States-
   Department of Wisconsin
c/o Wayne Woodman, Chair
Frank Brown Scholarships
701 Wolcott Street
Sparta, WI 54656
(608) 269-0214   E-mail: h2boivert@yahoo.com
Web: vfwwi.org/di/vfw/v2/default.asp?pid=6763

Summary To provide financial assistance to veterans who are attending college in Wisconsin to prepare for a career as a teacher.
Eligibility This program is open to veterans of the U.S. armed forces who have completed at least their first year of study at a college or university in Wisconsin. Applicants must have a declared major in education. Along with their application, they must submit transcripts, documentation of veteran status, information on membership in any veteran organization, a list of community service activities, and documentation of financial need. Membership in the Veterans of Foreign Wars of the United States (VFW) or VFW Auxiliary is not required.
Financial data A stipend is awarded (amount not specified).
Duration 1 year.
Number awarded Varies each year.
Deadline May of each year.

[69]
G. RAY EKENSTAM MEMORIAL SCHOLARSHIP

Institute of Electrical and Electronics Engineers
Attn: Power and Energy Society
445 Hoes Lane
P.O. Box 1331
Piscataway, NJ 08855-1331
(732) 562-3883   Fax: (732) 562-3881
E-mail: pes-awardsadmin@ieee.org
Web: www.ieee-pes.org

Summary To provide financial assistance to veterans working on an electrical engineering degree in the field of power.
Eligibility This program is open to honorably-discharged veterans enrolled full time at accredited colleges, universities, and community colleges in the United States. Applicants must be U.S. citizens or permanent residents working toward a bachelor's degree in electrical engineering as preparation for a career in electric power and energy engineering. They must have a GPA of 3.0 or higher. Financial need is not considered in the selection process.
Financial data The stipend is $5,000. A 1-year student membership in the Institute of Electrical and Electronics Engineers (IEEE) and a travel grant of $500 to attend the IEEE Power and Energy Society General Meeting are also provided.
Duration 1 year.
Additional information This program began in 2009.
Number awarded 1 each year.
Deadline June of each year.

[70]
GEN. JACK N. MERRITT SCHOLARSHIP

Association of the United States Army
Attn: Scholarships
2425 Wilson Boulevard
Arlington, VA 22201
(703) 841-4300   Toll Free: (800) 336-4570
E-mail: scholarships@ausa.org
Web: www.ausa.org/resources/scholarships

Summary To provide financial assistance to members of the Association of the United States Army (AUSA) who are interested in attending college.
Eligibility This program is open to AUSA members who are enrolled or accepted at an accredited college or university to work on a degree in any field. Along with their application, they must submit a 1-page autobiography, 2 letters of recommendation, a letter describing their career aspirations (including their course of study and plans for completion of a degree), and a transcript of high school or college grades (depending on which they are currently attending). Selection is based on academic merit and personal achievement.

Financial need is not normally a selection criterion but in some cases of extreme need it may be used as a factor; the lack of financial need, however, is never a cause for non-selection.
Financial data The stipend is $5,000; funds are sent directly to the recipient's college or university.
Duration 1 year.
Additional information Membership in the AUSA is open to everyone who supports a strong national defense, with special concern for the Army. That includes Regular Army, National Guard, Army Reserve, government civilians, retired soldiers, Wounded Warriors, veterans, concerned citizens and family members.
Number awarded 2 each year.
Deadline June of each year.

[71]
GEORGE L. PATT SCHOLARSHIP FUND
Illinois Association of Realtors
Attn: Illinois Real Estate Educational Foundation
522 South Fifth Street
P.O. Box 2607
Springfield, IL 62708
Toll Free: (866) 854-REEF   Fax: (217) 529-5893
E-mail: lclayton@ilreef.org
Web: www.ilreef.org/scholarships

Summary To provide financial assistance to veterans and Reservists in Illinois who are preparing for a career in real estate at a college or university in the state.
Eligibility This program is open to residents of Illinois enrolled at a school in the state. Applicants must be either 1) veterans working on an undergraduate college or university degree in the field of real estate; or 2) active Reservists or Guard members studying real estate administration to establish themselves as an association executive in a realtor organization. Along with their application, they must submit a 1,000-word statement of their general activities and intellectual interests, employment (if any), contemplated line of study, and career they expect to follow. Selection is based on the applicant's record of military service, record of academic achievement, course of study and career goals, references and recommendations, and financial need. Finalists are interviewed.
Financial data The stipend is $1,000.
Duration 1 year.
Number awarded 1 each year.
Deadline March of each year.

[72]
GEORGE WASHINGTON CHAPTER AUSA SCHOLARSHIPS
Association of the United States Army-George
   Washington Chapter
c/o Col (Ret.) William G. Yarborough, Jr., Scholarship
   Committee
P.O. Box 828
McLean, VA 22101-0828
(703) 748-1717   E-mail: wgyarc@aol.com
Web: www.ausa.org/chapters/george-washington-chapter

Summary To provide financial assistance for undergraduate or graduate study at a school in any state to members of the George Washington Chapter of the Association of the United States Army (AUSA) and their families.
Eligibility This program is open to active members of the AUSA George Washington Chapter and the spouses, children, and grandchildren of active members. Applicants must have a GPA of 2.5 or higher and be working on an undergraduate or graduate degree at a college or university in any state. Along with their application, they must submit a letter describing any family circumstances they believe are relevant and explaining why they deserve the scholarship. Members must also submit a favorable recommendation from their supervisor. Membership in AUSA is open to Army personnel (including Reserves and National Guard) who are either active or retired, ROTC cadets, or civilian employees of the Army.
Financial data Stipends range up to $1,000.
Duration 1 year.
Additional information This program includes the following named awards: the Ed Dauksz Scholarship Award, the Major General Harry Greene STEM Scholarship Award, and the Major General Carl F. McNair Jr. Scholarship Award. The George Washington Chapter serves Washington, D.C.; the Virginia counties of Alexandria, Clarke, Fairfax, Frederick, Loudoun, and Prince William; and the Maryland counties of Calvert, Charles, Montgomery, Prince George's, and St. Mary's.
Number awarded Varies each year; recently, 45 were awarded.
Deadline April of each year.

[73]
GLADYS MCPARTLAND SCHOLARSHIPS
United States Marine Corps Combat Correspondents
   Association
Attn: Scholarship Committee
385 S.W. 254th Street
Newberry, FL 32669
(352) 448-9167   E-mail: hq@usmccca.org
Web: www.usmccca.org/awards/gladys

Summary To provide financial assistance to members of the U.S. Marine Corps Combat Correspondents Association (USMCCCA) or their dependents and Marines in specified occupational fields who are interested in studying any field in college.
Eligibility This program is open to members of USMCCCA who have been members for at least 2 years and their dependents of such members, including children of deceased members. Applications are also accepted from active-duty Marines in occupational field 4300 or 4600 who are enrolled in government-sponsored degree completion programs, whose tuition is not paid from other sources, and who agree to become USMCCA members upon award of a scholarship. Applicants must be enrolled or planning to enroll in an undergraduate program in any field. Along with their application, they must submit 500-word essays on 1) their noteworthy achievements and long-range goals; and 2) "The United States I want to see in 15 years and my role in the transformation." Financial need is not considered in the selection process.
Financial data Stipends for full-time study range up to $3,000; part-time stipends range from $250 to $500. Funds are disbursed directly to recipients to be used exclusively for tuition, books, and/or fees.

Duration 1 year; may be renewed up to 3 additional years.
Number awarded 1 or more each year.
Deadline May of each year.

[74]
GOOGLE-SVA SCHOLARSHIP

Student Veterans of America
Attn: Scholarship Committee
1012 14th Street, N.W., Suite 1200
Washington, DC 20005
(202) 223-4710
E-mail: scholarships@studentveterans.org
Web: www.studentveterans.org/programs/scholarships

Summary To provide financial assistance to veterans and current military personnel who are working on a bachelor's or graduate degree in a computer-related field.

Eligibility This program is open to sophomores, juniors, seniors, and graduate students at 4-year colleges and universities who are veterans of any branch of service, including Reserves and National Guard, and were honorably discharged or are active-duty military personnel still in good standing with their branch of service. Applicants must be working full time on a degree in computer science, computer engineering, or a closely-related technical field (e.g., software engineering, electrical engineering with a heavy computer science course load, information systems, information technology, applied networking, system administration). Along with their application, they must submit essays of 300 to 500 words each on 1) what sparked their interest in computer science; 2) examples of how they have exhibited leadership; 3) a significant challenge that they believe student veterans in the field of technology face and how they see themselves as being part of the solution(s) to that challenge; and 4) the impact receiving this scholarship would have on their education. Financial need is not considered in the selection process.

Financial data The stipend is $10,000.
Duration 1 year.
Additional information This program is sponsored by Google and administered by Student Veterans of America (SVA).
Number awarded 8 each year.
Deadline November of each year.

[75]
GROGAN MEMORIAL SCHOLARSHIP

American Academy of Physician Assistants-Veterans
  Caucus
Attn: Scholarship Program
P.O. Box 362
Ossining, NY 10562
(803) 328-1864   Fax: (704) 838-8494
E-mail: rmunsee@veteranscaucus.org
Web: www.veteranscaucus.org/scholarships

Summary To provide financial assistance to veterans and their dependents who are studying to become physician assistants.

Eligibility This program is open to U.S. citizens who are currently enrolled in a physician assistant program. Applicants must be honorably discharged members of any branch of the military or the dependents of those members. Along with their application, they must submit a personal statement about what led them to attend PA school; their background, present, and future intentions; and why they deserve to receive a scholarship. Selection is based on military honors and awards received, civic and college honors and awards received, professional memberships and activities, potential for future achievement, and GPA.

Financial data The stipend is $2,000.
Duration 1 year.
Number awarded 1 each year.
Deadline February of each year.

[76]
HAMMER FAMILY SCHOLARSHIPS

Marines' Memorial Association
c/o Marines Memorial Club and Hotel
609 Sutter Street
San Francisco, CA 94102
(415) 673-6672, ext. 293   Toll Free: (800) 5-MARINE
Fax: (415) 441-3649
E-mail: scholarship@marineclub.com
Web: www.marinesmemorial.org

Summary To provide financial assistance to veterans who are interested in attending college to major in a field of science, engineering, or mathematics.

Eligibility This program is open to veterans who have served since 2009 and received an honorable discharge. Applicants must be interested in working on a bachelor's degree in a field of science, engineering, or mathematics. Membership in the sponsoring organization is not required. Along with their application, they must submit an essay of up to 500 words on why they chose their specific path of study, what they hope to accomplish after graduation with their degree, and how their efforts will benefit others in their community. Applicants entering college as freshmen must submit a high school transcript and SAT or ACT scores; continuing college students must submit a college transcript. Selection is based on the essay, academic merit, references, and financial need.

Financial data The stipend is $5,000 per year.
Duration 1 year; recipients may reapply for up to 3 additional years.
Number awarded 1 each year.
Deadline April of each year.

[77]
HAZLEWOOD ACT EXEMPTIONS FOR VETERANS

Texas Veterans Commission
1700 North Congress Avenue, Suite 800
P.O. Box 12277
Austin, TX 78711-2277
(512) 463-3168   Toll Free: (800) 252-VETS
Fax: (512) 475-2395   E-mail: hazlewood@tvc.texas.gov
Web: www.tvc.texas.gov/education/hazlewood

Summary To exempt Texas veterans from payment of tuition for undergraduate or graduate study at public universities in the state.

Eligibility This program is open to veterans who are current residents of Texas and were legal residents of the state at the time they entered the U.S. armed forces and served for at least 181 days of active military duty, excluding basic training, during specified periods of wartime. Applicants must have received an honorable discharge or separation or a general discharge under honorable conditions. They must be enrolled at a public college or university in Texas and all their other federal veterans' education benefits (not including Pell and SEOG grants) may not exceed the value of this exemption.

Financial data Veterans who are eligible for this benefit are entitled to free tuition and fees at state-supported colleges and universities in Texas.

Duration Exemptions may be claimed up to a cumulative total of 150 credit hours, including undergraduate and graduate study.

Additional information This program was previously administered by the Texas Higher Education Coordinating Board but was transferred to the Texas Veterans Commission in 2013.

Number awarded Varies each year; recently, 8,612 veterans received $44,631,752 in support at 4-year institutions and 9,637 veterans received $14,080,701 in support at 2-year colleges.

Deadline Deadline not specified.

[78]
HELEN DYAR KING SCHOLARSHIP

Arizona Community Foundation
Attn: Director of Scholarships
2201 East Camelback Road, Suite 405B
Phoenix, AZ 85016
(602) 381-1400   Toll Free: (800) 222-8221
Fax: (602) 381-1575
E-mail: scholarship@azfoundation.org
Web: azfoundation.academicworks.com/opportunities/4156

Summary To provide financial assistance to high school seniors and current college students from Arizona who are members or dependents of members of the armed services or a law enforcement agency and are interested in attending college in any state.

Eligibility This program is open to residents of Arizona who are graduating high school seniors or current full-time students at colleges or universities in any state. Applicants must be an active-duty or retired member or dependent of such a member of the armed services (Air Force, Army, Coast Guard, Marine Corps, National Guard, Navy) or public service agency (police, fire, or other departments). Students entering or enrolled at a 2-year community college must have a GPA of 2.75 or higher; students entering or enrolled at a 4-year college or university must have a GPA of 3.0 or higher. Financial need is considered in the selection process.

Financial data The stipend is $2,000 for students at 2-year colleges or $4,000 for students at 4-year colleges and universities.

Duration 1 year.

Number awarded Varies each year.

Deadline May of each year.

[79]
HELPING HEROES GRANTS OF TENNESSEE

Tennessee Student Assistance Corporation
312 Rosa Parks Boulevard, Ninth Floor
Nashville, TN 37243
(615) 741-1346   Toll Free: (800) 342-1663
Fax: (615) 741-6101   E-mail: TSAC.Aidinfo@tn.gov
Web: www.tn.gov

Summary To provide financial assistance to veterans and current Reservists or National Guard members who are residents of Tennessee and enrolled at a college or university in the state.

Eligibility This program is open to residents of Tennessee who are veterans honorably discharged from the U.S. armed forces and former or current members of a Reserve or Tennessee National Guard unit who were called into active military service. Applicants must have been awarded, on or after September 11, 2001, the Iraq Campaign Medal, the Afghanistan Campaign Medal, or the Global War on Terrorism Expeditionary Medal. They must be enrolled at least half time at an eligible college or university in Tennessee and receive no final failing grade in any course. No academic standard or financial need requirements apply.

Financial data Grants are $1,000 per semester for full-time study or $500 per semester for part-time study. Funds are awarded after completion of each semester of work.

Duration Grants are awarded until completion of the equivalent of 8 full semesters of work, completion of a baccalaureate degree, or the eighth anniversary of honorable discharge from military service, whichever comes first.

Additional information This program was added as a component of the Tennessee Education Lottery Scholarship Program in 2005.

Number awarded Varies each year; recently, 486 students received approximately $734,000 in scholarships through this program.

Deadline August of each year for fall enrollment, January of each year for spring, or April of each year for summer.

[80]
HENRY J. REILLY SCHOLARSHIPS

Reserve Officers Association of the United States
Attn: Scholarship Program
One Constitution Avenue, N.E.
Washington, DC 20002-5618
(202) 646-7758   Toll Free: (800) 809-9448
E-mail: scholarship@roa.org
Web: www.roa.org/page/Scholarships

Summary To provide financial assistance for college or graduate school to members of the Reserve Officers Association (ROA) and their children or grandchildren.

Eligibility Applicants for this scholarship must be active or associate members of the association or their children or grandchildren (under the age of 26). Children, age 21 or under, of deceased members who were active and paid up at the time of their death are also eligible. Spouses are not eligible, unless they are members of the association. ROTC members do not qualify as sponsors. Entering and continuing undergraduates must provide evidence of full-time enrollment at a regionally-accredited 4-year college or university, demonstrate leadership qualities, have earned a GPA of 3.3 or higher in high school and 3.0 or higher in college, have scored at least 1875 on the SAT or 55 on the English/math ACT, and (if appropriate) have registered for the draft. Applicants for a master's degree must have earned a GPA of 3.2 or higher as an undergraduate; applicants for a doctoral degree must have received a master's degree or been accepted into a doctoral program. All applicants must submit a 500-word essay on career goals. Selection is based on that essay, aca-

demic excellence, extracurricular activities and leadership, and letters of recommendation.
Financial data The stipend is $2,500 per year.
Duration 1 year; may be renewed.
Number awarded Up to 20 each year.
Deadline April of each year.

[81]
HILL & PONTON VETERANS SCHOLARSHIPS
Hill & Ponton, P.A.
1607 South State Road 15A, Suite 12
P.O. Box 449
Deland, FL 32721
Toll Free: (888) 373-9436
Web: www.hillandponton.com/veterans-scholarship

Summary To provide financial assistance for college to veterans who demonstrate an interest in helping other veterans.
Eligibility This program is open to veterans who are enrolled or planning to enroll at a college or university in any state. Applicants must submit a 300-word essay on how they plan to use their education to help fellow veterans.
Financial data The stipend is $1,000.
Duration 1 year.
Additional information This program began in 2015.
Number awarded 4 each year: 2 in fall and 2 in spring.
Deadline April of each year for fall; October of each year for spring.

[82]
HOMEGROWN BY HEROES SCHOLARSHIPS
Arkansas Agriculture Department
Attn: Homegrown by Heroes Program
1 Natural Resources Drive
Little Rock, AR 72205
(501) 225-1598
E-mail: amy.lyman@agriculture.arkansas.gov
Web: www.agriculture.arkansas.gov/aad-programs

Summary To provide financial assistance to veterans, current military personnel, and their spouses and children in Arkansas who are interested in working on a degree in agriculture at a college in any state.
Eligibility This program is open to residents of Arkansas who are military veterans, currently serving military personnel, and their spouses or children. Applicants must be enrolled or planning to enroll at a college or university in any state to working on a degree in agriculture or a related field. Selection is based on academic achievement, community involvement, extracurricular activities, family circumstances, and financial need. Preference is given to farmers and their families who participate in Homegrown by Heroes, a program of the Arkansas Agriculture Department that helps veterans market their local agricultural products by labeling them as veteran-produced.
Financial data The stipend is $1,000.
Duration 1 year.
Additional information This program is funded by Farm Credit of Western Arkansas, AgHeritage Farm Credit Services, and Farm Credit Midsouth.
Number awarded 8 each year.
Deadline March of each year.

[83]
HONORABLY DISCHARGED GRADUATE ASSISTANCE PROGRAM
Florida Department of Education
Attn: Office of Student Financial Assistance
State Scholarship and Grant Programs
325 West Gaines Street, Suite 1314
Tallahassee, FL 32399-0400
(850) 410-5160   Toll Free: (888) 827-2004
Fax: (850) 487-1809   E-mail: osfa@fldoe.org
Web: www.floridastudentfinancialaidsg.org

Summary To provide funding to active-duty and veterans in Florida who need assistance for payment of living expenses during holiday and semester breaks from college.
Eligibility This program is open to residents of Florida who are active-duty or honorably discharged members of the armed forces, served on or after September 11, 2001, and are currently enrolled in a program of study at a postsecondary institution in the state. Applicants must be able to demonstrate a financial need for assistance in payment of living expenses during holiday and semester breaks, including, but not limited to, food, shelter, utilities, and personal care products.
Financial data Support is limited to $50 per day. The total award may not exceed the student's unmet need.
Duration Up to 20 days per academic year.
Additional information This program began in 2014.
Number awarded Varies each year; recently, 1,236 initial and 467 renewal scholarships were awarded.
Deadline Applications may be submitted at any time.

[84]
IDAHO LEGION AUXILIARY GENERAL STUDIES NON-TRADITIONAL SCHOLARSHIP
American Legion Auxiliary
Department of Idaho
905 Warren Street
Boise, ID 83706-3825
(208) 342-7066   Fax: (208) 342-7066
E-mail: idalegionaux@msn.com
Web: www.idahoala.org/14301.html

Summary To provide financial assistance to members of American Legion organizations in Idaho who are interested in attending college in any state and majoring in any field.
Eligibility This program is open to residents of Idaho who are members of the American Legion, American Legion Auxiliary, or Sons of the American Legion. Applicants must be nontraditional students who are returning to the classroom after some period of time during which their formal education was interrupted or beginning postsecondary education at a later point in life. Along with their application, they must submit brief statements describing any circumstances that may affect support for their college education, community service activities, the major they plan to pursue in college and why, the college or university they plan to attend any why, and who or what inspired them to seek a college degree.
Financial data The stipend is $1,000. Funds are paid directly to the school.
Duration 1 year.
Number awarded 1 each year.
Deadline April of each year.

[85]
IDAHO LEGION AUXILIARY NON-TRADITIONAL NURSES SCHOLARSHIP

American Legion Auxiliary
Department of Idaho
905 Warren Street
Boise, ID 83706-3825
(208) 342-7066   Fax: (208) 342-7066
E-mail: idalegionaux@msn.com
Web: www.idahoala.org/14301.html

Summary To provide financial assistance to Idaho veterans and their descendants who are interested in studying nursing at a school in any state.

Eligibility This program is open to residents of Idaho who are wartime veterans or the children or grandchildren of such veterans. Applicants must be attending or planning to attend a school of nursing in any state. They must be nontraditional students who have been out of high school more than 2 years. Along with their application, they must submit a letter describing their career goals and experience, 2 letters of recommendation, a resume that includes their work history, their most recent high school or college transcripts including ACT or SAT scores, and documentation of financial need.

Financial data The stipend is $1,000. Funds are paid directly to the school.

Duration 1 year.

Number awarded 1 each year.

Deadline April of each year.

[86]
ILLINOIS AMERICAN LEGION AUXILIARY PAST PRESIDENTS PARLEY NURSES SCHOLARSHIP

American Legion Auxiliary
Department of Illinois
2720 East Lincoln Street
P.O. Box 1426
Bloomington, IL 61702-1426
(309) 663-9366   Fax: (309) 663-5827
E-mail: karen.boughan@ilala.org
Web: www.ilala.org/education.html

Summary To provide financial assistance to Illinois veterans and their descendants who are attending college in any state to prepare for a career as a nurse.

Eligibility This program is open to veterans who served during designated periods of wartime and their children, grandchildren, and great-grandchildren. Applicants must be currently enrolled full time at a college or university in any state and studying nursing. They must be residents of Illinois or members of the American Legion Family, Department of Illinois. Selection is based on commitment to a nursing career (25%) character (25%), academic rating (20%), and financial need (30%).

Financial data The stipend is $1,000.

Duration 1 year.

Additional information Applications may be obtained only from a local unit of the American Legion Auxiliary.

Number awarded 1 or more each year.

Deadline April of each year.

[87]
ILLINOIS AMVETS SERVICE FOUNDATION VETERANS SCHOLARSHIPS

AMVETS-Department of Illinois
2200 South Sixth Street
Springfield, IL 62703
(217) 528-4713   Toll Free: (800) 638-VETS (within IL)
Fax: (217) 528-9896   E-mail: info@ilamvets.org
Web: www.ilamvets.org

Summary To provide financial assistance for college to veterans in Illinois.

Eligibility This program is open to residents of Illinois who are honorably discharged veterans. Applicants must be enrolled or planning to enroll full or part time at a 2- or 4-year college, university, or vocational/technical school in the state. Selection is based on merit and financial need.

Financial data The stipend is $2,000 per year.

Duration 1 year; may be renewed up to 3 additional years, provided the recipient maintains a GPA of 3.0 or higher.

Number awarded 1 or more each year.

Deadline February of each year.

[88]
ILLINOIS NATIONAL GUARD GRANT PROGRAM

Illinois Student Assistance Commission
Attn: Scholarship and Grant Services
1755 Lake Cook Road
Deerfield, IL 60015-5209
(847) 948-8550   Toll Free: (800) 899-ISAC
Fax: (847) 831-8549   TDD: (800) 526-0844
E-mail: isac.studentservices@illinois.gov
Web: www.isac.org

Summary To provide financial assistance to current or former members of the Illinois National Guard who are interested in attending college or graduate school in the state.

Eligibility This program is open to members of the Illinois National Guard who 1) are currently active and have completed at least 1 full year of service; or 2) have been active for at least 5 consecutive years, have had their studies interrupted by being called to federal active duty for at least 6 months, and are within 12 months after their discharge date. Applicants must also be enrolled at an Illinois public 2- or 4-year college or university.

Financial data Recipients are eligible for payment of tuition and some fees for either undergraduate or graduate study at an Illinois state-supported college or university.

Duration This assistance extends for 4 academic years of full-time study (or the equivalent in part-time study) for Guard members with less than 10 years of active duty service. For Guard members with 10 years or more of active duty service, assistance is available for up to the equivalent of 6 academic years of full-time study.

Number awarded Varies each year.

Deadline September of each year for the academic year; February of each year for spring semester, winter quarter, or spring quarter; June of each year for summer term.

[89]
ILLINOIS VETERAN GRANT PROGRAM

Illinois Student Assistance Commission
Attn: Scholarship and Grant Services
1755 Lake Cook Road
Deerfield, IL 60015-5209
(847) 948-8550   Toll Free: (800) 899-ISAC
Fax: (847) 831-8549   TDD: (800) 526-0844
E-mail: isac.studentservices@illinois.gov
Web: www.isac.org

Summary To provide financial assistance to Illinois veterans who are interested in attending college or graduate school in the state.

Eligibility This program is open to Illinois residents who served in the U.S. armed forces (including members of the Reserves and the Illinois National Guard called to federal active duty) for at least 1 year on active duty and have been honorably discharged. The 1-year service requirement does not apply to veterans who 1) served in a foreign country in a time of hostilities in that country; 2) were medically discharged for service-related reasons; or 3) were discharged prior to August 11, 1967. Illinois residency may be established in 1 of the following ways: 1) currently residing in the state, except those who are serving federal active duty service at the time of enrollment in college or residing with a spouse in continued military service who is currently stationed outside of Illinois; 2) resided in Illinois at the time of entering federal active duty service or within 6 months prior to entering the service or were a student at an Illinois public 2- or 4-year college at the time of entering federal active duty service; or 3) established, or, if on federal active duty service, plan to establish, Illinois residency within 6 months after leaving federal active duty service. Students who cannot establish residency by 1 of those 3 methods may do so if they reside in Illinois at the time of application and at the time of receiving benefits and, at some point after leaving federal active duty service, have been a resident of Illinois for at least 15 consecutive years. Current members of the Reserve Officer Training Corps are not eligible.

Financial data This program pays all tuition and mandatory fees at all Illinois public colleges, universities, and community colleges.

Duration This scholarship may be used for the equivalent of up to 4 years of full-time enrollment at the undergraduate or graduate level, provided the recipient maintains the minimum GPA required by their college or university.

Additional information This is an entitlement program; once eligibility has been established, no further applications are necessary.

Number awarded Varies each year.

Deadline Applications may be submitted at any time.

[90]
IMAGINE AMERICA MILITARY AWARD PROGRAM

Imagine America Foundation
Attn: Student Services Representative
14200 Park Meadow Drive, Suite 117S
Chantilly, VA 20151
(571) 267-3015   Fax: (866) 734-5812
E-mail: studentservices@imagine-america.org
Web: www.imagine-america.org

Summary To provide financial assistance to veterans and military personnel interested in attending a participating career college.

Eligibility This program is open to active-duty, reservist, honorably-discharged, and retired veterans of a U.S. military service branch. Applicants must be interested in attending 1 of more than 550 participating career colleges. All applications are submitted online to the college where the student wishes to enroll. Selection is based on the likelihood of successfully completing postsecondary education and financial need.

Financial data The stipend is $1,000. Funds must be used for payment of tuition at a participating career college.

Duration 1 year.

Additional information The Imagine America Foundation (originally known as the Career College Foundation) established this program in 2004. Its membership includes 550 career colleges.

Number awarded Varies each year.

Deadline Deadline not specified.

[91]
INDIANA PURPLE HEART RECIPIENT VETERAN PROGRAM

Indiana Commission for Higher Education
Attn: Financial Aid and Student Support Services
101 West Ohio Street, Suite 300
Indianapolis, IN 46204-4206
(317) 232-1023   Toll Free: (888) 528-4719 (within IN)
Fax: (317) 232-3260   E-mail: Scholars@che.in.gov
Web: www.in.gov/che/4521.htm

Summary To provide financial assistance to veterans from Indiana who received a Purple Heart and are interested in attending college or graduate school in the state.

Eligibility This program is open to veterans who entered active-duty service from a permanent home address in Indiana, received an honorable discharge, and received the Purple Heart decoration for that active-duty service. Applicants must be interested in working on an undergraduate, graduate, or professional degree at an eligible institution in Indiana.

Financial data Qualified applicants receive a 100% remission of tuition and all mandatory fees for undergraduate, graduate, or professional degrees at eligible postsecondary schools and universities in Indiana. Support is not provided for such fees as room and board.

Duration Up to 124 semester hours of study, provided the recipient maintains satisfactory academic progress. If the veteran initially enlisted on or before June 30, 2011, there is no time limit to use those hours. If the veteran initially enlisted after June 30, 2011, the allotted 124 credit hours must be used within 8 years after the date of initial application.

Number awarded Varies each year.

Deadline Applications must be submitted at least 30 days before the start of the college term.

[92]
JACK E. BARGER, SR. MEMORIAL NURSING SCHOLARSHIPS

Nursing Foundation of Pennsylvania
3605 Vartan Way, Suite 204
Harrisburg, PA 17110
(717) 827-4369 Toll Free: (888) 707-7762
Fax: (717) 657-3796 E-mail: info@theNFP.org
Web: www.thenfp.org/scholarships

Summary To provide financial assistance to veterans, military personnel, and their dependents who are studying nursing in Pennsylvania.

Eligibility This program is open to veterans, active-duty military personnel, and the children and spouses of veterans and active-duty military personnel. Applicants must be residents of Pennsylvania and currently enrolled in an undergraduate professional school of nursing in the state. Recipients are selected by lottery from among the qualified applicants.

Financial data The stipend is $1,000.

Duration 1 year.

Additional information This program is sponsored by the Department of Pennsylvania of Veterans of Foreign Wars (VFW). Recipients must attend the VFW Convention to accept the scholarship; travel, meals, and overnight expenses are paid by the VFW.

Number awarded 6 each year.

Deadline March of each year.

[93]
JAMES JOSEPH DAVIS MEMORIAL SCHOLARSHIP

American Society of Safety Professionals
Attn: ASSP Foundation
Scholarship Award Program
520 North Northwest Highway
Park Ridge, IL 60068-2538
(847) 699-2929 Fax: (847) 296-3769
E-mail: asspfoundation@assp.org
Web: foundation.assp.org/scholarships-and-grants

Summary To provide financial assistance to students, especially those who have served in the military, who are working on a degree related to occupational safety.

Eligibility This program is open to students, including international students, who are working full or part time on an undergraduate or graduate degree in occupational safety, health, environment, or a closely-related field. Priority is given to students who have served in the military. Associate degree students must have completed at least 24 semester hours and bachelor's degree students at least 60 semester hours. Membership in the American Society of Safety Professionals (ASSP) is not required, but members receive priority. Applicants must have a GPA of 3.0 or higher as an undergraduate or 3.5 or higher as a graduate student. Along with their application, they must submit 5 short essays of up to 500 words each on the following topics: 1) what drew them to the field of safety and how their education has affected their views of the field; 2) their goals and plans for reaching those; 3) their leadership and volunteer positions within the safety community; 4) the greatest takeaway from their current year in school; and 5) what makes them stand out as an applicant. Selection is based on academic performance, leadership activity in ASSP and the broader safety community, motivations for entering the field, and letters of recommendation.(e.g., industrial or environmental engineering).

Financial data The stipend is $10,000.

Duration 1 year.

Additional information This program is sponsored by Applications International Corporation.

Number awarded 1 each year.

Deadline November of each year.

[94]
JEWISH WAR VETERANS NATIONAL ACHIEVEMENT PROGRAM

Jewish War Veterans of the U.S.A.
Attn: National Achievement Program
1811 R Street, N.W.
Washington, DC 20009-1659
(202) 265-6280 Fax: (202) 234-5662
E-mail: jwv@jwv.org
Web: www.jwvusafoundation.org

Summary To recognize and reward veterans and current servicemembers who are currently enrolled in college or graduate school and submit outstanding essays on their military experience.

Eligibility This competition is open to veterans and current servicemembers who are enrolled or planning to enroll in an accredited associate, bachelor's, nursing, or graduate degree program. All veterans are eligible, regardless of race, religion, creed, or culture. Applicants must submit an essay of 500 to 750 words on their military experience and how it will help them pursue their academic studies. Selection is based on answering the essay question (50%), logic and coherence of the essay's organization (25%), and description of relevant military experience (25%).

Financial data Awards range from $1,000 to $5,000.

Duration The awards are presented annually.

Additional information This program includes the Robert M. Zweiman Memorial Award, the Sidney Lieppe Memorial Grant, the Charles Kosmutza Memorial Grant, the Max R. and Irene Rubenstein Memorial Grant, and the Leon Brooks Memorial Grant.

Number awarded 6 each year: 2 at $5,000, 1 at $2,500, 1 at $1,500, and 2 at $1,000.

Deadline May of each year.

[95]
JOHN KEYS KENTUCKY SONS OF THE AMERICAN LEGION SCHOLARSHIP

Sons of the American Legion
Detachment of Kentucky
Independence Squadron 275
P.O. Box 18791
Erlanger, KY 41018-0791
E-mail: SAL275@fuse.net

Summary To provide financial assistance for college in any state to members of Kentucky squadrons of the Sons of the American Legion and to veterans who are residents of Kentucky.

Eligibility This program is open to 1) members of the Sons of the American Legion who belong to a squadron in Kentucky; and 2) honorably-discharged veterans of the U.S. armed forces who are residents of Kentucky (regardless of

length or period of service). Applicants must be enrolled at a postsecondary institution in any state. Along with their application, they must submit a letter explaining their background, career objectives, current educational program, and financial need.
Financial data The stipend varies, depending on the availability of funds; recently, they averaged $1,000. Awards are made directly to the recipient's institution.
Duration 1 year.
Additional information This program began in 1988.
Number awarded 1 or 2 each year; since the program began, it has awarded more than 60 scholarships.
Deadline Applications may be submitted at any time.

[96]
JOSEPH P. AND HELEN T. CRIBBINS SCHOLARSHIP
Association of the United States Army
Attn: Scholarships
2425 Wilson Boulevard
Arlington, VA 22201
(703) 841-4300   Toll Free: (800) 336-4570
E-mail: scholarships@ausa.org
Web: www.ausa.org/resources/scholarships

Summary To provide financial assistance to members of the Association of the United States Army (AUSA) who are interested in studying a field of STEM in college.
Eligibility This program is open to AUSA members who are enrolled or accepted at an accredited college or university to work on a degree in a field of STEM. Along with their application, they must submit a 1-page autobiography, 2 letters of recommendation, a letter describing their career aspirations (including their course of study and plans for completion of a degree), and a transcript of high school or college grades (depending on which they are currently attending). Selection is based on academic merit and personal achievement. Financial need is not normally a selection criterion but in some cases of extreme need it may be used as a factor; the lack of financial need, however, is never a cause for nonselection.
Financial data The stipend is $10,000; funds are sent directly to the recipient's college or university.
Duration 1 year.
Additional information Membership in the AUSA is open to everyone who supports a strong national defense, with special concern for the Army. That includes Regular Army, National Guard, Army Reserve, government civilians, retired soldiers, Wounded Warriors, veterans, concerned citizens and family members.
Number awarded 2 each year.
Deadline June of each year.

[97]
KANSAS MILITARY SERVICE SCHOLARSHIPS
Kansas Board of Regents
Attn: Student Financial Aid
1000 S.W. Jackson Street, Suite 520
Topeka, KS 66612-1368
(785) 430-4255   Fax: (785) 430-4233
E-mail: scholars@ksbor.org
Web: www.kansasregents.org/scholarships_and_grants

Summary To provide financial assistance for college to residents of Kansas who have served or are still serving in the military.
Eligibility This program is open to students who graduated from high school in Kansas or received a GED credential and have been a resident of the state for at least 2 years. Applicants must have served in the U.S. armed forces in international waters or on foreign soil in support of military operations for at least 90 days after September 11, 2001 or for less than 90 days because of injuries received during such service. They must still be in military service or have received an honorable discharge with orders that indicate they served after September 11, 2001 in any operation for which they received hostile fire pay. Qualified veterans and military personnel may enroll full or part time at a public postsecondary institution in Kansas, including area vocational schools, area vocational/technical schools, community colleges, the municipal university, state educational institutions, or technical colleges. In the selection process, priority is given to applicants who can demonstrate financial need.
Financial data Qualifying students are permitted to enroll at an approved Kansas institution without payment of tuition or fees. If they receive any federal military tuition assistance, that money must be applied to their tuition and fees and they are eligible only for the remaining balance in scholarship assistance.
Duration 1 year; may be renewed for a total of 10 semesters as long as the recipient remains in good academic standing.
Additional information This program began in 2007.
Number awarded Varies each year.
Deadline April of each year.

[98]
KANSAS WAIVER OF TUITION AND FEES FOR PRISONERS OF WAR
Kansas Board of Regents
Attn: Student Financial Aid
1000 S.W. Jackson Street, Suite 520
Topeka, KS 66612-1368
(785) 430-4255   Fax: (785) 430-4233
E-mail: scholars@ksbor.org
Web: www.kansasregents.org/scholarships_and_grants

Summary To provide financial assistance for college to residents of Kansas who have been a prisoner of war.
Eligibility This program is open to current residents of Kansas who entered active service in the U.S. armed forces as a resident of the state. Applicants must have been declared a prisoner of war after January 1, 1960 while serving in the armed forces. They must be enrolled or planning to enroll at a public educational institution in Kansas, including area vocational/technical schools and colleges, community colleges, the state universities, and Washburn University.
Financial data Qualifying students are permitted to enroll at an approved Kansas institution without payment of tuition or fees. They are responsible for other costs, such as books, room, and board.
Duration 1 year; may be renewed for a total of 10 semesters of undergraduate study.
Additional information This program began in 2005.
Number awarded Varies each year.
Deadline Deadline not specified.

[99] LANCASTER SCHOLARSHIP

VisionCorps Foundation
244 North Queen Street
Lancaster, PA 17603
(717) 291-5951   E-mail: info@visioncorps.net
Web: www.visioncorps.net

Summary To provide financial assistance to Pennsylvania residents who are legally blind veterans and interested in working on a degree at any level at a college in any state.

Eligibility This program is open to veterans who are residents of Pennsylvania and legally blind. Applicants must be attending or planning to attend an institution of higher education at any level in any state. Along with their application, they must submit a brief description of their career goal. Financial need is considered in the selection process. U.S. citizenship is required.

Financial data The stipend is $1,000 per year.

Duration 1 year; may be renewed up to 3 additional years.

Additional information This sponsor was formerly the Susquehanna Foundation for the Blind.

Number awarded 1 or more each year.

Deadline January of each year.

[100] LILLIAN CAMPBELL MEDICAL SCHOLARSHIP

VFW Auxiliary-Department of Wisconsin
c/o Donna Butler, Department Scholarship Chair
522 Topaz Lane
Madison, WI 53714
(608) 695-0261   E-mail: butlerdonna999@yahoo.com
Web: www.wivfwaux.org/department-scholarships.html

Summary To provide financial assistance to students working on a degree in a medical field in Wisconsin who served in the military or are related to a person who did.

Eligibility This program is open to students who have completed at least 1 year of study in Wisconsin in a program in 1) a medical field, including nursing, pharmacy, physician assistant, medical or surgical technology, physical or occupational therapy, dental hygiene, radiology, or other related medical profession; or 2) an emergency medical technician field (EMT), including paramedic studies. Applicants or a member of their immediate family (parent, sibling, child, spouse, or grandparent) must have served in the military. They must have a high school diploma or GED but may be of any age. Along with their application, they must submit a 200-word essay on why they are studying this medical profession. Financial need is considered in the selection process.

Financial data The stipend is $1,000 for students in a medical field or $750 for EMT students.

Duration 1 year.

Number awarded 1 for a student in a medical field and 1 for an EMT student.

Deadline March of each year.

[101] LOUIS J. SCHOBER MEMORIAL SCHOLARSHIP

Society of American Military Engineers-Louisiana Post
c/o Chris Dunn, Young Members Committee Chair
U.S. Army Corps of Engineers, New Orleans District
7400 Leake Avenue
P.O. Box 60267
New Orleans, LA 70160
(504) 862-1799
E-mail: Christopher.L.Dunn@usace.army.mil
Web: www.same.org

Summary To provide financial assistance to engineering students at universities in Louisiana and to children of members of the Louisiana Post of the Society of American Military Engineers (SAME) at schools in any state.

Eligibility This program is open to students currently working on an undergraduate degree in engineering. Applicants must be either 1) enrolled at a college or university in Louisiana; or 2) the children of a member of the SAME Louisiana Post (who may be studying at a college or university in any state). Graduate students are not eligible; high school seniors may be considered if no suitable college students apply. Selection is based primarily on academic record and demonstration of leadership characteristics; other factors considered are participation in SAME posts and activities, enrollment in an ROTC program, former or current military service, and participation in school and community activities.

Financial data The stipend is $2,000.

Duration 1 year; nonrenewable.

Number awarded 1 or more each year.

Deadline April of each year.

[102] LOWE'S AMVETS TECHNOLOGY SCHOLARSHIPS

AMVETS National Headquarters
Attn: National Programs Director
4647 Forbes Boulevard
Lanham, MD 20706-3807
(301) 459-9600   Toll Free: (877) 7-AMVETS, ext. 4027
Fax: (301) 459-7924   E-mail: klathroum@amvets.org
Web: www.amvets.org

Summary To provide financial assistance to veterans, military personnel, and their spouses who are working on a degree in computer sciences.

Eligibility This program is open to veterans, active-duty military members, and their spouses who are U.S. citizens; children are not eligible. Applicants must be enrolled as sophomores, juniors, or seniors at a college or university and working on a degree in computer science. They must have a GPA of 3.0 or higher.

Financial data Stipends range up to $5,000.

Duration 1 year.

Additional information This program is supported by Lowe's.

Number awarded 10 each year.

Deadline July of each year.

[103]
LT RUTH CORTES MEMORIAL SCHOLARSHIP
American Academy of Physician Assistants-Veterans Caucus
Attn: Scholarship Program
P.O. Box 362
Ossining, NY 10562
(803) 328-1864   Fax: (704) 838-8494
E-mail: rmunsee@veteranscaucus.org
Web: www.veteranscaucus.org/scholarships

Summary To provide financial assistance to female veterans who are studying to become physician assistants.

Eligibility This program is open to U.S. citizens who are currently enrolled in a physician assistant program. Applicants must be women who are honorably discharged members of any branch of the uniformed services. Along with their application, they must submit a personal statement about what led them to attend PA school; their background, present, and future intentions; and why they deserve to receive a scholarship. Selection is based on honors and awards received, civic and college honors and awards received, professional memberships and activities, potential for future achievement, and GPA.

Financial data The stipend is $2,000.
Duration 1 year.
Number awarded 1 each year.
Deadline February of each year.

[104]
LUCILE PARRISH WARD VETERAN'S AWARD
National Federation of Music Clubs
1646 West Smith Valley Road
Greenwood, IN 46142
(317) 882-4003   Fax: (317) 882-4019
E-mail: info@nfmc-music.org
Web: www.nfmc-music.org

Summary To provide financial assistance to music students whose careers have been delayed or interrupted as a result of their service in the U.S. armed forces.

Eligibility This program is open to undergraduate and graduate students who are majoring in music and whose musical careers were interrupted by service in the armed forces. Veterans who served overseas receive preference. Applicants must be U.S. citizens, but membership in the National Federation of Music Clubs (NFMC) is not required. They must submit a 30-minute performance/audition recording. Selection is based on worthiness, character, background, musical talent, potential ability, and financial need.

Financial data The stipend is $2,250.
Duration 1 year; may be renewed if the recipient maintains a GPA of 3.0 or higher.
Additional information The entry fee is $20.
Number awarded 1 each year.
Deadline April of each year.

[105]
MAINE VIETNAM VETERANS SCHOLARSHIP FUND
Maine Community Foundation
Attn: Program Director
245 Main Street
Ellsworth, ME 04605
(207) 667-9735   Toll Free: (877) 700-6800
Fax: (207) 667-0447   E-mail: info@mainecf.org
Web: www.mainecf.org

Summary To provide financial assistance for college or graduate school to Vietnam veterans or the dependents of Vietnam or other veterans in Maine.

Eligibility This program is open to residents of Maine who are Vietnam veterans or the descendants of veterans who served in the Vietnam Theater. As a second priority, children of veterans from other time periods are also considered. Graduating high school seniors, nontraditional students, undergraduates, and graduate students are eligible to apply. Selection is based on financial need, extracurricular activities, work experience, academic achievement, and a personal statement of career goals and how the applicant's educational plans relate to them.

Financial data The stipend is $1,000 per year.
Duration 1 year.
Additional information This program began in 1985. There is a $3 processing fee.
Number awarded 3 to 6 each year.
Deadline April of each year.

[106]
MAJOR GENERAL DUANE L. "DUKE" CORNING MEMORIAL SCHOLARSHIP
South Dakota National Guard Enlisted Association
c/o Derek Jaeger, Scholarship Chair
7713 West 53rd Street
Sioux Falls, SD 57106
E-mail: derek.e.jaeger.mil@mail.mil
Web: sdngea.com/programs/scholarships

Summary To provide financial assistance to current and retired members of the South Dakota National Guard Enlisted Association (SDNGEA), the National Guard Association of South Dakota (NGASD), or their dependents who are interested in attending college in any state.

Eligibility This program is open to current and retired members of the SDNGEA and the NGASD and the dependents of current and retired members of those associations. Applicants must be graduating high school seniors or full-time undergraduate students at a college or university in any state. They must submit a 300-page autobiography that includes their experiences to date and their hopes and plans for the future. Selection is based on the essay; awards, honors, and offices in high school, college, or trade school; GPA and ACT/SAT scores; letters of recommendation; and extracurricular and community activities and honors.

Financial data The stipend is $1,000.
Duration 1 year; nonrenewable.
Number awarded 2 each year.
Deadline March of each year.

[107]
MAJOR RICHARD L. RIDDER MEMORIAL SCHOLARSHIP

Central Indiana Community Foundation
Attn: Scholarship Program
615 North Alabama Street, Suite 119
Indianapolis, IN 46204-1498
(317) 634-2423   Fax: (317) 684-0943
E-mail: scholarships@cicf.org
Web: www.cicf.org/scholarships

Summary To provide financial assistance to children of current or former members of the Indiana National Guard who are interested in attending college in the state.

Eligibility This program is open to seniors graduating from high schools in Indiana who are a current or former member of the Indiana National Guard or the child of such a member. Applicants must be planning to attend a college, university, or vocational/technical school in any state. They must have a GPA of 2.0 or higher and be able to demonstrate financial need or other significant barrier to completing a postsecondary degree.

Financial data The stipend is at least $1,000.

Duration 1 year.

Number awarded 1 or more each year.

Deadline February of each year.

[108]
MARCELLA ARNOLD NURSING SCHOLARSHIP

VFW Auxiliary-Department of Minnesota
Attn: Scholarship Committee
20 West 12th Street, Floor 3
St. Paul, MN 55155-2002
(651) 291-1759   Fax: (661) 291-7932
E-mail: vfwamn@vfwamn.org

Summary To provide financial assistance to residents of Minnesota who are either eligible for membership in the Veterans of Foreign Wars (VFW) or the VFW Auxiliary or the child or grandchild of a member and interested in studying nursing at a school in the state.

Eligibility This program is open to residents of Minnesota enrolled full time at a school or nursing in the state and working on an associate degree, bachelor's degree, or L.P.N. certificate; the scholarship is designed to help fund the final year of study. Applicants must be eligible to join the VFW or the VFW Auxiliary or be the child or grandchild of a VFW or Auxiliary member. Along with their application, they must submit essays on how the scholarship will make a difference for them and if they would be willing to work at a Veterans Administration medical center or veterans home.

Financial data A stipend is awarded (amount not specified).

Duration 1 year.

Additional information This program began in 1981.

Number awarded 1 each year.

Deadline March of each year for fall; September of each year for spring.

[109]
MARGUERITE MC'ALPIN MEMORIAL SCHOLARSHIP

American Legion Auxiliary
Department of Washington
Attn: Education Chair
3600 Ruddell Road S.E.
P.O. Box 5867
Lacey, WA 98509-5867
(360) 456-5995   Fax: (360) 491-7442
E-mail: secretary@walegion-aux.org
Web: www.walegion-aux.org/EducationScholarships.html

Summary To provide financial assistance to Washington veterans or their descendants who are interested in working on an undergraduate or graduate degree in nursing at a school in any state.

Eligibility This program is open to residents of Washington who are veterans or the children, grandchildren, and great-grandchildren of veterans. Applicants must be interested in studying nursing on the undergraduate or graduate level at a school in any state. Selection is based on a 300-word essay on their desire to study nursing, character, leadership, scholastic history, and financial need.

Financial data The stipend is $1,000.

Duration 1 year.

Number awarded 1 each year.

Deadline February of each year.

[110]
MARIA C. JACKSON/GENERAL GEORGE A. WHITE SCHOLARSHIP

Oregon Office of Student Access and Completion
Attn: Scholarships
1500 Valley River Drive, Suite 100
Eugene, OR 97401-2146
(541) 687-7400   Toll Free: (800) 452-8807
Fax: (541) 687-7414   TDD: (800) 735-2900
E-mail: osac@hecc.oregon.gov
Web: app.oregonstudentaid.gov/Catalog/Default.aspx

Summary To provide financial assistance to veterans and children of veterans and military personnel in Oregon who are interested in attending college or graduate school in the state.

Eligibility This program is open to residents of Oregon who served, or whose parents are serving or have served, in the U.S. armed forces. Applicants or their parents must have resided in Oregon at the time of enlistment. They must be enrolled or planning to enroll at a college or graduate school in the state. College and university undergraduates must have a GPA of 3.75 or higher, but there is no minimum GPA requirement for graduate students or those attending a technical school. Selection is based on scholastic ability and financial need.

Financial data Stipends for scholarships offered by the Oregon Office of Student Access and Completion (OSAC) range from $1,000 to $10,000 but recently averaged $4,710.

Duration 1 year.

Number awarded Varies each year.

Deadline February of each year.

SCHOLARSHIPS: VETERANS

[111]
MARILYN HAINES MUSIC SCHOLARSHIP
Veterans of Foreign Wars of the United States-
   Department of Nebraska
Attn: Scholarship Chair
2431 North 48th Street
Lincoln, NE 68504
(402) 464-0674   Fax: (402) 464-0675
E-mail: Johnl@vfwne.org
Web: vfwne.com/di/vfw/v2/default.asp?pid=6204

Summary To provide financial assistance to members of the Veterans of Foreign Wars (VFW), the VFW Auxiliary, and their families in Nebraska who wish to study music at a college in the state.

Eligibility This program is open to members of the Nebraska chapter of the VFW, the VFW Auxiliary, and their spouses, children, stepchildren, and grandchildren. Applicants must be majoring in music and have completed at least 1 year of full-time study at a college or university in Nebraska. They must be able to demonstrate financial need.

Financial data A stipend is awarded (amount not specified).

Duration 1 year.

Number awarded 1 or more each year.

Deadline March of each year.

[112]
MARINE CORPS LEAGUE SCHOLARSHIPS
Marine Corps League
Attn: Foundation
2904 Cross Creek Drive
Cumming, GA 30040
(404) 547-6631   E-mail: jerryholt813@gmail.com
Web: www.mclfoundation.org/scholarship-program

Summary To provide college aid to students whose parents served in the Marines and to members of the Marine Corps League or Marine Corps League Auxiliary.

Eligibility This program is open to 1) children of Marines, Navy FMF Corpsmen, and Navy Chaplains serving with Marine Units who were killed in action; 2) spouses, children, grandchildren, great-grandchildren, and stepchildren of active Marine Corps League and/or Auxiliary members; and 3) members of the Marine Corps League and/or Marine Corps League. Applicants must be seeking further education and training as a full-time student and be recommended by the commandant of an active chartered detachment of the Marine Corps League or the president of an active chartered unit of the Auxiliary. They must have a GPA of 3.0 or higher. Financial need is not considered in the selection process.

Financial data A stipend is awarded (amount not specified). Funds are paid directly to the recipient.

Duration 1 year; may be renewed up to 3 additional years upon reapplication.

Number awarded Varies, depending upon the amount of funds available each year.

Deadline July of each year.

[113]
MARINES' MEMORIAL FAMILY SCHOLARSHIPS
Marines' Memorial Association
c/o Marines Memorial Club and Hotel
609 Sutter Street
San Francisco, CA 94102
(415) 673-6672, ext. 293   Toll Free: (800) 5-MARINE
Fax: (415) 441-3649
E-mail: scholarship@marineclub.com
Web: www.marinesmemorial.org/members/scholarships

Summary To provide financial assistance for college to members of the Marines' Memorial Association from all branches of the armed forces and their descendants.

Eligibility This program is open to active members of the association and their children and grandchildren. Applicants must be high school seniors or students currently enrolled full time in an undergraduate degree program in any field at a college or university. Along with their application, they must submit an essay of up to 500 words on why they chose their specific path of study, what they hope to accomplish after graduation with their degree, and how their efforts will benefit others in their community. Graduating high school seniors must submit a high school transcript and SAT or ACT scores; continuing college students must submit a college transcript. Selection is based on the essay, academic merit, references, and financial need.

Financial data The stipend ranges from $2,500 to $5,000 per year.

Duration 1 year; recipients may reapply for up to 3 additional years.

Additional information Membership in the association is open to veterans of the Marines, Army, Navy, Air Force, or Coast Guard and to personnel currently serving in a branch of the armed forces.

Number awarded 8 each year.

Deadline April of each year.

[114]
MARINES' MEMORIAL TRIBUTE SCHOLARSHIPS
Marines' Memorial Association
c/o Marines Memorial Club and Hotel
609 Sutter Street
San Francisco, CA 94102
(415) 673-6672, ext. 293   Toll Free: (800) 5-MARINE
Fax: (415) 441-3649
E-mail: scholarship@marineclub.com
Web: www.marinesmemorial.org

Summary To provide financial assistance to military personnel who are transitioning from active duty to civilian or Reserve status and wish to attend college.

Eligibility This program is open to military personnel who have separated from full-time active duty to civilian or Reserve status within the past 3 years. Applicants must be enrolled or planning to enroll full time in an accredited undergraduate or graduate degree program in any field at a college or university. Membership in the sponsoring organization is not required. Along with their application, they must submit an essay of up to 500 words on why they chose their specific path of study, what they hope to accomplish after graduation with their degree, and how their efforts will benefit others in their community. Applicants entering college as freshmen must submit a high school transcript and SAT or ACT scores;

continuing college students must submit a college transcript. Selection is based on the essay, academic merit, references, and financial need.
Financial data The stipend ranges from $2,500 to $5,000 per year.
Duration 1 year; recipients may reapply for up to 3 additional years.
Number awarded 8 each year.
Deadline April of each year.

[115]
MARYLAND VETERANS OF AFGHANISTAN AND IRAQ CONFLICTS SCHOLARSHIP PROGRAM
Maryland Higher Education Commission
Attn: Office of Student Financial Assistance
6 North Liberty Street, Ground Suite
Baltimore, MD 21201
(410) 767-3300   Toll Free: (800) 974-0203
Fax: (410) 332-0250   TDD: (800) 735-2258
E-mail: osfamail.mhec@maryland.gov
Web: www.mhec.maryland.gov

Summary To provide financial assistance for college to residents of Maryland who served in the armed forces in Afghanistan or Iraq and their children and spouses.
Eligibility This program is open to Maryland residents who are 1) a veteran who served at least 60 days in Afghanistan on or after October 24, 2001 or in Iraq on or after March 19, 2003; 2) an active-duty member of the armed forces who served at least 60 days in Afghanistan or Iraq on or after those dates; 3) a member of a Reserve component of the armed forces or the Maryland National Guard who was activated as a result of the Afghanistan or Iraq conflicts and served at least 60 days; and 4) the children and spouses of such veterans, active-duty armed forces personnel, or members of Reserve forces or Maryland National Guard. Applicants must be enrolled or accepted for enrollment in a regular undergraduate program at an eligible Maryland institution. In the selection process, veterans are given priority over dependent children and spouses.
Financial data The stipend is equal to 50% of the annual tuition, mandatory fees, and room and board of a resident undergraduate at a 4-year public institution within the University System of Maryland, currently capped at $7,316 per year for students who live on campus, at $4,570 for students who live with their parents, or at %5,140 for students who live off campus.
Duration 1 year; may be renewed for an additional 3 years of full-time study or 7 years of part-time study, provided the recipient remains enrolled in an eligible program with a GPA of 2.5 or higher.
Number awarded Varies each year.
Deadline February of each year.

[116]
MERRILYN STOCK/EVELYN OLIVER MEMORIAL SCHOLARSHIP
American Legion Auxiliary
Department of Alaska
Attn: Barb Nath, Secretary
P.O. Box 242304
Anchorage, AK 99524
(907) 277-8169   E-mail: aladofak@gmail.com
Web: www.alaskalegionauxiliary.org/Education.htm

Summary To provide financial assistance to nontraditional students in Alaska who have a tie to the American Legion.
Eligibility This program is open to residents of Alaska who are members or children of members of the American Legion, American Legion Auxiliary, or Sons of the American Legion. Applicants must be nontraditional students accepted or enrolled at an accredited college, university, or vocational/technical institution in any state to enhance their job skills so they can enter or reenter the work field at a higher level. Along with their application, they must submit brief essays on why receiving this scholarship would be important to them; the course of study they plan to pursue and why; their involvement in school, church, and community activities; and why they think United States patriotic organizations, such as the American Legion, are important to the world today. Selection is based on character (25%), Americanism (25%), leadership (25%), and financial need (25%).
Financial data A stipend is awarded (amount not specified).
Duration 1 year.
Number awarded 1 each year.
Deadline Applications must be submitted to the unit president by February of each year.

[117]
MG BENJAMIN J. BUTLER "CENTURY DIVISION" SCHOLARSHIP PROGRAM
Association of the Century, Inc.
Attn: Scholarship Committee
P.O. Box 34393
Louisville, KY 40232
Web: www.the-century.org/scholarship.htm

Summary To provide financial assistance for college to members of the United States Army 100th Infantry Division and their descendants.
Eligibility This program is open to active, retired, or former members of the Army 100th Infantry Division (or any of its successor designations), their direct lineal descendants, and their adopted dependents. Applicants must be enrolled or planning to enroll at an accredited college or university. They must have a GPA of 2.5 or higher. Along with their application, they must submit a 250-word essay on how this scholarship will help them achieve their goals. Selection is based on academic excellence, qualities of good citizenship and patriotism, letters of recommendation, and financial need.
Financial data The stipend is $1,000 per year.
Duration 1 year; may be renewed 1 additional year.
Additional information This program, which began in 2008, is managed by the Community Foundation of Louisville.

Number awarded Varies each year; recently, 5 were awarded.
Deadline June of each year.

[118]
MILDRED R. KNOLES SCHOLARSHIPS
American Legion Auxiliary
Department of Illinois
2720 East Lincoln Street
P.O. Box 1426
Bloomington, IL 61702-1426
(309) 663-9366   Fax: (309) 663-5827
E-mail: karen.boughan@ilala.org
Web: www.ilala.org/education.html

Summary To provide financial assistance to Illinois veterans and their descendants who are attending college in any state.
Eligibility This program is open to veterans who served during designated periods of wartime and their children, grandchildren, and great-grandchildren. Applicants must be currently enrolled at a college or university in any state and studying any field except nursing. They must be residents of Illinois or members of the American Legion Family, Department of Illinois. Along with their application, they must submit a 1,000-word essay on "What My Education Will Do for Me." Selection is based on that essay (25%) character and leadership (25%), scholarship (25%), and financial need (25%).
Financial data The stipend is $1,000.
Duration 1 year.
Number awarded 1 or more each year.
Deadline March of each year.

[119]
MILITARY BENEFIT ASSOCIATION SCHOLARSHIPS
Military Benefit Association
Attn: Member Services Department
14605 Avion Parkway
P.O. Box 221110
Chantilly, VA 20153-1110
(703) 968-6200   Toll Free: (800) 336-0100
Fax: (703) 968-6423
Web: www.militarybenefit.org

Summary To provide financial assistance for college to children of insured members of the Military Benefit Association (MBA).
Eligibility This program is open to 1) unmarried dependent children under 26 years of age of insured MBA members; 2) MBA sponsored spouse members or dependent spouses of MBA members; 3) MBA members who are National Guard members or Reservists; and 4) MBA members who are Veterans. Applicants must be enrolled or planning to enroll as a full-time undergraduate student at an accredited 2- or 4-year college, university, or vocational/technical school. They must have a GPA of 2.5 or higher.
Financial data The stipend is $2,300.
Duration 1 year.
Additional information The MBA is an organization that provides insurance to active-duty and retired servicemembers, full-time federal government employees, honorably discharged servicemembers, National Guard, Reservists, uniformed officers of the United States Public Health Service or National Oceanic and Atmospheric Administration, cadets and midshipmen at the military academies, and the spouses of all those categories. This program is administered by Scholarship Management Services, a division of Scholarship America.
Number awarded 20 each year.
Deadline February of each year.

[120]
MILITARY COLLEGE SCHOLARSHIP
Low VA Rates
384 South 400 West, Suite 100
Lindon, UT 84042
Toll Free: (855) 581-7341   E-mail: hr@lowvarates.com
Web: www.lowvarates.com/scholarship

Summary To provide financial assistance for college to military personnel, veterans, and children of military personnel.
Eligibility This program is open to students who are nominated by a family member, a friend, or the student themselves. Nominees must be active service military members, veterans, or children with a parent serving in a branch of the U.S. armed forces. Along with their application, they must submit brief statements on how they are associated with the military, why they feel they qualify for this scholarship, their educational and career goals and what they plan to do with their degree, and how the military has positively impacted their life.
Financial data The stipend is $1,250 per semester.
Duration 1 semester.
Number awarded 2 each year: 1 from the winter applications and 1 from the fall applications.
Deadline December of each year for the winter application; August of each year for the fall application.

[121]
MILITARY INTELLIGENCE CORPS ASSOCIATION SCHOLARSHIPS
Military Intelligence Corps Association
Attn: Scholarship Committee
P.O. Box 13020
Fort Huachuca, AZ 85670-3020
(520) 227-3894   E-mail: dfa@micorps.org
Web: www.mica-national.org/category/press-release

Summary To provide financial assistance for college to members of the Military Intelligence Corps Association (MICA) and their immediate family.
Eligibility This program is open to active-duty, Reserve, National Guard, and retired military intelligence soldiers who are MICA members and to their immediate family (spouses, children, or other relatives living with and supported by the MICA member). Applicants must be attending or accepted for attendance at an accredited college, university, vocational school, or technical institution. Along with their application, they must submit a 1-page essay on their educational goals and program of study. Financial need is not considered in the selection process.
Financial data Stipend amounts vary depending on the availability of funds and the number of qualified applicants, but recently were $5,000. Funds are to be used for tuition, books, and classroom fees; support is not provided for housing, board, travel, or administrative purposes.
Duration 1 year; recipients may reapply.

Number awarded 10 each year.
Deadline May of each year.

[122]
MILITARY ORDER OF THE PURPLE HEART SCHOLARSHIP PROGRAM

Military Order of the Purple Heart
Attn: Scholarship Manager
5413-B Backlick Road
Springfield, VA 22151-3960
(703) 642-5360   Toll Free: (888) 668-1656
Fax: (703) 642-2054
E-mail: scholarship@purpleheart.org
Web: www.purpleheart.org

Summary To provide financial assistance for college or graduate school to members of the Military Order of the Purple Heart (MOPH) and their families.
Eligibility This program is open to 1) members of the MOPH who received a Purple Heart; 2) spouses and widows of MOPH members; 3) direct descendants (children, stepchildren, adopted children, and grandchildren) of veterans who are MOPH members or were members at the time of death; and 4) spouses, widows, widowers, and direct descendants of veterans killed in action or who died of wounds. Applicants must be graduating seniors or graduates of an accredited high school who are enrolled or accepted for enrollment in a full-time program of study in a college, university, or trade school. They must have a GPA of 2.75 or higher. U.S. citizenship is required. Along with their application, they must submit an essay of 200 to 300 words on a topic that changes annually but recently asked how they will use their education to serve their country and its citizens. Financial need is not considered in the selection process.
Financial data The stipend is approximately $2,500 per year.
Duration 1 year; may be renewed up to 2 additional years.
Additional information Membership in MOPH is open to all veterans who received a Purple Heart Medal and were discharged under conditions other than dishonorable. This program includes the Navy SEAL LT Michael Murphy Memorial Award. A processing fee of $15 is required.
Number awarded Approximately 8 each year.
Deadline January of each year.

[123]
MILITARY SCHOLARSHIP ESSAY CONTEST

EducationDynamics, LLC
Attn: eLearners
111 River Street, Tenth Floor
Hoboken, NJ 07030
(201) 377-3000   Toll Free: (888) 567-2008
Web: www.elearners.com

Summary To recognize and reward, with college scholarships, veterans, military personnel, and their spouses who submit outstanding essays on the effect of their military service.
Eligibility This competition is open to active-duty servicemembers, veterans, and their spouses who are enrolled or planning to enroll at an accredited college, university, or trade school. Applicants must submit a 250-word essay on how their military service has better prepared them to enhance their education. The winner is selected on the basis of writing ability (25%), creativity (25%), originality (25%), and overall excellence (25%).
Financial data The award is a $1,000 scholarship.
Duration The competition is held annually.
Number awarded 1 each year.
Deadline February of each year.

[124]
MILITARY VETERAN AUTOMOTIVE TECHNICIAN SCHOLARSHIP

CPS Products
1010 East 31st Street
Hialeah, FL 33013
(305) 687-4121   Toll Free: (800) 277-3808
Fax: (305) 687-3743   E-mail: cs@cpsproducts.com
Web: www.StarEnviroTech.com

Summary To provide financial assistance to military veterans who interested in studying automotive technology.
Eligibility This program is open to active, retired, or otherwise honorably discharged U.S. military veterans from any branch of service. Applicants must be enrolled or planning to enroll at an automotive, heavy-duty, or diesel technician training program at a college, university, or certified automotive vocational program. They must have a GPA of 2.5 or higher. Selection is based on military service, academic achievement, career goals, recommendations, and financial need.
Financial data The stipend is $1,000.
Duration 1 year.
Additional information This program was established by Star EnviroTech, which was acquired by CPS Products in 2016. Applications are submitted through the website of the University of the Aftermarket Foundation.
Number awarded 1 each year.
Deadline March of each year.

[125]
MINNESOTA G.I. BILL PROGRAM

Minnesota Department of Veterans Affairs
Attn: Programs and Services Division
20 West 12th Street, Room 206
St. Paul, MN 55155
(651) 296-2562   Toll Free: (888) LINK-VET
Fax: (651) 296-3954   TDD: (800) 627-3529
E-mail: MNGIBill@state.mn.us
Web: www.mn.gov

Summary To provide financial assistance for college or graduate school in the state to residents of Minnesota who served in the military after September 11, 2001 and the families of deceased or disabled military personnel.
Eligibility This program is open to residents of Minnesota enrolled at colleges and universities in the state as undergraduate or graduate students. Applicants must be 1) a veteran who is serving or has served honorably in a branch of the U.S. armed forces at any time; 2) a non-veteran who has served honorably for a total of 5 years or more cumulatively as a member of the Minnesota National Guard or other active or Reserve component of the U.S. armed forces, and any part of that service occurred on or after September 11, 2001; or 3) a surviving child or spouse of a person who has served in the military at any time and who has died or has a total and permanent disability as a result of that military service. They may be attending college in the state or participating in an appren-

ticeship or on-the-job (OJT) training program. Financial need is also considered in the selection process.
Financial data The college stipend is $1,000 per semester for full-time study or $500 per semester for part-time study. The maximum award is $3,000 per academic year or $10,000 per lifetime. Apprenticeship and OJT students are eligible for up to $2,000 per fiscal year. Approved employers are eligible to receive $1,000 placement credit payable upon hiring a person under this program and another $1,000 after 12 consecutive months of employment. No more than $3,000 in aggregate benefits under this paragraph may be paid to or on behalf of an individual in one fiscal year, and not more than $9,000 over any period of time.
Duration 1 year; may be renewed, provided the recipient continues to make satisfactory academic progress.
Additional information This program was established by the Minnesota Legislature in 2007.
Number awarded At least 1,000 each year.
Deadline Deadline not specified.

[126]
MINNESOTA NATIONAL GUARD ENLISTED ASSOCIATION AUXILIARY MINUTEMAN SCHOLARSHIPS
Minnesota National Guard Enlisted Association Auxiliary
c/o Carol Benda, Treasurer and Scholarship Chair
3280 30th Street
Slayton, MN 56172
E-mail: cbenda@mchsi.com
Web: www.mngea.com/minuteman-scholarship

Summary To provide financial assistance to members of the Minnesota National Guard Enlisted Association (MNGEA), its Auxiliary, and the families of the Association and Auxiliary who are interested in attending college in any state.
Eligibility This program is open to high school seniors, GED recipients, and students currently enrolled at colleges and universities in any state. Applicants must be active annual or life MNGEA members, active MNGEA Auxiliary members, or the unmarried children, stepchildren, or grandchildren under 26 years of age of those members. They must have a GPA of 2.5 or higher for their most recent academic term. Along with their application, they must submit an essay on their educational goals and how this scholarship will benefit those.
Financial data Stipends are $1,000 or $500.
Duration 1 year; nonrenewable.
Additional information The $1,000 scholarship is sponsored by USAA Insurance Corporation.
Number awarded Varies each year; recently, 4 were awarded.
Deadline March of each year.

[127]
MINNESOTA NATIONAL GUARD EXTENDED STATE TUITION REIMBURSEMENT
Minnesota National Guard
Attn: Education Office
600 Cedar Street
St. Paul, MN 5510-2509
(651) 282-4589   Toll Free: (800) 657-3848
Fax: (651) 282-4694
E-mail: ng.mn.mnarng.mbx.assets-education@mail.mil
Web: minnesotanationalguard.ng.mil/education

Summary To provide financial assistance for college or graduate school to former members of the Minnesota National Guard.
Eligibility Eligible for this program are former members of the Minnesota Army or Air National Guard who have satisfactorily completed their service contract or the portions of it involving selective reserve status, of which any part of that service was spent in federal active service or federally-funded state active duty after September 11, 2001. Applicants must be enrolled as undergraduate or graduate students at colleges or universities in Minnesota. Reimbursement is provided for undergraduate courses completed with a grade of "C" or better or for graduate courses completed with a grade of "B" or better. Eligibility extends for 2 years after honorable completion of the National Guard service contract, plus an amount of time equal to the duration of active service. For Guard members who served honorably and were separated or discharged because of a service-connected injury, disease, or illness, eligibility is extended for 8 years beyond the date of separation.
Financial data The maximum reimbursement rate is 100% of the tuition rate at the University of Minnesota Twin Cities campus for undergraduate study or 50% for graduate work, with a maximum benefit of $18,000 per fiscal year for undergraduate course work or $20,000 per fiscal year for graduate course work.
Duration 1 semester, to a maximum of 18 credits per semester; may be renewed until completion of an associate, bachelor's, master's, or doctoral degree or 144 semester credits, whichever comes first.
Number awarded Varies each year.
Deadline Deadline not specified.

[128]
MISSOURI AMERICAN LEGION COMMANDER'S SCHOLARSHIPS
American Legion
Department of Missouri
3341 American Avenue
P.O. Box 179
Jefferson City, MO 65102-0179
(573) 893-2353   Toll Free: (800) 846-9023
Fax: (573) 893-2980   E-mail: info@missourilegion.org
Web: www.missourilegion.org/scholarships

Summary To provide financial assistance to veterans in Missouri who are interested in attending college in the state.
Eligibility This program is open to residents of Missouri who served at least 90 days in the U.S. armed forces and received an honorable discharge. Applicants must be enrolled or planning to enroll full time at an accredited vocational/technical school, college, or university in Missouri.

Financial data The stipend is $1,000.
Duration 1 year.
Number awarded 2 each year.
Deadline April of each year.

[129]
MONTANA HONORABLY DISCHARGED VETERAN WAIVER
Office of the Commissioner of Higher Education
Attn: Montana University System
State Scholarship Coordinator
560 North Park Avenue, Fourth Floor
P.O. Box 203201
Helena, MT 59620-3201
(406) 449-9168   Toll Free: (800) 537-7508
Fax: (406) 449-9171
E-mail: mtscholarships@montana.edu
Web: www.mus.edu

Summary To provide financial assistance for undergraduate or graduate studies to selected Montana veterans.
Eligibility This program is open to honorably-discharged veterans who served with the U.S. armed forces and who are residents of Montana. Only veterans who at some time qualified for U.S. Department of Veterans Affairs (VA) educational benefits, but who are no longer eligible or have exhausted their benefits, are entitled to this waiver. Veterans who served any time prior to May 8, 1975 are eligible to work on undergraduate or graduate degrees. Veterans whose service began after May 7, 1975 are eligible only to work on their first undergraduate degree. They must have received an Armed Forces Expeditionary Medal for service in Lebanon, Grenada, or Panama; served in a combat theater in the Persian Gulf between August 2, 1990 and April 11, 1991 and received the Southwest Asia Service Medal; were awarded the Kosovo Campaign Medal; or served in a combat theater in Afghanistan or Iraq after September 11, 2001 and received the Global War on Terrorism Expeditionary Medal, the Afghanistan Campaign Medal, or the Iraq Campaign Medal. Financial need must be demonstrated.
Financial data Veterans eligible for this benefit are entitled to attend any unit of the Montana University System without payment of registration or incidental fees.
Duration Students are eligible for continued fee waiver as long as they make reasonable academic progress as full-time students.
Number awarded Varies each year.
Deadline Deadline not specified.

[130]
MONTGOMERY GI BILL (ACTIVE DUTY)
Department of Veterans Affairs
Attn: Veterans Benefits Administration
810 Vermont Avenue, N.W.
Washington, DC 20420
(202) 418-4343   Toll Free: (888) 442-4551
Web: www.va.gov

Summary To provide financial assistance for college, graduate school, and other types of postsecondary schools to new enlistees in any of the armed forces after they have completed their service obligation.
Eligibility This program is open to veterans who received an honorable discharge and have a high school diploma, a GED, or, in some cases, up to 12 hours of college credit; veterans who already have a bachelor's degree are eligible to work on a master's degree or higher. Applicants must have had their military pay reduced by $100 per month for the first 12 months of service. They must also meet the detailed requirements of 4 special categories; for specifics, contact the Department of Veterans Affairs (VA). Following completion of their service obligation, participants may enroll in colleges or universities for associate, bachelor, or graduate degrees; in courses leading to a certificate or diploma from business, technical, or vocational schools; for apprenticeships or on-the-job training programs; in correspondence courses; in flight training; for preparatory courses necessary for admission to a college or graduate school; for licensing and certification tests approved for veterans; or in state-approved teacher certification programs.
Financial data Stipends depend on the length of service, the type of education or training program, and the special category in which the veteran falls. Recently, basic rates for institutional raining for veterans who completed an enlistment of 3 or more years was $2,050 per month and for those with an enlistment of less than 3 years $1,664 per month. Rates for other types of training were generally lower.
Duration 36 months; active-duty servicemembers must utilize the funds within 10 years of leaving the armed services; Reservists may draw on their funds while still serving.
Additional information Further information is available from local armed forces recruiters. This was the basic VA education program, referred to as Chapter 30, until the passage of the Post-9/11 GI Bill in 2009. Veterans who have remaining benefits available from this program may utilize those or transfer to the new program.
Number awarded Varies each year.
Deadline Deadline not specified.

[131]
MSSDAR VETERANS SCHOLARSHIP
Daughters of the American Revolution-Missouri State Society
c/o Patsy West, Veterans Scholarship Committee Chair
24 Willow Hill Road
St. Louis, MO 63124-2055
(314) 503-3271   E-mail: DAR@websitewiz.com
Web: www.mssdar.org/state-scholarships

Summary To provide financial assistance to veterans from Missouri who are interested in attending college in the state.
Eligibility This program is open to residents of Missouri who are military veterans, including Guard and Reserve members. Applicants must have served for at least 90 days and been honorably discharged. They must have a high school diploma or GED and be enrolled or planning to enroll at an accredited Missouri college or university. Along with their application, they must submit a resume detailing military duty and awards, volunteer activities, community service, and employment during the past 3 years, along with a 250-word essay on their career goal. U.S. citizenship is required.
Financial data The stipend is $1,000.
Duration 1 year.
Number awarded 1 or more each year.
Deadline January of each year.

SCHOLARSHIPS: VETERANS

[132]
NANCY AND BARRY CARLSON SCHOLARSHIP
American Welding Society
Attn: AWS Foundation, Inc.
8669 N.W. 36th Street, Suite 130
Doral, FL 33166-6672
(305) 443-9353   Toll Free: (800) 443-9353, ext. 250
Fax: (305) 443-7559   E-mail: foundation@aws.org
Web: www.aws.org

Summary To provide financial assistance to veterans who are studying welding.

Eligibility This program is open to honorably-discharged veterans who are enrolled full time in at least the second year of a 2- or 4-year welding-related program. They must be U.S. citizens and have a GPA of 2.8 or higher.

Financial data The stipend is $2,500 per year; funds are paid directly to the educational institution.

Duration 1 year; may be renewed for 1 additional year of a 2-year program or 3 additional years of a 4-year program.

Additional information This program began in 2013.

Number awarded 1 each year.

Deadline February of each year.

[133]
NATIONAL 4TH INFANTRY (IVY) DIVISION ASSOCIATION ANNUAL EDUCATIONAL SCHOLARSHIP
National 4th Infantry (IVY) Division Association
c/o Don Kelby, Executive Director
P.O. Box 1914
St. Peters, MO 63376-0035
(314) 606-1969   E-mail: 4thidaed@swbell.net
Web: www.4thinfantry.org/content/scholarships-donations

Summary To provide financial assistance for college to members of the National 4th Infantry (IVY) Division Association and their families.

Eligibility This program is open to 1) association members in good standing; 2) children and grandchildren of members; and 3) spouses of members while the member is a soldier on active duty. Recipients are chosen by lottery.

Financial data The stipend is $2,000.

Duration 1 year; may be renewed.

Additional information The trust fund from which these scholarships are awarded was created by the officers and enlisted men of the 4th Infantry Division as a living memorial to the men of the division who died in Vietnam. Originally, it was only open to children of members of the division who died in the line of duty while serving in Vietnam between August 1, 1966 and December 31, 1977. When all those eligible had completed college, it adopted its current requirements.

Number awarded Up to 10 each year.

Deadline June of each year.

[134]
NATIONAL GUARD ASSOCIATION OF CALIFORNIA SCHOLARSHIPS
National Guard Association of California
Attn: Executive Director
3336 Bradshaw Road, Suite 230
Sacramento, CA 95827-2615
(916) 362-3411   Toll Free: (800) 647-0018
Fax: (916) 362-3707
Web: www.ngac.org/ngac-scholarship-program-2

Summary To provide financial assistance to members of the National Guard Association of California (NGAC) and their dependents who are interested in attending college in any state.

Eligibility This program is open to 1) current members of the NGAC; 2) dependents of NGAC members; and 3) dependents of retired California National Guard servicemembers who are life members of the NGAC. Applicants must be attending or planning to attend a college, university, or trade school in any state. Along with their application, they must submit a 500-word essay on the greatest challenge they have faced and how it has impacted them. Selection is based on that essay; unweighted GPA; extracurricular activities, honors, and/or awards; letters of recommendation; and (for high school seniors and college students with less than 2 semesters of completed courses) SAT or ACT scores.

Financial data Stipends range from $250 to $1,000. Funds are paid directly to the recipient.

Duration 1 year.

Number awarded Varies each year; recently, 19 were awarded.

Deadline May of each year.

[135]
NATIONAL GUARD ASSOCIATION OF MARYLAND SCHOLARSHIPS
National Guard Association of Maryland
Attn: Scholarship Committee
P.O. Box 16675
Baltimore, MD 21221-0675
(410) 557-2606   Toll Free: (800) 844-1394
Fax: (410) 893-7529
E-mail: nationalguardassociationmd@gmail.com
Web: www.ngam.net/scholarship-application

Summary To provide financial assistance to members of the National Guard Association of Maryland (NGAM) and their family members who are interested in attending college in any state.

Eligibility This program is open to NGAM members (including current and former members of the National Guard) and their spouses and children. Applicants must be enrolled or planning to enroll full or part time at an accredited college, university, or vocational/technical school in any state. They must submit a resume in which they outline their academic background, activities in which they have participated, and honors they have received; 3 letters of recommendation; an essay on their goals and how this scholarship will assist them; and information on financial need.

Financial data The stipend is $1,000. Funds are paid directly to the recipient's university to be used for tuition, fees, and books.

Duration 1 year; recipients may reapply.

Number awarded Varies each year; recently, 11 were awarded.
Deadline March of each year.

[136]
NATIONAL GUARD ASSOCIATION OF MINNESOTA SCHOLARSHIPS

National Guard Association of Minnesota
Attn: Executive Director
P.O. Box 131766
St. Paul, MN 55113-0020
(651) 503-7993   E-mail: director@ngamn.org
Web: www.ngamn.org/scholarships

Summary To provide financial assistance to current and retired members of the National Guard Association of Minnesota (NGAMN) and their families who are interested in working on an undergraduate or graduate degree at a school in any state.

Eligibility This program is open to active members and retired life members of NGAMN and their spouses, children, and grandchildren. Applicants must be high school seniors or students currently enrolled at least half time at an accredited institution of higher learning in any state and working on a 4-year bachelor's or graduate degree. They must have a GPA of 2.75 or higher. Along with their application, they must submit an essay on a topic that describes a value of the Army or Air Force, rotating among loyalty, duty, respect, selfless service, honor, integrity, personal courage, commitment, and excellence. Financial need is not considered in the selection process.

Financial data Stipends are $1,000 or $500. Funds are paid directly to the recipient.

Duration 1 year. Recipients may reapply after 3 years.

Additional information The $1,000 scholarship is sponsored by McGough Construction Company. This program began in 2008.

Number awarded 3 each year: 1 at $1,000 and 2 at $500 (1 to a member or retired member and 1 to a spouse, child, or grandchild).

Deadline June of each year.

[137]
NATIONAL GUARD ASSOCIATION OF NEW HAMPSHIRE SCHOLARSHIPS

National Guard Association of New Hampshire
Attn: Scholarship Committee
P.O. Box 22031
Portsmouth, NH 03802-2031
(603) 227-1597   E-mail: nganhscholarship@gmail.com
Web: www.nganh.org/benefits

Summary To provide financial assistance to members of the National Guard Association of New Hampshire and their dependents who are interested in attending college or graduate school in any state.

Eligibility This program is open to current members of the National Guard Association of New Hampshire (officer, enlisted, or retired), their spouses, and their dependent children. Applicants must be enrolled or planning to enroll full or part time in an associate, bachelor's, graduate, professional, or doctoral degree program at an accredited college or university in any state. Along with their application, they must submit a 1-page essay on a topic that changes annually; recently, they were asked to describe what citizen service means to them.

Financial data The stipend is $1,000.
Duration 1 year.
Number awarded 1 each year.
Deadline April of each year.

[138]
NATIONAL GUARD ASSOCIATION OF TEXAS SCHOLARSHIP PROGRAM

National Guard Association of Texas
Attn: Education Committee
3706 Crawford Avenue
Austin, TX 78731-6803
(512) 454-7300   Toll Free: (800) 252-NGAT
Fax: (512) 467-6803   E-mail: tbz@ngat.org
Web: www.ngat.org/education.htm

Summary To provide financial assistance to members and dependents of members of the National Guard Association of Texas who are interested in attending college or graduate school in any state.

Eligibility This program is open to annual and life members of the association and their spouses and children (associate members and their dependents are not eligible). Applicants may be high school seniors, undergraduate students, or graduate students, either enrolled or planning to enroll at an institution of higher education in any state. Along with their application, they must submit an essay on their desire to continue their education. Selection is based on scholarship, citizenship, and leadership.

Financial data Stipends range from $500 to $5,000.
Duration 1 year (nonrenewable).

Additional information This program includes the Len and Jean Tallas Memorial Scholarship, the Texas Capital Area Chapter of the AUSA Scholarship, the Lewis O. King Memorial Scholarship, the Gloria Jenell and Marlin E. Mote Endowed Scholarship, the LTC Gary Parrish Memorial Scholarship, the TXNG Retirees Endowed Scholarship, and 2 scholarships sponsored by USAA Insurance Corporation.

Number awarded Varies each year; recently, 8 were awarded: 1 at $5,000, 1 at $4,000, 1 at $2,000, 1 at $1,250, 3 at $1,000, and 1 at $500.

Deadline February of each year.

[139]
NAVAL HELICOPTER ASSOCIATION SCHOLARSHIPS

Naval Helicopter Association
Attn: Scholarship Fund
P.O. Box 180578
Coronado, CA 92178-0578
(619) 435-7139   Fax: (619) 435-7354
E-mail: pres@nhascholarshipfund.org
Web: www.nhascholarshipfund.org/about/scholarships

Summary To provide financial assistance for college or graduate school to members of the Naval Helicopter Association (NHA) and their families.

Eligibility This program is open to NHA members and their spouses, children, and grandchildren. Membership in the NHA is open to active-duty and retired U.S. Navy, U.S. Marine Corps, and U.S. Coast Guard helicopter pilots, aircrew, and maintenance professionals. Applicants must be working on or planning to work on an undergraduate or graduate degree in any field. Along with their application, they must submit a personal statement on their academic and career aspirations. Selection is based on that statement, academic proficiency, scholastic achievements and awards, extracurricular activities, employment history, and letters of recommendation. The program includes scholarships 1) reserved for NHA family members; 2) reserved for active-duty personnel; 3) sponsored by private corporations; 4) named as memorials in honor of distinguished individuals; and 5) awarded on a regional basis.

Financial data Stipends are approximately $2,000.
Duration 1 year.
Additional information Corporate sponsors have included FLIR Systems, D.P. Associates, L-3 Communications, CAE, Raytheon Corporation, Lockheed Martin (designated the Sergei Sikorsky Scholarship), and Northrop Grumman. Memorial Scholarships have included the Edward and Veronica Ream Memorial Scholarship, the CDR Mort McCarthy Memorial Scholarship, the Charles Karman Memorial Scholarship, the LT Christian "Horse" Hescock Memorial Scholarship, and the Captain Mark Starr Memorial Scholarship.
Number awarded Varies each year; recently, 17 were awarded: 1 graduate student family member, 3 active-duty graduate students, 1 active-duty undergraduate student, 4 sponsored by corporate donors, 4 memorial scholarships, and 4 regional scholarships.
Deadline January of each year.

[140]
NBCUNIVERSAL-SVA SCHOLARSHIPS

Student Veterans of America
Attn: Scholarship Committee
1012 14th Street, N.W., Suite 1200
Washington, DC 20005
(202) 223-4710
E-mail: scholarships@studentveterans.org
Web: www.studentveterans.org

Summary To provide financial assistance to veterans who are working on an undergraduate or graduate degree in a field related to the media and entertainment industry.
Eligibility This program is open to veterans who are currently enrolled at an accredited institution of higher education. Applicants must be working on an associate, bachelor's, or graduate degree in film, media, television, journalism, or communications. They must be U.S. citizens or eligible to work in the United States. Along with their application, they must submit essays of 300 to 500 words on 1) their previous leadership experiences during their military service and beyond and how they have carried those experiences forward in the classroom or in other university activities; and 2) why they are interested in NBCUniversal and a career in the entertainment industry. Financial need is not considered in the selection process.
Financial data The stipend is $12,000.
Duration 1 year.
Additional information This program, which began in 2014, is supported by NBCUniversal and administered by Student Veterans of America (SVA).
Number awarded 2 each year.
Deadline November of each year.

[141]
NEW MEXICO VIETNAM VETERAN SCHOLARSHIPS

New Mexico Department of Veterans' Services
Attn: State Benefits
407 Galisteo Street, Room 134
P.O. Box 2324
Santa Fe, NM 87504-2324
(505) 383-2400   Toll Free: (866) 433-VETS
Fax: (505) 827-6372 E-mail: JosephM.Dorn@state.nm.us
Web: www.nmdvs.org/state-benefits

Summary To provide financial assistance to Vietnam veterans in New Mexico who are interested in working on an undergraduate or master's degree at a public college in the state.
Eligibility This program is open to Vietnam veterans who have been residents of New Mexico for at least 10 years. Applicants must have been honorably discharged and have been awarded the Vietnam Service Medal or the Vietnam Campaign Medal. They must be planning to attend a state-supported college, university, or community college in New Mexico to work on an undergraduate or master's degree. Awards are granted on a first-come, first-served basis.
Financial data The scholarships provide full payment of tuition and purchase of required books at any state-funded postsecondary institution in New Mexico.
Duration 1 year.
Number awarded Varies each year.
Deadline Deadline not specified.

[142]
NEW MEXICO WARTIME VETERAN SCHOLARSHIP FUND

New Mexico Department of Veterans' Services
Attn: State Benefits
407 Galisteo Street, Room 134
P.O. Box 2324
Santa Fe, NM 87504-2324
(505) 383-2400   Toll Free: (866) 433-VETS
Fax: (505) 827-6372 E-mail: JosephM.Dorn@state.nm.us
Web: www.nmdvs.org/state-benefits

Summary To provide financial assistance to residents of New Mexico who served in the military after 1990 and are interested in working on an undergraduate or master's degree at a public college in the state.
Eligibility This program is open to veterans who have been residents of New Mexico for at least 10 years and have been awarded the Southwest Asia Service Medal, Global War on Terrorism Expeditionary Medal, Iraq Campaign Medal, Afghanistan Campaign Medal, or any other medal issued for service in the U.S. armed forces in support of any U.S. military campaign or armed conflict as defined by Congress or presidential executive order for service after August 1, 1990. Applicants must have exhausted all available federal G.I. education benefits. They must be interested in attending a state-supported college, university, or community college in New Mexico to work on an undergraduate or master's degree. Awards are granted on a first-come, first-served basis.
Financial data The scholarships provide full payment of tuition and purchase of required books at any state-funded postsecondary institution in New Mexico.
Duration 1 year.

Number awarded Varies each year.
Deadline Deadline not specified.

[143]
NEW YORK MILITARY ENHANCED RECOGNITION INCENTIVE AND TRIBUTE (MERIT) SCHOLARSHIPS

New York State Higher Education Services Corporation
Attn: Student Information
99 Washington Avenue
Albany, NY 12255
(518) 473-1574   Toll Free: (888) NYS-HESC
Fax: (518) 473-3749   TDD: (800) 445-5234
E-mail: scholarships@hesc.com
Web: www.hesc.ny.gov

Summary To provide financial assistance to disabled veterans and the family members of deceased or disabled veterans who are residents of New York and interested in attending college in the state.

Eligibility This program is open to New York residents who served in the armed forces of the United States or state organized militia at any time on or after August 2, 1990 and became severely and permanently disabled as a result of injury or illness suffered or incurred in a combat theater or combat zone or during military training operations in preparation for duty in a combat theater or combat zone of operations. Also eligible are the children, spouses, or financial dependents of members of the armed forces of the United States or state organized militia who at any time after August 2, 1990 1) died, became severely and permanently disabled as a result of injury or illness suffered or incurred, or are classified as missing in action in a combat theater or combat zone of operations; 2) died as a result of injuries incurred in those designated areas; or 3) died or became severely and permanently disabled as a result of injury or illness suffered or incurred during military training operations in preparation for duty in a combat theater or combat zone of operations. Applicants must be attending or accepted at an approved program of study as full-time undergraduates at a public college or university or private institution in New York.

Financial data At public colleges and universities, this program provides payment of actual tuition and mandatory educational fees; actual room and board charged to students living on campus or an allowance for room and board for commuter students; and allowances for books, supplies, and transportation. At private institutions, the award is equal to the amount charged at the State University of New York (SUNY) for 4-year tuition and average mandatory fees (or the student's actual tuition and fees, whichever is less) plus allowances for room, board, books, supplies, and transportation. Recently, maximum awards were $24,250 for students living on campus or $15,750 for commuter students.

Duration This program is available for 4 years of full-time undergraduate study (or 5 years in an approved 5-year bachelor's degree program).

Additional information This program was previously known as the New York State Military Service Recognition Scholarships (MSRS).

Number awarded Varies each year; recently, 134 students received more than $2.1 million from this program.

Deadline April of each year.

[144]
NEW YORK VETERANS TUITION AWARDS

New York State Higher Education Services Corporation
Attn: Student Information
99 Washington Avenue
Albany, NY 12255
(518) 473-1574   Toll Free: (888) NYS-HESC
Fax: (518) 473-3749   TDD: (800) 445-5234
E-mail: scholarships@hesc.com
Web: www.hesc.ny.gov

Summary To provide tuition assistance to eligible veterans enrolled in an undergraduate or graduate program in New York.

Eligibility This program is open to veterans who served in the U.S. armed forces in 1) Indochina between February 1, 1961 and May 7, 1975; 2) hostilities that occurred after February 28, 1961 as evidenced by receipt of an Armed Forces Expeditionary Medal, Navy Expeditionary Medal, or Marine Corps Expeditionary Medal; 3) the Persian Gulf on or after August 2, 1990; or 4) Afghanistan on or after September 11, 2001. Applicants must have been discharged from the service under honorable conditions, must be a New York resident, must be a U.S. citizen or eligible noncitizen, must be enrolled full or part time at an undergraduate or graduate degree-granting institution in New York or in an approved vocational training program in the state, must be charged at least $200 tuition per year, and must apply for a New York Tuition Assistance Program (TAP) award.

Financial data For full-time study, the maximum stipend is equivalent to tuition charged to New York residents at the State University of New York (SUNY) or actual tuition charged, whichever is less. For part-time study, the stipend is based on the number of credits certified and the student's actual part-time tuition.

Duration For full-time undergraduate study, up to 8 semesters, or up to 10 semesters for a program requiring 5 years for completion; for full-time graduate study, up to 6 semesters; for full-time vocational programs, up to 4 semesters. Awards for part-time undergraduate study are available for up to 16 semesters, or 20 semesters for a 5-year program; for part-time graduate study, up to 12 semesters; for part-time vocational study, up to 8 semesters.

Additional information If a TAP award is also received, the combined academic year award cannot exceed tuition costs. If it does, the TAP award will be reduced accordingly.

Number awarded Varies each year; recently, 738 veterans received more than $2.7 million from this program.

Deadline April of each year.

[145]
NGAI MEMBER EDUCATIONAL GRANTS

National Guard Association of Indiana
Attn: Educational Grant Committee
2002 South Holt Road, Building 5
Indianapolis, IN 46241-4839
(317) 247-3196   Toll Free: (800) 219-2173
Fax: (317) 247-3575   E-mail: membership@ngai.net
Web: www.myngai.org/benefits-2/grants

Summary To provide financial assistance to members of the National Guard Association of Indiana (NGAI) and their dependents who plan to attend college in any state.

SCHOLARSHIPS: VETERANS

Eligibility This program is open to NGAI members and their dependents who are currently serving in the Indiana National Guard or are retired members of the Indiana National Guard. Applicants must be attending or planning to attend a college or university in any state. Along with their application, they must submit 2 letters of recommendation, a copy of high school or college transcripts, SAT or ACT scores (if taken), a letter of acceptance from a college or university (if not currently attending college), and a 2-page essay on the educational program they intend to pursue and the goals they wish to attain. Selection is based on academic achievement, commitment and desire to achieve, extracurricular activities, accomplishments, goals, and financial need.
Financial data The stipend is $1,000.
Duration 1 year; may be renewed up to 3 additional years.
Number awarded 10 each year: 5 for members and 5 for dependents.
Deadline March of each year.

[146]
NGAOK SCHOLARSHIPS
National Guard Association of Oklahoma
c/o Scholarship Foundation
Attn: Rosemary Masters, Scholarship Chair
3501 Military Circle
Oklahoma City, OK 73111
(405) 823-0799   E-mail: ngaok.scholarship@gmail.com
Web: www.ngaok.org/benefits

Summary To provide financial assistance to members of the National Guard Association of Oklahoma (NGAOK) and their dependents who are interested in attending college in any state.
Eligibility This program is open to NGAOK members and their dependent children and spouses who are enrolled or planning to enroll full or part time in an undergraduate or graduate program at a college or university in any state. The primary next of kin of members of the Oklahoma National Guard killed in action after September 11, 2001 are considered life members of NGAOK. Applicants must submit transcripts that include ACT and/or SAT scores; lists of awards and recognitions, community and volunteer services, and extracurricular and sports activities; and a 500-word essay about how they exemplify the traits of selfless service, leadership, character, and their aspirations. Financial need is not considered in the selection process.
Financial data Stipends are $500 or $1,000.
Duration 1 year.
Number awarded 20 to 25 each year.
Deadline January of each year.

[147]
NGARI SCHOLARSHIP PROGRAM
National Guard Association of Rhode Island
Attn: Scholarship Committee
645 New London Avenue
Cranston, RI 02920-3097
(401) 228-6586   Fax: (401) 541-9182
E-mail: ngarinews@gmail.com
Web: www.ngari.org/scholarships

Summary To provide financial assistance to current and former members of the Rhode Island National Guard and their children who plan to attend college in any state.
Eligibility This program is open to active and retired members of the Rhode Island National Guard and their children. Applicants must be high school seniors, high school graduates, or undergraduate students. They must be attending or accepted at an accredited college, university, or vocational/technical school in any state. As part of their application, they must describe any needs, goals, and other factors that may help the selection committee.
Financial data The stipend is $1,000.
Duration 1 year; nonrenewable.
Number awarded Varies each year; recently, 4 were awarded.
Deadline May of each year.

[148]
NICHOLAS D. CHABRAJA SCHOLARSHIP
Association of the United States Army
Attn: Scholarships
2425 Wilson Boulevard
Arlington, VA 22201
(703) 841-4300   Toll Free: (800) 336-4570
E-mail: scholarships@ausa.org
Web: www.ausa.org/resources/scholarships

Summary To provide financial assistance to members of the Association of the United States Army (AUSA) who are interested in studying a field of STEM in college.
Eligibility This program is open to AUSA members who are enrolled or accepted at an accredited college or university to work on a degree in a field of STEM. Along with their application, they must submit a 1-page autobiography, 2 letters of recommendation, a letter describing their career aspirations (including their course of study and plans for completion of a degree), and a transcript of high school or college grades (depending on which they are currently attending). Selection is based on academic merit and personal achievement. Financial need is not normally a selection criterion but in some cases of extreme need it may be used as a factor; the lack of financial need, however, is never a cause for nonselection.
Financial data The stipend is $5,000; funds are sent directly to the recipient's college or university.
Duration 1 year.
Additional information Membership in the AUSA is open to everyone who supports a strong national defense, with special concern for the Army. That includes Regular Army, National Guard, Army Reserve, government civilians, retired soldiers, Wounded Warriors, veterans, concerned citizens and family members.
Number awarded 6 each year.
Deadline June of each year.

[149]
NJ HIMSS VETERANS AWARD

Healthcare Information and Management Systems
  Society-New Jersey Chapter
c/o Jim Hennessy, Scholarship Committee Chair
e4 Services, LLC
139 West Market Street, Suite C
West Chester, PA 19382
(610) 247-4951   Toll Free: (888) 443-4782
Fax: (888) 521-7874
E-mail: jhennessy@e4-services.com
Web: www.njhimss.org/scholarship

Summary To provide financial assistance to veterans from New Jersey who are working on an undergraduate or graduate degree in a field related to health care information and management.

Eligibility This program is open to veterans who are residents of New Jersey attending college in any state or residents of other states attending college in New Jersey. Applicants must be working on an undergraduate or graduate degree in a field related to health care information and management, such as health care informatics, health care computer science and information systems, health care policy, and quantitative programs in business administration or hospital administration. They must have a GPA of 3.0 or higher. Along with their application, they must submit a 500-word essay on how they will impact the arena of health care informatics and/or health care technology.

Financial data The stipend is $4,000.
Duration 1 year.
Number awarded 1 each year.
Deadline May of each year.

[150]
NORTH CAROLINA NATIONAL GUARD ASSOCIATION ACADEMIC EXCELLENCE AND LEADERSHIP SCHOLARSHIPS

North Carolina National Guard Association
Attn: Educational Foundation, Inc.
7410 Chapel Hill Road
Raleigh, NC 27607-5047
(919) 851-3390, ext. 5
Toll Free: (800) 821-6159 (within NC)
Fax: (919) 859-4990   E-mail: edfoundation@ncnga.org
Web: www.edfoundationofncnga.org

Summary To provide financial assistance to members and dependents of members of the North Carolina National Guard Association who demonstrate academic excellence and are attending college in any state.

Eligibility This program is open to active and associate members of the association as well as the spouses, children, grandchildren, and legal dependents of active, associate, or deceased members. Applicants must be high school seniors or students currently attending a 4-year college or university in any state and have a GPA of 3.5 or higher. Selection is based on academic and leadership achievements.

Financial data The stipend is $1,200.
Duration 1 year; may be renewed.
Number awarded 2 each year: 1 to a high school senior and 1 to a current college student.
Deadline January of each year for high school graduates and college students; February of each year for high school seniors.

[151]
NORTH CAROLINA NATIONAL GUARD ASSOCIATION CITIZENSHIP SCHOLARSHIPS

North Carolina National Guard Association
Attn: Educational Foundation, Inc.
7410 Chapel Hill Road
Raleigh, NC 27607-5047
(919) 851-3390, ext. 5
Toll Free: (800) 821-6159 (within NC)
Fax: (919) 859-4990   E-mail: edfoundation@ncnga.org
Web: www.edfoundationofncnga.org

Summary To provide financial assistance to members and dependents of members of the North Carolina National Guard Association who demonstrate outstanding achievement in citizenship and are attending college in any state.

Eligibility This program is open to active and associate members of the association as well as the spouses, children, grandchildren, and legal dependents of active, associate, or deceased members. Applicants must be high school seniors or students currently attending a 4-year college or university in any state. Selection is based on achievements and activities that contribute to their schools and communities.

Financial data The stipend is $1,200.
Duration 1 year; may be renewed.
Number awarded 2 each year: 1 to a high school senior and 1 to a current college student.
Deadline January of each year for high school graduates and college students; February of each year for high school seniors.

[152]
NORTH CAROLINA NATIONAL GUARD ASSOCIATION SCHOLARSHIPS

North Carolina National Guard Association
Attn: Educational Foundation, Inc.
7410 Chapel Hill Road
Raleigh, NC 27607-5047
(919) 851-3390, ext. 5
Toll Free: (800) 821-6159 (within NC)
Fax: (919) 859-4990   E-mail: edfoundation@ncnga.org
Web: www.edfoundationofncnga.org

Summary To provide financial assistance to members and dependents of members of the North Carolina National Guard Association who plan to attend college in any state.

Eligibility This program is open to active and associate members of the association as well as the spouses, children, grandchildren, and legal dependents of active, associate, or deceased members. Applicants must be high school seniors, high school graduates, or students currently enrolled at a college or university in any state. Selection is based on financial need, academic achievement, citizenship, leadership, and other application information. The most outstanding applicants receive scholarships provided by the SECU Foundation. Applicants who meet specified additional requirements qualify for various memorial and special scholarships.

Financial data Stipends are $10,000 or $5,000 for the SECU Foundation Scholarships, $1,200 for scholarships to 4-year universities, or $600 for community college scholarships.
Duration 1 year; may be renewed.
Additional information This program, which began in 1968, includes a number of named memorial and special scholarships. Other scholarships are funded by the SECU Foundation of the State Employees' Credit Union and the USAA Insurance Corporation.
Number awarded Varies each year; recently, 46 with a value of $67,800 were awarded. Since this program was established, it has awarded 1,918 scholarships worth more than $1.5 million.
Deadline January of each year for high school graduates and college students; February of each year for high school seniors.

[153]
NORTH CAROLINA VIETNAM VETERANS SCHOLARSHIP PROGRAM

North Carolina Vietnam Veterans, Inc.
Attn: Scholarship Administrator
7316 Ray Road
Raleigh, NC 27613
E-mail: bkuhr@nc.rr.com
Web: www.ncvvi.org

Summary To provide financial assistance to North Carolina residents who are Vietnam veterans or the dependents of veterans and interested in attending college in any state.
Eligibility This program is open to current residents of Chatham, Durham, Franklin, Granville, Harnett, Johnston, Nash, or Wake counties in North Carolina who are either a Vietnam veteran or the veteran's spouse, child, foster child, adopted child, or grandchild. Families of members of North Carolina Vietnam Veterans, Inc. (NCVVI) who live in any county of the state are also eligible. Applicants must be attending or planning to attend a college, university, community college, or trade school in any state. They must submit a copy of the Department of Defense Form DD214 to document Vietnam service; a birth certificate and/or marriage license (as needed); a personal statement about themselves, including work experience, anticipated career, and goals; a list of current activities and awards; and an essay of 600 to 900 words on a topic that changes annually; recently, the topic related to the impact of the draft on the country during the Vietnam War.
Financial data Stipends range from $250 to $1,500. Funds are paid directly to the recipients on a reimbursement basis (presentation of paid receipts for tuition, fees, and/or books).
Duration 1 year.
Additional information This program includes the Mike Hooks Memorial Scholarship.
Number awarded 1 or more each year.
Deadline March of each year.

[154]
NORTHAMERICAN.COM MILITARY SCHOLARSHIP

North American Van Lines
One Parkview Plaza
Oakbrook Terrace, IL 60180
Toll Free: (800) 228-3092
Web: www.northamerican.com/military-scholarship

Summary To provide financial assistance to current and former military personnel and their families who are interested in attending college to study fields related to logistics.
Eligibility This program is open to current and honorably discharged members of the military, their spouses, and their children under 21 years of age or (if currently attending college) under 23 years of age. Applicants must be enrolled or planning to enroll full time at a 4-year college or university and major in military logistics, supply chain management, or operational management. They must be U.S. citizens or permanent residents and have a GPA of 2.5 or higher. Along with their application, they must submit an essay of 400 to 800 words on why a career in logistics/supply chain management is their college major of choice. Financial need is not considered in the selection process.
Financial data The stipend is $1,000.
Duration 1 year.
Additional information This program began in 2015.
Number awarded 2 each year.
Deadline September of each year.

[155]
NORTHROP RICE FOUNDATION VETERAN SCHOLARSHIP

Northrop Rice Foundation
12502 Brantly Avenue
Houston, TX 77034
(713) 644-6616   Fax: (281) 334-0335
E-mail: awards@northropricefoundation.org
Web: www.northropricefoundation.org

Summary To provide funding to veterans who are interested in preparing for a career as a civilian aviation maintenance technician.
Eligibility This program is open to honorably discharged veterans whose service experience included aircraft maintenance. First priority is given to applicants approved by the FAA to take the airframe and/or powerplant (A&P) written examinations. They must submit an essay that describes the aircraft and equipment on which they worked while they were in the military, their duties in aviation maintenance, the FAA written examinations they plan to take, and what they have done to prepare for the examinations. Second priority is given to honorably-discharged veterans working on an A&P license at an FAA-approved Part 147 school. Those applicants must submit a 5-paragraph essay: 1) general aviation goals and financial need; 2) desired future involvement in aviation; 3) how the award is needed by and will benefit the applicant; 4) involvement in school, employment, and community extracurricular activities; and 5) any other information the applicant would like considered.
Financial data The stipend is $1,000; funds may be used to cover the cost of reference text books, study guides, or test fees related to the FAA airframe and/or powerplant (A&P) written examinations.
Duration This is a 1-time award.

Number awarded Up to 2 each year.
Deadline January of each year.

[156]
OHIO AMVETS SERVICE FOUNDATION SCHOLARSHIPS

AMVETS-Department of Ohio
Attn: Service Foundation
1395 East Dublin Granville Road, Suite 222
Columbus, OH 43229-3314
(614) 431-6990　　　　Toll Free: (800) 642-6838
Fax: (614) 431-6991　　E-mail: admin@ohamvets.org
Web: www.ohamvets.org/forms

Summary To provide financial assistance for college in any state to veterans and their families from Ohio.

Eligibility This program is open to residents of Ohio who are veterans, the children or grandchildren of veterans, or the spouses of veterans. Applicants must be graduating high school seniors or students currently enrolled at a college or university in any state. They must have a GPA of 2.5 or higher. Along with their application, they must submit an autobiographical statement that includes why they desire this scholarship and their projected goals in life. Selection is based on academic aptitude and financial need.

Financial data The stipend is $1,000.
Duration 1 year; nonrenewable.
Number awarded 10 each year.
Deadline March of each year.

[157]
OHIO LEGION AUXILIARY DEPARTMENT PRESIDENT'S SCHOLARSHIP

American Legion Auxiliary
Department of Ohio
1100 Brandywine Boulevard, Suite D
P.O. Box 2760
Zanesville, OH 43702-2760
(740) 452-8245　　　　Fax: (740) 452-2620
E-mail: kelly@alaohio.org
Web: www.alaohio.org/Scholarships

Summary To provide financial assistance to veterans and their descendants in Ohio who are interested in attending college in any state.

Eligibility This program is open to honorably-discharged veterans and the children, grandchildren, and great-grandchildren of living, deceased, or disabled honorably-discharged veterans who served during designated periods of wartime. Applicants must be residents of Ohio, seniors at an accredited high school, planning to enter a college in any state, and sponsored by an American Legion Auxiliary Unit. Along with their application, they must submit an original article (up to 500 words) written by the applicant on a topic that changes annually. Recently, students were asked to write on "Education and the American Dream." Selection is based on character, Americanism, leadership, scholarship, and financial need.

Financial data Stipends are $1,500 or $1,000. Funds are paid to the recipient's school.
Duration 1 year.
Number awarded 2 each year: 1 at $1,500 and 1 at $1,000.
Deadline March of each year.

[158]
OHIO LEGION MEMBER/MILITARY VETERAN SCHOLARSHIP

American Legion
Department of Ohio
60 Big Run Road
P.O. Box 8007
Delaware, OH 43015
(740) 362-7478　　　　Fax: (740) 362-1429
E-mail: legion@ohiolegion.com
Web: www.ohiolegion.com/programs/scholarships

Summary To provide financial assistance to residents of Ohio who are members of the American Legion, veterans, or current military personnel and interested in attending college in any state.

Eligibility This program is open to residents of Ohio who are 1) members of the American Legion; 2) honorably discharged members of the armed forces; or 3) currently on active duty or a member of the National Guard or Reserves. Applicants must be attending or planning to attend colleges, universities, or other approved postsecondary schools in any state as an undergraduate or graduate student. They must have a GPA of 3.5 or higher and an ACT score of at least 25. Along with their application, they must submit a personal statement of 500 to 550 words on their career objectives. Selection is based on academic achievement as measured by course grades, ACT scores, difficulty of curriculum, participation in school and outside activities, and the judging committee's general impression.

Financial data Stipends are normally at least $2,000.
Duration 1 year.
Number awarded 1 each year.
Deadline April of each year.

[159]
PAST NATIONAL COMMANDER MICHAEL J. KOGUTEK SCHOLARSHIP

Erie County American Legion
Attn: Scholarship Committee
609 City Hall
65 Niagara Square
Buffalo, NY 14202
(716) 852-6500　　　　Fax: (716) 852-4664
E-mail: veteran14202@verizon.net
Web: www.eriecountyal.org

Summary To provide financial assistance to New York residents who are veterans, their families, or other students interested in attending college in any state.

Eligibility This program is open to residents of New York who are veterans, their families, or other students who share the values of the American Legion. Applicants must be enrolled or planning to enroll at a college or university in any state. Students entering from high school must enroll full time, but veterans and other students may enroll part time. Along with their application, they must submit a 500-word essay describing their proposed course of study, their career objectives and how this scholarship would help them attain those, and what they have achieved and learned through their studies and activities. Selection is based on academic ability, realistic goals, extracurricular activities, community involvement, and financial need.

Financial data The stipend is $1,500.

Duration 1 year.
Number awarded 2 each year.
Deadline April of each year.

[160]
PATRIOT EDUCATION FUND SCHOLARSHIPS

Patriot Education Fund
312 Park Avenue, Suite 31
Clarendon Hills, IL 60514
(773) 273-9601 E-mail: info@patrioteducationfund.org
Web: www.patrioteducationfund.secure-platform.com/a

Summary To provide financial assistance to enlisted veterans, their spouses, or their dependent children and interested in attending a college or university in any state.

Eligibility This program is open to enlisted veterans (E1-E5) who served after September 11, 2001, the spouses of those veterans, and the dependent children of those veterans. Applicants must be enrolled or planning to enroll full time at a college, university, or vocational/trade school in any state. They must be eligible to receive Post-9/11 GI Bill benefits but be able to demonstrate that they still have financial need because of a gap between the available benefits and the actual costs of tuition.

Financial data The amount of the assistance depends on the financial gap facing the veteran or family member. Funds are sent directly to the recipient's institution.

Duration Funding is provided until completion of a degree or certificate.

Additional information This program began in 2011.

Number awarded Varies each year; since the program began, it has awarded 122 scholarships.

Deadline March of each year.

[161]
PERSONAL MONEY SERVICE SCHOLARSHIP FOR VETERANS

Personal Money Service
1001 Bayhill Drive, Suite 200
San Bruno, CA 94066
Toll Free: (888) 373-0748
E-mail: admin@personalmoneyservice.com
Web: www.personalmoneyservice.com

Summary To provide financial assistance to military personnel and veterans who are interested in attending college in any state.

Eligibility This program is open to active-duty members of the U.S. military service and veterans. Applicants must be high school seniors or high school graduates who are enrolled or planning to enroll at a college or university in any state. They must be U.S. citizens or permanent residents. As part of the selection process, they must write a post that explains why they should be awarded this scholarship. They then make this post public on their Facebook or YouTube account with a link to Personal Money Service.

Financial data The stipend is $1,000.

Duration 1 year.

Number awarded 1 each year.

Deadline December of each year.

[162]
PETER CONNACHER MEMORIAL SCHOLARSHIPS

Oregon Office of Student Access and Completion
Attn: Scholarships
1500 Valley River Drive, Suite 100
Eugene, OR 97401-2146
(541) 687-7400 Toll Free: (800) 452-8807
Fax: (541) 687-7414 TDD: (800) 735-2900
E-mail: osac@hecc.oregon.gov
Web: app.oregonstudentaid.gov/Catalog/Default.aspx

Summary To provide financial assistance for college or graduate school to ex-prisoners of war and their descendants.

Eligibility Applicants must be U.S. citizens who 1) were military or civilian prisoners of war; or 2) are the descendants of ex-prisoners of war. They must be full-time undergraduate or graduate students. A copy of the ex-prisoner of war's discharge papers from the U.S. armed forces must accompany the application. In addition, written proof of POW status must be submitted, along with a statement of the relationship between the applicant and the ex-prisoner of war (father, grandfather, etc.). Selection is based on academic record and financial need. Preference is given to Oregon residents or their dependents.

Financial data Stipends for scholarships offered by the Oregon Office of Student Access and Completion (OSAC) range from $1,000 to $10,000 but recently averaged $4,710.

Duration 1 year; may be renewed for up to 3 additional years for undergraduate students or 2 additional years for graduate students. Renewal is dependent on evidence of continued financial need and satisfactory academic progress.

Additional information This program is administered by the OSAC with funds provided by the Oregon Community Foundation and by the Columbia River Chapter of American Ex-prisoners of War, Inc.

Number awarded Varies each year; recently, 4 were awarded.

Deadline February of each year.

[163]
PHILLIP COON SCHOLARSHIP

Muscogee (Creek) Nation of Oklahoma
Attn: Scholarship Foundation
P.O. Box 580
Okmulgee, OK 74447
(918) 732-7754 Toll Free: (800) 482-1979, ext. 7754
Fax: (918) 732-7756 E-mail: RWahnee@mcn-nsn.gov
Web: www.creeknationfoundation.org/scholarships

Summary To provide financial assistance to citizens of the Muscogee (Creek) Nation who are veterans and are interested in attending college in any state.

Eligibility This program is open to enrolled citizens of the Muscogee (Creek) Nation who are currently enrolled full time at an institution of higher education or entering as a first-time student. Applicants must be veterans and able to demonstrate financial need. Along with their application, they must submit transcripts and a 1-page statement on their goals, career choice, tribal community involvement, and how this scholarship will affect their college education.

Financial data The stipend is $1,000 per semester.

Duration 1 semester.

Number awarded 1 or more each year.
Deadline May of each year for fall semester; December of each year for spring semester.

[164]
PISCATAQUA POST SAME SCHOLARSHIPS
Society of American Military Engineers-Piscataqua Post
PWD Maine Building 59
Portsmouth, NH 03804
E-mail: samepiscataquapost@gmail.com
Web: www.same.org

Summary To provide financial assistance to high school seniors in Maine, Massachusetts, and New Hampshire, especially those interested in joining ROTC or with ties to the military, who are planning to attend college in any state to major in engineering or the physical sciences.
Eligibility This program is open to seniors graduating from high schools in Maine, Massachusetts, or New Hampshire and planning to attend a college or university in any state. Applicants must be interested in majoring in engineering or the physical sciences and enrolling in ROTC, especially if they do not receive an ROTC scholarship. They should be willing to attend meetings of the Society of American Military Engineers (SAME) to receive their scholarship and share their learning experiences. Preference is given to members and children of members of the Piscataqua Post of SAME, students who are enrolled in ROTC (preferably not ROTC scholarship recipients), and individuals with prior or current U.S. military service and their children.
Financial data The stipend is $1,500.
Duration 1 year.
Number awarded Up to 2 each year.
Deadline March or June of each year.

[165]
PORTLAND POST SOCIETY OF AMERICAN MILITARY ENGINEERS SCHOLARSHIP
Oregon Office of Student Access and Completion
Attn: Scholarships
1500 Valley River Drive, Suite 100
Eugene, OR 97401-2146
(541) 687-7400   Toll Free: (800) 452-8807
Fax: (541) 687-7414   TDD: (800) 735-2900
E-mail: osac@hecc.oregon.gov
Web: app.oregonstudentaid.gov/Catalog/Default.aspx

Summary To provide financial assistance to engineering students at public colleges in Oregon who have ties to the military.
Eligibility This program is open to residents of Oregon who will be entering their sophomore year of higher of full-time students of aeronautical, biomedical, chemical, civil, electrical, or mechanical engineering at a public college or university in the state. Applicants must have a GPA of 3.0 or higher. Along with their application, they must submit a 1-page essay on how their future career as an engineer integrates with the mission of the Society of American Military Engineers (SAME) to identify and resolve national security infrastructure-related challenges and the steps they have taken to prepare themselves for this challenge. Preference is given to ROTC students, National Guard Reservists, and prior service veterans. Financial need may or may not be considered in the selection process.
Financial data Stipends for scholarships offered by the Oregon Office of Student Access and Completion (OSAC) range from $1,000 to $10,000 but recently averaged $4,710.
Duration 1 year; may be renewed up to 3 additional years.
Additional information This program is sponsored by the SAME Portland Post.
Number awarded Varies each year.
Deadline February of each year.

[166]
POST-9/11 GI BILL
Department of Veterans Affairs
Attn: Veterans Benefits Administration
810 Vermont Avenue, N.W.
Washington, DC 20420
(202) 418-4343   Toll Free: (888) 442-4551
Web: www.va.gov/education/about-gi-bill-benefits/post-9-11

Summary To provide financial assistance to veterans or military personnel who entered service on or after September 11, 2001.
Eligibility This program is open to current and former military personnel who 1) served on active duty for at least 90 aggregate days after September 11, 2001; 2) were discharged with a service-connected disability after 30 days; or 3) received a Purple Heart on or after September 11, 2001 and were discharged after any length of service. Applicants must be planning to enroll in an educational program, including work on an undergraduate or graduate degree, vocational/technical training, on-the-job training, flight training, correspondence training, licensing and national testing programs, entrepreneurship training, and tutorial assistance.
Financial data Participants working on an undergraduate or graduate degree at public institutions in their state receive full payment of tuition and fees. For participants who attend private institutions in most states, tuition and fee reimbursement is capped at $25,162.14 per academic year. Benefits for other types of training programs depend on the amount for which the veteran qualified under prior educational programs. Veterans also receive a monthly housing allowance that is 1) based on the Department of Defense Basic Allowance for Housing (BAH) for an E-5 with dependents (which depends on the location of the school but ranges from approximately $1,000 per month to approximately $2,500 per month); 2) $1,789 per month at schools in foreign countries; or 3) $894.50 per month for online training classes. They also receive an annual book allowance of $1,000 and (for participants who live in a rural county remote from an educational institution) a rural benefit payment of $500 per year.
Duration Most participants receive up to 36 months of entitlement under this program. Benefits are payable for up to 15 years following release from active duty.
Additional information This program, referred to as Chapter 33, began in 2009 as a replacement for previous educational programs for veterans and military personnel (e.g., Montgomery GI Bill, REAP). Current participants in those programs may be able to transfer benefits from those programs to this new plan. To qualify for 100% of Post 9/11-GI Bill benefits, transferees must have at least 36 months of active-duty service. Transferees with less service are entitled to smaller percentages of benefits, ranging down to 40% for those with only 90 days of service.

SCHOLARSHIPS: VETERANS

Number awarded Varies each year; recently, approximately 700,000 veterans received $10.7 billion on benefits through this program.
Deadline Deadline not specified.

[167] PROVETS MILITARY SCHOLARSHIPS

ProNet International Gifts and Scholarships, Inc.
P.O. Box 31578
St. Louis, MO 63131
(636) 227-2471   Fax: (636) 391-3903
E-mail: info@pronetscholarships.org
Web: www.pronetscholarships.org/scholarships.htm

Summary To provide financial assistance for college to veterans and their children, especially those interested in studying ethics or preparing for a career in the insurance industry.
Eligibility This program is open to U.S. citizens who rank in the upper 20% of their high school class and have been admitted to a postsecondary educational program. Applicants must have served in the military or have a parent who served in the military. Preference is given to 1) veterans of a foreign war or the children of a veteran of a foreign war; or 2) plan to prepare for a career in the insurance industry and/or the study of ethics. Along with their application, they must submit a 1-page essay explaining their reasons for applying for this scholarship, the challenges they face, how the receipt of this funds will help them to attain their educational and/or career goals, and how they will benefit from this program. Financial need is considered in the selection process.
Financial data A stipend is awarded (amount not specified).
Duration 1 year.
Additional information This program includes the following named awards: the Carol Anne Abrams Memorial Scholarship, the William E. Brand, Jr. Memorial Scholarship, the Joseph P. Joseph Memorial Scholarship, the John D. Perrey, Sr. Memorial Scholarship, the Sgt. Lonnie Stephenson Memorial Scholarship, and the Arthur Robert "Bob" Troutt Memorial Scholarship.
Number awarded Varies each year.
Deadline Deadline not specified.

[168] PVA EDUCATIONAL SCHOLARSHIP PROGRAM

Paralyzed Veterans of America
Attn: Membership Department
801 18th Street, N.W.
Washington, DC 20006-3517
(202) 416-7776   Toll Free: (800) 424-8200, ext. 776
Fax: (202) 416-1250   TDD: (800) 795-HEAR
E-mail: members@pva.org
Web: www.pva.org/membership/scholarship-program

Summary To provide financial assistance for college to members of the Paralyzed Veterans of America (PVA) and their families.
Eligibility This program is open to PVA members, spouses of members, and unmarried dependent children of members under 24 years of age. Applicants must be attending or planning to attend an accredited U.S. college or university as a full- or part-time student. They must be U.S. citizens. Along with their application, they must submit a personal statement explaining why they wish to further their education, short- and long-term academic goals, how this will meet their career objectives, and how it will affect the PVA membership. Selection is based on that statement, academic records, letters of recommendation, and extracurricular and community activities.
Financial data The stipend is $1,000 for full-time students or $500 for part-time students.
Duration 1 year.
Additional information This program began in 1986.
Number awarded Varies each year; recently 11 were awarded.
Deadline June of each year.

[169] RANGER MEMORIAL SCHOLARSHIPS

National Ranger Memorial Foundation
Attn: Executive Secretary
P.O. Box 53369
Fort Benning, GA 31995
(706) 687-0906   E-mail: rangermemorial@gmail.com
Web: www.rangermemorial.com/scholarship

Summary To provide financial assistance for college to U.S. Army Rangers and their descendants.
Eligibility This program is open to Rangers from any era and their descendants; some awards (those offered by the Ranger Battalions Association of WWII) are limited to descendants of Rangers who served during the World War II era. Applicants must be graduating high school seniors or students currently enrolled at an accredited 2- or 4-year educational or technical institution. They must have a GPA of 3.0 or higher. Along with their application, they must submit information on their leadership activities, future goals and how they plan to attain those, and honors and awards received to date. Financial need is not considered in the selection process.
Financial data The stipend is $1,000.
Duration 1 year.
Additional information The National Ranger Memorial Foundation began awarding scholarships in 1999. The Ranger Battalions Association of WWII became a partner in 2007 and offered additional scholarships to descendants of World War II era Rangers.
Number awarded 49 each year: 45 offered by the National Ranger Memorial Foundation and 4 by the Ranger Battalions Association of WWII.
Deadline May of each year.

[170] RAYTHEON SPY-6 SCHOLARSHIPS

Student Veterans of America
Attn: Scholarship Committee
1012 14th Street, N.W., Suite 1200
Washington, DC 20005
(202) 223-4710
E-mail: scholarships@studentveterans.org
Web: www.studentveterans.org

Summary To provide financial assistance to U.S. Navy veterans who are working on an undergraduate or graduate degree in any field.
Eligibility This program is open to U.S. Navy veterans who have been honorably discharged and are currently enrolled

full-time at a 4-year college or university as an entering sophomore, junior, senior, or graduate student. Applicants may be working on a degree in any field. Along with their application, they must submit essays on 1) what they hope to accomplish with their degree; and 2) if they served on a Navy ship, an explanation of their experience. Financial need is not considered in the selection process.
Financial data The stipend is $10,000.
Duration 1 year.
Additional information This program, which began in 2013, is supported by Raytheon Company and administered by Student Veterans of America (SVA).
Number awarded 2 each year.
Deadline April of each year.

[171]
RECYCLING RESEARCH FOUNDATION VETERANS SCHOLARSHIP PROGRAM

Institute of Scrap Recycling Industries
Attn: Recycling Research Foundation, Inc.
1250 H Street, N.W., Suite 400
Washington, DC 20005
(202) 662-8524   Fax: (202) 624-9256
E-mail: ngrant@isri.org
Web: www.isri.org/about-isri/recycling-research-foundation

Summary To provide financial assistance to veterans interested in working on an undergraduate degree.
Eligibility This program is open to veterans who served at least 2 years on active duty or at least 4 years in a reserve capacity. Although the program is focused on those who have completed military service, it does not exclude members of the Ready Reserve who are in a non-drill pay or non-drill status. Applicants must be interested in enrolling at an accredited 4-year college or university, community college, or trade or vocational school. They must be U.S. citizens. Along with their application, they must submit essays on 1) how their military service changed their life; and 2) their professional goals and how this scholarship will help them achieve those.
Financial data The stipend is $2,000 per year. Funds are paid directly to the recipient's school.
Duration 1 year; may be renewed up to 3 additional years, provided the recipient maintains a GPA of 2.5 or higher.
Additional information This program began in 2013.
Number awarded 1 or more each year.
Deadline May of each year.

[172]
REES SCHOLARSHIP FOUNDATION VETERANS PROGRAM

Clifford H. "Ted" Rees, Jr. Scholarship Foundation
Attn: Mishi Adams
2111 Wilson Boulevard, Suite 200
Arlington, VA 22201
(703) 293-4854   E-mail: Madams@ahrinet.org
Web: www.reesscholarship.org/site/292/Apply

Summary To provide financial assistance to veterans preparing for a career in the heating, ventilation, air conditioning, and refrigeration (HVACR) industry.
Eligibility This program is open to veterans currently enrolled in an accredited HVACR training program. Applicants must submit transcripts, 2 letters of recommendation, documentation of veteran status, and a 500-word essay on why they should receive this scholarship, why they are interested in the HVACR field, and how they plan to use what they will learn to make an impact in Florida.
Financial data Stipends range up to $2,000. Funds are paid directly to the school's accounting department.
Duration Up to 1 year.
Number awarded Varies each year; recently 3 were awarded.
Deadline May of each year for fall semester; September of each year for spring semester.

[173]
RICHARD AND SUSAN BRAUN FAMILY SCHOLARSHIP

Marines' Memorial Association
c/o Marines Memorial Club and Hotel
609 Sutter Street
San Francisco, CA 94102
(415) 673-6672, ext. 293   Toll Free: (800) 5-MARINE
Fax: (415) 441-3649
E-mail: scholarship@marineclub.com
Web: www.marinesmemorial.org

Summary To provide financial assistance to veterans who are interested in attending college to major in any field.
Eligibility This program is open to veterans who have served in any branch of the U.S. armed forces and received an honorable discharge. Applicants must be interested in working full time on an undergraduate degree in any field. Membership in the sponsoring organization is not required. Along with their application, they must submit an essay of up to 500 words on why they chose their specific path of study, what they hope to accomplish after graduation with their degree, and how their efforts will benefit others in their community. Applicants entering college as freshmen must submit a high school transcript and SAT or ACT scores; continuing college students must submit a college transcript. Selection is based on the essay, academic merit, references, and financial need.
Financial data The stipend is $5,000 per year.
Duration 1 year; recipients may reapply for up to 3 additional years.
Number awarded 1 each year.
Deadline April of each year.

[174]
RICK HOPCRAFT MEMORIAL SCHOLARSHIP FOR VETERANS

Orange County Community Foundation
Attn: Scholarship Officer
4041 MacArthur Boulevard, Suite 510
Newport Beach, CA 92660
(949) 553-4202, ext. 246   Fax: (949) 553-4211
E-mail: mabril@oc-cf.org
Web: oc-cf.academicworks.com/opportunities/1546

Summary To provide financial assistance to veterans who are interested in attending specified universities in southern California to prepare for a career in commercial real estate.
Eligibility This program is open to veterans of service in the U.S. military who received an honorable discharge. Applicants must be enrolled or accepted for enrollment at Chapman University, California State University at Fullerton, the

SCHOLARSHIPS: VETERANS

University of California at Irvine, the University of Southern California, Pepperdine University, the University of California at San Diego, or a community college in Orange County. They must be preparing for a career in commercial real estate in Orange County and have a GPA of 2.5 or higher. Along with their application, they must submit a brief essay describing their military experience and their current academic interests and plans.
Financial data A stipend is awarded (amount not specified).
Duration 1 year.
Number awarded 1 or more each year.
Deadline March of each year.

[175]
RON PACE MEMORIAL SCHOLARSHIP
American Academy of Physician Assistants
Attn: Physician Assistant Foundation
2318 Mill Road, Suite 1300
Alexandria, VA 22314-6868
(571) 319-4510   E-mail: pafoundation@aapa.org
Web: app.smarterselect.com

Summary To provide financial assistance to student members of the American Academy of Physician Assistants (AAPA) who are veterans from Florida.
Eligibility This program is open to student members of the Florida Academy of Physician Assistants who have completed at least 1 semester of an accredited physician assistant program in Florida. Applicants must be veterans or dependent children of veterans.
Financial data The stipend is $1,000.
Duration 1 year; nonrenewable.
Number awarded 1 each year.
Deadline May of each year.

[176]
ROSAMOND P. HAEBERLE MEMORIAL SCHOLARSHIP
Daughters of the American Revolution-Michigan State Society
c/o LuDean Peters, Memorial Scholarship Committee
18403 Doris Street
Livonia, MI 48152
(248) 478-1345   E-mail: lu85lar@hotmail.com
Web: www.michdar.org

Summary To provide financial assistance to Michigan veterans and military personnel interested in attending college in the state.
Eligibility This program is open to residents of Michigan who have served on active duty in the U.S. armed forces (including Reserves and National Guard) for at least 6 continuous months and are either currently serving in the armed forces or have received a separation from active duty under honorable conditions. Applicants must be currently accepted to and/or enrolled at a 2- or 4-year accredited college, university, or trade/technical school in Michigan. They must be enrolled at least half time and have a cumulative high school or undergraduate GPA of 2.5 or higher. Along with their application, they must submit a 1-page essay on what serving their country has meant to them and how it has influenced their future goals and priorities. Selection is based on academic performance, extracurricular activities, community service, potential to succeed in an academic environment, financial need, and military service record.
Financial data The stipend is $1,500.
Duration 1 year.
Additional information This program began in 2007.
Number awarded At least 1 each year.
Deadline January of each year.

[177]
RUARK-WIGHT FAMILY SCHOLARSHIP
Marines' Memorial Association
c/o Marines Memorial Club and Hotel
609 Sutter Street
San Francisco, CA 94102
(415) 673-6672, ext. 293   Toll Free: (800) 5-MARINE
Fax: (415) 441-3649
E-mail: scholarship@marineclub.com
Web: www.marinesmemorial.org/members/scholarships

Summary To provide financial assistance to veterans, military personnel, and their families who are interested in attending college or graduate school to work on a degree in any field.
Eligibility This program is open to students who meet 1 of the following requirements: 1) have served honorably or is currently serving in any branch of the U.S. armed forces; or 2) is the spouse or child of a person who served honorably or is currently serving in any branch of the U.S. armed forces. Applicants must be enrolled as full-time sophomores, juniors, seniors or graduate students working on a degree in any field. They must have a GPA of 2.5 or higher. Membership in the sponsoring organization is not required for student veterans. Along with their application, they must submit an essay of up to 500 words on why they chose their specific path of study, what they hope to accomplish after graduation with their degree, and how their efforts will benefit others in their community. Selection is based on the essay, academic merit, references, and financial need.
Financial data The stipend is $5,000 per year.
Duration 1 year; recipients may reapply for up to 3 additional years.
Number awarded 1 each year.
Deadline April of each year.

[178]
RUBY GONZALES SCHOLARSHIP
Louisiana National Guard Enlisted Association Auxiliary
c/o Cheryl L. McGlothin, Scholarship Committee
2911 Effie Highway
Deville, LA 71328
(318) 253-8834
Web: www.langea.org/langea-auxiliary

Summary To provide financial assistance to members of the Louisiana National Guard Enlisted Association (LANGEA) and their dependents who plan to attend college in any state.
Eligibility This program is open to LANGEA members, their spouses and unmarried dependent children, and the unmarried spouses and unmarried dependent children of deceased members who were in good standing at the time of their death. Applicants must be enrolled or planning to enroll full time at an accredited college, university, trade school, or business school in any state. Along with their application,

they must submit a letter specifying their reasons for their desire to continue their education and why they need financial assistance.

Financial data The stipend is $2,000.
Duration 1 year; nonrenewable.
Number awarded 2 each year.
Deadline February of each year.

[179]
SAPA ANNUAL SCHOLARSHIP AWARDS

Society of Army Physician Assistants
Attn: Scholarship Committee
P.O. Box 623
Monmouth, IL 61462
(309) 734-5446   Fax: (309) 734-4489
E-mail: orpotter@aol.com
Web: www.sapa.org/scholarships

Summary To provide financial assistance to members of the Society of Army Physician Assistants (SAPA) and their families interested in attending college in any state to major in any field.
Eligibility This program is open to SAPA members, spouses of SAPA members, dependent children under 24 years of age of SAPA members, and spouses and children of deceased SAPA members. Applicants must be high school seniors or students currently enrolled at a college, university, or vocational school and working on a degree in any field or a license or certificate to practice a trade. There is no application form; interested parties submit a letter of introduction that includes why the grant is needed, educational goals, goals for the future, and anything else they feel would be of interest to the selection committee; a letter of acceptance from a school; a list of activities and achievements; and transcripts.
Financial data The stipend is $1,000.
Duration 1 year.
Additional information This program began in 2012. Membership in SAPA is open to graduates of approved physician assistant training programs commissioned as a physician assistant in the Active Duty Army, Army National Guard, Army Reserve, or honorably retired from those branches of service; they must also be members of the American Academy of Physician Assistants who have designated SAPA as their constituent chapter.
Number awarded 3 each year.
Deadline January of each year.

[180]
SCHNEIDER-EMANUEL AMERICAN LEGION SCHOLARSHIPS

American Legion
Department of Wisconsin
2930 American Legion Drive
P.O. Box 388
Portage, WI 53901-0388
(608) 745-1090   Fax: (608) 745-0179
E-mail: info@wilegion.org
Web: www.wilegion.org

Summary To provide financial assistance to members of the American Legion in Wisconsin and their children or grandchildren who plan to attend college in any state.
Eligibility This program is open to seniors and graduates from accredited Wisconsin high schools. Applicants must be at least 1 of the following 1) a child whose father, mother, or legal guardian is a member of the Department of Wisconsin of the American Legion, American Legion Auxiliary, or Sons of the American Legion; 2) a grandchild whose grandfather, grandmother, or legal guardian is a member of the Department of Wisconsin of the American Legion, American Legion Auxiliary, or Sons of the American Legion; 3) a member of the Sons of the American Legion, American Legion Auxiliary, or Junior American Legion Auxiliary; or 4) a veteran and an American Legion member in Wisconsin. Applicants must have participated in Legion and Auxiliary youth programs. They must be planning to attend a college or university in any state to work on a baccalaureate degree. Selection is based on moral character; scholastic excellence (GPA of 3.0 or higher); participation and accomplishment in American Legion affiliated activities; and personality, leadership, and participation in general extracurricular activities.
Financial data The stipend is $1,000.
Duration 1 year.
Additional information This program began in 1968.
Number awarded 3 each year.
Deadline February of each year.

[181]
SENATOR DANIEL K. INOUYE MEMORIAL SCHOLARSHIP

Japanese American Veterans Association
Attn: Chris DeRosa, Scholarship Committee Chair
P.O. Box 341198
Bethesda, MD 20827
E-mail: javascholarship222@gmail.com
Web: www.java.wildapricot.org

Summary To provide financial assistance for college or graduate school to relatives of Japanese American veterans who plan a career in the military or public service.
Eligibility This program is open to students who 1) have completed at least 1 year of an undergraduate program or are currently enrolled in graduate school and are preparing for a career in the military or public service; 2) are currently enrolled in a university or college ROTC program or the U.S. Marine Corps Platoon Leaders Course but are not receiving an ROTC scholarship; or 3) are disabled veterans. Applicants must also be 1) a direct or collateral descendant of a person who served with the 442nd Regimental Combat Team, the 100th Infantry Battalion, Military Intelligence Service, 1399th Engineering Construction Battalion, or other unit associated with those during or after World War II; or 2) a member or child of a member of the Japanese American Veterans Association (JAVA) whose membership extends back at least 1 year. Along with their application, they must submit a 500-word essay on their plan and vision to serve America through public service or the military.
Financial data The stipend is $5,000.
Duration 1 year.
Number awarded 1 each year.
Deadline March of each year.

[182]
SFC CURTIS MANCINI MEMORIAL SCHOLARSHIPS

Association of the United States Army-Rhode Island Chapter
c/o LTC Robert A. Galvanin, President
31 Canoe River Drive
Mansfield, MA 02048
(508) 339-5301   E-mail: bpje5310@verizon.net
Web: www.riroa.org/ausari/scholarship.htm

Summary To provide financial assistance to members of the Rhode Island Chapter of the Association of the United States Army (AUSA) and their families who are interested in attending college or graduate school in any state.

Eligibility This program is open to members of the AUSA Rhode Island Chapter and their family members (spouses, children, and grandchildren). Applicants must be high school seniors or graduates accepted at an accredited college, university, or vocational/technical school in any state or current undergraduate or graduate students. Along with their application, they must submit a 250-word essay on why they feel their achievements should qualify them for this award. Selection is based on academic and individual achievements; financial need is not considered. Special consideration is given to students or graduates of Lincoln High School in Lincoln, Rhode Island (the alma mater of this program's namesake), especially those preparing for a career in law enforcement or enrolled or planning to enroll in Army ROTC.

Financial data The stipend is $1,000.

Duration 1 year.

Additional information Membership in the AUSA is open to everyone who supports a strong national defense, with special concern for the Army. That includes Regular Army, National Guard, Army Reserve, government civilians, retired soldiers, Wounded Warriors, veterans, concerned citizens and family members.

Number awarded Several each year.

Deadline April of each year.

[183]
SGT. FREDERICK C. BRACE, JR. MEMORIAL SCHOLARSHIP

American Academy of Physician Assistants-Veterans Caucus
Attn: Scholarship Program
P.O. Box 362
Ossining, NY 10562
(803) 328-1864   Fax: (704) 838-8494
E-mail: rmunsee@veteranscaucus.org
Web: www.veteranscaucus.org/scholarships

Summary To provide financial assistance to Air Force veterans and their dependents who are studying to become physician assistants.

Eligibility This program is open to U.S. citizens who are currently enrolled in a physician assistant program. Applicants must be honorably discharged members of the United States Air Force or the dependent of an Air Force veteran. Along with their application, they must submit a personal statement about what led them to attend PA school; their background, present, and future intentions; and why they deserve to receive a scholarship. Selection is based on military honors and awards received, civic and college honors and awards received, professional memberships and activities, potential for future achievement, and GPA.

Financial data The stipend is $2,000.

Duration 1 year.

Number awarded 1 each year.

Deadline February of each year.

[184]
SIGMA CHI MILITARY SERVICE SCHOLARSHIPS

Sigma Chi Foundation
Attn: Scholarship Committee
1714 Hinman Avenue
Evanston, IL 60201
(847) 869-3655, ext. 270   Fax: (847) 869-4906
E-mail: foundation@sigmachi.org
Web: www.sigmachi.org

Summary To provide financial assistance to undergraduate and graduate student members of Sigma Chi who are serving or have served in the military.

Eligibility This program is open to undergraduate and graduate brothers of the fraternity who are currently serving or have served in the military (Army, Navy, Air Force, Marines, Coast Guard, or National Guard). They must have earned a GPA of 2.5 or higher and have completed at least 2 semesters of undergraduate study. ROTC students are not eligible.

Financial data The stipend is $1,000. Funds are to be used for tuition/fees only and are paid directly to the recipient's school.

Duration 1 year.

Number awarded Varies each year; recently, 9 were awarded.

Deadline May of each year.

[185]
SMA LEON VAN AUTREVE SCHOLARSHIPS

Association of the United States Army
Attn: Scholarships
2425 Wilson Boulevard
Arlington, VA 22201
(703) 841-4300   Toll Free: (800) 336-4570
E-mail: scholarships@ausa.org
Web: www.ausa.org/resources/scholarships

Summary To provide financial assistance to members of the Association of the United States Army (AUSA) who are interested in attending college.

Eligibility This program is open to AUSA members who are enrolled or accepted at an accredited college or university to work on a degree in any field. Along with their application, they must submit a 1-page autobiography, 2 letters of recommendation, a letter describing their career aspirations (including their course of study and plans for completion of a degree), and a transcript of high school or college grades (depending on which they are currently attending). Selection is based on academic merit and personal achievement. Financial need is not normally a selection criterion but in some cases of extreme need it may be used as a factor; the lack of financial need, however, is never a cause for non-selection.

Financial data The stipend ranges from $2,000 to $25,000; funds are sent directly to the recipient's college or university.

Duration 1 year.
Additional information Membership in the AUSA is open to everyone who supports a strong national defense, with special concern for the Army. That includes Regular Army, National Guard, Army Reserve, government civilians, retired soldiers, Wounded Warriors, veterans, concerned citizens and family members. This program is sponsored by the USAA Foundation.
Number awarded Varies each year; recently, 1 at $25,000, 1 at $10,000, 1 at $5,000, and 5 at $2,000 were awarded.
Deadline June of each year.

[186]
SMSGT. NATHAN L. LIPSCOMB, SR. MEMORIAL SCHOLARSHIP

American Academy of Physician Assistants-Veterans Caucus
Attn: Scholarship Program
P.O. Box 362
Ossining, NY 10562
(803) 328-1864   Fax: (704) 838-8494
E-mail: rmunsee@veteranscaucus.org
Web: www.veteranscaucus.org/scholarships

Summary To provide financial assistance to Air Force veterans and their dependents who are studying to become physician assistants.
Eligibility This program is open to U.S. citizens who are currently enrolled in a physician assistant program. Applicants must be honorably discharged members of the United States Air Force or the dependent of an Air Force veteran. Along with their application, they must submit a personal statement about what led them to attend PA school; their background, present, and future intentions; and why they deserve to receive a scholarship. Selection is based on military honors and awards received, civic and college honors and awards received, professional memberships and activities, potential for future achievement, and GPA.
Financial data The stipend is $2,000.
Duration 1 year.
Number awarded 1 each year.
Deadline February of each year.

[187]
SOCIETY OF AIR FORCE PHYSICIAN ASSISTANTS MEMORIAL SCHOLARSHIP

American Academy of Physician Assistants-Veterans Caucus
Attn: Scholarship Program
P.O. Box 362
Ossining, NY 10562
(803) 328-1864   Fax: (704) 838-8494
E-mail: rmunsee@veteranscaucus.org
Web: www.veteranscaucus.org/scholarships

Summary To provide financial assistance to Air Force veterans who are studying to become physician assistants.
Eligibility This program is open to U.S. citizens who are currently enrolled in a physician assistant program. Applicants must be honorably discharged members of the United States Air Force. Along with their application, they must submit a personal statement about what led them to attend PA school; their background, present, and future intentions; and why they deserve to receive a scholarship. Selection is based on military honors and awards received, civic and college honors and awards received, professional memberships and activities, potential for future achievement, and GPA.
Financial data The stipend is $2,000.
Duration 1 year.
Number awarded 1 each year.
Deadline February of each year.

[188]
SOCIETY OF ARMY PHYSICIAN ASSISTANTS MEMORIAL SCHOLARSHIP

American Academy of Physician Assistants-Veterans Caucus
Attn: Scholarship Program
P.O. Box 362
Ossining, NY 10562
(803) 328-1864   Fax: (704) 838-8494
E-mail: rmunsee@veteranscaucus.org
Web: www.veteranscaucus.org/scholarships

Summary To provide financial assistance to Army veterans who are studying to become physician assistants.
Eligibility This program is open to U.S. citizens who are currently enrolled in a physician assistant program. Applicants must be honorably discharged members of the United States Army. Along with their application, they must submit a personal statement about what led them to attend PA school; their background, present, and future intentions; and why they deserve to receive a scholarship. Selection is based on military honors and awards received, civic and college honors and awards received, professional memberships and activities, potential for future achievement, and GPA.
Financial data The stipend is $2,000.
Duration 1 year.
Number awarded 1 each year.
Deadline February of each year.

[189]
SOUTH DAKOTA AMERICAN LEGION EDUCATIONAL SCHOLARSHIP

American Legion
Department of South Dakota
14 First Avenue S.E.
P.O. Box 67
Watertown, SD 57201-0067
(605) 886-3604   Fax: (605) 886-2870
E-mail: sdlegion@dailypost.com
Web: www.sdlegion.org/scholarship-information

Summary To provide financial assistance to children and grandchildren of South Dakota veterans who are interested in attending college in the state.
Eligibility This program is open to residents of South Dakota who are wartime veterans or their children or grandchildren; wartime veterans include those eligible for membership in the American Legion (although Legion membership is not required). Applicants must be interested in attending a South Dakota college or technical school (unless no school in the state offers the professional or technical degree being sought). They must be high school graduates or GED recipients and have completed at least 16 hours of postsecondary credits. Along with their application, they must submit 2 essays of up to 500 words each on 1) how they have pre-

pared for higher education; and 2) which of the 10 clauses of the American Legion Preamble is the most meaningful to them and why.
Financial data The stipend ranges up to $2,500 per year.
Duration 1 year.
Additional information This program began in 1956 as a loan fund for the children of veterans. It was expanded in 2002 to include veterans themselves and in 2006 to include grandchildren of veterans. In 2019, it was converted to a scholarship.
Number awarded Varies each year.
Deadline December of each year.

[190]
SPORTS CLIPS HELP A HERO SCHOLARSHIPS

Veterans of Foreign Wars of the United States
Attn: National Military Services
406 West 34th Street, Suite 216
Kansas City, MO 64111
(816) 756-3390   Toll Free: (866) 789-NEED
E-mail: HelpAHero@vfw.org
Web: www.vfw.org/assistance/student-veterans-support

Summary To provide financial assistance to military personnel and veterans who are interested in attending college.
Eligibility This program is open to military personnel on active duty, retired and honorably discharged veterans, and members of the National Guard or Reserves who have completed basic training and follow-on training. Applicants must be U.S. citizens at the rank of E-5 or below and be able to demonstrate financial need. They must be enrolled or planning to enroll at a VA-approved program or institution of higher education.
Financial data The stipend is $5,000. Funds are paid directly to the recipient's institution.
Duration 1 year.
Additional information This program began in 2014 with support from Sports Clips, Inc.
Number awarded This program attempts to provide support to 115 veterans and military members each year.
Deadline April of each year for fall semester; November of each year for spring semester.

[191]
SR EDUCATION GROUP MILITARY SCHOLARSHIPS

SR Education Group
123 Lake Street South, Site B-1
Kirkland, WA 98033-6401
(425) 605-8898
Web: www.sreducationgroup.org

Summary To provide financial assistance to veterans and active military members and their families who are currently enrolled in college and have high financial need.
Eligibility This program is open to legal residents of any state except Rhode Island who are 1) veterans or active members of the U.S. military; 2) children or spouses of veterans or active military members; or 3) children and spouses of deceased veterans or military members. Children must be younger than 21 years of age or, if enrolled full time, younger than 23. Applicants must be currently enrolled at a college or university and able to demonstrate high financial need. Along with their application, they must submit 3 essays of 300 to 500 words each on 1) how they will apply their degree in the future and what they anticipate for their first 5 years beyond college; 2) their involvement with the military and how it has influenced their personal development; and 3) any special or family circumstances affecting their financial need.
Financial data The stipend is $5,000.
Duration 1 year.
Additional information This program began in 2010.
Number awarded 4 each year. Since the program began, this sponsor has awarded a total of $547,000 to 141 students at 113 colleges.
Deadline December of each year.

[192]
SSGT. ROBERT V. MILNER MEMORIAL SCHOLARSHIP

American Academy of Physician Assistants-Veterans Caucus
Attn: Scholarship Program
P.O. Box 362
Ossining, NY 10562
(803) 328-1864   Fax: (704) 838-8494
E-mail: rmunsee@veteranscaucus.org
Web: www.veteranscaucus.org/scholarships

Summary To provide financial assistance to Air Force veterans and their dependents who are studying to become physician assistants.
Eligibility This program is open to U.S. citizens who are currently enrolled in a physician assistant program. Applicants must be honorably discharged members of the United States Air Force or the dependent of an Air Force veteran. Along with their application, they must submit a personal statement about what led them to attend PA school; their background, present, and future intentions; and why they deserve to receive a scholarship. Selection is based on military honors and awards received, civic and college honors and awards received, professional memberships and activities, potential for future achievement, and GPA.
Financial data The stipend is $2,000.
Duration 1 year.
Number awarded 1 each year.
Deadline February of each year.

[193]
TAILHOOK EDUCATIONAL FOUNDATION SCHOLARSHIPS

Tailhook Educational Foundation
9696 Business Park Avenue
San Diego, CA 92131-1643
(858) 689-9223   Toll Free: (800) 322-4665
Fax: (858) 578-8839   E-mail: bethr@tailhook.net
Web: www.tailhook.net/A_Foundation_Index.html

Summary To provide financial assistance for college to personnel associated with naval aviation and their children.
Eligibility This program is open to 1) the children (natural, step, and adopted) and grandchildren of current or former U.S. Navy, Coast Guard, or Marine Corps personnel who served as an aviator, flight officer, or air crewman; or 2) personnel and children and grandchildren of personnel who are serving or have served on board a U.S. Navy aircraft carrier as a member of the ship's company or air wing. Applicants must be enrolled or accepted for enrollment at an accredited

college or university. Selection is based on educational and extracurricular achievements, merit, and citizenship.
Financial data The stipend ranges from $2,500 to $15,000.
Duration 1 to 2 years.
Number awarded Varies; usually, more than 100 are awarded each year.
Deadline February of each year.

[194]
TEXAS STATE COUNCIL VIETNAM VETERANS OF AMERICA SCHOLARSHIPS
Vietnam Veterans of America-Texas State Council
Attn: Percilla Newberry, Scholarship Committee Co-Chair
100 Elmwood Street
Fritch, TX 79036
(806) 857-2261
Web: vvatsc.org/vvatsc-committees

Summary To provide financial assistance to Vietnam veterans and their families in Texas who are interested in attending college in the state.
Eligibility This program is open to residents of Texas who are veterans of the Vietnam War or their children, stepchildren, grandchildren, current spouses, and unremarried widows. Applicants must be high school seniors planning to enroll or students currently enrolled full time at an accredited college or university in the state. High school seniors must submit transcripts showing a GPA of 2.5 or higher and ACT/SAT scores. College students must have completed at least 12 college credit hours during the preceding 12-month period. They must submit a letter on their career ambition following completion of their degree. All applicants must submit an essay of at least 1,500 words based on an interview of a Vietnam veteran.
Financial data A stipend is awarded (amount not specified).
Duration 1 year.
Additional information This program is comprised of the following named awards: the Don Carlos Kennedy Memorial Scholarship, the Alberto Rodriquez Memorial Scholarship, and the Robert Dale Spencer Memorial Scholarship.
Number awarded 3 each year.
Deadline February of each year.

[195]
THE AMERICAN COLLEGE SCHOLARSHIPS
First Command Educational Foundation
Attn: Scholarship Programs Manager
1 FirstComm Plaza
Fort Worth, TX 76109-4999
(817) 569-2940   Toll Free: (877) 872-8289
Fax: (817) 569-2970   E-mail: scholarships@fcef.com
Web: www.fcef.com/scholarships

Summary To provide financial assistance to veterans and their families working on a financial services professional career.
Eligibility This program is open to military veterans and dependent family members. Applicants must be seeking funding to pay for professional certification as a financial services professional.
Financial data The stipend is $5,000. Funds may be used to cover the costs of professional certification.
Duration 1 year.
Additional information This program, which began in 2016, is sponsored by The American College of Financial Services.
Number awarded 3 each year.
Deadline Deadline not specified.

[196]
THE PFC ROGER W. CUMMINS MEMORIAL SCHOLARSHIP
American Academy of Physician Assistants-Veterans Caucus
Attn: Scholarship Program
P.O. Box 362
Ossining, NY 10562
(803) 328-1864   Fax: (704) 838-8494
E-mail: rmunsee@veteranscaucus.org
Web: www.veteranscaucus.org/scholarships

Summary To provide financial assistance to Marine Corps and Navy service members or veterans or family members who are studying to become physician assistants.
Eligibility This program is open to U.S. citizens who are currently enrolled in a physician assistant program. Applicants must be active-duty members of the U.S. Marine Corps or Navy Corpsmen who have served with the Marine Corps, veterans of those services, or their spouses or children. Along with their application, they must submit a personal statement about what led them to attend PA school; their background, present, and future intentions; and why they deserve to receive a scholarship. Selection is based on military honors and awards received, civic and college honors and awards received, professional memberships and activities, potential for future achievement, and GPA.
Financial data The stipend is $2,000.
Duration 1 year.
Number awarded 1 each year.
Deadline February of each year.

[197]
TILLMAN MILITARY SCHOLARS PROGRAM
Pat Tillman Foundation
222 North Merchandise Mart Plaza, Suite 1212
Chicago, IL 60654
(773) 360-5277
E-mail: scholarships@pattillmanfoundation.org
Web: www.pattillmanfoundation.org/apply-to-be-a-scholar

Summary To provide financial assistance to veterans, active servicemembers, and their spouses who are interested in working on an undergraduate or graduate degree.
Eligibility This program is open to veterans and active servicemembers of all branches of the armed forces from both the pre- and post-September 11 era and their spouses; children are not eligible. Applicants must be enrolled or planning to enroll full time at a 4-year public or private college or university to work on an undergraduate, graduate, or postgraduate degree. Current and former servicemembers must submit 400-word essays on 1) their motivation and decision to serve in the U.S. military and how that decision and experience has changed their life and ambitions; and 2) their educational and career goals, how they will incorporate their military service

experience into those goals, and how they intend to continue their service to others and the community. Spouses must submit 400-word essays on 1) their previous service to others and the community; and 2) their educational and career goals, how they will incorporate their service experiences and the impact of their spouse's military service into those goals, and how they intend to continue their service to others and the community. Selection is based on those essays, educational and career ambitions, record of military service, record of personal achievement, demonstration of service to others in the community, desire to continue such service, and leadership potential.

Financial data The stipend depends on the need of the recipient and the availability of funds; recently, stipends averaged approximately $11,000 per year.

Duration 1 year; may be renewed, provided the recipient maintains a GPA of 3.0 or higher, remains enrolled full time, and documents participation in civic action or community service.

Additional information This program began in 2009.

Number awarded Approximately 60 each year. Since the program began, it has awarded more than $15 million to 580 scholars.

Deadline February of each year.

[198]
TONALAW VETERAN'S SCHOLARSHIP

TonaLaw
152 Islip Avenue, Suite 18
Islip, NY 11751
(631) 780-5355   Toll Free: (844) TONA-LAW
Fax: (631) 780-5685   E-mail: contact@tonalaw.com
Web: www.tonalaw.com/scholarship

Summary To provide financial assistance to veterans who are interested in attending college of law school in any state.

Eligibility This program is open to veterans of all branches of the U.S. armed forces. Applicants must be enrolled at an accredited college or law school in any state or accepted for enrollment to begin within 6 months of application. Along with their application, they must submit an essay of 300 to 600 words on how their military service has made an impact on their life, how it has prepared them for college, and what they plan to do after they complete their education.

Financial data The stipend is $1,000.

Duration 1 year.

Number awarded 2 each year: 1 each semester.

Deadline July of each year for fall semester; November of each year for spring semester.

[199]
TONY LOPEZ SCHOLARSHIP PROGRAM

Louisiana National Guard Enlisted Association
c/o CMSgt John M. Roach, Executive Director
5445 Point Clair Road
Carville, LA 70721
Web: www.geauxlangea.org/about/langea

Summary To provide financial assistance to members of the Louisiana National Guard Enlisted Association (LANGEA) and their dependents who plan to attend college in any state.

Eligibility This program is open to members of the association, their spouses and unmarried dependent children, and the unremarried spouses and unmarried dependent children of deceased members who were in good standing at the time of their death. The qualifying LANGEA members must have at least 1 year remaining on their enlistment following completion of the school year for which the application is submitted or have served 20 years of more in the Louisiana National Guard. Applicants must be enrolled or planning to enroll full time at an accredited college, university, trade school, or business school in any state. Graduate students are not eligible. Selection is based on academic achievement, character, leadership, and financial need.

Financial data The stipend is $2,000.

Duration 1 year; nonrenewable.

Number awarded 2 each year.

Deadline April of each year.

[200]
TVSHKA (WARRIOR) SCHOLARSHIP

Chahta Foundation
Attn: Scholarship Director
P.O. Box 1849
Durant, OK 74702
(580) 924-8280, ext. 2546
Toll Free: (800) 522-6170, ext. 2546
Fax: (580) 745-9023
E-mail: scholarship@chahtafoundation.com
Web: www.chahtafoundation.com/scholarship/veterans

Summary To provide financial assistance to Choctaw Indians who are serving or have served in the armed services and are planning to attend college or graduate school in any state.

Eligibility This program is open to Choctaw students who are active duty or retired U.S. armed services veterans. Applicants be enrolled or planning to enroll full time in an undergraduate or graduate degree program at a college or university in any state. They must have a GPA of 2.5 or higher. Along with their application, they must submit essays on assigned topics, transcripts, 2 letters of recommendation, a resume, and documentation of financial need.

Financial data The stipend is $3,000.

Duration 1 year.

Additional information This program began in 2016.

Number awarded 1 or more each year.

Deadline March of each year.

[201]
UNIFIED ARIZONA VETERANS SCHOLARSHIPS

Unified Arizona Veterans, Inc.
Attn: Scholarship Committee
P.O. Box 34338
Phoenix, AZ 85067
E-mail: scholarships@azuav.org
Web: www.azuav.org

Summary To provide financial assistance to veterans and military personnel in Arizona who are interested in attending college in the state.

Eligibility This program is open to residents of Arizona who are 1) honorably discharged veterans; 2) currently on active duty, including service members in good standing with a Reserve or Guard components; or 3) immediate family members of an Arizona veteran killed in action or by an act of terror. Applicants must be enrolled at an institution of higher

learning in Arizona and working on a bachelor's or master's degree in any field. Along with their application, they must submit 1) a 1-page essay on why they chose their current academic program and how they plan to use their degree, certificate, or license; 2) letters of recommendation; 3) verification of enrollment and Arizona residency; and 4) documentation of financial need.
Financial data Stipends range up to $5,000.
Duration 1 year.
Number awarded 1 or more each year.
Deadline February of each year.

[202]
UNITED AIRLINES VETERAN SCHOLARSHIP
Northrop Rice Foundation
12502 Brantly Avenue
Houston, TX 77034
(713) 644-6616 Fax: (281) 334-0335
E-mail: awards@northropricefoundation.org
Web: www.northropricefoundation.org
Summary To provide funding to veterans who are interested in preparing for a career as a civilian aviation maintenance technician.
Eligibility This program is open to honorably discharged veterans whose service experience included aircraft maintenance. Applicants must be enrolled at an FAA-approved Part 147 school for aviation maintenance technicians. They must submit a 5-paragraph essay: 1) general aviation goals and financial need; 2) desired future involvement in aviation; 3) how the award is needed by and will benefit the applicant; 4) involvement in school, employment, and community extracurricular activities; and 5) any other information the applicant would like considered.
Financial data The stipend is $1,500; funds may be applied toward tuition, books, or tools.
Duration This is a 1-time award.
Additional information This program is sponsored by United Airlines.
Number awarded 1 each year.
Deadline January of each year.

[203]
UTAH TUITION WAIVER FOR PURPLE HEART RECIPIENTS
Utah Department of Veterans and Military Affairs
Attn: Director
550 Foothill Boulevard, Suite 105
Salt Lake City, UT 84113
(801) 326-2372 Toll Free: (800) 894-9497 (within UT)
Fax: (801) 326-2369 E-mail: veterans@utah.gov
Web: veterans.utah.gov/state-education-benefits
Summary To provide a tuition waiver to veterans in Utah who received a Purple Heart award and are attending a public institution in the state.
Eligibility This program is open to residents of Utah who received a Purple Heart award as a result of military service. Applicants must be working on an undergraduate or master's degree at a public college or university in the state.
Financial data Tuition at the rate for residents of the state is waived for qualified veterans.
Duration Tuition is waived until completion of a bachelor's or master's degree.
Number awarded Varies each year.
Deadline Deadline not specified.

[204]
UTAH VETERAN TUITION GAP PROGRAM
Utah Department of Veterans and Military Affairs
Attn: Director
550 Foothill Boulevard, Suite 105
Salt Lake City, UT 84113
(801) 326-2372 Toll Free: (800) 894-9497 (within UT)
Fax: (801) 326-2369 E-mail: veterans@utah.gov
Web: veterans.utah.gov/state-education-benefits
Summary To provide financial assistance to veterans in Utah who are entering their final year of study at a public institution in the state but who have exhausted all federal benefits.
Eligibility This program is open to residents of Utah who are entering the final year of a bachelor's degree program at a public college or university in the state. Applicants must be veterans who have exhausted all federal educational funding.
Financial data Tuition is waived for qualified veterans.
Duration 1 year.
Additional information This program began in 2014.
Number awarded Varies each year.
Deadline September of each year.

[205]
VAN HIPP HEROES SCHOLARSHIP
National Guard Educational Foundation
Attn: Scholarship Fund
One Massachusetts Avenue, N.W.
Washington, DC 20001
(202) 789-0031 Fax: (202) 682-9358
E-mail: ngef@ngaus.org
Web: www.ngef.org/the-van-hipp-heroes-scholarship-fund
Summary To provide financial assistance for college to members of the National Guard who were wounded in service.
Eligibility This program is open to current and former National Guard members who were wounded in an operational or training mission in support of Operation Enduring Freedom, Operation Iraqi Freedom, or Operation New Dawn. Applicants must be attending or planning to attend an accredited college, university, or community college located in the 50 states, the District of Columbia, Puerto Rico, the U.S. Virgin Islands, or Guam. Along with their application, they must submit a 1-page essay on how their National Guard service has shaped their life.
Financial data The stipend is $1,000 per year.
Duration 1 year; may be renewed up to 3 additional years, provided the recipient maintains a GPA of 2.5 or higher.
Additional information This program was established in 2017 by Van Hipp, author of *The New Terrorism: How to Fight It and Defeat It*. All the proceeds from sale of the book go to support this program.
Number awarded Up to 10 each year.
Deadline June of each year.

[206]
VETERANS IN PLUMBING, HEATING, COOLING AND ELECTRICAL SCHOLARSHIP

Nexstar Legacy Foundation
Attn: Explore the Trades
101 East Fifth Street, Suite 2100
St. Paul, MN 55101
(651) 789-8518   Fax: (651) 789-8519
E-mail: info@explorethetrades.org
Web: www.explorethetrades.org

Summary To provide financial assistance to veterans who are interested in preparing for a career in designated residential service trades.

Eligibility This program is open to veterans who have been honorably discharged from the U.S. or Canadian military. Applicants must be enrolled or registered to enroll in a trade school or apprenticeship program in a plumbing, heating/ventilating/air conditioning (HVAC), or electrical training program. Selection is based on academic achievement, character, leadership, financial need, and commitment to advancing the plumbing, HVAC, and electrical trades.

Financial data The stipend is $5,000.
Duration 1 year; nonrenewable.
Number awarded 1 each year.
Deadline July of each year.

[207]
VETERANS MAKE GREAT STEM TEACHERS PROGRAM

International Technology and Engineering Educators Association
Attn: Foundation for Technology and Engineering Educators
1914 Association Drive, Suite 201
Reston, VA 20191-1539
(703) 860-2100   Fax: (703) 860-0353
E-mail: iteea@iteea.org
Web: www.iteea.org

Summary To provide financial assistance to veterans who are working on an undergraduate or graduate degree as a technology and engineering teacher.

Eligibility This program is open to veterans of any branch of the military who are enrolled full time as an undergraduate or graduate student at an accredited institution of higher education. Applicants must be preparing for a career as a technology and engineering teacher and have a GPA of 3.0 or higher. They must be members of the International Technology and Engineering Educators Association (ITEEA).

Financial data The stipend is $1,000 for freshmen and sophomores or $3,000 for juniors, seniors, and graduate students. Funds are provided directly to the recipient.
Duration 1 year.
Additional information This program, which began in 2018, is sponsored by CNC Mastercam.
Number awarded 2 each year: 1 to a freshman or sophomore and 1 to a junior, senior, or graduate student.
Deadline November of each year.

[208]
VETERANS PURSUING A CAREER IN LAW SCHOLARSHIP

Friedl Richardson Trial Lawyers
Attn: Scholarship Coordinator
13633 North Cave Creek Road
Phoenix, AZ 85022
(602) 553-2220   E-mail: randy@friedlrichardson.com
Web: www.friedlrichardson.com

Summary To provide financial assistance for college to veterans who are preparing for a career in the law.

Eligibility This program is open to veterans who are transitioning from military service into academics and eventually into a career in law. Applicants must provide proof of service in the armed forces and enrollment at a college or university of their choice for the coming academic year. They must be U.S. citizens and have a GPA of 2.8 or higher. Along with their application, they must submit an essay or video explaining why they are an excellent candidate for this scholarship.

Financial data The stipend is $1,000.
Duration 1 year.
Number awarded 1 each year.
Deadline July of each year.

[209]
VETERANS TUITION WAIVER PROGRAM OF MASSACHUSETTS

Massachusetts Office of Student Financial Assistance
75 Pleasant Street
Malden, MA 02148
(617) 391-6070   Fax: (617) 727-0667
E-mail: osfa@osfa.mass.edu
Web: www.mass.edu/osfa/programs/categorical.asp

Summary To provide financial assistance for college to Massachusetts residents who are veterans.

Eligibility Applicants for these scholarships must have been permanent legal residents of Massachusetts for at least 1 year and veterans who served actively during the Spanish-American War, World War I, World War II, Korea, Vietnam, the Lebanese peace keeping force, the Grenada rescue mission, the Panamanian intervention force, the Persian Gulf, or Operation Restore Hope in Somalia. They may not be in default on any federal student loan. U.S. citizenship or permanent resident status is required.

Financial data Eligible veterans are exempt from any tuition payments for an undergraduate degree or certificate program at public colleges or universities in Massachusetts.
Duration Up to 4 academic years, for a total of 130 semester hours.
Additional information Recipients may enroll either part or full time in a Massachusetts publicly-supported institution.
Number awarded Varies each year.
Deadline Deadline not specified.

[210]
VICE ADMIRAL ROBERT L. WALTERS SCHOLARSHIP

Surface Navy Association
Attn: Scholarship Coordinator
6564 Loisdale Court, Suite 318
Springfield, VA 22150
(703) 960-6800   Toll Free: (800) NAVY-SNA
Fax: (703) 960-6807   E-mail: navysna@aol.com
Web: www.navysna.org/scholarship/information.html

Summary To provide financial assistance for college or graduate school to members of the Surface Navy Association (SNA) and their dependents.

Eligibility This program is open to SNA members and their children, stepchildren, wards, and spouses. The SNA member must 1) be in the second or subsequent consecutive year of membership; 2) be serving, retired, or honorably discharged; 3) be a Surface Warfare Officer or Enlisted Surface Warfare Specialist; and 4) have served for at least 3 years on a surface ship of the U.S. Navy or Coast Guard (the 3 years need not have been consecutive but must have been served on active duty). Applicants must be enrolled or planning to enroll full time at an accredited undergraduate or graduate institution; the full-time requirement may be waived for spouses. Along with their application, they must submit a 500-word essay about themselves and why they should be selected to receive this scholarship. High school seniors should also include a transcript of high school grades and a copy of ACT or SAT scores. Current college students should also include a transcript of the grades from their most recent 4 semesters of school. Selection is based on academic proficiency, non-scholastic activities, scholastic and non-scholastic awards, character, and financial need.

Financial data The stipend is $2,000 per year.

Duration 4 years, provided the recipient maintains a GPA of 3.0 or higher.

Number awarded Varies each year.

Deadline February of each year.

[211]
VII CORPS DESERT STORM VETERANS ASSOCIATION SCHOLARSHIP

VII Corps Desert Storm Veterans Association
Attn: Scholarship Committee
c/o BG (Ret) Edward Dyer
12888 Coco Plum Lane
Naples, FL 34119
E-mail: viicorpsdsva@gmail.com
Web: www.desertstormvets.org/scholarships

Summary To provide financial assistance for college to students who served, or are the spouses or other family members of individuals who served, with VII Corps in Operations Desert Shield, Desert Storm, or related activities.

Eligibility Applicants must have served, or be a family member of those who served, with VII Corps in Operations Desert Shield/Desert Storm, Provide Comfort, or 1 of the support base activities. Scholarships are limited to students entering or enrolled full or part time at accredited 2- and 4-year colleges, universities, and technical schools. Selection is not based solely on academic standing; consideration is also given to extracurricular activities, community activities and/or involvement, professional organizations, high school organizations and/or activities, and other self-development skills and abilities obtained through on-the-job training or correspondence courses. Priority is given to survivors of VII Corps soldiers who died during Operations Desert Shield/Desert Storm or Provide Comfort, veterans who are also members of the VII Corps Desert Storm Veterans Association, and family members of veterans who are also members of the VII Corps Desert Storm Veterans Association.

Financial data The stipend ranges from $1,000 to $5,000 per year. Funds are paid to the recipients upon proof of admission or registration at an accredited institution, college, or university.

Duration 1 year; recipients may reapply.

Additional information This program began in 1998.

Number awarded 15 to 20 each year; since this program began, it has awarded more than $350,000 in scholarships.

Deadline December of each year.

[212]
WAPA VETERAN SCHOLARSHIPS

Washington Academy of Physician Assistants
Attn: Veterans Committee
2001 Sixth Avenue, Suite 2700
Seattle, WA 98121
(206) 956-3624   Toll Free: (800) 552-0612, ext. 3006
Fax: (206) 441-5863   E-mail: wapa@wapa.com
Web: www.wapa.com/scholarship-information

Summary To provide financial assistance for college or graduate school to members of the Washington Academy of Physician Assistants (WAPA) who are veterans.

Eligibility This program is open to WAPA members who are veterans working on an undergraduate or graduate degree in a physician assistant program in Washington. Applicants must submit a 1- to 2-page narrative on why they chose the physician assistant profession, their community involvement, their plans for future involvement in WAPA, and how the scholarship will benefit them.

Financial data A stipend is awarded (amount not specified).

Duration 1 year.

Number awarded 1 each year.

Deadline April of each year.

[213]
WELLS FARGO VETERANS SCHOLARSHIP PROGRAM

Scholarship America
Attn: Scholarship Management Services
One Scholarship Way
P.O. Box 297
St. Peter, MN 56082
(507) 931-1682   Toll Free: (844) 402-0357
Fax: (507) 931-9168
E-mail: wellsfargoveterans@scholarshipamerica.org
Web: www.scholarsapply.org/wellsfargoveterans

Summary To provide financial assistance to veterans and the spouses of disabled veterans who are interested in attending college.

Eligibility This program is open to honorably-discharged (no longer drilling) veterans and the spouses of disabled veterans of the U.S. armed forces, including the Reserves and National Guard. Applicants must be enrolled or planning to

SCHOLARSHIPS: VETERANS

enroll full time at an accredited 2- or 4-year college, university, or vocational/technical school to work on a bachelor's or master's degree. They must have a GPA of 2.5 or higher and be able to demonstrate financial need. Along with their application, they must submit essays on 1) their military service and career and educational goals and objectives; and 2) any personal or financial challenges that may be barriers to completing postsecondary education. Selection is based on those essays, academic performance, demonstrated leadership, participation in school and community activities, work experience, and financial need.

Financial data The amount of the initial stipend depends on an analysis of the recipient's military education benefits, institutional grants, and other scholarships. If renewed, the stipend increases by $1,000 each year.

Duration 1 year; scholarships may be renewed up to 3 additional years or until completion of a degree, whichever occurs firsts. Renewal depends on the recipient's maintaining satisfactory academic progress and full-time enrollment.

Additional information This trustee for this program is Wells Fargo Bank and the administrator is Scholarship America.

Number awarded Varies each year.

Deadline February of each year.

[214]
WESLEY HAMMON LEACH SCHOLARSHIPS

Marines' Memorial Association
c/o Marines Memorial Club and Hotel
609 Sutter Street
San Francisco, CA 94102
(415) 673-6672, ext. 293   Toll Free: (800) 5-MARINE
Fax: (415) 441-3649
E-mail: scholarship@marineclub.com
Web: www.marinesmemorial.org

Summary To provide financial assistance to members of the Marines' Memorial Association from all branches of the armed forces and their descendants who are interested in studying at a career school or college.

Eligibility This program is open to active members of the association (including student veterans) and their children and grandchildren. Applicants must be high school seniors or students currently enrolled at an accredited trade or vocational school. They must have a field of study that will lead to a viable career; preference is given to students with a medical or nursing focus. Along with their application, they must submit an essay of up to 500 words on why they chose their specific path of study, what they hope to accomplish after graduation with their degree, and how their efforts will benefit others in their community. Selection is based on the essay, academic merit, references, and financial need.

Financial data The stipend is $2,500.

Duration 1 year.

Additional information Membership in the association is open to veterans of the Marines, Army, Navy, Air Force, or Coast Guard and to personnel currently serving in a branch of the armed forces. This program began in 2017.

Number awarded 3 each year.

Deadline April of each year.

[215]
WEST VIRGINIA VETERAN'S REEDUCATION SCHOLARSHIP PROGRAM

West Virginia Department of Veteran's Assistance
Attn: Office of the Cabinet Secretary
1900 Kanawha Boulevard East, Building 5, Suite 205
Charleston, WV 25305
(304) 558-3661   Toll Free: (866) WV4-VETS (within WV)
Fax: (304) 558-3662   E-mail: dennis.e.davis@wv.gov
Web: veterans.wv.gov/Benefits/Pages/default.aspx

Summary To provide financial assistance to veterans in West Virginia who wish to return to college after completing their military service.

Eligibility This program is open to residents of West Virginia who have been honorably discharged after at least 181 consecutive days of military service; Reservists with active duty for training only are not eligible. Applicants must be eligible for federal Pell Grants or be unemployed and have exhausted all federal educational benefits from the Department of Veterans Affairs (VA). They must be attending or planning to attend a college or university in West Virginia and apply through their institution.

Financial data The stipend is $500 per term for full-time students or $250 per term for part-time students. The maximum award per calendar year is $1,500. Funds may be used for tuition assistance, tests associated with professional licensure or certification, or other training materials.

Duration 1 year; may be renewed upon reapplication if the student maintains a cumulative GPA of at least 2.0.

Number awarded Varies each year.

Deadline Applications may be submitted at any time, but they should be received at least 6 weeks before the beginning of class.

[216]
WILMA D. HOYAL/MAXINE CHILTON SCHOLARSHIPS

American Legion Auxiliary
Department of Arizona
4701 North 19th Avenue, Suite 100
Phoenix, AZ 85015-3727
(602) 241-1080   Fax: (602) 604-9640
E-mail: secretary@aladeptaz.org
Web: www.aladeptaz.org/member-resources.html

Summary To provide financial assistance to veterans, the dependents of veterans, and other students who are majoring in selected subjects at Arizona public universities.

Eligibility This program is open to second-year or upper-division full-time students majoring in political science, public programs, or special education at public universities in Arizona (the University of Arizona, Northern Arizona University, or Arizona State University). Applicants must have been Arizona residents for at least 1 year. They must have a GPA of 3.0 or higher. U.S. citizenship is required. Honorably-discharged veterans and immediate family members of veterans receive preference. Selection is based on scholarship (25%), financial need (40%), character (20%), and leadership (15%).

Financial data The stipend is $1,000.

Duration 1 year; renewable.

Number awarded 3 each year: 1 to each of the 3 universities.

Deadline May of each year.

[217]
WISCONSIN G.I. BILL TUITION REMISSION PROGRAM

Wisconsin Department of Veterans Affairs
2135 Rimrock Road
P.O. Box 7843
Madison, WI 53707-7843
(608) 266-1311   Toll Free: (800) WIS-VETS
Fax: (608) 267-0403   E-mail: WDVAInfo@dva.state.wi.us
Web: dva.wi.gov

Summary To provide financial assistance for college or graduate school to Wisconsin veterans and their dependents.

Eligibility This program is open to current residents of Wisconsin who 1) were residents of the state when they entered or reentered active duty in the U.S. armed forces; or 2) have moved to the state and have been residents for at least 5 consecutive years after entry or reentry into service. Applicants must have served on active duty for at least 2 continuous years or for at least 90 days during specified wartime periods. Also eligible are 1) qualifying children and unremarried surviving spouses of Wisconsin veterans who died in the line of duty or as the direct result of a service-connected disability; and 2) children and spouses of Wisconsin veterans who have a service-connected disability rated by the U.S. Department of Veterans Affairs as 30% or greater. Children must be between 17 and 25 years of age (regardless of the date of the veteran's death or initial disability rating) and be a Wisconsin resident for tuition purposes. Spouses remain eligible for 10 years following the date of the veteran's death or initial disability rating; they must be Wisconsin residents for tuition purposes, but they may enroll full or part time. Students may attend any institution, center, or school within the University of Wisconsin (UW) System or the Wisconsin Technical College System (WCTS). There are no income limits, delimiting periods following military service during which the benefit must be used, or limits on the level of study (e.g., vocational, undergraduate, professional, or graduate).

Financial data Veterans who qualify as a Wisconsin resident for tuition purposes are eligible for a remission of 100% of standard academic fees and segregated fees at a UW campus or 100% of program and material fees at a WCTS institution. Veterans who qualify as a Wisconsin veteran for purposes of this program but for other reasons fail to meet the definition of a Wisconsin resident for tuition purposes at the UW system are eligible for a remission of 100% of non-resident fees. Spouses and children of deceased or disabled veterans are entitled to a remission of 100% of tuition and fees at a UW or WCTS institution.

Duration Up to 8 semesters or 128 credits, whichever is greater.

Additional information This program began in 2005 as a replacement for Wisconsin Tuition and Fee Reimbursement Grants.

Number awarded Varies each year.

Deadline Applications must be submitted within 14 days from the office start of the academic term: in October for fall, March for spring, or June for summer.

[218]
WOMEN IN DEFENSE PALMETTO CHAPTER HORIZONS SCHOLARSHIP

Women in Defense-Palmetto Chapter
c/o Rachel Link, Vice President
Maga Design
913 Bowman Road, Suite 102
Mount Pleasant, SC 29464
E-mail: outreach@widpalmettochapter.org
Web: www.widpalmettochapter.org/scholarship-program

Summary To provide financial assistance to women, including those with ties to the military, who are working on an undergraduate degree in a field of science, technology, engineering, or mathematics (STEM) at a college in South Carolina.

Eligibility This program is open to women currently enrolled full time at a college or university in South Carolina and working on a degree in STEM. Applicants must be working on a field of STEM and have a GPA of 2.5 or higher if entering their sophomore year, 2.75 or higher as an entering junior, or 3.0 or higher as an entering senior. They must be U.S. citizens and able to demonstrate financial need. The program includes women who are current or former U.S. military active duty, retired, Reserve, or Guard members or are currently enrolled in an ROTC program.

Financial data The stipend is $2,500.

Duration 1 year.

Number awarded 2 each year, of which 1 is reserved for a woman with ties to the military.

Deadline November of each year.

[219]
WOMEN MARINES ASSOCIATION SCHOLARSHIP PROGRAM

Women Marines Association
120 State Avenue, Suite 303
Olympia, WA 98501
Toll Free: (888) 525-1943
E-mail: scholarship@womenmarines.org
Web: www.womenmarines.org/scholarships

Summary To provide financial assistance for college or graduate school to students sponsored by members of the Women Marines Association (WMA).

Eligibility Applicants must be sponsored by a WMA member and fall into 1 of the following categories: 1) have served or are serving in the U.S. Marine Corps, regular or Reserve; 2) are a direct descendant by blood or legal adoption or a stepchild of a Marine on active duty or who has served honorably in the U.S. Marine Corps, regular or Reserve; 3) are a sibling or a descendant of a sibling by blood or legal adoption or a stepchild of a Marine on active duty or who has served honorably in the U.S. Marine Corps, regular or Reserve; 4) be a spouse of a Marine; or 5) have completed 2 years in a Marine Corps JROTC program. WMA members may sponsor an unlimited number of applicants per year. High school seniors must submit transcripts (GPA of 3.0 or higher) and SAT or ACT scores. Undergraduate and graduate students must have a GPA of 3.0 or higher. Along with their application, they must submit 1-page statements on 1) the Marine to whom they are related; 2) their community service; and 3) their goals after college.

SCHOLARSHIPS: MILITARY PERSONNEL

Financial data Stipends range from $500 to $5,000 per year.
Duration 1 year; may be renewed 1 additional year.
Additional information This program includes the following named scholarships: the WMA Memorial Scholarships, the Lily H. Gridley Memorial Scholarship, the Ethyl and Armin Wiebke Memorial Scholarship, the Maj. Megan McClung Memorial Scholarship, the Agnes Sopcak Memorial Scholarship, the Virginia Guveyan Memorial Scholarship, the LaRue A. Ditmore Music Scholarships, the Fallen Warrior Scholarship, and the Margaret Apel Scholarship. Applicants must know a WMA member to serve as their sponsor; the WMA will not supply listings of the names or addresses of chapters or individual members.
Number awarded Varies each year.
Deadline February of each year.

[220]
WOMEN MILITARY AVIATORS DREAM OF FLIGHT SCHOLARSHIP

Women in Aviation International
Attn: Scholarships
Morningstar Airport
3647 State Route 503 South
West Alexandria, OH 45381-9354
(937) 839-4647   Fax: (937) 839-4645
E-mail: scholarships@wai.org
Web: www.wai.org/education/scholarships

Summary To provide financial assistance to members of Women in Aviation International (WAI) who have military experience and are interested in flight training or academic study.
Eligibility This program is open to WAI members who have military experience and are enrolled at an accredited academic institution or an FAA Part 141 approved flight school. Applicants must be seeking flight ratings in order to pursue opportunities in aviation. Along with their application, they must submit 1) a 500-word essay and professional resume that include their aviation history and goals, what they have done for themselves to achieve their goals, where they see themselves in 5 and 10 years, involvement in aviation activities, how the scholarship will help them achieve their objectives, and their present financial need; and 2) a narrative addressing their demonstrated persistence and determination to fly, ability to complete their current training program with 1 year, and their interest and/or participation in military aviation.
Financial data The stipend is $2,500. A 1-year membership in Women Military Aviators (WMA) is also provided.
Duration Recipients must be able to complete training within 1 year.
Additional information WAI is a nonprofit professional organization dedicated to encouraging women to consider an aviation career and to providing educational outreach activities and networking resources to women active in the industry. WMA established this program in 2005 to honor the women aviators who were serving or had served in Iraq and Afghanistan.
Number awarded 1 each year.
Deadline November of each year.

[221]
YELLOW RIBBON PROGRAM OF THE POST-9/11 GI BILL

Department of Veterans Affairs
Attn: Veterans Benefits Administration
810 Vermont Avenue, N.W.
Washington, DC 20420
(202) 418-4343   Toll Free: (888) 442-4551
Web: www.va.gov

Summary To provide financial assistance to veterans and their dependents who qualify for the Post-9/11 GI Bill and wish to attend a high cost private or out-of-state public institution.
Eligibility Maximum Post-9/11 GI Bill benefits are available to veterans who 1) served on active duty for at least 36 aggregate months after September 11, 2001; or 2) received a Purple Heart on or after September 11, 2001 and were honorably discharged after any length of service; or 3) received a Fry Scholarship on or after August 1, 2018 and/or are currently receiving that scholarship; or 4) were honorably discharged after 60 days for a service-connected disability and served at least 30 continuous days after September 11, 2001. Military personnel currently on active duty and their spouses may qualify for Post-9/11 GI Bill benefits but are not eligible for the Yellow Ribbon Program. This program is available to veterans who qualify for those benefits at the 100% rate, the children and spouses of those veterans to whom they wish to transfer their benefits, and the children of active-duty personnel who qualify for benefits at the 100% rate to whom they wish to transfer those benefits. Applicants must be working on or planning to work on an undergraduate or graduate degree at a private or out-of-state public institution that charges tuition in excess of the $25,162.14 cap imposed by the Post-9/11 GI Bill and that has agreed with the Department of Veterans Affairs (VA) to participate in this program.
Financial data Colleges and universities that charge more than $25,162.14 per academic year in tuition and fees may agree to waive tuition (up to 50%) for qualifying veterans and dependents. The amount that the college or university waives is matched by VA.
Duration Most participants receive up to 36 months of entitlement under this program. Benefits are payable for up to 15 years following release from active duty.
Number awarded Varies each year.
Deadline Deadline not specified.

Military Personnel

[222]
10TH MOUNTAIN DIVISION (LIGHT INFANTRY) SCHOLARSHIPS

Northern New York Community Foundation, Inc.
131 Washington Street
Watertown, NY 13601
(315) 782-7110   Fax: (315) 782-0047
E-mail: info@nnycf.org
Web: www.nnycf.org/scholarships/scholarships-available

Summary To provide financial assistance for college to current and former members of the 10th Mountain Division and their dependents.
Eligibility This program is open to current and former members of the 10th Mountain Division and their dependents (children and spouses). Applicants must be high school seniors applying for the freshmen year or traditional or non-traditional students enrolled as full-time undergraduates in any year of college or technical school. They must also be members of the 10th Mountain Division Association. Along with their application, they must submit a 150-word essay on the character traits that have contributed the most to their success, how they have contributed to their success, and how each will contribute to their success in life. High school juniors who will graduate early because they are in an advanced placement program may also apply. Interviews are required. Selection is based on academic achievement, personal data, and financial need.
Financial data The stipend is $5,000 per year.
Duration 1 year; recipients may reapply.
Number awarded Varies each year; recently, 8 were awarded.
Deadline March of each year.

[223]
3M "HIRE OUR HEROES" SCHOLARSHIPS AND TOOL GRANTS

Collision Repair Education Foundation
Attn: Administrative Coordinator
5125 Trillium Boulevard
Hoffman Estates, IL 60192
(847) 463-5283   Toll Free: (888) 722-3787
Fax: (847) 463-5483
E-mail: Janet.Marczyk@ed-foundation.org
Web: www.collisioneducationfoundation.org

Summary To provide financial assistance, in the form of scholarships and tool grants, to veterans and their families preparing for a career in automotive collision repair.
Eligibility This program is open to collision repair students who are currently serving or have recently served in the military, as well as their immediate family. Applicants must have completed at least 1 semester at a school that offers an auto collision/auto body repair program. Selection is based on past academic achievement, future plans, and financial need.
Financial data Recently, the program offered stipends of $2,000 to veterans and military personnel, $2,500 to family members, and tool grants to veterans.
Duration 1 year.
Additional information This program is sponsored by 3M Company.
Number awarded Varies each year; recently, the program awarded 12 scholarships to veterans and military personnel, 7 scholarships to family members, and 40 tool kit grants to veterans.
Deadline February of each year.

[224]
AEA CONGRESSMAN DAVID L. HOBSON STEM SCHOLARSHIP

Army Engineer Association
Attn: Director Washington DC Operations
P.O. Box 30260
Alexandria, VA 22310-8260
(703) 428-7084   Fax: (703) 428-6043
E-mail: xd@armyengineer.com
Web: www.armyengineer.com/scholarships

Summary To provide financial assistance to members of the Army Engineer Association (AEA) and their families interested in studying a field of STEM in college.
Eligibility This program is open to AEA members and their families who are U.S. citizens. Applicants must be enrolled full time at an accredited college or university and working on a bachelor's degree in a field of STEM. Along with their application, they must submit a 600-word essay on how their STEM degree will advance their academic/professional goals. Selection is based on that essay, scholastic aptitude, and letters of recommendation.
Financial data The stipend is $3,000.
Duration 1 year; nonrenewable.
Additional information This program is sponsored by the engineering firm, Trimble.
Number awarded Up to 3 each year.
Deadline February of each year.

[225]
AFBA NGAUS ACTIVE LIFE MEMBER SCHOLARSHIP

National Guard Association of the United States
Attn: Scholarship
One Massachusetts Avenue, N.W.
Washington, DC 20001
(202) 789-0031   Fax: (202) 682-9358
E-mail: ngaus@ngaus.org
Web: www.ngaus.org

Summary To provide financial assistance to members of the National Guard Association of the United States (NGAUS) and their dependents who are interested in working on an undergraduate or graduate degree.
Eligibility This program is open to active life NGAUS members and their dependents. Applicants must be enrolled or planning to enroll full time at a college or university in any state to work on an undergraduate or graduate degree. Along with their application, they must submit their college acceptance letter, SAT and/or ACT scores, high school or undergraduate transcripts, a publicity photograph, and an essay up to 300 words in length on an experience with the National Guard and how it has shaped their development and goals.
Financial data The stipend is $5,000.
Duration 1 year.
Additional information This program is sponsored by the Armed Forces Benefit Association (AFBA).
Number awarded 2 each year.
Deadline May of each year.

SCHOLARSHIPS: MILITARY PERSONNEL

[226]
AFCEA ROTC SCHOLARSHIPS
Armed Forces Communications and Electronics
   Association
Attn: AFCEA Educational Foundation
4114 Legato Road, Suite 1000
Fairfax, VA 22033-3342
(703) 631-6147   Toll Free: (800) 336-4583, ext. 6147
Fax: (703) 631-4693   E-mail: edfoundation@afcea.org
Web: www.afcea.org

Summary To provide financial assistance for college to outstanding ROTC cadets who are majoring in specified fields.

Eligibility This program is open to U.S. citizens who are enrolled in the ROTC detachment at an accredited college or university in any state. Applicants must have a GPA of 3.0 or higher. They must be enrolled as sophomores or juniors and working on a degree in biometrics, computer forensics science, computer programming, computer science, cyber security, engineering (computer, electrical, electronics, network, robotics, telecommunications), geospatial science, information technology, information resources management, mathematics, network security, operations research, physics, robotics, statistics, or strategic intelligence. Majors related to medicine, nursing, political science, psychology, and other fields of engineering (e.g., aerospace, chemical, civil, mechanical) are not eligible. Their application must be endorsed by the professor of aviation science at their institution. Selection is based on demonstrated dedication, superior performance, potential to serve as an officer in the armed forces, and financial need.

Financial data Stipends range from $2,000 to $3,000. Funds are paid directly to the recipient.

Duration 1 year.

Number awarded At least 3 each year: normally, 1 each for Army, Navy (including Marine Corps option), and Air Force ROTC.

Deadline April of each year.

[227]
AFCEA WAR VETERANS SCHOLARSHIPS
Armed Forces Communications and Electronics
   Association
Attn: AFCEA Educational Foundation
4114 Legato Road, Suite 1000
Fairfax, VA 22033-3342
(703) 631-6147   Toll Free: (800) 336-4583, ext. 6147
Fax: (703) 631-4693   E-mail: edfoundation@afcea.org
Web: www.afcea.org

Summary To provide financial assistance to veterans and military personnel who served in designated Overseas Contingency Operations and are working on an undergraduate degree in fields related to the support of U.S. intelligence enterprises.

Eligibility This program is open to active-duty and honorably discharged U.S. military members (including Reservists and National Guard personnel) who served in Operation Enduring Freedom, Operation Iraqi Freedom, Operation New Dawn, Operation Inherent Resolve, or Operation Freedom's Sentinel. Applicants must be enrolled as full- or part-time sophomores or juniors at a 4-year institution in the United States and working on an undergraduate degree in biometrics, computer forensics science, computer programming, computer science, cyber security, engineering (computer, electrical, electronics, network, robotics, telecommunications), geospatial science, information technology, information resources management, mathematics, network security, operations research, physics, robotics, statistics, or strategic intelligence at a school in any state. They must have a GPA of 3.0 or higher. Selection is based on merit.

Financial data The stipend is $2,500.

Duration 1 year.

Additional information This program began in 2005 as the Afghanistan and Iraq War Veterans Scholarships with funding from the Northern Virginia Chapter of AFCEA.

Number awarded Up to 12 each year: 6 for the fall semester and 6 for the spring semester.

Deadline April of each year for fall semester; November of each year for spring semester.

[228]
AIR FORCE CLUB SCHOLARSHIP PROGRAM
Air Force Services Agency
Attn: HQ AFPC/SVOFT
10100 Reunion Place, Suite 501
San Antonio, TX 78216-4138
(210) 395-7351   Toll Free: (800) 443-4834
E-mail: clubs@myairforcelife.com
Web: www.myairforcelife.com/Clubs

Summary To recognize and reward, with academic scholarships, Air Force Club members and their families who submit outstanding essays.

Eligibility This program is open to Air Force Club members and their spouses, children, stepchildren, or grandchildren who have been accepted by or are enrolled at an accredited college or university. Applicants may be traditional (graduating high school seniors) or nontraditional (all other club members). They must submit either 1) an essay of 980 to 1020 words on a topic that changes annually; or 2) a video of 4 minutes 30 seconds to 5 minutes 30 seconds on the same topic. Essays and videos must relate to a topic that changes annually; recently, students were asked to write about the core values of the U.S. Air Force. Applicants must also include a 1-page summary of their long-term career and life goals and previous accomplishments, including civic, athletic, and academic awards.

Financial data Awards for both traditional and nontraditional applicants are presented as scholarships of $7,000 for first, $5,000 for second, $3,000 for third, $2,000 for fourth, and $1,000 for honorable mention.

Duration The competition is held annually.

Additional information This competition was first held in 1997.

Number awarded 10 each year: 5 for traditional applicants and 5 for nontraditional.

Deadline May of each year.

[229]
AIR FORCE RESERVE TUITION ASSISTANCE
U.S. Air Force Reserve
Attn: Air Reserve Recruiting Service
180 Page Road, Building 208
Robins, AFB GA 31098-1815
Toll Free: (800) 257-1212
Web: www.afreserve.com/benefits

Summary To provide financial assistance for college or graduate school to members of the Air Force Reserve.

Eligibility This program is open to Air Force Reserve members interested in working on an undergraduate or graduate degree either through distance learning or on-campus courses from an accredited postsecondary institution. Applicants must be actively participating (for pay and points) and in good standing (not have a UIF, not placed on a control roster, not pending or issued an Article 15, and/or not pending court martial). They must submit a degree plan specifying all classes for which they are seeking assistance. Enlisted students must have retainability that extends beyond the last course approved for assistance or they must extend or re-enlist; commissioned officers must have a mandatory separation date of not less than 48 months of service commitment starting at the end of the last course completed.

Financial data Airmen receive 100% of tuition for undergraduate or graduate study, to a maximum of $250 per semester hour or $4,500 per year.

Duration 1 year; may be renewed.

Number awarded Varies each year.

Deadline Applications may be submitted at any time.

[230]
AIR FORCE ROTC HIGH SCHOOL SCHOLARSHIPS
U.S. Air Force
Attn: Headquarters AFROTC/RRUC
60 West Maxwell Boulevard, Building 835
Maxwell AFB, AL 36112-6501
(334) 953-3490   Toll Free: (866) 4-AFROTC
Fax: (334) 953-6167
E-mail: AFROTC.collegescholarshipprogram@us.af.mil
Web: www.afrotc.com/scholarships/high-school/types

Summary To provide financial assistance to high school seniors or graduates who are interested in joining Air Force ROTC in college and are willing to serve as Air Force officers following completion of their bachelor's degree.

Eligibility This program is open to high school seniors who are U.S. citizens at least 17 years of age and have been accepted at a college or university with an Air Force ROTC unit on campus or a college with a cross-enrollment agreement with such a college. Applicants must have a cumulative GPA of 3.0 or higher and an ACT composite score of 26 or higher or an SAT score of 1240 or higher. They must agree to serve for at least 4 years as active-duty Air Force officers following graduation from college. Recently, first priority was given to students planning to major in the science and technical fields of architecture, chemistry, computer science, engineering (aeronautical, aerospace, architectural, astronautical, civil, computer, electrical, environmental, mechanical, or nuclear), mathematics, meteorology and atmospheric sciences, nuclear physics, operations research, or physic. Second priority was given to students planning to major in foreign languages (Arabic, Baluchi, Chinese (Amoy, Cantonese, Mandarin, and Wu), Indonesian, Japanese, Javanese, Korean, Pashto-Afghan, Persian-Afghan, Persian-Iranian, Punjabi, Russian, Somali, Turkish, or Turkmen). Students could major in any other field, although most scholarships were offered for technical or language programs.

Financial data Type 1 scholarships provide payment of full tuition and most laboratory fees, as well as $900 per year for books. Type 2 scholarships pay the same benefits except tuition is capped at $18,000 per year; students who attend an institution where tuition exceeds $18,000 must pay the difference. Type 7 scholarships pay full tuition and most laboratory fees, but students must attend a public college or university where they qualify for the in-state tuition rate or a college or university where the tuition is less than the in-state rate; they may not attend an institution with higher tuition and pay the difference. Approximately 5% of scholarship offers are for Type 1, approximately 15% are for Type 2, and approximately 80% are for Type 7. All recipients are also awarded a tax-free subsistence allowance for 10 months of each year that is $300 per month as a freshman, $350 per month as a sophomore, $450 per month as a junior, and $500 per month as a senior.

Duration 4 years.

Additional information While scholarship recipients can major in any subject, they must enroll in 4 years of aerospace studies courses at 1 of the 1,100 colleges and universities that have an Air Force ROTC unit on campus or that have cross-enrollment agreements with the institutions that have an Air Force ROTC unit on campus. Recipients must attend a 4-week summer training camp at an Air Force base, usually between their sophomore and junior years. Most cadets incur a 4-year active-duty commitment.

Number awarded Approximately 2,000 each year.

Deadline January of each year.

[231]
AIR FORCE ROTC NURSING SCHOLARSHIPS
U.S. Air Force
Attn: Headquarters AFROTC/RRUC
60 West Maxwell Boulevard, Building 835
Maxwell AFB, AL 36112-6501
(334) 953-3490   Toll Free: (866) 4-AFROTC
Fax: (334) 953-6167
E-mail: AFROTC.collegescholarshipprogram@us.af.mil
Web: www.afrotc.com/scholarships/college/types

Summary To provide financial assistance to college students who are interested in a career as a nurse, are interested in joining Air Force ROTC, and are willing to serve as Air Force officers following completion of their bachelor's degree.

Eligibility This program is open to U.S. citizens who are freshmen or sophomores in college and interested in a career as a nurse. Applicants must have a cumulative GPA of 2.5 or higher at the end of their freshman year and meet all other academic and physical requirements for participation in AFROTC. They must be interested in working on a nursing degree from an accredited program. At the time of Air Force commissioning, they may be no more than 31 years of age. They must be able to pass the Air Force Officer Qualifying Test (AFOQT) and the Air Force ROTC Physical Fitness Test.

Financial data Awards are type 2 AFROTC scholarships that provide for payment of tuition and fees up to $18,000 per

year; students who attend an institution where tuition exceeds $18,000 must pay the difference. All recipients are also awarded an annual book allowance of $900 and a tax-free subsistence allowance for 10 months of each year that is $350 per month during their sophomore year, $450 during their junior year, and $500 during their senior year.
Duration 2 or 3 years, provided the recipient maintains a GPA of 2.5 or higher.
Additional information Recipients must also complete 4 years of aerospace studies courses at 1 of the 143 colleges and universities that have an Air Force ROTC unit on campus or 1 of the 850 colleges that have cross-enrollment agreements with those institutions. They must also attend a 4-week summer training camp at an Air Force base, usually between their sophomore and junior years. Following completion of their bachelor's degree, scholarship recipients earn a commission as a second lieutenant in the Air Force and serve at least 4 years.
Number awarded Varies each year.
Deadline June of each year.

[232]
AIR FORCE TUITION ASSISTANCE PROGRAM
U.S. Air Force
Attn: Air Force Personnel Center
Headquarters USAF/DPPAT
550 C Street West, Suite 10
Joint Base San Antonio-Randolph, TX 78150-4712
Toll Free: (800) 525-0102   Fax: (210) 565-2328
E-mail: afpc.pa.task@us.af.mil
Web: www.afpc.af.mil
Summary To provide financial assistance for college or graduate school to active-duty Air Force personnel.
Eligibility Eligible to apply for this program are active-duty Air Force personnel who have completed 2 years of their service obligation.
Financial data Air Force personnel chosen for participation in this program continue to receive their regular Air Force pay. The Air Force will pay 100% of the tuition costs in an approved program, to a maximum of $4,500 per year or $250 per semester hour, whichever is less. Funding is available only for tuition, not fees or other associated expenses.
Duration Up to 124 semester hours for a bachelor's degree or up to 42 semester hours for a graduate degree. Undergraduates must complete all courses with a grade of "C" or better; graduate students must complete classes with a grade of "B" of better. If recipients fail to achieve those grades, they must reimburse the Air Force for all funds received.
Additional information Applications and further information about this program are available from counselors at the education centers on Air Force bases. Most Air Force personnel who receive tuition assistance participate in the Community College of the Air Force; there, participants earn a 2-year associate degree by combining on-the-job technical training or attendance at Air Force schools with enrollment in college courses at a civilian institution during off-duty hours. In addition, each Air Force base offers at least 4 subject areas in which selected Air Force personnel can receive tuition assistance for study leading to a bachelor's degree, and 2 disciplines in which they can pursue graduate study.
Number awarded Varies each year.
Deadline Deadline not specified.

[233]
AIRMAN SCHOLARSHIP AND COMMISSIONING PROGRAM
U.S. Air Force
Attn: Headquarters AFROTC/RRUE
Jeanne M. Holm Center for Officer Accession and Citizen Development
60 West Maxwell Boulevard, Building 835
Maxwell AFB, AL 36112-6501
(334) 953-5122   Toll Free: (866) 4-AFROTC
Fax: (334) 953-6167   E-mail: afrotc.rrue@us.af.mil
Web: www.afrotc.com/scholarships/enlisted/ascp-soar
Summary To allow selected enlisted Air Force personnel to separate from the Air Force and earn a bachelor's degree in approved majors by providing financial assistance for full-time college study, especially in designated fields.
Eligibility This program is open to active-duty enlisted members of the Air Force who have completed at least 1 year of continuous active duty and at least 1 year on station. Applicants normally must have completed at least 24 semester hours of graded college credit with a cumulative college GPA of 2.5 or higher. If they have not completed 24 hours of graded college credit, they must have an ACT score of 26 or higher or an SAT score of 1240 or higher. They must also have scores on the Air Force Officer Qualifying Test (AFOQT) of 55 or more and be able to pass the Air Force ROTC Physical Fitness Test. Applicants must have been accepted at a college or university (including cross-town schools) offering the AFROTC 4-year program. When they complete the program and receive their commission, they may not be 31 years of age or older. They must complete 24 semesters of mathematics and physical sciences or 4 semesters of a foreign language and major in an approved field; for a list of currently-approved majors, contact the program. U.S. citizenship is required.
Financial data Awards are type 2 AFROTC scholarships that provide for payment of tuition and fees, to a maximum of $18,000 per year, plus an annual book allowance of $900. All recipients are also awarded a tax-free subsistence allowance of $300 to $500 per month.
Duration 2 to 4 years, until completion of a bachelor's degree.
Additional information Selectees separate from the active-duty Air Force, join an AFROTC detachment, and become full-time students. Upon completing their degree, they are commissioned as officers and returned to active duty in the Air Force with a service obligation of 4 years of active duty and 4 years of Reserves. Further information is available from base education service officers or an Air Force ROTC unit.
Number awarded Varies each year.
Deadline October of each year.

[234]
ALABAMA NATIONAL GUARD EDUCATIONAL ASSISTANCE PROGRAM

Alabama Commission on Higher Education
Attn: Grants Coordinator
100 North Union Street
P.O. Box 302000
Montgomery, AL 36130-2000
(334) 242-2273 Fax: (334) 242-0268
E-mail: cheryl.newton@ache.alabama.gov
Web: www.ache.edu/StudentAsst.aspx

Summary To provide financial assistance to members of the Alabama National Guard interested in attending college or graduate school in the state.

Eligibility This program is open to Alabama residents who are enrolled in an associate, baccalaureate, master's, or doctoral program at a public college, university, community college, technical college, or junior college in the state; are making satisfactory academic progress as determined by the eligible institution; and are members in good standing of the Alabama National Guard who have completed basic training and advanced individual training. Applicants may be receiving federal veterans benefits, but they must show a cost less aid amount of at least $25.

Financial data Scholarships cover tuition, educational fees, books, and supplies, up to a maximum of $5,406 per semester ($10,812 per year). All Alabama Student Grant program proceeds for which the student is eligible are deducted from this award.

Duration Up to 12 years after the date of the first grant payment to the student through this program.

Number awarded Varies each year; recently, 653 were awarded. Awards are determined on a first-in, first-out basis as long as funds are available.

Deadline July of each year.

[235]
ALASKA NATIONAL GUARD STATE TUITION REIMBURSEMENT PROGRAM

Alaska National Guard
Attn: Education Services Office
Army Guard Road, Building 49000
P.O. Box 5800
Joint Base Elmendorf-Richardson, AK 99505-5800
(907) 428-6477 Fax: (907) 428-6929
E-mail: maria.j.alvarez10.mil@mail.mil
Web: www.dmva.alaska.gov/FamilyServices/Education

Summary To provide financial assistance to current and former members of the Alaska National Guard who wish to attend a college or university in the state.

Eligibility This program is open to members of the Alaska National Guard (Air and Army) and Naval Militia who have a rating of E-1 through O-5, including warrant officers, and are attending a university program in Alaska. Eligibility extends to members who 1) have satisfactorily completed their service contract and who served honorably in federal active service or federally-funded state active service after September 11, 2001; or 2) have been separated or discharged from the Guard because of a service-connected injury, disease, or disability. First priority is given to undergraduates; if funding is available, students working on a second bachelor's degree or a master's degree may be supported. Non-prior servicemembers must complete Initial Active Duty for Training (IADT); prior servicemembers are eligible immediately.

Financial data Recipients are entitled to reimbursement equivalent to 100% of the cost of tuition and fees at the University of Alaska, to a maximum of $4,500 per fiscal year.

Duration 1 semester; may be renewed for a total of 144 semester credits.

Number awarded Varies each year.

Deadline Applications may be submitted at any time, but they must be received at least 90 days after the last official day of the class or term.

[236]
ALBERT M. BECKER MEMORIAL MILITARY SCHOLARSHIP

New York American Legion Press Association
Attn: Scholarship Chair
P.O. Box 424
Sanborn, NY 14132
E-mail: jackbutton@hotmail.com
Web: nyalpa.webs.com/pubslinksannualevents.htm

Summary To provide financial assistance to veterans and specified military personnel from New York who are interested in careers in communications.

Eligibility This program is open to New York residents who are 1) veterans with an honorable discharge; or 2) currently-serving members of the National Guard or military Reserve. Membership in the American Legion family is not required, but extra credit is given for membership. Applicants must be enrolled or planning to enroll full time at an accredited college, university, or trade school in any school to work on a degree in communications (including public relations, journalism, reprographics, newspaper design or management, web page design, video design, social media communications, photojournalism, American history, political science, public communications, or other field of study related to the goals of the sponsor or the American Legion family). Along with their application, they must submit a 500-word essay on their field of study, the reasons for choosing their field of study, and their goals upon completion of study. Financial need and class standing are not considered. U.S. citizenship is required.

Financial data The stipend is $1,000.

Duration 1 year.

Number awarded 1 each year.

Deadline April of each year.

[237]
ALLIED.COM MILITARY SCHOLARSHIP

Allied Van Lines
One Parkview Plaza
Oakbrook Terrace, IL 60180
Toll Free: (800) 689-8684
Web: www.allied.com/military-scholarship

Summary To provide financial assistance to current and former military personnel and their families who are interested in attending college to study fields related to logistics.

Eligibility This program is open to current and honorably discharged members of the military, their spouses, and their children under 21 years of age or (if currently attending college) under 23 years of age. Applicants must be enrolled or planning to enroll full time at a 4-year college or university and major in military logistics, supply chain management, or oper-

ational management. They must be U.S. citizens or permanent residents. Along with their application, they must submit an essay of 400 to 800 words on why a career in logistics/supply chain management is their college major of choice. Financial need is not considered in the selection process.
Financial data The stipend is $1,000.
Duration 1 year.
Additional information This program began in 2015.
Number awarded 2 each year.
Deadline September of each year.

[238]
ANGEA SCHOLARSHIP
Alaska National Guard Enlisted Association
Attn: Scholarship Program
P.O. Box 5302
Joint Base Elmendorf-Richardson, AK 99505-5302
E-mail: akenlisted@angea.org
Web: www.angea.org

Summary To provide financial assistance to members of the Alaska National Guard Enlisted Association (ANGEA) and their families who are interested in attending college in any state.
Eligibility This program is open to current and retired members of the Alaska Air and Army National Guard who are current members of ANGEA and their dependents. Applicants must be enrolled or planning to enroll at an accredited college, university, or vocational/technical school in any state. Along with their application, they must submit a letter that includes their educational and career goals; a list of awards, honors, extracurricular activities, and organizational involvement; information on their civic involvement, moral leadership, or other constructive characteristics demonstrating commitment to community, state, and/or country; and a statement on their financial need.
Financial data A stipend is awarded (amount not specified).
Duration 1 year.
Number awarded 1 or more each year.
Deadline March of each year.

[239]
ARKANSAS NATIONAL GUARD TUITION WAIVER PROGRAM
Arkansas National Guard
Attn: Education Services Office
DCSPER-ED
Camp Robinson
North Little Rock, AR 72199-9600
(501) 212-4021   Fax: (501) 212-5449
E-mail: ng.ar.ararng.list.education-office@mail.mil
Web: arkansas.nationalguard.mil

Summary To provide financial assistance to members of the Arkansas National Guard who are interested in attending a public college in the state.
Eligibility This program is open to members of the Arkansas National Guard who have completed Initial Active Duty Training (IADT) and are not currently flagged for misconduct. Applicants must be enrolled or accepted for enrollment in an undergraduate program at a public college or university in Arkansas.
Financial data The program provides full payment of tuition and mandatory fees, but not books, other fees, or other educational expenses.
Duration 1 semester; may be renewed for up to 120 credit hours or completion of a bachelor's degree, whichever comes first.
Additional information This program began in 2017 as a replacement for the Arkansas National Guard Tuition Incentive Program (GTIP).
Number awarded Varies each year.
Deadline Applications are accepted from 60 days prior to until 30 days after the start of the semester.

[240]
ARMED FORCES TUITION WAIVER PROGRAM OF MASSACHUSETTS
Massachusetts Office of Student Financial Assistance
75 Pleasant Street
Malden, MA 02148
(617) 391-6070   Fax: (617) 727-0667
E-mail: osfa@osfa.mass.edu
Web: www.mass.edu/osfa/programs/categorical.asp

Summary To waive tuition at Massachusetts public colleges and universities for members of the armed forces.
Eligibility Applicants for this assistance must have been permanent legal residents of Massachusetts for at least 1 year and stationed in Massachusetts as members of the Army, Navy, Marine Corps, Air Force, or Coast Guard. They may not be in default on any federal student loan. They must enroll in at least 3 undergraduate credits per semester. U.S. citizenship or permanent resident status is required.
Financial data Eligible military personnel are exempt from any tuition payments toward an undergraduate degree or certificate program at public colleges or universities in Massachusetts.
Duration Up to 4 academic years, for a total of 130 semester hours.
Additional information Recipients may enroll either part or full time in a Massachusetts publicly-supported institution.
Number awarded Varies each year.
Deadline April of each year.

[241]
ARMY AVIATION ASSOCIATION OF AMERICA SCHOLARSHIPS
Army Aviation Association of America Scholarship Foundation
Attn: AAAA Scholarship Foundation
593 Main Street
Monroe, CT 06468-2806
(203) 268-2450   Fax: (203) 268-5870
E-mail: scholarship@quad-a.org
Web: www.quad-a.org/Scholarship/Scholarship/about.aspx

Summary To provide financial aid for undergraduate or graduate study to members of the Army Aviation Association of America (AAAA) and their relatives.
Eligibility This program is open to current AAAA members and the spouses, children, grandchildren, and unmarried siblings of current or deceased members. Applicants must be enrolled or accepted for enrollment as an undergraduate or graduate student at an accredited college or university. They must include a 300-word essay on their life experiences, work

history, and aspirations. Some scholarships are specifically reserved for enlisted, warrant officer, company grade, and Department of the Army civilian members. Selection is based on academic merit and personal achievement.
Financial data Stipends range from $1,000 to $5,000 per year.
Duration Scholarships may be for 1 year, 2 years, or 4 years.
Number awarded Varies each year; recently, $516,000 in scholarships was awarded to 304 students. Since the program began in 1963, the foundation has awarded more than $4 million to more than 4,100 qualified applicants.
Deadline Interested students must submit a pre-qualifying form by March of each year. The final application is due in April.

[242]
ARMY NATIONAL GUARD FEDERAL TUITION ASSISTANCE
U.S. Army National Guard
Education Support Center
Camp Joseph T. Robinson
Building 5400 Box 46
North Little Rock, AR 72199-9600
Toll Free: (866) 628-5999 Fax: (501) 212-4928
E-mail: esc@ng.army.mil
Web: www.nationalguard.com

Summary To provide financial assistance for college or graduate school to members of the Army National Guard in each state.
Eligibility This program is open to members of the Army National Guard in every state who are interested in attending a college, community college, or university within the state. Applicants must have sufficient time to complete the course before their Expiration Time of Service (ETS) date. They must be interested in working on a high school diploma or equivalent (GED), certificate, associate degree, bachelor's degree, master's degree, or first professional degree, including those in architecture, Certified Public Accountant (C.P.A.), podiatry, dentistry (D.D.S. or D.M.D.), medicine (M.D.), optometry, osteopathic medicine, pharmacy (Pharm.D.), or theology (M.Div. or M.H.L.). Commissioned officers must agree to remain in the Guard for at least 4 years following completion of the course for which assistance is provided, unless they are involuntarily separated from the service.
Financial data Assistance provides up to 100% of tuition (to a maximum of $250 per semester hour or $4,500 per person per fiscal year).
Duration Participants in Officer Candidate School (OCS), Warrant Officer Candidate School (WOCS), and ROTC Simultaneous Membership Program (SMP) may enroll in up to 15 semester hours per year until completion of a baccalaureate degree. Warrant Officers are funded to complete an associate degree.
Additional information Tuition assistance may be used along with federal Pell Grants but not with Montgomery GI Bill benefits. State tuition assistance programs can be used concurrently with this program, but not to exceed 100% of tuition costs.
Number awarded Varies each year; recently, more than 22,000 Guard members received tuition assistance.
Deadline Deadline not specified.

[243]
ARMY NURSE CORPS ASSOCIATION SCHOLARSHIPS
Army Nurse Corps Association
Attn: Scholarship Program
8000 IH-10 West, Suite 600
San Antonio, TX 78230-3887
(210) 650-3534 Toll Free: (888) 742-9910
E-mail: education@e-anca.org
Web: www.e-anca.org/Scholarships

Summary To provide financial assistance to students who have a connection to the Army and are interested in working on an undergraduate or graduate degree in nursing.
Eligibility This program is open to U.S. citizens attending colleges or universities that have accredited programs offering undergraduate or graduate degrees in nursing. Applicants must be 1) students currently enrolled in an accredited baccalaureate or advanced nursing or nurse anesthesia program who are serving or have served (and received an honorable discharge) in any branch and at any rank of a component of the Active Army, Army National Guard, or Army Reserve; or 2) nursing or anesthesia students whose parent(s), spouse, or child(ren) are serving or have served in a component of the Active Army, Army National Guard, or Army Reserve. Along with their application, they must submit a personal statement on their professional career objectives, reasons for applying for this scholarship, financial need, special considerations, personal and academic interests, and why they are preparing for a nursing career. Students who are receiving any support from any branch of the military, including ROTC scholarships, are not eligible.
Financial data The stipend is $3,000. Funds are sent directly to the recipient's school.
Duration 1 year.
Additional information Although the sponsoring organization is made up of current, retired, and honorably discharged officers of the Army Nurse Corps, it does not have an official affiliation with the Army. Therefore, students who receive these scholarships do not incur any military service obligation.
Number awarded Varies each year.
Deadline March of each year.

[244]
ARMY RESERVE TUITION ASSISTANCE
U.S. Army Reserve
Attn: Director, USAR Education
ARPC-PS
1 Reserve Way
St. Louis, MO 63132-5200
Toll Free: (800) 452-0201
Web: myarmybenefits.us.army.mil

Summary To provide financial assistance for college or graduate school to specified members of the U.S. Army Reserve (USAR).
Eligibility This program is open to drilling USAR soldiers in good standing. Applicants must be working on their first bachelor's or master's degree and be able to declare an educational goal after completing 15 credit hours. Enlisted members and warrant officers must be able to complete the program under their current term of service or reenlist. Commis-

sioned officers must have at last 4 years of remaining service obligation from the date or course completion.
Financial data Assistance is provided at the rate of $250 per credit hour, to a maximum of $4,500 per fiscal year.
Duration 1 year; may be renewed.
Number awarded Varies each year.
Deadline Applications may be submitted at any time.

[245]
ARMY ROTC 4-YEAR HIGH SCHOOL SCHOLARSHIPS
U.S. Army
Attn: U.S. Army Cadet Command
G2 Incentives Division
1307 Third Avenue
Fort Knox, KY 40121-2725
(502) 624-7371   Toll Free: (888) 550-ARMY
Fax: (502) 624-1120
E-mail: usarmy.knox.usacc.mbx.train2lead@mail.mil
Web: www.goarmy.com

Summary To provide financial assistance to high school seniors or graduates who are interested in enrolling in Army ROTC in college.
Eligibility Applicants for this program must 1) be U.S. citizens; 2) be between 17 and 26 years of age; 3) score at least 1000 on the SAT or 19 on the ACT; 4) have a high school GPA of 2.5 or higher; and 5) meet medical and other regulatory requirements. Current college or university students may apply if their school considers them beginning freshmen with 4 academic years remaining for a bachelor's degree.
Financial data This scholarship provides financial assistance of up to $20,000 per year for college tuition and educational fees or for room and board, whichever the student selects. In addition, a flat rate of $1,200 per year is provided for the purchase of textbooks, classroom supplies, and equipment. Recipients are also awarded a stipend of $420 per month for up to 10 months of each year.
Duration 4 years, until completion of a baccalaureate degree.
Additional information Scholarship recipients participate in the Army ROTC program as part of their college curriculum by enrolling in 4 years of military science classes and attending a 6-week Cadet Leadership Course (CLC) between the junior and senior years. Following graduation, they receive a commission as a Regular Army, Army Reserve, or Army National Guard officer. Scholarship winners must serve in the Army for 8 years, including 4 years of full-time service and 4 years in the Individual Ready Reserve (IRR). They may elect to serve part time in the Army Reserve or Army National Guard while pursuing a civilian career.
Number awarded Approximately 1,500 each year.
Deadline January of each year.

[246]
ARMY ROTC COLLEGE SCHOLARSHIP PROGRAM
U.S. Army
Attn: U.S. Army Cadet Command
G2 Incentives Division
1307 Third Avenue
Fort Knox, KY 40121-2725
(502) 624-7371   Toll Free: (888) 550-ARMY
Fax: (502) 624-6937
E-mail: usarmy.knox.usacc.mbx.train2lead@mail.mil
Web: www.goarmy.com/rotc/college-students.html

Summary To provide financial assistance to students who are or will be enrolled in Army ROTC.
Eligibility This program is open to U.S. citizens between 17 and 26 years of age who have already completed 1 or 2 years in a college or university with an Army ROTC unit on campus or in a college with a cross-enrollment agreement with a college with an Army ROTC unit on campus. Applicants must have 2 or 3 years remaining for their bachelor's degree (or 4 years of a 5-year bachelor's program) and must be able to complete that degree before their 31st birthday. They must have a high school GPA of 2.5 or higher and scores of at least 1000 on the SAT or 19 on the ACT.
Financial data These scholarships provide financial assistance for college tuition and educational fees, up to an annual amount of $20,000. In addition, a flat rate of $1,200 is provided for the purchase of textbooks, classroom supplies, and equipment. Recipients are also awarded a stipend of $420 per month for up to 10 months of each year.
Additional information Applications must be made through professors of military science at 1 of the schools hosting the Army ROTC program. Preference is given to students who have already enrolled as non-scholarship students in military science classes at 1 of the more than 270 institutions with an Army ROTC unit on campus, at 1 of the 75 college extension centers, or at 1 of the more than 1,000 colleges with cross-enrollment or extension agreements with 1 of the colleges with an Army ROTC unit. Scholarship winners must serve full time in the Army for 4 years. They may elect to serve part time in the Army Reserve or Army National Guard while pursuing a civilian career.
Number awarded Varies each year; a recent allocation provided for 700 4-year scholarships, 1,800 3-year scholarships, and 2,800 2-year scholarships.
Deadline December of each year.

[247]
ARMY ROTC NURSE PROGRAM
U.S. Army
Attn: U.S. Army Cadet Command
G2 Incentives Division
1307 Third Avenue
Fort Knox, KY 40121-2725
(502) 624-6298   Toll Free: (888) 550-ARMY
Fax: (502) 624-6937
E-mail: usarmy.knox.usacc.mbx.train2lead@mail.mil
Web: www.goarmy.com

Summary To provide financial assistance to high school seniors or graduates who are interested in enrolling in Army ROTC and majoring in nursing in college.
Eligibility Applicants for the Army Reserve Officers' Training Corps (ROTC) Nurse program must 1) be U.S. citizens; 2)

be at least 17 years of age by October of the year in which they are seeking a scholarship; 3) be no more than 27 years of age when they graduate from college after 4 years; 4) score at least 920 on the combined mathematics and critical reading SAT or 19 on the ACT; 5) have a high school GPA of 2.5 or higher; and 6) meet medical and other regulatory requirements. This program is open to ROTC scholarship applicants who wish to enroll in a nursing program at 1 of approximately 100 designated partner colleges and universities and become Army nurses after graduation.

Financial data This scholarship provides financial assistance toward college tuition and educational fees up to an annual amount of $20,000. In addition, a flat rate of $1,200 is provided for the purchase of textbooks, classroom supplies, and equipment. Recipients are also awarded a stipend of $420 per month for up to 10 months of each year.

Duration 4 years, until completion of a baccalaureate degree. A limited number of 2-year and 3-year scholarships are also available to students who are already attending an accredited B.S.N. program on a campus affiliated with ROTC.

Additional information This program began in 1996 to ensure that ROTC cadets seeking nursing careers would be admitted to the upper-level division of a baccalaureate program. The 56 partnership nursing schools affiliated with Army ROTC have agreed to guarantee upper-level admission to students who maintain an established GPA during their first 2 years. During the summer, recipients have the opportunity to participate in the Nurse Summer Training Program, a paid 3- to 4-week clinical elective at an Army hospital in the United States, Germany, or Korea. Following completion of their baccalaureate degree, participants become commissioned officers in the Army Nurse Corps. Scholarship winners must serve in the military for 8 years. That service obligation may be fulfilled 1) by serving on active duty for 4 years followed by service in the Army National Guard (ARNG), the United States Army Reserve (USAR), or the Inactive Ready Reserve (IRR) for the remainder of the 8 years; or 2) by serving 8 years in an ARNG or USAR troop program unit that includes a 3- to 6-month active-duty period for initial training.

Number awarded A limited number each year.
Deadline November of each year.

[248]
ARMY SPECIALIZED TRAINING ASSISTANCE PROGRAM (STRAP)

U.S. Army National Guard
Education Support Center
Camp Joseph T. Robinson
Building 5400 Box 46
North Little Rock, AR 72199-9600
Toll Free: (866) 628-5999   Fax: (501) 212-4928
E-mail: esc@ng.army.mil
Web: www.nationalguard.com

Summary To provide funding for service to members of the United States Army Reserve (USAR) or Army National Guard (ARNG) who are engaged in additional training in designated health care fields that are considered critical for wartime medical needs.

Eligibility This program is open to members of the USAR or ARNG who are 1) medical residents (currently in orthopedic surgery, family practice, emergency medicine, general surgery, obstetrics/gynecology, or internal medicine); 2) dental residents (currently in general dentistry, oral surgery, prosthodontics, or comprehensive dentistry); 3) nursing students working on a master's degree (currently in community health, psychiatric nurse practitioner, or nurse anesthesia; or 4) associate degree or diploma nurses working on a bachelor's degree. Applicants must agree to a service obligation of 1 year for every 6 months of support received.

Financial data This program pays a stipend of at least $2,300 per month.

Duration 1 year; may be renewed.

Additional information During their obligated period of service, participants must attend Extended Combat Training (ECT) at least 12 days each year and complete the Officer Basic Leadership Course (OBLC) within the first year.

Number awarded Varies each year.
Deadline Applications may be submitted at any time.

[249]
ARMY TUITION ASSISTANCE BENEFITS

U.S. Army
Human Resources Command
AHRC-PDE-EI
Attn: Education Incentives and Counseling Branch
1600 Spearhead Division Avenue
Fort Knox, KY 40122-5408
Toll Free: (800) 872-8272
E-mail: usarmy.knox.hrc.mbx.tagd-pdeei@mail.mil
Web: myarmybenefits.us.army.mil

Summary To provide financial assistance to Army personnel interested in working on an undergraduate or master's degree.

Eligibility This program is open to active-duty Army personnel, including members of the Army National Guard and Army Reserve on active duty, who have completed at least 1 year of service after graduation from AIT, OCS, or BOLC; graduate students must have completed 10 years of service. Applicants must first visit an education counselor to declare an educational goal and establish an educational plan. They may enroll in up to 16 semester hours of academic courses. Support is not provided for a second equivalent degree or for first professional degrees (e.g., Ph.D., M.D., or J.D.).

Financial data Those selected for participation in this program receive their regular Army pay and 100% of tuition at the postsecondary educational institution of their choice, but capped at $4,500 per year or $250 per semester hour, whichever is less. Funding is available only for tuition, not fees or other associated expenses.

Duration Up to 130 semester hours for completion of a bachelor's degree or up to 39 semester hours for completion of a master's degree. Undergraduates must complete all courses with a grade of "C" or better; graduate students must complete classes with a grade of "B" of better. If recipients fail to achieve those grades, they must reimburse the Army for all funds received.

Additional information This program is part of the Army Continuing Education System (ACES). Further information is available from counselors at the education centers at all Army installations with a troop strength of 750 or more. Officers incur a service obligation of 2 years for active duty or 4 years for Reserve and National Guard.

Number awarded Varies each year; recently, this program funded completion of 8,525 degree for active soldiers, 1,359 for Guard soldiers, and 1,469 for Reserve soldiers.
Deadline Deadline not specified.

[250]
ARMY WOMEN'S FOUNDATION LEGACY SCHOLARSHIPS

Army Women's Foundation
Attn: Scholarship Committee
P.O. Box 5030
Fort Lee, VA 23801-0030
(804) 734-3078   E-mail: info@awfdn.org
Web: www.awfdn.org/scholarships/general-information

Summary To provide financial assistance for college or graduate school to women who are serving or have served in the Army and their children.
Eligibility This program is open to 1) women who have served or are serving honorably in the U.S. Army, U.S. Army Reserve, or Army National Guard; and 2) children of those women. Applicants must be 1) high school graduates or GED recipients enrolled at a community college or technical certificate program who have a GPA of 2.5 or higher; 2) sophomores or higher at an accredited college or university who have a GPA of 3.0 or higher; or 3) students enrolled in or accepted to a graduate program who have a GPA of 3.0 or higher. Along with their application, they must submit a 2-page essay on why they should be considered for this scholarship; their future plans as related to their program of study; their community service, activities, and work experience; and how the Army has impacted their life and/or goals. Selection is based on merit, academic potential, community service, and financial need.
Financial data The stipend is $2,500 for college and graduate students or $1,000 for community college and certificate students.
Duration 1 year; recipients may reapply.
Number awarded Varies each year; recently, 21 soldiers and 10 children received these scholarships.
Deadline January of each year.

[251]
ARNOLD AIR SOCIETY AND SILVER WINGS ACADEMIC SCHOLARSHIP PROGRAM

Arnold Air Society-Silver Wings
c/o Executive Management Center
1501 Lee Highway, Suite 400
Arlington, VA 22209
(202) 999-5173   E-mail: mgmt.center@arnold-air.org
Web: www.aas-sw.org/grants-and-internships

Summary To provide financial assistance for continuing college education to members of Arnold Air Society and Silver Wings.
Eligibility This program is open to 1) non-graduating AS200, AS300, and AS400 Arnold Air Society and Silver Wings cadets in Air Force ROTC; and 2) Silver Wings civilian sophomores, juniors, and non-graduating seniors. Each AFROTC Detachment Commander may nominate 1 Arnold Air Society member from each class and 1 Silver Wings member from each class. Applicants must have a GPA of 2.5 or higher and be able to demonstrate financial need. Along with their application, they must submit a 3-page essay on either air mobility or the impact of technology on today's air operations. Selection is based primarily on the essay's content and strength of supporting arguments (40%), originality of thought (25%), conformance with accepted English composition and bibliographic standards (10%), and conformance with formatting instructions (5%); other factors considered include demonstration of leadership and service (10%) and demonstration of financial need (10%).
Financial data Stipends range from $2,500 to $10,000.
Duration 1 year.
Additional information This program is supported by the Airlift Tanker Association (ATA) and the George and Vicki Muellner Foundation.
Number awarded 17 each year: 1 at $10,000, 1 at $8,000, 2 at $5,000, and 13 at $2,500.
Deadline November of each year.

[252]
ARNOLD AIR SOCIETY AND SILVER WINGS FLYING SCHOLARSHIPS

Arnold Air Society-Silver Wings
c/o Executive Management Center
1501 Lee Highway, Suite 400
Arlington, VA 22209
(202) 999-5173   E-mail: mgmt.center@arnold-air.org
Web: www.aas-sw.org/grants-and-internships

Summary To provide financial assistance for flight training to members of Arnold Air Society and Silver Wings, including women and African Americans.
Eligibility This program is open to all active members of the Arnold Air Society and Silver Wings, including those with and without flight experience. Applicants must be interested in enrolling in flight training at a local airport of their choice. They must have a GPA of 2.5 or higher. Along with their application, they must submit a 300-word essay explaining why they desire to receive flight training. Financial need is not considered in the selection process. The program includes scholarships designated for women and for African Americans.
Financial data The stipend is $1,500. Funds are sent directly to the flight training center.
Duration Training must be completed within 6 months after the award.
Additional information This program receives support from the Airpower Foundation, Lockheed Martin, USAA, Boeing, Southwest Airlines, the Airlift Tanker Association, and the Air Force Association. It includes 1 of the scholarships for all students named in honor of General (Ret.) Craig R. McKinley and 2 named in honor of Herb Kelleher, founder of Southwest Airlines, including 1 of the scholarships for women and 1 for African Americans.
Number awarded 30 each year: 10 available for all students, 10 available for women, and 10 available for African Americans.
Deadline October of each year.

[253]
ASMC MEMBERS' CONTINUING EDUCATION GRANTS

American Society of Military Comptrollers
Attn: National Awards Committee
415 North Alfred Street
Alexandria, VA 22314
(703) 549-0360   Toll Free: (800) 462-5637
Fax: (703) 549-3181   E-mail: awards@asmconline.org
Web: asmc.secure-platform.com/a

Summary To provide financial assistance for continuing education to members of the American Society of Military Comptrollers (ASMC).

Eligibility Applicants for this assistance must have been members of the society for at least 2 full years and must have been active in the local chapter at some level (e.g., board member, committee chair or member, volunteer for chapter events), They must be enrolled or planning to enroll at an academic institution in a field of study directly related to military comptrollership, including business administration, economics, public administration, accounting, or finance. Selection is based on individual merit.

Financial data Stipends are $3,000 or $1,500.

Duration 1 year.

Additional information The ASMC is open to all financial management professionals employed by the U.S. Department of Defense or Coast Guard, both civilian and military. The applicant whose service to the society is judged the most exceptional is designated the Dick Vincent Scholarship winner.

Number awarded 11 each year: 1 at $3,000 (the Dick Vincent Scholarship) and 10 at $1,500.

Deadline March of each year.

[254]
ASSOCIATION OF THE UNITED STATES NAVY SCHOLARSHIP PROGRAM

Association of the United States Navy
Attn: Scholarship Program
3601 Eisenhower Avenue, Suite 110
Alexandria, VA 22304
(703) 548-5800   Toll Free: (877) NAVY-411
Fax: (703) 683-3647   E-mail: Membership@ausn.org
Web: ausn.org/members/scholarships

Summary To provide financial assistance for college to members and dependents of members of the Association of the United States Navy (AUSN).

Eligibility This program is open to AUSN members, children and grandchildren of members, and surviving spouses of deceased members. Applicants must be enrolled or planning to enroll full time at a college, university, or technical school. Along with their application, they must submit a 1-page autobiography that includes the things that have influenced their life, including memberships, accomplishments, hobbies, and goals. Selection is based on academic and leadership ability, potential, character, personal qualities, and financial need.

Financial data Stipends range from $1,000 to $2,000 per year.

Duration 1 year; may be renewed 1 additional year, provided the recipient maintains a GPA of 2.5 or higher.

Additional information The AUSN was formed in 2009 as a successor to the Naval Reserve Association.

Number awarded Varies each year.

Deadline May of each year.

[255]
BG BENJAMIN B. TALLEY SCHOLARSHIP

Society of American Military Engineers-Anchorage Post
c/o Thomas Fenoseff
Anchorage School District
Senior Director, Capital Planning and Construction
1301 Labar Street
Anchorage, AK 99515-3517
(907) 348-5223   Fax: (901) 348-5227
E-mail: Fenoseff_Thomas@askd12.org
Web: www.sameanchorage.org/wp/scholarship-information

Summary To provide financial assistance to student members of the Society of American Military Engineers (SAME) from Alaska who are working on a bachelor's or master's degree in designated fields of engineering or the natural sciences.

Eligibility This program is open to members of the Anchorage Post of SAME who are residents of Alaska, attending college in Alaska, an active-duty military member stationed in Alaska, or a dependent of an active-duty military member stationed in Alaska. Applicants must be 1) sophomores, juniors, or seniors majoring in engineering, architecture, construction or project management, natural sciences, physical sciences, applied sciences, or mathematics at an accredited college or university; or 2) students working on a master's degree in those fields. They must have a GPA of 2.5 or higher. U.S. citizenship is required. Along with their application, they must submit an essay of 250 to 500 words on their career goals. Selection is based on that essay, academic achievement, participation in school and community activities, and work/family activities; financial need is not considered.

Financial data Stipends range up to $3,000.

Duration 1 year.

Additional information This program began in 1997.

Number awarded Several each year; at least 1 scholarship is reserved for a master's degree student.

Deadline December of each year.

[256]
BOSTON POST SAME SCHOLARSHIPS

Society of American Military Engineers-Boston Post
c/o Lisa Branson, Scholarship Committee Chair
CDM Smith
75 State Street, Suite 701
Boston, MA 02109
(617) 901-8281   Fax: (617) 345-3901
E-mail: brandonlo@cdmsmith.com
Web: www.same.org

Summary To provide financial assistance to residents of New England majoring in a program related to construction at a college in any state.

Eligibility This program is open to residents of New England who are currently enrolled in an accepted engineering or architecture program, preferably in civil engineering, environmental engineering, architecture, or other construction-related program, at a college or university in any state. Applicants must have completed at least 1 academic year and have at least 1 year remaining. They must be nominated by their institution. Along with their application, they must submit a resume describing their academic and career objectives, extracurricular and community activities, work experience, and special interests or hobbies; transcripts; documentation of financial need; and a personal letter describing their qualifications and needs. An interview is required. Selection is based on academic achievement, financial need, extracurricular and community activities, the letter, and the interview. Preference is given to applicants who are enrolled in ROTC (preferably not a recipient of an ROTC scholarship), have current or prior service in the U.S. armed forces, are interested in the U.S. Public Health Service, and/or are interested in other public service with federal, state, or local government. U.S. citizenship is required.

Financial data The stipend averages approximately $4,000 per year.

Duration 1 year.

Number awarded Approximately 25 each year.

Deadline February of each year.

[257]
BRAXTON BRAGG CHAPTER AUSA SCHOLARSHIPS

Association of the United States Army-Braxton Bragg Chapter
Attn: Vice President for Scholarship Programs
P.O. Box 70036
Fort Bragg, NC 28307
(910) 396-3755   E-mail: hbraxtonbraggc@nc.rr.com
Web: www.ausa.org/chapters/braxton-bragg-chapter

Summary To provide financial assistance to members of the Braxton Bragg Chapter of the Association of the United States Army (AUSA) in North Carolina and their dependents who are interested in attending college or graduate school in any state.

Eligibility This program is open to chapter members and their families in North Carolina who are working on or planning to work on an undergraduate, graduate, or technical degree at a college or technical school in any state. Applicants must submit a 500-word essay on a topic that changes annually (recently, students were asked to explain how a person makes a difference in our world); letters of recommendation; a list of personal accomplishments; and a transcript that includes their ACT or SAT score. Selection is based on academic achievement (50%), participation in extracurricular activities at school (25%), and participation in community service activities (25%).

Financial data The stipend is $1,000.

Duration 1 year; recipients may reapply.

Additional information Membership in the Braxton Bragg Chapter is open to all Army active, National Guard, and Reserve members in North Carolina, along with Department of the Army civilians, retirees, concerned citizens, and family members.

Number awarded Varies each year; recently, 15 were awarded.

Deadline April of each year.

[258]
BRIGADIER GENERAL JOHN F. KINNEY FELLOWSHIP

Alpha Tau Omega
Attn: Foundation
333 North Alabama Street, Suite 220
Indianapolis, IN 46204
(317) 684-1865   E-mail: info@ato.org
Web: www.ato.org/home/ato-scholarships

Summary To provide financial assistance to members of Alpha Tau Omega fraternity who are serving in the military or an ROTC unit while they attend college.

Eligibility This program is open to members of the fraternity who have a GPA of 3.5 or higher. Applicants must be serving in a National Guard or Reserve component of the military or enrolled in an ROTC training program. They must be planning to serve on active duty in the National Guard, the Reserves, or the active armed forces following graduation. Selection is based on academic achievement (40%), demonstrated leadership in the fraternity (30%), and demonstrated initiative on campus and in the community (30%).

Financial data A stipend is awarded (amount not specified).

Duration 1 year.

Number awarded 1 each year.

Deadline March of each year.

[259]
BRIGADIER GENERAL ROBERT L. DENIG FOUNDATION SCHOLARSHIP

United States Marine Corps Combat Correspondents Association
Attn: Scholarship Committee
385 S.W. 254th Street
Newberry, FL 32669
(352) 448-9167   E-mail: hq@usmccca.org
Web: www.usmccca.org/awards/gladys

Summary To provide financial assistance to members of the U.S. Marine Corps Combat Correspondents Association (USMCCCA) or their dependents and Marines in specified occupational fields who are interested in studying communications in college.

Eligibility This program is open to members of USMCCCA who have been members for at least 2 years and their dependents of such members, including children of deceased members. Applications are also accepted from active-duty Marines in occupational field 4300 or 4600 who are enrolled in government-sponsored degree completion programs, whose tuition is not paid from other sources, and who agree to become USMCCA members upon award of a scholarship. Applicants must be enrolled or planning to enroll in an undergraduate program in communications. Along with their application, they must submit 500-word essays on 1) their noteworthy achievements and long-range goals; and 2) "The United States I want to see in 15 years and my role in the transformation." Financial need is not considered in the selection process.

Financial data Stipends for full-time study range up to $3,000; part-time stipends range from $250 to $500. Funds are disbursed directly to recipients to be used exclusively for tuition, books, and/or fees.

Duration 1 year; may be renewed up to 3 additional years.

Additional information This program was previously named the USMCCCA Scholarship.
Number awarded 1 or more each year.
Deadline May of each year.

[260]
BRIGADIER GENERAL ROSCOE C. CARTWRIGHT AWARDS

The ROCKS, Inc.
c/o WSC Associates, LLP
P.O. Box 47435
Forestville, MD 20753
(301) 423-5500 E-mail: rocksnationalboard@gmail.com
Web: www.rocksinc.org

Summary To provide financial assistance to students enrolled in ROTC programs at Historically Black Colleges and Universities (HBCUs).
Eligibility This program is open to Army and Air Force Cadets and Navy Midshipmen at HBCUs at the MS I, MS II, or MS III level. Applicants must be planning to enter military service as officers following graduation from college. They must submit 1) a 1-page paper on a topic related to leadership or mentorship; and 2) a letter of recommendation from their professor of military science evaluating their appearance, attitude, APFT score, dedication, initiative, integrity, judgment, leadership potential, and written and oral communication ability. Financial need is not considered in the selection process.
Financial data The stipend is $2,000 or $1,300.
Duration 1 year.
Additional information This program began in 1974.
Number awarded Varies each year; recently, 4 were awarded: 2 at $2,000 and 2 at $1,300.
Deadline December of each year.

[261]
CALIFORNIA ENLISTED ASSOCIATION OF THE NATIONAL GUARD OF THE UNITED STATES SCHOLARSHIP PROGRAM

California Enlisted Association of the National Guard of
  the United States
c/o CMSgt Steven W. Taber, Executive Director
14779 Echo Ridge Road
Nevada City, CA 95959
E-mail: tabers52@comcast.net
Web: www.caleangus.org

Summary To provide financial assistance to enlisted members of the California National Guard who are interested in obtaining additional education.
Eligibility This program is open to members of the California Army and Air National Guards who have completed at least 1 year of military service. The program supports 2 categories of applicants: Category A for those who hold a military rank of E-3 to E-6 and Category B for those who hold a military rank of E-7 to E-9. Applicants must be enrolled in an educational program whose goal is an associate or bachelor's degree or certification in a subject matter that will enhance their ability to support the unit's mission and goals. Along with their application, they must submit a personal statement that discusses how they plan to apply their educational accomplishments to their civilian and military professional and career goals; a current transcript, and a letter of endorsement from their commanding officer. Awards are granted first to Category A applicants; if funding is sufficient, applicants in Category B are considered.
Financial data The stipend is $1,000.
Duration 1 year; may be renewed for 1 additional year.
Number awarded Varies each year; recently, 3 were awarded.
Deadline July of each year.

[262]
CALIFORNIA LEGION AUXILIARY SCHOLARSHIPS FOR CONTINUING AND/OR REENTRY STUDENTS

American Legion Auxiliary
Department of California
401 Van Ness Avenue, Suite 319
San Francisco, CA 94102-4570
(415) 861-5092   Fax: (415) 861-8365
E-mail: calegionaux@calegionaux.org
Web: www.calegionaux.org/scholarships.htm

Summary To provide financial assistance to California residents who are active-duty military personnel, veterans, or children of veterans and require assistance to continue their education.
Eligibility This program is open to California residents who are 1) active-duty military personnel; 2) veterans of World War I, World War II, Korea, Vietnam, Grenada/Lebanon, Panama, or Desert Shield/Desert Storm; and 3) children of veterans who served during those periods of war. Applicants must be continuing or reentry students at a college, university, or business/trade school in California. Selection is based on the application (25%), scholarship (25%), character and leadership (25%), and financial need (25%).
Financial data The stipend is $1,000 or $500.
Duration 1 year.
Additional information This program includes 1 scholarship designated as the Mel Foronda Memorial Scholarship.
Number awarded 5 each year: 3 at $1,000 and 2 at $500.
Deadline March of each year.

[263]
CALIFORNIA MILITARY DEPARTMENT GI BILL AWARD PROGRAM

California State Military Department
Joint Force Headquarters
Attn: Civilian Education Office
CAAD-G1-CE, Box 26
9800 Goethe Road
Sacramento, CA 95826
(916) 854-4446   Fax: (916) 854-3259
E-mail: ng.ca.caarng.list.cn6-eaap-mailbox-access@mail.mil
Web: www.calguard.ca.gov/education

Summary To provide financial assistance to members of services within the California Military Department who are interested in attending college or graduate school in the state.
Eligibility This program is open to residents of California who are active members of the California Army or Air National Guard, the California State Guard, or the California Naval Militia. Applicants must be planning to attend a college, university, or community college in the state to obtain a certificate, degree (associate, bachelor's, master's, or doctoral) or diploma that they do not currently hold. They must agree to

remain an active member of the National Guard, State Guard, or Naval Militia for at least 2 years after they complete participation in the program.
Financial data The program pays up to 100% of tuition at branches of the University of California, branches of the California State University system, or community colleges. Graduate students receive an additional stipend of $500 for books and supplies.
Duration 1 year; may be renewed, provided the recipient maintains a GPA of 2.0 or higher.
Additional information This program was formerly named the California National Guard Education Assistance Award Program.
Number awarded Up to 1,000 each year.
Deadline The priority deadline for new applications is April of each year.

[264]
CALIFORNIA NON-RESIDENT COLLEGE FEE WAIVER PROGRAM FOR MILITARY PERSONNEL AND DEPENDENTS
California Department of Veterans Affairs
Attn: Division of Veterans Services
1227 O Street, Room 101
P.O. Box 942895
Sacramento, CA 94295
(916) 653-2573   Toll Free: (800) 952-5626
Fax: (916) 653-2563   TDD: (800) 324-5966
Web: www.calvet.ca.gov

Summary To waive non-resident fees at public institutions in California for undergraduate or graduate students from other states who are active-duty military personnel, recently-discharged veterans, or dependents of active-duty military personnel.
Eligibility This program is open to residents of states outside California who are 1) veterans of the U.S. armed forces who spent more than 1 year on active duty in California immediately prior to being discharged; 2) members of the U.S. armed forces stationed in California on active duty; or 3) the natural or adopted child, stepchild, or spouse of a member of the U.S. armed forces stationed in California on active duty. Applicants must be attending or planning to attend a community college, branch of the California State University system, or campus of the University of California as an undergraduate or graduate student.
Financial data This program waives non-resident fees of qualifying military personnel, veterans, and families who attend publicly-supported community or state colleges or universities in California.
Duration 1 year; may be renewed until completion of an undergraduate degree or for 1 additional year for military personnel working on a graduate degree; nonrenewable for graduate students who are children or spouses.
Number awarded Varies each year.
Deadline Deadline not specified.

[265]
CAPTAIN SEAN P. GRIMES PHYSICIAN ASSISTANT EDUCATIONAL SCHOLARSHIP AWARD
Society of Army Physician Assistants
Attn: Scholarship Committee
P.O. Box 623
Monmouth, IL 61462
(309) 734-5446   Fax: (309) 734-4489
E-mail: orpotter@aol.com
Web: www.sapa.org/scholarships

Summary To provide financial assistance to current and former Army personnel interested in attending a college or university to become a physician assistant.
Eligibility This program is open to Army personnel who are currently on active duty, in the Reserves or National Guard, or veterans with any MOS and in pay grades E-5 through O-4. Applicants must be interested in attending an accredited college or university in order to either 1) gain initial training as a physician assistant; or 2) if already a physician assistant, work on a bachelor's, master's, or doctoral degree. They must have a GPA of 2.5 or higher and be able to demonstrate financial need. Selection is based on academic record, community and professional activities, future goals as a physician assistant, and financial need.
Financial data The stipend is $6,000.
Duration 1 year.
Additional information This program began in 2006.
Number awarded 1 each year.
Deadline January of each year.

[266]
CARROLL H. PAYNE MEMORIAL SCHOLARSHIP ENDOWMENT
First Command Educational Foundation
Attn: Scholarship Programs Manager
1 FirstComm Plaza
Fort Worth, TX 76109-4999
(817) 569-2940   Toll Free: (877) 872-8289
Fax: (817) 569-2970   E-mail: scholarships@fcef.com
Web: www.fcef.com/scholarships

Summary To provide financial assistance to college students who have ties to the military.
Eligibility This program is open to college-bound high school students, current college students, and adults seeking advanced education. Applicants must have a tie to the military. They must apply through a local military organization that supports military families, such as a DoD school, officers' spouses' club, National Guard organization, or veteran organization. Individuals who have received military academy appointments or ROTC scholarships are also eligible. The organization must normally agree to provide half the cost of the scholarship and apply to this sponsor for the balance. Partner organizations select the recipients.
Financial data Each partner organization may apply for up to $2,000 in matching funds from this sponsor. Individual scholarships range from $1,000 to $4,000 but may be greater if the partner organization agrees to pay all the additional cost.
Duration 1 year; recipients may reapply.
Additional information This sponsor was established in 1983 as the nonprofit affiliate of First Command Financial Services, Inc.

Number awarded Varies each year; recently, this sponsor partnered with 50 community organizations to award $81,030 in scholarships to 61 students.
Deadline Each partner organization sets its own deadline.

[267]
CIVIL ENGINEER CORPS COLLEGIATE PROGRAM
U.S. Navy
Bureau of Navy Personnel
BUPERS-314E
5720 Integrity Drive
Millington, TN 38055-4630
(901) 874-4034   Toll Free: (866) CEC-NAVY
Fax: (901) 874-2681   E-mail: p4413d@persnet.navy.mil
Web: www.navycs.com/officer/civilengineerofficer.html

Summary To provide financial assistance to undergraduate and graduate students in architecture and engineering who are interested in serving in the Navy's Civil Engineer Corps (CEC) following graduation.
Eligibility This program is open to bachelor's and master's degree students who are U.S. citizens between 19 and 35 years of age. Applicants must be enrolled in an engineering program accredited by the Accreditation Board for Engineering and Technology (ABET) or an architecture program accredited by the National Architectural Accrediting Board (NAAB) and have a GPA of 2.7 or higher overall and 3.0 or higher in science and technical courses. They may be civilians, enlisted personnel of the regular Navy and the Naval Reserve, or enlisted personnel of other branches of the armed services with a conditional release from their respective service. Eligible majors include civil engineering, construction engineering, electrical engineering, environmental engineering, industrial engineering, mechanical engineering, ocean engineering, or architecture. Preference is given to applicants who have engineering or architecture work experience and registration as a Professional Engineer (P.E.) or Engineer-in-Training (EIT). Applicants must also be able to meet the Navy's physical fitness requirements.
Financial data While attending classes, students are assigned to the Naval Reserve and receive the standard pay at E-3 level (approximately $2,042.70 per month) as an undergraduate or E-5 (approximately $2,467.50 per month) as a graduate student.
Duration Up to 24 months.
Additional information While in college, selectees have no uniforms, drills, or military duties. After graduation with a bachelor's or master's degree, they enter the Navy and attend 13 weeks at Officer Candidate School (OCS) in Pensacola, Florida, followed by 15 weeks at Civil Engineer Corps Officers School (CECOS) in Port Hueneme, California. They then serve 4 years in the CEC, rotating among public works, contract management, and the Naval Construction Force (Seabees).
Number awarded Varies each year.
Deadline Deadline not specified.

[268]
CIVIL ENGINEER CORPS OPTION OF THE SEAMAN TO ADMIRAL-21 PROGRAM
U.S. Navy
Attn: Commander, Naval Service Training Command
250 Dallas Street, Suite A
Pensacola, FL 32508-5268
(850) 452-9433   Fax: (850) 452-2486
E-mail: PNSC_STA21@navy.mil
Web: www.public.navy.mil

Summary To allow outstanding enlisted Navy personnel to attend a college or university with an NROTC unit, complete a bachelor's degree, and receive a commission in the Civil Engineer Corps (CEC).
Eligibility This program is open to U.S. citizens who are currently serving on active duty in the Navy as enlisted personnel in any rating. Applicants must have completed at least 4 years of active duty, of which at least 3 years were in an other than formal training environment. They must be high school graduates (or GED recipients) who are able to complete requirements for a professional Accreditation Board for Engineering and Technology (ABET) engineering degree or National Architectural Accrediting Board (NAAB) architectural degree within 36 months or less. Preferred specialties are civil, electrical, mechanical, or ocean engineering. When applicants complete their degree requirements, they must be younger than 42 years of age. Within the past 3 years, they must have taken the SAT (and achieved scores of at least 500 on the mathematics section and 500 on the evidence based reading and writing or critical reading section) or the ACT (and achieved a score of at least 21 on the mathematics portion and 20 on the English portion).
Financial data Awardees continue to receive their regular Navy pay and allowances while they attend college on a full-time basis. They also receive reimbursement for tuition, fees, and books up to $10,000 per year. If base housing is available, they are eligible to live there. Participants are not eligible to receive benefits under the Navy's Tuition Assistance Program (TA), the Montgomery GI Bill (MGIB), the Navy College Fund, or the Veterans Educational Assistance Program (VEAP).
Duration Selectees are supported for up to 36 months of full-time, year-round study or completion of a bachelor's degree, as long as they maintain a GPA of 3.0 or higher.
Additional information This program began in 2001 as a replacement for the Civil Engineer Corps Enlisted Commissioning Program (CECECP). Upon acceptance into the program, selectees attend the Naval Science Institute (NSI) in Newport, Rhode Island for an 8-week program in the fundamental core concepts of being a naval officer (navigation, engineering, weapons, military history and justice, etc.). They then enter a college or university with an NROTC unit that is designated for the CEC to work full time on a bachelor's degree. They become members of and drill with the NROTC unit. When they complete their degree, they are commissioned as ensigns in the United States Naval Reserve and assigned to initial training as an officer in the CEC. After commissioning, 5 years of active service are required.
Number awarded Varies each year.
Deadline June of each year.

SCHOLARSHIPS: MILITARY PERSONNEL

[269]
CMSGT GERALD R. GUILD MEMORIAL SCHOLARSHIPS

Enlisted Association National Guard of Arizona
Attn: Scholarship Chair
5636 East McDowell Road
Phoenix, AZ 85008-3495
(602) 267-2467   Fax: (602) 267-2509
E-mail: scholarship@eanga.org
Web: www.eanga.org/scholarship-information

Summary To provide financial assistance to members of the Enlisted Association National Guard of Arizona (EANGA) and to members of their families who plan to attend college in any state.

Eligibility This program is open to EANGA members, the unmarried children of EANGA members, the spouses of EANGA members, and the unremarried spouses and unmarried dependent children of deceased EANGA members (who were in good standing at their time of death). Qualifying EANGA members must have at least 1 year remaining on their enlistment or have served 20 or more years of service. Applicants may be high school seniors or current college students who are enrolled or planning to enroll full time at a college or university in any state. Graduate students are not eligible. Selection is based on academic record, character, leadership, and financial need.

Financial data The stipend is $1,000. Funds are made payable to the recipient's school and sent directly to the recipient.

Duration 1 year; nonrenewable.

Number awarded 1 each year.

Deadline April of each year.

[270]
COAST GUARD RESERVE FAMILIES SCHOLARSHIPS

Coast Guard Foundation
Attn: Scholarships
394 Taugwonk Road
Stonington, CT 06378
(860) 535-0786   Fax: (860) 535-0944
E-mail: swilliams@coastguardfoundation.org
Web: www.coastguardfoundation.org

Summary To provide financial assistance for postsecondary education to members of the Coast Guard Reserve and their families.

Eligibility This program is open to members of the Coast Guard Reserve and their families. Applicants must be enrolled at an accredited institution and working on a degree, professional development course, licensing course, or certification. Selection is based on academic promise, motivation, moral character, good citizenship, leadership qualities, and financial need.

Financial data Grants up to $1,000 per calendar year are available. Funds may be used for reimbursement of required educational expenses not funded through other resources (e.g., books, school fees, transportation, child care).

Duration 1 year; may be renewed.

Additional information This program is sponsored by USAA.

Number awarded Varies each year; recently, 8 were awarded.

Deadline August of each year.

[271]
COAST GUARD TUITION ASSISTANCE PROGRAM

U.S. Coast Guard
Attn: Force Readiness Command (FORCECOM)
Tuition Assistance and Grants Division
300 East Main Street, Room 233
Norfolk, VA 23510
(757) 756-5300   E-mail: ETQC-SMB-TAG@uscg.mil
Web: www.forcecom.uscg.mil

Summary To provide financial assistance to members and employees of the Coast Guard who are interested in pursuing additional education during their off-duty hours.

Eligibility This program is open to Coast Guard members on active duty and Reservists on long-term orders greater than 180 days. Applicants must be interested in working on their first associate, bachelor's, or master's degree. Civilian employees with at least 90 days of Coast Guard service are also eligible. Enlisted members must complete the course before their enlistment ends or they retire. Active-duty officers must agree to fulfill a 2-year service obligation following completion of the course; officers of the selected reserve must agree to fulfill a 4-year service obligation following completion of the course. Civilian employees must agree to retain employment with the Coast Guard for 1 month for each completed course credit hour. For military personnel, the command education services officer (ESO) must certify that the course of instruction is Coast Guard mission or career related. The supervisor of civilian employees must certify that the education is career related. All courses must be related to the mission of the Coast Guard or the individual's career or professional development.

Financial data The program reimburses 75% of the cost of tuition, to a maximum of $250 per semester hour (of which the Coast Guard share is $187.50) or $3,000 per fiscal year (of which the Coast Guard share is $2,250). Funding is available only for tuition, not fees or other associated expenses.

Duration Until completion of an associate, bachelor's, or master's degree. Undergraduates must complete all courses with a grade of "C" or better; graduate students must complete classes with a grade of "B" of better. If recipients fail to achieve those grades, they must reimburse the Coast Guard for all funds received.

Number awarded Varies each year; recently, more than 10,000 Coast Guard personnel received tuition assistance worth approximately $14.5 million.

Deadline Applications may be submitted at any time.

[272]
COLD WAR VETERANS ENGINEERING AND SCIENCE SCHOLARSHIPS

Marines' Memorial Association
c/o Marines Memorial Club and Hotel
609 Sutter Street
San Francisco, CA 94102
(415) 673-6672, ext. 293   Toll Free: (800) 5-MARINE
Fax: (415) 441-3649
E-mail: scholarship@marineclub.com
Web: www.marinesmemorial.org

Summary To provide financial assistance to members of the Marines' Memorial Association from all branches of the armed forces and their descendants who are interested in studying a field of STEM in college.
Eligibility This program is open to active members of the association and their children and grandchildren. Applicants must be high school seniors or students currently enrolled full time in an undergraduate degree program in a field of STEM. Along with their application, they must submit an essay of up to 500 words on why they chose their specific path of study, what they hope to accomplish after graduation with their degree, and how their efforts will benefit others in their community. Graduating high school seniors must submit a high school transcript and SAT or ACT scores; continuing college students must submit a college transcript. Selection is based on the essay, academic merit, references, and financial need.
Financial data The stipend is $2,500 per year.
Duration 1 year; recipients may reapply for up to 3 additional years.
Additional information Membership in the association is open to veterans of the Marines, Army, Navy, Air Force, or Coast Guard and to personnel currently serving in a branch of the armed forces. This program began in 2014.
Number awarded 3 each year.
Deadline April of each year.

[273]
COLLEGE STUDENT PRE-COMMISSIONING INITIATIVE
U.S. Coast Guard
Attn: Recruiting Command
2703 Martin Luther King, Jr. Avenue, S.E., Stop 7419
Washington, DC 20593-7200
(202) 795-6864
Web: www.gocoastguard.com

Summary To provide financial assistance to college students at minority or other designated institutions who are willing to serve in the Coast Guard following graduation.
Eligibility This program is open to students entering their junior or senior year at a college or university designated as an Historically Black College or University (HBCU), Predominantly Black Institution (PBI), Hispanic Serving Institution (HSI), Asian American and Native American Pacific Islander-Serving Institution, American Indian Tribally Controlled College or University (TCU), Alaska Native Serving Institution (ANSI), or Native American Serving, Non-Tribal Institution. Applicants must be U.S. citizens; have a GPA of 2.5 or higher; have scores of 1100 or higher on the SAT, 23 or higher on the ACT, or 109 or higher General Technical score on the ASVAB; be between 19 and 28 years of age; and meet all physical requirements for a Coast Guard commission. They must agree to attend the Coast Guard Officer Candidate School following graduation and serve on active duty as an officer for at least 3 years.
Financial data Those selected to participate receive full payment of tuition, books, and fees; monthly housing and food allowances; medical and life insurance; special training in leadership, management, law enforcement, navigation, and marine science; 30 days of paid vacation per year; and a Coast Guard monthly salary of approximately $1,800.
Duration Up to 2 years.

Number awarded Varies each year; recently, 38 were awarded.
Deadline September or January of each year.

[274]
COLONEL JOHN D. HEDGES MEMORIAL SCHOLARSHIP
Order of Daedalians
Attn: Daedalian Foundation
55 Main Circle (Building 676)
P.O. Box 249
Joint Base San Antonio-Randolph, TX 78148-0249
(210) 945-2113   Fax: (210) 945-2112
E-mail: info@daedalians.org
Web: www.daedalians.org/programs/scholarships

Summary To provide financial assistance to Air Force ROTC students from specified states who wish to become military pilots.
Eligibility This program is open to students who are currently enrolled in an Air Force ROTC program at a college or university in Alaska, Arkansas, Tennessee, or Texas. Applicants must be interested in preparing for a career as a military pilot. They must apply through their ROTC detachment. Selection is based on intention to pursue a career as a military pilot, demonstrated moral character and patriotism, scholastic and military standing and aptitude, and physical condition and aptitude for flight. Financial need may also be considered.
Financial data The stipend is $1,000.
Duration 1 year.
Number awarded 1 each year.
Deadline December of each year.

[275]
COLONEL RICHARD HALLOCK SCHOLARSHIPS
Marines' Memorial Association
c/o Marines Memorial Club and Hotel
609 Sutter Street
San Francisco, CA 94102
(415) 673-6672, ext. 293   Toll Free: (800) 5-MARINE
Fax: (415) 441-3649
E-mail: scholarship@marineclub.com
Web: www.marinesmemorial.org

Summary To provide financial assistance for college to members of the Marines' Memorial Association from all branches of the armed forces and their descendants.
Eligibility This program is open to active members of the association and their children and grandchildren. Applicants must be high school seniors or students currently enrolled full time in an undergraduate degree program in any field at a college or university. Along with their application, they must submit an essay of up to 500 words on why they chose their specific path of study, what they hope to accomplish after graduation with their degree, and how their efforts will benefit others in their community. Graduating high school seniors must submit a high school transcript and SAT or ACT scores; continuing college students must submit a college transcript. Selection is based on the essay, academic merit, references, and financial need.
Financial data The stipend is $2,500 per year.
Duration 1 year; recipients may reapply for up to 3 additional years.

Additional information Membership in the association is open to veterans of the Marines, Army, Navy, Air Force, or Coast Guard and to personnel currently serving in a branch of the armed forces.
Number awarded 2 each year.
Deadline April of each year.

[276]
COLORADO NATIONAL GUARD STATE TUITION ASSISTANCE
Department of Military and Veterans Affairs
Attn: Colorado State Tuition Assistance Office
6848 South Revere Parkway
Centennial, CO 80112-6703
(720) 250-1550   Fax: (720) 250-1559
E-mail: tuition@dmva.state.co.us
Web: www.colorado.gov/pacific/dmva/tuition-assistance

Summary To provide financial assistance for college or graduate school to members of the Colorado National Guard.
Eligibility This program is open to members of the Colorado National Guard who have served at least 6 months. Applicants must be enrolled or planning to enroll at a public institution of higher education in Colorado to work on a vocational certificate or associate, bachelor's, or master's degree. They must have a GPA of 2.5 or higher. Enlisted personnel must complete courses before their expiration term of service date. Commissioned officers must agree to remain in the Guard for at least 4 years following completion of the course.
Financial data This program provides payment of up to $5,000 per semester.
Duration 1 semester; may be renewed as long as the recipient remains an active member of the Guard and maintains a GPA of 2.0 or higher, to a maximum of 132 semester hours or 8 years.
Number awarded Varies each year.
Deadline July of each year for the fall semester; November of each year for the spring semester; April of each year for the summer term.

[277]
CONNECTICUT NATIONAL GUARD EDUCATIONAL ASSISTANCE PROGRAM
Connecticut National Guard
Attn: Education Service Officer
360 Broad Street
Hartford, CT 06105-3795
(860) 524-4816
Web: ct.ng.mil/Careers/Pages/ArmyRec_Education.aspx

Summary To provide financial assistance for college to members of the Connecticut National Guard.
Eligibility This program is open to active members of the Connecticut National Guard who are interested in working on an undergraduate degree at any branch of the University of Connecticut, any of the 4 state universities, or any of the 13 community/technical colleges in Connecticut. Applicants must have been residents of the state and a satisfactory Guard participant for at least 12 months.
Financial data The program provides a full waiver of tuition at state colleges or universities in Connecticut.
Duration 1 year; may be renewed.

Number awarded Varies each year.
Deadline Deadline not specified.

[278]
CONNECTICUT NATIONAL GUARD FOUNDATION SCHOLARSHIPS
Connecticut National Guard Foundation, Inc.
Attn: Scholarship Committee
360 Broad Street
Hartford, CT 06105-3795
(860) 241-1550   Fax: (860) 293-2929
E-mail: ctngfi@sbcglobal.net
Web: www.ctngfi.org/scholarships

Summary To provide financial assistance for college to members of the Connecticut National Guard and their families.
Eligibility This program is open to members of the Connecticut Army National Guard and Organized Militia, their children, their spouses, and children of Connecticut National Guard retirees. Applicants must be enrolled or planning to enroll at an accredited college or technical program in any state. Along with their application, they must submit a letter of recommendation, a list of extracurricular activities, high school or college transcripts, and a 200-word statement on their educational and future goals. Selection is based on achievement and citizenship.
Financial data The stipend is $2,000.
Duration 1 year.
Number awarded 5 each year.
Deadline April of each year.

[279]
CONNECTICUT TUITION WAIVER FOR VETERANS
Connecticut State Universities and Colleges
61 Woodland Street
Hartford, CT 06105
(860) 723-0013   E-mail: fitzgeralde@ct.edu
Web: www.ct.edu/admission/veterans

Summary To provide financial assistance for college to certain Connecticut veterans and military personnel and their dependents.
Eligibility This program is open to 1) honorably-discharged Connecticut veterans who served at least 90 days during specified periods of wartime; 2) active members of the Connecticut Army or Air National Guard; 3) Connecticut residents who are a dependent child or surviving spouse of a member of the armed forces killed in action on or after September 11, 2001 who was also a Connecticut resident; and 4) Connecticut residents who are a dependent child or surviving spouse of a person officially declared missing in action or a prisoner of war while serving in the armed forces after January 1, 1960. Applicants must be attending or planning to attend a public college or university in the state.
Financial data The program provides a waiver of 100% of tuition for general fund courses at the 4 campuses of Connecticut State University, 50% of tuition for extension and summer courses at campuses of Connecticut State University, 100% of tuition at the 12 Connecticut community colleges, and 50% of fees at Charter Oak State College.
Duration Up to 4 years.

Additional information This is an entitlement program; applications are available at the respective college financial aid offices.
Number awarded Varies each year.
Deadline Deadline not specified.

[280]
CSM HARRY AND MARY HENSELL SCHOLARSHIP PROGRAM

Enlisted Association National Guard of Arizona
Attn: Scholarship Chair
5636 East McDowell Road
Phoenix, AZ 85008-3495
(602) 267-2467   Fax: (602) 267-2509
E-mail: scholarship@eanga.org
Web: www.eanga.org/scholarship-information

Summary To provide financial assistance to members of the Enlisted Association National Guard of Arizona (EANGA) and to members of their families who plan to attend college in any state.
Eligibility This program is open to EANGA members, the unmarried children of EANGA members, the spouses of EANGA members, and the unremarried spouses and unmarried dependent children of deceased EANGA members (who were in good standing at their time of death). Qualifying EANGA members must have at least 1 year remaining on their enlistment or have served 20 or more years of service. Applicants may be high school seniors or current college students who are enrolled or planning to enroll full time at a college or university in any state. Graduate students are not eligible. Selection is based on academic record, character, leadership, and financial need.
Financial data The stipend is $1,000. Funds are made payable to the recipient's school and sent directly to the recipient.
Duration 1 year; nonrenewable.
Additional information This program, sponsored by USAA Insurance Corporation, was established in 1998 and given its current name in 2009.
Number awarded 1 each year.
Deadline April of each year.

[281]
CSM LEONARD MAGLIONE MEMORIAL SCHOLARSHIPS

Association of the United States Army-Rhode Island Chapter
c/o LTC Robert A. Galvanin, President
31 Canoe River Drive
Mansfield, MA 02048
(508) 339-5301   E-mail: bpje5310@verizon.net
Web: www.rioa.org/ausari/scholarship.htm

Summary To provide financial assistance to members of the Rhode Island Chapter of the Association of the United States Army (AUSA) and their families who are interested in attending college or graduate school in any state.
Eligibility This program is open to members of the AUSA Rhode Island Chapter and their family members (spouses, children, and grandchildren). Applicants must be high school seniors or graduates accepted at an accredited college, university, or vocational/technical school in any state or current undergraduate or graduate students. Along with their application, they must submit a 250-word essay on why they feel their achievements should qualify them for this award. Selection is based on academic and individual achievements; financial need is not considered. Special consideration is given to students or graduates of LaSalle Academy in Providence (the alma mater of this program's namesake), especially those preparing for a career in the arts or engineering or enrolled or planning to enroll in Army ROTC.
Financial data The stipend is $1,000.
Duration 1 year.
Additional information Membership in the AUSA is open to everyone who supports a strong national defense, with special concern for the Army. That includes Regular Army, National Guard, Army Reserve, government civilians, retired soldiers, Wounded Warriors, veterans, concerned citizens and family members.
Number awarded Several each year.
Deadline April of each year.

[282]
CSM ROBERT W. ELKEY SCHOLARSHIP

Army Engineer Association
Attn: Director Washington DC Operations
P.O. Box 30260
Alexandria, VA 22310-8260
(703) 428-7084   Fax: (703) 428-6043
E-mail: xd@armyengineer.com
Web: www.armyengineer.com/scholarships

Summary To provide financial assistance for college or graduate school to enlisted members of the Army Engineer Association (AEA).
Eligibility This program is open to AEA members serving in an active, Reserve, or National Guard component Army Engineer unit, school, or organization within the Corps of Engineers of the United States Army. Applicants must be enlisted personnel (PVT, PFC, SPC, CPL, SGT, or SSG). They must be working on or planning to work on an associate, bachelor's, or master's degree at an accredited college or university. Along with their application, they must submit a 1-page essay outlining why they should be selected for an award, including a paragraph on their financial need and their evaluation of their potential for success.
Financial data The stipend is $1,000.
Duration 1 year.
Number awarded 3 each year.
Deadline June of each year.

[283]
CSM VIRGIL R. WILLIAMS SCHOLARSHIP PROGRAM

Enlisted Association of the National Guard of the United States
1 Massachusetts Avenue, N.W., Suite 880
Washington, DC 20001
Toll Free: (800) 234-EANG   Fax: (703) 519-3849
E-mail: eangus@eangus.org
Web: www.eangus.org/scholarship-information

Summary To provide financial assistance to National Guard members and their dependents who are members of the Enlisted Association of the National Guard of the United States (EANGUS) and entering or continuing in college.

SCHOLARSHIPS: MILITARY PERSONNEL

Eligibility This program is open to high school seniors and current college students who are enrolled or planning to enroll as full-time undergraduate students. They must be 1) National Guard members who belong to EANGUS; 2) unmarried sons and daughters of EANGUS members; 3) spouses of EANGUS members; or 4) unremarried spouses and unmarried dependent children of deceased EANGUS members who were in good standing at the time of their death. Honorary, associate, or corporate membership alone does not qualify. Applicants must submit a copy of their school transcript, 3 letters of recommendation, a letter of academic reference (from their principal, dean, or counselor), a photocopy of the qualifying state and/or national membership card (parent's, spouse's or applicant's), and a personal letter with specific facts as to their desire to continue their education and why financial assistance is necessary. Application packets must be submitted to the state EANGUS association; acceptable packets are then sent to the national offices for judging. Selection is based on academic achievement, character, leadership, and financial need.
Financial data The stipend is $2,000.
Duration 1 year; nonrenewable.
Additional information Recent sponsors of this program included USAA Insurance Corporation and the Armed Forces Benefit Association.
Number awarded Varies each year; recently, 9 were awarded.
Deadline Applications must first be verified by the state office and then submitted by May to the national office.

[284]
DAEDALIAN ACADEMIC MATCHING SCHOLARSHIP PROGRAM

Order of Daedalians
Attn: Daedalian Foundation
55 Main Circle (Building 676)
P.O. Box 249
Joint Base San Antonio-Randolph, TX 78148-0249
(210) 945-2113   Fax: (210) 945-2112
E-mail: info@daedalians.org
Web: www.daedalians.org/programs/scholarships

Summary To provide financial assistance to ROTC and other college students who wish to become military pilots.
Eligibility Eligible are students who are attending or have been accepted at an accredited 4-year college or university and have demonstrated the desire and potential to become a commissioned military pilot. Usually, students in ROTC units of all services apply to local chapters (Flights) of Daedalian; if the Flight awards a scholarship, the application is forwarded to the Daedalian Foundation for 1 of these matching scholarships. College students not part of a ROTC program are eligible to apply directly to the Foundation if their undergraduate goals and performance are consistent with Daedalian criteria. Selection is based on intention to pursue a career as a military pilot, demonstrated moral character and patriotism, scholastic and military standing and aptitude, and physical condition and aptitude for flight. Financial need may also be considered. Additional eligibility criteria may be set by a Flight Scholarship Selection Board.
Financial data The amount awarded varies but is intended to serve as matching funds for the Flight scholarship. Generally, the maximum awarded is $2,000.
Duration 1 year.
Number awarded Up to 99 each year.
Deadline Students who are members of Daedalian Flights must submit their applications by November of each year; students who apply directly to the Daedalian Foundation must submit their applications by July of each year.

[285]
DALE SPENCER SCHOLARSHIP FUND

Arizona Community Foundation
Attn: Director of Scholarships
2201 East Camelback Road, Suite 405B
Phoenix, AZ 85016
(602) 381-1400   Toll Free: (800) 222-8221
Fax: (602) 381-1575
E-mail: scholarship@azfoundation.org
Web: www.azfoundation.academicworks.com

Summary To provide financial assistance to residents of Arizona who are veterans or current military personnel and interested in attending college in the state.
Eligibility This program is open to veterans and current active duty members of the U.S. armed forces in Arizona. Applicants must be able to demonstrate significant financial need. Preference is given to those who are current or former participants in the foster care system.
Financial data The stipend is $1,000.
Duration 1 year; nonrenewable.
Number awarded Varies each year.
Deadline May of each year.

[286]
DEDICATED ARMY NATIONAL GUARD (DEDARNG) SCHOLARSHIPS

U.S. Army National Guard
Education Support Center
Camp Joseph T. Robinson
Building 5400 Box 46
North Little Rock, AR 72199-9600
Toll Free: (866) 628-5999   Fax: (501) 212-4928
E-mail: esc@ng.army.mil
Web: www.nationalguard.com/tools/guard-scholarships

Summary To provide financial assistance to college and graduate students who are interested in enrolling in Army ROTC and serving in the Army National Guard following graduation.
Eligibility This program is open to full-time students entering their sophomore or junior year of college with a GPA of 2.5 or higher. Applicants must have a GPA of 2.5 or higher and scores of at least 19 on the ACT or 1000 on the SAT. Graduate students may also be eligible if they have only 2 years remaining for completion of their degree. Students who have been awarded an ROTC campus-based scholarship may apply to convert to this program during their freshman year. Applicants must meet all medical and moral character requirements for enrollment in Army ROTC. They must be willing to enroll in the Simultaneous Membership Program (SMP) of an ROTC unit on their campus; the SMP requires simultaneous membership in Army ROTC and the Army National Guard.
Financial data Participants receive full reimbursement of tuition up to $10,000 per year, a grant of $1,200 per year for books, plus an ROTC stipend for 10 months of the year at

$420 per month, and weekend drill pay at the pay grade of a sergeant (approximately $319 per month) while participating in the SMP.

Duration 2 or 3 years.

Additional information After graduation, participants serve 3 to 6 months on active duty in the Officer Basic Course (OBC). Following completion of OBC, they are released from active duty and are obligated to serve 8 years in the Army National Guard.

Number awarded Approximately 600 each year.

Deadline Deadline not specified.

[287]
DELAWARE NATIONAL GUARD EDUCATION ASSISTANCE PROGRAM

Delaware National Guard
Attn: Education Services Officer
State Tuition Reimbursement Program
First Regiment Road
Wilmington, DE 19808-2191
(302) 326-7044   Fax: (302) 326-7029
Web: www.de.ng.mil

Summary To provide financial assistance to members of the Delaware National Guard who plan to attend college in the state.

Eligibility This program is open to active members of the Delaware National Guard who are interested in working on an associate or bachelor's degree at a school in Delaware. Applicants must have made satisfactory progress in their assigned military career field, may not have missed more than 6 periods of scheduled unit training assembly periods in the preceding 12 months, and must have avoided all adverse personnel actions. They must earn a grade of 2.0 or higher in all courses to qualify for tuition reimbursement.

Financial data Participants receive reimbursement of 100% of the tuition at state-supported colleges and universities in Delaware, to a maximum of $1,236 per semester at Delaware Technical and Community college, $4,270 per semester at the University of Delaware, or $3,240.50 per semester at Delaware State University. Students who attend a Delaware private college are reimbursed up to $243 per credit hour. If total funding appropriated by the legislature is insufficient for all qualified applicants, the available funds are distributed among recipients according to a maximum allowable fair percentage formula. Recipients must complete 6 years of satisfactory membership in the Delaware National Guard (before, during, and after participation in the program) or repay the funds received.

Duration 1 semester; may be renewed. Guard members are eligible for this assistance only for 10 years after the date on which they begin the first course for which reimbursement was granted.

Number awarded Varies each year; recently, a total of $490,000 was available for this program.

Deadline September of each year for fall semester; January of each year for winter semester; March of each year for spring semester; June of each year for summer semester.

[288]
DELTA DENTAL GRANTS

Air Force Association
Attn: Scholarships
1501 Lee Highway
Arlington, VA 22209-1198
(703) 247-5800, ext. 4868
Toll Free: (800) 727-3337, ext. 4868
Fax: (703) 247-5853   E-mail: scholarships@afa.org
Web: www.app.smarterselect.com

Summary To provide financial assistance to spouses and dependents of military personnel who are interested in further training related to oral health and wellness.

Eligibility This program is open to military spouses, dependents, and transitioning service members who are interested in training, certification, or a degree related to oral health and wellness. Eligible areas of study include dentistry, nursing, home health care aid, or caregiver training. Applicants must submit a statement of purpose describing how the grant will assist in meeting their educational goals.

Financial data The stipend is $2,000.

Duration 1 year.

Additional information This program is sponsored by Delta Dental.

Number awarded 5 each year.

Deadline April of each year.

[289]
DELTA DENTAL ORAL HEALTH AND WELLNESS SCHOLARSHIP

Association of the United States Army
Attn: Scholarships
2425 Wilson Boulevard
Arlington, VA 22201
(703) 841-4300   Toll Free: (800) 336-4570
E-mail: scholarships@ausa.org
Web: www.ausa.org/resources/scholarships

Summary To provide financial assistance to Army family members and transitioning soldiers who are interested in studying a field related to oral health and wellness in college.

Eligibility This program is open to Army family members and transitioning soldiers who are members of the Association of the United States Army and enrolled or accepted at an accredited college, university, or certificate program. Applicants must be studying dentistry, nursing, home health care aid, caregiver training, or other field related to oral health and wellness. Along with their application, they must submit a 1-page autobiography, 2 letters of recommendation, a letter describing their career aspirations (including their course of study and plans for completion of a certificate or degree), and a transcript of high school or college grades (depending on which they are currently attending). Selection is based on academic merit and personal achievement. Financial need is not normally a selection criterion but in some cases of extreme need it may be used as a factor; the lack of financial need, however, is never a cause for non-selection.

Financial data The stipend is $2,000; funds are sent directly to the recipient's institution.

Duration 1 year.

Additional information Membership in the AUSA is open to everyone who supports a strong national defense, with special concern for the Army. That includes Regular Army,

National Guard, Army Reserve, government civilians, retired soldiers, Wounded Warriors, veterans, concerned citizens and family members. This program is sponsored by Delta Dental.

Number awarded 10 each year.
Deadline June of each year.

[290]
DISTRICT OF COLUMBIA NATIONAL GUARD STATE TUITION ASSISTANCE REIMBURSEMENT

District of Columbia National Guard
Attn: Education Services Office
2001 East Capitol Street, S.E.
Washington, DC 20001
(202) 685-9862   Fax: (202) 685-9815
E-mail: sherry.d.mitchell3.mil@mail.mil
Web: dc.ng.mil/Resources/Education/

Summary To provide financial assistance for college or graduate school to current members of the District of Columbia National Guard.

Eligibility This program is open to traditional, technician, and AGR members of the District of Columbia Air and Army National Guard. Applicants must have a high school diploma or equivalency and currently be working on an associate, bachelor's, or master's degree at an accredited postsecondary education institution. In some instances, support may also be available for an M.D., D.O., P.A., or J.D. degree.

Financial data Army National Guard members are eligible for up to $4,500 per year in federal tuition assistance; they may supplement that with up to $2,000 per year in District tuition assistance plus up to $500 for fees. Air National Guard members do not have access to federal tuition assistance, so they may receive up to $6,000 in District tuition assistance. Funds must be used to pay for tuition, fees, and/or books.

Duration 1 semester; recipients may reapply.
Number awarded Varies each year.
Deadline Applications must be submitted between 45 days after the start of the semester and 60 days after the end of the semester.

[291]
DIVISION COMMANDER'S HIP POCKET SCHOLARSHIPS

U.S. Army
Attn: U.S. Army Cadet Command
G2 Incentives Division
1307 Third Avenue
Fort Knox, KY 40121-2725
(502) 624-7371   Toll Free: (888) 550-ARMY
Fax: (502) 624-6937
E-mail: usarmy.knox.usacc.mbx.train2lead@mail.mil
Web: www.goarmy.com

Summary To enable soldiers who are nominated by their Division Commanding General to obtain an early discharge from the Army and return to college to participate in the Army Reserve Officers' Training Corps (ROTC).

Eligibility Enlisted soldiers who have served at least 2 but less than 10 years on active duty are eligible for this program. They must be nominated by their Division Commanding General to obtain an early discharge in order to enroll in a baccalaureate degree program. Nominees must have a cumulative high school or college GPA of 3.0 or higher, a score of at least 21 on the ACT or 1100 on the SAT, a General Technical (GT) score of 110 or higher, and an Army Physical Fitness Test (APFT) score of 270 or higher, including 90 in each event. They may not have a spouse who is also in the military or dependent children under 18 years of age (those requirements may be waived). Waivers may be granted to applicants who have a GPA of 2.5 or higher, scores of 19 on the ACT or 1000 on the SAT, and APFT scores of 180, including 60 in each event. At the time they graduate and are commissioned, they must be under 31 years of age. Selection is made by the Division Commanding General; no additional review is made by Cadet Command Headquarters.

Financial data Scholarship winners receive full payment of tuition, a grant of $1,200 per year for books and supplies, a monthly stipend of $420 per month for 10 months per year, and pay for attending the 6-week Cadet Leadership Course (CLC) during the summer between the junior and senior year of college.

Duration 2, 3, or 4 years.

Additional information Recipients who had previously qualified for benefits from the Army College Fund and/or the Montgomery GI Bill are still entitled to receive those in addition to any benefits from this program. Upon graduation from college, scholarship winners are commissioned as second lieutenants and are required to serve in the military for 8 years. That obligation may be fulfilled by serving 4 years on active duty followed by 4 years in the Inactive Ready Reserve (IRR).

Number awarded Varies each year; recently, 117 were awarded.
Deadline March of each year.

[292]
DONALDSON D. FRIZZELL MEMORIAL SCHOLARSHIPS

First Command Educational Foundation
Attn: Scholarship Programs Manager
1 FirstComm Plaza
Fort Worth, TX 76109-4999
(817) 569-2940   Toll Free: (877) 872-8289
Fax: (817) 569-2970   E-mail: scholarships@fcef.com
Web: www.fcef.com/scholarships

Summary To provide financial assistance to students, especially those with ties to the military, entering or attending college or graduate school.

Eligibility This program is open to 1) members of a U.S. uniformed service (active, Guard, Reserve, retired, or non-retired veteran) and their spouses and dependents; 2) clients of First Command Financial Services and their family members; 3) dependent family members of First Command Advisors or field office staff members; or 4) non-contractual ROTC students. Applicants may be traditional students (high school seniors and students already enrolled at a college, university, or accredited trade school) or nontraditional students (those defined by their institution as nontraditional and adult students planning to return to a college, university, or accredited trade school). They must have a GPA of 3.0 or higher and be working on a trade school certification or associate, undergraduate, or graduate degree. Applicants must submit 1-page essays on 1) their active involvement in community service programs; 2) the impact of financial literacy on their future;

and 3) why they need this scholarship. Selection is based primarily on the essays, academic merit, and financial need.
Financial data The stipend is $3,000. Funds are disbursed directly to the recipient's college, university, or trade school.
Duration 1 year.
Additional information The sponsoring organization was formerly known as the USPA & IRA Educational Foundation, founded in 1983 to provide scholarships to the children of active, retired, or deceased military personnel.
Number awarded Varies each year; recently, 10 were awarded.
Deadline The online application process begins in February of each year and continues until April or until 2,500 applications have been received.

[293]
DR. AILEEN WEBB TOBIN SCHOLARSHIP PROGRAM

U.S. Army Ordnance Corps Association
Attn: Scholarship
P.O. Box 5251
Fort Lee, VA 23801
(804) 733-5596   Fax: (804) 733-5599
E-mail: usaoca@usaocaweb.ort
Web: www.usaoca.org/index.php/scholarship-information

Summary To provide financial assistance for college to soldiers serving in the U.S. Army Ordnance Corps and members of the U.S. Army Ordnance Corps Association (OCA) and their families.
Eligibility This program is open to Ordnance soldiers (active and reserve), OCA members, and immediate family of OCA members. Applicants must be entering or attending a college or university to work on an associate or baccalaureate degree. Along with their application, they must submit 1) an essay of 1,000 to 1,500 words on life-long learning as it applies to the U.S. Army Ordnance Corps; and 2) an essay of 300 to 500 words on their educational and career goals. Selection is based on the essays, scholastic aptitude, and grades.
Financial data The stipend is $1,000.
Duration 1 year.
Additional information This program began in 2014.
Number awarded Varies each year; recently, 4 were awarded.
Deadline June of each year.

[294]
DR. AURELIO M. CACCCOMO FAMILY FOUNDATION MEMORIAL SCHOLARSHIP

AMVETS National Headquarters
Attn: National Programs Director
4647 Forbes Boulevard
Lanham, MD 20706-3807
(301) 459-9600   Toll Free: (877) 7-AMVETS, ext. 4027
Fax: (301) 459-7924   E-mail: klathroum@amvets.org
Web: www.amvets.org/scholarships

Summary To provide financial assistance for college to veterans, National Guard members, and Reservists.
Eligibility This program is open to U.S. citizens who are veterans or members of the National Guard or Reserves. Applicants must be interested in working full or part time on an undergraduate degree or certification from an accredited trade/technical school. They must have exhausted all other government aid. Selection is based on financial need, academic promise, military duty and awards, volunteer activities, community services, jobs held during the past 4 years, and an essay of 50 to 100 words on "This award will help me achieve my career/vocational goal, which is..."
Financial data The stipend is $3,000.
Duration 1 year; nonrenewable.
Number awarded 2 each year.
Deadline April of each year.

[295]
DR. NANCY M. SCHONHER SCHOLARSHIP

Marines' Memorial Association
c/o Marines Memorial Club and Hotel
609 Sutter Street
San Francisco, CA 94102
(415) 673-6672, ext. 293   Toll Free: (800) 5-MARINE
Fax: (415) 441-3649
E-mail: scholarship@marineclub.com
Web: www.marinesmemorial.org

Summary To provide financial assistance to women who have a tie to the military and are interested in working on a degree in a health-related field.
Eligibility This program is open to women who 1) are active-duty service members or reservists in the U.S. armed forces; 2) have separated honorably from the U.S. armed forces within the past 6 years; 3) are a current or former corpsman or medic in any branch of the U.S. armed forces; or 4) are the child or grandchild of an active member of the Marines' Memorial Association. Applicants must be planning to enroll in 1) an advanced medical program with the goal of becoming a nurse, nurse practitioner, physician's assistant, or medical doctor (M.D. or O.D.) from an accredited American college or university; or 2) an accredited paramedic program (must have completed the EMT Basic training program, have taken the National Registry EMT Examination, hold an EMT Certificate, and have at least 6 months' work experience). Membership in the sponsoring organization is not required. Along with their application, they must submit an essay of up to 500 words on why they chose their specific path of study, what they hope to accomplish after graduation with their degree, and how their efforts will benefit others in their community. Selection is based on the essay, academic merit, references, and financial need. Preference is given to Navy Corpsmen.
Financial data The stipend is $5,000.
Duration 1 year.
Additional information Membership in the association is open to veterans of the Marines, Army, Navy, Air Force, or Coast Guard and to personnel currently serving in a branch of the armed forces. This program began in 2017.
Number awarded 1 each year.
Deadline April of each year.

SCHOLARSHIPS: MILITARY PERSONNEL

[296]
D.W. STEELE CHAPTER AFA STEM SCHOLARSHIPS
Air Force Association-Donald W. Steele, Sr. Chapter
c/o Sonya Yelbert
8704 Ashby Court
Upper Marlboro, MD 20772
E-mail: VA239.STEELE@afa.org
Web: www.dwsteele.org

Summary To provide financial assistance to Air Force personnel and their families from the greater Washington, D.C. area who are interested in attending college in any state to major in a field of STEM.

Eligibility This program is open to 1) members of the Air Force (active, Guard, or Reserve) assigned to the greater Washington, D.C. area who are also members of the Air Force Association; and 2) their spouses and children. Applicants must be enrolled to planning to enroll at a college or university in any state. Selection is based on academic achievement, demonstrated leadership, community involvement, and a 1-page essay on their academic and career goals.

Financial data Stipends are $2,000 or $1,000.

Duration 1 year.

Number awarded 3 each year; recently, 2 at $2,000 and 1 at $1,000.

Deadline May of each year.

[297]
EANGMT USAA SCHOLARSHIPS
Enlisted Association of the National Guard of Montana
c/o Will Frank, Scholarship Chair
P.O. Box 33
Fort Harrison, MT 59636
Web: www.mteang.org/scholarships

Summary To provide financial assistance to members of the Enlisted Association of the National Guard of Montana (EANGMT) and their dependents who are interested in attending college in any state.

Eligibility This program is open to current dues-paying members of the EANGMT and their dependents who are attending or planning to attend a college, university, or vocational/technical school in any state. Applicants must submit a current grade transcript; 3 to 4 short paragraphs on their goals in life, the type of degree they are seeking, any community service they have performed and what it meant to them, and any awards earned; and a letter of recommendation.

Financial data The stipend is $1,000.

Duration 1 year; nonrenewable.

Additional information This program is supported in part by USAA Insurance Corporation.

Number awarded 2 each year: usually, 1 is awarded to an Army Guard applicant and 1 to an Air Guard applicant.

Deadline March of each year.

[298]
EANGNJ SCHOLARSHIP PROGRAM
Enlisted Association National Guard of New Jersey
Attn: Corresponding Secretary
3650 Saylors Pond Road
Joint Base McGuire-Dix-Lakehurst, NJ 08640-5606
(530) 329-6813
Web: www.eangnj.org

Summary To provide financial assistance to New Jersey National Guard members and their children who are interested in attending college in any state.

Eligibility This program is open to 1) spouses, children, stepchildren, and grandchildren of New Jersey National Guard members (active, inactive, or retired) who are also members of the Enlisted Association National Guard of New Jersey; 2) drilling Guard members who are also members of the Association; and 3) spouses, children, stepchildren, and grandchildren of deceased members who were in good standing at the time of their death. Applicants must be attending or planning to attend a college or university in any state. Along with their application, they must submit 1) information on their church, school, and community activities; 2) a list of honors they have received; 3) letters of recommendation; 4) transcripts; 5) a letter with specific reasons for their education and why financial assistance is required; and 6) a 500-word essay about the importance of education.

Financial data The stipend is $1,000.

Duration 1 year.

Additional information This program includes the CSM Vincent Baldassari Memorial Scholarships, the CSM John H. Humphreys Jr. Memorial Scholarship, the CMSgt Richard W. Spencer Scholarship, and a scholarship sponsored by USAA Insurance Corporation.

Number awarded Varies each year; recently, 7 were awarded.

Deadline June of each year.

[299]
EANGTN SCHOLARSHIP PROGRAM
Enlisted Association of the National Guard of Tennessee
Attn: Scholarship Committee
4332 Kenilwood Drive, Suite B
Nashville, TN 37204-4401
(615) 620-7255   Fax: (615) 620-7256
E-mail: melissa@eangtn.org
Web: www.eangtn.org/scholarships

Summary To provide financial assistance to members of the Enlisted Association of the National Guard of Tennessee (EANGTN) and to their dependents who are interested in attending college in any state.

Eligibility This program is open to students who are members of both the Tennessee National Guard and EANGTN or the dependent son, daughter, or spouse of a member in good standing. Children must be unmarried, unless they are also a member of the National Guard. Applicants must be entering or continuing at a college or university in any state. Along with their application, they must submit a transcript, a letter with specific facts as to their desire to continue their education and why financial assistance is required, 3 letters of recommendation, and a letter of academic reference.

Financial data The stipend is $1,000. Funds are paid to the recipient's school once enrollment is confirmed.

Duration 1 year.

Additional information In 1985, the National Guard Association of Tennessee (NGAT) agreed that the EANGTN would fund the scholarships of both associations. Additional funding is also provided by USAA Insurance Corporation.

Number awarded 4 each year, of which 1 is funded by USAA.

Deadline March of each year.

[300]
EANGUS PATRIOTS SCHOLARSHIPS

Enlisted Association of the National Guard of the United States
1 Massachusetts Avenue, N.W., Suite 880
Washington, DC 20001
Toll Free: (800) 234-EANG   Fax: (703) 519-3849
E-mail: eangus@eangus.org
Web: www.eangus.org/scholarship-information

Summary To provide financial assistance to National Guard members and their dependents who are members of the Enlisted Association of the National Guard of the United States (EANGUS) and entering or continuing in college.

Eligibility This program is open to high school seniors and current college students who are enrolled or planning to enroll as full-time undergraduate students. They must be 1) National Guard members who belong to EANGUS; 2) unmarried sons and daughters of EANGUS members; 3) spouses of EANGUS members; or 4) unremarried spouses and unmarried dependent children of deceased EANGUS members who were in good standing at the time of their death. Honorary, associate, or corporate membership alone does not qualify. Applicants must submit a copy of their school transcript, 3 letters of recommendation, a letter of academic reference (from their principal, dean, or counselor), a photocopy of the qualifying state and/or national membership card (parent's, spouse's or applicant's), and a personal letter with specific facts as to their desire to continue their education and why financial assistance is necessary. Application packets must be submitted to the state EANGUS association; acceptable packets are then sent to the national offices for judging. Selection is based on academic achievement, character, leadership, and financial need.

Financial data The stipend is $1,000.

Duration 1 year; nonrenewable.

Additional information This program began in 2018.

Number awarded Varies each year; recently, 5 were awarded.

Deadline Applications must first be verified by the state office and then submitted by May to the national office.

[301]
EANGUT SCHOLARSHIPS

Enlisted Association of the National Guard of Utah
Attn: Scholarship Committee
12953 South Minuteman Drive
P.O. Box 1776
Draper, UT 84020
(801) 699-1680   E-mail: scholarships@eangut.com
Web: www.eangut.org/eangut-scholarship-application

Summary To provide financial assistance to National Guard members who are active members of the Enlisted Association National Guard of Utah (EANGUT) and their families entering or continuing in college in the state.

Eligibility This program is open to members of EANGUT, their spouses, their children, and the spouses and unmarried dependent children of deceased members. Applicants must be attending or planning to attend a college, university, or vocational/technical school in Utah. EANGUT members must have at least 1 year remaining on their enlistment or have completed 20 or more years of service. Along with their application, they must submit 4 essays on 1) their educational and career goals; 2) how the military has influenced their life; 3) their extracurricular activities and the leadership positions they have held; and 4) their financial need.

Financial data The stipend ranges from $1,000 to $3,000.

Duration 1 year.

Additional information This program receives support from the USAA Insurance Corporation.

Number awarded Varies each year: recently, 1 at $3,000, 1 at $2,000, 2 at $1,500, and 4 at $1,000 were awarded.

Deadline July of each year.

[302]
EANYNG EDUCATION AWARDS

Enlisted Association of the New York National Guard, Inc.
Attn: Education Awards Chair
330 Old Niskayuna Road
Latham, NY 12110-2224
(518) 344-2670   E-mail: awards@eanyng.org
Web: www.eanyng.org/awards

Summary To provide financial assistance to members of the Enlisted Association of the New York National Guard (EANYNG) and their families who are interested in attending college in any state.

Eligibility This program is open to EANYNG members and their spouses, children, and grandchildren. Applicants must be high school seniors or current undergraduates at a college or university in any state. The applicant or sponsor must have belonged to EANYNG for more than 30 days for the $500 awards or than 1 year for the larger awards. Membership in EANYNG is limited to enlisted personnel in the New York Air or Army National Guard. Selection is based on academic achievement, community service, extracurricular activities, and leadership abilities.

Financial data The stipend ranges from $500 to $3,000.

Duration 1 year; nonrenewable.

Additional information This program includes the Robert H. Connal Scholarship, the EANYNG Memorial Scholarship, the EANYNG Patriot Scholarship, and a scholarship sponsored by the USAA Insurance Corporation.

Number awarded Varies each year; 1 at $3,000, 1 at $1,500, 1 at $1,000, and 2 at $500.

Deadline July of each year.

SCHOLARSHIPS: MILITARY PERSONNEL

[303]
EDMUND K. GROSS EDUCATION SCHOLARSHIP
Marines' Memorial Association
c/o Marines Memorial Club and Hotel
609 Sutter Street
San Francisco, CA 94102
(415) 673-6672, ext. 293   Toll Free: (800) 5-MARINE
Fax: (415) 441-3649
E-mail: scholarship@marineclub.com
Web: www.marinesmemorial.org

Summary To provide financial assistance to members of the Marines' Memorial Association from all branches of the armed forces and their descendants who are interested in studying education in college.

Eligibility This program is open to active members of the association and their children and grandchildren. Applicants must be enrolled or planning to enroll full time in an undergraduate degree program in education at a college or university. Along with their application, they must submit an essay of up to 500 words on why they chose their specific path of study, what they hope to accomplish after graduation with their degree, and how their efforts will benefit others in their community. Graduating high school seniors must submit a high school transcript and SAT or ACT scores; continuing college students must submit a college transcript. Selection is based on the essay, academic merit, references, and financial need.

Financial data The stipend is $2,500 per year.

Duration 1 year; recipients may reapply for up to 3 additional years.

Additional information Membership in the association is open to veterans of the Marines, Army, Navy, Air Force, or Coast Guard and to personnel currently serving in a branch of the armed forces.

Number awarded 1 each year.

Deadline April of each year.

[304]
EDUCATION FOUNDATION FOR THE COLORADO NATIONAL GUARD GRANTS
National Guard Association of Colorado
Attn: Education Foundation, Inc.
P.O. Box 440889
Aurora, CO 80044-0889
(303) 909-6369   Fax: (720) 535-5925
E-mail: BernieRogoff@comcast.net
Web: www.efcong.org

Summary To provide financial assistance to members of the Colorado National Guard and their families who are interested in attending college or graduate school in any state.

Eligibility This program is open to current and retired members of the Colorado National Guard and their dependent unmarried children and spouses. Applicants must be enrolled or planning to enroll full or part time at a college, university, trade school, business school, or graduate school in any state. Along with their application, they must submit an essay, up to 2 pages in length, on their desire to continue their education, what motivates them, their financial need, their commitment to academic excellence, and their current situation. Selection is based on academic achievement, community involvement, and financial need.

Financial data Stipends are generally at least $1,000 per year.

Duration 1 year; may be renewed.

Number awarded Normally, 15 to 25 of these grants are awarded each semester.

Deadline July of each year for fall semester; January of each year for spring semester.

[305]
EGAN ROTC SCHOLARSHIPS
Order of Daedalians
Attn: Daedalian Foundation
55 Main Circle (Building 676)
P.O. Box 249
Joint Base San Antonio-Randolph, TX 78148-0249
(210) 945-2113   Fax: (210) 945-2112
E-mail: info@daedalians.org
Web: www.daedalians.org/programs/scholarships

Summary To provide financial assistance to ROTC students who wish to become military pilots.

Eligibility This program is open to students who are currently enrolled in an ROTC program at their college or university. Applicants must be interested in preparing for a career as a military pilot. They must apply through their ROTC detachment. Selection is based on intention to pursue a career as a military pilot, demonstrated moral character and patriotism, scholastic and military standing and aptitude, and physical condition and aptitude for flight. Financial need may also be considered.

Financial data The stipend is $2,500.

Duration 1 year.

Number awarded 19 each year: 13 for Air Force ROTC cadets, 3 for Army ROTC cadets, and 3 for Navy/Marine ROTC midshipmen.

Deadline December of each year.

[306]
EILEEN M. BONNER SCHOLARSHIP AWARD FOR MEDICAL EXCELLENCE
Reserve Officers Association of the United States
Attn: Scholarship Program
One Constitution Avenue, N.E.
Washington, DC 20002-5618
(202) 646-7758   Toll Free: (800) 809-9448
E-mail: scholarship@roa.org
Web: www.roa.org/page/Scholarships

Summary To provide financial assistance to members of Reserve components of the uniformed services who are working on a health-related degree.

Eligibility This program is open to drilling Reserve component personnel studying a field of health care (e.g., medicine, nursing, physical therapy, occupational therapy, respiratory therapy, nutrition/dietetics, laboratory sciences, physician assistant). Their program of study must enhance their civilian occupation and/or their military career. Along with their application, they must submit 1) a 250-word description of an activity in which they engaged within the past 2 years, was part of their Reserve duties, and which they consider worthy of recognition; and 2) a 500-word essay on their choice of a health care career and how they will use this scholarship in their academic pursuit to impact their military and/or civilian career.

Financial data The stipend is $1,000.
Duration 1 year.
Number awarded 1 or more each year.
Deadline June of each year.

[307]
ENLISTED ASSOCIATION OF THE NATIONAL GUARD OF GEORGIA SCHOLARSHIPS

Enlisted Association of the National Guard of Georgia
Attn: Executive Director
P.O. Box 602
Ellenwood, GA 30294
(678) 644-9245   Fax: (770) 719-9791
E-mail: csmharper@comcast.net
Web: www.eangga.com/eangga-scholarship

Summary To provide financial assistance to members of the Enlisted Association of the National Guard of Georgia (EANGGA) and their families who are interested in attending college in any state.
Eligibility This program is open to members of EANGGA who have been in good standing for at least 1 year and to their children and spouses. Applicants must be enrolled or planning to enroll at a college or university in any state. Selection is based primarily on an essay, up to 5 paragraphs in length, on a patriotic theme (e.g., heritage of the U.S. flag, history of the National Guard or a National Guard unit, acts of heroism by American patriots, our Constitution or Bill of Rights, civil liberties and other issues in a democratic state).
Financial data The stipend is $1,000.
Duration 1 year.
Number awarded 3 each year, of which 1 is sponsored by USAA Insurance Corporation.
Deadline April of each year.

[308]
ENLISTED ASSOCIATION OF THE NATIONAL GUARD OF IOWA AUXILIARY SCHOLARSHIP PROGRAM

Enlisted Association of the National Guard of Iowa Auxiliary
c/o Lori Waters, President
1005 Second Street S.W.
Altoona, IA 50009
(515) 490-3202   E-mail: bullriderfan@msn.com
Web: www.eangi.org/auxiliary-scholarship

Summary To provide financial assistance to members of the Enlisted Association of the National Guard of Iowa (EANIG) Auxiliary and their families who are interested in attending college in any state.
Eligibility This program is open to EANGI Auxiliary members and their spouses, dependents, and grandchildren. Applicants must be enrolled, accepted for enrollment, or in the process of applying to a college or vocational/technical school as a full-time undergraduate or graduate student. Along with their application, they must submit a letter describing specific fats about their desire to continue their education and why they need financial assistance. Selection is based on character, leadership, and need.
Financial data The stipend is $1,000.
Duration 1 year; recipients may reapply.

Number awarded 2 each year.
Deadline February of each year.

[309]
ENLISTED ASSOCIATION OF THE NATIONAL GUARD OF KANSAS SCHOLARSHIPS

Enlisted Association of the National Guard of Kansas
Attn: Scholarship Program
125 S.E. Airport Drive
Topeka, KS 66619
(785) 242-5678   Fax: (785) 242-3765
E-mail: scholarship/eangks.org
Web: www.eangks.org

Summary To provide financial assistance to members of the Enlisted Association National Guard of Kansas and their families who are interested in attending college in any state.
Eligibility This program is open to members of the association who are also currently serving in the Kansas National Guard and their children and grandchildren. Spouses and dependents of associate members are not eligible. Applicants must submit high school and/or college transcripts (including SAT and/or ACT scores); letters of recommendation; information on their awards and recognition, community service, extracurricular activities, and work experience; documentation of financial need; and a brief essay on their goals and career objectives. They must be enrolled or planning to enroll full time at an accredited institution of higher learning in any state.
Financial data The stipend ranges up to $1,000.
Duration 1 year.
Additional information This program includes 1 scholarship supported by USAA Insurance Corporation.
Number awarded Varies each year.
Deadline April of each year.

[310]
EVELYN B. HAMILTON HEALTH CARE SCHOLARSHIP

Marines' Memorial Association
c/o Marines Memorial Club and Hotel
609 Sutter Street
San Francisco, CA 94102
(415) 673-6672, ext. 293   Toll Free: (800) 5-MARINE
Fax: (415) 441-3649
E-mail: scholarship@marineclub.com
Web: www.marinesmemorial.org

Summary To provide financial assistance to members of the Marines' Memorial Association from all branches of the armed forces and their descendants who are interested in studying health care in college.
Eligibility This program is open to active members of the association and their children and grandchildren. Applicants must be high school seniors or students currently enrolled in an undergraduate degree program in a discipline within the field of health care. Along with their application, they must submit an essay of up to 500 words on why they chose their specific path of study, what they hope to accomplish after graduation with their degree, and how their efforts will benefit others in their community. Graduating high school seniors must submit a high school transcript and SAT or ACT scores; continuing college students must submit a college transcript.

Selection is based on the essay, academic merit, references, and financial need.
Financial data The stipend is $2,500 per year.
Duration 1 year; recipients may reapply for up to 3 additional years.
Additional information Membership in the association is open to veterans of the Marines, Army, Navy, Air Force, or Coast Guard and to personnel currently serving in a branch of the armed forces.
Number awarded 1 each year.
Deadline April of each year.

[311]
EXPLOSIVE ORDNANCE DISPOSAL OPTION OF THE SEAMAN TO ADMIRAL-21 PROGRAM

U.S. Navy
Attn: Commander, Naval Service Training Command
250 Dallas Street, Suite A
Pensacola, FL 32508-5268
(850) 452-9563   Fax: (850) 452-2486
E-mail: PNSC_STA21@navy.mil
Web: www.public.navy.mil

Summary To allow outstanding enlisted Navy personnel to attend a college or university with an NROTC unit, complete a bachelor's degree, and receive a commission as an explosive ordnance disposal (EOD) officer.
Eligibility This program is open to U.S. citizens who are currently serving on active duty in the U.S. Navy or Naval Reserve, including Full Time Support (FTS), Selected Reserves (SELRES), and Navy Reservists on active duty, except for those on active duty for training (ACDUTRA). Applicants must have 1 of the following NECs: 5332, 5333, 5334, 5335, 5336, 5337, 5342, 5343, 5931, 5932, and 8493 or 8494. They must be high school graduates (or GED recipients) who are able to complete requirements for a baccalaureate degree in 36 months or less. When they complete their degree requirements, they must be younger than 29 years of age. That age limitation may be adjusted upward for active service on a month-for-month basis up to 24 months, and waivers are considered for enlisted personnel who possess particularly exceptional qualifications if they can complete their degree prior to their 35th birthday. Within the past 3 years, they must have taken the SAT (and achieved scores of at least 500 on the mathematics section and 500 on the evidence based reading and writing or critical reading section) or the ACT (and achieved a score of at least 21 on the mathematics portion and 20 on the English portion). They must also meet physical regulations that include qualification for diving duty and/or combat swimmer. Preference is given to applicants who plan to major in a technical field (e.g., chemistry, computer science, engineering, mathematics, oceanography, operations analysis, physical sciences, or physics).
Financial data Awardees continue to receive their regular Navy pay and allowances while they attend college on a full-time basis. They also receive reimbursement for tuition, fees, and books up to $10,000 per year. If base housing is available, they are eligible to live there. Participants are not eligible to receive benefits under the Navy's Tuition Assistance Program (TA), the Montgomery GI Bill (MGIB), the Navy College Fund, or the Veterans Educational Assistance Program (VEAP).
Duration Selectees are supported for up to 36 months of full-time, year-round study or completion of a bachelor's degree, as long as they maintain a GPA of 2.5 or higher.
Additional information This program began in 2001 as a replacement for the Seaman to Admiral Program (established in 1994), the Enlisted Commissioning Program, and other specialized programs for sailors to earn a commission. Upon acceptance into the program, selectees attend the Naval Science Institute (NSI) in Newport, Rhode Island for an 8-week program in the fundamental core concepts of being a naval officer (navigation, engineering, weapons, military history and justice, etc.). They then enter a college or university with an NROTC unit or affiliation to work full time on a bachelor's degree. They become members of and drill with the NROTC unit. When they complete their degree, they are commissioned as ensigns in the United States Naval Reserve and assigned to initial training as an EOD officer. After commissioning, 5 years of active service are required.
Number awarded Varies each year.
Deadline June of each year.

[312]
FIRST CAVALRY DIVISION ASSOCIATION SCHOLARSHIPS

First Cavalry Division Association
Attn: Foundation
302 North Main Street
Copperas Cove, TX 76522-1703
(254) 547-6537   Fax: (254) 547-8853
E-mail: firstcav@1cda.org
Web: www.1cda.org/scholarships/foundation

Summary To provide financial assistance for undergraduate education to soldiers currently or formerly assigned to the First Cavalry Division and their families.
Eligibility This program is open to children of soldiers who died or have been declared totally and permanently disabled from injuries incurred while serving with the First Cavalry Division during any armed conflict; children of soldiers who died while serving in the First Cavalry Division during peacetime; and active-duty soldiers currently assigned or attached to the First Cavalry Division and their spouses and children.
Financial data The stipend is $1,200 per year. The checks are made out jointly to the student and the school and may be used for whatever the student needs, including tuition, books, and clothing.
Duration 1 year; may be renewed up to 3 additional years.
Number awarded Varies each year.
Deadline July of each year.

[313]
FIRST LIEUTENANT MICHAEL LICALZI MEMORIAL SCHOLARSHIP

Marine Corps Tankers Association
c/o Dan Miller, Scholarship Chair
8212 West Fourth Place
Kennewick, WA 99336
E-mail: dmiller@msn.com
Web: www.usmctankers.org/pageScholarship

Summary To provide financial assistance for college or graduate school to children and grandchildren of members of the Marine Corps Tankers Association and to Marine and Navy personnel currently serving in tank units.

Eligibility This program is open to high school seniors and graduates who are children, grandchildren, or under the guardianship of an active, Reserve, retired, or honorably discharged Marine who served in a tank unit. Marine or Navy Corpsmen currently assigned to tank units are also eligible. Applicants must be enrolled or planning to enroll full time at a college or graduate school. Their parent or grandparent must be a member of the Marine Corps Tankers Association or, if not a member, must join if the application is accepted. Along with their application, they must submit a 500-word essay that explains their reason for seeking this scholarship, their educational goals, and their plans for post-graduation life. Selection is based on that essay, academic record, school activities, leadership potential, and community service.
Financial data The stipend is $3,000.
Duration 1 year.
Number awarded Varies each year; recently, 6 were awarded.
Deadline March of each year.

[314]
FLEET RESERVE ASSOCIATION MEMBER SCHOLARSHIPS
Fleet Reserve Association
Attn: FRA Education Foundation
125 North West Street
Alexandria, VA 22314-2754
(703) 683-1400   Toll Free: (800) FRA-1924
Fax: (703) 549-6610   E-mail: scholars@fra.org
Web: www.fra.org

Summary To provide financial assistance for college or graduate school to members of the Fleet Reserve Association (FRA) and their families.
Eligibility This program is open to members of the FRA and the children, grandchildren, great-grandchildren, and spouses of living or deceased members. Applicants must be enrolled or planning to enroll as full-time undergraduate or graduate students. Along with their application, they must submit transcripts that include (for high school students and college freshmen) SAT and/or ACT scores; a list of school and community activities; at least 2 letters of recommendation; and an essay on why they want to go to college and what they intend to accomplish with their degree. Selection is based on academic record, financial need, extracurricular activities, leadership skills, and participation in community activities. U.S. citizenship is required.
Financial data Stipends range from $1,000 to $5,000.
Duration 1 year; may be renewed.
Additional information Membership in the FRA is open to current and former enlisted members of the Navy, Marine Corps, and Coast Guard. This program includes awards designated as the MCPO Ken E. Blair Scholarship, the Robert M. Treadwell Annual Scholarship, the Donald Bruce Pringle Family Scholarship, the Tom and Karen Snee Scholarship, the Angelo and Mildred Nunez Scholarships, the Express Scripts Scholarships, the US Family Health Scholarship, and the Navy Department Branch 181 Scholarship.
Number awarded Varies each year; recently, 10 were awarded: 6 at $5,000, 2 at $4,000, 1 at $3,000, and 1 at $2,000.
Deadline April of each year.

[315]
FLEET RESERVE ASSOCIATION NON-MEMBER SCHOLARSHIPS
Fleet Reserve Association
Attn: FRA Education Foundation
125 North West Street
Alexandria, VA 22314-2754
(703) 683-1400   Toll Free: (800) FRA-1924
Fax: (703) 549-6610   E-mail: scholars@fra.org
Web: www.fra.org

Summary To provide financial assistance for college or graduate school to sea service personnel and their families.
Eligibility This program is open to 1) active-duty, Reserve, honorably-discharged veterans, and retired members of the U.S. Navy, Marine Corps, and Coast Guard; and 2) their spouses, children, grandchildren, and great-grandchildren. Applicants must be enrolled or planning to enroll as full-time undergraduate or graduate students, but neither they nor their family member are required to be members of the sponsoring organization. Along with their application, they must submit transcripts that include (for high school students and college freshmen) SAT and/or ACT scores; a list of school and community activities; at least 2 letters of recommendation; and an essay on why they want to go to college and what they intend to accomplish with their degree. Selection is based on academic record, financial need, extracurricular activities, leadership skills, and participation in community activities. U.S. citizenship is required.
Financial data Stipends range up to $5,000 per year.
Duration 1 year; may be renewed.
Additional information This program includes the GEICO Scholarship and the Rosemary Posekany Memorial Scholarship.
Number awarded Varies each year; recently, 6 were awarded: 5 at $5,000 and 1 at $1,000.
Deadline April of each year.

[316]
FLORIDA NATIONAL GUARD EDUCATIONAL DOLLARS FOR DUTY (EDD) PROGRAM
Department of Military Affairs
Attn: State Education Program Administrator
82 Marine Street
St. Augustine, FL 32084
(904) 823-0339   Toll Free: (800) 342-6528
E-mail: ng.fl.flarng.list.ngfl-edd-office@mail.mil
Web: fl.ng.mil

Summary To provide financial assistance for college or graduate school to members of the Florida National Guard.
Eligibility This program is open to current members of the Florida National Guard. Applicants must be attending or planning to attend a college or university in Florida to work on an undergraduate or master's degree. College preparatory and vocational/technical programs also qualify. Guard members who already have a master's degree are not eligible.
Financial data The program provides for payment of 100% of tuition and fees at a public college or university or an equivalent amount at a private institution.
Duration 1 year; may be renewed.

SCHOLARSHIPS: MILITARY PERSONNEL

Number awarded Varies each year; recently, approximately 765 Florida National Guard members utilized this program.
Deadline Applications may be submitted at any time, but they must be received at least 90 days prior to the start of the class.

[317]
FLORIDA NAVY NURSE CORPS ASSOCIATION SCHOLARSHIPS

Florida Navy Nurse Corps Association
c/o Margaret Holder, Scholarship Committee
1033 Inverness Drive
St. Augustine, FL 32092
E-mail: maholder@me.com
Web: www.nnca.org/join-nnca-2/local-chapters/fnnca

Summary To provide financial assistance to undergraduate and graduate nursing students, especially residents of Florida with ties to the military.
Eligibility This program is open to students, including registered nursing continuing their studies, who are working on a baccalaureate or graduate degree in nursing. Applicants must have completed at least 1 clinical nursing course and have a GPA of 3.0 or higher. They may be full- or part-time students. Along with their application, they must submit an essay, up to 500 words in length, on the reasons they are qualified for the scholarship, how it will benefit them, career goals, and potential for contribution to the profession. Preference is given in order to current active-duty and Reserve service members, veterans of military service, family members of current or former military service personnel, civil service employees, and residents of Florida. Financial need is considered in the selection process.
Financial data The stipend is $1,500. Funds are paid directly to the student.
Duration 1 year.
Number awarded 2 each year.
Deadline October of each year.

[318]
FORCE RECON ASSOCIATION SCHOLARSHIPS

Force Recon Association
c/o Al Sniadecki, Scholarship Committee Chair
2928 Cambridgeshire Drive
Carrollton, TX 75007
E-mail: commchief@forcerecon.com
Web: www.forcerecon.com/join.htm

Summary To provide financial assistance for college to members of the Force Recon Association and their dependents.
Eligibility This program is open to members of the Force Recon Association and family members of a relative who served both in the U.S. Marine Corps and was or is assigned to a Force Reconnaissance Company. The relative must be either an active or deceased member of the Force Recon Association. Family members include wives and widows, sons and daughters (including adopted and stepchildren), grandchildren, and great-grandchildren. Applicants may be pursuing scholastic, vocational, or technical education. Along with their application, they must submit a personal statement on why they desire this scholarship, their proposed course of study, their progress in their current course of study, and their long-range career goals. Selection is based on academic achievement, letters of recommendation, demonstrated character, and the written statements.
Financial data A stipend is awarded (amount not specified).
Duration 1 year; may be renewed.
Number awarded 1 or more each year.
Deadline June of each year.

[319]
FORT WORTH POST SAME SCHOLARSHIP

Society of American Military Engineers-Fort Worth Post
c/o J.B. West, Scholarship Chair
Halff Associates
4000 Fossil Creek Boulevard
Fort Worth, TX 76137
(817) 205-7981   E-mail: warwagon16@gmail.com
Web: www.samefortworth.org/scholarship-application

Summary To provide financial assistance to engineering, architecture, and science college and graduate students, especially those at colleges and universities in Texas.
Eligibility This program is open to U.S. citizens who are currently enrolled in college or graduate school; preference is given to students at colleges and universities in Texas. Applicants must be working full time on a degree in an engineering, architecture, or science-related field. Along with their application, they must submit a 500-word essay that covers why they are preparing for a career in engineering, architecture, or a related science, their understanding of the Society of American Military Engineers (SAME) and how involvement with the organization will help them to achieve their academic and professional aspirations and objectives, and what distinguishes them from other candidates. Selection is based on academic achievement, character, personal merit, and commitment to the field of engineering. Special consideration is given to veterans and students enrolled in ROTC.
Financial data The stipend for the highest-ranked student enrolled in engineering and ROTC is $2,000. Other stipend amounts vary.
Duration 1 year.
Number awarded Varies each year.
Deadline April of each year.

[320]
FREDERICK C. BRANCH MARINE CORPS LEADERSHIP SCHOLARSHIPS

U.S. Navy
Attn: Naval Service Training Command Officer
 Development
NAS Pensacola
250 Dallas Street
Pensacola, FL 32508-5220
(850) 452-4941, ext. 29395
Toll Free: (800) NAV-ROTC, ext. 29395
Fax: (850) 452-2486
E-mail: pnsc_nrotc.scholarship@navy.mil
Web: www.nrotc.navy.mil/marine_2_2.html

Summary To provide financial assistance to students who are entering or enrolled at specified Historically Black Colleges or Universities (HBCUs) and interested in joining Navy ROTC to prepare for service as an officer in the U.S. Marine Corps.

Eligibility This program is open to students attending or planning to attend 1 of 17 specified HBCUs with a Navy ROTC unit on campus. Applicants may either apply through their local Marine recruiter for a 4-year scholarship or be nominated by the professor of naval science at their institution and meet academic requirements set by each school for 2- or 3-year scholarships. They must be U.S. citizens between 17 and 23 years of age who are willing to serve for 4 years as active-duty Marine Corps officers following graduation from college. They must not have reached their 27th birthday by the time of college graduation and commissioning; applicants who have prior active-duty military service may be eligible for age adjustments for the amount of time equal to their prior service, up to a maximum of 36 months. The qualifying scores are 1000 composite on the SAT or 22 composite on the ACT. Current enlisted and former military personnel are also eligible if they will complete the program by the age of 30.

Financial data These scholarships provide payment of full tuition and required educational fees, as well as $750 per year for textbooks, supplies, and equipment. The program also provides a stipend for 10 months of the year that is $250 per month as a freshman, $300 per month as a sophomore, $350 per month as a junior, and $400 per month as a senior.

Duration Scholarships are available for 2-, 3-, or 4-year terms.

Additional information Recipients must complete 4 years of study in naval science classes as students at 1 of the following HBCUs: Allen University, Clark Atlanta University, Dillard University, Florida A&M University, Hampton University, Howard University, Huston-Tillotson University, Morehouse College, Norfolk State University, Prairie View A&M University, Savannah State University, Southern University and A&M College, Spelman College, Tennessee State University, Texas Southern University, Tuskegee University, or Xavier University. After completing the program, all participants are commissioned as second lieutenants in the Marine Corps Reserve with an 8-year service obligation, including 4 years of active duty. Current military personnel who are accepted into this program are released from active duty and are not eligible for active-duty pay and allowances, medical benefits, or other active-duty entitlements.

Number awarded Varies each year.

Deadline January of each year for students applying for a 4-year scholarship through their local Marine recruiter; July of each year if applying for a 2- or 3-year scholarship through the Navy ROTC unit at their institution.

[321]
GEN. JACK N. MERRITT SCHOLARSHIP

Association of the United States Army
Attn: Scholarships
2425 Wilson Boulevard
Arlington, VA 22201
(703) 841-4300   Toll Free: (800) 336-4570
E-mail: scholarships@ausa.org
Web: www.ausa.org/resources/scholarships

Summary To provide financial assistance to members of the Association of the United States Army (AUSA) who are interested in attending college.

Eligibility This program is open to AUSA members who are enrolled or accepted at an accredited college or university to work on a degree in any field. Along with their application, they must submit a 1-page autobiography, 2 letters of recommendation, a letter describing their career aspirations (including their course of study and plans for completion of a degree), and a transcript of high school or college grades (depending on which they are currently attending). Selection is based on academic merit and personal achievement. Financial need is not normally a selection criterion but in some cases of extreme need it may be used as a factor; the lack of financial need, however, is never a cause for nonselection.

Financial data The stipend is $5,000; funds are sent directly to the recipient's college or university.

Duration 1 year.

Additional information Membership in the AUSA is open to everyone who supports a strong national defense, with special concern for the Army. That includes Regular Army, National Guard, Army Reserve, government civilians, retired soldiers, Wounded Warriors, veterans, concerned citizens and family members.

Number awarded 2 each year.

Deadline June of each year.

[322]
GENERAL PEDRO DEL VALLE LEADERSHIP SCHOLARSHIPS

U.S. Navy
Attn: Naval Service Training Command Officer
    Development
NAS Pensacola
250 Dallas Street
Pensacola, FL 32508-5220
(850) 452-4941, ext. 29395
Toll Free: (800) NAV-ROTC, ext. 29395
Fax: (850) 452-2486
E-mail: pnsc_nrotc.scholarship@navy.mil
Web: www.nrotc.navy.mil/marine_2_3.html

Summary To provide financial assistance to students who are entering or enrolled at specified Hispanic Serving Institutions (HSIs) and interested in joining Navy ROTC to prepare for service as an officer in the U.S. Marine Corps.

Eligibility This program is open to students attending or planning to attend 1 of 3 specified HSIs with a Navy ROTC unit on campus. Applicants may either apply through their local Marine recruiter for a 4-year scholarship or be nominated by the professor of naval science at their institution and meet academic requirements set by each school for 2- or 3-year scholarships. They must be U.S. citizens between 17 and 23 years of age who are willing to serve for 4 years as active-duty Marine Corps officers following graduation from college. They must not have reached their 27th birthday by the time of college graduation and commissioning; applicants who have prior active-duty military service may be eligible for age adjustments for the amount of time equal to their prior service, up to a maximum of 36 months. The qualifying scores are 1000 composite on the SAT or 22 composite on the ACT. Current enlisted and former military personnel are also eligible if they will complete the program by the age of 30.

Financial data These scholarships provide payment of full tuition and required educational fees, as well as $750 per year for textbooks, supplies, and equipment. The program

also provides a stipend for 10 months of the year that is $250 per month as a freshman, $300 per month as a sophomore, $350 per month as a junior, and $400 per month as a senior.
Duration Scholarships are available for 2-, 3-, or 4-year terms.
Additional information Recipients must complete 4 years of study in naval science classes as students at 1 of the following HSIs: California State University at San Marcos, University of New Mexico, or San Diego State University. After completing the program, all participants are commissioned as second lieutenants in the Marine Corps Reserve with an 8-year service obligation, including 4 years of active duty. Current military personnel who are accepted into this program are released from active duty and are not eligible for active-duty pay and allowances, medical benefits, or other active-duty entitlements.
Number awarded Varies each year.
Deadline January of each year for students applying for a 4-year scholarship through their local Marine recruiter; July of each year if applying for a 2- or 3-year scholarship through the Navy ROTC unit at their institution.

[323]
GEORGE L. PATT SCHOLARSHIP FUND

Illinois Association of Realtors
Attn: Illinois Real Estate Educational Foundation
522 South Fifth Street
P.O. Box 2607
Springfield, IL 62708
Toll Free: (866) 854-REEF Fax: (217) 529-5893
E-mail: lclayton@ilreef.org
Web: www.ilreef.org/scholarships

Summary To provide financial assistance to veterans and Reservists in Illinois who are preparing for a career in real estate at a college or university in the state.
Eligibility This program is open to residents of Illinois enrolled at a school in the state. Applicants must be either 1) veterans working on an undergraduate college or university degree in the field of real estate; or 2) active Reservists or Guard members studying real estate administration to establish themselves as an association executive in a realtor organization. Along with their application, they must submit a 1,000-word statement of their general activities and intellectual interests, employment (if any), contemplated line of study, and career they expect to follow. Selection is based on the applicant's record of military service, record of academic achievement, course of study and career goals, references and recommendations, and financial need. Finalists are interviewed.
Financial data The stipend is $1,000.
Duration 1 year.
Number awarded 1 each year.
Deadline March of each year.

[324]
GEORGE WASHINGTON CHAPTER AUSA SCHOLARSHIPS

Association of the United States Army-George Washington Chapter
c/o Col (Ret.) William G. Yarborough, Jr., Scholarship Committee
P.O. Box 828
McLean, VA 22101-0828
(703) 748-1717 E-mail: wgyarc@aol.com
Web: www.ausa.org/chapters/george-washington-chapter

Summary To provide financial assistance for undergraduate or graduate study at a school in any state to members of the George Washington Chapter of the Association of the United States Army (AUSA) and their families.
Eligibility This program is open to active members of the AUSA George Washington Chapter and the spouses, children, and grandchildren of active members. Applicants must have a GPA of 2.5 or higher and be working on an undergraduate or graduate degree at a college or university in any state. Along with their application, they must submit a letter describing any family circumstances they believe are relevant and explaining why they deserve the scholarship. Members must also submit a favorable recommendation from their supervisor. Membership in AUSA is open to Army personnel (including Reserves and National Guard) who are either active or retired, ROTC cadets, or civilian employees of the Army.
Financial data Stipends range up to $1,000.
Duration 1 year.
Additional information This program includes the following named awards: the Ed Dauksz Scholarship Award, the Major General Harry Greene STEM Scholarship Award, and the Major General Carl F. McNair Jr. Scholarship Award. The George Washington Chapter serves Washington, D.C.; the Virginia counties of Alexandria, Clarke, Fairfax, Frederick, Loudoun, and Prince William; and the Maryland counties of Calvert, Charles, Montgomery, Prince George's, and St. Mary's.
Number awarded Varies each year; recently, 45 were awarded.
Deadline April of each year.

[325]
GEORGIA HERO SCHOLARSHIP PROGRAM

Georgia Student Finance Commission
Attn: Scholarships and Grants Division
2082 East Exchange Place, Suite 200
Tucker, GA 30084-5305
(770) 724-9249 Toll Free: (800) 505-GSFC
Fax: (770) 724-9089 E-mail: GAfutures@gsfc.org
Web: www.gafutures.org

Summary To provide financial assistance for college to members of the National Guard or Reserves in Georgia and their children and spouses.
Eligibility This program is open to Georgia residents who are active members of the Georgia National Guard or U.S. Military Reserves, were deployed outside the United States for active-duty service on or after February 1, 2003 to a location designated as a combat zone, and served in that combat zone for at least 181 consecutive days. Also eligible are 1) the children, younger than 25 years of age, of Guard and Reserve members who completed at least 1 term of service

(of 181 days each) overseas on or after February 1, 2003; 2) the children, younger than 25 years of age, of Guard and Reserve members who were killed or totally disabled during service overseas on or after February 1, 2003, regardless of their length of service; and 3) the spouses of Guard and Reserve members who were killed in a combat zone, died as a result of injuries, or became 100% disabled as a result of injuries received in a combat zone during service overseas on or after February 1, 2003, regardless of their length of service. Applicants must be interested in attending a unit of the University System of Georgia, a unit of the Technical College System of Georgia, or an eligible private college or university in Georgia.
Financial data The stipend for full-time study is $2,000 per academic year, not to exceed $8,000 during an entire program of study. The stipend for part-time study is prorated appropriately.
Duration 1 year; may be renewed (if satisfactory progress is maintained) for up to 3 additional years.
Additional information This program, which stands for Helping Educate Reservists and their Offspring, was established in 2005.
Number awarded Varies each year.
Deadline June of each year.

[326]
GEORGIA NATIONAL GUARD SERVICE CANCELABLE LOAN
Georgia Student Finance Commission
Attn: Scholarships and Grants Division
2082 East Exchange Place, Suite 200
Tucker, GA 30084-5305
(770) 724-9249   Toll Free: (800) 505-GSFC
Fax: (770) 724-9089   E-mail: GAfutures@gsfc.org
Web: www.gafutures.org
Summary To provide loans for service to members of the Georgia National Guard who are interested in attending college in the state.
Eligibility This program is open to Georgia residents who are serving members of the Georgia National Guard. Applicants must be enrolled at least half time at public or approved private universities in the state. U.S. citizenship or eligible noncitizen status is required.
Financial data At public institutions, the loan is equivalent to the standard undergraduate tuition at that school. At private institutions, the maximum loan is $2,174 for full-time study or $1,087 for half-time study. To repay the loan by service, the recipient must remain in good standing as a member of the Georgia National Guard and in good academic standing at the college or university. Loans not repaid by service must be repaid in cash, plus interest.
Duration 1 semester; may be renewed for up to 9 additional semesters, provided the recipient remains enrolled at least half time and maintains a GPA of 2.0 or higher.
Number awarded Varies each year.
Deadline Loans are granted on a first-come, first-served basis until funds are exhausted.

[327]
GLADYS MCPARTLAND SCHOLARSHIPS
United States Marine Corps Combat Correspondents Association
Attn: Scholarship Committee
385 S.W. 254th Street
Newberry, FL 32669
(352) 448-9167   E-mail: hq@usmccca.org
Web: www.usmccca.org/awards/gladys
Summary To provide financial assistance to members of the U.S. Marine Corps Combat Correspondents Association (USMCCCA) or their dependents and Marines in specified occupational fields who are interested in studying any field in college.
Eligibility This program is open to members of USMCCCA who have been members for at least 2 years and their dependents of such members, including children of deceased members. Applications are also accepted from active-duty Marines in occupational field 4300 or 4600 who are enrolled in government-sponsored degree completion programs, whose tuition is not paid from other sources, and who agree to become USMCCCA members upon award of a scholarship. Applicants must be enrolled or planning to enroll in an undergraduate program in any field. Along with their application, they must submit 500-word essays on 1) their noteworthy achievements and long-range goals; and 2) "The United States I want to see in 15 years and my role in the transformation." Financial need is not considered in the selection process.
Financial data Stipends for full-time study range up to $3,000; part-time stipends range from $250 to $500. Funds are disbursed directly to recipients to be used exclusively for tuition, books, and/or fees.
Duration 1 year; may be renewed up to 3 additional years.
Number awarded 1 or more each year.
Deadline May of each year.

[328]
GOOGLE-SVA SCHOLARSHIP
Student Veterans of America
Attn: Scholarship Committee
1012 14th Street, N.W., Suite 1200
Washington, DC 20005
(202) 223-4710
E-mail: scholarships@studentveterans.org
Web: www.studentveterans.org/programs/scholarships
Summary To provide financial assistance to veterans and current military personnel who are working on a bachelor's or graduate degree in a computer-related field.
Eligibility This program is open to sophomores, juniors, seniors, and graduate students at 4-year colleges and universities who are veterans of any branch of service, including Reserves and National Guard, and were honorably discharged or are active-duty military personnel still in good standing with their branch of service. Applicants must be working full time on a degree in computer science, computer engineering, or a closely-related technical field (e.g., software engineering, electrical engineering with a heavy computer science course load, information systems, information technology, applied networking, system administration). Along with their application, they must submit essays of 300 to 500 words each on 1) what sparked their interest in computer sci-

ence; 2) examples of how they have exhibited leadership; 3) a significant challenge that they believe student veterans in the field of technology face and how they see themselves as being part of the solution(s) to that challenge; and 4) the impact receiving this scholarship would have on their education. Financial need is not considered in the selection process.

Financial data The stipend is $10,000.

Duration 1 year.

Additional information This program is sponsored by Google and administered by Student Veterans of America (SVA).

Number awarded 8 each year.

Deadline November of each year.

[329]
GREEN TO GOLD NON-SCHOLARSHIP PROGRAM

U.S. Army
Attn: U.S. Army Cadet Command
G2 Incentives Division
1307 Third Avenue
Fort Knox, KY 40121-2725
(502) 624-7371   Toll Free: (888) 550-ARMY
Fax: (502) 624-6937
E-mail: usarmy.knox.usacc.mbx.train2lead@mail.mil
Web: www.goarmy.com

Summary To provide financial assistance to soldiers who wish to obtain an early discharge from the Army and return to college to participate in the Army Reserve Officers' Training Corps (ROTC).

Eligibility This program is open to enlisted soldiers who have served from 2 to 10 years on active duty and have also completed at least 2 years of college with a GPA of 2.0 or higher. Applicants must be under 30 years of age when they graduate (waivers up to 42 years of age are available). They apply for this program to obtain an early discharge from active duty in order to enroll in a baccalaureate degree program.

Financial data Cadets receive a stipend for 10 months of the year that is $450 per month during their junior year and $500 per month during their senior year, as well as pay for attending the 6-week Cadet Leadership Course (CLC) during the summer between the junior and senior year of college.

Duration 2 years.

Additional information Cadets who had previously qualified for benefits from the Army College Fund and/or the Montgomery GI Bill are still entitled to receive those in addition to any benefits from this program. Cadets are also entitled to participate in the Simultaneous Membership Program and serve with pay in a drilling unit of the Army Reserve or Army National Guard. Upon graduation from college, cadets are commissioned as second lieutenants and are required to serve in the military for 8 years. That obligation may be fulfilled by serving 3 years on active duty and 5 years in the Inactive Ready Reserve (IRR).

Number awarded Varies each year.

Deadline March or September of each year.

[330]
GREEN TO GOLD SCHOLARSHIP PROGRAM

U.S. Army
Attn: U.S. Army Cadet Command
G2 Incentives Division
1307 Third Avenue
Fort Knox, KY 40121-2725
(502) 624-7371   Toll Free: (888) 550-ARMY
Fax: (502) 624-6937
E-mail: usarmy.knox.usacc.mbx.train2lead@mail.mil
Web: www.goarmy.com

Summary To provide scholarships and other payments to soldiers who wish to obtain an early discharge from the Army and return to college to participate in the Army Reserve Officers' Training Corps (ROTC).

Eligibility This program is open to enlisted soldiers who are younger than 31 years of age and have served at least 2 years on active duty plus 3 months of active duty for each month of specialized training. Applicants must have a cumulative high school or college GPA of 2.5 or higher, scores of at least 1000 on the SAT or 19 on the ACT, a General Technical (GT) score of 110 or higher, and a recent (within the past 6 months) Army Physical Fitness Test (APFT) score of 180 or higher (including 60 points in each event). They may have no more than 3 dependents including a spouse (that requirement may be waived) and must be under 31 years of age when they graduate and are commissioned. They must have been accepted at a college or university offering Army ROTC. U.S. citizenship is required.

Financial data Scholarship winners receive up to $20,000 per year as support for tuition and fees or for room and board, whichever the recipient selects; additional support up to $1,200 per year for textbooks, supplies, and equipment; a stipend for 10 months of the year that is $350 per month during their sophomore year, $450 per month during their junior year, and $500 per month during their senior year; and pay for attending the 6-week Cadet Leadership Course (CLC) during the summer between the junior and senior year of college.

Duration Scholarships are for 2, 3, or 4 years; soldiers without prior college credit or whose colleges accept them as academic freshmen are eligible for 4-year scholarships; soldiers with 1 year of college completed are eligible for 3-year scholarships; soldiers with 2 years of college completed are eligible for 2-year scholarships.

Additional information Recipients who had previously qualified for benefits from the Army College Fund and/or the Montgomery GI Bill are still entitled to receive those in addition to any benefits from this program. Upon graduation from college, scholarship winners are commissioned as second lieutenants and are required to serve in the military for 8 years. That obligation may be fulfilled by serving 4 years on active duty followed by 4 years in the Inactive Ready Reserve (IRR).

Number awarded Varies each year.

Deadline November of each year.

[331]
GUARANTEED RESERVE FORCES DUTY (GRFD) SCHOLARSHIPS

U.S. Army National Guard
Education Support Center
Camp Joseph T. Robinson
Building 5400 Box 46
North Little Rock, AR 72199-9600
Toll Free: (866) 628-5999　　　Fax: (501) 212-4928
E-mail: esc@ng.army.mil
Web: www.nationalguard.com/tools/guard-scholarships

Summary To provide financial assistance to college students who are willing to enroll in Army ROTC and serve in a Reserve component of the Army following graduation.

Eligibility This program is open to full-time students entering their junior year of college who have a GPA of 2.5 or higher and scores of 1000 on the SAT or 19 on the ACT. Applicants must meet all other medical and moral character requirements for enrollment in Army ROTC and be able to complete the basic course requirements or basic training. They must be willing to enroll in the Simultaneous Membership Program (SMP) of an ROTC unit on their campus; the SMP requires simultaneous membership in Army ROTC and either the Army National Guard or Army Reserve.

Financial data Participants receive full reimbursement of tuition up to $10,000 per year, a grant of $1,200 per year for books, an ROTC stipend for 10 months of the year at $420 per month, and weekend drill pay at the pay grade of a sergeant (approximately $319 per month) while participating in the SMP.

Duration 2 years.

Additional information After graduation, participants serve 3 to 6 months on active duty in the Officer Basic Course (OBC). Following completion of OBC, they are released from active duty and are obligated to serve 8 years in the Army National Guard or Army Reserve.

Number awarded Approximately 400 each year.

Deadline Deadline not specified.

[332]
HAROLD C. PIERCE JR. SCHOLARSHIP PROGRAM

Enlisted Association of the National Guard of West Virginia
c/o WVAR-CSM
1703 Coonskin Drive
Charleston, WV 25311-1085
(304) 561-6314　　　E-mail: scholarship@eangus.org
Web: www.eangwv.org/category/benefits

Summary To provide financial assistance to the children and spouses of current or deceased members of the Enlisted Association of the National Guard of West Virginia (EANGWV) who are interested in attending college in any state.

Eligibility This program is open EANGWV members, their dependent unmarried children, and their spouses; unremarried spouses and unmarried dependent children of deceased EANGWV members who were in good standing at the time of their death are also eligible. Applicants must be enrolled full time at a college, university, trade school, or business school in any state; graduate students are not eligible. Along with their application, they must submit a copy of their high school or college transcript; a letter with personal, specific facts on their desire to continue their education; 3 letters of recommendation; a letter of academic reference; and a photocopy of the qualifying membership card. Selection is based on scholarship, character, leadership, and merit; financial need is not considered.

Financial data The stipend is $1,000. Funds are sent directly to the recipient's school.

Duration 1 year; nonrenewable.

Number awarded 1 or more each year.

Deadline June of each year.

[333]
HAWAII ALOHA CHAPTER MOAA SCHOLARSHIP FUND

Military Officers Association of America-Hawaii Aloha Chapter
Attn: John Ma, Scholarship Fund Chair
P.O. Box 201441
Honolulu, HI 96820-1356
(808) 486-4805　　　E-mail: john.ma08@yahoo.com
Web: www.moaa-hawaii.org/Bylaws_Scholarship_Fund.htm

Summary To provide financial assistance to residents of Hawaii who have ties to the military and are interested in attending college in any state.

Eligibility This program is open to residents of Hawaii who are 1) members of the Military Officers Association of America (MOAA) and their spouses, children, or grandchildren; 2) children of parents currently serving in any of the uniformed services; 3) currently serving in any of the uniformed services; or 4) enrolled in a Junior ROTC program at a high school in Hawaii or in an ROTC program at a college or university in Hawaii. Applicants must be enrolled or planning to enroll at an accredited college or university in Hawaii or, if eligible, in any state. Selection is based on academic ability or potential, character, personal qualities, and financial need.

Financial data Stipends are $1,000 or $500.

Duration 1 year.

Number awarded Varies each year; recently, 23 were awarded: 2 at $1,000 each to ROTC students at the University of Hawaii and 21 at $500 each to JROTC students at high schools in Hawaii. Since this program began, it has awarded 1,300 scholarships worth more than $120,000.

Deadline Deadline not specified.

[334]
HELEN DYAR KING SCHOLARSHIP

Arizona Community Foundation
Attn: Director of Scholarships
2201 East Camelback Road, Suite 405B
Phoenix, AZ 85016
(602) 381-1400　　　Toll Free: (800) 222-8221
Fax: (602) 381-1575
E-mail: scholarship@azfoundation.org
Web: azfoundation.academicworks.com/opportunities/4156

Summary To provide financial assistance to high school seniors and current college students from Arizona who are members or dependents of members of the armed services or a law enforcement agency and are interested in attending college in any state.

Eligibility This program is open to residents of Arizona who are graduating high school seniors or current full-time students at colleges or universities in any state. Applicants

must be an active-duty or retired member or dependent of such a member of the armed services (Air Force, Army, Coast Guard, Marine Corps, National Guard, Navy) or public service agency (police, fire, or other departments). Students entering or enrolled at a 2-year community college must have a GPA of 2.75 or higher; students entering or enrolled at a 4-year college or university must have a GPA of 3.0 or higher. Financial need is considered in the selection process.
Financial data The stipend is $2,000 for students at 2-year colleges or $4,000 for students at 4-year colleges and universities.
Duration 1 year.
Number awarded Varies each year.
Deadline May of each year.

[335]
HELPING HEROES GRANTS OF TENNESSEE
Tennessee Student Assistance Corporation
312 Rosa Parks Boulevard, Ninth Floor
Nashville, TN 37243
(615) 741-1346   Toll Free: (800) 342-1663
Fax: (615) 741-6101   E-mail: TSAC.Aidinfo@tn.gov
Web: www.tn.gov

Summary To provide financial assistance to veterans and current Reservists or National Guard members who are residents of Tennessee and enrolled at a college or university in the state.
Eligibility This program is open to residents of Tennessee who are veterans honorably discharged from the U.S. armed forces and former or current members of a Reserve or Tennessee National Guard unit who were called into active military service. Applicants must have been awarded, on or after September 11, 2001, the Iraq Campaign Medal, the Afghanistan Campaign Medal, or the Global War on Terrorism Expeditionary Medal. They must be enrolled at least half time at an eligible college or university in Tennessee and receive no final failing grade in any course. No academic standard or financial need requirements apply.
Financial data Grants are $1,000 per semester for full-time study or $500 per semester for part-time study. Funds are awarded after completion of each semester of work.
Duration Grants are awarded until completion of the equivalent of 8 full semesters of work, completion of a baccalaureate degree, or the eighth anniversary of honorable discharge from military service, whichever comes first.
Additional information This program was added as a component of the Tennessee Education Lottery Scholarship Program in 2005.
Number awarded Varies each year; recently, 486 students received approximately $734,000 in scholarships through this program.
Deadline August of each year for fall enrollment, January of each year for spring, or April of each year for summer.

[336]
HENRY J. REILLY SCHOLARSHIPS
Reserve Officers Association of the United States
Attn: Scholarship Program
One Constitution Avenue, N.E.
Washington, DC 20002-5618
(202) 646-7758   Toll Free: (800) 809-9448
E-mail: scholarship@roa.org
Web: www.roa.org/page/Scholarships

Summary To provide financial assistance for college or graduate school to members of the Reserve Officers Association (ROA) and their children or grandchildren.
Eligibility Applicants for this scholarship must be active or associate members of the association or their children or grandchildren (under the age of 26). Children, age 21 or under, of deceased members who were active and paid up at the time of their death are also eligible. Spouses are not eligible, unless they are members of the association. ROTC members do not qualify as sponsors. Entering and continuing undergraduates must provide evidence of full-time enrollment at a regionally-accredited 4-year college or university, demonstrate leadership qualities, have earned a GPA of 3.3 or higher in high school and 3.0 or higher in college, have scored at least 1875 on the SAT or 55 on the English/math ACT, and (if appropriate) have registered for the draft. Applicants for a master's degree must have earned a GPA of 3.2 or higher as an undergraduate; applicants for a doctoral degree must have received a master's degree or been accepted into a doctoral program. All applicants must submit a 500-word essay on career goals. Selection is based on that essay, academic excellence, extracurricular activities and leadership, and letters of recommendation.
Financial data The stipend is $2,500 per year.
Duration 1 year; may be renewed.
Number awarded Up to 20 each year.
Deadline April of each year.

[337]
HOMEGROWN BY HEROES SCHOLARSHIPS
Arkansas Agriculture Department
Attn: Homegrown by Heroes Program
1 Natural Resources Drive
Little Rock, AR 72205
(501) 225-1598
E-mail: amy.lyman@agriculture.arkansas.gov
Web: www.agriculture.arkansas.gov/aad-programs

Summary To provide financial assistance to veterans, current military personnel, and their spouses and children in Arkansas who are interested in working on a degree in agriculture at a college in any state.
Eligibility This program is open to residents of Arkansas who are military veterans, currently serving military personnel, and their spouses or children. Applicants must be enrolled or planning to enroll at a college or university in any state to working on a degree in agriculture or a related field. Selection is based on academic achievement, community involvement, extracurricular activities, family circumstances, and financial need. Preference is given to farmers and their families who participate in Homegrown by Heroes, a program of the Arkansas Agriculture Department that helps veterans market their local agricultural products by labeling them as veteran-produced.

Financial data The stipend is $1,000.
Duration 1 year.
Additional information This program is funded by Farm Credit of Western Arkansas, AgHeritage Farm Credit Services, and Farm Credit Midsouth.
Number awarded 8 each year.
Deadline March of each year.

[338]
HONORABLY DISCHARGED GRADUATE ASSISTANCE PROGRAM

Florida Department of Education
Attn: Office of Student Financial Assistance
State Scholarship and Grant Programs
325 West Gaines Street, Suite 1314
Tallahassee, FL 32399-0400
(850) 410-5160   Toll Free: (888) 827-2004
Fax: (850) 487-1809   E-mail: osfa@fldoe.org
Web: www.floridastudentfinancialaidsg.org

Summary To provide funding to active-duty and veterans in Florida who need assistance for payment of living expenses during holiday and semester breaks from college.
Eligibility This program is open to residents of Florida who are active-duty or honorably discharged members of the armed forces, served on or after September 11, 2001, and are currently enrolled in a program of study at a postsecondary institution in the state. Applicants must be able to demonstrate a financial need for assistance in payment of living expenses during holiday and semester breaks, including, but not limited to, food, shelter, utilities, and personal care products.
Financial data Support is limited to $50 per day. The total award may not exceed the student's unmet need.
Duration Up to 20 days per academic year.
Additional information This program began in 2014.
Number awarded Varies each year; recently, 1,236 initial and 467 renewal scholarships were awarded.
Deadline Applications may be submitted at any time.

[339]
HOWARD R. HARPER SCHOLARSHIP

Enlisted Association of the National Guard of Iowa
c/o Michelle E. Hartwell, Scholarship Chair
1780 N.W. 32nd Lane, Apartment 21
Ankeny, IA 50023
(319) 350-6167   E-mail: meaberle@yahoo.com
Web: www.eangi.org/howard-r-harper-scholarship

Summary To provide financial assistance to members of the Enlisted Association of the National Guard of Iowa (EANGI) and their spouses, children, and grandchildren who are interested in attending college in any state.
Eligibility This program is open to members in good standing of the EANGI and their spouses, children, and grandchildren. Applicants must be attending or accepted for attendance at a VA-approved college or technical school. Along with their application, they must submit a letter with specific information about their desire to continue their education and why they require financial assistance.
Financial data The stipend is $1,500.
Duration 1 year; recipients may reapply.

Number awarded 3 each year.
Deadline February of each year.

[340]
ILLINOIS NATIONAL GUARD GRANT PROGRAM

Illinois Student Assistance Commission
Attn: Scholarship and Grant Services
1755 Lake Cook Road
Deerfield, IL 60015-5209
(847) 948-8550   Toll Free: (800) 899-ISAC
Fax: (847) 831-8549   TDD: (800) 526-0844
E-mail: isac.studentservices@illinois.gov
Web: www.isac.org

Summary To provide financial assistance to current or former members of the Illinois National Guard who are interested in attending college or graduate school in the state.
Eligibility This program is open to members of the Illinois National Guard who 1) are currently active and have completed at least 1 full year of service; or 2) have been active for at least 5 consecutive years, have had their studies interrupted by being called to federal active duty for at least 6 months, and are within 12 months after their discharge date. Applicants must also be enrolled at an Illinois public 2- or 4-year college or university.
Financial data Recipients are eligible for payment of tuition and some fees for either undergraduate or graduate study at an Illinois state-supported college or university.
Duration This assistance extends for 4 academic years of full-time study (or the equivalent in part-time study) for Guard members with less than 10 years of active duty service. For Guard members with 10 years or more of active duty service, assistance is available for up to the equivalent of 6 academic years of full-time study.
Number awarded Varies each year.
Deadline September of each year for the academic year; February of each year for spring semester, winter quarter, or spring quarter; June of each year for summer term.

[341]
IMAGINE AMERICA MILITARY AWARD PROGRAM

Imagine America Foundation
Attn: Student Services Representative
14200 Park Meadow Drive, Suite 117S
Chantilly, VA 20151
(571) 267-3015   Fax: (866) 734-5812
E-mail: studentservices@imagine-america.org
Web: www.imagine-america.org

Summary To provide financial assistance to veterans and military personnel interested in attending a participating career college.
Eligibility This program is open to active-duty, reservist, honorably-discharged, and retired veterans of a U.S. military service branch. Applicants must be interested in attending 1 of more than 550 participating career colleges. All applications are submitted online to the college where the student wishes to enroll. Selection is based on the likelihood of successfully completing postsecondary education and financial need.
Financial data The stipend is $1,000. Funds must be used for payment of tuition at a participating career college.
Duration 1 year.

SCHOLARSHIPS: MILITARY PERSONNEL

Additional information The Imagine America Foundation (originally known as the Career College Foundation) established this program in 2004. Its membership includes 550 career colleges.
Number awarded Varies each year.
Deadline Deadline not specified.

[342] INDIANA NATIONAL GUARD SUPPLEMENTAL GRANT PROGRAM

Indiana Commission for Higher Education
Attn: Financial Aid and Student Support Services
101 West Ohio Street, Suite 300
Indianapolis, IN 46204-4206
(317) 232-1023   Toll Free: (888) 528-4719 (within IN)
Fax: (317) 232-3260   E-mail: Scholars@che.in.gov
Web: www.in.gov/che/4516.htm

Summary To provide financial assistance to members of the Indiana National Guard who are interested in attending public colleges in the state.
Eligibility This program is open to members of the Indiana Air and Army National Guard who are in active drilling status and have not been AWOL at any time during the preceding 12 months. Applicants must be high school graduates seeking their first associate or bachelor's degree at a public college or university in the state. Allowances may be made for students who earned a GED certificate or were home schooled, but only on a case-by-case basis following a written appeal. As part of the application process, students must file the Free Application for Federal Student Aid (FAFSA). If they qualify as dependent students based on FAFSA data, their parents must be residents of Indiana; if the FAFSA standards define them as independent students, they must be Indiana residents.
Financial data The award provides payment of 100% of the tuition costs at state-funded colleges and universities in Indiana. No funding is provided for books, room, or board.
Duration 1 year; may be renewed.
Number awarded Varies each year.
Deadline March of each year.

[343] IOWA NATIONAL GUARD EDUCATIONAL ASSISTANCE PROGRAM

Iowa National Guard
Joint Forces Headquarters Iowa
Attn: Education Services Officer
7105 N.W. 70th Avenue
Johnston, IA 50131-1824
(515) 252-4468   Toll Free: (800) 294-6607, ext. 4468
Fax: (515) 252-4025
E-mail: ng.ia.iaarng.list.g1-education-services@mail.mil
Web: www.iowanationalguard.com

Summary To provide financial assistance to members of the Iowa National Guard who wish to attend college.
Eligibility This program is open to residents of Iowa who are members of an Iowa Army or Air National Guard unit. Applicants must have satisfactorily completed Initial Entry Training (Basic Training and Advanced Individual Training), have maintained satisfactory performance of duty (including attending a minimum 90% of scheduled drill dates and scheduled annual training in the preceding 12 months), have maintained satisfactory academic progress as determined by their academic institution, and have not completed their baccalaureate degree. They may be seeking to attend a state-supported university, community college, or participating private accredited institution of postsecondary education located in Iowa.
Financial data Recently, available funding permitted payment of 100% of the tuition rate at Iowa Regents institutions, or a maximum of $7,725 per year for full-time enrollment. Funds may be used for any educational expense, including tuition, room, board, supplies, books, fees, and other associated costs.
Duration 1 year; may be renewed for up to 120 credit hours of undergraduate study.
Additional information This program began in 1999.
Number awarded Varies each year; recently, a total of $5,100,233 was available for this program statewide. Assistance is provided on a first-come, first-served basis.
Deadline June of each year for fall term or November of each year for spring term.

[344] JACK E. BARGER, SR. MEMORIAL NURSING SCHOLARSHIPS

Nursing Foundation of Pennsylvania
3605 Vartan Way, Suite 204
Harrisburg, PA 17110
(717) 827-4369   Toll Free: (888) 707-7762
Fax: (717) 657-3796   E-mail: info@theNFP.org
Web: www.thenfp.org/scholarships

Summary To provide financial assistance to veterans, military personnel, and their dependents who are studying nursing in Pennsylvania.
Eligibility This program is open to veterans, active-duty military personnel, and the children and spouses of veterans and active-duty military personnel. Applicants must be residents of Pennsylvania and currently enrolled in an undergraduate professional school of nursing in the state. Recipients are selected by lottery from among the qualified applicants.
Financial data The stipend is $1,000.
Duration 1 year.
Additional information This program is sponsored by the Department of Pennsylvania of Veterans of Foreign Wars (VFW). Recipients must attend the VFW Convention to accept the scholarship; travel, meals, and overnight expenses are paid by the VFW.
Number awarded 6 each year.
Deadline March of each year.

[345] JEWISH WAR VETERANS NATIONAL ACHIEVEMENT PROGRAM

Jewish War Veterans of the U.S.A.
Attn: National Achievement Program
1811 R Street, N.W.
Washington, DC 20009-1659
(202) 265-6280   Fax: (202) 234-5662
E-mail: jwv@jwv.org
Web: www.jwvusafoundation.org

Summary To recognize and reward veterans and current servicemembers who are currently enrolled in college or

graduate school and submit outstanding essays on their military experience.
Eligibility This competition is open to veterans and current servicemembers who are enrolled or planning to enroll in an accredited associate, bachelor's, nursing, or graduate degree program. All veterans are eligible, regardless of race, religion, creed, or culture. Applicants must submit an essay of 500 to 750 words on their military experience and how it will help them pursue their academic studies. Selection is based on answering the essay question (50%), logic and coherence of the essay's organization (25%), and description of relevant military experience (25%).
Financial data Awards range from $1,000 to $5,000.
Duration The awards are presented annually.
Additional information This program includes the Robert M. Zweiman Memorial Award, the Sidney Lieppe Memorial Grant, the Charles Kosmutza Memorial Grant, the Max R. and Irene Rubenstein Memorial Grant, and the Leon Brooks Memorial Grant.
Number awarded 6 each year: 2 at $5,000, 1 at $2,500, 1 at $1,500, and 2 at $1,000.
Deadline May of each year.

[346]
JOAN BOWDEN SCHOLARSHIP
Armed Forces Communications and Electronics Association
Attn: AFCEA Educational Foundation
4114 Legato Road, Suite 1000
Fairfax, VA 22033-3342
(703) 631-6147   Toll Free: (800) 336-4583, ext. 6147
Fax: (703) 631-4693   E-mail: edfoundation@afcea.org
Web: www.afcea.org

Summary To provide financial assistance for college to outstanding Air Force ROTC cadets in designated states.
Eligibility This program is open to U.S. citizens who are enrolled in the Air Force ROTC detachment at an accredited college or university in Alabama, Louisiana, Mississippi, or the northwest panhandle of Florida. Applicants must be enrolled as sophomores or juniors and working on a degree in biometrics, computer forensics science, computer programming, computer science, cyber security, engineering (computer, electrical, electronics, network, robotics, telecommunications), geospatial science, information technology, information resources management, mathematics, network security, operations research, physics, robotics, statistics, or strategic intelligence. Majors related to medicine, nursing, political science, psychology, and other fields of engineering (e.g., aerospace, chemical, civil, mechanical) are not eligible. Their application must be endorsed by the professor of aviation science at their institution. They must have a GPA of 3.0 or higher. Selection is based on demonstrated dedication, superior performance, potential to serve as an officer in the United States Air Force, and financial need.
Financial data The stipend is $3,000. Funds are paid directly to the recipient.
Duration 1 year.
Additional information This program began in 1987 with support from the Montgomery Chapter of the Armed Forces Communications and Electronics Association (AFCEA).
Number awarded 1 each year.
Deadline April of each year.

[347]
JOE KING SCHOLARSHIPS
Council of College and Military Educators
c/o Jim Yeonopolus, Scholarship Committee Chair
Central Texas College
P.O. Box 1800
Killeen, TX 76540-1800
(254) 526-1781   Fax: (254) 526-1750
E-mail: jim.yeonopolus@ctcd.edu
Web: www.ccmeonline.org/scholarships

Summary To provide financial assistance to members of the armed services who are interested in working on an undergraduate or master's degree.
Eligibility This program is open to members of the uniformed services currently on active duty. Applicants must be currently enrolled full time at an accredited institution that is a member of the Council of College and Military Educators (CCME) and working on an associate, bachelor's, or master's degree. Undergraduates must have a GPA of 2.5 or higher and graduate students must have a GPA of 3.0 or higher. Along with their application, they must submit an essay of 400 to 750 words on how they would describe military leadership. Financial need is not considered in the selection process.
Financial data The stipend is $1,000. Funds are paid directly to the student.
Duration 1 year; nonrenewable.
Number awarded 5 each year.
Deadline September of each year.

[348]
JOHN AND ALICE EGAN MULTI-YEAR SCHOLARSHIPS
Order of Daedalians
Attn: Daedalian Foundation
55 Main Circle (Building 676)
P.O. Box 249
Joint Base San Antonio-Randolph, TX 78148-0249
(210) 945-2113   Fax: (210) 945-2112
E-mail: info@daedalians.org
Web: www.daedalians.org/programs/scholarships

Summary To provide financial assistance to college students who are participating in a ROTC program and wish to become military pilots.
Eligibility This program is open to students who are sophomores through seniors at an accredited 4-year college or university and have a GPA of 3.0 or higher. Applicants must be participating in an ROTC program and be medically qualified for flight training. They must plan to apply for and be awarded a military pilot training allocation at the appropriate juncture in their ROTC program. Selection is based on intention to prepare for a career as a military pilot, demonstrated moral character and patriotism, scholastic and military standing and aptitude, and physical condition and aptitude for flight. Financial need may also be considered.
Financial data The stipend is $2,500 per year, including $500 provided by a local Flight of the organization and $2,000 as a matching award provided by the foundation.
Duration 1 year; may be renewed up to 2 or 3 additional years, provided the recipient maintains a GPA of 3.0 or higher and is enrolled in an undergraduate program.
Additional information This program began in 2003. It includes a mentoring component.

Number awarded Up to 11 each year.
Deadline July of each year.

[349]
JOHN CORNELIUS/MAX ENGLISH MEMORIAL SCHOLARSHIP

Marine Corps Tankers Association
c/o Dan Miller, Scholarship Chair
8212 West Fourth Place
Kennewick, WA 99336
E-mail: dmiller@msn.com
Web: www.usmctankers.org/pageScholarship

Summary To provide financial assistance for college or graduate school to children and grandchildren of members of the Marine Corps Tankers Association and to Marine and Navy personnel currently serving in tank units.

Eligibility This program is open to high school seniors and graduates who are children, grandchildren, or under the guardianship of an active, Reserve, retired, or honorably discharged Marine who served in a tank unit. Marine or Navy Corpsmen currently assigned to tank units are also eligible. Applicants must be enrolled or planning to enroll full time at a college or graduate school. Their parent or grandparent must be a member of the Marine Corps Tankers Association or, if not a member, must join if the application is accepted. Along with their application, they must submit a 500-word essay that explains their reason for seeking this scholarship, their educational goals, and their plans for post-graduation life. Selection is based on that essay, academic record, school activities, leadership potential, and community service.

Financial data The stipend is at least $2,000 per year.
Duration 1 year; recipients may reapply.
Number awarded Varies each year; recently, 4 were awarded.
Deadline March of each year.

[350]
JOSEPH P. AND HELEN T. CRIBBINS SCHOLARSHIP

Association of the United States Army
Attn: Scholarships
2425 Wilson Boulevard
Arlington, VA 22201
(703) 841-4300   Toll Free: (800) 336-4570
E-mail: scholarships@ausa.org
Web: www.ausa.org/resources/scholarships

Summary To provide financial assistance to members of the Association of the United States Army (AUSA) who are interested in studying a field of STEM in college.

Eligibility This program is open to AUSA members who are enrolled or accepted at an accredited college or university to work on a degree in a field of STEM. Along with their application, they must submit a 1-page autobiography, 2 letters of recommendation, a letter describing their career aspirations (including their course of study and plans for completion of a degree), and a transcript of high school or college grades (depending on which they are currently attending). Selection is based on academic merit and personal achievement. Financial need is not normally a selection criterion but in some cases of extreme need it may be used as a factor; the lack of financial need, however, is never a cause for non-selection.

Financial data The stipend is $10,000; funds are sent directly to the recipient's college or university.
Duration 1 year.
Additional information Membership in the AUSA is open to everyone who supports a strong national defense, with special concern for the Army. That includes Regular Army, National Guard, Army Reserve, government civilians, retired soldiers, Wounded Warriors, veterans, concerned citizens and family members.
Number awarded 2 each year.
Deadline June of each year.

[351]
KANSAS MILITARY SERVICE SCHOLARSHIPS

Kansas Board of Regents
Attn: Student Financial Aid
1000 S.W. Jackson Street, Suite 520
Topeka, KS 66612-1368
(785) 430-4255   Fax: (785) 430-4233
E-mail: scholars@ksbor.org
Web: www.kansasregents.org/scholarships_and_grants

Summary To provide financial assistance for college to residents of Kansas who have served or are still serving in the military.

Eligibility This program is open to students who graduated from high school in Kansas or received a GED credential and have been a resident of the state for at least 2 years. Applicants must have served in the U.S. armed forces in international waters or on foreign soil in support of military operations for at least 90 days after September 11, 2001 or for less than 90 days because of injuries received during such service. They must still be in military service or have received an honorable discharge with orders that indicate they served after September 11, 2001 in any operation for which they received hostile fire pay. Qualified veterans and military personnel may enroll full or part time at a public postsecondary institution in Kansas, including area vocational schools, area vocational/technical schools, community colleges, the municipal university, state educational institutions, or technical colleges. In the selection process, priority is given to applicants who can demonstrate financial need.

Financial data Qualifying students are permitted to enroll at an approved Kansas institution without payment of tuition or fees. If they receive any federal military tuition assistance, that money must be applied to their tuition and fees and they are eligible only for the remaining balance in scholarship assistance.

Duration 1 year; may be renewed for a total of 10 semesters as long as the recipient remains in good academic standing.
Additional information This program began in 2007.
Number awarded Varies each year.
Deadline April of each year.

[352]
KANSAS NATIONAL GUARD EDUCATIONAL ASSISTANCE

Kansas Board of Regents
Attn: Student Financial Aid
1000 S.W. Jackson Street, Suite 520
Topeka, KS 66612-1368
(785) 430-4255   Fax: (785) 430-4233
E-mail: scholars@ksbor.org
Web: www.kansasregents.org/scholarships_and_grants

Summary To provide scholarship/loans to members of the Kansas National Guard who wish to take additional college courses.

Eligibility This program is open to enlisted members of the Kansas National Guard (Air or Army) who are interested in working on a vocational, associate, or bachelor's degree. Non-commissioned officers must have less than 20 years of service. All applicants must agree to complete their current service obligation plus 24 months of additional service. Full-time enrollment is not required.

Financial data The program reimburses a percentage, up to 100%, of tuition and fees at public and designated private institutions in Kansas. The actual percentage reimbursed depends on the number of eligible students and available appropriations.

Duration 1 semester; may be renewed.

Additional information Recipients who fail to comply with the additional service requirement must repay all funds received.

Number awarded Varies each year; recently, approximately 300 were granted each semester.

Deadline August of each year for the fall semester; January of each year for spring semester only.

[353]
KANSAS ROTC SERVICE SCHOLARSHIP

Kansas Army National Guard
Attn: Education Services Officer
5920 S.E. Coyote Drive, Suite A101
Topeka, KS 66619
(785) 646-0156   Fax: (785) 646-1609
E-mail: steven.n.harmon.mil@mail.mil
Web: www.kansastag.gov/NGUARD.asp?PageID=500

Summary To provide financial assistance to Army ROTC students in Kansas.

Eligibility This program is open to non-scholarship Army ROTC students planning to enroll full time at a state university in Kansas. Applicants must be U.S. citizens and residents of Kansas eligible for in-state tuition. They must have an ACT score of 19 or higher, be able to meet medical and physical fitness requirements for military service, and be able to complete all requirements for a college degree and a commission while they are younger than 30 years of age (may be extended to 40 years of age upon petition). Selection is based on scholastic potential and achievement, participation in extracurricular activities, demonstrated leadership, interest in service with the Kansas Army National Guard, and an interview.

Financial data This program provides free tuition at the participating schools (where there are Army ROTC programs). Beginning with their fifth semester in the program, recipients also are given a stipend of $450 per month. Recipients must agree to become a commissioned officer and serve at least 8 years in the military after completing ROTC and graduating from college. That service includes at least 4 years in the Kansas Army National Guard, 2 years with a Reserve component unit, and 2 years in the Individual Ready Reserves (IRR). If they fail to graduate or fulfill the military service obligation, they must either repay all funds received or serve 4 years as an enlisted member of the Kansas Army National Guard.

Duration 4 years, or until the recipient completes the baccalaureate degree.

Number awarded 40 each year.

Deadline January of each year.

[354]
KENTUCKY NATIONAL GUARD TUITION AWARD PROGRAM

Kentucky Higher Education Assistance Authority
Attn: Student Aid Branch
100 Airport Road
P.O. Box 798
Frankfort, KY 40602-0798
(502) 696-7392   Toll Free: (800) 928-8926, ext. 7392
Fax: (502) 696-7373   TDD: (800) 855-2880
E-mail: studentaid@kheaa.com
Web: www.kheaa.com/website/kheaa/military_ky?main=7

Summary To provide financial assistance for college or graduate school to members of the Kentucky National Guard.

Eligibility This program is open to active enlisted members of the Kentucky National Guard who are interested in working full or part time on an undergraduate or graduate degree. Applicants must have maintained standards of satisfactory membership in the Guard, including passing the most recent physical fitness test, meeting the height-weight standard, meeting attendance standards, having no unsatisfactory performance or absence-without-leave records, and having no other restrictions on their personnel file. Preference is given to applicants working on their first undergraduate degree.

Financial data The program provides payment of full tuition and fees at any state-supported university, community college, or vocational or technical school in Kentucky.

Duration 1 semester; may be renewed.

Number awarded Varies each year.

Deadline March of each year for summer or fall terms; September of each year for spring term.

[355]
KIMBERLY KAY CLARK MEMORIAL SCHOLARSHIP

Oklahoma City Community Foundation
Attn: Scholarship Coordinator
1000 North Broadway
P.O. Box 1146
Oklahoma City, OK 73101-1146
(405) 606-2907   Fax: (405) 235-5612
E-mail: w.minter@occf.org
Web: occf.academicworks.com/opportunities/3002

Summary To provide financial assistance for college to enlisted members of the Naval Reserves in any state.

Eligibility This program is open to drilling enlisted Naval Reservists actively working on a degree at an accredited institution of higher education in any state. Applicants may not have a pay grade higher than E-6. They must submit 1) a

summary of their military career to date; and 2) a statement on how this scholarship will advance their military and/or civilian career.
Financial data The stipend is $2,000.
Duration 1 year.
Number awarded 1 or more each year.
Deadline June of each year.

[356]
LARRY STRICKLAND MEMORIAL FUND AND SCHOLARSHIP

Association of the United States Army
Attn: Scholarships
2425 Wilson Boulevard
Arlington, VA 22201
(703) 841-4300   Toll Free: (800) 336-4570
E-mail: scholarships@ausa.org
Web: www.ausa.org/resources/scholarships

Summary To recognize and reward, with funding for additional education, Army non-commissioned officers who demonstrate outstanding leadership.
Eligibility This award is presented to non-commissioned officers who best exemplify "the Army's vision and influence others in shaping future leaders." Candidates must also be interested in obtaining additional education.
Financial data The award consists of a plaque and $4,000 to assist in covering educational costs that Army tuition assistance does not pay, such as instructional fees, laboratory fees, and books.
Duration The award is presented annually.
Additional information This award was established in 2003 to honor SGM Larry L. Strickland, who was killed in the Pentagon on September 11, 2001.
Number awarded 2 each year.
Deadline June of each year.

[357]
LOS ANGELES CHAPTER AFCEA SCHOLARSHIPS

Armed Forces Communications and Electronics
  Association-Los Angeles Chapter
c/o Steve Staso, Scholarships Vice President
Hewlett Packard Enterprise
P.O. Box 1227
El Segundo, CA 90245
(310) 748-3059   E-mail: vpcomm@afcea-la.org
Web: www.afcea-la.org/scholarships

Summary To provide financial assistance to ROTC students at colleges and universities in the greater Los Angeles area.
Eligibility This program is open to ROTC cadets and midshipmen enrolled at colleges and universities in the greater Los Angeles area. Preference is given to applicants majoring in science, mathematics, engineering, computer science, or natural sciences.
Financial data A stipend is awarded (amount not specified).
Duration 1 year.
Number awarded Varies each year; a total of $8,000 is available for this program annually.
Deadline March of each year.

[358]
LOUIS J. SCHOBER MEMORIAL SCHOLARSHIP

Society of American Military Engineers-Louisiana Post
c/o Chris Dunn, Young Members Committee Chair
U.S. Army Corps of Engineers, New Orleans District
7400 Leake Avenue
P.O. Box 60267
New Orleans, LA 70160
(504) 862-1799
E-mail: Christopher.L.Dunn@usace.army.mil
Web: www.same.org

Summary To provide financial assistance to engineering students at universities in Louisiana and to children of members of the Louisiana Post of the Society of American Military Engineers (SAME) at schools in any state.
Eligibility This program is open to students currently working on an undergraduate degree in engineering. Applicants must be either 1) enrolled at a college or university in Louisiana; or 2) the children of a member of the SAME Louisiana Post (who may be studying at a college or university in any state). Graduate students are not eligible; high school seniors may be considered if no suitable college students apply. Selection is based primarily on academic record and demonstration of leadership characteristics; other factors considered are participation in SAME posts and activities, enrollment in an ROTC program, former or current military service, and participation in school and community activities.
Financial data The stipend is $2,000.
Duration 1 year; nonrenewable.
Number awarded 1 or more each year.
Deadline April of each year.

[359]
LOUISIANA NATIONAL GUARD STATE TUITION EXEMPTION PROGRAM

Louisiana National Guard
Attn: State Tuition Exemption Manager
Public Affairs Office
6400 St. Claude Avenue
New Orleans, LA 70117
(504) 278-8273   Toll Free: (800) 899-6355
E-mail: leonard.c.acker.civ@mail.mil
Web: www.geauxguard.la.gov/education

Summary To provide financial assistance to members of the Louisiana National Guard who are interested in attending college or graduate school in the state.
Eligibility This program is open to active drilling members of the Louisiana Army National Guard or Air National Guard. Guard members are ineligible if they have been disqualified by their unit commander for any adverse action, have already obtained a bachelor's degree, are placed on academic probation or suspension, test positive on a drug/alcohol test or declare themselves as a self-referral, are separated or transfer to the Inactive National Guard, or have 9 or more AWOLs. Applicants must have been accepted for admission or be enrolled in a Louisiana public institution of higher learning, either part time or full time, to work on an associate, bachelor's, or master's degree.
Financial data Recipients are exempt from all tuition charges at Louisiana state-funded colleges, universities, or community colleges.

Duration The exemption may be claimed for 5 separate academic years or until the receipt of a degree, whichever occurs first.
Additional information The state legislature established this program in 1974.
Number awarded Varies each year.
Deadline Deadline not specified.

[360]
LOWE'S AMVETS TECHNOLOGY SCHOLARSHIPS

AMVETS National Headquarters
Attn: National Programs Director
4647 Forbes Boulevard
Lanham, MD 20706-3807
(301) 459-9600   Toll Free: (877) 7-AMVETS, ext. 4027
Fax: (301) 459-7924   E-mail: klathroum@amvets.org
Web: www.amvets.org

Summary To provide financial assistance to veterans, military personnel, and their spouses who are working on a degree in computer sciences.
Eligibility This program is open to veterans, active-duty military members, and their spouses who are U.S. citizens; children are not eligible. Applicants must be enrolled as sophomores, juniors, or seniors at a college or university and working on a degree in computer science. They must have a GPA of 3.0 or higher.
Financial data Stipends range up to $5,000.
Duration 1 year.
Additional information This program is supported by Lowe's.
Number awarded 10 each year.
Deadline July of each year.

[361]
LT. PAUL (JAY) SMITH MEMORIAL ENDOWMENT SCHOLARSHIP

First Command Educational Foundation
Attn: Scholarship Programs Manager
1 FirstComm Plaza
Fort Worth, TX 76109-4999
(817) 569-2940   Toll Free: (877) 872-8289
Fax: (817) 569-2970   E-mail: scholarships@fcef.com
Web: www.fcef.com

Summary To provide financial assistance to outstanding Air Force ROTC cadets.
Eligibility This program is open to students enrolled as cadets in the Air Force ROTC unit at their college or university. Selection is based on "leadership and dedicated service to community and country."
Financial data The stipend is $2,000 or $1,000.
Duration 1 year.
Additional information This program began in 1996 and was transferred to First Command Educational Foundation in 2007.
Number awarded 2 each year: 1 at $2,000 and 1 at $1,000.
Deadline Applications must be submitted to the Air Force ROTC unit, each of which sets its own deadline.

[362]
LTC MICHAEL WARREN MEMORIAL SCHOLARSHIPS

National Guard Association of Arizona
Attn: Scholarship Committee
5640 East McDowell Road
Phoenix, AZ 85008
(602) 275-8305   Fax: (602) 275-9254
E-mail: ngaofaz@aol.com
Web: www.ngaaz.org

Summary To provide financial assistance to students at colleges and universities in Arizona who have a connection to the National Guard and the National Guard Association of Arizona (NGAAZ).
Eligibility This program is open to full-time students at colleges, universities, and community colleges in Arizona. Applicants must be a member of 1 of the following categories: 1) a current enlisted member of the Arizona National Guard; 2) a current officer member of the Arizona National Guard who is also a member of the NGAAZ; or 3) a child or spouse of an NGAAZ member. Applicants must submit 2 letters of recommendation and verification of good standing from the first commander in the chain of command of the Arizona National Guard. Selection is based on GPA (25%), community service (15%), letters of recommendation (15%), knowledge of National Guard philosophy (15%), and financial need (30%).
Financial data The stipend is $1,000.
Duration 1 year; nonrenewable.
Number awarded 3 each year: 1 to each category of applicant.
Deadline March of each year.

[363]
LTG EDWARD HONOR SCHOLARSHIP AWARD

The ROCKS, Inc.
c/o WSC Associates, LLP
P.O. Box 47435
District Heights, MD 20753
(301) 423-5500   E-mail: rocksnationalboard@gmail.com
Web: natlrocks.clubexpress.com

Summary To provide financial assistance to college seniors who have participated in ROTC programs at Historically Black Colleges and Universities (HBCUs).
Eligibility This award is available to graduating seniors who are Army or Air Force Cadets or Navy Midshipmen at HBCUs at the MS IV level. Applicants must submit 1) a 1-page paper on a topic related to leadership or mentorship; and 2) a letter of recommendation from their professor of military science evaluating their appearance, attitude, APFT score, dedication, initiative, integrity, judgment, leadership potential, and written and oral communication ability.
Financial data The award is $3,000.
Duration The award is presented annually.
Number awarded 1 each year.
Deadline December of each year.

SCHOLARSHIPS: MILITARY PERSONNEL

[364] M. ALICE KONECNY MEMORIAL ENDOWMENT SCHOLARSHIP

First Command Educational Foundation
Attn: Scholarship Programs Manager
1 FirstComm Plaza
Fort Worth, TX 76109-4999
(817) 569-2940   Toll Free: (877) 872-8289
Fax: (817) 569-2970   E-mail: scholarships@fcef.com
Web: www.fcef.com

Summary To provide financial assistance for study of nursing to outstanding Air Force ROTC cadets.

Eligibility This program is open to students enrolled as cadets in the Air Force ROTC unit at their college or university. Applicants must be working on a during degree.

Financial data The stipend is $2,000 or $1,000.

Duration 1 year.

Additional information This program began in 2011.

Number awarded 2 each year: 1 at $2,000 and 1 at $1,000.

Deadline Applications must be submitted to the Air Force ROTC unit, each of which sets its own deadline.

[365] MAINE NATIONAL GUARD TUITION ASSISTANCE

Bureau of Veterans' Services
117 State House Station
Augusta, ME 04333-0117
(207) 430-6035   Toll Free: (800) 345-0116 (within ME)
Fax: (207) 626-4471   E-mail: mainebvs@maine.gov
Web: www.maine.gov

Summary To provide financial assistance for college in the state to members of the Maine National Guard.

Eligibility This program is open to members of the Maine National Guard who have a record of satisfactory participation. Applicants must be enrolled or planning to enroll full or part time at a state postsecondary education institution to work on a baccalaureate degree, associate degree, or certificate and licensure. They must agree to serve in the Maine National Guard for at least 1 year beyond the end of the term for which these benefits are awarded.

Financial data Recipients are entitled to free tuition at institutions of higher education supported by the state of Maine.

Duration 1 semester; may be renewed until completion of a degree or certificate.

Number awarded Varies each year.

Deadline Deadline not specified.

[366] MAJOR ELBERT A. WELSH EDUCATION AWARDS (ROTC)

Society of American Military Engineers-Detroit Post
c/o Gregory M. Mausolf, Post Secretary
U.S. Army Corps of Engineers
477 Michigan Avenue, Seventh Floor
Detroit, MI 48226
(313) 226-3389   Fax: (313) 226-2013
E-mail: Gregory.M.Mausolf@usace.army.mil
Web: www.same.org

Summary To provide financial assistance to ROTC cadets or midshipmen who are majoring in engineering, architecture, construction management, or a related science at a college in the area served by the Detroit Post of the Society of American Military Engineers (SAME).

Eligibility This program is open to ROTC cadets or midshipmen who are sophomores or juniors at a college or university in the area of the SAME Detroit Post (the entire state of Michigan and Toledo, Ohio). Applicants must be working on a bachelor's degree in engineering, architecture, construction management, or a related science. Along with their nomination form, they must submit a 1-page statement describing their scholastic and career goals. Selection is based on that statement (30 points); academic record and the nature of the course load (30 points); ROTC class ranking (10 points); recommendation from ROTC staff adviser (10 points); experience in wage-earning or volunteer employment (10 points); participation in academic, business, or social organizations, committees, societies, and activities (20 points); and academic honors and awards (10 points). U.S. citizenship is required.

Financial data The stipend is $2,000.

Duration 1 year.

Additional information This program began in 1975. The recipient is also given a 1-year student membership to the Society of American Military Engineers through the Detroit Post.

Number awarded 2 each year.

Deadline January of each year.

[367] MAJOR GENERAL DUANE L. "DUKE" CORNING MEMORIAL SCHOLARSHIP

South Dakota National Guard Enlisted Association
c/o Derek Jaeger, Scholarship Chair
7713 West 53rd Street
Sioux Falls, SD 57106
E-mail: derek.e.jaeger.mil@mail.mil
Web: sdngea.com/programs/scholarships

Summary To provide financial assistance to current and retired members of the South Dakota National Guard Enlisted Association (SDNGEA), the National Guard Association of South Dakota (NGASD), or their dependents who are interested in attending college in any state.

Eligibility This program is open to current and retired members of the SDNGEA and the NGASD and the dependents of current and retired members of those associations. Applicants must be graduating high school seniors or full-time undergraduate students at a college or university in any state. They must submit a 300-page autobiography that includes their experiences to date and their hopes and plans for the future. Selection is based on the essay; awards, honors, and offices in high school, college, or trade school; GPA and ACT/SAT scores; letters of recommendation; and extracurricular and community activities and honors.

Financial data The stipend is $1,000.

Duration 1 year; nonrenewable.

Number awarded 2 each year.

Deadline March of each year.

[368]
MAJOR RICHARD L. RIDDER MEMORIAL SCHOLARSHIP

Central Indiana Community Foundation
Attn: Scholarship Program
615 North Alabama Street, Suite 119
Indianapolis, IN 46204-1498
(317) 634-2423   Fax: (317) 684-0943
E-mail: scholarships@cicf.org
Web: www.cicf.org/scholarships

Summary To provide financial assistance to children of current or former members of the Indiana National Guard who are interested in attending college in the state.

Eligibility This program is open to seniors graduating from high schools in Indiana who are a current or former member of the Indiana National Guard or the child of such a member. Applicants must be planning to attend a college, university, or vocational/technical school in any state. They must have a GPA of 2.0 or higher and be able to demonstrate financial need or other significant barrier to completing a postsecondary degree.

Financial data The stipend is at least $1,000.

Duration 1 year.

Number awarded 1 or more each year.

Deadline February of each year.

[369]
MARINE CORPS TUITION ASSISTANCE PROGRAM

U.S. Marine Corps
c/o Naval Education and Training Professional
  Development and Technology Command
Code N814
6490 Saufley Field Road
Pensacola, FL 32509-5241
(850) 452-1001   Toll Free: (877) 838-1659
Fax: (850) 473-6401   E-mail: SFLY_TA.Marine@navy.mil
Web:

Summary To provide financial assistance for undergraduate or graduate study to Marine Corps personnel.

Eligibility Eligible for assistance under this program are active-duty Marines who wish to take college courses for academic credit during off-duty time. Funding is available for vocational/technical, undergraduate, graduate, undergraduate development, independent study, and distance learning programs. Applicants must have completed at least 2 years of service, be eligible for promotion, and have completed designated military training courses. Commissioned officers must agree to remain on active duty for 2 years after the completion of any funded courses. Enlisted Marines must have an end of active duty status (EAS) of at least 60 days beyond the completion date of the course. All students must successfully complete their courses with a satisfactory grade.

Financial data Those selected for participation in this program receive their regular Marine Corps pay and 100% of tuition at the postsecondary educational institution of their choice, but capped at $4,500 per year or $250 per semester hour, whichever is less. Funding is available only for tuition, not fees or other associated expenses.

Duration Until completion of a bachelor's or graduate degree. Undergraduates must complete all courses with a grade of "C" or better; graduate students must complete classes with a grade of "B" of better. If recipients fail to achieve those grades, they must reimburse the Marine Corps for all funds received.

Number awarded Varies each year; in recent years, approximately 20,000 Marines availed themselves of this funding.

Deadline Applications must be submitted within 30 days of the start date of the class.

[370]
MARINES' MEMORIAL FAMILY SCHOLARSHIPS

Marines' Memorial Association
c/o Marines Memorial Club and Hotel
609 Sutter Street
San Francisco, CA 94102
(415) 673-6672, ext. 293   Toll Free: (800) 5-MARINE
Fax: (415) 441-3649
E-mail: scholarship@marineclub.com
Web: www.marinesmemorial.org/members/scholarships

Summary To provide financial assistance for college to members of the Marines' Memorial Association from all branches of the armed forces and their descendants.

Eligibility This program is open to active members of the association and their children and grandchildren. Applicants must be high school seniors or students currently enrolled full time in an undergraduate degree program in any field at a college or university. Along with their application, they must submit an essay of up to 500 words on why they chose their specific path of study, what they hope to accomplish after graduation with their degree, and how their efforts will benefit others in their community. Graduating high school seniors must submit a high school transcript and SAT or ACT scores; continuing college students must submit a college transcript. Selection is based on the essay, academic merit, references, and financial need.

Financial data The stipend ranges from $2,500 to $5,000 per year.

Duration 1 year; recipients may reapply for up to 3 additional years.

Additional information Membership in the association is open to veterans of the Marines, Army, Navy, Air Force, or Coast Guard and to personnel currently serving in a branch of the armed forces.

Number awarded 8 each year.

Deadline April of each year.

[371]
MARINES' MEMORIAL TRIBUTE SCHOLARSHIPS

Marines' Memorial Association
c/o Marines Memorial Club and Hotel
609 Sutter Street
San Francisco, CA 94102
(415) 673-6672, ext. 293   Toll Free: (800) 5-MARINE
Fax: (415) 441-3649
E-mail: scholarship@marineclub.com
Web: www.marinesmemorial.org

Summary To provide financial assistance to military personnel who are transitioning from active duty to civilian or Reserve status and wish to attend college.

Eligibility This program is open to military personnel who have separated from full-time active duty to civilian or Reserve status within the past 3 years. Applicants must be enrolled or planning to enroll full time in an accredited undergraduate or graduate degree program in any field at a college or university. Membership in the sponsoring organization is not required. Along with their application, they must submit an essay of up to 500 words on why they chose their specific path of study, what they hope to accomplish after graduation with their degree, and how their efforts will benefit others in their community. Applicants entering college as freshmen must submit a high school transcript and SAT or ACT scores; continuing college students must submit a college transcript. Selection is based on the essay, academic merit, references, and financial need.

Financial data The stipend ranges from $2,500 to $5,000 per year.

Duration 1 year; recipients may reapply for up to 3 additional years.

Number awarded 8 each year.

Deadline April of each year.

[372]
MARYLAND NATIONAL GUARD STATE TUITION ASSISTANCE REIMBURSEMENT (STAR)

Maryland National Guard
Attn: Education Services Office
Fifth Regiment Armory
29th Division Street, Room B-23
Baltimore, MD 21201-2288
(410) 576-1499   Toll Free: (800) 492-2526
Fax: (410) 576-6082
E-mail: mdng_education@md.ngb.army.mil
Web: military.maryland.gov

Summary To provide partial tuition reimbursement to members of the Maryland National Guard working on an undergraduate degree at a college in the state.

Eligibility This program is open to members of the Maryland National Guard in pay grades E-1 through O-4. Applicants must be attending or planning to attend designated "Partners in Education" institutions in the state (all 5 branches of the University of Maryland, 8 other public colleges and universities, 13 community colleges, 5 private universities, and 4 private career education institutions). They must have at least a 2-year obligation remaining from the course start date. Partial reimbursement of tuition is provided for courses completed with a grade of "C" or above.

Financial data This program provides reimbursement of all tuition charges not covered by other state or federal tuition assistance programs.

Duration 1 semester; recipients may reapply.

Additional information Individuals must submit their grades within 60 days after their course is completed.

Number awarded Varies each year.

Deadline Applications must be submitted within 45 days after the start of the semester.

[373]
MARYLAND NATIONAL GUARD STATE TUITION WAIVER (STW)

Maryland National Guard
Attn: Education Services Office
Fifth Regiment Armory
29th Division Street, Room B-23
Baltimore, MD 21201-2288
(410) 576-1499   Toll Free: (800) 492-2526
Fax: (410) 576-6082
E-mail: mdng_education@md.ngb:army.mil
Web: military.maryland.gov

Summary To waive tuition for members of the Maryland National Guard at colleges and universities in the state.

Eligibility This program is open to members of the Maryland National Guard who wish to attend designated "Partners in Education" institutions in the state. That includes all 5 branches of the University of Maryland, 8 other public colleges and universities, 13 community colleges, 5 private universities, and 4 private career education institutions that have agreed to waive part of the tuition charges for National Guard members. Applicants must have a 2-year obligation remaining from the course start date.

Financial data The amount of the waiver ranges from 25% to 50%. Most 4-year colleges waive 50% of tuition for up to 6 credits per semester.

Duration 1 semester; recipients may reapply.

Additional information Some schools also limit the number of credits for which a Guard member can receive waivers during any semester.

Number awarded Varies each year.

Deadline Deadline not specified.

[374]
MARYLAND VETERANS OF AFGHANISTAN AND IRAQ CONFLICTS SCHOLARSHIP PROGRAM

Maryland Higher Education Commission
Attn: Office of Student Financial Assistance
6 North Liberty Street, Ground Suite
Baltimore, MD 21201
(410) 767-3300   Toll Free: (800) 974-0203
Fax: (410) 332-0250   TDD: (800) 735-2258
E-mail: osfamail.mhec@maryland.gov
Web: www.mhec.maryland.gov

Summary To provide financial assistance for college to residents of Maryland who served in the armed forces in Afghanistan or Iraq and their children and spouses.

Eligibility This program is open to Maryland residents who are 1) a veteran who served at least 60 days in Afghanistan on or after October 24, 2001 or in Iraq on or after March 19, 2003; 2) an active-duty member of the armed forces who served at least 60 days in Afghanistan or Iraq on or after those dates; 3) a member of a Reserve component of the armed forces or the Maryland National Guard who was activated as a result of the Afghanistan or Iraq conflicts and served at least 60 days; and 4) the children and spouses of such veterans, active-duty armed forces personnel, or members of Reserve forces or Maryland National Guard. Applicants must be enrolled or accepted for enrollment in a regular undergraduate program at an eligible Maryland institution. In the selection process, veterans are given priority over dependent children and spouses.

Financial data The stipend is equal to 50% of the annual tuition, mandatory fees, and room and board of a resident undergraduate at a 4-year public institution within the University System of Maryland, currently capped at $7,316 per year for students who live on campus, at $4,570 for students who live with their parents, or at %5,140 for students who live off campus.
Duration 1 year; may be renewed for an additional 3 years of full-time study or 7 years of part-time study, provided the recipient remains enrolled in an eligible program with a GPA of 2.5 or higher.
Number awarded Varies each year.
Deadline February of each year.

[375]
MASSACHUSETTS NATIONAL GUARD TUITION WAIVER PROGRAM

Massachusetts National Guard
Attn: Education Services Officer
2 Randolph Road
Hanscom AFB, MA 01731
(339) 202-3199 Fax: (339) 202-0109
E-mail: ng.ma.maarng.mbx.education-ma@mail.mil
Web: www.massnationalguard.org

Summary To provide financial assistance to members of the Massachusetts National Guard interested in working on an undergraduate or graduate degree at a college in the state.
Eligibility This program is open to actively participating members of the Army or Air National Guard in Massachusetts. Applicants must have less than 9 AWOLs (Absence Without Leave) at all times and must not ETS (Expiration of Term of Service) during the period enrolled. They must be accepted for admission or enrolled at 1 of 28 Massachusetts public colleges, universities, or community colleges and working on an associate, bachelor's, master's, or doctoral degree. The institution must have a vacancy after all tuition-paying students and all students who are enrolled under any scholarship or tuition waiver provisions have enrolled.
Financial data Eligible Guard members are exempt from any tuition payments at colleges or universities operated by the Commonwealth of Massachusetts and funded by the Massachusetts Board of Higher Education.
Duration Up to a total of 130 semester hours.
Additional information Recipients may enroll either part or full time in a Massachusetts state-supported institution. This program is funded through the Massachusetts Board of Higher Education.
Number awarded Varies each year.
Deadline Deadline not specified.

[376]
MEDICAL SERVICE CORPS INSERVICE PROCUREMENT PROGRAM (MSC-IPP)

U.S. Navy
Attn: Navy Medicine Professional Development Center
Code O3C HMDT
8955 Wood Road, 16th Floor
Bethesda, MD 20889-5611
(301) 319-4520 Fax: (301) 295-1783
E-mail: beverly.d.kemp.civ@mail.mil
Web: www.navyadvancement.com

Summary To provide funding to Navy and Marine enlisted personnel who wish to earn an undergraduate or graduate degree in selected health care specialties while continuing to receive their regular pay and allowances.
Eligibility This program is open to enlisted personnel who are serving on active duty in any rating in pay grade E-4 through E-9 of the U.S. Navy, U.S. Marine Corps, or the Marine Corps Reserve serving on active duty (including Full Time Support of the Reserve). Applicants must be interested in working on a degree to become commissioned in the following medical specialties: entomology, environmental health, health care administration industrial hygiene, occupational therapy, pharmacy, physician assistant radiation health, or social work. If they plan to work on a graduate degree, they must have scores of at least 300 on the GRE or 525 on the GMAT; if they plan to work on a bachelor's or physician assistant degree, they must have scores of at least 1000 on the SAT (including 460 on the mathematics portion) or 42 on the ACT (21 on the English portion, 21 on the mathematics portion). They must be U.S. citizens who can be commissioned before they reach their 42nd birthday.
Financial data Participants receive payment of tuition, mandatory fees, a book allowance, and full pay and allowances for their enlisted pay grade. They are eligible for advancement while in college.
Duration 24 to 48 months of full-time, year-round study, until completion of a relevant degree.
Additional information Following graduation, participants are commissioned in the Medical Service Corps and attend Officer Indoctrination School. They incur an 8-year military service obligation, including at least 3 years served on active duty.
Number awarded Varies each year; recently, 36 were awarded.
Deadline August of each year.

[377]
MG BENJAMIN J. BUTLER "CENTURY DIVISION" SCHOLARSHIP PROGRAM

Association of the Century, Inc.
Attn: Scholarship Committee
P.O. Box 34393
Louisville, KY 40232
Web: www.the-century.org/scholarship.htm

Summary To provide financial assistance for college to members of the United States Army 100th Infantry Division and their descendants.
Eligibility This program is open to active, retired, or former members of the Army 100th Infantry Division (or any of its successor designations), their direct lineal descendants, and their adopted dependents. Applicants must be enrolled or planning to enroll at an accredited college or university. They must have a GPA of 2.5 or higher. Along with their application, they must submit a 250-word essay on how this scholarship will help them achieve their goals. Selection is based on academic excellence, qualities of good citizenship and patriotism, letters of recommendation, and financial need.
Financial data The stipend is $1,000 per year.
Duration 1 year; may be renewed 1 additional year.
Additional information This program, which began in 2008, is managed by the Community Foundation of Louisville.

SCHOLARSHIPS: MILITARY PERSONNEL

Number awarded Varies each year; recently, 5 were awarded.
Deadline June of each year.

[378] MG LEIF J. SVERDRUP SCHOLARSHIP

Army Engineer Association
Attn: Director Washington DC Operations
P.O. Box 30260
Alexandria, VA 22310-8260
(703) 428-7084   Fax: (703) 428-6043
E-mail: xd@armyengineer.com
Web: www.armyengineer.com/scholarships

Summary To provide financial assistance for college or graduate school to officers who are members of the Army Engineer Association (AEA).
Eligibility This program is open to AEA members serving in an active, Reserve, or National Guard component Army Engineer unit, school, or organization within the Corps of Engineers of the United States Army. Applicants must be commissioned officers (2LT, 1LT, or CPT) or warrant officers (WO1 or WO2). They must be working on or planning to work on an associate, bachelor's, or master's degree at an accredited college or university. Along with their application, they must submit a 1-page essay outlining why they should be selected for an award, including a paragraph on their financial need and their evaluation of their potential for success.
Financial data The stipend is $1,000.
Duration 1 year.
Number awarded 2 each year: 1 to a commissioned officer and 1 to a warrant officer.
Deadline June of each year.

[379] MICHIGAN NATIONAL GUARD STATE TUITION ASSISTANCE PROGRAM

Department of Military and Veterans Affairs
Attn: State Operations-Budget Office
3423 North Martin Luther King Boulevard
Lansing, MI 48906
(517) 481-7640   Toll Free: (800) 481-7644
E-mail: MINGSTAP@michigan.gov
Web: ww.michigan.gov

Summary To provide financial assistance to members of the Michigan National Guard who are enrolled at a college in the state.
Eligibility This program is open to all members of the Michigan National Guard who are in good standing with their unit and have completed basic training. Applicants must be enrolled at a college, university, vocational/technical institution, or trade school in the state and working on a certificate, associate degree, bachelor's degree, master's degree, or professional degree.
Financial data Grants provide up to $600 per credit hour or up to $6,000 per year for tuition and fees.
Duration Guard members may receive tuition assistance for up to 144 hours of undergraduate credit or completion of a baccalaureate degree, whichever comes first. If they continue on for a master's or professional degree, they may receive up to 42 credit hours of additional tuition assistance.
Additional information This program began in 2014.

Number awarded Varies each year.
Deadline Applications may be submitted at any time, but they must be received no earlier than 60 calendar days before and no later than 14 calendar days after the course start date.

[380] MILITARY BENEFIT ASSOCIATION SCHOLARSHIPS

Military Benefit Association
Attn: Member Services Department
14605 Avion Parkway
P.O. Box 221110
Chantilly, VA 20153-1110
(703) 968-6200   Toll Free: (800) 336-0100
Fax: (703) 968-6423
Web: www.militarybenefit.org

Summary To provide financial assistance for college to children of insured members of the Military Benefit Association (MBA).
Eligibility This program is open to 1) unmarried dependent children under 26 years of age of insured MBA members; 2) MBA sponsored spouse members or dependent spouses of MBA members; 3) MBA members who are National Guard members or Reservists; and 4) MBA members who are Veterans. Applicants must be enrolled or planning to enroll as a full-time undergraduate student at an accredited 2- or 4-year college, university, or vocational/technical school. They must have a GPA of 2.5 or higher.
Financial data The stipend is $2,300.
Duration 1 year.
Additional information The MBA is an organization that provides insurance to active-duty and retired servicemembers, full-time federal government employees, honorably discharged servicemembers, National Guard, Reservists, uniformed officers of the United States Public Health Service or National Oceanic and Atmospheric Administration, cadets and midshipmen at the military academies, and the spouses of all those categories. This program is administered by Scholarship Management Services, a division of Scholarship America.
Number awarded 20 each year.
Deadline February of each year.

[381] MILITARY COLLEGE SCHOLARSHIP

Low VA Rates
384 South 400 West, Suite 100
Lindon, UT 84042
Toll Free: (855) 581-7341   E-mail: hr@lowvarates.com
Web: www.lowvarates.com/scholarship

Summary To provide financial assistance for college to military personnel, veterans, and children of military personnel.
Eligibility This program is open to students who are nominated by a family member, a friend, or the student themselves. Nominees must be active service military members, veterans, or children with a parent serving in a branch of the U.S. armed forces. Along with their application, they must submit brief statements on how they are associated with the military, why they feel they qualify for this scholarship, their educational and career goals and what they plan to do with their degree, and how the military has positively impacted their life.
Financial data The stipend is $1,250 per semester.

Duration 1 semester.
Number awarded 2 each year: 1 from the winter applications and 1 from the fall applications.
Deadline December of each year for the winter application; August of each year for the fall application.

[382]
MILITARY INTELLIGENCE CORPS ASSOCIATION SCHOLARSHIPS

Military Intelligence Corps Association
Attn: Scholarship Committee
P.O. Box 13020
Fort Huachuca, AZ 85670-3020
(520) 227-3894   E-mail: dfa@micorps.org
Web: www.mica-national.org/category/press-release

Summary To provide financial assistance for college to members of the Military Intelligence Corps Association (MICA) and their immediate family.
Eligibility This program is open to active-duty, Reserve, National Guard, and retired military intelligence soldiers who are MICA members and to their immediate family (spouses, children, or other relatives living with and supported by the MICA member). Applicants must be attending or accepted for attendance at an accredited college, university, vocational school, or technical institution. Along with their application, they must submit a 1-page essay on their educational goals and program of study. Financial need is not considered in the selection process.
Financial data Stipend amounts vary depending on the availability of funds and the number of qualified applicants, but recently were $5,000. Funds are to be used for tuition, books, and classroom fees; support is not provided for housing, board, travel, or administrative purposes.
Duration 1 year; recipients may reapply.
Number awarded 10 each year.
Deadline May of each year.

[383]
MILITARY SCHOLARSHIP ESSAY CONTEST

EducationDynamics, LLC
Attn: eLearners
111 River Street, Tenth Floor
Hoboken, NJ 07030
(201) 377-3000   Toll Free: (888) 567-2008
Web: www.elearners.com

Summary To recognize and reward, with college scholarships, veterans, military personnel, and their spouses who submit outstanding essays on the effect of their military service.
Eligibility This competition is open to active-duty servicemembers, veterans, and their spouses who are enrolled or planning to enroll at an accredited college, university, or trade school. Applicants must submit a 250-word essay on how their military service has better prepared them to enhance their education. The winner is selected on the basis of writing ability (25%), creativity (25%), originality (25%), and overall excellence (25%).
Financial data The award is a $1,000 scholarship.
Duration The competition is held annually.
Number awarded 1 each year.
Deadline February of each year.

[384]
MINNESOTA G.I. BILL PROGRAM

Minnesota Department of Veterans Affairs
Attn: Programs and Services Division
20 West 12th Street, Room 206
St. Paul, MN 55155
(651) 296-2562   Toll Free: (888) LINK-VET
Fax: (651) 296-3954   TDD: (800) 627-3529
E-mail: MNGIBill@state.mn.us
Web: www.mn.gov

Summary To provide financial assistance for college or graduate school in the state to residents of Minnesota who served in the military after September 11, 2001 and the families of deceased or disabled military personnel.
Eligibility This program is open to residents of Minnesota enrolled at colleges and universities in the state as undergraduate or graduate students. Applicants must be 1) a veteran who is serving or has served honorably in a branch of the U.S. armed forces at any time; 2) a non-veteran who has served honorably for a total of 5 years or more cumulatively as a member of the Minnesota National Guard or other active or Reserve component of the U.S. armed forces, and any part of that service occurred on or after September 11, 2001; or 3) a surviving child or spouse of a person who has served in the military at any time and who has died or has a total and permanent disability as a result of that military service. They may be attending college in the state or participating in an apprenticeship or on-the-job (OJT) training program. Financial need is also considered in the selection process.
Financial data The college stipend is $1,000 per semester for full-time study or $500 per semester for part-time study. The maximum award is $3,000 per academic year or $10,000 per lifetime. Apprenticeship and OJT students are eligible for up to $2,000 per fiscal year. Approved employers are eligible to receive $1,000 placement credit payable upon hiring a person under this program and another $1,000 after 12 consecutive months of employment. No more than $3,000 in aggregate benefits under this paragraph may be paid to or on behalf of an individual in one fiscal year, and not more than $9,000 over any period of time.
Duration 1 year; may be renewed, provided the recipient continues to make satisfactory academic progress.
Additional information This program was established by the Minnesota Legislature in 2007.
Number awarded At least 1,000 each year.
Deadline Deadline not specified.

[385]
MINNESOTA NATIONAL GUARD ENLISTED ASSOCIATION AUXILIARY MINUTEMAN SCHOLARSHIPS

Minnesota National Guard Enlisted Association Auxiliary
c/o Carol Benda, Treasurer and Scholarship Chair
3280 30th Street
Slayton, MN 56172
E-mail: cbenda@mchsi.com
Web: www.mngea.com/minuteman-scholarship

Summary To provide financial assistance to members of the Minnesota National Guard Enlisted Association (MNGEA), its Auxiliary, and the families of the Association and Auxiliary who are interested in attending college in any state.

Eligibility This program is open to high school seniors, GED recipients, and students currently enrolled at colleges and universities in any state. Applicants must be active annual or life MNGEA members, active MNGEA Auxiliary members, or the unmarried children, stepchildren, or grandchildren under 26 years of age of those members. They must have a GPA of 2.5 or higher for their most recent academic term. Along with their application, they must submit an essay on their educational goals and how this scholarship will benefit those.
Financial data Stipends are $1,000 or $500.
Duration 1 year; nonrenewable.
Additional information The $1,000 scholarship is sponsored by USAA Insurance Corporation.
Number awarded Varies each year; recently, 4 were awarded.
Deadline March of each year.

[386]
MINNESOTA NATIONAL GUARD STATE TUITION REIMBURSEMENT

Minnesota National Guard
Attn: Education Office
600 Cedar Street
St. Paul, MN 5510-2509
(651) 282-4589   Toll Free: (800) 657-3848
Fax: (651) 282-4694
E-mail: ng.mn.mnarng.mbx.assets-education@mail.mil
Web: minnesotanationalguard.ng.mil/education

Summary To provide financial assistance for college or graduate school to current members of the Minnesota National Guard.
Eligibility Eligible for this program are members of the Minnesota Army or Air National Guard who are currently serving in grades E-1 through O-5 (including warrant officers) and are enrolled as undergraduate or graduate students at colleges or universities in Minnesota. Reimbursement is provided only for undergraduate courses completed with a grade of "C" or better or for graduate courses completed with a grade of "B" or better. Applicants must be serving satisfactorily according to National Guard standards.
Financial data The maximum reimbursement rate is 100% of the tuition rate at the University of Minnesota Twin Cities campus for undergraduate study or 50% for graduate work, with a maximum benefit of $18,000 per fiscal year for undergraduate course work or $20,000 per fiscal year for graduate course work.
Duration 1 semester, to a maximum of 18 credits per semester; may be renewed until completion of an associate, bachelor's, master's, or doctoral degree or 144 semester credits, whichever comes first.
Number awarded Varies each year.
Deadline Deadline not specified.

[387]
MINORITY SERVING INSTITUTION SCHOLARSHIP PROGRAM

U.S. Navy
Attn: Naval Service Training Command Officer
  Development
NAS Pensacola
250 Dallas Street
Pensacola, FL 32508-5220
(850) 452-4941, ext. 29395
Toll Free: (800) NAV-ROTC, ext. 29395
Fax: (850) 452-2486
E-mail: pnsc_nrotc.scholarship@navy.mil
Web: www.public.navy.mil/netc/nstc/nrotc/MSI.aspx

Summary To provide financial assistance to students at specified minority institutions who are interested in joining Navy ROTC to prepare for service as an officer in the U.S. Navy.
Eligibility This program is open to students attending or planning to attend 1 of 17 specified Historically Black Colleges or Universities (HBCUs), 1 of 3 High Hispanic Enrollment (HHE) schools, or 1 other minority institution, all of which have a Navy ROTC unit on campus. Applicants must be nominated by the professor of naval science at their institution and meet academic requirements set by each school. They must be U.S. citizens between 17 and 23 years of age who are willing to serve for 4 years as active-duty Navy officers following graduation from college. They must not have reached their 27th birthday by the time of college graduation and commissioning; applicants who have prior active-duty military service may be eligible for age adjustments for the amount of time equal to their prior service, up to a maximum of 36 months. The qualifying scores are 550 verbal/critical reading and 540 mathematics on the SAT or 22 on English and 21 on mathematics on the ACT. Current enlisted and former military personnel are also eligible if they will complete the program by the age of 30.
Financial data These scholarships provide payment of full tuition and required educational fees, as well as $750 per year for textbooks, supplies, and equipment. The program also provides a stipend for 10 months of the year that is $250 per month as a freshman, $300 per month as a sophomore, $350 per month as a junior, and $400 per month as a senior.
Duration Up to 4 years.
Additional information The eligible HBCUs are Allen University, Clark Atlanta University, Dillard University, Florida A&M University, Hampton University, Howard University, Huston-Tillotson University, Morehouse College, Norfolk State University, Prairie View A&M University, Savannah State University, Southern University and A&M College, Spelman College, Tennessee State University, Texas Southern University, Tuskegee University, and Xavier University. The eligible HHEs are Central New Mexico Community College, Pima Community College, and the University of New Mexico. The other minority institution is Kennedy King College. After completing the program, all participants are commissioned as ensigns in the Naval Reserve with an 8-year service obligation, including 4 years of active duty. Current military personnel who are accepted into this program are released from active duty and are not eligible for active-duty pay and allowances, medical benefits, or other active-duty entitlements.

Number awarded Varies each year.
Deadline December of each year.

[388]
MISSISSIPPI NATIONAL GUARD STATE EDUCATIONAL ASSISTANCE PROGRAM
Mississippi Military Department
Attn: Education Services and Incentives Office
JFH-MS-J1-ED
1410 Riverside Drive
P.O. Box 5027
Jackson, MS 39296-5027
(601) 313-6248   Fax: (601) 313-6151
E-mail: msedu@ng.army.mil
Web: ms.ng.mil/resources/education/Pages/SEAP.aspx

Summary To provide financial assistance to members of the Mississippi National Guard who are interested in attending college in the state.
Eligibility This program is open to members of the Mississippi Army or Air National Guard who have completed basic training and are in good standing. Applicants must be registered to vote in Mississippi and be enrolled or accepted for enrollment at an accredited college or university (public or private) in the state. They may not currently be receiving federal tuition assistance.
Financial data Stipends cover the actual cost of tuition, to a maximum of $4,500 per year or $250 per semester hour.
Duration 1 year; may be renewed until the Guard member earns a bachelor's degree, as long as the member maintains a minimum GPA of 2.0. The full benefit must be utilized within a 10-year period.
Number awarded Varies each year.
Deadline Applications must be submitted not later than 2 weeks after the start date of the semester.

[389]
MISSOURI NATIONAL GUARD ASSOCIATION SCHOLARSHIPS
Missouri National Guard Association
Attn: Scholarship Committee Chair
c/o Ike Skelton Training Center
2302 Militia Drive
Jefferson City, MO 65101-1203
(573) 632-4240
Web: www.mongaonline.com/page/Scholarship

Summary To provide financial assistance to members of the Missouri National Guard Association (MoNGA) and their dependents who are interested in attending college in any state.
Eligibility This program is open to annual, associate, and lifetime members of the association and their dependents. Applicants must be interested in working on a degree at an accredited junior college or 4-year college or university in any state. They must submit high school or college transcripts, 3 letters of recommendation, and a letter describing their desire to continue their education, why they need financial assistance, and how they have demonstrated the traits (scholarship, citizenship, and leadership) upon which selection is based.
Financial data Stipends for MoNGA members are $1,000. Stipends for dependents are $750 or $500. In addition, USAA Insurance Corporation sponsors a $1,000 scholarship for enlisted MoNGA members. Funds are paid directly to the recipient's college or university.
Duration 1 year.
Number awarded 6 each year: 2 for MoNGA members (at $1,000), 3 for dependents (2 at $750 and 1 at $500), and 1 USAA scholarship.
Deadline March of each year.

[390]
MISSOURI NATIONAL GUARD STATE TUITION ASSISTANCE PROGRAM
Office of the Adjutant General
Attn: NGMO-PER-INC (State TA)
2302 Militia Drive
Jefferson City, MO 65101-1203
(573) 638-9500, ext. 37689   Toll Free: (888) 526-MONG
Fax: (573) 638-9822
E-mail: ng.mo.moarng.mbx.per-inc-stateta@mail.mil
Web: www.moguard.ngb.mil

Summary To provide financial assistance for college to members of the Missouri National Guard.
Eligibility This program is open to members of the Missouri National Guard who are participating satisfactorily in required training. Applicants must be enrolled or accepted for enrollment as a full-time or part-time undergraduate at an approved public or private institution of higher learning. Army members must apply for Federal Tuition Assistance before being awarded support from this program. Study leading to a degree in theology or divinity is not eligible.
Financial data The program provides 100% tuition assistance, paid at the rate at the University of Missouri (recently, $284.80 per semester hour) and may not exceed 39 hours per state fiscal year (15 hours in the fall, 15 hours in the spring, and 9 hours in the summer).
Duration Support is provided for up to 39 hours per state fiscal year (15 hours in the fall, 15 hours in the spring, and 9 hours in the summer). The lifetime maximum is 150 credit hours or completion of a bachelor's degree, whichever comes first. Recipients must maintain a GPA of 2.5 or higher.
Additional information This program began in 1998.
Number awarded Varies each year, depending on the availability of funds.
Deadline Applications must be submitted before the start date of class; preference is given to applications received at least 10 days prior to the start.

[391]
MONTANA NATIONAL GUARD SCHOLARSHIPS
Montana National Guard
Attn: Education Service Officer
P.O. Box 4789
Fort Harrison, MT 59636-4789
(406) 324-3236   E-mail: Julie.benson1@us.army.mil
Web: www.montanaguard.net/education-overview

Summary To provide financial assistance for college to members of the Montana National Guard.
Eligibility This program is open to members of the Montana National Guard who are enrolled or accepted for enrollment at a college, university, vocational/technical college, or other VA-approved training program in the state. Applicants must be in pay grades E-1 through E-7, W-01 through CW-3, or O-1 through O-2; have completed Initial Active Duty for

SCHOLARSHIPS: MILITARY PERSONNEL

Training; have a high school diploma or GED; be eligible for Montgomery GI Bill Selected Reserve Benefits or be under a 6-year obligation to the Montana National Guard; and not have completed more than 16 years of military service. Funds are awarded on a first-come, first-served basis until exhausted.

Financial data Stipends are $1,200 per semester for study at a college or university or $400 per semester at a community college.

Duration 1 year; may be renewed.

Number awarded Varies each year.

Deadline Deadline not specified.

[392]
MONTGOMERY GI BILL (SELECTED RESERVE)
Department of Veterans Affairs
Attn: Veterans Benefits Administration
810 Vermont Avenue, N.W.
Washington, DC 20420
(202) 418-4343   Toll Free: (888) 442-4551
Web: www.va.gov

Summary To provide financial assistance for college or graduate school to members of the Reserves or National Guard.

Eligibility Eligible to apply are members of the Reserve elements of the Army, Navy, Air Force, Marine Corps, and Coast Guard, as well as the Army National Guard and the Air National Guard. To be eligible, a Reservist must 1) have a 6-year obligation to serve in the Selected Reserves signed after June 30, 1985 (or, if an officer, to agree to serve 6 years in addition to the original obligation); 2) complete Initial Active Duty for Training (IADT); 3) meet the requirements for a high school diploma or equivalent certificate before completing IADT; and 4) remain in good standing in a drilling Selected Reserve unit. Reservists who enlisted after June 30, 1985 can receive benefits for undergraduate degrees, graduate training, or technical courses leading to certificates at colleges and universities. Reservists whose 6-year commitment began after September 30, 1990 may also use these benefits for a certificate or diploma from business, technical, or vocational schools; cooperative training; apprenticeship or on-the-job training; correspondence courses; independent study programs; tutorial assistance; remedial, deficiency, or refresher training; flight training; or state-approved alternative teacher certification programs.

Financial data The current monthly rate is $392 for full-time study, $293 for three-quarter time study, $195 for half-time study, or $98 for less than half-time study. For apprenticeship and on-the-job training, the monthly stipend is $294 for the first 6 months, $215.60 for the second 6 months, and $137.20 for the remainder of the program. Other rates apply for cooperative education, correspondence courses, and flight training.

Duration Up to 36 months for full-time study, 48 months for three-quarter study, 72 months for half-time study, or 144 months for less than half-time study. Benefits end 10 years from the date the Reservist became eligible for the program.

Additional information This program is frequently referred to as Chapter 1606 (formerly Chapter 106).

Number awarded Varies each year.

Deadline Applications may be submitted at any time.

[393]
MORT MARKS SCHOLARSHIP
Armed Forces Communications and Electronics
  Association
Attn: AFCEA Educational Foundation
4114 Legato Road, Suite 1000
Fairfax, VA 22033-3342
(703) 631-6147   Toll Free: (800) 336-4583, ext. 6147
Fax: (703) 631-4693   E-mail: edfoundation@afcea.org
Web: www.afcea.org

Summary To provide financial assistance for college to outstanding Navy ROTC cadets in designated states who are majoring in specified fields.

Eligibility This program is open to U.S. citizens who are enrolled in the Navy (including Marine Corps option) ROTC detachment at an accredited college or university in Alabama, Louisiana, Mississippi, or the northwest panhandle of Florida. Applicants must be enrolled as sophomores or juniors and working on a degree in biometrics, computer forensics science, computer programming, computer science, cyber security, engineering (computer, electrical, electronics, network, robotics, telecommunications), geospatial science, information technology, information resources management, mathematics, network security, operations research, physics, robotics, statistics, or strategic intelligence. Majors related to medicine, nursing, political science, psychology, and other fields of engineering (e.g., aerospace, chemical, civil, mechanical) are not eligible. Their application must be endorsed by the professor of aviation science at their institution. They must have a GPA of 3.0 or higher. Selection is based on demonstrated dedication, superior performance, potential to serve as an officer in the U.S. Navy or Marine Corps, and financial need.

Financial data The stipend is $3,000. Funds are paid directly to the recipient.

Duration 1 year.

Additional information This program began in 2010 with support from the Montgomery Chapter of the Armed Forces Communications and Electronics Association (AFCEA).

Number awarded 1 each year.

Deadline April of each year.

[394]
NATIONAL CALL TO SERVICE PROGRAM
Department of Veterans Affairs
Attn: Veterans Benefits Administration
810 Vermont Avenue, N.W.
Washington, DC 20420
(202) 418-4343   Toll Free: (844) 698-2311
Web: www.va.gov

Summary To provide educational or other benefits to military personnel who have completed their initial enlistment and agree to additional service in the military.

Eligibility This program is open to military personnel who 1) completed their initial entry training and then continued to serve on active duty for 15 months in an approved military occupational specialty; 2) without a break in service, they served either an additional period of approved active duty or a period of 24 months in active status in the Selected Reserved; and 3) spend the rest of their obligated service on active duty, in the selected reserve, in the individual ready reserve, or in AmeriCorps or another domestic national service program.

Financial data Participants who complete the required service may choose to receive 1) a cash bonus of $5,000; 2) repayment of qualifying student loans up to $18,000; 3) entitlement to the full-time educational allowance established by the Montgomery GI Bill for 3-year enlistees (currently $2,050 per month); or 4) entitlement to 50% of the educational allowance established by the Montgomery GI Bill for less than 3-year enlistees (currently $832 per month).

Duration The cash bonus and loan repayment are 1-time benefits. Educational assistance is provided for up to 12 months at the 3-year enlistee rate or up to 36 months at the less than 3-year enlistee rate.

Additional information This program, which began in 2003, is a Department of Defense program but administered by the Department of Veterans Affairs.

Number awarded Varies each year.

Deadline Applications may be submitted at any time.

[395]
NATIONAL GUARD ASSOCIATION OF CALIFORNIA SCHOLARSHIPS

National Guard Association of California
Attn: Executive Director
3336 Bradshaw Road, Suite 230
Sacramento, CA 95827-2615
(916) 362-3411   Toll Free: (800) 647-0018
Fax: (916) 362-3707
Web: www.ngac.org/ngac-scholarship-program-2

Summary To provide financial assistance to members of the National Guard Association of California (NGAC) and their dependents who are interested in attending college in any state.

Eligibility This program is open to 1) current members of the NGAC; 2) dependents of NGAC members; and 3) dependents of retired California National Guard servicemembers who are life members of the NGAC. Applicants must be attending or planning to attend a college, university, or trade school in any state. Along with their application, they must submit a 500-word essay on the greatest challenge they have faced and how it has impacted them. Selection is based on that essay; unweighted GPA; extracurricular activities, honors, and/or awards; letters of recommendation; and (for high school seniors and college students with less than 2 semesters of completed courses) SAT or ACT scores.

Financial data Stipends range from $250 to $1,000. Funds are paid directly to the recipient.

Duration 1 year.

Number awarded Varies each year; recently, 19 were awarded.

Deadline May of each year.

[396]
NATIONAL GUARD ASSOCIATION OF MARYLAND SCHOLARSHIPS

National Guard Association of Maryland
Attn: Scholarship Committee
P.O. Box 16675
Baltimore, MD 21221-0675
(410) 557-2606   Toll Free: (800) 844-1394
Fax: (410) 893-7529
E-mail: nationalguardassociationmd@gmail.com
Web: www.ngam.net/scholarship-application

Summary To provide financial assistance to members of the National Guard Association of Maryland (NGAM) and their family members who are interested in attending college in any state.

Eligibility This program is open to NGAM members (including current and former members of the National Guard) and their spouses and children. Applicants must be enrolled or planning to enroll full or part time at an accredited college, university, or vocational/technical school in any state. They must submit a resume in which they outline their academic background, activities in which they have participated, and honors they have received; 3 letters of recommendation; an essay on their goals and how this scholarship will assist them; and information on financial need.

Financial data The stipend is $1,000. Funds are paid directly to the recipient's university to be used for tuition, fees, and books.

Duration 1 year; recipients may reapply.

Number awarded Varies each year; recently, 11 were awarded.

Deadline March of each year.

[397]
NATIONAL GUARD ASSOCIATION OF MICHIGAN EDUCATIONAL GRANTS

National Guard Association of Michigan
Attn: Educational Grants
P.O. Box 14095
Lansing, MI 48901
(517) 668-6673
E-mail: ExecutiveDirector_NGAM@outlook.com
Web: www.ngam.org/site/?page_id=23

Summary To provide financial assistance to members of the National Guard Association of Michigan who are interested in attending college in any state.

Eligibility This program is open to members of the association who are also current members of the Michigan National Guard. Applicants may be enlisted members of any rank, warrant officers through CW3, or commissioned officers through O-3. They must be attending or planning to attend a college, university, or trade school in any state. Along with their application, they must submit a 100-word statement on their educational and military goals. Financial need is not considered in the selection process.

Financial data A stipend is awarded (amount not specified).

Duration 1 semester; may be renewed.

Number awarded Varies each year; recently, 6 were awarded.

Deadline June of each year for fall semester; November of each year for winter/spring semester.

[398]
NATIONAL GUARD ASSOCIATION OF MINNESOTA SCHOLARSHIPS

National Guard Association of Minnesota
Attn: Executive Director
P.O. Box 131766
St. Paul, MN 55113-0020
(651) 503-7993   E-mail: director@ngamn.org
Web: www.ngamn.org/scholarships

Summary To provide financial assistance to current and retired members of the National Guard Association of Minnesota (NGAMN) and their families who are interested in working on an undergraduate or graduate degree at a school in any state.

Eligibility This program is open to active members and retired life members of NGAMN and their spouses, children, and grandchildren. Applicants must be high school seniors or students currently enrolled at least half time at an accredited institution of higher learning in any state and working on a 4-year bachelor's or graduate degree. They must have a GPA of 2.75 or higher. Along with their application, they must submit an essay on a topic that describes a value of the Army or Air Force, rotating among loyalty, duty, respect, selfless service, honor, integrity, personal courage, commitment, and excellence. Financial need is not considered in the selection process.

Financial data Stipends are $1,000 or $500. Funds are paid directly to the recipient.

Duration 1 year. Recipients may reapply after 3 years.

Additional information The $1,000 scholarship is sponsored by McGough Construction Company. This program began in 2008.

Number awarded 3 each year: 1 at $1,000 and 2 at $500 (1 to a member or retired member and 1 to a spouse, child, or grandchild).

Deadline June of each year.

[399]
NATIONAL GUARD ASSOCIATION OF NEW HAMPSHIRE SCHOLARSHIPS

National Guard Association of New Hampshire
Attn: Scholarship Committee
P.O. Box 22031
Portsmouth, NH 03802-2031
(603) 227-1597   E-mail: nganhscholarship@gmail.com
Web: www.nganh.org/benefits

Summary To provide financial assistance to members of the National Guard Association of New Hampshire and their dependents who are interested in attending college or graduate school in any state.

Eligibility This program is open to current members of the National Guard Association of New Hampshire (officer, enlisted, or retired), their spouses, and their dependent children. Applicants must be enrolled or planning to enroll full or part time in an associate, bachelor's, graduate, professional, or doctoral degree program at an accredited college or university in any state. Along with their application, they must submit a 1-page essay on a topic that changes annually; recently, they were asked to describe what citizen service means to them.

Financial data The stipend is $1,000.

Duration 1 year.

Number awarded 1 each year.

Deadline April of each year.

[400]
NATIONAL GUARD ASSOCIATION OF NEW JERSEY SCHOLARSHIP PROGRAM

National Guard Association of New Jersey
Attn: Scholarship Committee
P.O. Box 266
Wrightstown, NJ 08562
(848) 480-3441   E-mail: scholarship@nganj.org
Web: www.nganj.org/awards-scholarships

Summary To provide financial assistance to members of the National Guard Association of New Jersey (NGANJ) or their dependents who are interested in attending college or graduate school in any state.

Eligibility This program is open to 1) active members of the NGANJ currently enrolled full time at an approved community college, school of nursing, or 4-year college in any state; and 2) the spouses, children, and grandchildren of active, retired, or deceased members entering or attending a 4-year college or university in any state. Applicants must submit transcripts, information on the civic and academic activities in which they have participated, and a list of offices, honors, awards, and special recognitions they have received. Selection is based on academic accomplishment, leadership, and citizenship.

Financial data Stipends up to $1,000 are available.

Duration 1 year; nonrenewable.

Number awarded Varies each year; recently, 5 were awarded.

Deadline February of each year.

[401]
NATIONAL GUARD ASSOCIATION OF TEXAS SCHOLARSHIP PROGRAM

National Guard Association of Texas
Attn: Education Committee
3706 Crawford Avenue
Austin, TX 78731-6803
(512) 454-7300   Toll Free: (800) 252-NGAT
Fax: (512) 467-6803   E-mail: tbz@ngat.org
Web: www.ngat.org/education.htm

Summary To provide financial assistance to members and dependents of members of the National Guard Association of Texas who are interested in attending college or graduate school in any state.

Eligibility This program is open to annual and life members of the association and their spouses and children (associate members and their dependents are not eligible). Applicants may be high school seniors, undergraduate students, or graduate students, either enrolled or planning to enroll at an institution of higher education in any state. Along with their application, they must submit an essay on their desire to continue their education. Selection is based on scholarship, citizenship, and leadership.

Financial data Stipends range from $500 to $5,000.

Duration 1 year (nonrenewable).

Additional information This program includes the Len and Jean Tallas Memorial Scholarship, the Texas Capital Area Chapter of the AUSA Scholarship, the Lewis O. King Memorial Scholarship, the Gloria Jenell and Marlin E. Mote

Endowed Scholarship, the LTC Gary Parrish Memorial Scholarship, the TXNG Retirees Endowed Scholarship, and 2 scholarships sponsored by USAA Insurance Corporation.
Number awarded Varies each year; recently, 8 were awarded: 1 at $5,000, 1 at $4,000, 1 at $2,000, 1 at $1,250, 3 at $1,000, and 1 at $500.
Deadline February of each year.

[402]
NATIONAL GUARD ASSOCIATION OF VERMONT SCHOLARSHIPS

National Guard Association of Vermont
Attn: Scholarships
P.O. Box 694
Essex Junction, VT 05453
(802) 999-7675   E-mail: ngavtpresident@gmail.com
Web: www.ngavt.org/scholarships

Summary To provide financial assistance to members of the Vermont National Guard (VTNG) or the National Guard Association of Vermont (NGA-VT) and their children or spouses who are interested in attending college or graduate school in any state.
Eligibility This program is open to current members of the VTNG or the NGA-VT, their spouses, and their unmarried children. Applicants must be working, or planning to work, on an associate, undergraduate, technical, or graduate degree as a full-time student at a school in any state. Along with their application, they must submit an essay on their commitment to selfless public service or their plan for pursuing it in the future. Selection is based on academic performance and overall potential for a commitment to selfless public service.
Financial data The stipend is $1,000. Funds are sent directly to the recipient.
Duration 1 year; recipients may reapply.
Additional information This program is sponsored by the New England Federal Credit Union.
Number awarded 4 undergraduate and 1 graduate scholarship are awarded each year.
Deadline January of each year.

[403]
NATIONAL GUARD OF GEORGIA SCHOLARSHIP FUND FOR COLLEGES OR UNIVERSITIES

Georgia Guard Insurance Trust
3 Central Plaza, Suite 356
Rome, GA 30161
(770) 739-9651   Toll Free: (800) 229-1053
Fax: (770) 745-0673   E-mail: director@ngaga.org
Web: www.ngaga.org

Summary To provide financial assistance to members of the Georgia National Guard and their spouses, children, and grandchildren who are interested in attending college in any state.
Eligibility This program is open to policyholders with the Georgia Guard Insurance Trust (GGIT) who are members of the National Guard Association of Georgia (NGAGA) or the Enlisted Association of the National Guard of Georgia (EANGGA); spouses, children, and grandchildren of NGAGA and EANGGA members are also eligible. Applicants must be enrolled or planning to enroll as undergraduate students at a college or university in any state and have received an academic honor while in high school; family members must be enrolled full time but drilling Guard members may be enrolled half time. Graduating high school seniors must have an SAT score of at least 1000, an ACT score of at least 19, or a GPA of 3.0 or higher. Students already enrolled at a college or university must have a cumulative GPA of 3.0 or higher. Along with their application, they must submit transcripts, a letter with personal specific facts regarding their desire to continue their education, 2 letters of recommendation, a letter of academic reference, and an agreement to retain insurance with the GGIT for at least 2 years following completion of the school year for which the scholarship is awarded. Selection is based on academics, character, and moral and personal traits.
Financial data Stipends are $3,000 or $1,000.
Duration 1 year.
Number awarded Up to 10 each year at $3,000; the number of $1,000 scholarships varies each year; recently, 23 were awarded.
Deadline April of each year.

[404]
NATIONAL GUARD OF GEORGIA SCHOLARSHIP FUND FOR VOCATIONAL OR BUSINESS SCHOOLS

Georgia Guard Insurance Trust
3 Central Plaza, Suite 356
Rome, GA 30161
(770) 739-9651   Toll Free: (800) 229-1053
Fax: (770) 745-0673   E-mail: director@ngaga.org
Web: www.ngaga.org

Summary To provide financial assistance to members of the Georgia National Guard and their spouses, children, and grandchildren who are interested in attending business or vocational school in any state.
Eligibility This program is open to policyholders with the Georgia Guard Insurance Trust (GGIT) who are members of the National Guard Association of Georgia (NGAGA) or the Enlisted Association of the National Guard of Georgia (EANGGA); spouses, children, and grandchildren of NGAGA and EANGGA members are also eligible. Applicants must be interested in enrolling at least half time in day or evening classes at a business or vocational school in any state. They must be able to meet program-specific admission standards and institutional requirements and complete all admission procedures for admission to a degree/diploma program in regular program status. Along with their application, they must submit transcripts, a letter with personal specific facts regarding their desire to continue their education, 2 letters of recommendation, and an agreement to retain insurance with the GGIT for at least 2 years following completion of the school year for which the scholarship is awarded. Selection is based on academics, character, and moral and personal traits.
Financial data The stipend is $1,000.
Duration 1 year.
Number awarded 1 or 2 each year.
Deadline April of each year.

[405]
NATIONAL GUARD TUITION WAIVER PROGRAM OF OKLAHOMA

Oklahoma State Regents for Higher Education
Attn: Director of Scholarship and Grant Programs
655 Research Parkway, Suite 200
P.O. Box 108850
Oklahoma City, OK 73101-8850
(405) 225-9239   Toll Free: (800) 858-1840
Fax: (405) 225-9230   E-mail: studentinfo@osrhe.edu
Web: secure.okcollegestart.org

Summary To provide financial assistance to members of the Oklahoma National Guard who plan to attend college in the state.

Eligibility This program is open to current members in good standing of the Oklahoma National Guard who do not have any other baccalaureate or graduate degree. Applicants must be attending or planning to attend a state-supported college or university in Oklahoma to work on an associate or baccalaureate degree. They must have submitted a plan for completion of their degree to the Guard. Courses leading to a certification, continuing education courses, and career technology courses that are not counted towards a degree at another institution are not covered.

Financial data Under this program, all tuition is waived for up to 18 credit hours per semester.

Duration 1 year; may be renewed as long as the Guard member remains in good standing both in the unit and in the college or university, to a maximum of 6 years from the date of first application.

Number awarded Varies each year.

Deadline August of each year for fall semester; January of each year for spring semester, June of each year for summer semester.

[406]
NAVAL FLIGHT OFFICER OPTION OF THE SEAMAN TO ADMIRAL-21 PROGRAM

U.S. Navy
Attn: Commander, Naval Service Training Command
250 Dallas Street, Suite A
Pensacola, FL 32508-5268
(850) 452-9563   Fax: (850) 452-2486
E-mail: PNSC_STA21@navy.mil
Web: www.public.navy.mil

Summary To allow outstanding enlisted Navy personnel to attend a college or university with an NROTC unit, complete a bachelor's degree, and receive a commission as a naval flight officer (NFO).

Eligibility This program is open to U.S. citizens who are currently serving on active duty in the U.S. Navy or Naval Reserve, including Full Time Support (FTS), Selected Reserves (SELRES), and Navy Reservists on active duty, except for those on active duty for training (ACDUTRA). Applicants must be high school graduates (or GED recipients) who are able to complete requirements for a baccalaureate degree in 36 months or less. When they complete their degree requirements, they must be younger than 27 years of age (may be adjusted to 31 years of age for prior active-duty service). Within the past 3 years, they must have taken the SAT (and achieved scores of at least 500 on the mathematics section and 500 on the evidence based reading and writing or critical reading section) or the ACT (and achieved a score of at least 21 on the mathematics portion and 20 on the English portion). They must also achieve a score on the Aviation Selection Test Battery of at least 5 on the Academic Qualifications Rating (AQR) and 6 on the Flight Officer Aptitude Rating (PFAR).

Financial data Awardees continue to receive their regular Navy pay and allowances while they attend college on a full-time basis. They also receive reimbursement for tuition, fees, and books up to $10,000 per year. If base housing is available, they are eligible to live there. Participants are not eligible to receive benefits under the Navy's Tuition Assistance Program (TA), the Montgomery GI Bill (MGIB), the Navy College Fund, or the Veterans Educational Assistance Program (VEAP).

Duration Selectees are supported for up to 36 months of full-time, year-round study or completion of a bachelor's degree, as long as they maintain a GPA of 2.5 or higher.

Additional information This program began in 2001 as a replacement for the Aviation Enlisted Commissioning Program (AECP). Upon acceptance into the program, selectees attend the Naval Science Institute (NSI) in Newport, Rhode Island for an 8-week program in the fundamental core concepts of being a naval officer (navigation, engineering, weapons, military history and justice, etc.). They then enter a college or university with an NROTC unit or affiliation to work full time on a bachelor's degree. They become members of and drill with the NROTC unit. When they complete their degree, they are commissioned as ensigns in the United States Naval Reserve and assigned to flight training. After commissioning, participants incur an active-duty obligation of 6 years after designation as a Naval Flight Officer or 6 years from the date of disenrollment from flight training.

Number awarded Varies each year.

Deadline June of each year.

[407]
NAVAL HELICOPTER ASSOCIATION SCHOLARSHIPS

Naval Helicopter Association
Attn: Scholarship Fund
P.O. Box 180578
Coronado, CA 92178-0578
(619) 435-7139   Fax: (619) 435-7354
E-mail: pres@nhascholarshipfund.org
Web: www.nhascholarshipfund.org/about/scholarships

Summary To provide financial assistance for college or graduate school to members of the Naval Helicopter Association (NHA) and their families.

Eligibility This program is open to NHA members and their spouses, children, and grandchildren. Membership in the NHA is open to active-duty and retired U.S. Navy, U.S. Marine Corps, and U.S. Coast Guard helicopter pilots, aircrew, and maintenance professionals. Applicants must be working on or planning to work on an undergraduate or graduate degree in any field. Along with their application, they must submit a personal statement on their academic and career aspirations. Selection is based on that statement, academic proficiency, scholastic achievements and awards, extracurricular activities, employment history, and letters of recommendation. The program includes scholarships 1) reserved for NHA family members; 2) reserved for active-duty personnel; 3) spon-

sored by private corporations; 4) named as memorials in honor of distinguished individuals; and 5) awarded on a regional basis.
Financial data Stipends are approximately $2,000.
Duration 1 year.
Additional information Corporate sponsors have included FLIR Systems, D.P. Associates, L-3 Communications, CAE, Raytheon Corporation, Lockheed Martin (designated the Sergei Sikorsky Scholarship), and Northrop Grumman. Memorial Scholarships have included the Edward and Veronica Ream Memorial Scholarship, the CDR Mort McCarthy Memorial Scholarship, the Charles Karman Memorial Scholarship, the LT Christian "Horse" Hescock Memorial Scholarship, and the Captain Mark Starr Memorial Scholarship.
Number awarded Varies each year; recently, 17 were awarded: 1 graduate student family member, 3 active-duty graduate students, 1 active-duty undergraduate student, 4 sponsored by corporate donors, 4 memorial scholarships, and 4 regional scholarships.
Deadline January of each year.

[408]
NAVY NURSE CANDIDATE PROGRAM
U.S. Navy
Attn: Navy Bureau of Medicine and Surgery
Accessions Department
8955 Wood Road, Suite 13132
Bethesda, MD 20889-5628
(301) 295-1217   Toll Free: (800) USA-NAVY
Fax: (301) 295-6865   E-mail: usn.ohstudent@mail.mil
Web: www.med.navy.mil

Summary To provide financial assistance for nursing education to students interested in serving in the Navy.
Eligibility This program is open to full-time students in a bachelor of science in nursing program who are U.S. citizens under 40 years of age. Prior to or during their junior year of college, applicants must enlist in the U.S. Navy Nurse Corps Reserve. Following receipt of their degree, they must be willing to serve on active duty as a nurse in the Navy.
Financial data This program pays a $10,000 initial grant upon enlistment (paid in 2 installments of $5,000 each) and a stipend of $1,000 per month. Students are responsible for paying all school expenses.
Duration Up to 24 months.
Additional information Students who receive support from this program for 1 to 12 months incur an active-duty service obligation of 4 years; students who receive support for 13 to 24 months have a service obligation of 5 years.
Number awarded Varies each year.
Deadline Deadline not specified.

[409]
NAVY NURSE CORPS NROTC SCHOLARSHIP PROGRAM
U.S. Navy
Attn: Naval Service Training Command Officer Development
NAS Pensacola
250 Dallas Street
Pensacola, FL 32508-5220
(850) 452-4941, ext. 29395
Toll Free: (800) NAV-ROTC, ext. 29395
Fax: (850) 452-2486
E-mail: pnsc_nrotc.scholarship@navy.mil
Web: www.public.navy.mil

Summary To provide financial assistance to graduating high school seniors who are interested in joining Navy ROTC and majoring in nursing in college.
Eligibility Eligible to apply for these scholarships are graduating high school seniors who have been accepted at a college with a Navy ROTC unit on campus or a college with a cross-enrollment agreement with such a college. Applicants must be U.S. citizens between the ages of 17 and 23 who plan to study nursing in college and are willing to serve for 4 years as active-duty Navy officers in the Navy Nurse Corps following graduation from college. They must not have reached their 27th birthday by the time of college graduation and commissioning; applicants who have prior active-duty military service may be eligible for age adjustments for the amount of time equal to their prior service, up to a maximum of 36 months. They must have minimum SAT scores of 550 in critical reading and 540 in mathematics with a combined score of 1150 or higher or minimum ACT scores of 22 in English and 21 in mathematics and a combined score of 47 or higher.
Financial data This scholarship provides payment of full tuition and required educational fees, as well as $375 per semester for textbooks, supplies, and equipment. The program also provides a stipend for 10 months of the year that is $250 per month as a freshman, $300 per month as a sophomore, $350 per month as a junior, and $400 per month as a senior.
Duration 4 years.
Number awarded Varies each year.
Deadline December of each year.

[410]
NAVY SEAL FOUNDATION SCHOLARSHIPS
Navy Seal Foundation
Attn: Chief Financial Officer
1619 D Street, Building 5326
Virginia Beach, VA 23459
(757) 744-5326   Fax: (757) 363-7491
E-mail: info@navysealfoundation.org
Web: www.navysealfoundation.org

Summary To provide financial assistance for college or graduate school to Naval Special Warfare (NSW) personnel and their families.
Eligibility This program is open to active-duty Navy SEALS, Special Warfare Combatant-craft Crewmen (SWCC), and military personnel assigned to other NSW commands. Their dependent children and spouses are also eligible. Applicants must be entering or continuing full or part-time stu-

dents working on an associate or bachelor's degree. Active-duty and spouses, but not dependent children, may also work on a graduate degree. Selection is based on GPA, SAT scores, class ranking, extracurricular activities, volunteer community involvement, leadership positions held, military service record, and employment (as appropriate).
Financial data Stipends are $15,000, $7,500, or $5,000 per year.
Duration 1 year; may be renewed.
Number awarded Varies each year; recently, the Navy Seal Foundation awarded 16 scholarships for all of its programs: 3 for 4 years at $15,000 per year to high school seniors and graduates, 3 for 1 year at $7,500 to high school seniors and graduates, 3 for 1 year at $15,000 to current college students, 3 for 1 year at $7,500 to current college students, and 4 for 1 year at $5,000 to spouses.
Deadline February of each year.

[411]
NAVY TUITION ASSISTANCE PROGRAM
U.S. Navy
Attn: Navy College Virtual Education Center
1155 Nider Boulevard, Building 3510, Room 100
Virginia Beach, VA 23459-2732
(703) 604-5256 Toll Free: (877) 838-1659
E-mail: james.p.johnson@navy.mil
Web: www.navycollege.navy.mil

Summary To provide financial assistance for high school, vocational, undergraduate, or graduate studies to Navy personnel.
Eligibility This program is open to active-duty Navy officers and enlisted personnel with at least 2 years of service, including Naval Reservists on continuous active duty, enlisted Naval Reservists ordered to active duty for 120 days or more, and Naval Reservist officers ordered to active duty for 2 years or more. Applicants must register to take courses at accredited civilian schools during off-duty time. They must be working on their first associate, bachelor's, master's, doctoral, or professional degree. Tuition assistance is provided for courses taken at accredited colleges, universities, vocational/technical schools, private schools, and through independent study/distance learning (but not for flight training).
Financial data Those selected for participation in this program receive their regular Navy pay and 100% of tuition at the postsecondary educational institution of their choice, but capped at $250 per semester hour and 12 semester hours per fiscal year, or a total of $3,000 per fiscal year. Funding is available only for tuition, not fees or other associated expenses.
Duration The lifetime limit is 120 semester hours. Undergraduates must complete all courses with a grade of "C" or better; graduate students must complete classes with a grade of "B" of better. If recipients fail to achieve those grades, they must reimburse the Navy for all funds received.
Additional information Officers must agree to remain on active duty for at least 2 years after completion of courses funded by this program.
Number awarded Varies each year.
Deadline Deadline not specified.

[412]
NAVY-MARINE CORPS RELIEF SOCIETY EDUCATION ASSISTANCE
Navy-Marine Corps Relief Society
Attn: Education Division
875 North Randolph Street, Suite 225
Arlington, VA 22203-1757
(703) 696-4960 Toll Free: (800) 654-8364
Fax: (703) 696-0144 E-mail: education@nmcrs.org
Web: www.nmcrs.org

Summary To provide grants and interest-free loans for college to the spouses and children of Navy and Marine Corps personnel and to Navy and Marine Corps personnel in designated programs.
Eligibility This program is open to Navy and Marine Corps personnel and their families, including 1) dependent children under 23 years of age of sailors and Marines who are active-duty, retired (including retired Reservists drawing military retirement pay), or deceased (died on active duty or after retirement); 2) spouses of sailors and Marines who are active-duty or retired; or 3) active-duty members of the Navy or Marine Corps selected for or enrolled in the Marine Enlisted Commissioning Education Program (MECEP) or the Navy's Medical Enlisted Commissioning Program (MECP). Applicants must be enrolled or planning to enroll as a full-time undergraduate student at an accredited college, university, or vocational/technical school; be registered at the Defense Eligibility Enrollment Reporting System (DEERS); have a GPA of 2.0 or higher; and be able to demonstrate financial need. They must be seeking grants or interest-free grants.
Financial data Grants and interest-free loans range from $500 to $3,000 per academic year. Funds are disbursed directly to the recipient's academic institution. Loans to children and spouses must be repaid within 24 months by allotment of pay, at a monthly rate of at least $50. Loans to MECEP and MECP students must be repaid within 48 months following commissioning.
Duration Recipients may reapply.
Additional information Recently, this program included the following named grants: the Gold Star Scholarship Programs (limited to children and spouses of sailors and Marines who died as a result of specified military engagements; the Joseph A. McAlinden Divers Scholarship (limited to sailors and Marines serving on active duty as divers and their families); and the RADM Courtney G. Clegg and Mrs. Margaret H. Clegg Scholarship. Loan programs included the Vice Admiral E.P. Travers Loan Program and the Admiral Mike Boorda Loan Program (limited to MECEP and MECP students).
Number awarded Varies each year.
Deadline May of each year.

[413]
NAVY-MARINE CORPS ROTC 2- AND 3-YEAR SCHOLARSHIPS

U.S. Navy
Attn: Naval Service Training Command Officer Development
NAS Pensacola
250 Dallas Street
Pensacola, FL 32508-5220
(850) 452-4941, ext. 29395
Toll Free: (800) NAV-ROTC, ext. 29395
Fax: (850) 452-2486
E-mail: pnsc_nrotc.scholarship@navy.mil
Web: www.public.navy.mil

Summary To provide financial assistance to students currently enrolled in college who are interested in joining Navy ROTC.

Eligibility This program is open to students who have completed at least 30 semester hours of college and have a GPA of 2.5 or higher overall. Preference is given to students at colleges with a Navy ROTC unit on campus or at colleges with a cross-enrollment agreement with a college with an NROTC unit. Applicants must be U.S. citizens between the ages of 17 and 21 who plan to pursue an approved course of study in college and complete their degree before they reach the age of 27. Former and current enlisted military personnel are also eligible if they will complete the program by the age of 30.

Financial data These scholarships provide payment of full tuition and required educational fees, as well as $750 per year for textbooks, supplies, and equipment. The program also provides a stipend for 10 months of the year that is 300 per month as a sophomore, $350 per month as a junior, and $400 per month as a senior.

Duration 2 or 3 years, until the recipient completes the bachelor's degree.

Additional information Applications must be made through professors of naval science at 1 of the schools hosting the Navy ROTC program. Prior to final selection, applicants must attend, at Navy expense, a 6-week summer training course at the Naval Science Institute at Newport, Rhode Island. Recipients must also complete 4 years of study in naval science classes as students either at 1 of the 74 colleges with NROTC units or at 1 of the more than 100 institutions with cross-enrollment agreements (in which case they attend their home college for their regular academic courses but attend naval science classes at a nearby school with an NROTC unit). After completing the program, all participants are commissioned as ensigns in the Naval Reserve with an 8-year service obligation, including 4 years of active duty.

Number awarded Approximately 800 each year.
Deadline December of each year.

[414]
NAVY-MARINE CORPS ROTC COLLEGE PROGRAM

U.S. Navy
Attn: Naval Service Training Command Officer Development
NAS Pensacola
250 Dallas Street
Pensacola, FL 32508-5220
(850) 452-4941, ext. 29395
Toll Free: (800) NAV-ROTC, ext. 29395
Fax: (850) 452-2486
E-mail: PNSC_NROTC.scholarship@navy.mil
Web: www.public.navy.mil

Summary To provide financial assistance to lower-division students who are interested in joining Navy ROTC in college.

Eligibility Applicants must be U.S. citizens between the ages of 17 and 21 who are already enrolled as non-scholarship students in naval science courses at a college or university with a Navy ROTC program on campus. They must apply before the spring of their sophomore year. All applications must be submitted through the professors of naval science at the college or university attended.

Financial data Participants in this program receive free naval science textbooks, all required uniforms, and a stipend for 10 months of the year that is $350 per month as a junior and $400 per month as a senior.

Duration 2 or 4 years.

Additional information Following acceptance into the program, participants attend the Naval Science Institute in Newport, Rhode Island for 6 and a half weeks during the summer between their sophomore and junior year. During the summer between their junior and senior year, they participate in an additional training program, usually at sea for Navy midshipmen or at Quantico, Virginia for Marine Corps midshipmen. After graduation from college, they are commissioned ensigns in the Naval Reserve or second lieutenants in the Marine Corps Reserve with an 8-year service obligation, including 3 years of active duty.

Number awarded Varies each year.
Deadline December of each year.

[415]
NAVY-MARINE CORPS ROTC NATIONAL SCHOLARSHIPS

U.S. Navy
Attn: Naval Service Training Command Officer Development
NAS Pensacola
250 Dallas Street
Pensacola, FL 32508-5220
(850) 452-4941, ext. 29395
Toll Free: (800) NAV-ROTC, ext. 29395
Fax: (850) 452-2486
E-mail: pnsc_nrotc.scholarship@navy.mil
Web: www.public.navy.mil

Summary To provide financial assistance to graduating high school seniors who are interested in joining Navy ROTC in college.

Eligibility This program is open to graduating high school seniors who have been accepted at a college with a Navy ROTC unit on campus or a college with a cross-enrollment agreement with such a college. Applicants must be U.S. citizens between 17 and 23 years of age who are willing to serve for 4 years as active-duty Navy officers following graduation from college. They must not have reached their 27th birthday by the time of college graduation and commissioning; applicants who have prior active-duty military service may be eligible for age adjustments for the amount of time equal to their prior service, up to a maximum of 36 months. The qualifying scores for the Navy option are minimum SAT scores of 550 in critical reading and 540 in mathematics with a combined score of 1150 or higher or minimum ACT scores of 22 in English and 21 in mathematics and a combined score of 47 or higher; for the Marine Corps option they are 1000 composite on the SAT or 22 composite on the ACT. Eligible academic majors are classified as Tier 1 for engineering programs of Navy interest (aerospace, aeronautical, astronautical, chemical, electrical, mechanical, naval, nuclear, ocean, and systems); Tier 2 for other engineering, mathematics, and science programs (e.g., general engineering and other engineering specialties; biochemistry and other specialties within biology; chemistry; mathematics; oceanography; pharmacology and toxicology; physics; quantitative economics; physics); or Tier 3 for selected regional and cultural area studies, designated foreign languages, or other academic majors.

Financial data These scholarships provide payment of full tuition and required educational fees, as well as $750 per year for textbooks, supplies, and equipment. The program also provides a stipend for 10 months of the year that is $250 per month as a freshman, $300 per month as a sophomore, $350 per month as a junior, and $400 per month as a senior.

Duration 4 years.

Additional information Students may apply for either a Navy or Marine Corps option scholarship but not for both. Navy option applicants apply through Navy recruiting offices; Marine Corps applicants apply through Marine Corps recruiting offices. Recipients must also complete 4 years of study in naval science classes as students either at 1 of the 74 colleges, universities, and maritime institutes with NROTC units or at 1 of the approximately 100 institutions with cross-enrollment agreements (in which case they attend their home college for their regular academic courses but attend naval science classes at a nearby school with an NROTC unit). After completing the program, all participants are commissioned as ensigns in the Naval Reserve or second lieutenants in the Marine Corps Reserve with an 8-year service obligation, including 4 years of active duty. Current military personnel who are accepted into this program are released from active duty and are not eligible for active-duty pay and allowances, medical benefits, or other active-duty entitlements.

Number awarded Approximately 2,200 each year; approximately 85% of the scholarships are awarded to students with Tier 1 or 2 majors.

Deadline December of each year.

[416]
NEBRASKA NATIONAL GUARD STATE TUITION ASSISTANCE PROGRAM

Nebraska Military Department
Attn: Nebraska National Guard
2433 N.W. 24th Street
Lincoln, NE 68524
(402) 309-8210
Web: ne.ng.mil/Resource/Pages/TA-Register.aspx

Summary To provide an opportunity for enlisted members of the Nebraska National Guard to pursue additional education.

Eligibility Eligible for this benefit are enlisted members of the Nebraska National Guard who are enrolled in a Nebraska university, college, or community college. Commissioned and warrant officers are not eligible, nor are enlisted personnel who already have a baccalaureate degree. Guard members must apply for this assistance within 10 years of the date of initial enlistment. The credit is not available for graduate study or non-credit courses. Priority is given to Guard members who have previously received these benefits.

Financial data Students at state-supported institutions are exempted from payment of the tuition charges at their schools. Students at independent, nonprofit, accredited colleges and universities in Nebraska receive a credit equal to the amount they would receive if they attended the University of Nebraska at Lincoln. All funds are paid directly to the school.

Duration 1 year; may be renewed.

Additional information Any member of the Nebraska National Guard who receives this assistance must agree to serve in the Guard for 3 years after completion of the courses for which assistance was given.

Number awarded Up to 1,200 each year.

Deadline June of each year for academic terms beginning between July and September; September of each year for academic terms beginning between October and December; December of each year for academic terms beginning between January and March; March of each year for academic terms beginning between April and June.

[417]
NEBRASKA RESERVIST TUITION CREDIT

Department of Veterans' Affairs
State Office Building
301 Centennial Mall South, Fourth Floor
P.O. Box 95083
Lincoln, NE 68509-5083
(402) 471-2458　　　　　　　　Fax: (402) 742-1142
E-mail: ndva@nebraska.gov
Web: www.veterans.nebraska.gov/reservist-tuition

Summary To provide financial assistance for college to members of Nebraska units of the active Reserves.

Eligibility Nebraska residents who are enlisted members of a Nebraska-based unit of the active selected Reserve are eligible for this benefit. They must have at least 2 years remaining on their enlistment, have agreed to serve at least 3 years in the Reserves, not have completed the tenth year of total service in the U.S. armed forces (including active and Reserve time), and be working on a degree at a state-supported college or university or an equivalent level of study in a technical community college.

Financial data Reservists who meet the requirements may receive a credit for 50% of the tuition charges at any state-supported university or college in Nebraska, including any technical community college.

Duration 1 year; may be renewed until receipt of the degree or completion of the course of study.

Number awarded Varies each year; the program is limited to 200 new applications per calendar year.

Deadline Deadline not specified.

[418]
NERA/USAA COLLEGE SCHOLARSHIP PROGRAM

Naval Enlisted Reserve Association
Attn: Scholarship Committee
8116 Arlington Boulevard
Falls Church, VA 22042
(703) 534-1329　　　　　Toll Free: (800) 776-9020
Fax: (703) 534-3617　　　E-mail: members@nera.org
Web: www.nera.org

Summary To provide financial assistance for college to members of the Naval Enlisted Reserve Association (NERA) and their families.

Eligibility This program is open to students enrolled or entering a college or university to work full or part time on an associate degree, vocational or trade school certificate, bachelor's degree, master's degree, or doctoral degree. Applicants or their sponsor must be a member of NERA in good standing. They must have a GPA of 3.0 or higher. Along with their application, they must submit an essay of 500 to 600 words on 1) their aspirations and course of study; and 2) the role of the Reservist in America and the importance of the Reserves to our national defense. In the selection process, priority is given in the following order: 1) currently serving Reserve, active and IRR members of the U.S. armed forces; 2) children and spouses of those currently serving in the U.S. armed forces; and 3) spouses, children, or grandchildren sponsored by any NERA member. Financial need is not considered in the selection process.

Financial data The stipend is $2,000.

Duration 1 year.

Additional information This program is funded in part by USAA Insurance Corporation. Regular membership in NERA is open to enlisted members of the Navy, Marine Corps, and Coast Guard Reserve components, including FTS, IRR, VTU, and retirees; associate membership is open to anyone who wishes to support NERA.

Number awarded 5 each year.

Deadline June of each year.

[419]
NEVADA NATIONAL GUARD STATE TUITION WAIVER PROGRAM

Nevada National Guard
Attn: Education Services Officer
2460 Fairview Drive
Carson City, NV 89701-6807
(775) 887-7326　　　　　Fax: (775) 887-7279
E-mail: NV-TSC@ng.army.mil
Web: nv.ng.mil/Pages/Departments/Education.aspx

Summary To provide financial assistance to Nevada National Guard members who are interested in attending college or graduate school in the state.

Eligibility This program is open to active members of the Nevada National Guard who are interested in attending a public community college, 4-year college, or university in the state. Applicants must be residents of Nevada. Independent study, correspondence courses, and study at the William S. Boyd School of Law, the University of Nevada School of Medicine, and the UNLV School of Dental Medicine are not eligible.

Financial data This program provides a waiver of 100% of tuition at state-supported community colleges, colleges, or universities in Nevada.

Duration 1 year; may be renewed.

Additional information This program was established on a pilot basis in 2003 and became permanent in 2005. Recipients must attain a GPA of at least 2.0 or refund all tuition received.

Number awarded Varies each year.

Deadline Applications must be received at least 3 weeks prior to the start of classes.

[420]
NEW HAMPSHIRE NATIONAL GUARD TUITION WAIVER PROGRAM

Office of the Adjutant General
Attn: Education Services Officer
1 Minuteman Way
Building 1, Room 125
Concord, NH 03301
(603) 225-1207　　　　　Fax: (603) 225-1257
TDD: (800) 735-2964
E-mail: sukari.d.stattonbill.mil@mail.mil
Web: www.nh.ngb.army.mil/members/education

Summary To provide financial assistance to members of the New Hampshire National Guard who are interested in attending college or graduate school in the state.

Eligibility This program is open to active members of the New Hampshire National Guard who have completed advanced individual training or commissioning and have at least a 90% attendance rate at annual training and drill assemblies. Applicants may be working on any type of academic degree at public institutions in New Hampshire. They must apply for financial aid from their school, for the New Hampshire National Guard Scholarship Program, and for federal tuition assistance.

Financial data The program provides full payment of tuition.

Duration 1 year; may be renewed.

Additional information This program began in 1996.

Number awarded Varies each year, depending on availability of space.

Deadline Deadline not specified.

[421]
NEW JERSEY NATIONAL GUARD TUITION PROGRAM

New Jersey Department of Military and Veterans Affairs
Attn: New Jersey Army National Guard Education
　Services Officer
Second Floor, B204
3650 Saylors Pond Road
Fort Dix, NJ 08640-7600
(609) 562-0975　　　　　Toll Free: (888) 859-0352
Fax: (609) 562-0188
E-mail: benjamin.j.stoner.mil@mail.mil
Web: education.njarmyguard.com/njngtp

Summary To provide financial assistance for college or graduate school to New Jersey National Guard members and the surviving spouses and children of deceased members.

Eligibility This program is open to active members of the New Jersey National Guard who have completed Initial Active

Duty for Training (IADT). Applicants must be New Jersey residents who have been accepted into a program of undergraduate or graduate study at any of 30 public institutions of higher education in the state. The surviving spouses and children of deceased members of the Guard who had completed IADT and were killed in the performance of their duties while a member of the Guard are also eligible if the school has classroom space available.
Financial data Tuition for up to 16 credits per semester is waived for full-time recipients in state-supported colleges or community colleges in New Jersey.
Duration 1 semester; may be renewed.
Number awarded Varies each year.
Deadline Deadline not specified.

[422]
NEW YORK RECRUITMENT INCENTIVE AND RETENTION PROGRAM
New York State Division of Military and Naval Affairs
Attn: New York National Guard Education Services
Recruitment Incentive and Retention Program
330 Old Niskayuna Road
Latham, NY 12110-3514
(518) 786-0464　E-mail: ng.ny.nyarng.mbx.rirpny@mail.mil
Web: dmna.ny.gov/education/?id=rirp

Summary To provide financial assistance to members of the New York State Military Forces who are interested in attending college in the state.
Eligibility This program is open to members of the New York Army National Guard, New York Air National Guard, and New York Naval Militia in good military and academic standing. Applicants must have been enrolled in a degree program for a minimum of 6 credit hours per semester, have been legal residents of New York for at least 186 days prior to using the program for the first time and 186 days per year (excluding periods of active federal service), and be enrolled in their first baccalaureate degree program. They must have completed Initial Active Duty for Training (IADT), naval enlisted code (NEC) training, or a commissioning program.
Financial data The program pays for the cost of tuition (up to the maximum cost of the State University of New York undergraduate tuition) for credit bearing courses, or courses that are required as a prerequisite within the declared degree program.
Duration Up to 8 semesters of full-time study, or the equivalent of 4 academic years, are supported; if the undergraduate program normally requires 5 academic years of full-time study, then this program will support 10 semesters of full-time study or the equivalent of 5 academic years. For part-time (from 6 to 11 semester hours per semester) study, the program provides up to 16 semesters of support.
Additional information This program became effective in 1997.
Number awarded Varies each year.
Deadline August of each year for fall semester; December of each year for spring semester.

[423]
NGAI MEMBER EDUCATIONAL GRANTS
National Guard Association of Indiana
Attn: Educational Grant Committee
2002 South Holt Road, Building 5
Indianapolis, IN 46241-4839
(317) 247-3196　　　　　　　Toll Free: (800) 219-2173
Fax: (317) 247-3575　　　　E-mail: membership@ngai.net
Web: www.myngai.org/benefits-2/grants

Summary To provide financial assistance to members of the National Guard Association of Indiana (NGAI) and their dependents who plan to attend college in any state.
Eligibility This program is open to NGAI members and their dependents who are currently serving in the Indiana National Guard or are retired members of the Indiana National Guard. Applicants must be attending or planning to attend a college or university in any state. Along with their application, they must submit 2 letters of recommendation, a copy of high school or college transcripts, SAT or ACT scores (if taken), a letter of acceptance from a college or university (if not currently attending college), and a 2-page essay on the educational program they intend to pursue and the goals they wish to attain. Selection is based on academic achievement, commitment and desire to achieve, extracurricular activities, accomplishments, goals, and financial need.
Financial data The stipend is $1,000.
Duration 1 year; may be renewed up to 3 additional years.
Number awarded 10 each year: 5 for members and 5 for dependents.
Deadline March of each year.

[424]
NGAMA SCHOLARSHIP PROGRAM
National Guard Association of Massachusetts
Attn: Education Services Office
2 Randolph Road, Building 1505
Hanscom AFB 01731-3001
E-mail: ngama.scholarship@gmail.com
Web: www.ngama.org/scholarships

Summary To provide financial assistance to members of the Massachusetts National Guard and their dependents who are interested in attending college in any state.
Eligibility This program is open to 1) current members of the Massachusetts National Guard; 2) children and spouses of current members of the National Guard Association of Massachusetts (NGAMA); and 3) children and spouses of current members of the Massachusetts National Guard. Applicants must be enrolled in or planning to enroll in an accredited college or technical program in any state. Along with their application, they must submit a letter of recommendation, a list of extracurricular activities and other significant accomplishments, high school or college transcripts, and an essay on a topic that changes annually but relates to the National Guard and leadership.
Financial data Stipend amounts vary, but generally range from $1,000 to $2,500.
Duration 1 year.
Number awarded Varies each year; recently, 1 at $2,020 (to recognize Boston as host of the 2020 general conference of the National Guard Association of the United States) and 1

at $1,636 (to recognize the date of the first muster of the Massachusetts militia) were awarded.
Deadline February of each year.

[425]
NGAOK SCHOLARSHIPS
National Guard Association of Oklahoma
c/o Scholarship Foundation
Attn: Rosemary Masters, Scholarship Chair
3501 Military Circle
Oklahoma City, OK 73111
(405) 823-0799   E-mail: ngaok.scholarship@gmail.com
Web: www.ngaok.org/benefits

Summary To provide financial assistance to members of the National Guard Association of Oklahoma (NGAOK) and their dependents who are interested in attending college in any state.

Eligibility This program is open to NGAOK members and their dependent children and spouses who are enrolled or planning to enroll full or part time in an undergraduate or graduate program at a college or university in any state. The primary next of kin of members of the Oklahoma National Guard killed in action after September 11, 2001 are considered life members of NGAOK. Applicants must submit transcripts that include ACT and/or SAT scores; lists of awards and recognitions, community and volunteer services, and extracurricular and sports activities; and a 500-word essay about how they exemplify the traits of selfless service, leadership, character, and their aspirations. Financial need is not considered in the selection process.

Financial data Stipends are $500 or $1,000.
Duration 1 year.
Number awarded 20 to 25 each year.
Deadline January of each year.

[426]
NGARI SCHOLARSHIP PROGRAM
National Guard Association of Rhode Island
Attn: Scholarship Committee
645 New London Avenue
Cranston, RI 02920-3097
(401) 228-6586   Fax: (401) 541-9182
E-mail: ngarinews@gmail.com
Web: www.ngari.org/scholarships

Summary To provide financial assistance to current and former members of the Rhode Island National Guard and their children who plan to attend college in any state.

Eligibility This program is open to active and retired members of the Rhode Island National Guard and their children. Applicants must be high school seniors, high school graduates, or undergraduate students. They must be attending or accepted at an accredited college, university, or vocational/technical school in any state. As part of their application, they must describe any needs, goals, and other factors that may help the selection committee.

Financial data The stipend is $1,000.
Duration 1 year; nonrenewable.
Number awarded Varies each year; recently, 4 were awarded.
Deadline May of each year.

[427]
NGATN FOUNDATION LEGACY SCHOLARSHIP
National Guard Association of Tennessee
Attn: Foundation
4332 Kenilwood Drive
Nashville, TN 37204-4401
(615) 833-9100   Toll Free: (888) 642-8448 (within TN)
Fax: (615) 833-9173   E-mail: byron@ngatn.org
Web: www.ngatn.org/scholarships

Summary To provide financial assistance for college to members of the Tennessee National Guard whose parent or parents were (or are still serving as) members of the Guard.

Eligibility This program is open to current active members of the Tennessee Army or Air National Guard whose parent or parents also were or still are members of the Guard. Applicants must also be annual members of the Enlisted Association of the National Guard of Tennessee (EANGTN) or the National Guard Association of Tennessee (NGATN). They must be high school seniors or students currently enrolled at a college or university in any state. Along with their application, they must submit transcripts, letters of recommendation, and a letter on their desire to continue their education.

Financial data The stipend is $4,000.
Duration 1 year.
Number awarded 1 each year.
Deadline February of each year.

[428]
NGAUT "MINUTEMAN" SCHOLARSHIPS
National Guard Association of Utah
12953 South Minuteman Drive, Room 19835
P.O. Box 435
Draper, UT 84020
(801) 599-7869   E-mail: ngautah@ngaut.org
Web: www.ngaut.org/scholarship.php

Summary To provide financial assistance to members and dependents of members of the National Guard Association of Utah (NGAAUT) who are interested in attending college in any state.

Eligibility This program is open to members and dependents of members of NGAUT who are high school seniors or students enrolled for at least 6 credit hours at a college or university in any state. Applicants must submit 1) a 200-word description of their educational and career goals; 2) a 200-word description of leadership and extracurricular activities that they may have had or currently enjoy; 3) a 300-word essay on how the military has influenced their life; 4) a 1-page cover letter or resume; and 5) 2 letters of reference.

Financial data Stipends are $1,500 or $1,000. Funds are sent to the recipient's school and must be used for tuition, laboratory fees, and curriculum-required books and supplies.
Duration 1 year; nonrenewable.
Number awarded 10 each year: 2 at $1,500 and 8 at $1,000.
Deadline January of each year.

SCHOLARSHIPS: MILITARY PERSONNEL

[429]
NGAW SCHOLARSHIP PROGRAM
National Guard Association of Washington
Attn: Scholarship Committee
P.O. Box 5144
Camp Murray
Tacoma, WA 98430-5144
(253) 584-5411   Toll Free: (800) 588-6420
Fax: (253) 582-9521   E-mail: ngaw@ngaw.org
Web: www.ngaw.org/scholarships-2

Summary To provide financial assistance to members of the Washington National Guard and their dependents who are interested in attending college in the state.

Eligibility This program is open to members of the Washington National Guard and their dependents who are enrolled at an accredited college, university, or trade school in the state. Guard members may be full-time or part-time students; dependents must be enrolled full time. Applicants do not need to be members of the National Guard Association of Washington (NGAW) although members are eligible for larger awards. Along with their application, they must submit a statement that covers their educational goals, academic credits completed, honors and awards, participation in National Guard, plans for the future in the National Guard, participation in school extracurricular activities, participation in volunteer civic and community events, and financial need.

Financial data The stipend ranges from $500 to $1,000.

Duration 1 year.

Number awarded 7 each year: 1 at $1,000 (designated the Lowenberg Scholarship and reserved for a Guard member) and 6 at either $750 (if the recipient is an NGAW member) or $500 (if the recipient is not a member).

Deadline May of each year.

[430]
NGOA-FL AND ENGAF SCHOLARSHIP PROGRAM
National Guard Association of Florida
Attn: Scholarship Committee
P.O. Box 3446
St. Augustine, FL 32085-3446
(904) 823-0629   Fax: (904) 839-2068
E-mail: ngafl1903@floridaguard.org
Web: www.floridaguard.org/scholarships

Summary To provide financial assistance to members of the Florida National Guard and their families who are also members of either the National Guard Officers Association of Florida (NGOA-FL) or the Enlisted National Guard Association of Florida (ENGAF) and interested in attending college in the state.

Eligibility This program is open to active members of the Florida National Guard (enlisted, officer, and warrant officer), their spouses, and children, but preference is given to Guard members. Applicants must be residents of Florida attending or planning to attend an accredited college, university, or vocational/technical school in the state. They must also be a member, spouse of a member, or child of a member of their respective association. Selection is based on academic achievement, civic and moral leadership, character, and financial need.

Financial data Scholarships are $1,000 for full-time students or $500 for part-time students; funds are paid directly to the recipient's institution.

Duration 1 year; may be renewed.

Additional information This program is jointly sponsored by the respective associations.

Number awarded 15 each year.

Deadline May of each year.

[431]
NICHOLAS D. CHABRAJA SCHOLARSHIP
Association of the United States Army
Attn: Scholarships
2425 Wilson Boulevard
Arlington, VA 22201
(703) 841-4300   Toll Free: (800) 336-4570
E-mail: scholarships@ausa.org
Web: www.ausa.org/resources/scholarships

Summary To provide financial assistance to members of the Association of the United States Army (AUSA) who are interested in studying a field of STEM in college.

Eligibility This program is open to AUSA members who are enrolled or accepted at an accredited college or university to work on a degree in a field of STEM. Along with their application, they must submit a 1-page autobiography, 2 letters of recommendation, a letter describing their career aspirations (including their course of study and plans for completion of a degree), and a transcript of high school or college grades (depending on which they are currently attending). Selection is based on academic merit and personal achievement. Financial need is not normally a selection criterion but in some cases of extreme need it may be used as a factor; the lack of financial need, however, is never a cause for non-selection.

Financial data The stipend is $5,000; funds are sent directly to the recipient's college or university.

Duration 1 year.

Additional information Membership in the AUSA is open to everyone who supports a strong national defense, with special concern for the Army. That includes Regular Army, National Guard, Army Reserve, government civilians, retired soldiers, Wounded Warriors, veterans, concerned citizens and family members.

Number awarded 6 each year.

Deadline June of each year.

[432]
NORTH CAROLINA NATIONAL GUARD ASSOCIATION ACADEMIC EXCELLENCE AND LEADERSHIP SCHOLARSHIPS
North Carolina National Guard Association
Attn: Educational Foundation, Inc.
7410 Chapel Hill Road
Raleigh, NC 27607-5047
(919) 851-3390, ext. 5
Toll Free: (800) 821-6159 (within NC)
Fax: (919) 859-4990   E-mail: edfoundation@ncnga.org
Web: www.edfoundationofncnga.org

Summary To provide financial assistance to members and dependents of members of the North Carolina National Guard Association who demonstrate academic excellence and are attending college in any state.

Eligibility This program is open to active and associate members of the association as well as the spouses, children, grandchildren, and legal dependents of active, associate, or

deceased members. Applicants must be high school seniors or students currently attending a 4-year college or university in any state and have a GPA of 3.5 or higher. Selection is based on academic and leadership achievements.
Financial data The stipend is $1,200.
Duration 1 year; may be renewed.
Number awarded 2 each year: 1 to a high school senior and 1 to a current college student.
Deadline January of each year for high school graduates and college students; February of each year for high school seniors.

[433]
NORTH CAROLINA NATIONAL GUARD ASSOCIATION CITIZENSHIP SCHOLARSHIPS

North Carolina National Guard Association
Attn: Educational Foundation, Inc.
7410 Chapel Hill Road
Raleigh, NC 27607-5047
(919) 851-3390, ext. 5
Toll Free: (800) 821-6159 (within NC)
Fax: (919) 859-4990   E-mail: edfoundation@ncnga.org
Web: www.edfoundationofncnga.org

Summary To provide financial assistance to members and dependents of members of the North Carolina National Guard Association who demonstrate outstanding achievement in citizenship and are attending college in any state.
Eligibility This program is open to active and associate members of the association as well as the spouses, children, grandchildren, and legal dependents of active, associate, or deceased members. Applicants must be high school seniors or students currently attending a 4-year college or university in any state. Selection is based on achievements and activities that contribute to their schools and communities.
Financial data The stipend is $1,200.
Duration 1 year; may be renewed.
Number awarded 2 each year: 1 to a high school senior and 1 to a current college student.
Deadline January of each year for high school graduates and college students; February of each year for high school seniors.

[434]
NORTH CAROLINA NATIONAL GUARD ASSOCIATION SCHOLARSHIPS

North Carolina National Guard Association
Attn: Educational Foundation, Inc.
7410 Chapel Hill Road
Raleigh, NC 27607-5047
(919) 851-3390, ext. 5
Toll Free: (800) 821-6159 (within NC)
Fax: (919) 859-4990   E-mail: edfoundation@ncnga.org
Web: www.edfoundationofncnga.org

Summary To provide financial assistance to members and dependents of members of the North Carolina National Guard Association who plan to attend college in any state.
Eligibility This program is open to active and associate members of the association as well as the spouses, children, grandchildren, and legal dependents of active, associate, or deceased members. Applicants must be high school seniors, high school graduates, or students currently enrolled at a college or university in any state. Selection is based on financial need, academic achievement, citizenship, leadership, and other application information. The most outstanding applicants receive scholarships provided by the SECU Foundation. Applicants who meet specified additional requirements qualify for various memorial and special scholarships.
Financial data Stipends are $10,000 or $5,000 for the SECU Foundation Scholarships, $1,200 for scholarships to 4-year universities, or $600 for community college scholarships.
Duration 1 year; may be renewed.
Additional information This program, which began in 1968, includes a number of named memorial and special scholarships. Other scholarships are funded by the SECU Foundation of the State Employees' Credit Union and the USAA Insurance Corporation.
Number awarded Varies each year; recently, 46 with a value of $67,800 were awarded. Since this program was established, it has awarded 1,918 scholarships worth more than $1.5 million.
Deadline January of each year for high school graduates and college students; February of each year for high school seniors.

[435]
NORTH CAROLINA NATIONAL GUARD TUITION ASSISTANCE PROGRAM

North Carolina National Guard
Attn: Education Services Office
1636 Gold Star Drive
Raleigh, NC 27607
(919) 664-6272   Toll Free: (800) 621-4136
Fax: (919) 664-6520
E-mail: ng.nc.ncarng.mbx.education-service-office@mail.mil
Web: nc.ng.mil/ESO/Pages/New-Students.aspx

Summary To provide financial assistance to members of the North Carolina National Guard who plan to attend college or graduate school in the state.
Eligibility This program is open to active members of the North Carolina National Guard (officer, warrant officer, or enlisted) who have at least 2 years of enlistment remaining after the end of the academic period for which tuition assistance is provided. Applicants must be enrolled in an eligible business or trade school, private institution, or public college/university in North Carolina. They may be working on a vocational, undergraduate, graduate, or doctoral degree.
Financial data The maximum stipend is currently $4,515 per academic year.
Duration 1 year; may be renewed.
Additional information This program is administered by the North Carolina State Education Assistance Authority.
Number awarded Varies each year; recently, 763 of these grants, with a value of $2,062,815, were awarded.
Deadline Applications must be submitted prior to the start of the term.

[436]
NORTH DAKOTA NATIONAL GUARD ENLISTED ASSOCIATION SCHOLARSHIPS

North Dakota National Guard Enlisted Association
c/o CSM Joe Lovelace, Scholarship Chair
4900 107th Avenue S.E.
Minot, ND 58701-9207
(701) 420-5841   E-mail: joseph.m.lovelace.mil@mail.mil
Web: www.ndngea.org/helpful-documents

Summary To provide financial assistance to members of the North Dakota National Guard Enlisted Association (NDNGEA) and their families who are interested in attending college in any state.

Eligibility This program is open to association members who have at least 1 year remaining on their enlistment or have completed 20 or more years in service. Also eligible are their unmarried dependent children and spouses and the unremarried spouses and unmarried dependent children of deceased NDNGEA members who were in good standing at the time of death. Applicants must be enrolled or planning to enroll full time at a university, college, or trade/business school in any state. Graduate students are not eligible. Selection is based on academic achievement, leadership, character, and financial need.

Financial data The stipend is $1,000. Funds are sent directly to the school in the recipient's name.

Duration 1 year.

Number awarded 2 each year: 1 to an NDNGEA member and 1 to a child or spouse.

Deadline November of each year.

[437]
NORTH DAKOTA NATIONAL GUARD TUITION ASSISTANCE PROGRAM

North Dakota National Guard
Attn: State Tuition Assistance Program
4200 East Divide Avenue
P.O. Box 5511
Bismarck, ND 58506-5511
(701) 333-3008
E-mail: ng.nd.ndarng.list.state-tuition-assistance@mail.mil
Web: www.ndguard.nd.gov/education-services

Summary To provide financial assistance to members of the North Dakota National Guard who plan to attend college or graduate school in the state.

Eligibility This program is open to members of the North Dakota National Guard who have a record of satisfactory participation (no more than 9 unexcused absences in the past 12 months) and service remaining after completion of the class for which they are requesting assistance. Applicants must be seeking support for trade or vocational training or work on an associate, baccalaureate, or graduate degree. They must be attending or planning to attend a North Dakota higher education public institution or a participating private institution (currently, Jamestown College, University of Mary in Bismarck, MedCenter One College of Nursing, Rasmussen College, or Trinity Bible College). Full-time AGR personnel do not qualify for this program. This is an entitlement program, provided all requirements are met.

Financial data Participating colleges and universities waive 25% of tuition for eligible courses (undergraduate only), up to 25% of the tuition at the University of North Dakota. Through this program, the National Guard provides reimbursement of the remaining 75% of tuition for eligible courses (undergraduate and graduate), or up to 75% of the tuition at the University of North Dakota. The program also reimburses 100% of all regular fees, not to exceed 100% of the regular fees charged by the University of North Dakota. State reimbursements are paid directly to the student in the form of a check, based upon the number of credit hours successfully completed.

Duration Benefits are available for up to 144 semester credit hours or the completion of an undergraduate or graduate degree, provided the recipient earns a grade of "C" or higher in each undergraduate course or "B" or higher in each graduate course.

Number awarded Varies each year.

Deadline August of each year for fall; January of each year for spring; June of each year for summer.

[438]
NORTH DAKOTA TUITION AND FEE WAIVERS

North Dakota University System
Attn: Financial Aid Office
State Capitol, Tenth Floor
600 East Boulevard Avenue, Department 215
Bismarck, ND 58505-0230
(701) 328-2964   Fax: (701) 328-2979
E-mail: ndfinaid@ndus.edu
Web: www.ndus.edu

Summary To reduce tuition and fees for designated categories of students at public institutions in North Dakota.

Eligibility This program is open to residents of North Dakota who are law enforcement officers; National Guard members; surviving dependents of POW/MIA veterans who were killed in action, died of service-related causes, were prisoners of war, have 100% service-connected disability, or who were declared missing in action; surviving spouses and children of firefighters, emergency medical services personnel, and peace officers who died as a direct result of injuries received in the performance of official duties; and senior citizens. Applicants must be attending or planning to attend a public college or university in North Dakota.

Financial data North Dakota public colleges and universities have the authority to provide partial or full reductions in tuition and fees for qualified students.

Duration 1 academic year; renewable.

Number awarded Varies each year.

Deadline Deadline not specified.

[439]
NORTHAMERICAN.COM MILITARY SCHOLARSHIP

North American Van Lines
One Parkview Plaza
Oakbrook Terrace, IL 60180
Toll Free: (800) 228-3092
Web: www.northamerican.com/military-scholarship

Summary To provide financial assistance to current and former military personnel and their families who are interested in attending college to study fields related to logistics.

Eligibility This program is open to current and honorably discharged members of the military, their spouses, and their children under 21 years of age or (if currently attending col-

lege) under 23 years of age. Applicants must be enrolled or planning to enroll full time at a 4-year college or university and major in military logistics, supply chain management, or operational management. They must be U.S. citizens or permanent residents and have a GPA of 2.5 or higher. Along with their application, they must submit an essay of 400 to 800 words on why a career in logistics/supply chain management is their college major of choice. Financial need is not considered in the selection process.
Financial data The stipend is $1,000.
Duration 1 year.
Additional information This program began in 2015.
Number awarded 2 each year.
Deadline September of each year.

[440]
NORTHERN NEW JERSEY CHAPTER ROTC SCHOLARSHIPS
Military Officers Association of America-Northern New Jersey Chapter
Attn: MAJ George Paffendorf, Scholarships
US Army ARDEC
Building 121
Picatinny Arsenal, NJ 07806-5000
(908) 619-4463   E-mail: majorgwp@aol.com
Web: www.nnj-moaa.org/activities

Summary To provide financial assistance to residents of New Jersey who are enrolled in an ROTC program at a college in any state.
Eligibility This program is open to residents of New Jersey who are attending a college or university in the state. Applicants must be preparing for a military career through the ROTC program at their institution.
Financial data The stipend is $1,000.
Duration 1 year.
Number awarded 3 each year.
Deadline Deadline not specified.

[441]
NUCLEAR PROPULSION OFFICER CANDIDATE (NUPOC) PROGRAM
U.S. Navy
Attn: Navy Personnel Command
5722 Integrity Drive
Millington, TN 38054-5057
(901) 874-3070   Toll Free: (888) 633-9674
Fax: (901) 874-2651
E-mail: nukeprograms@cnrc.navy.mil
Web: www.navycs.com/officer/nupoc.html

Summary To provide financial assistance to college juniors and seniors who wish to serve in the Navy's nuclear propulsion training program following graduation.
Eligibility This program is open to U.S. citizens who are entering their junior or senior year of college as a full-time student. Strong technical majors (mathematics, physics, chemistry, or an engineering field) are encouraged. Applicants must have completed at least 1 year of calculus and 1 year of physics and must have earned a grade of "C" or better in all mathematics, science, and technical courses. They must be younger than 29 years of age.

Financial data Participants become Active Reserve enlisted Navy personnel and receive a basic salary of an Officer Candidate (E-6, or $2,693.70 per month); the exact amount depends on the local cost of living and other factors.
Duration Up to 30 months, until completion of a bachelor's degree.
Additional information Following graduation, participants attend Officer Candidate School in Pensacola, Florida for 4 months and receive their commissions. They have a service obligation of 8 years (of which at least 5 years must be on active duty), beginning with 6 months at the Navy Nuclear Power Training Command in Charleston, South Carolina and 6 more months of hands-on training at a nuclear reactor facility.
Number awarded Varies each year.
Deadline Deadline not specified.

[442]
NUCLEAR (SUBMARINE AND SURFACE) OPTION OF THE SEAMAN TO ADMIRAL-21 PROGRAM
U.S. Navy
Attn: Commander, Naval Service Training Command
250 Dallas Street, Suite A
Pensacola, FL 32508-5268
(850) 452-9563   Fax: (850) 452-2486
E-mail: PNSC_STA21@navy.mil
Web: www.public.navy.mil

Summary To allow outstanding enlisted Navy personnel to attend a college or university with an NROTC unit, complete a bachelor's degree, and receive a commission in the nuclear officer community.
Eligibility This program is open to U.S. citizens who are currently serving on active duty in the U.S. Navy or Naval Reserve, including Full Time Support (FTS), Selected Reserves (SELRES), and Navy Reservists on active duty, except for those on active duty for training (ACDUTRA). Only personnel 1) currently enrolled in the Naval Nuclear Training Pipeline (i.e., Nuclear Field A-School, Naval Nuclear Power School or Naval Nuclear Power Training Unit); or 2) who have completed the naval nuclear power training pipeline, hold a nuclear NEC (335X, 336X, 338X, or 339X), and are stationed at any command. Applicants must be high school graduates (or GED recipients) who are able to complete requirements for a baccalaureate degree in 36 months or less. When they complete their degree requirements, they must be younger than 31 years of age. Sea returnee staff instructors must finish prior to their 31st birthday. Applicants must have taken the SAT or ACT within the past 3 years and achieved a score of 1140 or higher on the SAT or 50 or higher on the ACT. Their proposed college major must be in a technical area.
Financial data Awardees continue to receive their regular Navy pay and allowances while they attend college on a full-time basis. They also receive reimbursement for tuition, fees, and books up to $10,000 per year. If base housing is available, they are eligible to live there. Participants are not eligible to receive benefits under the Navy's Tuition Assistance Program (TA), the Montgomery GI Bill (MGIB), the Navy College Fund, or the Veterans Educational Assistance Program (VEAP).
Duration Selectees are supported for up to 36 months of full-time, year-round study or completion of a bachelor's degree, as long as they maintain a GPA of 3.0 or higher.

Additional information This program began in 2001 as a replacement for the Nuclear Enlisted Commissioning Program (NECP). Upon acceptance into the program, selectees attend the Naval Science Institute (NSI) in Newport, Rhode Island for an 8-week program in the fundamental core concepts of being a naval officer (navigation, engineering, weapons, military history and justice, etc.). They then enter 1 of 22 universities with an NROTC nuclear unit (University of Arizona, Auburn University, The Citadel, Columbia University, University of Idaho, University of Illinois, Iowa State University, University of Kansas, University of Missouri, University of New Mexico, North Carolina State University, Old Dominion University, Oregon State University, Pennsylvania State University, Purdue University, Southern University and A&M College, SUNY Maritime College, University of South Carolina, University of Texas, University of Utah, University of Washington, or University of Wisconsin) to work full time on a bachelor's degree. They become members of and drill with the NROTC unit. When they complete their degree, they are commissioned as ensigns in the United States Naval Reserve and assigned to initial training for their nuclear officer community. After commissioning, participants incur an active-duty obligation of 5 years.

Number awarded Varies each year.
Deadline June of each year.

[443]
NURSE CORPS OPTION OF THE SEAMAN TO ADMIRAL-21 PROGRAM

U.S. Navy
Attn: Commander, Naval Service Training Command
250 Dallas Street, Suite A
Pensacola, FL 32508-5268
(850) 452-9563   Fax: (850) 452-2486
E-mail: PNSC_STA21@navy.mil
Web: www.public.navy.mil

Summary To allow outstanding enlisted Navy personnel to attend a college or university with an NROTC unit, complete a bachelor's degree, and receive a commission in the Nurse Corps.

Eligibility This program is open to U.S. citizens who are currently serving on active duty in the U.S. Navy or Naval Reserve, including Full Time Support (FTS), Selected Reserves (SELRES), and Navy Reservists on active duty, except for those on active duty for training (ACDUTRA). Applicants must be high school graduates (or GED recipients) who are able to complete requirements for a baccalaureate degree in nursing in 36 months or less. They must have completed at least 30 semester units in undergraduate nursing prerequisite courses with a GPA of 2.5 or higher. They must be at least 18 years of age and able to complete degree requirements and be commissioned prior to age 42. Within the past 3 years, they must have taken the SAT (and achieved scores of at least 500 on the mathematics section and 500 on the evidence based reading and writing or critical reading section) or the ACT (and achieved a score of at least 21 on the mathematics portion and 20 on the English portion).

Financial data Awardees continue to receive their regular Navy pay and allowances while they attend college on a full-time basis. They also receive reimbursement for tuition, fees, and books up to $10,000 per year. If base housing is available, they are eligible to live there. Participants are not eligible to receive benefits under the Navy's Tuition Assistance Program (TA), the Montgomery GI Bill (MGIB), the Navy College Fund, or the Veterans Educational Assistance Program (VEAP).

Duration Selectees are supported for up to 36 months of full-time, year-round study or completion of a bachelor's degree, as long as they maintain a GPA of 2.5 or higher.

Additional information This program began in 2001 as a replacement for the Fleet Accession to Naval Reserve Officer Training Corps (NROTC) Nurse Option. Upon acceptance into the program, selectees attend the Naval Science Institute (NSI) in Newport, Rhode Island for an 8-week program in the fundamental core concepts of being a naval officer (navigation, engineering, weapons, military history and justice, etc.). They then enter an NROTC affiliated college or university with a nursing program that confers an accredited baccalaureate degree in nursing to pursue full-time study. They become members of and drill with the NROTC unit. When they complete their bachelor's degree in nursing, they must successfully pass the National Council Licensing Examination-Registered Nurse (NCLEX-RN) and then be commissioned as ensigns in the United States Naval Reserve and assigned to initial training as an officer in the Nurse Corps. After commissioning, 5 years of active service are required.

Number awarded Varies each year.
Deadline June of each year.

[444]
OHIO LEGION MEMBER/MILITARY VETERAN SCHOLARSHIP

American Legion
Department of Ohio
60 Big Run Road
P.O. Box 8007
Delaware, OH 43015
(740) 362-7478   Fax: (740) 362-1429
E-mail: legion@ohiolegion.com
Web: www.ohiolegion.com/programs/scholarships

Summary To provide financial assistance to residents of Ohio who are members of the American Legion, veterans, or current military personnel and interested in attending college in any state.

Eligibility This program is open to residents of Ohio who are 1) members of the American Legion; 2) honorably discharged members of the armed forces; or 3) currently on active duty or a member of the National Guard or Reserves. Applicants must be attending or planning to attend colleges, universities, or other approved postsecondary schools in any state as an undergraduate or graduate student. They must have a GPA of 3.5 or higher and an ACT score of at least 25. Along with their application, they must submit a personal statement of 500 to 550 words on their career objectives. Selection is based on academic achievement as measured by course grades, ACT scores, difficulty of curriculum, participation in school and outside activities, and the judging committee's general impression.

Financial data Stipends are normally at least $2,000.
Duration 1 year.
Number awarded 1 each year.
Deadline April of each year.

[445]
OHIO NATIONAL GUARD SCHOLARSHIP PROGRAM

Adjutant General's Department
Attn: ONG Scholarship Program Office
2825 West Dublin Granville Road
Columbus, OH 43235-2789
(614) 336-7143   Toll Free: (888) 400-6484
Fax: (614) 336-7318
E-mail: ng.oh.oharng.mbx.ong-scholarship@mail.mil
Web: www.ong.ohio.gov/scholarship_index.html

Summary To provide financial assistance to members of the Ohio National Guard (ONG) interested in working on a college degree.

Eligibility This program is open to members of the Ohio Army and Air National Guard attending a 2- or 4-year public college or university in the state. Applicants may be 1) those with a 6-year enlistment in the Ohio Guard; 2) active-duty, prior-service members with an enlistment of 3 to 6 years in the Ohio Guard; or 3) non-prior service ONG members in an active 3-year enlistment. New enlistees must complete basic training and obtain a military job skill.

Financial data The program covers 100% of the tuition and general fee charges at state-assisted 2- and 4-year colleges and universities in Ohio or an equivalent sum at private and proprietary institutions.

Duration The grant is limited to 96 credit units for 6-year enlistments or 48 credit hours for active-duty prior-service members and those with 3-year enlistments. Participants must remain enrolled as a full-time undergraduate student for that time. Enrollment in the institution of higher education must begin no later than 12 months after the completion of Initial Active Duty for Training (IADT), or date of reenlistment, or date of extension of current enlistment.

Additional information This program began in 1999. Grant assistance is not available for an additional baccalaureate degree, for postgraduate courses, or for courses not applicable to a degree.

Number awarded Grants are limited to the annual average student load of 4,000 full-time equivalent students per term.

Deadline June for fall term; October for winter quarter or spring semester; January for spring quarter; or March for summer term.

[446]
ONGA LEADERSHIP GRANTS

Ohio National Guard Association
Attn: Leadership Grant Committee
1299 Virginia Avenue
Columbus, OH 43212
(614) 486-4186   E-mail: ongaedkelly@gmail.com
Web: www.ngaoh.org/salon-services

Summary To provide financial assistance to members of the Ohio National Guard Association (ONGA) and their families who are interested in attending college in any state.

Eligibility This program is open to active members (either officers or warrant officers) of the ONGA and the dependents of active, life, retired, or deceased members. Applicants must be enrolled or planning to enroll at a college or university in any state. Along with their application, they must submit transcripts, SAT/ACT scores, and a 2-page essay explaining why they should be selected to receive a grant. Selection is based on grades, future plans, membership and leadership, honors and awards, need, and overall impression.

Financial data A stipend is awarded (amount not specified).

Duration 1 year; nonrenewable.

Additional information This program began in 1996.

Number awarded Varies each year; recently, 5 were awarded.

Deadline November of each year.

[447]
OREGON NATIONAL GUARD ASSOCIATION SCHOLARSHIPS

Oregon National Guard Association
c/o Oregon National Guard Charitable Education Fund, Inc.
Attn: Scholarship Review Committee
10705 S.W. Black Diamond Way
Tigard, OR 97223
(503) 584-3030   Fax: (503) 584-3052
E-mail: rhansjan@outlook.com
Web: www.ornga.org/scholarships

Summary To provide financial assistance to members of the Oregon National Guard, the Oregon National Guard Association (ORNGA), and their children and spouses who are interested in attending college in any state.

Eligibility This program is open to active members of the Oregon Army and Air National Guard, members of the ORNGA, and their children and spouses. Applicants must be high school seniors, graduates, or GED recipients and interested in working on an undergraduate degree at a college, university, or trade school in any state. The parent, spouse, or applicant must have an ETS date beyond the end of the academic year for which the scholarship is used. Selection is based on demonstrated qualities of leadership, civic action, and academic achievement.

Financial data The stipend is $1,500.

Duration 1 year.

Number awarded Up to 10 each year.

Deadline March of each year.

[448]
PENNSYLVANIA NATIONAL GUARD EDUCATIONAL ASSISTANCE PROGRAM (EAP)

Pennsylvania Higher Education Assistance Agency
Attn: State Grant and Special Programs
1200 North Seventh Street
P.O. Box 8157
Harrisburg, PA 17105-8157
(717) 720-2800   Toll Free: (800) 692-7392
Fax: (717) 720-3786   TDD: (800) 654-5988
E-mail: info@pheaa.org
Web: www.pheaa.org

Summary To provide scholarship/loans for college or graduate school to Pennsylvania National Guard members.

Eligibility This program is open to active members of the Pennsylvania National Guard who are Pennsylvania residents and serving as enlisted personnel, warrant officers, or commissioned officers of any grade. Applicants must accept an obligation to serve in the Pennsylvania National Guard for a period of 6 years from the date of entry into the program. Students who do not possess a baccalaureate degree must

SCHOLARSHIPS: MILITARY PERSONNEL

be enrolled full or part time in an approved program of education at an approved institution of higher learning in Pennsylvania. Master's degree students are supported on a part-time basis only. Guard members receiving an ROTC scholarship of any type are not eligible.

Financial data Full-time undergraduate students receive the lesser of 100% of tuition plus technology fee at the institution where they are enrolled or the annual tuition rate and technology fee charged to a Pennsylvania resident at a state-owned university. Part-time undergraduates receive the lesser of 100% of the tuition plus technology fee for a part-time course of study at their institution or the per credit tuition rate charged to a Pennsylvania resident at a state-owned university plus the technology fee. Graduate students receive the lesser of 100% of the tuition plus technology fee charged for a part-time course of study at their institution or the per credit tuition rate charged to a Pennsylvania resident at a state-owned university. Recipients who fail to fulfill the service obligation must repay all funds received, plus interest.

Duration Up to 5 years.

Additional information This program, first offered in 1997, is jointly administered by the Pennsylvania Department of Military and Veterans Affairs and the Pennsylvania Higher Education Assistance Agency. Support for summer and graduate school is available only if funding permits.

Number awarded Varies each year; recently, 1,789 members of the Pennsylvania National Guard were enrolled in this program.

Deadline Deadline not specified.

[449]
PENNSYLVANIA NATIONAL GUARD SCHOLARSHIP FUND

Pennsylvania National Guard Associations
Attn: Pennsylvania National Guard Scholarship Fund
Biddle Hall (Building 9-109)
Fort Indiantown Gap
Annville, PA 17003-5002
(717) 861-6696   Toll Free: (800) 997-8885
Fax: (717) 861-5560   E-mail: kristi.a.carlsen.civ@mail.mil
Web: www.pngas.org/page/3

Summary To provide financial assistance to Pennsylvania National Guard members and the children of disabled or deceased members who are interested in attending college in any state.

Eligibility This program is open to active members of the Pennsylvania Army or Air National Guard. Children of members of the Guard who died or were permanently disabled while on Guard duty are also eligible. Applicants must be entering their first year of higher education as a full-time student or presently attending a college or vocational school in any state as a full-time student. Along with their application, they must submit an essay that outlines their military and civilian plans for the future. Selection is based on academic potential, military commitment, extracurricular activities, and Guard participation.

Financial data Stipends range from $500 to $2,000.

Duration 1 year.

Additional information The sponsoring organization includes the National Guard Association of Pennsylvania (NGAP) and the Pennsylvania National Guard Enlisted Association (PNGEA). This program, which began in 1977, currently receives support from the USAA Insurance Corporation and the 28th Infantry Division Association.

Number awarded Varies each year; recently, 14 were awarded: 2 at $2,000, 1 at $1,500, 3 at $1,000, 1 at $750, and 7 at $500.

Deadline June of each year.

[450]
PERSONAL MONEY SERVICE SCHOLARSHIP FOR VETERANS

Personal Money Service
1001 Bayhill Drive, Suite 200
San Bruno, CA 94066
Toll Free: (888) 373-0748
E-mail: admin@personalmoneyservice.com
Web: www.personalmoneyservice.com

Summary To provide financial assistance to military personnel and veterans who are interested in attending college in any state.

Eligibility This program is open to active-duty members of the U.S. military service and veterans. Applicants must be high school seniors or high school graduates who are enrolled or planning to enroll at a college or university in any state. They must be U.S. citizens or permanent residents. As part of the selection process, they must write a post that explains why they should be awarded this scholarship. They then make this post public on their Facebook or YouTube account with a link to Personal Money Service.

Financial data The stipend is $1,000.

Duration 1 year.

Number awarded 1 each year.

Deadline December of each year.

[451]
PILOT OPTION OF THE SEAMAN TO ADMIRAL-21 PROGRAM

U.S. Navy
Attn: Commander, Naval Service Training Command
250 Dallas Street, Suite A
Pensacola, FL 32508-5268
(850) 452-9563   Fax: (850) 452-2486
E-mail: PNSC_STA21@navy.mil
Web: www.public.navy.mil

Summary To allow outstanding enlisted Navy personnel to attend a college or university with an NROTC unit, complete a bachelor's degree, and receive a commission as a pilot.

Eligibility This program is open to U.S. citizens who are currently serving on active duty in the U.S. Navy or Naval Reserve, including Full Time Support (FTS), Selected Reserves (SELRES), and Navy Reservists on active duty, except for those on active duty for training (ACDUTRA). Applicants must be high school graduates (or GED recipients) who are at least 19 years of age and able to complete requirements for a baccalaureate degree in 36 months or less. When they complete their degree requirements, they must be younger than 27 years of age (may be adjusted to 29 years of age for prior active-duty service). Within the past 3 years, they must have taken the SAT (and achieved scores of at least 500 on the mathematics section and 500 on the evidence based reading and writing or critical reading section) or the ACT (and achieved a score of at least 21 on the mathematics portion and 20 on the English portion). They must

also achieve a score on the Aviation Selection Test Battery (ASTB) of at least 5 on the Academic Qualifications Rating (AQR) and 6 on the Pilot Flight Aptitude Rating.
Financial data Awardees continue to receive their regular Navy pay and allowances while they attend college on a full-time basis. They also receive reimbursement for tuition, fees, and books up to $10,000 per year. If base housing is available, they are eligible to live there. Participants are not eligible to receive benefits under the Navy's Tuition Assistance Program (TA), the Montgomery GI Bill (MGIB), the Navy College Fund, or the Veterans Educational Assistance Program (VEAP).
Duration Selectees are supported for up to 36 months of full-time, year-round study or completion of a bachelor's degree, as long as they maintain a GPA of 2.5 or higher.
Additional information This program began in 2001 as a replacement for the Aviation Enlisted Commissioning Program (AECP). Upon acceptance into the program, selectees attend the Naval Science Institute (NSI) in Newport, Rhode Island for an 8-week program in the fundamental core concepts of being a naval officer (navigation, engineering, weapons, military history and justice, etc.). They then enter a college or university with an NROTC unit or affiliation to work full time on a bachelor's degree. They become members of and drill with the NROTC unit. When they complete their degree, they are commissioned as ensigns in the United States Naval Reserve and assigned to flight training. After commissioning, participants incur an active-duty obligation of 8 years after designation as a Naval Aviator or 6 years from the date of disenrollment from flight training.
Number awarded Varies each year.
Deadline June of each year.

[452]
PISCATAQUA POST SAME SCHOLARSHIPS

Society of American Military Engineers-Piscataqua Post
PWD Maine Building 59
Portsmouth, NH 03804
E-mail: samepiscataquapost@gmail.com
Web: www.same.org

Summary To provide financial assistance to high school seniors in Maine, Massachusetts, and New Hampshire, especially those interested in joining ROTC or with ties to the military, who are planning to attend college in any state to major in engineering or the physical sciences.
Eligibility This program is open to seniors graduating from high schools in Maine, Massachusetts, or New Hampshire and planning to attend a college or university in any state. Applicants must be interested in majoring in engineering or the physical sciences and enrolling in ROTC, especially if they do not receive an ROTC scholarship. They should be willing to attend meetings of the Society of American Military Engineers (SAME) to receive their scholarship and share their learning experiences. Preference is given to members and children of members of the Piscataqua Post of SAME, students who are enrolled in ROTC (preferably not ROTC scholarship recipients), and individuals with prior or current U.S. military service and their children.
Financial data The stipend is $1,500.
Duration 1 year.
Number awarded Up to 2 each year.
Deadline March or June of each year.

[453]
PORTLAND POST SOCIETY OF AMERICAN MILITARY ENGINEERS SCHOLARSHIP

Oregon Office of Student Access and Completion
Attn: Scholarships
1500 Valley River Drive, Suite 100
Eugene, OR 97401-2146
(541) 687-7400   Toll Free: (800) 452-8807
Fax: (541) 687-7414   TDD: (800) 735-2900
E-mail: osac@hecc.oregon.gov
Web: app.oregonstudentaid.gov/Catalog/Default.aspx

Summary To provide financial assistance to engineering students at public colleges in Oregon who have ties to the military.
Eligibility This program is open to residents of Oregon who will be entering their sophomore year of higher of full-time students of aeronautical, biomedical, chemical, civil, electrical, or mechanical engineering at a public college or university in the state. Applicants must have a GPA of 3.0 or higher. Along with their application, they must submit a 1-page essay on how their future career as an engineer integrates with the mission of the Society of American Military Engineers (SAME) to identify and resolve national security infrastructure-related challenges and the steps they have taken to prepare themselves for this challenge. Preference is given to ROTC students, National Guard Reservists, and prior service veterans. Financial need may or may not be considered in the selection process.
Financial data Stipends for scholarships offered by the Oregon Office of Student Access and Completion (OSAC) range from $1,000 to $10,000 but recently averaged $4,710.
Duration 1 year; may be renewed up to 3 additional years.
Additional information This program is sponsored by the SAME Portland Post.
Number awarded Varies each year.
Deadline February of each year.

[454]
POST-9/11 GI BILL

Department of Veterans Affairs
Attn: Veterans Benefits Administration
810 Vermont Avenue, N.W.
Washington, DC 20420
(202) 418-4343   Toll Free: (888) 442-4551
Web: www.va.gov/education/about-gi-bill-benefits/post-9-11

Summary To provide financial assistance to veterans or military personnel who entered service on or after September 11, 2001.
Eligibility This program is open to current and former military personnel who 1) served on active duty for at least 90 aggregate days after September 11, 2001; 2) were discharged with a service-connected disability after 30 days; or 3) received a Purple Heart on or after September 11, 2001 and were discharged after any length of service. Applicants must be planning to enroll in an educational program, including work on an undergraduate or graduate degree, vocational/technical training, on-the-job training, flight training, correspondence training, licensing and national testing programs, entrepreneurship training, and tutorial assistance.
Financial data Participants working on an undergraduate or graduate degree at public institutions in their state receive full payment of tuition and fees. For participants who attend

private institutions in most states, tuition and fee reimbursement is capped at $25,162.14 per academic year. Benefits for other types of training programs depend on the amount for which the veteran qualified under prior educational programs. Veterans also receive a monthly housing allowance that is 1) based on the Department of Defense Basic Allowance for Housing (BAH) for an E-5 with dependents (which depends on the location of the school but ranges from approximately $1,000 per month to approximately $2,500 per month); 2) $1,789 per month at schools in foreign countries; or 3) $894.50 per month for online training classes. They also receive an annual book allowance of $1,000 and (for participants who live in a rural county remote from an educational institution) a rural benefit payment of $500 per year.

Duration Most participants receive up to 36 months of entitlement under this program. Benefits are payable for up to 15 years following release from active duty.

Additional information This program, referred to as Chapter 33, began in 2009 as a replacement for previous educational programs for veterans and military personnel (e.g., Montgomery GI Bill, REAP). Current participants in those programs may be able to transfer benefits from those programs to this new plan. To qualify for 100% of Post 9/11-GI Bill benefits, transferees must have at least 36 months of active-duty service. Transferees with less service are entitled to smaller percentages of benefits, ranging down to 40% for those with only 90 days of service.

Number awarded Varies each year; recently, approximately 700,000 veterans received $10.7 billion on benefits through this program.

Deadline Deadline not specified.

[455]
PROFESSIONAL OFFICER COURSE EARLY RELEASE PROGRAM
U.S. Air Force
Attn: Headquarters AFROTC/RRUE
Jeanne M. Holm Center for Officer Accession and Citizen Development
60 West Maxwell Boulevard, Building 835
Maxwell AFB, AL 36112-6501
(334) 953-5122   Toll Free: (866) 4-AFROTC
Fax: (334) 953-6167   E-mail: afrotc.rrue@us.af.mil
Web: www.afrotc.com/scholarships/enlisted/poc-erp

Summary To allow selected enlisted Air Force personnel to earn a baccalaureate degree by providing financial assistance for full-time college study as an ROTC cadet.

Eligibility Eligible to participate in this program are enlisted members of the Air Force under the age of 30 (or otherwise able to be commissioned before becoming 35 years of age) who have completed at least 1 year on continuous active duty, have served on station for at least 1 year, and have no more than 2 years remaining to complete their initial baccalaureate degree. Scholarship applicants must be younger than 31 years of age when they graduate and earn their commission. All applicants must have been accepted at a college or university offering the AFROTC 4-year program and must have a cumulative college GPA of 2.5 or higher. Their Air Force Officer Qualifying Test (AFOQT) scores must be at least 15 on the verbal and 10 on the quantitative. Applicants who have not completed 24 units of college work must have an ACT composite score of 26 or higher or an SAT score of 1240 or higher. U.S. citizenship is required. All academic majors are eligible.

Financial data Participants receive a stipend of $450 to $500 per month and an allowance of $900 per year for books. No other scholarship funding is provided.

Duration 2 years (no more and no less).

Additional information Upon completing their degree, selectees are commissioned as officers in the Air Force with a 4-year service obligation. Further information is available from base education service officers or an Air Force ROTC unit. Recipients must attend a school with annual tuition and fees less than $18,000 per year. They are not allowed to pay the difference to attend a higher cost school.

Number awarded Varies each year.

Deadline October of each year.

[456]
RANGER MEMORIAL SCHOLARSHIPS
National Ranger Memorial Foundation
Attn: Executive Secretary
P.O. Box 53369
Fort Benning, GA 31995
(706) 687-0906   E-mail: rangermemorial@gmail.com
Web: www.rangermemorial.com/scholarship

Summary To provide financial assistance for college to U.S. Army Rangers and their descendants.

Eligibility This program is open to Rangers from any era and their descendants; some awards (those offered by the Ranger Battalions Association of WWII) are limited to descendants of Rangers who served during the World War II era. Applicants must be graduating high school seniors or students currently enrolled at an accredited 2- or 4-year educational or technical institution. They must have a GPA of 3.0 or higher. Along with their application, they must submit information on their leadership activities, future goals and how they plan to attain those, and honors and awards received to date. Financial need is not considered in the selection process.

Financial data The stipend is $1,000.

Duration 1 year.

Additional information The National Ranger Memorial Foundation began awarding scholarships in 1999. The Ranger Battalions Association of WWII became a partner in 2007 and offered additional scholarships to descendants of World War II era Rangers.

Number awarded 49 each year: 45 offered by the National Ranger Memorial Foundation and 4 by the Ranger Battalions Association of WWII.

Deadline May of each year.

[457]
RECYCLING RESEARCH FOUNDATION VETERANS SCHOLARSHIP PROGRAM
Institute of Scrap Recycling Industries
Attn: Recycling Research Foundation, Inc.
1250 H Street, N.W., Suite 400
Washington, DC 20005
(202) 662-8524   Fax: (202) 624-9256
E-mail: ngrant@isri.org
Web: www.isri.org/about-isri/recycling-research-foundation

Summary To provide financial assistance to veterans interested in working on an undergraduate degree.

Eligibility This program is open to veterans who served at least 2 years on active duty or at least 4 years in a reserve capacity. Although the program is focused on those who have completed military service, it does not exclude members of the Ready Reserve who are in a non-drill pay or non-drill status. Applicants must be interested in enrolling at an accredited 4-year college or university, community college, or trade or vocational school. They must be U.S. citizens. Along with their application, they must submit essays on 1) how their military service changed their life; and 2) their professional goals and how this scholarship will help them achieve those.
Financial data The stipend is $2,000 per year. Funds are paid directly to the recipient's school.
Duration 1 year; may be renewed up to 3 additional years, provided the recipient maintains a GPA of 2.5 or higher.
Additional information This program began in 2013.
Number awarded 1 or more each year.
Deadline May of each year.

[458]
RHODE ISLAND NATIONAL GUARD STATE TUITION ASSISTANCE PROGRAM

Rhode Island National Guard
Joint Force Headquarters
Attn: Education Office
645 New London Avenue
Cranston, RI 02920-3097
(401) 275-4039 Fax: (401) 275-4014
E-mail: christopher.a.toti.mil@mail.mil
Web: www.vets.ri.gov/includes/benefits/education/stap.php

Summary To provide financial support to members of the National Guard in Rhode Island interested in attending college or graduate school in the state.
Eligibility This program is open to active members of the Rhode Island National Guard in good standing who are currently satisfactorily participating in all unit training assemblies and annual training periods. Applicants must have at least 1 year of service remaining. They must be enrolled in or planning to enroll in an associate, bachelor's, or master's degree program at a public institution in the state.
Financial data Qualified Guard members are exempt from payment of tuition for up to 5 courses per semester.
Duration 1 semester; may be renewed.
Additional information This program began in 1999. The designated institutions are the University of Rhode Island, Rhode Island College, and the Community College of Rhode Island.
Number awarded Varies each year.
Deadline Deadline not specified.

[459]
RICHARD W. COLLINS III LEADERSHIP WITH HONOR SCHOLARSHIPS

Maryland Higher Education Commission
Attn: Office of Student Financial Assistance
6 North Liberty Street, Ground Suite
Baltimore, MD 21201
(410) 767-3300 Toll Free: (800) 974-0203
Fax: (410) 332-0250 TDD: (800) 735-2258
E-mail: osfamail.mhec@maryland.gov
Web: www.mhec.maryland.gov

Summary To provide financial assistance to minority students who are enrolled in ROTC programs at designated universities in Maryland.
Eligibility This program is open to full-time students participating in an ROTC program at Bowie State University, Coppin State University, Morgan State University, or University of Maryland Eastern Shore. Applicants must be a member of a minority group or another group historically underrepresented in ROTC programs. They must be able to qualify for in-state tuition.
Financial data The stipend is at least $1,000 per year.
Duration 1 year; may be renewed up to 3 additional years, provided the recipient remains eligible for in-state tuition and meets satisfactory academic progress requirements.
Number awarded Varies each year.
Deadline July of each year.

[460]
ROBERT W. BRUNSMAN MEMORIAL SCHOLARSHIP

International Military Community Executives' Association
Attn: Scholarship Committee
14080 Nacogdoches Road, Suite 329
San Antonio, TX 78247-1944
(940) 463-5145 Fax: (866) 369-2435
E-mail: imcea@imcea.org
Web: www.imcea.org/awards/scholarship-info

Summary To provide financial assistance to members of the International Military Community Executives' Association (IMCEA) who are working in the field of military morale, welfare, and recreation (MWR) and currently enrolled in college or graduate school.
Eligibility This program is open to regular IMCEA members who are currently employed in the field of military MWR. Applicants must be already enrolled at a college or university, either on-campus or online, and taking undergraduate or graduate courses related to MWR. Along with their application, they must submit a 2-page essay comparing other professional organizations with which they have been involved, the value they think IMCEA provides, and how IMCEA can continue to fulfill their professional needs and provide outstanding service in the coming years. Selection is based on that essay, participation in IMCEA activities, and involvement in military MWR services.
Financial data The stipend is $1,000.
Duration 1 year.
Additional information Regular membership in IMCEA is open to Army, Air Force, Navy, Marine Corps, and Coast Guard personnel who provide MWR services at military installations and bases worldwide.
Number awarded 1 each year.
Deadline June of each year.

SCHOLARSHIPS: MILITARY PERSONNEL

[461]
ROSAMOND P. HAEBERLE MEMORIAL SCHOLARSHIP

Daughters of the American Revolution-Michigan State Society
c/o LuDean Peters, Memorial Scholarship Committee
18403 Doris Street
Livonia, MI 48152
(248) 478-1345   E-mail: lu85lar@hotmail.com
Web: www.michdar.org

Summary To provide financial assistance to Michigan veterans and military personnel interested in attending college in the state.

Eligibility This program is open to residents of Michigan who have served on active duty in the U.S. armed forces (including Reserves and National Guard) for at least 6 continuous months and are either currently serving in the armed forces or have received a separation from active duty under honorable conditions. Applicants must be currently accepted to and/or enrolled at a 2- or 4-year accredited college, university, or trade/technical school in Michigan. They must be enrolled at least half time and have a cumulative high school or undergraduate GPA of 2.5 or higher. Along with their application, they must submit a 1-page essay on what serving their country has meant to them and how it has influenced their future goals and priorities. Selection is based on academic performance, extracurricular activities, community service, potential to succeed in an academic environment, financial need, and military service record.

Financial data The stipend is $1,500.
Duration 1 year.
Additional information This program began in 2007.
Number awarded At least 1 each year.
Deadline January of each year.

[462]
RUARK-WIGHT FAMILY SCHOLARSHIP

Marines' Memorial Association
c/o Marines Memorial Club and Hotel
609 Sutter Street
San Francisco, CA 94102
(415) 673-6672, ext. 293   Toll Free: (800) 5-MARINE
Fax: (415) 441-3649
E-mail: scholarship@marineclub.com
Web: www.marinesmemorial.org/members/scholarships

Summary To provide financial assistance to veterans, military personnel, and their families who are interested in attending college or graduate school to work on a degree in any field.

Eligibility This program is open to students who meet 1 of the following requirements: 1) have served honorably or is currently serving in any branch of the U.S. armed forces; or 2) is the spouse or child of a person who served honorably or is currently serving in any branch of the U.S. armed forces. Applicants must be enrolled as full-time sophomores, juniors, seniors or graduate students working on a degree in any field. They must have a GPA of 2.5 or higher. Membership in the sponsoring organization is not required for student veterans. Along with their application, they must submit an essay of up to 500 words on why they chose their specific path of study, what they hope to accomplish after graduation with their degree, and how their efforts will benefit others in their community. Selection is based on the essay, academic merit, references, and financial need.

Financial data The stipend is $5,000 per year.
Duration 1 year; recipients may reapply for up to 3 additional years.
Number awarded 1 each year.
Deadline April of each year.

[463]
RUBY GONZALES SCHOLARSHIP

Louisiana National Guard Enlisted Association Auxiliary
c/o Cheryl L. McGlothin, Scholarship Committee
2911 Effie Highway
Deville, LA 71328
(318) 253-8834
Web: www.langea.org/langea-auxiliary

Summary To provide financial assistance to members of the Louisiana National Guard Enlisted Association (LANGEA) and their dependents who plan to attend college in any state.

Eligibility This program is open to LANGEA members, their spouses and unmarried dependent children, and the unmarried spouses and unmarried dependent children of deceased members who were in good standing at the time of their death. Applicants must be enrolled or planning to enroll full time at an accredited college, university, trade school, or business school in any state. Along with their application, they must submit a letter specifying their reasons for their desire to continue their education and why they need financial assistance.

Financial data The stipend is $2,000.
Duration 1 year; nonrenewable.
Number awarded 2 each year.
Deadline February of each year.

[464]
SAN ANTONIO POST SAME SCHOLARSHIPS

Society of American Military Engineers-San Antonio Post
Attn: Scholarship Awards Committee
20770 U.S. Highway 281 N, Suite 108
PMB 451
San Antonio, TX 78258-7500
(210) 355-1355   E-mail: dlg@mocasystems.com
Web: www.same-satx.org

Summary To provide financial assistance to students (especially those participating in ROTC) who are majoring in designated fields at colleges and universities in Texas.

Eligibility This program is open to full-time students majoring in architecture, community planning, construction science or management, or a field of science, technology, engineering, or mathematics (STEM) at a college or university in Texas. Applicants must have a GPA of 2.0 or higher. Preference is given to students participating in an ROTC program and planning a career in the U.S. Army, Navy, Marine Corps, Coast Guard, or Air Force. Selection is based on academic achievement, leadership, and active participation in social, community, and extracurricular activities. Financial need is not considered, but students receiving a full scholarship from another source are not eligible.

Financial data Stipends are $5,000 for the named awards or from $1,000 to $4,000 for the general scholarships.

Duration 1 year; named awards are nonrenewable, but all recipients may reapply for general scholarships.
Additional information This program includes the following named awards: the General Edgar Jadwin Scholarship, the Brigadier General Hubert O. "Hub" Johnson Scholarship, the Colonel William "Bill" Myers Scholarship, the John Hill Carruth Scholarship, the Larry Martin Small Business Scholarship, and the Thomas Russell Scholarship. Recipients are asked to join the Society of American Military Engineers (SAME) as a student member.
Number awarded Varies each year; recently, this program awarded the 6 named scholarships at $5,000 each and 5 other scholarships that provided a total of $10,500.
Deadline October of each year.

[465]
SAPA ANNUAL SCHOLARSHIP AWARDS

Society of Army Physician Assistants
Attn: Scholarship Committee
P.O. Box 623
Monmouth, IL 61462
(309) 734-5446   Fax: (309) 734-4489
E-mail: orpotter@aol.com
Web: www.sapa.org/scholarships

Summary To provide financial assistance to members of the Society of Army Physician Assistants (SAPA) and their families interested in attending college in any state to major in any field.
Eligibility This program is open to SAPA members, spouses of SAPA members, dependent children under 24 years of age of SAPA members, and spouses and children of deceased SAPA members. Applicants must be high school seniors or students currently enrolled at a college, university, or vocational school and working on a degree in any field or a license or certificate to practice a trade. There is no application form; interested parties submit a letter of introduction that includes why the grant is needed, educational goals, goals for the future, and anything else they feel would be of interest to the selection committee; a letter of acceptance from a school; a list of activities and achievements; and transcripts.
Financial data The stipend is $1,000.
Duration 1 year.
Additional information This program began in 2012. Membership in SAPA is open to graduates of approved physician assistant training programs commissioned as a physician assistant in the Active Duty Army, Army National Guard, Army Reserve, or honorably retired from those branches of service; they must also be members of the American Academy of Physician Assistants who have designated SAPA as their constituent chapter.
Number awarded 3 each year.
Deadline January of each year.

[466]
SCHOLARSHIPS FOR OUTSTANDING AIRMEN TO ROTC (SOAR)

U.S. Air Force
Attn: Headquarters AFROTC/RRUE
Jeanne M. Holm Center for Officer Accession and Citizen Development
60 West Maxwell Boulevard, Building 835
Maxwell AFB, AL 36112-6501
(334) 953-5122   Toll Free: (866) 4-AFROTC
Fax: (334) 953-6167   E-mail: afrotc.rrue@us.af.mil
Web: www.afrotc.com/scholarships/enlisted/ascp-soar

Summary To allow selected enlisted Air Force personnel to earn a bachelor's degree by providing financial assistance for full-time college study.
Eligibility Eligible to participate in this program are enlisted members of the Air Force who have completed from 1 to 6 years of active duty and have at least 1 year time-on-station. Candidates must be nominated by their commanding officers and be accepted at a college or university offering the AFROTC 4-year program. Airmen with 24 semester hours or more of graded college credit must have a cumulative GPA of 2.5 or higher; airmen with less than 24 semester hours must have an ACT score of 26 or higher or an SAT score of 1240 or higher. All applicants must earn Air Force Officer Qualifying Test (AFOQT) scores of 15 or more on the verbal scale and 10 or more on the quantitative scale. They must complete 24 semesters of mathematics and physical sciences or 4 semesters of a foreign language and major in an approved field; for a list of currently-approved majors, contact the program. U.S. citizenship is required. When the recipients complete the program, they may be no more than 31 years of age.
Financial data Selectees receive a tuition and fees scholarship of up to $18,000 per year, an annual textbook allowance of $900, and a monthly non-taxable stipend of $300 to $500.
Duration 2 to 4 years.
Additional information Upon completing their degree, selectees are commissioned as officers in the Air Force with a 4-year service obligation. Further information is available from base education service officers or an Air Force ROTC unit.
Number awarded 51 each year.
Deadline October of each year.

[467]
SCNGF ACADEMIC EXCELLENCE LEADERSHIP SCHOLARSHIPS

National Guard Association of South Carolina
Attn: South Carolina National Guard Foundation
132 Pickens Street
P.O. Box 7606
Columbia, SC 29202
(803) 254-8456   Toll Free: (800) 822-3235
Fax: (803) 254-3869   E-mail: dianne@scngf.org
Web: www.scngf.org/scngfscholarshipapplication

Summary To provide financial assistance to South Carolina National Guard members and their dependents who are interested in attending college or graduate school in any state.
Eligibility This program is open to members of the South Carolina National Guard and dependents of active or retired

members. Applicants must be enrolled or planning to enroll full time at a 4-year college or university in any state as an undergraduate student. Guard members, but not dependents, are also eligible to attend graduate school. Applicants must have a GPA of 3.5 or higher and a record of involvement and leadership in school, civic, and/or community activities. Selection is based on excellence in academics and leadership; financial need is not considered.
Financial data The stipend is $1,500 per year. Funds are disbursed directly to the recipient's institution.
Duration 1 year; may be renewed up to 3 additional years.
Number awarded Varies each year; recently, this sponsor awarded a total of 75 scholarships through both of its programs.
Deadline February of each year.

[468]
SCNGF FINANCIAL NEED/ACADEMIC ACHIEVEMENT SCHOLARSHIPS
National Guard Association of South Carolina
Attn: South Carolina National Guard Foundation
132 Pickens Street
P.O. Box 7606
Columbia, SC 29202
(803) 254-8456   Toll Free: (800) 822-3235
Fax: (803) 254-3869   E-mail: dianne@scngf.org
Web: www.scngf.org/scngfscholarshipapplication
Summary To provide financial assistance to South Carolina National Guard members and their dependents who are interested in attending college or graduate school in any state and can demonstrate financial need.
Eligibility This program is open to members of the South Carolina National Guard and dependents of active or retired members. Applicants must be enrolled or planning to enroll full time at a college or university in any state as an undergraduate student. Guard members, but not dependents, are also eligible to attend graduate school. Applicants must have a GPA of 2.5 or higher and a record of involvement and leadership in school, civic, and/or community activities. High school seniors must also submit SAT and/or ACT scores. Selection is based on excellence in academics and leadership and on financial need.
Financial data The stipend is $1,000 per year. Funds are disbursed directly to the recipient's institution.
Duration 1 year; may be renewed up to 3 additional years.
Number awarded Varies each year; recently, this sponsor awarded a total of 75 scholarships through both of its programs.
Deadline February of each year.

[469]
SDNGEA AUXILIARY SCHOLARSHIPS
South Dakota National Guard Enlisted Association Auxiliary
c/o Alicia Engebretson, Scholarship Committee
7321 West 66th Street
Sioux Falls, SD 57106
(605) 413-7395   E-mail: alicia.engebretson@poet.com
Web: sdngea.com/auxiliary/scholarships
Summary To provide financial assistance to members of the South Dakota National Guard Enlisted Association (SDN-GEA) Auxiliary and their dependents who are interested in attending college in any state.
Eligibility This program is open to current members of the SDNGEA Auxiliary, their unmarried children and grandchildren up to 26 years of age, and their spouses. Applicants must be graduating high school seniors or undergraduate students at a college, university, or vocational school in any state. They must submit a letter outlining specific goals to continue their education and why aid is required. Selection is based on academic achievement, character, leadership characteristics, and financial need.
Financial data The stipend is $1,000. Funds are paid directly to the recipient's school.
Duration 1 year; nonrenewable.
Number awarded 2 each year.
Deadline March of each year.

[470]
SEAMAN TO ADMIRAL-21 CORE PROGRAM
U.S. Navy
Attn: Commander, Naval Service Training Command
250 Dallas Street, Suite A
Pensacola, FL 32508-5268
(850) 452-9563   Fax: (850) 452-2486
E-mail: PNSC_STA21@navy.mil
Web: www.public.navy.mil
Summary To allow outstanding enlisted Navy personnel to attend a college or university with an NROTC unit, complete a bachelor's degree, and receive a commission.
Eligibility This program is open to U.S. citizens who are currently serving on active duty in the U.S. Navy or Naval Reserve, including Full Time Support (FTS), Selected Reserves (SELRES), and Navy Reservists on active duty, except for those on active duty for training (ACDUTRA). Applicants must be high school graduates (or GED recipients) who are able to complete requirements for a baccalaureate degree in 36 months or less. They may apply to the core program or a target group option. The core program allows participants the most flexibility in selecting a major and requesting schools to attend. When they complete their degree requirements, they must be younger than 31 years of age. Within the past 3 years, they must have taken the SAT (and achieved scores of at least 500 on the mathematics section and 500 on the evidence based reading and writing or critical reading section) or the ACT (and achieved a score of at least 21 on the mathematics portion and 20 on the English portion).
Financial data Awardees continue to receive their regular Navy pay and allowances while they attend college on a full-time basis. They also receive reimbursement for tuition, fees, and books up to $10,000 per year. If base housing is available, they are eligible to live there. Participants are not eligible to receive benefits under the Navy's Tuition Assistance Program (TA), the Montgomery GI Bill (MGIB), the Navy College Fund, or the Veterans Educational Assistance Program (VEAP).
Duration Selectees are supported for up to 36 months of full-time, year-round study or completion of a bachelor's degree, as long as they maintain a GPA of 2.5 or higher.
Additional information This program began in 2001 as a replacement for the Seaman to Admiral Program (established in 1994), the Enlisted Commissioning Program, and other

specialized programs for sailors to earn a commission. Upon acceptance into the program, selectees attend the Naval Science Institute (NSI) in Newport, Rhode Island for an 8-week program in the fundamental core concepts of being a naval officer (navigation, engineering, weapons, military history and justice, etc.). They then enter a college or university with an NROTC unit or affiliation to work full time on a bachelor's degree. They become members of and drill with the NROTC unit. When core program participants complete their degree, they are commissioned as ensigns in the United States Naval Reserve and assigned to an Unrestricted Line (URL) Navy officer designator upon commissioning. After commissioning, 5 years of active service are required.

Number awarded Varies each year.

Deadline June of each year.

[471]
SENATOR DANIEL K. INOUYE MEMORIAL SCHOLARSHIP

Japanese American Veterans Association
Attn: Chris DeRosa, Scholarship Committee Chair
P.O. Box 341198
Bethesda, MD 20827
E-mail: javascholarship222@gmail.com
Web: www.java.wildapricot.org

Summary To provide financial assistance for college or graduate school to relatives of Japanese American veterans who plan a career in the military or public service.

Eligibility This program is open to students who 1) have completed at least 1 year of an undergraduate program or are currently enrolled in graduate school and are preparing for a career in the military or public service; 2) are currently enrolled in a university or college ROTC program or the U.S. Marine Corps Platoon Leaders Course but are not receiving an ROTC scholarship; or 3) are disabled veterans. Applicants must also be 1) a direct or collateral descendant of a person who served with the 442nd Regimental Combat Team, the 100th Infantry Battalion, Military Intelligence Service, 1399th Engineering Construction Battalion, or other unit associated with those during or after World War II; or 2) a member or child of a member of the Japanese American Veterans Association (JAVA) whose membership extends back at least 1 year. Along with their application, they must submit a 500-word essay on their plan and vision to serve America through public service or the military.

Financial data The stipend is $5,000.

Duration 1 year.

Number awarded 1 each year.

Deadline March of each year.

[472]
SFC CURTIS MANCINI MEMORIAL SCHOLARSHIPS

Association of the United States Army-Rhode Island
   Chapter
c/o LTC Robert A. Galvanin, President
31 Canoe River Drive
Mansfield, MA 02048
(508) 339-5301   E-mail: bpje5310@verizon.net
Web: www.riroa.org/ausari/scholarship.htm

Summary To provide financial assistance to members of the Rhode Island Chapter of the Association of the United States Army (AUSA) and their families who are interested in attending college or graduate school in any state.

Eligibility This program is open to members of the AUSA Rhode Island Chapter and their family members (spouses, children, and grandchildren). Applicants must be high school seniors or graduates accepted at an accredited college, university, or vocational/technical school in any state or current undergraduate or graduate students. Along with their application, they must submit a 250-word essay on why they feel their achievements should qualify them for this award. Selection is based on academic and individual achievements; financial need is not considered. Special consideration is given to students or graduates of Lincoln High School in Lincoln, Rhode Island (the alma mater of this program's namesake), especially those preparing for a career in law enforcement or enrolled or planning to enroll in Army ROTC.

Financial data The stipend is $1,000.

Duration 1 year.

Additional information Membership in the AUSA is open to everyone who supports a strong national defense, with special concern for the Army. That includes Regular Army, National Guard, Army Reserve, government civilians, retired soldiers, Wounded Warriors, veterans, concerned citizens and family members.

Number awarded Several each year.

Deadline April of each year.

[473]
SGM DAWN KILPATRICK MEMORIAL AUSA SCHOLARSHIP

Association of the United States Army
Attn: Scholarships
2425 Wilson Boulevard
Arlington, VA 22201
(703) 841-4300   Toll Free: (800) 336-4570
E-mail: scholarships@ausa.org
Web: www.ausa.org/resources/scholarships

Summary To recognize and reward, with funding for additional education, Army mid-level and senior non-commissioned officers who demonstrate outstanding leadership.

Eligibility This award is presented to Army personnel in the Active component, Army Reserve or Army National Guard. Applicants must be a CMF 46 sergeant to sergeant major with fewer than 18 years of active service; hold a primary MOS of 46Q, 46R, or 46Z; and have at least 3 years of service remaining after receipt of the scholarship. They must exemplify "the Army's vision and influence others in shaping future leaders." Along with their application, they must submit 1) a 1,000-word essay on the future of Army Public Affairs and how the NCO can impact it; 2) a letter of recommendation from their supervisor explaining how they best exemplify the Army's vision, care for soldiers, and work toward shaping our future leaders; and 3) their enlisted record brief.

Financial data The award consists of $4,000 to assist in covering educational costs that Army tuition assistance does not pay, such as instructional fees, laboratory fees, and books.

Duration The award is presented annually.

Additional information This award was established in 1999.

Number awarded 1 each year.

Deadline June of each year.

[474]
SIGMA CHI MILITARY SERVICE SCHOLARSHIPS
Sigma Chi Foundation
Attn: Scholarship Committee
1714 Hinman Avenue
Evanston, IL 60201
(847) 869-3655, ext. 270   Fax: (847) 869-4906
E-mail: foundation@sigmachi.org
Web: www.sigmachi.org

Summary To provide financial assistance to undergraduate and graduate student members of Sigma Chi who are serving or have served in the military.

Eligibility This program is open to undergraduate and graduate brothers of the fraternity who are currently serving or have served in the military (Army, Navy, Air Force, Marines, Coast Guard, or National Guard). They must have earned a GPA of 2.5 or higher and have completed at least 2 semesters of undergraduate study. ROTC students are not eligible.

Financial data The stipend is $1,000. Funds are to be used for tuition/fees only and are paid directly to the recipient's school.

Duration 1 year.

Number awarded Varies each year; recently, 9 were awarded.

Deadline May of each year.

[475]
SIMULTANEOUS MEMBERSHIP PROGRAM (SMP)
U.S. Army
Attn: U.S. Army Cadet Command
G2 Incentives Division
1307 Third Avenue
Fort Knox, KY 40121-2725
(502) 624-7371   Toll Free: (888) 550-ARMY
Fax: (502) 624-6937
E-mail: usarmy.knox.usacc.mbx.train2lead@mail.mil
Web: www.goarmy.com/rotc/enroll/enlisted.html

Summary To provide financial assistance to individuals who serve simultaneously in the Army National Guard or Army Reserve and the Army Reserve Officers' Training Corps (ROTC) while they are in college.

Eligibility Students who are members of the Army National Guard or the Army Reserve and Army ROTC at the same time are eligible for this assistance. Applicants must have completed basic training or the equivalent, have at least 4 years remaining on their current military obligation, be full-time college juniors, have a GPA of 2.0 or higher, and be U.S. citizens.

Financial data Advanced ROTC Simultaneous Membership Program (SMP) participants are paid at the rate of at least a Sergeant E-5 for their Guard or Reserve training assemblies (recently, $329 to $412.60 per month, depending on the number of years of service), plus an ROTC stipend for 10 months of the year at $450 per month during their junior year and $500 per month during their senior year.

Duration Up to 2 years.

Additional information Participants serve as officer trainees in their Guard or Reserve units and, under the close supervision of a commissioned officer, perform duties commensurate with those of a second lieutenant. Cadets who successfully complete the SMP program graduate with a commission as a second lieutenant. Once commissioned, they may continue to serve in their Guard or Reserve units, or they may apply for active duty in the U.S. Army.

Number awarded Varies each year.

Deadline Deadline not specified.

[476]
SMA LEON VAN AUTREVE SCHOLARSHIPS
Association of the United States Army
Attn: Scholarships
2425 Wilson Boulevard
Arlington, VA 22201
(703) 841-4300   Toll Free: (800) 336-4570
E-mail: scholarships@ausa.org
Web: www.ausa.org/resources/scholarships

Summary To provide financial assistance to members of the Association of the United States Army (AUSA) who are interested in attending college.

Eligibility This program is open to AUSA members who are enrolled or accepted at an accredited college or university to work on a degree in any field. Along with their application, they must submit a 1-page autobiography, 2 letters of recommendation, a letter describing their career aspirations (including their course of study and plans for completion of a degree), and a transcript of high school or college grades (depending on which they are currently attending). Selection is based on academic merit and personal achievement. Financial need is not normally a selection criterion but in some cases of extreme need it may be used as a factor; the lack of financial need, however, is never a cause for non-selection.

Financial data The stipend ranges from $2,000 t0 $25,000; funds are sent directly to the recipient's college or university.

Duration 1 year.

Additional information Membership in the AUSA is open to everyone who supports a strong national defense, with special concern for the Army. That includes Regular Army, National Guard, Army Reserve, government civilians, retired soldiers, Wounded Warriors, veterans, concerned citizens and family members. This program is sponsored by the USAA Foundation.

Number awarded Varies each year; recently, 1 at $25,000, 1 at $10,000, 1 at $5,000, and 5 at $2,000 were awarded.

Deadline June of each year.

[477]
SOUTH CAROLINA NATIONAL GUARD COLLEGE ASSISTANCE PROGRAM
South Carolina Commission on Higher Education
Attn: Director, Student Affairs
1122 Lady Street, Suite 300
Columbia, SC 29201
(803) 737-2244   Toll Free: (877) 349-7183
Fax: (803) 737-2297   E-mail: kwoodfaulk@che.sc.gov
Web: www.che.sc.gov

Summary To provide financial assistance to members of the South Carolina National Guard who are interested in attending college in the state.

Eligibility This program is open to members of the South Carolina National Guard who are in good standing and have not already received a bachelor's or graduate degree. Applicants must be admitted, enrolled, and classified as a degree-seeking full- or part-time student at an eligible institution in South Carolina. They may not be taking continuing education or graduate course work. U.S. citizenship or permanent resident status is required.

Financial data This program provides full payment of the cost of attendance, including tuition, fees, and textbooks, to a maximum of $9,000 per year for members of the Air National Guard or $4,500 for members of the Army National Guard. The cumulative total of all benefits received from this program may not exceed $18,000.

Duration Support is provided for up to 130 semester hours of study, provided the Guard member maintains satisfactory academic progress as defined by the institution.

Additional information This program is administered by the South Carolina Commission on Higher Education in consultation with the state Adjutant General. The General Assembly established this program in 2007 as a replacement for the South Carolina National Guard Student Loan Repayment Program. Enlisted personnel are required to continue their service in the National Guard during all terms of courses covered by the benefit received. Officers must continue their service with the National Guard for at least 4 years after completion of the most recent award or degree completion.

Number awarded Varies each year.

Deadline Deadline not specified.

[478]
SOUTH DAKOTA USAA SCHOLARSHIP

South Dakota National Guard Enlisted Association
c/o Derek Jaeger, Scholarship Chair
7713 West 53rd Street
Sioux Falls, SD 57106
E-mail: derek.e.jaeger.mil@mail.mil
Web: sdngea.com/programs/scholarships

Summary To provide financial assistance to members of the South Dakota National Guard Enlisted Association (SDNGEA) and their dependents who are interested in attending college in any state.

Eligibility This program is open to current members of the SDNGEA and their dependents. Applicants must be graduating high school seniors or full-time undergraduate students at a college or university in any state. They must submit a 300-page autobiography that includes their experiences to date and their hopes and plans for the future. Selection is based on the essay; awards, honors, and offices in high school, college, or trade school; GPA and ACT/SAT scores; letters of recommendation; and extracurricular and community activities and honors.

Financial data The stipend is $1,000.

Duration 1 year.

Additional information This program is sponsored by the USAA Insurance Corporation.

Number awarded 1 each year.

Deadline March of each year.

[479]
SPECIAL DUTY OFFICER (INFORMATION PROFESSIONAL) OPTION OF THE SEAMAN TO ADMIRAL-21 PROGRAM

U.S. Navy
Attn: Commander, Naval Service Training Command
250 Dallas Street, Suite A
Pensacola, FL 32508-5268
(850) 452-9563   Fax: (850) 452-2486
E-mail: PNSC_STA21@navy.mil
Web: www.public.navy.mil

Summary To allow outstanding enlisted Navy personnel to attend a college or university with an NROTC unit, complete a bachelor's degree, and receive a commission as a special duty officer (information professional).

Eligibility This program is open to U.S. citizens who are currently serving on active duty in the U.S. Navy or Naval Reserve, including Full Time Support (FTS), Selected Reserves (SELRES), and Navy Reservists on active duty, except for those on active duty for training (ACDUTRA). Applicants must be high school graduates (or GED recipients) who are at least 18 years of age and able to complete requirements for a baccalaureate degree in 36 months or less. Sailors in all ratings are eligible. When they complete their degree requirements, they must be younger than 35 years of age. Within the past 3 years, they must have taken the SAT (and achieved scores of at least 500 on the mathematics section and 500 on the evidence based reading and writing or critical reading section) or the ACT (and achieved a score of at least 21 on the mathematics portion and 20 on the English portion). They must also meet relevant medical standards. Only the following fields of study qualify: information technology, information management, computer science, computer network administration, information assurance, information security, electronic engineering technology, or computer/software programming.

Financial data Awardees continue to receive their regular Navy pay and allowances while they attend college on a full-time basis. They also receive reimbursement for tuition, fees, and books up to $10,000 per year. If base housing is available, they are eligible to live there. Participants are not eligible to receive benefits under the Navy's Tuition Assistance Program (TA), the Montgomery GI Bill (MGIB), the Navy College Fund, or the Veterans Educational Assistance Program (VEAP).

Duration Selectees are supported for up to 36 months of full-time, year-round study or completion of a bachelor's degree, as long as they maintain a GPA of 2.5 or higher.

Additional information This program began in 2001 as a replacement for the Seaman to Admiral Program (established in 1994), the Enlisted Commissioning Program, and other specialized programs for sailors to earn a commission. Upon acceptance into the program, selectees attend the Naval Science Institute (NSI) in Newport, Rhode Island for an 8-week program in the fundamental core concepts of being a naval officer (navigation, engineering, weapons, military history and justice, etc.). They then enter a college or university with an NROTC unit or affiliation to work full time on a bachelor's degree. They become members of and drill with the NROTC unit. When they complete their degree, they are commissioned as ensigns in the United States Naval Reserve and assigned to initial training as a special duty officer (information warfare); that designation was formerly special duty officer (cryptologic). After commissioning, 5 years of active service are required.

Number awarded Varies each year.

Deadline June of each year.

[480]
SPECIAL WARFARE OPTION OF THE SEAMAN TO ADMIRAL-21 PROGRAM

U.S. Navy
Attn: Commander, Naval Service Training Command
250 Dallas Street, Suite A
Pensacola, FL 32508-5268
(850) 452-9563   Fax: (850) 452-2486
E-mail: PNSC_STA21@navy.mil
Web: www.public.navy.mil

Summary To allow outstanding enlisted Navy personnel to attend a college or university with an NROTC unit, complete a bachelor's degree, and receive a commission as a special warfare officer.

Eligibility This program is open to U.S. citizens who are currently serving on active duty in the U.S. Navy or Naval Reserve, including Full Time Support (FTS), Selected Reserves (SELRES), and Navy Reservists on active duty, except for those on active duty for training (ACDUTRA). Only males are eligible for this option. They must be a member of the SEAL community. Applicants must be high school graduates (or GED recipients) who are able to complete requirements for a baccalaureate degree in 36 months or less. When they complete their degree requirements, they must be younger than 29 years of age. That age limitation may be adjusted upward for active service on a month-for-month basis up to 24 months, and waivers are considered for enlisted personnel who possess particularly exceptional qualifications if they can complete their degree prior to their 35th birthday. Within the past 3 years, they must have taken the SAT (and achieved scores of at least 500 on the mathematics section and 500 on the evidence based reading and writing or critical reading section) or the ACT (and achieved a score of at least 21 on the mathematics portion and 20 on the English portion). They must also meet physical regulations that include qualification for diving duty and/or combat swimmer. Preference is given to applicants who plan to major in a technical field (e.g., chemistry, computer science, engineering, mathematics, oceanography, operations analysis, physical sciences, or physics).

Financial data Awardees continue to receive their regular Navy pay and allowances while they attend college on a full-time basis. They also receive reimbursement for tuition, fees, and books up to $10,000 per year. If base housing is available, they are eligible to live there. Participants are not eligible to receive benefits under the Navy's Tuition Assistance Program (TA), the Montgomery GI Bill (MGIB), the Navy College Fund, or the Veterans Educational Assistance Program (VEAP).

Duration Selectees are supported for up to 36 months of full-time, year-round study or completion of a bachelor's degree, as long as they maintain a GPA of 2.5 or higher.

Additional information This program began in 2001 as a replacement for the Seaman to Admiral Program (established in 1994), the Enlisted Commissioning Program, and other specialized programs for sailors to earn a commission. Upon acceptance into the program, selectees attend the Naval Science Institute (NSI) in Newport, Rhode Island for an 8-week program in the fundamental core concepts of being a naval officer (navigation, engineering, weapons, military history and justice, etc.). They then enter a college or university with an NROTC unit or affiliation to work full time on a bachelor's degree. They become members of and drill with the NROTC unit. When they complete their degree, they are commissioned as ensigns in the United States Naval Reserve and assigned to initial training as a special warfare officer. After commissioning, 5 years of active service are required.

Number awarded Varies each year.

Deadline June of each year.

[481]
SPORTS CLIPS HELP A HERO SCHOLARSHIPS

Veterans of Foreign Wars of the United States
Attn: National Military Services
406 West 34th Street, Suite 216
Kansas City, MO 64111
(816) 756-3390   Toll Free: (866) 789-NEED
E-mail: HelpAHero@vfw.org
Web: www.vfw.org/assistance/student-veterans-support

Summary To provide financial assistance to military personnel and veterans who are interested in attending college.

Eligibility This program is open to military personnel on active duty, retired and honorably discharged veterans, and members of the National Guard or Reserves who have completed basic training and follow-on training. Applicants must be U.S. citizens at the rank of E-5 or below and be able to demonstrate financial need. They must be enrolled or planning to enroll at a VA-approved program or institution of higher education.

Financial data The stipend is $5,000. Funds are paid directly to the recipient's institution.

Duration 1 year.

Additional information This program began in 2014 with support from Sports Clips, Inc.

Number awarded This program attempts to provide support to 115 veterans and military members each year.

Deadline April of each year for fall semester; November of each year for spring semester.

[482]
SR EDUCATION GROUP MILITARY SCHOLARSHIPS

SR Education Group
123 Lake Street South, Site B-1
Kirkland, WA 98033-6401
(425) 605-8898
Web: www.sreducationgroup.org

Summary To provide financial assistance to veterans and active military members and their families who are currently enrolled in college and have high financial need.

Eligibility This program is open to legal residents of any state except Rhode Island who are 1) veterans or active members of the U.S. military; 2) children or spouses of veterans or active military members; or 3) children and spouses of deceased veterans or military members. Children must be younger than 21 years of age or, if enrolled full time, younger than 23. Applicants must be currently enrolled at a college or university and able to demonstrate high financial need. Along with their application, they must submit 3 essays of 300 to 500 words each on 1) how they will apply their degree in the

future and what they anticipate for their first 5 years beyond college; 2) their involvement with the military and how it has influenced their personal development; and 3) any special or family circumstances affecting their financial need.
Financial data The stipend is $5,000.
Duration 1 year.
Additional information This program began in 2010.
Number awarded 4 each year. Since the program began, this sponsor has awarded a total of $547,000 to 141 students at 113 colleges.
Deadline December of each year.

[483]
STATE TUITION ASSISTANCE PROGRAM OF THE TEXAS NATIONAL GUARD

Texas Military Department
Attn: State Tuition Assistance Program
2200 West 35th Street, Building 10
P.O. Box 5218
Austin, TX 78703
(512) 782-5515   E-mail: ng.tx.txarng.mbx.pao@mail.mil
Web: tmd.texas.gov/state-tuition-assistance-program

Summary To provide financial assistance for college or graduate school to members of the Texas National Guard.
Eligibility This program is open to Texas residents who are active, drilling members of the Texas National Guard, the Texas Air Guard, or the State Guard in enlisted pay grades E-1 through E-9, officers 0-1 through O-5, or warrant officers W-1 through W-3. Applicants may be undergraduate or graduate students attending or planning to attend a public or private college or university in Texas. They may qualify for a high need exemption if they meet 1 of the following requirements: non-scholarship ROTC cadet, in first year of undergraduate school with fewer than 30 hours of credit toward an associate or bachelor's degree, not eligible for any other financial aid, or enrolled at a private institution.
Financial data Eligible Guard members receive exemption from up to 6 hours of tuition and mandatory fees at Texas colleges and universities, to a maximum of $2,250 per semester. Guard members who qualify for the high need exemption receive up to 12 hours of tuition and mandatory fees, to a maximum of $4,500 per semester.
Duration Tuition assistance is available for up to 10 semesters or 5 academic years, whichever occurs first.
Number awarded Varies each year; recently, 864 Guard members participated in this program.
Deadline For spring semester, the primary deadline is November of each year (required for high need exemption); the extended deadline is January of each year. For fall semester, the primary deadline is August of each year; the extended deadline is in September.

[484]
SURFACE WARFARE OFFICER OPTION OF THE SEAMAN TO ADMIRAL-21 PROGRAM

U.S. Navy
Attn: Commander, Naval Service Training Command
250 Dallas Street, Suite A
Pensacola, FL 32508-5268
(850) 452-9563   Fax: (850) 452-2486
E-mail: PNSC_STA21@navy.mil
Web: www.public.navy.mil

Summary To allow outstanding enlisted Navy personnel to attend a college or university with an NROTC unit, complete a bachelor's degree, and receive a commission as a surface warfare officer (SWO).
Eligibility This program is open to U.S. citizens who are currently serving on active duty in the U.S. Navy or Naval Reserve, including Full Time Support (FTS), Selected Reserves (SELRES), and Navy Reservists on active duty, except for those on active duty for training (ACDUTRA). Applicants must be high school graduates (or GED recipients) who are able to complete requirements for a baccalaureate degree in 36 months or less. When they complete their degree requirements, they must be younger than 31 years of age. Within the past 3 years, they must have taken the SAT (and achieved scores of at least 500 on the mathematics section and 500 on the evidence based reading and writing or critical reading section) or the ACT (and achieved a score of at least 21 on the mathematics portion and 20 on the English portion). They must also meet relevant medical standards. Preference is given to applicants who plan to major in a technical field (e.g., chemistry, computer science, engineering, mathematics, oceanography, operations analysis, physical sciences, or physics).
Financial data Awardees continue to receive their regular Navy pay and allowances while they attend college on a full-time basis. They also receive reimbursement for tuition, fees, and books up to $10,000 per year. If base housing is available, they are eligible to live there. Participants are not eligible to receive benefits under the Navy's Tuition Assistance Program (TA), the Montgomery GI Bill (MGIB), the Navy College Fund, or the Veterans Educational Assistance Program (VEAP).
Duration Selectees are supported for up to 36 months of full-time, year-round study or completion of a bachelor's degree, as long as they maintain a GPA of 2.5 or higher.
Additional information This program began in 2001 as a replacement for the Seaman to Admiral Program (established in 1994), the Enlisted Commissioning Program, and other specialized programs for sailors to earn a commission. Upon acceptance into the program, selectees attend the Naval Science Institute (NSI) in Newport, Rhode Island for an 8-week program in the fundamental core concepts of being a naval officer (navigation, engineering, weapons, military history and justice, etc.). They then enter a college or university with an NROTC unit or affiliation to work full time on a bachelor's degree. They become members of and drill with the NROTC unit. When they complete their degree, they are commissioned as ensigns in the United States Naval Reserve and assigned to initial training as a surface warfare officer. After commissioning, 5 years of active service are required.
Number awarded Varies each year.
Deadline June of each year.

[485]
TAILHOOK EDUCATIONAL FOUNDATION SCHOLARSHIPS

Tailhook Educational Foundation
9696 Business Park Avenue
San Diego, CA 92131-1643
(858) 689-9223   Toll Free: (800) 322-4665
Fax: (858) 578-8839   E-mail: bethr@tailhook.net
Web: www.tailhook.net/A_Foundation_Index.html

Summary To provide financial assistance for college to personnel associated with naval aviation and their children.
Eligibility This program is open to 1) the children (natural, step, and adopted) and grandchildren of current or former U.S. Navy, Coast Guard, or Marine Corps personnel who served as an aviator, flight officer, or air crewman; or 2) personnel and children and grandchildren of personnel who are serving or have served on board a U.S. Navy aircraft carrier as a member of the ship's company or air wing. Applicants must be enrolled or accepted for enrollment at an accredited college or university. Selection is based on educational and extracurricular achievements, merit, and citizenship.
Financial data The stipend ranges from $2,500 to $15,000.
Duration 1 to 2 years.
Number awarded Varies; usually, more than 100 are awarded each year.
Deadline February of each year.

[486]
TEXAS ARMED SERVICES SCHOLARSHIP PROGRAM

Texas Higher Education Coordinating Board
Attn: Hinson-Hazlewood College Student Loan Program
1200 East Anderson Lane
P.O. Box 12788
Austin, TX 78711-2788
(512) 427-6340   Toll Free: (800) 242-3062
Fax: (512) 427-6420   E-mail: grantinfo@thecb.state.tx.us
Web: www.hhloans.com

Summary To provide scholarship/loans to high school seniors in Texas who plan to participate in an ROTC program at a college in the state and then serve in the U.S. armed forces, the Texas National Guard, or the Texas Air National Guard.
Eligibility This program is open to seniors graduating from high schools in Texas who can meet any 2 of the following requirements: 1) are on track to graduate with the Distinguished Achievement Program (DAP) or International Baccalaureate (IB) Program; 2) have a high school GPA of 3.0 or higher; 3) have an SAT score of 1070 or higher or an ACT score of 23 or higher; or 4) rank in the top third of their class. Applicants must plan to attend a public or private college or university in Texas and enter into a written agreement to complete 4 years of ROTC training, graduate within 6 years, and serve 4 years as a member of the Texas Army or Air Force National Guard, Texas State Guard, United States Coast Guard, Merchant Marine, or as a commissioned officer in the U.S. armed services. They must apply through their state senator or representative.
Financial data The program provides payment of the student's cost of attendance or $10,000, whichever is smaller. If the student fails to comply with the service agreement, the scholarship converts to a loan that must be repaid within 15 years with interest.
Duration 1 year; may be renewed up to 3 additional years.
Additional information This program began in 2010.
Number awarded Varies each year; recently, 246 students received $1,758,369 in assistance from this program.
Deadline Legislators must submit nominations by August of each year.

[487]
THE PFC ROGER W. CUMMINS MEMORIAL SCHOLARSHIP

American Academy of Physician Assistants-Veterans Caucus
Attn: Scholarship Program
P.O. Box 362
Ossining, NY 10562
(803) 328-1864   Fax: (704) 838-8494
E-mail: rmunsee@veteranscaucus.org
Web: www.veteranscaucus.org/scholarships

Summary To provide financial assistance to Marine Corps and Navy service members or veterans or family members who are studying to become physician assistants.
Eligibility This program is open to U.S. citizens who are currently enrolled in a physician assistant program. Applicants must be active-duty members of the U.S. Marine Corps or Navy Corpsmen who have served with the Marine Corps, veterans of those services, or their spouses or children. Along with their application, they must submit a personal statement about what led them to attend PA school; their background, present, and future intentions; and why they deserve to receive a scholarship. Selection is based on military honors and awards received, civic and college honors and awards received, professional memberships and activities, potential for future achievement, and GPA.
Financial data The stipend is $2,000.
Duration 1 year.
Number awarded 1 each year.
Deadline February of each year.

[488]
TILLMAN MILITARY SCHOLARS PROGRAM

Pat Tillman Foundation
222 North Merchandise Mart Plaza, Suite 1212
Chicago, IL 60654
(773) 360-5277
E-mail: scholarships@pattillmanfoundation.org
Web: www.pattillmanfoundation.org/apply-to-be-a-scholar

Summary To provide financial assistance to veterans, active servicemembers, and their spouses who are interested in working on an undergraduate or graduate degree.
Eligibility This program is open to veterans and active servicemembers of all branches of the armed forces from both the pre- and post-September 11 era and their spouses; children are not eligible. Applicants must be enrolled or planning to enroll full time at a 4-year public or private college or university to work on an undergraduate, graduate, or postgraduate degree. Current and former servicemembers must submit 400-word essays on 1) their motivation and decision to serve in the U.S. military and how that decision and experience has changed their life and ambitions; and 2) their educational and career goals, how they will incorporate their military service experience into those goals, and how they intend to continue their service to others and the community. Spouses must submit 400-word essays on 1) their previous service to others and the community; and 2) their educational and career goals, how they will incorporate their service experiences and the impact of their spouse's military service into those goals, and how they intend to continue their service to others and the community. Selection is based on those essays, educational and career ambitions, record of military service, record

of personal achievement, demonstration of service to others in the community, desire to continue such service, and leadership potential.
Financial data The stipend depends on the need of the recipient and the availability of funds; recently, stipends averaged approximately $11,000 per year.
Duration 1 year; may be renewed, provided the recipient maintains a GPA of 3.0 or higher, remains enrolled full time, and documents participation in civic action or community service.
Additional information This program began in 2009.
Number awarded Approximately 60 each year. Since the program began, it has awarded more than $15 million to 580 scholars.
Deadline February of each year.

[489]
TONY LOPEZ SCHOLARSHIP PROGRAM
Louisiana National Guard Enlisted Association
c/o CMSgt John M. Roach, Executive Director
5445 Point Clair Road
Carville, LA 70721
Web: www.geauxlangea.org/about/langea

Summary To provide financial assistance to members of the Louisiana National Guard Enlisted Association (LANGEA) and their dependents who plan to attend college in any state.
Eligibility This program is open to members of the association, their spouses and unmarried dependent children, and the unremarried spouses and unmarried dependent children of deceased members who were in good standing at the time of their death. The qualifying LANGEA members must have at least 1 year remaining on their enlistment following completion of the school year for which the application is submitted or have served 20 years of more in the Louisiana National Guard. Applicants must be enrolled or planning to enroll full time at an accredited college, university, trade school, or business school in any state. Graduate students are not eligible. Selection is based on academic achievement, character, leadership, and financial need.
Financial data The stipend is $2,000.
Duration 1 year; nonrenewable.
Number awarded 2 each year.
Deadline April of each year.

[490]
TVSHKA (WARRIOR) SCHOLARSHIP
Chahta Foundation
Attn: Scholarship Director
P.O. Box 1849
Durant, OK 74702
(580) 924-8280, ext. 2546
Toll Free: (800) 522-6170, ext. 2546
Fax: (580) 745-9023
E-mail: scholarship@chahtafoundation.com
Web: www.chahtafoundation.com/scholarship/veterans

Summary To provide financial assistance to Choctaw Indians who are serving or have served in the armed services and are planning to attend college or graduate school in any state.
Eligibility This program is open to Choctaw students who are active duty or retired U.S. armed services veterans. Applicants be enrolled or planning to enroll full time in an undergraduate or graduate degree program at a college or university in any state. They must have a GPA of 2.5 or higher. Along with their application, they must submit essays on assigned topics, transcripts, 2 letters of recommendation, a resume, and documentation of financial need.
Financial data The stipend is $3,000.
Duration 1 year.
Additional information This program began in 2016.
Number awarded 1 or more each year.
Deadline March of each year.

[491]
UNIFIED ARIZONA VETERANS SCHOLARSHIPS
Unified Arizona Veterans, Inc.
Attn: Scholarship Committee
P.O. Box 34338
Phoenix, AZ 85067
E-mail: scholarships@azuav.org
Web: www.azuav.org

Summary To provide financial assistance to veterans and military personnel in Arizona who are interested in attending college in the state.
Eligibility This program is open to residents of Arizona who are 1) honorably discharged veterans; 2) currently on active duty, including service members in good standing with a Reserve or Guard components; or 3) immediate family members of an Arizona veteran killed in action or by an act of terror. Applicants must be enrolled at an institution of higher learning in Arizona and working on a bachelor's or master's degree in any field. Along with their application, they must submit 1) a 1-page essay on why they chose their current academic program and how they plan to use their degree, certificate, or license; 2) letters of recommendation; 3) verification of enrollment and Arizona residency; and 4) documentation of financial need.
Financial data Stipends range up to $5,000.
Duration 1 year.
Number awarded 1 or more each year.
Deadline February of each year.

[492]
UNITED STATES FIELD ARTILLERY ASSOCIATION SCHOLARSHIPS
United States Field Artillery Association
Attn: Scholarship Committee
Building 758, McNair Avenue
P.O. Box 33027
Fort Sill, OK 73503-0027
(580) 355-4677   Toll Free: (866) 355-4677
Fax: (580) 355-8745   E-mail: suzette@fieldartillery.org
Web: www.fieldartillery.org/usfaa-scholarships

Summary To provide financial assistance for college to members of the United States Field Artillery Association (USFAA) and their immediate family.
Eligibility This program is open to 3 categories of students: USFAA members (officer or enlisted), immediate family of enlisted members, and immediate family of officer members. Applicants must have been accepted for admission as an undergraduate at an accredited college, university, or vocational program. Along with their application, they must submit an essay explaining their educational goals and how

this scholarship will help meet those goals. Financial need is also considered in the selection process.
Financial data Stipends range from $2,500 to $5,000.
Duration 1 year.
Additional information The USFAA services the field artillery branch of the military.
Number awarded Varies each year; recently, 1 at $5,000, 3 at $3,000, and 1 at $2,500 were awarded.
Deadline April of each year.

[493]
U.S. ARMY HEALTH CARE ENLISTED COMMISSIONING PROGRAM (AECP)
U.S. Army
Attn: Recruiting Command, RCHS-AN-AECP
1307 Third Avenue
Fort Knox, KY 40121-2726
(502) 626-0361   Toll Free: (800) 223-3735, ext. 60361
Fax: (502) 626-1916
E-mail: usarmy.knox.usarec.mbx.hsd-aecp@mail.mil
Web: www.goarmy.com

Summary To provide financial assistance to enlisted Army personnel who are interested in completing a bachelor's degree in nursing and becoming a commissioned officer.
Eligibility This program is open to enlisted Army personnel of grade E-4 or above in the active component, National Guard, or Reserves who have at least 3 but no more than 12 years of active federal service. Applicants must be interested in enrolling full time at an accredited school of nursing to work on a bachelor's degree and becoming a licensed registered nurse. They must be U.S. citizens, have a GPA of 3.0 or higher, have SAT scores of at least 450 in critical reading and 450 in mathematics, have an enrollment GT score of 110 or higher, be able to complete a bachelor's degree in nursing within 24 calendar months, be between 21 and 41 years of age, be eligible to become a commissioned officer in the active component following licensure, and agree to fulfill a 4-year additional service obligation.
Financial data The stipend is $9,000 per year for tuition and $1,000 for books. Participants are not allowed to attend a school whose tuition exceeds $9,000. They continue to draw their regular pay and allowances while attending nursing school.
Duration Participants must be able to complete all degree requirements in 24 consecutive months or less.
Number awarded Up to 100 each year.
Deadline June of each year.

[494]
USAA/EANGKY SCHOLARSHIP
Enlisted Association National Guard of Kentucky
Attn: Scholarship Committee
P.O. Box 1992
Louisville, KY 40259
(502) 314-4005   E-mail: eangky2@gmail.com
Web: www.eangky.org/scholarship-application

Summary To provide financial assistance to members of the Enlisted Association National Guard of Kentucky (EANGKY) and their families who are interested in attending college in any state.
Eligibility This program is open to EANGKY members and their dependent children and spouses; children of deceased members who were in good standing at the time of their death are also eligible. Applicants must be attending or planning to attend a college, university, or trade school in any state. Along with their application, they must submit transcripts, letters of recommendation, and a 1-page statement describing their long-range personal educational goals and explaining why they need the scholarship assistance.
Financial data The stipend is $1,000.
Duration 1 year.
Additional information This program is sponsored by USAA Insurance Corporation.
Number awarded 1 or more each year.
Deadline April of each year.

[495]
UTAH NATIONAL GUARD STATE TUITION ASSISTANCE PROGRAM
Utah Army National Guard
Attn: UT-G1-ESO
12953 South Minuteman Drive
P.O. Box 1776
Draper, UT 84020-1776
(801) 432-4354
E-mail: ng.ut.utarng.list.education-office@mail.mil
Web: ut.ng.mil/Resources/Education-Services

Summary To provide tuition assistance to currently-enrolled members of the Utah National Guard.
Eligibility This program is open to Utah residents who are MOS/AFSC qualified members of the Utah National Guard. Applicants must be seeking funding to obtain a 1) high school diploma or GED certification; 2) undergraduate, graduate, vocational, technical, or licensure certificate; 3) associate degree; 4) baccalaureate degree; or 5) master's degree. Support is not provided for doctoral or first professional degrees, such as architecture, certified public accountant, podiatry (D.P.M.), dentistry (D.D.S. or D.M.D.), medicine (M.D.), optometry (O.D.), osteopathic medicine (D.O.), pharmacy (Pharm.D.), law (J.D.), or theology (M.Div. or M.H.L.). Enlisted personnel must have remaining obligation on their existing enlistment contract that will extend to or beyond the last date of course enrollment for these funds. Officers must have at least 4 years of Selected Reserve service remaining from the date of completion of the course for which this funding is provided.
Financial data Support is provided for 100% of the cost of tuition, to a maximum of $250 per hour or a maximum of $6,000 per year combined with federal tuition assistance. Soldiers and airmen majoring in cyber studies or a field of STEM are eligible for up t $7,000 per year.
Duration 1 semester; recipients may renew.
Additional information Recipients of this funding may continue to receive any GI Bill funding to which they are entitled.
Number awarded Varies each year; recently, a total of $750,000 was available for this program.
Deadline Applications must be received at least 3 weeks prior to the course start date. They are processed on a first-come, first-served basis.

[496]
UTAH NATIONAL GUARD STATE TUITION WAIVER

Utah Army National Guard
Attn: UT-G1-ESO
12953 South Minuteman Drive
P.O. Box 1776
Draper, UT 84020-1776
(801) 432-4354
E-mail: ng.ut.utarng.list.education-office@mail.mil
Web: ut.ng.mil/Resources/Education-Services

Summary To waive tuition for members of the Utah National Guard at public institutions in the state.

Eligibility This program is open to Utah residents who are MOS/AFSC qualified members of the Utah National Guard. Applicants must have been accepted as a full-time student at a public college or university in the state. They may not currently be on active duty and may not already have a 4-year degree. Along with their application, they must submit a short essay on their military goals and how their civilian education will assist them in achieving those goals.

Financial data This program provides waiver of 100% of tuition at Utah public colleges and universities.

Duration 1 semester; recipients may renew.

Additional information Recipients of these waivers may continue to receive any GI Bill funding to which they are entitled and they may utilize state Tuition Assistance or federal Tuition Assistance to pay for fees or credits not covered by this program.

Number awarded Varies each year. Each Utah public college and university is required to set aside 2.5% of its scholarship funds for members of the National Guard.

Deadline April of each year.

[497]
VADM JON L. BOYES, VICE ADMIRAL, USN (RET.) MEMORIAL SCHOLARSHIP

Armed Forces Communications and Electronics
   Association
Attn: AFCEA Educational Foundation
4114 Legato Road, Suite 1000
Fairfax, VA 22033-3342
(703) 631-6147   Toll Free: (800) 336-4583, ext. 6147
Fax: (703) 631-4693   E-mail: edfoundation@afcea.org
Web: www.afcea.org

Summary To provide financial assistance to Navy ROTC midshipmen who are majoring in electrical engineering.

Eligibility This program is open to Navy ROTC midshipmen enrolled full time at an accredited degree-granting 4-year college or university in the United States. Applicants must be sophomores or juniors at the time of application and have a GPA of 3.0 or higher with a major in electrical engineering. Their application must be endorsed by the professor of naval science at their institution. Selection is based on demonstrated dedication, superior performance, potential to serve as an officer in the United States Navy, and financial need.

Financial data The stipend is $3,000.

Duration 1 year.

Number awarded 1 each year.

Deadline April of each year.

[498]
VAN HIPP HEROES SCHOLARSHIP

National Guard Educational Foundation
Attn: Scholarship Fund
One Massachusetts Avenue, N.W.
Washington, DC 20001
(202) 789-0031   Fax: (202) 682-9358
E-mail: ngef@ngaus.org
Web: www.ngef.org/the-van-hipp-heroes-scholarship-fund

Summary To provide financial assistance for college to members of the National Guard who were wounded in service.

Eligibility This program is open to current and former National Guard members who were wounded in an operational or training mission in support of Operation Enduring Freedom, Operation Iraqi Freedom, or Operation New Dawn. Applicants must be attending or planning to attend an accredited college, university, or community college located in the 50 states, the District of Columbia, Puerto Rico, the U.S. Virgin Islands, or Guam. Along with their application, they must submit a 1-page essay on how their National Guard service has shaped their life.

Financial data The stipend is $1,000 per year.

Duration 1 year; may be renewed up to 3 additional years, provided the recipient maintains a GPA of 2.5 or higher.

Additional information This program was established in 2017 by Van Hipp, author of *The New Terrorism: How to Fight It and Defeat It*. All the proceeds from sale of the book go to support this program.

Number awarded Up to 10 each year.

Deadline June of each year.

[499]
VERMONT NATIONAL GUARD TUITION BENEFIT PROGRAM

Vermont Student Assistance Corporation
Attn: Scholarship Programs
10 East Allen Street
P.O. Box 2000
Winooski, VT 05404-2601
(802) 654-3798   Toll Free: (888) 253-4819
Fax: (802) 654-3765   TDD: (800) 281-3341 (within VT)
E-mail: info@vsac.org
Web: www.vsac.org

Summary To provide forgivable loans to members of the Vermont National Guard (VTNG) who are attending college in the state.

Eligibility This program is open to residents of Vermont who are active members of the VTNG but have exhausted other sources of post September 11 financial aid and federal tuition assistance. Applicants must plan to enroll in a certificate or degree program at an accredited postsecondary school in any state.

Financial data Students receive a loan that may be applied to tuition only. The amount of the loan depends on the recipient's enrollment status and college. Loans are forgiven at the rate of 2 years of service in the VTNG for each full-time academic year paid for by this program.

Duration 1 year; may be renewed.

Number awarded Varies each year.

Deadline Applications may be submitted at any time; they are considered on a first-come, first-served basis.

SCHOLARSHIPS: MILITARY PERSONNEL

[500]
VICE ADMIRAL ROBERT L. WALTERS SCHOLARSHIP

Surface Navy Association
Attn: Scholarship Coordinator
6564 Loisdale Court, Suite 318
Springfield, VA 22150
(703) 960-6800   Toll Free: (800) NAVY-SNA
Fax: (703) 960-6807   E-mail: navysna@aol.com
Web: www.navysna.org/scholarship/information.html

Summary To provide financial assistance for college or graduate school to members of the Surface Navy Association (SNA) and their dependents.

Eligibility This program is open to SNA members and their children, stepchildren, wards, and spouses. The SNA member must 1) be in the second or subsequent consecutive year of membership; 2) be serving, retired, or honorably discharged; 3) be a Surface Warfare Officer or Enlisted Surface Warfare Specialist; and 4) have served for at least 3 years on a surface ship of the U.S. Navy or Coast Guard (the 3 years need not have been consecutive but must have been served on active duty). Applicants must be enrolled or planning to enroll full time at an accredited undergraduate or graduate institution; the full-time requirement may be waived for spouses. Along with their application, they must submit a 500-word essay about themselves and why they should be selected to receive this scholarship. High school seniors should also include a transcript of high school grades and a copy of ACT or SAT scores. Current college students should also include a transcript of the grades from their most recent 4 semesters of school. Selection is based on academic proficiency, non-scholastic activities, scholastic and non-scholastic awards, character, and financial need.

Financial data The stipend is $2,000 per year.

Duration 4 years, provided the recipient maintains a GPA of 3.0 or higher.

Number awarded Varies each year.

Deadline February of each year.

[501]
VIRGINIA NATIONAL GUARD ASSOCIATION SCHOLARSHIP

Virginia National Guard Association
Attn: Scholarship Committee Chair
11518 Hardwood Drive
Midlothian, VA 23114
(804) 350-0175   E-mail: scholarship@vnga.us
Web: www.vnga.us/scholarship

Summary To provide financial assistance to members of the Virginia National Guard Association (VNGA) and their families who are interested in attending college in any state.

Eligibility Applicants must have been enrolled at a college or university in any state for 1 year and qualify under 1 of the following conditions: 1) an officer or warrant officer in the Virginia National Guard and a VNGA member; 2) a dependent child or spouse of an officer or warrant officer in the Virginia National Guard who is a VNGA member; 3) a dependent child or spouse of a retired officer or warrant officer who is a VNGA member; 4) a dependent child or spouse of a deceased retired officer or warrant officer; or 5) a dependent child or spouse of a Virginia National Guard officer or warrant officer who died while actively serving in the Virginia National Guard. Along with their application, they must submit a brief description of their educational and/or military objectives, a list of their leadership positions and honors, and a brief statement of their financial need.

Financial data A stipend is awarded; the amount is determined annually.

Duration 1 year; may be renewed for 2 additional years.

Additional information This program includes scholarships designated the CW4 William C. Singletary Scholarship and the Colonel Joseph "Ed" Galloway Scholarship.

Number awarded Varies each year.

Deadline September of each year.

[502]
VIRGINIA NATIONAL GUARD TUITION ASSISTANCE PROGRAM

Virginia National Guard
Attn: Educational Services Officer
Fort Pickett, Building 316
Blackstone, VA 23824-6316
(434) 298-6155   Toll Free: (888) 483-2682
Fax: (434) 298-6296 E-mail: vickie.a.kegley2.nfg@mail.mil
Web: vaguard.dodlive.mil/tuitionassistance

Summary To provide financial assistance to members of the Virginia National Guard who are interested in attending college or graduate school in the state.

Eligibility This program is open to active members of the Virginia National Guard who are residents of Virginia and interested in attending college or graduate school in the state. Awards are presented in the following priority order: 1) enlisted personnel who have previously received assistance through this program; 2) officers who need to complete a bachelor's degree in order to be eligible for promotion to captain; 3) warrant officers working on an associate or bachelor's degree; 4) any member working on an undergraduate degree; and 4) any member working on a graduate degree.

Financial data The program provides reimbursement of tuition at approved colleges, universities, and vocational/technical schools in Virginia, to a maximum of $7,000 per year.

Duration 1 semester; may be renewed.

Additional information This program began in 1983. Recipients must remain in the Guard for at least 2 years after being funded.

Number awarded Varies each year.

Deadline June of each year for fall semester; October of each year for spring semester; March of each year for summer session.

[503]
VTNGEA SCHOLARSHIPS

Vermont National Guard Enlisted Association
Attn: Scholarship Committee
P.O. Box 7
Essex Junction, VT 05452-0007
Web: www.vtngea.org/vtngea-scholarships/

Summary To provide financial assistance to members and dependents of members of the Enlisted Association of the National Guard of the United States (EANGUS) who reside in Vermont and are interested in attending college in any state.

Eligibility This program is open to members of the Vermont chapter of EANGUS and their dependents. Applicants

must be enrolled or planning to enroll at a college or university in any state. Along with their application, they must submit transcripts, letters of recommendation, and a 1-page essay describing their desire to continue their education and why financial assistance is required.
Financial data A stipend is awarded (amount not specified).
Duration 1 year.
Additional information This program receives support from Jolley Associates and USAA Insurance Corporation.
Number awarded Multiple scholarships are awarded each year.
Deadline July of each year.

[504]
WALTER BEALL SCHOLARSHIP
Walter Beall Scholarship Foundation
c/o PNP Jim Scarbo
613 Hillwell Road
Chesapeake, VA 23322-3812
E-mail: jimscarbo@cox.net
Web: www.walterbeallscholarship.org

Summary To provide financial assistance to members of the Fleet Reserve Association (FRA) and their families who are interested in studying engineering, aeronautical engineering, or aviation in college.
Eligibility This program is open to FRA members who have been in good standing for at least the past 2 consecutive years and their spouses, children, and grandchildren. Students in a Reserve officer candidate program receiving aid or attending a military academy are not eligible. Applicants must be enrolled at an accredited college, university, or technical institution in the United States in a program related to general engineering, aviation, or aeronautical engineering. Selection is based on GPA, scholastic aptitude test scores, curriculum goals, interests, community activities, awards, and financial need. U.S. citizenship is required.
Financial data The amounts of the awards depend on the availability of funds and the need of the recipients; they normally range from $2,000 to $5,000.
Duration 1 year; recipients may reapply.
Additional information The Walter Beall Scholarship Foundation is sponsored by the Past Regional Presidents Club of the Fleet Reserve Association. Membership in the FRA is restricted to active-duty, retired, and Reserve members of the Navy, Marine Corps, and Coast Guard.
Number awarded 1 or more each year.
Deadline Requests for applications must be received by March of each year.

[505]
WASHINGTON NATIONAL GUARD POSTSECONDARY EDUCATION GRANT
Washington Student Achievement Council
917 Lakeridge Way
P.O. Box 43430
Olympia, WA 98504-3430
(360) 753-7850   Toll Free: (888) 535-0747
Fax: (360) 753-7808   TDD: (360) 753-7809
E-mail: nationalguard@wsac.wa.gov
Web: www.wsac.wa.gov/national-guard

Summary To provide forgivable loans to members of the Washington National Guard who wish to attend college in the state.
Eligibility This program is open to active drilling members of the Washington National Guard who are attending or planning to attend an accredited college in the state as an undergraduate student. Applicants must agree to serve an additional year in the Guard for each year of funding they receive through this program.
Financial data Grants cover tuition and fees at approved colleges in Washington, as well as a portion of books and materials. Recipients who fail to meet the service requirement must repay all funds received, plus interest and fees.
Duration 1 year; may be renewed.
Additional information This program began in 2020 as a replacement for the former Washington National Guard Conditional Scholarship Program.
Number awarded Varies each year.
Deadline Deadline not specified.

[506]
WESLEY HAMMON LEACH SCHOLARSHIPS
Marines' Memorial Association
c/o Marines Memorial Club and Hotel
609 Sutter Street
San Francisco, CA 94102
(415) 673-6672, ext. 293   Toll Free: (800) 5-MARINE
Fax: (415) 441-3649
E-mail: scholarship@marineclub.com
Web: www.marinesmemorial.org

Summary To provide financial assistance to members of the Marines' Memorial Association from all branches of the armed forces and their descendants who are interested in studying at a career school or college.
Eligibility This program is open to active members of the association (including student veterans) and their children and grandchildren. Applicants must be high school seniors or students currently enrolled at an accredited trade or vocational school. They must have a field of study that will lead to a viable career; preference is given to students with a medical or nursing focus. Along with their application, they must submit an essay of up to 500 words on why they chose their specific path of study, what they hope to accomplish after graduation with their degree, and how their efforts will benefit others in their community. Selection is based on the essay, academic merit, references, and financial need.
Financial data The stipend is $2,500.
Duration 1 year.
Additional information Membership in the association is open to veterans of the Marines, Army, Navy, Air Force, or Coast Guard and to personnel currently serving in a branch of the armed forces. This program began in 2017.
Number awarded 3 each year.
Deadline April of each year.

[507]
WEST VIRGINIA NATIONAL GUARD EDUCATIONAL ENCOURAGEMENT PROGRAM

Office of the Adjutant General
Attn: Education Services Office
1703 Coonskin Drive
Charleston, WV 25311-1085
(304) 561-6306   Toll Free: (866) 986-4326
Fax: (304) 561-6463   E-mail: valerie.j.lambing.nfg@mail.mil
Web: www.wv.ng.mil/Education

Summary To provide financial assistance to members of the National Guard in West Virginia who are interested in attending college or graduate school in the state.

Eligibility This program is open to active members of the West Virginia National Guard who are residents of West Virginia and interested in attending a public or private college in the state. Applicants must have maintained satisfactory participation in the Guard. They must be interested in working on a vocational, associate, bachelor's, or master's degree. In some instances, support may also be available to Guard members who are interested in working on an M.D., D.O., P.A., or J.D. degree.

Financial data The program provides payment of 100% of the tuition and fees at participating colleges and universities in West Virginia, to a maximum of $7,000 per year.

Duration 1 academic year; may be renewed, provided the recipient maintains a GPA of 2.0 or higher as an undergraduate or 3.0 or higher as a graduate student.

Number awarded Varies each year.

Deadline April of each year for fall, October of each year for spring, or 60 days prior to class start for nontraditional programs and/or cohorts.

[508]
WISCONSIN NATIONAL GUARD ASSOCIATION EDUCATION GRANT

Wisconsin National Guard Association, Inc.
Attn: Awards, Gifts, and Grants Committee
2400 Wright Street, Room 151
Madison, WI 53704-2572
(608) 242-3114   Fax: (608) 242-3513
E-mail: info@winga.org
Web: www.winga.org/html/members/scholarships.html

Summary To provide financial assistance to members of the Wisconsin National Guard Association (WINGA), their spouses, and their unmarried children who are interested in attending college in any state.

Eligibility This program is open to WINGA members and their spouses and unmarried dependent children. Applicants must have completed at least 1 year of college. They must be enrolled full time at an accredited college, university, technical institute, or trade or business school in any state. High school seniors and graduate students are not eligible. Selection is based on academic record (GPA of 3.0 or higher), extracurricular activities, community involvement, work experience, and goals.

Financial data The stipend is $1,000. Funds are paid to the recipient's school upon proof of enrollment.

Duration 1 year; may be renewed for 1 additional year.

Additional information This grant was first awarded in 1992. Graduate education is not supported.

Number awarded Varies each year; recently, 10 were awarded.

Deadline June of each year.

[509]
WISCONSIN NATIONAL GUARD ENLISTED ASSOCIATION COLLEGE GRANT PROGRAM

Wisconsin National Guard Enlisted Association
Attn: Executive Director
2400 Wright Street
Madison, WI 53704-2572
(608) 242-3112   E-mail: WNGEA@yahoo.com
Web: wngea.org/scholarships

Summary To provide financial assistance to members of the Wisconsin National Guard Enlisted Association (WNGEA) and their spouses and children who are interested in attending college or graduate school in any state.

Eligibility This program is open to WNGEA members, the unmarried children and spouses of WNGEA members, and the unmarried children and spouses of deceased WNGEA members. Applicants must be enrolled full or part time at a college, university, graduate school, trade school, or business school in any state. Along with their application, they must submit a letter explaining their desire to continue their education; why financial assistance is needed; awards received, accomplishments, volunteerism, and hours volunteered per week or month; and WNGEA membership and role in the organization. Selection is based on financial need, leadership, and moral character.

Financial data Stipends are $1,000 or $500 per year.

Duration 1 year; recipients may not reapply for 2 years.

Additional information This program includes 1 scholarship sponsored by the USAA Insurance Corporation.

Number awarded Varies each year; recently, 6 were awarded: the Raymond A. Matera Scholarship at $1,000, a grant of $1,000 sponsored by USAA, and 4 others (1 reserved for a graduate student) at $500 each.

Deadline May of each year.

[510]
WISCONSIN NATIONAL GUARD TUITION GRANT

Wisconsin Department of Military Affairs
Attn: Grant Specialist
WIAR-G1-ED
2400 Wright Street
P.O. Box 8111
Madison, WI 53708-8111
(608) 242-3159   Toll Free: (800) 335-5147
Fax: (608) 242-3154
E-mail: jessica.wagner@wisconsin.gov
Web: dma.wi.gov/DMA/support/education

Summary To provide financial assistance for college to members of the Wisconsin National Guard.

Eligibility Eligible to apply for these grants are enlisted members and warrant officers in good standing in the Wisconsin National Guard who wish to work on an undergraduate degree. Applicants may not have been flagged for unexcused absences or failing to meet Guard standards. They must be attending or planning to attend an extension division or campus of the University of Wisconsin system, a campus of the Wisconsin Technical College System, an accredited private institution of higher education located within Wiscon-

sin, a campus of the University of Minnesota system, a campus of the Minnesota State Community and Technical College system, or a few other institutions in neighboring states with which Wisconsin has reciprocity agreements.
Financial data This program offers assistance based on the undergraduate tuition rate of the University of Wisconsin at Madison (recently, that was $10,555 per year for full-time study).
Duration 8 semesters of full-time study or completion of a bachelor's degree, provided the recipient maintains a GPA of 2.0 or higher.
Number awarded Varies each year.
Deadline Applications may be submitted at any time, but they must be received at least 90 days after completion of the course.

[511]
WOMEN IN DEFENSE PALMETTO CHAPTER HORIZONS SCHOLARSHIP
Women in Defense-Palmetto Chapter
c/o Rachel Link, Vice President
Maga Design
913 Bowman Road, Suite 102
Mount Pleasant, SC 29464
E-mail: outreach@widpalmettochapter.org
Web: www.widpalmettochapter.org/scholarship-program

Summary To provide financial assistance to women, including those with ties to the military, who are working on an undergraduate degree in a field of science, technology, engineering, or mathematics (STEM) at a college in South Carolina.
Eligibility This program is open to women currently enrolled full time at a college or university in South Carolina and working on a degree in STEM. Applicants must be working on a field of STEM and have a GPA of 2.5 or higher if entering their sophomore year, 2.75 or higher as an entering junior, or 3.0 or higher as an entering senior. They must be U.S. citizens and able to demonstrate financial need. The program includes women who are current or former U.S. military active duty, retired, Reserve, or Guard members or are currently enrolled in an ROTC program.
Financial data The stipend is $2,500.
Duration 1 year.
Number awarded 2 each year, of which 1 is reserved for a woman with ties to the military.
Deadline November of each year.

[512]
WOMEN MARINES ASSOCIATION SCHOLARSHIP PROGRAM
Women Marines Association
120 State Avenue, Suite 303
Olympia, WA 98501
Toll Free: (888) 525-1943
E-mail: scholarship@womenmarines.org
Web: www.womenmarines.org/scholarships

Summary To provide financial assistance for college or graduate school to students sponsored by members of the Women Marines Association (WMA).
Eligibility Applicants must be sponsored by a WMA member and fall into 1 of the following categories: 1) have served or are serving in the U.S. Marine Corps, regular or Reserve; 2) are a direct descendant by blood or legal adoption or a stepchild of a Marine on active duty or who has served honorably in the U.S. Marine Corps, regular or Reserve; 3) are a sibling or a descendant of a sibling by blood or legal adoption or a stepchild of a Marine on active duty or who has served honorably in the U.S. Marine Corps, regular or Reserve; 4) be a spouse of a Marine; or 5) have completed 2 years in a Marine Corps JROTC program. WMA members may sponsor an unlimited number of applicants per year. High school seniors must submit transcripts (GPA of 3.0 or higher) and SAT or ACT scores. Undergraduate and graduate students must have a GPA of 3.0 or higher. Along with their application, they must submit 1-page statements on 1) the Marine to whom they are related; 2) their community service; and 3) their goals after college.
Financial data Stipends range from $500 to $5,000 per year.
Duration 1 year; may be renewed 1 additional year.
Additional information This program includes the following named scholarships: the WMA Memorial Scholarships, the Lily H. Gridley Memorial Scholarship, the Ethyl and Armin Wiebke Memorial Scholarship, the Maj. Megan McClung Memorial Scholarship, the Agnes Sopcak Memorial Scholarship, the Virginia Guveyan Memorial Scholarship, the LaRue A. Ditmore Music Scholarships, the Fallen Warrior Scholarship, and the Margaret Apel Scholarship. Applicants must know a WMA member to serve as their sponsor; the WMA will not supply listings of the names or addresses of chapters or individual members.
Number awarded Varies each year.
Deadline February of each year.

[513]
WOMEN MILITARY AVIATORS DREAM OF FLIGHT SCHOLARSHIP
Women in Aviation International
Attn: Scholarships
Morningstar Airport
3647 State Route 503 South
West Alexandria, OH 45381-9354
(937) 839-4647   Fax: (937) 839-4645
E-mail: scholarships@wai.org
Web: www.wai.org/education/scholarships

Summary To provide financial assistance to members of Women in Aviation International (WAI) who have military experience and are interested in flight training or academic study.
Eligibility This program is open to WAI members who have military experience and are enrolled at an accredited academic institution or an FAA Part 141 approved flight school. Applicants must be seeking flight ratings in order to pursue opportunities in aviation. Along with their application, they must submit 1) a 500-word essay and professional resume that include their aviation history and goals, what they have done for themselves to achieve their goals, where they see themselves in 5 and 10 years, involvement in aviation activities, how the scholarship will help them achieve their objectives, and their present financial need; and 2) a narrative addressing their demonstrated persistence and determination to fly, ability to complete their current training program with 1 year, and their interest and/or participation in military aviation.

Financial data The stipend is $2,500. A 1-year membership in Women Military Aviators (WMA) is also provided.
Duration Recipients must be able to complete training within 1 year.
Additional information WAI is a nonprofit professional organization dedicated to encouraging women to consider an aviation career and to providing educational outreach activities and networking resources to women active in the industry. WMA established this program in 2005 to honor the women aviators who were serving or had served in Iraq and Afghanistan.
Number awarded 1 each year.
Deadline November of each year.

[514]
WOMEN'S OVERSEAS SERVICE LEAGUE SCHOLARSHIPS FOR WOMEN

Women's Overseas Service League
Attn: Scholarship Committee
P.O. Box 124
Cedar Knolls, NJ 07927-0124
E-mail: kelsey@openix.com
Web: www.wosl.org/scholarships

Summary To provide financial assistance for college to women who are committed to a military or other public service career.
Eligibility This program is open to women who are committed to a military or other public service career. Applicants must have completed at least 12 semester hours of postsecondary study with a GPA of 2.5 or higher. They must be working on an academic degree (the program may be professional or technical in nature) and must agree to enroll for at least 6 semester hours of study each academic period. Along with their application, they must submit a 250-word essay on their career goals. Financial need is considered in the selection process.
Financial data Stipends range from $500 to $1,000 per year.
Duration 1 year; may be renewed 1 additional year.
Additional information The Women's Overseas Service League is a national organization of women who have served overseas in or with the armed forces.
Number awarded Varies each year.
Deadline February of each year.

[515]
WOMEN'S SCUBA ASSOCIATION DIVE TRAINING GRANT

Women Divers Hall of Fame
Attn: Bonnie Toth
503 Via Florida
San Clemente, CA 92672
E-mail: wdhofgrants@gmail.com
Web: www.wdhof.org/wdhof-scholarshipDesc.aspx

Summary To provide financial assistance for dive training to students who are currently enrolled in designated military-associated programs.
Eligibility This program is open to males and females who are enrolled in an ROTC or JROTC program, at a military academy, in Sea Cadets, on in Sea Scouts. Applicants must wish to begin or further their dive education or training.

Financial data The grant is $1,000, including $500 for the training and $500 for equipment. Funds are paid directly to the training facility.
Duration Training must be completed within 1 year.
Number awarded 1 each year.
Deadline October of each year.

[516]
WYOMING NATIONAL GUARD ASSOCIATION SCHOLARSHIPS

Wyoming National Guard Association
Attn: Scholarships
P.O. Box 2615
Cheyenne, WY 82003-2615
(307) 630-9502   E-mail: janetlcowley@gmail.com
Web: www.wynga.org

Summary To provide financial assistance to members of the Wyoming National Guard Association (WYNGA) and their families who are interested in attending college in any state.
Eligibility This program is open to enlisted and officer members of the WYNGA and their spouses and unmarried children. Applicants must be attending or planning to attend an accredited institution of higher education in any state. Along with their application, they must submit a cover letter that includes information on their educational career goals, their need for this scholarship, their family involvement in WYNGA, and a list of awards, honors, extracurricular activities, and organizations in which they have participated.
Financial data A stipend is awarded (amount not specified).
Duration 1 year.
Additional information This program includes the following named scholarships: the MG Charles J. Wing Family Program Scholarship, the Mrs. Beverly Holmes Scholarship, the Wyoming Army National Guard Combined Club Scholarship, and the USAA Insurance Corporation Scholarship.
Number awarded Varies each year; recently, 7 were awarded.
Deadline April of each year.

[517]
WYOMING NATIONAL GUARD EDUCATIONAL ASSISTANCE PLAN

Wyoming National Guard
Attn: Education Services Officer
5410 Bishop Boulevard
Cheyenne, WY 82009
(307) 777-8160   Fax: (307) 777-8105
E-mail: jenna.chapin@wyo.gov
Web: veteranseducation.wyo.gov/state-tuition-assistance

Summary To provide financial assistance to members of the Wyoming National Guard who are interested in attending college or graduate school in the state.
Eligibility This program is open to members of the Wyoming Army National Guard and the Wyoming Air National Guard who have spent at least 6 years in the Guard or are currently serving under their initial 6-year enlistment period. New enlistees who commit to serving 6 years are also eligible. Applicants may be pursuing, or planning to pursue, a degree at any level at the University of Wyoming, a Wyoming community college, or an approved technical institution in Wyoming.

Financial data The program provides full payment of tuition at eligible institutions.
Duration Guard members may continue to receive these benefits as long as they maintain a GPA of 2.0 or higher, keep up with Guard standards for drill attendance, and remain in good standing with the Guard.
Additional information The Wyoming legislature created this program in 2001. Recipients must agree to serve in the Guard for at least 2 years after they graduate or stop using the plan.
Number awarded Varies each year.
Deadline September of each year.

Family Members

[518]
100TH INFANTRY BATTALION MEMORIAL SCHOLARSHIP FUND
Hawai'i Community Foundation
Attn: Scholarship Department
827 Fort Street Mall
Honolulu, HI 96813
(808) 566-5570   Toll Free: (888) 731-3863
Fax: (808) 521-6286
E-mail: scholarships@hcf-hawaii.org
Web: hcf.scholarships.ngwebsolutions.com

Summary To provide financial assistance for college or graduate school to descendants of 100th Infantry Battalion World War II veterans.
Eligibility This program is open to entering and continuing full-time undergraduate and graduate students at 2- and 4-year colleges and universities. Applicants must be a direct descendant of a World War II veteran of the 100th Infantry Battalion (which was comprised of Americans of Japanese descent). They must be able to demonstrate academic achievement (GPA of 3.0 or higher), an active record of extracurricular activities and community service (especially volunteer work connected with the activities of the 100th Infantry Battalion Veterans organization), and a willingness to promote the legacy of the 100th Infantry Battalion of World War II. Along with their application, they must submit personal statements that include 1) 900 words each on their reasons for attending college, why they chose their course of study, and their career goals; and 2) 600 words on how they plan to give back to Hawaii. They must also submit a separate essay on the historical significance of the 100th Infantry Battalion and what the stories of those soldiers have to teach all American citizens. Neither current residency in Hawaii nor financial need is required.
Financial data The amounts of the awards depend on the availability of funds and the need of the recipient. Recently, the average value of the scholarships awarded by the foundation was approximately $2,500.
Duration 1 year.
Additional information This program began in 2006.
Number awarded Varies each year; recently, 2 were awarded.
Deadline February of each year.

[519]
100TH INFANTRY BATTALION VETERANS STANLEY IZUMIGAWA SCHOLARSHIP FUND
Hawai'i Community Foundation
Attn: Scholarship Department
827 Fort Street Mall
Honolulu, HI 96813
(808) 566-5570   Toll Free: (888) 731-3863
Fax: (808) 521-6286
E-mail: scholarships@hcf-hawaii.org
Web: hcf.scholarships.ngwebsolutions.com

Summary To provide financial assistance for college or graduate school to descendants of 100th Infantry Battalion World War II veterans.
Eligibility This program is open to entering and continuing full-time undergraduate and graduate students at 2- and 4-year colleges and universities. Applicants must be a direct descendant of a World War II veteran of the 100th Infantry Battalion (which was comprised of Americans of Japanese descent). They must be able to demonstrate academic achievement (GPA of 3.0 or higher), an active record of extracurricular activities and community service, especially volunteer work connected with the activities of the 100th Infantry Battalion Veterans organization, including (but not limited to) educational programs, memorial services, and the anniversary banquet. Along with their application, they must submit a personal statement that includes 1) 900 words each on their reasons for attending college, why they chose their course of study, and their career goals; and 2) 600 words on how they plan to give back to Hawaii. They must also submit a separate essay on the historical significance of the 100th Infantry Battalion and what the stories of those soldiers have to teach all American citizens. Neither current residency in Hawaii nor financial need is required.
Financial data The amounts of the awards depend on the availability of funds and the need of the recipient. Recently, the average value of the scholarships awarded by the foundation was approximately $2,500.
Duration 1 year.
Additional information This program began in 2014.
Number awarded 1 or more each year.
Deadline February of each year.

[520]
10TH MOUNTAIN DIVISION (LIGHT INFANTRY) SCHOLARSHIPS
Northern New York Community Foundation, Inc.
131 Washington Street
Watertown, NY 13601
(315) 782-7110   Fax: (315) 782-0047
E-mail: info@nnycf.org
Web: www.nnycf.org/scholarships/scholarships-available

Summary To provide financial assistance for college to current and former members of the 10th Mountain Division and their dependents.
Eligibility This program is open to current and former members of the 10th Mountain Division and their dependents (children and spouses). Applicants must be high school

seniors applying for the freshmen year or traditional or non-traditional students enrolled as full-time undergraduates in any year of college or technical school. They must also be members of the 10th Mountain Division Association. Along with their application, they must submit a 150-word essay on the character traits that have contributed the most to their success, how they have contributed to their success, and how each will contribute to their success in life. High school juniors who will graduate early because they are in an advanced placement program may also apply. Interviews are required. Selection is based on academic achievement, personal data, and financial need.

Financial data The stipend is $5,000 per year.
Duration 1 year; recipients may reapply.
Number awarded Varies each year; recently, 8 were awarded.
Deadline March of each year.

[521]
11TH ARMORED CAVALRY VETERANS OF VIETNAM AND CAMBODIA SCHOLARSHIP

11th Armored Cavalry Veterans of Vietnam and Cambodia
c/o Mike "Doc" Rafferty, Scholarship Chair
5837 Habanero Drive
P.O. Box 13188
Las Cruces, NM 88013
(915) 792-2804 E-mail: platoonmedic36@gmail.com
Web: www.11thcavnam.com/scholarship/scholar.html

Summary To provide financial assistance for college to children and grandchildren of veterans who served with the 11th Armored Cavalry Regiment during combat in Vietnam and Cambodian.
Eligibility This program is open to 1) children and grandchildren of current life members of the 11th Armored Cavalry Veterans of Vietnam and Cambodia (11ACVVC); 2) children and grandchildren of deceased life members of the 11th Armored Cavalry Veterans of Vietnam and Cambodia (11ACVVC); and 3) children and grandchildren of 11th Armored Cavalry Regiment troopers who were killed in action in Vietnam or Cambodia. Applicants must be enrolled or planning to enroll as an undergraduate student. They must have a GPA of 3.0 or higher. Along with their application, they must submit a brief essay on their extracurricular and volunteer activities.
Financial data The stipend is $4,000; funds are paid directly to the recipient's school, in 2 equal installments.
Duration 1 year; nonrenewable.
Additional information This program began in 1997. Recipients must use the awarded money within 44 months of being notified.
Number awarded Varies each year; recently, 45 were awarded. Since the program was established, it has awarded 375 scholarships worth more than $1.2 million.
Deadline May of each year.

[522]
173RD AIRBORNE BRIGADE COMBAT TEAM HONORARY SCHOLARSHIP

Army Scholarship Foundation
11700 Preston Road, Suite 660-301
Dallas, TX 75230
E-mail: ContactUs@armyscholarshipfoundation.org
Web: www.armyscholarshipfoundation.org

Summary To provide financial assistance for undergraduate study to the children and spouses of Army personnel who are serving or have served in the 173rd Airborne Brigade.
Eligibility This program is open to children and spouses of enlisted soldiers who are current members or veterans of the 173rd Airborne Brigade. Applicants must be high school seniors, high school graduates, or undergraduates enrolled at an accredited college, university, or vocational/technical institute. They must be U.S. citizens and have a GPA of 2.0 or higher; children must be younger than 24 years of age. Financial need is considered in the selection process.
Financial data The stipend ranges from $500 to $2,000 per year.
Duration 1 year; recipients may reapply.
Additional information The Army Scholarship Foundation was established in 2001. This program is sponsored by the 173rd Airborne Brigade.
Number awarded 1 each year.
Deadline April of each year.

[523]
1ST LT. DIMITRI DEL CASTILLO SCHOLARSHIPS

U.S. Army Ranger Association
Attn: Scholarship Fund
P.O. Box 52126
Fort Benning, GA 31995-2126
Web: www.ranger.org/Scholarships

Summary To provide financial assistance for college to children and spouses of deceased soldiers recognized by the Army as Rangers.
Eligibility This program is open to the unmarried children under 23 years of age and unremarried spouses of deceased tabbed Rangers (graduated from Ranger school and awarded the Ranger Tab) or scrolled Rangers (served with the 75th Ranger Regiment in a Ranger slot). The parent or spouse must have been killed in action or during training or have died in a hospital as a result of critical wounds related to combat or training. Applicants must be attending or planning to attend an accredited college, university, or technical school. They must enroll full time and have a GPA of 2.0 or higher.
Financial data The stipend is $5,000; funds are disbursed directly to the recipient's institution.
Duration 1 year.
Number awarded Varies each year; recently, 3 were awarded.
Deadline April of each year.

[524]
3/26 SCHOLARSHIP FUND
3rd Battalion 26th Marines (Vietnam)
c/o Marine Corps Scholarship Foundation
909 North Washington Street, Suite 400
Alexandria, VA 22314
(703) 549-0060　　　　　Toll Free: (866) 496-5462
Fax: (703) 549-9474　　　E-mail: students@mcsf.org
Web: www.326marines.org/326_scholarship

Summary To provide financial assistance for college to the children and grandchildren of veterans who served with the Third Battalion of 26th Marines during Vietnam.

Eligibility This program is open to children and grandchildren of veterans who served honorably with the Battalion during Vietnam or died in service. Applicants must be high school seniors, high school graduates, or current college students. Along with their application, they must submit academic transcripts, a copy of their grandparent's honorable discharge, and a 500-word essay on a topic that changes periodically. Only undergraduate study is supported. The family income of applicants must be less than $93,000 per year.

Financial data Stipends depend on the need of the recipient and the availability of funds, but generally range from $2,000 to $3,000.

Duration 1 year.

Number awarded 1 each year.

Deadline February of each year.

[525]
37TH DIVISION VETERANS SCHOLARSHIP GRANT
37th Division Veterans Association
c/o Mandy Oberyszyn, Executive Director
312 Ridge Side Drive
Powell, OH 43065
(614) 228-3788　　　　　Fax: (614) 228-3793
E-mail: mandy@37thdva.org
Web: www.37thdva.org/grants

Summary To provide financial assistance for college to members of the 37th Division Veterans Association and their descendants.

Eligibility This program is open to veterans and descendants of veterans who served honorably with a unit of the 37th Infantry Division until its deactivation in 1968. The veteran must be an active or life member of the association or, if deceased, must have been a member at the time of his death. Applicants may be seniors in high school or already enrolled in a college program. They must have a GPA of 2.25 or higher. Along with their application, they must submit transcripts that include ACT and/or SAT scores, a statement of future educational and career goals, and a 2-page essay on why they should be selected to receive this grant. Financial need is not considered in the selection process.

Financial data The stipend is $1,000.

Duration 1 year.

Number awarded Varies each year.

Deadline April of each year.

[526]
3M "HIRE OUR HEROES" SCHOLARSHIPS AND TOOL GRANTS
Collision Repair Education Foundation
Attn: Administrative Coordinator
5125 Trillium Boulevard
Hoffman Estates, IL 60192
(847) 463-5283　　　　　Toll Free: (888) 722-3787
Fax: (847) 463-5483
E-mail: Janet.Marczyk@ed-foundation.org
Web: www.collisioneducationfoundation.org

Summary To provide financial assistance, in the form of scholarships and tool grants, to veterans and their families preparing for a career in automotive collision repair.

Eligibility This program is open to collision repair students who are currently serving or have recently served in the military, as well as their immediate family. Applicants must have completed at least 1 semester at a school that offers an auto collision/auto body repair program. Selection is based on past academic achievement, future plans, and financial need.

Financial data Recently, the program offered stipends of $2,000 to veterans and military personnel, $2,500 to family members, and tool grants to veterans.

Duration 1 year.

Additional information This program is sponsored by 3M Company.

Number awarded Varies each year; recently, the program awarded 12 scholarships to veterans and military personnel, 7 scholarships to family members, and 40 tool kit grants to veterans.

Deadline February of each year.

[527]
43D INFANTRY DIVISION VETERANS ASSOCIATION SCHOLARSHIPS
43d Infantry Division Veterans Association
c/o David Thiede, Secretary/Treasurer
P.O. Box 7281
Berlin, CT 06037
E-mail: 43rdvets@gmail.com
Web: www.43rd-infantry-division.org

Summary To provide financial assistance for college to members of the 43d Infantry Division Veterans Association and their families.

Eligibility This program is open to members of the association; the wives, children, grandchildren, and great-grandchildren of members; and the widows, children, grandchildren, and great-grandchildren of deceased members who were in good standing at the time of their death. Descendants of members of the 43d Infantry Division who died on active duty with the division during World War II are also eligible. Financial need is considered in the selection process.

Financial data The stipend is $1,000.

Duration 1 year.

Number awarded 4 each year.

Deadline May of each year.

[528]
506TH AIRBORNE INFANTRY REGIMENT ASSOCIATION SCHOLARSHIP

506th Airborne Infantry Regiment Association
c/o Alfred May, Scholarship Committee
30 Sweetman Lane
West Milford, NJ 07480-2933
(973) 728-1458 E-mail: alfredmay@aol.com
Web: www.506infantry.org

Summary To provide financial assistance for college or graduate school to former members of the 506th Airborne Infantry Regiment and their families.

Eligibility This program is open to veterans who served with the 506th Airborne Infantry Regiment and their children, grandchildren, spouses, and siblings. Applicants must be entering or attending an undergraduate or graduate program at a college or university in the United States. They must submit a statement describing their personal achievements and career objectives. Selection is based on academic excellence, quality of the institution the applicant has chosen to attend, and financial need.

Financial data The stipend is $1,500 or $1,000.

Duration 1 year; nonrenewable.

Additional information This program includes the Currahee Scholarship Award, the Marcia and John Lally Scholarship Award, the Eugene and Marilyn Overton Scholarship Award, the SPC Edwin Roodhouse Memorial Scholarship Award, the NAVILLUS Award, and the CPT Luke Wullenwaber Memorial Scholarship Award.

Number awarded 3 at $1,500 and 3 at $1,000 each year.

Deadline April of each year.

[529]
531 GRAY GHOST SQUADRON ASSOCIATION SCHOLARSHIP

531 Gray Ghost Squadron Association
c/o Marine Corps Scholarship Foundation
Attn: Scholarship Office
909 North Washington Street, Suite 400
Alexandria, VA 22314
(703) 549-0060 Toll Free: (866) 496-5462
Fax: (703) 549-9474 E-mail: students@mcsf.org
Web: sites.google.com/site/531grayghostsquadron/main

Summary To provide financial assistance for college to the children and grandchildren of veterans who served with the 531 Gray Ghost Squadron of Marines.

Eligibility This program is open to children grandchildren of veterans who served with the 531 Gray Ghost Squadron and are or were members of its association. Applicants must be high school seniors, high school graduates, or current college students. Along with their application, they must submit academic transcripts, a copy of their grandparent's honorable discharge, and a 500-word essay on a topic that changes periodically. Only undergraduate study is supported. The family income of applicants must be less than $96,000 per year.

Financial data Stipends depend on the need of the recipient and the availability of funds, but generally range from $500 to $2,500 per year.

Duration 1 year; may be renewed for up to 3 additional years.

Number awarded Varies each year; recently, 2 were awarded.

Deadline February of each year.

[530]
82ND AIRBORNE DIVISION ASSOCIATION AWARDS

82nd Airborne Division Association
Attn: Educational Fund Treasurer
P.O. Box 87482
Fayetteville, NC 28304-7482
(281) 814-2377 E-mail: patrickcopening@gmail.com
Web: www.82ndairborneassociation.org

Summary To provide financial assistance for college to members of the 82d Airborne Division Association and their dependent children.

Eligibility Eligible to apply for this award are 1) dependent children of 82nd Airborne Division Association voting members; 2) dependent children of 82nd Airborne servicemen killed in combat; 3) dependent children of deceased Life or All American members of the 82nd Airborne Division Association; and 4) former active-duty 82nd Airborne Division troopers who are association members, are within 2 years of honorable discharge, and served no more than 2 enlistments. Applicants must be enrolled full time in an accredited university or college. Selection is based on academic achievement and financial need. In years when a suitable candidate applies, 1 of these awards for dependent children is designated the General Mathew B. Ridgeway Scholarship and 1 for former troopers as the Past President Herb Altman Memorial Scholarship.

Financial data The stipend is $2,000 per year. Recipients of the Ridgeway and Alman scholarships, if awarded, receive an additional $1,500. Funds are paid to the recipient's college or university.

Duration 1 semester (the second in a school year); recipients may reapply for up to 3 additional annual awards.

Additional information Membership in the association is open to anyone who ever served in the 82nd Airborne Division, anyone who is currently serving on active duty in jump status, and anyone who has ever served in any of the uniformed services on either jump or glider status and was honorably discharged.

Number awarded Varies each year; recently, 36 were awarded. In the past 15 years, this program has awarded $2,143,800 in scholarships.

Deadline October of each year.

[531]
95TH DIVISION SCHOLARSHIP

Oklahoma City Community Foundation
Attn: Scholarship Coordinator
1000 North Broadway
P.O. Box 1146
Oklahoma City, OK 73101-1146
(405) 606-2907 Fax: (405) 235-5612
E-mail: w.minter@occf.org
Web: occf.academicworks.com/opportunities/2822

Summary To provide financial assistance for college to high school seniors in any state who are descendants of members of the 95th Division.

Eligibility This program is open to high school seniors who are descendants of members of the various components of the 95th Division, including its World War II service or various transitions as part of the Army Reserves. Applicants must be planning to enroll at an accredited 2- or 4-year college, university, or vocational school in any state. They must have a GPA of 2.5 or higher. Along with their application, they must submit a statement on their higher education goals and how life events or experiences have led them to those goals. Preference is given to students who can demonstrate financial need.

Financial data The stipend is $2,000 per year.
Duration 1 year; recipients may reapply for up to 3 additional years.
Number awarded 1 or more each year.
Deadline April of each year.

[532]
A-7 CORSAIR ASSOCIATION SCHOLARSHIP

Wings Over America Scholarship Foundation
Attn: Scholarship Administrator
770 Lynnhaven Parkway, Suite 155
Virginia Beach, VA 23452
(757) 228-3532
E-mail: scholarship@wingsoveramerica.us
Web: www.wingsoveramerica.us/scholarships/administered

Summary To provide financial assistance for college to dependents of U.S. Air Force and Air National Guard personnel who are members of the A-7 Corsair Association.
Eligibility This program is open to 1) children of a military sponsor who are graduating high school seniors planning to enroll in college full time to work on a bachelor's degree or who are already enrolled in such a program; and 2) spouses of a military sponsor currently enrolled full or part time and working on an associate or bachelor's degree at an accredited college or university. Children must be unmarried and younger than 22 years of age. The military sponsor must be a current or deceased member of the A-7 Corsair Association. The minimum GPA is 3.0 for high school seniors or 2.5 for college students (children and spouses). Selection is based on academic achievement, extracurricular activities, work/internships, community service, recommendations, and an essay.
Financial data The basic stipend is $3,800.
Duration 1 year.
Additional information This program is funded by the A-7 Corsair Association.
Number awarded 1 or more each year.
Deadline Pre-qualification forms must be submitted by January of each year.

[533]
ADA MUCKLESTONE MEMORIAL SCHOLARSHIPS

American Legion Auxiliary
Department of Illinois
2720 East Lincoln Street
P.O. Box 1426
Bloomington, IL 61702-1426
(309) 663-9366   Fax: (309) 663-5827
E-mail: karen.boughan@ilala.org
Web: www.ilala.org/education.html

Summary To provide financial assistance to high school seniors in Illinois who are the descendants of veterans and planning to attend college in any state.

Eligibility This program is open to the children, grandchildren, or great-grandchildren of veterans who served during eligibility dates for membership in the American Legion. Applicants must be high school seniors or graduates who have not yet attended an institution of higher learning and are planning to attend college in any state. They must be residents of Illinois or members of the American Legion Family, Department of Illinois. Along with their application, they must submit a 1,000-word essay on "What My Education Will Do for Me." Selection is based on that essay (25%), character and leadership (25%), scholarship (25%), and financial need (25%).
Financial data The stipend is $1,000.
Duration 1 year.
Number awarded Varies each year.
Deadline March of each year.

[534]
ADRIAN AND CORENA SWANIER EDUCATION SCHOLARSHIPS

Ketia4Kidz Foundation
3012 Gold Creek Drive
Villa Rica, GA 30180
(706) 577-1731   Fax: (770) 456-9766
E-mail: kswanier@ketia4kidz.org
Web: www.ketia4kidz.org

Summary To provide financial assistance for college to children of active-duty, retired, and deceased military personnel.
Eligibility This program is open to unmarried children younger than 23 years of age of active-duty personnel, military veterans, deceased members, and Guard and Reserve personnel. Applicants must be enrolled or planning to enroll full time at an accredited college or university to work on a 4-year degree and have a GPA of 2.5 or higher. They may attend a community, vocational, technical, or junior college if they are enrolled in a program of studies designed to allow them to transfer directly into a 4-year program. Along with their application, they must submit a 2-page essay about their experience as a military brat.
Financial data The stipend is $1,000.
Duration 1 year.
Additional information This program began in 2010.
Number awarded Varies each year; recently, 4 were awarded.
Deadline Deadline not specified.

[535]
ADRIENNE ALIX SCHOLARSHIP

American Legion Auxiliary
Department of New Hampshire
Attn: Department Auxiliary Secretary
121 South Fruit Street, Suite 103
Concord, NH 03301-2412
(603) 856-8942   E-mail: nhalasec@legionnh.org
Web: www.legionnh.org

Summary To provide financial assistance to New Hampshire residents, including those recently discharged from the military, who wish to refresh or upgrade their skills at a school in any state.
Eligibility This program is open to New Hampshire residents and to members of a unit of the American Legion Aux-

SCHOLARSHIPS: FAMILY MEMBERS

iliary, Department of New Hampshire, who have been members for at least 3 consecutive years. Applicants must be 1) reentering the workforce or upgrading skills; 2) displaced from the workforce; or 3) recently discharged honorably from the military. They must be interested in taking a refresher course or advancing their knowledge or techniques needed in today's workforce at a school in any state. Along with their application, they must submit a 500-word essay explaining their career goals and objectives.
Financial data The stipend is $1,000.
Duration 1 year.
Number awarded 1 each year.
Deadline March of each year.

[536]
AEA CONGRESSMAN DAVID L. HOBSON STEM SCHOLARSHIP

Army Engineer Association
Attn: Director Washington DC Operations
P.O. Box 30260
Alexandria, VA 22310-8260
(703) 428-7084   Fax: (703) 428-6043
E-mail: xd@armyengineer.com
Web: www.armyengineer.com/scholarships

Summary To provide financial assistance to members of the Army Engineer Association (AEA) and their families interested in studying a field of STEM in college.
Eligibility This program is open to AEA members and their families who are U.S. citizens. Applicants must be enrolled full time at an accredited college or university and working on a bachelor's degree in a field of STEM. Along with their application, they must submit a 600-word essay on how their STEM degree will advance their academic/professional goals. Selection is based on that essay, scholastic aptitude, and letters of recommendation.
Financial data The stipend is $3,000.
Duration 1 year; nonrenewable.
Additional information This program is sponsored by the engineering firm, Trimble.
Number awarded Up to 3 each year.
Deadline February of each year.

[537]
AFAS MERIT SCHOLARSHIPS

Air Force Aid Society
Attn: Education Assistance Department
1550 Crystal Drive, Suite 809
Arlington, VA 22202
(703) 972-2647   Toll Free: (866) 896-5637
Fax: (703) 972-2646   E-mail: ed@afas-hq.org
Web: www.afas.org/how-we-help/afas-merit-scholarship

Summary To provide merit-based financial assistance for college to dependents of active-duty, retired, disabled, or deceased Air Force personnel who demonstrate outstanding academic achievement.
Eligibility This program is open to dependent children of Air Force personnel who are active duty, Title 10 Reservists on extended active duty, Title 32 Guard performing full-time active-duty service, retired due to length of active-duty service or disability, or deceased while on active duty or in retired status. Applicants must be entering their freshman year as full-time undergraduate students at an accredited college, university, or vocational/trade school. Selection is based on cumulative GPA, SAT/ACT scores, transcripts, extracurricular activities, volunteer and/or work experience, a resume, and an essay on a specified topic.
Financial data The stipend is $5,000.
Duration 1 year.
Number awarded 10 each year.
Deadline March of each year.

[538]
AFBA NGAUS ACTIVE LIFE MEMBER SCHOLARSHIP

National Guard Association of the United States
Attn: Scholarship
One Massachusetts Avenue, N.W.
Washington, DC 20001
(202) 789-0031   Fax: (202) 682-9358
E-mail: ngaus@ngaus.org
Web: www.ngaus.org

Summary To provide financial assistance to members of the National Guard Association of the United States (NGAUS) and their dependents who are interested in working on an undergraduate or graduate degree.
Eligibility This program is open to active life NGAUS members and their dependents. Applicants must be enrolled or planning to enroll full time at a college or university in any state to work on an undergraduate or graduate degree. Along with their application, they must submit their college acceptance letter, SAT and/or ACT scores, high school or undergraduate transcripts, a publicity photograph, and an essay up to 300 words in length on an experience with the National Guard and how it has shaped their development and goals.
Financial data The stipend is $5,000.
Duration 1 year.
Additional information This program is sponsored by the Armed Forces Benefit Association (AFBA).
Number awarded 2 each year.
Deadline May of each year.

[539]
AFCEA DC STEM SCHOLARSHIPS

Armed Forces Communications and Electronics
    Association-Washington D.C. Chapter
Attn: Vice President, STEM
1700 Diagonal Road, Suite 450
Alexandria, VA 22314
(703) 660-4835
E-mail: scholarships@dc.afceachapters.org
Web: dc.afceachapters.org/content/chapter-scholarships

Summary To provide financial assistance to residents of the metropolitan Washington, D.C. area who are interested in majoring in fields of STEM in college.
Eligibility This program is open to residents of the metropolitan Washington, D.C. area who are U.S. citizens or permanent residents. Applicants may be either high school seniors or second-year students at a community college, but they must have been accepted as a full-time student at an accredited 4-year college or university in the United States. They must be planning to major in chemistry, computer science, cyber security, electronics, engineering (aerospace, chemical, computer, electrical, or systems), mathematics, management information systems, or physics. Applications

are especially encouraged from students whose family includes current members of the military, veterans, and members of the Washington, D.C. chapter of the Armed Forces Communications and Electronics Association (AFCEA). Selection is based on academic achievement, school activities, letters of recommendation, and financial need.
Financial data The stipend is $5,000.
Duration 1 year; nonrenewable.
Additional information This program was established in 1989. The metropolitan Washington, D.C. area is defined to include the District of Columbia; the Maryland counties of Charles, Frederick, Montgomery, and Prince George's; the Virginia counties of Arlington, Fairfax, Loudoun, and Prince William; and the Virginia cities of Alexandria, Fairfax, Falls Church, Manassas, and Manassas Park.
Number awarded Varies each year; recently, 20 were awarded. Since the program was established, it has awarded more than $2,500,000 to 420 students.
Deadline April of each year.

[540]
AFSA SCHOLARSHIP PROGRAM
Air Force Sergeants Association
Attn: Membership and Field Relations
5211 Auth Road
Suitland, MD 20746
(301) 899-3500 Toll Free: (800) 638-0594
Fax: (301) 899-8136 E-mail: staff@hqafsa.org
Web: www.hqafsa.org/scholarships.html

Summary To provide financial assistance for undergraduate education to the dependent children of Air Force enlisted personnel.
Eligibility This program is open to the unmarried children (including stepchildren and legally adopted children) of active-duty, retired, or veteran members of the U.S. Air Force, Air National Guard, or Air Force Reserves. Applicants must be attending or planning to attend an accredited academic institution. They must have an unweighted GPA of 3.5 or higher. Their parent must be a member of the Air Force Sergeants Association or its auxiliary. Along with their application, they must submit information on their future plans, activities and work experience during the past 4 years, the academic or other experience that has given them the greatest satisfaction, books and significant articles they have read in the past year, and films they have seen in the past year. High school seniors must also submit a transcript of all high school grades and a record of their SAT or ACT scores. Selection is based on academic record, character, leadership skills, writing ability, versatility, and potential for success. Financial need is not a consideration.
Financial data Stipends recently ranged from $1,500 to $2,500 per year. Funds may be used for tuition, room and board, fees, books, supplies, and transportation.
Duration 1 year; may be renewed if the student maintains full-time enrollment.
Additional information This program began in 1968.
Number awarded Varies each year; recently, 12 worth $23,500 were awarded: 4 at $2,500, 3 at $2,000, and 5 at $1,500. Since the program began, it has awarded 617 scholarships worth more than $920,100.
Deadline March of each year.

[541]
AHIMA VETERANS SCHOLARSHIP
American Health Information Management Association
Attn: AHIMA Foundation
233 North Michigan Avenue, 21st Floor
Chicago, IL 60601-5809
(312) 233-1131 Fax: (312) 233-1537
E-mail: info@ahimafoundation.org
Web: www.ahimafoundation.org

Summary To provide financial assistance to veterans and spouses of veterans and active-duty service personnel who are interested in working on an undergraduate or graduate degree in health information management (HIM) or health information technology (HIT).
Eligibility This program is open to 1) veterans of the armed forces, including Army, Navy, Air Force, Marine Corps, Coast Guard, Reserves, and National Guard; and 2) spouses and surviving spouses of servicemembers, including active-duty military, retirees, veterans, and wounded warriors. Applicants must be working full time on a degree in HIM or HIT at the associate, bachelor's, post-baccalaureate, master's, or doctoral level. They must have at least 6 credit hours remaining after the date of the award. Along with their application, they must submit an essay of 250 to 400 words on their educational and career ambitions, record of military service, record of personal achievement, community service, desire to serve others and make a positive community impact, and leadership potential. In the selection process, preference is given to 1) physically wounded or disabled veterans; 2) surviving spouses; and 3) those who served in a combat tour of duty.
Financial data Stipends are $1,000 for associate degree students, $1,500 for bachelor's degree or post-baccalaureate certificate students, $2,000 for master's degree students, or $2,500 for doctoral degree students.
Duration 1 year.
Additional information Effective in 2018, this program includes the John Kloss Memorial Veteran Scholarship and other scholarships supported by Nuance Communications and the Walter Reed Society.
Number awarded 4 each year.
Deadline September of each year.

[542]
AIR FORCE CLUB SCHOLARSHIP PROGRAM
Air Force Services Agency
Attn: HQ AFPC/SVOFT
10100 Reunion Place, Suite 501
San Antonio, TX 78216-4138
(210) 395-7351 Toll Free: (800) 443-4834
E-mail: clubs@myairforcelife.com
Web: www.myairforcelife.com/Clubs

Summary To recognize and reward, with academic scholarships, Air Force Club members and their families who submit outstanding essays.
Eligibility This program is open to Air Force Club members and their spouses, children, stepchildren, or grandchildren who have been accepted by or are enrolled at an accredited college or university. Applicants may be traditional (graduating high school seniors) or nontraditional (all other club members). They must submit either 1) an essay of 980 to 1020 words on a topic that changes annually; or 2) a video of 4 minutes 30 seconds to 5 minutes 30 seconds on the same

topic. Essays and videos must relate to a topic that changes annually; recently, students were asked to write about the core values of the U.S. Air Force. Applicants must also include a 1-page summary of their long-term career and life goals and previous accomplishments, including civic, athletic, and academic awards.
Financial data Awards for both traditional and nontraditional applicants are presented as scholarships of $7,000 for first, $5,000 for second, $3,000 for third, $2,000 for fourth, and $1,000 for honorable mention.
Duration The competition is held annually.
Additional information This competition was first held in 1997.
Number awarded 10 each year: 5 for traditional applicants and 5 for nontraditional.
Deadline May of each year.

[543]
AIR FORCE SERGEANTS ASSOCIATION INTERNATIONAL AUXILIARY EDUCATION GRANTS
Air Force Sergeants Association
Attn: Membership and Field Relations
5211 Auth Road
Suitland, MD 20746
(301) 899-3500   Toll Free: (800) 638-0594
Fax: (301) 899-8136   E-mail: staff@hqafsa.org
Web: www.hqafsa.org/scholarships.html

Summary To provide financial assistance for college to members of the Air Force Sergeants Association (AFSA) Auxiliary.
Eligibility This program is open to AFSA Auxiliary members who need assistance to enhance their income potential through formal education and/or training. Applicants must be seeking to obtain effective education and/or training to acquire improved marketable skills. They must be 19 years of age or older and have been members for at least 1 year. Financial need is considered in the selection process.
Financial data Stipends are $2,000 per year. Funds are sent directly to the recipient's school to be used for tuition, room and board, fees, books, supplies, child care, meals, and transportation.
Duration 1 year; may be renewed if the student maintains full-time enrollment.
Additional information This program began in 1990.
Number awarded Varies each year; recently, 5 were awarded. Since the program began, it has awarded more than 170 grants worth more than $165,700.
Deadline March of each year.

[544]
AL AND WILLAMARY VISTE SCHOLARSHIP PROGRAM
101st Airborne Division Association
32 Screaming Eagle Boulevard
P.O. Box 929
Fort Campbell, KY 42223-0929
(931) 431-0199   Fax: (931) 431-0195
E-mail: 101exec@screamingeagle.org
Web: www.screamingeaglefoundation.org

Summary To provide financial assistance to the spouses, children, and grandchildren of members of the 101st Airborne Division Association who are upper-division or graduate students working on a degree in science.
Eligibility This program is open to college juniors, seniors, and graduate students who maintained a GPA of 3.75 or higher during the preceding school year and whose parent, grandparent, or spouse is (or, if deceased, was) a regular or life (not associate) member of the 101st Airborne Division. Preference is given to students working on a degree in a physical science, medical science, or other scientific research field. Applicants must submit an essay of 500 to 550 words on the importance of the U.S. constitution and their long-term goals, career objectives, community service, hobbies, interests, personal achievements, and how a higher education for them in their chosen field can benefit our nation. Financial need is not considered in the selection process.
Financial data A stipend is awarded (amount not specified).
Duration 1 year; may be renewed.
Number awarded At least 1 each year.
Deadline May of each year.

[545]
ALABAMA G.I. DEPENDENTS' SCHOLARSHIP PROGRAM
Alabama Department of Veterans Affairs
100 North Union Street, Suite 850
Montgomery, AL 36104
(334) 242-5077   Fax: (334) 242-5102
Web: www.va.alabama.gov/gi_dep_scholarship.aspx

Summary To provide educational benefits to the dependents of disabled, deceased, and other Alabama veterans.
Eligibility This program is open to children, spouses, and unremarried widow(er)s of veterans who are currently rated as 40% or more service-connected disabled or were so rated at time of death, were a former prisoner of war, have been declared missing in action, died as the result of a service-connected disability, or died while on active military duty in the line of duty. The veteran must have been a permanent civilian resident of Alabama for at least 1 year prior to entering active military service and served honorably for at least 90 days during wartime (or less, in case of death or service-connected disability). They must also have been a resident of Alabama for at least 2 years prior to applying, have been discharged within the last 12 months, or filed a resident Alabama income tax return for the past 10 consecutive years. Veterans who were not Alabama residents at the time of entering active military service may also qualify if they have a 100% disability and were permanent residents of Alabama for at least 5 years prior to filing the application for this program or prior to death, if deceased. Children and stepchildren must be under the age of 26, but spouses and widow(er)s may be of any age. Spouses cease to be eligible if they become divorced from the qualifying veteran. Widow(er)s cease to be eligible if they remarry.
Financial data This program provides payment of tuition at public universities in Alabama, to a maximum of $250 per semester hour. Purchase of required textbooks and payment of fees are supported at the rate of $1,000 per semester.
Duration This is an entitlement program for 5 years of full-time undergraduate or graduate study or part-time equivalent for all qualifying children and for spouses and unremarried widow(er)s who veteran spouse is or was rated 100% dis-

abled or meets other qualifying requirements. Spouses and unremarried widow(er)s whose veteran spouse is or was rated between 40% and 90% disabled may attend only 3 standard academic years.
Number awarded Varies each year.
Deadline Applications may be submitted at any time.

[546]
ALASKA SEA SERVICES SCHOLARSHIPS
Navy League of the United States
Attn: Scholarships
2300 Wilson Boulevard, Suite 200
Arlington, VA 22201-5424
(703) 528-1775 Toll Free: (800) 356-5760
Fax: (703) 528-2333
E-mail: scholarships@navyleague.org
Web: /www.navyleague.org/programs/scholarships

Summary To provide financial assistance to spouses and dependent children of naval personnel in Alaska who are interested in attending college in any state.
Eligibility This program is open to U.S. citizens who are 1) dependents or direct descendants of an active, Reserve, retired, or honorably discharged member of the U.S. sea service (including the Navy, Marine Corps, Coast Guard, or Merchant Marine); or 2) currently an active member of the Naval Sea Cadet Corps. Applicants must be high school seniors in Alaska entering their freshman year at an accredited college or university. They must have a GPA of 3.0 or higher. Along with their application, they must submit transcripts, 2 letters of recommendation, SAT/ACT scores, documentation of financial need, proof of qualifying sea service duty, and a 1-page personal statement on why they should be considered for this scholarship.
Financial data The stipend is $1,000; funds are paid directly to the academic institution for tuition, books, and fees.
Duration 1 year.
Additional information This program began in 1986 with funds originally raised as a War Bond during World War II to honor the sailors of USS Juneau.
Number awarded 6 each year.
Deadline February of each year.

[547]
ALBERT M. BECKER MEMORIAL YOUTH SCHOLARSHIP
New York American Legion Press Association
Attn: Scholarship Chair
P.O. Box 424
Sanborn, NY 14132
E-mail: jackbutton@hotmail.com
Web: nyalpa.webs.com/pubslinksannualevents.htm

Summary To provide financial assistance to residents of New York who have a connection with veterans and are interested in careers in communications.
Eligibility This program is open to New York residents younger than 23 years of age who are 1) members of the American Legion, American Legion Auxiliary, or Sons of the American Legion; 2) children or grandchildren of members of those organizations; 3) children of a 50% or more disabled veteran; 4) children of a currently-serving member of the National Guard or military Reserves; or 4) children of a deceased veteran. Applicants must be enrolled or planning to enroll full time at an accredited college, university, or trade school in any school to work on a degree in communications (including public relations, journalism, reprographics, newspaper design or management, web page design, video design, social media communications, photojournalism, American history, political science, public communications, or other field of study related to the goals of the sponsor or the American Legion family). Along with their application, they must submit a 500-word essay on their field of study, the reasons for choosing their field of study, and their goals upon completion of study. Financial need and class standing are not considered. U.S. citizenship is required.
Financial data The stipend is $1,000.
Duration 1 year.
Number awarded 1 each year.
Deadline April of each year.

[548]
ALBERT M. LAPPIN SCHOLARSHIP
American Legion
Department of Kansas
1314 S.W. Topeka Boulevard
Topeka, KS 66612-1886
(785) 232-9315 Fax: (785) 232-1399
Web: www.ksamlegion.org

Summary To provide financial assistance to the children of members of the Kansas American Legion or American Legion Auxiliary who plan to attend college in the state.
Eligibility This program is open to high school seniors and college freshmen and sophomores who are attending or planning to attend an approved Kansas college, university, or trade school. At least 1 of their parents must be a veteran and have been a member of an American Legion Post or Auxiliary in Kansas for the past 3 consecutive years. Along with their application, they must submit an essay of 250 to 500 words on "Why I Want to Go to College." Financial need is also considered in the selection process.
Financial data The stipend is $1,000.
Duration 1 year.
Number awarded 1 each year.
Deadline February of each year.

[549]
ALBERT T. MARCOUX MEMORIAL SCHOLARSHIP
American Legion
Department of New Hampshire
121 South Fruit Street
Concord, NH 03301
(603) 856-8951 Fax: (603) 856-8943
E-mail: adjutantnh@nhlegion.com
Web: www.legionnh.org

Summary To provide financial assistance to the children of members of the New Hampshire Department of the American Legion or American Legion Auxiliary who are interested in studying any field at a college in any state.
Eligibility This program is open to residents of New Hampshire who are entering their first year at an accredited 4-year college or university in any state to work on a bachelor's degree in any field. Applicant's parent must be a member of the American Legion or its Auxiliary (or if deceased have been a member at time of death). They must have a GPA of

3.0 or higher in their junior and senior high school years. Financial need is considered in the selection process.
Financial data The stipend is $2,000.
Duration 1 year.
Number awarded 1 each year.
Deadline April of each year.

[550]
ALEXANDER KREIGLOWA NAVY AND MARINE CORPS DEPENDENTS EDUCATION FOUNDATION SCHOLARSHIP
Navy League of the United States-San Diego Council
Attn: Scholarship Committee
2115 Park Boulevard
San Diego, CA 92101
(619) 230-0301   Fax: (619) 230-0302
Web: www.navyleague-sd.com/scholarship-program

Summary To provide financial assistance to high school seniors in California who are children of Naval Service personnel and interested in attending college in any state.
Eligibility This program is open to seniors graduating from high schools in California in the top 10% of their class or with a GPA of 3.6 or higher. Applicants must be the dependent child of an active-duty, retired, or deceased member of the Naval Service (U.S. Navy or U.S. Marine Corps). They must be planning to enroll at an accredited 4-year college or university in any state. Along with their application, they must submit a 1-page essay outlining their college and future plans, including how life and transitions as a military dependent have contributed. Financial need is considered in the selection process.
Financial data The stipend ranges up to $15,000 per year.
Duration 1 year; may be renewed up to 3 additional years.
Number awarded 1 each year.
Deadline April of each year.

[551]
ALLIE MAE ODEN MEMORIAL SCHOLARSHIP
Ladies Auxiliary of the Fleet Reserve Association
c/o Amanda Murray, National Scholarship Chair
512 Hyde Park Road
Norfolk, VA 23503-5514
(757) 588-6125   E-mail: sairockstar@gmail.com
Web: www.la-fra.org/scholarship.html

Summary To provide financial assistance for college to the children and grandchildren of members of the Fleet Reserve Association (FRA) or its Ladies Auxiliary (LA).
Eligibility This program is open to the children and grandchildren of FRA or LA FRA members. Applicants must submit an essay on why they want to go to college and what they intend to accomplish with their degree, including life experiences, career objectives, and what motivated them to select those objectives. Selection is based on academic record, financial need, extracurricular activities, leadership skills, and participation in community activities. U.S. citizenship is required.
Financial data The stipend is $2,500.
Duration 1 year; may be renewed.
Additional information Membership in the FRA is open to current and former enlisted members of the Navy, Marine Corps, and Coast Guard.
Number awarded 1 each year.
Deadline April of each year.

[552]
ALLIED.COM MILITARY SCHOLARSHIP
Allied Van Lines
One Parkview Plaza
Oakbrook Terrace, IL 60180
Toll Free: (800) 689-8684
Web: www.allied.com/military-scholarship

Summary To provide financial assistance to current and former military personnel and their families who are interested in attending college to study fields related to logistics.
Eligibility This program is open to current and honorably discharged members of the military, their spouses, and their children under 21 years of age or (if currently attending college) under 23 years of age. Applicants must be enrolled or planning to enroll full time at a 4-year college or university and major in military logistics, supply chain management, or operational management. They must be U.S. citizens or permanent residents. Along with their application, they must submit an essay of 400 to 800 words on why a career in logistics/supply chain management is their college major of choice. Financial need is not considered in the selection process.
Financial data The stipend is $1,000.
Duration 1 year.
Additional information This program began in 2015.
Number awarded 2 each year.
Deadline September of each year.

[553]
ALOHA SCHOLARSHIP
American Legion Auxiliary
Department of Montana
Attn: Mechelle Holmes, Education Chair
1956 Mt Majo
Fort Harrison, MT 59636
(406) 324-3989
Web: www.mtlegion.org/forms/scholarships.html

Summary To provide financial assistance to descendants of Montana members of the American Legion Auxiliary who plan to study nursing at a school in any state.
Eligibility This program is open to the children, grandchildren, or great-grandchildren of living or deceased members in Montana of the American Legion Auxiliary. Applicants must be residents of Montana who are accepted or enrolled at an accredited school of nursing in any state. Along with their application, they must submit an essay of 300 to 500 words on a phase of nursing as a profession and their reason for wishing to enter the profession. Selection is based 50% on the essay and 50% on the character, aptitude, scholarship, and need of the applicant.
Financial data A stipend is awarded (amount not specified).
Duration 1 year.
Number awarded 1 each year.
Deadline March of each year.

[554]
AMERICAL SCHOLARSHIP PROGRAM
Americal Division Veterans Association
Attn: American Legacy Foundation
c/o William Bruinsma, Scholarship Program Chair
5425 Parmalee Road
Middleville, MI 49333
(269) 795-5237　　　　　E-mail: wb3379@gmail.com
Web: www.americalfoundation.org/cmsalf/scholarship.html

Summary To provide financial assistance for college to the dependents of members of the Americal Division Veterans Association.

Eligibility This program is open to the children and grandchildren of members of the Americal Division Veterans Association and to the children of Americal Division veterans who were killed in action or died while on active duty with the Division. Applicants must be attending or planning to attend a college or vocational school. Along with their application, they must submit an essay of 200 to 300 words on a topic that changes annually but related to loyalty to the nation. Financial need is considered in the selection process.

Financial data Recently, stipends ranged from $500 to $3,500 per year.

Duration 1 year; recipients may reapply.

Number awarded Varies each year; approximately $30,000 in scholarships are awarded annually.

Deadline April of each year.

[555]
AMERICAN LEGION AUXILIARY EMERGENCY FUND
American Legion Auxiliary
Attn: AEF Program Case Manager
3450 Founders Road
Indianapolis, IN 46268
(317) 569-4544　　　　　Fax: (317) 569-4502
E-mail: aef@alaforveterans.org
Web: www.alaforveterans.org/about/Brochures

Summary To provide funding to members of the American Legion Auxiliary who are facing temporary emergency needs.

Eligibility This program is open to members of the American Legion Auxiliary who have maintained their membership for the immediate past 2 consecutive years and have paid their dues for the current year. Applicants must need emergency assistance for the following purposes: 1) food, shelter, and utilities during a time of financial crisis; 2) food and shelter because of weather-related emergencies and natural disasters; or 3) educational training for eligible members who lack the necessary skills for employment or to upgrade competitive workforce skills. They must have exhausted all other sources of financial assistance, including funds and/or services available through the local Post and/or Unit, appropriate community welfare agencies, or state and federal financial aid for education. Grants are not available to settle already existing or accumulated debts, handle catastrophic illness, resettle disaster victims, or other similar problems.

Financial data The maximum grant is $2,400. Payments may be made directly to the member or to the mortgage company or utility. Educational grants may be paid directly to the educational institution.

Duration Grants are expended over no more than 3 months.

Additional information This program began in 1969. In 1981, it was expanded to include the Displaced Homemaker Fund (although that title is no longer used).

Number awarded Varies each year.

Deadline Applications may be submitted at any time.

[556]
AMERICAN LEGION AUXILIARY JUNIOR MEMBER LOYALTY SCHOLARSHIP
American Legion Auxiliary
3450 Founders Road
Indianapolis, IN 46268
(317) 569-4500　　　　　Fax: (317) 569-4502
E-mail: alahq@alaforveterans.org
Web: www.alaforveterans.org

Summary To provide financial assistance to junior members of the American Legion Auxiliary who are enrolled in college.

Eligibility Applicants for this scholarship must have been junior members of the Auxiliary for at least the past 3 years. They must have completed at least the first semester at a college or technical school. They must have a GPA of 3.0 or higher. Along with their application, they must submit a 1,000-word essay on a topic that changes annually; recently, students were asked to write on how their membership as a Junior in the American Legion Auxiliary contributed to their leadership skills and educational success as a senior member. Selection is based on leadership, character, and participation in the Auxiliary as presented in the essay (50%), academic achievement (25%), and completed application (25%).

Financial data The stipend is $2,500.

Duration 1 year.

Additional information Applications are available from the president of the candidate's own unit or from the secretary or education chair of the department.

Number awarded 10 each year: 2 in each division of the American Legion Auxiliary.

Deadline Applications must be submitted to the unit president by February of each year.

[557]
AMERICAN LEGION AUXILIARY SCHOLARSHIP FOR NON-TRADITIONAL STUDENTS
American Legion Auxiliary
3450 Founders Road
Indianapolis, IN 46268
(317) 569-4500　　　　　Fax: (317) 569-4502
E-mail: alahq@alaforveterans.org
Web: www.alaforveterans.org

Summary To provide financial assistance for college to nontraditional students affiliated with the American Legion.

Eligibility This program is open to members of the American Legion, American Legion Auxiliary, or Sons of the American Legion who have paid dues for the 2 preceding years and the calendar year in which application is being made. Applicants must be nontraditional students who are either 1) returning to school after some period of time during which their formal education was interrupted; or 2) just beginning their education at a later point in life. Each department (state) of the American Legion Auxiliary may nominate 1 student for this scholarship. Selection is based on academic achieve-

ment (25%), character and leadership (25%), initiative and goals (25%), and financial need (25%).
Financial data The stipend is $2,000, paid directly to the school.
Duration 1 year.
Additional information Applications are available from the president of the candidate's own unit or from the secretary or education chair of the department.
Number awarded 5 each year: 1 in each division of the American Legion Auxiliary.
Deadline Applications must be submitted to the unit president by February of each year.

[558]
AMERICAN LEGION LEGACY SCHOLARSHIPS
American Legion
Attn: Americanism and Children & Youth Division
700 North Pennsylvania Street
P.O. Box 1055
Indianapolis, IN 46206-1055
(317) 630-1212 Fax: (317) 630-1223
E-mail: scholarships@legion.org
Web: www.legion.org/scholarships/legacy

Summary To provide financial assistance for college to children of U.S. military personnel killed on active duty or disabled on or after September 11, 2001.
Eligibility This program is open to the children (including adopted children and stepchildren) of active-duty U.S. military personnel (including federalized National Guard and Reserve members) who died on active duty or became 50% or more disabled on or after September 11, 2001. Applicants must be high school seniors or graduates planning to enroll full time at an accredited institution of higher education in the United States. Selection is based on academic achievement, school and community activities, leadership skills, and financial need.
Financial data Stipends range up to $20,000.
Duration 1 year; may be renewed.
Additional information This program began in 2003.
Number awarded Varies each year; recently, 57, with a total value of $1,122,624, were awarded. Since the program began, it has awarded more than $3 million to more than 360 students.
Deadline April of each year.

[559]
AMERICAN PATRIOT SCHOLARSHIPS
Military Officers Association of America
Attn: Educational Assistance Program
201 North Washington Street
Alexandria, VA 22314-2539
(703) 549-2311 Toll Free: (800) 234-MOAA
Fax: (703) 838-5819 E-mail: edassist@moaa.org
Web: www.moaa.org

Summary To provide financial assistance for undergraduate education to children of members of the uniformed services who have died or suffered a traumatic injury.
Eligibility This program is open to children under 24 years of age of active, Reserve, and National Guard uniformed service personnel (Army, Navy, Air Force, Marines, Coast Guard, Public Health Service, or National Oceanographic and Atmospheric Administration) whose parent has died on active service or is receiving Traumatic Servicemembers' Group Life Insurance (T-SGLI) payments. Applicants must be working on an undergraduate degree. They must have a GPA of 3.0 or higher. Selection is based on scholastic ability (33%)), extracurricular activities (33%), and financial need (33%).
Financial data The stipend is currently $7,000 per year.
Duration 1 year; may be renewed up to 4 additional years.
Additional information The MOAA was formerly named The Retired Officers Association (TROA). It established this program in 2002 in response to the tragic events of September 11, 2001.
Number awarded Varies each year.
Deadline February of each year.

[560]
AMERICAN STATES UTILITY SERVICES SCHOLARSHIP PROGRAM
American States Utility Services, Inc.
630 East Foothill Boulevard
San Dimas, CA 91773
(909) 306-2400 Fax: (909) 394-0711
E-mail: contactus@asusinc.com
Web: www.asusinc.com/responsibility/scholarship_program

Summary To provide financial assistance to high school seniors who are children of military personnel assigned to designated bases and interested in studying specified fields at colleges in any state.
Eligibility This program is open to high school seniors who are dependent children of active military personnel assigned to the following military locations: Eglin Air Force Base (Okaloosa County, Florida); Fort Bliss (El Paso, Texas); Fort Bragg (Cumberland, Harnett, Hoke, and Moore counties, North Carolina); Fort Eustis (Virginia); Fort Jackson (Columbia, South Carolina); Fort Lee (Virginia); Fort Riley (Geary and Riley counties, Kansas); Fort Story (Virginia); and Joint Base Andrews (National Capital Region). Dependent children of honorable discharged U.S. military veterans living within those locations are also eligible. Applicants must be planning to enroll full time at a 2- or 4-year college, university, or vocational/technical school in any state and major in acquisition and contract management, biology, business management, chemistry, environmental engineering, environmental science, mathematical sciences, medical sciences, or technology.
Financial data The stipend is $2,500 per year.
Duration 1 year; may be renewed up to 3 additional years or completion of a bachelor's degree, whichever occurs first. Renewal requires that the recipient continue to meet eligibility requirements and maintains a GPA of 2.5 or higher.
Additional information This program is administered by Scholarship Management Services, a division of Scholarship America.
Number awarded Up to 7 each year.
Deadline March of each year.

[561]
AMVETS GENERATION T SCHOLARSHIPS
AMVETS National Headquarters
Attn: National Programs Director
4647 Forbes Boulevard
Lanham, MD 20706-3807
(301) 459-9600   Toll Free: (877) 7-AMVETS, ext. 4027
Fax: (301) 459-7924   E-mail: klathroum@amvets.org
Web: www.amvets.org/amvets-generation-t-scholarships

Summary To provide financial assistance for trade school to veterans and their spouses.
Eligibility This program is open to veterans and their spouses who are U.S. citizens; children are not eligible. Applicants must have completed high school or a GED program and be enrolled in an eligible construction trade program.
Financial data Stipends range up to $5,000.
Duration 1 year.
Additional information This program is supported by the Generation T program of Lowe's.
Number awarded Approximately 75 each year.
Deadline April or July of each year.

[562]
AMVETS JROTC SCHOLARSHIPS
AMVETS National Headquarters
Attn: National Programs Director
4647 Forbes Boulevard
Lanham, MD 20706-3807
(301) 459-9600   Toll Free: (877) 7-AMVETS, ext. 4027
Fax: (301) 459-7924   E-mail: klathroum@amvets.org
Web: www.amvets.org/scholarships

Summary To provide financial assistance for college to the children and grandchildren of veterans or active military servicemembers who have participated in Junior Reserve Officers' Training Corps (JROTC) in high school.
Eligibility This program is open to graduating high school seniors who are JROTC cadets and the children or grandchildren of a veteran (living or deceased) or an active military servicemember. Applicants must be interested in working full time on an undergraduate degree at an accredited college, university, or trade/technical school. They must be U.S. citizens and have a GPA of 3.0 or higher. Selection is based on financial need, academic promise, and merit.
Financial data The stipend is $1,000.
Duration 1 year; nonrenewable.
Number awarded 1 each year.
Deadline April of each year.

[563]
AMVETS NATIONAL LADIES AUXILIARY SCHOLARSHIPS
AMVETS National Ladies Auxiliary
Attn: Scholarship Officer
4647 Forbes Boulevard
Lanham, MD 20706-4380
(301) 459-6255   Fax: (301) 459-5403
E-mail: auxhdqs@amvets.org
Web: www.amvetsaux.org/scholarships.html

Summary To provide financial assistance to members and certain dependents of members of AMVETS National Ladies Auxiliary who are already enrolled in college.
Eligibility Applicants must belong to AMVETS Auxiliary or be the child or grandchild of a member. They must be in at least the second year of undergraduate study at an accredited college or university. Applications must include 3 letters of recommendation and an essay (from 200 to 500 words) about their past accomplishments, career and educational goals, and objectives for the future. Selection is based on the letters of reference (15%), academic record (15%), the essay (25%), and financial need (45%).
Financial data Stipends are $1,000 or $750.
Duration 1 year.
Number awarded Up to 7 each year: 2 at $1,000 and 5 at $750.
Deadline June of each year.

[564]
AMVETS NATIONAL SCHOLARSHIPS FOR HIGH SCHOOL SENIORS
AMVETS National Headquarters
Attn: National Programs Director
4647 Forbes Boulevard
Lanham, MD 20706-3807
(301) 459-9600   Toll Free: (877) 7-AMVETS, ext. 4027
Fax: (301) 459-7924   E-mail: klathroum@amvets.org
Web: www.amvets.org

Summary To provide financial assistance to the children and grandchildren of veterans and active military servicemembers who are entering college.
Eligibility This program is open to graduating high school seniors who are the children or grandchildren of veterans (living or deceased) or active military servicemembers. Applicants must be planning to enroll full time at a college, university, or accredited trade/technical school. They must be U.S. citizens and have a GPA of 3.0 or higher. Selection is based on financial need, academic promise, and merit.
Financial data The stipend is $1,000 per year.
Duration 4 years (provided the recipient maintains a GPA of 2.0 or higher).
Number awarded 6 each year: 1 in each AMVETS national district.
Deadline April of each year.

[565]
ANCHOR SCHOLARSHIPS
Anchor Scholarship Foundation
Attn: Executive Director
138 South Rosemont Road, Suite 206
Virginia Beach, VA 23452
(757) 777-4724
E-mail: Joy.Eyrolles@anchorscholarship.com
Web: www.anchorscholarship.com/scholarships.html

Summary To provide financial assistance for college to dependents of current or former personnel serving in the Naval Surface Forces.
Eligibility This program is open to dependent children and spouses of active-duty, honorably-discharged, or retired personnel who have served at least 6 years (need not be consecutive) in a unit under the administrative control of Commander, Naval Surface Forces, U.S. Atlantic Fleet or U.S. Pacific Fleet. Children must be high school seniors or students already attending an accredited 4-year college or university and working on a bachelor's degree as a full-time stu-

dent. Spouses are eligible if they are working full time on an associate or first bachelor's degree. The sponsor must have a Surface Warfare qualification (SWO/ESWS). Selection is based on academic performance, extracurricular activities, character, and financial need.
Financial data Stipends of renewable scholarships are $2,500 per year; stipends of nonrenewable scholarships are $2,000.
Duration 1 year; may be renewed.
Additional information This foundation was established in 1980 and limited to personnel who had served in the Atlantic Fleet. Its program was originally known as the SURFLANT Scholarship Foundation Award. In 2004, the program was expanded to include those who served in the Pacific Fleet and the current name was adopted.
Number awarded Varies each year; recently, 6 renewable and 27 nonrenewable scholarships were awarded.
Deadline February of each year.

[566]
ANGEA SCHOLARSHIP
Alaska National Guard Enlisted Association
Attn: Scholarship Program
P.O. Box 5302
Joint Base Elmendorf-Richardson, AK 99505-5302
E-mail: akenlisted@angea.org
Web: www.angea.org

Summary To provide financial assistance to members of the Alaska National Guard Enlisted Association (ANGEA) and their families who are interested in attending college in any state.
Eligibility This program is open to current and retired members of the Alaska Air and Army National Guard who are current members of ANGEA and their dependents. Applicants must be enrolled or planning to enroll at an accredited college, university, or vocational/technical school in any state. Along with their application, they must submit a letter that includes their educational and career goals; a list of awards, honors, extracurricular activities, and organizational involvement; information on their civic involvement, moral leadership, or other constructive characteristics demonstrating commitment to community, state, and/or country; and a statement on their financial need.
Financial data A stipend is awarded (amount not specified).
Duration 1 year.
Number awarded 1 or more each year.
Deadline March of each year.

[567]
AREA SCHOLARSHIP PROGRAM
Army and Air Force Exchange Service
Attn: Retired Employees Association
Scholarship Program
P.O. Box 380614
Duncanville, TX 75138-0614
E-mail: scholarships@aafesretired.com
Web: www.aafes.com

Summary To provide financial assistance for college to children of employees (civilian and military) of Army and Air Force Exchange Service (AAFES) personnel.

Eligibility This program is open to college-bound high school seniors who 1) are the natural, adopted, or custodial children of active, retired, or deceased AAFES U.S. payroll employees or assigned military personnel; or 2) work for AAFES themselves and have been paid on its regular U.S. payroll for at least 12 months. Applicants must be planning to attend an accredited college, university, or military academy. They must have a score of at least 23 on the ACT or 1200 on the SAT. If their sponsor is a military retiree, the parent must have retired while on assignment with AAFES and must be an active member of the AAFES Retired Employees Association (AREA). If their sponsor is deceased, the parent must have died while an active or retired employee. All parents must have had at least 12 consecutive months of employment or military assignment. Selection is based on an essay on why they feel they should be awarded this scholarship, academic honors and other recognition, school activity participation, outside activities and hobbies, and letters of recommendation.
Financial data Stipends are $5,000 or $3,000.
Duration 1 year.
Additional information This program began in 1985.
Number awarded Varies each year; recently, 2 at $5,000 and 11 at $3,000 were awarded. Since the program began, it has awarded 371 scholarships worth $827,795.
Deadline March of each year.

[568]
ARIZONA VFW AUXILIARY EDUCATIONAL GRANT
VFW Auxiliary-Department of Arizona
c/o Brenda Kinghorn, Scholarship Chair
P.O. Box 1108
Pinetop, AZ 85935
(928) 205-1066   E-mail: breadfriend@msn.com
Web: www.azvfwaux.org/scholarship-program

Summary To provide financial assistance to members of the VFW Auxiliary in Arizona who are interested in returning to college in any state.
Eligibility This program is open to residents of Arizona who are 18 years of age or older. Applicants must be members of a VFW Auxiliary. They must be interested in working on a degree or career credential at a college, university, or vocational/technical school in any state. Along with their application, they must submit 300-word essays on 1) their commitment to their goals and how this scholarship will help them attain those goals; and 2) how being a VFW Auxiliary member has had an influence in their life.
Financial data The stipend is $1,000.
Duration 1 year.
Additional information Until 2015, the VFW Auxiliary was named the Ladies Auxiliary to the Veterans of Foreign Wars.
Number awarded 1 each year.
Deadline March of each year.

[569]
ARIZONA VFW AUXILIARY MERIT SCHOLARSHIP
VFW Auxiliary-Department of Arizona
c/o Brenda Kinghorn, Scholarship Chair
P.O. Box 1108
Pinetop, AZ 85935
(928) 205-1066 E-mail: breadfriend@msn.com
Web: www.azvfwaux.org/scholarship-program

Summary To provide financial assistance to high school seniors in Arizona who are related to a member of the Veterans of Foreign Wars (VFW) or the VFW Auxiliary and planning to attend college in any state.

Eligibility This program is open to seniors graduating from high schools in Arizona who are the sibling, child, or grandchild of a member of the VFW or the VFW Auxiliary. Applicants must be planning to attend a college, university, or vocational school in any state. Along with their application, they must submit an essay that includes their goals and aspirations in life, why they should receive this scholarship, and how their relationship to a VFW or Auxiliary member has had a positive effect on their life.

Financial data The stipend is at least $1,000.

Duration 1 year.

Additional information Until 2015, the VFW Auxiliary was named the Ladies Auxiliary to the Veterans of Foreign Wars.

Number awarded 1 or more each year.

Deadline March of each year.

[570]
ARKANSAS AMERICAN LEGION AUXILIARY ACADEMIC SCHOLARSHIP
American Legion Auxiliary
Department of Arkansas
Attn: Department Secretary
1415 West Seventh Street
Little Rock, AR 72201-2903
(501) 374-5836 Fax: (501) 372-0855
E-mail: arkaux@att.net
Web: www.auxiliary.arlegion.org

Summary To provide financial assistance to descendants of veterans who are high school seniors in Arkansas and planning to attend college in any state.

Eligibility This program is open to the descendants of veterans in Arkansas who served during eligibility dates for membership in the American Legion. Both the student and the parent must be residents of Arkansas. Their total family income must be less than $75,000. The student must be a high school senior planning to attend college in any state. Along with their application, they must submit an essay that covers 1) why receiving this scholarship would be important to them; 2) the course of study they plan to pursue and why; 3) their involvement in school, church, and community activities; and 4) why they think the United States' patriotic organizations, such as the American Legion Auxiliary, are important to the world today. Selection is based on that essay (25%), character and leadership (25%), academic achievement (25%), and financial need (25%).

Financial data The stipend is $1,000; funds are paid in 2 equal installments.

Duration 1 year.

Number awarded 1 each year.

Deadline May of each year.

[571]
ARKANSAS MILITARY DEPENDENTS SCHOLARSHIP PROGRAM
Arkansas Department of Higher Education
Attn: Financial Aid Division
423 Main Street, Suite 400
Little Rock, AR 72201-3801
(501) 371-2050 Toll Free: (800) 54-STUDY
Fax: (501) 371-2001 E-mail: finaid@adhe.edu
Web: scholarships.adhe.edu

Summary To provide financial assistance for educational purposes to dependents of certain categories of Arkansas veterans.

Eligibility This program is open to the natural children, adopted children, stepchildren, and spouses of Arkansas residents who have been declared to be a prisoner of war, killed in action, missing in action, killed on ordnance delivery, or 100% totally and permanently disabled during, or as a result of, active military service. Applicants and their parent or spouse must be residents of Arkansas. They must be working on, or planning to work on, a bachelor's degree or certificate of completion at a public college, university, or technical school in Arkansas.

Financial data The program pays for tuition, general registration fees, special course fees, activity fees, room and board (if provided in campus facilities), and other charges associated with earning a degree or certificate.

Duration 1 year; participants may obtain renewal provided they make satisfactory progress toward a baccalaureate degree.

Additional information This program began in 1973 as the Arkansas Missing in Action/Killed in Action Dependents Scholarship Program to provide assistance to the dependents of veterans killed in action, missing in action, or declared a prisoner of war. In 2005, it was amended to include dependents of disabled veterans and given its current name. Applications must be submitted to the financial aid director at an Arkansas state-supported institution of higher education or state-supported vocational/technical school.

Number awarded Varies each year; recently, 4 were awarded.

Deadline May of each year.

[572]
ARKANSAS SERVICE MEMORIAL SCHOLARSHIPS
Arkansas Community Foundation
5 Allied Drive, Suite 51110
Building 5, llth Floor
Little Rock, AR 72201
(501) 372-1116 Toll Free: (800) 220-ARCF
Fax: (501) 372-1166 E-mail: arcf@arcf.org
Web: www.arcf.org/about/funds

Summary To provide financial assistance to children of deceased veterans or other government officials in Arkansas who plan to attend college in the state.

Eligibility This program is open to seniors graduating from high schools in Arkansas whose parent died in service to the community, state, or nation. Applicants must be planning to attend an accredited 2- or 4-year college in Arkansas on a

full-time basis. Selection is based on academics, leadership, and financial need.
Financial data The stipend is $2,500 per year.
Duration 1 year; may be renewed for up to 3 additional years, provided the recipient maintains a GPA of 2.5 or higher.
Additional information This program began in 1984.
Number awarded Varies each year; since this program was established, it has awarded 127 scholarships worth more than $15,000.
Deadline March of each year.

[573]
ARK-LA-TEX CHAPTER MOAA ACADEMIC SCHOLARSHIPS
Military Officers Association of America-Ark-La-Tex Chapter
c/o Lt. Colonel (Ret.) George Finck, Scholarship Chair
167 Beaver Lane
Benton, LA 771006
(318) 965-4124 E-mail: gfincksr@gmail.com

Summary To provide financial assistance to descendants of members of the Ark-La-Tex Chapter of the Military Officers Association of America (MOAA) who are high school seniors planning to attend college in any state.
Eligibility This program is open to graduating high school seniors who are the children, grandchildren, or great-grandchildren of a member of the Ark-La-Tex Chapter of MOAA. Applicants may be attending high school in any state, as long as they are sponsored by a chapter member who is their parent, grandparent, or great-grandparent. They must be planning to attend a college or university in any state. Along with their application, they must submit a resume, a letter of recommendation, and transcripts that include ACT/SAT test scores. Selection is based on academic performance, earned honors, involvement in school and community activities, and leadership.
Financial data The stipend is $1,000.
Duration 1 year.
Number awarded At least 16 each year.
Deadline April of each year.

[574]
ARMY AVIATION ASSOCIATION OF AMERICA SCHOLARSHIPS
Army Aviation Association of America Scholarship Foundation
Attn: AAAA Scholarship Foundation
593 Main Street
Monroe, CT 06468-2806
(203) 268-2450 Fax: (203) 268-5870
E-mail: scholarship@quad-a.org
Web: www.quad-a.org/Scholarship/Scholarship/about.aspx

Summary To provide financial aid for undergraduate or graduate study to members of the Army Aviation Association of America (AAAA) and their relatives.
Eligibility This program is open to current AAAA members and the spouses, children, grandchildren, and unmarried siblings of current or deceased members. Applicants must be enrolled or accepted for enrollment as an undergraduate or graduate student at an accredited college or university. They must include a 300-word essay on their life experiences, work history, and aspirations. Some scholarships are specifically reserved for enlisted, warrant officer, company grade, and Department of the Army civilian members. Selection is based on academic merit and personal achievement.
Financial data Stipends range from $1,000 to $5,000 per year.
Duration Scholarships may be for 1 year, 2 years, or 4 years.
Number awarded Varies each year; recently, $516,000 in scholarships was awarded to 304 students. Since the program began in 1963, the foundation has awarded more than $4 million to more than 4,100 qualified applicants.
Deadline Interested students must submit a pre-qualifying form by March of each year. The final application is due in April.

[575]
ARMY NURSE CORPS ASSOCIATION SCHOLARSHIPS
Army Nurse Corps Association
Attn: Scholarship Program
8000 IH-10 West, Suite 600
San Antonio, TX 78230-3887
(210) 650-3534 Toll Free: (888) 742-9910
E-mail: education@e-anca.org
Web: www.e-anca.org/Scholarships

Summary To provide financial assistance to students who have a connection to the Army and are interested in working on an undergraduate or graduate degree in nursing.
Eligibility This program is open to U.S. citizens attending colleges or universities that have accredited programs offering undergraduate or graduate degrees in nursing. Applicants must be 1) students currently enrolled in an accredited baccalaureate or advanced nursing or nurse anesthesia program who are serving or have served (and received an honorable discharge) in any branch and at any rank of a component of the Active Army, Army National Guard, or Army Reserve; or 2) nursing or anesthesia students whose parent(s), spouse, or child(ren) are serving or have served in a component of the Active Army, Army National Guard, or Army Reserve. Along with their application, they must submit a personal statement on their professional career objectives, reasons for applying for this scholarship, financial need, special considerations, personal and academic interests, and why they are preparing for a nursing career. Students who are receiving any support from any branch of the military, including ROTC scholarships, are not eligible.
Financial data The stipend is $3,000. Funds are sent directly to the recipient's school.
Duration 1 year.
Additional information Although the sponsoring organization is made up of current, retired, and honorably discharged officers of the Army Nurse Corps, it does not have an official affiliation with the Army. Therefore, students who receive these scholarships do not incur any military service obligation.
Number awarded Varies each year.
Deadline March of each year.

[576]
ARMY SCHOLARSHIP FOUNDATION SCHOLARSHIPS

Army Scholarship Foundation
11700 Preston Road, Suite 660-301
Dallas, TX 75230
E-mail: ContactUs@armyscholarshipfoundation.org
Web: www.armyscholarshipfoundation.org

Summary To provide financial assistance for undergraduate study to the children and spouses of Army personnel.

Eligibility This program is open to 1) children of regular active-duty, active-duty Reserve, and active-duty Army National Guard members in good standing; 2) spouses of serving enlisted regular active-duty, active-duty Reserve, and active-duty Army National Guard members in good standing; and 3) children of former U.S. Army members who received an honorable or medical discharge or were killed while serving in the U.S. Army. Applicants must be high school seniors, high school graduates, or undergraduates enrolled at an accredited college, university, or vocational/technical institute. They must be U.S. citizens and have a GPA of 2.0 or higher; children must be younger than 24 years of age. Financial need is considered in the selection process.

Financial data The stipend ranges from $500 to $2,000 per year.

Duration 1 year; recipients may reapply.

Additional information The Army Scholarship Foundation was established in 2001. Among the general scholarships offered by the foundation are those designated the Captain Jennifer Shafer Odom Memorial Scholarship, the Lieutenant Colonel Walter R. Bowie Memorial Scholarship, the Alan Robert and Veronica Lenox Cotarlu Memorial Scholarship, the Lieutenant J. Allan Green Memorial Scholarship, the Johnny Mac Soldiers Fund Scholarships, the Lieutenant Keirn C. Brown Memorial Scholarship, the Staff Sergeant John F. Kusior Memorial Scholarship, the Colonel Urey Woodson Alexander Memorial Scholarship, the Perot Family Scholarship, and the Lieutenant General Jack Costello Memorial Scholarship. The program also includes programs sponsored by BAE Systems, Bell Helicopter, Fluor Corporation, General Dynamics, KBR, Northrop Grumman, Raytheon, and USAA.

Number awarded Varies each year; recently, 278 were awarded.

Deadline April of each year.

[577]
ARMY WOMEN'S FOUNDATION LEGACY SCHOLARSHIPS

Army Women's Foundation
Attn: Scholarship Committee
P.O. Box 5030
Fort Lee, VA 23801-0030
(804) 734-3078   E-mail: info@awfdn.org
Web: www.awfdn.org/scholarships/general-information

Summary To provide financial assistance for college or graduate school to women who are serving or have served in the Army and their children.

Eligibility This program is open to 1) women who have served or are serving honorably in the U.S. Army, U.S. Army Reserve, or Army National Guard; and 2) children of those women. Applicants must be 1) high school graduates or GED recipients enrolled at a community college or technical certificate program who have a GPA of 2.5 or higher; 2) sophomores or higher at an accredited college or university who have a GPA of 3.0 or higher; or 3) students enrolled in or accepted to a graduate program who have a GPA of 3.0 or higher. Along with their application, they must submit a 2-page essay on why they should be considered for this scholarship; their future plans as related to their program of study; their community service, activities, and work experience; and how the Army has impacted their life and/or goals. Selection is based on merit, academic potential, community service, and financial need.

Financial data The stipend is $2,500 for college and graduate students or $1,000 for community college and certificate students.

Duration 1 year; recipients may reapply.

Number awarded Varies each year; recently, 21 soldiers and 10 children received these scholarships.

Deadline January of each year.

[578]
ASSOCIATION OF AVIATION ORDNANCEMEN EDUCATIONAL FOUNDATION SCHOLARSHIPS

Association of Aviation Ordnancemen
Attn: Robert L. Crow Scholarship Foundation
c/o Rick Garza, Committee Chair
10213 Rolling Green Way
Fort Washington, MD 20744
Web: www.aaoweb.org/AAO/Scholar

Summary To provide financial assistance to members of the Association of Aviation Ordnancemen, their families, and dependents of deceased aviation ordnancemen of the Navy or Marine Corps.

Eligibility This program is open to 1) regular and associate members of the Association of Aviation Ordnancemen; 2) dependents and immediate relatives (siblings, grandchildren) of regular and associate members; and 3) dependents of deceased aviation ordnancemen of the U.S. Navy or Marine Corps. Applicants must be enrolled or planning to enroll at a college, university, trade/technical school, or postsecondary specialty school in any state. Selection is based on academic record, goals, eligibility for and award of other scholarships and educational grants, and financial need.

Financial data Stipends recently ranged from $2,000 to $4,000 per year.

Duration 1 year; recipients may reapply.

Additional information This program began in 1979. It currently consists of scholarships designated as Robert L. Crow Awards and others named after current donors.

Number awarded Varies each year; recently, 5 were awarded: 1 each at $4,000, $3,000, and $2,500 (the Robert L. Crow Awards) and 2 at $2,000 (the Ed Scott Memorial Scholarship and the award In Memory of James E. Thompson).

Deadline June of each year.

[579]
ASSOCIATION OF COMMISSIONED OFFICERS SCHOLARSHIPS

NOAA Officers' Family Association
Attn: National ACO Scholarships, Inc.
P.O. Box 13083
Silver Spring, MD 20911-3083
(301) 921-6357   E-mail: kmpdhp@comcast.net
Web: www.nofaweb.org/resources

Summary To provide financial assistance for college to students with any major sponsored by an officer of the National Oceanic and Atmospheric Administration (NOAA) Commissioned Officer Corps.

Eligibility This program is open to graduating high school seniors and continuing undergraduate students. Applicants must be sponsored by a member of the NOAA Commissioned Officer Corps. Along with their application, they must submit brief statements of why they chose their particular college or other institution, why they are a good candidate for this scholarship, their goals in life, and why they chose their major field of study. Financial need is not considered in the selection process.

Financial data The stipend is $1,500.

Duration 1 year.

Additional information National ACO Scholarships, Inc. is a project of the National Association of Commissioned Officers. Originally, its scholarships were limited to NOAA Commissioned Corps officers, but eligibility has been expanded to include other deserving students.

Number awarded 2 each year.

Deadline April of each year.

[580]
ASSOCIATION OF THE UNITED STATES NAVY SCHOLARSHIP PROGRAM

Association of the United States Navy
Attn: Scholarship Program
3601 Eisenhower Avenue, Suite 110
Alexandria, VA 22304
(703) 548-5800   Toll Free: (877) NAVY-411
Fax: (703) 683-3647   E-mail: Membership@ausn.org
Web: ausn.org/members/scholarships

Summary To provide financial assistance for college to members and dependents of members of the Association of the United States Navy (AUSN).

Eligibility This program is open to AUSN members, children and grandchildren of members, and surviving spouses of deceased members. Applicants must be enrolled or planning to enroll full time at a college, university, or technical school. Along with their application, they must submit a 1-page autobiography that includes the things that have influenced their life, including memberships, accomplishments, hobbies, and goals. Selection is based on academic and leadership ability, potential, character, personal qualities, and financial need.

Financial data Stipends range from $1,000 to $2,000 per year.

Duration 1 year; may be renewed 1 additional year, provided the recipient maintains a GPA of 2.5 or higher.

Additional information The AUSN was formed in 2009 as a successor to the Naval Reserve Association.

Number awarded Varies each year.

Deadline May of each year.

[581]
AUSTAL USA STEM SCHOLARSHIP

Anchor Scholarship Foundation
Attn: Executive Director
138 South Rosemont Road, Suite 206
Virginia Beach, VA 23452
(757) 777-4724
E-mail: Joy.Eyrolles@anchorscholarship.com
Web: www.anchorscholarship.com

Summary To provide financial assistance for college to dependents of current or former personnel serving in the Naval Surface Forces who live in designated areas and plan to study a field of STEM.

Eligibility This program is open to dependent children of active-duty, honorably-discharged, or retired personnel who have served at least 6 years (need not be consecutive) in a unit under the administrative control of Commander, Naval Surface Forces, U.S. Atlantic Fleet or U.S. Pacific Fleet. Applicants must be high school seniors planning to attend an accredited 4-year college or university and work full time on a bachelor's degree in a field of STEM. They must be residents of the greater Washington, D.C. area, San Diego County in California, or the state of Alabama. The sponsor must have a Surface Warfare qualification (SWO/ESWS). Selection is based on academic performance, extracurricular activities, character, and financial need.

Financial data The stipend is $4,500.

Duration 1 year; nonrenewable.

Additional information This program, which began in 2019, is supported by Austal USA.

Number awarded 1 each year.

Deadline February of each year.

[582]
BG BENJAMIN B. TALLEY SCHOLARSHIP

Society of American Military Engineers-Anchorage Post
c/o Thomas Fenoseff
Anchorage School District
Senior Director, Capital Planning and Construction
1301 Labar Street
Anchorage, AK 99515-3517
(907) 348-5223   Fax: (901) 348-5227
E-mail: Fenoseff_Thomas@askd12.org
Web: www.sameanchorage.org/wp/scholarship-information

Summary To provide financial assistance to student members of the Society of American Military Engineers (SAME) from Alaska who are working on a bachelor's or master's degree in designated fields of engineering or the natural sciences.

Eligibility This program is open to members of the Anchorage Post of SAME who are residents of Alaska, attending college in Alaska, an active-duty military member stationed in Alaska, or a dependent of an active-duty military member stationed in Alaska. Applicants must be 1) sophomores, juniors, or seniors majoring in engineering, architecture, construction or project management, natural sciences, physical sciences, applied sciences, or mathematics at an accredited college or university; or 2) students working on a master's degree in those fields. They must have a GPA of 2.5 or higher. U.S. cit-

izenship is required. Along with their application, they must submit an essay of 250 to 500 words on their career goals. Selection is based on that essay, academic achievement, participation in school and community activities, and work/family activities; financial need is not considered.
Financial data Stipends range up to $3,000.
Duration 1 year.
Additional information This program began in 1997.
Number awarded Several each year; at least 1 scholarship is reserved for a master's degree student.
Deadline December of each year.

[583]
BILL CREECH SCHOLARSHIP
Second Indianhead Division Association
P.O. Box 218
Fox Lake, IL 60020-0218
(224) 225-1202   E-mail: 2idahq@comcast.net
Web: www.2ida.org/Scholarship.htm

Summary To provide financial assistance for college to children and grandchildren of members of the Second Indianhead Division Association.
Eligibility This program is open to 1) children and grandchildren of veterans who have been members of the association for the past 3 years and have a current membership; and 2) children and grandchildren of men or women killed in action while serving with the Second Division. Applicants may be high school seniors or currently-enrolled college students. They must submit a personal letter giving reasons for the request and plans for the future; a high school and, if appropriate, college transcript; ACT or SAT test scores; a statement from their school principal attesting to their character and involvement in extracurricular activities; 2 letters of recommendation from current teachers or professors; a 200- to 300-word essay on such subjects as "What Being an American Means to Me," "Why I Should Receive This Scholarship," or "What Significant Part of U.S. Army History Has the Second Infantry Division Contributed;" and a statement from their parents or guardians on the financial support they will be able to provide the applicant.
Financial data The stipend is usually $1,000 per year.
Duration 1 year; may be renewed.
Number awarded 1 or more each year.
Deadline May of each year.

[584]
BLACKHORSE SCHOLARSHIPS
Blackhorse Association
c/o Murphy Gagne, Scholarship Committee Chair
5521 Keltonburg Road
Smithville, TN 37166
(615) 597-9603   E-mail: allonsllc@gmail.com
Web: www.blackhorse.org/scholarships

Summary To provide financial assistance for college to children of members of the Blackhorse Association who are currently serving or have served with the 11th Armored Cavalry Regiment (ACR).
Eligibility This program is open to the natural and adopted children of current or former 11th ACR solders who are also members of the association. Applicants must be attending or planning to attend college. Along with their application, they must submit a 250-word essay on their ambitions and goals; a 250-word essay on 2 persons in their chosen field who have most influenced them and why; a list of activities, training, and awards received in high school; 2 letters of recommendation; and transcripts that include SAT and/or ACT scores. In the selection process, first priority is given to children who lost a parent in service of the regiment; second priority is given to children of those incapacitated by wounds or injury while serving the regiment; third priority is given based on financial need of the applicant and family.
Financial data The stipend is $3,000 per year.
Duration 1 year; may be renewed up to 3 additional years.
Additional information The Blackhorse Association was founded in 1970 by veterans of the 11th ACR who had served in Vietnam.
Number awarded Varies each year; recently, 20 were awarded. Since this program was established, it has awarded more than $700,000 in scholarships.
Deadline March of each year.

[585]
BOWFIN MEMORIAL SCHOLARSHIPS
Pacific Fleet Submarine Memorial Association
USS Bowfin Submarine Museum and Park
11 Arizona Memorial Drive
Honolulu, HI 96818
(808) 423-1341   Fax: (808) 422-5201
E-mail: info@bowfin.org
Web: www.bowfin.org/scholarship

Summary To provide financial assistance to the children of submarine force personnel who live in Hawaii and plan to attend college in any state.
Eligibility This program is open to the children of submarine force personnel (active duty, retired, or deceased) who are under 23 years of age. Applicants may attend school anywhere in the United States, but their submarine sponsor or surviving parent must live in Hawaii. Along with their application, they must submit a 1-page essay on their current or anticipated major or field of study, why they picked this field of study, and their goals and career aspirations. Selection is based on academic performance, demonstrated potential, extracurricular activities, and financial need.
Financial data The stipend recently was $5,000 per year.
Duration 1 year; may be renewed upon annual reapplication.
Additional information This program began in 1985 to honor the 3,505 submariners and 52 submarines lost during World War II. It is currently administered in partnership with the Hawai'i Community Foundation.
Number awarded Varies each year; recently, 12 were awarded.
Deadline March of each year.

[586]
BRAXTON BRAGG CHAPTER AUSA SCHOLARSHIPS
Association of the United States Army-Braxton Bragg Chapter
Attn: Vice President for Scholarship Programs
P.O. Box 70036
Fort Bragg, NC 28307
(910) 396-3755   E-mail: hbraxtonbraggc@nc.rr.com
Web: www.ausa.org/chapters/braxton-bragg-chapter

Summary To provide financial assistance to members of the Braxton Bragg Chapter of the Association of the United States Army (AUSA) in North Carolina and their dependents who are interested in attending college or graduate school in any state.
Eligibility This program is open to chapter members and their families in North Carolina who are working on or planning to work on an undergraduate, graduate, or technical degree at a college or technical school in any state. Applicants must submit a 500-word essay on a topic that changes annually (recently, students were asked to explain how a person makes a difference in our world); letters of recommendation; a list of personal accomplishments; and a transcript that includes their ACT or SAT score. Selection is based on academic achievement (50%), participation in extracurricular activities at school (25%), and participation in community service activities (25%).
Financial data The stipend is $1,000.
Duration 1 year; recipients may reapply.
Additional information Membership in the Braxton Bragg Chapter is open to all Army active, National Guard, and Reserve members in North Carolina, along with Department of the Army civilians, retirees, concerned citizens, and family members.
Number awarded Varies each year; recently, 15 were awarded.
Deadline April of each year.

[587]
BRIGADIER GENERAL ROBERT L. DENIG FOUNDATION SCHOLARSHIP

United States Marine Corps Combat Correspondents Association
Attn: Scholarship Committee
385 S.W. 254th Street
Newberry, FL 32669
(352) 448-9167   E-mail: hq@usmccca.org
Web: www.usmccca.org/awards/gladys

Summary To provide financial assistance to members of the U.S. Marine Corps Combat Correspondents Association (USMCCCA) or their dependents and Marines in specified occupational fields who are interested in studying communications in college.
Eligibility This program is open to members of USMCCCA who have been members for at least 2 years and their dependents of such members, including children of deceased members. Applications are also accepted from active-duty Marines in occupational field 4300 or 4600 who are enrolled in government-sponsored degree completion programs, whose tuition is not paid from other sources, and who agree to become USMCCA members upon award of a scholarship. Applicants must be enrolled or planning to enroll in an undergraduate program in communications. Along with their application, they must submit 500-word essays on 1) their noteworthy achievements and long-range goals; and 2) "The United States I want to see in 15 years and my role in the transformation." Financial need is not considered in the selection process.
Financial data Stipends for full-time study range up to $3,000; part-time stipends range from $250 to $500. Funds are disbursed directly to recipients to be used exclusively for tuition, books, and/or fees.
Duration 1 year; may be renewed up to 3 additional years.
Additional information This program was previously named the USMCCCA Scholarship.
Number awarded 1 or more each year.
Deadline May of each year.

[588]
BUCKINGHAM MEMORIAL SCHOLARSHIPS

Air Traffic Control Association
Attn: Scholarship Fund
225 Reinekers Lane, Suite 400
Alexandria, VA 22314
(703) 299-2430   Fax: (703) 299-2437
E-mail: info@atca.org
Web: www.atca.org/scholarship

Summary To provide financial assistance for college or graduate school to children of current or former air traffic control specialists.
Eligibility This program is open to U.S. citizens who are the children, natural or adopted, of a person currently or formerly serving as an air traffic control specialist with the U.S. government, with the U.S. military, or in a private facility in the United States. Applicants must be enrolled or planning to enroll at least half time in a baccalaureate or graduate program at an accredited college or university and have at least 30 semester hours to be completed before graduation. Along with their application, they must submit a 500-word essay on how they see your career unfolding, especially how they will blend their career with community service in their adult life. Financial need is considered in the selection process.
Financial data A stipend is awarded; recently, scholarships awarded by this sponsor averaged more than $7,000.
Duration 1 year; may be renewed.
Additional information This program was formerly known as the Children of Air Traffic Control Specialists Scholarship Program.
Number awarded Varies each year; recently, 4 were awarded.
Deadline April of each year.

[589]
CALIFORNIA COLLEGE FEE WAIVER PROGRAM FOR CHILDREN OF VETERANS

California Department of Veterans Affairs
Attn: Division of Veterans Services
1227 O Street, Room 105
P.O. Box 942895
Sacramento, CA 94295
(916) 653-2573   Toll Free: (800) 952-5626
Fax: (916) 653-2563   TDD: (800) 324-5966
Web: www.calvet.ca.gov

Summary To provide financial assistance for college to the children of disabled or deceased veterans in California.
Eligibility Eligible for this program are the children of veterans who 1) died of a service-connected disability; 2) had a service-connected disability at the time of death; or 3) currently have a service-connected disability of any level of severity. Applicants must plan to attend a community college in California, branch of the California State University system, or campus of the University of California. Their income, including the value of support received from parents, cannot exceed a specified level (recently, $13,064). The veteran is

not required to have a connection to California for this program. Dependents in college who are eligible to receive federal education benefits from the U.S. Department of Veterans Affairs are not eligible for these fee waivers.
Financial data This program provides for waiver of registration fees to students attending any publicly-supported community or state college or university in California.
Duration 1 year; may be renewed.
Number awarded Varies each year.
Deadline Deadline not specified.

[590]
CALIFORNIA FEE WAIVER PROGRAM FOR DEPENDENTS OF DECEASED OR DISABLED NATIONAL GUARD MEMBERS
California Department of Veterans Affairs
Attn: Division of Veterans Services
1227 O Street, Room 105
P.O. Box 942895
Sacramento, CA 94295
(916) 653-2573   Toll Free: (800) 952-5626
Fax: (916) 653-2563   TDD: (800) 324-5966
Web: www.calvet.ca.gov

Summary To provide financial assistance for college to dependents of disabled and deceased members of the California National Guard.
Eligibility Eligible for this program are dependents, unremarried surviving spouses, and current registered domestic partners (RDPs) of members of the California National Guard who, in the line of duty and in the active service of the state, were killed, died of a disability, or became permanently disabled. Applicants must be attending or planning to attend a community college, branch of the California State University system, or campus of the University of California.
Financial data Full-time college students receive a waiver of tuition and registration fees at any publicly-supported community or state college or university in California.
Duration 1 year; may be renewed.
Number awarded Varies each year.
Deadline Deadline not specified.

[591]
CALIFORNIA FEE WAIVER PROGRAM FOR DEPENDENTS OF TOTALLY DISABLED VETERANS
California Department of Veterans Affairs
Attn: Division of Veterans Services
1227 O Street, Room 105
P.O. Box 942895
Sacramento, CA 94295
(916) 653-2573   Toll Free: (800) 952-5626
Fax: (916) 653-2563   TDD: (800) 324-5966
Web: www.calvet.ca.gov

Summary To provide financial assistance for college to dependents of disabled and other California veterans.
Eligibility Eligible for this program are spouses, children, and unremarried spouses or registered domestic partners (RDPs) of veterans who are currently totally service-connected disabled (or are being compensated for a service-connected disability at a rate of 100%) or who died of a service-connected cause or disability. The veteran parent must have served during a qualifying war period and must have been discharged or released from military service under honorable conditions. Children must be younger than 27 years of age (extended to 30 if the child is a veteran); there are no age restrictions for spouses, surviving spouses, or RDPs. This program does not have an income limit. Dependents in college are not eligible if they are qualified to receive educational benefits from the U.S. Department of Veterans Affairs. Applicants must be attending or planning to attend a community college, branch of the California State University system, or campus of the University of California.
Financial data Full-time college students receive a waiver of tuition and registration fees at any publicly-supported community or state college or university in California.
Duration Children of eligible veterans may receive postsecondary benefits until the needed training is completed or until the dependent reaches 27 years of age (extended to 30 if the dependent serves in the armed forces). Spouses and surviving spouses are limited to a maximum of 48 months' full-time training or the equivalent in part-time training.
Number awarded Varies each year.
Deadline Deadline not specified.

[592]
CALIFORNIA FEE WAIVER PROGRAM FOR RECIPIENTS OF THE MEDAL OF HONOR AND THEIR CHILDREN
California Department of Veterans Affairs
Attn: Division of Veterans Services
1227 O Street, Room 101
P.O. Box 942895
Sacramento, CA 94295
(916) 653-2573   Toll Free: (800) 952-5626
Fax: (916) 653-2563   TDD: (800) 324-5966
Web: www.calvet.ca.gov

Summary To provide financial assistance for college to veterans in California who received the Medal of Honor and their children.
Eligibility This program is open to recipients of the Medal of Honor and their children younger than 27 years of age who are residents of California. Applicants must be attending or planning to attend a community college, branch of the California State University system, or campus of the University of California.
Financial data Full-time college students receive a waiver of tuition and registration fees at any publicly-supported community or state college or university in California.
Duration 1 year; may be renewed.
Number awarded Varies each year.
Deadline Deadline not specified.

[593]
CALIFORNIA LEGION AUXILIARY EDUCATIONAL ASSISTANCE GENERAL SCHOLARSHIPS
American Legion Auxiliary
Department of California
401 Van Ness Avenue, Suite 319
San Francisco, CA 94102-4570
(415) 861-5092   Fax: (415) 861-8365
E-mail: calegionaux@calegionaux.org
Web: www.calegionaux.org/scholarships.htm

Summary To provide financial assistance to high school seniors in California who are the children of veterans or military personnel and require assistance to continue their education.

Eligibility This program is open to seniors graduating from high schools in California who are the children of active-duty military personnel or veterans who served during wartime. Applicants must be planning to continue their education at a college, university, or business/trade school in California. Each high school in California may nominate only 1 student for these scholarships; the faculty selects the nominee if more than 1 student wishes to apply. Selection is based on the application (25%), scholarship (25%), character and leadership (25%), and financial need (25%).

Financial data Stipends are $1,000 or $500 per year.

Duration 1 year; 1 of the scholarships may be renewed 1 additional year.

Number awarded 8 each year: 1 at $1,000 per year that may be renewed 1 additional year, 4 at $1,000 that are nonrenewable, and 3 at $500 that are nonrenewable.

Deadline March of each year.

[594]
CALIFORNIA LEGION AUXILIARY PAST DEPARTMENT PRESIDENT'S JUNIOR SCHOLARSHIP

American Legion Auxiliary
Department of California
401 Van Ness Avenue, Suite 319
San Francisco, CA 94102-4570
(415) 861-5092   Fax: (415) 861-8365
E-mail: calegionaux@calegionaux.org
Web: www.calegionaux.org/scholarships.htm

Summary To provide financial assistance for college to the daughters and other female descendants of California veterans who are active in the American Legion Junior Auxiliary.

Eligibility This program is open to the daughters, granddaughters, and great-granddaughters of veterans who served during wartime. Applicants must be in their senior year at an accredited high school, must have been members of the Junior Auxiliary for at least 3 consecutive years, and must be residents of California (if eligibility for Junior Auxiliary membership is by a current member of the American Legion or Auxiliary in California, the applicant may reside elsewhere). They must be planning to attend college in California. Selection is based on scholastic merit (20%); active participation in Junior Auxiliary (15%); record of service or volunteerism within the applicant's community, school, and/or unit (35%); a brief description of the applicant's desire to pursue a higher education (15%); and 3 letters of reference (15%).

Financial data The stipend depends on the availability of funds but ranges from $300 to $1,000.

Duration 1 year.

Number awarded 1 each year.

Deadline March of each year.

[595]
CALIFORNIA LEGION AUXILIARY PAST PRESIDENTS' PARLEY NURSING SCHOLARSHIPS

American Legion Auxiliary
Department of California
401 Van Ness Avenue, Suite 319
San Francisco, CA 94102-4570
(415) 861-5092   Fax: (415) 861-8365
E-mail: calegionaux@calegionaux.org
Web: www.calegionaux.org/scholarships.htm

Summary To provide financial assistance to California residents who are veterans or members of their families and interested in studying nursing at a school in the state.

Eligibility This program is open to California residents who are veterans with wartime service or the spouse, widow(er), or child of such a veteran. Applicants must be entering or currently enrolled in an accredited nursing school in California and working on a licensed vocational nurse, registered nurse, or other recognized nursing degree. Selection is based on the application (25%), scholarship (25%), character and leadership (25%), and financial need (25%).

Financial data The stipend is $2,000.

Duration 1 year.

Number awarded 1 each year.

Deadline March of each year.

[596]
CALIFORNIA LEGION AUXILIARY SCHOLARSHIPS FOR CONTINUING AND/OR REENTRY STUDENTS

American Legion Auxiliary
Department of California
401 Van Ness Avenue, Suite 319
San Francisco, CA 94102-4570
(415) 861-5092   Fax: (415) 861-8365
E-mail: calegionaux@calegionaux.org
Web: www.calegionaux.org/scholarships.htm

Summary To provide financial assistance to California residents who are active-duty military personnel, veterans, or children of veterans and require assistance to continue their education.

Eligibility This program is open to California residents who are 1) active-duty military personnel; 2) veterans of World War I, World War II, Korea, Vietnam, Grenada/Lebanon, Panama, or Desert Shield/Desert Storm; and 3) children of veterans who served during those periods of war. Applicants must be continuing or reentry students at a college, university, or business/trade school in California. Selection is based on the application (25%), scholarship (25%), character and leadership (25%), and financial need (25%).

Financial data The stipend is $1,000 or $500.

Duration 1 year.

Additional information This program includes 1 scholarship designated as the Mel Foronda Memorial Scholarship.

Number awarded 5 each year: 3 at $1,000 and 2 at $500.

Deadline March of each year.

[597]
CALIFORNIA NON-RESIDENT COLLEGE FEE WAIVER PROGRAM FOR MILITARY PERSONNEL AND DEPENDENTS

California Department of Veterans Affairs
Attn: Division of Veterans Services
1227 O Street, Room 101
P.O. Box 942895
Sacramento, CA 94295
(916) 653-2573   Toll Free: (800) 952-5626
Fax: (916) 653-2563   TDD: (800) 324-5966
Web: www.calvet.ca.gov

Summary To waive non-resident fees at public institutions in California for undergraduate or graduate students from other states who are active-duty military personnel, recently-discharged veterans, or dependents of active-duty military personnel.

Eligibility This program is open to residents of states outside California who are 1) veterans of the U.S. armed forces who spent more than 1 year on active duty in California immediately prior to being discharged; 2) members of the U.S. armed forces stationed in California on active duty; or 3) the natural or adopted child, stepchild, or spouse of a member of the U.S. armed forces stationed in California on active duty. Applicants must be attending or planning to attend a community college, branch of the California State University system, or campus of the University of California as an undergraduate or graduate student.

Financial data This program waives non-resident fees of qualifying military personnel, veterans, and families who attend publicly-supported community or state colleges or universities in California.

Duration 1 year; may be renewed until completion of an undergraduate degree or for 1 additional year for military personnel working on a graduate degree; nonrenewable for graduate students who are children or spouses.

Number awarded Varies each year.

Deadline Deadline not specified.

[598]
CAPITOL AREA CHAPTER MOAA COLLEGE SCHOLARSHIP PROGRAM

Military Officers Association of America-Capitol Area
    Chapter
c/o Major DeLee M. Dankenbring, Treasurer
992 Pennine Ridge Way
Grand Ledge, MI 48837-9809
(517) 614-6090
Web: www.cacmoaa.org/Scholarships.aspx

Summary To provide financial assistance for college or graduate school in any state to residents of Michigan who are disabled veterans, members of the Military Officers Association of America (MOAA) or their children or grandchildren, or children of deceased or disabled servicemembers.

Eligibility This program is open to 1) disabled military servicemembers who entered service after September 11, 2001 and whose home of record is Michigan; 2) members of the national and Capitol Area Chapter of the MOAA and their children and grandchildren; and 3) children of servicemembers who entered the armed forces from Michigan and died or were disabled in the line of duty. Applicants must be enrolled or planning to enroll in a program of college or university study, job training, or graduate school. They must have a GPA of 2.0 or higher. Along with their application they must submit transcripts (that include SAT/ACT scores for high school seniors), a list of honors and awards that includes any ROTC or military training, a 200-word essay on their career goals, and a brief explanation of their financial need.

Financial data The stipend ranges from $1,000 to $1,250 per year.

Duration 1 year; recipients may reapply.

Number awarded Varies each year.

Deadline March of each year.

[599]
CAPT ERNEST G. "SCOTTY" CAMPBELL, USN (RET) AND RENEE CAMPBELL SCHOLARSHIP

Navy League of the United States
Attn: Scholarships
2300 Wilson Boulevard, Suite 200
Arlington, VA 22201-5424
(703) 528-1775   Toll Free: (800) 356-5760
Fax: (703) 528-2333
E-mail: scholarships@navyleague.org
Web: www.navyleague.org/programs/scholarships

Summary To provide financial assistance for college to dependent children of sea service personnel, especially those interested in majoring in mathematics, engineering, and/or the sciences.

Eligibility This program is open to U.S. citizens who are 1) dependents or direct descendants of an active, Reserve, retired, or honorably discharged member of the U.S. sea service (including the Navy, Marine Corps, Coast Guard, or Merchant Marine); or 2) currently an active member of the Naval Sea Cadet Corps. Applicants must be high school seniors entering their freshman year at an accredited college or university. They must have a GPA of 3.0 or higher. Along with their application, they must submit transcripts, 2 letters of recommendation, SAT/ACT scores, documentation of financial need, proof of qualifying sea service duty, and a 1-page personal statement on why they should be considered for this scholarship. Preference is given to students who have demonstrated an interest in and an intention to continue their education in mathematics, engineering, and/or the sciences.

Financial data The stipend is $2,500 per year.

Duration 4 years, provided the recipient maintains a GPA of 3.0 or higher.

Number awarded 1 each year.

Deadline February of each year.

[600]
CAPTAIN CALIENDO COLLEGE ASSISTANCE FUND SCHOLARSHIP

U.S. Coast Guard Chief Petty Officers Association
Attn: CCCAF Scholarship Committee
5520-G Hempstead Way
Springfield, VA 22151-4009
(703) 941-0395   Fax: (703) 941-0397
E-mail: coastguardcpoa@gmail.com
Web: www.uscgcpoa.org/resources/cccaf

Summary To recognize and reward, with college scholarships, children of members or deceased members of the U.S. Coast Guard Chief Petty Officers Association (CPOA) or the

Coast Guard Enlisted Association (CGEA) who submit outstanding essays.

Eligibility This competition is open to children of members or deceased members of the CPOA or CGEA who are attending or planning to attend a college, university, or vocational school. Applicants may not be older than 24 years of age (the age limit does not apply to disabled children). They must submit an essay, up to 500 words, on a topic that changes annually; recently, students were asked whether automatic safety features in automobiles enhance safety or encourage distracted driving and a further erosion of basic driving skill. The authors of essays judged most outstanding receive these scholarships.

Financial data The awards are scholarships of $5,000 for first, $2,500 for second, and $1,000 for third.

Duration The competition is held annually.

Number awarded 3 each year.

Deadline March of each year.

[601]
CAPTAIN FREDERICK C. BRACE III MEMORIAL SCHOLARSHIP

American Academy of Physician Assistants-Veterans Caucus
Attn: Scholarship Program
P.O. Box 362
Ossining, NY 10562
(803) 328-1864 Fax: (704) 838-8494
E-mail: rmunsee@veteranscaucus.org
Web: www.veteranscaucus.org/scholarships

Summary To provide financial assistance to Air Force veterans and their dependents who are studying to become physician assistants.

Eligibility This program is open to U.S. citizens who are currently enrolled in a physician assistant program. Applicants must be honorably discharged members of the United States Air Force or the dependent of an Air Force veteran. Along with their application, they must submit a personal statement about what led them to attend PA school; their background, present, and future intentions; and why they deserve to receive a scholarship. Selection is based on military honors and awards received, civic and college honors and awards received, professional memberships and activities, potential for future achievement, and GPA.

Financial data The stipend is $2,000.

Duration 1 year.

Number awarded 1 each year.

Deadline February of each year.

[602]
CARROLL H. PAYNE MEMORIAL SCHOLARSHIP ENDOWMENT

First Command Educational Foundation
Attn: Scholarship Programs Manager
1 FirstComm Plaza
Fort Worth, TX 76109-4999
(817) 569-2940 Toll Free: (877) 872-8289
Fax: (817) 569-2970 E-mail: scholarships@fcef.com
Web: www.fcef.com/scholarships

Summary To provide financial assistance to college students who have ties to the military.

Eligibility This program is open to college-bound high school students, current college students, and adults seeking advanced education. Applicants must have a tie to the military. They must apply through a local military organization that supports military families, such as a DoD school, officers' spouses' club, National Guard organization, or veteran organization. Individuals who have received military academy appointments or ROTC scholarships are also eligible. The organization must normally agree to provide half the cost of the scholarship and apply to this sponsor for the balance. Partner organizations select the recipients.

Financial data Each partner organization may apply for up to $2,000 in matching funds from this sponsor. Individual scholarships range from $1,000 to $4,000 but may be greater if the partner organization agrees to pay all the additional cost.

Duration 1 year; recipients may reapply.

Additional information This sponsor was established in 1983 as the nonprofit affiliate of First Command Financial Services, Inc.

Number awarded Varies each year; recently, this sponsor partnered with 50 community organizations to award $81,030 in scholarships to 61 students.

Deadline Each partner organization sets its own deadline.

[603]
CHAPPIE HALL MEMORIAL SCHOLARSHIP PROGRAM

101st Airborne Division Association
32 Screaming Eagle Boulevard
P.O. Box 929
Fort Campbell, KY 42223-0929
(931) 431-0199 Fax: (931) 431-0195
E-mail: 101exec@screamingeagle.org
Web: www.screamingeaglefoundation.org

Summary To provide financial assistance for college to the spouses, children, and grandchildren of members of the 101st Airborne Division Association.

Eligibility This program is open to graduating high school seniors and current college students who maintained a GPA of 3.0 or higher during the preceding school year and whose parent, grandparent, or spouse is (or, if deceased, was) a regular or life (not associate) member of the 101st Airborne Division. Applicants must submit a letter on their career objectives, community service, hobbies, interests, personal achievements, and how a higher education for them in their chosen field can benefit our nation. High school seniors must also submit an essay of 250 to 300 words on patriotism. College students must submit an essay of 500 to 550 words on the importance of the U.S. constitution. Financial need is not considered in the selection process.

Financial data A stipend is awarded (amount not specified).

Duration 1 year; may be renewed.

Additional information This program includes the Pratt Scholarships, the Lencioni Family Scholarship, the Catherine and Charles Kratz Scholarships, the Laverne and Phillip Blottenberger Scholarship, the 327th REG Scholarship, the Bill Nelson Scholarship, the William Latta Scholarship, and the Ron Gillette Scholarship.

Number awarded Varies each year; recently, 21 were awarded.
Deadline May of each year.

[604]
CHARLES KOSMUTZA SCHOLARSHIP FUND

Disabled American Veterans-Department of New Jersey
Attn: Scholarship Committee
171 Jersey Street, Building 5, Second Floor
Trenton, NJ 08611
(609) 396-2885　　　　　　　　Fax: (609) 396-9562
Web: www.davnj.org

Summary To provide financial assistance to high school seniors who are the children or grandchildren of members of the Disabled American Veterans (DAV) in New Jersey and planning to attend college in any state.

Eligibility This program is open to seniors graduating from high schools in New Jersey and planning to attend a college, university, community college, or trade school in any state. Applicants must be the natural or adopted descendant (child, grandchild, niece, nephew, cousin) of a member of the DAV Department of New Jersey. Along with their application, they must submit a 500-word essay on a topic that changes annually; recently, students were asked to write on what they would do to make this country a better and safer place to live. Financial need is not considered in the selection process.

Financial data The stipend is $1,500.
Duration 1 year.
Number awarded 3 each year: 1 in each region (north, central, and south) of the state.
Deadline May of each year.

[605]
CHARLES W. AND ANNETTE HILL SCHOLARSHIP FUND

American Legion
Department of Kansas
1314 S.W. Topeka Boulevard
Topeka, KS 66612-1886
(785) 232-9315　　　　　　　　Fax: (785) 232-1399
Web: www.ksamlegion.org

Summary To provide financial assistance to the children of members of the Kansas American Legion, particularly those interested in majoring in science, engineering, or business at a college in the state.

Eligibility This program is open to graduating seniors at high schools in Kansas and freshmen and sophomores at colleges in the state. Applicants must be a descendant of a member of the American Legion and have a GPA of 3.0 or higher. Preference is given to applicants planning to major in science, engineering, or business administration at a Kansas college, university, junior college, or trade school. Selection is based on high school transcripts, 3 letters of recommendation, an essay of 250 to 500 words on "Why I Want to Go to College," and financial need.

Financial data The stipend is $1,000.
Duration 1 year; nonrenewable.
Number awarded 1 each year.
Deadline February of each year.

[606]
CHARLIE CORN SCHOLARSHIPS

Society of American Military Engineers-Guam Post
c/o Tor Gudmundsen, Scholarship Chair
TG Engineers, PC
101 First Street, Tiyan
Barrigada, GU 96913
(671) 647-0808　　　　　　　　Fax: (671) 647-0886
E-mail: admin@tg-engr.com
Web: www.same.org

Summary To provide financial assistance to residents of Guam and Micronesia who are interested in majoring in engineering or architecture in college.

Eligibility This program is open to 1) residents of Guam and neighboring islands of Micronesia (Commonwealth of the Northern Mariana Islands, Federated States of Micronesia, and Republic of Palau); and 2) dependents of active-duty or Reserve military personnel from those islands. Applicants must be high school seniors or college students enrolled or planning to enroll full time at a college or university approved by the sponsor to work on a bachelor's degree in engineering or architecture. They must demonstrate a sincere interest in returning to Guam or Micronesia after graduation to begin a professional career. Selection is based on that interest as well as scholastic achievement, aptitude, attitude, character, and financial need.

Financial data The stipend is $3,500 for high school seniors and college freshmen and $5,000 for upper-division students.
Duration 1 year; may be renewed if the recipient maintains full-time enrollment and a GPA of 3.0 or higher.
Number awarded Varies each year.
Deadline January of each year.

[607]
CHIEF MASTER SERGEANT OF THE AIR FORCE SCHOLARSHIP PROGRAM

Air Force Sergeants Association
Attn: Membership and Field Relations
5211 Auth Road
Suitland, MD 20746
(301) 899-3500　　　　　　　　Toll Free: (800) 638-0594
Fax: (301) 899-8136　　　　　E-mail: staff@hqafsa.org
Web: www.hqafsa.org/scholarships.html

Summary To provide financial assistance for college to the dependent children of enlisted Air Force personnel.

Eligibility This program is open to the unmarried children (including stepchildren and legally adopted children) of enlisted active-duty, retired, or veteran members of the U.S. Air Force, Air National Guard, or Air Force Reserves. Applicants must be attending or planning to attend an accredited academic institution. They must have an unweighted GPA of 3.5 or higher. Along with their application, they must submit 1) a paragraph on their life objectives and what they plan to do with the education they receive; and 2) an essay on the most urgent problem facing society today. High school seniors must also submit a transcript of all high school grades and a record of their SAT or ACT scores. Selection is based on academic record, character, leadership skills, writing ability, versatility, and potential for success. Financial need is not a consideration. A unique aspect of these scholarships is that applicants may supply additional information regarding cir-

cumstances that entitle them to special consideration; examples of such circumstances include student disabilities, financial hardships, parent disabled and unable to work, parent missing in action/killed in action/prisoner of war, or other unusual extenuating circumstances.
Financial data Stipends range from $1,000 to $3,500; funds may be used for tuition, room and board, fees, books, supplies, and transportation.
Duration 1 year; may be renewed if the recipient maintains full-time enrollment.
Additional information The Air Force Sergeants Association administers this program on behalf of the Airmen Memorial Foundation. It was established in 1987 and named in honor of CMSAF Richard D. Kisling, the late third Chief Master Sergeant of the Air Force. In 1997, following the deaths of CMSAF's (Retired) Andrews and Harlow, it was given its current name. The highest-ranked applicant receives the Paul W. Airey Memorial Scholarship, sponsored by GEICO Insurance.
Number awarded Varies each year; recently, 11 worth $16,500 were awarded: 1 at $3,500, 1 at $2,500, 1 at $2,000, 1 at $1,500, and 7 at $1,000. Since this program began, it has awarded more than 303 scholarships valued at more than $433,000.
Deadline March of each year.

[608]
CHIEF PETTY OFFICER SCHOLARSHIPS

Chief Petty Officer Scholarship Fund
328 Office Square Lane, Suite 101A
Virginia Beach, VA 23462
(757) 233-9136   E-mail: admin@cposf.org
Web: www.cposf.org/scholarship

Summary To provide financial assistance for college to the dependents of Navy Chief Petty Officers (CPOs).
Eligibility This program is open to the non-uniformed spouses and children (natural born, adopted, or step) of active, Reserve, honorably retired, honorably discharged, or deceased Navy Chief, Senior Chief, or Master Chief Petty Officers. Applicants must be high school seniors or students currently enrolled at a college, university, or vocational/technical school with the goal of obtaining an associate or bachelor's degree or certificate. Along with their application, they must submit an autobiographical essay of 200 to 500 words that discusses their significant experiences, community involvement, and qualities of character and leadership important in achieving their goals. Selection is based on the essay, honors and awards received during high school, extracurricular activities, community activities, and employment experience; financial need is not considered. Members of the armed services are not eligible. The highest-ranked applicants receive named scholarships designated the Thomas Crow Memorial Scholarship and the MCPON Walker Honorary Scholarship.
Financial data The stipend is $5,000 for the named scholarships or $2,000 for the others.
Duration 1 year.
Additional information This program began in 1998. The MCPON Thomas Crow Memorial Scholarship was established in 2010 and the MCPON Walker Honorary Scholarship in 2012.

Number awarded Varies each year; recently, 37 were awarded, including the 2 named awards.
Deadline March of each year.

[609]
CHILDREN AND SPOUSES OF INDIANA NATIONAL GUARD PROGRAM

Indiana Commission for Higher Education
Attn: Financial Aid and Student Support Services
101 West Ohio Street, Suite 300
Indianapolis, IN 46204-4206
(317) 232-1023   Toll Free: (888) 528-4719 (within IN)
Fax: (317) 232-3260   E-mail: Scholars@che.in.gov
Web: www.in.gov/che/4523.htm

Summary To provide financial assistance to residents of Indiana who are children or spouses of deceased members of the National Guard and interested in attending college or graduate school in the state.
Eligibility This program is open to residents of Indiana whose father, mother, or spouse was a member of the Indiana National Guard and suffered a service-connected death while serving on state active duty. Applicants must be interested in working on an undergraduate, graduate, or professional degree at an eligible institution in Indiana.
Financial data Qualified applicants receive a 100% remission of tuition and all mandatory fees for undergraduate, graduate, or professional degrees at eligible postsecondary schools and universities in Indiana. Support is not provided for such fees as room and board.
Duration Up to 124 semester hours of study.
Number awarded Varies each year.
Deadline Applications must be submitted at least 30 days before the start of the college term.

[610]
CHILDREN OF COAST GUARD MEMBERS SCHOLARSHIPS

Coast Guard Foundation
Attn: Scholarships
394 Taugwonk Road
Stonington, CT 06378
(860) 535-0786   Fax: (860) 535-0944
E-mail: swilliams@coastguardfoundation.org
Web: www.coastguardfoundation.org

Summary To provide financial assistance for college to the dependent children of Coast Guard personnel.
Eligibility This program is open to the dependent children of officers, chief warrant officers, and enlisted members of the U.S. Coast Guard on active duty, retired, or deceased, and of enlisted personnel in the Coast Guard Reserve currently on extended active duty 180 days or more. Applicants must be high school seniors or current undergraduates enrolled or planning to enroll full-time at a 4-year college, university, or vocational school. They must be under 24 years of age and registered in the Defense Enrollment Eligibility Reporting System (DEERS) system. Along with their application, they must submit their SAT or ACT scores, a letter of recommendation, transcripts, a financial information statement, and a 500-word essay on their personal and academic achievements, extracurricular activities, contributions to the community, and academic plans and career goals.

Financial data The stipend is $2,500 for children of officers and chief warrant officers and from $1,000 to $5,000 per year for children of enlisted personnel.
Duration 1 year; some scholarships may be renewed up to 3 additional years.
Number awarded Varies each year; recently, 182 were awarded.
Deadline March of each year.

[611]
CHILDREN OF FALLEN COAST GUARD HEROES SCHOLARSHIPS

Coast Guard Foundation
Attn: Scholarships
394 Taugwonk Road
Stonington, CT 06378
(860) 535-0786   Fax: (860) 535-0944
E-mail: swilliams@coastguardfoundation.org
Web: www.coastguardfoundation.org

Summary To provide financial assistance for college to the dependent children of Coast Guard personnel who lost their lives while on duty.
Eligibility This program is open to the dependent children of members of the U.S. Coast Guard who lost their lives in Coast Guard land, air, or sea operations. Applicants must be high school seniors or current undergraduates enrolled or planning to enroll full-time at a college, university, or technical school. They must be under 23 years of age and registered in the Defense Enrollment Eligibility Reporting System (DEERS) system. Along with their application, they must submit their SAT or ACT scores, a letter of recommendation, transcripts, a financial information statement, and a 500-word essay on their personal and academic achievements, extracurricular activities, contributions to the community, and academic plans and career goals.
Financial data The program covers 100% of higher education expenses.
Duration 1 year; may be renewed up to 3 additional years.
Number awarded Varies each year; recently, 2 were awarded.
Deadline Applications may be submitted at any time.

[612]
CHILDREN OF FALLEN IOWA SERVICE MEMBERS SCHOLARSHIP

Iowa Department of Veterans Affairs
Attn: Trust Fund and Grants Administrator
Camp Dodge, Building 3465
7105 N.W. 70th Avenue
Johnston, IA 50131-1824
(515) 727-3443   Toll Free: (800) VET-IOWA
Fax: (515) 727-3713   E-mail: missy.miller@iowa.gov
Web: www.va.iowa.gov/benefits

Summary To provide financial assistance for college in Iowa to children and siblings of members of the armed forces from that state who died in active service after September 11, 2001.
Eligibility This program is open to children and siblings of military personnel who died in active service or as a result of such service after September 11, 2001. The deceased servicemember must have been 1) a resident of Iowa at the time of entering into active military service; 2) assigned to a unit based in Iowa at the time of death; or 3) a resident of Iowa at the time of death. The death does not have to be combat-related. Active military status includes federal service in the armed forces, National Guard, or Reserves. Students must be attending or planning to attend a postsecondary institution located within Iowa. They must be able to demonstrate financial need.
Financial data Stipends are awarded (amount not specified); funds are to be used to subsidize the costs of tuition, books, fees, housing, special tools and equipment required for course work, school-approved tutoring, and any other required educational expenses. Once all educational expenses are met, any remaining funds will be released to the student to cover other expenses as needed.
Duration 1 year.
Additional information Governor Terry E. Branstad and Lieutenant Governor Kim Reynolds established this program as part of the Branstad-Reynolds Scholarship Fund in 2010. It is funded through the Community Foundation of Greater Des Moines.
Number awarded Varies each year; recently, 2 were awarded.
Deadline December of each year.

[613]
CHILDREN OF FALLEN PATRIOTS SCHOLARSHIP

Children of Fallen Patriots Foundation
44900 Prentice Drive
Dulles, VA 20166
Toll Free: (866) 917-CFPF   Fax: (703) 935-4751
E-mail: contact@fallenpatriots.org
Web: www.fallenpatriots.org/faqs-for-families

Summary To provide financial assistance to the children of military personnel killed in combat or training.
Eligibility This program is open to the children (natural, by marriage, or adopted) of military personnel who died in the line of duty. Applicants must be enrolled or planning to enroll at a college, university, community college, or vocational school. They must submit documentation of their relationship to the deceased military member, bills or receipts for all covered expenses, transcripts that include GPA, and information on their U.S. Department of Veterans Affairs benefits.
Financial data The foundation attempts to pay for all costs of higher education not covered by other grants or scholarships.
Duration 1 year; may be renewed up to 3 additional years.
Additional information This program began in 1990.
Number awarded Varies each year; since the program began, it has awarded more than $35 million to more than 1,700 recipients.
Deadline Applications may be submitted at any time.

[614]
CHILDREN OF FALLEN SOLDIERS RELIEF FUND COLLEGE GRANTS

Children of Fallen Soldiers Relief Fund
P.O. Box 1099
Temple Hills, MD 20757
(301) 685-3421   Toll Free: (888) 805-7383
Fax: (301) 685-3271   E-mail: yellowribbon7@msn.com
Web: www.cfsrf.org/ourprograms.html

Summary To provide financial assistance for college to children and spouses of military personnel killed or severely disabled during service in Iraq or Afghanistan.
Eligibility This program is open to spouses and children of military personnel killed or severely disabled as a result of service in Operation Iraqi Freedom or Operation Enduring Freedom. Applicants must be enrolled or planning to enroll at a college or university. They must have a GPA of 2.75 or higher and be able to demonstrate financial need.
Financial data The stipend is $3,500 per semester ($7,000 per year).
Duration 1 semester; may be renewed.
Additional information This organization was founded in 2003.
Number awarded Varies each year; since the organization was founded, it has awarded more than $4,800,000 in grants to more than 800 military children for all forms of assistance.
Deadline April of each year for fall; October of each year for spring.

[615] CHILDREN OF POW/MIA SOLDIERS OF PENNSYLVANIA GRANTS

Pennsylvania Higher Education Assistance Agency
Attn: Special Programs
1200 North Seventh Street
P.O. Box 8157
Harrisburg, PA 17105-8157
(717) 720-2800   Toll Free: (800) 692-7392
Fax: (717) 720-3786   TDD: (800) 654-5988
E-mail: info@pheaa.org
Web: www.pheaa.org

Summary To provide financial assistance for college to the children of POWs/MIAs from Pennsylvania.
Eligibility This program is open to dependent children of members or former members of the U.S. armed services who served on active duty after January 31, 1955, who are or have been prisoners of war or are or have been listed as missing in action, and who were residents of Pennsylvania for at least 12 months preceding service on active duty. Eligible children must be enrolled in a program of at least 1 year in duration on at least a half-time basis at an approved school. Financial need is not considered in the selection process.
Financial data The maximum grant is $1,200.
Duration 1 year; may be renewed for 3 additional years.
Additional information With certain exceptions, recipients may attend any accredited college in the United States. Excluded from coverage are 2-year public colleges located outside Pennsylvania and schools in states bordering Pennsylvania that do not allow their state grant recipients to attend Pennsylvania schools (i.e., New York, Maryland, and New Jersey).
Number awarded Varies each year.
Deadline April of each year for students at colleges, universities, and transferable programs at community colleges; July of each year for students at business schools, trade/technical schools, hospital schools of nursing, and non-transferable programs at community colleges.

[616] CHILDREN OF WARRIORS NATIONAL PRESIDENTS' SCHOLARSHIP

American Legion Auxiliary
3450 Founders Road
Indianapolis, IN 46268
(317) 569-4500   Fax: (317) 569-4502
E-mail: alahq@alaforveterans.org
Web: www.alaforveterans.org

Summary To provide financial assistance for college to the descendants of war veterans.
Eligibility This program is open to children, stepchildren, grandchildren, and great-grandchildren of veterans who served during wartime. Applicants must be high school seniors who have completed at least 50 hours of volunteer service within their community and plan to attend an accredited 4-year college or university. Each Department (state) organization of the American Legion Auxiliary nominates 1 candidate for this scholarship annually. Nominees must submit a 1,000-word essay on a topic that changes annually; recently, students were asked to write on "How can education, both private and public, help prevent homelessness in our country, particularly that of our veteran population?" Selection is based on the essay (25%), character and leadership (25%), academic achievement, (25%), and financial need (25%).
Financial data The stipend is $5,000. Funds are paid directly to the recipient's school.
Duration 1 year; recipients may not reapply.
Additional information Applications are available from the local Unit or from the Department Secretary or Department Education Chair of the state in which the applicant resides. This program was previously named the American Legion Auxiliary National President's Scholarship.
Number awarded 15 each year: 3 in each of the 5 divisions of the Auxiliary.
Deadline Applications must be submitted to the local American Legion Auxiliary unit by February of each year.

[617] CLAIRE OLIPHANT MEMORIAL SCHOLARSHIP

American Legion Auxiliary
Department of New Jersey
Attn: Secretary
1540 Kuser Road, Suite A-8
Hamilton, NJ 08619
(609) 581-9580   Fax: (609) 581-8429
E-mail: newjerseyala2@optimum.net
Web: www.alanj.org/index.php/scholarshipsgrants

Summary To provide financial assistance to New Jersey residents who are the descendants of veterans and planning to attend college in any state.
Eligibility This program is open to the children, grandchildren, and great-grandchildren of veterans who served in the U.S. armed forces during specified periods of wartime. Applicants must be graduating high school seniors who have been residents of New Jersey for at least 2 years. They must be planning to attend a college or university in any state. Along with their application, they must submit a 1,000-word essay on a topic that changes annually; recently, students were asked to write on the topic, "How Pride in country, community, school and family directs my daily life." Selection is based on

academic achievement (40%), character (15%), leadership (15%), Americanism (15%), and financial need (15%).
Financial data The stipend is $2,500.
Duration 1 year.
Number awarded 1 each year.
Deadline February each year.

[618]
CMSGT GERALD R. GUILD MEMORIAL SCHOLARSHIPS

Enlisted Association National Guard of Arizona
Attn: Scholarship Chair
5636 East McDowell Road
Phoenix, AZ 85008-3495
(602) 267-2467   Fax: (602) 267-2509
E-mail: scholarship@eanga.org
Web: www.eanga.org/scholarship-information

Summary To provide financial assistance to members of the Enlisted Association National Guard of Arizona (EANGA) and to members of their families who plan to attend college in any state.
Eligibility This program is open to EANGA members, the unmarried children of EANGA members, the spouses of EANGA members, and the unremarried spouses and unmarried dependent children of deceased EANGA members (who were in good standing at their time of death). Qualifying EANGA members must have at least 1 year remaining on their enlistment or have served 20 or more years of service. Applicants may be high school seniors or current college students who are enrolled or planning to enroll full time at a college or university in any state. Graduate students are not eligible. Selection is based on academic record, character, leadership, and financial need.
Financial data The stipend is $1,000. Funds are made payable to the recipient's school and sent directly to the recipient.
Duration 1 year; nonrenewable.
Number awarded 1 each year.
Deadline April of each year.

[619]
COAST GUARD EXCHANGE SCHOLARSHIP PROGRAM

Coast Guard Exchange
Attn: Scholarship Committee
Battlefield Technology Center 1
510 Independence Parkway, Suite 500
Chesapeake, VA 23320-5191
(757) 842-4793
E-mail: CGEScholarship@cgexchange.org
Web: www.dcms.uscg.mil

Summary To provide financial assistance to the children of Coast Guard personnel who are high school seniors entering college.
Eligibility This program is open to high school seniors who are dependent children of Coast Guard active duty, reserve, and military retired members; current civilian employees in both non-appropriated funds (NAF) and appropriated funds (APF) categories; and current Coast Guard Auxiliarists. Home-school students are eligible if they submit standardized test results. Applicants must be planning to enroll at an accredited college or university in an undergraduate degree program. Along with their application, they must submit a 1-page essay on what they hope to achieve in their college career, including educational, professional, and personal goals. Selection is based on that essay, SAT and/or ACT scores, GPA, letters of recommendation, participation in extracurricular activities, demonstrated leadership qualities, and personal accomplishments and interests.
Financial data The stipend is $2,000.
Duration 1 year.
Number awarded Varies each year.
Deadline February of each year.

[620]
COAST GUARD RESERVE FAMILIES SCHOLARSHIPS

Coast Guard Foundation
Attn: Scholarships
394 Taugwonk Road
Stonington, CT 06378
(860) 535-0786   Fax: (860) 535-0944
E-mail: swilliams@coastguardfoundation.org
Web: www.coastguardfoundation.org

Summary To provide financial assistance for postsecondary education to members of the Coast Guard Reserve and their families.
Eligibility This program is open to members of the Coast Guard Reserve and their families. Applicants must be enrolled at an accredited institution and working on a degree, professional development course, licensing course, or certification. Selection is based on academic promise, motivation, moral character, good citizenship, leadership qualities, and financial need.
Financial data Grants up to $1,000 per calendar year are available. Funds may be used for reimbursement of required educational expenses not funded through other resources (e.g., books, school fees, transportation, child care).
Duration 1 year; may be renewed.
Additional information This program is sponsored by USAA.
Number awarded Varies each year; recently, 8 were awarded.
Deadline August of each year.

[621]
COL CARL F. BASWELL FALLEN ENGINEER MEMORIAL SCHOLARSHIP

Army Engineer Association
Attn: Director Washington DC Operations
P.O. Box 30260
Alexandria, VA 22310-8260
(703) 428-7084   Fax: (703) 428-6043
E-mail: xd@armyengineer.com
Web: www.armyengineer.com/scholarships

Summary To provide financial assistance for college to children and spouses of U.S. Army Engineers who were killed in Iraq or Afghanistan.
Eligibility This program is open to the children and spouses of U.S. Army Engineers who were killed in combat during Operation Iraqi Freedom or Operation Enduring Freedom. Applicants must be working on or planning to work on an associate, bachelor's, or master's degree at an accredited college or university. Along with their application, they must

submit a 1-page essay outlining why they should be selected for an award, including a paragraph on their financial need and their evaluation of their potential for success.
Financial data The stipend is $2,500.
Duration 1 year.
Additional information This program began in 2010.
Number awarded 1 each year.
Deadline June of each year.

[622]
COLD WAR VETERANS ENGINEERING AND SCIENCE SCHOLARSHIPS

Marines' Memorial Association
c/o Marines Memorial Club and Hotel
609 Sutter Street
San Francisco, CA 94102
(415) 673-6672, ext. 293   Toll Free: (800) 5-MARINE
Fax: (415) 441-3649
E-mail: scholarship@marineclub.com
Web: www.marinesmemorial.org

Summary To provide financial assistance to members of the Marines' Memorial Association from all branches of the armed forces and their descendants who are interested in studying a field of STEM in college.
Eligibility This program is open to active members of the association and their children and grandchildren. Applicants must be high school seniors or students currently enrolled full time in an undergraduate degree program in a field of STEM. Along with their application, they must submit an essay of up to 500 words on why they chose their specific path of study, what they hope to accomplish after graduation with their degree, and how their efforts will benefit others in their community. Graduating high school seniors must submit a high school transcript and SAT or ACT scores; continuing college students must submit a college transcript. Selection is based on the essay, academic merit, references, and financial need.
Financial data The stipend is $2,500 per year.
Duration 1 year; recipients may reapply for up to 3 additional years.
Additional information Membership in the association is open to veterans of the Marines, Army, Navy, Air Force, or Coast Guard and to personnel currently serving in a branch of the armed forces. This program began in 2014.
Number awarded 3 each year.
Deadline April of each year.

[623]
COLONEL AARON BURGSTEIN MEMORIAL SCHOLARSHIP

Air Force Association
Attn: Scholarships
1501 Lee Highway
Arlington, VA 22209-1198
(703) 247-5800, ext. 4868
Toll Free: (800) 727-3337, ext. 4868
Fax: (703) 247-5853   E-mail: scholarships@afa.org
Web: www.app.smarterselect.com

Summary To provide financial assistance to dependents of military personnel who are high school seniors or current college undergraduates working on a degree in any field.

Eligibility This program is open to dependents of (officer or enlisted) active duty, retired, or prior service members of all branches; Reserve; or National Guard personnel. Applicants must be graduating high school seniors or current undergraduates enrolled or planning to enroll at an accredited 2- or 4-year college or university to work on an undergraduate degree in any field. They must have a GPA of 2.5 or higher. Along with their application, they must submit a 600-word essay on their academic and personal achievements and goals and how this scholarship will help them accomplish their goals. Priority is given to applicants whose parent or guardian served for 8 or more years, has had a parent die while serving on or in an active-duty status, or has a parent who has been classified as a wounded warrior through the Air Force Wounded Warrior program.
Financial data The stipend is $1,000.
Duration 1 year; nonrenewable.
Number awarded 1 or 2 each year.
Deadline April of each year.

[624]
COLONEL CHARLES L. SCHMIDT LEADERSHIP SCHOLARSHIP

11th Armored Cavalry Veterans of Vietnam and Cambodia
c/o Mike "Doc" Rafferty, Scholarship Chair
5837 Habanero Drive
P.O. Box 13188
Las Cruces, NM 88013
(915) 792-2804   E-mail: platoonmedic36@gmail.com
Web: www.11thcavnam.com/scholarship/scholar.html

Summary To provide financial assistance for college to children and grandchildren of veterans who served with the 11th Armored Cavalry Regiment during combat in Vietnam and Cambodia and who demonstrate leadership.
Eligibility This program is open to 1) children and grandchildren of current life members of the 11th Armored Cavalry Veterans of Vietnam and Cambodia (11ACVVC); 2) children and grandchildren of deceased life members of the 11th Armored Cavalry Veterans of Vietnam and Cambodia (11ACVVC); and 3) children and grandchildren of 11th Armored Cavalry Regiment troopers who were killed in action in Vietnam or Cambodia. Applicants must be enrolled or planning to enroll as an undergraduate student. They must have a GPA of 3.0 or higher. Along with their application, they must submit a brief essay on their extracurricular and volunteer activities. Selection is based on criteria established by members of Colonel Schmidt's family and may change each year, but emphasis is given to demonstrated leadership.
Financial data The stipend is $1,000 in addition to the $4,000 paid for all the sponsor's scholarships; funds are paid directly to the recipient's school, in 2 equal installments.
Duration 1 year; nonrenewable.
Additional information This program began in 2008. Recipients must use the awarded money within 44 months of being notified.
Number awarded 1 each year.
Deadline May of each year.

[625]
COLONEL HAROLD M. BEARDSLEE MEMORIAL SCHOLARSHIP AWARDS

Army Engineer Association
Attn: Director Washington DC Operations
P.O. Box 30260
Alexandria, VA 22310-8260
(703) 428-7084   Fax: (703) 428-6043
E-mail: xd@armyengineer.com
Web: www.armyengineer.com/scholarships

Summary To provide financial assistance for college to children and spouses of members of the Army Engineer Association (AEA).

Eligibility This program is open to spouses and children of AEA members in the following 4 categories: 1) graduating high school seniors who are children of active-duty or civilian members (including active-duty retired); 2) graduating high school seniors who are children of Reserve or National Guard members (including Reserve or National Guard retired); 3) children and spouses of members in the second, third, or fourth year of a baccalaureate degree program; and 4) the next best qualified applicant, regardless of category, not receiving any of those awards. Applicants must be enrolled or planning to enroll full time at an accredited college or university. Along with their application, they must submit an essay on their reasons for seeking this award. Selection is based on the essay, scholastic aptitude, and letters of recommendation.

Financial data The stipend is $1,000.
Duration 1 year; nonrenewable.
Number awarded 4 each year: 1 in each category.
Deadline April of each year.

[626]
COLONEL HAZEL BENN, USMC, SCHOLARSHIP

Fleet Reserve Association
Attn: FRA Education Foundation
125 North West Street
Alexandria, VA 22314-2754
(703) 683-1400   Toll Free: (800) FRA-1924
Fax: (703) 549-6610   E-mail: scholars@fra.org
Web: www.fra.org

Summary To provide financial assistance for college to children of members of the Fleet Reserve Association (FRA) serving in the Navy as an enlisted medical rating assigned to the United States Marine Corps (USMC).

Eligibility This program is open to the dependent children of members of the association or persons who were members at the time of death. Applicants must be entering their freshman or sophomore year of college as a full-time student. Their parent must be serving or have served in the U.S. Navy as an enlisted medical rating assigned to the USMC. Along with their application, they must submit transcripts that include SAT and/or ACT scores, an essay of any length about their sponsor's military career, a list of school and community activities, and at least 2 letters of recommendation. Selection is based on academic record, financial need, extracurricular activities, leadership skills, and participation in community activities. U.S. citizenship is required.

Financial data The stipend is $2,000.
Duration 1 year.

Additional information Membership in the FRA is open to current and former enlisted members of the Navy, Marine Corps, and Coast Guard.
Number awarded 2 each year.
Deadline April of each year.

[627]
COLONEL RICHARD HALLOCK SCHOLARSHIPS

Marines' Memorial Association
c/o Marines Memorial Club and Hotel
609 Sutter Street
San Francisco, CA 94102
(415) 673-6672, ext. 293   Toll Free: (800) 5-MARINE
Fax: (415) 441-3649
E-mail: scholarship@marineclub.com
Web: www.marinesmemorial.org

Summary To provide financial assistance for college to members of the Marines' Memorial Association from all branches of the armed forces and their descendants.

Eligibility This program is open to active members of the association and their children and grandchildren. Applicants must be high school seniors or students currently enrolled full time in an undergraduate degree program in any field at a college or university. Along with their application, they must submit an essay of up to 500 words on why they chose their specific path of study, what they hope to accomplish after graduation with their degree, and how their efforts will benefit others in their community. Graduating high school seniors must submit a high school transcript and SAT or ACT scores; continuing college students must submit a college transcript. Selection is based on the essay, academic merit, references, and financial need.

Financial data The stipend is $2,500 per year.
Duration 1 year; recipients may reapply for up to 3 additional years.
Additional information Membership in the association is open to veterans of the Marines, Army, Navy, Air Force, or Coast Guard and to personnel currently serving in a branch of the armed forces.
Number awarded 2 each year.
Deadline April of each year.

[628]
COLORADO DEPENDENTS TUITION ASSISTANCE PROGRAM

Colorado Commission on Higher Education
1600 Broadway, Suite 2200
Denver, CO 80202
(303) 862-3001   Fax: (303) 996-1329
E-mail: cche@state.co.us
Web: highered.colorado.gov

Summary To provide financial assistance for college to the dependents of disabled or deceased Colorado National Guardsmen, law enforcement officers, and firefighters.

Eligibility Eligible for the program are dependents of Colorado law enforcement officers, firefighters, and National Guardsmen disabled or killed in the line of duty, as well as dependents of prisoners of war or service personnel listed as missing in action. Students must be Colorado residents under 22 years of age enrolled at 1) a state-supported 2- or 4-year Colorado college or university; 2) a private college, university, or vocational school in Colorado approved by the commission; or 3) an out-of-state 4-year college. Financial need is considered in the selection process.

Financial data Eligible students receive free tuition at Colorado public institutions of higher education. If the recipient wishes to attend a private college, university, or proprietary school, the award is limited to the amount of tuition at a comparable state-supported institution. Students who have applied to live in a dormitory, but have not been accepted because there is not enough space, may be provided supplemental assistance. Students who choose to live off-campus are not eligible for room reimbursement or a meal plan. Students who attend a non-residential Colorado institution and do not live at home are eligible for a grant of $1,000 per semester to assist with living expenses. Students who attend an out-of-state institution are eligible for the amount of tuition equivalent to that at a comparable Colorado public institution, but they are not eligible for room and board.

Duration Up to 6 years or until completion of a bachelor's degree, provided the recipient maintains a GPA of 2.5 or higher.

Additional information Recipients must attend accredited postsecondary institutions in Colorado.

Number awarded Varies each year; recently, nearly $672,000 was allocated to this program.

Deadline Deadline not specified.

[629]
COLORADO LEGION AUXILIARY DEPARTMENT PRESIDENT'S SCHOLARSHIP FOR JUNIOR AUXILIARY MEMBERS

American Legion Auxiliary
Department of Colorado
7465 East First Avenue, Suite D
Denver, CO 80230
(303) 367-5388   Fax: (303) 367-5388
E-mail: dept-sec@alacolorado.com
Web: www.alacolorado.com/scholarships.html

Summary To provide financial assistance to junior members of the American Legion Auxiliary in Colorado who plan to attend college in the state.

Eligibility This program is open to seniors at high schools in Colorado who have been junior members of the auxiliary for the past 3 years. Applicants must be Colorado residents planning to attend college in the state. Along with their application, they must submit a 1,000-word essay on a topic that changes annually; recently, students were asked to write on, "How Military Families are Keeping the Promise to Preserve our Freedom." Selection is based on character (20%), Americanism (20%), leadership (20%), scholarship (20%), and financial need (20%).

Financial data The stipend is $1,000.

Duration 1 year; nonrenewable.

Number awarded 3 each year.

Deadline Applications must be submitted to the unit president by February of each year.

[630]
COLORADO LEGION AUXILIARY DEPARTMENT PRESIDENT'S SCHOLARSHIPS

American Legion Auxiliary
Department of Colorado
7465 East First Avenue, Suite D
Denver, CO 80230
(303) 367-5388   Fax: (303) 367-5388
E-mail: dept-sec@alacolorado.com
Web: www.alacolorado.com/scholarships.html

Summary To provide financial assistance to children and grandchildren of veterans in Colorado who plan to attend college in the state.

Eligibility This program is open to children and grandchildren of veterans who served in the armed forces during wartime eligibility dates for membership in the American Legion. Applicants must be residents of Colorado who are high school seniors planning to attend a college in the state. Along with their application, they must submit a 1,000-word essay on a topic that changes annually; recently, students were asked to write on, "How Military Families are Keeping the Promise to Preserve our Freedom." Selection is based on character (20%), Americanism (20%), leadership (20%), scholarship (20%), and financial need (20%).

Financial data The stipend is $1,000 or $500.

Duration 1 year.

Number awarded 3 each year: 1 at $1,000 and 2 at 4500.

Deadline Applications must be submitted to the unit president by February of each year.

[631]
COLORADO LEGION AUXILIARY DEPARTMENT SCHOLARSHIP FOR NON-TRADITIONAL STUDENTS

American Legion Auxiliary
Department of Colorado
7465 East First Avenue, Suite D
Denver, CO 80230
(303) 367-5388   Fax: (303) 367-5388
E-mail: dept-sec@alacolorado.com
Web: www.alacolorado.com/scholarships.html

Summary To provide financial assistance to nontraditional students who are members of American Legion organizations in Colorado and interested in attending college in the state.

Eligibility This program is open to members of the American Legion, American Legion Auxiliary, or Sons of the American Legion in Colorado who have been members for the past 2 years and the current year. Applicants must be 1) nontraditional students returning to the classroom after some period of time in which their formal education was interrupted; or 2) nontraditional students who are just beginning their education at a later point in life or continuing to work on a degree. Selection is based on character and leadership (25%), an essay and the application (25%), scholarship and grades (25%), and financial need (25%).

Financial data The stipend is $2,000.

Duration 1 year; nonrenewable.

Number awarded 1 each year.

Deadline Applications must be submitted to the unit president by February of each year.

[632]
COLORADO LEGION AUXILIARY PAST PRESIDENT'S PARLEY HEALTH PROFESSIONAL SCHOLARSHIP

American Legion Auxiliary
Department of Colorado
7465 East First Avenue, Suite D
Denver, CO 80230
(303) 367-5388 Fax: (303) 367-5388
E-mail: dept-sec@alacolorado.com
Web: www.alacolorado.com/scholarships.html

Summary To provide financial assistance to wartime veterans and their descendants in Colorado who are interested in attending school in the state to prepare for a career in nursing.

Eligibility This program is open to 1) daughters, sons, spouses, granddaughters, and great-granddaughters of veterans; and 2) veterans who served in the armed forces during eligibility dates for membership in the American Legion. Applicants must be Colorado residents who are seeking training in any field of health at a school in the state. Along with their application, they must submit a 500-word essay on the topic, "Americanism." Selection is based on that essay (25%), scholastic ability (25%), financial need (25%), references (13%), and dedication to medical field (12%).

Financial data Stipends range from $500 to $1,000.

Duration 1 year; nonrenewable.

Number awarded Varies each year, depending on the availability of funds.

Deadline April of each year.

[633]
COMMANDER WILLIAM S. STUHR SCHOLARSHIPS

Commander William S. Stuhr Scholarship Fund
Attn: Executive Director
3292 Thompson Bridge Road, Suite 120
Gainesville, GA 30506
E-mail: stuhrstudents@earthlink.net

Summary To provide financial assistance for college to the dependent children of retired or active-duty military personnel.

Eligibility This program is open to the dependent children of military personnel who are serving on active duty or retired with pay after 20 years' service (not merely separated from service). Applicants must be high school seniors who rank in the top 10% of their class and have an SAT score of at least 1900 or an ACT score of at least 27. They must plan to attend a 4-year accredited college. Selection is based on academic performance, extracurricular activities, demonstrated leadership potential, and financial need.

Financial data The stipend ranges up to $4,500 per year.

Duration 4 years, provided the recipient makes the dean's list at their college at least once during their first 2 years.

Additional information This program began in 1965. Recipients and their families attend a scholarship awards function in late May or early June; the fund pays air transportation to the event. Applications may be obtained only by writing and enclosing a self-addressed stamped envelope. The fund does not respond to telephone, fax, or email inquiries.

Number awarded 6 each year: 1 for a child of a military servicemember from each of the 6 branches (Air Force, Army, Coast Guard, Marine Corps, Navy, and Reserves/National Guard).

Deadline February of each year.

[634]
COMMISSIONED OFFICERS' ASSOCIATION DEPENDENT SCHOLARSHIPS

PHS Commissioned Officers Foundation for the Advancement of Public Health
8201 Corporate Drive, Suite 1170
Landover, MD 20785
(301) 731-9080 Fax: (301) 731-9084
E-mail: scholarship@coausphs.org
Web: www.phscof.org/dependent-scholarship.html

Summary To provide financial assistance for college or graduate school to dependents of officers of the United States Public Health Service (USPHS) Commissioned Corps who are also members of the Commissioned Officers' Association (COA).

Eligibility This program is open to dependent children, grandchildren, and spouses of active-duty, retired, or deceased officers of the USPHS Commissioned Corps who are also COA members. Applicants must be entering or continuing full-time students at a college or graduate school and prepare for a career in an area of focus of the USPHS (clinical and rehabilitation therapists, dentist, dietitian, engineer, environmental health, health services, nurse, pharmacist, physician, science and research health professional, or veterinarian). They must be U.S. citizens and have a GPA of 3.0 or higher. Along with their application, they must submit a 3,000-character essay on what they intend to accomplish with their degree and how your area of focus relates to any of the USPHS categories. Financial need is not considered in the selection process.

Financial data Stipends range up to $1,000.

Duration 1 year.

Number awarded Varies each year; recently, 10 were awarded.

Deadline July of each year.

[635]
CONNECTICUT BETTER BUSINESS BUREAU MILITARY LINE STUDENT ETHICS SCHOLARSHIP

Better Business Bureau Serving Connecticut
Attn: Student Ethics Award Entry Committee
29 Berlin Road
Cromwell, CT 06416
(860) 740-4500, ext. 123 Fax: (860) 740-4515
E-mail: events@ct.bbb.org
Web: www.bbb.org

Summary To provide financial assistance for college in any state to Connecticut residents who are children or spouses of military personnel and demonstrate high ethical standards.

Eligibility This program is open to residents of Connecticut who are children or spouses of a military member. Applications are accepted as early as their junior year of high school or as late as the end of college freshman year. Applicants must be attending or planning to attend an accredited institution of higher education in any state. Applicants must be able to demonstrate high ethical standards. Along with their application, they must submit a 500-word essay related to their understanding of the concept of "character ethics" and how

their qualities, principles, and actions have helped build their character. Selection is based on that essay, academic accomplishments, personal integrity, contributions to their communities and schools, and leadership.
Financial data The stipend is $2,500; funds are disbursed directly to the recipient's college to be applied toward such school-related expenses as tuition, books, room, and/or board.
Duration 1 year.
Number awarded 1 each year.
Deadline July of each year.

[636]
CONNECTICUT NATIONAL GUARD FOUNDATION SCHOLARSHIPS
Connecticut National Guard Foundation, Inc.
Attn: Scholarship Committee
360 Broad Street
Hartford, CT 06105-3795
(860) 241-1550   Fax: (860) 293-2929
E-mail: ctngfi@sbcglobal.net
Web: www.ctngfi.org/scholarships

Summary To provide financial assistance for college to members of the Connecticut National Guard and their families.
Eligibility This program is open to members of the Connecticut Army National Guard and Organized Militia, their children, their spouses, and children of Connecticut National Guard retirees. Applicants must be enrolled or planning to enroll at an accredited college or technical program in any state. Along with their application, they must submit a letter of recommendation, a list of extracurricular activities, high school or college transcripts, and a 200-word statement on their educational and future goals. Selection is based on achievement and citizenship.
Financial data The stipend is $2,000.
Duration 1 year.
Number awarded 5 each year.
Deadline April of each year.

[637]
CONNECTICUT TUITION WAIVER FOR VETERANS
Connecticut State Universities and Colleges
61 Woodland Street
Hartford, CT 06105
(860) 723-0013   E-mail: fitzgeralde@ct.edu
Web: www.ct.edu/admission/veterans

Summary To provide financial assistance for college to certain Connecticut veterans and military personnel and their dependents.
Eligibility This program is open to 1) honorably-discharged Connecticut veterans who served at least 90 days during specified periods of wartime; 2) active members of the Connecticut Army or Air National Guard; 3) Connecticut residents who are a dependent child or surviving spouse of a member of the armed forces killed in action on or after September 11, 2001 who was also a Connecticut resident; and 4) Connecticut residents who are a dependent child or surviving spouse of a person officially declared missing in action or a prisoner of war while serving in the armed forces after January 1, 1960. Applicants must be attending or planning to attend a public college or university in the state.
Financial data The program provides a waiver of 100% of tuition for general fund courses at the 4 campuses of Connecticut State University, 50% of tuition for extension and summer courses at campuses of Connecticut State University, 100% of tuition at the 12 Connecticut community colleges, and 50% of fees at Charter Oak State College.
Duration Up to 4 years.
Additional information This is an entitlement program; applications are available at the respective college financial aid offices.
Number awarded Varies each year.
Deadline Deadline not specified.

[638]
CONNIE SETTLES SCHOLARSHIP
American Legion Auxiliary
Department of California
401 Van Ness Avenue, Suite 319
San Francisco, CA 94102-4570
(415) 861-5092   Fax: (415) 861-8365
E-mail: calegionaux@calegionaux.org
Web: www.calegionaux.org/scholarships.htm

Summary To provide financial assistance to members of the American Legion Auxiliary in California who are attending college or graduate school in the state.
Eligibility This program is open to residents of California who are currently working on an undergraduate or graduate degree at a college or university in the state. Applicants must have been members of the American Legion Auxiliary for at least the 2 preceding years and be current members. Each unit of the Auxiliary may nominate only 1 member. Selection is based on transcripts, 2 letters of recommendation, a letter from the applicant about themselves and their goals, and financial need. Support is not provided for programs of study deemed to be nonessential (e.g., sewing classes, aerobics, sculpting).
Financial data The stipend is $5,000. Funds are paid directly to the recipient's college or university.
Duration 1 year.
Number awarded 1 each year.
Deadline Applications must be submitted to Auxiliary units by February of each year.

[639]
CORVIAS FOUNDATION SCHOLARSHIPS FOR MILITARY SPOUSES
Corvias Foundation
1405 South County Trail, Suite 530
East Greenwich, RI 02818
(401) 228-2836   Fax: (401) 336-2523
E-mail: info@CorviasFoundation.org
Web: www.corvias.com

Summary To provide financial assistance to spouses of designated categories of military personnel working on professional certifications or licenses.
Eligibility This program is open to students who are 1) spouses of members of the 7 uniformed services who have a valid military ID; 2) married to an active-duty, Reserve, Guard, retired, medically retired, wounded, or fallen service member (must be a service-related wound, illness, injury, or death that took place after September 11, 2001); 3) a dual service military spouse; or 4) a divorced spouse who is receiving 20/20/

20 benefits. Applicants must be enrolled or planning to enroll in a program for procurement of professional certification or license in any state. Selection is based on academic performance, community involvement, an essay on an assigned topic, and financial need.
Financial data The stipend is $5,000.
Duration 1 year; nonrenewable.
Additional information This program operates in partnership with the National Military Family Association.
Number awarded Varies each year; recently, 5 were awarded.
Deadline Applications may be submitted at any time.

[640]
COUDRET TRUST SCHOLARSHIPS

American Legion
Department of Arkansas
702 Victory Street
P.O. Box 3280
Little Rock, AR 72203
(501) 375-1104　　　　　Toll Free: (877) 243-9799
Fax: (501) 375-4236　　　E-mail: alegion@swbell.net
Web: www.arlegion.org

Summary To provide financial assistance to descendants of members of the American Legion in Arkansas who are interested in attending college in any state.
Eligibility This program is open to the children, grandchildren, and great-grandchildren of living or deceased members of the American Legion in Arkansas. The Legionnaire must have been a member for at least 2 years. Applicants must be high school seniors or graduates of a 2-year college in Arkansas and planning to attend an institution of higher learning in any state. They must sign a drug free pledge and a declaration of support for the Preamble to the Constitution of the American Legion. Selection is based on American spirit, character, leadership quality, scholastic endeavor, and financial need.
Financial data The stipend is $1,000.
Duration 1 year; nonrenewable.
Number awarded 4 each year.
Deadline March of each year.

[641]
CPT JAMES AND RUBY EHEMAN MEMORIAL SCHOLARSHIP

Army Scholarship Foundation
11700 Preston Road, Suite 660-301
Dallas, TX 75230
E-mail: ContactUs@armyscholarshipfoundation.org
Web: www.armyscholarshipfoundation.org/eheman.html

Summary To provide financial assistance for undergraduate study to the children and spouses of Army personnel who major in a field of STEM.
Eligibility This program is open to 1) children of regular active-duty, active-duty Reserve, and active-duty Army National Guard members in good standing; 2) spouses of serving enlisted regular active-duty, active-duty Reserve, and active-duty Army National Guard members in good standing; and 3) children of former U.S. Army members who received an honorable or medical discharge or were killed while serving in the U.S. Army. Applicants must be high school seniors, high school graduates, or undergraduates enrolled at an accredited college, university, or vocational/technical institute and majoring or planning to major in a field of STEM. They must be U.S. citizens and have a GPA of 2.0 or higher; children must be younger than 24 years of age. Financial need is considered in the selection process.
Financial data The stipend ranges from $500 to $2,000 per year.
Duration 1 year; recipients may reapply.
Additional information The Army Scholarship Foundation was established in 2001.
Number awarded 1 each year.
Deadline April of each year.

[642]
CSM HARRY AND MARY HENSELL SCHOLARSHIP PROGRAM

Enlisted Association National Guard of Arizona
Attn: Scholarship Chair
5636 East McDowell Road
Phoenix, AZ 85008-3495
(602) 267-2467　　　　　Fax: (602) 267-2509
E-mail: scholarship@eanga.org
Web: www.eanga.org/scholarship-information

Summary To provide financial assistance to members of the Enlisted Association National Guard of Arizona (EANGA) and to members of their families who plan to attend college in any state.
Eligibility This program is open to EANGA members, the unmarried children of EANGA members, the spouses of EANGA members, and the unremarried spouses and unmarried dependent children of deceased EANGA members (who were in good standing at their time of death). Qualifying EANGA members must have at least 1 year remaining on their enlistment or have served 20 or more years of service. Applicants may be high school seniors or current college students who are enrolled or planning to enroll full time at a college or university in any state. Graduate students are not eligible. Selection is based on academic record, character, leadership, and financial need.
Financial data The stipend is $1,000. Funds are made payable to the recipient's school and sent directly to the recipient.
Duration 1 year; nonrenewable.
Additional information This program, sponsored by USAA Insurance Corporation, was established in 1998 and given its current name in 2009.
Number awarded 1 each year.
Deadline April of each year.

[643]
CSM LEONARD MAGLIONE MEMORIAL SCHOLARSHIPS

Association of the United States Army-Rhode Island
　Chapter
c/o LTC Robert A. Galvanin, President
31 Canoe River Drive
Mansfield, MA 02048
(508) 339-5301　　　　　E-mail: bpje5310@verizon.net
Web: www.riroa.org/ausari/scholarship.htm

Summary To provide financial assistance to members of the Rhode Island Chapter of the Association of the United

States Army (AUSA) and their families who are interested in attending college or graduate school in any state.

Eligibility This program is open to members of the AUSA Rhode Island Chapter and their family members (spouses, children, and grandchildren). Applicants must be high school seniors or graduates accepted at an accredited college, university, or vocational/technical school in any state or current undergraduate or graduate students. Along with their application, they must submit a 250-word essay on why they feel their achievements should qualify them for this award. Selection is based on academic and individual achievements; financial need is not considered. Special consideration is given to students or graduates of LaSalle Academy in Providence (the alma mater of this program's namesake), especially those preparing for a career in the arts or engineering or enrolled or planning to enroll in Army ROTC.

Financial data The stipend is $1,000.

Duration 1 year.

Additional information Membership in the AUSA is open to everyone who supports a strong national defense, with special concern for the Army. That includes Regular Army, National Guard, Army Reserve, government civilians, retired soldiers, Wounded Warriors, veterans, concerned citizens and family members.

Number awarded Several each year.

Deadline April of each year.

[644]
CSM VIRGIL R. WILLIAMS SCHOLARSHIP PROGRAM

Enlisted Association of the National Guard of the United States
1 Massachusetts Avenue, N.W., Suite 880
Washington, DC 20001
Toll Free: (800) 234-EANG   Fax: (703) 519-3849
E-mail: eangus@eangus.org
Web: www.eangus.org/scholarship-information

Summary To provide financial assistance to National Guard members and their dependents who are members of the Enlisted Association of the National Guard of the United States (EANGUS) and entering or continuing in college.

Eligibility This program is open to high school seniors and current college students who are enrolled or planning to enroll as full-time undergraduate students. They must be 1) National Guard members who belong to EANGUS; 2) unmarried sons and daughters of EANGUS members; 3) spouses of EANGUS members; or 4) unremarried spouses and unmarried dependent children of deceased EANGUS members who were in good standing at the time of their death. Honorary, associate, or corporate membership alone does not qualify. Applicants must submit a copy of their school transcript, 3 letters of recommendation, a letter of academic reference (from their principal, dean, or counselor), a photocopy of the qualifying state and/or national membership card (parent's, spouse's or applicant's), and a personal letter with specific facts as to their desire to continue their education and why financial assistance is necessary. Application packets must be submitted to the state EANGUS association; acceptable packets are then sent to the national offices for judging. Selection is based on academic achievement, character, leadership, and financial need.

Financial data The stipend is $2,000.

Duration 1 year; nonrenewable.

Additional information Recent sponsors of this program included USAA Insurance Corporation and the Armed Forces Benefit Association.

Number awarded Varies each year; recently, 9 were awarded.

Deadline Applications must first be verified by the state office and then submitted by May to the national office.

[645]
CWOA LT ART AND ELEANOR COLONA SCHOLARSHIP GRANT

Chief Warrant and Warrant Officers Association, USCG
12 Brookley Avenue, S.W.
Bolling AFB, DC 20032-7733
(202) 554-7753   E-mail: cwoauscg@cwoauscg.org
Web: www.cwoauscg.org/colona-scholarship

Summary To provide financial assistance for college to children of active or retired enlisted personnel of the U.S. Coast Guard.

Eligibility This program is open to the dependent children of members of the U.S. Coast Guard (active duty, retired, or Reserve). Applicants must be high school seniors or currently-enrolled full-time college students and have at least a 2.0 GPA. Along with their application, they must submit transcripts, a letter of acceptance, an essay on their reasons for attending or desiring to attend an accredited institution of higher learning, support documentation if applicable, and a photograph (optional). Their parents' financial status is not considered in the selection process.

Financial data The stipend is $1,000 per year.

Duration 1 year; may be renewed up to 3 additional years.

Number awarded 1 or more each year.

Deadline May of each year.

[646]
DAEDALIAN FOUNDATION DESCENDANTS' SCHOLARSHIP PROGRAM

Order of Daedalians
Attn: Daedalian Foundation
55 Main Circle (Building 676)
P.O. Box 249
Joint Base San Antonio-Randolph, TX 78148-0249
(210) 945-2113   Fax: (210) 945-2112
E-mail: info@daedalians.org
Web: www.daedalians.org/programs/scholarships

Summary To provide financial assistance to descendants of members of the Order of Daedalians who wish to prepare for a career in military aviation or space.

Eligibility This program is open to descendants of members of the order who are working on or planning to work on a baccalaureate or higher degree. Applicants must be interested in and willing to commit to a career as a commissioned military pilot, flight crew member, astronaut, or commissioned officer in 1 of the armed forces of the United States in a discipline directly supporting aeronautics or astronautics. They must be physically and mentally qualified for flight and/or space; if they intend to pursue a non-flying career as a commissioned officer in a scientific or engineering discipline supporting aviation or space, they must pass a physical examination qualifying for active commissioned duty in the U.S. armed forces. Nominations must be submitted by a local chapter

(Flight) of Daedalian. Selection is based on academic achievement and recognition, extracurricular activities, honors, and employment experience. Financial need may be considered if all other factors are equal.
Financial data The stipend is $2,000.
Duration 1 year.
Additional information The Order of Daedalians was founded in 1934 as an organization of the nearly 14,000 aviators who served as military pilots during World War I and are still listed and designated as Founder Members. In the 1950s, the organization expanded eligibility to include 1) on a sponsorship basis, current and former commissioned military pilots from all services; and 2) on a hereditary basis, descendants of Founder Members.
Number awarded Up to 3 each year.
Deadline July of each year.

[647]
DANIEL DREVNICK MEMORIAL FUND SCHOLARSHIPS
Daniel Drevnick Memorial Fund
P.O. Box 251566
Woodbury, MN 55125-6566
(651) 324-2122   Fax: (651) 730-7467
E-mail: Ken@HeroAtHome.org
Web: www.heroathome.org/apply-for-a-scholarship
Summary To provide financial assistance to veterans in Iowa, Minnesota, and Wisconsin who are studying law enforcement at a technical college or university in the state.
Eligibility This program is open to residents of Iowa, Minnesota, and Wisconsin who served in the military any time after September 11, 2001. Applicants must have completed Basic and Advanced Individual Training and have been honorably discharged. They must be enrolled in a law enforcement program at a technical college or university in their state. Current and widowed spouses and children of veterans from Iowa, Minnesota, or Wisconsin are also eligible. Along with their application, they must submit an essay on why they feel they should be considered for a scholarship.
Financial data The stipend is $1,000.
Duration 1 year.
Additional information This program began in 2012.
Number awarded 10 each year.
Deadline Deadline not specified.

[648]
DANIEL E. LAMBERT MEMORIAL SCHOLARSHIP
American Legion
Department of Maine
5 Verti Drive
Winslow, ME 04901-0727
(207) 873-3229   Fax: (207) 872-0501
E-mail: legionme@mainelegion.org
Web: www.mainelegion.org
Summary To provide financial assistance to the children of veterans in Maine who plan to attend college in any state.
Eligibility This program is open to residents of Maine who are the child or grandchild of a veteran. Applicants must be attending or planning to attend an accredited college or vocational/technical school in any state. They must have demonstrated, by their past behavior, that they believe in the American way of life. U.S. citizenship is required. Financial need is considered in the selection process.
Financial data The stipend is $1,000.
Duration 1 year.
Number awarded 1 or 2 each year.
Deadline April of each year.

[649]
DANIEL GEIGER SCHOLARSHIP
Veterans of Foreign Wars of the United States-
  Department of Pennsylvania
Attn: Scholarship
4002 Fenton Avenue
Harrisburg, PA 17109-5943
(717) 234-7927   Fax: (717) 234-1955
E-mail: quartermaster@vfwpahq.org
Web: www.vfwpahq.org
Summary To provide financial assistance to children and grandchildren of veterans in Pennsylvania who are high school seniors planning to attend college in any state.
Eligibility This program is open to seniors graduating from high schools in Pennsylvania and planning to enroll at a college or university in any state. Applicants must be the child or grandchild of a Pennsylvania veteran. Along with their application, they must submit 1) a resume that including high school transcripts, letters of recommendation, certificates of appreciation or commendation, and a copy of a letter of acceptance to college or other higher level of education; 2) a letter of endorsement from the VFW Post Commander; and 3) a letter from the applicant describing financial need and/or family hardship.
Financial data The stipend is $1,000.
Duration 1 year.
Number awarded 1 each year.
Deadline March of each year.

[650]
DAUGHTERS OF THE CINCINNATI SCHOLARSHIP PROGRAM
Daughters of the Cincinnati
Attn: Scholarship Administrator
271 Madison Avenue, Suite 1408
New York, NY 10016
(212) 991-9945
E-mail: scholarships@daughters1894.org
Web: www.daughters1894.org/scholarship
Summary To provide financial assistance for college to high school seniors who are the daughters of active-duty, deceased, or retired military officers.
Eligibility This program is open to high school seniors who are the daughters of career commissioned officers of the regular Army, Navy, Air Force, Coast Guard, or Marine Corps on active duty, deceased, or retired. Applicants must be planning to enroll in an undergraduate program at a college or university in any state. Along with their application, they must submit an official school transcript, SAT or ACT scores, a letter of recommendation, an essay on their choice of 3 assigned topics, and documentation of financial need.
Financial data Scholarship amounts have ranged from $4,000 to $5,000 per year. Funds are paid directly to the college of the student's choice.

Duration 1 year; may be renewed up to 3 additional years, provided the recipient remains in good academic standing.
Additional information This program was originally established in 1906.
Number awarded Approximately 12 each year.
Deadline March of each year.

[651]
DELAWARE EDUCATIONAL BENEFITS FOR CHILDREN OF DECEASED VETERANS AND OTHERS

Delaware Department of Education
Attn: Higher Education Office
401 Federal Street, Suite 2
Dover, DE 19901-3639
(302) 735-4120 Toll Free: (800) 292-7935
Fax: (302) 739-5894 E-mail: dheo@doe.k12.de.us
Web: www.doe.k12.de.us/Page/1005

Summary To provide financial assistance for undergraduate education to dependents of deceased Delaware veterans, state police officers, and Department of Transportation employees and members of the armed forces declared prisoners of war or missing in action.
Eligibility Applicants for this assistance must have been Delaware residents for at least 3 consecutive years and be the children, between 16 and 24 years of age, of members of the armed forces 1) whose cause of death was service-related; 2) who are being held or were held as a prisoner of war; or 3) who are officially declared missing in action. The parent must have been a resident of Delaware at the time of death or declaration of missing in action or prisoner of war status. Also eligible are children of Delaware state police officers whose cause of death was service-related and employees of the state Department of Transportation routinely employed in job-related activities upon the state highway system whose cause of death was job related. U.S. citizenship or eligible noncitizen status is required.
Financial data Eligible students receive full tuition at any state-supported institution in Delaware or, if the desired educational program is not available at a state-supported school, at any private institution in Delaware. If the desired educational program is not offered at either a public or private institution in Delaware, this program pays the full cost of tuition at the out-of-state school the recipient attends. Students who wish to attend a private or out-of-state school even though their program is offered at a Delaware public institution receive the equivalent of the average tuition and fees at the state school.
Duration 1 year; may be renewed for 3 additional years.
Number awarded Varies each year.
Deadline Applications may be submitted at any time, but they must be received 6 to 8 weeks before the beginning of classes.

[652]
DELLA VAN DEUREN MEMORIAL SCHOLARSHIPS

American Legion Auxiliary
Department of Wisconsin
Attn: Education Chair
2930 American Legion Drive
P.O. Box 140
Portage, WI 53901-0140
(608) 745-0124 Toll Free: (866) 664-3863
Fax: (608) 745-1947
E-mail: deptsec@amlegionauxwi.org
Web: www.amlegionauxwi.org/scholarships

Summary To provide financial assistance to Wisconsin residents who are members or children of members of the American Legion Auxiliary and interested in attending college in any state.
Eligibility This program is open to members and children of members of the American Legion Auxiliary in Wisconsin. Applicants must be high school seniors or graduates and attending or planning to attend a college or university in any state. They must have a GPA of 3.5 or higher and be able to demonstrate financial need. Along with their application, they must submit a 300-word essay on "Education—An Investment in the Future."
Financial data The stipend is $1,000.
Duration 1 year; nonrenewable.
Number awarded 2 each year.
Deadline March of each year.

[653]
DELTA DENTAL GRANTS

Air Force Association
Attn: Scholarships
1501 Lee Highway
Arlington, VA 22209-1198
(703) 247-5800, ext. 4868
Toll Free: (800) 727-3337, ext. 4868
Fax: (703) 247-5853 E-mail: scholarships@afa.org
Web: www.app.smarterselect.com

Summary To provide financial assistance to spouses and dependents of military personnel who are interested in further training related to oral health and wellness.
Eligibility This program is open to military spouses, dependents, and transitioning service members who are interested in training, certification, or a degree related to oral health and wellness. Eligible areas of study include dentistry, nursing, home health care aid, or caregiver training. Applicants must submit a statement of purpose describing how the grant will assist in meeting their educational goals.
Financial data The stipend is $2,000.
Duration 1 year.
Additional information This program is sponsored by Delta Dental.
Number awarded 5 each year.
Deadline April of each year.

[654]
DELTA DENTAL ORAL HEALTH AND WELLNESS SCHOLARSHIP

Association of the United States Army
Attn: Scholarships
2425 Wilson Boulevard
Arlington, VA 22201
(703) 841-4300   Toll Free: (800) 336-4570
E-mail: scholarships@ausa.org
Web: www.ausa.org/resources/scholarships

Summary To provide financial assistance to Army family members and transitioning soldiers who are interested in studying a field related to oral health and wellness in college.

Eligibility This program is open to Army family members and transitioning soldiers who are members of the Association of the United States Army and enrolled or accepted at an accredited college, university, or certificate program. Applicants must be studying dentistry, nursing, home health care aid, caregiver training, or other field related to oral health and wellness. Along with their application, they must submit a 1-page autobiography, 2 letters of recommendation, a letter describing their career aspirations (including their course of study and plans for completion of a certificate or degree), and a transcript of high school or college grades (depending on which they are currently attending). Selection is based on academic merit and personal achievement. Financial need is not normally a selection criterion but in some cases of extreme need it may be used as a factor; the lack of financial need, however, is never a cause for non-selection.

Financial data The stipend is $2,000; funds are sent directly to the recipient's institution.

Duration 1 year.

Additional information Membership in the AUSA is open to everyone who supports a strong national defense, with special concern for the Army. That includes Regular Army, National Guard, Army Reserve, government civilians, retired soldiers, Wounded Warriors, veterans, concerned citizens and family members. This program is sponsored by Delta Dental.

Number awarded 10 each year.

Deadline June of each year.

[655]
DENNIS COMAI SCHOLARSHIPS

Sons of the American Legion
Detachment of Vermont
c/o Henry Cleveland, Scholarship Chair
1212 Coburn Hill Road
Craftsbury, VT 05826
Web: www.salvermont.com/forms.html

Summary To provide financial assistance to high school seniors in Vermont whose family has a connection to the American Legion and who are planning to attend a trade/technical school in any state.

Eligibility This program is open to seniors graduating from high schools in Vermont whose grandparent, parent, or sibling is a member of the American Legion, American Legion Auxiliary, or Sons of the American Legion. Applicants must be planning to attend a trade school or technical college in any state. Along with their application, they must submit a brief essay on what the American veteran means to them. Financial need is considered in the selection process.

Financial data Stipends are $1,000 or $500.

Duration 1 year.

Number awarded 4 each year: 2 at $1,000 (1 in the northern part of the state and 1 in the southern part of the state) and 2 at $500 (1 in the northern part of the state and 1 in the southern part of the state).

Deadline April of each year.

[656]
DEPARTMENT OF NEBRASKA VFW STATE SCHOLARSHIPS

Veterans of Foreign Wars of the United States-
    Department of Nebraska
Attn: Scholarship Chair
2431 North 48th Street
Lincoln, NE 68504
(402) 464-0674   Fax: (402) 464-0675
E-mail: Johnl@vfwne.org
Web: vfwne.com/di/vfw/v2/default.asp?pid=6204

Summary To provide financial assistance to members of the Veterans of Foreign Wars (VFW), the VFW Auxiliary, and their families in Nebraska who wish to attend college in the state.

Eligibility This program is open to members of the Nebraska chapter of the VFW, the VFW Auxiliary, and their spouses, children, stepchildren, and grandchildren. Applicants must have completed at least 1 year of full-time study at a college or university in Nebraska. They must be able to demonstrate financial need.

Financial data A stipend is awarded (amount not specified).

Duration 1 year.

Additional information This program includes named awards designated as the Past State Commanders Scholarship, the Darrell Thibault VFW State Memorial Scholarship, the Nathan Grossman VFW State Memorial Scholarship, the Phillips Scholarship, and the Connie Liebsack Memorial Scholarship.

Number awarded At least 5 each year.

Deadline March of each year.

[657]
DFC SOCIETY WARD MACAULEY SCHOLARSHIPS

Distinguished Flying Cross Society
Attn: Scholarship Program
P.O. Box 502408
San Diego, CA 92150
Toll Free: (866) 332-6332
E-mail: mepark@dfcsociety.org
Web: www.dfcsociety.org

Summary To provide financial assistance for college to descendants of members of the Distinguished Flying Cross Society (DFCS).

Eligibility This program is open to descendants (including legally adopted children) of DFCS members. Applicants must be working on an undergraduate degree at an accredited institution of higher education. Along with their application, they must submit a list of memberships in school-related organizations, a list of elected leadership positions they have held, information on activities that demonstrate community involvement, transcripts (including SAT and/or ACT scores), and a 500-word essay on 1 of the following topics: 1) why they deserve this scholarship; 2) their life aspirations, including whether they plan a military career; or 3) the role of patriotism in their life and American society.

Financial data The stipend is $1,000.

Duration 1 year.

Additional information Membership in the sponsoring organization, founded in 1994, is limited to members of the U.S. armed forces who have been awarded the Distinguished Flying Cross as a result of deeds accomplished during aerial flight.

Number awarded Varies each year; recently, 5 were awarded.

Deadline June of each year.

[658]
DISABLED AMERICAN VETERANS AUXILIARY NATIONAL EDUCATION SCHOLARSHIP FUND

Disabled American Veterans Auxiliary
Attn: National Education Scholarship Fund
3725 Alexandria Pike
Cold Spring, KY 41076
(859) 441-7300   Toll Free: (877) 426-2838, ext. 4020
Fax: (859) 442-2095   E-mail: dava@davmail.org
Web: auxiliary.dav.org/membership/programs

Summary To provide financial assistance to members of the Disabled American Veterans (DAV) Auxiliary who are interested in attending college or graduate school.

Eligibility This program is open to paid life members of the auxiliary who are attending or planning to attend a college, university, or vocational school as a full- or part-time undergraduate or graduate student. Applicants must be at least seniors in high school, but there is no maximum age limit. Along with their application, they must submit a 500-word essay on their personal or career goals and how their education will help them reach those goals. Selection is based on that essay (35 points), academic information (10 points), DAV membership activities (10 points), participation in DAV activities or projects to benefit veterans or their families (15 points), participation in other extracurricular or volunteer activities (15 points), and financial need (10 points).

Financial data Stipends are $1,500 per year for full-time students or $750 per year for part-time students.

Duration 1 year; may be renewed for up to 4 additional years, provided the recipient maintains a GPA of 2.5 or higher.

Additional information Membership in the DAV Auxiliary is available to extended family members of veterans eligible for membership in Disabled American Veterans (i.e., any man or woman who served in the armed forces during a period of war or under conditions simulating war and was wounded, disabled to any degree, or left with long-term illness as a result of military service and was discharged or retired from military service under honorable conditions). This program was established in September 2010 as a replacement for the educational loan program that the DAV Auxiliary operated from 1931 until August 2010.

Number awarded Varies each year.

Deadline March of each year.

[659]
DISTRICT 8 ALR SCHOLARSHIPS

District 8 American Legion Riders
c/o Tom Coons, Director
P.O. Box 3029
Dickinson, ND 58602
(701) 225-9130   E-mail: tcoons@ravendrillingllc.com

Summary To provide financial assistance to children of veterans in North Dakota who are interested in attending college in any state.

Eligibility This program is open to residents of North Dakota who are children of military veterans, wounded warriors, disabled veterans, or service members killed in action. Applicants must be enrolled or planning to enroll at a college or trade school in any state. Along with their application, they are encouraged to submit an essay on their educational goals, career objectives, life experiences that made them who they are today, and how their choice of school will help them in achieving their goals.

Financial data The stipend is $1,000.

Duration 1 year.

Number awarded 10 each year.

Deadline April of each year.

[660]
DKF VETERANS ASSISTANCE FOUNDATION SCHOLARSHIPS

DKF Veterans Assistance Foundation
P.O. Box 7166
San Carlos, CA 94070
(650) 595-3896   E-mail: admin@dkfveterans.com
Web: www.dkfveterans.com/apply.html

Summary To provide financial assistance for college in any state to California residents who are veterans of Operation Enduring Freedom (OEF) in Afghanistan or Operation Iraqi Freedom (OIF) or the dependents of deceased or disabled veterans of those actions.

Eligibility This program is open to 1) veterans of the U.S. armed forces (including the Coast Guard) who served in support of OEF or OIF within the central command area of responsibility; and 2) dependents of those veterans who were killed in action or incurred disabilities rated as 75% or more. Applicants must be residents of California enrolled or planning to enroll full time at a college, university, community college, or trade institution in any state. Along with their application, they must submit a cover letter introducing themselves and their educational goals.

Financial data The stipend is $5,000 per year for students at universities and state colleges or $1,500 per year for students at community colleges and trade institutions.

Duration 1 year; may be renewed up to 3 additional years, provided the recipient maintains a GPA of 3.0 or higher.

Additional information This foundation was established in 2005.

Number awarded A limited number of these scholarships are awarded each year.

Deadline Deadline not specified.

[661]
DOL1 SCHOLARSHIP

Green Beret Foundation
14402 Blanco Road, Suite 101
San Antonio, TX 78216
(910) 787-3309　　　　　Toll Free: (844) 287-7133
E-mail: support@greenberetfoundation.org
Web: www.greenberetfoundation.org/scholarships

Summary To provide financial assistance for college to children of non-commissioned officers assigned to Special Forces.

Eligibility This program is open to children and other legal dependents of non-commissioned officers who have served or are serving in Special Forces. Applicants must be enrolled or planning to enroll at a college or university. They must have a GPA of 2.5 or higher. Along with their application, they must submit transcripts that include SAT and/or ACT scores; a 1-page resume with information about their extracurricular activities, honors, employment, community service, and special skills; and an essay of 500 to 1,000 words explaining their need, intended use of the scholarship, and how their experiences or their family member's experiences in the Special Forces have affected them.

Financial data A stipend is awarded (amount not specified).

Duration 1 year.

Number awarded 1 or more each year.

Deadline June of each year.

[662]
DOL2 SCHOLARSHIP

Green Beret Foundation
14402 Blanco Road, Suite 101
San Antonio, TX 78216
(910) 787-3309　　　　　Toll Free: (844) 287-7133
E-mail: support@greenberetfoundation.org
Web: www.greenberetfoundation.org/scholarships

Summary To provide financial assistance for college to children of warrant officers assigned to Special Forces.

Eligibility This program is open to children and other legal dependents of warrant officers who have served or are serving in Special Forces. Applicants must be enrolled or planning to enroll at a college or university. They must have a GPA of 2.5 or higher. Along with their application, they must submit transcripts that include SAT and/or ACT scores; a 1-page resume with information about their extracurricular activities, honors, employment, community service, and special skills; and an essay of 500 to 1,000 words explaining their need, intended use of the scholarship, and how their experiences or their family member's experiences in the Special Forces have affected them.

Financial data A stipend is awarded (amount not specified).

Duration 1 year.

Number awarded 1 or more each year.

Deadline June of each year.

[663]
DOL3 SCHOLARSHIP

Green Beret Foundation
14402 Blanco Road, Suite 101
San Antonio, TX 78216
(910) 787-3309　　　　　Toll Free: (844) 287-7133
E-mail: support@greenberetfoundation.org
Web: www.greenberetfoundation.org/scholarships

Summary To provide financial assistance for college to children of commissioned officers assigned to Special Forces.

Eligibility This program is open to children and other legal dependents of commissioned officers who have served or are serving in Special Forces. Applicants must be enrolled or planning to enroll at a college or university. They must have a GPA of 2.5 or higher. Along with their application, they must submit transcripts that include SAT and/or ACT scores; a 1-page resume with information about their extracurricular activities, honors, employment, community service, and special skills; and an essay of 500 to 1,000 words explaining their need, intended use of the scholarship, and how their experiences or their family member's experiences in the Special Forces have affected them.

Financial data A stipend is awarded (amount not specified).

Duration 1 year.

Number awarded 1 or more each year.

Deadline June of each year.

[664]
DOLPHIN SCHOLARSHIPS

Dolphin Scholarship Foundation
Attn: Scholarship Administrator
4966 Euclid Road, Suite 109
Virginia Beach, VA 23462
(757) 671-3200　　　　　Fax: (757) 671-3330
E-mail: scholarship@dolphinscholarship.org
Web: www.dolphinscholarship.org

Summary To provide financial assistance for college to the children of members or former members of the Submarine Force.

Eligibility This program is open to the unmarried children and stepchildren under 24 years of age of 1) members or former members of the Submarine Force who qualified in submarines and served in the submarine force for at least 8 years; 2) Navy members who served in submarine support activities for at least 10 years; and 3) Submarine Force members who died on active duty. Applicants must be working or intending to work full time toward an associate or bachelor's degree at an accredited 2- or 4-year college or university. Spouses are also eligible; they may be of any age and be enrolled full or part time. Selection is based on academic proficiency, commitment and excellence in school and community activities, and financial need.

Financial data The stipend is $3,400 per year.

Duration 1 year; may be renewed for up to 3 additional years.

Additional information Since this program was established in 1961, it has awarded more than $12 million to more than 1,300 students. It includes awards previously offered by U.S. Submarine Veterans of World War II. In 1991, that organization agreed to turn over its funds to the Dolphin Scholarship Foundation with the stipulation that it would award 3 scholarships each year, designated the U.S. Submarine Veterans of World War II Scholarship, the Wives of the U.S. Submarine Veterans of World War II Scholarship, and the Arnold Krippendorf Scholarship.

Number awarded 25 to 30 each year.

Deadline March of each year.

[665]
DONALDSON D. FRIZZELL MEMORIAL SCHOLARSHIPS

First Command Educational Foundation
Attn: Scholarship Programs Manager
1 FirstComm Plaza
Fort Worth, TX 76109-4999
(817) 569-2940   Toll Free: (877) 872-8289
Fax: (817) 569-2970   E-mail: scholarships@fcef.com
Web: www.fcef.com/scholarships

Summary To provide financial assistance to students, especially those with ties to the military, entering or attending college or graduate school.

Eligibility This program is open to 1) members of a U.S. uniformed service (active, Guard, Reserve, retired, or non-retired veteran) and their spouses and dependents; 2) clients of First Command Financial Services and their family members; 3) dependent family members of First Command Advisors or field office staff members; or 4) non-contractual ROTC students. Applicants may be traditional students (high school seniors and students already enrolled at a college, university, or accredited trade school) or nontraditional students (those defined by their institution as nontraditional and adult students planning to return to a college, university, or accredited trade school). They must have a GPA of 3.0 or higher and be working on a trade school certification or associate, undergraduate, or graduate degree. Applicants must submit 1-page essays on 1) their active involvement in community service programs; 2) the impact of financial literacy on their future; and 3) why they need this scholarship. Selection is based primarily on the essays, academic merit, and financial need.

Financial data The stipend is $3,000. Funds are disbursed directly to the recipient's college, university, or trade school.

Duration 1 year.

Additional information The sponsoring organization was formerly known as the USPA & IRA Educational Foundation, founded in 1983 to provide scholarships to the children of active, retired, or deceased military personnel.

Number awarded Varies each year; recently, 10 were awarded.

Deadline The online application process begins in February of each year and continues until April or until 2,500 applications have been received.

[666]
DOUGLAS SCHOLARSHIP FOR MILITARY CHILDREN

Foundation for the Carolinas
Attn: Scholarships Department
220 North Tryon Street
Charlotte, NC 28202
(704) 973-4535   Toll Free: (800) 973-7244
Fax: (704) 973-4935   E-mail: scholars@fftc.org
Web: fftcscholarships.communityforce.com

Summary To provide financial assistance for college to high school seniors who are children of current or former military personnel.

Eligibility This program is open to graduating high school seniors who are the dependent unmarried children of active-duty personnel, Reserve and Guard members, retired military members, survivors of service members who died while on active duty, or survivors of individuals who died while receiving pay from the military. Applicants must be planning to enroll at a college or university and have a GPA of 3.0 or higher. They must be able to demonstrate significant financial need.

Financial data A stipend is awarded (amount not specified). Funds are paid directly to the recipient's school to be used for tuition, required fees, books, and supplies.

Duration 1 year.

Number awarded 1 or more each year.

Deadline February of each year.

[667]
DR. KATE WALLER BARRETT GRANT

American Legion Auxiliary
Department of Virginia
Attn: Education Chair
1708 Commonwealth Avenue
Richmond, VA 23230
(804) 355-6410   Fax: (804) 353-5246
Web: www.vaauxiliary.org/site2/index.php/scholarships

Summary To provide financial assistance to Virginia residents who are children of veterans or of members of the American Legion Auxiliary and planning to attend college in any state.

Eligibility This program is open to the children of veterans or of members of the American Legion Auxiliary who are high school seniors in Virginia planning to enroll full time at an accredited educational institution in any state. Along with their application, they must submit transcripts with SAT or ACT scores, 4 letters of recommendation, and a 500-word essay on their responsibilities as a citizen of the United States.

Financial data The stipend is $1,000.

Duration 1 year.

Number awarded 3 each year: 1 in each of the Auxiliary's zones.

Deadline March of each year.

[668]
DR. NANCY M. SCHONHER SCHOLARSHIP

Marines' Memorial Association
c/o Marines Memorial Club and Hotel
609 Sutter Street
San Francisco, CA 94102
(415) 673-6672, ext. 293   Toll Free: (800) 5-MARINE
Fax: (415) 441-3649
E-mail: scholarship@marineclub.com
Web: www.marinesmemorial.org

Summary To provide financial assistance to women who have a tie to the military and are interested in working on a degree in a health-related field.

Eligibility This program is open to women who 1) are active-duty service members or reservists in the U.S. armed forces; 2) have separated honorably from the U.S. armed forces within the past 6 years; 3) are a current or former corpsman or medic in any branch of the U.S. armed forces; or 4) are the child or grandchild of an active member of the Marines' Memorial Association. Applicants must be planning to enroll in 1) an advanced medical program with the goal of becoming a nurse, nurse practitioner, physician's assistant, or medical doctor (M.D. or O.D.) from an accredited American college or university; or 2) an accredited paramedic program (must have completed the EMT Basic training program, have taken the National Registry EMT Examination, hold an EMT Certificate, and have at least 6 months' work experience). Membership in the sponsoring organization is not required. Along with their application, they must submit an essay of up to 500 words on why they chose their specific path of study, what they hope to accomplish after graduation with their degree, and how their efforts will benefit others in their community. Selection is based on the essay, academic merit, references, and financial need. Preference is given to Navy Corpsmen.

Financial data The stipend is $5,000.
Duration 1 year.
Additional information Membership in the association is open to veterans of the Marines, Army, Navy, Air Force, or Coast Guard and to personnel currently serving in a branch of the armed forces. This program began in 2017.
Number awarded 1 each year.
Deadline April of each year.

[669]
DR. SYDELL PERLMUTTER GOLD MEMORIAL SCHOLARSHIPS

Air Force Association
Attn: Scholarships
1501 Lee Highway
Arlington, VA 22209-1198
(703) 247-5800, ext. 4868
Toll Free: (800) 727-3337, ext. 4868
Fax: (703) 247-5853   E-mail: scholarships@afa.org
Web: www.app.smarterselect.com

Summary To provide financial assistance to high school seniors who are daughters of Air Force personnel and planning to attend college to major in a field of STEM.

Eligibility This program is open to female dependents of Air Force active duty, retired, or deceased personnel who are graduating high school seniors. Applicants must be planning to enroll at an accredited 4-year college or university to work on a bachelor's degree in a field of STEM. Preference is given to applicants who are first-generation college students or who can demonstrate financial need.

Financial data The stipend is $5,000 per year.
Duration 4 years.
Number awarded 1 each year.
Deadline April of each year.

[670]
D.W. STEELE CHAPTER AFA STEM SCHOLARSHIPS

Air Force Association-Donald W. Steele, Sr. Chapter
c/o Sonya Yelbert
8704 Ashby Court
Upper Marlboro, MD 20772
E-mail: VA239.STEELE@afa.org
Web: www.dwsteele.org

Summary To provide financial assistance to Air Force personnel and their families from the greater Washington, D.C. area who are interested in attending college in any state to major in a field of STEM.

Eligibility This program is open to 1) members of the Air Force (active, Guard, or Reserve) assigned to the greater Washington, D.C. area who are also members of the Air Force Association; and 2) their spouses and children. Applicants must be enrolled to planning to enroll at a college or university in any state. Selection is based on academic achievement, demonstrated leadership, community involvement, and a 1-page essay on their academic and career goals.

Financial data Stipends are $2,000 or $1,000.
Duration 1 year.
Number awarded 3 each year; recently, 2 at $2,000 and 1 at $1,000.
Deadline May of each year.

[671]
E.A. BLACKMORE SCHOLARSHIP

American Legion
Department of Wyoming
1320 Hugur Avenue
Cheyenne, WY 82001-4817
(307) 634-3035   Fax: (307) 635-7093
E-mail: adjutant@wylegion.org
Web: mobile.wyolegion.net/ea-blackmore-scholarship.shtml

Summary To provide financial assistance to the children and grandchildren of members of the American Legion in Wyoming who are interested in attending college in any state.

Eligibility This program is open to the children and grandchildren of members and deceased members of the American Legion in Wyoming. Applicants must rank in the top 20% of their high school graduating class and be able to demonstrate financial need. They must be attending or planning to attend a college or university in any state.

Financial data The stipend is $1,000 per year. Funds are paid directly to the recipient's school to be used for tuition, room and board, textbooks, and other fees.
Duration 1 year; may be renewed up to 3 additional years.
Number awarded 1 each year.
Deadline May of each year.

[672]
EANGMT USAA SCHOLARSHIPS
Enlisted Association of the National Guard of Montana
c/o Will Frank, Scholarship Chair
P.O. Box 33
Fort Harrison, MT 59636
Web: www.mteang.org/scholarships

Summary To provide financial assistance to members of the Enlisted Association of the National Guard of Montana (EANGMT) and their dependents who are interested in attending college in any state.

Eligibility This program is open to current dues-paying members of the EANGMT and their dependents who are attending or planning to attend a college, university, or vocational/technical school in any state. Applicants must submit a current grade transcript; 3 to 4 short paragraphs on their goals in life, the type of degree they are seeking, any community service they have performed and what it meant to them, and any awards earned; and a letter of recommendation.

Financial data The stipend is $1,000.

Duration 1 year; nonrenewable.

Additional information This program is supported in part by USAA Insurance Corporation.

Number awarded 2 each year: usually, 1 is awarded to an Army Guard applicant and 1 to an Air Guard applicant.

Deadline March of each year.

[673]
EANGNJ SCHOLARSHIP PROGRAM
Enlisted Association National Guard of New Jersey
Attn: Corresponding Secretary
3650 Saylors Pond Road
Joint Base McGuire-Dix-Lakehurst, NJ 08640-5606
(530) 329-6813
Web: www.eangnj.org

Summary To provide financial assistance to New Jersey National Guard members and their children who are interested in attending college in any state.

Eligibility This program is open to 1) spouses, children, stepchildren, and grandchildren of New Jersey National Guard members (active, inactive, or retired) who are also members of the Enlisted Association National Guard of New Jersey; 2) drilling Guard members who are also members of the Association; and 3) spouses, children, stepchildren, and grandchildren of deceased members who were in good standing at the time of their death. Applicants must be attending or planning to attend a college or university in any state. Along with their application, they must submit 1) information on their church, school, and community activities; 2) a list of honors they have received; 3) letters of recommendation; 4) transcripts; 5) a letter with specific reasons for their education and why financial assistance is required; and 6) a 500-word essay about the importance of education.

Financial data The stipend is $1,000.

Duration 1 year.

Additional information This program includes the CSM Vincent Baldassari Memorial Scholarships, the CSM John H. Humphreys Jr. Memorial Scholarship, the CMSgt Richard W. Spencer Scholarship, and a scholarship sponsored by USAA Insurance Corporation.

Number awarded Varies each year; recently, 7 were awarded.

Deadline June of each year.

[674]
EANGTN SCHOLARSHIP PROGRAM
Enlisted Association of the National Guard of Tennessee
Attn: Scholarship Committee
4332 Kenilwood Drive, Suite B
Nashville, TN 37204-4401
(615) 620-7255   Fax: (615) 620-7256
E-mail: melissa@eangtn.org
Web: www.eangtn.org/scholarships

Summary To provide financial assistance to members of the Enlisted Association of the National Guard of Tennessee (EANGTN) and to their dependents who are interested in attending college in any state.

Eligibility This program is open to students who are members of both the Tennessee National Guard and EANGTN or the dependent son, daughter, or spouse of a member in good standing. Children must be unmarried, unless they are also a member of the National Guard. Applicants must be entering or continuing at a college or university in any state. Along with their application, they must submit a transcript, a letter with specific facts as to their desire to continue their education and why financial assistance is required, 3 letters of recommendation, and a letter of academic reference.

Financial data The stipend is $1,000. Funds are paid to the recipient's school once enrollment is confirmed.

Duration 1 year.

Additional information In 1985, the National Guard Association of Tennessee (NGAT) agreed that the EANGTN would fund the scholarships of both associations. Additional funding is also provided by USAA Insurance Corporation.

Number awarded 4 each year, of which 1 is funded by USAA.

Deadline March of each year.

[675]
EANGUS AUXILIARY SCHOLARSHIP PROGRAM
Enlisted Association of the National Guard of the United States
Attn: Auxiliary
c/o Liz Bryant, Scholarship Committee Co-Chair
1 C Camino de Pinones
Glorieta, NM 87535
(505) 699-4081   E-mail: labrab0704@gamil.com
Web: www.eangusauxiliary.org/scholarships-2

Summary To provide financial assistance to members of the Auxiliary of the Enlisted Association of the National Guard of the United States (EANGUS) and their dependents who are entering or continuing in college.

Eligibility This program is open to high school seniors and currently-enrolled college students who are EANGUS Auxiliary members, their unmarried children or grandchildren younger than 26 years of age, or their spouses. Applicants must be enrolled or planning to enroll at a college, university, business school, or trade school and taking at least 8 accredited hours. Graduate students are not eligible. Along with their application, they must submit a copy of their school transcript, 3 letters of recommendation, a letter of academic reference (from their principal, dean, or counselor), and a letter of 350 to 500 words with specific goals for continuing their education and why financial assistance is necessary. The sponsor's State Auxiliary must have made a donation to the EANGUS Auxiliary Scholarship fund for the current and prior years. Selection is based on academic achievement, character, leadership, and financial need. The highest-ranked applicant receives a scholarship donated by USAA Insurance Corporation.

Financial data Stipends range from $1,000 to $3,000.
Duration 1 year; nonrenewable.
Additional information This program includes 1 scholarship donated by USAA Insurance Corporation.
Number awarded 5 each year: 1 at $3,000 (supported by USAA Insurance Corporation), 1 at $2,000, 1 at $1,500, and 2 at $1,000.
Deadline June of each year.

[676]
EANGUS PATRIOTS SCHOLARSHIPS

Enlisted Association of the National Guard of the United States
1 Massachusetts Avenue, N.W., Suite 880
Washington, DC 20001
Toll Free: (800) 234-EANG   Fax: (703) 519-3849
E-mail: eangus@eangus.org
Web: www.eangus.org/scholarship-information

Summary To provide financial assistance to National Guard members and their dependents who are members of the Enlisted Association of the National Guard of the United States (EANGUS) and entering or continuing in college.
Eligibility This program is open to high school seniors and current college students who are enrolled or planning to enroll as full-time undergraduate students. They must be 1) National Guard members who belong to EANGUS; 2) unmarried sons and daughters of EANGUS members; 3) spouses of EANGUS members; or 4) unremarried spouses and unmarried dependent children of deceased EANGUS members who were in good standing at the time of their death. Honorary, associate, or corporate membership alone does not qualify. Applicants must submit a copy of their school transcript, 3 letters of recommendation, a letter of academic reference (from their principal, dean, or counselor), a photocopy of the qualifying state and/or national membership card (parent's, spouse's or applicant's), and a personal letter with specific facts as to their desire to continue their education and why financial assistance is necessary. Application packets must be submitted to the state EANGUS association; acceptable packets are then sent to the national offices for judging. Selection is based on academic achievement, character, leadership, and financial need.
Financial data The stipend is $1,000.
Duration 1 year; nonrenewable.
Additional information This program began in 2018.
Number awarded Varies each year; recently, 5 were awarded.
Deadline Applications must first be verified by the state office and then submitted by May to the national office.

[677]
EANGUT SCHOLARSHIPS

Enlisted Association of the National Guard of Utah
Attn: Scholarship Committee
12953 South Minuteman Drive
P.O. Box 1776
Draper, UT 84020
(801) 699-1680   E-mail: scholarships@eangut.com
Web: www.eangut.org/eangut-scholarship-application

Summary To provide financial assistance to National Guard members who are active members of the Enlisted Association National Guard of Utah (EANGUT) and their families entering or continuing in college in the state.
Eligibility This program is open to members of EANGUT, their spouses, their children, and the spouses and unmarried dependent children of deceased members. Applicants must be attending or planning to attend a college, university, or vocational/technical school in Utah. EANGUT members must have at least 1 year remaining on their enlistment or have completed 20 or more years of service. Along with their application, they must submit 4 essays on 1) their educational and career goals; 2) how the military has influenced their life; 3) their extracurricular activities and the leadership positions they have held; and 4) their financial need.
Financial data The stipend ranges from $1,000 to $3,000.
Duration 1 year.
Additional information This program receives support from the USAA Insurance Corporation.
Number awarded Varies each year: recently, 1 at $3,000, 1 at $2,000, 2 at $1,500, and 4 at $1,000 were awarded.
Deadline July of each year.

[678]
EANYNG EDUCATION AWARDS

Enlisted Association of the New York National Guard, Inc.
Attn: Education Awards Chair
330 Old Niskayuna Road
Latham, NY 12110-2224
(518) 344-2670   E-mail: awards@eanyng.org
Web: www.eanyng.org/awards

Summary To provide financial assistance to members of the Enlisted Association of the New York National Guard (EANYNG) and their families who are interested in attending college in any state.
Eligibility This program is open to EANYNG members and their spouses, children, and grandchildren. Applicants must be high school seniors or current undergraduates at a college or university in any state. The applicant or sponsor must have belonged to EANYNG for more than 30 days for the $500 awards or than 1 year for the larger awards. Membership in EANYNG is limited to enlisted personnel in the New York Air or Army National Guard. Selection is based on academic achievement, community service, extracurricular activities, and leadership abilities.
Financial data The stipend ranges from $500 to $3,000.
Duration 1 year; nonrenewable.
Additional information This program includes the Robert H. Connal Scholarship, the EANYNG Memorial Scholarship, the EANYNG Patriot Scholarship, and a scholarship sponsored by the USAA Insurance Corporation.

Number awarded Varies each year; 1 at $3,000, 1 at $1,500, 1 at $1,000, and 2 at $500.
Deadline July of each year.

[679]
EARLINE MAYBERRY SCHOLARSHIP

VFW Auxiliary-Department of North Carolina
c/o Farres Upton, Scholarship Chair
653 Haynes Road
High Point, NC 27262
(336) 889-4133 E-mail: farresupton@aol.com
Web: vfwauxnc.org/di/vfw/v2/default.asp?pid=71857

Summary To provide financial assistance to children and grandchildren of members of the Veterans of Foreign Wars (VFW) and the VFW Auxiliary in North Carolina who plan to attend college in the state.
Eligibility This program is open to seniors graduating from high schools in North Carolina and planning to enroll at a 2- or 4-year college in the state. Applicants must be the child, grandchild, or stepchild of a member of the VFW or the VFW Auxiliary, or, if deceased, was a member at time of death.
Financial data The stipend is $1,000 per year. Funds are paid directly to the recipient's institution.
Duration 1 year; may be renewed up to 3 additional years.
Additional information This program began in 1971.
Number awarded 4 each year.
Deadline February of each year.

[680]
EASTERN REGION KOREAN WAR VETERAN DESCENDANT SCHOLARSHIPS

Korean American Scholarship Foundation
Eastern Region
1952 Gallows Road, Suite 310
Vienna, VA 22182
(703) 748-5935 Fax: (703) 748-1874
E-mail: erc.scholarship@kasf.org
Web: www.kasf.org/apply-erc

Summary To provide financial assistance to the descendants of the Korean War from any state who are working on an undergraduate or graduate degree in any field at a school in eastern states.
Eligibility This program is open to direct descendants of veterans who served in Korea from June 25, 1950 to January 31, 1955. Applicants may reside in any state, but they must be enrolled as full-time undergraduate or graduate students at a college or university in Delaware, District of Columbia, Kentucky, Maryland, North Carolina, Pennsylvania, Virginia, or West Virginia. They must have a GPA of 3.0 or higher. Selection is based on academic achievement, an essay, extracurricular activities, and recommendations.
Financial data Stipends range from $500 to $5,000.
Duration 1 year.
Additional information This program began in 2013.
Number awarded Varies each year; recently, 3 were awarded.
Deadline June of each year.

[681]
EDMUND K. GROSS EDUCATION SCHOLARSHIP

Marines' Memorial Association
c/o Marines Memorial Club and Hotel
609 Sutter Street
San Francisco, CA 94102
(415) 673-6672, ext. 293 Toll Free: (800) 5-MARINE
Fax: (415) 441-3649
E-mail: scholarship@marineclub.com
Web: www.marinesmemorial.org

Summary To provide financial assistance to members of the Marines' Memorial Association from all branches of the armed forces and their descendants who are interested in studying education in college.
Eligibility This program is open to active members of the association and their children and grandchildren. Applicants must be enrolled or planning to enroll full time in an undergraduate degree program in education at a college or university. Along with their application, they must submit an essay of up to 500 words on why they chose their specific path of study, what they hope to accomplish after graduation with their degree, and how their efforts will benefit others in their community. Graduating high school seniors must submit a high school transcript and SAT or ACT scores; continuing college students must submit a college transcript. Selection is based on the essay, academic merit, references, and financial need.
Financial data The stipend is $2,500 per year.
Duration 1 year; recipients may reapply for up to 3 additional years.
Additional information Membership in the association is open to veterans of the Marines, Army, Navy, Air Force, or Coast Guard and to personnel currently serving in a branch of the armed forces.
Number awarded 1 each year.
Deadline April of each year.

[682]
EDUCATION FOUNDATION FOR THE COLORADO NATIONAL GUARD GRANTS

National Guard Association of Colorado
Attn: Education Foundation, Inc.
P.O. Box 440889
Aurora, CO 80044-0889
(303) 909-6369 Fax: (720) 535-5925
E-mail: BernieRogoff@comcast.net
Web: www.efcong.org

Summary To provide financial assistance to members of the Colorado National Guard and their families who are interested in attending college or graduate school in any state.
Eligibility This program is open to current and retired members of the Colorado National Guard and their dependent unmarried children and spouses. Applicants must be enrolled or planning to enroll full or part time at a college, university, trade school, business school, or graduate school in any state. Along with their application, they must submit an essay, up to 2 pages in length, on their desire to continue their education, what motivates them, their financial need, their commitment to academic excellence, and their current situation. Selection is based on academic achievement, community involvement, and financial need.

Financial data Stipends are generally at least $1,000 per year.
Duration 1 year; may be renewed.
Number awarded Normally, 15 to 25 of these grants are awarded each semester.
Deadline July of each year for fall semester; January of each year for spring semester.

[683]
EDUCATIONAL GRATUITY OF THE PENNSYLVANIA DEPARTMENT OF MILITARY AND VETERANS AFFAIRS

Pennsylvania Department of Military and Veterans Affairs
Attn: Educational Gratuity
Building 0-47
Fort Indiantown Gap
Annville, PA 17003-5002
(717) 861-8910   Toll Free: (800) 547-2838
Fax: (717) 861-8589   E-mail: ra-eg@pa.gov
Web: www.dmva.pa.gov

Summary To provide financial assistance to residents of Pennsylvania who are the child of a deceased or disabled veteran and wish to attend college in the state.
Eligibility This program is open to students between 16 and 23 years of age who have been residents of Pennsylvania for at least 5 years. Applicants must be the child of a veteran who 1) died in service during a period of war or armed conflict; or 2) received an honorable discharge, served during established dates of war, and has a 100% permanent and total service-connected disability. They must be enrolled or planning to enroll at a college or university in Pennsylvania. Financial need is considered in the selection process.
Financial data The stipend is $500 per semester. Funds are paid directly to the educational institution.
Duration 1 semester; may be renewed up to 7 additional semesters.
Number awarded Varies each year.
Deadline Deadline not specified.

[684]
EDWARD O. NESHEIM MEMORIAL SCHOLARSHIP

American Legion
Department of North Dakota
405 West Main Street, Suite 4A
P.O. Box 5057
West Fargo, ND 58078
(701) 293-3120   Fax: (701) 293-9951
E-mail: Programs@ndlegion.org
Web: www.ndlegion.org/scholarships

Summary To provide financial assistance to high school seniors in North Dakota who are direct descendants of veterans and interested in attending college in the state to study specified fields.
Eligibility This program is open to seniors graduating from high schools in North Dakota who have a GPA of 2.75 or higher. Applicants must be the children, grandchildren, or great- grandchildren of veterans who served honorably in the U.S. armed forces. They must be planning to attend a college or university in North Dakota to work on a degree in agriculture, human nutrition, or a medical field (e.g., pre-medicine, physician assistant, dentistry, dental hygiene, pharmacy, chiropractic). Along with their application, they must submit an essay of 500 to 750 words on their educational and career goals, how they plan to accomplish those goals, the part their education will play in attaining those goals, where they plan to attend college and why they chose that institution, and how their secondary education helped prepare them for their choice of college, their life, and their career. Financial need is considered in the selection process.
Financial data The stipend is $1,500 per year.
Duration 1 year; recipients may reapply, provided they have a GPA of 2.5 or higher for the preceding year of college study.
Additional information This program began in 2008.
Number awarded 1 each year.
Deadline March of each year.

[685]
ENLISTED ASSOCIATION OF THE NATIONAL GUARD OF GEORGIA SCHOLARSHIPS

Enlisted Association of the National Guard of Georgia
Attn: Executive Director
P.O. Box 602
Ellenwood, GA 30294
(678) 644-9245   Fax: (770) 719-9791
E-mail: csmharper@comcast.net
Web: www.eangga.com/eangga-scholarship

Summary To provide financial assistance to members of the Enlisted Association of the National Guard of Georgia (EANGGA) and their families who are interested in attending college in any state.
Eligibility This program is open to members of EANGGA who have been in good standing for at least 1 year and to their children and spouses. Applicants must be enrolled or planning to enroll at a college or university in any state. Selection is based primarily on an essay, up to 5 paragraphs in length, on a patriotic theme (e.g., heritage of the U.S. flag, history of the National Guard or a National Guard unit, acts of heroism by American patriots, our Constitution or Bill of Rights, civil liberties and other issues in a democratic state).
Financial data The stipend is $1,000.
Duration 1 year.
Number awarded 3 each year, of which 1 is sponsored by USAA Insurance Corporation.
Deadline April of each year.

[686]
ENLISTED ASSOCIATION OF THE NATIONAL GUARD OF IOWA AUXILIARY SCHOLARSHIP PROGRAM

Enlisted Association of the National Guard of Iowa Auxiliary
c/o Lori Waters, President
1005 Second Street S.W.
Altoona, IA 50009
(515) 490-3202   E-mail: bullriderfan@msn.com
Web: www.eangi.org/auxiliary-scholarship

Summary To provide financial assistance to members of the Enlisted Association of the National Guard of Iowa (EANIG) Auxiliary and their families who are interested in attending college in any state.
Eligibility This program is open to EANGI Auxiliary members and their spouses, dependents, and grandchildren. Applicants must be enrolled, accepted for enrollment, or in

the process of applying to a college or vocational/technical school as a full-time undergraduate or graduate student. Along with their application, they must submit a letter describing specific fats about their desire to continue their education and why they need financial assistance. Selection is based on character, leadership, and need.
Financial data The stipend is $1,000.
Duration 1 year; recipients may reapply.
Number awarded 2 each year.
Deadline February of each year.

[687]
ENLISTED ASSOCIATION OF THE NATIONAL GUARD OF KANSAS SCHOLARSHIPS
Enlisted Association of the National Guard of Kansas
Attn: Scholarship Program
125 S.E. Airport Drive
Topeka, KS 66619
(785) 242-5678   Fax: (785) 242-3765
E-mail: scholarship/eangks.org
Web: www.eangks.org

Summary To provide financial assistance to members of the Enlisted Association National Guard of Kansas and their families who are interested in attending college in any state.
Eligibility This program is open to members of the association who are also currently serving in the Kansas National Guard and their children and grandchildren. Spouses and dependents of associate members are not eligible. Applicants must submit high school and/or college transcripts (including SAT and/or ACT scores); letters of recommendation; information on their awards and recognition, community service, extracurricular activities, and work experience; documentation of financial need; and a brief essay on their goals and career objectives. They must be enrolled or planning to enroll full time at an accredited institution of higher learning in any state.
Financial data The stipend ranges up to $1,000.
Duration 1 year.
Additional information This program includes 1 scholarship supported by USAA Insurance Corporation.
Number awarded Varies each year.
Deadline April of each year.

[688]
EOD WARRIOR FOUNDATION SCHOLARSHIPS
EOD Warrior Foundation
Attn: Executive Director
716 Crestview Avenue
Niceville, FL 32578
(850) 729-2336
E-mail: scholarship@eodwarriorfoundation.org
Web: www.eodwarriorfoundation.org/scholarship-program

Summary To provide financial assistance for college to spouses and other family members of technicians or military officers who have worked in explosive ordnance disposal (EOD).
Eligibility This program is open to children, stepchildren, spouses, grandchildren, and other recognized dependents of graduates of Naval School Explosive Ordnance Disposal (NAVSCOLEOD) who served or are serving in the Army, Navy, Air Force, or Marine Corps. Active-duty personnel and NAVSCOLEOD graduates are not eligible. Children or other dependents must be 23 years of age or younger; spouses may be of any age. Selection is based on GPA, community involvement and volunteerism, extracurricular activities, awards, paid employment, an essay, future goals, letters of recommendation, and overall impression. Priority is given to members of Gold Star and Wounded Warrior families.
Financial data A stipend is awarded (amount not specified). Funds are paid directly to the academic institution for the student's tuition, books, fees, and on-campus housing.
Duration 1 year; may be renewed up to 3 additional years.
Additional information This sponsor was formerly named the Explosive Ordnance Disposal Memorial Foundation.
Number awarded Varies each year; recently, 42 were awarded.
Deadline February of each year.

[689]
E.R. SMITH MEMORIAL SCHOLARSHIP
National 4th Infantry (IVY) Division Association
c/o Don Kelby, Executive Director
P.O. Box 1914
St. Peters, MO 63376-0035
(314) 606-1969   E-mail: 4thidaed@swbell.net
Web: www.4thinfantry.org/content/scholarships-donations

Summary To provide financial assistance for college to descendants of soldiers who were killed while serving in the Fourth Infantry Division in the Global War on Terror (GWOT).
Eligibility This program is open to the children, stepchildren, and adopted children of soldiers who were killed while serving with the Fourth Infantry Division in Iraq, Afghanistan, and/or the GWOT. Membership in the sponsoring organization is not required. Recipients are chosen by lottery. Eligibility ends when the child reaches 25 years of age.
Financial data The stipend is $2,000.
Duration 1 year.
Number awarded 1 or more each year.
Deadline June of each year.

[690]
ERNEST AND GISELA HALE SCHOLARSHIPS
The Marlee Foundation
809 Country Way
Scituate, MA 02066
(781) 264-0092   E-mail: info@MarleeFoundation.com
Web: www.marleefoundation.com/eghs-scholarship1.html

Summary To provide financial assistance to the children of members of U.S. military Special Forces.
Eligibility This program is open to students younger than 23 years of age entering or enrolled at an accredited college or university. Applicants must be the children of U.S. Special Forces members. Along with their application, they must submit essays up to 1 page in length on assigned topics that change annually; recently students were asked to write on the following: 1) the kindest person they have ever met; 2) the percentage of media coverage that should be factual vs. op-ed and why; 3) their thoughts on whether universities should promote free speech and open discussions of different points of view; and 4) the 2 things that they feel could improve our county's military readiness. Selection is based on those essays, transcripts that include SAT and/or ACT scores, 2 letters of recommendation, and financial need.

Financial data Stipends range from $200 to $5,000. Funds are paid directly to the recipient's university.
Duration 1 year.
Additional information This program began in 2017 in cooperation with the Navy Seal Museum Foundation and the Army Unit Scholarship Fund.
Number awarded Varies each year; recently, 31 were awarded: 10 at $5,000, 9 at $2,600, 5 at $750, 5 at $500, and 2 at $200.
Deadline May of each year.

[691]
ERNIE WILSON JR. SCHOLARSHIP
Sons of the American Legion
Detachment of New Jersey
171 Jersey Street, Building 5, Second Floor
Trenton, NJ 08611
Web: www.njsal.org/forms

Summary To provide financial assistance to members of the Sons of the American Legion who are high school seniors in New Jersey and planning to attend college in any state.
Eligibility This program is open to seniors graduating from high schools in New Jersey who are members of the Sons of the American Legion. Applicants must be planning to enroll at a college or university in any state. Along with their application, they must submit a 500-word essay describing a person or event that impacted their life, transcripts, letters of recommendation, a brief letter describing their reasons for their choice of vocation, and documentation of financial need. Selection is based on scholarship (20%), character (20%), leadership (20%), Americanism and community service (20%), and financial need (20%).
Financial data The stipend is $3,500.
Duration 1 year.
Number awarded 1 each year.
Deadline April of each year.

[692]
EVELYN B. HAMILTON HEALTH CARE SCHOLARSHIP
Marines' Memorial Association
c/o Marines Memorial Club and Hotel
609 Sutter Street
San Francisco, CA 94102
(415) 673-6672, ext. 293   Toll Free: (800) 5-MARINE
Fax: (415) 441-3649
E-mail: scholarship@marineclub.com
Web: www.marinesmemorial.org

Summary To provide financial assistance to members of the Marines' Memorial Association from all branches of the armed forces and their descendants who are interested in studying health care in college.
Eligibility This program is open to active members of the association and their children and grandchildren. Applicants must be high school seniors or students currently enrolled in an undergraduate degree program in a discipline within the field of health care. Along with their application, they must submit an essay of up to 500 words on why they chose their specific path of study, what they hope to accomplish after graduation with their degree, and how their efforts will benefit others in their community. Graduating high school seniors must submit a high school transcript and SAT or ACT scores; continuing college students must submit a college transcript. Selection is based on the essay, academic merit, references, and financial need.
Financial data The stipend is $2,500 per year.
Duration 1 year; recipients may reapply for up to 3 additional years.
Additional information Membership in the association is open to veterans of the Marines, Army, Navy, Air Force, or Coast Guard and to personnel currently serving in a branch of the armed forces.
Number awarded 1 each year.
Deadline April of each year.

[693]
EXEMPTION FROM TUITION FEES FOR DEPENDENTS OF KENTUCKY VETERANS
Kentucky Department of Veterans Affairs
Attn: Tuition Waiver Coordinator
1111B Louisville Road
Frankfort, KY 40601
(502) 564-9203   Toll Free: (800) 572-6245 (within KY)
Fax: (502) 564-9240   E-mail: kdva.tuitionwaiver@ky.gov
Web: www.veterans.ky.gov

Summary To provide financial assistance for undergraduate or graduate studies to family of deceased Kentucky veterans.
Eligibility This program is open to the children, stepchildren, adopted children, and unremarried widows or widowers of veterans who were residents of Kentucky when they entered military service or joined the Kentucky National Guard. The qualifying veteran must have been killed in action during a wartime period or died as a result of a service-connected disability incurred during a wartime period. Applicants must be attending or planning to attend a state-supported college or university in Kentucky to work on an undergraduate or graduate degree.
Financial data Eligible dependents and survivors are exempt from tuition and matriculation fees at any state-supported institution of higher education in Kentucky.
Duration The exemption continues until completion of an undergraduate or graduate degree. There are no age or time limits.
Number awarded Varies each year.
Deadline Deadline not specified.

[694]
FIFTH MARINE DIVISION ASSOCIATION SCHOLARSHIP
Fifth Marine Division Association Scholarship Fund
c/o Marine Corps Scholarship Foundation
909 North Washington Street, Suite 400
Alexandria, VA 22314
(703) 549-0060   Toll Free: (866) 496-5462
Fax: (703) 549-9474   E-mail: students@mcsf.org
Web: www.mcsf.org/apply/eligibility

Summary To provide financial assistance for college to the grandchildren of veterans who served with the Fifth Marine Division.
Eligibility This program is open to grandchildren of veterans who served with the Fifth Marine Division during World War II or Vietnam and are or were members of the Fifth Marine Division Association. Applicants must be high school

seniors, high school graduates, or current college students. Along with their application, they must submit academic transcripts, a copy of their grandparent's honorable discharge, and a 500-word essay on a topic that changes periodically. The family income of applicants must be less than $103,000 per year.
Financial data Stipends range from $1,500 to $10,000 per year.
Duration 1 year; may be renewed for up to 3 additional years.
Additional information Recipients may also accept scholarship aid from other sources.
Number awarded Varies each year; recently, 3 were awarded.
Deadline February of each year.

[695]
FIRST CAVALRY DIVISION ASSOCIATION SCHOLARSHIPS
First Cavalry Division Association
Attn: Foundation
302 North Main Street
Copperas Cove, TX 76522-1703
(254) 547-6537   Fax: (254) 547-8853
E-mail: firstcav@1cda.org
Web: www.1cda.org/scholarships/foundation

Summary To provide financial assistance for undergraduate education to soldiers currently or formerly assigned to the First Cavalry Division and their families.
Eligibility This program is open to children of soldiers who died or have been declared totally and permanently disabled from injuries incurred while serving with the First Cavalry Division during any armed conflict; children of soldiers who died while serving in the First Cavalry Division during peacetime; and active-duty soldiers currently assigned or attached to the First Cavalry Division and their spouses and children.
Financial data The stipend is $1,200 per year. The checks are made out jointly to the student and the school and may be used for whatever the student needs, including tuition, books, and clothing.
Duration 1 year; may be renewed up to 3 additional years.
Number awarded Varies each year.
Deadline July of each year.

[696]
FIRST LIEUTENANT MICHAEL LICALZI MEMORIAL SCHOLARSHIP
Marine Corps Tankers Association
c/o Dan Miller, Scholarship Chair
8212 West Fourth Place
Kennewick, WA 99336
E-mail: dmiller@msn.com
Web: www.usmctankers.org/pageScholarship

Summary To provide financial assistance for college or graduate school to children and grandchildren of members of the Marine Corps Tankers Association and to Marine and Navy personnel currently serving in tank units.
Eligibility This program is open to high school seniors and graduates who are children, grandchildren, or under the guardianship of an active, Reserve, retired, or honorably discharged Marine who served in a tank unit. Marine or Navy Corpsmen currently assigned to tank units are also eligible.

Applicants must be enrolled or planning to enroll full time at a college or graduate school. Their parent or grandparent must be a member of the Marine Corps Tankers Association or, if not a member, must join if the application is accepted. Along with their application, they must submit a 500-word essay that explains their reason for seeking this scholarship, their educational goals, and their plans for post-graduation life. Selection is based on that essay, academic record, school activities, leadership potential, and community service.
Financial data The stipend is $3,000.
Duration 1 year.
Number awarded Varies each year; recently, 6 were awarded.
Deadline March of each year.

[697]
FIRST LIEUTENANT SCOTT MCCLEAN LOVE MEMORIAL SCHOLARSHIP
Army Scholarship Foundation
11700 Preston Road, Suite 660-301
Dallas, TX 75230
E-mail: ContactUs@armyscholarshipfoundation.org
Web: www.armyscholarshipfoundation.org/love.html

Summary To provide financial assistance for undergraduate study to the children and spouses of Army personnel, especially those who major in the fine arts.
Eligibility This program is open to 1) children of regular active-duty, active-duty Reserve, and active-duty Army National Guard members in good standing; 2) spouses of serving enlisted regular active-duty, active-duty Reserve, and active-duty Army National Guard members in good standing; and 3) children of former U.S. Army members who received an honorable or medical discharge or were killed while serving in the U.S. Army. Preference is given to students who are majoring or planning to major in the fine arts. Applicants must be high school seniors, high school graduates, or undergraduates enrolled at an accredited college, university, or vocational/technical institute. They must be U.S. citizens and have a GPA of 2.0 or higher; children must be younger than 24 years of age. Financial need is considered in the selection process.
Financial data The stipend ranges from $500 to $2,000 per year.
Duration 1 year; recipients may reapply.
Additional information The Army Scholarship Foundation was established in 2001.
Number awarded 1 each year.
Deadline April of each year.

[698]
FIRST MARINE DIVISION ASSOCIATION SCHOLARSHIPS
First Marine Division Association
P.O. Box 9000, Box 902
Oceanside, CA 92051
(760) 763-3268   E-mail: june.oldbreed@fmda.us
Web: www.firstmardivassoc.com/fmda-scholarships

Summary To provide financial assistance for college to dependents of deceased or disabled veterans of the First Marine Division.
Eligibility This program is open to dependents of veterans who served in the First Marine Division or in a unit attached to

that Division, are honorably discharged, and now are either totally and permanently disabled or deceased from any cause. Applicants must be attending or planning to attend an accredited college, university, or trade school as a full-time undergraduate student. Graduate students and students still in high school or prep school are not eligible.

Financial data The stipend is $2,500 per year.

Duration 1 year; may be renewed up to 3 additional years.

Additional information This program began in 1953.

Number awarded Varies each year; recently, 23 were awarded.

Deadline Deadline not specified.

[699]
FLEET RESERVE ASSOCIATION MEMBER SCHOLARSHIPS

Fleet Reserve Association
Attn: FRA Education Foundation
125 North West Street
Alexandria, VA 22314-2754
(703) 683-1400   Toll Free: (800) FRA-1924
Fax: (703) 549-6610   E-mail: scholars@fra.org
Web: www.fra.org

Summary To provide financial assistance for college or graduate school to members of the Fleet Reserve Association (FRA) and their families.

Eligibility This program is open to members of the FRA and the children, grandchildren, great-grandchildren, and spouses of living or deceased members. Applicants must be enrolled or planning to enroll as full-time undergraduate or graduate students. Along with their application, they must submit transcripts that include (for high school students and college freshmen) SAT and/or ACT scores; a list of school and community activities; at least 2 letters of recommendation; and an essay on why they want to go to college and what they intend to accomplish with their degree. Selection is based on academic record, financial need, extracurricular activities, leadership skills, and participation in community activities. U.S. citizenship is required.

Financial data Stipends range from $1,000 to $5,000.

Duration 1 year; may be renewed.

Additional information Membership in the FRA is open to current and former enlisted members of the Navy, Marine Corps, and Coast Guard. This program includes awards designated as the MCPO Ken E. Blair Scholarship, the Robert M. Treadwell Annual Scholarship, the Donald Bruce Pringle Family Scholarship, the Tom and Karen Snee Scholarship, the Angelo and Mildred Nunez Scholarships, the Express Scripts Scholarships, the US Family Health Scholarship, and the Navy Department Branch 181 Scholarship.

Number awarded Varies each year; recently, 10 were awarded: 6 at $5,000, 2 at $4,000, 1 at $3,000, and 1 at $2,000.

Deadline April of each year.

[700]
FLEET RESERVE ASSOCIATION NON-MEMBER SCHOLARSHIPS

Fleet Reserve Association
Attn: FRA Education Foundation
125 North West Street
Alexandria, VA 22314-2754
(703) 683-1400   Toll Free: (800) FRA-1924
Fax: (703) 549-6610   E-mail: scholars@fra.org
Web: www.fra.org

Summary To provide financial assistance for college or graduate school to sea service personnel and their families.

Eligibility This program is open to 1) active-duty, Reserve, honorably-discharged veterans, and retired members of the U.S. Navy, Marine Corps, and Coast Guard; and 2) their spouses, children, grandchildren, and great-grandchildren. Applicants must be enrolled or planning to enroll as full-time undergraduate or graduate students, but neither they nor their family member are required to be members of the sponsoring organization. Along with their application, they must submit transcripts that include (for high school students and college freshmen) SAT and/or ACT scores; a list of school and community activities; at least 2 letters of recommendation; and an essay on why they want to go to college and what they intend to accomplish with their degree. Selection is based on academic record, financial need, extracurricular activities, leadership skills, and participation in community activities. U.S. citizenship is required.

Financial data Stipends range up to $5,000 per year.

Duration 1 year; may be renewed.

Additional information This program includes the GEICO Scholarship and the Rosemary Posekany Memorial Scholarship.

Number awarded Varies each year; recently, 6 were awarded: 5 at $5,000 and 1 at $1,000.

Deadline April of each year.

[701]
FLORENCE LEMKE MEMORIAL SCHOLARSHIP IN FINE ARTS

American Legion Auxiliary
Department of Washington
Attn: Education Chair
3600 Ruddell Road S.E.
P.O. Box 5867
Lacey, WA 98509-5867
(360) 456-5995   Fax: (360) 491-7442
E-mail: secretary@walegion-aux.org
Web: www.walegion-aux.org/EducationScholarships.html

Summary To provide financial assistance to descendants of Washington veterans who are interested in studying the fine arts at a college in any state.

Eligibility This program is open to residents of Washington who are high school seniors and the children, grandchildren, or great-grandchildren of veterans. Applicants must be interested in studying fine arts (including painting, drawing, photography, literature, architecture, sculpture, poetry, music, dance, or drama) at a college in any state. Selection is based on a 300-word essay on their proposed course of study and educational goals in the field of fine arts, character, leadership, academic record, and financial need.

Financial data The stipend is $1,000.

Duration 1 year.
Number awarded 1 each year.
Deadline February of each year.

[702]
FLORIDA AMERICAN LEGION GENERAL SCHOLARSHIPS

American Legion
Department of Florida
Attn: Programs Director
1912A Lee Road
P.O. Box 547859
Orlando, FL 32854-7859
(407) 295-2631, ext. 235
Toll Free: (800) 393-3378 (within FL)
Fax: (407) 299-0901
E-mail: scholarships@legionmail.org
Web: www.floridalegion.org/programs-services/scholarships

Summary To provide financial assistance to the descendants of American Legion members in Florida who plan to attend college in any state.

Eligibility This program is open to the direct descendants (children, grandchildren, great-grandchildren, and legally adopted children) of 1) a member of the American Legion's Department of Florida; 2) a veteran eligible for membership in the American Legion; or 3) a deceased U.S. veteran who would have been eligible for membership in the American Legion. Applicants must be seniors graduating from a Florida high school and planning to attend an accredited college or university in any state. Along with their application, they must submit essays on 1) the career for which they plan to prepare when they enter postsecondary education; 2) why they are seeking higher education; 3) how their area of study will contribute to their immediate or long-range career plans; 4) the community service activities in which they have been involved during their high school career; 5) what they consider to be the single most important societal problem; and 6) an experience from their own life and how it has influenced their development. Financial need is not considered in the selection process.

Financial data Stipends are $2,500, $1,500, $1,000, or $500.
Duration 1 year; nonrenewable.
Number awarded 7 each year: 1 at $2,500, 1 at $1,500, 1 at $1,000, and 4 at $500.
Deadline February of each year.

[703]
FLORIDA LEGION AUXILIARY DEPARTMENT SCHOLARSHIP

American Legion Auxiliary
Department of Florida
1912A Lee Road
P.O. Box 547917
Orlando, FL 32854-7917
(407) 293-7411   Toll Free: (866) 710-4192
Fax: (407) 299-0901   E-mail: contact@alafl.org
Web: www.alafl.org/programs/education/scholarships

Summary To provide financial assistance to the children of Florida veterans who are interested in attending college in the state.

Eligibility This program is open to children and stepchildren of honorably-discharged veterans who are Florida residents. Applicants must be enrolled or planning to enroll full time at a postsecondary school in the state. Financial need is considered in the selection process.

Financial data The stipends are up to $2,000 for a 4-year university or up to $1,000 for a community college or vocational/technical school. All funds are paid directly to the institution.

Duration 1 year; may be renewed if the recipient needs further financial assistance and has maintained a GPA of 2.5 or higher.

Number awarded Varies each year, depending on the availability of funds.

Deadline January of each year.

[704]
FLORIDA LEGION AUXILIARY MEMORIAL SCHOLARSHIP

American Legion Auxiliary
Department of Florida
1912A Lee Road
P.O. Box 547917
Orlando, FL 32854-7917
(407) 293-7411   Toll Free: (866) 710-4192
Fax: (407) 299-0901   E-mail: contact@alafl.org
Web: www.alafl.org/programs/education/scholarships

Summary To provide financial assistance to members and female dependents of members of the Florida American Legion Auxiliary who are interested in attending college in any state.

Eligibility Applicants must be members of the Florida Auxiliary or daughters or granddaughters of members who have at least 3 years of continuous membership. They must be sponsored by their local units, be Florida residents, and be enrolled or planning to enroll full time at a college, university, community college, or vocational/technical school in any state. Selection is based on academic record and financial need.

Financial data The stipends are up to $2,000 for a 4-year university or up to $1,000 for a community college or vocational/technical school. All funds are paid directly to the institution.

Duration 1 year; may be renewed if the recipient needs further financial assistance and has maintained at least a 2.5 GPA.

Number awarded Varies each year, depending on the availability of funds.

Deadline January of each year.

[705]
FLORIDA NAVY NURSE CORPS ASSOCIATION SCHOLARSHIPS

Florida Navy Nurse Corps Association
c/o Margaret Holder, Scholarship Committee
1033 Inverness Drive
St. Augustine, FL 32092
E-mail: maholder@me.com
Web: www.nnca.org/join-nnca-2/local-chapters/fnnca

Summary To provide financial assistance to undergraduate and graduate nursing students, especially residents of Florida with ties to the military.

Eligibility This program is open to students, including registered nursing continuing their studies, who are working on a baccalaureate or graduate degree in nursing. Applicants must have completed at least 1 clinical nursing course and have a GPA of 3.0 or higher. They may be full- or part-time students. Along with their application, they must submit an essay, up to 500 words in length, on the reasons they are qualified for the scholarship, how it will benefit them, career goals, and potential for contribution to the profession. Preference is given in order to current active-duty and Reserve service members, veterans of military service, family members of current or former military service personnel, civil service employees, and residents of Florida. Financial need is considered in the selection process.
Financial data The stipend is $1,500. Funds are paid directly to the student.
Duration 1 year.
Number awarded 2 each year.
Deadline October of each year.

[706]
FLORIDA SCHOLARSHIPS FOR CHILDREN AND SPOUSES OF DECEASED OR DISABLED VETERANS
Florida Department of Education
Attn: Office of Student Financial Assistance
State Scholarship and Grant Programs
325 West Gaines Street, Suite 1314
Tallahassee, FL 32399-0400
(850) 410-5160   Toll Free: (888) 827-2004
Fax: (850) 487-1809   E-mail: osfa@fldoe.org
Web: www.floridastudentfinancialaidsg.org

Summary To provide financial assistance for college to the children and spouses of Florida veterans who are disabled, deceased, or officially classified as prisoners of war (POW) or missing in action (MIA).
Eligibility This program is open to residents of Florida who are U.S. citizens or eligible noncitizens and the dependent children or spouses of veterans or servicemembers who 1) died as a result of service-connected injuries, diseases, or disabilities sustained while on active duty; 2) have a service-connected 100% total and permanent disability; or 3) were classified as POW or MIA by the U.S. armed forces or as civilian personnel captured while serving with the consent or authorization of the U.S. government during wartime service. The veteran or servicemember must have been a U.S. citizen or eligible noncitizens and a resident of Florida for at least 1 year before death, disability, or POW/MIA status. Children must be between 16 and 22 years of age. Spouses of deceased veterans or servicemembers must be unremarried and must apply within 5 years of their spouse's death. Spouses of disabled veterans must have been married for at least 1 year.
Financial data Students at public institutions receive full payment of tuition and fees. Students at 4-year private institutions receive $211 per semester credit hour. Students at 2-year private institutions receive $104 per semester credit hour.
Duration 1 quarter or semester; may be renewed for up to 110% of the required credit hours of an initial associate, baccalaureate, diploma, or certificate program, provided the student maintains a GPA of 2.0 or higher.

Number awarded Varies each year; recently, 658 initial and 1,026 renewal scholarships were awarded.
Deadline March of each year.

[707]
FOLDED FLAG FOUNDATION SCHOLARSHIPS AND GRANTS
Folded Flag Foundation
1550 South Pavilion Center Drive
Las Vegas, NV 89135
Toll Free: (844) 204-2856
E-mail: scholarships@foldedflagfoundation.org
Web: www.foldedflagfoundation.org/how-to-apply

Summary To provide financial assistance for education at any level to spouses and children of military and civilian personnel who lost their lives in combat.
Eligibility This program is open to spouses and children of 1) members of the U.S. military who died as a result of hostile action or in an accident related to U.S. combat operations; and 2) employees of the U.S. government who died as a result of hostile action or in an accident related to U.S. combat operations. Applicants may be any age younger than 26. They may apply for 1) a children's education scholarship, which supplies funds for K-12 students to cover private school tuition and fees, tutoring, after-school programs, summer camps, or other related educational expenses; 2) a college or trade/technical school scholarship, to cover tuition and fees, books, computers, living expenses (including child care for students with young children), tutoring, test preparation, and career preparation (e.g., internships, resume writing workshops, interview preparation training). Financial need is considered in the selection process.
Financial data A stipend is provided (amount not specified). Recently, stipends averaged nearly $7,500.
Duration 1 year.
Additional information This program began in 2014.
Number awarded Varies each year; recently, 347 scholarships (167 new and 180 renewal) worth $2.6 million were awarded. Since the program began, it has awarded more than $6 million to more than 400 spouses and children.
Deadline May of each year.

[708]
FOLDS OF HONOR HIGHER EDUCATION SCHOLARSHIPS
Folds of Honor
8551 North 125 East Avenue, Suite 100
Owasso, OK 74055
(918) 274-4700   E-mail: scholarships@foldsofhonor.org
Web: www.foldsofhonor.org

Summary To provide financial assistance for college to the children and spouses of deceased or disabled current and former military personnel.
Eligibility This program is open to dependent children under 24 years of age and spouses of any age of military personnel. The military family member must have 1) been killed in action; 2) suffered the loss of a limb in service; 3) died of any cause while on active duty or after having been classified as having a service-connected disability; 4) sustained a service-connected disability of 10% or higher; or 5) received a Purple Heart of loss of limb (if still on active duty). Applicants

must be enrolled or planning to enroll at an accredited 2- or 4-year college, university, or vocational school.
Financial data Stipends range up to $5,000 per year, depending on the need of the recipient.
Duration 1 year; may be renewed up to 3 additional years.
Number awarded Varies each year.
Deadline March of each year.

[709]
FORCE RECON ASSOCIATION SCHOLARSHIPS
Force Recon Association
c/o Al Sniadecki, Scholarship Committee Chair
2928 Cambridgeshire Drive
Carrollton, TX 75007
E-mail: commchief@forcerecon.com
Web: www.forcerecon.com/join.htm

Summary To provide financial assistance for college to members of the Force Recon Association and their dependents.
Eligibility This program is open to members of the Force Recon Association and family members of a relative who served both in the U.S. Marine Corps and was or is assigned to a Force Reconnaissance Company. The relative must be either an active or deceased member of the Force Recon Association. Family members include wives and widows, sons and daughters (including adopted and stepchildren), grandchildren, and great-grandchildren. Applicants may be pursuing scholastic, vocational, or technical education. Along with their application, they must submit a personal statement on why they desire this scholarship, their proposed course of study, their progress in their current course of study, and their long-range career goals. Selection is based on academic achievement, letters of recommendation, demonstrated character, and the written statements.
Financial data A stipend is awarded (amount not specified).
Duration 1 year; may be renewed.
Number awarded 1 or more each year.
Deadline June of each year.

[710]
FOURTH MARINE DIVISION ASSOCIATION OF WWII SCHOLARSHIP
Fourth Marine Division Association of WWII
c/o Marine Corps Scholarship Foundation
909 North Washington Street, Suite 400
Alexandria, VA 22314
(703) 549-0060   Toll Free: (866) 496-5462
Fax: (703) 549-9474   E-mail: students@mcsf.org
Web: www.mcsf.org/apply/eligibility

Summary To provide financial assistance for college to the grandchildren of veterans who served with the Fourth Marine Division during World War II.
Eligibility This program is open to grandchildren of veterans who served with the Fourth Marine Division during World War II and are or were members of the Fourth Marine Division Association of World War II. Applicants must be high school seniors, high school graduates, or current college students. Along with their application, they must submit academic transcripts, a copy of their grandparent's honorable discharge, and a 500-word essay on a topic that changes periodically. Only undergraduate study is supported. The family income of applicants must be less than $103,000 per year.
Financial data Stipends depend on the need of the recipient and the availability of funds, but generally range from $1,500 to $10,000 per year.
Duration 1 year; may be renewed for up to 3 additional years.
Additional information The highest-ranked applicant receives an award that is designated the Thomas W. Morrow Scholarship.
Number awarded Varies each year; recently, 6 were awarded.
Deadline February of each year.

[711]
FRANCISCO GARCIA SCHOLARSHIPS
Air Force Association-Rocky Mountain Region
c/o Don Kidd, President
Excellence in Defense Consulting, LLC
9105 Melbourne Drive
Colorado Springs, CO 80920
(719) 660-1187   E-mail: don.kidd@comcast.net
Web: www.lancepsijanafa.org/scholarship-winners

Summary To provide financial assistance to children of Air Force personnel in Colorado who plan to study an aerospace-related field at a college in any state.
Eligibility This program is open to high school seniors and current college students who are children of active duty and retired Air Force, Air Force Reserve, and Air National Guard members in Colorado. Each chapter of the Air Force Association in Colorado may designate 1 student. Applicants must be attending or planning to attend a college or university in any state and major in an aerospace-related field. They must submit an essay of 500 to 1,000 words on a topic that changes annually; recently, students were asked to present their opinion on whether women should have to register for the draft. Selection is based on writing skills as demonstrated in the essay, academic achievement, community service, and demonstrated leadership responsibilities.
Financial data The stipend is $1,000.
Duration 1 year.
Number awarded Varies each year; recently, 2 were awarded.
Deadline April of each year.

[712]
FREEDOM ALLIANCE SCHOLARSHIPS
Freedom Alliance
Attn: Scholarship Fund
22570 Markey Court, Suite 240
Dulles, VA 20166-6915
(703) 444-7940   Toll Free: (800) 475-6620
Fax: (703) 444-9893   E-mail: info@freedomalliance.org
Web: www.fascholarship.com

Summary To provide financial assistance for college to the children of deceased and disabled military personnel.
Eligibility This program is open to high school seniors, high school graduates, and undergraduate students under 26 years of age who are dependent children of military personnel (soldier, sailor, airman, Marine, or Guardsman). The military parent must have 1) been killed in action; 2) become 100% totally and permanently disabled as a direct result of an

operational or combat mission or suffered a major limb amputation due to enemy action; 3) been classified as a POW or MIA; 4) been awarded the Medal of Honor, the Navy Cross, the Distinguished Service Cross, the Air Force Cross, or the Coast Guard Cross; or 5) been involved in a training accident that resulted in the death of the service member or cause an immediate inability to continue serving. Applicants must submit a 500-word essay on what their parent's service means to them.
Financial data The stipend depends on the need of the recipient.
Duration 1 year; may be renewed up to 3 additional years, provided the recipient remains enrolled full time with a GPA of 2.0 or higher.
Number awarded Varies each year; recently, 240 were awarded. Since the program was established, it has awarded more than $7 million in scholarships.
Deadline July of each year.

[713]
FUND A SCHOLAR PROGRAM
A Million Thanks, Inc.
Attn: Armed Forces Children's Education Fund
4590 MacArthur Boulevard, Suite 500
Newport Beach, CA 92660
Toll Free: (844) MILL THX
E-mail: Info@amillionthanks.org
Web: www.amillionthanks.org/scholar/apply

Summary To provide financial assistance for college to children of military personnel who have died on active duty since October 7, 2001.
Eligibility This program is open to children of military personnel who died in the course of their active duties while enlisted, warranted, or commissioned in the armed forces, including activated National Guard and Reserve personnel, on or after October 7, 2001. Applicants must be enrolled or planning to enroll at an accredited postsecondary educational institution. Along with their application, they must submit information on financial need and a 500-word essay on why continued education is important for them and how it fits into the plan they have for their life.
Financial data Awards provide partial or full payment of tuition.
Duration 1 year; recipients may reapply.
Number awarded Varies each year.
Deadline March or October of each year.

[714]
GAMEWARDENS ASSOCIATION SCHOLARSHIP
Gamewardens Association, Vietnam to Present
c/o Glen Slay, Scholarship Program
1074 Buena Vista Drive
La Selva Beach, CA 95076
E-mail: scholarship@tf116.org
Web: www.tf116.org

Summary To provide financial assistance for college to the children or grandchildren of members of Gamewardens Association, Vietnam to Present.
Eligibility This program is open to the children and grandchildren of living or deceased members of Gamewardens Association, Vietnam to Present. High school students (under 21 years of age) planning to enter college as full-time students and students already enrolled in college (under 23 years of age) are eligible. Selection is based on SAT or ACT scores, extracurricular activities, leadership positions held, work or volunteer experience, and financial need.
Financial data Stipends are $2,000. Funds are paid directly to the college the student is attending.
Duration 1 year.
Additional information Membership in Gamewardens Association, Vietnam to Present is open to 1) veterans who served in Vietnam in Task Force 116 or in support of Task Force 116, River Patrol Force; or 2) veterans or current Navy personnel serving as a Special Warfare Combatant-craft Crewman (SWCC) or Riverine Operator in any operation subsequent to Vietnam (including in Iraq). This program includes the YNC John Williams Scholarship and the RIVDIV 534/551 Scholarship.
Number awarded Up to 3 each year.
Deadline July of each year.

[715]
GARNER TRUST SCHOLARSHIPS
American Legion
Department of Arkansas
702 Victory Street
P.O. Box 3280
Little Rock, AR 72203
(501) 375-1104 Toll Free: (877) 243-9799
Fax: (501) 375-4236 E-mail: alegion@swbell.net
Web: www.arlegion.org

Summary To provide financial assistance to descendants of members of the American Legion in Arkansas who are interested in attending college in the state.
Eligibility This program is open to the children, grandchildren, and great-grandchildren of living or deceased members of the American Legion in Arkansas. The Legionnaire must have been a member for at least 2 years. Applicants must be high school seniors or graduates of a 2-year college in Arkansas and planning to attend a college, university, or trade/technical school in the state. They must sign a drug free pledge and a declaration of support for the Preamble to the Constitution of the American Legion. Selection is based on American spirit, character, leadership quality, scholastic endeavor, and financial need.
Financial data The stipend is $2,500.
Duration 1 year; nonrenewable.
Number awarded 4 each year.
Deadline March of each year.

[716]
GEN. JACK N. MERRITT SCHOLARSHIP
Association of the United States Army
Attn: Scholarships
2425 Wilson Boulevard
Arlington, VA 22201
(703) 841-4300 Toll Free: (800) 336-4570
E-mail: scholarships@ausa.org
Web: www.ausa.org/resources/scholarships

Summary To provide financial assistance to members of the Association of the United States Army (AUSA) who are interested in attending college.
Eligibility This program is open to AUSA members who are enrolled or accepted at an accredited college or university

to work on a degree in any field. Along with their application, they must submit a 1-page autobiography, 2 letters of recommendation, a letter describing their career aspirations (including their course of study and plans for completion of a degree), and a transcript of high school or college grades (depending on which they are currently attending). Selection is based on academic merit and personal achievement. Financial need is not normally a selection criterion but in some cases of extreme need it may be used as a factor; the lack of financial need, however, is never a cause for non-selection.

Financial data The stipend is $5,000; funds are sent directly to the recipient's college or university.

Duration 1 year.

Additional information Membership in the AUSA is open to everyone who supports a strong national defense, with special concern for the Army. That includes Regular Army, National Guard, Army Reserve, government civilians, retired soldiers, Wounded Warriors, veterans, concerned citizens and family members.

Number awarded 2 each year.

Deadline June of each year.

[717]
GENERAL AND MRS. CHARLES C. BLANTON AFBA FAMILY SURVIVOR COLLEGE SCHOLARSHIP

Armed Forces Benefit Association
AFBA Building
909 North Washington Street
Alexandria, VA 22314-1556
(703) 549-4455   Toll Free: (800) 776-2322
Fax: (703) 706-5961   E-mail: info@afba.com
Web: www.afba.com/about-afba/scholarship

Summary To provide financial assistance for college to surviving spouses and children of members of the Armed Forces Benefit Association (AFBA) who were killed on duty.

Eligibility This program is open to surviving spouses and children of deceased members of AFBA. Membership in AFBA is open to active-duty, National Guard, or Reserve members of the armed forces; those who are retired or separated from service; and emergency service providers (law enforcement officers, firefighters, and emergency medical service providers). The AFBA member's death must have been in a combat zone, as a result of combat action, as a result of acts of foreign or domestic terrorism, or at an event to which an emergency service provider is dispatched in a situation where there is the potential for loss of life. Applicants must be attending or planning to attend an undergraduate college or university.

Financial data The stipend is $10,000 per year.

Duration 1 year; may be renewed for up to 3 additional years.

Number awarded 1 or more each year.

Deadline Deadline not specified.

[718]
GENERAL HENRY H. ARNOLD EDUCATION GRANT PROGRAM

Air Force Aid Society
Attn: Education Assistance Department
1550 Crystal Drive, Suite 809
Arlington, VA 22202
(703) 972-2647   Toll Free: (866) 896-5637
Fax: (703) 972-2646   E-mail: ed@afas-hq.org
Web: www.afas.org

Summary To provide need-based financial assistance for college to dependents of active-duty, retired, disabled, or deceased Air Force personnel.

Eligibility This program is open to 1) dependent children of Air Force personnel who are active duty, Title 10 Reservists on extended active duty, Title 32 Guard performing full-time active-duty service, retired due to length of active-duty service or disability, or deceased while on active duty or in retired status; 2) spouses of active-duty Air Force members and Title 10 Reservists on extended active duty; and 3) surviving spouses of Air Force members who died while on active duty or in retired status. Applicants must be enrolled or planning to enroll as full-time undergraduate students at an accredited college, university, or vocational/trade school. Spouses must be attending school within the 48 contiguous states. Selection is based on family income and education costs.

Financial data Stipends range from $500 to $4,000.

Duration 1 year; may be renewed if the recipient maintains a GPA of 2.0 or higher.

Additional information Since this program was established in the 1988-89 academic year, it has awarded more than 100,000 grants.

Number awarded Varies each year.

Deadline April of each year.

[719]
GENERAL JIM AND PAT BOSWELL MERIT SCHOLARSHIP PROGRAM

7th Infantry Regiment Association
c/o David Spanburg
P.O. Box 3181
Merrifield, VA 22116
(570) 409-9265   E-mail: edajack@ptd.net
Web: www.cottonbalers.com

Summary To provide financial assistance for college to descendants of members of the 7th Infantry Regiment Association.

Eligibility This program is open to the children, grandchildren, and great grandchildren of members of the association who served a duty assignment with the 7th Infantry Regiment or a component or attached unit while on active duty in the United States Army and who has been a member of the association in good standing for at least the past year. Applicants must be enrolled or planning to enroll full time in an undergraduate program. They must be U.S. citizens and have a cumulative GPA of 2.5 or higher. Along with their application, they must submit a resume, transcripts, ACT or SAT scores, 3 letters of recommendation, and a 1-page essay on why they want and/or deserve this scholarship. Selection is based on academic excellence, leadership, and demonstrated achievement.

Financial data A stipend is awarded (amount not specified).
Duration 1 year; recipients may reapply for 1 additional year.
Number awarded 1 or more each year.
Deadline April of each year.

[720]
GENERAL JOHN PAUL RATAY EDUCATIONAL FUND GRANTS

Military Officers Association of America
Attn: Educational Assistance Program
201 North Washington Street
Alexandria, VA 22314-2539
(703) 549-2311   Toll Free: (800) 234-MOAA
Fax: (703) 838-5819   E-mail: edassist@moaa.org
Web: www.moaa.org

Summary To provide financial assistance to dependent children of deceased members of Military Officers Association of America (MOAA) who are working on an undergraduate degree.
Eligibility This program is open to children whose military parent retired and subsequently died. The parent must have been eligible for MOAA membership or been an active-duty, Reserve, National Guard, or retired enlisted military member. Applicants must be younger than 24 years of age. Selection is based on scholastic ability (33%)), extracurricular activities (33%), and financial need (33%).
Financial data The stipend is $5,000 per year.
Duration 1 year; may be renewed for up to 4 additional years if the recipient remains enrolled full time and has not yet graduated.
Additional information The MOAA was formerly named The Retired Officers Association (TROA). No grants are made for graduate study.
Number awarded Varies each year.
Deadline February of each year.

[721]
GENERAL LAWSON MEMORIAL SCHOLARSHIP

Iowa National Guard Officers Auxiliary
c/o Jeanine Schochenmaier, Scholarship Chair
7739 43rd Avenue
Prole, IA 50229
E-mail: ingoaaux@gmail.com
Web: www.ingoaux.com/ingoauxscholarship

Summary To provide financial assistance to dependents and spouses of Iowa National Guard members who are currently enrolled in a non-degree program in any state.
Eligibility This program is open to residents of Iowa who are working on a licensure program, certificate program, CEU, or non-degree education in any state. Applicants must be a dependent or spouse of an Iowa National Guard member, current or retired. Along with their application, they must submit 1) transcripts; 2) a 1-paragraph autobiography; 3) a 500-word essay describing the most important thing they have learned from the National Guard member in their life; 4) letters of recommendation; and 5) a list of curricular and extracurricular activities in which they have participated.
Financial data A stipend is awarded (amount not specified).
Duration 1 year.
Number awarded 1 or more each year.
Deadline January of each year.

[722]
GENERAL WILLIAM E. DEPUY MEMORIAL SCHOLARSHIP PROGRAM

Society of the First Infantry Division
Attn: 1st Infantry Division Foundation
P.O. Box 607
Ambler, PA 19002
(215) 740-0669   E-mail: 1stidfdnpa@gmail.com
Web: www.1stid.org/scholarships

Summary To provide financial assistance for college to the children of certain deceased members of the First Infantry Division.
Eligibility This program is open to the children of soldiers who served in the First Infantry Division and were killed while serving in combat with the Division or in peacetime training accidents. This is an entitlement program. All eligible applicants receive an award.
Financial data The stipend is $2,500 per year.
Duration 1 year; may be renewed up to 3 additional years.
Additional information This program was established during the Vietnam war to provide scholarships to children of soldiers killed while on duty with the active division; more than 1,300 children whose fathers died while serving in Vietnam have received these scholarships.
Number awarded Varies each year.
Deadline Deadline not specified.

[723]
GENWORTH FOUNDATION VETERANS SCHOLARSHIPS

Great Aspirations Scholarship Program, Inc.
Attn: Scholarship Coordinator
4551 Cox Road, Suite 115
Glen Allen, VA 23060
(804) 527-7726   Fax: (804) 527-7750
E-mail: scholarships@grasp4virginia.com
Web: www.grasp4va.org/scholarships

Summary To provide financial assistance to seniors at selected high schools in Virginia who are children of current or former members of the U.S. military and plan to attend college in any state, especially to study business or fields of science, technology, engineering, or mathematics (STEM).
Eligibility This program is open to seniors graduating from high schools in Virginia that participate in activities of the Great Aspirations Scholarship Program (GRASP). Applicants must have met with their high school GRASP adviser during their senior year and be able to demonstrate financial need. They must be the child of a current or former member of the U.S. military. Preference is given to students planning to major in business or a field of STEM. As part of the application process, they must conduct an interview of their veteran parent to gain an understanding of the challenges and sacrifices made by veterans while serving their country. Along with their application, they must submit 500-word essays on the following topics: 1) how they have impacted their community in an area of service, leadership, or values; 2) how this scholarship would impact their educational and career goals; and 3) after completing their veteran interview, what they believe

is the value that veterans bring to their communities and why it is important to honor their service to our country.
Financial data The stipend is $5,000.
Duration 1 year; nonrenewable.
Additional information This program is supported by the Genworth Foundation. The sponsor began in 1983 as the Greater Richmond Area Scholarship Programs but in 2009 adopted its current name and expanded its activities to all of Virginia. It currently serves 76 high schools throughout the state.
Number awarded 2 each year.
Deadline March of each year.

[724]
GEORGE WASHINGTON CHAPTER AUSA SCHOLARSHIPS

Association of the United States Army-George Washington Chapter
c/o Col (Ret.) William G. Yarborough, Jr., Scholarship Committee
P.O. Box 828
McLean, VA 22101-0828
(703) 748-1717   E-mail: wgyarc@aol.com
Web: www.ausa.org/chapters/george-washington-chapter

Summary To provide financial assistance for undergraduate or graduate study at a school in any state to members of the George Washington Chapter of the Association of the United States Army (AUSA) and their families.
Eligibility This program is open to active members of the AUSA George Washington Chapter and the spouses, children, and grandchildren of active members. Applicants must have a GPA of 2.5 or higher and be working on an undergraduate or graduate degree at a college or university in any state. Along with their application, they must submit a letter describing any family circumstances they believe are relevant and explaining why they deserve the scholarship. Members must also submit a favorable recommendation from their supervisor. Membership in AUSA is open to Army personnel (including Reserves and National Guard) who are either active or retired, ROTC cadets, or civilian employees of the Army.
Financial data Stipends range up to $1,000.
Duration 1 year.
Additional information This program includes the following named awards: the Ed Dauksz Scholarship Award, the Major General Harry Greene STEM Scholarship Award, and the Major General Carl F. McNair Jr. Scholarship Award. The George Washington Chapter serves Washington, D.C.; the Virginia counties of Alexandria, Clarke, Fairfax, Frederick, Loudoun, and Prince William; and the Maryland counties of Calvert, Charles, Montgomery, Prince George's, and St. Mary's.
Number awarded Varies each year; recently, 45 were awarded.
Deadline April of each year.

[725]
GEORGIA DEPARTMENT AMERICAN LEGION SCHOLARSHIP

American Legion
Department of Georgia
Attn: Scholarship Award Program
3035 Mt. Zion Road
Stockbridge, GA 30281-4101
(678) 289-8883   Fax: (678) 289-8885
E-mail: amerlegga@bellsouth.net
Web: www.galegion.org/forms.html

Summary To provide financial assistance to children and grandchildren of members of the American Legion in Georgia who plan to attend college in any state.
Eligibility This program is open to seniors graduating from high schools in Georgia who have a GPA of 3.0 or higher in core subjects. Applicants must be children or grandchildren of members of the American Legion in the Department of Georgia who served in the military. They must be sponsored by a Georgia post of the American Legion. Financial need is not considered in the selection process.
Financial data The stipend is $1,000.
Duration 1 year.
Number awarded 6 each year.
Deadline June of each year.

[726]
GEORGIA HERO SCHOLARSHIP PROGRAM

Georgia Student Finance Commission
Attn: Scholarships and Grants Division
2082 East Exchange Place, Suite 200
Tucker, GA 30084-5305
(770) 724-9249   Toll Free: (800) 505-GSFC
Fax: (770) 724-9089   E-mail: GAfutures@gsfc.org
Web: www.gafutures.org

Summary To provide financial assistance for college to members of the National Guard or Reserves in Georgia and their children and spouses.
Eligibility This program is open to Georgia residents who are active members of the Georgia National Guard or U.S. Military Reserves, were deployed outside the United States for active-duty service on or after February 1, 2003 to a location designated as a combat zone, and served in that combat zone for at least 181 consecutive days. Also eligible are 1) the children, younger than 25 years of age, of Guard and Reserve members who completed at least 1 term of service (of 181 days each) overseas on or after February 1, 2003; 2) the children, younger than 25 years of age, of Guard and Reserve members who were killed or totally disabled during service overseas on or after February 1, 2003, regardless of their length of service; and 3) the spouses of Guard and Reserve members who were killed in a combat zone, died as a result of injuries, or became 100% disabled as a result of injuries received in a combat zone during service overseas on or after February 1, 2003, regardless of their length of service. Applicants must be interested in attending a unit of the University System of Georgia, a unit of the Technical College System of Georgia, or an eligible private college or university in Georgia.
Financial data The stipend for full-time study is $2,000 per academic year, not to exceed $8,000 during an entire pro-

gram of study. The stipend for part-time study is prorated appropriately.
Duration 1 year; may be renewed (if satisfactory progress is maintained) for up to 3 additional years.
Additional information This program, which stands for Helping Educate Reservists and their Offspring, was established in 2005.
Number awarded Varies each year.
Deadline June of each year.

[727]
GEORGIA LEGION AUXILIARY PAST DEPARTMENT PRESIDENTS SCHOLARSHIPS

American Legion Auxiliary
Department of Georgia
Attn: Department Secretary/Treasurer
3035 Mt. Zion Road
Stockbridge, GA 30281-4101
(678) 289-8446 Fax: (678) 289-9496
E-mail: secretary@galegionaux.org
Web: www.galegionaux.org

Summary To provide financial assistance to descendants of veterans in Georgia who are interested in attending college in any state to major in any field.
Eligibility This program is open to Georgia residents who are the descendants of veterans who served during specified periods of wartime. Applicants must be sponsored by a local unit of the American Legion Auxiliary. Selection is based on a statement explaining why they want to further their education and why they need a scholarship, a transcript of all high school or college grades, a 500-word essay on a topic of their choice, and 4 letters of recommendation (1 from a high school principal or superintendent, 1 from the sponsoring American Legion Auxiliary local unit, and 2 from other responsible people).
Financial data The stipend is $1,000.
Duration 1 year.
Number awarded 2 each year.
Deadline May of each year.

[728]
GEORGIA LEGION AUXILIARY PAST PRESIDENT PARLEY NURSING SCHOLARSHIP

American Legion Auxiliary
Department of Georgia
Attn: Department Secretary/Treasurer
3035 Mt. Zion Road
Stockbridge, GA 30281-4101
(678) 289-8446 Fax: (678) 289-9496
E-mail: secretary@galegionaux.org
Web: www.galegionaux.org

Summary To provide financial assistance to descendants of veterans in Georgia who are interested in attending college in any state to prepare for a career in nursing.
Eligibility This program is open to Georgia residents who are 1) interested in nursing education; and 2) the descendants of veterans. Applicants must be sponsored by a local unit of the American Legion Auxiliary. Selection is based on a statement explaining why they want to become a nurse and why they need a scholarship, a transcript of all high school or college grades, and 4 letters of recommendation (1 from a high school principal or superintendent, 1 from the sponsoring American Legion Auxiliary local unit, and 2 from other responsible people).
Financial data The amount of the award depends on the availability of funds.
Duration 1 year.
Number awarded Varies each year, depending upon availability of funds.
Deadline May of each year.

[729]
GERALDINE K. MORRIS AWARD

Army Engineer Spouses' Club
Attn: Kara Anderson, Awards Chair
P.O. Box 6332
Alexandria, VA 22306-6332
E-mail: awardsapplication@armyengineerspouses.com
Web: www.armyengineerspouses.com

Summary To provide financial assistance to the children of officers and civilians who served in the Army Corps of Engineers and are interested in studying nursing in college.
Eligibility This program is open to children of 1) U.S. Army Corps of Engineers officers and warrant officers who are on active duty, retired, or deceased while on active duty or after retiring from active duty; or 2) current Department of the Army employees of the U.S. Army Corps of Engineers. Applicants must be high school seniors planning to enroll in a program leading to a nursing degree or certification. They must also have a parent who is a member of the Army Engineer Spouses' Club. Along with their application, they must submit an essay of 300 to 400 words on what intrigues them the most about a career in nursing and their experience in the field. Selection is based on that essay and academic and extracurricular achievement during high school. U.S. citizenship is required.
Financial data The stipend is $1,000.
Duration 1 year; may be renewed, provided the recipient remains enrolled full time in a nursing program.
Additional information This program began in 2006.
Number awarded 1 each year.
Deadline February of each year.

[730]
GLADYS MCPARTLAND SCHOLARSHIPS

United States Marine Corps Combat Correspondents Association
Attn: Scholarship Committee
385 S.W. 254th Street
Newberry, FL 32669
(352) 448-9167 E-mail: hq@usmccca.org
Web: www.usmccca.org/awards/gladys

Summary To provide financial assistance to members of the U.S. Marine Corps Combat Correspondents Association (USMCCCA) or their dependents and Marines in specified occupational fields who are interested in studying any field in college.
Eligibility This program is open to members of USMCCCA who have been members for at least 2 years and their dependents of such members, including children of deceased members. Applications are also accepted from active-duty Marines in occupational field 4300 or 4600 who are enrolled in government-sponsored degree completion programs, whose tuition is not paid from other sources, and who agree

to become USMCCA members upon award of a scholarship. Applicants must be enrolled or planning to enroll in an undergraduate program in any field. Along with their application, they must submit 500-word essays on 1) their noteworthy achievements and long-range goals; and 2) "The United States I want to see in 15 years and my role in the transformation." Financial need is not considered in the selection process.

Financial data Stipends for full-time study range up to $3,000; part-time stipends range from $250 to $500. Funds are disbursed directly to recipients to be used exclusively for tuition, books, and/or fees.

Duration 1 year; may be renewed up to 3 additional years.

Number awarded 1 or more each year.

Deadline May of each year.

[731]
GROGAN MEMORIAL SCHOLARSHIP

American Academy of Physician Assistants-Veterans Caucus
Attn: Scholarship Program
P.O. Box 362
Ossining, NY 10562
(803) 328-1864   Fax: (704) 838-8494
E-mail: rmunsee@veteranscaucus.org
Web: www.veteranscaucus.org/scholarships

Summary To provide financial assistance to veterans and their dependents who are studying to become physician assistants.

Eligibility This program is open to U.S. citizens who are currently enrolled in a physician assistant program. Applicants must be honorably discharged members of any branch of the military or the dependents of those members. Along with their application, they must submit a personal statement about what led them to attend PA school; their background, present, and future intentions; and why they deserve to receive a scholarship. Selection is based on military honors and awards received, civic and college honors and awards received, professional memberships and activities, potential for future achievement, and GPA.

Financial data The stipend is $2,000.

Duration 1 year.

Number awarded 1 each year.

Deadline February of each year.

[732]
HAD RICHARDS UDT-SEAL MEMORIAL SCHOLARSHIP

Navy Seal Foundation
Attn: Chief Financial Officer
1619 D Street, Building 5326
Virginia Beach, VA 23459
(757) 744-5326   Fax: (757) 363-7491
E-mail: info@navysealfoundation.org
Web: www.navysealfoundation.org

Summary To provide financial assistance for college to children of members of the UDT-SEAL Association.

Eligibility This program is open to children of members who are single, under 24 years of age, and a dependent of a sponsoring member of the association. Sponsors must be serving or have served in the armed forces and the Naval Special Warfare Community, been an association member for the last 4 consecutive years, and paid their dues for the current year. Applicants may be high school seniors, high school graduates, or full-time undergraduate students. Selection is based on GPA, SAT scores, class ranking, extracurricular activities, volunteer community involvement, leadership positions held, military service record, and employment (as appropriate).

Financial data Stipends are $15,000 or $7,500 per year.

Duration 1 year; may be renewed.

Additional information Membership in the association is open to all officers and enlisted personnel of the armed forces (active, retired, discharged, or separated) who have served with a Navy Combat Demolition Unit (NCDU), Underwater Demolition Team (UDT), or SEAL Team.

Number awarded Varies each year; recently, the Navy Seal Foundation awarded 12 dependent scholarships for all of its programs: 3 for 4 years at $15,000 per year to high school seniors and graduates, 3 for 1 year at $7,500 to high school seniors and graduates, 3 for 1 year at $15,000 to current college students, and 3 for 1 year at $7,500 to current college students.

Deadline February of each year.

[733]
HAROLD C. PIERCE JR. SCHOLARSHIP PROGRAM

Enlisted Association of the National Guard of West Virginia
c/o WVAR-CSM
1703 Coonskin Drive
Charleston, WV 25311-1085
(304) 561-6314   E-mail: scholarship@eangus.org
Web: www.eangwv.org/category/benefits

Summary To provide financial assistance to the children and spouses of current or deceased members of the Enlisted Association of the National Guard of West Virginia (EANGWV) who are interested in attending college in any state.

Eligibility This program is open EANGWV members, their dependent unmarried children, and their spouses; unremarried spouses and unmarried dependent children of deceased EANGWV members who were in good standing at the time of their death are also eligible. Applicants must be enrolled full time at a college, university, trade school, or business school in any state; graduate students are not eligible. Along with their application, they must submit a copy of their high school or college transcript; a letter with personal, specific facts on their desire to continue their education; 3 letters of recommendation; a letter of academic reference; and a photocopy of the qualifying membership card. Selection is based on scholarship, character, leadership, and merit; financial need is not considered.

Financial data The stipend is $1,000. Funds are sent directly to the recipient's school.

Duration 1 year; nonrenewable.

Number awarded 1 or more each year.

Deadline June of each year.

[734]
HATTIE TEDROW MEMORIAL FUND SCHOLARSHIP

American Legion
Department of North Dakota
405 West Main Street, Suite 4A
P.O. Box 5057
West Fargo, ND 58078
(701) 293-3120   Fax: (701) 293-9951
E-mail: Programs@ndlegion.org
Web: www.ndlegion.org/scholarships

Summary To provide financial assistance to high school seniors in North Dakota who are direct descendants of veterans and interested in attending college in any state.

Eligibility This program is open to seniors graduating from high schools in North Dakota and planning to attend a college, university, trade school, or technical school in any state. Applicants must be the children, grandchildren, or great-grandchildren of veterans who served honorably in the U.S. armed forces. Along with their application, they must submit a 500-word essay on why they should receive this scholarship. Selection is based on the essay and academic performance; financial need is not considered.

Financial data The stipend is $2,000.

Duration 1 year; nonrenewable.

Number awarded 1 each year.

Deadline April of each year.

[735]
HAWAII ALOHA CHAPTER MOAA SCHOLARSHIP FUND

Military Officers Association of America-Hawaii Aloha Chapter
Attn: John Ma, Scholarship Fund Chair
P.O. Box 201441
Honolulu, HI 96820-1356
(808) 486-4805   E-mail: john.ma08@yahoo.com
Web: www.moaa-hawaii.org/Bylaws_Scholarship_Fund.htm

Summary To provide financial assistance to residents of Hawaii who have ties to the military and are interested in attending college in any state.

Eligibility This program is open to residents of Hawaii who are 1) members of the Military Officers Association of America (MOAA) and their spouses, children, or grandchildren; 2) children of parents currently serving in any of the uniformed services; 3) currently serving in any of the uniformed services; or 4) enrolled in a Junior ROTC program at a high school in Hawaii or in an ROTC program at a college or university in Hawaii. Applicants must be enrolled or planning to enroll at an accredited college or university in Hawaii or, if eligible, in any state. Selection is based on academic ability or potential, character, personal qualities, and financial need.

Financial data Stipends are $1,000 or $500.

Duration 1 year.

Number awarded Varies each year; recently, 23 were awarded: 2 at $1,000 each to ROTC students at the University of Hawaii and 21 at $500 each to JROTC students at high schools in Hawaii. Since this program began, it has awarded 1,300 scholarships worth more than $120,000.

Deadline Deadline not specified.

[736]
HAZLEWOOD ACT FOR SPOUSE/CHILD

Texas Veterans Commission
1700 North Congress Avenue, Suite 800
P.O. Box 12277
Austin, TX 78711-2277
(512) 463-3168   Toll Free: (800) 252-VETS
Fax: (512) 475-2395   E-mail: hazlewood@tvc.texas.gov
Web: www.tvc.texas.gov/education/hazlewood

Summary To exempt children and spouses of disabled or deceased U.S. veterans from payment of tuition at public universities in Texas.

Eligibility This program is open to residents of Texas whose parent or spouse was a resident of the state at the time of entry into the U.S. armed forces, the Texas National Guard, or the Texas Air National Guard. The veteran parent or spouse must have died as a result of service-related injuries or illness, be missing in action, or have become totally disabled as a result of service-related injury or illness. Applicants must have no remaining federal education benefits. They must be attending or planning to attend a public college or university in the state and have no available federal veterans educational benefits. Children of veterans must be 25 years of age or younger.

Financial data Eligible students are exempt from payment of tuition, dues, fees, and charges at state-supported colleges and universities in Texas.

Duration 1 year; may be renewed.

Additional information This program was previously administered by the Texas Higher Education Coordinating Board but was transferred to the Texas Veterans Commission in 2013.

Number awarded Varies each year; recently, 2,197 children received $15,651,842 in support at 4-year institutions and 1,021 children received $2,291,562 in support at 2-year colleges; 219 spouses received $1,076,957 in support at 4-year institutions and 185 spouses received $392,593 in support at 2-year colleges.

Deadline Deadline not specified.

[737]
HAZLEWOOD LEGACY ACT (CHILD)

Texas Veterans Commission
1700 North Congress Avenue, Suite 800
P.O. Box 12277
Austin, TX 78711-2277
(512) 463-3168   Toll Free: (800) 252-VETS
Fax: (512) 475-2395   E-mail: hazlewood@tvc.texas.gov
Web: www.tvc.texas.gov/education/hazlewood

Summary To exempt the children of certain Texas veterans from payment of tuition for undergraduate or graduate study at public universities in the state.

Eligibility This program is open to the dependent children under 25 years of age of veterans who are current residents of Texas and were legal residents of the state at the time they entered the U.S. armed forces and served for at least 181 days of active military duty, excluding basic training, during specified periods of wartime. The veteran parent must have received an honorable discharge or separation or a general discharge under honorable conditions. They must have unused hours of exemption from tuition under the Hazlewood Act that they can assign to a dependent child. The dependent children must be enrolled or planning to enroll at a public college or university in Texas and all their other federal veterans' education benefits (not including Pell and SEOG grants) may not exceed the value of this exemption.

Financial data Dependent children who are eligible for this benefit are entitled to free tuition and fees at state-supported colleges and universities in Texas.

Duration The combined exemptions for veteran and child may be claimed up to a cumulative total of 150 credit hours, including undergraduate and graduate study.

Additional information This program was previously administered by the Texas Higher Education Coordinating Board but was transferred to the Texas Veterans Commission in 2013.

Number awarded Varies each year; recently, 16,958 eligible children received $132,471,254 in support at 4-year institutions and 5,727 eligible children received $10,991,860 in support at 2-year colleges.

Deadline Deadline not specified.

[738]
HELEN DYAR KING SCHOLARSHIP

Arizona Community Foundation
Attn: Director of Scholarships
2201 East Camelback Road, Suite 405B
Phoenix, AZ 85016
(602) 381-1400   Toll Free: (800) 222-8221
Fax: (602) 381-1575
E-mail: scholarship@azfoundation.org
Web: azfoundation.academicworks.com/opportunities/4156

Summary To provide financial assistance to high school seniors and current college students from Arizona who are members or dependents of members of the armed services or a law enforcement agency and are interested in attending college in any state.

Eligibility This program is open to residents of Arizona who are graduating high school seniors or current full-time students at colleges or universities in any state. Applicants must be an active-duty or retired member or dependent of such a member of the armed services (Air Force, Army, Coast Guard, Marine Corps, National Guard, Navy) or public service agency (police, fire, or other departments). Students entering or enrolled at a 2-year community college must have a GPA of 2.75 or higher; students entering or enrolled at a 4-year college or university must have a GPA of 3.0 or higher. Financial need is considered in the selection process.

Financial data The stipend is $2,000 for students at 2-year colleges or $4,000 for students at 4-year colleges and universities.

Duration 1 year.

Number awarded Varies each year.

Deadline May of each year.

[739]
HELEN KLIMEK STUDENT SCHOLARSHIP

American Legion Auxiliary
Department of New York
1580 Columbia Turnpike
Building 1, Suite 3
Castleton-On-Hudson, NY 12033
(518) 463-1162   Toll Free: (800) 421-6348
Fax: (518) 449-5406   E-mail: nyaladeptoffice@gmail.com
Web: www.deptny.org/?page_id=2128

Summary To provide financial assistance to New York residents who are the descendants of veterans and interested in attending college in any state.

Eligibility This program is open to residents of New York who are high school seniors or graduates and attending or planning to attend an accredited college or university in any state. Applicants must be the children, grandchildren, or great-grandchildren of veterans who served during specified periods of wartime. Along with their application they must submit a 700-word statement on the significance or value of volunteerism as a resource towards the positive development of their personal and professional future. Selection is based on character (15%), Americanism (15%), community involvement (15%), leadership (15%), scholarship (20%), and financial need (20%). U.S. citizenship is required.

Financial data The stipend is $1,000. Funds are paid directly to the recipient's school.

Duration 1 year.

Number awarded 1 each year.

Deadline February of each year.

[740]
HENRY J. REILLY SCHOLARSHIPS

Reserve Officers Association of the United States
Attn: Scholarship Program
One Constitution Avenue, N.E.
Washington, DC 20002-5618
(202) 646-7758   Toll Free: (800) 809-9448
E-mail: scholarship@roa.org
Web: www.roa.org/page/Scholarships

Summary To provide financial assistance for college or graduate school to members of the Reserve Officers Association (ROA) and their children or grandchildren.

Eligibility Applicants for this scholarship must be active or associate members of the association or their children or grandchildren (under the age of 26). Children, age 21 or under, of deceased members who were active and paid up at the time of their death are also eligible. Spouses are not eligible, unless they are members of the association. ROTC members do not qualify as sponsors. Entering and continuing undergraduates must provide evidence of full-time enrollment at a regionally-accredited 4-year college or university, demonstrate leadership qualities, have earned a GPA of 3.3 or higher in high school and 3.0 or higher in college, have scored at least 1875 on the SAT or 55 on the English/math ACT, and (if appropriate) have registered for the draft. Applicants for a master's degree must have earned a GPA of 3.2 or higher as an undergraduate; applicants for a doctoral degree must have received a master's degree or been accepted into a doctoral program. All applicants must submit a 500-word essay on career goals. Selection is based on that essay, aca-

demic excellence, extracurricular activities and leadership, and letters of recommendation.
Financial data The stipend is $2,500 per year.
Duration 1 year; may be renewed.
Number awarded Up to 20 each year.
Deadline April of each year.

[741]
HEROES' LEGACY SCHOLARSHIPS
Fisher House Foundation
12300 Twinbrook Parkway, Suite 410
Rockville, MD 20852
Toll Free: (888) 294-8560
E-mail: bgawne@fisherhouse.org
Web: www.militaryscholar.org/legacy/index.html

Summary To provide financial assistance for college to the children of deceased and disabled veterans and military personnel.
Eligibility This program is open to the unmarried sons and daughters of U.S. military servicemembers (including active duty, retirees, Guard/Reserves, and survivors) who are high school seniors or full-time students at an accredited college, university, or community college and younger than 23 years of age. Applicants must have at least 1 parent who, while serving on active duty after September 11, 2001, either died or became disabled, defined as qualified for receipt of Traumatic Servicemembers Group Life Insurance (TSGLI) or rated as 100% permanently and totally disabled by the U.S. Department of Veterans Affairs. High school applicants must have a GPA of 3.0 or higher and college applicants must have a GPA of 2.5 or higher. Along with their application, they must submit a 500-word essay on a topic that changes annually; recently, students were asked to write on the greatest challenge military families face. Selection is based on that essay, academic achievement, work experience, and participation in school, community, and volunteer activities.
Financial data The stipend is $5,000 per year.
Duration 1 year; recipients may reapply.
Additional information This program began in 2010 with proceeds from the sale of the book *Of Thee I Sing: A Letter to My Daughters* by President Barack Obama.
Number awarded Varies each year, depending on the availability of funds. In its first 3 years, the program awarded 130 scholarships.
Deadline February of each year.

[742]
HEROES PROMISE SCHOLARSHIP OF OKLAHOMA
Oklahoma State Regents for Higher Education
Attn: Director of Scholarship and Grant Programs
655 Research Parkway, Suite 200
P.O. Box 108850
Oklahoma City, OK 73101-8850
(405) 225-9131   Toll Free: (800) 858-1840
Fax: (405) 225-9230   E-mail: studentinfo@osrhe.edu
Web: secure.okcollegestart.org

Summary To provide financial assistance for college to children of Oklahoma military personnel who were killed in action.
Eligibility This program is open to Oklahoma residents who are the child of a person killed after January 1, 2000 in the line of duty in a branch of the U.S. armed forces or who died after January 1, 2000 as a result of an injury sustained in the line of duty. Applicants must enroll at a college or university in Oklahoma prior to reaching 21 years of age. Their parent must have filed an individual or joint Oklahoma resident income tax return for the year prior to their death.
Financial data The program pays the tuition at a public community college or university in the state or a comparable amount at an accredited Oklahoma private college or university.
Duration Assistance continues for 5 years or until receipt of a bachelor's degree, whichever occurs first.
Additional information This program was established in 2011 as a replacement for the former program named the Oklahoma Tuition Waiver for Prisoners of War, Persons Missing in Action, and Dependents.
Number awarded Varies each year.
Deadline Deadline not specified.

[743]
HEROES TRIBUTE SCHOLARSHIP PROGRAM FOR CHILDREN OF THE FALLEN
Marine Corps Scholarship Foundation, Inc.
Attn: Scholarship Office
909 North Washington Street, Suite 400
Alexandria, VA 22314
(703) 549-0060   Toll Free: (866) 496-5462
Fax: (703) 549-9474   E-mail: students@mcsf.org
Web: www.mcsf.org/apply/eligibility

Summary To provide financial assistance for college to the children of Marines and Navy personnel serving with the Marines who were killed on September 11, 2001 or in combat or combat-related training since that date.
Eligibility This program is open to the children of 1) Marines and former Marines killed in the terrorist attacks on September 11, 2001; 2) Marines who were killed in combat or during a Department of Defense operation, training exercise, or domestic terrorist incident on or after September 11, 2001; 3) Navy Corpsmen, Chaplains, or Navy Religious Program Specialists attached to a Marine unit who were killed in combat or during a Department of Defense operation, training exercise, or domestic terrorist incident on or after September 11, 2001; and 4) Marines, Navy Corpsmen, Chaplains, or Religious Program Specialists attached to a Marine unit whose parent died by suicide as a result of combat related Post-Traumatic Stress Disorder. Applicants must be high school seniors, high school graduates, or current undergraduates in an accredited college, university, or postsecondary vocational/technical school. They must submit academic transcripts (GPA of 2.0 or higher), documentation of their parent's service, and a 500-word essay on a topic that changes periodically. Only undergraduate study is supported. There is no maximum family income limitation. All qualified applicants receive scholarships.
Financial data The stipend is $7,500 per year.
Duration 4 years.
Number awarded Varies each year; recently, 4 were awarded.
Deadline February of each year.

SCHOLARSHIPS: FAMILY MEMBERS

[744]
HEROES TRIBUTE SCHOLARSHIP PROGRAM FOR CHILDREN OF THE WOUNDED

Marine Corps Scholarship Foundation, Inc.
Attn: Scholarship Office
909 North Washington Street, Suite 400
Alexandria, VA 22314
(703) 549-0060   Toll Free: (866) 496-5462
Fax: (703) 549-9474   E-mail: students@mcsf.org
Web: www.mcsf.org/apply/eligibility

Summary To provide financial assistance for college to the children of Marines and Navy personnel serving with the Marines who were wounded in action.

Eligibility This program is open to the children of Marines and Navy Corpsmen, Chaplains, or Religious Program Specialists serving with the Marines 1) who were wounded in action in any war or conflict; 2) who were permanently retired from the Marine Corps or Navy as a result of their service-related injury; or 3) whose parent is currently ill or injured and serving with Wounded Warrior Regiment/Battalion. Applicants must be high school seniors, high school graduates, or current undergraduates in an accredited college, university, or postsecondary vocational/technical school. They must submit academic transcripts (GPA of 2.0 or higher), documentation of their parent's service, and a 500-word essay on a topic that changes periodically. Only undergraduate study is supported. There is no maximum family income limitation. All qualified applicants receive scholarships.

Financial data The stipend ranges from $1,500 to $10,000 per year.

Duration 4 years.

Number awarded 1 or more each year.

Deadline February of each year.

[745]
HOMEGROWN BY HEROES SCHOLARSHIPS

Arkansas Agriculture Department
Attn: Homegrown by Heroes Program
1 Natural Resources Drive
Little Rock, AR 72205
(501) 225-1598
E-mail: amy.lyman@agriculture.arkansas.gov
Web: www.agriculture.arkansas.gov/aad-programs

Summary To provide financial assistance to veterans, current military personnel, and their spouses and children in Arkansas who are interested in working on a degree in agriculture at a college in any state.

Eligibility This program is open to residents of Arkansas who are military veterans, currently serving military personnel, and their spouses or children. Applicants must be enrolled or planning to enroll at a college or university in any state to working on a degree in agriculture or a related field. Selection is based on academic achievement, community involvement, extracurricular activities, family circumstances, and financial need. Preference is given to farmers and their families who participate in Homegrown by Heroes, a program of the Arkansas Agriculture Department that helps veterans market their local agricultural products by labeling them as veteran-produced.

Financial data The stipend is $1,000.

Duration 1 year.

Additional information This program is funded by Farm Credit of Western Arkansas, AgHeritage Farm Credit Services, and Farm Credit Midsouth.

Number awarded 8 each year.

Deadline March of each year.

[746]
HOWARD R. HARPER SCHOLARSHIP

Enlisted Association of the National Guard of Iowa
c/o Michelle E. Hartwell, Scholarship Chair
1780 N.W. 32nd Lane, Apartment 21
Ankeny, IA 50023
(319) 350-6167   E-mail: meaberle@yahoo.com
Web: www.eangi.org/howard-r-harper-scholarship

Summary To provide financial assistance to members of the Enlisted Association of the National Guard of Iowa (EANGI) and their spouses, children, and grandchildren who are interested in attending college in any state.

Eligibility This program is open to members in good standing of the EANGI and their spouses, children, and grandchildren. Applicants must be attending or accepted for attendance at a VA-approved college or technical school. Along with their application, they must submit a letter with specific information about their desire to continue their education and why they require financial assistance.

Financial data The stipend is $1,500.

Duration 1 year; recipients may reapply.

Number awarded 3 each year.

Deadline February of each year.

[747]
H.S. AND ANGELINE LEWIS SCHOLARSHIPS

American Legion Auxiliary
Department of Wisconsin
Attn: Education Chair
2930 American Legion Drive
P.O. Box 140
Portage, WI 53901-0140
(608) 745-0124   Toll Free: (866) 664-3863
Fax: (608) 745-1947
E-mail: deptsec@amlegionauxwi.org
Web: www.amlegionauxwi.org/scholarships

Summary To provide financial assistance to Wisconsin residents who are related to veterans and interested in working on an undergraduate or graduate degree at a school in any state.

Eligibility This program is open to residents of Wisconsin who are the children, grandchildren, great-grandchildren, wives, or widows of veterans. Students who are members of the Wisconsin American Legion family may live in any state. Applicants must be enrolled or planning to enroll as an undergraduate or graduate students at a college or university in any state. They must have a GPA of 3.5 or higher and be able to demonstrate financial need. Along with their application, they must submit a 300-word essay on "Education—An Investment in the Future."

Financial data The stipend is $1,000.

Duration 1 year; nonrenewable.

Number awarded 6 each year: 1 to a graduate student and 5 to undergraduates.

Deadline March of each year.

[748]
IA DRANG SCHOLARSHIP PROGRAM
First Cavalry Division Association
Attn: Foundation
302 North Main Street
Copperas Cove, TX 76522-1703
(254) 547-6537　　　　　　　　　Fax: (254) 547-8853
E-mail: firstcav@1cda.org
Web: www.1cda.org/scholarships/ia-drang

Summary To provide financial assistance for undergraduate education to descendants of Army and Air Force personnel who fought in the battle of Ia Drang in 1965.

Eligibility This program is open to the children and grandchildren of members of designated Army and Air Force units who actually fought in the battle of the Ia Drang valley from November 3 through 19, 1965. For a list of the qualifying units, contact the sponsor. Children and grandchildren of personnel who were assigned to a unit that fought in the battles but were themselves at other locations during the specified dates are not eligible.

Financial data The stipend is $1,200 per year. The checks are made out jointly to the student and the school and may be used for whatever the student needs, including tuition, books, and clothing.

Duration 1 year; may be renewed up to 3 additional years.

Additional information This program began in 1994.

Number awarded 1 or more each year.

Deadline July of each year.

[749]
IDAHO ARMED FORCES AND PUBLIC SAFETY OFFICER SCHOLARSHIPS
Idaho State Board of Education
Attn: Scholarships Program Manager
650 West State Street, Room 307
P.O. Box 83720
Boise, ID 83720-0037
(208) 334-2270　　　　　　　　　Fax: (208) 334-2632
E-mail: scholarshiphelp@osbe.idaho.gov
Web: boardofed.idaho.gov

Summary To provide financial assistance for college in Idaho to dependents of certain members of the armed forces and of disabled or deceased public safety officers.

Eligibility This program is open to spouses and children of 1) Idaho residents determined by the federal government to have been prisoners of war, missing in action, or killed in action or died of injuries or wounds sustained in any area of armed conflict to which the United States was a party; 2) any member of the armed forces stationed in Idaho and deployed from Idaho to any area of armed conflict to which the United States was a party and who has been determined by the federal government to be a prisoner of war or missing in action or to have died of or become totally and permanently disabled by injuries or wounds sustained in action as a result of such deployment; or 3) full- or part-time Idaho public safety officers (peace officer, firefighter, paramedic, or EMT) employed by or volunteering for the state or a political subdivision who were killed or totally and permanently disabled in the line of duty. Applicants must be Idaho residents enrolled or planning to enroll at a public institution of higher education in the state.

Financial data Each scholarship provides a full waiver of tuition and fees at public institutions of higher education or public vocational schools within Idaho, an allowance of $500 per semester for books, on-campus housing, and a campus meal plan.

Duration Benefits are available for a maximum of 36 months (4 academic years).

Number awarded Varies each year.

Deadline Applications may be submitted at any time.

[750]
IDAHO LEGION AUXILIARY GENERAL STUDIES NON-TRADITIONAL SCHOLARSHIP
American Legion Auxiliary
Department of Idaho
905 Warren Street
Boise, ID 83706-3825
(208) 342-7066　　　　　　　　　Fax: (208) 342-7066
E-mail: idalegionaux@msn.com
Web: www.idahoala.org/14301.html

Summary To provide financial assistance to members of American Legion organizations in Idaho who are interested in attending college in any state and majoring in any field.

Eligibility This program is open to residents of Idaho who are members of the American Legion, American Legion Auxiliary, or Sons of the American Legion. Applicants must be nontraditional students who are returning to the classroom after some period of time during which their formal education was interrupted or beginning postsecondary education at a later point in life. Along with their application, they must submit brief statements describing any circumstances that may affect support for their college education, community service activities, the major they plan to pursue in college and why, the college or university they plan to attend any why, and who or what inspired them to seek a college degree.

Financial data The stipend is $1,000. Funds are paid directly to the school.

Duration 1 year.

Number awarded 1 each year.

Deadline April of each year.

[751]
IDAHO LEGION AUXILIARY GENERAL STUDIES TRADITIONAL SCHOLARSHIP
American Legion Auxiliary
Department of Idaho
905 Warren Street
Boise, ID 83706-3825
(208) 342-7066　　　　　　　　　Fax: (208) 342-7066
E-mail: idalegionaux@msn.com
Web: www.idahoala.org/14301.html

Summary To provide financial assistance to residents of Idaho who are descendants of wartime veterans and interested in attending college in any state to majoring in any field.

Eligibility This program is open to residents of Idaho who are high school seniors or graduates within the past 2 years. Applicants must be the children, grandchildren, or great-grandchildren of veterans who served during specified dates of wartime. They must be planning to attend a college or university in any state and major in any field. Along with their application, they must submit a letter of application, 3 letters of recommendation, high school transcripts including ACT or SAT scores, and documentation of financial need.

Financial data The stipend is $1,000. Funds are paid directly to the school.
Duration 1 year.
Number awarded 1 each year.
Deadline April of each year.

[752]
IDAHO LEGION AUXILIARY NON-TRADITIONAL NURSES SCHOLARSHIP

American Legion Auxiliary
Department of Idaho
905 Warren Street
Boise, ID 83706-3825
(208) 342-7066   Fax: (208) 342-7066
E-mail: idalegionaux@msn.com
Web: www.idahoala.org/14301.html

Summary To provide financial assistance to Idaho veterans and their descendants who are interested in studying nursing at a school in any state.
Eligibility This program is open to residents of Idaho who are wartime veterans or the children or grandchildren of such veterans. Applicants must be attending or planning to attend a school of nursing in any state. They must be nontraditional students who have been out of high school more than 2 years. Along with their application, they must submit a letter describing their career goals and experience, 2 letters of recommendation, a resume that includes their work history, their most recent high school or college transcripts including ACT or SAT scores, and documentation of financial need.
Financial data The stipend is $1,000. Funds are paid directly to the school.
Duration 1 year.
Number awarded 1 each year.
Deadline April of each year.

[753]
IDAHO LEGION AUXILIARY TRADITIONAL NURSES SCHOLARSHIP

American Legion Auxiliary
Department of Idaho
905 Warren Street
Boise, ID 83706-3825
(208) 342-7066   Fax: (208) 342-7066
E-mail: idalegionaux@msn.com
Web: www.idahoala.org/14301.html

Summary To provide financial assistance to descendants of Idaho veterans who are interested in studying nursing at a school in any state.
Eligibility This program is open to residents of Idaho who are high school seniors or graduates within the past 2 years. Applicants must be the children, grandchildren, or great-grandchildren of veterans who served during specified dates of wartime. They must be planning to attend a school of nursing in any state. Along with their application, they must submit a letter of application, 3 letters of recommendation, high school transcripts including ACT or SAT scores, and documentation of financial need.
Financial data The stipend is $1,000. Funds are paid directly to the school.
Duration 1 year.
Number awarded 1 each year.
Deadline April of each year.

[754]
ILLINOIS AMERICAN LEGION AUXILIARY PAST PRESIDENTS PARLEY NURSES SCHOLARSHIP

American Legion Auxiliary
Department of Illinois
2720 East Lincoln Street
P.O. Box 1426
Bloomington, IL 61702-1426
(309) 663-9366   Fax: (309) 663-5827
E-mail: karen.boughan@ilala.org
Web: www.ilala.org/education.html

Summary To provide financial assistance to Illinois veterans and their descendants who are attending college in any state to prepare for a career as a nurse.
Eligibility This program is open to veterans who served during designated periods of wartime and their children, grandchildren, and great-grandchildren. Applicants must be currently enrolled full time at a college or university in any state and studying nursing. They must be residents of Illinois or members of the American Legion Family, Department of Illinois. Selection is based on commitment to a nursing career (25%) character (25%), academic rating (20%), and financial need (30%).
Financial data The stipend is $1,000.
Duration 1 year.
Additional information Applications may be obtained only from a local unit of the American Legion Auxiliary.
Number awarded 1 or more each year.
Deadline April of each year.

[755]
ILLINOIS AMERICAN LEGION SCHOLARSHIPS

American Legion
Department of Illinois
Attn: Education and Scholarship Committee
2720 East Lincoln Street
P.O. Box 2910
Bloomington, IL 61702-2910
(309) 663-0361   Fax: (309) 663-5783
E-mail: hdqs@illegion.org
Web: www.illegion.org

Summary To provide financial assistance to the children and grandchildren of members of the American Legion in Illinois who plan to attend college in any state.
Eligibility This program is open to students graduating from high schools in Illinois who plan to further their education at an accredited college, university, technical school, or trade school in any state. Applicants must be the children or grandchildren of living or deceased members of American Legion Posts in Illinois. Selection is based on academic performance and financial need. U.S. citizenship is required.
Financial data The stipend is $1,000.
Duration 1 year; nonrenewable.
Number awarded 25 each year: 5 in each of the Illinois department's 5 divisions.
Deadline March of each year.

[756]
ILLINOIS AMERICAN LEGION TRADE SCHOOL SCHOLARSHIPS

American Legion
Department of Illinois
Attn: Education and Scholarship Committee
2720 East Lincoln Street
P.O. Box 2910
Bloomington, IL 61702-2910
(309) 663-0361   Fax: (309) 663-5783
E-mail: hdqs@illegion.org
Web: www.illegion.org

Summary To provide financial assistance to the children and grandchildren of members of the American Legion in Illinois who plan to attend trade school in any state.

Eligibility This program is open to students graduating from high schools in Illinois who plan to further their education through a private career school, on-the-job training, apprenticeship, or cooperative training at a program in any state. Applicants must be the children or grandchildren of members of American Legion Posts in Illinois. Selection is based on academic performance and financial need.

Financial data The stipend is $1,000.

Duration 1 year; nonrenewable.

Number awarded 5 each year: 1 in each of the Illinois department's 5 divisions.

Deadline March of each year.

[757]
ILLINOIS AMVETS JUNIOR ROTC SCHOLARSHIPS

AMVETS-Department of Illinois
2200 South Sixth Street
Springfield, IL 62703
(217) 528-4713   Toll Free: (800) 638-VETS (within IL)
Fax: (217) 528-9896   E-mail: info@ilamvets.org
Web: www.ilamvets.org

Summary To provide financial assistance for college to high school seniors in Illinois who have participated in Junior ROTC (JROTC) and are children or grandchildren of veterans or military personnel.

Eligibility This program is open to seniors graduating from high schools in Illinois who have taken the ACT or SAT and have participated in the JROTC program. Applicants must be the child or grandchild of a veteran or the child of a military person on active duty. They must be planning to attend a college or university in any state. Along with their application, they must submit a 100-word essay on why they should be selected to receive this scholarship. Financial need is considered in the selection process.

Financial data The stipend is $1,000.

Duration 1 year; nonrenewable.

Number awarded Up to 5 each year: 1 in each of the sponsor's divisions.

Deadline February of each year.

[758]
ILLINOIS AMVETS LADIES AUXILIARY MEMORIAL SCHOLARSHIP

AMVETS-Department of Illinois
2200 South Sixth Street
Springfield, IL 62703
(217) 528-4713   Toll Free: (800) 638-VETS (within IL)
Fax: (217) 528-9896   E-mail: info@ilamvets.org
Web: www.ilamvets.org

Summary To provide financial assistance for college to high school seniors in Illinois who are children or grandchildren of veterans or military personnel.

Eligibility This program is open to high school seniors in Illinois who have taken the SAT or ACT. Applicants must be children or grandchildren of veterans who served after September 15, 1940 and were honorably discharged or are presently serving in the military. They must be planning to attend a college or university in any state. Financial need is considered in the selection process.

Financial data The stipend varies each year.

Duration 1 year; nonrenewable.

Number awarded 1 or more each year.

Deadline February of each year.

[759]
ILLINOIS AMVETS SERVICE FOUNDATION SCHOLARSHIPS

AMVETS-Department of Illinois
2200 South Sixth Street
Springfield, IL 62703
(217) 528-4713   Toll Free: (800) 638-VETS (within IL)
Fax: (217) 528-9896   E-mail: info@ilamvets.org
Web: www.ilamvets.org

Summary To provide financial assistance for college to high school seniors in Illinois who are children or grandchildren of veterans or military personnel.

Eligibility This program is open to seniors graduating from high schools in Illinois who have taken the ACT or SAT. Applicants must be the child or grandchild of a veteran or the child of a military person on active duty. They must be planning to attend a college or university in any state. Along with their application, they must submit a 100-word essay on why they should be selected to receive this scholarship. Financial need is considered in the selection process.

Financial data The stipend is $1,000.

Duration 1 year; nonrenewable.

Number awarded Up to 30 each year: 6 in each of the sponsor's 5 divisions.

Deadline February of each year.

[760]
ILLINOIS AMVETS TRADE SCHOOL SCHOLARSHIPS

AMVETS-Department of Illinois
2200 South Sixth Street
Springfield, IL 62703
(217) 528-4713   Toll Free: (800) 638-VETS (within IL)
Fax: (217) 528-9896   E-mail: info@ilamvets.org
Web: www.ilamvets.org

Summary To provide financial assistance to high school seniors in Illinois who are children or grandchildren of veter-

ans or military personnel and interested in attending trade school.
Eligibility This program is open to seniors graduating from high schools in Illinois who have been accepted at an approved trade school. Applicants must be the child or grandchild of a veteran or the child of a military person on active duty. Along with their application, they must submit a 100-word essay on why they should be selected to receive this scholarship. Financial need is considered in the selection process.
Financial data The stipend is $1,000.
Duration 1 year; nonrenewable.
Number awarded Up to 5 each year: 1 in each of the sponsor's divisions.
Deadline February of each year.

[761]
ILLINOIS CHILDREN OF VETERANS SCHOLARSHIPS
University of Illinois at Urbana-Champaign
Attn: Office of Student Financial Aid
Student Services Arcade
620 East John Street, MC-303
Champaign, IL 61820
(217) 333-0100   Fax: (217) 265-5516
E-mail: finaid@illinois.edu
Web: www.osfa.illinois.edu

Summary To provide financial assistance for college to the children of Illinois veterans (with preference given to the children of disabled or deceased veterans).
Eligibility Each county in the state is entitled to award an honorary scholarship to children of veterans of World War II, the Korean Conflict, the Vietnam Conflict, the Siege of Beirut, the Grenada Conflict, the Southwest Asia Conflict, Operation Enduring Freedom, or Operation Iraqi Freedom. Applicants must be working on an undergraduate, graduate, or professional degree at a branch of the University of Illinois. Preference is given to applications received before the priority deadline.
Financial data Students selected for this program receive free tuition at a branch of the University of Illinois.
Duration Up to 4 years.
Number awarded Each county in Illinois is entitled to award 3 scholarships.
Deadline The priority deadline is December of each year.

[762]
ILLINOIS FALLEN HEROES SCHOLARSHIP
Office of the Illinois State Treasurer
Attn: Fallen Heroes Scholarship
100 West Randolph Street, Suite 15-600
Chicago, IL 60601
Toll Free: (866) 465-9724
E-mail: fallenheroes@IllinoisTreasurer.gov
Web: www.illinoistreasurer.gov/Individuals/Fallen_Heroes

Summary To provide financial assistance for college to the children of Illinois servicemembers killed in Iraq.
Eligibility This program is open to the children of fallen Illinois servicemembers who served in Operation Iraqi Freedom or Operation Enduring Freedom. Applicants must be U.S. citizens of any age under 30 years. They may be planning to attend an accredited college or university anywhere in the United States or at selected institutions abroad. Children of all Illinois active and Reserve servicemen and women are eligible as well as firefighters, law enforcement officers, and paramedics who have died while serving their state or country.
Financial data The stipend is $1,000. Funds are deposited into an age-based Bright Start portfolio (the Illinois 529 program) and are available when the student reaches college age. The older the child, the more conservative the investment becomes. Funds may be used only for tuition, fees, room, and board, and must be spent before the child reaches 30 years of age.
Duration 1 year.
Additional information This program began in 2008.
Number awarded Varies each year.
Deadline July of each year.

[763]
ILLINOIS MIA/POW SCHOLARSHIP
Illinois Department of Veterans' Affairs
833 South Spring Street
P.O. Box 19432
Springfield, IL 62794-9432
(217) 782-3564   Toll Free: (800) 437-9824 (within IL)
Fax: (217) 524-8493   TDD: (217) 524-4645
E-mail: webmail@dva.state.il.us
Web: www2.illinois.gov

Summary To provide financial assistance for undergraduate education to Illinois dependents of disabled or deceased veterans or those listed as prisoners of war or missing in action.
Eligibility This program is open to the spouses, natural children, legally adopted children, or stepchildren of a veteran or servicemember who 1) has been declared by the U.S. Department of Veterans Affairs to be permanently and 100% disabled from service-connected causes, deceased as the result of a service-connected disability, a prisoner of war, or missing in action; and 2) at the time of entering service was an Illinois resident or was an Illinois resident within 6 months of entering such service.
Financial data An eligible dependent is entitled to full payment of tuition and certain fees at any Illinois state-supported college, university, or community college. The total benefit cannot exceed the cost equivalent of 4 calendar years of full-time enrollment, including summer terms, at the University of Illinois.
Duration This scholarship may be used for a period equivalent to 4 calendar years, including summer terms. Dependents have 12 years from the initial term of study to complete the equivalent of 4 calendar years.
Number awarded Varies each year.
Deadline Deadline not specified.

[764]
ILLINOIS SCHOLARSHIPS FOR JUNIOR MEMBERS

American Legion Auxiliary
Department of Illinois
2720 East Lincoln Street
P.O. Box 1426
Bloomington, IL 61702-1426
(309) 663-9366   Fax: (309) 663-5827
E-mail: karen.boughan@ilala.org
Web: www.ilala.org/education.html

Summary To provide financial assistance to high school seniors or graduates in Illinois who are junior members of the American Legion Auxiliary and planning to attend college in any state.

Eligibility This program is open to junior members of the Illinois American Legion Auxiliary who are daughters, granddaughters, great-granddaughters, or sisters of veterans who served during eligibility dates for membership in the American Legion. Applicants must have been members for at least 3 years. They must be high school seniors or graduates who have not yet attended an institution of higher learning and are planning to attend college in any state. Along with their application, they must submit a 1,000-word essay on "The Veteran in My Life." Selection is based on that essay (25%) character and leadership (25%), scholarship (25%), and financial need (25%).

Financial data The stipend is $1,000.
Duration 1 year.
Number awarded Varies each year.
Deadline March of each year.

[765]
INDIANA AMERICAN LEGION FAMILY SCHOLARSHIP

American Legion
Department of Indiana
Attn: Programs Coordinator
5440 Herbert Lord Road
Indianapolis, IN 46216-2119
(317) 630-1391   Fax: (317) 237-9891
E-mail: bmiller@indianalegion.org
Web: www.indianalegion.org/scholarships—awards.html

Summary To provide financial assistance to children and grandchildren of members of the American Legion family in Indiana who are interested in attending college in the state.

Eligibility This program is open to residents of Indiana who are the children or grandchildren of members of the American Legion, American Legion Auxiliary, Sons of the American Legion, or deceased members of those organizations who, at the time of death, were in current paid status. Applicants must be enrolled or accepted for enrollment at an Indiana college, university, junior college, community college, or technical school. Along with their application, they must submit a 500-word essay describing the reasons they wish to be considered for this scholarship, the purpose to which the funds will be put, their relationship to the Legion family and what it has meant to them, and how the citizens of Indiana and the members of the American Legion family will benefit in the future from their having achieved their educational goals with the assistance of this scholarship. Financial need is not considered in the selection process.

Financial data The stipend is $1,500.
Duration 1 year.
Number awarded 8 each year.
Deadline March of each year.

[766]
INDIANA CHILDREN OF DECEASED OR DISABLED VETERANS PROGRAM

Indiana Commission for Higher Education
Attn: Financial Aid and Student Support Services
101 West Ohio Street, Suite 300
Indianapolis, IN 46204-4206
(317) 232-1023   Toll Free: (888) 528-4719 (within IN)
Fax: (317) 232-3260   E-mail: Scholars@che.in.gov
Web: www.in.gov/che/4517.htm

Summary To provide financial assistance to residents of Indiana who are the children of deceased or disabled veterans and interested in attending college in the state.

Eligibility This program is open to residents of Indiana whose parent served in the U.S. armed forces during a war or performed duty equally hazardous that was recognized by the award of a U.S. service or campaign medal, suffered a service-connected death or disability, and received a discharge or separation other than dishonorable. Applicants must be the biological child of the veteran or legally adopted prior to their 24th birthday; stepchildren are not eligible. Parents who enlisted on or before June 30, 2011 must have resided in Indiana for at least 36 consecutive months during their lifetime. Parents who enlisted after June 30, 2011 must have designated Indiana as home of record at the time of enlistment or resided in that state at least 5 years before the child first applies for the benefit.

Financial data If the veterans parent initially enlisted on or before June 30, 2011, the child receives a 100% remission of tuition and all mandatory fees for undergraduate, graduate, or professional degrees at eligible postsecondary schools and universities in Indiana. If the veteran parent initially enlisted after June 30, 2011 and suffered a disability with a rating of 80% or more, the child receives a 100% remission of tuition and all mandatory fees for undergraduate or professional degrees at eligible postsecondary schools and universities in Indiana. If the veteran parent initially enlisted after June 30, 2011 and suffered a disability with a rating less than 80%, the rate of remission for tuition and regularly assessed fees is 20% plus the disability rating. Support is not provided for such fees as room and board.

Duration Up to 124 semester hours of study. If the veteran parent initially enlisted on or before June 30, 2011, there is no time limit to use those hours. If the veteran parent initially enlisted after June 30, 2011, the allotted 124 credit hours must be used within 8 years after the date the child first applied.

Number awarded Varies each year.
Deadline Applications must be submitted at least 30 days before the start of the college term.

[767]
INDIANA CHILDREN OF FORMER POW/MIA PROGRAM

Indiana Commission for Higher Education
Attn: Financial Aid and Student Support Services
101 West Ohio Street, Suite 300
Indianapolis, IN 46204-4206
(317) 232-1023   Toll Free: (888) 528-4719 (within IN)
Fax: (317) 232-3260   E-mail: Scholars@che.in.gov
Web: www.in.gov/che/4517.htm

Summary To provide financial assistance to residents of Indiana who are the children of former POW/MIA veterans and are interested in attending college in the state.

Eligibility This program is open to residents of Indiana whose parent was a resident of Indiana at the time of entry into the U.S. armed forces and was declared a POW or MIA while serving after January 1, 1960. Applicants must be younger than 32 years of age. They must be the biological child of the veteran or legally adopted prior to their 24th birthday; stepchildren are not eligible.

Financial data Qualified applicants receive a 100% remission of tuition and all mandatory fees for undergraduate or professional degrees at eligible postsecondary schools and universities in Indiana. Support is not provided for such fees as room and board.

Duration Up to 124 semester hours of study. Students who first enrolled in college after June 30, 2011 and whose parent enlisted after that date must maintain satisfactory academic progress. If the veteran parent initially enlisted on or before June 30, 2011, there is no time limit to use those hours. If the veteran parent initially enlisted after June 30, 2011, the allotted 124 credit hours must be used within 8 years after the date the child first applied.

Number awarded Varies each year.

Deadline Applications must be submitted at least 30 days before the start of the college term.

[768]
INDIANA CHILDREN OF PURPLE HEART RECIPIENTS PROGRAM

Indiana Commission for Higher Education
Attn: Financial Aid and Student Support Services
101 West Ohio Street, Suite 300
Indianapolis, IN 46204-4206
(317) 232-1023   Toll Free: (888) 528-4719 (within IN)
Fax: (317) 232-3260   E-mail: Scholars@che.in.gov
Web: www.in.gov/che/4517.htm

Summary To provide financial assistance to residents of Indiana who are the children of veterans who received the Purple Heart decoration and are interested in attending college in the state.

Eligibility This program is open to residents of Indiana whose parent served in the U.S. armed forces during a war or performed duty equally hazardous that was recognized by the award of a U.S. service or campaign medal, received the Purple Heart decoration or wounds as a result of enemy action, and received a discharge or separation other than dishonorable. Applicants must be the biological child of the veteran or legally adopted prior to their 24th birthday; stepchildren are not eligible. Parents who enlisted on or before June 30, 2011 must have resided in Indiana for at least 36 consecutive months during their lifetime. Parents who enlisted after June 30, 2011 must have designated Indiana as home of record at the time of enlistment or resided in that state at least 5 years before the child first applies for the benefit.

Financial data Qualified applicants receive a 100% remission of tuition and all mandatory fees for undergraduate or professional degrees at eligible postsecondary schools and universities in Indiana. Support is not provided for such fees as room and board.

Duration Up to 124 semester hours of study. If the veteran parent initially enlisted on or before June 30, 2011, there is no time limit to use those hours. If the veteran parent initially enlisted after June 30, 2011, the allotted 124 credit hours must be used within 8 years after the date the child first applied.

Number awarded Varies each year.

Deadline Applications must be submitted at least 30 days before the start of the college term.

[769]
IOWA NATIONAL GUARD OFFICERS AUXILIARY SPOUSE SCHOLARSHIP

Iowa National Guard Officers Auxiliary
c/o Jeanine Schochenmaier, Scholarship Chair
7739 43rd Avenue
Prole, IA 50229
E-mail: ingoaaux@gmail.com
Web: www.ingoaux.com/ingoauxscholarship

Summary To provide financial assistance to spouses of Iowa National Guard members who are currently enrolled at a college in any state.

Eligibility This program is open to residents of Iowa who are working on an associate, bachelor's or other postsecondary degree at a continuing education institution in any state. Applicants must be a spouse of an Iowa National Guard member, current or retired. Along with their application, they must submit 1) transcripts; 2) a 1-paragraph autobiography; 3) a 500-word essay describing the most important thing they have learned from the National Guard member in their life; 4) letters of recommendation; and 5) a list of curricular and extracurricular activities in which they have participated.

Financial data A stipend is awarded (amount not specified).

Duration 1 year.

Number awarded 1 or more each year.

Deadline January of each year.

[770]
IOWA NATIONAL GUARD OFFICERS AUXILIARY STUDENT SCHOLARSHIP

Iowa National Guard Officers Auxiliary
c/o Jeanine Schochenmaier, Scholarship Chair
7739 43rd Avenue
Prole, IA 50229
E-mail: ingoaaux@gmail.com
Web: www.ingoaux.com/ingoauxscholarship

Summary To provide financial assistance to children of Iowa National Guard members who are high school seniors or entering freshmen at a college in any state.

Eligibility This program is open to residents of Iowa who are graduating high school seniors or incoming freshmen at 2- and 4-year colleges and universities in any state. Applicants must be a dependent of an Iowa National Guard mem-

ber, current or retired. Along with their application, they must submit 1) transcripts; 2) a 1-paragraph autobiography; 3) a 500-word essay describing the most important thing they have learned from the National Guard member in their life; 4) letters of recommendation; and 5) a list of curricular and extracurricular activities in which they have participated.
Financial data A stipend is awarded (amount not specified).
Duration 1 year.
Number awarded 1 or more each year.
Deadline January of each year.

[771]
IOWA WAR ORPHAN TUITION ASSISTANCE
Iowa Department of Veterans Affairs
Attn: Trust Fund and Grants Administrator
Camp Dodge, Building 3465
7105 N.W. 70th Avenue
Johnston, IA 50131-1824
(515) 727-3443 Toll Free: (800) VET-IOWA
Fax: (515) 727-3713 E-mail: missy.miller@iowa.gov
Web: www.va.iowa.gov/benefits

Summary To provide financial assistance for college in Iowa to children of members of the armed forces from that state who died in active service during specified periods of war.
Eligibility This program is open to children of military personnel who died in active service or as a result of such service during specified wartime periods (including Persian Gulf conflict from August 2, 1990 through the present). Also eligible are former members of the Reserve forces of the United States and of the Iowa National Guard who served at least 20 years after January 28, 1973 and were honorably discharged or who served at least 90 days of active federal service and were honorably discharged. Applicants must have lived in Iowa for at least 2 years prior to applying and must be attending or planning to attend a college, university, junior college, school of nursing, business school, or trade school within Iowa.
Financial data For children of veterans killed in action prior to September 11, 2001, the stipend is $600 per year. For children of veterans killed in action after September 11, 2001, the maximum stipend is $11,844 per year.
Duration 1 year; may be renewed up to 4 additional years.
Number awarded Varies each year.
Deadline Deadline not specified.

[772]
IRAQ AND AFGHANISTAN SERVICE GRANTS
Department of Education
Attn: Federal Student Aid Information Center
P.O. Box 84
Washington, DC 20044-0084
(319) 337-5665 Toll Free: (800) 4-FED-AID
TDD: (800) 730-8913
Web: www.studentaid.gov

Summary To provide financial assistance for undergraduate education to students whose parent was killed as a result of service in Iraq or Afghanistan.
Eligibility This program is open to students younger than 24 years of age whose parent or guardian was a member of the U.S. armed forces and died as a result of service performed in Iraq or Afghanistan after September 11, 2001. Applicants must be enrolled at least part time. The program is designed for students who do not qualify for federal Pell Grants because of their family's financial situation.
Financial data The amount of the grant ranges up to that of a federal Pell Grant, currently $6,345 per year.
Duration Up to 5 years of undergraduate study.
Number awarded Varies each year; recently, approximately 1,000 students qualified for this program.
Deadline Students may submit applications between January of the current year through June of the following year.

[773]
ISABELLA M. GILLEN MEMORIAL SCHOLARSHIP
Aviation Boatswain's Mates Association
c/o Terry L. New, Scholarship Chair
3193 Glastonbury Drive
Virginia Beach, VA 23453
E-mail: airbosn1@msn.com
Web: www.abma-usn.org/scholarships

Summary To provide financial assistance for college to family of members of the Aviation Boatswains Mates Association (ABMA).
Eligibility This program is open to children, grandchildren, and spouses of active, dues-paying members of the ABMA who have been members for at least 2 years. Children and grandchildren must be younger than 26 years of age. Applicants must prepare a statement describing their vocational or professional goals and relating how their past, present, and future activities make the accomplishment of those goals probable. Other submissions include transcripts, SAT or ACT scores, letters of recommendation, and honors received in scholarship, leadership, athletics, dramatics, community service, or other activities. Selection is based on financial need, character, leadership, and academic achievement.
Financial data The stipend is $3,500 per year.
Duration 1 year; may be renewed.
Additional information This program began in 1976. Membership in ABMA is open to all U.S. Navy personnel (active, retired, discharged, or separated) who hold or held the rating of aviation boatswains mate.
Number awarded 1 or 2 each year.
Deadline May of each year.

[774]
JACK E. BARGER, SR. MEMORIAL NURSING SCHOLARSHIPS
Nursing Foundation of Pennsylvania
3605 Vartan Way, Suite 204
Harrisburg, PA 17110
(717) 827-4369 Toll Free: (888) 707-7762
Fax: (717) 657-3796 E-mail: info@theNFP.org
Web: www.thenfp.org/scholarships

Summary To provide financial assistance to veterans, military personnel, and their dependents who are studying nursing in Pennsylvania.
Eligibility This program is open to veterans, active-duty military personnel, and the children and spouses of veterans and active-duty military personnel. Applicants must be residents of Pennsylvania and currently enrolled in an undergraduate professional school of nursing in the state. Recipients are selected by lottery from among the qualified applicants.

Financial data The stipend is $1,000.
Duration 1 year.
Additional information This program is sponsored by the Department of Pennsylvania of Veterans of Foreign Wars (VFW). Recipients must attend the VFW Convention to accept the scholarship; travel, meals, and overnight expenses are paid by the VFW.
Number awarded 6 each year.
Deadline March of each year.

[775]
JAPANESE AMERICAN VETERANS ASSOCIATION MEMORIAL SCHOLARSHIPS

Japanese American Veterans Association
Attn: Chris DeRosa, Scholarship Committee Chair
P.O. Box 341198
Bethesda, MD 20827
E-mail: javascholarship222@gmail.com
Web: www.java.wildapricot.org

Summary To provide financial assistance for college to high school seniors who are relatives of Japanese American veterans.
Eligibility This program is open to graduating high school seniors planning to work on an undergraduate degree at a college, university, or school of specialized study. Applicants must be 1) a direct or collateral descendant of a person who served with the 442nd Regimental Combat Team, the 100th Infantry Battalion, Military Intelligence Service, 1399th Engineering Construction Battalion, or other unit associated with those during or after World War II; or 2) a member or child of a member of the Japanese American Veterans Association (JAVA) whose membership extends back at least 1 year. Along with their application, they must submit a 500-word essay on what winning this scholarship will mean to them.
Financial data The stipend is $1,500.
Duration 1 year.
Additional information This program, which began in 2008, includes the following named awards: the CW04 Mitsugi Kasai Scholarship, the Teru and Victor Matsui Scholarship, the Robert Nakamoto Scholarship, the Betty Shima Scholarship, the Orville Shirey Scholarship, the Dr. Americo Bugliani Scholarship, the Ranger Grant Hirabayashi Scholarship, the Colonel Jimmie Kanaya Scholarship, the Ben Kuroki Scholarship, and the Major Muneo "Mike" Okusa Scholarship.
Number awarded Varies each year; recently, 10 were awarded.
Deadline March of each year.

[776]
JAVA FOUNDERS' SCHOLARSHIP

Japanese American Veterans Association
Attn: Chris DeRosa, Scholarship Committee Chair
P.O. Box 341198
Bethesda, MD 20827
E-mail: javascholarship222@gmail.com
Web: www.java.wildapricot.org

Summary To provide financial assistance for college or graduate school to relatives of Japanese American veterans.
Eligibility This program is open to students who have completed at least 2 years of an undergraduate program or are currently enrolled in graduate school. Applicants must be 1) a direct or collateral descendant of a person who served with the 442nd Regimental Combat Team, the 100th Infantry Battalion, Military Intelligence Service, 1399th Engineering Construction Battalion, or other unit associated with those during or after World War II; or 2) a member or child of a member of the Japanese American Veterans Association (JAVA) whose membership extends back at least 1 year. Along with their application, they must submit a 500-word essay on what winning this scholarship will mean to them.
Financial data The stipend is $3,000.
Duration 1 year.
Number awarded 1 each year.
Deadline March of each year.

[777]
JEWELL HILTON BONNER SCHOLARSHIP

Navy League of the United States
Attn: Scholarships
2300 Wilson Boulevard, Suite 200
Arlington, VA 22201-5424
(703) 528-1775   Toll Free: (800) 356-5760
Fax: (703) 528-2333
E-mail: scholarships@navyleague.org
Web: www.navyleague.org/programs/scholarships

Summary To provide financial assistance for college to dependent children of sea service personnel, especially Native Americans.
Eligibility This program is open to U.S. citizens who are 1) dependents or direct descendants of an active, Reserve, retired, or honorably discharged member of the U.S. sea service (including the Navy, Marine Corps, Coast Guard, or Merchant Marines); or 2) current active members of the Naval Sea Cadet Corps. Applicants must be entering their freshman year at an accredited college or university. They must have a GPA of 3.0 or higher. Along with their application, they must submit transcripts, 2 letters of recommendation, SAT/ACT scores, documentation of financial need, proof of qualifying sea service duty, and a 1-page personal statement on why they should be considered for this scholarship. Preference is given to applicants of Native American heritage.
Financial data The stipend is $2,500 per year.
Duration 4 years, provided the recipient maintains a GPA of 3.0 or higher.
Number awarded 1 each year.
Deadline February of each year.

[778]
JEWISH WAR VETERANS NATIONAL YOUTH ACHIEVEMENT PROGRAM

Jewish War Veterans of the U.S.A.
1811 R Street, N.W.
Washington, DC 20009-1659
(202) 265-6280   Fax: (202) 234-5662
E-mail: jwv@jwv.org
Web: www.jwvusafoundation.org

Summary To provide financial assistance for college to descendants of members of the Jewish War Veterans of the U.S.A.
Eligibility This program is open to children, grandchildren, and great-grandchildren of members or of deceased members of Jewish War Veterans in good standing who are high school seniors. Applicants must have been accepted by an accredited college, university, community college, or hospital

school of nursing as a freshman. They must have a GPA of 3.7 or higher unweighted to 4.5 or higher weighted, an SAT score of at least 735 average or 1470 cumulative, and/or an ACT score of 31 or higher. Selection is based on academic achievement, class standing, and extracurricular and community activities.
Financial data Grants are $1,250 or $1,000.
Duration 1 year; nonrenewable.
Additional information This program currently includes the Cliford Lee Kristal Education Grant, the Bernard Rotberg Memorial Grant, and the Edith, Louis, and Max S. Millen Memorial Athletic Grant.
Number awarded 3 each year: 1 at $1,250 and 2 at $1,000.
Deadline Applications must be submitted to the department commander by May of each year.

[779]
JOHN A. HIGH CHILD WELFARE SCHOLARSHIP ENDOWMENT FUND
American Legion
Department of New Hampshire
121 South Fruit Street
Concord, NH 03301
(603) 856-8951   Fax: (603) 856-8943
E-mail: adjutantnh@nhlegion.com
Web: www.legionnh.org

Summary To provide financial assistance to the sons of members of the New Hampshire Department of the American Legion or American Legion Auxiliary who plan to attend college in any state.
Eligibility This program is open to male seniors graduating from high schools in New Hampshire who plan to attend college in any state. Applicants must be the son of a deceased veteran or of parents who have been members of the American Legion or the American Legion Auxiliary in New Hampshire for 3 continuous years. Along with their application, they must submit a 300-word essay on what this scholarship would mean to them. Selection is based on academic record (20%), Americanism (10%), financial need (50%), and character (20%).
Financial data The stipend is $2,000.
Duration 1 year.
Number awarded 1 each year.
Deadline April of each year.

[780]
JOHN C. AND BLANCHE LEE LINDSAY MEMORIAL SCHOLARSHIP
Air Force Association
Attn: Scholarships
1501 Lee Highway
Arlington, VA 22209-1198
(703) 247-5800, ext. 4868
Toll Free: (800) 727-3337, ext. 4868
Fax: (703) 247-5853   E-mail: scholarships@afa.org
Web: www.app.smarterselect.com

Summary To provide financial assistance to children of active and retired Air Force personnel who are interested in attending college.
Eligibility This program is open to children of Air Force (officer or enlisted) active duty, veteran, retired, Reserve, or Air National Guard personnel who are enrolled or planning to enroll at an accredited college or university. Applicants must submit a statement of purpose describing how the scholarship will assist in meeting their educational goals. Preference is given to applicants who 1) are majoring in a field of STEM; or 2) have at least 1 parent member of the Air Force Association (AFA).
Financial data The stipend is $2,500.
Duration 1 year; nonrenewable.
Number awarded 1 each year.
Deadline April of each year.

[781]
JOHN CASEY SCHOLARSHIP
American Legion
Department of New Jersey
Attn: Adjutant
171 Jersey Street
Building 5, Second Floor
Trenton, NJ 08611
(609) 695-5418   Fax: (609) 394-1532
E-mail: adjutant@njamericanlegion.org
Web: www.njamericanlegion.org

Summary To provide financial assistance for college in any state to the descendants of combat-wounded members of the New Jersey Department of the American Legion.
Eligibility This program is open to high school seniors who are the natural or adopted children, grandchildren, or great-grandchildren of living or deceased members of the American Legion's New Jersey Department. Applicants must be planning to attend a college or university in any state. Their ancestor must have been wounded in combat. Along with their application, they must submit a brief statement on the reasons for their choice of vocation. Selection is based on character (20%), Americanism and community service (20%), leadership (20%), scholarship (20%), and financial need (20%).
Financial data The stipend is $1,500.
Duration 1 year.
Number awarded 1 each year.
Deadline February of each year.

[782]
JOHN CORNELIUS/MAX ENGLISH MEMORIAL SCHOLARSHIP
Marine Corps Tankers Association
c/o Dan Miller, Scholarship Chair
8212 West Fourth Place
Kennewick, WA 99336
E-mail: dmiller@msn.com
Web: www.usmctankers.org/pageScholarship

Summary To provide financial assistance for college or graduate school to children and grandchildren of members of the Marine Corps Tankers Association and to Marine and Navy personnel currently serving in tank units.
Eligibility This program is open to high school seniors and graduates who are children, grandchildren, or under the guardianship of an active, Reserve, retired, or honorably discharged Marine who served in a tank unit. Marine or Navy Corpsmen currently assigned to tank units are also eligible. Applicants must be enrolled or planning to enroll full time at a college or graduate school. Their parent or grandparent must

be a member of the Marine Corps Tankers Association or, if not a member, must join if the application is accepted. Along with their application, they must submit a 500-word essay that explains their reason for seeking this scholarship, their educational goals, and their plans for post-graduation life. Selection is based on that essay, academic record, school activities, leadership potential, and community service.

Financial data The stipend is at least $2,000 per year.
Duration 1 year; recipients may reapply.
Number awarded Varies each year; recently, 4 were awarded.
Deadline March of each year.

[783]
JOHN KEYS KENTUCKY SONS OF THE AMERICAN LEGION SCHOLARSHIP

Sons of the American Legion
Detachment of Kentucky
Independence Squadron 275
P.O. Box 18791
Erlanger, KY 41018-0791
E-mail: SAL275@fuse.net

Summary To provide financial assistance for college in any state to members of Kentucky squadrons of the Sons of the American Legion and to veterans who are residents of Kentucky.
Eligibility This program is open to 1) members of the Sons of the American Legion who belong to a squadron in Kentucky; and 2) honorably-discharged veterans of the U.S. armed forces who are residents of Kentucky (regardless of length or period of service). Applicants must be enrolled at a postsecondary institution in any state. Along with their application, they must submit a letter explaining their background, career objectives, current educational program, and financial need.
Financial data The stipend varies, depending on the availability of funds; recently, they averaged $1,000. Awards are made directly to the recipient's institution.
Duration 1 year.
Additional information This program began in 1988.
Number awarded 1 or 2 each year; since the program began, it has awarded more than 60 scholarships.
Deadline Applications may be submitted at any time.

[784]
JOSEPH P. AND HELEN T. CRIBBINS SCHOLARSHIP

Association of the United States Army
Attn: Scholarships
2425 Wilson Boulevard
Arlington, VA 22201
(703) 841-4300   Toll Free: (800) 336-4570
E-mail: scholarships@ausa.org
Web: www.ausa.org/resources/scholarships

Summary To provide financial assistance to members of the Association of the United States Army (AUSA) who are interested in studying a field of STEM in college.
Eligibility This program is open to AUSA members who are enrolled or accepted at an accredited college or university to work on a degree in a field of STEM. Along with their application, they must submit a 1-page autobiography, 2 letters of recommendation, a letter describing their career aspirations (including their course of study and plans for completion of a degree), and a transcript of high school or college grades (depending on which they are currently attending). Selection is based on academic merit and personal achievement. Financial need is not normally a selection criterion but in some cases of extreme need it may be used as a factor; the lack of financial need, however, is never a cause for non-selection.
Financial data The stipend is $10,000; funds are sent directly to the recipient's college or university.
Duration 1 year.
Additional information Membership in the AUSA is open to everyone who supports a strong national defense, with special concern for the Army. That includes Regular Army, National Guard, Army Reserve, government civilians, retired soldiers, Wounded Warriors, veterans, concerned citizens and family members.
Number awarded 2 each year.
Deadline June of each year.

[785]
JOSEPH P. GAVENONIS SCHOLARSHIPS

American Legion
Department of Pennsylvania
Attn: Scholarship Endowment Fund
P.O. Box 2324
Harrisburg, PA 17105-2324
(717) 730-9100   Fax: (717) 975-2836
E-mail: hq@pa-legion.com
Web: www.pa-legion.com

Summary To provide financial assistance to the children and grandchildren of members of the American Legion in Pennsylvania who plan to attend college in the state.
Eligibility This program is open to seniors at high schools in Pennsylvania who are planning to attend a 4-year college or university in the state. Applicants must have a parent or grandparent who has been in the military or is in the military and is a member of an American Legion Post in Pennsylvania. First preference is given to the children of Legion members who are deceased, killed in action, or missing in action. Financial need is considered in the selection process.
Financial data The stipend is $1,000 per year. Funds are sent directly to the student.
Duration 4 years, provided the recipient maintains a GPA of 2.5 or higher each semester.
Number awarded 1 or more each year.
Deadline May of each year.

[786]
JUDITH HAUPT MEMBER'S CHILD SCHOLARSHIP

Navy Wives Clubs of America
c/o NSA Mid-South
Attn: Melissa Worthey, National President
P.O. Box 54022
Millington, TN 38054-0022
Toll Free: (866) 511-NWCA
E-mail: nwca@navywivesclubsofamerica.org
Web: www.navywivesclubsofamerica.org/scholarships

Summary To provide financial assistance for college to the children of members of the Navy Wives Clubs of America (NWCA).

Eligibility This program is open to students currently enrolled at accredited college or university whose parent has been an NWCA member for at least 1 year. Along with their application, they must submit a brief statement on why they feel they should be awarded this scholarship and any special circumstances (financial or other) they wish to have considered. Financial need is also considered in the selection process.
Financial data A stipend is provided (amount not specified).
Duration 1 year.
Additional information Membership in the NWCA is open to spouses of enlisted personnel serving in the Navy, Marine Corps, Coast Guard, and the active Reserve units of those services; spouses of enlisted personnel who have been honorably discharged, retired, or transferred to the Fleet Reserve on completion of duty; and widows of enlisted personnel in those services.
Number awarded 1 each year.
Deadline March of each year.

[787]
KANSAS TUITION WAIVER FOR DEPENDENTS AND SPOUSES OF DECEASED MILITARY PERSONNEL
Kansas Board of Regents
Attn: Student Financial Aid
1000 S.W. Jackson Street, Suite 520
Topeka, KS 66612-1368
(785) 430-4255   Fax: (785) 430-4233
E-mail: scholars@ksbor.org
Web: www.kansasregents.org/scholarships_and_grants

Summary To provide financial assistance for college to residents of Kansas whose parent or spouse died on active military service after September 11, 2001.
Eligibility This program is open to residents of Kansas who are the dependent children or spouses of members of the U.S. armed forces who died on or after September 11, 2001 while, and as a result of, serving on active military duty. The deceased military member must have been a resident of Kansas at the time of death. Applicants must be enrolled or planning to enroll at a public educational institution in Kansas, including area vocational/technical schools and colleges, community colleges, the state universities, and Washburn University.
Financial data Qualifying students are permitted to enroll at an approved Kansas institution without payment of tuition or fees. They are responsible for other costs, such as books, room, and board.
Duration 1 year; may be renewed for a total of 10 semesters of undergraduate study.
Additional information This program began in 2005.
Number awarded Varies each year.
Deadline Deadline not specified.

[788]
KANSAS VFW ENDOWMENT SCHOLARSHIP
Veterans of Foreign Wars of the United States- Department of Kansas
Attn: VFW Endowment Association
115 S.W. Gage Boulevard
P.O. Box 1008
Topeka, KS 66601-1008
(785) 272-6463   Fax: (785) 272-2629
E-mail: ksvfwhq@kvfw.kscoxmail.com
Web: www.ksvfw.org/programs.html

Summary To provide financial assistance to residents of Kansas who are related to members of the Veterans of Foreign Wars (VFW) or the VFW Auxiliary and interested in attending college in any state.
Eligibility This program is open to residents of Kansas who are graduating high school seniors, holders of a high school diploma equivalent, or students already enrolled at a college, university, or vocational school in any state. Applicants must be the child or grandchild of an active or deceased member of the VFW or the VFW Auxiliary. Along with their application, they must submit transcripts that include ACT scores (the ACT score requirement may be waived if the applicant is 25 years of age or older), information on extracurricular activities, statements on their career plans reasons for furthering their education, and documentation of financial need.
Financial data Stipends range from $500 to $2,000 per year.
Duration 1 year; may be renewed up to 3 additional years.
Number awarded 1 or more each year.
Deadline January of each year.

[789]
KATHERN F. GRUBER SCHOLARSHIPS
Blinded Veterans Association
Attn: Scholarship Coordinator
125 North West Street, Third Floor
Alexandria, VA 22314
(202) 371-8880, ext. 330   Toll Free: (800) 669-7079
Fax: (202) 371-8258   E-mail: bjones@bva.org
Web: www.bva.org

Summary To provide financial assistance for undergraduate or graduate study to immediate family of blinded veterans and servicemembers.
Eligibility This program is open to dependent children, grandchildren, and spouses of blinded veterans and active-duty blinded servicemembers of the U.S. armed forces. The veteran or servicemember must be legally blind; the blindness may be either service-connected or nonservice-connected. Applicants must have been accepted or be currently enrolled as a full-time student in an undergraduate or graduate program at an accredited institution of higher learning. Along with their application, they must submit a 300-word essay on their career goals and aspirations. Financial need is not considered in the selection process.
Financial data The stipend is $2,000; funds are intended to be used to cover the student's expenses, including tuition, other academic fees, books, dormitory fees, and cafeteria fees. Funds are paid directly to the recipient's school.
Duration 1 year; recipients may reapply for up to 3 additional years.

Number awarded 6 each year.
Deadline April of each year.

[790]
KENTUCKY VETERANS TUITION WAIVER PROGRAM

Kentucky Department of Veterans Affairs
Attn: Tuition Waiver Coordinator
1111B Louisville Road
Frankfort, KY 40601
(502) 564-9203 Toll Free: (800) 572-6245 (within KY)
Fax: (502) 564-9240 E-mail: kdva.tuitionwaiver@ky.gov
Web: www.veterans.ky.gov

Summary To provide financial assistance for college to the children, spouses, or unremarried widows or widowers of disabled or deceased Kentucky veterans.

Eligibility This program is open to the children, stepchildren, spouses, and unremarried widows or widowers of veterans who are residents of Kentucky (or were residents at the time of their death). The qualifying veteran must meet 1 of the following conditions: 1) died on active duty (regardless of wartime service); 2) died as a result of a service-connected disability (regardless of wartime service); 3) has a 100% service-connected disability; 4) is totally disabled (nonservice-connected) with wartime service; or 5) is deceased and served during wartime. The military service may have been as a member of the U.S. armed forces, the Kentucky National Guard, or a Reserve component; service in the Guard or Reserves must have been on state active duty, active duty for training, inactive duty training, or active duty with the U.S. armed forces. Children of veterans must be under 26 years of age; no age limit applies to spouses or unremarried widows or widowers. All applicants must be attending or planning to attend a 2-year, 4-year, or vocational technical school operated and funded by the Kentucky Department of Education.

Financial data Eligible dependents and survivors are exempt from tuition and matriculation fees at any state-supported institution of higher education in Kentucky.

Duration Tuition is waived until the recipient completes 45 months of training, receives a college degree, or (in the case of children of veterans) reaches 26 years of age, whichever comes first. Spouses and unremarried widows or widowers are not subject to the age limitation.

Number awarded Varies each year.
Deadline Deadline not specified.

[791]
KIYOKO TSUBOI TAUBKIN LEGACY SCHOLARSHIP

Japanese American Veterans Association
Attn: Chris DeRosa, Scholarship Committee Chair
P.O. Box 341198
Bethesda, MD 20827
E-mail: javascholarship222@gmail.com
Web: www.java.wildapricot.org

Summary To provide financial assistance for college to relatives of Japanese American veterans.

Eligibility This program is open to students who have completed at least 1 year of an undergraduate program at a 4-year college or university. Applicants must be 1) a direct or collateral descendant of a person who served with the 442nd Regimental Combat Team, the 100th Infantry Battalion, Military Intelligence Service, 1399th Engineering Construction Battalion, or other unit associated with those during or after World War II; or 2) a member or child of a member of the Japanese American Veterans Association (JAVA) whose membership extends back at least 1 year. Along with their application, they must submit a 500-word essay on what winning this scholarship will mean to them.

Financial data The stipend is $2,000.
Duration 1 year.
Number awarded 1 each year.
Deadline March of each year.

[792]
KOREA VETERANS SCHOLARSHIP PROGRAM

Korean War Veterans Association
Attn: American Veterans of Korea Foundation
Scholarship Selection Committee
635 Glover Drive
Lancaster, PA 17601-4110
Web: www.kwva.us/?page=blog

Summary To provide financial assistance to high school seniors and current undergraduate and graduate students who are the descendants of Korean War veterans.

Eligibility This program is open to U.S. citizens who are working full time on an associate, bachelor's, or advanced degree in any discipline. Applicants must be the child, grandchild, or great-grandchild of a veteran who served in Korea and is a regular member of the Korean War Veterans Association. They must have a GPA of 3.5 or higher. Along with their application, they must submit an essay of 300 to 400 words on a topic that changes annually; recently, students were asked to write on the historical lessons learned from the Korean War. Selection is based on scholastic activities, extracurricular activities, community activities, and employment history (including military service).

Financial data The stipend is $2,000 per year.
Duration 1 year; recipients may reapply.
Number awarded Varies each year.
Deadline June of each year.

[793]
KOREAN WAR VETERANS ASSOCIATION SCHOLARSHIPS

Korean War Veterans Association
Attn: Scholarship Coordinator
13730 Loumont Street
Whittier, CA 90601

Summary To provide financial assistance for college to descendants of Army veterans who served in Korea during or prior to the war there.

Eligibility This program is open to the children, grandchildren, and great-grandchildren of veterans who served on active duty in the U.S. Army in Korea between August 15, 1945 and December 31, 1955. Applicants must be attending or planning to attend an accredited college or university. Along with their application, they must submit an essay describing their educational and career goals, why they think they should receive this scholarship, and where they learned about it. Selection is based on academic achievement (GPA of 2.75 or higher), extracurricular activities, and financial need.

Financial data The stipend depends on the need of the recipient, to a maximum of $5,000 per year.

Duration 1 year; may be renewed up to 3 additional years or until completion of a bachelor's degree.
Number awarded Varies each year; recently, 5 were awarded.
Deadline April of each year.

[794]
KOREAN WAR VETERAN'S CHILDREN'S CC SCHOLARSHIP

Hawai'i Community Foundation
Attn: Scholarship Department
827 Fort Street Mall
Honolulu, HI 96813
(808) 566-5570   Toll Free: (888) 731-3863
Fax: (808) 521-6286
E-mail: scholarships@hcf-hawaii.org
Web: hcf.scholarships.ngwebsolutions.com

Summary To provide financial assistance to descendants of veterans, especially those who served during the Korean War, and are attending a community college in any state.
Eligibility This program is open to residents of any state who are direct descendants of, in order of preference, 1) Korean War veterans who died in combat; 2) veterans who served during the Korean War; and 3) veterans who either died or served in a foreign war. Applicants must be enrolled full time at an accredited 2-year college in the United States (including U.S. territories). They must have a GPA of 3.0 or higher and be able to demonstrate financial need. Along with their application, they must submit a personal statement that includes 1) 900 words each on their reasons for attending college, why they chose their course of study, and their career goals; and 2) 600 words on how they plan to give back to Hawaii.
Financial data The amounts of the awards depend on the availability of funds and the need of the recipient. Recently, the average value of the scholarships awarded by the foundation was approximately $2,500.
Duration 1 year.
Additional information This program began in 2012.
Number awarded 1 or more each year.
Deadline February of each year.

[795]
KOREAN WAR VETERAN'S CHILDREN'S SCHOLARSHIP

Hawai'i Community Foundation
Attn: Scholarship Department
827 Fort Street Mall
Honolulu, HI 96813
(808) 566-5570   Toll Free: (888) 731-3863
Fax: (808) 521-6286
E-mail: scholarships@hcf-hawaii.org
Web: hcf.scholarships.ngwebsolutions.com

Summary To provide financial assistance to descendants of veterans, especially those who served during the Korean War, and are attending a college or university in any state.
Eligibility This program is open to residents of any state who are direct descendants of, in order of preference, 1) Korean War veterans who died in combat; 2) veterans who served during the Korean War; and 3) veterans who either died or served in a foreign war. Applicants must be enrolled full time at an accredited 4-year college or university in the United States (including U.S. territories). They must have a GPA of 3.0 or higher and be able to demonstrate financial need. Along with their application, they must submit a personal statement that includes 1) 900 words each on their reasons for attending college, why they chose their course of study, and their career goals; and 2) 600 words on how they plan to give back to Hawaii.
Financial data The amounts of the awards depend on the availability of funds and the need of the recipient. Recently, the average value of the scholarships awarded by the foundation was approximately $2,500.
Duration 1 year.
Additional information This program began in 2012.
Number awarded 1 or more each year.
Deadline February of each year.

[796]
LA FRA NATIONAL PRESIDENT'S SCHOLARSHIP

Ladies Auxiliary of the Fleet Reserve Association
c/o Amanda Murray, National Scholarship Chair
512 Hyde Park Road
Norfolk, VA 23503-5514
(757) 588-6125   E-mail: sairockstar@gmail.com
Web: www.la-fra.org/scholarship.html

Summary To provide financial assistance for college to the children and grandchildren of living or deceased members of the Fleet Reserve Association (FRA) or its Ladies Auxiliary (LA).
Eligibility This program is open to the children and grandchildren of FRA or LA FRA members or deceased members. Applicants must submit an essay on their life experiences, career objectives, and what motivated them to select those objectives. Selection is based on academic record, financial need, extracurricular activities, leadership skills, and participation in community activities. U.S. citizenship is required.
Financial data The stipend is $2,500.
Duration 1 year; may be renewed.
Additional information Membership in the FRA is open to current and former enlisted members of the Navy, Marine Corps, and Coast Guard.
Number awarded 1 each year.
Deadline April of each year.

[797]
LA FRA SCHOLARSHIP

Ladies Auxiliary of the Fleet Reserve Association
c/o Amanda Murray, National Scholarship Chair
512 Hyde Park Road
Norfolk, VA 23503-5514
(757) 588-6125   E-mail: sairockstar@gmail.com
Web: www.la-fra.org/scholarship.html

Summary To provide financial assistance for college to the children and grandchildren of members of the Fleet Reserve Association (FRA) or its Ladies Auxiliary (LA).
Eligibility This program is open to the children and grandchildren of FRA or LA FRA members. Applicants must submit an essay on their life experiences, career objectives, and what motivated them to select those objectives. Selection is based on academic record, financial need, extracurricular activities, leadership skills, and participation in community activities. U.S. citizenship is required.

Financial data The stipend is $2,500.
Duration 1 year; may be renewed.
Additional information Membership in the FRA is open to current and former enlisted members of the Navy, Marine Corps, and Coast Guard.
Number awarded 1 each year.
Deadline April of each year.

[798]
LAURA BLACKBURN MEMORIAL SCHOLARSHIP

American Legion Auxiliary
Department of Kentucky
134 Walnut Street
Frankfort, KY 40601
(502) 352-2380   Fax: (502) 352-2381
E-mail: aladeptaux@yahoo.com
Web: www.kyamlegionaux.org/scholarships

Summary To provide financial assistance to descendants of veterans in Kentucky who plan to attend college in any state.
Eligibility This program is open to the children, grandchildren, and great-grandchildren of veterans who served in the armed forces during eligibility dates for membership in the American Legion. Applicants must be Kentucky residents enrolled in their senior year at an accredited high school. They must be planning to attend a college or university in any state. Along with their application, they must submit transcripts that include SAT and/or ACT scores, letters of recommendation, a copy of the veteran's discharge papers, and a 1,000-word essay on the value of education in a democratic society. Selection is based on academic achievement (40%), character (20%), leadership (20%), and Americanism (20%).
Financial data The stipend is $1,000.
Duration 1 year.
Number awarded 1 each year.
Deadline March of each year.

[799]
LEIDOS STEM SCHOLARSHIP

Anchor Scholarship Foundation
Attn: Executive Director
138 South Rosemont Road, Suite 206
Virginia Beach, VA 23452
(757) 777-4724
E-mail: Joy.Eyrolles@anchorscholarship.com
Web: www.anchorscholarship.com

Summary To provide financial assistance for college to dependents of current or former personnel serving in the Naval Surface Forces who plan to study a field of STEM.
Eligibility This program is open to dependent children of active-duty, honorably-discharged, or retired personnel who have served at least 6 years (need not be consecutive) in a unit under the administrative control of Commander, Naval Surface Forces, U.S. Atlantic Fleet or U.S. Pacific Fleet. Applicants must be high school seniors planning to attend an accredited 4-year college or university and work full time on a bachelor's degree in a field of STEM. The sponsor must have a Surface Warfare qualification (SWO/ESWS). Selection is based on academic performance, extracurricular activities, character, and financial need.
Financial data The stipend is $6,000.

Duration 1 year; nonrenewable.
Additional information This program is supported by Leidos.
Number awarded 1 each year.
Deadline February of each year.

[800]
LEO A. SEIGEL-DR. PHILIP SHAPIRO EDUCATION GRANT

Jewish War Veterans of the U.S.A.-New Jersey Chapter
Attn: Grant Committee
171 Jersey Street, Building 5, Room 232
Trenton, NJ 08611-3111
(609) 396-2508   Fax: (609) 571-3767
E-mail: JWVDeptNJ@gmail.com
Web: www.jwv-nj.org/?page_id=31

Summary To provide financial assistance to high school seniors in New Jersey who are descendants of members of the Jewish War Veterans (JWV) of the U.S.A and planning to attend college in any state.
Eligibility This program is open to seniors graduating from public or private high schools in New Jersey and planning to attend an accredited college, university, community college, or hospital school of nursing in any state. Applicants must be the child, grandchild, or great-grandchild of a veteran who has been a JWV member for at least 3 consecutive years or, if deceased, was a member at time of death. They must rank in the top 25% of their class. Selection is based on class standing, SAT or ACT scores, GPA, and participation in extracurricular activities (school, Jewish community, and community at large).
Financial data Stipends are $2,000, $1,500, or $1,000.
Duration 1 year.
Number awarded 3 each year: 1 each at $2,000, $1,500, and $1,000.
Deadline May of each year.

[801]
LEONARDO DRS GUARDIAN SCHOLARSHIP

National Guard Educational Foundation
Attn: Scholarship Fund
One Massachusetts Avenue, N.W.
Washington, DC 20001
(202) 789-0031   Fax: (202) 682-9358
E-mail: ngef@ngaus.org
Web: www.ngef.org

Summary To provide financial assistance for college to children of members of the National Guard who died in service.
Eligibility This program is open to 1) high school juniors and seniors who have been accepted to an accredited community college, technical school, or 4-year college or university and have a GPA of 3.0 or higher; and 2) students who are currently enrolled full time at an accredited community college, technical school, or 4-year college or university and have a GPA of 2.5 or higher. Applicants must be the dependent child of a National Guard member who died in an operational or training mission in support of Operation Enduring Freedom, Operation Iraqi Freedom, or Operation New Dawn. The educational institution they are attending or planning to attend must be located in the 50 states, the District of Columbia, Puerto Rico, the U.S. Virgin Islands, or Guam. Along with

their application, they must submit a 1-page essay on their deceased parent, transcripts, and documentation of financial need.

Financial data The stipend is $6,250 per year.

Duration 1 year; may be renewed 1 additional year by students at community colleges and technical schools and up to 3 additional years by students at 4-year colleges and universities.

Additional information This program was established in 2011 by DRS Technologies, Inc., a defense contractor headquartered in Arlington, Virginia.

Number awarded Varies each year; recently, 7 new and 5 renewal scholarships were awarded. Since the program began, it has awarded scholarships to 80 students.

Deadline June of each year.

[802]
LIEUTENANT GENERAL CLARENCE L. HUEBNER SCHOLARSHIPS

Society of the First Infantry Division
Attn: 1st Infantry Division Foundation
P.O. Box 607
Ambler, PA 19002
(215) 740-0669   E-mail: 1stidfdnpa@gmail.com
Web: www.1stid.org/scholarships

Summary To provide financial support for college to the children or grandchildren of members of the First Infantry Division.

Eligibility This program is open to high school seniors who are the children, grandchildren, or great-grandchildren of soldiers who served in the First Infantry Division of the U.S. Army. Applicants must submit academic transcripts, letters of recommendation, and a personal statement of their career objectives, goals, and why they should be awarded this scholarship. Selection is based on the essay, academic achievement, extracurricular activities, community service, and work experience.

Financial data The stipend is $2,500 per year, payable to the recipient's school annually.

Duration 4 years.

Number awarded Varies each year; recently, 5 were awarded.

Deadline May of each year.

[803]
LILLIAN CAMPBELL MEDICAL SCHOLARSHIP

VFW Auxiliary-Department of Wisconsin
c/o Donna Butler, Department Scholarship Chair
522 Topaz Lane
Madison, WI 53714
(608) 695-0261   E-mail: butlerdonna999@yahoo.com
Web: www.wivfwaux.org/department-scholarships.html

Summary To provide financial assistance to students working on a degree in a medical field in Wisconsin who served in the military or are related to a person who did.

Eligibility This program is open to students who have completed at least 1 year of study in Wisconsin in a program in 1) a medical field, including nursing, pharmacy, physician assistant, medical or surgical technology, physical or occupational therapy, dental hygiene, radiology, or other related medical profession; or 2) an emergency medical technician field (EMT), including paramedic studies. Applicants or a member of their immediate family (parent, sibling, child, spouse, or grandparent) must have served in the military. They must have a high school diploma or GED but may be of any age. Along with their application, they must submit a 200-word essay on why they are studying this medical profession. Financial need is considered in the selection process.

Financial data The stipend is $1,000 for students in a medical field or $750 for EMT students.

Duration 1 year.

Number awarded 1 for a student in a medical field and 1 for an EMT student.

Deadline March of each year.

[804]
LILLIE LOIS FORD SCHOLARSHIPS

American Legion
Department of Missouri
3341 American Avenue
P.O. Box 179
Jefferson City, MO 65102-0179
(573) 893-2353   Toll Free: (800) 846-9023
Fax: (573) 893-2980   E-mail: info@missourilegion.org
Web: www.missourilegion.org/scholarships

Summary To provide financial assistance for college to descendants of Missouri veterans who have participated in specified American Legion programs.

Eligibility This program is open to the unmarried children, grandchildren, and great-grandchildren under 21 years of age of honorably-discharged Missouri veterans who served at least 90 days on active duty. Applicants must be enrolled or planning to enroll at an accredited college or university in any state as a full-time student. Boys must have attended a complete session of Missouri Boys State or Cadet Patrol Academy. Girls must have attended a complete session of Missouri Girls State or Cadet Patrol Academy. Financial need is considered in the selection process.

Financial data The stipend is $1,000.

Duration 1 year (the first year of college).

Number awarded 2 each year: 1 for a boy and 1 for a girl.

Deadline April of each year.

[805]
LORETTA CORNETT-HUFF SCHOLARSHIPS

Council of College and Military Educators
c/o Jim Yeonopolus, Scholarship Committee Chair
Central Texas College
P.O. Box 1800
Killeen, TX 76540-1800
(254) 526-1781   Fax: (254) 526-1750
E-mail: jim.yeonopolus@ctcd.edu
Web: www.ccmeonline.org/scholarships

Summary To provide financial assistance to spouses of members of the armed services who are interested in working on an undergraduate or master's degree.

Eligibility This program is open to spouses of members of the uniformed services, including active, National Guard, and Reserves. Applicants must be currently enrolled full time at an accredited institution that is a member of the Council of College and Military Educators (CCME) and working on an associate, bachelor's, or master's degree. Undergraduates must have a GPA of 2.5 or higher and graduate students must have a GPA of 3.0 or higher. Along with their application, they

must submit an essay of 400 to 750 words on their most meaningful achievements and how those relate to their field of study and their future goals. Financial need is not considered in the selection process.
Financial data The stipend is $1,000.
Duration 1 year.
Number awarded 5 each year.
Deadline September of each year.

[806]
LOUIS J. SCHOBER MEMORIAL SCHOLARSHIP
Society of American Military Engineers-Louisiana Post
c/o Chris Dunn, Young Members Committee Chair
U.S. Army Corps of Engineers, New Orleans District
7400 Leake Avenue
P.O. Box 60267
New Orleans, LA 70160
(504) 862-1799
E-mail: Christopher.L.Dunn@usace.army.mil
Web: www.same.org

Summary To provide financial assistance to engineering students at universities in Louisiana and to children of members of the Louisiana Post of the Society of American Military Engineers (SAME) at schools in any state.
Eligibility This program is open to students currently working on an undergraduate degree in engineering. Applicants must be either 1) enrolled at a college or university in Louisiana; or 2) the children of a member of the SAME Louisiana Post (who may be studying at a college or university in any state). Graduate students are not eligible; high school seniors may be considered if no suitable college students apply. Selection is based primarily on academic record and demonstration of leadership characteristics; other factors considered are participation in SAME posts and activities, enrollment in an ROTC program, former or current military service, and participation in school and community activities.
Financial data The stipend is $2,000.
Duration 1 year; nonrenewable.
Number awarded 1 or more each year.
Deadline April of each year.

[807]
LOUISIANA TITLE 29 DEPENDENTS' EDUCATIONAL ASSISTANCE
Louisiana Department of Veterans Affairs
Attn: Education Program
602 North Fifth Street
Baton Rouge, LA 70802
(225) 219-5000   Toll Free: (877) GEAUX-VA
Fax: (225) 219-5590   E-mail: veteran@la.gov
Web: www.vetaffairs.la.gov/benefit-category/education

Summary To provide financial assistance to children, spouses, and surviving spouses of certain disabled or deceased Louisiana veterans who plan to attend college in the state.
Eligibility This program is open to children (between 16 and 25 years of age), spouses, or surviving spouses of veterans who served during specified periods of wartime and 1) were killed in action or died in active service; 2) died of a service-connected disability; 3) are missing in action (MIA) or a prisoner of war (POW); 4) sustained a disability rated as 90% or more by the U.S. Department of Veterans Affairs; or 5) have been determined to be unemployable as a result of a service-connected disability. Deceased, MIA, and POW veterans must have resided in Louisiana for at least 12 months prior to entry into service. Living disabled veterans must have resided in Louisiana for at least 24 months prior to the child's or spouse's admission into the program.
Financial data Eligible persons accepted as full-time students at Louisiana state-supported colleges, universities, trade schools, or vocational/technical schools are admitted free and are exempt from payment of tuition, laboratory, athletic, medical, and other special fees. Free registration does not cover books, supplies, room and board, or fees assessed by the student body on themselves (such as yearbooks and weekly papers).
Duration Support is provided for a maximum of 4 school years, to be completed in not more than 5 years from date of original entry.
Additional information Attendance must be on a full-time basis. Surviving spouses must remain unremarried and must take advantage of the benefit within 10 years after eligibility is established.
Number awarded Varies each year.
Deadline Applications must be received no later than 3 months prior to the beginning of a semester.

[808]
LOWE'S AMVETS TECHNOLOGY SCHOLARSHIPS
AMVETS National Headquarters
Attn: National Programs Director
4647 Forbes Boulevard
Lanham, MD 20706-3807
(301) 459-9600   Toll Free: (877) 7-AMVETS, ext. 4027
Fax: (301) 459-7924   E-mail: klathroum@amvets.org
Web: www.amvets.org

Summary To provide financial assistance to veterans, military personnel, and their spouses who are working on a degree in computer sciences.
Eligibility This program is open to veterans, active-duty military members, and their spouses who are U.S. citizens; children are not eligible. Applicants must be enrolled as sophomores, juniors, or seniors at a college or university and working on a degree in computer science. They must have a GPA of 3.0 or higher.
Financial data Stipends range up to $5,000.
Duration 1 year.
Additional information This program is supported by Lowe's.
Number awarded 10 each year.
Deadline July of each year.

[809]
LT. COL. ROMEO AND JOSEPHINE BASS FERRETTI SCHOLARSHIP
Air Force Association
Attn: Scholarships
1501 Lee Highway
Arlington, VA 22209-1198
(703) 247-5800, ext. 4868
Toll Free: (800) 727-3337, ext. 4868
Fax: (703) 247-5853   E-mail: scholarships@afa.org
Web: www.app.smarterselect.com

Summary To provide financial assistance to dependents of Air Force enlisted personnel who are high school seniors planning to attend college to major in a field of STEM.
Eligibility This program is open to dependents of Air Force active duty, Reserve, or Air National Guard enlisted personnel who are graduating high school seniors. Applicants must be planning to enroll full time at an accredited institute of higher education to work on an undergraduate degree in a field of STEM. Along with their application, they must submit a 600-word essay on their academic and personal achievements and goals and how this scholarship will help them accomplish their goals. Selection is based on academic achievement, character, and financial need.
Financial data The stipend is $5,000.
Duration 1 year; nonrenewable.
Number awarded 1 each year.
Deadline April of each year.

[810]
LT. JON C. LADDA MEMORIAL FOUNDATION SCHOLARSHIP

Lt. Jon C. Ladda Memorial Foundation
7 Gillette Way
Farmington, CT 06032
E-mail: info@jonladda.org
Web: www.jonladda.org/scholarship.htm

Summary To provide financial assistance for college to children of deceased and disabled U.S. Naval Academy graduates and members of the Navy submarine service.
Eligibility This program is open to children of U.S. Naval Academy graduates and members of the U.S. Navy submarine service. The parent must have died on active duty or been medically retired with a 100% disability. Applicants must be enrolled or accepted at a 4-year college or university, including any of the service academies. Along with their application, they must submit an essay on a topic that changes annually. Selection is based on academic achievement, financial need, and merit.
Financial data A stipend is awarded (amount not specified). Funds are disbursed directly to the recipient's institution.
Duration 1 year; may be renewed.
Number awarded 1 or more each year.
Deadline March of each year.

[811]
LTC MICHAEL WARREN MEMORIAL SCHOLARSHIPS

National Guard Association of Arizona
Attn: Scholarship Committee
5640 East McDowell Road
Phoenix, AZ 85008
(602) 275-8305   Fax: (602) 275-9254
E-mail: ngaofaz@aol.com
Web: www.ngaaz.org

Summary To provide financial assistance to students at colleges and universities in Arizona who have a connection to the National Guard and the National Guard Association of Arizona (NGAAZ).
Eligibility This program is open to full-time students at colleges, universities, and community colleges in Arizona. Applicants must be a member of 1 of the following categories: 1) a current enlisted member of the Arizona National Guard; 2) a current officer member of the Arizona National Guard who is also a member of the NGAAZ; or 3) a child or spouse of an NGAAZ member. Applicants must submit 2 letters of recommendation and verification of good standing from the first commander in the chain of command of the Arizona National Guard. Selection is based on GPA (25%), community service (15%), letters of recommendation (15%), knowledge of National Guard philosophy (15%), and financial need (30%).
Financial data The stipend is $1,000.
Duration 1 year; nonrenewable.
Number awarded 3 each year: 1 to each category of applicant.
Deadline March of each year.

[812]
LUCIAN BUTLER AMERICAN LEGION SCHOLARSHIP FUND

American Legion
Department of Virginia
1708 Commonwealth Avenue
Richmond, VA 23230
(804) 353-6606   Fax: (804) 358-1940
E-mail: eeccleston@valegion.org
Web: www.valegion.org

Summary To provide financial assistance to high school seniors in Virginia who are descendants of members of the American Legion family and planning to attend college in any state.
Eligibility This program is open to seniors graduating from high schools in Virginia and planning to enroll at an accredited 4-year college or university in any state. Applicants must be the child, stepchild, or grandchild of members of the American Legion family. Along with their application, they must submit brief statements on their job or work experiences, their most significant challenge or accomplishment and its value to their life, their long-range goals for school and career, the specific skills and personal values they want to foster in themselves to achieve those goals, any circumstances that may affect their family's ability to provide for their college education, their community service and volunteer work, and school and non-school activities and awards.
Financial data The stipend is $2,000 per year.
Duration 1 year; may be renewed, provided the recipient maintains a GPA of 3.5 or higher.
Number awarded Varies each year; recently, 2 were awarded.
Deadline February of each year.

[813]
MAINE VETERANS DEPENDENTS EDUCATIONAL BENEFITS

Bureau of Veterans' Services
117 State House Station
Augusta, ME 04333-0117
(207) 430-6035   Toll Free: (800) 345-0116 (within ME)
Fax: (207) 626-4471   E-mail: mainebvs@maine.gov
Web: www.maine.gov

Summary To provide financial assistance for undergraduate or graduate education to dependents of disabled and other Maine veterans.

Eligibility Applicants for these benefits must be children (high school seniors or graduates under 22 years of age), non-divorced spouses, or unremarried widow(er)s of veterans who meet 1 or more of the following requirements: 1) living and determined to have a total permanent disability resulting from a service-connected cause; 2) killed in action; 3) died from a service-connected disability; 4) died while totally and permanently disabled due to a service-connected disability but whose death was not related to the service-connected disability; or 5) a member of the armed forces on active duty who has been listed for more than 90 days as missing in action, captured, forcibly detained, or interned in the line of duty by a foreign government or power. The veteran parent must have been a resident of Maine at the time of entry into service or a resident of Maine for 5 years preceding application for these benefits. Children may be working on a certificate, associate degree, or bachelor's degree. Spouses, widows, and widowers may work on a certificate or an associate, bachelor's, or master's degree.
Financial data Recipients are entitled to free tuition at institutions of higher education supported by the state of Maine.
Duration Recipients are entitled to receive up to 120 credit hours of educational benefits and have 10 years from the date of first entrance to complete their program.
Additional information College preparatory schooling and correspondence courses are not supported under this program.
Number awarded Varies each year.
Deadline Deadline not specified.

[814]
MAINE VIETNAM VETERANS SCHOLARSHIP FUND
Maine Community Foundation
Attn: Program Director
245 Main Street
Ellsworth, ME 04605
(207) 667-9735
Toll Free: (877) 700-6800
Fax: (207) 667-0447
E-mail: info@mainecf.org
Web: www.mainecf.org

Summary To provide financial assistance for college or graduate school to Vietnam veterans or the dependents of Vietnam or other veterans in Maine.
Eligibility This program is open to residents of Maine who are Vietnam veterans or the descendants of veterans who served in the Vietnam Theater. As a second priority, children of veterans from other time periods are also considered. Graduating high school seniors, nontraditional students, undergraduates, and graduate students are eligible to apply. Selection is based on financial need, extracurricular activities, work experience, academic achievement, and a personal statement of career goals and how the applicant's educational plans relate to them.
Financial data The stipend is $1,000 per year.
Duration 1 year.
Additional information This program began in 1985. There is a $3 processing fee.
Number awarded 3 to 6 each year.
Deadline April of each year.

[815]
MAJOR GENERAL DUANE L. "DUKE" CORNING MEMORIAL SCHOLARSHIP
South Dakota National Guard Enlisted Association
c/o Derek Jaeger, Scholarship Chair
7713 West 53rd Street
Sioux Falls, SD 57106
E-mail: derek.e.jaeger.mil@mail.mil
Web: sdngea.com/programs/scholarships

Summary To provide financial assistance to current and retired members of the South Dakota National Guard Enlisted Association (SDNGEA), the National Guard Association of South Dakota (NGASD), or their dependents who are interested in attending college in any state.
Eligibility This program is open to current and retired members of the SDNGEA and the NGASD and the dependents of current and retired members of those associations. Applicants must be graduating high school seniors or full-time undergraduate students at a college or university in any state. They must submit a 300-page autobiography that includes their experiences to date and their hopes and plans for the future. Selection is based on the essay; awards, honors, and offices in high school, college, or trade school; GPA and ACT/SAT scores; letters of recommendation; and extracurricular and community activities and honors.
Financial data The stipend is $1,000.
Duration 1 year; nonrenewable.
Number awarded 2 each year.
Deadline March of each year.

[816]
MAJOR RICHARD L. RIDDER MEMORIAL SCHOLARSHIP
Central Indiana Community Foundation
Attn: Scholarship Program
615 North Alabama Street, Suite 119
Indianapolis, IN 46204-1498
(317) 634-2423
Fax: (317) 684-0943
E-mail: scholarships@cicf.org
Web: www.cicf.org/scholarships

Summary To provide financial assistance to children of current or former members of the Indiana National Guard who are interested in attending college in the state.
Eligibility This program is open to seniors graduating from high schools in Indiana who are a current or former member of the Indiana National Guard or the child of such a member. Applicants must be planning to attend a college, university, or vocational/technical school in any state. They must have a GPA of 2.0 or higher and be able to demonstrate financial need or other significant barrier to completing a postsecondary degree.
Financial data The stipend is at least $1,000.
Duration 1 year.
Number awarded 1 or more each year.
Deadline February of each year.

[817]
MANUELA NEHLS RE-ENTRY SCHOLARSHIPS
American GI Forum Colorado State Women
Attn: Kathleen Clenin, Scholarship Committee Chair
P.O. Box 11784
Denver, CO 80211
(303) 458-1700   Toll Free: (866) 244-3628
Fax: (303) 458-1634   E-mail: kathyclenin@comcast.net
Web: www.agifco.org

Summary To provide financial assistance to women from Colorado who are members of the American GI Forum and interested in attending college.

Eligibility This program is open to female residents of Colorado who have been members of the American GI Forum for at least 18 months. Applicants must be enrolled or planning to enroll in a certificate, vocational, or degree program at a school in any state. Along with their application, they must submit an essay of 250 to 500 words on their educational and career goals, why they should be selected to receive this award, and what they know about the American GI Forum. Selection is based on that essay, academic goals, extracurricular activities, and community service.

Financial data A stipend is awarded (amount not specified).

Duration 1 year; recipients may reapply.

Additional information The American GI Forum is the largest federally-chartered Hispanic veterans' organization in the United States.

Number awarded 1 or more each year.

Deadline April of each year.

[818]
MARC PURPLE HEART ENDOWMENT SCHOLARSHIP
Epsilon Sigma Alpha International
Attn: ESA Foundation
363 West Drake Road
Fort Collins, CO 80526
(970) 223-2824   Fax: (970) 223-4456
E-mail: esainfo@epsilonsigmaalpha.org
Web: scholarship.epsilonsigmaalpha.org

Summary To provide financial assistance for college to residents of any state who are relatives of recipients of a U.S. Armed Forces Purple Heart Medal.

Eligibility This program is open to residents of any state who are 1) graduating high school seniors with a GPA of 3.0 or higher; 2) enrolled in college with a GPA of 3.0 or higher; 3) enrolled at a technical school or returning to school after an absence for retraining of job skills or obtaining a degree; or 4) engaged in online study through an accredited college, university, or vocational school. Applicants must be the child, adopted child, stepchild, grandchild, or surviving spouse of a Purple Heart Medal recipient. They may be attending or planning to attend a school in any state and major in any field. Selection is based on service and leadership (50 points), financial need (20 points), and scholastic ability (20 points).

Financial data The stipend is $1,200.

Duration 1 year; may be renewed.

Additional information Epsilon Sigma Alpha (ESA) is a women's service organization, but scholarships are available to both men and women. This program was established by the Midwest Area Regional Council (MARC) of ESA, but it is available to residents of all states. A $5 processing fee is required. Completed applications must be submitted to the ESA state counselor who then verifies the information before forwarding them to the scholarship director.

Number awarded 1 each year.

Deadline January of each year.

[819]
MARCELLA ARNOLD NURSING SCHOLARSHIP
VFW Auxiliary-Department of Minnesota
Attn: Scholarship Committee
20 West 12th Street, Floor 3
St. Paul, MN 55155-2002
(651) 291-1759   Fax: (661) 291-7932
E-mail: vfwamn@vfwamn.org

Summary To provide financial assistance to residents of Minnesota who are either eligible for membership in the Veterans of Foreign Wars (VFW) or the VFW Auxiliary or the child or grandchild of a member and interested in studying nursing at a school in the state.

Eligibility This program is open to residents of Minnesota enrolled full time at a school or nursing in the state and working on an associate degree, bachelor's degree, or L.P.N. certificate; the scholarship is designed to help fund the final year of study. Applicants must be eligible to join the VFW or the VFW Auxiliary or be the child or grandchild of a VFW or Auxiliary member. Along with their application, they must submit essays on how the scholarship will make a difference for them and if they would be willing to work at a Veterans Administration medical center or veterans home.

Financial data A stipend is awarded (amount not specified).

Duration 1 year.

Additional information This program began in 1981.

Number awarded 1 each year.

Deadline March of each year for fall; September of each year for spring.

[820]
MARGENE MOGAN PROCTOR AND GENERAL JERRY WYATT MEMORIAL SCHOLARSHIP
National Guard Association of Tennessee Auxiliary
Attn: Scholarship Committee
4332 Kenilwood Drive
Nashville, TN 37204-4401
(615) 833-9100   Toll Free: (888) 642-8448 (within TN)
Fax: (615) 833-9173   E-mail: ngatnauxiliary@gmail.com

Summary To provide financial assistance to spouses of members of the Tennessee National Guard who are interested in attending college in any state.

Eligibility This program is open to spouses of current members of the Tennessee National Guard who are attending or planning to attend college in any state. Preference is given to members of the National Guard Association of Tennessee Auxiliary. Applicants must submit a personal statement on their reason for requesting the scholarship, their educational and career goals, and how this award can help them attain those goals. Financial need is also considered in the selection process.

Financial data The stipend is $1,500. Funds are sent directly to the recipient's institution.

Duration 1 year.

SCHOLARSHIPS: FAMILY MEMBERS

Number awarded 1 or more each year.
Deadline July of each year.

[821]
MARGUERITE MC'ALPIN MEMORIAL SCHOLARSHIP

American Legion Auxiliary
Department of Washington
Attn: Education Chair
3600 Ruddell Road S.E.
P.O. Box 5867
Lacey, WA 98509-5867
(360) 456-5995   Fax: (360) 491-7442
E-mail: secretary@walegion-aux.org
Web: www.walegion-aux.org/EducationScholarships.html

Summary To provide financial assistance to Washington veterans or their descendants who are interested in working on an undergraduate or graduate degree in nursing at a school in any state.

Eligibility This program is open to residents of Washington who are veterans or the children, grandchildren, and great-grandchildren of veterans. Applicants must be interested in studying nursing on the undergraduate or graduate level at a school in any state. Selection is based on a 300-word essay on their desire to study nursing, character, leadership, scholastic history, and financial need.

Financial data The stipend is $1,000.
Duration 1 year.
Number awarded 1 each year.
Deadline February of each year.

[822]
MARIA C. JACKSON/GENERAL GEORGE A. WHITE SCHOLARSHIP

Oregon Office of Student Access and Completion
Attn: Scholarships
1500 Valley River Drive, Suite 100
Eugene, OR 97401-2146
(541) 687-7400   Toll Free: (800) 452-8807
Fax: (541) 687-7414   TDD: (800) 735-2900
E-mail: osac@hecc.oregon.gov
Web: app.oregonstudentaid.gov/Catalog/Default.aspx

Summary To provide financial assistance to veterans and children of veterans and military personnel in Oregon who are interested in attending college or graduate school in the state.

Eligibility This program is open to residents of Oregon who served, or whose parents are serving or have served, in the U.S. armed forces. Applicants or their parents must have resided in Oregon at the time of enlistment. They must be enrolled or planning to enroll at a college or graduate school in the state. College and university undergraduates must have a GPA of 3.75 or higher, but there is no minimum GPA requirement for graduate students or those attending a technical school. Selection is based on scholastic ability and financial need.

Financial data Stipends for scholarships offered by the Oregon Office of Student Access and Completion (OSAC) range from $1,000 to $10,000 but recently averaged $4,710.
Duration 1 year.
Number awarded Varies each year.
Deadline February of each year.

[823]
MARIE KLUGOW MEMORIAL SCHOLARSHIPS

VFW Auxiliary-Department of California
Attn: Youth Activities Chair
9136 Elk Grove Boulevard
Elk Grove, CA 95624
(916) 509-8724   Fax: (916) 509-8754
E-mail: vfwauxca@gmail.com
Web: vfwauxca.org/di/vfw/v2/default.asp?pid=69480

Summary To provide financial assistance to children and grandchildren of members of the Veterans of Foreign Wars (VFW) or the VFW Auxiliary in California who are interested in attending college or nursing school in any state.

Eligibility This program is open to the children and grandchildren of members in good standing in a California VFW Post or VFW Auxiliary and to members of an Auxiliary. Applicants may be 1) graduating high school seniors; 2) students graduating from a community college or continuing as a full-time student at a 4-year college or university in any state; or 3) students preparing for a nursing career. They must have a GPA of 2.5 or higher and not have received a failing grade in any class. Graduating high school seniors must submit their SAT and/or ACT scores. Financial need is considered in the selection process. U.S. citizenship is required.

Financial data The stipend is $2,000 per year.
Duration 1 year; recipients may reapply for 1 additional year.
Additional information Until 2015, the VFW Auxiliary was named the Ladies Auxiliary to the Veterans of Foreign Wars.
Number awarded 3 each year: 1 to a graduating high school senior, 1 to a community college graduate or continuing university student, and 1 to a nursing student.
Deadline April of each year.

[824]
MARILYN HAINES MUSIC SCHOLARSHIP

Veterans of Foreign Wars of the United States-
  Department of Nebraska
Attn: Scholarship Chair
2431 North 48th Street
Lincoln, NE 68504
(402) 464-0674   Fax: (402) 464-0675
E-mail: Johnl@vfwne.org
Web: vfwne.com/di/vfw/v2/default.asp?pid=6204

Summary To provide financial assistance to members of the Veterans of Foreign Wars (VFW), the VFW Auxiliary, and their families in Nebraska who wish to study music at a college in the state.

Eligibility This program is open to members of the Nebraska chapter of the VFW, the VFW Auxiliary, and their spouses, children, stepchildren, and grandchildren. Applicants must be majoring in music and have completed at least 1 year of full-time study at a college or university in Nebraska. They must be able to demonstrate financial need.

Financial data A stipend is awarded (amount not specified).
Duration 1 year.
Number awarded 1 or more each year.
Deadline March of each year.

[825]
MARINE CORPS COUNTERINTELLIGENCE ASSOCIATION SCHOLARSHIPS

Marine Corps Counterintelligence Association
c/o Mike Dubrule, Scholarship Committee Chair
6818 South Dauphin Avenue
Tamps, FL 33611
E-mail: michaeldubrule@hotmail.com
Web: www.mccia.org/scholarship

Summary To provide financial assistance for college to dependents of members of the Marine Corps Counterintelligence Association (MCCIA).
Eligibility This program is open to children, grandchildren, and spouses of 1) current MCCIA members; 2) deceased Marines who were MCCIA members at the time of death; and 3) counterintelligence Marines who lost their lives in the line of duty (whether they were a member of MCCIA or not). Children and grandchildren must be younger than 25 years of age (may be extended 1 year for each year up to 5 years of active-duty military service). Spouses of deceased Marines must also be MCCIA Auxiliary members. Applicants must be enrolled or planning to enroll as a full-time undergraduate student at an accredited college or university and have a GPA of 3.0 or higher. Along with their application, they must submit a 1-page essay that describes their personal and professional goals and objectives, letters of recommendation, SAT or ACT scores, transcripts, copies of awards and other honors, and evidence of acceptance at a college or university. Financial need is not considered.
Financial data Stipends range up to $1,000. Funds must be used to help pay for tuition, books, fees, and materials; they may not be used for personal or living expenses.
Duration 1 year; may be renewed up to 4 additional years (need not be consecutive).
Number awarded Varies each year; recently, 6 were awarded.
Deadline June of each year.

[826]
MARINE CORPS LEAGUE SCHOLARSHIPS

Marine Corps League
Attn: Foundation
2904 Cross Creek Drive
Cumming, GA 30040
(404) 547-6631   E-mail: jerryholt813@gmail.com
Web: www.mclfoundation.org/scholarship-program

Summary To provide college aid to students whose parents served in the Marines and to members of the Marine Corps League or Marine Corps League Auxiliary.
Eligibility This program is open to 1) children of Marines, Navy FMF Corpsmen, and Navy Chaplains serving with Marine Units who were killed in action; 2) spouses, children, grandchildren, great-grandchildren, and stepchildren of active Marine Corps League and/or Auxiliary members; and 3) members of the Marine Corps League and/or Marine Corps League. Applicants must be seeking further education and training as a full-time student and be recommended by the commandant of an active chartered detachment of the Marine Corps League or the president of an active chartered unit of the Auxiliary. They must have a GPA of 3.0 or higher. Financial need is not considered in the selection process.
Financial data A stipend is awarded (amount not specified). Funds are paid directly to the recipient.
Duration 1 year; may be renewed up to 3 additional years upon reapplication.
Number awarded Varies, depending upon the amount of funds available each year.
Deadline July of each year.

[827]
MARINE CORPS SCHOLARSHIPS

Marine Corps Scholarship Foundation, Inc.
Attn: Scholarship Office
909 North Washington Street, Suite 400
Alexandria, VA 22314
(703) 549-0060   Toll Free: (866) 496-5462
Fax: (703) 549-9474   E-mail: students@mcsf.org
Web: www.mcsf.org/apply/eligibility

Summary To provide financial assistance for college to the children of present or former members of the U.S. Marine Corps.
Eligibility This program is open to the children of 1) Marines on active duty or in the Reserves; 2) veteran Marines who have received an honorable discharge or were killed while serving in the U.S. Marines; 3) active-duty, Reserve, or veteran U.S. Navy Corpsmen who are serving or have served with a U.S. Marine unit or were killed while serving with a Marine Corps unit; and 4) U.S. Navy Chaplains or Religious Program Specialists who are serving or have served with a U.S. Marine unit and have received an honorable discharge or were killed while serving with a Marine Corps unit. Applicants must be high school seniors, high school graduates, or current undergraduates in an accredited college, university, or postsecondary vocational/technical school. They must submit academic transcripts (GPA of 2.0 or higher); a written statement of service from their parent's commanding officer or a copy of their parent's honorable discharge; and a 500-word essay on a topic that changes periodically. Only undergraduate study is supported. The family income of applicants must be less than $103,000 per year.
Financial data Stipends range from $1,500 to $10,000 per year. Recently, awards averaged $3,470 per year.
Duration 1 year; may be renewed upon reapplication.
Additional information This program began in 1962.
Number awarded Varies each year; recently 2,360, worth more than $8,200,000, were awarded. Since the program began, it has awarded more than 40,000 scholarships, worth more than $135,000,000.
Deadline February of each year for college scholarships. Career and technical scholarships may be submitted at any time; they are processed monthly.

[828]
MARINE GUNNERY SERGEANT JOHN DAVID FRY SCHOLARSHIP

Department of Veterans Affairs
Attn: Veterans Benefits Administration
810 Vermont Avenue, N.W.
Washington, DC 20420
(202) 418-4343   Toll Free: (844) 698-2311
Web: www.va.gov

Summary To provide financial assistance to children and surviving spouses of military personnel who died in the line of duty on or after September 11, 2001.

Eligibility This program is open to the children and surviving spouses of active-duty members of the Armed Forces who have died in the line of duty on or after September 11, 2001. Applicants must be planning to enroll as undergraduates at a college or university. They must be at least 18 years of age, even if they have completed high school. Children are eligible until they reach 33 years of age. Spouses are eligible for 15 years after the death of the servicemember or until they remarry.

Financial data Eligible students receive full payment of tuition and fees at public schools in their state of residence. For students attending a private or foreign university, the maximum payment for tuition and fees is $22,805.34. A monthly living stipend based on the military housing allowance for the zip code where the school is located and an annual book and supplies allowance of $1,000 are also provided.

Duration Participants receive up to 36 months of entitlement.

Additional information This program began in 2009 as a component of the Post-9/11 GI Bill.

Number awarded Varies each year.

Deadline Deadline not specified.

[829]
MARINES' MEMORIAL FAMILY SCHOLARSHIPS

Marines' Memorial Association
c/o Marines Memorial Club and Hotel
609 Sutter Street
San Francisco, CA 94102
(415) 673-6672, ext. 293   Toll Free: (800) 5-MARINE
Fax: (415) 441-3649
E-mail: scholarship@marineclub.com
Web: www.marinesmemorial.org/members/scholarships

Summary To provide financial assistance for college to members of the Marines' Memorial Association from all branches of the armed forces and their descendants.

Eligibility This program is open to active members of the association and their children and grandchildren. Applicants must be high school seniors or students currently enrolled full time in an undergraduate degree program in any field at a college or university. Along with their application, they must submit an essay of up to 500 words on why they chose their specific path of study, what they hope to accomplish after graduation with their degree, and how their efforts will benefit others in their community. Graduating high school seniors must submit a high school transcript and SAT or ACT scores; continuing college students must submit a college transcript. Selection is based on the essay, academic merit, references, and financial need.

Financial data The stipend ranges from $2,500 to $5,000 per year.

Duration 1 year; recipients may reapply for up to 3 additional years.

Additional information Membership in the association is open to veterans of the Marines, Army, Navy, Air Force, or Coast Guard and to personnel currently serving in a branch of the armed forces.

Number awarded 8 each year.

Deadline April of each year.

[830]
MARION J. BAGLEY SCHOLARSHIP

American Legion Auxiliary
Department of New Hampshire
Attn: Department Auxiliary Secretary
121 South Fruit Street, Suite 103
Concord, NH 03301-2412
(603) 856-8942   E-mail: nhalasec@legionnh.org
Web: www.legionnh.org

Summary To provide financial assistance to members of the New Hampshire American Legion Auxiliary who plan to attend college in any state.

Eligibility This program is open to graduating high school seniors, graduates of a high school or equivalent, or students currently attending an institution of higher learning in any state. Applicants must be a resident of New Hampshire or have been a member of a unit of the American Legion Auxiliary in that state for at least 3 years. Along with their application, they must submit 3 letters of recommendation; a list of school, church, and community activities or organizations in which they have participated; transcripts; and a 1,000-word essay on "My Obligations as an American." Financial need is considered in the selection process.

Financial data The stipend is $1,000.

Duration 1 year.

Number awarded 1 each year.

Deadline March of each year.

[831]
MARITIME PATROL ASSOCIATION SCHOLARSHIPS

Wings Over America Scholarship Foundation
Attn: Scholarship Administrator
770 Lynnhaven Parkway, Suite 155
Virginia Beach, VA 23452
(757) 228-3532
E-mail: scholarship@wingsoveramerica.us
Web: www.wingsoveramerica.us/scholarships/administered

Summary To provide financial assistance for college to dependents of Navy personnel who have served or are serving in the Maritime Patrol and Reconnaissance community.

Eligibility This program is open to 1) children of a military sponsor who are graduating high school seniors planning to enroll in college full time to work on a bachelor's degree or who are already enrolled in such a program; and 2) spouses of a military sponsor currently enrolled full or part time and working on an associate or bachelor's degree at an accredited college or university. Children must be unmarried and younger than 22 years of age. The military sponsor must have completed at least 8 years of active-duty service in the Maritime Patrol and Reconnaissance community and be currently on active duty, honorably discharged, retired, or deceased. The minimum GPA is 3.0 for high school seniors or 2.5 for college students (children and spouses). Selection is based on academic achievement, extracurricular activities, work/internships, community service, recommendations, and an essay.

Financial data The basic stipend is $3,800.

Duration 1 year.

Additional information This program, which began in 2013, is sponsored by the Maritime Patrol Association.
Number awarded Varies each year; recently, 13 were awarded.
Deadline Pre-qualification forms must be submitted by January of each year.

[832]
MARK FORESTER SCHOLARSHIP
Combat Control Association
Attn: Foundation
P.O. Box 432
Mary Esther, FL 32569-0432
E-mail: admin@usafcca.org
Web: www.usafcca.org/wp/scholar

Summary To provide financial assistance for college to dependents of members of the Combat Control Association (CCA).
Eligibility This program is open to dependents of CCA members who are former, retired, or active duty/Guard/Reserve Air Force personnel who are serving or have served as a combat controller, combat control officer, or special tactics officer. Applicants must be working on an associate or bachelor's degree at an institution of higher learning and have a GPA of 2.5 or higher. Selection is based on academic achievement, extracurricular activities, and interests.
Financial data The stipend is $2,500.
Duration 1 year.
Number awarded 4 each year.
Deadline July of each year.

[833]
MARY BARRETT MARSHALL SCHOLARSHIP
American Legion Auxiliary
Department of Kentucky
134 Walnut Street
Frankfort, KY 40601
(502) 352-2380   Fax: (502) 352-2381
E-mail: aladeptaux@yahoo.com
Web: www.kyamlegionaux.org/scholarships

Summary To provide financial assistance to female dependents of veterans in Kentucky who plan to attend college in the state.
Eligibility This program is open to the daughters, wives, sisters, widows, granddaughters, or great-granddaughters of veterans eligible for membership in the American Legion who are high school seniors or graduates and 5-year residents of Kentucky. Applicants must be planning to attend a college or university in Kentucky.
Financial data The stipend is $1,000. The funds may be used for tuition, registration fees, laboratory fees, and books, but not for room and board.
Duration 1 year.
Number awarded 1 each year.
Deadline March of each year.

[834]
MARY PAOLOZZI MEMBER'S SCHOLARSHIP
Navy Wives Clubs of America
c/o NSA Mid-South
Attn: Melissa Worthey, National President
P.O. Box 54022
Millington, TN 38054-0022
Toll Free: (866) 511-NWCA
E-mail: nwca@navywivesclubsofamerica.org
Web: www.navywivesclubsofamerica.org/scholarships

Summary To provide financial assistance for undergraduate or graduate study to members of the Navy Wives Clubs of America (NWCA).
Eligibility This program is open to NWCA members who can demonstrate financial need. Applicants must be 1) a high school graduate or senior planning to attend college full time next year; 2) currently enrolled in an undergraduate program and planning to continue as a full-time undergraduate; 3) a college graduate or senior planning to be a full-time graduate student next year; or 4) a high school graduate or GED recipient planning to attend vocational or business school next year. Along with their application, they must submit a brief statement on why they feel they should be awarded this scholarship and any special circumstances (financial or other) they wish to have considered. Financial need is also considered in the selection process.
Financial data Stipends range from $500 to $1,000 each year (depending upon the donations from the NWCA chapters).
Duration 1 year.
Additional information Membership in the NWCA is open to spouses of enlisted personnel serving in the Navy, Marine Corps, Coast Guard, and the active Reserve units of those services; spouses of enlisted personnel who have been honorably discharged, retired, or transferred to the Fleet Reserve on completion of duty; and widows of enlisted personnel in those services.
Number awarded 1 each year.
Deadline March of each year.

[835]
MARY ROWENA COOPER SCHOLARSHIP
Winston-Salem Foundation
Attn: Student Aid Department
751 West Fourth Street, Suite 200
Winston-Salem, NC 27101-2702
(336) 714-3445   Toll Free: (866) 227-1209
Fax: (336) 727-0581
E-mail: StudentAid@wsfoundation.org
Web: www.wsfoundation.org/document.doc?id=170

Summary To provide financial assistance for college to children of veterans who served in Vietnam.
Eligibility This program is open to students currently enrolled at least half time at an accredited 2- or 4-year college, university, or vocational/technical school. Applicants must be the child of a living or deceased veteran who served in Vietnam. They must have a GPA of 2.0 or higher and be able to demonstrate financial need. U.S. citizenship is required.
Financial data A stipend is awarded (amount not specified).
Duration 1 year; nonrenewable.

Additional information This program began in 1991.
Number awarded 1 or more each year.
Deadline July of each year.

[836]
MARYANN K. MURTHA MEMORIAL SCHOLARSHIP

American Legion Auxiliary
Department of New York
1580 Columbia Turnpike
Building 1, Suite 3
Castleton-On-Hudson, NY 120330
(518) 463-1162   Toll Free: (800) 421-6348
Fax: (518) 449-5406 E-mail: nyaladeptoffice@gmail.com
Web: www.deptny.org/?page_id=2128

Summary To provide financial assistance to New York residents who are the descendants of veterans and interested in attending college in any state.
Eligibility This program is open to residents of New York who are high school seniors or graduates and attending or planning to attend an accredited college or university in any state. Applicants must be the children, grandchildren, or great-grandchildren of veterans who served during specified periods of wartime. Along with their application, they must submit a 700-word article describing their plans and goals for the future and how they hope to use their talent and education to help others. Selection is based on character (15%), Americanism (15%), community involvement (15%), leadership (15%), scholarship (20%), and financial need (20%). U.S. citizenship is required.
Financial data The stipend is $1,000. Funds are paid directly to the recipient's school.
Duration 1 year.
Number awarded 1 each year.
Deadline February of each year.

[837]
MARYLAND AMERICAN LEGION GENERAL SCHOLARSHIPS

American Legion
Department of Maryland
War Memorial Building
101 North Gay Street, Room E
Baltimore, MD 21202
(410) 752-1405   Fax: (410) 752-3822
E-mail: execsec@mdlegion.org
Web: www.mdlegion.org/formspage.htm

Summary To provide financial assistance to Maryland residents who are the children or grandchildren of veterans and interested in attending college in any state.
Eligibility This program is open to Maryland residents who are the children or grandchildren of veterans and younger than 20 years of age. Applicants must intend to enroll full time at a college or university in any state. Along with their application, they must submit a high school transcript that includes SAT scores and GPA, 3 letters of reference, and a brief essay describing their career objectives, why they require further education, and any extenuating circumstances. Financial need is not considered in the selection process.
Financial data Stipends are $1,500, $1,000, or $500.
Duration 1 year.

Number awarded Up to 11 each year: 1 at $1,500, 1 at $1,000, and 9 at $500.
Deadline April of each year.

[838]
MARYLAND VETERANS OF AFGHANISTAN AND IRAQ CONFLICTS SCHOLARSHIP PROGRAM

Maryland Higher Education Commission
Attn: Office of Student Financial Assistance
6 North Liberty Street, Ground Suite
Baltimore, MD 21201
(410) 767-3300   Toll Free: (800) 974-0203
Fax: (410) 332-0250   TDD: (800) 735-2258
E-mail: osfamail.mhec@maryland.gov
Web: www.mhec.maryland.gov

Summary To provide financial assistance for college to residents of Maryland who served in the armed forces in Afghanistan or Iraq and their children and spouses.
Eligibility This program is open to Maryland residents who are 1) a veteran who served at least 60 days in Afghanistan on or after October 24, 2001 or in Iraq on or after March 19, 2003; 2) an active-duty member of the armed forces who served at least 60 days in Afghanistan or Iraq on or after those dates; 3) a member of a Reserve component of the armed forces or the Maryland National Guard who was activated as a result of the Afghanistan or Iraq conflicts and served at least 60 days; and 4) the children and spouses of such veterans, active-duty armed forces personnel, or members of Reserve forces or Maryland National Guard. Applicants must be enrolled or accepted for enrollment in a regular undergraduate program at an eligible Maryland institution. In the selection process, veterans are given priority over dependent children and spouses.
Financial data The stipend is equal to 50% of the annual tuition, mandatory fees, and room and board of a resident undergraduate at a 4-year public institution within the University System of Maryland, currently capped at $7,316 per year for students who live on campus, at $4,570 for students who live with their parents, or at %5,140 for students who live off campus.
Duration 1 year; may be renewed for an additional 3 years of full-time study or 7 years of part-time study, provided the recipient remains enrolled in an eligible program with a GPA of 2.5 or higher.
Number awarded Varies each year.
Deadline February of each year.

[839]
MASTER SERGEANT NEAL BENSON ELBIT HONORARY SCHOLARSHIP

Army Scholarship Foundation
11700 Preston Road, Suite 660-301
Dallas, TX 75230
E-mail: ContactUs@armyscholarshipfoundation.org
Web: www.armyscholarshipfoundation.org/elbit.html

Summary To provide financial assistance for undergraduate study to the children and spouses of Army personnel who major in a field of STEM.
Eligibility This program is open to 1) children of regular active-duty, active-duty Reserve, and active-duty Army National Guard members in good standing; 2) spouses of serving enlisted regular active-duty, active-duty Reserve, and

active-duty Army National Guard members in good standing; and 3) children of former U.S. Army members who received an honorable or medical discharge or were killed while serving in the U.S. Army. Applicants must be high school seniors, high school graduates, or undergraduates enrolled at an accredited college, university, or vocational/technical institute and majoring or planning to major in a field of STEM. They must be U.S. citizens and have a GPA of 2.0 or higher; children must be younger than 24 years of age. Financial need is considered in the selection process.

Financial data The stipend ranges from $500 to $2,000 per year.

Duration 1 year; recipients may reapply.

Additional information The Army Scholarship Foundation was established in 2001. This program is sponsored by Elbit Systems of America, LLC.

Number awarded 1 each year.

Deadline April of each year.

[840]
MATTHEWS AND SWIFT EDUCATIONAL TRUST SCHOLARSHIPS

Knights of Columbus
Attn: Department of Scholarships
1 Columbus Plaza
P.O. Box 1670
New Haven, CT 06507-0901
(203) 752-4332   Fax: (203) 752-4103
E-mail: scholarships@kofc.org
Web: www.kofc.org

Summary To provide financial assistance at Catholic colleges or universities in any country to children of disabled or deceased veterans, law enforcement officers, or firemen who are/were also Knights of Columbus members.

Eligibility This program is open to children of members of the sponsoring organization who are high school seniors in any country planning to attend a 4-year Catholic college or university in their country. The parent must be a member of Knights of Columbus who 1) was serving in the military forces of their country and was killed by hostile action or wounded by hostile action, resulting within 2 years in permanent and total disability; 2) was a full-time law enforcement officer who died as a result of criminal violence; or 3) was a firefighter who died in the line of duty.

Financial data The amounts of the awards vary but are designed to cover tuition, to a maximum of $25,000 per year, at the Catholic college or university of the recipient's choice in the country of their residence. Funds are not available for room, board, books, fees, transportation, dues, computers, or supplies.

Duration 1 year; may be renewed up to 3 additional years.

Additional information This program began in 1944 to provide scholarships to the children of Knights who became totally and permanently disabled through service during World War II. It has been modified on many occasions, most recently in 2007 to its current requirements.

Number awarded Varies each year.

Deadline February of each year.

[841]
M.D. "JACK" MURPHY MEMORIAL NURSES TRAINING SCHOLARSHIP

American Legion
Department of Missouri
3341 American Avenue
P.O. Box 179
Jefferson City, MO 65102-0179
(573) 893-2353   Toll Free: (800) 846-9023
Fax: (573) 893-2980 E-mail: info@missourilegion.org
Web: www.missourilegion.org/scholarships

Summary To provide financial assistance to residents of Missouri who are the descendants of veterans and interested in studying nursing at a school in any state.

Eligibility This program is open to residents of Missouri who are high school seniors or current college students working on or planning to work on a program of training to become a registered nurse. Applicants must graduate in the top 40% of their high school class. They must be 1) the child, grandchild, or great-grandchild of a veteran who served 90 days on active duty in the Air Force, Army, Coast Guard, Marine Corps, or Navy of the United States and received an honorable discharge; 2) unmarried; 3) under 21 years of age; and 4) attending or planning to attend an accredited college or university in any state as a full-time student. Financial need is considered in the selection process.

Financial data The stipend is $1,000 per year, payable in 2 equal installments.

Duration 1 year; may be renewed for 1 additional year.

Number awarded 1 each year.

Deadline April of each year.

[842]
MEMORIAL SIBLING SCHOLARSHIP

The Matthew Freeman Project
Attn: Sibling Scholarships
P.O. Box 1608
Richmond Hill, GA 31324
E-mail: lfreeman@freemanproject.org
Web: www.imaginenet.us

Summary To provide financial assistance to siblings of military personnel who were killed in action.

Eligibility This program is open to students entering or attending a college or university. Applicants must be the sibling of a fallen military member who was killed while deployed to a combat zone. Along with their application, they must submit an essay describing their relationship with their sibling, how their death affected them, and how it disrupted their education. Selection is based on that essay, transcripts, and 3 letters of recommendation.

Financial data The stipend is $1,000.

Duration 1 year.

Additional information This program began in 2012.

Number awarded 1 or 2 each year.

Deadline January of each year.

SCHOLARSHIPS: FAMILY MEMBERS

[843]
MERRILYN STOCK/EVELYN OLIVER MEMORIAL SCHOLARSHIP

American Legion Auxiliary
Department of Alaska
Attn: Barb Nath, Secretary
P.O. Box 242304
Anchorage, AK 99524
(907) 277-8169   E-mail: aladofak@gmail.com
Web: www.alaskalegionauxiliary.org/Education.htm

Summary To provide financial assistance to nontraditional students in Alaska who have a tie to the American Legion.

Eligibility This program is open to residents of Alaska who are members or children of members of the American Legion, American Legion Auxiliary, or Sons of the American Legion. Applicants must be nontraditional students accepted or enrolled at an accredited college, university, or vocational/technical institution in any state to enhance their job skills so they can enter or reenter the work field at a higher level. Along with their application, they must submit brief essays on why receiving this scholarship would be important to them; the course of study they plan to pursue and why; their involvement in school, church, and community activities; and why they think United States patriotic organizations, such as the American Legion, are important to the world today. Selection is based on character (25%), Americanism (25%), leadership (25%), and financial need (25%).

Financial data A stipend is awarded (amount not specified).

Duration 1 year.

Number awarded 1 each year.

Deadline Applications must be submitted to the unit president by February of each year.

[844]
MG BENJAMIN J. BUTLER "CENTURY DIVISION" SCHOLARSHIP PROGRAM

Association of the Century, Inc.
Attn: Scholarship Committee
P.O. Box 34393
Louisville, KY 40232
Web: www.the-century.org/scholarship.htm

Summary To provide financial assistance for college to members of the United States Army 100th Infantry Division and their descendants.

Eligibility This program is open to active, retired, or former members of the Army 100th Infantry Division (or any of its successor designations), their direct lineal descendants, and their adopted dependents. Applicants must be enrolled or planning to enroll at an accredited college or university. They must have a GPA of 2.5 or higher. Along with their application, they must submit a 250-word essay on how this scholarship will help them achieve their goals. Selection is based on academic excellence, qualities of good citizenship and patriotism, letters of recommendation, and financial need.

Financial data The stipend is $1,000 per year.

Duration 1 year; may be renewed 1 additional year.

Additional information This program, which began in 2008, is managed by the Community Foundation of Louisville.

Number awarded Varies each year; recently, 5 were awarded.

Deadline June of each year.

[845]
MG JAMES URSANO SCHOLARSHIP FUND

Army Emergency Relief
2530 Crystal Drive, Suite 13161
Arlington, VA 22202
Toll Free: (866) 878-6378   Fax: (888) 965-2462
E-mail: scholarships@aerhq.org
Web: www.armyemergencyrelief.org/scholarships/child

Summary To provide financial assistance for college to the dependent children of Army personnel.

Eligibility This program is open to dependent unmarried children under 23 years of age (including stepchildren and legally adopted children) of soldiers on active duty, retired, or deceased while on active duty or after retirement. Applicants must be working or planning to work full time on a 4-year degree at an accredited college or university. They must have a GPA of 2.0 or higher. Selection is based primarily on financial need, but academic achievements and individual accomplishments are also considered.

Financial data Stipends recently ranged from $500 to $3,400 per academic year.

Duration 1 year; may be renewed for up to 3 additional years, provided the recipient maintains a GPA of 2.0 or higher.

Additional information Army Emergency Relief is a private nonprofit organization dedicated to "helping the Army take care of its own." Its primary mission is to provide financial assistance to Army people and their dependents in time of valid emergency need; its educational program was established as a secondary mission to meet a need of Army people for their dependents to pursue vocational training, preparation for acceptance by service academies, or an undergraduate education. It established this program in 1976.

Number awarded Varies each year; recently, 3,094 were awarded.

Deadline March of each year.

[846]
MICHIGAN CHAPTER NDIA STEM SCHOLARSHIP PROGRAM

National Defense Industrial Association-Michigan Chapter
Attn: Patricia Lopez, STEM Program
Rose-A-Lee Technologies, Inc.
6550 Sims Drive
Sterling Heights, MI 48313
(586) 799-4555   E-mail: stem@nida-mich.org
Web: www.ndia-mich.org/stem/scholarships

Summary To provide financial assistance to high school seniors in Michigan who plan to major in a field of STEM at a college in the state.

Eligibility This program is open to high school seniors who are either residents of Michigan or have an active military parent serving in the state. Applicants must be planning to work on a bachelor's degree in a field of STEM at a college or university in Michigan. They must be U.S. citizens and have a GPA of 3.0 or higher.

Financial data The stipend is $1,000.

Duration 1 year.

Additional information This program began in 2010.
Number awarded Varies each year; recently, 9 were awarded.
Deadline March of each year.

[847]
MICHIGAN CHILDREN OF VETERANS TUITION GRANTS

Michigan Department of Treasury
Attn: Office of Postsecondary Financial Planning
P.O. Box 30462
Lansing, MI 48909-7962
(517) 373-0457 Toll Free: (888) 4-GRANTS
Fax: (517) 241-5835 E-mail: mistudentaid@michigan.gov
Web: www.michigan.gov

Summary To provide financial assistance for college to the children of Michigan veterans who are totally disabled or deceased as a result of service-connected causes.

Eligibility This program is open to natural and adopted children of veterans who have been totally and permanently disabled as a result of a service-connected illness or injury prior to death and have now died, have died or become totally and permanently disabled as a result of a service-connected illness or injury, have been killed in action or died from another cause while serving in a war or war condition, or are listed as missing in action in a foreign country. The veteran must have been a legal resident of Michigan immediately before entering military service and did not reside outside of Michigan for more than 2 years, or must have established legal residency in Michigan after entering military service. Applicants must be between 16 and 26 years of age and must have lived in Michigan at least 12 months prior to the date of application. They must be enrolled or planning to enroll at least half time at a community college, public university, or independent degree-granting college or university in Michigan. U.S. citizenship or permanent resident status is required.

Financial data Full-time recipients are exempt from payment of the first $2,800 per year of tuition or any other fee that takes the place of tuition. Prorated exemptions apply to three-quarter time and half-time students.

Duration 1 year; may be renewed for up to 3 additional years if the recipient maintains full-time enrollment and a GPA of 2.25 or higher.

Additional information This program was formerly known as the Michigan Veterans Trust Fund Tuition Grants, administered by the Michigan Veterans Trust Fund within the Department of Military and Veterans Affairs. It was transferred to the Office of Postsecondary Financial Planning in 2006.

Number awarded Varies each year; recently, 414 of these grants, worth $967,853, were awarded.
Deadline Deadline not specified.

[848]
MIDWESTERN REGION KOREAN WAR VETERAN DESCENDANT SCHOLARSHIPS

Korean American Scholarship Foundation
Midwestern Region
c/o Jane Lee-Kwon, Scholarship Committee Chair
5903 North Campbell Avenue, Apartment 2
Chicago, IL 60659
E-mail: mwrc.scholarship@kasf.org
Web: www.kasf.org/apply-mwrc

Summary To provide financial assistance to the descendants of the Korean War from any state who are working on an undergraduate or graduate degree in any field at a school in eastern states.

Eligibility This program is open to direct descendants of veterans who served in Korea from June 25, 1950 to January 31, 1955. Applicants may reside in any state, but they must be enrolled as full-time undergraduate or graduate students at a college or university in in Illinois, Indiana, Iowa, Michigan, Minnesota, Missouri, North Dakota, Ohio, South Dakota, or Wisconsin. They must have a GPA of 3.0 or higher. Selection is based on academic achievement, extracurricular activities, an essay, and recommendations.

Financial data Stipends range from $500 to $5,000.
Duration 1 year.
Number awarded 1 or more each year.
Deadline June of each year.

[849]
MIKE AND GAIL DONLEY SPOUSE SCHOLARSHIPS

Air Force Association
Attn: Scholarships
1501 Lee Highway
Arlington, VA 22209-1198
(703) 247-5800, ext. 4868
Toll Free: (800) 727-3337, ext. 4868
Fax: (703) 247-5853 E-mail: scholarships@afa.org
Web: www.app.smarterselect.com

Summary To provide financial assistance for undergraduate or graduate study to spouses of Air Force members.

Eligibility This program is open to spouses of active-duty Air Force, Air National Guard, Air Force Reserve members, or Department of the Air Force civilian employee. Spouses who are themselves military members or in ROTC are not eligible. Applicants must have a GPA of 3.5 or higher in college (or high school if entering college for the first time) and be able to provide proof of acceptance into an accredited undergraduate or graduate degree program. They must submit a 2-page essay on their academic and career goals, the motivation that led them to that decision, and how Air Force and other local community activities in which they are involved will enhance their goals. Selection is based on the essay and 2 letters of recommendation.

Financial data The stipend is $2,500; funds are sent to the recipients' schools to be used for any reasonable cost related to working on a degree.
Duration 1 year; nonrenewable.
Additional information This program began in 1995.
Number awarded Varies each year; recently, 3 were awarded.
Deadline April of each year.

SCHOLARSHIPS: FAMILY MEMBERS

[850]
MILDRED R. KNOLES SCHOLARSHIPS
American Legion Auxiliary
Department of Illinois
2720 East Lincoln Street
P.O. Box 1426
Bloomington, IL 61702-1426
(309) 663-9366 Fax: (309) 663-5827
E-mail: karen.boughan@ilala.org
Web: www.ilala.org/education.html

Summary To provide financial assistance to Illinois veterans and their descendants who are attending college in any state.

Eligibility This program is open to veterans who served during designated periods of wartime and their children, grandchildren, and great-grandchildren. Applicants must be currently enrolled at a college or university in any state and studying any field except nursing. They must be residents of Illinois or members of the American Legion Family, Department of Illinois. Along with their application, they must submit a 1,000-word essay on "What My Education Will Do for Me." Selection is based on that essay (25%) character and leadership (25%), scholarship (25%), and financial need (25%).

Financial data The stipend is $1,000.

Duration 1 year.

Number awarded 1 or more each year.

Deadline March of each year.

[851]
MILITARY BENEFIT ASSOCIATION SCHOLARSHIPS
Military Benefit Association
Attn: Member Services Department
14605 Avion Parkway
P.O. Box 221110
Chantilly, VA 20153-1110
(703) 968-6200 Toll Free: (800) 336-0100
Fax: (703) 968-6423
Web: www.militarybenefit.org

Summary To provide financial assistance for college to children of insured members of the Military Benefit Association (MBA).

Eligibility This program is open to 1) unmarried dependent children under 26 years of age of insured MBA members; 2) MBA sponsored spouse members or dependent spouses of MBA members; 3) MBA members who are National Guard members or Reservists; and 4) MBA members who are Veterans. Applicants must be enrolled or planning to enroll as a full-time undergraduate student at an accredited 2- or 4-year college, university, or vocational/technical school. They must have a GPA of 2.5 or higher.

Financial data The stipend is $2,300.

Duration 1 year.

Additional information The MBA is an organization that provides insurance to active-duty and retired servicemembers, full-time federal government employees, honorably discharged servicemembers, National Guard, Reservists, uniformed officers of the United States Public Health Service or National Oceanic and Atmospheric Administration, cadets and midshipmen at the military academies, and the spouses of all those categories. This program is administered by Scholarship Management Services, a division of Scholarship America.

Number awarded 20 each year.

Deadline February of each year.

[852]
MILITARY COLLEGE SCHOLARSHIP
Low VA Rates
384 South 400 West, Suite 100
Lindon, UT 84042
Toll Free: (855) 581-7341 E-mail: hr@lowvarates.com
Web: www.lowvarates.com/scholarship

Summary To provide financial assistance for college to military personnel, veterans, and children of military personnel.

Eligibility This program is open to students who are nominated by a family member, a friend, or the student themselves. Nominees must be active service military members, veterans, or children with a parent serving in a branch of the U.S. armed forces. Along with their application, they must submit brief statements on how they are associated with the military, why they feel they qualify for this scholarship, their educational and career goals and what they plan to do with their degree, and how the military has positively impacted their life.

Financial data The stipend is $1,250 per semester.

Duration 1 semester.

Number awarded 2 each year: 1 from the winter applications and 1 from the fall applications.

Deadline December of each year for the winter application; August of each year for the fall application.

[853]
MILITARY COMMANDERS' SCHOLARSHIP FUND
Scholarship America
Attn: Scholarship Management Services
One Scholarship Way
P.O. Box 297
St. Peter, MN 56082
(507) 931-1682 Toll Free: (800) 537-4180
Fax: (507) 931-9168
Web: sms.scholarshipamerica.org/militarycommanders

Summary To provide financial assistance for college to children of active and retired military personnel.

Eligibility This program is open to children of active-duty, Reserve, National Guard, and retired members of the U.S. military. Applicants must be high school seniors or graduates who plan to enroll full time as entering freshmen at an accredited 2- or 4-year college or university. They must have a cumulative GPA of 3.5 or higher. Selection is based on academic record, demonstrated leadership and participation in school and community activities, honors, work experience, a statement of goals and aspirations, unusual personal or family circumstances, an outside appraisal, and financial need.

Financial data The stipend is $5,000.

Duration 1 year; nonrenewable.

Additional information This program is administered by Scholarship Management Services of Scholarship America on behalf of the New York Chapter of the American Logistics Association.

Number awarded 10 each year: 2 from each branch of the armed forces (Air Force, Army, Coast Guard, Marines, Navy).

Deadline February of each year.

[854]
MILITARY FAMILY SUPPORT TRUST SCHOLARSHIPS

Military Family Support Trust
1010 American Eagle Boulevard, Suite 301
Sun City Center, FL 33573
(813) 634-4675   Fax: (813) 419-4944
E-mail: president@mfst.us
Web: www.mfst.us/our-programs/scholarships

Summary To provide financial assistance for college to children and grandchildren of retired and deceased officers who served in the military.

Eligibility This program is open to graduating high school seniors who have a GPA of 3.0 and a minimum score of 21 on the ACT or 1000 on the 2-part SAT. Applicants must have a parent, guardian, grandparent, or great-grandparent who is 1) a retired active-duty, National Guard, or Reserve officer or former officer of the U.S. Army, Navy, Marine Corps, Air Force, Coast Guard, Public Health Service, or National Oceanic and Atmospheric Administration, at the rank of O-1 through O-10, WO-1 through WO-5, or E-5 through E-9; 2) an officer who died while on active duty in service to the country; 3) a recipient of the Purple Heart, regardless of pay grade or length of service; 4) a World War II combat veteran of the Merchant Marine; 5) an honorably discharged or retired foreign military officer of friendly nations meeting the service and disability retirement criteria of the respective country and living in the United States; or 6) cadets in Florida JROTC programs. Applicants must have been accepted to an accredited program at a college or university. Along with their application, they must submit an essay of 400 to 600 words on their professional goal and how their past, present, and future activities make the accomplishment of that goal probable; their plans for enrollment in an accredited American college or university; and their involvement in volunteer organizations and positions held in gainful employment. Selection is based on leadership, scholarship, and financial need.

Financial data Stipends range from $500 to $3,000 per year.

Duration 4 years, provided the recipient maintains a GPA of 3.0 or higher.

Additional information This foundation was established in 1992 as the Military Officers' Benevolent Corporation. It changed its name in 2008 to the current usage.

Number awarded 16 each year.

Deadline January of each year.

[855]
MILITARY INTELLIGENCE CORPS ASSOCIATION SCHOLARSHIPS

Military Intelligence Corps Association
Attn: Scholarship Committee
P.O. Box 13020
Fort Huachuca, AZ 85670-3020
(520) 227-3894   E-mail: dfa@micorps.org
Web: www.mica-national.org/category/press-release

Summary To provide financial assistance for college to members of the Military Intelligence Corps Association (MICA) and their immediate family.

Eligibility This program is open to active-duty, Reserve, National Guard, and retired military intelligence soldiers who are MICA members and to their immediate family (spouses, children, or other relatives living with and supported by the MICA member). Applicants must be attending or accepted for attendance at an accredited college, university, vocational school, or technical institution. Along with their application, they must submit a 1-page essay on their educational goals and program of study. Financial need is not considered in the selection process.

Financial data Stipend amounts vary depending on the availability of funds and the number of qualified applicants, but recently were $5,000. Funds are to be used for tuition, books, and classroom fees; support is not provided for housing, board, travel, or administrative purposes.

Duration 1 year; recipients may reapply.

Number awarded 10 each year.

Deadline May of each year.

[856]
MILITARY ORDER OF THE PURPLE HEART SCHOLARSHIP PROGRAM

Military Order of the Purple Heart
Attn: Scholarship Manager
5413-B Backlick Road
Springfield, VA 22151-3960
(703) 642-5360   Toll Free: (888) 668-1656
Fax: (703) 642-2054
E-mail: scholarship@purpleheart.org
Web: www.purpleheart.org

Summary To provide financial assistance for college or graduate school to members of the Military Order of the Purple Heart (MOPH) and their families.

Eligibility This program is open to 1) members of the MOPH who received a Purple Heart; 2) spouses and widows of MOPH members; 3) direct descendants (children, stepchildren, adopted children, and grandchildren) of veterans who are MOPH members or were members at the time of death; and 4) spouses, widows, widowers, and direct descendants of veterans killed in action or who died of wounds. Applicants must be graduating seniors or graduates of an accredited high school who are enrolled or accepted for enrollment in a full-time program of study in a college, university, or trade school. They must have a GPA of 2.75 or higher. U.S. citizenship is required. Along with their application, they must submit an essay of 200 to 300 words on a topic that changes annually but recently asked how they will use their education to serve their country and its citizens. Financial need is not considered in the selection process.

Financial data The stipend is approximately $2,500 per year.

Duration 1 year; may be renewed up to 2 additional years.

Additional information Membership in MOPH is open to all veterans who received a Purple Heart Medal and were discharged under conditions other than dishonorable. This program includes the Navy SEAL LT Michael Murphy Memorial Award. A processing fee of $15 is required.

Number awarded Approximately 8 each year.

Deadline January of each year.

[857]
MILITARY SCHOLARSHIP ESSAY CONTEST

EducationDynamics, LLC
Attn: eLearners
111 River Street, Tenth Floor
Hoboken, NJ 07030
(201) 377-3000   Toll Free: (888) 567-2008
Web: www.elearners.com

Summary To recognize and reward, with college scholarships, veterans, military personnel, and their spouses who submit outstanding essays on the effect of their military service.

Eligibility This competition is open to active-duty servicemembers, veterans, and their spouses who are enrolled or planning to enroll at an accredited college, university, or trade school. Applicants must submit a 250-word essay on how their military service has better prepared them to enhance their education. The winner is selected on the basis of writing ability (25%), creativity (25%), originality (25%), and overall excellence (25%).

Financial data The award is a $1,000 scholarship.

Duration The competition is held annually.

Number awarded 1 each year.

Deadline February of each year.

[858]
MILITARY SPOUSE AND CAREGIVER NEW BEGINNINGS SCHOLARSHIP

Hope for the Warriors
Attn: Scholarship Committee
5518 Port Royal Road
Springfield, VA 22151
(703) 321-0588   Toll Free: (877) 2HOPE4W
Fax: (703) 256-3702
E-mail: scholarships@hopeforthewarriors.org
Web: www.hopeforthewarriors.org

Summary To provide financial assistance for entry-level study or training to spouses and caregivers of deceased and disabled veterans who served after September 11, 2001.

Eligibility This program is open to spouses and caregivers of military personnel who were killed or became disabled as a result of service after September 11, 2001. Applicants must be enrolled or planning to enroll in entry-level classes or training at an accredited college, university, or trade school in any state. Along with their application, they must submit an essay on their academic achievement and personal goals. Financial need is not considered in the selection process.

Financial data The stipend is at least $2,000.

Duration 1 year.

Additional information This program began in 2008.

Number awarded Normally, 2 each year (1 each semester).

Deadline May of each year for fall semester; October of each year for spring semester.

[859]
MILITARY SPOUSE CAREER ADVANCEMENT ACCOUNTS (MYCAA) PROGRAM

Department of Defense
Attn: Spouse Education and Career Opportunities Program
1400 Defense Pentagon
Washington, DC 20301-1400
(703) 253-7599   Toll Free: (800) 342-9647
TDD: (866) 607-6794
E-mail: MyCAAHELP@militaryonesource.com
Web: mycaa.militaryonesource.mil/mycaa

Summary To provide financial assistance to military spouses who are interested in obtaining additional education that will improve their employment opportunities.

Eligibility This program is open to military spouses who are enrolled or planning to enroll in educational or training courses that lead to an associate degree, license, certificate, or certification at an accredited college, university, or technical school in the United States or an approved testing organization that expands employment or portable career opportunities for military spouses. Applicants must be spouses of servicemembers on active duty in pay grades E-1 to E-5, W-1 to W-2, or O-1 to O-2 who can start and complete their course work while their military sponsor is on Title 10 military orders, including spouses married to members of the National Guard and Reserve components. Support is not available for non-academic credit or ungraded courses; academic credit by examination courses; general studies, liberal arts, or interdisciplinary associate degrees that do not have a concentration; personal enrichment courses; transportation, lodging, child care, or medical services; study abroad programs; or high school completion programs. Spouses who are themselves in the military or married to members of the Coast Guard are not eligible.

Financial data The maximum support per fiscal year is $2,000; spouses may receive a lifetime total of $4,000 from this program. Funds are paid directly to schools.

Duration Associate degrees must be completed in 12 months and licenses and certificates within 18 months. The times of study may be extended over a 3-year period.

Additional information This program began in March 2009 but was suspended in February 2010 when an unexpected large number of spouses applied. It was resumed for spouses who had already applied in March 2010 and for new enrollees in October 2010.

Number awarded More than 136,000 military spouses and more than 3,000 schools are currently participating in this program.

Deadline Applications may be submitted at any time.

[860]
MILITARY SPOUSE SCHOLARSHIPS

National Military Family Association, Inc.
Attn: Spouse Scholarship Program
2800 Eisenhower Avenue, Suite 250
Alexandria, VA 22314
(703) 931-NMFA   Toll Free: (800) 260-0218
Fax: (703) 931-4600
E-mail: scholarships@militaryfamily.org
Web: www.scholarships.militaryfamily.org

Summary To provide financial assistance for postsecondary study to spouses of active and retired military personnel.
Eligibility This program is open to students who are 1) spouses of members of the 7 uniformed services who have a valid military ID; 2) married to an active-duty, Reserve, Guard, retired, medically retired, wounded, or fallen service member (must be a service-related wound, illness, injury, or death that took place after September 11, 2001); 3) a dual service military spouse; or 4) a divorced spouse who is receiving 20/20/20 benefits. Applicants must be enrolled or planning to enroll in a program for procurement of professional certification or license in any state. Applicants must be attending or planning to attend an accredited postsecondary institution to work on an undergraduate or graduate degree, professional certification, vocational training, licensure, or other postsecondary training. They may enroll part or full time and on-campus or online. Along with their application, they must submit an essay on a question that changes annually; recently, applicants were asked to write about what they like most about the health care they are receiving as a military family member, what they like the least, and what they would recommend to change it. Selection is based on that essay, community involvement, and academic achievement.
Financial data The stipend is $1,000. Funds are paid directly to the educational institution to be used for tuition, fees, and school room and board. Support is not provided for books, rent, or previous education loans.
Duration 1 year; recipients may reapply.
Additional information This program began in 2004.
Number awarded Varies each year.
Deadline Applications may be submitted at any time.

[861]
MINNESOTA G.I. BILL PROGRAM
Minnesota Department of Veterans Affairs
Attn: Programs and Services Division
20 West 12th Street, Room 206
St. Paul, MN 55155
(651) 296-2562   Toll Free: (888) LINK-VET
Fax: (651) 296-3954   TDD: (800) 627-3529
E-mail: MNGIBill@state.mn.us
Web: www.mn.gov

Summary To provide financial assistance for college or graduate school in the state to residents of Minnesota who served in the military after September 11, 2001 and the families of deceased or disabled military personnel.
Eligibility This program is open to residents of Minnesota enrolled at colleges and universities in the state as undergraduate or graduate students. Applicants must be 1) a veteran who is serving or has served honorably in a branch of the U.S. armed forces at any time; 2) a non-veteran who has served honorably for a total of 5 years or more cumulatively as a member of the Minnesota National Guard or other active or Reserve component of the U.S. armed forces, and any part of that service occurred on or after September 11, 2001; or 3) a surviving child or spouse of a person who has served in the military at any time and who has died or has a total and permanent disability as a result of that military service. They may be attending college in the state or participating in an apprenticeship or on-the-job (OJT) training program. Financial need is also considered in the selection process.

Financial data The college stipend is $1,000 per semester for full-time study or $500 per semester for part-time study. The maximum award is $3,000 per academic year or $10,000 per lifetime. Apprenticeship and OJT students are eligible for up to $2,000 per fiscal year. Approved employers are eligible to receive $1,000 placement credit payable upon hiring a person under this program and another $1,000 after 12 consecutive months of employment. No more than $3,000 in aggregate benefits under this paragraph may be paid to or on behalf of an individual in one fiscal year, and not more than $9,000 over any period of time.
Duration 1 year; may be renewed, provided the recipient continues to make satisfactory academic progress.
Additional information This program was established by the Minnesota Legislature in 2007.
Number awarded At least 1,000 each year.
Deadline Deadline not specified.

[862]
MINNESOTA LEGION AUXILIARY DEPARTMENT SCHOLARSHIPS
American Legion Auxiliary
Department of Minnesota
State Veterans Service Building
20 West 12th Street, Room 314
St. Paul, MN 55155-2069
(651) 224-7634   Toll Free: (888) 217-9598
Fax: (651) 224-5243   E-mail: deptoffice@mnala.org
Web: www.mnala.org/scholarships

Summary To provide financial assistance to the children and grandchildren of Minnesota veterans who are interested in attending college in the state.
Eligibility This program is open to the children and grandchildren of veterans who served since December 7, 1941. Applicants must be a resident of Minnesota or a member of an American Legion Post, American Legion Auxiliary unit, or Sons of the American Legion detachment in the Department of Minnesota. They must be high school seniors or graduates, have a GPA of 2.0 or higher, be able to demonstrate financial need, and be planning to attend a vocational or business school, college, or university in Minnesota. Along with their application, they must submit an essay up to 1,000 words in length telling of their plans for college, career goals, extracurricular and community activities, and financial need.
Financial data The stipend is $1,000. Funds are to be used to pay for tuition or books and are sent directly to the recipient's school.
Duration 1 year.
Number awarded 8 each year.
Deadline March of each year.

SCHOLARSHIPS: FAMILY MEMBERS

[863]
MINNESOTA LEGION AUXILIARY PAST PRESIDENTS PARLEY HEALTH CARE SCHOLARSHIP

American Legion Auxiliary
Department of Minnesota
State Veterans Service Building
20 West 12th Street, Room 314
St. Paul, MN 55155-2069
(651) 224-7634   Toll Free: (888) 217-9598
Fax: (651) 224-5243   E-mail: deptoffice@mnala.org
Web: www.mnala.org/scholarships

Summary To provide financial assistance for education in health care fields to members of the American Legion Auxiliary in Minnesota.
Eligibility This program is open to residents of Minnesota who have been members of the American Legion Auxiliary for at least 3 years. Applicants must have a GPA of 2.0 or higher and be planning to study in Minnesota. They must be preparing for a career in a phase of health care, including nursing assistant, registered nurse, licensed practical nurse, X-ray or other technician, dietician, physical or other therapist, dental hygienist, or dental assistant. Along with their application, they must submit an essay on their plans for higher education, career goals, and need for financial assistance/.
Financial data The stipend is $1,000. Funds are sent directly to the recipient's school after satisfactory completion of the first quarter.
Duration 1 year.
Number awarded Up to 10 each year.
Deadline March of each year.

[864]
MINNESOTA NATIONAL GUARD ENLISTED ASSOCIATION AUXILIARY MINUTEMAN SCHOLARSHIPS

Minnesota National Guard Enlisted Association Auxiliary
c/o Carol Benda, Treasurer and Scholarship Chair
3280 30th Street
Slayton, MN 56172
E-mail: cbenda@mchsi.com
Web: www.mngea.com/minuteman-scholarship

Summary To provide financial assistance to members of the Minnesota National Guard Enlisted Association (MNGEA), its Auxiliary, and the families of the Association and Auxiliary who are interested in attending college in any state.
Eligibility This program is open to high school seniors, GED recipients, and students currently enrolled at colleges and universities in any state. Applicants must be active annual or life MNGEA members, active MNGEA Auxiliary members, or the unmarried children, stepchildren, or grandchildren under 26 years of age of those members. They must have a GPA of 2.5 or higher for their most recent academic term. Along with their application, they must submit an essay on their educational goals and how this scholarship will benefit those.
Financial data Stipends are $1,000 or $500.
Duration 1 year; nonrenewable.
Additional information The $1,000 scholarship is sponsored by USAA Insurance Corporation.
Number awarded Varies each year; recently, 4 were awarded.
Deadline March of each year.

[865]
MINNESOTA NATIONAL GUARD SURVIVOR ENTITLEMENT TUITION REIMBURSEMENT PROGRAM

Minnesota National Guard
Attn: Education Office
600 Cedar Street
St. Paul, MN 5510-2509
(651) 282-4589   Toll Free: (800) 657-3848
Fax: (651) 282-4694
E-mail: ng.mn.mnarng.mbx.assets-education@mail.mil
Web: minnesotanationalguard.ng.mil/education

Summary To provide financial assistance for college or graduate school to survivors of members of the Minnesota National Guard who were killed on active duty.
Eligibility This program is open to surviving spouses and children of members of the Minnesota Army or Air National Guard who were killed while performing military duty. Dependent children are eligible until their 24th birthday; surviving spouses are eligible regardless of age or remarriage; all survivors remain eligible even if they move out of state and become residents of another state. The Guard member's death must have occurred within the scope of assigned duties while in a federal duty status or on state active service. Applicants must be enrolled as undergraduate or graduate students at colleges or universities in Minnesota. Reimbursement is provided only for undergraduate courses completed with a grade of "C" or better or for graduate courses completed with a grade of "B" or better.
Financial data The maximum reimbursement rate is 100% of the tuition rate at the University of Minnesota Twin Cities campus for undergraduate study or 50% for graduate work, with a maximum benefit of $18,000 per fiscal year for undergraduate course work or $20,000 per fiscal year for graduate course work.
Duration 1 academic term, to a maximum of 18 credits per term; may be renewed for a total of 144 semester credits or 208 quarter credits.
Additional information This program became effective in 1992.
Number awarded Varies each year.
Deadline Participants must request reimbursement within 90 days of the last official day of the term.

[866]
MISSISSIPPI EDUCATIONAL ASSISTANCE FOR MIA/POW DEPENDENTS

Mississippi State Veterans Affairs Board
660 North Street, Suite 200
P.O. Box 5947
Jackson, MS 39202
(601) 576-4850   Toll Free: (877) 203-5632
Fax: (601) 576-4868
Web: www.vab.ms.gov

Summary To provide financial assistance for college to the children of Mississippi residents who are POWs or MIAs.
Eligibility This entitlement program is open to the children of members of the armed services whose official home of

record and residence is in Mississippi and who are officially reported as being either a prisoner of a foreign government or missing in action. Applicants must be attending or planning to attend a state-supported college or university in Mississippi.
Financial data This assistance covers all costs of college attendance.
Duration Up to 8 semesters.
Number awarded Varies each year.
Deadline Deadline not specified.

[867]
MISSISSIPPI NATIONAL GUARD NCO ASSOCIATION SCHOLARSHIPS
Mississippi National Guard NCO Association
Attn: Executive Director
P.O. Box 48
Lauderdale, MS 39335
(601) 632-4535   E-mail: msccm10@gmail.com
Web: www.msncoa.org/scholarship-program

Summary To provide financial assistance to dependents of members of the Mississippi National Guard NCO Association who are interested in attending college in any state.
Eligibility This program is open to the unmarried dependent children and spouses of annual, enlisted, retired, and life members of the association and of deceased members who were annual, enlisted, retired, or life members at the time of death. Applicants must be high school seniors or undergraduate students with at least 1 full semester remaining before graduation. They must be attending or planning to attend an accredited university, college, community college, vocational/technical, business, or trade school in any state. Along with their application, they must submit a letter on their desire to continue their education and why financial assistance is required. Selection is based on that letter (20%), GPA (25%), ACT score (25%), honors (10%), school, community, church, and social activities (10%), and letters of recommendation (10%).
Financial data A stipend is awarded (amount not specified).
Duration 1 year.
Number awarded Varies each year.
Deadline January of each year.

[868]
MISSOURI NATIONAL GUARD ASSOCIATION SCHOLARSHIPS
Missouri National Guard Association
Attn: Scholarship Committee Chair
c/o Ike Skelton Training Center
2302 Militia Drive
Jefferson City, MO 65101-1203
(573) 632-4240
Web: www.mongaonline.com/page/Scholarship

Summary To provide financial assistance to members of the Missouri National Guard Association (MoNGA) and their dependents who are interested in attending college in any state.
Eligibility This program is open to annual, associate, and lifetime members of the association and their dependents. Applicants must be interested in working on a degree at an accredited junior college or 4-year college or university in any state. They must submit high school or college transcripts, 3 letters of recommendation, and a letter describing their desire to continue their education, why they need financial assistance, and how they have demonstrated the traits (scholarship, citizenship, and leadership) upon which selection is based.
Financial data Stipends for MoNGA members are $1,000. Stipends for dependents are $750 or $500. In addition, USAA Insurance Corporation sponsors a $1,000 scholarship for enlisted MoNGA members. Funds are paid directly to the recipient's college or university.
Duration 1 year.
Number awarded 6 each year: 2 for MoNGA members (at $1,000), 3 for dependents (2 at $750 and 1 at $500), and 1 USAA scholarship.
Deadline March of each year.

[869]
MISSOURI PAST NATIONAL PRESIDENTS' SCHOLARSHIP
VFW Auxiliary-Department of Missouri
c/o Sheila Allen, Department Scholarship Chair
1119 County Road 391
Whitewater, MO 63785
(573) 576-0768   E-mail: satch319@yahoo.com
Web: www.movfwaux.org/scholarship

Summary To provide financial assistance to high school seniors in Missouri who have a tie to the Veterans of Foreign Wars (VFW) or the VFW Auxiliary and plan to attend college in any state.
Eligibility This program is open to seniors graduating from high schools in Missouri who are the children, grandchildren, or great-grandchildren of current or deceased VFW or VFW Auxiliary members. Applicants must be planning to enroll at a college, university, or vocational/technical school in any state. Along with their application, they must submit a 300-word essay on their community involvement, their volunteer activities, the honors they have received, and organizations outside of school in which they participate.
Financial data Stipends are $1,800 or $1,200.
Duration 1 year.
Number awarded 2 each year: 1 at $1,800 and 1 at $1,200.
Deadline April of each year.

[870]
MISSOURI PATRIOT GUARD RIDERS SCHOLARSHIP
Missouri Patriot Guard Riders
c/o R.J. Bailey
P.O. Box 914
Carl Junction, MO 64834

Summary To provide financial assistance to college to students from Missouri who are children of deceased or disabled veterans or first responders.
Eligibility This program is open to Missouri students who are children of 1) military personnel, law enforcement officers, or firefighters who gave their lives in the line of duty; 2) honorably-discharged veterans who died after their term of service; or 3) veterans, law enforcement officers, or firefighters disabled in the line of duty. Applicants must submit documentation of the status of their disabled or deceased parent; information on their financial status; a list of extracurricular activi-

ties or organizations to which they belong; a list of any honors, recognitions, or awards they have received; a letter of recommendation; and a brief essay on why this scholarship would be of assistance to them.
Financial data The stipend is $2,500.
Duration 1 year; nonrenewable.
Number awarded 1 each year.
Deadline March of each year.

[871]
MISSOURI WARTIME VETERAN'S SURVIVOR GRANT PROGRAM

Missouri Department of Higher Education and Workforce Development
Attn: Grants and Scholarships
301 West High Street
P.O. Box 1469
Jefferson City, MO 65102-1469
(573) 751-2361   Toll Free: (800) 473-6757
Fax: (573) 751-6635   E-mail: info@dhewd.mo.gov
Web: dhewd.mo.gov/ppc/grants/wartimevetsurvivor.php

Summary To provide financial assistance to survivors of deceased or disabled Missouri post-September 11, 2001 veterans who plan to attend college in the state.
Eligibility This program is open to spouses and children of veterans whose deaths or injuries were a result of combat action or were attributed to an illness that was contracted while serving in combat action, or who became at least 80% disabled as a result of injuries or accidents sustained in combat action after September 11, 2001. The veteran must have been a Missouri resident when first entering military service or at the time of death or injury. The spouse or child must be a U.S. citizen or permanent resident or otherwise lawfully present in the United States; children of veterans must be younger than 25 years of age. All applicants must be enrolled or accepted for enrollment at least half time at participating public college or university in Missouri.
Financial data The maximum annual grant is the lesser of 1) the actual tuition charged at the school where the recipient is enrolled; or 2) the amount of tuition charged to a Missouri resident enrolled in the same number of hours at the University of Missouri at Columbia. Additional allowances provide up to $2,000 per semester for room and board and the lesser of the actual cost for books or $500.
Duration 1 year. May be renewed, provided the recipient maintains a GPA of 2.5 or higher and makes satisfactory academic progress; children of veterans are eligible until they turn 25 years of age or receive their first bachelor's degree, whichever occurs first.
Number awarded Up to 25 each year.
Deadline There is no application deadline, but early submission of the completed application is encouraged.

[872]
MONTANA WAR ORPHANS WAIVER

Office of the Commissioner of Higher Education
Attn: Montana University System
State Scholarship Coordinator
560 North Park Avenue, Fourth Floor
P.O. Box 203201
Helena, MT 59620-3201
(406) 449-9168   Toll Free: (800) 537-7508
Fax: (406) 449-9171
E-mail: mtscholarships@montana.edu
Web: www.mus.edu

Summary To provide financial assistance for undergraduate education to the children of Montana veterans who died in the line of duty or as a result of service-connected disabilities.
Eligibility This program is open to children of members of the U.S. armed forces who served on active duty during World War II, the Korean Conflict, the Vietnam Conflict, the Afghanistan Conflict, or the Iraq Conflict; were legal residents of Montana at the time of entry into service; and were killed in action or died as a result of injury, disease, or other disability while in the service. Applicants must be no older than 25 years of age. Financial need is considered in the selection process.
Financial data Students eligible for this benefit are entitled to attend any unit of the Montana University System without payment of undergraduate registration or incidental fees.
Duration Undergraduate students are eligible for continued fee waiver as long as they maintain reasonable academic progress as full-time students.
Number awarded Varies each year.
Deadline Deadline not specified.

[873]
MRS. PATTY SHINSEKI SPOUSE SCHOLARSHIP PROGRAM

Army Emergency Relief
2530 Crystal Drive, Suite 13161
Arlington, VA 22202
Toll Free: (866) 878-6378   Fax: (888) 965-2462
E-mail: Spouse@aerhq.org
Web: www.armyemergencyrelief.org/scholarships/spouse

Summary To provide financial assistance for college to the dependent spouses of Army personnel.
Eligibility This program is open to spouses of Army soldiers on active duty, widow(er)s of soldiers who died while on active duty, spouses of retired soldiers, and widow(er)s of soldiers who died while in a retired status. Applicants may not be members of the National Guard, Reserves, or other military branch. They must be working full or part time on a 4-year college degree and have a GPA of 2.0 or higher. Study for a second undergraduate or graduate degree is not supported. Selection is based primarily on financial need.
Financial data Stipends recently ranged from $500 to $1,900 per academic year.
Duration 1 year; may be renewed up to 3 additional years of full-time study or up to 7 additional years of part-time study.
Additional information This program began in 1976 and was given its current name in December 2019.

Number awarded Varies each year; recently, 1,055 spouses received support.
Deadline Applications may be submitted at any time of each year; they are reviewed approximately monthly.

[874]
MSON DEPENDENT CHILD SCHOLARSHIP

Military Spouses of Newport
Attn: Scholarship Committee
P.O. Box 5115
Newport, RI 02841
(401) 366-4823
E-mail: scholarships@milspousesnewport.org
Web: www.milspousenewport.org/Scholarships

Summary To provide financial assistance to residents of Rhode Island whose parent has a tie to a military base in the state and who are currently enrolled at a college in any state.
Eligibility This program is open to residents of Rhode Island currently enrolled at an accredited 2- or 4-year college or university in any state. Applicants must be dependent children possessing a valid military ID card of 1) active-duty military personnel (any branch, officer or enlisted) attached to a base in Rhode Island); 2) retired military (any branch, officer or enlisted) who resides in Rhode Island; or 3) deceased military, while on active duty or paid retired status (any branch, officer or enlisted) who resided in Rhode Island. Along with their application, they must submit 1) a 500-word essay on their favorite literary or historical quote and how the quote impacts or defines them; and 2) a 250-word essay on how being part of a military family has impacted their life. Selection is based on the essays; academic achievement (based on transcripts with a GPA of 2.5); school-sponsored extracurricular activities; community service; achievements and leadership qualities; and letters of recommendation.
Financial data A stipend is awarded (amount not specified).
Duration 1 year.
Number awarded Varies each year.
Deadline April of each year.

[875]
MSON FRESHMAN SCHOLARSHIP

Military Spouses of Newport
Attn: Scholarship Committee
P.O. Box 5115
Newport, RI 02841
(401) 366-4823
E-mail: scholarships@milspousesnewport.org
Web: www.milspousenewport.org/Scholarships

Summary To provide financial assistance for college in any state to high school seniors in Rhode Island whose parent has a tie to a military base in the state.
Eligibility This program is open to graduating high school seniors who plan to enroll at an accredited 2- or 4-year college or university in any state. Applicants must be dependent children possessing a valid military ID card of 1) active-duty military personnel (any branch, officer or enlisted) attached to a base in Rhode Island); 2) retired military (any branch, officer or enlisted) who resides in Rhode Island; or 3) deceased military, while on active duty or paid retired status (any branch, officer or enlisted) who resided in Rhode Island. Along with their application, they must submit 1) a 500-word essay on the advice they would give to an incoming high school freshman and how they would encourage them to make the most of their time in high school; and 2) a 250-word essay on how being part of a military family has impacted their life. Selection is based on the essays; academic achievement (based on transcripts with a GPA of 2.5 or higher and ACT/SAT scores); school-sponsored extracurricular activities; community service; achievements and leadership qualities; and letters of recommendation.
Financial data A stipend is awarded (amount not specified).
Duration 1 year.
Number awarded Varies each year.
Deadline April of each year.

[876]
MSON SPOUSE SCHOLARSHIPS

Military Spouses of Newport
Attn: Scholarship Committee
P.O. Box 5115
Newport, RI 02841
(401) 366-4823
E-mail: scholarships@milspousesnewport.org
Web: www.milspousenewport.org/Scholarships

Summary To provide financial assistance for college in any state to residents of Rhode Island whose spouse has a tie to a military base in the state.
Eligibility This program is open to residents of Rhode Island whose spouse is an active duty servicemember (any branch, officer or enlisted) and assigned to a base in Rhode Island. Applicants must be enrolled or planning to enroll at an accredited postsecondary institution or certification program in any state. They must be a high school graduate or GED recipient and have a GPA of 2.5 or higher. Along with their application, they must submit 1) a 250-word essay on how life as a military spouse has positively affected them; and 2) a 500-word essay on what they have learned as a military spouse and what advice would they give to a new spouse that they wish someone had given to them. Selection is based on those essays, academic achievement, school-sponsored extracurricular activities, community service, achievements and leadership qualities, and letters of recommendation.
Financial data A stipend is awarded (amount not specified).
Duration 1 year.
Number awarded Varies each year.
Deadline April of each year.

[877]
NANNIE NORFLEET EDUCATIONAL SCHOLARSHIP

American Legion Auxiliary
Department of North Carolina
2940 Falstaff Road
P.O. Box 25726
Raleigh, NC 27611-5726
(984) 206-4404 E-mail: ncala-membership@nclegion.org
Web: www.alanorthcarolina.com/resources

Summary To provide financial assistance to members of the American Legion Auxiliary in North Carolina and their children and grandchildren who plan to attend college in any state.

Eligibility This program is open to North Carolina residents who are either adult members of the American Legion Auxiliary or high school seniors (with preference to the children and grandchildren of members). Applicants must be interested in attending college in any state. They must be able to demonstrate at least 50 hours of community service. Along with their application, they must submit an essay up to 1,000 words in length on the value of volunteering in their community. Selection is based on academics (40%), character (15%), Americanism (15%), leadership (15%), and financial need (15%).
Financial data The stipend is $1,000.
Duration 1 year.
Number awarded 1 each year.
Deadline March of each year.

[878]
NATIONAL 4TH INFANTRY (IVY) DIVISION ASSOCIATION ANNUAL EDUCATIONAL SCHOLARSHIP

National 4th Infantry (IVY) Division Association
c/o Don Kelby, Executive Director
P.O. Box 1914
St. Peters, MO 63376-0035
(314) 606-1969   E-mail: 4thidaed@swbell.net
Web: www.4thinfantry.org/content/scholarships-donations

Summary To provide financial assistance for college to members of the National 4th Infantry (IVY) Division Association and their families.
Eligibility This program is open to 1) association members in good standing; 2) children and grandchildren of members; and 3) spouses of members while the member is a soldier on active duty. Recipients are chosen by lottery.
Financial data The stipend is $2,000.
Duration 1 year; may be renewed.
Additional information The trust fund from which these scholarships are awarded was created by the officers and enlisted men of the 4th Infantry Division as a living memorial to the men of the division who died in Vietnam. Originally, it was only open to children of members of the division who died in the line of duty while serving in Vietnam between August 1, 1966 and December 31, 1977. When all those eligible had completed college, it adopted its current requirements.
Number awarded Up to 10 each year.
Deadline June of each year.

[879]
NATIONAL GUARD ASSOCIATION OF CALIFORNIA SCHOLARSHIPS

National Guard Association of California
Attn: Executive Director
3336 Bradshaw Road, Suite 230
Sacramento, CA 95827-2615
(916) 362-3411   Toll Free: (800) 647-0018
Fax: (916) 362-3707
Web: www.ngac.org/ngac-scholarship-program-2

Summary To provide financial assistance to members of the National Guard Association of California (NGAC) and their dependents who are interested in attending college in any state.

Eligibility This program is open to 1) current members of the NGAC; 2) dependents of NGAC members; and 3) dependents of retired California National Guard servicemembers who are life members of the NGAC. Applicants must be attending or planning to attend a college, university, or trade school in any state. Along with their application, they must submit a 500-word essay on the greatest challenge they have faced and how it has impacted them. Selection is based on that essay; unweighted GPA; extracurricular activities, honors, and/or awards; letters of recommendation; and (for high school seniors and college students with less than 2 semesters of completed courses) SAT or ACT scores.
Financial data Stipends range from $250 to $1,000. Funds are paid directly to the recipient.
Duration 1 year.
Number awarded Varies each year; recently, 19 were awarded.
Deadline May of each year.

[880]
NATIONAL GUARD ASSOCIATION OF MARYLAND SCHOLARSHIPS

National Guard Association of Maryland
Attn: Scholarship Committee
P.O. Box 16675
Baltimore, MD 21221-0675
(410) 557-2606   Toll Free: (800) 844-1394
Fax: (410) 893-7529
E-mail: nationalguardassociationmd@gmail.com
Web: www.ngam.net/scholarship-application

Summary To provide financial assistance to members of the National Guard Association of Maryland (NGAM) and their family members who are interested in attending college in any state.
Eligibility This program is open to NGAM members (including current and former members of the National Guard) and their spouses and children. Applicants must be enrolled or planning to enroll full or part time at an accredited college, university, or vocational/technical school in any state. They must submit a resume in which they outline their academic background, activities in which they have participated, and honors they have received; 3 letters of recommendation; an essay on their goals and how this scholarship will assist them; and information on financial need.
Financial data The stipend is $1,000. Funds are paid directly to the recipient's university to be used for tuition, fees, and books.
Duration 1 year; recipients may reapply.
Number awarded Varies each year; recently, 11 were awarded.
Deadline March of each year.

[881]
NATIONAL GUARD ASSOCIATION OF MINNESOTA SCHOLARSHIPS

National Guard Association of Minnesota
Attn: Executive Director
P.O. Box 131766
St. Paul, MN 55113-0020
(651) 503-7993   E-mail: director@ngamn.org
Web: www.ngamn.org/scholarships

Summary To provide financial assistance to current and retired members of the National Guard Association of Minnesota (NGAMN) and their families who are interested in working on an undergraduate or graduate degree at a school in any state.
Eligibility This program is open to active members and retired life members of NGAMN and their spouses, children, and grandchildren. Applicants must be high school seniors or students currently enrolled at least half time at an accredited institution of higher learning in any state and working on a 4-year bachelor's or graduate degree. They must have a GPA of 2.75 or higher. Along with their application, they must submit an essay on a topic that describes a value of the Army or Air Force, rotating among loyalty, duty, respect, selfless service, honor, integrity, personal courage, commitment, and excellence. Financial need is not considered in the selection process.
Financial data Stipends are $1,000 or $500. Funds are paid directly to the recipient.
Duration 1 year. Recipients may reapply after 3 years.
Additional information The $1,000 scholarship is sponsored by McGough Construction Company. This program began in 2008.
Number awarded 3 each year: 1 at $1,000 and 2 at $500 (1 to a member or retired member and 1 to a spouse, child, or grandchild).
Deadline June of each year.

[882]
NATIONAL GUARD ASSOCIATION OF NEW HAMPSHIRE SCHOLARSHIPS

National Guard Association of New Hampshire
Attn: Scholarship Committee
P.O. Box 22031
Portsmouth, NH 03802-2031
(603) 227-1597   E-mail: nganhscholarship@gmail.com
Web: www.nganh.org/benefits

Summary To provide financial assistance to members of the National Guard Association of New Hampshire and their dependents who are interested in attending college or graduate school in any state.
Eligibility This program is open to current members of the National Guard Association of New Hampshire (officer, enlisted, or retired), their spouses, and their dependent children. Applicants must be enrolled or planning to enroll full or part time in an associate, bachelor's, graduate, professional, or doctoral degree program at an accredited college or university in any state. Along with their application, they must submit a 1-page essay on a topic that changes annually; recently, they were asked to describe what citizen service means to them.
Financial data The stipend is $1,000.
Duration 1 year.
Number awarded 1 each year.
Deadline April of each year.

[883]
NATIONAL GUARD ASSOCIATION OF NEW JERSEY SCHOLARSHIP PROGRAM

National Guard Association of New Jersey
Attn: Scholarship Committee
P.O. Box 266
Wrightstown, NJ 08562
(848) 480-3441   E-mail: scholarship@nganj.org
Web: www.nganj.org/awards-scholarships

Summary To provide financial assistance to members of the National Guard Association of New Jersey (NGANJ) or their dependents who are interested in attending college or graduate school in any state.
Eligibility This program is open to 1) active members of the NGANJ currently enrolled full time at an approved community college, school of nursing, or 4-year college in any state; and 2) the spouses, children, and grandchildren of active, retired, or deceased members entering or attending a 4-year college or university in any state. Applicants must submit transcripts, information on the civic and academic activities in which they have participated, and a list of offices, honors, awards, and special recognitions they have received. Selection is based on academic accomplishment, leadership, and citizenship.
Financial data Stipends up to $1,000 are available.
Duration 1 year; nonrenewable.
Number awarded Varies each year; recently, 5 were awarded.
Deadline February of each year.

[884]
NATIONAL GUARD ASSOCIATION OF SOUTH CAROLINA AUXILIARY COLLEGE SCHOLARSHIP GRANT

National Guard Association of South Carolina Auxiliary
P.O. Box 281
Irmo, SC 29063
E-mail: info@ngasca.org
Web: www.ngasca.org/scholarship

Summary To provide financial assistance to members of the National Guard Association of South Carolina Auxiliary (NGASCA) and their dependents who are interested in attending college in any state.
Eligibility This program is open to members of the auxiliary and their dependents or spouses who are related to an active, retired, or deceased member of the NGASCA. Applicants must be attending or planning to attend a college or university in any state. Along with their application, they must submit transcripts and documentation of financial need.
Financial data A stipend is awarded (amount not specified).
Duration 1 year; recipients may reapply for up to 3 additional years.
Number awarded Varies each year; recently, 6 were awarded.
Deadline January of each year.

SCHOLARSHIPS: FAMILY MEMBERS

[885]
NATIONAL GUARD ASSOCIATION OF TEXAS SCHOLARSHIP PROGRAM
National Guard Association of Texas
Attn: Education Committee
3706 Crawford Avenue
Austin, TX 78731-6803
(512) 454-7300   Toll Free: (800) 252-NGAT
Fax: (512) 467-6803   E-mail: tbz@ngat.org
Web: www.ngat.org/education.htm

Summary To provide financial assistance to members and dependents of members of the National Guard Association of Texas who are interested in attending college or graduate school in any state.

Eligibility This program is open to annual and life members of the association and their spouses and children (associate members and their dependents are not eligible). Applicants may be high school seniors, undergraduate students, or graduate students, either enrolled or planning to enroll at an institution of higher education in any state. Along with their application, they must submit an essay on their desire to continue their education. Selection is based on scholarship, citizenship, and leadership.

Financial data Stipends range from $500 to $5,000.

Duration 1 year (nonrenewable).

Additional information This program includes the Len and Jean Tallas Memorial Scholarship, the Texas Capital Area Chapter of the AUSA Scholarship, the Lewis O. King Memorial Scholarship, the Gloria Jenell and Marlin E. Mote Endowed Scholarship, the LTC Gary Parrish Memorial Scholarship, the TXNG Retirees Endowed Scholarship, and 2 scholarships sponsored by USAA Insurance Corporation.

Number awarded Varies each year; recently, 8 were awarded: 1 at $5,000, 1 at $4,000, 1 at $2,000, 1 at $1,250, 3 at $1,000, and 1 at $500.

Deadline February of each year.

[886]
NATIONAL GUARD ASSOCIATION OF VERMONT SCHOLARSHIPS
National Guard Association of Vermont
Attn: Scholarships
P.O. Box 694
Essex Junction, VT 05453
(802) 999-7675   E-mail: ngavtpresident@gmail.com
Web: www.ngavt.org/scholarships

Summary To provide financial assistance to members of the Vermont National Guard (VTNG) or the National Guard Association of Vermont (NGA-VT) and their children or spouses who are interested in attending college or graduate school in any state.

Eligibility This program is open to current members of the VTNG or the NGA-VT, their spouses, and their unmarried children. Applicants must be working, or planning to work, on an associate, undergraduate, technical, or graduate degree as a full-time student at a school in any state. Along with their application, they must submit an essay on their commitment to selfless public service or their plan for pursuing it in the future. Selection is based on academic performance and overall potential for a commitment to selfless public service.

Financial data The stipend is $1,000. Funds are sent directly to the recipient.

Duration 1 year; recipients may reapply.

Additional information This program is sponsored by the New England Federal Credit Union.

Number awarded 4 undergraduate and 1 graduate scholarship are awarded each year.

Deadline January of each year.

[887]
NATIONAL GUARD OF GEORGIA SCHOLARSHIP FUND FOR COLLEGES OR UNIVERSITIES
Georgia Guard Insurance Trust
3 Central Plaza, Suite 356
Rome, GA 30161
(770) 739-9651   Toll Free: (800) 229-1053
Fax: (770) 745-0673   E-mail: director@ngaga.org
Web: www.ngaga.org

Summary To provide financial assistance to members of the Georgia National Guard and their spouses, children, and grandchildren who are interested in attending college in any state.

Eligibility This program is open to policyholders with the Georgia Guard Insurance Trust (GGIT) who are members of the National Guard Association of Georgia (NGAGA) or the Enlisted Association of the National Guard of Georgia (EANGGA); spouses, children, and grandchildren of NGAGA and EANGGA members are also eligible. Applicants must be enrolled or planning to enroll as undergraduate students at a college or university in any state and have received an academic honor while in high school; family members must be enrolled full time but drilling Guard members may be enrolled half time. Graduating high school seniors must have an SAT score of at least 1000, an ACT score of at least 19, or a GPA of 3.0 or higher. Students already enrolled at a college or university must have a cumulative GPA of 3.0 or higher. Along with their application, they must submit transcripts, a letter with personal specific facts regarding their desire to continue their education, 2 letters of recommendation, a letter of academic reference, and an agreement to retain insurance with the GGIT for at least 2 years following completion of the school year for which the scholarship is awarded. Selection is based on academics, character, and moral and personal traits.

Financial data Stipends are $3,000 or $1,000.

Duration 1 year.

Number awarded Up to 10 each year at $3,000; the number of $1,000 scholarships varies each year; recently, 23 were awarded.

Deadline April of each year.

[888]
NATIONAL GUARD OF GEORGIA SCHOLARSHIP FUND FOR VOCATIONAL OR BUSINESS SCHOOLS
Georgia Guard Insurance Trust
3 Central Plaza, Suite 356
Rome, GA 30161
(770) 739-9651   Toll Free: (800) 229-1053
Fax: (770) 745-0673   E-mail: director@ngaga.org
Web: www.ngaga.org

Summary To provide financial assistance to members of the Georgia National Guard and their spouses, children, and grandchildren who are interested in attending business or vocational school in any state.

Eligibility This program is open to policyholders with the Georgia Guard Insurance Trust (GGIT) who are members of the National Guard Association of Georgia (NGAGA) or the Enlisted Association of the National Guard of Georgia (EANGGA); spouses, children, and grandchildren of NGAGA and EANGGA members are also eligible. Applicants must be interested in enrolling at least half time in day or evening classes at a business or vocational school in any state. They must be able to meet program-specific admission standards and institutional requirements and complete all admission procedures for admission to a degree/diploma program in regular program status. Along with their application, they must submit transcripts, a letter with personal specific facts regarding their desire to continue their education, 2 letters of recommendation, and an agreement to retain insurance with the GGIT for at least 2 years following completion of the school year for which the scholarship is awarded. Selection is based on academics, character, and moral and personal traits.

Financial data The stipend is $1,000.

Duration 1 year.

Number awarded 1 or 2 each year.

Deadline April of each year.

[889]
NAVAL CRYPTOLOGIC VETERANS ASSOCIATION SCHOLARSHIPS

Naval Cryptologic Veterans Association
c/o Bill Hickey, Executive Director
156 Barcelona Drive
Boulder, CO 80303-4938
E-mail: wa3h@hotmail.com
Web: www.usncva.org

Summary To provide financial assistance to high school seniors and college students who are sponsored by a member of the Naval Cryptologic Veterans Association (NCVA).

Eligibility This program is open to graduating high school seniors and students currently or previously enrolled in college. Applicants must be sponsored by an NCVA member who submits their application on their behalf, although they do not need to be related to the sponsor. Along with their application, they must submit a brief written statement on their current and future educational goals, any special circumstances they wish to have considered, and the nature of their financial need.

Financial data Stipends range from $2,000 to $3,000.

Duration 1 year.

Number awarded Varies each year; recently, 3 were awarded: 1 each at $3,000, $2,500, and $2,000.

Deadline June of each year.

[890]
NAVAL HELICOPTER ASSOCIATION SCHOLARSHIPS

Naval Helicopter Association
Attn: Scholarship Fund
P.O. Box 180578
Coronado, CA 92178-0578
(619) 435-7139   Fax: (619) 435-7354
E-mail: pres@nhascholarshipfund.org
Web: www.nhascholarshipfund.org/about/scholarships

Summary To provide financial assistance for college or graduate school to members of the Naval Helicopter Association (NHA) and their families.

Eligibility This program is open to NHA members and their spouses, children, and grandchildren. Membership in the NHA is open to active-duty and retired U.S. Navy, U.S. Marine Corps, and U.S. Coast Guard helicopter pilots, aircrew, and maintenance professionals. Applicants must be working on or planning to work on an undergraduate or graduate degree in any field. Along with their application, they must submit a personal statement on their academic and career aspirations. Selection is based on that statement, academic proficiency, scholastic achievements and awards, extracurricular activities, employment history, and letters of recommendation. The program includes scholarships 1) reserved for NHA family members; 2) reserved for active-duty personnel; 3) sponsored by private corporations; 4) named as memorials in honor of distinguished individuals; and 5) awarded on a regional basis.

Financial data Stipends are approximately $2,000.

Duration 1 year.

Additional information Corporate sponsors have included FLIR Systems, D.P. Associates, L-3 Communications, CAE, Raytheon Corporation, Lockheed Martin (designated the Sergei Sikorsky Scholarship), and Northrop Grumman. Memorial Scholarships have included the Edward and Veronica Ream Memorial Scholarship, the CDR Mort McCarthy Memorial Scholarship, the Charles Karman Memorial Scholarship, the LT Christian "Horse" Hescock Memorial Scholarship, and the Captain Mark Starr Memorial Scholarship.

Number awarded Varies each year; recently, 17 were awarded: 1 graduate student family member, 3 active-duty graduate students, 1 active-duty undergraduate student, 4 sponsored by corporate donors, 4 memorial scholarships, and 4 regional scholarships.

Deadline January of each year.

[891]
NAVAL SPECIAL WARFARE DEVELOPMENT GROUP SCHOLARSHIPS

Navy Seal Foundation
Attn: DEVGRU Scholarship Committee
1619 D Street, Building 5326
Virginia Beach, VA 23459
(757) 744-5326   Fax: (757) 363-7491
E-mail: info@navysealfoundation.org
Web: www.navysealfoundation.org

Summary To provide financial assistance for college to the children and spouses of personnel assigned to the Naval Special Warfare Development Group (DEVGRU).

Eligibility This program is open to the dependent children and spouses of former and present Navy SEAL, Special Warfare Combatant-craft Crewmen (SWCC), or Military Direct Support person who are or have been assigned to DEVGRU. Applicants must be enrolled or planning to enroll at a trade school, vocational/technical institute, or undergraduate college. Spouses may also apply for graduate school. Along with their application, they must submit an essay on their plans as related to their educational and career objectives and long-term goals. Selection is based on merit (as measured by GPA, SAT scores, class rank, extracurricular activities, volun-

teer community involvement, leadership positions held, military service record, and after school employment, as appropriate) and academic potential.
Financial data Stipends are $15,000, $7,500, or $5,000 per year.
Duration 1 year; may be renewed.
Number awarded Varies each year; recently, the Navy Seal Foundation awarded 16 scholarships for all of its programs: 3 for 4 years at $15,000 per year to high school seniors and graduates, 3 for 1 year at $7,500 to high school seniors and graduates, 3 for 1 year at $15,000 to current college students, 3 for 1 year at $7,500 to current college students, and 4 for 1 year at $5,000 to spouses.
Deadline January of each year.

[892]
NAVY LEAGUE FOUNDATION SCHOLARSHIPS
Navy League of the United States
Attn: Scholarships
2300 Wilson Boulevard, Suite 200
Arlington, VA 22201-5424
(703) 528-1775   Toll Free: (800) 356-5760
Fax: (703) 528-2333
E-mail: scholarships@navyleague.org
Web: www.navyleague.org/programs/scholarships

Summary To provide financial assistance for college to dependent children of sea service personnel.
Eligibility This program is open to U.S. citizens who are 1) dependents or direct descendants of an active, Reserve, retired, or honorably discharged member of the U.S. sea service (including the Navy, Marine Corps, Coast Guard, or Merchant Marine); or 2) currently an active member of the Naval Sea Cadet Corps. Applicants must be high school seniors entering their freshman year at an accredited college or university. They must have a GPA of 3.0 or higher. Along with their application, they must submit transcripts, 2 letters of recommendation, SAT/ACT scores, documentation of financial need, proof of qualifying sea service duty, and a 1-page personal statement on why they should be considered for this scholarship.
Financial data The stipend is $5,000 or $2,500 per year.
Duration 4 years, provided the recipient maintains a GPA of 3.0 or higher.
Additional information This program includes the following named awards (not all of which are awarded each year): the Jack and Eileen Anderson Scholarship, the John G. Brokaw Scholarship, the Wesley C. Cameron Scholarship, the Ann E. Clark Foundation Scholarship, the CAPT Winifred Quick Collins, USN (Ret) Scholarship, the Albert Levinson Scholarship, the Gladys Ann Smith Greater Los Angeles Women's Council Scholarship, the Gloria and J. Michael McGrath Scholarship, the John J. Schiff Scholarship, the Harold Wirth Scholarship, and the United Armed Forces Association Scholarship.1.
Number awarded Varies each year; recently, 1 at $5,000 per year and 7 at $2,500 per year were awarded.
Deadline February of each year.

[893]
NAVY SEAL FOUNDATION SCHOLARSHIPS
Navy Seal Foundation
Attn: Chief Financial Officer
1619 D Street, Building 5326
Virginia Beach, VA 23459
(757) 744-5326   Fax: (757) 363-7491
E-mail: info@navysealfoundation.org
Web: www.navysealfoundation.org

Summary To provide financial assistance for college or graduate school to Naval Special Warfare (NSW) personnel and their families.
Eligibility This program is open to active-duty Navy SEALS, Special Warfare Combatant-craft Crewmen (SWCC), and military personnel assigned to other NSW commands. Their dependent children and spouses are also eligible. Applicants must be entering or continuing full or part-time students working on an associate or bachelor's degree. Active-duty and spouses, but not dependent children, may also work on a graduate degree. Selection is based on GPA, SAT scores, class ranking, extracurricular activities, volunteer community involvement, leadership positions held, military service record, and employment (as appropriate).
Financial data Stipends are $15,000, $7,500, or $5,000 per year.
Duration 1 year; may be renewed.
Number awarded Varies each year; recently, the Navy Seal Foundation awarded 16 scholarships for all of its programs: 3 for 4 years at $15,000 per year to high school seniors and graduates, 3 for 1 year at $7,500 to high school seniors and graduates, 3 for 1 year at $15,000 to current college students, 3 for 1 year at $7,500 to current college students, and 4 for 1 year at $5,000 to spouses.
Deadline February of each year.

[894]
NAVY SUPPLY CORPS FOUNDATION MEMORIAL SCHOLARSHIPS
Navy Supply Corps Foundation
Attn: Administrator
2061 Experiment Station Road, Suite 301
PMB 423
Watkinsville, GA 30677
(706) 354-4111   Fax: (706) 354-0334
E-mail: foundationadmin@usnscf.com
Web: www.usnscf.com

Summary To provide financial assistance for college to children of Navy Supply Corps personnel who died on active duty.
Eligibility This program is open to children of Navy Supply Corps personnel who died on active duty after 2001. The program applies to Active Duty Supply Corps Officers as well as Reserve Supply Corps Officers in the following categories: Mobilization, Active Duty for Special Work (ADSW), Active Duty for Training (ADT), Annual Training (AT), and Inactive Duty for Training (IDT). Applicants must be attending or planning to attend a 2- or 4-year accredited college on a full-time basis and have a GPA of 2.5 or higher in high school and/or college. Selection is based on character, demonstrated leadership or leadership potential, academic achievement, extracurricular activities, and financial need.
Financial data The stipend is $2,500.

Duration 1 year.
Number awarded Varies each year; recently, 4 were awarded.
Deadline February of each year.

[895]
NAVY SUPPLY CORPS FOUNDATION SCHOLARSHIPS

Navy Supply Corps Foundation
Attn: Administrator
2061 Experiment Station Road, Suite 301
PMB 423
Watkinsville, GA 30677
(706) 354-4111   Fax: (706) 354-0334
E-mail: foundationadmin@usnscf.com
Web: www.usnscf.com

Summary To provide financial assistance for college to relatives of current or former Navy Supply Corps personnel.
Eligibility This program is open to 1) children, grandchildren, and spouses of living or deceased regular, retired, Reserve, or prior service Navy Supply Corps officer; and 2) children and spouses of active or retired enlisted members with ratings of AK (Aviation Storekeeper), SK (Storekeeper), MS (Mess Specialist), DK (Disbursing Clerk), SH (Ship Serviceman), LI (Lithographer), or PC (Postal Clerk). Applicants must be attending or planning to attend a 2- or 4-year accredited college on a full-time basis and have a GPA of 2.5 or higher in high school and/or college. Selection is based on character, demonstrated leadership or leadership potential, academic achievement, extracurricular activities, and financial need.
Financial data Stipends range from $1,000 to $12,500 per year.
Duration 1 year; some scholarships may be renewed for 3 additional years.
Additional information This program began in 1971.
Number awarded Varies each year; recently, the foundation awarded 46 new scholarships (worth $102,000) and 34 renewal scholarships (worth $115,000). Since the program was established, it has awarded 2,431 scholarships with a total value of more than $5,764,000.
Deadline February of each year.

[896]
NAVY WIVES CLUBS OF AMERICA SCHOLARSHIP FOUNDATION DEPENDENT CHILD SCHOLARSHIP

Navy Wives Clubs of America
c/o NSA Mid-South
Attn: Lois Wilber, Scholarship Director
4368 Water Briar Road
P.O. Box 54022
Millington, TN 38054-0022
Toll Free: (866) 511-NWCA
E-mail: nwca@navywivesclubsofamerica.org
Web: www.navywivesclubsofamerica.org/scholarships

Summary To provide financial assistance for college or graduate school to the children of naval personnel.
Eligibility Applicants for these scholarships must be the children (natural born, legally adopted, or stepchildren) of enlisted members of the Navy, Marine Corps, or Coast Guard on active duty, retired with pay, or deceased. Applicants must be attending or planning to attend an accredited college or university as a full-time undergraduate or graduate student. They must have a GPA of 2.5 or higher. Along with their application, they must submit an essay on their career objectives and the reasons they chose those objectives. Selection is based on academic standing, moral character, and financial need. Some scholarships are reserved for students majoring in special education, medical students, and children of members of Navy Wives Clubs of America (NWCA).
Financial data The stipend is $1,500.
Duration 1 year; may be renewed up to 3 additional years.
Additional information Membership in the NWCA is open to spouses of enlisted personnel serving in the Navy, Marine Corps, Coast Guard, and the active Reserve units of those services; spouses of enlisted personnel who have been honorably discharged, retired, or transferred to the Fleet Reserve on completion of duty; and widows of enlisted personnel in those services.
Number awarded 30 each year, including at least 4 to freshmen, 4 to current undergraduates applying for the first time, 2 to medical students, 1 to a student majoring in special education, and 4 to children of NWCA members.
Deadline March of each year.

[897]
NAVY-MARINE CORPS RELIEF SOCIETY EDUCATION ASSISTANCE

Navy-Marine Corps Relief Society
Attn: Education Division
875 North Randolph Street, Suite 225
Arlington, VA 22203-1757
(703) 696-4960   Toll Free: (800) 654-8364
Fax: (703) 696-0144   E-mail: education@nmcrs.org
Web: www.nmcrs.org

Summary To provide grants and interest-free loans for college to the spouses and children of Navy and Marine Corps personnel and to Navy and Marine Corps personnel in designated programs.
Eligibility This program is open to Navy and Marine Corps personnel and their families, including 1) dependent children under 23 years of age of sailors and Marines who are active-duty, retired (including retired Reservists drawing military retirement pay), or deceased (died on active duty or after retirement); 2) spouses of sailors and Marines who are active-duty or retired; or 3) active-duty members of the Navy or Marine Corps selected for or enrolled in the Marine Enlisted Commissioning Education Program (MECEP) or the Navy's Medical Enlisted Commissioning Program (MECP). Applicants must be enrolled or planning to enroll as a full-time undergraduate student at an accredited college, university, or vocational/technical school; be registered at the Defense Eligibility Enrollment Reporting System (DEERS); have a GPA of 2.0 or higher; and be able to demonstrate financial need. They must be seeking grants or interest-free grants.
Financial data Grants and interest-free loans range from $500 to $3,000 per academic year. Funds are disbursed directly to the recipient's academic institution. Loans to children and spouses must be repaid within 24 months by allotment of pay, at a monthly rate of at least $50. Loans to MECEP and MECP students must be repaid within 48 months following commissioning.
Duration Recipients may reapply.

Additional information Recently, this program included the following named grants: the Gold Star Scholarship Programs (limited to children and spouses of sailors and Marines who died as a result of specified military engagements; the Joseph A. McAlinden Divers Scholarship (limited to sailors and Marines serving on active duty as divers and their families); and the RADM Courtney G. Clegg and Mrs. Margaret H. Clegg Scholarship. Loan programs included the Vice Admiral E.P. Travers Loan Program and the Admiral Mike Boorda Loan Program (limited to MECEP and MECP students).
Number awarded Varies each year.
Deadline May of each year.

[898]
ND DEPENDENT TUITION WAIVER

North Dakota Department of Veterans Affairs
4201 38th Street South, Suite 104
Fargo, ND 58104-7535
(701) 239-7165   Toll Free: (866) 634-8387
Fax: (701) 239-7166
Web: www.nd.gov

Summary To provide financial assistance for college to the spouses, widow(er)s, and children of disabled and other North Dakota veterans and military personnel.
Eligibility This program is open to the spouses, widow(er)s, and dependent children of veterans who were killed in action, died from wounds or other service-connected causes, were totally disabled as a result of service-connected causes, died from service-connected disabilities, were a prisoner of war, or were declared missing in action. Veteran parents must have been born in and lived in North Dakota until entrance into the armed forces (or must have resided in the state for at least 6 months prior to entrance into military service) and must have served during wartime.
Financial data Eligible dependents receive free tuition and are exempt from fees at any state-supported institution of higher education, technical school, or vocational school in North Dakota.
Duration Up to 45 months or 10 academic semesters.
Number awarded Varies each year.
Deadline Deadline not specified.

[899]
NEBRASKA WAIVER OF TUITION FOR VETERANS' DEPENDENTS

Department of Veterans' Affairs
State Office Building
301 Centennial Mall South, Fourth Floor
P.O. Box 95083
Lincoln, NE 68509-5083
(402) 471-2458   Fax: (402) 742-1142
E-mail: ndva@nebraska.gov
Web: www.veterans.nebraska.gov/waiver

Summary To provide financial assistance for college to dependents of deceased and disabled veterans and military personnel in Nebraska.
Eligibility Eligible are spouses, widow(er)s, and children who are residents of Nebraska and whose parent, stepparent, or spouse was a member of the U.S. armed forces and 1) died of a service-connected disability; 2) died subsequent to discharge as a result of injury or illness sustained while in service; 3) is permanently and totally disabled as a result of military service; or 4) is classified as missing in action or as a prisoner of war during armed hostilities. Applicants must be attending or planning to attend a branch of the University of Nebraska, a state college, or a community college in Nebraska.
Financial data Tuition is waived at public institutions in Nebraska.
Duration Spouses may receive support until completion of a bachelor's degree; children are eligible until the complete a bachelor's degree or reach 26 years of age.
Additional information Applications may be submitted through 1 of the recognized veterans' organizations or any county service officer.
Number awarded Varies each year; recently, 311 were awarded.
Deadline Deadline not specified.

[900]
NERA/USAA COLLEGE SCHOLARSHIP PROGRAM

Naval Enlisted Reserve Association
Attn: Scholarship Committee
8116 Arlington Boulevard
Falls Church, VA 22042
(703) 534-1329   Toll Free: (800) 776-9020
Fax: (703) 534-3617   E-mail: members@nera.org
Web: www.nera.org

Summary To provide financial assistance for college to members of the Naval Enlisted Reserve Association (NERA) and their families.
Eligibility This program is open to students enrolled or entering a college or university to work full or part time on an associate degree, vocational or trade school certificate, bachelor's degree, master's degree, or doctoral degree. Applicants or their sponsor must be a member of NERA in good standing. They must have a GPA of 3.0 or higher. Along with their application, they must submit an essay of 500 to 600 words on 1) their aspirations and course of study; and 2) the role of the Reservist in America and the importance of the Reserves to our national defense. In the selection process, priority is given in the following order: 1) currently serving Reserve, active and IRR members of the U.S. armed forces; 2) children and spouses of those currently serving in the U.S. armed forces; and 3) spouses, children, or grandchildren sponsored by any NERA member. Financial need is not considered in the selection process.
Financial data The stipend is $2,000.
Duration 1 year.
Additional information This program is funded in part by USAA Insurance Corporation. Regular membership in NERA is open to enlisted members of the Navy, Marine Corps, and Coast Guard Reserve components, including FTS, IRR, VTU, and retirees; associate membership is open to anyone who wishes to support NERA.
Number awarded 5 each year.
Deadline June of each year.

[901]
NEW HAMPSHIRE CHAPTER MOAA SCHOLARSHIP LOAN PROGRAM

Military Officers Association of America-New Hampshire Chapter
c/o Col. Joe DiChiaro
P.O. Box 865
Londonderry, NH 03050
(603) 363-2396 E-mail: j.dichiaro@comcast.net
Web: www.moaa-nh.org/Chapter_News.html#Scholarship

Summary To provide financial assistance for college in any state to the children and grandchildren of members of the New Hampshire Chapter of the Military Officers Association of America (MOAA).

Eligibility This program is open to children and grandchildren of members of the chapter who are attending or planning to attend college in any state. Selection is based on merit, not need.

Financial data Loans recently were $2,000 for first-year students or $3,000 for continuing students. Repayment is expected to begin 6 months after completion of the recipient's academic program at the rate of 2% of the loan per month. No interest is charged. Portions of a loan may be forgiven, based on academic performance, at the discretion of the sponsor.

Duration 1 year; may be renewed.

Additional information This program began in 1985.

Number awarded Varies each year; recently, 9 were granted.

Deadline May of each year.

[902]
NEW HAMPSHIRE HIGHER EDUCATION SCHOLARSHIPS FOR ORPHANS OF VETERANS

New Hampshire Department of Education
Attn: Division of Higher Education
Higher Education Commission
101 Pleasant Street
Concord, NH 03301-3860
(603) 271-8508 Fax: (603) 271-1953
TDD: (800) 735-2964 E-mail: patricia.edes@doe.nh.gov
Web: www.education.nh.gov

Summary To provide financial assistance for college in the state to the children of New Hampshire veterans who died of service-connected causes.

Eligibility This program is open to New Hampshire residents between 16 and 25 years of age whose parent(s) died while on active duty or as a result of a service-related disability incurred during World War II, the Korean Conflict, the southeast Asian Conflict (Vietnam), or the Gulf Wars. Parents must have been residents of New Hampshire at the time of death. Applicants must be enrolled at least half time as undergraduate students at a public college or university in New Hampshire. Financial need is not considered in the selection process.

Financial data The stipend is $2,500 per year, to be used for the payment of room, board, books, and supplies. Recipients are also eligible to receive a tuition waiver from the institution.

Duration 1 year; may be renewed for up to 3 additional years.

Additional information This program began in 1943.

Number awarded Varies each year; recently, 2 were awarded.

Deadline August of each year.

[903]
NEW JERSEY AMERICAN LEGION SCHOLARSHIPS

American Legion
Department of New Jersey
Attn: Adjutant
171 Jersey Street
Building 5, Second Floor
Trenton, NJ 08611
(609) 695-5418 Fax: (609) 394-1532
E-mail: adjutant@njamericanlegion.org
Web: www.njamericanlegion.org

Summary To provide financial assistance to the descendants of members of the New Jersey Department of the American Legion who plan to attend college in any state.

Eligibility This program is open to high school seniors who are the natural or adopted children, grandchildren, or great-grandchildren of living or deceased members of the American Legion's New Jersey Department. Applicants must be planning to attend a college or university in any state. Along with their application, they must submit a brief statement on the reasons for their choice of vocation. Selection is based on character (20%), Americanism and community service (20%), leadership (20%), scholarship (20%), and financial need (20%).

Financial data The stipend is $1,000 per year.

Duration These scholarships are for 4 years, 2 years, or 1 year.

Additional information These scholarships were formerly designated the Lawrence Luterman Memorial Scholarships and the Stutz Memorial Scholarship.

Number awarded 8 each year: 2 at $1,000 per year for 4 years, 4 at $1,000 per year for 2 years, and 2 at $1,000 for 1 year.

Deadline February of each year.

[904]
NEW JERSEY BANKERS EDUCATION FOUNDATION SCHOLARSHIPS

New Jersey Bankers Association
Attn: New Jersey Bankers Charitable Foundation, Inc.
411 North Avenue East
Cranford, NJ 07016-2436
(908) 272-8500, ext. 627 Fax: (908) 272-6626
E-mail: j.mcweeney@njbankers.com
Web: www.njbankers.com

Summary To provide financial assistance to dependents of deceased and disabled military personnel who have a connection to New Jersey and are interested in attending college in any state.

Eligibility This program is open to the spouses, children, stepchildren, and grandchildren of members of the armed services who died or became disabled while on active duty; it is not required that the military person died in combat. Applicants must have a high school or equivalency diploma and be attending college in any state. Adult dependents who wish to obtain a high school equivalency diploma are also eligible. Either the dependent or the servicemember must have a connection to New Jersey; the applicant's permanent address

must be in New Jersey or the servicemember's last permanent address or military base must have been in the state. Financial need is considered in the selection process.
Financial data A stipend is awarded (amount not specified).
Duration 1 year; may be renewed if the recipient maintains a "C" average.
Additional information This program began in 2005.
Number awarded 1 or more each year.
Deadline June of each year.

[905]
NEW JERSEY LEGION AUXILIARY PAST PRESIDENTS' PARLEY NURSING GRANT
American Legion Auxiliary
Department of New Jersey
Attn: Secretary
1540 Kuser Road, Suite A-8
Hamilton, NJ 08619
(609) 581-9580   Fax: (609) 581-8429
E-mail: newjerseyala2@optimum.net
Web: www.alanj.org/index.php/scholarshipsgrants

Summary To provide financial assistance to New Jersey residents who are the descendants of veterans and interested in studying nursing at a school in any state.
Eligibility This program is open to the children, grandchildren, and great-grandchildren of veterans who served in the U.S. armed forces since December 7, 1941. Applicants must be graduating high school seniors who have been residents of New Jersey for at least 2 years. They must be planning to study nursing at a school in any state. Along with their application, they must submit a 1,000-word essay on the topic, "How Pride in country, community, school and family directs my daily life." Selection is based on academic achievement (40%), character (15%), leadership (15%), Americanism (15%), and financial need (15%).
Financial data A stipend is awarded (amount not specified).
Duration 1 year.
Number awarded 1 or more each year.
Deadline February of each year.

[906]
NEW JERSEY NATIONAL GUARD TUITION PROGRAM
New Jersey Department of Military and Veterans Affairs
Attn: New Jersey Army National Guard Education
  Services Officer
Second Floor, B204
3650 Saylors Pond Road
Fort Dix, NJ 08640-7600
(609) 562-0975   Toll Free: (888) 859-0352
Fax: (609) 562-0188
E-mail: benjamin.j.stoner.mil@mail.mil
Web: education.njarmyguard.com/njngtp

Summary To provide financial assistance for college or graduate school to New Jersey National Guard members and the surviving spouses and children of deceased members.
Eligibility This program is open to active members of the New Jersey National Guard who have completed Initial Active Duty for Training (IADT). Applicants must be New Jersey residents who have been accepted into a program of undergraduate or graduate study at any of 30 public institutions of higher education in the state. The surviving spouses and children of deceased members of the Guard who had completed IADT and were killed in the performance of their duties while a member of the Guard are also eligible if the school has classroom space available.
Financial data Tuition for up to 16 credits per semester is waived for full-time recipients in state-supported colleges or community colleges in New Jersey.
Duration 1 semester; may be renewed.
Number awarded Varies each year.
Deadline Deadline not specified.

[907]
NEW JERSEY POW/MIA TUITION BENEFIT PROGRAM
New Jersey Department of Military and Veterans Affairs
Attn: Veterans Benefits Bureau
101 Eggert Crossing Road
P.O. Box 340
Trenton, NJ 08625-0340
(609) 530-6949   Toll Free: (888) 8NJ-VETS (within NJ)
Fax: (609) 530-7075   E-mail: vbb@dmava.nj.gov
Web: www.nj.gov/military/veterans/benefits-resources

Summary To provide financial assistance for college to the children of New Jersey military personnel reported as missing in action or prisoners of war during the southeast Asian conflict.
Eligibility Eligible to apply for this assistance are New Jersey residents attending or accepted at a New Jersey public or independent postsecondary institution whose parents were military service personnel officially declared prisoners of war or missing in action after January 1, 1960.
Financial data This program entitles recipients to full undergraduate tuition at any public or independent postsecondary educational institution in New Jersey.
Duration Assistance continues until completion of a bachelor's degree.
Number awarded Varies each year.
Deadline September of each year for fall; February of each year for spring.

[908]
NEW MEXICO CHILDREN OF DECEASED MILITARY PERSONNEL SCHOLARSHIPS
New Mexico Department of Veterans' Services
Attn: State Benefits
407 Galisteo Street, Room 134
P.O. Box 2324
Santa Fe, NM 87504-2324
(505) 383-2400   Toll Free: (866) 433-VETS
Fax: (505) 827-6372 E-mail: JosephM.Dorn@state.nm.us
Web: www.nmdvs.org/state-benefits

Summary To provide financial assistance for college or graduate school to the children of deceased military personnel in New Mexico.
Eligibility This program is open to the children of military personnel killed in action or as a result of such action during a period of armed conflict. Applicants must be between the ages of 16 and 26 and enrolled in a state-supported school in New Mexico. Selection is based on merit and financial need.

Financial data The scholarships provide full waiver of tuition at state-funded postsecondary schools in New Mexico. A stipend of $150 per semester ($300 per year) provides assistance with books and fees.
Duration 1 year; may be renewed.
Number awarded Varies each year.
Deadline Deadline not specified.

[909]
NEW YORK LEGION AUXILIARY DEPARTMENT SCHOLARSHIP
American Legion Auxiliary
Department of New York
1580 Columbia Turnpike
Building 1, Suite 3
Castleton-On-Hudson, NY 12033
(518) 463-1162   Toll Free: (800) 421-6348
Fax: (518) 449-5406   E-mail: nyaladeptoffice@gmail.com
Web: www.deptny.org/?page_id=2128

Summary To provide financial assistance to New York residents who are the descendants of veterans and interested in attending college in any state.
Eligibility This program is open to residents of New York who are high school seniors or graduates and attending or planning to attend an accredited college or university in any state. Applicants must be the children, grandchildren, or great-grandchildren of veterans who served during specified periods of wartime. Along with their application, they must submit a 500-word essay on a subject of their choice. Selection is based on character (30%), Americanism (20%), leadership (10%), scholarship (20%), and financial need (20%). U.S. citizenship is required.
Financial data The stipend is $1,000. Funds are paid directly to the recipient's school.
Duration 1 year.
Number awarded 1 each year.
Deadline February of each year.

[910]
NEW YORK LEGION AUXILIARY DISTRICT SCHOLARSHIPS
American Legion Auxiliary
Department of New York
1580 Columbia Turnpike
Building 1, Suite 3
Castleton-On-Hudson, NY 12033
(518) 463-1162   Toll Free: (800) 421-6348
Fax: (518) 449-5406   E-mail: nyaladeptoffice@gmail.com
Web: www.deptny.org/?page_id=2128

Summary To provide financial assistance to descendants of veterans in New York who are interested in attending college in any state.
Eligibility This program is open to residents of New York who are high school seniors or graduates and attending or planning to attend an accredited college or university in any state. Applicants must be the children, grandchildren, or great-grandchildren of veterans who served during specified periods of wartime. Along with their application, they must submit a 500-word essay on a topic of their choice. Selection is based on character (30%), Americanism (20%), leadership (10%), scholarship (20%), and financial need (20%). U.S. citizenship is required.
Financial data The stipend is $1,000. Funds are paid directly to the recipient's school.
Duration 1 year.
Number awarded 10 each year: 1 in each of the 10 judicial districts in New York.
Deadline February of each year.

[911]
NEW YORK LEGION AUXILIARY PAST PRESIDENTS PARLEY STUDENT SCHOLARSHIP IN MEDICAL FIELD
American Legion Auxiliary
Department of New York
1580 Columbia Turnpike
Building 1, Suite 3
Castleton-On-Hudson, NY 12033
(518) 463-1162   Toll Free: (800) 421-6348
Fax: (518) 449-5406   E-mail: nyaladeptoffice@gmail.com
Web: www.deptny.org/?page_id=2128

Summary To provide financial assistance to descendants of wartime veterans in New York who are interested in attending college in any state to prepare for a career in a medical field.
Eligibility This program is open to residents of New York who are high school seniors or graduates and attending or planning to attend an accredited college or university in any state to prepare for a career in a medical field. Applicants must be the children, grandchildren, or great-grandchildren of veterans who served during specified periods of wartime. Along with their application, they must submit a 500-word essay on why they selected the medical field. Selection is based on character (30%), Americanism (20%), leadership (10%), scholarship (20%), and financial need (20%). U.S. citizenship is required.
Financial data The stipend is $1,000. Funds are paid directly to the recipient's school.
Duration 1 year.
Number awarded 2 each year.
Deadline February of each year.

[912]
NEW YORK MILITARY ENHANCED RECOGNITION INCENTIVE AND TRIBUTE (MERIT) SCHOLARSHIPS
New York State Higher Education Services Corporation
Attn: Student Information
99 Washington Avenue
Albany, NY 12255
(518) 473-1574   Toll Free: (888) NYS-HESC
Fax: (518) 473-3749   TDD: (800) 445-5234
E-mail: scholarships@hesc.com
Web: www.hesc.ny.gov

Summary To provide financial assistance to disabled veterans and the family members of deceased or disabled veterans who are residents of New York and interested in attending college in the state.
Eligibility This program is open to New York residents who served in the armed forces of the United States or state organized militia at any time on or after August 2, 1990 and became severely and permanently disabled as a result of injury or illness suffered or incurred in a combat theater or combat zone or during military training operations in preparation for duty in a combat theater or combat zone of opera-

SCHOLARSHIPS: FAMILY MEMBERS

tions. Also eligible are the children, spouses, or financial dependents of members of the armed forces of the United States or state organized militia who at any time after August 2, 1990 1) died, became severely and permanently disabled as a result of injury or illness suffered or incurred, or are classified as missing in action in a combat theater or combat zone of operations; 2) died as a result of injuries incurred in those designated areas; or 3) died or became severely and permanently disabled as a result of injury or illness suffered or incurred during military training operations in preparation for duty in a combat theater or combat zone of operations. Applicants must be attending or accepted at an approved program of study as full-time undergraduates at a public college or university or private institution in New York.

Financial data At public colleges and universities, this program provides payment of actual tuition and mandatory educational fees; actual room and board charged to students living on campus or an allowance for room and board for commuter students; and allowances for books, supplies, and transportation. At private institutions, the award is equal to the amount charged at the State University of New York (SUNY) for 4-year tuition and average mandatory fees (or the student's actual tuition and fees, whichever is less) plus allowances for room, board, books, supplies, and transportation. Recently, maximum awards were $24,250 for students living on campus or $15,750 for commuter students.

Duration This program is available for 4 years of full-time undergraduate study (or 5 years in an approved 5-year bachelor's degree program).

Additional information This program was previously known as the New York State Military Service Recognition Scholarships (MSRS).

Number awarded Varies each year; recently, 134 students received more than $2.1 million from this program.

Deadline April of each year.

[913]
NEXT GEN SCHOLARS PROGRAM

U.S. Navy
Attn: Navy Exchange Service Command
3280 Virginia Beach Boulevard
Virginia Beach, VA 23452-5724
Toll Free: (800) NAV-EXCH
Web: www.mynavyexchange.com

Summary To provide financial assistance for college to children of active and retired military personnel who shop at Navy Exchange (NEX) stores.

Eligibility This program is open to dependent children of active-duty military members, Reservists, and military retirees who are enrolled in grades 1-12 and have a GPA of 3.0 or higher. Applicants submit an entry at the service desk of their NEX store. Winners are selected in a drawing.

Financial data Winners receive savings bonds for $2,500, $1,500, $1,000, or $500. Funds are intended to help pay expenses of college.

Duration Drawings are held 4 times a year (in February, May, August, and November).

Additional information This program began in 1997 as the A-OK Student Reward Program.

Number awarded 16 each year: at each drawing, 1 savings bond for each of the 4 denominations is awarded.

Deadline Deadline not specified.

[914]
NGAI MEMBER EDUCATIONAL GRANTS

National Guard Association of Indiana
Attn: Educational Grant Committee
2002 South Holt Road, Building 5
Indianapolis, IN 46241-4839
(317) 247-3196   Toll Free: (800) 219-2173
Fax: (317) 247-3575   E-mail: membership@ngai.net
Web: www.myngai.org/benefits-2/grants

Summary To provide financial assistance to members of the National Guard Association of Indiana (NGAI) and their dependents who plan to attend college in any state.

Eligibility This program is open to NGAI members and their dependents who are currently serving in the Indiana National Guard or are retired members of the Indiana National Guard. Applicants must be attending or planning to attend a college or university in any state. Along with their application, they must submit 2 letters of recommendation, a copy of high school or college transcripts, SAT or ACT scores (if taken), a letter of acceptance from a college or university (if not currently attending college), and a 2-page essay on the educational program they intend to pursue and the goals they wish to attain. Selection is based on academic achievement, commitment and desire to achieve, extracurricular activities, accomplishments, goals, and financial need.

Financial data The stipend is $1,000.

Duration 1 year; may be renewed up to 3 additional years.

Number awarded 10 each year: 5 for members and 5 for dependents.

Deadline March of each year.

[915]
NGAMA SCHOLARSHIP PROGRAM

National Guard Association of Massachusetts
Attn: Education Services Office
2 Randolph Road, Building 1505
Hanscom AFB 01731-3001
E-mail: ngama.scholarship@gmail.com
Web: www.ngama.org/scholarships

Summary To provide financial assistance to members of the Massachusetts National Guard and their dependents who are interested in attending college in any state.

Eligibility This program is open to 1) current members of the Massachusetts National Guard; 2) children and spouses of current members of the National Guard Association of Massachusetts (NGAMA); and 3) children and spouses of current members of the Massachusetts National Guard. Applicants must be enrolled in or planning to enroll in an accredited college or technical program in any state. Along with their application, they must submit a letter of recommendation, a list of extracurricular activities and other significant accomplishments, high school or college transcripts, and an essay on a topic that changes annually but relates to the National Guard and leadership.

Financial data Stipend amounts vary, but generally range from $1,000 to $2,500.

Duration 1 year.

Number awarded Varies each year; recently, 1 at $2,020 (to recognize Boston as host of the 2020 general conference of the National Guard Association of the United States) and 1

at $1,636 (to recognize the date of the first muster of the Massachusetts militia) were awarded.
Deadline February of each year.

[916]
NGAOK SCHOLARSHIPS
National Guard Association of Oklahoma
c/o Scholarship Foundation
Attn: Rosemary Masters, Scholarship Chair
3501 Military Circle
Oklahoma City, OK 73111
(405) 823-0799 E-mail: ngaok.scholarship@gmail.com
Web: www.ngaok.org/benefits

Summary To provide financial assistance to members of the National Guard Association of Oklahoma (NGAOK) and their dependents who are interested in attending college in any state.

Eligibility This program is open to NGAOK members and their dependent children and spouses who are enrolled or planning to enroll full or part time in an undergraduate or graduate program at a college or university in any state. The primary next of kin of members of the Oklahoma National Guard killed in action after September 11, 2001 are considered life members of NGAOK. Applicants must submit transcripts that include ACT and/or SAT scores; lists of awards and recognitions, community and volunteer services, and extracurricular and sports activities; and a 500-word essay about how they exemplify the traits of selfless service, leadership, character, and their aspirations. Financial need is not considered in the selection process.

Financial data Stipends are $500 or $1,000.
Duration 1 year.
Number awarded 20 to 25 each year.
Deadline January of each year.

[917]
NGARI SCHOLARSHIP PROGRAM
National Guard Association of Rhode Island
Attn: Scholarship Committee
645 New London Avenue
Cranston, RI 02920-3097
(401) 228-6586 Fax: (401) 541-9182
E-mail: ngarinews@gmail.com
Web: www.ngari.org/scholarships

Summary To provide financial assistance to current and former members of the Rhode Island National Guard and their children who plan to attend college in any state.

Eligibility This program is open to active and retired members of the Rhode Island National Guard and their children. Applicants must be high school seniors, high school graduates, or undergraduate students. They must be attending or accepted at an accredited college, university, or vocational/technical school in any state. As part of their application, they must describe any needs, goals, and other factors that may help the selection committee.

Financial data The stipend is $1,000.
Duration 1 year; nonrenewable.
Number awarded Varies each year; recently, 4 were awarded.
Deadline May of each year.

[918]
NGATN FOUNDATION DEPENDENT SCHOLARSHIPS
National Guard Association of Tennessee
Attn: Foundation
4332 Kenilwood Drive
Nashville, TN 37204-4401
(615) 833-9100 Toll Free: (888) 642-8448 (within TN)
Fax: (615) 833-9173 E-mail: byron@ngatn.org
Web: www.ngatn.org/scholarships

Summary To provide financial assistance for college to children and spouses of members of the National Guard Association of Tennessee (NGATN).

Eligibility This program is open to children and spouses of annual active members or retired life members of NGATN. Applicants must be high school seniors or students currently enrolled at a college or university in any state. Along with their application, they must submit transcripts, letters of recommendation, a letter on their desire to continue their education and a 2-page essay on how their parent's service in the National Guard has affected their life.

Financial data The stipend is $3,000.
Duration 1 year.
Number awarded 7 each year.
Deadline February of each year.

[919]
NGATN FOUNDATION LEGACY SCHOLARSHIP
National Guard Association of Tennessee
Attn: Foundation
4332 Kenilwood Drive
Nashville, TN 37204-4401
(615) 833-9100 Toll Free: (888) 642-8448 (within TN)
Fax: (615) 833-9173 E-mail: byron@ngatn.org
Web: www.ngatn.org/scholarships

Summary To provide financial assistance for college to members of the Tennessee National Guard whose parent or parents were (or are still serving as) members of the Guard.

Eligibility This program is open to current active members of the Tennessee Army or Air National Guard whose parent or parents also were or still are members of the Guard. Applicants must also be annual members of the Enlisted Association of the National Guard of Tennessee (EANGTN) or the National Guard Association of Tennessee (NGATN). They must be high school seniors or students currently enrolled at a college or university in any state. Along with their application, they must submit transcripts, letters of recommendation, and a letter on their desire to continue their education.

Financial data The stipend is $4,000.
Duration 1 year.
Number awarded 1 each year.
Deadline February of each year.

[920]
NGAUT "MINUTEMAN" SCHOLARSHIPS
National Guard Association of Utah
12953 South Minuteman Drive, Room 19835
P.O. Box 435
Draper, UT 84020
(801) 599-7869 E-mail: ngautah@ngaut.org
Web: www.ngaut.org/scholarship.php

Summary To provide financial assistance to members and dependents of members of the National Guard Association of Utah (NGAAUT) who are interested in attending college in any state.
Eligibility This program is open to members and dependents of members of NGAUT who are high school seniors or students enrolled for at least 6 credit hours at a college or university in any state. Applicants must submit 1) a 200-word description of their educational and career goals; 2) a 200-word description of leadership and extracurricular activities that they may have had or currently enjoy; 3) a 300-word essay on how the military has influenced their life; 4) a 1-page cover letter or resume; and 5) 2 letters of reference.
Financial data Stipends are $1,500 or $1,000. Funds are sent to the recipient's school and must be used for tuition, laboratory fees, and curriculum-required books and supplies.
Duration 1 year; nonrenewable.
Number awarded 10 each year: 2 at $1,500 and 8 at $1,000.
Deadline January of each year.

[921]
NGAW SCHOLARSHIP PROGRAM
National Guard Association of Washington
Attn: Scholarship Committee
P.O. Box 5144
Camp Murray
Tacoma, WA 98430-5144
(253) 584-5411 Toll Free: (800) 588-6420
Fax: (253) 582-9521 E-mail: ngaw@ngaw.org
Web: www.ngaw.org/scholarships-2

Summary To provide financial assistance to members of the Washington National Guard and their dependents who are interested in attending college in the state.
Eligibility This program is open to members of the Washington National Guard and their dependents who are enrolled at an accredited college, university, or trade school in the state. Guard members may be full-time or part-time students; dependents must be enrolled full time. Applicants do not need to be members of the National Guard Association of Washington (NGAW) although members are eligible for larger awards. Along with their application, they must submit a statement that covers their educational goals, academic credits completed, honors and awards, participation in National Guard, plans for the future in the National Guard, participation in school extracurricular activities, participation in volunteer civic and community events, and financial need.
Financial data The stipend ranges from $500 to $1,000.
Duration 1 year.
Number awarded 7 each year: 1 at $1,000 (designated the Lowenberg Scholarship and reserved for a Guard member) and 6 at either $750 (if the recipient is an NGAW member) or $500 (if the recipient is not a member).
Deadline May of each year.

[922]
NGOA-FL AND ENGAF SCHOLARSHIP PROGRAM
National Guard Association of Florida
Attn: Scholarship Committee
P.O. Box 3446
St. Augustine, FL 32085-3446
(904) 823-0629 Fax: (904) 839-2068
E-mail: ngafl1903@floridaguard.org
Web: www.floridaguard.org/scholarships

Summary To provide financial assistance to members of the Florida National Guard and their families who are also members of either the National Guard Officers Association of Florida (NGOA-FL) or the Enlisted National Guard Association of Florida (ENGAF) and interested in attending college in the state.
Eligibility This program is open to active members of the Florida National Guard (enlisted, officer, and warrant officer), their spouses, and children, but preference is given to Guard members. Applicants must be residents of Florida attending or planning to attend an accredited college, university, or vocational/technical school in the state. They must also be a member, spouse of a member, or child of a member of their respective association. Selection is based on academic achievement, civic and moral leadership, character, and financial need.
Financial data Scholarships are $1,000 for full-time students or $500 for part-time students; funds are paid directly to the recipient's institution.
Duration 1 year; may be renewed.
Additional information This program is jointly sponsored by the respective associations.
Number awarded 15 each year.
Deadline May of each year.

[923]
NICHOLAS D. CHABRAJA SCHOLARSHIP
Association of the United States Army
Attn: Scholarships
2425 Wilson Boulevard
Arlington, VA 22201
(703) 841-4300 Toll Free: (800) 336-4570
E-mail: scholarships@ausa.org
Web: www.ausa.org/resources/scholarships

Summary To provide financial assistance to members of the Association of the United States Army (AUSA) who are interested in studying a field of STEM in college.
Eligibility This program is open to AUSA members who are enrolled or accepted at an accredited college or university to work on a degree in a field of STEM. Along with their application, they must submit a 1-page autobiography, 2 letters of recommendation, a letter describing their career aspirations (including their course of study and plans for completion of a degree), and a transcript of high school or college grades (depending on which they are currently attending). Selection is based on academic merit and personal achievement. Financial need is not normally a selection criterion but in some cases of extreme need it may be used as a factor; the lack of financial need, however, is never a cause for non-selection.
Financial data The stipend is $5,000; funds are sent directly to the recipient's college or university.
Duration 1 year.

Additional information Membership in the AUSA is open to everyone who supports a strong national defense, with special concern for the Army. That includes Regular Army, National Guard, Army Reserve, government civilians, retired soldiers, Wounded Warriors, veterans, concerned citizens and family members.
Number awarded 6 each year.
Deadline June of each year.

[924]
NMCCG ENLISTED DEPENDENT SPOUSE SCHOLARSHIP
Navy Wives Clubs of America
c/o NSA Mid-South
Attn: Allison Barnes, National Vice President
8885 Bass Road
P.O. Box 54022
Millington, TN 38054-0022
Toll Free: (866) 511-NWCA
E-mail: nwca@navywivesclubsofamerica.org
Web: www.navywivesclubsofamerica.org/scholarships

Summary To provide financial assistance for undergraduate or graduate study to spouses of naval personnel.
Eligibility This program is open to Navy, Marine Corps, or Coast Guard dependent spouse: active duty, retired, widow, or widower. Applicants must be 1) a high school graduate or senior planning to attend college full time next year; 2) currently enrolled in an undergraduate program and planning to continue as a full-time undergraduate; 3) a college graduate or senior planning to be a full-time graduate student next year; or 4) a high school graduate or GED recipient planning to attend vocational or business school next year. Along with their application, they must submit a brief statement on why they feel they should be awarded this scholarship and any special circumstances (financial or other) they wish to have considered. Financial need is also considered in the selection process.
Financial data The stipends range from $500 to $1,000 each year (depending upon the donations from chapters of the Navy Wives Clubs of America).
Duration 1 year.
Additional information This program includes the Cecilia Clark Scholarship.
Number awarded 2 each year.
Deadline March of each year.

[925]
NO ANGEL LEFT BEHIND SCHOLARSHIP
No Angel Left Behind
c/o Aerial Construction
3062 Anderson Street
Bonita, CA 91902
(619) 990-1007   Toll Free: (888) 502-9688
Fax: (619) 434-5374
Web: www.noangelsleftbehind.org/scholarship

Summary To provide financial assistance for to children of military personnel killed or disabled in service.
Eligibility This program is open to graduating high school seniors and graduates between 16 and 25 years of age who are attending or planning to attend an accredited college or university in their state. Priority is given in order to applicants who have at least 1 parent who was 1) killed in active duty on foreign soil; 2) killed in active duty by friendly fire; 3) accidentally killed while serving; 4) died while in service; or 5) maimed or disabled while in the service. Applicants must be planning to study economics, education, engineering, finance, liberal arts, or science. They must have a GPA of 2.8 or higher and scores of at least 1450 on the SAT or 20 on the ACT. Financial need is considered in the selection process.
Financial data Stipends range from $1,000 to $5,000 per year.
Duration 1 year; may be renewed up to 3 additional years, provided the recipient demonstrates satisfactory academic performance and maintains a high level of community commitment and involvement.
Number awarded Varies each year.
Deadline July or December of each year.

[926]
NO GREATER SACRIFICE SCHOLARSHIP
No Greater Sacrifice
Attn: Foundation
1101 Pennsylvania Avenue, N.W. Suite 300
Washington, DC 20004
(202) 756-1980   E-mail: info@nogreatersacrifice.org
Web: www.nogreatersacrifice.org/who-we-help

Summary To provide financial assistance for college to children of deceased and disabled veterans who served after September 11, 2001.
Eligibility This program is open to children up to 26 years of age whose parent or legal guardian has fallen or suffered from a wound, illness, or injury in the line of duty while serving in the United States military after September 11, 2001. Living parents must have a Veterans Affairs disability rating of 60% or more or active duty equivalent.
Financial data The program pays benefits up to the amount of the Post-9/11 GI Bill (recently, that was full payment of tuition and fees at public institutions in the student's home state or up to $25,162.14 at private institutions).
Duration 1 year; may be renewed for up to 36 additional months or until completion of an associate or bachelor's degree.
Additional information This program began in 2008.
Number awarded Varies each year; recently, 44, worth $1.7 million, were awarded. Since the program began, it has awarded more than $12.5 million to 206 students.
Deadline April of each year.

[927]
NORTH CAROLINA NATIONAL GUARD ASSOCIATION ACADEMIC EXCELLENCE AND LEADERSHIP SCHOLARSHIPS
North Carolina National Guard Association
Attn: Educational Foundation, Inc.
7410 Chapel Hill Road
Raleigh, NC 27607-5047
(919) 851-3390, ext. 5
Toll Free: (800) 821-6159 (within NC)
Fax: (919) 859-4990   E-mail: edfoundation@ncnga.org
Web: www.edfoundationofncnga.org

Summary To provide financial assistance to members and dependents of members of the North Carolina National Guard Association who demonstrate academic excellence and are attending college in any state.

Eligibility This program is open to active and associate members of the association as well as the spouses, children, grandchildren, and legal dependents of active, associate, or deceased members. Applicants must be high school seniors or students currently attending a 4-year college or university in any state and have a GPA of 3.5 or higher. Selection is based on academic and leadership achievements.
Financial data The stipend is $1,200.
Duration 1 year; may be renewed.
Number awarded 2 each year: 1 to a high school senior and 1 to a current college student.
Deadline January of each year for high school graduates and college students; February of each year for high school seniors.

[928]
NORTH CAROLINA NATIONAL GUARD ASSOCIATION CITIZENSHIP SCHOLARSHIPS
North Carolina National Guard Association
Attn: Educational Foundation, Inc.
7410 Chapel Hill Road
Raleigh, NC 27607-5047
(919) 851-3390, ext. 5
Toll Free: (800) 821-6159 (within NC)
Fax: (919) 859-4990   E-mail: edfoundation@ncnga.org
Web: www.edfoundationofncnga.org
Summary To provide financial assistance to members and dependents of members of the North Carolina National Guard Association who demonstrate outstanding achievement in citizenship and are attending college in any state.
Eligibility This program is open to active and associate members of the association as well as the spouses, children, grandchildren, and legal dependents of active, associate, or deceased members. Applicants must be high school seniors or students currently attending a 4-year college or university in any state. Selection is based on achievements and activities that contribute to their schools and communities.
Financial data The stipend is $1,200.
Duration 1 year; may be renewed.
Number awarded 2 each year: 1 to a high school senior and 1 to a current college student.
Deadline January of each year for high school graduates and college students; February of each year for high school seniors.

[929]
NORTH CAROLINA NATIONAL GUARD ASSOCIATION SCHOLARSHIPS
North Carolina National Guard Association
Attn: Educational Foundation, Inc.
7410 Chapel Hill Road
Raleigh, NC 27607-5047
(919) 851-3390, ext. 5
Toll Free: (800) 821-6159 (within NC)
Fax: (919) 859-4990   E-mail: edfoundation@ncnga.org
Web: www.edfoundationofncnga.org
Summary To provide financial assistance to members and dependents of members of the North Carolina National Guard Association who plan to attend college in any state.
Eligibility This program is open to active and associate members of the association as well as the spouses, children, grandchildren, and legal dependents of active, associate, or deceased members. Applicants must be high school seniors, high school graduates, or students currently enrolled at a college or university in any state. Selection is based on financial need, academic achievement, citizenship, leadership, and other application information. The most outstanding applicants receive scholarships provided by the SECU Foundation. Applicants who meet specified additional requirements qualify for various memorial and special scholarships.
Financial data Stipends are $10,000 or $5,000 for the SECU Foundation Scholarships, $1,200 for scholarships to 4-year universities, or $600 for community college scholarships.
Duration 1 year; may be renewed.
Additional information This program, which began in 1968, includes a number of named memorial and special scholarships. Other scholarships are funded by the SECU Foundation of the State Employees' Credit Union and the USAA Insurance Corporation.
Number awarded Varies each year; recently, 46 with a value of $67,800 were awarded. Since this program was established, it has awarded 1,918 scholarships worth more than $1.5 million.
Deadline January of each year for high school graduates and college students; February of each year for high school seniors.

[930]
NORTH CAROLINA SCHOLARSHIPS FOR CHILDREN OF WAR VETERANS
North Carolina Department of Military and Veterans Affairs
413 North Salisbury Street
4001 Mail Service Center
Raleigh, NC 27699-4001
(984) 204-2981   Toll Free: (844) 624-8387
Fax: (984) 204-8343
E-mail: ncdmva.scholarships@milvets.nc.gov
Web: scholarships.milvets.nc.gov/Pages/Help.aspx
Summary To provide financial assistance to the children of disabled and other classes of North Carolina veterans who plan to attend college in the state.
Eligibility Eligible applicants come from 5 categories: Class I-A: the veteran parent died in wartime service or as a result of a service-connected condition incurred in wartime service; Class I-B: the veteran parent is rated by the U.S. Department of Veterans Affairs (VA) as 100% disabled as a result of wartime service and currently or at the time of death was drawing compensation for such disability; Class II: the veteran parent is rated by the VA as much as 20% but less than 100% disabled due to wartime service, or was awarded a Purple Heart medal for wounds received, and currently or at the time of death drawing compensation for such disability; Class III: the veteran parent is currently or was at the time of death receiving a VA pension for total and permanent disability, or the veteran parent is deceased but does not qualify under any other provisions, or the veteran parent served in a combat zone or waters adjacent to a combat zone and received a campaign badge or medal but does not qualify under any other provisions; Class IV: the veteran parent was a prisoner of war or missing in action. For all classes, applicants must 1) be under 25 years of age and have a veteran parent who was a resident of North Carolina at the time of entrance into the armed forces; or 2) be the natural child, or

adopted child prior to age 15, who was born in North Carolina, has been a resident of the state continuously since birth, and is the child of a veteran whose disabilities occurred during a period of war.

Financial data Students in Classes I-A, II, III, and IV receive $7,000 per academic year if they attend a private college or junior college; if attending a public postsecondary institution, they receive free tuition, a room allowance, a board allowance, and exemption from certain mandatory fees. Students in Class I-B receive $2,800 per academic year if they attend a private college or junior college; if attending a public postsecondary institution, they receive free tuition and exemption from certain mandatory fees.

Duration 4 academic years, used within an 8-year period. Renewal of scholarships for Classes II and III require the recipient to maintain a GPA of 2.0 or higher.

Number awarded An unlimited number of awards are made under Classes I-A, I-B, and IV. Classes II and III are limited to 100 awards each year in each class.

Deadline Applications for Classes I-A, I-B, and IV must be submitted by May or November of each year; applications for Classes II and III must be submitted by February of each year.

[931]
NORTH CAROLINA VIETNAM VETERANS SCHOLARSHIP PROGRAM

North Carolina Vietnam Veterans, Inc.
Attn: Scholarship Administrator
7316 Ray Road
Raleigh, NC 27613
E-mail: bkuhr@nc.rr.com
Web: www.ncvvi.org

Summary To provide financial assistance to North Carolina residents who are Vietnam veterans or the dependents of veterans and interested in attending college in any state.

Eligibility This program is open to current residents of Chatham, Durham, Franklin, Granville, Harnett, Johnston, Nash, or Wake counties in North Carolina who are either a Vietnam veteran or the veteran's spouse, child, foster child, adopted child, or grandchild. Families of members of North Carolina Vietnam Veterans, Inc. (NCVVI) who live in any county of the state are also eligible. Applicants must be attending or planning to attend a college, university, community college, or trade school in any state. They must submit a copy of the Department of Defense Form DD214 to document Vietnam service; a birth certificate and/or marriage license (as needed); a personal statement about themselves, including work experience, anticipated career, and goals; a list of current activities and awards; and an essay of 600 to 900 words on a topic that changes annually; recently, the topic related to the impact of the draft on the country during the Vietnam War.

Financial data Stipends range from $250 to $1,500. Funds are paid directly to the recipients on a reimbursement basis (presentation of paid receipts for tuition, fees, and/or books).

Duration 1 year.

Additional information This program includes the Mike Hooks Memorial Scholarship.

Number awarded 1 or more each year.

Deadline March of each year.

[932]
NORTH DAKOTA DOLLARS FOR SCHOLARS MILITARY SCHOLARSHIPS

North Dakota Dollars for Scholars
Attn: State Director
P.O. Box 5509
Bismarck, ND 58506-5509
(701) 328-5702   Toll Free: (888) 592-8540
E-mail: statedirector@nddfs.org
Web: www.northdakota.dollarsforscholars.org

Summary To provide financial assistance to high school seniors and college students who are dependents of military personnel in North Dakota.

Eligibility This program is open to graduating high school seniors and college students enrolled or planning to enroll full time at a college or university. Applicants must be dependents of a North Dakota military unit or installation. They must have a GPA of 2.5 or higher.

Financial data The stipend is $1,000.

Duration 1 year.

Number awarded Varies each year; recently, 2 were awarded.

Deadline March of each year.

[933]
NORTH DAKOTA NATIONAL GUARD ENLISTED ASSOCIATION SCHOLARSHIPS

North Dakota National Guard Enlisted Association
c/o CSM Joe Lovelace, Scholarship Chair
4900 107th Avenue S.E.
Minot, ND 58701-9207
(701) 420-5841   E-mail: joseph.m.lovelace.mil@mail.mil
Web: www.ndngea.org/helpful-documents

Summary To provide financial assistance to members of the North Dakota National Guard Enlisted Association (NDNGEA) and their families who are interested in attending college in any state.

Eligibility This program is open to association members who have at least 1 year remaining on their enlistment or have completed 20 or more years in service. Also eligible are their unmarried dependent children and spouses and the unremarried spouses and unmarried dependent children of deceased NDNGEA members who were in good standing at the time of death. Applicants must be enrolled or planning to enroll full time at a university, college, or trade/business school in any state. Graduate students are not eligible. Selection is based on academic achievement, leadership, character, and financial need.

Financial data The stipend is $1,000. Funds are sent directly to the school in the recipient's name.

Duration 1 year.

Number awarded 2 each year: 1 to an NDNGEA member and 1 to a child or spouse.

Deadline November of each year.

[934]
NORTH DAKOTA TUITION AND FEE WAIVERS
North Dakota University System
Attn: Financial Aid Office
State Capitol, Tenth Floor
600 East Boulevard Avenue, Department 215
Bismarck, ND 58505-0230
(701) 328-2964 Fax: (701) 328-2979
E-mail: ndfinaid@ndus.edu
Web: www.ndus.edu

Summary To reduce tuition and fees for designated categories of students at public institutions in North Dakota.

Eligibility This program is open to residents of North Dakota who are law enforcement officers; National Guard members; surviving dependents of POW/MIA veterans who were killed in action, died of service-related causes, were prisoners of war, have 100% service-connected disability, or who were declared missing in action; surviving spouses and children of firefighters, emergency medical services personnel, and peace officers who died as a direct result of injuries received in the performance of official duties; and senior citizens. Applicants must be attending or planning to attend a public college or university in North Dakota.

Financial data North Dakota public colleges and universities have the authority to provide partial or full reductions in tuition and fees for qualified students.

Duration 1 academic year; renewable.

Number awarded Varies each year.

Deadline Deadline not specified.

[935]
NORTHAMERICAN.COM MILITARY SCHOLARSHIP
North American Van Lines
One Parkview Plaza
Oakbrook Terrace, IL 60180
Toll Free: (800) 228-3092
Web: www.northamerican.com/military-scholarship

Summary To provide financial assistance to current and former military personnel and their families who are interested in attending college to study fields related to logistics.

Eligibility This program is open to current and honorably discharged members of the military, their spouses, and their children under 21 years of age or (if currently attending college) under 23 years of age. Applicants must be enrolled or planning to enroll full time at a 4-year college or university and major in military logistics, supply chain management, or operational management. They must be U.S. citizens or permanent residents and have a GPA of 2.5 or higher. Along with their application, they must submit an essay of 400 to 800 words on why a career in logistics/supply chain management is their college major of choice. Financial need is not considered in the selection process.

Financial data The stipend is $1,000.

Duration 1 year.

Additional information This program began in 2015.

Number awarded 2 each year.

Deadline September of each year.

[936]
NORTHEASTERN REGION KOREAN WAR VETERAN DESCENDANT SCHOLARSHIPS
Korean American Scholarship Foundation
Northeastern Region
Attn: Scholarship Committee Chair
By Design, LLC
463 Seventh Avenue, Suite 200
New York, NY 10018
E-mail: nerc.scholarship@kasf.org
Web: www.kasf.org/apply-nerc

Summary To provide financial assistance to the descendants of the Korean War from any state who are working on an undergraduate or graduate degree in any field at a school in northeastern states.

Eligibility This program is open to direct descendants of veterans who served in Korea from June 25, 1950 to January 31, 1955. Applicants may reside in any state, but they must be enrolled as full-time undergraduate or graduate students at a college or university in Connecticut, Maine, Massachusetts, New Hampshire, New Jersey, New York, Rhode Island, or Vermont. They must have a GPA of 3.0 or higher. Selection is based on academic achievement, an essay, extracurricular activities, and recommendations.

Financial data Stipends range from $500 to $5,000.

Duration 1 year.

Number awarded 1 or more each year.

Deadline June of each year.

[937]
NVC/WAC SCHOLARSHIP
Nisei Veterans Committee
Attn: NVC Foundation
1212 South King Street
Seattle, WA 98144-2025
(206) 322-1122 E-mail: education@nvcfoundation.org
Web: www.nvcfoundation.org/education/scholarship/

Summary To provide financial assistance to high school seniors and current college students who are related to a member of the Nisei Veterans Committee or the NVC Foundation.

Eligibility This program is open to high school seniors and current college students who are relatives of members of the Nisei Veterans Committee (an organization of Japanese American veterans) or of the NVC Foundation. Applicants must be planning to attend a college or university. Along with their application, they must submit essays on 1) what the Nisei veterans' legacy means to them; and 2) their future aspirations and life plans. Special consideration is given to students who have helped support the NVC organization. Financial need is considered in the selection process.

Financial data The stipend is $3,000.

Duration 1 year.

Additional information This program honors the NVC and the former Women's Auxiliary Club (WAC).

Number awarded 1 each year.

Deadline January of each year.

[938]
OHIO AMVETS SERVICE FOUNDATION SCHOLARSHIPS

AMVETS-Department of Ohio
Attn: Service Foundation
1395 East Dublin Granville Road, Suite 222
Columbus, OH 43229-3314
(614) 431-6990   Toll Free: (800) 642-6838
Fax: (614) 431-6991   E-mail: admin@ohamvets.org
Web: www.ohamvets.org/forms

Summary To provide financial assistance for college in any state to veterans and their families from Ohio.
Eligibility This program is open to residents of Ohio who are veterans, the children or grandchildren of veterans, or the spouses of veterans. Applicants must be graduating high school seniors or students currently enrolled at a college or university in any state. They must have a GPA of 2.5 or higher. Along with their application, they must submit an autobiographical statement that includes why they desire this scholarship and their projected goals in life. Selection is based on academic aptitude and financial need.
Financial data The stipend is $1,000.
Duration 1 year; nonrenewable.
Number awarded 10 each year.
Deadline March of each year.

[939]
OHIO LEGION AUXILIARY DEPARTMENT PRESIDENT'S SCHOLARSHIP

American Legion Auxiliary
Department of Ohio
1100 Brandywine Boulevard, Suite D
P.O. Box 2760
Zanesville, OH 43702-2760
(740) 452-8245   Fax: (740) 452-2620
E-mail: kelly@alaohio.org
Web: www.alaohio.org/Scholarships

Summary To provide financial assistance to veterans and their descendants in Ohio who are interested in attending college in any state.
Eligibility This program is open to honorably-discharged veterans and the children, grandchildren, and great-grandchildren of living, deceased, or disabled honorably-discharged veterans who served during designated periods of wartime. Applicants must be residents of Ohio, seniors at an accredited high school, planning to enter a college in any state, and sponsored by an American Legion Auxiliary Unit. Along with their application, they must submit an original article (up to 500 words) written by the applicant on a topic that changes annually. Recently, students were asked to write on "Education and the American Dream." Selection is based on character, Americanism, leadership, scholarship, and financial need.
Financial data Stipends are $1,500 or $1,000. Funds are paid to the recipient's school.
Duration 1 year.
Number awarded 2 each year: 1 at $1,500 and 1 at $1,000.
Deadline March of each year.

[940]
OHIO LEGION COLLEGE OR UNIVERSITY SCHOLARSHIPS

American Legion
Department of Ohio
60 Big Run Road
P.O. Box 8007
Delaware, OH 43015
(740) 362-7478   Fax: (740) 362-1429
E-mail: legion@ohiolegion.com
Web: www.ohiolegion.com/programs/scholarships

Summary To provide financial assistance to residents of Ohio who are descendants of members of the American Legion and attending college in any state.
Eligibility This program is open to residents of Ohio who are children, grandchildren or great-grandchildren of living or deceased Legionnaires. Applicants must be attending colleges, universities, or other approved postsecondary schools in any state as undergraduate or graduate students. They must have a high school and college GPA of 3.5 or higher and an ACT score of at least 25. Along with their application, they must submit a personal statement of 500 to 550 words on their career objectives. Selection is based on academic achievement as measured by course grades, ACT scores, difficulty of curriculum, participation in school and outside activities, and the judging committee's general impression.
Financial data Stipends are normally at least $2,000.
Duration 1 year.
Number awarded 1 or more each year.
Deadline April of each year.

[941]
OHIO LEGION HIGH SCHOOL SCHOLARSHIPS

American Legion
Department of Ohio
60 Big Run Road
P.O. Box 8007
Delaware, OH 43015
(740) 362-7478   Fax: (740) 362-1429
E-mail: legion@ohiolegion.com
Web: www.ohiolegion.com/programs/scholarships

Summary To provide financial assistance to high school seniors in Ohio who are descendants of members of the American Legion and interested in attending college in any state.
Eligibility This program is open to seniors graduating from high schools in Ohio who are children, grandchildren, or great-grandchildren of living or deceased Legionnaires. Applicants must be planning to attend colleges, universities, or other approved postsecondary schools in any state with a vocational objective. They must have a GPA of 3.5 or higher and an ACT score of at least 25. Along with their application, they must submit a personal statement of 500 to 550 words on their career objectives. Selection is based on academic achievement as measured by course grades, ACT scores, difficulty of curriculum, participation in school and outside activities, and the judging committee's general impression.
Financial data Stipends are normally at least $2,000.
Duration 1 year.
Number awarded 1 or more each year.
Deadline April of each year.

[942]
OHIO LEGION SURVIVING SPOUSE OR CHILD SCHOLARSHIPS

American Legion
Department of Ohio
60 Big Run Road
P.O. Box 8007
Delaware, OH 43015
(740) 362-7478　　　　　　　Fax: (740) 362-1429
E-mail: legion@ohiolegion.com
Web: www.ohiolegion.com/programs/scholarships

Summary To provide financial assistance to residents of Ohio who are surviving spouses or children of deceased service members and interested in attending college in any state.

Eligibility This program is open to residents of Ohio who are surviving spouses or children of service members who died on active duty or from injuries received on active duty Applicants must be attending or planning to attend colleges, universities, or other approved postsecondary schools in any state as an undergraduate or graduate student. They must have a GPA of 3.5 or higher and an ACT score of at least 25. Along with their application, they must submit a personal statement of 500 to 550 words on their career objectives. Selection is based on academic achievement as measured by course grades, ACT scores, difficulty of curriculum, participation in school and outside activities, and the judging committee's general impression.

Financial data Stipends are normally at least $2,000.
Duration 1 year.
Number awarded 1 or more each year.
Deadline April of each year.

[943]
OHIO SAFETY OFFICERS COLLEGE MEMORIAL FUND

Ohio Department of Higher Education
Attn: State Grants and Scholarships Department
25 South Front Street
Columbus, OH 43215-3414
(614) 628-8862　　　　　　Toll Free: (888) 833-1133
Fax: (614) 466-5866　E-mail: tbraswell@highered.ohio.gov
Web: www.ohiohighered.org/safety-officers-college-fund

Summary To provide financial assistance to Ohio residents who are interested in attending college in the state and whose parent or spouse was killed in the line of duty as a safety officer or member of the armed forces.

Eligibility This program is open to Ohio residents whose parent or spouse was 1) a peace officer, firefighter, or other safety officer killed in the line of duty anywhere in the United States; or 2) a member of the U.S. armed forces killed in the line of duty during Operation Enduring Freedom, Operation Iraqi Freedom, or other designated combat zone. Applicants must be interested in enrolling full or part time at a participating Ohio college or university. Children of military personnel are eligible for this program only if they do not qualify for the Ohio War Orphan Scholarship.

Financial data At Ohio public colleges and universities, the program provides full payment of tuition. At Ohio private colleges and universities, the stipend is equivalent to the average amounts paid to students attending public institutions, currently $7,942 per year.

Duration 1 year; may be renewed up to 4 additional years.
Additional information Eligible institutions are Ohio state-assisted colleges and universities and Ohio institutions approved by the Board of Regents. This program was established in 1980.
Number awarded Varies each year; recently, 54 students received benefits from this program.
Deadline Application deadlines are established by each participating college and university.

[944]
OHIO WAR ORPHAN AND SEVERELY DISABLED VETERANS' CHILDREN SCHOLARSHIP

Ohio Department of Higher Education
Attn: State Grants and Scholarships Department
25 South Front Street
Columbus, OH 43215-3414
(614) 752-9528　　　　　　Toll Free: (888) 833-1133
Fax: (614) 752-5903　E-mail: rchurch@highered.ohio.gov
Web: www.ohiohighered.org/ohio-war-orphans

Summary To provide financial assistance to the children of deceased or disabled Ohio veterans who plan to attend college in the state.

Eligibility This program is open to residents of Ohio who are under 25 years of age and interested in enrolling full time at an eligible college or university in the state. Applicants must be the child of a veteran who 1) was a member of the U.S. armed forces, including the organized Reserves and Ohio National Guard, for a period of 90 days or more (or discharged because of a disability incurred after less than 90 days of service); 2) served during specified periods of wartime; 3) entered service as a resident of Ohio; and 4) as a result of that service, either was killed or became at least 60% service-connected disabled. Also eligible are children of veterans who have a permanent and total nonservice-connected disability and are receiving disability benefits from the U.S. Department of Veterans Affairs. If the veteran parent served only in the organized Reserves or Ohio National Guard, the parent must have been killed or became permanently and totally disabled while at a scheduled training assembly, field training period (of any duration or length), or active duty for training, pursuant to bona fide orders issued by a competent authority. Financial need is considered in the selection process.

Financial data At Ohio public colleges and universities, the program currently provides payment of 100% of tuition and fees. At Ohio private colleges and universities, the stipend is $7,044 per year.

Duration 1 year; may be renewed up to 4 additional years, provided the recipient maintains a GPA of 2.0 or higher.

Additional information Eligible institutions are Ohio state-assisted colleges and universities and Ohio institutions approved by the Board of Regents. This program was established in 1957.

Number awarded Varies, depending upon the funds available. If sufficient funds are available, all eligible applicants are given a scholarship. Recently, 861 students received benefits from this program.

Deadline May of each year.

[945]
ONGA LEADERSHIP GRANTS
Ohio National Guard Association
Attn: Leadership Grant Committee
1299 Virginia Avenue
Columbus, OH 43212
(614) 486-4186   E-mail: ongaedkelly@gmail.com
Web: www.ngaoh.org/salon-services

Summary To provide financial assistance to members of the Ohio National Guard Association (ONGA) and their families who are interested in attending college in any state.

Eligibility This program is open to active members (either officers or warrant officers) of the ONGA and the dependents of active, life, retired, or deceased members. Applicants must be enrolled or planning to enroll at a college or university in any state. Along with their application, they must submit transcripts, SAT/ACT scores, and a 2-page essay explaining why they should be selected to receive a grant. Selection is based on grades, future plans, membership and leadership, honors and awards, need, and overall impression.

Financial data A stipend is awarded (amount not specified).

Duration 1 year; nonrenewable.

Additional information This program began in 1996.

Number awarded Varies each year; recently, 5 were awarded.

Deadline November of each year.

[946]
OREGON NATIONAL GUARD ASSOCIATION SCHOLARSHIPS
Oregon National Guard Association
c/o Oregon National Guard Charitable Education Fund, Inc.
Attn: Scholarship Review Committee
10705 S.W. Black Diamond Way
Tigard, OR 97223
(503) 584-3030   Fax: (503) 584-3052
E-mail: rhansjan@outlook.com
Web: www.ornga.org/scholarships

Summary To provide financial assistance to members of the Oregon National Guard, the Oregon National Guard Association (ORNGA), and their children and spouses who are interested in attending college in any state.

Eligibility This program is open to active members of the Oregon Army and Air National Guard, members of the ORNGA, and their children and spouses. Applicants must be high school seniors, graduates, or GED recipients and interested in working on an undergraduate degree at a college, university, or trade school in any state. The parent, spouse, or applicant must have an ETS date beyond the end of the academic year for which the scholarship is used. Selection is based on demonstrated qualities of leadership, civic action, and academic achievement.

Financial data The stipend is $1,500.

Duration 1 year.

Number awarded Up to 10 each year.

Deadline March of each year.

[947]
OTIS N. BROWN/BILLY RAY CAMERON SCHOLARSHIPS
Veterans of Foreign Wars of the United States-
  Department of North Carolina
Attn: Scholarship Committee
917 New Bern Avenue
P.O. Box 25337
Raleigh, NC 27611
(919) 828-5058   Fax: (919) 261-6771
E-mail: qm@nc.vfwweb.mail.com
Web: vfwnc.com/di/vfw/v2/default.asp?pid=5708

Summary To provide financial assistance to children and grandchildren of members of the Veterans of Foreign Wars (VFW) and the VFW Auxiliary in North Carolina who plan to attend college in the state.

Eligibility This program is open to seniors graduating from high schools in North Carolina and planning to enroll at a junior or senior college in the state. Applicants must be the child, grandchild, or stepchild of a member of the VFW or the VFW Auxiliary, or, if deceased, was a member at time of death.

Financial data The stipend is $1,000 per year. Funds are paid directly to the recipient's institution.

Duration 1 year; may be renewed up to 3 additional years.

Number awarded 2 each year.

Deadline February of each year.

[948]
PAST NATIONAL COMMANDER MICHAEL J. KOGUTEK SCHOLARSHIP
Erie County American Legion
Attn: Scholarship Committee
609 City Hall
65 Niagara Square
Buffalo, NY 14202
(716) 852-6500   Fax: (716) 852-4664
E-mail: veteran14202@verizon.net
Web: www.eriecountyal.org

Summary To provide financial assistance to New York residents who are veterans, their families, or other students interested in attending college in any state.

Eligibility This program is open to residents of New York who are veterans, their families, or other students who share the values of the American Legion. Applicants must be enrolled or planning to enroll at a college or university in any state. Students entering from high school must enroll full time, but veterans and other students may enroll part time. Along with their application, they must submit a 500-word essay describing their proposed course of study, their career objectives and how this scholarship would help them attain those, and what they have achieved and learned through their studies and activities. Selection is based on academic ability, realistic goals, extracurricular activities, community involvement, and financial need.

Financial data The stipend is $1,500.

Duration 1 year.

Number awarded 2 each year.

Deadline April of each year.

SCHOLARSHIPS: FAMILY MEMBERS

[949]
PATRIOT EDUCATION FUND SCHOLARSHIPS
Patriot Education Fund
312 Park Avenue, Suite 31
Clarendon Hills, IL 60514
(773) 273-9601   E-mail: info@patrioteducationfund.org
Web: www.patrioteducationfund.secure-platform.com/a

Summary To provide financial assistance to enlisted veterans, their spouses, or their dependent children and interested in attending a college or university in any state.

Eligibility This program is open to enlisted veterans (E1-E5) who served after September 11, 2001, the spouses of those veterans, and the dependent children of those veterans. Applicants must be enrolled or planning to enroll full time at a college, university, or vocational/trade school in any state. They must be eligible to receive Post-9/11 GI Bill benefits but be able to demonstrate that they still have financial need because of a gap between the available benefits and the actual costs of tuition.

Financial data The amount of the assistance depends on the financial gap facing the veteran or family member. Funds are sent directly to the recipient's institution.

Duration Funding is provided until completion of a degree or certificate.

Additional information This program began in 2011.

Number awarded Varies each year; since the program began, it has awarded 122 scholarships.

Deadline March of each year.

[950]
PATRIOT SCHOLARSHIP OF THE UNIVERSITY INTERSCHOLASTIC LEAGUE
University Interscholastic League
Attn: Texas Interscholastic League Foundation
1701 Manor Road
P.O. Box 151027
Austin, TX 78715-1027
(512) 382-0916   Fax: (512) 382-0377
E-mail: info@tilfoundation.org
Web: www.tilfoundation.org/scholarships/list

Summary To provide financial assistance to high school seniors who participate in programs of the Texas Interscholastic League Foundation (TILF), are children of veterans, and plan to attend college in the state.

Eligibility This program is open to seniors graduating from high schools in Texas who have competed in a University Interscholastic League (UIL) academic state meet (participation in athletic or music contests does not qualify). Applicants must be the child of a veteran, rank in the top 25% of their class, and have a GPA of 2.5 or higher. They must be planning to enroll full time at a college or university in the state and major in any field. Along with their application, they must submit high school transcripts that include SAT and/or ACT scores and documentation of financial need. Preference is given to children of injured veterans.

Financial data The stipend is $2,000.

Duration 1 year; nonrenewable.

Number awarded 1 or more each year.

Deadline May of each year.

[951]
PAULINE LANGKAMP MEMORIAL SCHOLARSHIP
Navy Wives Clubs of America
c/o NSA Mid-South
Attn: Melissa Worthey, National President
P.O. Box 54022
Millington, TN 38053-6022
Toll Free: (866) 511-NWCA
E-mail: nwca@navywivesclubsofamerica.org
Web: www.navywivesclubsofamerica.org/scholarships

Summary To provide financial assistance for college to the adult children of members of the Navy Wives Clubs of America (NWCA).

Eligibility This program is open to children of NWCA members who no longer carry a military ID card because they have reached adult status. Applicants must be attending or planning to attend an accredited college or university. Along with their application, they must submit a brief statement on why they feel they should be awarded this scholarship and any special circumstances (financial or other) they wish to have considered. Financial need is also considered in the selection process.

Financial data A stipend is provided (amount not specified).

Duration 1 year.

Additional information Membership in the NWCA is open to spouses of enlisted personnel serving in the Navy, Marine Corps, Coast Guard, and the active Reserve units of those services; spouses of enlisted personnel who have been honorably discharged, retired, or transferred to the Fleet Reserve on completion of duty; and widows of enlisted personnel in those services.

Number awarded 1 each year.

Deadline March of each year.

[952]
PENNSYLVANIA NATIONAL GUARD MILITARY FAMILY EDUCATION PROGRAM (MFEP)
Pennsylvania Higher Education Assistance Agency
Attn: State Grant and Special Programs
1200 North Seventh Street
P.O. Box 8157
Harrisburg, PA 17105-8157
(717) 720-2800   Toll Free: (800) 692-7392
Fax: (717) 720-3786   TDD: (800) 654-5988
E-mail: info@pheaa.org
Web: www.pheaa.org

Summary To provide financial assistance for college or graduate school to dependents of Pennsylvania National Guard members who agree to an additional service commitment.

Eligibility This program is open to children and spouses of members of the Pennsylvania National Guard who have completed an initial service obligation and reenlist for a period of 6 years. Applicants must be enrolled or planning to enroll full or part time in an approved undergraduate or graduate program of education at an approved institution of higher learning in Pennsylvania. Children can use this benefit up to reaching 26 years of age. Spouses can use the benefit up to 6 years after the Guard member's separation from the Guard. The Guard member can assign the entire benefit to 1 dependent or a portion of the benefit to more than 1 dependent.

Financial data Full-time students receive the lesser of 100% of tuition plus technology fee at the institution where they are enrolled or the annual tuition rate and technology fee charged to a Pennsylvania resident at a state-owned university. Part-time students receive the lesser of 100% of the tuition plus technology fee for a part-time course of study at their institution or the per credit tuition rate charged to a Pennsylvania resident at a state-owned university plus the technology fee. The Guard member must honor the service commitment or repay all funds received, plus interest.
Duration Up to 5 years.
Additional information This program, first offered in 2020, is jointly administered by the Pennsylvania Department of Military and Veterans Affairs and the Pennsylvania Higher Education Assistance Agency.
Number awarded Varies each year.
Deadline Deadline not specified.

[953]
PENNSYLVANIA NATIONAL GUARD SCHOLARSHIP FUND

Pennsylvania National Guard Associations
Attn: Pennsylvania National Guard Scholarship Fund
Biddle Hall (Building 9-109)
Fort Indiantown Gap
Annville, PA 17003-5002
(717) 861-6696   Toll Free: (800) 997-8885
Fax: (717) 861-5560   E-mail: kristi.a.carlsen.civ@mail.mil
Web: www.pngas.org/page/3

Summary To provide financial assistance to Pennsylvania National Guard members and the children of disabled or deceased members who are interested in attending college in any state.
Eligibility This program is open to active members of the Pennsylvania Army or Air National Guard. Children of members of the Guard who died or were permanently disabled while on Guard duty are also eligible. Applicants must be entering their first year of higher education as a full-time student or presently attending a college or vocational school in any state as a full-time student. Along with their application, they must submit an essay that outlines their military and civilian plans for the future. Selection is based on academic potential, military commitment, extracurricular activities, and Guard participation.
Financial data Stipends range from $500 to $2,000.
Duration 1 year.
Additional information The sponsoring organization includes the National Guard Association of Pennsylvania (NGAP) and the Pennsylvania National Guard Enlisted Association (PNGEA). This program, which began in 1977, currently receives support from the USAA Insurance Corporation and the 28th Infantry Division Association.
Number awarded Varies each year; recently, 14 were awarded: 2 at $2,000, 1 at $1,500, 3 at $1,000, 1 at $750, and 7 at $500.
Deadline June of each year.

[954]
PENNSYLVANIA POSTSECONDARY EDUCATIONAL GRATUITY PROGRAM

Pennsylvania Higher Education Assistance Agency
Attn: State Grant and Special Programs
1200 North Seventh Street
P.O. Box 8157
Harrisburg, PA 17105-8157
(717) 720-2800   Toll Free: (800) 692-7392
Fax: (717) 720-3786   TDD: (800) 654-5988
E-mail: pegp@pheaa.org
Web: www.pheaa.org

Summary To provide financial assistance for college to the children of Pennsylvania public service personnel who died in the line of service.
Eligibility This program is open to residents of Pennsylvania who are the children of 1) Pennsylvania police officers, firefighters, rescue and ambulance squad members, corrections facility employees, or National Guard members who died in the line of duty after January 1, 1976; or 2) Pennsylvania sheriffs, deputy sheriffs, National Guard members, and certain other individuals on federal or state active military duty who died after September 11, 2001 as a direct result of performing their official duties. Applicants must be 25 years of age or younger and enrolled or accepted at a Pennsylvania community college, state-owned institution, or state-related institution as a full-time student working on an associate or baccalaureate degree. They must have already applied for other scholarships, including state and federal grants and financial aid from the postsecondary institution to which they are applying.
Financial data Grants cover tuition, fees, room, and board charged by the institution, less awarded scholarships and federal and state grants.
Duration Up to 5 years.
Additional information This program began in the 1998-99 winter/spring term to cover service personnel who died after January 1, 1976. It was amended in 2004 to cover additional service personnel who died after September 11, 2001.
Number awarded Varies each year.
Deadline March of each year.

[955]
PETE FREEMAN MEMORIAL SCHOLARSHIP

Marine Corps Aviation Association-Donald E. Davis Squadron
Attn: Col. Kevin McCutcheon, Executive Officer
P.O. Box 22
Chatham, MI 49816
(828) 443-1560   E-mail: kevinmccutcheon76@gmail.com
Web: www.avlogmarines.org/scholarship

Summary To provide financial assistance to dependents of Marine Corps Aviation Logisticians who are interested in attending college in any state.
Eligibility This program is open to dependents (spouses, children, grandchildren) of Aviation Logisticians (aircraft maintenance, aviation ordnance, avionics, or aviation supply) who are active-duty, Reserve, retired, or former Marines. Applicants must be enrolled or planning to enroll at a college or university in any state. Selection is based on past academic accomplishments and desire to further excel in academics.

Financial data Stipends normally range up to $1,000.
Duration 1 year.
Additional information This program receives support from Lockheed Martin, Andromeda Systems Incorporated, and Robbins-Giola LLC. The sponsoring organization is headquartered in North Carolina, but it serves Marine aviators in all states.
Number awarded Varies each year; recently, 17 scholarships, worth $15,250, were awarded.
Deadline Deadline not specified.

[956]
PETER CONNACHER MEMORIAL SCHOLARSHIPS

Oregon Office of Student Access and Completion
Attn: Scholarships
1500 Valley River Drive, Suite 100
Eugene, OR 97401-2146
(541) 687-7400   Toll Free: (800) 452-8807
Fax: (541) 687-7414   TDD: (800) 735-2900
E-mail: osac@hecc.oregon.gov
Web: app.oregonstudentaid.gov/Catalog/Default.aspx

Summary To provide financial assistance for college or graduate school to ex-prisoners of war and their descendants.
Eligibility Applicants must be U.S. citizens who 1) were military or civilian prisoners of war; or 2) are the descendants of ex-prisoners of war. They must be full-time undergraduate or graduate students. A copy of the ex-prisoner of war's discharge papers from the U.S. armed forces must accompany the application. In addition, written proof of POW status must be submitted, along with a statement of the relationship between the applicant and the ex-prisoner of war (father, grandfather, etc.). Selection is based on academic record and financial need. Preference is given to Oregon residents or their dependents.
Financial data Stipends for scholarships offered by the Oregon Office of Student Access and Completion (OSAC) range from $1,000 to $10,000 but recently averaged $4,710.
Duration 1 year; may be renewed for up to 3 additional years for undergraduate students or 2 additional years for graduate students. Renewal is dependent on evidence of continued financial need and satisfactory academic progress.
Additional information This program is administered by the OSAC with funds provided by the Oregon Community Foundation and by the Columbia River Chapter of American Ex-prisoners of War, Inc.
Number awarded Varies each year; recently, 4 were awarded.
Deadline February of each year.

[957]
PHS COMMISSIONED OFFICERS FOUNDATION DEPENDENT SCHOLARSHIP PROGRAM

Commissioned Officers Association of the U.S. Public Health Service
Attn: PHS Commissioned Officers Foundation for the Advancement of Public Health
8201 Corporate Drive, Suite 200
Landover, MD 20785
(301) 731-9080   Fax: (301) 731-9084
E-mail: scholarship@coausphs.org
Web: www.phscof.org/education/cof-scholarship-program

Summary To provide financial assistance to spouses and descendants of members of the Commissioned Officers Association of the U.S. Public Health Service (COA) who are interested in working on an undergraduate or graduate degree in any of the Public Health Service (PHS) categories.
Eligibility This program is open to high school seniors, undergraduates, and graduate students who are the spouse, child, or grandchild of an active-duty or retired COA member. Applicants must be preparing for a career in a PHS category (e.g., dentist, dietician, engineer, nurse, pharmacist, physician, clinical or rehabilitation therapist, veterinarian). Along with their application, they must submit a 1-page essay on what they intend to accomplish with their degrees and how their area of focus may relate to any of the PHS professional categories.
Financial data The stipend is approximately $1,000.
Duration 1 year.
Number awarded Varies each year; recently, 18 were awarded.
Deadline June of each year.

[958]
PISCATAQUA POST SAME SCHOLARSHIPS

Society of American Military Engineers-Piscataqua Post
PWD Maine Building 59
Portsmouth, NH 03804
E-mail: samepiscataquapost@gmail.com
Web: www.same.org

Summary To provide financial assistance to high school seniors in Maine, Massachusetts, and New Hampshire, especially those interested in joining ROTC or with ties to the military, who are planning to attend college in any state to major in engineering or the physical sciences.
Eligibility This program is open to seniors graduating from high schools in Maine, Massachusetts, or New Hampshire and planning to attend a college or university in any state. Applicants must be interested in majoring in engineering or the physical sciences and enrolling in ROTC, especially if they do not receive an ROTC scholarship. They should be willing to attend meetings of the Society of American Military Engineers (SAME) to receive their scholarship and share their learning experiences. Preference is given to members and children of members of the Piscataqua Post of SAME, students who are enrolled in ROTC (preferably not ROTC scholarship recipients), and individuals with prior or current U.S. military service and their children.
Financial data The stipend is $1,500.
Duration 1 year.
Number awarded Up to 2 each year.
Deadline March or June of each year.

[959]
PLANNING SYSTEMS INCORPORATED SCIENCE AND ENGINEERING SCHOLARSHIP

Navy League of the United States
Attn: Scholarships
2300 Wilson Boulevard, Suite 200
Arlington, VA 22201-5424
(703) 528-1775   Toll Free: (800) 356-5760
Fax: (703) 528-2333
E-mail: scholarships@navyleague.org
Web: www.navyleague.org/programs/scholarships

Summary To provide financial assistance for college to dependent children of sea service personnel, especially those interested in majoring in engineering and/or the sciences.

Eligibility This program is open to U.S. citizens who are 1) dependents or direct descendants of an active, Reserve, retired, or honorably discharged member of the U.S. sea service (including the Navy, Marine Corps, Coast Guard, or Merchant Marine); or 2) currently an active member of the Naval Sea Cadet Corps. Applicants must be high school seniors entering their freshman year at an accredited college or university. They must have a GPA of 3.0 or higher. Along with their application, they must submit transcripts, 2 letters of recommendation, SAT/ACT scores, documentation of financial need, proof of qualifying sea service duty, and a 1-page personal statement on why they should be considered for this scholarship. Preference is given to students who have demonstrated an interest in and an intention to continue their education in engineering and/or the sciences.

Financial data The stipend is $2,500 per year.

Duration 4 years, provided the recipient maintains a GPA of 3.0 or higher.

Number awarded 1 each year.

Deadline February of each year.

[960]
POP-A-SMOKE SCHOLARSHIPS
USMC/Combat Helicopter & Tiltrotor Association
Attn: Scholarships
2394 West Oak Bridge Way, N.E.
Leland, NC 28451-8835
E-mail: admin@popasmoke.com
Web: www.popasmoke.com/scholarships

Summary To provide financial assistance for college to the children, grandchildren, and spouses of members of the USMC/Combat Helicopter & Tiltrotor Association.

Eligibility This program is open to 1) children and grandchildren of regular and associate members of the USMC/Combat Helicopter & Tiltrotor Association who are 24 years of age or younger (associate members must have prior Marine Corps/Navy service or be a spouse of a deceased member); and 2) spouses of active-duty Marine or Navy personnel who are members of the association. Children and grandchildren must be high school seniors or undergraduates who have a GPA of 2.0 or higher and are enrolled or planning to enroll fulltime at an accredited 2- or 4-year college, university, or vocational/technical school; spouses may be enrolled full or part time in a degree program or a non-degree licensure/certification program, even if they already have a bachelor's degree. Along with their application, they must submit a 500-word essay on how their family and/or significant persons have influenced their desire to pursue higher education, including the influence their parent's or grandparent's Marine Corps or Navy career has had on them and any special circumstances (military deployments, unemployment, other situations) have affected their life and inspired their decision to further their academic or technical career.

Financial data Stipends range from $500 to $1,000 per year.

Duration 1 year; may be renewed for up to 3 additional years.

Additional information This program includes the Corporal Ernesto "Gooie" Gomez Memorial Scholarship, the Master Gunnery Sergeant and Mrs. Dot Easter Scholarship, the Colonel Bruce and Mrs. Jeanne Colbert Scholarship, and the Morphine 1 2 Memorial Scholarship.

Number awarded 5 each year.

Deadline September of each year.

[961]
PRAIRIE MINUTEMAN SCHOLARSHIP
National Guard Association of Illinois
Attn: Executive Director
1301 North MacArthur Boulevard
Springfield, IL 62702-2317
(630) 864-1843   E-mail: execdir@ngai.com
Web: www.ngai.com/scholarships

Summary To provide financial assistance to dependents of members of the National Guard Association of Illinois (NGAI) who are interested in attending college in any state.

Eligibility This program is open to dependents (children and spouses) of NGAI members in good standing. Applicants may be high school seniors, high school graduates, or currently-enrolled students at a college or university in any state. They must submit a completed application form, official transcripts, 2 letters of recommendation, a verified copy of their ACT/SAT scores, and a 250-word essay on their scholastic and professional goals and aspirations. Financial need is also considered in the selection process.

Financial data The stipend is $2,500 or $1,000.

Duration 1 year.

Number awarded 4 each year: 1 at $2,500 to an Illinois Army National Guard dependent, 1 at $2,500 to an Illinois Air National Guard dependent, 1 at $2,500 to an "at large" dependent of an Illinois National Guard soldier or airman; and 1 (sponsored by USAA Insurance Corporation) to a dependent of an enlisted Illinois National Guard member.

Deadline May of each year.

[962]
PROVETS MILITARY SCHOLARSHIPS
ProNet International Gifts and Scholarships, Inc.
P.O. Box 31578
St. Louis, MO 63131
(636) 227-2471   Fax: (636) 391-3903
E-mail: info@pronetscholarships.org
Web: www.pronetscholarships.org/scholarships.htm

Summary To provide financial assistance for college to veterans and their children, especially those interested in studying ethics or preparing for a career in the insurance industry.

Eligibility This program is open to U.S. citizens who rank in the upper 20% of their high school class and have been admitted to a postsecondary educational program. Applicants must have served in the military or have a parent who served in the military. Preference is given to 1) veterans of a foreign war or the children of a veteran of a foreign war; or 2) plan to prepare for a career in the insurance industry and/or the study of ethics. Along with their application, they must submit a 1-page essay explaining their reasons for applying for this scholarship, the challenges they face, how the receipt of this funds will help them to attain their educational and/or career goals, and how they will benefit from this program. Financial need is considered in the selection process.

Financial data A stipend is awarded (amount not specified).
Duration 1 year.
Additional information This program includes the following named awards: the Carol Anne Abrams Memorial Scholarship, the William E. Brand, Jr. Memorial Scholarship, the Joseph P. Joseph Memorial Scholarship, the John D. Perrey, Sr. Memorial Scholarship, the Sgt. Lonnie Stephenson Memorial Scholarship, and the Arthur Robert "Bob" Troutt Memorial Scholarship.
Number awarded Varies each year.
Deadline Deadline not specified.

[963]
PVA EDUCATIONAL SCHOLARSHIP PROGRAM
Paralyzed Veterans of America
Attn: Membership Department
801 18th Street, N.W.
Washington, DC 20006-3517
(202) 416-7776 Toll Free: (800) 424-8200, ext. 776
Fax: (202) 416-1250 TDD: (800) 795-HEAR
E-mail: members@pva.org
Web: www.pva.org/membership/scholarship-program

Summary To provide financial assistance for college to members of the Paralyzed Veterans of America (PVA) and their families.
Eligibility This program is open to PVA members, spouses of members, and unmarried dependent children of members under 24 years of age. Applicants must be attending or planning to attend an accredited U.S. college or university as a full- or part-time student. They must be U.S. citizens. Along with their application, they must submit a personal statement explaining why they wish to further their education, short- and long-term academic goals, how this will meet their career objectives, and how it will affect the PVA membership. Selection is based on that statement, academic records, letters of recommendation, and extracurricular and community activities.
Financial data The stipend is $1,000 for full-time students or $500 for part-time students.
Duration 1 year.
Additional information This program began in 1986.
Number awarded Varies each year; recently 11 were awarded.
Deadline June of each year.

[964]
RANGER MEMORIAL SCHOLARSHIPS
National Ranger Memorial Foundation
Attn: Executive Secretary
P.O. Box 53369
Fort Benning, GA 31995
(706) 687-0906 E-mail: rangermemorial@gmail.com
Web: www.rangermemorial.com/scholarship

Summary To provide financial assistance for college to U.S. Army Rangers and their descendants.
Eligibility This program is open to Rangers from any era and their descendants; some awards (those offered by the Ranger Battalions Association of WWII) are limited to descendants of Rangers who served during the World War II era. Applicants must be graduating high school seniors or students currently enrolled at an accredited 2- or 4-year educational or technical institution. They must have a GPA of 3.0 or higher. Along with their application, they must submit information on their leadership activities, future goals and how they plan to attain those, and honors and awards received to date. Financial need is not considered in the selection process.
Financial data The stipend is $1,000.
Duration 1 year.
Additional information The National Ranger Memorial Foundation began awarding scholarships in 1999. The Ranger Battalions Association of WWII became a partner in 2007 and offered additional scholarships to descendants of World War II era Rangers.
Number awarded 49 each year: 45 offered by the National Ranger Memorial Foundation and 4 by the Ranger Battalions Association of WWII.
Deadline May of each year.

[965]
RAYMOND P. GIEHLL, IV MEMORIAL SCHOLARSHIP
Sons of the American Legion
Detachment of Indiana
Attn: Scholarship Chair
5440 Herbert Lord Road
Indianapolis, IN 46216
(317) 630-1300 Fax: (317) 237-9891
Web: www.indianasal.org

Summary To provide financial assistance to members of the Sons of the American Legion in Indiana who are interested in attending college in the state.
Eligibility This program is open to active members of a Squadron within the Indiana Detachment of the Sons of the American Legion. Applicants must be 1) seniors graduating from high school and planning to attend an accredited college, university, or trade school in Indiana; or 2) high school graduates attending or planning to attend an accredited college, university, or trade school in the state. Along with their application, they must submit an essay (up to 1,800 words) on the reasons why they feel they should receive this scholarship. Selection is based entirely on involvement in activities of the Sons of the American Legion.
Financial data The stipend is $1,000.
Duration 1 year; nonrenewable.
Number awarded 1 each year.
Deadline May of each year.

[966]
RAYMOND T. WELLINGTON, JR. MEMORIAL SCHOLARSHIP
American Legion Auxiliary
Department of New York
1580 Columbia Turnpike
Building 1, Suite 3
Castleton-On-Hudson, NY 12033
(518) 463-1162 Toll Free: (800) 421-6348
Fax: (518) 449-5406 E-mail: nyaladeptoffice@gmail.com
Web: www.deptny.org/?page_id=2128

Summary To provide financial assistance to New York residents who are the descendants of veterans and interested in attending college in any state.

Eligibility This program is open to residents of New York who are high school seniors or graduates and attending or planning to attend an accredited college or university in any state. Applicants must be the children, grandchildren, or great-grandchildren of veterans who served during specified periods of wartime. Along with their application, they must submit a 700-word autobiography that includes their interests, experiences, long-range plans, and goals. Selection is based on character (15%), Americanism (15%), community involvement (15%), leadership (15%), scholarship (20%), and financial need (20%). U.S. citizenship is required.
Financial data The stipend is $1,000. Funds are paid directly to the recipient's school.
Duration 1 year.
Number awarded 1 each year.
Deadline February of each year.

[967]
RAYTHEON-ZUMWALT ENDOWED SCHOLARSHIP

Anchor Scholarship Foundation
4966 Euclid Road, Suite 109
Virginia Beach, VA 23462
(757) 671-3200   Fax: (757) 671-3300
E-mail: scholarshipadmin@anchorscholarship.com
Web: www.anchorscholarship.com

Summary To provide financial assistance for college to dependents of current or former personnel serving in the Naval Surface Forces who plan to study a field of STEM.
Eligibility This program is open to dependent children of active-duty, honorably-discharged, or retired personnel (officer or enlisted) who have served at least 6 years (need not be consecutive) in a unit under the administrative control of Commander, Naval Surface Forces, U.S. Atlantic Fleet or U.S. Pacific Fleet. Applicants must be high school seniors planning to attend an accredited 4-year college or university and work full time on a bachelor's degree in a field of STEM. The sponsor must have a Surface Warfare qualification (SWO/ESWS). Selection is based on academic performance, extracurricular activities, character, and financial need.
Financial data The stipend is $5,000 per year.
Duration 4 years, provided the recipient continues to meet eligibility requirements and maintains a GPA of 3.0 or higher.
Additional information This program is supported by an endowment from Raytheon.
Number awarded 1 each year.
Deadline February of each year.

[968]
REBECCA POST SIKES MEMORIAL SCHOLARSHIP

Operation Once in a Lifetime
P.O. Box 797052
Dallas, TX 75379
(214) 263-9880
E-mail: contact@operationonceinalifetime.com
Web: www.operationonceinalifetime.com

Summary To provide financial assistance for college to spouses of active duty military members and veterans.
Eligibility This program is open to spouses of active duty military members and veterans who are attending an accredited public or nonprofit independent college. Applicants may be working on an undergraduate or graduate degree. They must have a GPA of 2.0 or higher.

Financial data A stipend is awarded (amount not specified).
Duration 1 year.
Number awarded 1 or more each year.
Deadline Deadline not specified.

[969]
RED RIVER VALLEY FIGHTER PILOTS ASSOCIATION KINSHIP SCHOLARSHIP GRANT PROGRAM

Red River Valley Association Foundation
Attn: Executive Director
1376 Needham Circle West
York, PA 17404
(717) 505-8529   E-mail: ExecDir@river-rats.org
Web: www.river-rats.org/about-us/scholarship-program.html

Summary To provide financial assistance for college or graduate school to the spouses and children of selected service personnel and members of the Red River Valley Fighter Pilots Association.
Eligibility This program is open to the spouses and children of 1) U.S. aircrew members missing in action (MIA) or killed in action (KIA) in combat situations involving U.S. military forces from August 1964 through the present; 2) U.S. military aircrew members killed in a non-combat aircraft accident in which they were performing aircrew duties; and 3) current members of the association and deceased members who were in good standing at the time of their death. Applicants must be enrolled or planning to enroll full or part time at an accredited college, university, vocational/technical institute, or career school to work on an undergraduate or graduate degree. Selection is based on demonstrated academic achievement, SAT or ACT scores, financial need, and accomplishments in school, church, civic, and social activities.
Financial data The amount awarded varies, depending upon the need of the recipient. Recently, undergraduate stipends have ranged from $500 to $3,500 and averaged $1,725; graduate stipends have ranged from $500 to $2,000 and averaged $1,670. Funds are paid directly to the recipient's institution and are to be used for tuition, fees, books, and room and board for full-time students.
Duration 1 year; may be renewed if the recipient maintains a GPA of 2.0 or higher.
Additional information This program began in 1970, out of concern for the families of aircrews (known as "River Rats") who were killed or missing in action in the Red River Valley of North Vietnam.
Number awarded Varies each year; since this program was established, it has awarded more than 1,130 scholarships worth more than $2,300,000.
Deadline June of each year.

[970]
REMEMBERING MARINE SSGT MARK ANTHONY WOJCIECHOWSKI "TONY WOJO" SCHOLARSHIP

Cincinnati Scholarship Foundation
602 Main Street, Suite 1000
Cincinnati, OH 45202
(513) 345-6701   Fax: (513) 345-6705
E-mail: info@cincinnatischolarshipfoundation.org
Web: www.cincinnatischolarshipfoundation.org

Summary To provide financial assistance to high school seniors and current college students who are relatives of veterans and active-duty military personnel.
Eligibility This program is open to college-bound high school seniors and students enrolled in a non-proprietary college or university in any state. Applicants must be a relative (defined as children, grandchildren, step-children, adopted children, siblings, nephews, nieces, cousins, aunts, or uncles) of an active-duty U.S. service member or a U.S. service member veteran. Along with their application, they must submit a 2-page essay on the topic, "What it Means to me that Servicemen like SSGT Mark Anthony Wojciechowski ("Wojo") are Willing to Serve and Protect Our Country and Our Way of Life."
Financial data A stipend is awarded (amount not specified).
Duration 1 year.
Number awarded 1 or more each year.
Deadline April of each year.

[971]
RENEE FELDMAN SCHOLARSHIPS
Blinded Veterans Association Auxiliary
c/o Lottie Davis, Scholarship Chair
615 South Adams Street
Arlington, VA 22204-2112
(703) 521-3745
Web: www.nbvaaux.org

Summary To provide financial assistance for college to spouses and children of blinded veterans.
Eligibility This program is open to children and spouses of blinded veterans who are enrolled or planning to enroll full time at a college, university, community college, or vocational school. Grandchildren are not eligible. The veteran's blindness may be service-connected or non-service connected. The veteran is not required to be a member of the Blinded Veterans Association. Applicants must submit a 300-word essay on their career goals and aspirations. Selection is based on that essay, academic achievement, and financial need.
Financial data Stipends are $2,000 or $1,000 per year. Funds are paid directly to the recipient's school to be applied to tuition, books, and general fees.
Duration 1 year; may be renewed up to 3 additional years.
Number awarded 3 each year: 2 at $2,000 and 1 at $1,000.
Deadline April of each year.

[972]
REOC CHARITABLE FUND SCHOLARSHIP
San Antonio Area Foundation
Attn: Philanthropic Advisor, Scholarships
303 Pearl Parkway, Suite 114
San Antonio, TX 78215-1285
(210) 228-3759 Fax: (210) 225-1980
E-mail: scholarships@ssafdn.org
Web: www.saafdn.org/Scholarships/Apply-for-a-Scholarship

Summary To provide financial assistance for college to the children of armed services members who were killed in action, lost limbs, or suffered a serious traumatic injury.
Eligibility This program is open to seniors graduating from high schools in any state who are the child of an American service man or woman who has been killed in action, lost limbs, or suffered a serious traumatic injury. Applicants must be planning to attend an accredited college, university, or vocational school in any state and major in any field. They must have a GPA of 2.5 or higher.
Financial data A stipend is awarded (amount not specified).
Duration 1 year; may be renewed.
Number awarded 1 or more each year.
Deadline February of each year.

[973]
RESTORING FAMILY SCHOLARSHIP
Hope for the Warriors
Attn: Scholarship Committee
5518 Port Royal Road
Springfield, VA 22151
(703) 321-0588 Toll Free: (877) 2HOPE4W
Fax: (703) 256-3702
E-mail: scholarships@hopeforthewarriors.org
Web: www.hopeforthewarriors.org

Summary To provide financial assistance for college or graduate school to spouses and caregivers of deceased veterans who served after September 11, 2001.
Eligibility This program is open to spouses and caregivers of military personnel who were killed as a result of service after September 11, 2001. Applicants must be enrolled or planning to enroll at an accredited college, university, or trade school in any state. They must be working on an undergraduate or graduate degree in any field. Along with their application, they must submit an essay on their academic achievement and personal goals. Financial need is not considered in the selection process.
Financial data The stipend is at least $2,000.
Duration 1 year.
Additional information This program began in 2008.
Number awarded Normally, 2 each year (1 each semester).
Deadline May of each year for fall semester; October of each year for spring semester.

[974]
RESTORING SELF SCHOLARSHIP
Hope for the Warriors
Attn: Scholarship Committee
5518 Port Royal Road
Springfield, VA 22151
(703) 321-0588 Toll Free: (877) 2HOPE4W
Fax: (703) 256-3702
E-mail: scholarships@hopeforthewarriors.org
Web: www.hopeforthewarriors.org

Summary To provide financial assistance for undergraduate study to spouses and caregivers of deceased and disabled veterans who served after September 11, 2001.
Eligibility This program is open to spouses and caregivers of military personnel who were killed or became disabled as a result of service after September 11, 2001. Applicants must be enrolled or planning to enroll at an accredited college, university, or trade school in any state to work on an undergraduate degree in any field. Along with their application, they must submit an essay on their academic achievement and

personal goals. Financial need is not considered in the selection process.
Financial data The stipend is at least $2,000.
Duration 1 year.
Additional information This program began in 2008.
Number awarded Normally, 2 each year (1 each semester).
Deadline May of each year for fall semester; October of each year for spring semester.

[975]
RICHARD M. PEDRO MEMORIAL SCHOLARSHIP
American Legion
Department of New York
1304 Park Boulevard
Troy, NY 12180
(518) 463-2215   Toll Free: (800) 253-4466
Fax: (518) 427-8443   E-mail: info@nylegion.org
Web: www.nylegion.net

Summary To provide financial assistance to descendants of members of the American Legion in New York who are interested in attending college in any state.
Eligibility This program is open to seniors graduating from high schools in New York and planning to enroll at a college or university in any state. Applicants must be 1) a child, grandchild, or great-grandchild of a New York State Legionnaire; 2) a child, grandchild, or great-grandchild of a deceased New York State Legionnaire; or 3) a child of a New York service member who was killed as a result of the war on terrorism, including the World Trade Center, the Pentagon, or the wars in Iraq or Afghanistan. Along with their application, they must submit a 500-word essay or video on the importance of the American Legion in their community.
Financial data The stipend is $1,000.
Duration 1 year.
Number awarded 1 each year.
Deadline June of each year.

[976]
RICHARD T. NUSKE MEMORIAL SCHOLARSHIPS
Vietnam Veterans of America-Wisconsin State Council
c/o Virginia Nuske, Scholarship Committee Chair
N5448 Broder Road
Shawano, WI 54166
(715) 524-2487   E-mail: nuskerv@gmail.com
Web: www.vvawi.org/wsc-committees/scholarship/

Summary To recognize and reward high school seniors in Wisconsin who submit outstanding essays based on an interview of a Vietnam veteran, especially if the veteran is a relative.
Eligibility This competition is open to seniors graduating from high schools in Wisconsin who plan to attend an accredited institution of higher education in any state. Applicants must submit an essay, from 3 to 5 pages in length, based on an interview of a veteran of any branch who served on active duty anywhere in the world during the Vietnam War (from January 1, 1959 to May 7, 1975). Essays are judged on originality, appearance, and elements of grammar; up to 35 points may be awarded, depending on the quality of the essay. An additional 10 points are awarded if the student is the child or grandchild of the veteran; an additional 5 points are awarded if the student is another relative (niece, cousin) of the veteran.
Financial data The award is a $1,500 scholarship that may be used at a college or university in Wisconsin.
Duration The awards are presented annually.
Number awarded 3 each year.
Deadline February of each year.

[977]
ROCKWELL COLLINS NAVY LEAGUE SCHOLARSHIP
Navy League of the United States
Attn: Scholarships
2300 Wilson Boulevard, Suite 200
Arlington, VA 22201-5424
(703) 528-1775   Toll Free: (800) 356-5760
Fax: (703) 528-2333
E-mail: scholarships@navyleague.org
Web: www.navyleague.org/programs/scholarships

Summary To provide financial assistance for college to dependent children of sea service personnel who are interested in majoring in aviation, engineering, and/or the sciences.
Eligibility This program is open to U.S. citizens who are 1) dependents or direct descendants of an active, Reserve, retired, or honorably discharged member of the U.S. sea service (including the Navy, Marine Corps, Coast Guard, or Merchant Marine); or 2) currently an active member of the Naval Sea Cadet Corps. Applicants must be high school seniors entering their freshman year at an accredited college or university and planning to major in aviation, engineering, and/or the sciences. They must have a GPA of 3.0 or higher. Along with their application, they must submit transcripts, 2 letters of recommendation, SAT/ACT scores, documentation of financial need, proof of qualifying sea service duty, and a 1-page personal statement on why they should be considered for this scholarship.
Financial data The stipend is $2,500.
Duration 1 year.
Additional information This program is sponsored by Rockwell Collins.
Number awarded 1 each year.
Deadline February of each year.

[978]
ROLLS-ROYCE STEM SCHOLARSHIP
Anchor Scholarship Foundation
Attn: Executive Director
138 South Rosemont Road, Suite 206
Virginia Beach, VA 23452
(757) 777-4724
E-mail: Joy.Eyrolles@anchorscholarship.com
Web: www.anchorscholarship.com

Summary To provide financial assistance for college to dependents of current or former personnel serving in the Naval Surface Forces who plan to study a field of STEM.
Eligibility This program is open to dependent children of active-duty, honorably-discharged, or retired personnel who have served at least 6 years (need not be consecutive) in a unit under the administrative control of Commander, Naval Surface Forces, U.S. Atlantic Fleet or U.S. Pacific Fleet. Applicants must be high school seniors planning to attend an

accredited 4-year college or university and work full time on a bachelor's degree in a field of STEM. The sponsor must have a Surface Warfare qualification (SWO/ESWS). Selection is based on academic performance, extracurricular activities, character, and financial need.

Financial data The stipend is $4,500.

Duration 1 year; nonrenewable.

Additional information This program is supported by Rolls-Royce Marine North America Inc.

Number awarded 1 each year.

Deadline February of each year.

[979]
RON PACE MEMORIAL SCHOLARSHIP

American Academy of Physician Assistants
Attn: Physician Assistant Foundation
2318 Mill Road, Suite 1300
Alexandria, VA 22314-6868
(571) 319-4510   E-mail: pafoundation@aapa.org
Web: app.smarterselect.com

Summary To provide financial assistance to student members of the American Academy of Physician Assistants (AAPA) who are veterans from Florida.

Eligibility This program is open to student members of the Florida Academy of Physician Assistants who have completed at least 1 semester of an accredited physician assistant program in Florida. Applicants must be veterans or dependent children of veterans.

Financial data The stipend is $1,000.

Duration 1 year; nonrenewable.

Number awarded 1 each year.

Deadline May of each year.

[980]
ROSEDALE POST 346 SCHOLARSHIP FUND

American Legion
Department of Kansas
1314 S.W. Topeka Boulevard
Topeka, KS 66612-1886
(785) 232-9315   Fax: (785) 232-1399
Web: www.ksamlegion.org

Summary To provide financial assistance to the children of members of the Kansas American Legion or American Legion Auxiliary who are interested in attending college in any state.

Eligibility This program is open to high school seniors and college freshmen and sophomores who are attending or planning to attend an approved college, university, junior college, or trade school in any state. Applicants must have an average or better academic record. At least 1 of their parents must be a veteran and have been a member of an American Legion Post or Auxiliary in Kansas for at least 3 consecutive years. Along with their application, they must submit an essay of 250 to 500 words on "Why I Want to Go to College." Financial need is also considered in the selection process.

Financial data The stipend is $1,500.

Duration 1 year; nonrenewable.

Number awarded 2 each year.

Deadline February of each year.

[981]
ROY C. AND DOROTHY JEAN OLSON MEMORIAL SCHOLARSHIP

International Military Community Executives' Association
Attn: Scholarship Committee
14080 Nacogdoches Road, Suite 329
San Antonio, TX 78247-1944
(940) 463-5145   Fax: (866) 369-2435
E-mail: imcea@imcea.org
Web: www.imcea.org/awards/scholarship-info

Summary To provide financial assistance to children of members of the International Military Community Executives' Association (IMCEA) who are interested in attending college.

Eligibility This program is open to dependent children of regular IMCEA members who are graduating from high school or already enrolled at a college or university. Along with their application, they must submit a 2-page essay on how they have demonstrated leadership ability, both in and out of school. Selection is based on that essay, participation in extracurricular activities over the past 4 years, participation in community activities over the past 4 year, and commendations and honors received during the past 4 years.

Financial data The stipend is $1,000.

Duration 1 year.

Additional information Regular membership in IMCEA is open to Army, Air Force, Navy, Marine Corps, and Coast Guard personnel who provide MWR services at military installations and bases worldwide.

Number awarded 1 each year.

Deadline June of each year.

[982]
RUARK-WIGHT FAMILY SCHOLARSHIP

Marines' Memorial Association
c/o Marines Memorial Club and Hotel
609 Sutter Street
San Francisco, CA 94102
(415) 673-6672, ext. 293   Toll Free: (800) 5-MARINE
Fax: (415) 441-3649
E-mail: scholarship@marineclub.com
Web: www.marinesmemorial.org/members/scholarships

Summary To provide financial assistance to veterans, military personnel, and their families who are interested in attending college or graduate school to work on a degree in any field.

Eligibility This program is open to students who meet 1 of the following requirements: 1) have served honorably or is currently serving in any branch of the U.S. armed forces; or 2) is the spouse or child of a person who served honorably or is currently serving in any branch of the U.S. armed forces. Applicants must be enrolled as full-time sophomores, juniors, seniors or graduate students working on a degree in any field. They must have a GPA of 2.5 or higher. Membership in the sponsoring organization is not required for student veterans. Along with their application, they must submit an essay of up to 500 words on why they chose their specific path of study, what they hope to accomplish after graduation with their degree, and how their efforts will benefit others in their community. Selection is based on the essay, academic merit, references, and financial need.

Financial data The stipend is $5,000 per year.

Duration 1 year; recipients may reapply for up to 3 additional years.
Number awarded 1 each year.
Deadline April of each year.

[983]
RUBY GONZALES SCHOLARSHIP
Louisiana National Guard Enlisted Association Auxiliary
c/o Cheryl L. McGlothin, Scholarship Committee
2911 Effie Highway
Deville, LA 71328
(318) 253-8834
Web: www.langea.org/langea-auxiliary

Summary To provide financial assistance to members of the Louisiana National Guard Enlisted Association (LANGEA) and their dependents who plan to attend college in any state.
Eligibility This program is open to LANGEA members, their spouses and unmarried dependent children, and the unremarried spouses and unmarried dependent children of deceased members who were in good standing at the time of their death. Applicants must be enrolled or planning to enroll full time at an accredited college, university, trade school, or business school in any state. Along with their application, they must submit a letter specifying their reasons for their desire to continue their education and why they need financial assistance.
Financial data The stipend is $2,000.
Duration 1 year; nonrenewable.
Number awarded 2 each year.
Deadline February of each year.

[984]
SAD SACKS NURSING SCHOLARSHIP
AMVETS-Department of Illinois
2200 South Sixth Street
Springfield, IL 62703
(217) 528-4713   Toll Free: (800) 638-VETS (within IL)
Fax: (217) 528-9896   E-mail: info@ilamvets.org
Web: www.ilamvets.org

Summary To provide financial assistance for nursing education to Illinois residents, especially descendants of disabled or deceased veterans.
Eligibility This program is open to seniors at high schools in Illinois who have been accepted to an approved nursing program and students already enrolled in an approved school of nursing in Illinois. Priority is given to dependents of deceased or disabled veterans. Selection is based on academic record, character, interest and activity record, and financial need. Preference is given to students in the following order: third-year students, second-year students, and first-year students.
Financial data The stipend varies annually.
Duration 1 year; nonrenewable.
Number awarded Varies each year; recently, 2 were awarded.
Deadline February of each year.

[985]
SAM ROSE MEMORIAL SCHOLARSHIP
Ladies Auxiliary of the Fleet Reserve Association
c/o Amanda Murray, National Scholarship Chair
512 Hyde Park Road
Norfolk, VA 23503-5514
(757) 588-6125   E-mail: sairockstar@gmail.com
Web: www.la-fra.org/scholarship.html

Summary To provide financial assistance for college to the children and grandchildren of deceased members of the Fleet Reserve Association (FRA).
Eligibility This program is open to children and grandchildren of deceased members of the association or those who were eligible to be members at the time of death. Applicants must submit an essay on their life experiences, career objectives, and what motivated them to select those objectives. Selection is based on academic record, financial need, extracurricular activities, leadership skills, and participation in community activities. U.S. citizenship is required.
Financial data The stipend is $2,500.
Duration 1 year.
Additional information Membership in the FRA is open to current and former enlisted members of the Navy, Marine Corps, and Coast Guard.
Number awarded 1 each year.
Deadline April of each year.

[986]
SAMSUNG AMERICAN LEGION SCHOLARSHIPS
American Legion
Attn: Americanism and Children & Youth Division
700 North Pennsylvania Street
P.O. Box 1055
Indianapolis, IN 46206-1055
(317) 630-1202   Fax: (317) 630-1223
E-mail: scholarships@legion.org
Web: www.legion.org/scholarships/samsung

Summary To provide financial assistance for college to descendants of veterans who participate in Girls State or Boys State.
Eligibility This program is open to students entering their senior year of high school who are selected to participate in Girls State or Boys State, sponsored by the American Legion Auxiliary or American Legion in their state. Applicants must be the child, grandchild, or great-grandchild of a veteran who saw active-duty service during specified periods of wartime. Finalists are chosen at each participating Girls and Boys State, and they are then nominated for the national awards. Selection is based on academic record, community service, involvement in school and community activities, and financial need. Special consideration is given to descendants of U.S. veterans of the Korean War.
Financial data Stipends are $10,000 for winners, $5,000 for runners-up, and $1,250 for other finalists.
Duration 4 years.
Additional information These scholarships were first presented in 1996, following a gift in July 1995 to the American Legion from Samsung Corporation of Korea, as an act of appreciation for U.S. involvement in the Korean War.
Number awarded 10 winners each year, 2 from each of 5 American Legion regions; 10 runners-up each year, 2 from each of 5 American Legion regions; and as many other final-

ists each year as are nominated in each state (recently, there were 79).
Deadline Deadline not specified.

[987]
SAPA ANNUAL SCHOLARSHIP AWARDS
Society of Army Physician Assistants
Attn: Scholarship Committee
P.O. Box 623
Monmouth, IL 61462
(309) 734-5446   Fax: (309) 734-4489
E-mail: orpotter@aol.com
Web: www.sapa.org/scholarships

Summary To provide financial assistance to members of the Society of Army Physician Assistants (SAPA) and their families interested in attending college in any state to major in any field.

Eligibility This program is open to SAPA members, spouses of SAPA members, dependent children under 24 years of age of SAPA members, and spouses and children of deceased SAPA members. Applicants must be high school seniors or students currently enrolled at a college, university, or vocational school and working on a degree in any field or a license or certificate to practice a trade. There is no application form; interested parties submit a letter of introduction that includes why the grant is needed, educational goals, goals for the future, and anything else they feel would be of interest to the selection committee; a letter of acceptance from a school; a list of activities and achievements; and transcripts.

Financial data The stipend is $1,000.
Duration 1 year.
Additional information This program began in 2012. Membership in SAPA is open to graduates of approved physician assistant training programs commissioned as a physician assistant in the Active Duty Army, Army National Guard, Army Reserve, or honorably retired from those branches of service; they must also be members of the American Academy of Physician Assistants who have designated SAPA as their constituent chapter.
Number awarded 3 each year.
Deadline January of each year.

[988]
SCHNEIDER-EMANUEL AMERICAN LEGION SCHOLARSHIPS
American Legion
Department of Wisconsin
2930 American Legion Drive
P.O. Box 388
Portage, WI 53901-0388
(608) 745-1090   Fax: (608) 745-0179
E-mail: info@wilegion.org
Web: www.wilegion.org

Summary To provide financial assistance to members of the American Legion in Wisconsin and their children or grandchildren who plan to attend college in any state.

Eligibility This program is open to seniors and graduates from accredited Wisconsin high schools. Applicants must be at least 1 of the following 1) a child whose father, mother, or legal guardian is a member of the Department of Wisconsin of the American Legion, American Legion Auxiliary, or Sons of the American Legion; 2) a grandchild whose grandfather, grandmother, or legal guardian is a member of the Department of Wisconsin of the American Legion, American Legion Auxiliary, or Sons of the American Legion; 3) a member of the Sons of the American Legion, American Legion Auxiliary, or Junior American Legion Auxiliary; or 4) a veteran and an American Legion member in Wisconsin. Applicants must have participated in Legion and Auxiliary youth programs. They must be planning to attend a college or university in any state to work on a baccalaureate degree. Selection is based on moral character; scholastic excellence (GPA of 3.0 or higher); participation and accomplishment in American Legion affiliated activities; and personality, leadership, and participation in general extracurricular activities.

Financial data The stipend is $1,000.
Duration 1 year.
Additional information This program began in 1968.
Number awarded 3 each year.
Deadline February of each year.

[989]
SCHOLARSHIPS FOR MILITARY CHILDREN
Fisher House Foundation
12300 Twinbrook Parkway, Suite 410
Rockville, MD 20852
Toll Free: (888) 294-8560
E-mail: bgawne@fisherhouse.org
Web: www.militaryscholar.org/sfmc

Summary To provide financial assistance for college to the children of veterans and military personnel.

Eligibility This program is open to sons and daughters of U.S. military servicemembers (including active duty, retirees, Guard/Reserves, and survivors of deceased members) who are enrolled or accepted for enrollment as a full-time undergraduate at a college or university. Applicants must be younger than 23 years of age and enrolled in the Defense Enrollment Eligibility Reporting System (DEERS). They must have a GPA of 3.0 or higher. Along with their application, they must submit a 500-word essay on a topic that changes annually; recently, students were asked to identify the 4 persons whose faces they would place on a 21st century Mount Rushmore type of monument and why. Selection is based on that essay, academic achievement, work experience, and participation in school, community, and volunteer activities.

Financial data The stipend is $2,000.
Duration 1 year; recipients may reapply.
Additional information This program, established in 2001, is administered by the Fisher House Foundation on behalf of the Defense Commissary Agency.
Number awarded At least 1 scholarship is allocated for each of the commissaries worldwide operated by the Defense Commissary Agency (DeCA); more than 1 scholarship per commissary may be available, depending on donations from suppliers and manufacturers whose products are sold at commissaries. Recently, the program awarded 500 scholarships. Since the program was established, it has awarded $19,126,000 to more than 11,300 students.
Deadline February of each year.

[990]
SCNGF ACADEMIC EXCELLENCE LEADERSHIP SCHOLARSHIPS

National Guard Association of South Carolina
Attn: South Carolina National Guard Foundation
132 Pickens Street
P.O. Box 7606
Columbia, SC 29202
(803) 254-8456　　　Toll Free: (800) 822-3235
Fax: (803) 254-3869　　　E-mail: dianne@scngf.org
Web: www.scngf.org/scngfscholarshipapplication

Summary To provide financial assistance to South Carolina National Guard members and their dependents who are interested in attending college or graduate school in any state.

Eligibility This program is open to members of the South Carolina National Guard and dependents of active or retired members. Applicants must be enrolled or planning to enroll full time at a 4-year college or university in any state as an undergraduate student. Guard members, but not dependents, are also eligible to attend graduate school. Applicants must have a GPA of 3.5 or higher and a record of involvement and leadership in school, civic, and/or community activities. Selection is based on excellence in academics and leadership; financial need is not considered.

Financial data The stipend is $1,500 per year. Funds are disbursed directly to the recipient's institution.

Duration 1 year; may be renewed up to 3 additional years.

Number awarded Varies each year; recently, this sponsor awarded a total of 75 scholarships through both of its programs.

Deadline February of each year.

[991]
SCNGF FINANCIAL NEED/ACADEMIC ACHIEVEMENT SCHOLARSHIPS

National Guard Association of South Carolina
Attn: South Carolina National Guard Foundation
132 Pickens Street
P.O. Box 7606
Columbia, SC 29202
(803) 254-8456　　　Toll Free: (800) 822-3235
Fax: (803) 254-3869　　　E-mail: dianne@scngf.org
Web: www.scngf.org/scngfscholarshipapplication

Summary To provide financial assistance to South Carolina National Guard members and their dependents who are interested in attending college or graduate school in any state and can demonstrate financial need.

Eligibility This program is open to members of the South Carolina National Guard and dependents of active or retired members. Applicants must be enrolled or planning to enroll full time at a college or university in any state as an undergraduate student. Guard members, but not dependents, are also eligible to attend graduate school. Applicants must have a GPA of 2.5 or higher and a record of involvement and leadership in school, civic, and/or community activities. High school seniors must also submit SAT and/or ACT scores. Selection is based on excellence in academics and leadership and on financial need.

Financial data The stipend is $1,000 per year. Funds are disbursed directly to the recipient's institution.

Duration 1 year; may be renewed up to 3 additional years.

Number awarded Varies each year; recently, this sponsor awarded a total of 75 scholarships through both of its programs.

Deadline February of each year.

[992]
SCOTT LUNDELL MILITARY SURVIVORS TUITION WAIVER

Utah Department of Veterans and Military Affairs
Attn: Director
550 Foothill Boulevard, Suite 105
Salt Lake City, UT 84113
(801) 326-2372　　　Toll Free: (800) 894-9497 (within UT)
Fax: (801) 326-2369　　　E-mail: veterans@utah.gov
Web: veterans.utah.gov/state-education-benefits

Summary To provide a tuition waiver to residents of Utah who are dependents of deceased military personnel and attending a public institution in the state.

Eligibility This program is open to residents of Utah who are dependents of military members, including the armed forces, the Reserve forces, and the Utah National Guard, killed in the line of duty after September 11, 2001. Applicants must be working on an undergraduate degree at a public college or university in the state.

Financial data Tuition is waived for qualified dependents.

Duration Tuition is waived until completion of a bachelor's degree.

Additional information This program began in 2007.

Number awarded Varies each year.

Deadline Deadline not specified.

[993]
SCREAMING EAGLE SURVIVING CHILDREN'S SCHOLARSHIP

101st Airborne Division Association
32 Screaming Eagle Boulevard
P.O. Box 929
Fort Campbell, KY 42223-0929
(931) 431-0199　　　Fax: (931) 431-0195
E-mail: 101exec@screamingeagle.org
Web: www.screamingeaglefoundation.org

Summary To provide financial assistance for college or graduate school to the children of soldiers of the 101st Airborne Division and Fort Campbell Units who have been killed or severely wounded since September 11, 2001.

Eligibility This program is open to dependent children of active-duty personnel who were assigned to the 101st Airborne Division or a tenant military organization assigned to Fort Campbell, Kentucky. The parent must have been killed, wounded, or injured while serving in support of the Global War on Terrorism on or after September 11, 2001. Applicants must be high school seniors or graduates up to 22 years of age, enrolled or planning to enroll full time at an accredited 2- or 4-year college, university, graduate program, or vocational/technical school. Along with their application, they must submit a 1-page letter on what this scholarship means to them.

Financial data The stipend is $2,500.

Duration 1 year.

Additional information This program is sponsored by the Screaming Eagle Foundation of the 101st Airborne Division Association in partnership with the Patriot Foundation.

SCHOLARSHIPS: FAMILY MEMBERS

Number awarded Varies each year.
Deadline March of each year.

[994]
SDNGEA AUXILIARY SCHOLARSHIPS

South Dakota National Guard Enlisted Association Auxiliary
c/o Alicia Engebretson, Scholarship Committee
7321 West 66th Street
Sioux Falls, SD 57106
(605) 413-7395   E-mail: alicia.engebretson@poet.com
Web: sdngea.com/auxiliary/scholarships

Summary To provide financial assistance to members of the South Dakota National Guard Enlisted Association (SDNGEA) Auxiliary and their dependents who are interested in attending college in any state.
Eligibility This program is open to current members of the SDNGEA Auxiliary, their unmarried children and grandchildren up to 26 years of age, and their spouses. Applicants must be graduating high school seniors or undergraduate students at a college, university, or vocational school in any state. They must submit a letter outlining specific goals to continue their education and why aid is required. Selection is based on academic achievement, character, leadership characteristics, and financial need.
Financial data The stipend is $1,000. Funds are paid directly to the recipient's school.
Duration 1 year; nonrenewable.
Number awarded 2 each year.
Deadline March of each year.

[995]
SEABEE MEMORIAL SCHOLARSHIP ASSOCIATION PROGRAM

Seabee Memorial Scholarship Association
P.O. Box 391
Springfield, VA 22150
(703) 690-SMSA   E-mail: smsa@seabee.org
Web: www.seabee.org/scholarship

Summary To provide financial assistance for college to the children or grandchildren of active or deceased members of the Naval Construction Battalion (Seabees) or Navy Civil Engineering Corps.
Eligibility This program is open to the children, stepchildren, and grandchildren of active, Reserve, retired, deceased, or honorably discharged officers and enlisted members who are now serving in or have served in the Naval Construction Force (Seabees) or Navy Civil Engineering Corps. Applicants may be high school seniors, high school graduates, or students currently enrolled full-time at a 2- or 4-year college or university. Along with their application, they must submit a 1-page essay on their future objectives and personal goals, how this scholarship will help them accomplish their objectives and goals, and the Seabee sponsor's role in their career objectives. Selection is based on financial need, citizenship and character, leadership, and scholastic record.
Financial data The stipend recently was $3,200 per year.
Duration 1 year; may be renewed for 3 additional years.

Number awarded Varies each year; recently, 25 new scholarships and 65 renewals were awarded through this program. The value was $319,500.
Deadline April of each year.

[996]
SEABEE WOUNDED IN ACTION SCHOLARSHIP

Seabee Memorial Scholarship Association
P.O. Box 391
Springfield, VA 22150
(703) 690-SMSA   E-mail: smsa@seabee.org
Web: www.seabee.org/scholarship

Summary To provide financial assistance for college to the children or grandchildren of active or deceased members of the Naval Construction Battalion (Seabees) or Navy Civil Engineering Corps who were wounded in action.
Eligibility This program is open to the children, stepchildren, and grandchildren of active, Reserve, retired, deceased, or honorably discharged officers and enlisted members who are now serving in or have served in the Naval Construction Force (Seabees) or Navy Civil Engineering Corps. The Seabee must have received a Purple Heart. Applicants may be high school seniors, high school graduates, or students currently enrolled full-time at a 2- or 4-year college or university. Along with their application, they must submit a 1-page essay on their future objectives and personal goals, how this scholarship will help them accomplish their objectives and goals, and the Seabee sponsor's role in their career objectives. Selection is based on financial need, citizenship and character, leadership, and scholastic record.
Financial data 1 stipend is awarded (amount not specified).
Duration 1 year; may be renewed for 3 additional years.
Number awarded 1 or more each year.
Deadline April of each year.

[997]
SENATOR DANIEL K. INOUYE MEMORIAL SCHOLARSHIP

Japanese American Veterans Association
Attn: Chris DeRosa, Scholarship Committee Chair
P.O. Box 341198
Bethesda, MD 20827
E-mail: javascholarship222@gmail.com
Web: www.java.wildapricot.org

Summary To provide financial assistance for college or graduate school to relatives of Japanese American veterans who plan a career in the military or public service.
Eligibility This program is open to students who 1) have completed at least 1 year of an undergraduate program or are currently enrolled in graduate school and are preparing for a career in the military or public service; 2) are currently enrolled in a university or college ROTC program or the U.S. Marine Corps Platoon Leaders Course but are not receiving an ROTC scholarship; or 3) are disabled veterans. Applicants must also be 1) a direct or collateral descendant of a person who served with the 442nd Regimental Combat Team, the 100th Infantry Battalion, Military Intelligence Service, 1399th Engineering Construction Battalion, or other unit associated with those during or after World War II; or 2) a member or child of a member of the Japanese American Veterans Association (JAVA) whose membership extends back at least 1

year. Along with their application, they must submit a 500-word essay on their plan and vision to serve America through public service or the military.
Financial data The stipend is $5,000.
Duration 1 year.
Number awarded 1 each year.
Deadline March of each year.

[998]
SERGEANT ANDREW EDMUND TOPHAM MEMORIAL SCHOLARSHIP

Army Scholarship Foundation
11700 Preston Road, Suite 660-301
Dallas, TX 75230
E-mail: ContactUs@armyscholarshipfoundation.org
Web: www.armyscholarshipfoundation.org/topham.html

Summary To provide financial assistance for undergraduate study to the children and spouses of Army personnel, especially those who served in the Global War on Terrorism.
Eligibility This program is open to 1) children of regular active-duty, active-duty Reserve, and active-duty Army National Guard members in good standing; 2) spouses of serving enlisted regular active-duty, active-duty Reserve, and active-duty Army National Guard members in good standing; and 3) children of former U.S. Army members who received an honorable or medical discharge or were killed while serving in the U.S. Army. Preference is given to students who are family members of soldiers who served in either Afghanistan or Iraq as part of the Global War on Terrorism. Applicants must be high school seniors, high school graduates, or undergraduates enrolled at an accredited college, university, or vocational/technical institute. They must be U.S. citizens and have a GPA of 2.0 or higher; children must be younger than 24 years of age. Financial need is considered in the selection process.
Financial data The stipend ranges from $500 to $2,000 per year.
Duration 1 year; recipients may reapply.
Additional information The Army Scholarship Foundation was established in 2001.
Number awarded 1 each year.
Deadline April of each year.

[999]
SERGEANT FELIX M. DELGRECO, JR. SCHOLARSHIP FUND

Connecticut Community Foundation
Attn: Senior Program and Scholarship Associate
43 Field Street
Waterbury, CT 06702-1906
(203) 753-1315, ext. 126   Fax: (203) 756-3054
E-mail: scholarships@conncf.org
Web: www.conncf.org/apply-for-scholarships

Summary To provide financial assistance to high school seniors and current college students whose parents are members of the Connecticut Army National Guard.
Eligibility This program is open to the children of members of the Connecticut Army National Guard who are attending or planning to attend college in any state. Applicants must have a GPA of 2.75 or higher. Selection is based on merit; financial need is not considered. U.S. citizenship is required.

Financial data The stipend is $4,000 per year. Funds are paid directly to the recipient's school.
Duration 1 year; recipients may reapply up to the minimum number of years required to complete an undergraduate degree in their course of study, provided they maintain a grade average of "C+" or higher.
Additional information This program is supported by the Connecticut National Guard Foundation.
Number awarded Varies each year.
Deadline March of each year.

[1000]
SFC CURTIS MANCINI MEMORIAL SCHOLARSHIPS

Association of the United States Army-Rhode Island Chapter
c/o LTC Robert A. Galvanin, President
31 Canoe River Drive
Mansfield, MA 02048
(508) 339-5301   E-mail: bpje5310@verizon.net
Web: www.riroa.org/ausari/scholarship.htm

Summary To provide financial assistance to members of the Rhode Island Chapter of the Association of the United States Army (AUSA) and their families who are interested in attending college or graduate school in any state.
Eligibility This program is open to members of the AUSA Rhode Island Chapter and their family members (spouses, children, and grandchildren). Applicants must be high school seniors or graduates accepted at an accredited college, university, or vocational/technical school in any state or current undergraduate or graduate students. Along with their application, they must submit a 250-word essay on why they feel their achievements should qualify them for this award. Selection is based on academic and individual achievements; financial need is not considered. Special consideration is given to students or graduates of Lincoln High School in Lincoln, Rhode Island (the alma mater of this program's namesake), especially those preparing for a career in law enforcement or enrolled or planning to enroll in Army ROTC.
Financial data The stipend is $1,000.
Duration 1 year.
Additional information Membership in the AUSA is open to everyone who supports a strong national defense, with special concern for the Army. That includes Regular Army, National Guard, Army Reserve, government civilians, retired soldiers, Wounded Warriors, veterans, concerned citizens and family members.
Number awarded Several each year.
Deadline April of each year.

[1001]
SGT. FREDERICK C. BRACE, JR. MEMORIAL SCHOLARSHIP

American Academy of Physician Assistants-Veterans Caucus
Attn: Scholarship Program
P.O. Box 362
Ossining, NY 10562
(803) 328-1864   Fax: (704) 838-8494
E-mail: rmunsee@veteranscaucus.org
Web: www.veteranscaucus.org/scholarships

SCHOLARSHIPS: FAMILY MEMBERS

Summary To provide financial assistance to Air Force veterans and their dependents who are studying to become physician assistants.
Eligibility This program is open to U.S. citizens who are currently enrolled in a physician assistant program. Applicants must be honorably discharged members of the United States Air Force or the dependent of an Air Force veteran. Along with their application, they must submit a personal statement about what led them to attend PA school; their background, present, and future intentions; and why they deserve to receive a scholarship. Selection is based on military honors and awards received, civic and college honors and awards received, professional memberships and activities, potential for future achievement, and GPA.
Financial data The stipend is $2,000.
Duration 1 year.
Number awarded 1 each year.
Deadline February of each year.

[1002]
SHIRO KASHINO MEMORIAL SCHOLARSHIPS
Nisei Veterans Committee
Attn: NVC Foundation
1212 South King Street
Seattle, WA 98144-2025
(206) 322-1122   E-mail: education@nvcfoundation.org
Web: www.nvcfoundation.org/education/scholarship/

Summary To provide financial assistance to high school seniors and current college students who are related to a member of the Nisei Veterans Committee or the NVC Foundation.
Eligibility This program is open to college-bound high school seniors and students who are already enrolled in college and are relatives of members of the Nisei Veterans Committee (an organization of Japanese American veterans) or of the NVC Foundation. Applicants must submit essays on 1) what the Nisei veterans' legacy means to them; and 2) their future aspirations and life plans. Special consideration is given to students who have helped support the NVC organization. Financial need is considered in the selection process.
Financial data The stipend is $3,000.
Duration 1 year.
Number awarded 3 each year.
Deadline January of each year.

[1003]
SIBLINGS OF COMBAT RELATED SUICIDE LOSS SCHOLARSHIP
The Matthew Freeman Project
Attn: Sibling Scholarships
P.O. Box 1608
Richmond Hill, GA 31324
E-mail: lfreeman@freemanproject.org
Web: www.imaginenet.us

Summary To provide financial assistance to siblings of military personnel lost through a combat-related death by suicide.
Eligibility This program is open to students entering or attending a college or university. Applicants must have lost a sibling through combat-related death by suicide. Along with their application, they must submit an essay describing their relationship with their sibling and how their death affected them. Selection is based on that essay, transcripts, and 3 letters of recommendation.
Financial data The stipend is $1,000.
Duration 1 year.
Additional information This program began in 2015.
Number awarded 1 or 2 each year.
Deadline January of each year.

[1004]
SMA LEON VAN AUTREVE SCHOLARSHIPS
Association of the United States Army
Attn: Scholarships
2425 Wilson Boulevard
Arlington, VA 22201
(703) 841-4300   Toll Free: (800) 336-4570
E-mail: scholarships@ausa.org
Web: www.ausa.org/resources/scholarships

Summary To provide financial assistance to members of the Association of the United States Army (AUSA) who are interested in attending college.
Eligibility This program is open to AUSA members who are enrolled or accepted at an accredited college or university to work on a degree in any field. Along with their application, they must submit a 1-page autobiography, 2 letters of recommendation, a letter describing their career aspirations (including their course of study and plans for completion of a degree), and a transcript of high school or college grades (depending on which they are currently attending). Selection is based on academic merit and personal achievement. Financial need is not normally a selection criterion but in some cases of extreme need it may be used as a factor; the lack of financial need, however, is never a cause for nonselection.
Financial data The stipend ranges from $2,000 t0 $25,000; funds are sent directly to the recipient's college or university.
Duration 1 year.
Additional information Membership in the AUSA is open to everyone who supports a strong national defense, with special concern for the Army. That includes Regular Army, National Guard, Army Reserve, government civilians, retired soldiers, Wounded Warriors, veterans, concerned citizens and family members. This program is sponsored by the USAA Foundation.
Number awarded Varies each year; recently, 1 at $25,000, 1 at $10,000, 1 at $5,000, and 5 at $2,000 were awarded.
Deadline June of each year.

[1005]
SMSGT. NATHAN L. LIPSCOMB, SR. MEMORIAL SCHOLARSHIP
American Academy of Physician Assistants-Veterans Caucus
Attn: Scholarship Program
P.O. Box 362
Ossining, NY 10562
(803) 328-1864   Fax: (704) 838-8494
E-mail: rmunsee@veteranscaucus.org
Web: www.veteranscaucus.org/scholarships

Summary To provide financial assistance to Air Force veterans and their dependents who are studying to become physician assistants.
Eligibility This program is open to U.S. citizens who are currently enrolled in a physician assistant program. Applicants must be honorably discharged members of the United States Air Force or the dependent of an Air Force veteran. Along with their application, they must submit a personal statement about what led them to attend PA school; their background, present, and future intentions; and why they deserve to receive a scholarship. Selection is based on military honors and awards received, civic and college honors and awards received, professional memberships and activities, potential for future achievement, and GPA.
Financial data The stipend is $2,000.
Duration 1 year.
Number awarded 1 each year.
Deadline February of each year.

[1006]
SOCIETY OF DAUGHTERS OF THE UNITED STATES ARMY SCHOLARSHIPS

Society of Daughters of the United States Army
c/o Jeanne Kunzig Anthony, President
6925 Espey Lane
McLean, VA 22101-5455
E-mail: DUSAscholarships@gmail.com
Web: www.armydaughters.org/scholarships

Summary To provide financial assistance for college to daughters and granddaughters of active, retired, or deceased career Army warrant and commissioned officers.
Eligibility This program is open to the daughters, adopted daughters, stepdaughters, or granddaughters of career commissioned officers or warrant officers of the U.S. Army (active, regular, or Reserve) who 1) are currently on active duty; 2) retired after 20 years of service; 3) was medically retired before 20 years of service; 4) died while on active duty; or 5) died after retiring from active duty with 20 or more years of service. Applicants must have at least a 3.0 GPA and be enrolled or planning to enroll full time at the undergraduate level. Selection is based on academic achievement, community involvement, and leadership potential; financial need is not considered.
Financial data Scholarships, to a maximum of $1,500, are paid directly to the college or school for tuition, laboratory fees, books, or other expenses.
Duration 1 year; may be renewed up to 4 additional years if the recipient maintains at least a 3.0 GPA.
Additional information Recipients may attend any accredited college, professional, or vocational school. This program includes named scholarships from the following funds: the Colonel Hayden W. Wagner Memorial Fund, the Eugenia Bradford Roberts Memorial Fund, the Daughters of the U.S. Army Scholarship Fund, the Gladys K. and John K. Simpson Scholarship Fund, and the Margaret M. Prickett Scholarship Fund.
Number awarded Up to 10 each year.
Deadline March of each year.

[1007]
SOCIETY OF THE 3RD INFANTRY DIVISION SCHOLARSHIPS

Society of the 3rd Infantry Division
Attn: Scholarship Foundation
2010 Worcester Lane
Garland, TX 75040-3331
(972) 495-1704   E-mail: ldball1@msn.com
Web: www.3idscholarshipfoundation.org

Summary To provide financial assistance for college to descendants of members of the Society of the 3rd Infantry Division and spouses of deceased 3rd Infantry Division members.
Eligibility This program is open to 1) children, grandchildren, and great-grandchildren of members of the society; and 2) children, grandchildren, and unremarried spouses of 3rd Infantry Division soldiers killed in action or died of wounds while on active duty. Applicants must be enrolled or planning to enroll as an undergraduate student. Along with their application, they must submit 1) an essay of 2 to 4 pages on the history of the 3rd Infantry Division, national pride, loyalty to the nation, patriotism, or a related subject; and 2) a personal statement of their goals after graduation, academic accomplishments, financial need, extracurricular activities (both in-school and out-of-school), community service involvement, and other activities that demonstrate personal character qualities as well as potential to succeed.
Financial data The stipend is $1,000.
Duration 1 year; recipients may reapply.
Additional information This program began in 2005.
Number awarded Varies each year; recently, 12 were awarded.
Deadline May of each year.

[1008]
SONS AND DAUGHTERS, PEARL HARBOR SURVIVORS SCHOLARSHIPS

Sons and Daughters, Pearl Harbor Survivors, Inc.
Attn: Carol Gladys, National Secretary
1122 Fox Run
Grafton, OH 44044
(850) 867-0645   E-mail: secretarysdphs@gmail.com
Web: www.sdphs.org/index.php/about/scholarships

Summary To provide financial assistance for college to members of Sons and Daughters, Pearl Harbor Survivors (SDPHS).
Eligibility This program is open to members of SDPHS who are enrolled or planning to enroll full time at an accredited college, university, or trade/technical school in any state. Applicants must be U.S. citizens and able to demonstrate financial need. Along with their application, they must submit essays, from 500 to 5,000 words each, on the following topics: 1) how they plan to participate in SDPHS activities to help meet its objectives and further its goals; 2) the person in their life who has been their biggest influence and why; and 3) how they have demonstrated leadership ability, both in and out of school.
Financial data The stipend is $1,000.
Duration 1 year.
Additional information This program began in 2012. Membership in SDPHS is open to sons and daughters (for direct lineage membership) and nieces and nephews (for col-

SCHOLARSHIPS: FAMILY MEMBERS

lateral membership) of descendants of members of the U.S. armed forces stationed on the island of Oahu or within 3 miles offshore at the time of the attack on Pearl Harbor on December 7, 1941.

Number awarded 1 each even-numbered year.
Deadline May of each even-numbered year.

[1009]
SONS OF UNION VETERANS OF THE CIVIL WAR SCHOLARSHIPS

Sons of Union Veterans of the Civil War
c/o Don Martin, Past Commander-in-Chief
6025 State Route 772
Chillicothe, OH 45601
E-mail: d76lm@yahoo.com
Web: www.suvcw.org/?page_id=807

Summary To provide financial assistance for college to descendants, males and females considered separately, of Union Civil War veterans.

Eligibility This program is open to high school seniors and students currently enrolled at a 4-year college or university. Applicants must 1) rank in the upper quarter of their high school graduating class (preferably in the upper tenth); 2) have a record of performance in school and community activities; 3) have an interest in and positive attitude toward college; 4) provide 3 letters of recommendation; and 5) submit an official grade transcript. Males must be a current member or associate of Sons of Union Veterans of the Civil War. Females must be the daughter or granddaughter of a current member or associate of Sons of Union Veterans of the Civil War and a current member of at least 1 of the following organizations: Woman's Relief Corps, Ladies of the Grand Army of the Republic, Daughters of Union Veterans of the Civil War 1861-1865, or Auxiliary to the Sons of Union Veterans of the Civil War. Financial need is not considered in the selection process.

Financial data The stipend is $2,500. Funds are to be used for tuition and books. Checks are mailed directly to the recipient's school.

Duration 1 year.
Number awarded 2 each year: 1 to a male and 1 to a female.
Deadline March of each year.

[1010]
SOUTH CAROLINA TUITION ASSISTANCE FOR CERTAIN WAR VETERANS CHILDREN

South Carolina Division of Veterans' Affairs
c/o VA Regional Office Building
6437 Garners Ferry Road, Suite 1126
Columbia, SC 29209
(803) 647-2434   Fax: (803) 647-2312
E-mail: va@admin.sc.gov
Web: va.sc.gov/benefits.html

Summary To provide free college tuition to the children of disabled and other South Carolina veterans.

Eligibility This program is open to the children of wartime veterans who were legal residents of South Carolina both at the time of entry into military or naval service and during service, or who have been residents of South Carolina for at least 1 year. Veteran parents must 1) be permanently and totally disabled as determined by the U.S. Department of Veterans Affairs; 2) have been a prisoner of war; 3) have been killed in action; 4) have died from other causes while in service; 5) have died of a disease or disability resulting from service; 6) be currently missing in action; 7) have received the Congressional Medal of Honor; 8) have received the Purple Heart Medal from wounds received in combat; or 9) now be deceased but qualified under categories 1 or 2 above. The veteran's child must be 26 years of age or younger and working on an undergraduate degree.

Financial data Children who qualify are eligible for free tuition at any South Carolina state-supported college, university, or postsecondary technical education institution. The waiver applies to tuition only. The costs of room and board, certain fees, and books are not covered.

Duration Students are eligible to receive this support as long as they are younger than 26 years of age and working on an undergraduate degree.

Number awarded Varies each year.
Deadline Deadline not specified.

[1011]
SOUTH DAKOTA AMERICAN LEGION EDUCATIONAL SCHOLARSHIP

American Legion
Department of South Dakota
14 First Avenue S.E.
P.O. Box 67
Watertown, SD 57201-0067
(605) 886-3604   Fax: (605) 886-2870
E-mail: sdlegion@dailypost.com
Web: www.sdlegion.org/scholarship-information

Summary To provide financial assistance to children and grandchildren of South Dakota veterans who are interested in attending college in the state.

Eligibility This program is open to residents of South Dakota who are wartime veterans or their children or grandchildren; wartime veterans include those eligible for membership in the American Legion (although Legion membership is not required). Applicants must be interested in attending a South Dakota college or technical school (unless no school in the state offers the professional or technical degree being sought). They must be high school graduates or GED recipients and have completed at least 16 hours of postsecondary credits. Along with their application, they must submit 2 essays of up to 500 words each on 1) how they have prepared for higher education; and 2) which of the 10 clauses of the American Legion Preamble is the most meaningful to them and why.

Financial data The stipend ranges up to $2,500 per year.
Duration 1 year.
Additional information This program began in 1956 as a loan fund for the children of veterans. It was expanded in 2002 to include veterans themselves and in 2006 to include grandchildren of veterans. In 2019, it was converted to a scholarship.

Number awarded Varies each year.
Deadline December of each year.

[1012]
SOUTH DAKOTA USAA SCHOLARSHIP
South Dakota National Guard Enlisted Association
c/o Derek Jaeger, Scholarship Chair
7713 West 53rd Street
Sioux Falls, SD 57106
E-mail: derek.e.jaeger.mil@mail.mil
Web: sdngea.com/programs/scholarships

Summary To provide financial assistance to members of the South Dakota National Guard Enlisted Association (SDNGEA) and their dependents who are interested in attending college in any state.

Eligibility This program is open to current members of the SDNGEA and their dependents. Applicants must be graduating high school seniors or full-time undergraduate students at a college or university in any state. They must submit a 300-page autobiography that includes their experiences to date and their hopes and plans for the future. Selection is based on the essay; awards, honors, and offices in high school, college, or trade school; GPA and ACT/SAT scores; letters of recommendation; and extracurricular and community activities and honors.

Financial data The stipend is $1,000.

Duration 1 year.

Additional information This program is sponsored by the USAA Insurance Corporation.

Number awarded 1 each year.

Deadline March of each year.

[1013]
SOUTHERN REGION KOREAN WAR VETERAN DESCENDANT SCHOLARSHIPS
Korean American Scholarship Foundation
Southern Region
Attn: Scholarship Committee Chair
P.O. Box 67
Duluth, GA 30097
E-mail: src.scholarship@kasf.org
Web: www.kasf.org/apply-src

Summary To provide financial assistance to the descendants of the Korean War from any state who are working on an undergraduate or graduate degree in any field at a school in southern states.

Eligibility This program is open to direct descendants of veterans who served in Korea from June 25, 1950 to January 31, 1955. Applicants may reside in any state, but they must be enrolled as full-time undergraduate or graduate students at a college or university in Alabama, Florida, Georgia, South Carolina, or Tennessee. They must have a GPA of 3.0 or higher. Selection is based on academic achievement, an essay, extracurricular activities, and recommendations.

Financial data Stipends range from $500 to $5,000.

Duration 1 year.

Number awarded Varies each year; recently, 15 were awarded.

Deadline June of each year.

[1014]
SPECIAL OPERATIONS WARRIOR FOUNDATION SCHOLARSHIPS
Special Operations Warrior Foundation
1137 Marbella Plaza Drive
P.O. Box 89367
Tampa, FL 33689
(813) 805-9400   Toll Free: (877) 337-7693
Fax: (813) 805-0567
E-mail: scholarships@specialops.org
Web: www.specialops.org/what-we-do/scholarship-program

Summary To provide financial assistance for college to the children of Special Operations personnel who died in training or operational missions.

Eligibility This program is open to the children of parents who served in Special Operations (Army, Air Force, Navy, or Marines) and were killed in a training accident or an operational mission. This is an entitlement program; all eligible students receive support.

Financial data The program ensures the full cost of a college education including tuition, fees, room and board, books, tutoring, computer, printer, supplies, transportation, college visits, and ACT/SAT preparation.

Duration 4 years or more.

Additional information This program began in 1980 because of the high casualty rates experienced by personnel of U.S. Special Operations Command.

Number awarded Varies each year; the program recently was supporting 153 surviving children in college.

Deadline Applications may be submitted at any time.

[1015]
SPECIAL OPS SURVIVORS EDUCATION AND CAREER ADVANCEMENT GRANTS
Special Ops Survivors
Attn: Executive Director
3022 South Morgan Point Road, Suite 276
Mt. Pleasant, SC 29466
(619) 437-1137 E-mail: contact@specialopssurvivors.org
Web: sos.memberclicks.net

Summary To provide financial assistance for college to the spouses of Special Operations military personnel killed in the line of duty after September 11, 2001.

Eligibility This program is open to the surviving spouses of soldiers, sailors, airmen, and marines who were serving under a U.S. military Special Operations command or directly supporting a Special Operations mission and were killed after September 11, 2001. Applicants must be enrolled or planning to enroll at an accredited college or technical school or in a professional licensure or certification program. They must have a GPA of 3.0 or higher. Along with their application, they must submit a 500-word essay explaining why they have chosen their intended program of study and how that program of study will contribute to their immediate or long-range career plans. Selection is based on the essay, merit, academic potential, and financial need.

Financial data The stipend is $2,500 per year. Funds are paid directly to the recipient to be used for payment of tuition, books, supplies, child care costs, and transportation expenses.

Duration 1 year; may be renewed up to 3 additional years.

Additional information This sponsor began in 2002 as the United Warrior Survivor Foundation. It adopted its current name in 2012.
Number awarded 1 or more each year.
Deadline June of each year.

[1016]
SPIRIT OF YOUTH SCHOLARSHIP FUND
American Legion Auxiliary
3450 Founders Road
Indianapolis, IN 46268
(317) 569-4500　　　　　　　　Fax: (317) 569-4502
E-mail: alahq@alaforveterans.org
Web: www.alaforveterans.org

Summary To provide financial assistance for college to junior members of the American Legion Auxiliary.
Eligibility Applicants for this scholarship must have been junior members of the Auxiliary for at least the past 3 years. They must be seniors at an accredited high school in the United States, have a GPA of 3.0 or higher, and be planning to enroll full time at an accredited 4-year institution of higher education. Along with their application, they must submit a 1,000-word essay on a topic that changes annually; recently, students were asked to write on "How can education, both private and public, help prevent homelessness in our country, particularly that of our women veteran population?" Selection is based on that essay (30%), character and leadership (30%), and academic achievement (40%). Each unit of the Auxiliary may select a candidate for application to the department level, and each department submits a candidate for the national award.
Financial data The stipend is $5,000.
Duration 1 year.
Additional information Applications are available from the president of the candidate's own unit or from the secretary or education chair of the department.
Number awarded 5 each year: 1 in each division of the American Legion Auxiliary.
Deadline Applications must be submitted to the unit president by February of each year.

[1017]
SR EDUCATION GROUP MILITARY SCHOLARSHIPS
SR Education Group
123 Lake Street South, Site B-1
Kirkland, WA 98033-6401
(425) 605-8898
Web: www.sreducationgroup.org

Summary To provide financial assistance to veterans and active military members and their families who are currently enrolled in college and have high financial need.
Eligibility This program is open to legal residents of any state except Rhode Island who are 1) veterans or active members of the U.S. military; 2) children or spouses of veterans or active military members; or 3) children and spouses of deceased veterans or military members. Children must be younger than 21 years of age or, if enrolled full time, younger than 23. Applicants must be currently enrolled at a college or university and able to demonstrate high financial need. Along with their application, they must submit 3 essays of 300 to 500 words each on 1) how they will apply their degree in the future and what they anticipate for their first 5 years beyond college; 2) their involvement with the military and how it has influenced their personal development; and 3) any special or family circumstances affecting their financial need.
Financial data The stipend is $5,000.
Duration 1 year.
Additional information This program began in 2010.
Number awarded 4 each year. Since the program began, this sponsor has awarded a total of $547,000 to 141 students at 113 colleges.
Deadline December of each year.

[1018]
SSGT. ROBERT V. MILNER MEMORIAL SCHOLARSHIP
American Academy of Physician Assistants-Veterans Caucus
Attn: Scholarship Program
P.O. Box 362
Ossining, NY 10562
(803) 328-1864　　　　　　　　Fax: (704) 838-8494
E-mail: rmunsee@veteranscaucus.org
Web: www.veteranscaucus.org/scholarships

Summary To provide financial assistance to Air Force veterans and their dependents who are studying to become physician assistants.
Eligibility This program is open to U.S. citizens who are currently enrolled in a physician assistant program. Applicants must be honorably discharged members of the United States Air Force or the dependent of an Air Force veteran. Along with their application, they must submit a personal statement about what led them to attend PA school; their background, present, and future intentions; and why they deserve to receive a scholarship. Selection is based on military honors and awards received, civic and college honors and awards received, professional memberships and activities, potential for future achievement, and GPA.
Financial data The stipend is $2,000.
Duration 1 year.
Number awarded 1 each year.
Deadline February of each year.

[1019]
STANLEY A. DORAN MEMORIAL SCHOLARSHIPS
Fleet Reserve Association
Attn: FRA Education Foundation
125 North West Street
Alexandria, VA 22314-2754
(703) 683-1400　　　　　　　Toll Free: (800) FRA-1924
Fax: (703) 549-6610　　　　　E-mail: scholars@fra.org
Web: www.fra.org

Summary To provide financial assistance for college or graduate school to children of members of the Fleet Reserve Association (FRA).
Eligibility This program is open to the dependent children of FRA members who are in good standing (or were at the time of death, if deceased). Applicants must be working on or planning to work full time on an undergraduate or graduate degree. Along with their application, they must submit transcripts that include (for high school students and college freshmen) SAT and/or ACT scores; a list of school and community activities; at least 2 letters of recommendation; and an essay on why they want to go to college and what they intend

to accomplish with their degree. Selection is based on academic record, financial need, extracurricular activities, leadership skills, and participation in community activities. U.S. citizenship is required.

Financial data The stipend is $5,000 per year.

Duration 1 year; may be renewed.

Additional information Membership in the FRA is open to current and former enlisted members of the Navy, Marine Corps, and Coast Guard.

Number awarded 1 each year.

Deadline April of each year.

[1020]
SUBIC BAY-CUBI POINT SCHOLARSHIP

Navy League of the United States
Attn: Scholarships
2300 Wilson Boulevard, Suite 200
Arlington, VA 22201-5424
(703) 528-1775   Toll Free: (800) 356-5760
Fax: (703) 528-2333
E-mail: scholarships@navyleague.org
Web: www.navyleague.org/programs/scholarships

Summary To provide financial assistance for college to dependent children of sea service personnel, especially to those who served in the Philippines.

Eligibility This program is open to U.S. citizens who are 1) dependents or direct descendants of an active, Reserve, retired, or honorably discharged member of the U.S. sea service (including the Navy, Marine Corps, Coast Guard, or Merchant Marine); or 2) currently an active member of the Naval Sea Cadet Corps. Applicants must be high school seniors entering their freshman year at an accredited college or university. They must have a GPA of 3.0 or higher. Along with their application, they must submit transcripts, 2 letters of recommendation, SAT/ACT scores, documentation of financial need, proof of qualifying sea service duty, and a 1-page personal statement on why they should be considered for this scholarship. Preference is given to dependents of sponsors who were permanently attached to the U.S. Naval Facility commands in the Philippines (Subic Bay, Cubi Point, or San Miguel) between January 1980 and December 1992.

Financial data The stipend is $2,500 per year.

Duration 4 years, provided the recipient maintains a GPA of 3.0 or higher.

Number awarded 1 each year.

Deadline February of each year.

[1021]
SURVIVING DEPENDENTS OF MONTANA NATIONAL GUARD MEMBER WAIVER

Office of the Commissioner of Higher Education
Attn: Montana University System
State Scholarship Coordinator
560 North Park Avenue, Fourth Floor
P.O. Box 203201
Helena, MT 59620-3201
(406) 449-9168   Toll Free: (800) 537-7508
Fax: (406) 449-9171
E-mail: mtscholarships@montana.edu
Web: www.umt.edu

Summary To provide financial assistance for undergraduate study to dependents of deceased National Guard members in Montana.

Eligibility Eligible for this benefit are residents of Montana who are surviving spouses or children of Montana National Guard members killed as a result of injury, disease, or other disability incurred in the line of duty while serving on state active duty. Financial need is considered.

Financial data Students eligible for this benefit are entitled to attend any unit of the Montana University System without payment of undergraduate registration or incidental fees.

Duration Undergraduate students are eligible for continued fee waiver as long as they maintain reasonable academic progress as full-time students.

Additional information The waiver does not apply if the recipient is eligible for educational benefits from any governmental or private program that provides comparable benefits.

Number awarded Varies each year.

Deadline Deadline not specified.

[1022]
SURVIVORS' AND DEPENDENTS' EDUCATIONAL ASSISTANCE PROGRAM

Department of Veterans Affairs
Attn: Veterans Benefits Administration
810 Vermont Avenue, N.W.
Washington, DC 20420
(202) 418-4343   Toll Free: (844) 698-2311
Web: www.va.gov

Summary To provide financial assistance for undergraduate or graduate study to children and spouses of deceased and disabled veterans, MIAs, and POWs.

Eligibility Eligible for this assistance are spouses and children of 1) veterans who died or are permanently and totally disabled as the result of active service in the armed forces; 2) veterans who died from any cause while rated permanently and totally disabled from a service-connected disability; 3) servicemembers listed as missing in action or captured in the line of duty by a hostile force; 4) servicemembers listed as forcibly detained or interned by a foreign government or power; and 5) servicemembers who are hospitalized or receiving outpatient treatment for a service-connected permanent and total disability and are likely to be discharged for that disability. Children must be between 18 and 26 years of age, although extensions may be granted. Spouses and children over 14 years of age with physical or mental disabilities are also eligible.

Financial data Monthly stipends for study at an academic institution are $1,248 for full time, $986 for three-quarter time, or $724 for half-time. Other rates apply for apprenticeship and on-the-job training, farm cooperative training, and special restorative training.

Duration Benefits are provided for up to 45 months (or the equivalent in part-time training). Some beneficiaries who qualify for more than 1 education program may be eligible for up to 81 months. Spouses must complete their training within 10 years of the date they are first found eligible. For spouses of servicemembers who died on active duty, benefits end 20 years from the date of death.

Additional information Benefits may be used to work on associate, bachelor's, or graduate degrees at colleges and universities, including independent study, cooperative train-

ing, and study abroad programs. Courses leading to a certificate or diploma from business, technical, or vocational schools may also be taken. Other eligible programs include apprenticeships, on-the-job training programs, farm cooperative courses, and correspondence courses (for spouses only). Remedial, deficiency, and refresher courses may be approved under certain circumstances.
Number awarded Varies each year.
Deadline Applications may be submitted at any time.

[1023]
T. NASH BROADDUS DECO SCHOLARSHIP

Anchor Scholarship Foundation
Attn: Executive Director
138 South Rosemont Road, Suite 206
Virginia Beach, VA 23452
(757) 777-4724
E-mail: Joy.Eyrolles@anchorscholarship.com
Web: www.anchorscholarship.com

Summary To provide financial assistance for college to dependents of current personnel serving in the Naval Surface Forces who plan to study engineering.
Eligibility This program is open to dependent children of active-duty enlisted personnel who have served at least 6 years (need not be consecutive) in a unit under the administrative control of Commander, Naval Surface Forces, U.S. Atlantic Fleet or U.S. Pacific Fleet. Applicants must be high school seniors planning to attend an accredited 4-year college or university and work full time on a bachelor's degree in engineering. The sponsor must have a Surface Warfare qualification (SWO/ESWS). Selection is based on academic performance, extracurricular activities, character, and financial need.
Financial data The stipend is $6,000.
Duration 1 year; nonrenewable.
Number awarded 2 each year.
Deadline February of each year.

[1024]
TAILHOOK EDUCATIONAL FOUNDATION SCHOLARSHIPS

Tailhook Educational Foundation
9696 Business Park Avenue
San Diego, CA 92131-1643
(858) 689-9223   Toll Free: (800) 322-4665
Fax: (858) 578-8839   E-mail: bethr@tailhook.net
Web: www.tailhook.net/A_Foundation_Index.html

Summary To provide financial assistance for college to personnel associated with naval aviation and their children.
Eligibility This program is open to 1) the children (natural, step, and adopted) and grandchildren of current or former U.S. Navy, Coast Guard, or Marine Corps personnel who served as an aviator, flight officer, or air crewman; or 2) personnel and children and grandchildren of personnel who are serving or have served on board a U.S. Navy aircraft carrier as a member of the ship's company or air wing. Applicants must be enrolled or accepted for enrollment at an accredited college or university. Selection is based on educational and extracurricular achievements, merit, and citizenship.
Financial data The stipend ranges from $2,500 to $15,000.
Duration 1 to 2 years.

Number awarded Varies; usually, more than 100 are awarded each year.
Deadline February of each year.

[1025]
TENNESSEE BOYS STATE SAMSUNG SCHOLARSHIP

American Legion
Department of Tennessee
318 Donelson Pike
Nashville, TN 37214
(615) 391-5088   Fax: (615) 391-5099
E-mail: debi@tnlegion.org
Web: www.tennesseelegion.org/index.php?id=100

Summary To provide financial assistance to the applicant for the Samsung American Legion Scholarship at Tennessee Boys State who is selected as the state candidate.
Eligibility This program is open to citizens of Tennessee Boys State who apply for the Samsung American Legion Scholarship. Applicants for that scholarship must be the child, grandchild, or great-grandchild of a veteran who saw active-duty service during specified periods of wartime. Selection is based on academic record, community service, involvement in school and community activities, and financial need. Special consideration is given to descendants of U.S. veterans of the Korean War. The Boys State citizen who is selected as Tennessee's candidate for the national award receives this scholarship.
Financial data The stipend is $1,000.
Duration 1 year.
Number awarded 1 each year.
Deadline Deadline not specified.

[1026]
TENTH MOUNTAIN DIVISION FOUNDATION COMMUNITY COLLEGE/PROFESSIONAL PROGRAM SCHOLARSHIP

Tenth Mountain Division Foundation
Attn: Scholarship Fund
133 South Van Gordon Street, Suite 200
Lakewood, CO 80228
(303) 756-8486   Fax: (303) 988-3005
E-mail: tenthmtnfdn@nsp.org
Web: www.10thmountainfoundation.org

Summary To provide financial assistance to descendants of former members of the 10th Mountain Division who are enrolled at a community college.
Eligibility This program is open to the descendants of veterans who served in the 10th Mountain Division during World War II. Applicants must have completed at least 12 credit hours at an accredited community college or comparable institution. They must be able to demonstrate financial need and a knowledge of the history of the Division and their ancestor's service in the Division during World War II.
Financial data The stipend is $500 per semester.
Duration Up to 4 semesters, provided the recipient remains enrolled full time.
Number awarded 1 or more each year.
Deadline April each year.

[1027]
TENTH MOUNTAIN DIVISION FOUNDATION SCHOLARSHIP

Tenth Mountain Division Foundation
Attn: Scholarship Fund
133 South Van Gordon Street, Suite 200
Lakewood, CO 80228
(303) 756-8486   Fax: (303) 988-3005
E-mail: tenthmtnfdn@nsp.org
Web: www.10thmountainfoundation.org

Summary To provide financial assistance for college or graduate school to descendants of former members of the 10th Mountain Division.

Eligibility This program is open to the descendants of veterans who served in the 10th Mountain Division during World War II. Applicants must be college juniors, seniors, or graduate students. They must be able to demonstrate financial need and a knowledge of the history of the Division and their ancestor's service in the Division during World War II. If there are more qualifying applicants than available scholarships, selection is based on a lottery.

Financial data The stipend is $5,000 per year.

Duration 1 year; may be renewed 1 additional year.

Number awarded Up to 5 each year.

Deadline April each year.

[1028]
TEXAS AMERICAN LEGION AUXILIARY PAST PRESIDENT'S PARLEY SCHOLARSHIPS

American Legion Auxiliary
Department of Texas
1624 East Anderson Lane
P.O. Box 140407
Austin, TX 78714-0407
(512) 476-7278   Fax: (512) 482-8391
E-mail: secretary@alatexas.org
Web: www.alatexas.org

Summary To provide financial assistance to descendants of Texas veterans who wish to study a field related to medicine at a school in the state.

Eligibility This program is open to the children, grandchildren, and great-grandchildren of veterans who served during specified periods of wartime. Applicants must be residents of Texas studying or planning to study a medical field at a postsecondary institution in the state. Selection is based on need, goals, character, citizenship, and objectives.

Financial data The stipend is $1,000.

Duration 1 year.

Additional information Applications for these scholarships must be submitted through local units of the American Legion Auxiliary in Texas.

Number awarded 1 or more each year.

Deadline April of each year.

[1029]
TEXAS CHILDREN OF U.S. MILITARY WHO ARE MISSING IN ACTION OR PRISONERS OF WAR EXEMPTION PROGRAM

Texas Higher Education Coordinating Board
Attn: Student Financial Aid Programs
1200 East Anderson Lane
P.O. Box 12788
Austin, TX 78711-2788
(512) 427-6366   Toll Free: (888) 311-8881
Fax: (512) 427-6570   E-mail: grantinfo@thecb.state.tx.us
Web: www.collegeforalltexans.com

Summary To provide educational assistance to the children of Texas military personnel declared prisoners of war or missing in action.

Eligibility Eligible are dependent children of Texas residents who are either prisoners of war or missing in action. Applicants must be under 21 years of age, or under 25 if they receive the majority of support from their parent(s).

Financial data Eligible students are exempted from the payment of all dues, fees, and tuition charges at publicly-supported colleges and universities in Texas.

Duration Up to 8 semesters, provided recipients maintain a GPA specified by their institution.

Number awarded Varies each year; recently, 3 of these exemptions, worth $1,909, were granted.

Deadline Deadline not specified.

[1030]
TEXAS STATE COUNCIL VIETNAM VETERANS OF AMERICA SCHOLARSHIPS

Vietnam Veterans of America-Texas State Council
Attn: Percilla Newberry, Scholarship Committee Co-Chair
100 Elmwood Street
Fritch, TX 79036
(806) 857-2261
Web: vvatsc.org/vvatsc-committees

Summary To provide financial assistance to Vietnam veterans and their families in Texas who are interested in attending college in the state.

Eligibility This program is open to residents of Texas who are veterans of the Vietnam War or their children, stepchildren, grandchildren, current spouses, and unremarried widows. Applicants must be high school seniors planning to enroll or students currently enrolled full time at an accredited college or university in the state. High school seniors must submit transcripts showing a GPA of 2.5 or higher and ACT/SAT scores. College students must have completed at least 12 college credit hours during the preceding 12-month period. They must submit a letter on their career ambition following completion of their degree. All applicants must submit an essay of at least 1,500 words based on an interview of a Vietnam veteran.

Financial data A stipend is awarded (amount not specified).

Duration 1 year.

Additional information This program is comprised of the following named awards: the Don Carlos Kennedy Memorial Scholarship, the Alberto Rodriguez Memorial Scholarship, and the Robert Dale Spencer Memorial Scholarship.

Number awarded 3 each year.

Deadline February of each year.

SCHOLARSHIPS: FAMILY MEMBERS

[1031]
THANKSUSA SCHOLARSHIPS
ThanksUSA
1390 Chain Bridge Road, Suite 260
McLean, VA 22101
(703) 375-9849   Toll Free: (888) 849-8720
E-mail: thanksusa@scholarshipamerica.org
Web: www.thanksusa.org/scholarships.html

Summary To provide financial assistance for college to children and spouses of military personnel who served after September 11, 2001.
Eligibility This program is open to dependent children 24 years of age or younger and spouses of active-duty, discharged, or retired military personnel. The parent or spouse must 1) have served on active duty for at least 180 days since September 11, 2001; 2) have been killed or wounded in action since that date; 3) be a member of the military Reserves activated to full-time duty; or 4) be a member of the National Guard who have been federalized. Children and spouses of retired or discharged service personnel are eligible if the parent or spouse served 180 days after September 11, 2011. Applicants must be entering or attending an accredited 2- or 4-year college, university, vocational school, or technical school as a full-time student. Spouses may use the award for non-degree licensure or certification programs and may enroll part time. All applicants must have a GPA of 2.0 or higher. Selection is based on financial need, academic record, a statement of goals, and demonstrated leadership and participation in school and community activities. Preference is given to children or spouses of service personnel killed or injured during active duty.
Financial data The stipend is $3,000.
Duration 1 year; recipients may reapply.
Additional information This program began in 2006. Selection of recipients is made by Scholarship Management Services, a division of Scholarship America.
Number awarded Up to 300 each year. Since the program was established, it has awarded more than 4,700 scholarships with a value of more than $15 million.
Deadline April of each year.

[1032]
THAT OTHERS MAY LIVE FOUNDATION SCHOLARSHIPS
That Others May Live Foundation
871 Coronado Center Drive, Suite 200
Henderson, NV 89052
Toll Free: (888) 474-7771   Fax: (702) 932-1978
E-mail: info@thatothersmaylive.org
Web: www.thatothersmaylive.org

Summary To provide financial assistance for college to dependents of members of Air Force rescue personnel.
Eligibility This program is open to children or grandchildren of current or former uniformed members of an Air Force Combat Rescue or rescue support organization. Applicants must be enrolled or planning to enroll at a college or university. Along with their application, they must submit academic information, financial information, a list of extracurricular activities, and a brief essay on their reasons for applying for this scholarship including the needs, anticipated cost, and any other pertinent information.
Financial data A stipend is awarded (amount not specified).
Duration 1 year.
Additional information As of 2019, this organization absorbed the resources of the former Jolly Green Association legacy program.
Number awarded Varies each year; recently, 6 were awarded.
Deadline April of each year.

[1033]
THE AMERICAN COLLEGE SCHOLARSHIPS
First Command Educational Foundation
Attn: Scholarship Programs Manager
1 FirstComm Plaza
Fort Worth, TX 76109-4999
(817) 569-2940   Toll Free: (877) 872-8289
Fax: (817) 569-2970   E-mail: scholarships@fcef.com
Web: www.fcef.com/scholarships

Summary To provide financial assistance to veterans and their families working on a financial services professional career.
Eligibility This program is open to military veterans and dependent family members. Applicants must be seeking funding to pay for professional certification as a financial services professional.
Financial data The stipend is $5,000. Funds may be used to cover the costs of professional certification.
Duration 1 year.
Additional information This program, which began in 2016, is sponsored by The American College of Financial Services.
Number awarded 3 each year.
Deadline Deadline not specified.

[1034]
THE PFC ROGER W. CUMMINS MEMORIAL SCHOLARSHIP
American Academy of Physician Assistants-Veterans Caucus
Attn: Scholarship Program
P.O. Box 362
Ossining, NY 10562
(803) 328-1864   Fax: (704) 838-8494
E-mail: rmunsee@veteranscaucus.org
Web: www.veteranscaucus.org/scholarships

Summary To provide financial assistance to Marine Corps and Navy service members or veterans or family members who are studying to become physician assistants.
Eligibility This program is open to U.S. citizens who are currently enrolled in a physician assistant program. Applicants must be active-duty members of the U.S. Marine Corps or Navy Corpsmen who have served with the Marine Corps, veterans of those services, or their spouses or children. Along with their application, they must submit a personal statement about what led them to attend PA school; their background, present, and future intentions; and why they deserve to receive a scholarship. Selection is based on military honors and awards received, civic and college honors and awards received, professional memberships and activities, potential for future achievement, and GPA.

Financial data The stipend is $2,000.
Duration 1 year.
Number awarded 1 each year.
Deadline February of each year.

[1035]
THIRD MARINE DIVISION ASSOCIATION MEMORIAL SCHOLARSHIP FUND

Third Marine Division Association, Inc.
c/o Patrick J. Conroy, Memorial Scholarship Fund
  Secretary
P.O. Box 2296
Stow, OH 44224
E-mail: ConroyPJ11@aol.com
Web: www.caltrap.org/3rd_MarDivAssoc/MSF.asp

Summary To provide financial assistance for college to descendants of members of the Third Marine Division Association.

Eligibility This program is open to dependent unmarried children, grandchildren, or great-grandchildren whose sponsor has been a member of the association for at least 2 years or, if deceased, had been a member for at least 2 years at the time of death. Dependent children, grandchildren, and great-grandchildren of military personnel who served in any Third Marine Division unit and lost their lives as a result of combat actions while serving in Vietnam or the operations known as Desert Shield, Desert Storm, Iraqi Freedom, Enduring Freedom, or any other operation anywhere in the world after August 2, 1990, are also eligible. Applicants must be interested in attending a college or university in any state and have a GPA of 2.5 or higher. They must be between 16 and 23 years of age and able to demonstrate financial need.

Financial data Stipends range from $500 to $1,500, depending upon need.

Duration 1 year; may be renewed for up to 3 additional years for undergraduate study or until the recipient reaches 26 years of age, provided a "C" average is maintained.

Additional information This program began in 1969.

Number awarded 20 to 25 each year. Since the program began, it has awarded more than $657,000 to more than 800 students.

Deadline May of each year.

[1036]
THOMAS H. MILLER SCHOLARSHIP

Blinded Veterans Association
Attn: Scholarship Coordinator
125 North West Street, Third Floor
Alexandria, VA 22314
(202) 371-8880, ext. 330   Toll Free: (800) 669-7079
Fax: (202) 371-8258   E-mail: bjones@bva.org
Web: www.bva.org

Summary To provide financial assistance for undergraduate or graduate study, especially of music or the fine arts, to immediate family of blinded veterans and servicemembers.

Eligibility This program is open to dependent children, grandchildren, and spouses of blinded veterans and active-duty blinded servicemembers of the U.S. armed forces. The veteran or servicemember must be legally blind; the blindness may be either service-connected or nonservice-connected. Applicants must have been accepted or be currently enrolled as a full-time student in an undergraduate or graduate program at an accredited institution of higher learning. Preference is given to students of music or the fine arts. Along with their application, they must submit a 300-word essay on their career goals and aspirations. Financial need is not considered in the selection process.

Financial data The stipend is $1,000; funds are intended to be used to cover the student's expenses, including tuition, other academic fees, books, dormitory fees, and cafeteria fees. Funds are paid directly to the recipient's school.

Duration 1 year; recipients may reapply for up to 3 additional years.

Number awarded 1 each year.

Deadline April of each year.

[1037]
TILLMAN MILITARY SCHOLARS PROGRAM

Pat Tillman Foundation
222 North Merchandise Mart Plaza, Suite 1212
Chicago, IL 60654
(773) 360-5277
E-mail: scholarships@pattillmanfoundation.org
Web: www.pattillmanfoundation.org/apply-to-be-a-scholar

Summary To provide financial assistance to veterans, active servicemembers, and their spouses who are interested in working on an undergraduate or graduate degree.

Eligibility This program is open to veterans and active servicemembers of all branches of the armed forces from both the pre- and post-September 11 era and their spouses; children are not eligible. Applicants must be enrolled or planning to enroll full time at a 4-year public or private college or university to work on an undergraduate, graduate, or postgraduate degree. Current and former servicemembers must submit 400-word essays on 1) their motivation and decision to serve in the U.S. military and how that decision and experience has changed their life and ambitions; and 2) their educational and career goals, how they will incorporate their military service experience into those goals, and how they intend to continue their service to others and the community. Spouses must submit 400-word essays on 1) their previous service to others and the community; and 2) their educational and career goals, how they will incorporate their service experiences and the impact of their spouse's military service into those goals, and how they intend to continue their service to others and the community. Selection is based on those essays, educational and career ambitions, record of military service, record of personal achievement, demonstration of service to others in the community, desire to continue such service, and leadership potential.

Financial data The stipend depends on the need of the recipient and the availability of funds; recently, stipends averaged approximately $11,000 per year.

Duration 1 year; may be renewed, provided the recipient maintains a GPA of 3.0 or higher, remains enrolled full time, and documents participation in civic action or community service.

Additional information This program began in 2009.

Number awarded Approximately 60 each year. Since the program began, it has awarded more than $15 million to 580 scholars.

Deadline February of each year.

SCHOLARSHIPS: FAMILY MEMBERS

[1038]
TONY LOPEZ SCHOLARSHIP PROGRAM
Louisiana National Guard Enlisted Association
c/o CMSgt John M. Roach, Executive Director
5445 Point Clair Road
Carville, LA 70721
Web: www.geauxlangea.org/about/langea

Summary To provide financial assistance to members of the Louisiana National Guard Enlisted Association (LANGEA) and their dependents who plan to attend college in any state.

Eligibility This program is open to members of the association, their spouses and unmarried dependent children, and the unremarried spouses and unmarried dependent children of deceased members who were in good standing at the time of their death. The qualifying LANGEA members must have at least 1 year remaining on their enlistment following completion of the school year for which the application is submitted or have served 20 years of more in the Louisiana National Guard. Applicants must be enrolled or planning to enroll full time at an accredited college, university, trade school, or business school in any state. Graduate students are not eligible. Selection is based on academic achievement, character, leadership, and financial need.

Financial data The stipend is $2,000.
Duration 1 year; nonrenewable.
Number awarded 2 each year.
Deadline April of each year.

[1039]
TRANSFER OF POST-9/11 GI-BILL BENEFITS TO DEPENDENTS
Department of Veterans Affairs
Attn: Veterans Benefits Administration
810 Vermont Avenue, N.W.
Washington, DC 20420
(202) 418-4343   Toll Free: (888) 442-4551
Web: www.va.gov

Summary To provide financial assistance to dependents of military personnel who qualify for Post-9/11 GI Bill benefits and agree to transfer unused benefits to their spouse or child.

Eligibility This program is open to dependents of current military personnel whose parent or spouse has at least 6 years of service in the armed forces (active duty and/or Selected Reserve) and agrees to serve 4 additional years. The military parent or spouse must agree to transfer unused months of educational benefits to a dependent while still serving on active duty. Dependents must be enrolled or planning to enroll in an educational program, including work on an undergraduate or graduate degree, vocational/technical training, on-the-job training, flight training, correspondence training, licensing and national testing programs, entrepreneurship training, and tutorial assistance.

Financial data Dependents working on an undergraduate or graduate degree at public institutions in their state receive full payment of tuition and fees. For dependents who attend private institutions in most states, tuition and fee reimbursement is capped at $25,162.14 per academic year. Benefits for other types of training programs depend on the amount for which the spouse or parent qualified under prior educational programs. Dependents also receive a monthly housing allowance that is 1) based on the Department of Defense Basic Allowance for Housing (BAH) for an E-5 with dependents (which depends on the location of the school but ranges from approximately $1,000 per month to approximately $2,500 per month); 2) $1,789 per month at schools in foreign countries; or 3) $894.50 per month for online training classes. They also receive an annual book allowance of $1,000 and (for participants who live in a rural county remote from an educational institution) a rural benefit payment of $500 per year.

Duration Military members may transfer all or a portion of their 36 months of entitlement to a dependent. Spouses may start to use the benefit immediately, but children may use the benefit only after they have completed high school (or equivalency certificate) or reached 18 years of age. They are not subject to the 15-year limit but may not use the benefit after reaching 26 years of age.

Additional information This supplement was added to the Post-9/11 GI Bill program as a result of legislation passed by Congress in 2010.

Number awarded Varies each year.
Deadline Deadline not specified.

[1040]
TREA MEMORIAL FOUNDATION SCHOLARSHIPS
The Enlisted Association
Attn: TREA Memorial Foundation
12200 East Briarwood Avenue, Suite 250
Centennial, CO 80112
(303) 752-0660   Toll Free: (800) 338-9337
Fax: (303) 752-0835   E-mail: treahq@trea.org
Web: voice.trea.org/forms-and-documents

Summary To provide financial assistance for college to the dependents of members of The Enlisted Association.

Eligibility This program is open to dependent children, grandchildren, and great-grandchildren of regular and associate members or deceased members who were in good standing at the time of their death. Applicants must be high school seniors or full-time college students and interested in attending a 2- or 4-year college or university. Along with their application, they must submit a 300-word essay on a topic that changes annually; recently, students were asked to explain what it means to them to attend college. Special consideration is given to students who can demonstrate financial need.

Financial data The stipend is $1,500 per year.
Duration 1 year; recipients may reapply.
Additional information The Enlisted Association began as The Retired Enlisted Association (TREA) in 1963. In 2012, it changed its name and opened regular membership to all enlisted personnel—retired, active duty, National Guard, and Reserves. Associate membership is open to widows and widowers of members and of non-members who were eligible for membership at the time of their death.
Number awarded 40 each year.
Deadline April of each year.

[1041]
TREA NATIONAL AUXILIARY SCHOLARSHIPS
The Enlisted Association
Attn: National Auxiliary Scholarship Chair
1101 Mercantile Lane, Suite 260
Upper Marlboro, MD 20774
(301) 583-8687   Toll Free: (800) 808-4517
Fax: (303) 583-8717
Web: www.trea.org

Summary To provide financial assistance for college to the dependents of members of TREA: The Enlisted Association National Auxiliary.

Eligibility This program is open to high school seniors, high school graduates, and full-time students currently enrolled at a college, university, or vocational/technical school. Applicants must have a parent or grandparent who is currently a member of TREA: The Enlisted Association National Auxiliary or was a member at the time of their death. Along with their application, they must submit an essay of at least 250 words on a topic that changes annually; recently, students were asked to give their opinion on the National Anthem Protest.

Financial data The stipend is $1,500 per year.

Duration 1 year; recipients may reapply.

Additional information The Enlisted Association began as The Retired Enlisted Association (TREA) in 1963. In 2012, it changed its name and opened regular membership to all enlisted personnel—retired, active duty, National Guard, and Reserves. Membership in its National Auxiliary is open to the spouses and survivors of retired enlisted personnel of all branches of the armed forces, including Reserve components.

Number awarded 15 each year.

Deadline May of each year.

[1042]
TUITION WAIVER FOR DISABLED CHILDREN OF KENTUCKY VETERANS
Kentucky Department of Veterans Affairs
Attn: Tuition Waiver Coordinator
1111B Louisville Road
Frankfort, KY 40601
(502) 564-9203   Toll Free: (800) 572-6245 (within KY)
Fax: (502) 564-9240   E-mail: kdva.tuitionwaiver@ky.gov
Web: www.veterans.ky.gov

Summary To provide financial assistance for college to the children of Kentucky veterans who have a disability related to their parent's military service.

Eligibility This program is open to the children of veterans who have acquired a disability as a direct result of their parent's military service. The disability must have been designated by the U.S. Department of Veterans Affairs as compensable (currently defined as spina bifida). The veteran parent must 1) have served on active duty with the U.S. armed forces or in the National Guard or Reserve component on state active duty, active duty for training, or inactive duty training; and 2) be (or if deceased have been) a resident of Kentucky. Applicants must have been admitted to a state-supported university, college, or vocational training institute in Kentucky.

Financial data Eligible children are exempt from payment of tuition at state-supported institutions of higher education in Kentucky.

Duration There are no age or time limits on the waiver.

Number awarded Varies each year.

Deadline Deadline not specified.

[1043]
UDT-SEAL SCHOLARSHIP
Navy Seal Foundation
Attn: Chief Financial Officer
1619 D Street, Building 5326
Virginia Beach, VA 23459
(757) 744-5326   Fax: (757) 363-7491
E-mail: info@navysealfoundation.org
Web: www.navysealfoundation.org

Summary To provide financial assistance for college to children of members of the UDT-SEAL Association.

Eligibility This program is open to children of members who are single, under 24 years of age, and a dependent of a sponsoring member of the association. Sponsors must be serving or have served in the armed forces and the Naval Special Warfare Community, have been an association member for the last 4 consecutive years, and have paid their dues for the current year. Applicants may be high school seniors, high school graduates, or full-time undergraduate students. Selection is based on GPA, SAT scores, class ranking, extracurricular activities, volunteer community involvement, leadership positions held, military service record, and employment (as appropriate).

Financial data Stipends are $15,000 or $7,500 per year.

Duration 1 year; may be renewed.

Additional information Membership in the association is open to all officers and enlisted personnel of the armed forces (active, retired, discharged, or separated) who have served with a Navy Combat Demolition Unit (NCDU), Underwater Demolition Team (UDT), or SEAL Team.

Number awarded Varies each year; recently, the Navy Seal Foundation awarded 12 dependent scholarships for all of its programs: 3 for 4 years at $15,000 per year to high school seniors and graduates, 3 for 1 year at $7,500 to high school seniors and graduates, 3 for 1 year at $15,000 to current college students, and 3 for 1 year at $7,500 to current college students.

Deadline February of each year.

[1044]
UNIFIED ARIZONA VETERANS SCHOLARSHIPS
Unified Arizona Veterans, Inc.
Attn: Scholarship Committee
P.O. Box 34338
Phoenix, AZ 85067
E-mail: scholarships@azuav.org
Web: www.azuav.org

Summary To provide financial assistance to veterans and military personnel in Arizona who are interested in attending college in the state.

Eligibility This program is open to residents of Arizona who are 1) honorably discharged veterans; 2) currently on active duty, including service members in good standing with a Reserve or Guard components; or 3) immediate family members of an Arizona veteran killed in action or by an act of

terror. Applicants must be enrolled at an institution of higher learning in Arizona and working on a bachelor's or master's degree in any field. Along with their application, they must submit 1) a 1-page essay on why they chose their current academic program and how they plan to use their degree, certificate, or license; 2) letters of recommendation; 3) verification of enrollment and Arizona residency; and 4) documentation of financial need.
Financial data Stipends range up to $5,000.
Duration 1 year.
Number awarded 1 or more each year.
Deadline February of each year.

[1045]
UNILEVER REWARDS OF CARING SCHOLARSHIP CONTEST
Army and Air Force Exchange Service
Attn: Scholarship Contest
P.O. Box 7778
Melville, NY 11775-7778
Web: www.flickr.com

Summary To recognize and reward, with college scholarships, students in middle school and high school who have a tie to the Army and Air Force Exchange Service (AAFES) and submit outstanding essays about their community service.
Eligibility This program is open to dependents of Army and Air Force personnel who are in grades 6-12 and utilize an AAFES facility in the United States or overseas. Applicants must have a GPA of 2.5 or higher. They must submit an essay, up to 500 words in length, explaining why their community and involvement in community service projects are important to them.
Financial data The award is a $2,000 scholarship.
Duration The competition is held annually.
Additional information This program, which began in 2014, is sponsored by Unilever. Further information is available at AAFES stores.
Number awarded 5 each year.
Deadline April of each year.

[1046]
UNITED STATES ARMY WARRANT OFFICERS ASSOCIATION SCHOLARSHIP PROGRAM
United States Army Warrant Officers Association
Attn: USAWOA Scholarship Foundation
462 Herndon Parkway, Suite 207
Herndon, VA 20170-5235
(703) 742-7727   Toll Free: (800) 5-USAWOA
Fax: (703) 742-7728   E-mail: usawoasf@cavetel.net
Web: www.usawoa.org/scholarship

Summary To provide financial assistance for college to dependents of members of the United States Army Warrant Officers Association (USAWOA).
Eligibility This program is open to children, grandchildren, and dependent stepchildren, under 23 years of age, of regular members of USAWOA. Spouses of members are also eligible. Applicants must be enrolled or planning to enroll full time at an accredited U.S. college, university, or vocational/technical institution. They must have a GPA of 3.0 or higher. Along with their application, they must submit transcripts, SAT/ACT scores, letters of recommendation, a list of extracurricular activities, information on any special circumstances that would impact their attending college, and an essay of 800 to 1,000 words describing their educational goals and how reaching those goals will benefit the world around them. Financial need is not considered in the selection process.
Financial data The stipend is at least $1,500.
Duration 1 year; may be renewed.
Additional information This program, which began in 2003, includes the John Allnatt Memorial Scholarship, the Jack B. Sacks Foundation Scholarship, the Pentagon Federal Credit Union Scholarship, and the RAO Freedom Scholarship.
Number awarded Varies each year; recently, 17 were awarded.
Deadline April of each year.

[1047]
UNITED STATES FIELD ARTILLERY ASSOCIATION SCHOLARSHIPS
United States Field Artillery Association
Attn: Scholarship Committee
Building 758, McNair Avenue
P.O. Box 33027
Fort Sill, OK 73503-0027
(580) 355-4677   Toll Free: (866) 355-4677
Fax: (580) 355-8745   E-mail: suzette@fieldartillery.org
Web: www.fieldartillery.org/usfaa-scholarships

Summary To provide financial assistance for college to members of the United States Field Artillery Association (USFAA) and their immediate family.
Eligibility This program is open to 3 categories of students: USFAA members (officer or enlisted), immediate family of enlisted members, and immediate family of officer members. Applicants must have been accepted for admission as an undergraduate at an accredited college, university, or vocational program. Along with their application, they must submit an essay explaining their educational goals and how this scholarship will help meet those goals. Financial need is also considered in the selection process.
Financial data Stipends range from $2,500 to $5,000.
Duration 1 year.
Additional information The USFAA services the field artillery branch of the military.
Number awarded Varies each year; recently, 1 at $5,000, 3 at $3,000, and 1 at $2,500 were awarded.
Deadline April of each year.

[1048]
U.S. MOUNTAIN RANGER ASSOCIATION SCHOLARSHIPS
U.S. Mountain Ranger Association
c/o Brian Cunningham
2805 Village Court
Gainesville, GA 30506
E-mail: brianc2327@me.com
Web: www.usmountainranger.org/scholar.php

Summary To provide financial assistance to children and grandchildren of members of the U.S. Mountain Ranger Association (USMRA) who are high school seniors planning to attend college.
Eligibility This program is open to the children and grandchildren of USMRA members (veterans who were assigned

to U.S. Army Ranger units for combat operations and/or have been awarded a Ranger Tab). Applicants must be high school seniors planning to attend an accredited college or other postsecondary institution. They must be nominated by a USMRA member. Along with their application, they must submit a list of extracurricular and other service activities, a statement from the nominating USMRA member explaining why they should be considered, and a 500-word essay on what they can do to be a better citizen. Financial need is not considered in the selection process.
Financial data The stipend is $2,000.
Duration 1 year.
Number awarded 2 each year.
Deadline March of each year.

[1049]
U.S. "UDIE" GRANT SCHOLARSHIP FUND
Sons of the American Legion
Detachment of Kansas
c/o American Legion Department of Kansas
1314 S.W. Topeka Boulevard
Topeka, KS 66612-1886
(785) 232-9315   Fax: (785) 232-1399
Web: www.ksamlegion.org

Summary To provide financial assistance for college to members of the Kansas Sons of the American Legion and their children and grandchildren.
Eligibility This program is open to high school seniors, college undergraduates, and adults holding high school diplomas and/or college credits who are attending or planning to attend an approved Kansas college, university, junior college, or trade school. Applicants must be a member of the Sons of the American Legion of the Detachment of Kansas or the child or grandchild of a member for at least the past 3 consecutive years. Along with their application, they must submit an essay of up to 250 words on what makes them proud of America. Financial need is also considered in the selection process.
Financial data The stipend is $1,000.
Duration 1 year; nonrenewable.
Number awarded 1 each year.
Deadline February of each year.

[1050]
USAA/EANGKY SCHOLARSHIP
Enlisted Association National Guard of Kentucky
Attn: Scholarship Committee
P.O. Box 1992
Louisville, KY 40259
(502) 314-4005   E-mail: eangky2@gmail.com
Web: www.eangky.org/scholarship-application

Summary To provide financial assistance to members of the Enlisted Association National Guard of Kentucky (EANGKY) and their families who are interested in attending college in any state.
Eligibility This program is open to EANGKY members and their dependent children and spouses; children of deceased members who were in good standing at the time of their death are also eligible. Applicants must be attending or planning to attend a college, university, or trade school in any state. Along with their application, they must submit transcripts, letters of recommendation, and a 1-page statement describing their long-range personal educational goals and explaining why they need the scholarship assistance.
Financial data The stipend is $1,000.
Duration 1 year.
Additional information This program is sponsored by USAA Insurance Corporation.
Number awarded 1 or more each year.
Deadline April of each year.

[1051]
USARA MICHAEL B. RANGER LEGACY SCHOLARSHIPS
U.S. Army Ranger Association
Attn: Scholarship Fund
P.O. Box 52126
Fort Benning, GA 31995-2126
Web: www.ranger.org/Scholarships

Summary To provide financial assistance for college to descendants of members of the U.S. Army Ranger Association (USARA).
Eligibility This program is open to the unmarried children, grandchildren, and great-grandchildren of USARA members who have been regular members of USARA for at least 1 year or are deceased members. Applicants must be younger than 23 years of age and attending or planning to attend an accredited college, university, or technical school. They must enroll full time and have a GPA of 2.0 or higher.
Financial data The stipend ranges from $1,000 to $3,000; funds are disbursed directly to the recipient's institution.
Duration 1 year.
Additional information Regular membership in USARA is open to veterans who have been awarded the Ranger Tab by the Department of the Army, or who served in a combat arms capacity in a recognized U.S. Army Ranger unit for at least 1 year, or (if less) were awarded the Combat Infantryman Badge or the Combat Medical Badge while serving in that unit.
Number awarded Varies each year; recently, 4 were awarded.
Deadline April of each year.

[1052]
USSV CF SCHOLARSHIP AWARDS
United States Submarine Veterans, Inc.
Attn: Charitable Foundation
c/o Robert Frick National Scholarship Committee Chair
15145 Fog Mountain Circle
Haymarket, VA 20169-8155
(703) 754-4959   E-mail: refrickussvcf@gmail.com
Web: www.ussvi.org/Scholarship.asp

Summary To provide financial assistance for college to the children and grandchildren of members of the United States Submarine Veterans, Inc. (USSVI).
Eligibility This program is open to children and grandchildren of USSVI members who are high school seniors planning to attend college or already enrolled as college students. Applicants must be unmarried and under 21 years of age (or 23 if currently enrolled in a full-time course of study). Along with their application, they must submit a 400-word essay on a topic that changes annually. Selection is based on that

essay, academic achievement, community service, academic potential, and financial need.
Financial data Stipends vary; recently, they averaged $1,150.
Duration 1 year; the Joe Henry Senft Scholarship may be renewed up to 3 additional years.
Number awarded Varies each year; recently, 24 were awarded for high school seniors and 26 to college students.
Deadline May of each year.

[1053]
VAW/VRC MEMORIAL SCHOLARSHIPS
VAW/VRC Officers' Spouses' Association
Attn: Scholarship Fund
P.O. Box 15322
Virginia Beach, VA 23511-0322
Web: vvosa.org/scholarships

Summary To provide financial assistance for college to dependents of deceased Navy personnel associated with the VAW/VRC community who were killed in an aviation-related accident.
Eligibility This program is open to children of 1) members of the VAW/VRC community who are lost as a result of a combat aircraft loss or as a result of a military aviation-related mishap; and 2) U.S. Navy enlisted personnel who are lost as a result of a combat aircraft loss or as a result of a military aviation-related mishap while assigned to a VAR or VRC squadron. All eligible children are entitled to this support.
Financial data Stipends provide payment of 100% of the average annual cost of college.
Duration Up to 4 years.
Additional information VAW is the US Navy designation for Squadrons of Carrier Airborne Early Warning Aircraft (AWACS). VRC is the designation for Carrier Reconnaissance Squadrons.
Number awarded Varies each year; recently, 3 students were eligible for these scholarships.
Deadline Eligibility must be established by January of each year.

[1054]
VAW/VRC MERIT SCHOLARSHIPS
Wings Over America Scholarship Foundation
Attn: Scholarship Administrator
770 Lynnhaven Parkway, Suite 155
Virginia Beach, VA 23452
(757) 228-3532
E-mail: scholarship@wingsoveramerica.us
Web: www.wingsoveramerica.us/scholarships/administered

Summary To provide financial assistance for college to dependents of Navy personnel who have been associated with the VAW/VRC community.
Eligibility This program is open to spouses and college-age children of current and former members of the VAW/VRC community who are working on or planning to work on their first undergraduate degree at a college, university, or vocational/technical school. Students enrolled in a Reserve Officer Candidate (ROTC) program are not eligible. Selection is based on merit.
Financial data Stipends range from $3,000 to $7,000 per year.
Duration 1 year may be renewed 1 additional year.
Additional information This program is funded by the VAW/VRC Officers' Spouses' Association (VVOSA) which joined with the Wings Over America Scholarship Foundation in 2016 to administer the program and enable students to apply for scholarships of both organizations. VAW is the US Navy designation for Squadrons of Carrier Airborne Early Warning Aircraft (AWACS). VRC is the designation for Carrier Reconnaissance Squadrons. The program recently included awards sponsored by Northrop Grumman, Lockheed Martin, and Merrill Lynch.
Number awarded Varies each year; recently, 8 were awarded 1 at $7,000, 1 at $5,000, and 6 at $3,000.
Deadline Pre-qualification forms must be submitted by January of each year.

[1055]
VERMONT ARMED SERVICES SCHOLARSHIP
Vermont Student Assistance Corporation
Attn: Scholarship Programs
10 East Allen Street
P.O. Box 2000
Winooski, VT 05404-2601
(802) 654-3798   Toll Free: (888) 253-4819
Fax: (802) 654-3765   TDD: (800) 281-3341 (within VT)
E-mail: info@vsac.org
Web: www.vsac.org

Summary To provide financial assistance to residents of Vermont whose parent or spouse was serving in the military and died on active or inactive duty.
Eligibility This program is open to residents of Vermont who are a child, stepchild, or spouse of 1) a member of the Vermont National Guard (VTNG) who since 1955 has been killed or who since January 1, 2001 has died while on active or inactive duty; 2) a member of the U.S. active Reserve forces who, since January 1, 2001 has died while on active or inactive duty and was a Vermont resident at the time of death; or 3) a member of the U.S. active armed forces who, since January 1, 2001, has died while on active duty and at the time of death was a Vermont resident, a nonresident member of the VTNG who was mobilized to active duty, or a nonresident active Reserve force member of a Vermont-based Reserve unit who was mobilized to active duty. Applicants must plan to enroll full time in a certificate or degree program at an accredited postsecondary school in the state.
Financial data Students receive full payment of tuition at public institutions or an equivalent amount at private institutions.
Duration 1 year; may be renewed until completion of a degree, to a maximum of 130 credits.
Number awarded Varies each year.
Deadline Applications may be submitted at any time; they are considered on a first-come, first-served basis.

FINANCIAL AID PROGRAMS

[1056]
VETERANS OF FOREIGN WARS OF MEXICAN ANCESTRY SCHOLARSHIP PROGRAM
Veterans of Foreign Wars of the United States of Mexican Ancestry
c/o Ramiro Puentes, Adjutant
17064 Pepper Brook Way
Hacienda Heights, CA 91745
(818) 216-7672   E-mail: puentes46@aol.com
Web: www.vfwofmexicanancestry.org/about

Summary To provide financial assistance for college in any state to Mexican American high school students, especially children of veterans, in California.

Eligibility This program is open to high school seniors of Mexican descent who reside in southern California and plan to attend college in any state. They must have earned a GPA of 2.8 or higher and need financial assistance to attend college. Preference is given to the children of veterans.

Financial data Stipends range are $1,500 or $1,000.

Duration 1 year.

Number awarded Varies each year; recently, 12 were awarded: 1 at $1,500 and 11 at $1,000.

Deadline March of each year.

[1057]
VETERANS OF FOREIGN WARS POST 81 TRUST FUND SCHOLARSHIP
Veterans of Foreign Wars of the United States-
  Department of Oregon
12440 N.E. Halsey Street
Portland, OR 97230
(503) 255-5808   Fax: (503) 255-5817
E-mail: admin@vfworegon.org
Web: vfwor.org/di/vfw/v2/default.asp?pid=20382

Summary To provide financial assistance to descendants of members of the Veterans of Foreign Wars (VFW) in Oregon who plan to attend college in any state.

Eligibility This program is open to seniors graduating from high schools in Oregon and planning to enroll full time at a 2- or 4-year college, university, or vocational school in any state. Applicants must be the child, grandchild, or great-grandchild of a VFW member who is presently, or was at the time of death, a member in good standing. They must have a GPA of 2.5 or higher and a record of involvement in community service activities. Along with their application, they must submit a 300-word essay on a patriotic topic that changes annually; recently, students were asked to write on "My Responsibility to America."

Financial data The stipend is $1,000.

Duration 1 year.

Additional information This program was previously known as the Edwin J. McGlothin Memorial Scholarship. It was established with funds recovered when the charter of Post 81 was revoked.

Number awarded Up to 5 each year.

Deadline February of each year.

[1058]
VETERANS UNITED FOUNDATION SCHOLARSHIPS
Veterans United Home Loans
Attn: Veterans United Foundation
1400 Veterans United Drive
Columbia, MO 65203
(573) 445-7999   Toll Free: (800) 884-5560
E-mail: customer_service@vu.com
Web: www.enhancelives.com/scholarships

Summary To provide financial assistance for college or graduate school to surviving children and spouses of deceased or disabled U.S. military veterans.

Eligibility This program is open to surviving spouses and children of deceased servicemembers from a service-related death or of a veteran with a 100% service-connected disability. Applicants must be attending or planning to attend a college or university to work on an associate, bachelor's, graduate, postgraduate, or doctoral degree. Along with their application, they must submit documentation of financial need; a list of community, church, sports, or school involvement or achievements; and an essay on their story, including how losing their spouse or parent has affected them, who they are, where their life has taken them, and what they hope to do with their college education and beyond.

Financial data The stipend ranges up to $20,000.

Duration 1 year; nonrenewable.

Additional information This program began in 2012.

Number awarded Up to 5 each year. Since the program began, it has awarded $200,000 in scholarships to 65 students.

Deadline October of each year. Only the first 250 applications received are accepted.

[1059]
VFW AUXILIARY CONTINUING EDUCATION SCHOLARSHIPS
VFW Auxiliary
Attn: Administrator of Programs
406 West 34th Street, Tenth Floor
Kansas City, MO 64111
(816) 561-8655   Fax: (816) 931-4753
E-mail: info@ladiesauxvfw.org
Web: www.vfwauxiliary.org

Summary To provide financial assistance for college to members of Ladies Auxiliary to the Veterans of Foreign Wars (VFW) and their families.

Eligibility This program is open to members of the Ladies Auxiliary VFW and their children and spouses. Applicants must be 18 years of age or older and planning to work on a college degree or a career direction at a technical school. Along with their application, they must submit a 300-word essay describing their commitment to their goals and how this scholarship will help them attain those goals. The qualifying member must have belonged to the Auxiliary for at least 1 year prior to application. Financial need is considered in the selection process.

Financial data The stipend is $1,000. Funds are paid directly to the college or vocational school.

Duration 1 year.

Additional information Until 2015, the VFW Auxiliary was named the Ladies Auxiliary to the Veterans of Foreign Wars.

SCHOLARSHIPS: FAMILY MEMBERS

Number awarded 4 each year: 1 in each VFW Auxiliary Conference.
Deadline February of each year.

[1060]
VICE ADMIRAL ROBERT L. WALTERS SCHOLARSHIP

Surface Navy Association
Attn: Scholarship Coordinator
6564 Loisdale Court, Suite 318
Springfield, VA 22150
(703) 960-6800   Toll Free: (800) NAVY-SNA
Fax: (703) 960-6807   E-mail: navysna@aol.com
Web: www.navysna.org/scholarship/information.html

Summary To provide financial assistance for college or graduate school to members of the Surface Navy Association (SNA) and their dependents.
Eligibility This program is open to SNA members and their children, stepchildren, wards, and spouses. The SNA member must 1) be in the second or subsequent consecutive year of membership; 2) be serving, retired, or honorably discharged; 3) be a Surface Warfare Officer or Enlisted Surface Warfare Specialist; and 4) have served for at least 3 years on a surface ship of the U.S. Navy or Coast Guard (the 3 years need not have been consecutive but must have been served on active duty). Applicants must be enrolled or planning to enroll full time at an accredited undergraduate or graduate institution; the full-time requirement may be waived for spouses. Along with their application, they must submit a 500-word essay about themselves and why they should be selected to receive this scholarship. High school seniors should also include a transcript of high school grades and a copy of ACT or SAT scores. Current college students should also include a transcript of the grades from their most recent 4 semesters of school. Selection is based on academic proficiency, non-scholastic activities, scholastic and non-scholastic awards, character, and financial need.
Financial data The stipend is $2,000 per year.
Duration 4 years, provided the recipient maintains a GPA of 3.0 or higher.
Number awarded Varies each year.
Deadline February of each year.

[1061]
VII CORPS DESERT STORM VETERANS ASSOCIATION SCHOLARSHIP

VII Corps Desert Storm Veterans Association
Attn: Scholarship Committee
c/o BG (Ret) Edward Dyer
12888 Coco Plum Lane
Naples, FL 34119
E-mail: viicorpsdsva@gmail.com
Web: www.desertstormvets.org/scholarships

Summary To provide financial assistance for college to students who served, or are the spouses or other family members of individuals who served, with VII Corps in Operations Desert Shield, Desert Storm, or related activities.
Eligibility Applicants must have served, or be a family member of those who served, with VII Corps in Operations Desert Shield/Desert Storm, Provide Comfort, or 1 of the support base activities. Scholarships are limited to students entering or enrolled full or part time at accredited 2- and 4-year colleges, universities, and technical schools. Selection is not based solely on academic standing; consideration is also given to extracurricular activities, community activities and/or involvement, professional organizations, high school organizations and/or activities, and other self-development skills and abilities obtained through on-the-job training or correspondence courses. Priority is given to survivors of VII Corps soldiers who died during Operations Desert Shield/Desert Storm or Provide Comfort, veterans who are also members of the VII Corps Desert Storm Veterans Association, and family members of veterans who are also members of the VII Corps Desert Storm Veterans Association.
Financial data The stipend ranges from $1,000 to $5,000 per year. Funds are paid to the recipients upon proof of admission or registration at an accredited institution, college, or university.
Duration 1 year; recipients may reapply.
Additional information This program began in 1998.
Number awarded 15 to 20 each year; since this program began, it has awarded more than $350,000 in scholarships.
Deadline December of each year.

[1062]
VIRGINIA MILITARY SURVIVORS AND DEPENDENTS EDUCATION PROGRAM

Virginia Department of Veterans Services
Attn: VMSDEP Coordinator
101 North 14th Street, 17th Floor
Richmond, VA 23219
(804) 225-2083   Fax: (804) 786-0809
E-mail: vmsdep@dvs.virginia.gov
Web: www.dvs.virginia.gov

Summary To provide educational assistance to the children and spouses of disabled and other Virginia veterans or service personnel.
Eligibility This program is open to residents of Virginia who are the child between 16 and 29 years of age or spouse of a current or former member of the U.S. armed forces. Applicants must be attending or planning to attend a public college or university in Virginia or Eastern Virginia Medical School as an undergraduate or graduate student. For Tier 1 support, applicants must be the child or spouse of a veteran who is rated totally and permanently disabled or at least 90% permanently disabled due to military service. For Tier 2 support, applicants must be the child or spouse of a military service member or veteran who is rated totally and permanently disabled or at least 90% permanently disabled due to direct involvement in covered military combat (includes military operation against terrorism; a peacekeeping mission; a terrorist act; or any armed conflict). The military service member's death or a veteran's total and permanent or at least 90% permanent disability must have been directly caused by the military service member's or veteran's involvement in military operations: 1) against terrorism; 2) on a peacekeeping mission; 3) as a result of a terrorist act; or 4) an armed conflict. The veteran must have been a resident of Virginia at the time of entry into active military service or for at least 5 consecutive years immediately prior to the date of application or death. Surviving spouses must have been residents of Virginia for at least 5 years prior to marrying the veteran or for at least 5 years immediately prior to the date on which the application was submitted.

Financial data Tier 1 support provides a waiver of tuition and all required fees at public institutions of higher education in Virginia. Tier 2 support includes a stipend to offset the costs of room, board, books, and supplies at those institutions; recently, the stipend for full-time study was $1,800 per academic year.
Duration Entitlement extends to a maximum of 36 months (4 years).
Additional information This program was formerly known as the Virginia War Orphans Education Program.
Number awarded Varies each year; recently, funding allowed for a total of 1,000 stipends.
Deadline April of each year for fall; August of each year for spring; December of each year for summer.

[1063]
VIRGINIA NATIONAL GUARD ASSOCIATION SCHOLARSHIP

Virginia National Guard Association
Attn: Scholarship Committee Chair
11518 Hardwood Drive
Midlothian, VA 23114
(804) 350-0175   E-mail: scholarship@vnga.us
Web: www.vnga.us/scholarship

Summary To provide financial assistance to members of the Virginia National Guard Association (VNGA) and their families who are interested in attending college in any state.
Eligibility Applicants must have been enrolled at a college or university in any state for 1 year and qualify under 1 of the following conditions: 1) an officer or warrant officer in the Virginia National Guard and a VNGA member; 2) a dependent child or spouse of an officer or warrant officer in the Virginia National Guard who is a VNGA member; 3) a dependent child or spouse of a retired officer or warrant officer who is a VNGA member; 4) a dependent child or spouse of a deceased retired officer or warrant officer; or 5) a dependent child or spouse of a Virginia National Guard officer or warrant officer who died while actively serving in the Virginia National Guard. Along with their application, they must submit a brief description of their educational and/or military objectives, a list of their leadership positions and honors, and a brief statement of their financial need.
Financial data A stipend is awarded; the amount is determined annually.
Duration 1 year; may be renewed for 2 additional years.
Additional information This program includes scholarships designated the CW4 William C. Singletary Scholarship and the Colonel Joseph "Ed" Galloway Scholarship.
Number awarded Varies each year.
Deadline September of each year.

[1064]
VTNGEA SCHOLARSHIPS

Vermont National Guard Enlisted Association
Attn: Scholarship Committee
P.O. Box 7
Essex Junction, VT 05452-0007
Web: www.vtngea.org/vtngea-scholarships/

Summary To provide financial assistance to members and dependents of members of the Enlisted Association of the National Guard of the United States (EANGUS) who reside in Vermont and are interested in attending college in any state.
Eligibility This program is open to members of the Vermont chapter of EANGUS and their dependents. Applicants must be enrolled or planning to enroll at a college or university in any state. Along with their application, they must submit transcripts, letters of recommendation, and a 1-page essay describing their desire to continue their education and why financial assistance is required.
Financial data A stipend is awarded (amount not specified).
Duration 1 year.
Additional information This program receives support from Jolley Associates and USAA Insurance Corporation.
Number awarded Multiple scholarships are awarded each year.
Deadline July of each year.

[1065]
WALTER BEALL SCHOLARSHIP

Walter Beall Scholarship Foundation
c/o PNP Jim Scarbo
613 Hillwell Road
Chesapeake, VA 23322-3812
E-mail: jimscarbo@cox.net
Web: www.walterbeallscholarship.org

Summary To provide financial assistance to members of the Fleet Reserve Association (FRA) and their families who are interested in studying engineering, aeronautical engineering, or aviation in college.
Eligibility This program is open to FRA members who have been in good standing for at least the past 2 consecutive years and their spouses, children, and grandchildren. Students in a Reserve officer candidate program receiving aid or attending a military academy are not eligible. Applicants must be enrolled at an accredited college, university, or technical institution in the United States in a program related to general engineering, aviation, or aeronautical engineering. Selection is based on GPA, scholastic aptitude test scores, curriculum goals, interests, community activities, awards, and financial need. U.S. citizenship is required.
Financial data The amounts of the awards depend on the availability of funds and the need of the recipients; they normally range from $2,000 to $5,000.
Duration 1 year; recipients may reapply.
Additional information The Walter Beall Scholarship Foundation is sponsored by the Past Regional Presidents Club of the Fleet Reserve Association. Membership in the FRA is restricted to active-duty, retired, and Reserve members of the Navy, Marine Corps, and Coast Guard.
Number awarded 1 or more each year.
Deadline Requests for applications must be received by March of each year.

[1066]
WALTER KEITH IRWIN MEMORIAL SCHOLARSHIP FUND

Arizona Community Foundation
Attn: Director of Scholarships
2201 East Camelback Road, Suite 405B
Phoenix, AZ 85016
(602) 381-1400   Toll Free: (800) 222-8221
Fax: (602) 381-1575
E-mail: scholarship@azfoundation.org
Web: azfoundation.academicworks.com/opportunities/4087

Summary To provide financial assistance to high school seniors in Arizona who are descendants of active or retired military personnel and interested in studying history or aviation at a college in the state.

Eligibility This program is open to seniors graduating from high schools in Arizona and planning to attend a college or university in the state to major in history or aviation. Applicants must reside with a familial guardian (e.g., parent, grandparent, uncle) who is an active-duty or retired member of any branch of the military. They must have a GPA of 2.5 or higher and be a U.S. citizen. Along with their application, they must submit a personal essay on their educational goals and the education program necessary to achieve those goals. Financial need is not required but may be considered in the selection process.

Financial data The stipend is $2,000.
Duration 1 year; may be renewed.
Number awarded Varies each year.
Deadline March of each year.

[1067]
WARREN-RAGAN JUNIOR SCHOLARSHIP FUND

American Legion Auxiliary
Department of North Carolina
2940 Falstaff Road
P.O. Box 25726
Raleigh, NC 27611-5726
(984) 206-4404   E-mail: ncala-membership@nclegion.org
Web: www.alanorthcarolina.com/resources

Summary To provide financial assistance to members of the American Legion Junior Auxiliary in North Carolina who plan to attend college in any state.

Eligibility This program is open to seniors graduating from high schools in North Carolina who are members of the American Legion Junior Auxiliary. Applicants must be interested in attending college in any state. Their unit must submit a letter about them, including their involvement in the unit and other accomplishments. Selection is based on academics, character, leadership, and financial need.

Financial data A stipend is awarded (amount not specified).
Duration 1 year.
Number awarded 1 each year.
Deadline March of each year.

[1068]
WARRIOR'S LEGACY SCHOLARSHIP FUND

Federal Resources Supply Company
Attn: Scholarship Committee
235G Log Canoe Circle
Stevensville, MD 21666
Toll Free: (800) 892-1099
E-mail: scholarships@federalresources.com
Web: www.federalresources.com/scholarship

Summary To provide financial assistance for college to the children of current and former military personnel, first responders, and law enforcement officers.

Eligibility This program is open to graduating high school seniors and current full-time college students who are the children of active or retired military personnel, first responders, or law enforcement officers. Applicants must be U.S. citizens or permanent residents and have a GPA of 3.0 or higher. Along with their application, they must submit a 500-word essay on how they have seen their parent contribute to society in their role as an active or retired service member and how that has inspired their educational and/or future career goals.

Financial data The stipend is $5,000.
Duration 1 year.
Additional information This program began in 2018.
Number awarded 2 each year.
Deadline May of each year.

[1069]
WASHINGTON LEGION CHILDREN AND YOUTH SCHOLARSHIPS

American Legion
Department of Washington
3600 Ruddell Road S.E.
P.O. Box 3917
Lacey, WA 98509-3917
(360) 491-4373   Fax: (360) 491-7442
E-mail: administrator@walegion.org
Web: www.walegion.org/index.php?id=109

Summary To provide financial assistance to the children of members of the American Legion or American Legion Auxiliary in Washington who plan to attend college in the state.

Eligibility This program is open to sons and daughters of Washington Legionnaires or Auxiliary members, living or deceased, who are high school seniors. Applicants must be planning to attend an accredited institution of higher education, trade, or vocational school in the state of Washington. Selection is based on presentation, initiative, goals, commitment to goals, and financial need.

Financial data The stipend is $2,500 or $1,500, payable in equal amounts per semester.
Duration 1 year.
Number awarded 2 each year: 1 at $2,500 and 1 at $1,500.
Deadline March of each year.

[1070]
WELLS FARGO VETERANS SCHOLARSHIP PROGRAM

Scholarship America
Attn: Scholarship Management Services
One Scholarship Way
P.O. Box 297
St. Peter, MN 56082
(507) 931-1682   Toll Free: (844) 402-0357
Fax: (507) 931-9168
E-mail: wellsfargoveterans@scholarshipamerica.org
Web: www.scholarsapply.org/wellsfargoveterans

Summary To provide financial assistance to veterans and the spouses of disabled veterans who are interested in attending college.

Eligibility This program is open to honorably-discharged (no longer drilling) veterans and the spouses of disabled veterans of the U.S. armed forces, including the Reserves and National Guard. Applicants must be enrolled or planning to enroll full time at an accredited 2- or 4-year college, university, or vocational/technical school to work on a bachelor's or master's degree. They must have a GPA of 2.5 or higher and be able to demonstrate financial need. Along with their application, they must submit essays on 1) their military service and career and educational goals and objectives; and 2) any personal or financial challenges that may be barriers to completing postsecondary education. Selection is based on those essays, academic performance, demonstrated leadership, participation in school and community activities, work experience, and financial need.

Financial data The amount of the initial stipend depends on an analysis of the recipient's military education benefits, institutional grants, and other scholarships. If renewed, the stipend increases by $1,000 each year.

Duration 1 year; scholarships may be renewed up to 3 additional years or until completion of a degree, whichever occurs firsts. Renewal depends on the recipient's maintaining satisfactory academic progress and full-time enrollment.

Additional information This trustee for this program is Wells Fargo Bank and the administrator is Scholarship America.

Number awarded Varies each year.

Deadline February of each year.

[1071]
WESLEY HAMMON LEACH SCHOLARSHIPS

Marines' Memorial Association
c/o Marines Memorial Club and Hotel
609 Sutter Street
San Francisco, CA 94102
(415) 673-6672, ext. 293   Toll Free: (800) 5-MARINE
Fax: (415) 441-3649
E-mail: scholarship@marineclub.com
Web: www.marinesmemorial.org

Summary To provide financial assistance to members of the Marines' Memorial Association from all branches of the armed forces and their descendants who are interested in studying at a career school or college.

Eligibility This program is open to active members of the association (including student veterans) and their children and grandchildren. Applicants must be high school seniors or students currently enrolled at an accredited trade or vocational school. They must have a field of study that will lead to a viable career; preference is given to students with a medical or nursing focus. Along with their application, they must submit an essay of up to 500 words on why they chose their specific path of study, what they hope to accomplish after graduation with their degree, and how their efforts will benefit others in their community. Selection is based on the essay, academic merit, references, and financial need.

Financial data The stipend is $2,500.

Duration 1 year.

Additional information Membership in the association is open to veterans of the Marines, Army, Navy, Air Force, or Coast Guard and to personnel currently serving in a branch of the armed forces. This program began in 2017.

Number awarded 3 each year.

Deadline April of each year.

[1072]
WEST VIRGINIA SONS OF THE AMERICAN LEGION SCHOLARSHIP

Sons of the American Legion
Detachment of West Virginia
Attn: Scholarship Committee
2016 Kanawha Boulevard, East
P.O. Box 3191
Charleston, WV 25332-3191
(304) 343-7591   Toll Free: (888) 534-4667
Fax: (304) 343-7592
Web: www.wvsal.org

Summary To provide financial assistance to high school seniors in West Virginia who have a family link to the American Legion and are planning to attend college in the state.

Eligibility This program is open to seniors graduating from high schools in West Virginia who are the child or grandchild of a member of the American Legion, American Legion Auxiliary, or Sons of the American Legion. Applicants must be planning to attend a college or university in West Virginia. Along with their application, they must submit an essay on a topic that changes annually; recently, students were asked to present their thoughts on the principle requirements of true leadership.

Financial data The stipend is $1,000 or $500. Funds are paid directly to the students, but only after they have completed their first semester of college.

Duration 1 year; nonrenewable.

Number awarded 2 each year: 1 at $1,000 and 1 at $500.

Deadline May of each year.

[1073]
WEST VIRGINIA STATE WAR ORPHANS EDUCATIONAL PROGRAM

West Virginia Department of Veteran's Assistance
Attn: Office of the Cabinet Secretary
1900 Kanawha Boulevard East, Building 5, Suite 205
Charleston, WV 25305
(304) 558-3661   Toll Free: (866) WV4-VETS (within WV)
Fax: (304) 558-3662   E-mail: dennis.e.davis@wv.gov
Web: veterans.wv.gov/Benefits/Pages/default.aspx

Summary To provide financial assistance for college to the children of deceased West Virginia veterans.

Eligibility This program is open to residents of West Virginia who are children between 16 and 25 years of age of

deceased veterans. The veteran must have entered service as a resident of West Virginia; served during specified periods of wartime; and died during that wartime period or, if subsequent to discharge, as a result of disability incurred in that wartime service. Applicants must be attending or planning to attend a public college or university in West Virginia.
Financial data Qualified children are exempt from payment of tuition and fees at public colleges and universities in West Virginia. They also receive a stipend of $1,000 per semester ($2,000 per year) to cover costs of room, board, books, and other living expenses.
Duration 1 year; may be renewed upon reapplication if the student maintains a cumulative GPA of at least 2.0.
Number awarded Varies each year.
Deadline August of each year for the fall semester; January of each year for the spring semester.

[1074]
WILLIAM P. O'CONNELL MEMORIAL VETERANS REHABILITATION SCHOLARSHIP
Sons of the American Legion
Detachment of New York
1304 Park Boulevard
Troy, NY 12180
(518) 463-2215   Fax: (518) 427-8443
E-mail: info@nylegion.org
Web: www.sonsdny.org

Summary To provide financial assistance to high school seniors and graduates in New York who are have been active in veterans rehabilitation activities of the Sons of the American Legion and plan to attend college in any state.
Eligibility This program is open to members of the Sons of the American Legion in New York who have been active in its veterans rehabilitation activities. Applicants must be high school seniors or graduates and planning to attend college or trade school in any state. Along with their application, they must submit a 200-word essay on what we can do for veterans' rehabilitation. Selection is based on academics (25%), character (25%), community service (25%), and participation in veterans rehabilitation activities (25%).
Financial data The stipend is $1,000.
Duration 1 year.
Number awarded 1 each year.
Deadline April of each year.

[1075]
WILLIAM W, BODDINGTON SCHOLARSHIP
Tenth Mountain Division Foundation
Attn: Scholarship Fund
133 South Van Gordon Street, Suite 200
Lakewood, CO 80228
(303) 756-8486   Fax: (303) 988-3005
E-mail: tenthmtnfdn@nsp.org
Web: www.tenthmountainfoundation.org/?page_id=18

Summary To provide financial assistance for college to descendants of former members of the 10th Mountain Division who demonstrate outstanding community service.
Eligibility This program is open to the descendants of veterans who served in the 10th Mountain Division during World War II. Applicants must have completed at least 60 credit hours of undergraduate study. Along with their application, they must submit an essay explaining how they emulate and put into practice the ideals and character traits of the program's namesake, along with documentation of their community service to support their essay.
Financial data The stipend is $1,250.
Duration 1 year; nonrenewable.
Number awarded 1 each year.
Deadline April each year.

[1076]
WILMA D. HOYAL/MAXINE CHILTON SCHOLARSHIPS
American Legion Auxiliary
Department of Arizona
4701 North 19th Avenue, Suite 100
Phoenix, AZ 85015-3727
(602) 241-1080   Fax: (602) 604-9640
E-mail: secretary@aladeptaz.org
Web: www.aladeptaz.org/member-resources.html

Summary To provide financial assistance to veterans, the dependents of veterans, and other students who are majoring in selected subjects at Arizona public universities.
Eligibility This program is open to second-year or upper-division full-time students majoring in political science, public programs, or special education at public universities in Arizona (the University of Arizona, Northern Arizona University, or Arizona State University). Applicants must have been Arizona residents for at least 1 year. They must have a GPA of 3.0 or higher. U.S. citizenship is required. Honorably-discharged veterans and immediate family members of veterans receive preference. Selection is based on scholarship (25%), financial need (40%), character (20%), and leadership (15%).
Financial data The stipend is $1,000.
Duration 1 year; renewable.
Number awarded 3 each year: 1 to each of the 3 universities.
Deadline May of each year.

[1077]
WINGS OVER AMERICA SCHOLARSHIPS
Wings Over America Scholarship Foundation
Attn: Scholarship Administrator
770 Lynnhaven Parkway, Suite 155
Virginia Beach, VA 23452
(757) 228-3532
E-mail: scholarship@wingsoveramerica.us
Web: www.wingsoveramerica.us/app/eligibilty

Summary To provide financial assistance for college to dependents of naval aviators.
Eligibility This program is open to 1) children of a military sponsor who are graduating high school seniors planning to enroll in college full time to work on a bachelor's degree or who are already enrolled in such a program; and 2) spouses of a military sponsor currently enrolled full or part time and working on an associate or bachelor's degree at an accredited college or university. Children must be unmarried and younger than 22 years of age. The military sponsor must have completed at least 8 years of active-duty service in a Naval air force or subordinate command and be currently on active duty, honorably discharged, retired, or deceased. Also eligible are children of members of the U.S. Navy who died while on active duty serving with a Naval air force unit, regardless of the length of service of the deceased parent.

The minimum GPA is 3.0 for high school seniors or 2.5 for college students (children and spouses). Selection is based on academic achievement, extracurricular activities, work/internships, community service, recommendations, and an essay.
Financial data The basic stipend is $3,800 per year.
Duration 1 year; may be renewed.
Additional information This program began in 1987. It currently includes scholarships sponsored by many individuals and corporations including Boeing, First Command, Lockheed Martin, Navy Federal Credit Union, and USAA.
Number awarded Varies each year; recently, 49 were awarded: 18 to high school seniors, 27 to children currently enrolled in college, and 4 to spouses. Since the program was established, it has awarded more than $1,600,000 in scholarships.
Deadline Pre-qualification forms must be submitted by January of each year.

[1078]
WISCONSIN G.I. BILL TUITION REMISSION PROGRAM

Wisconsin Department of Veterans Affairs
2135 Rimrock Road
P.O. Box 7843
Madison, WI 53707-7843
(608) 266-1311   Toll Free: (800) WIS-VETS
Fax: (608) 267-0403   E-mail: WDVAInfo@dva.state.wi.us
Web: dva.wi.gov

Summary To provide financial assistance for college or graduate school to Wisconsin veterans and their dependents.
Eligibility This program is open to current residents of Wisconsin who 1) were residents of the state when they entered or reentered active duty in the U.S. armed forces; or 2) have moved to the state and have been residents for at least 5 consecutive years after entry or reentry into service. Applicants must have served on active duty for at least 2 continuous years or for at least 90 days during specified wartime periods. Also eligible are 1) qualifying children and unremarried surviving spouses of Wisconsin veterans who died in the line of duty or as the direct result of a service-connected disability; and 2) children and spouses of Wisconsin veterans who have a service-connected disability rated by the U.S. Department of Veterans Affairs as 30% or greater. Children must be between 17 and 25 years of age (regardless of the date of the veteran's death or initial disability rating) and be a Wisconsin resident for tuition purposes. Spouses remain eligible for 10 years following the date of the veteran's death or initial disability rating; they must be Wisconsin residents for tuition purposes, but they may enroll full or part time. Students may attend any institution, center, or school within the University of Wisconsin (UW) System or the Wisconsin Technical College System (WCTS). There are no income limits, delimiting periods following military service during which the benefit must be used, or limits on the level of study (e.g., vocational, undergraduate, professional, or graduate).
Financial data Veterans who qualify as a Wisconsin resident for tuition purposes are eligible for a remission of 100% of standard academic fees and segregated fees at a UW campus or 100% of program and material fees at a WCTS institution. Veterans who qualify as a Wisconsin veteran for purposes of this program but for other reasons fail to meet the definition of a Wisconsin resident for tuition purposes at the UW system are eligible for a remission of 100% of non-resident fees. Spouses and children of deceased or disabled veterans are entitled to a remission of 100% of tuition and fees at a UW or WCTS institution.
Duration Up to 8 semesters or 128 credits, whichever is greater.
Additional information This program began in 2005 as a replacement for Wisconsin Tuition and Fee Reimbursement Grants.
Number awarded Varies each year.
Deadline Applications must be submitted within 14 days from the office start of the academic term: in October for fall, March for spring, or June for summer.

[1079]
WISCONSIN LEGION AUXILIARY DEPARTMENT PRESIDENT'S SCHOLARSHIP

American Legion Auxiliary
Department of Wisconsin
Attn: Education Chair
2930 American Legion Drive
P.O. Box 140
Portage, WI 53901-0140
(608) 745-0124   Toll Free: (866) 664-3863
Fax: (608) 745-1947
E-mail: deptsec@amlegionauxwi.org
Web: www.amlegionauxwi.org/scholarships

Summary To provide financial assistance to Wisconsin residents who are members or children of members of the American Legion Auxiliary and interested in attending college in any state.
Eligibility This program is open to members and children of members of the American Legion Auxiliary in Wisconsin. Applicants must be high school seniors or graduates and attending or planning to attend a college or university in any state. They must have a GPA of 3.5 or higher and be able to demonstrate financial need. Along with their application, they must submit a 300-word essay on "Education—An Investment in the Future."
Financial data The stipend is $1,000.
Duration 1 year.
Number awarded 3 each year.
Deadline March of each year.

[1080]
WISCONSIN LEGION AUXILIARY MERIT AND MEMORIAL SCHOLARSHIPS

American Legion Auxiliary
Department of Wisconsin
Attn: Education Chair
2930 American Legion Drive
P.O. Box 140
Portage, WI 53901-0140
(608) 745-0124   Toll Free: (866) 664-3863
Fax: (608) 745-1947
E-mail: deptsec@amlegionauxwi.org
Web: www.amlegionauxwi.org/scholarships

Summary To provide financial assistance to Wisconsin residents who are related to veterans and interested in working on an undergraduate degree at a school in any state.
Eligibility This program is open to residents of Wisconsin who are the children, grandchildren, great-grandchildren,

wives, or widows of veterans. Students who are also members of the Wisconsin American Legion family may live in any state. Applicants must be attending or entering a college or university in any state. They must have a GPA of 3.5 or higher and be able to demonstrate financial need. Along with their application, they must submit a 300-word essay on "Education—An Investment in the Future."

Financial data The stipend is $1,000.

Duration 1 year; nonrenewable.

Additional information This program includes the following named scholarships: the Harriet Hass Scholarship, the Adalin Macauley Scholarship, the Eleanor Smith Scholarship, the Pearl Behrend Scholarship, the Barbara Kranig Scholarship, the Diane Duscheck Scholarship, and the Jan Pulvermacher-Ryan Scholarship.

Number awarded Up to 8 each year.

Deadline March of each year.

[1081]
WISCONSIN LEGION AUXILIARY PAST PRESIDENTS PARLEY HEALTH CAREER SCHOLARSHIPS

American Legion Auxiliary
Department of Wisconsin
Attn: Education Chair
2930 American Legion Drive
P.O. Box 140
Portage, WI 53901-0140
(608) 745-0124   Toll Free: (866) 664-3863
Fax: (608) 745-1947
E-mail: deptsec@amlegionauxwi.org
Web: www.amlegionauxwi.org/scholarships

Summary To provide financial assistance to Wisconsin residents who are related to veterans and interested in working on a health-related degree at a school in any state.

Eligibility This program is open to residents of Wisconsin who are the children, grandchildren, great-grandchildren, wives, or widows of veterans. Students who are also members of the Wisconsin American Legion family may live in any state. Applicants must be attending or entering a hospital, university, or technical school in any state to prepare for a health-related career. They must have a GPA of 3.5 or higher and be able to demonstrate financial need. Along with their application, they must submit a 300-word essay on "The Importance of Health Careers Today."

Financial data The stipend is $1,000.

Duration 1 year; nonrenewable.

Number awarded 1 or 2 each year.

Deadline March of each year.

[1082]
WISCONSIN LEGION AUXILIARY PAST PRESIDENTS PARLEY REGISTERED NURSE SCHOLARSHIPS

American Legion Auxiliary
Department of Wisconsin
Attn: Education Chair
2930 American Legion Drive
P.O. Box 140
Portage, WI 53901-0140
(608) 745-0124   Toll Free: (866) 664-3863
Fax: (608) 745-1947
E-mail: deptsec@amlegionauxwi.org
Web: www.amlegionauxwi.org/scholarships

Summary To provide financial assistance to Wisconsin residents who are related to veterans and interested in working on a nursing degree at a school in any state.

Eligibility This program is open to residents of Wisconsin who are the children, grandchildren, great-grandchildren, wives, or widows of veterans. Students who are also members of the Wisconsin American Legion family may live in any state. Applicants must be enrolled or have been accepted in an accredited school of nursing in any state to prepare for a career as a registered nurse. They must have a GPA of 3.5 or higher and be able to demonstrate financial need. Along with their application, they must submit a 300-word essay on "The Need for Trained Nurses Today."

Financial data The stipend is $1,000.

Duration 1 year.

Number awarded 1 or 2 each year.

Deadline March of each year.

[1083]
WISCONSIN NATIONAL GUARD ASSOCIATION EDUCATION GRANT

Wisconsin National Guard Association, Inc.
Attn: Awards, Gifts, and Grants Committee
2400 Wright Street, Room 151
Madison, WI 53704-2572
(608) 242-3114   Fax: (608) 242-3513
E-mail: info@winga.org
Web: www.winga.org/html/members/scholarships.html

Summary To provide financial assistance to members of the Wisconsin National Guard Association (WINGA), their spouses, and their unmarried children who are interested in attending college in any state.

Eligibility This program is open to WINGA members and their spouses and unmarried dependent children. Applicants must have completed at least 1 year of college. They must be enrolled full time at an accredited college, university, technical institute, or trade or business school in any state. High school seniors and graduate students are not eligible. Selection is based on academic record (GPA of 3.0 or higher), extracurricular activities, community involvement, work experience, and goals.

Financial data The stipend is $1,000. Funds are paid to the recipient's school upon proof of enrollment.

Duration 1 year; may be renewed for 1 additional year.

Additional information This grant was first awarded in 1992. Graduate education is not supported.

Number awarded Varies each year; recently, 10 were awarded.
Deadline June of each year.

[1084]
WISCONSIN NATIONAL GUARD ENLISTED ASSOCIATION COLLEGE GRANT PROGRAM

Wisconsin National Guard Enlisted Association
Attn: Executive Director
2400 Wright Street
Madison, WI 53704-2572
(608) 242-3112   E-mail: WNGEA@yahoo.com
Web: wngea.org/scholarships

Summary To provide financial assistance to members of the Wisconsin National Guard Enlisted Association (WNGEA) and their spouses and children who are interested in attending college or graduate school in any state.
Eligibility This program is open to WNGEA members, the unmarried children and spouses of WNGEA members, and the unmarried children and spouses of deceased WNGEA members. Applicants must be enrolled full or part time at a college, university, graduate school, trade school, or business school in any state. Along with their application, they must submit a letter explaining their desire to continue their education; why financial assistance is needed; awards received, accomplishments, volunteerism, and hours volunteered per week or month; and WNGEA membership and role in the organization. Selection is based on financial need, leadership, and moral character.
Financial data Stipends are $1,000 or $500 per year.
Duration 1 year; recipients may not reapply for 2 years.
Additional information This program includes 1 scholarship sponsored by the USAA Insurance Corporation.
Number awarded Varies each year; recently, 6 were awarded: the Raymond A. Matera Scholarship at $1,000, a grant of $1,000 sponsored by USAA, and 4 others (1 reserved for a graduate student) at $500 each.
Deadline May of each year.

[1085]
WOMEN MARINES ASSOCIATION SCHOLARSHIP PROGRAM

Women Marines Association
120 State Avenue, Suite 303
Olympia, WA 98501
Toll Free: (888) 525-1943
E-mail: scholarship@womenmarines.org
Web: www.womenmarines.org/scholarships

Summary To provide financial assistance for college or graduate school to students sponsored by members of the Women Marines Association (WMA).
Eligibility Applicants must be sponsored by a WMA member and fall into 1 of the following categories: 1) have served or are serving in the U.S. Marine Corps, regular or Reserve; 2) are a direct descendant by blood or legal adoption or a stepchild of a Marine on active duty or who has served honorably in the U.S. Marine Corps, regular or Reserve; 3) are a sibling or a descendant of a sibling by blood or legal adoption or a stepchild of a Marine on active duty or who has served honorably in the U.S. Marine Corps, regular or Reserve; 4) be a spouse of a Marine; or 5) have completed 2 years in a Marine Corps JROTC program. WMA members may sponsor an unlimited number of applicants per year. High school seniors must submit transcripts (GPA of 3.0 or higher) and SAT or ACT scores. Undergraduate and graduate students must have a GPA of 3.0 or higher. Along with their application, they must submit 1-page statements on 1) the Marine to whom they are related; 2) their community service; and 3) their goals after college.
Financial data Stipends range from $500 to $5,000 per year.
Duration 1 year; may be renewed 1 additional year.
Additional information This program includes the following named scholarships: the WMA Memorial Scholarships, the Lily H. Gridley Memorial Scholarship, the Ethyl and Armin Wiebke Memorial Scholarship, the Maj. Megan McClung Memorial Scholarship, the Agnes Sopcak Memorial Scholarship, the Virginia Guveyan Memorial Scholarship, the LaRue A. Ditmore Music Scholarships, the Fallen Warrior Scholarship, and the Margaret Apel Scholarship. Applicants must know a WMA member to serve as their sponsor; the WMA will not supply listings of the names or addresses of chapters or individual members.
Number awarded Varies each year.
Deadline February of each year.

[1086]
WOMEN'S ARMY CORPS VETERANS' ASSOCIATION SCHOLARSHIP

Women's Army Corps Veterans' Association
P.O. Box 663
Weaver, AL 36277
(256) 820-6824   E-mail: info@armywomen.org
Web: www.armywomen.org

Summary To provide financial assistance for college to the relatives of Army military women.
Eligibility This program is open to high school seniors who are the children, grandchildren, nieces, or nephews of Army service women. Applicants must have a cumulative GPA of 3.5 or higher and be planning to enroll full time at an accredited college or university in the United States. They must submit a 500-word biographical sketch that includes their future goals and how the scholarship would be used. Selection is based on academic achievement, leadership ability as expressed through co-curricular activities and community involvement, the biographical sketch, and recommendations. Financial need is not considered. U.S. citizenship is required.
Financial data The stipend is $1,500.
Duration 1 year.
Number awarded 1 or more each year.
Deadline January of each year.

[1087]
WORCHID SCHOLARSHIP

AMVETS-Department of Illinois
2200 South Sixth Street
Springfield, IL 62703
(217) 528-4713   Toll Free: (800) 638-VETS (within IL)
Fax: (217) 528-9896   E-mail: info@ilamvets.org
Web: www.ilamvets.org

Summary To provide financial assistance for college in any state to the children of deceased veterans in Illinois.
Eligibility This program is open to high school seniors in Illinois who have taken the SAT or ACT and are planning to

attend college in any state. Applicants must be children of deceased veterans who served after September 15, 1940 and were honorably discharged. They need not have been killed in action or died as a result of a service-connected disability. Financial need is considered in the selection process.
Financial data The stipend varies annually.
Duration 1 year.
Number awarded 1 each year.
Deadline February of each year.

[1088]
WORLD WAR II ILLINOIS DESCENDANTS SCHOLARSHIP
Community Foundation for the Land of Lincoln
Attn: Scholarship Coordinator
205 South Fifth Street, Suite 530
Springfield, IL 62701
(217) 789-4431   Fax: (217) 789-4635
E-mail: scholarships@CFLL.org
Web: www.cfll.org

Summary To provide financial assistance to high school seniors in Illinois who are the direct descendant of a veteran of World War II and plan to attend college in any state.
Eligibility This program is open to seniors graduating from high schools in Illinois who are the direct descendant (i.e., grandchild or great-grandchild, but not a great niece or nephew) of an Illinois veteran of World War II. Applicants must be planning to enroll full time at an accredited community college or 4-year college or university in any state. They must have an unweighted GPA of 4.0 or be projected to be the valedictorian or salutatorian of their class.
Financial data The stipend is $1,000.
Duration 1 year.
Number awarded 2 each year.
Deadline February of each year.

[1089]
WYOMING ELKS ASSOCIATION ANGELS SCHOLARSHIP
Wyoming Elks Association
c/o Tom Hernandez, State Scholarship Chair
1613 Lewis Street
Riverton, WY 82501
E-mail: scholarshipwyoelks@gmail.com
Web: www.wyoelks.org/scholarships

Summary To provide financial assistance to residents of Wyoming whose parent was killed during the "War on Terror" and are interested in attending college in any state.
Eligibility This program is open to Wyoming residents who are the child, adopted child, or stepchild of a Wyoming veteran killed in the "War on Terror." Applicants must be enrolled or planning to enroll at an accredited institute of higher learning in any state. Along with their application, they must submit transcripts and documentation of their parent's death.
Financial data The stipend is $1,000 per year.
Duration 1 year; recipients may reapply.
Number awarded 1 or more each year.
Deadline May of each year.

[1090]
WYOMING LEGION AUXILIARY PAST PRESIDENT'S PARLEY FIELD OF HEALTH CARE SCHOLARSHIPS
American Legion Auxiliary
Department of Wyoming
c/o Peg Sullivan, Secretary
P.O. Box 186
Buffalo, WY 82834
(307) 684-2903   E-mail: deptaux@vcn.com
Web: www.wyamericanlegionauxiliary.org

Summary To provide financial assistance, preferably to the children of Wyoming veterans, who wish to study nursing or health care at a school in any state.
Eligibility This program is open to students who have completed at least 1 year of full-time training at a college or university in any state in nursing or health care studies (e.g., occupational therapy, optometry, pharmacy, physical therapy, respiratory therapy, speech therapy). Applicants must have a GPA of 3.0 or higher. Preference is given to descendants of veterans and members of the American Legion family in Wyoming. Financial need is considered in the selection process.
Financial data A stipend is awarded (amount not specified).
Duration 1 year.
Number awarded 1 each year.
Deadline May of each year.

[1091]
WYOMING NATIONAL GUARD ASSOCIATION SCHOLARSHIPS
Wyoming National Guard Association
Attn: Scholarships
P.O. Box 2615
Cheyenne, WY 82003-2615
(307) 630-9502   E-mail: janetlcowley@gmail.com
Web: www.wynga.org

Summary To provide financial assistance to members of the Wyoming National Guard Association (WYNGA) and their families who are interested in attending college in any state.
Eligibility This program is open to enlisted and officer members of the WYNGA and their spouses and unmarried children. Applicants must be attending or planning to attend an accredited institution of higher education in any state. Along with their application, they must submit a cover letter that includes information on their educational career goals, their need for this scholarship, their family involvement in WYNGA, and a list of awards, honors, extracurricular activities, and organizations in which they have participated.
Financial data A stipend is awarded (amount not specified).
Duration 1 year.
Additional information This program includes the following named scholarships: the MG Charles J. Wing Family Program Scholarship, the Mrs. Beverly Holmes Scholarship, the Wyoming Army National Guard Combined Club Scholarship, and the USAA Insurance Corporation Scholarship.
Number awarded Varies each year; recently, 7 were awarded.
Deadline April of each year.

[1092]
YELLOW RIBBON PROGRAM OF THE POST-9/11 GI BILL

Department of Veterans Affairs
Attn: Veterans Benefits Administration
810 Vermont Avenue, N.W.
Washington, DC 20420
(202) 418-4343   Toll Free: (888) 442-4551
Web: www.va.gov

Summary To provide financial assistance to veterans and their dependents who qualify for the Post-9/11 GI Bill and wish to attend a high cost private or out-of-state public institution.

Eligibility Maximum Post-9/11 GI Bill benefits are available to veterans who 1) served on active duty for at least 36 aggregate months after September 11, 2001; or 2) received a Purple Heart on or after September 11, 2001 and were honorably discharged after any length of service; or 3) received a Fry Scholarship on or after August 1, 2018 and/or are currently receiving that scholarship; or 4) were honorably discharged after 60 days for a service-connected disability and served at least 30 continuous days after September 11, 2001. Military personnel currently on active duty and their spouses may qualify for Post-9/11 GI Bill benefits but are not eligible for the Yellow Ribbon Program. This program is available to veterans who qualify for those benefits at the 100% rate, the children and spouses of those veterans to whom they wish to transfer their benefits, and the children of active-duty personnel who qualify for benefits at the 100% rate to whom they wish to transfer those benefits. Applicants must be working on or planning to work on an undergraduate or graduate degree at a private or out-of-state public institution that charges tuition in excess of the $25,162.14 cap imposed by the Post-9/11 GI Bill and that has agreed with the Department of Veterans Affairs (VA) to participate in this program.

Financial data Colleges and universities that charge more than $25,162.14 per academic year in tuition and fees may agree to waive tuition (up to 50%) for qualifying veterans and dependents. The amount that the college or university waives is matched by VA.

Duration Most participants receive up to 36 months of entitlement under this program. Benefits are payable for up to 15 years following release from active duty.

Number awarded Varies each year.

Deadline Deadline not specified.

Fellowships

- *Veterans*
- *Military Personnel*
- *Family Members*

Described here are 338 programs available to veterans, military personnel, and their family members who are or will be pursuing graduate or postdoctoral study or research in the United States. All of this is "free" money. Not one dollar will need to be repaid (provided, of course, that recipients meet all program requirements). Of these listings, 100 are set aside specifically for veterans, 122 for military personnel, and 116 for their family members (spouses, children, grandchildren, parents, and other relatives). If you are looking for a particular program and don't find it in this section, be sure to check the Program Title Index to see if it is covered elsewhere in the directory.

Veterans

[1093]
506TH AIRBORNE INFANTRY REGIMENT ASSOCIATION SCHOLARSHIP

506th Airborne Infantry Regiment Association
c/o Alfred May, Scholarship Committee
30 Sweetman Lane
West Milford, NJ 07480-2933
(973) 728-1458   E-mail: alfredmay@aol.com
Web: www.506infantry.org

Summary To provide financial assistance for college or graduate school to former members of the 506th Airborne Infantry Regiment and their families.
Eligibility This program is open to veterans who served with the 506th Airborne Infantry Regiment and their children, grandchildren, spouses, and siblings. Applicants must be entering or attending an undergraduate or graduate program at a college or university in the United States. They must submit a statement describing their personal achievements and career objectives. Selection is based on academic excellence, quality of the institution the applicant has chosen to attend, and financial need.
Financial data The stipend is $1,500 or $1,000.
Duration 1 year; nonrenewable.
Additional information This program includes the Currahee Scholarship Award, the Marcia and John Lally Scholarship Award, the Eugene and Marilyn Overton Scholarship Award, the SPC Edwin Roodhouse Memorial Scholarship Award, the NAVILLUS Award, and the CPT Luke Wullenwaber Memorial Scholarship Award.
Number awarded 3 at $1,500 and 3 at $1,000 each year.
Deadline April of each year.

[1094]
AAPA VETERANS CAUCUS SCHOLARSHIPS

American Academy of Physician Assistants-Veterans Caucus
Attn: Scholarship Program
P.O. Box 362
Ossining, NY 10562
(803) 328-1864   Fax: (704) 838-8494
E-mail: rmunsee@veteranscaucus.org
Web: www.veteranscaucus.org/scholarships

Summary To provide financial assistance to veterans of any of the uniformed services who are studying to become physician assistants.
Eligibility This program is open to U.S. citizens who are currently enrolled in a physician assistant program. Applicants must be honorably discharged members of 1 of the 7 uniformed services of the United States. Along with their application, they must submit a personal statement about what led them to attend PA school; their background, present, and future intentions; and why they deserve to receive a scholarship. Selection is based on military honors and awards received, civic and college honors and awards received, professional memberships and activities, potential for future achievement, and GPA.
Financial data The stipend is $2,000.
Duration 1 year.
Additional information This program includes the following named scholarships: the Albert T. Kissel Memorial Scholarship, the Donna Jones Moritsugu Memorial Scholarship, the SSGT Craig Ivory Memorial Scholarships, the Lt. Col. David Gwinn Memorial Scholarship, the Jesse Edwards Memorial Scholarship, and the Vicki Lianne Moritsugu Memorial Scholarship.
Number awarded Varies each year.
Deadline February of each year.

[1095]
AFCEA WAR VETERAN TEACHER CERTIFICATION PROGRAM

Armed Forces Communications and Electronics Association
Attn: AFCEA Educational Foundation
4114 Legato Road, Suite 1000
Fairfax, VA 22033-3342
(703) 631-6147   Toll Free: (800) 336-4583, ext. 6147
Fax: (703) 631-4693   E-mail: edfoundation@afcea.org
Web: www.afcea.org

Summary To provide financial assistance to veterans and military personnel who served in designated Overseas Contingency Operations and are interested in preparing for a career as a STEM teacher.
Eligibility This program is open to active-duty and honorably discharged U.S. military members (including Reservists and National Guard personnel) who served in Operation Enduring Freedom, Operation Iraqi Freedom, Operation New Dawn, Operation Inherent Resolve, or Operation Freedom's Sentinel. Applicants must have earned a bachelor's degree in a field of science and be working on a credential or license for the purpose of teaching STEM in a U.S. K-12 school. They must have a GPA of 3.0 or higher. Their expected date of graduation or certification cannot be in the same year as the award of the scholarship. Selection is based on merit.
Financial data The stipend is $2,500.
Duration 1 year.
Number awarded 1 or more each year.
Deadline November of each year.

[1096]
AHIMA VETERANS SCHOLARSHIP

American Health Information Management Association
Attn: AHIMA Foundation
233 North Michigan Avenue, 21st Floor
Chicago, IL 60601-5809
(312) 233-1131   Fax: (312) 233-1537
E-mail: info@ahimafoundation.org
Web: www.ahimafoundation.org

Summary To provide financial assistance to veterans and spouses of veterans and active-duty service personnel who are interested in working on an undergraduate or graduate degree in health information management (HIM) or health information technology (HIT).
Eligibility This program is open to 1) veterans of the armed forces, including Army, Navy, Air Force, Marine Corps, Coast Guard, Reserves, and National Guard; and 2) spouses and surviving spouses of servicemembers, including active-duty military, retirees, veterans, and wounded warriors. Applicants must be working full time on a degree in HIM or HIT at the

associate, bachelor's, post-baccalaureate, master's, or doctoral level. They must have at least 6 credit hours remaining after the date of the award. Along with their application, they must submit an essay of 250 to 400 words on their educational and career ambitions, record of military service, record of personal achievement, community service, desire to serve others and make a positive community impact, and leadership potential. In the selection process, preference is given to 1) physically wounded or disabled veterans; 2) surviving spouses; and 3) those who served in a combat tour of duty.
Financial data Stipends are $1,000 for associate degree students, $1,500 for bachelor's degree or post-baccalaureate certificate students, $2,000 for master's degree students, or $2,500 for doctoral degree students.
Duration 1 year.
Additional information Effective in 2018, this program includes the John Kloss Memorial Veteran Scholarship and other scholarships supported by Nuance Communications and the Walter Reed Society.
Number awarded 4 each year.
Deadline September of each year.

[1097]
AIR FORCE GRADUATE LAW PROGRAM
U.S. Air Force
Attn: HQ USAF/JAX
1500 West Perimeter Road, Suite 3330
Joint Base Andrews, MD 20762
Toll Free: (800) JAG-USAF
E-mail: airforcejagrecruiting@gmail.com
Web: www.airforce.com

Summary To provide financial assistance to first-year law students who are willing to join Air Force ROTC and serve as Air Force Judge Advocates following completion of their studies.
Eligibility This program is open to students in their first year at an ABA-approved law school that has, or is located near, an AFROTC detachment. Applicants must be in good academic standing and able to meet AFROTC entry standards (U.S. citizenship, weight and medical qualifications, and Air Force Officer Qualification Test minimum score). They must be younger than 40 years of age upon commissioning and entering active duty. Eligible students include veterans, current military personnel, and first-year law students without military experience. Selection is based on academic performance, extracurricular activities, community service, prior military record (if any), work experience, and a recommendation by a staff judge advocate following an interview.
Financial data Participants receive a stipend for 10 months of the year at $400 per month and a salary at pay grade E-5 during summer field training. No other scholarship assistance is available.
Duration 2 years.
Additional information Selectees with no prior military experience attend field training encampment during the summer prior to entering the AFROTC program as contract cadets. Upon completion of their degree, participants are commissioned as inactive second lieutenants in the Air Force Reserves. After passing legal licensing requirements, they enter active duty as first lieutenants in the U.S. Air Force Judge Advocate General's Department. The initial required active-duty service obligation is 4 years.

Number awarded Varies each year.
Deadline January of each year.

[1098]
ALASKA NATIONAL GUARD STATE TUITION REIMBURSEMENT PROGRAM
Alaska National Guard
Attn: Education Services Office
Army Guard Road, Building 49000
P.O. Box 5800
Joint Base Elmendorf-Richardson, AK 99505-5800
(907) 428-6477   Fax: (907) 428-6929
E-mail: maria.j.alvarez10.mil@mail.mil
Web: www.dmva.alaska.gov/FamilyServices/Education

Summary To provide financial assistance to current and former members of the Alaska National Guard who wish to attend a college or university in the state.
Eligibility This program is open to members of the Alaska National Guard (Air and Army) and Naval Militia who have a rating of E-1 through O-5, including warrant officers, and are attending a university program in Alaska. Eligibility extends to members who 1) have satisfactorily completed their service contract and who served honorably in federal active service or federally-funded state active service after September 11, 2001; or 2) have been separated or discharged from the Guard because of a service-connected injury, disease, or disability. First priority is given to undergraduates; if funding is available, students working on a second bachelor's degree or a master's degree may be supported. Non-prior servicemembers must complete Initial Active Duty for Training (IADT); prior servicemembers are eligible immediately.
Financial data Recipients are entitled to reimbursement equivalent to 100% of the cost of tuition and fees at the University of Alaska, to a maximum of $4,500 per fiscal year.
Duration 1 semester; may be renewed for a total of 144 semester credits.
Number awarded Varies each year.
Deadline Applications may be submitted at any time, but they must be received at least 90 days after the last official day of the class or term.

[1099]
AMVETS NATIONAL SCHOLARSHIPS FOR VETERANS
AMVETS National Headquarters
Attn: National Programs Director
4647 Forbes Boulevard
Lanham, MD 20706-3807
(301) 459-9600   Toll Free: (877) 7-AMVETS, ext. 4027
Fax: (301) 459-7924   E-mail: klathroum@amvets.org
Web: www.amvets.org/scholarships

Summary To provide financial assistance for college or graduate school to veterans.
Eligibility This program is open to veterans who are U.S. citizens. Applicants must be interested in working full or part time on an undergraduate degree, graduate degree, or certification from an accredited trade/technical school. They must have exhausted all other government aid. Selection is based on financial need, academic promise, military duty and awards, volunteer activities, community services, jobs held during the past 4 years, and an essay of 50 to 100 words on "What a Higher Education Means to Me."

Financial data The stipend is $1,000 per year.
Duration Up to 4 years.
Number awarded 3 each year.
Deadline April of each year.

[1100]
ANNE GANNETT VETERANS AWARD

National Federation of Music Clubs
1646 West Smith Valley Road
Greenwood, IN 46142
(317) 882-4003 Fax: (317) 882-4019
E-mail: info@nfmc-music.org
Web: www.nfmc-music.org

Summary To provide financial assistance for undergraduate education to music students whose careers have been delayed or interrupted as a result of their service in the U.S. armed forces.
Eligibility This program is open to veterans who are former music students but interrupted their education to serve in the U.S. Armed Forces and wish to resume music undergraduate or graduate study in pursuit of a career in music. Applicants must be U.S. citizens, but membership in the National Federation of Music Clubs (NFMC) is not required. Along with their application, they must submit a 30-minute recording of a musical performance or audition. Selection is based on worthiness, character, background, musical talent, potential ability, and financial need.
Financial data The stipend is $2,000.
Duration 1 year.
Additional information The application fee is $20.
Number awarded 1 each odd-numbered year.
Deadline April of each odd-numbered year.

[1101]
APPLICATIONS INTERNATIONAL CORPORATION IMPACT SCHOLARSHIPS

American Society of Safety Professionals
Attn: ASSP Foundation
Scholarship Award Program
520 North Northwest Highway
Park Ridge, IL 60068-2538
(847) 699-2929 Fax: (847) 296-3769
E-mail: asspfoundation@assp.org
Web: foundation.assp.org/scholarships-and-grants

Summary To provide financial assistance to students working on a degree related to occupational safety, especially those who have served in the military.
Eligibility This program is open to students, including international students, who are working full or part time on an undergraduate or graduate degree in occupational safety, health, environment, or a closely-related field. Priority is given to students who have served in the military. Associate degree students must have completed at least 24 semester hours and bachelor's degree students at least 60 semester hours. Membership in the American Society of Safety Professionals (ASSP) is not required, but members receive priority. Applicants must have a GPA of 3.0 or higher as an undergraduate or 3.5 or higher as a graduate student. Along with their application, they must submit 5 short essays of up to 500 words each on the following topics: 1) what drew them to the field of safety and how their education has affected their views of the field; 2) their goals and plans for reaching those; 3) their leadership and volunteer positions within the safety community; 4) the greatest takeaway from their current year in school; and 5) what makes them stand out as an applicant. Selection is based on academic performance, leadership activity in ASSP and the broader safety community, motivations for entering the field, and letters of recommendation.
Financial data The stipend is $15,000 or $10,000 per year.
Duration 1 year; recipients may reapply.
Additional information This program is sponsored by Applications International Corporation.
Number awarded 5 each year: 1 at $15,000 and 4 at $10,000.
Deadline November of each year.

[1102]
ARMY AVIATION ASSOCIATION OF AMERICA SCHOLARSHIPS

Army Aviation Association of America Scholarship Foundation
Attn: AAAA Scholarship Foundation
593 Main Street
Monroe, CT 06468-2806
(203) 268-2450 Fax: (203) 268-5870
E-mail: scholarship@quad-a.org
Web: www.quad-a.org/Scholarship/Scholarship/about.aspx

Summary To provide financial aid for undergraduate or graduate study to members of the Army Aviation Association of America (AAAA) and their relatives.
Eligibility This program is open to current AAAA members and the spouses, children, grandchildren, and unmarried siblings of current or deceased members. Applicants must be enrolled or accepted for enrollment as an undergraduate or graduate student at an accredited college or university. They must include a 300-word essay on their life experiences, work history, and aspirations. Some scholarships are specifically reserved for enlisted, warrant officer, company grade, and Department of the Army civilian members. Selection is based on academic merit and personal achievement.
Financial data Stipends range from $1,000 to $5,000 per year.
Duration Scholarships may be for 1 year, 2 years, or 4 years.
Number awarded Varies each year; recently, $516,000 in scholarships was awarded to 304 students. Since the program began in 1963, the foundation has awarded more than $4 million to more than 4,100 qualified applicants.
Deadline Interested students must submit a pre-qualifying form by March of each year. The final application is due in April.

[1103]
ARMY NURSE CORPS ASSOCIATION SCHOLARSHIPS

Army Nurse Corps Association
Attn: Scholarship Program
8000 IH-10 West, Suite 600
San Antonio, TX 78230-3887
(210) 650-3534 Toll Free: (888) 742-9910
E-mail: education@e-anca.org
Web: www.e-anca.org/Scholarships

Summary To provide financial assistance to students who have a connection to the Army and are interested in working on an undergraduate or graduate degree in nursing.
Eligibility This program is open to U.S. citizens attending colleges or universities that have accredited programs offering undergraduate or graduate degrees in nursing. Applicants must be 1) students currently enrolled in an accredited baccalaureate or advanced nursing or nurse anesthesia program who are serving or have served (and received an honorable discharge) in any branch and at any rank of a component of the Active Army, Army National Guard, or Army Reserve; or 2) nursing or anesthesia students whose parent(s), spouse, or child(ren) are serving or have served in a component of the Active Army, Army National Guard, or Army Reserve. Along with their application, they must submit a personal statement on their professional career objectives, reasons for applying for this scholarship, financial need, special considerations, personal and academic interests, and why they are preparing for a nursing career. Students who are receiving any support from any branch of the military, including ROTC scholarships, are not eligible.
Financial data The stipend is $3,000. Funds are sent directly to the recipient's school.
Duration 1 year.
Additional information Although the sponsoring organization is made up of current, retired, and honorably discharged officers of the Army Nurse Corps, it does not have an official affiliation with the Army. Therefore, students who receive these scholarships do not incur any military service obligation.
Number awarded Varies each year.
Deadline March of each year.

[1104]
ARMY WOMEN'S FOUNDATION LEGACY SCHOLARSHIPS

Army Women's Foundation
Attn: Scholarship Committee
P.O. Box 5030
Fort Lee, VA 23801-0030
(804) 734-3078   E-mail: info@awfdn.org
Web: www.awfdn.org/scholarships/general-information

Summary To provide financial assistance for college or graduate school to women who are serving or have served in the Army and their children.
Eligibility This program is open to 1) women who have served or are serving honorably in the U.S. Army, U.S. Army Reserve, or Army National Guard; and 2) children of those women. Applicants must be 1) high school graduates or GED recipients enrolled at a community college or technical certificate program who have a GPA of 2.5 or higher; 2) sophomores or higher at an accredited college or university who have a GPA of 3.0 or higher; or 3) students enrolled in or accepted to a graduate program who have a GPA of 3.0 or higher. Along with their application, they must submit a 2-page essay on why they should be considered for this scholarship; their future plans as related to their program of study; their community service, activities, and work experience; and how the Army has impacted their life and/or goals. Selection is based on merit, academic potential, community service, and financial need.
Financial data The stipend is $2,500 for college and graduate students or $1,000 for community college and certificate students.
Duration 1 year; recipients may reapply.
Number awarded Varies each year; recently, 21 soldiers and 10 children received these scholarships.
Deadline January of each year.

[1105]
AT&T WAR MEMORIAL SCHOLARSHIP

Arkansas Community Foundation
5 Allied Drive, Suite 51110
Building 5, llth Floor
Little Rock, AR 72201
(501) 372-1116   Toll Free: (800) 220-ARCF
Fax: (501) 372-1166   E-mail: arcf@arcf.org
Web: www.arcf.org/about/funds

Summary To provide financial assistance to veterans in Arkansas who plan to attend college in the state.
Eligibility This program is open to residents of Arkansas who are veterans of any branch of the armed services. Applicants must be attending or planning to attend an accredited 2- or 4-year college in Arkansas as an undergraduate or graduate student. Selection is based on financial need, community leadership, and potential to succeed in college.
Financial data The stipend is $2,500.
Duration 1 year.
Additional information This program is sponsored by AT&T.
Number awarded 1 each year.
Deadline March of each year.

[1106]
AVMA/AVMF SCHOLARSHIP FOR VETERANS

American Veterinary Medical Association
Attn: American Veterinary Medical Foundation
1931 North Meacham Road, Suite 100
Schaumburg, IL 60173-4360
(847) 285-6691   Toll Free: (800) 248-2862, ext. 6691
Fax: (847) 925-1329   E-mail: pgillespie@amva.org
Web: www.avmf.org/programs/avmf-scholarships

Summary To provide financial assistance to veterans currently enrolled at accredited colleges of veterinary medicine.
Eligibility This program is open to students entering the second, third, or fourth year at a veterinary school accredited by the American Veterinary Medical Association (AVMA). Applicants must be veterans of any branch of the U.S. military.
Financial data The stipend is $1,000.
Duration 1 year.
Additional information This program, sponsored by the AVMA and American Veterinary Medical Foundation (AVMF), began in 2016.
Number awarded Varies each year; recently, 4 were awarded.
Deadline May of each year.

[1107]
BRAXTON BRAGG CHAPTER AUSA SCHOLARSHIPS

Association of the United States Army-Braxton Bragg Chapter
Attn: Vice President for Scholarship Programs
P.O. Box 70036
Fort Bragg, NC 28307
(910) 396-3755   E-mail: hbraxtonbraggc@nc.rr.com
Web: www.ausa.org/chapters/braxton-bragg-chapter

Summary To provide financial assistance to members of the Braxton Bragg Chapter of the Association of the United States Army (AUSA) in North Carolina and their dependents who are interested in attending college or graduate school in any state.

Eligibility This program is open to chapter members and their families in North Carolina who are working on or planning to work on an undergraduate, graduate, or technical degree at a college or technical school in any state. Applicants must submit a 500-word essay on a topic that changes annually (recently, students were asked to explain how a person makes a difference in our world); letters of recommendation; a list of personal accomplishments; and a transcript that includes their ACT or SAT score. Selection is based on academic achievement (50%), participation in extracurricular activities at school (25%), and participation in community service activities (25%).

Financial data The stipend is $1,000.

Duration 1 year; recipients may reapply.

Additional information Membership in the Braxton Bragg Chapter is open to all Army active, National Guard, and Reserve members in North Carolina, along with Department of the Army civilians, retirees, concerned citizens, and family members.

Number awarded Varies each year; recently, 15 were awarded.

Deadline April of each year.

[1108]
CALIFORNIA NON-RESIDENT COLLEGE FEE WAIVER PROGRAM FOR MILITARY PERSONNEL AND DEPENDENTS

California Department of Veterans Affairs
Attn: Division of Veterans Services
1227 O Street, Room 101
P.O. Box 942895
Sacramento, CA 94295
(916) 653-2573   Toll Free: (800) 952-5626
Fax: (916) 653-2563   TDD: (800) 324-5966
Web: www.calvet.ca.gov

Summary To waive non-resident fees at public institutions in California for undergraduate or graduate students from other states who are active-duty military personnel, recently-discharged veterans, or dependents of active-duty military personnel.

Eligibility This program is open to residents of states outside California who are 1) veterans of the U.S. armed forces who spent more than 1 year on active duty in California immediately prior to being discharged; 2) members of the U.S. armed forces stationed in California on active duty; or 3) the natural or adopted child, stepchild, or spouse of a member of the U.S. armed forces stationed in California on active duty. Applicants must be attending or planning to attend a community college, branch of the California State University system, or campus of the University of California as an undergraduate or graduate student.

Financial data This program waives non-resident fees of qualifying military personnel, veterans, and families who attend publicly-supported community or state colleges or universities in California.

Duration 1 year; may be renewed until completion of an undergraduate degree or for 1 additional year for military personnel working on a graduate degree; nonrenewable for graduate students who are children or spouses.

Number awarded Varies each year.

Deadline Deadline not specified.

[1109]
CAPITOL AREA CHAPTER MOAA COLLEGE SCHOLARSHIP PROGRAM

Military Officers Association of America-Capitol Area Chapter
c/o Major DeLee M. Dankenbring, Treasurer
992 Pennine Ridge Way
Grand Ledge, MI 48837-9809
(517) 614-6090
Web: www.cacmoaa.org/Scholarships.aspx

Summary To provide financial assistance for college or graduate school in any state to residents of Michigan who are disabled veterans, members of the Military Officers Association of America (MOAA) or their children or grandchildren, or children of deceased or disabled servicemembers.

Eligibility This program is open to 1) disabled military servicemembers who entered service after September 11, 2001 and whose home of record is Michigan; 2) members of the national and Capitol Area Chapter of the MOAA and their children and grandchildren; and 3) children of servicemembers who entered the armed forces from Michigan and died or were disabled in the line of duty. Applicants must be enrolled or planning to enroll in a program of college or university study, job training, or graduate school. They must have a GPA of 2.0 or higher. Along with their application they must submit transcripts (that include SAT/ACT scores for high school seniors), a list of honors and awards that includes any ROTC or military training, a 200-word essay on their career goals, and a brief explanation of their financial need.

Financial data The stipend ranges from $1,000 to $1,250 per year.

Duration 1 year; recipients may reapply.

Number awarded Varies each year.

Deadline March of each year.

[1110]
CAPTAIN FREDERICK C. BRACE III MEMORIAL SCHOLARSHIP

American Academy of Physician Assistants-Veterans Caucus
Attn: Scholarship Program
P.O. Box 362
Ossining, NY 10562
(803) 328-1864   Fax: (704) 838-8494
E-mail: rmunsee@veteranscaucus.org
Web: www.veteranscaucus.org/scholarships

Summary To provide financial assistance to Air Force veterans and their dependents who are studying to become physician assistants.
Eligibility This program is open to U.S. citizens who are currently enrolled in a physician assistant program. Applicants must be honorably discharged members of the United States Air Force or the dependent of an Air Force veteran. Along with their application, they must submit a personal statement about what led them to attend PA school; their background, present, and future intentions; and why they deserve to receive a scholarship. Selection is based on military honors and awards received, civic and college honors and awards received, professional memberships and activities, potential for future achievement, and GPA.
Financial data The stipend is $2,000.
Duration 1 year.
Number awarded 1 each year.
Deadline February of each year.

[1111]
CAPTAIN MIKI IWATA MEMORIAL SCHOLARSHIP FOR ADVANCED PRACTICE

Florida Navy Nurse Corps Association
c/o Margaret Holder, Scholarship Committee
1033 Inverness Drive
St. Augustine, FL 32092
E-mail: maholder@me.com
Web: www.nnca.org/join-nnca-2/local-chapters/fnnca

Summary To provide financial assistance to advanced practice nursing students in Florida, especially those with ties to the military.
Eligibility This program is open to full- and part-time advanced practice nursing students in Florida. Applicants must have completed at least 1 clinical nursing course and have a current GPA of 3.0 or higher. Along with their application, they must submit an essay, up to 500 words in length, on the reasons they are qualified for the scholarship, how it will benefit them, career goals, and potential for contribution to the profession. Preference is given in the following order to current active-duty and Reserve service members, veterans of military service, family members of current or former military service personnel, civil service employees, and residents of Florida. Financial need is considered in the selection process.
Financial data The stipend is $1,500. Funds are paid directly to the student.
Duration 1 year.
Number awarded 1 each year.
Deadline October of each year.

[1112]
CAPTAIN SEAN P. GRIMES PHYSICIAN ASSISTANT EDUCATIONAL SCHOLARSHIP AWARD

Society of Army Physician Assistants
Attn: Scholarship Committee
P.O. Box 623
Monmouth, IL 61462
(309) 734-5446   Fax: (309) 734-4489
E-mail: orpotter@aol.com
Web: www.sapa.org/scholarships

Summary To provide financial assistance to current and former Army personnel interested in attending a college or university to become a physician assistant.
Eligibility This program is open to Army personnel who are currently on active duty, in the Reserves or National Guard, or veterans with any MOS and in pay grades E-5 through O-4. Applicants must be interested in attending an accredited college or university in order to either 1) gain initial training as a physician assistant; or 2) if already a physician assistant, work on a bachelor's, master's, or doctoral degree. They must have a GPA of 2.5 or higher and be able to demonstrate financial need. Selection is based on academic record, community and professional activities, future goals as a physician assistant, and financial need.
Financial data The stipend is $6,000.
Duration 1 year.
Additional information This program began in 2006.
Number awarded 1 each year.
Deadline January of each year.

[1113]
CHAPLAIN SAMUEL GROVER POWELL SCHOLARSHIP

United Methodist Higher Education Foundation
Attn: Scholarships Administrator
60 Music Square East, Suite 350
P.O. Box 340005
Nashville, TN 37203-0005
(615) 649-3990   Toll Free: (800) 811-8110
Fax: (615) 649-3980
E-mail: umhefscholarships@gbhem.org
Web: www.umhef.org

Summary To provide funding to students interested in preparing for a career as a military chaplain.
Eligibility This program is open to middlers and seniors at accredited theological seminaries who are either involved in the chaplain candidate (seminarian) program or serving in a military Reserve component after having completed an active-duty tour in 1 of the armed forces. Preference is given to students in their senior year who plan to serve in the U.S. Air Force. However, students preparing for chaplaincy in any branch of the military are considered. Applicants must submit a letter that includes a brief personal history and a statement about their decision to choose military chaplaincy as a career, a recent photograph, undergraduate and graduate transcripts, a financial statement, and a report on their ministry in the chaplain candidate (seminarian) program.
Financial data The stipend recently was $2,650. Funds must be used to pay for tuition. Checks are mailed to the recipient's school.
Duration 1 year; recipients may reapply for 1 additional year (but new applicants are given priority each year).
Additional information This program began in 1980. Recipients are expected to serve in the U.S. Military Chaplaincy upon completion of seminary and ordination. If this does not happen (due to factors within the recipient's control), the recipient may be asked to repay the scholarship.
Number awarded 1 or more each year.
Deadline June of each year.

[1114]
COL CARL F. BASWELL COMBAT WOUNDED ENGINEER SCHOLARSHIP

Army Engineer Association
Attn: Director Washington DC Operations
P.O. Box 30260
Alexandria, VA 22310-8260
(703) 428-7084　　　　　　　　Fax: (703) 428-6043
E-mail: xd@armyengineer.com
Web: www.armyengineer.com/scholarships

Summary To provide financial assistance for college to U.S. Army Engineers who were wounded in combat in Iraq or Afghanistan.

Eligibility This program is open to U.S. Army Engineers who were wounded in combat and received a Purple Heart during Operation Iraqi Freedom or Operation Enduring Freedom. Applicants must be working on or planning to work on an associate, bachelor's, or master's degree at an accredited college or university. Along with their application, they must submit a 1-page essay outlining why they should be selected for an award, including a paragraph on their financial need and their evaluation of their potential for success.

Financial data The stipend is $2,500.

Duration 1 year.

Additional information This program began in 2010.

Number awarded 1 each year.

Deadline June of each year.

[1115]
CONNECTICUT TUITION WAIVER FOR VETERANS

Connecticut State Universities and Colleges
61 Woodland Street
Hartford, CT 06105
(860) 723-0013　　　　　　　　E-mail: fitzgeralde@ct.edu
Web: www.ct.edu/admission/veterans

Summary To provide financial assistance for college to certain Connecticut veterans and military personnel and their dependents.

Eligibility This program is open to 1) honorably-discharged Connecticut veterans who served at least 90 days during specified periods of wartime; 2) active members of the Connecticut Army or Air National Guard; 3) Connecticut residents who are a dependent child or surviving spouse of a member of the armed forces killed in action on or after September 11, 2001 who was also a Connecticut resident; and 4) Connecticut residents who are a dependent child or surviving spouse of a person officially declared missing in action or a prisoner of war while serving in the armed forces after January 1, 1960. Applicants must be attending or planning to attend a public college or university in the state.

Financial data The program provides a waiver of 100% of tuition for general fund courses at the 4 campuses of Connecticut State University, 50% of tuition for extension and summer courses at campuses of Connecticut State University, 100% of tuition at the 12 Connecticut community colleges, and 50% of fees at Charter Oak State College.

Duration Up to 4 years.

Additional information This is an entitlement program; applications are available at the respective college financial aid offices.

Number awarded Varies each year.

Deadline Deadline not specified.

[1116]
COUNCIL OF COLLEGE AND MILITARY EDUCATORS VETERANS SCHOLARSHIPS

Council of College and Military Educators
c/o Jim Yeonopolus, Scholarship Committee Chair
Central Texas College
P.O. Box 1800
Killeen, TX 76540-1800
(254) 526-1781　　　　　　　　Fax: (254) 526-1750
E-mail: jim.yeonopolus@ctcd.edu
Web: www.ccmeonline.org/scholarships

Summary To provide financial assistance to veterans of the armed services who are interested in working on an undergraduate or master's degree.

Eligibility This program is open to veterans of the uniformed services who are currently enrolled full time at an accredited institution that is a member of the Council of College and Military Educators (CCME) and working on an associate, bachelor's, or master's degree. Undergraduates must have a GPA of 2.5 or higher and graduate students must have a GPA of 3.0 or higher. Along with their application, they must submit an essay of 400 to 750 words on how they would describe military leadership. Financial need is not considered in the selection process.

Financial data The stipend is $1,000. Funds are paid directly to the student.

Duration 1 year; nonrenewable.

Number awarded 5 each year.

Deadline October of each year.

[1117]
CSM LEONARD MAGLIONE MEMORIAL SCHOLARSHIPS

Association of the United States Army-Rhode Island
　Chapter
c/o LTC Robert A. Galvanin, President
31 Canoe River Drive
Mansfield, MA 02048
(508) 339-5301　　　　　　　　E-mail: bpje5310@verizon.net
Web: www.riroa.org/ausari/scholarship.htm

Summary To provide financial assistance to members of the Rhode Island Chapter of the Association of the United States Army (AUSA) and their families who are interested in attending college or graduate school in any state.

Eligibility This program is open to members of the AUSA Rhode Island Chapter and their family members (spouses, children, and grandchildren). Applicants must be high school seniors or graduates accepted at an accredited college, university, or vocational/technical school in any state or current undergraduate or graduate students. Along with their application, they must submit a 250-word essay on why they feel their achievements should qualify them for this award. Selection is based on academic and individual achievements; financial need is not considered. Special consideration is given to students or graduates of LaSalle Academy in Providence (the alma mater of this program's namesake), especially those preparing for a career in the arts or engineering or enrolled or planning to enroll in Army ROTC.

Financial data The stipend is $1,000.

Duration 1 year.

Additional information Membership in the AUSA is open to everyone who supports a strong national defense, with

special concern for the Army. That includes Regular Army, National Guard, Army Reserve, government civilians, retired soldiers, Wounded Warriors, veterans, concerned citizens and family members.
Number awarded Several each year.
Deadline April of each year.

[1118]
DARLENE HOOLEY SCHOLARSHIP FOR OREGON VETERANS

Oregon Community Foundation
Attn: Administrative Assistant for Scholarships
1221 S.W. Yamhill Street, Suite 100
Portland, OR 97205-2108
(503) 227-6846   Fax: (503) 274-7771
E-mail: opearsall@oregoncf.org
Web: www.oregoncf.org/grants-scholarships/scholarships

Summary To provide financial assistance to veterans in Oregon who served recently and are interested in working on an undergraduate or graduate degree at a college in the state.
Eligibility This program is open to Oregon National Guard members and Reservists who served after September 11, 2001; there is no minimum length of service requirement. Applicants must be enrolled or planning to enroll either full or part time as an undergraduate or graduate student at a college or university in Oregon. Along with their application, they must submit 150-word essays on the following topics: 1) their specific educational plans and career goals and what inspires them to achieve those; 2) a significant change or experience that has occurred in their life; 3) a personal accomplishment and the strengths and skills they used to achieve it; 4) what they have done for their family or community that they care about the most and why; and 5) their military service and the impact it had on their life.
Financial data Stipends of scholarships offered by this foundation range from $200 to $10,000 and average approximately $2,700.
Duration 1 year; may be renewed up to 5 additional years.
Number awarded Varies each year.
Deadline March of each year.

[1119]
DAVID AND REBECCA BARTEL VETERAN'S SCHOLARSHIP

Society of Exploration Geophysicists
Attn: SEG Foundation
8801 South Yale, Suite 500
P.O. Box 702740
Tulsa, OK 74170-2740
(918) 497-5500   Fax: (918) 497-5557
E-mail: scholarships@seg.org
Web: www.seg.org/scholarships

Summary To provide financial assistance to veterans who are interested in working on an undergraduate or graduate degree in applied geophysics or a related field.
Eligibility This program is open to retired or honorably discharged veterans of the armed forces (Army, Marine Corps, Navy, or Air Force), the National Guard (Army or Air), the U.S. Coast Guard, or the U.S. Merchant Marine. Preference is given to veterans who are medically disabled. Applicants must intend to work on an undergraduate or graduate degree directed toward a career in applied geophysics or a closely-related field (e.g., earth or environmental sciences, geology, geoscience, or physics). Along with their application, they must submit a 250-word essay on their interest in geophysics. Financial need is not considered in the selection process.
Financial data Stipends provided by this sponsor range from $500 to $10,000; recently, undergraduate stipends averaged more than $3,100 per year and graduate stipends averaged more than $4,500 per year.
Duration 1 academic year; may be renewable, based on scholastic standing, availability of funds, and continuance of a course of study leading to a career in applied geophysics.
Number awarded 1 each year.
Deadline February of each year.

[1120]
DONALDSON D. FRIZZELL MEMORIAL SCHOLARSHIPS

First Command Educational Foundation
Attn: Scholarship Programs Manager
1 FirstComm Plaza
Fort Worth, TX 76109-4999
(817) 569-2940   Toll Free: (877) 872-8289
Fax: (817) 569-2970   E-mail: scholarships@fcef.com
Web: www.fcef.com/scholarships

Summary To provide financial assistance to students, especially those with ties to the military, entering or attending college or graduate school.
Eligibility This program is open to 1) members of a U.S. uniformed service (active, Guard, Reserve, retired, or non-retired veteran) and their spouses and dependents; 2) clients of First Command Financial Services and their family members; 3) dependent family members of First Command Advisors or field office staff members; or 4) non-contractual ROTC students. Applicants may be traditional students (high school seniors and students already enrolled at a college, university, or accredited trade school) or nontraditional students (those defined by their institution as nontraditional and adult students planning to return to a college, university, or accredited trade school). They must have a GPA of 3.0 or higher and be working on a trade school certification or associate, undergraduate, or graduate degree. Applicants must submit 1-page essays on 1) their active involvement in community service programs; 2) the impact of financial literacy on their future; and 3) why they need this scholarship. Selection is based primarily on the essays, academic merit, and financial need.
Financial data The stipend is $3,000. Funds are disbursed directly to the recipient's college, university, or trade school.
Duration 1 year.
Additional information The sponsoring organization was formerly known as the USPA & IRA Educational Foundation, founded in 1983 to provide scholarships to the children of active, retired, or deceased military personnel.
Number awarded Varies each year; recently, 10 were awarded.
Deadline The online application process begins in February of each year and continues until April or until 2,500 applications have been received.

FELLOWSHIPS: VETERANS

[1121]
DR. NANCY M. SCHONHER SCHOLARSHIP
Marines' Memorial Association
c/o Marines Memorial Club and Hotel
609 Sutter Street
San Francisco, CA 94102
(415) 673-6672, ext. 293   Toll Free: (800) 5-MARINE
Fax: (415) 441-3649
E-mail: scholarship@marineclub.com
Web: www.marinesmemorial.org

Summary To provide financial assistance to women who have a tie to the military and are interested in working on a degree in a health-related field.
Eligibility This program is open to women who 1) are active-duty service members or reservists in the U.S. armed forces; 2) have separated honorably from the U.S. armed forces within the past 6 years; 3) are a current or former corpsman or medic in any branch of the U.S. armed forces; or 4) are the child or grandchild of an active member of the Marines' Memorial Association. Applicants must be planning to enroll in 1) an advanced medical program with the goal of becoming a nurse, nurse practitioner, physician's assistant, or medical doctor (M.D. or O.D.) from an accredited American college or university; or 2) an accredited paramedic program (must have completed the EMT Basic training program, have taken the National Registry EMT Examination, hold an EMT Certificate, and have at least 6 months' work experience). Membership in the sponsoring organization is not required. Along with their application, they must submit an essay of up to 500 words on why they chose their specific path of study, what they hope to accomplish after graduation with their degree, and how their efforts will benefit others in their community. Selection is based on the essay, academic merit, references, and financial need. Preference is given to Navy Corpsmen.
Financial data The stipend is $5,000.
Duration 1 year.
Additional information Membership in the association is open to veterans of the Marines, Army, Navy, Air Force, or Coast Guard and to personnel currently serving in a branch of the armed forces. This program began in 2017.
Number awarded 1 each year.
Deadline April of each year.

[1122]
EDUCATION FOUNDATION FOR THE COLORADO NATIONAL GUARD GRANTS
National Guard Association of Colorado
Attn: Education Foundation, Inc.
P.O. Box 440889
Aurora, CO 80044-0889
(303) 909-6369   Fax: (720) 535-5925
E-mail: BernieRogoff@comcast.net
Web: www.efcong.org

Summary To provide financial assistance to members of the Colorado National Guard and their families who are interested in attending college or graduate school in any state.
Eligibility This program is open to current and retired members of the Colorado National Guard and their dependent unmarried children and spouses. Applicants must be enrolled or planning to enroll full or part time at a college, university, trade school, business school, or graduate school in any state. Along with their application, they must submit an essay, up to 2 pages in length, on their desire to continue their education, what motivates them, their financial need, their commitment to academic excellence, and their current situation. Selection is based on academic achievement, community involvement, and financial need.
Financial data Stipends are generally at least $1,000 per year.
Duration 1 year; may be renewed.
Number awarded Normally, 15 to 25 of these grants are awarded each semester.
Deadline July of each year for fall semester; January of each year for spring semester.

[1123]
ELARY GROMOFF, JR. MILITARY VETERAN SCHOLARSHIP
The Aleut Corporation
Attn: Aleut Foundation
703 West Tudor Road, Suite 102
Anchorage, AK 99503-6650
(907) 646-1929   Toll Free: (800) 232-4882
Fax: (907) 646-1949   E-mail: taf@thealeutfoundation.org
Web: www.thealeutfoundation.org

Summary To provide financial assistance to Native Alaskans who are veterans and shareholders of The Aleut Corporation or their descendants working on a degree in any field at a school in any state.
Eligibility This program is open to Native Alaskans who are original enrollees or descendants of original enrollees of The Aleut Corporation (TAC). Applicants must have completed at least 1 year of a bachelor's, 2- or 4-year vocational, master's, or Ph.D. degree in any field at a school in any state. They must have served in the military, be enrolled full time and have a GPA of 3.0 or higher. Along with their application, they must include a letter of intent, up to 500 words in length, that describes their educational goals and objectives and their expected graduation date.
Financial data A stipend is awarded (amount not specified).
Duration 1 year.
Additional information The Aleut Corporation is 1 of 13 Alaska Native Regional Corporations created under the Alaska Native Claims Settlement Act of 1971.
Number awarded 1 each year.
Deadline June of each year.

[1124]
ENLISTED ASSOCIATION OF THE NATIONAL GUARD OF IOWA AUXILIARY SCHOLARSHIP PROGRAM
Enlisted Association of the National Guard of Iowa
  Auxiliary
c/o Lori Waters, President
1005 Second Street S.W.
Altoona, IA 50009
(515) 490-3202   E-mail: bullriderfan@msn.com
Web: www.eangi.org/auxiliary-scholarship

Summary To provide financial assistance to members of the Enlisted Association of the National Guard of Iowa (EANIG) Auxiliary and their families who are interested in attending college in any state.

Eligibility This program is open to EANGI Auxiliary members and their spouses, dependents, and grandchildren. Applicants must be enrolled, accepted for enrollment, or in the process of applying to a college or vocational/technical school as a full-time undergraduate or graduate student. Along with their application, they must submit a letter describing specific fats about their desire to continue their education and why they need financial assistance. Selection is based on character, leadership, and need.
Financial data The stipend is $1,000.
Duration 1 year; recipients may reapply.
Number awarded 2 each year.
Deadline February of each year.

[1125]
EPG VETERANS SCHOLARSHIPS
Energy Polymer Group
c/o David Nuss, Scholarship Committee Member
Akron Rubber Development Laboratory, Inc.
2887 Gilchrist Road
Akron, OH 44305
(330) 794-6600   Toll Free: (866) 778-ARDL
Fax: (330_ 794-6610   E-mail: david_nuss@ardl.com
Web: www.energypolymergroup.org

Summary To provide financial assistance to veterans in fields of interest to the Energy Polymer Group (EPG).
Eligibility This program is open to veterans who are working full time on a bachelor's or master's degree at an accredited 4-year college or university. Both members and non-members of the EPG are eligible. Selection is based on GPA, participation in activities, awards and honors received, work experience, and a statement of career objectives.
Financial data The stipend is $3,000 per year.
Duration 1 year; recipients may reapply.
Number awarded Varies each year; recently, 3 were awarded.
Deadline February of each year.

[1126]
FLEET RESERVE ASSOCIATION GRADUATE SCHOLARSHIPS
Fleet Reserve Association
Attn: FRA Education Foundation
125 North West Street
Alexandria, VA 22314-2754
(703) 683-1400   Toll Free: (800) FRA-1924
Fax: (703) 549-6610   E-mail: scholars@fra.org
Web: www.fra.org

Summary To provide financial assistance for graduate school to members of the Fleet Reserve Association (FRA) and their families.
Eligibility This program is open to members of the FRA and the dependent children, grandchildren, and spouses of living or deceased members. Applicants must be enrolled as full-time graduate students. Along with their application, they must submit an essay on why they want to go to college and what they intend to accomplish with their degree. Selection is based on academic record, financial need, extracurricular activities, leadership skills, and participation in community activities. U.S. citizenship is required.
Financial data The stipend is $5,000 per year.
Duration 1 year; may be renewed.
Additional information Membership in the FRA is open to current and former enlisted members of the Navy, Marine Corps, and Coast Guard. This program, established in 2001, includes the Glenn F. Glezen Scholarship, the Joseph R. Baranski Scholarship, and the Robert W. Nolan Scholarship.
Number awarded At least 3 each year.
Deadline April of each year.

[1127]
FLEET RESERVE ASSOCIATION MEMBER SCHOLARSHIPS
Fleet Reserve Association
Attn: FRA Education Foundation
125 North West Street
Alexandria, VA 22314-2754
(703) 683-1400   Toll Free: (800) FRA-1924
Fax: (703) 549-6610   E-mail: scholars@fra.org
Web: www.fra.org

Summary To provide financial assistance for college or graduate school to members of the Fleet Reserve Association (FRA) and their families.
Eligibility This program is open to members of the FRA and the children, grandchildren, great-grandchildren, and spouses of living or deceased members. Applicants must be enrolled or planning to enroll as full-time undergraduate or graduate students. Along with their application, they must submit transcripts that include (for high school students and college freshmen) SAT and/or ACT scores; a list of school and community activities; at least 2 letters of recommendation; and an essay on why they want to go to college and what they intend to accomplish with their degree. Selection is based on academic record, financial need, extracurricular activities, leadership skills, and participation in community activities. U.S. citizenship is required.
Financial data Stipends range from $1,000 to $5,000.
Duration 1 year; may be renewed.
Additional information Membership in the FRA is open to current and former enlisted members of the Navy, Marine Corps, and Coast Guard. This program includes awards designated as the MCPO Ken E. Blair Scholarship, the Robert M. Treadwell Annual Scholarship, the Donald Bruce Pringle Family Scholarship, the Tom and Karen Snee Scholarship, the Angelo and Mildred Nunez Scholarships, the Express Scripts Scholarships, the US Family Health Scholarship, and the Navy Department Branch 181 Scholarship.
Number awarded Varies each year; recently, 10 were awarded: 6 at $5,000, 2 at $4,000, 1 at $3,000, and 1 at $2,000.
Deadline April of each year.

[1128]
FLEET RESERVE ASSOCIATION NON-MEMBER SCHOLARSHIPS
Fleet Reserve Association
Attn: FRA Education Foundation
125 North West Street
Alexandria, VA 22314-2754
(703) 683-1400   Toll Free: (800) FRA-1924
Fax: (703) 549-6610   E-mail: scholars@fra.org
Web: www.fra.org

Summary To provide financial assistance for college or graduate school to sea service personnel and their families.
Eligibility This program is open to 1) active-duty, Reserve, honorably-discharged veterans, and retired members of the U.S. Navy, Marine Corps, and Coast Guard; and 2) their spouses, children, grandchildren, and great-grandchildren. Applicants must be enrolled or planning to enroll as full-time undergraduate or graduate students, but neither they nor their family member are required to be members of the sponsoring organization. Along with their application, they must submit transcripts that include (for high school students and college freshmen) SAT and/or ACT scores; a list of school and community activities; at least 2 letters of recommendation; and an essay on why they want to go to college and what they intend to accomplish with their degree. Selection is based on academic record, financial need, extracurricular activities, leadership skills, and participation in community activities. U.S. citizenship is required.
Financial data Stipends range up to $5,000 per year.
Duration 1 year; may be renewed.
Additional information This program includes the GEICO Scholarship and the Rosemary Posekany Memorial Scholarship.
Number awarded Varies each year; recently, 6 were awarded: 5 at $5,000 and 1 at $1,000.
Deadline April of each year.

[1129]
FLORIDA NAVY NURSE CORPS ASSOCIATION SCHOLARSHIPS
Florida Navy Nurse Corps Association
c/o Margaret Holder, Scholarship Committee
1033 Inverness Drive
St. Augustine, FL 32092
E-mail: maholder@me.com
Web: www.nnca.org/join-nnca-2/local-chapters/fnnca

Summary To provide financial assistance to undergraduate and graduate nursing students, especially residents of Florida with ties to the military.
Eligibility This program is open to students, including registered nursing continuing their studies, who are working on a baccalaureate or graduate degree in nursing. Applicants must have completed at least 1 clinical nursing course and have a GPA of 3.0 or higher. They may be full- or part-time students. Along with their application, they must submit an essay, up to 500 words in length, on the reasons they are qualified for the scholarship, how it will benefit them, career goals, and potential for contribution to the profession. Preference is given in order to current active-duty and Reserve service members, veterans of military service, family members of current or former military service personnel, civil service employees, and residents of Florida. Financial need is considered in the selection process.
Financial data The stipend is $1,500. Funds are paid directly to the student.
Duration 1 year.
Number awarded 2 each year.
Deadline October of each year.

[1130]
FORT WORTH POST SAME SCHOLARSHIP
Society of American Military Engineers-Fort Worth Post
c/o J.B. West, Scholarship Chair
Halff Associates
4000 Fossil Creek Boulevard
Fort Worth, TX 76137
(817) 205-7981   E-mail: warwagon16@gmail.com
Web: www.samefortworth.org/scholarship-application

Summary To provide financial assistance to engineering, architecture, and science college and graduate students, especially those at colleges and universities in Texas.
Eligibility This program is open to U.S. citizens who are currently enrolled in college or graduate school; preference is given to students at colleges and universities in Texas. Applicants must be working full time on a degree in an engineering, architecture, or science-related field. Along with their application, they must submit a 500-word essay that covers why they are preparing for a career in engineering, architecture, or a related science, their understanding of the Society of American Military Engineers (SAME) and how involvement with the organization will help them to achieve their academic and professional aspirations and objectives, and what distinguishes them from other candidates. Selection is based on academic achievement, character, personal merit, and commitment to the field of engineering. Special consideration is given to veterans and students enrolled in ROTC.
Financial data The stipend for the highest-ranked student enrolled in engineering and ROTC is $2,000. Other stipend amounts vary.
Duration 1 year.
Number awarded Varies each year.
Deadline April of each year.

[1131]
GEORGE WASHINGTON CHAPTER AUSA SCHOLARSHIPS
Association of the United States Army-George Washington Chapter
c/o Col (Ret.) William G. Yarborough, Jr., Scholarship Committee
P.O. Box 828
McLean, VA 22101-0828
(703) 748-1717   E-mail: wgyarc@aol.com
Web: www.ausa.org/chapters/george-washington-chapter

Summary To provide financial assistance for undergraduate or graduate study at a school in any state to members of the George Washington Chapter of the Association of the United States Army (AUSA) and their families.
Eligibility This program is open to active members of the AUSA George Washington Chapter and the spouses, children, and grandchildren of active members. Applicants must have a GPA of 2.5 or higher and be working on an undergraduate or graduate degree at a college or university in any state. Along with their application, they must submit a letter describing any family circumstances they believe are relevant and explaining why they deserve the scholarship. Members must also submit a favorable recommendation from their supervisor. Membership in AUSA is open to Army personnel (including Reserves and National Guard) who are either active or retired, ROTC cadets, or civilian employees of the Army.
Financial data Stipends range up to $1,000.

Duration 1 year.
Additional information This program includes the following named awards: the Ed Dauksz Scholarship Award, the Major General Harry Greene STEM Scholarship Award, and the Major General Carl F. McNair Jr. Scholarship Award. The George Washington Chapter serves Washington, D.C.; the Virginia counties of Alexandria, Clarke, Fairfax, Frederick, Loudoun, and Prince William; and the Maryland counties of Calvert, Charles, Montgomery, Prince George's, and St. Mary's.
Number awarded Varies each year; recently, 45 were awarded.
Deadline April of each year.

[1132]
GOOGLE-SVA SCHOLARSHIP
Student Veterans of America
Attn: Scholarship Committee
1012 14th Street, N.W., Suite 1200
Washington, DC 20005
(202) 223-4710
E-mail: scholarships@studentveterans.org
Web: www.studentveterans.org/programs/scholarships

Summary To provide financial assistance to veterans and current military personnel who are working on a bachelor's or graduate degree in a computer-related field.
Eligibility This program is open to sophomores, juniors, seniors, and graduate students at 4-year colleges and universities who are veterans of any branch of service, including Reserves and National Guard, and were honorably discharged or are active-duty military personnel still in good standing with their branch of service. Applicants must be working full time on a degree in computer science, computer engineering, or a closely-related technical field (e.g., software engineering, electrical engineering with a heavy computer science course load, information systems, information technology, applied networking, system administration). Along with their application, they must submit essays of 300 to 500 words each on 1) what sparked their interest in computer science; 2) examples of how they have exhibited leadership; 3) a significant challenge that they believe student veterans in the field of technology face and how they see themselves as being part of the solution(s) to that challenge; and 4) the impact receiving this scholarship would have on their education. Financial need is not considered in the selection process.
Financial data The stipend is $10,000.
Duration 1 year.
Additional information This program is sponsored by Google and administered by Student Veterans of America (SVA).
Number awarded 8 each year.
Deadline November of each year.

[1133]
GROGAN MEMORIAL SCHOLARSHIP
American Academy of Physician Assistants-Veterans Caucus
Attn: Scholarship Program
P.O. Box 362
Ossining, NY 10562
(803) 328-1864   Fax: (704) 838-8494
E-mail: rmunsee@veteranscaucus.org
Web: www.veteranscaucus.org/scholarships

Summary To provide financial assistance to veterans and their dependents who are studying to become physician assistants.
Eligibility This program is open to U.S. citizens who are currently enrolled in a physician assistant program. Applicants must be honorably discharged members of any branch of the military or the dependents of those members. Along with their application, they must submit a personal statement about what led them to attend PA school; their background, present, and future intentions; and why they deserve to receive a scholarship. Selection is based on military honors and awards received, civic and college honors and awards received, professional memberships and activities, potential for future achievement, and GPA.
Financial data The stipend is $2,000.
Duration 1 year.
Number awarded 1 each year.
Deadline February of each year.

[1134]
HAZLEWOOD ACT EXEMPTIONS FOR VETERANS
Texas Veterans Commission
1700 North Congress Avenue, Suite 800
P.O. Box 12277
Austin, TX 78711-2277
(512) 463-3168   Toll Free: (800) 252-VETS
Fax: (512) 475-2395   E-mail: hazlewood@tvc.texas.gov
Web: www.tvc.texas.gov/education/hazlewood

Summary To exempt Texas veterans from payment of tuition for undergraduate or graduate study at public universities in the state.
Eligibility This program is open to veterans who are current residents of Texas and were legal residents of the state at the time they entered the U.S. armed forces and served for at least 181 days of active military duty, excluding basic training, during specified periods of wartime. Applicants must have received an honorable discharge or separation or a general discharge under honorable conditions. They must be enrolled at a public college or university in Texas and all their other federal veterans' education benefits (not including Pell and SEOG grants) may not exceed the value of this exemption.
Financial data Veterans who are eligible for this benefit are entitled to free tuition and fees at state-supported colleges and universities in Texas.
Duration Exemptions may be claimed up to a cumulative total of 150 credit hours, including undergraduate and graduate study.
Additional information This program was previously administered by the Texas Higher Education Coordinating Board but was transferred to the Texas Veterans Commission in 2013.

Number awarded Varies each year; recently, 8,612 veterans received $44,631,752 in support at 4-year institutions and 9,637 veterans received $14,080,701 in support at 2-year colleges.
Deadline Deadline not specified.

[1135]
HENRY J. REILLY SCHOLARSHIPS

Reserve Officers Association of the United States
Attn: Scholarship Program
One Constitution Avenue, N.E.
Washington, DC 20002-5618
(202) 646-7758   Toll Free: (800) 809-9448
E-mail: scholarship@roa.org
Web: www.roa.org/page/Scholarships

Summary To provide financial assistance for college or graduate school to members of the Reserve Officers Association (ROA) and their children or grandchildren.
Eligibility Applicants for this scholarship must be active or associate members of the association or their children or grandchildren (under the age of 26). Children, age 21 or under, of deceased members who were active and paid up at the time of their death are also eligible. Spouses are not eligible, unless they are members of the association. ROTC members do not qualify as sponsors. Entering and continuing undergraduates must provide evidence of full-time enrollment at a regionally-accredited 4-year college or university, demonstrate leadership qualities, have earned a GPA of 3.3 or higher in high school and 3.0 or higher in college, have scored at least 1875 on the SAT or 55 on the English/math ACT, and (if appropriate) have registered for the draft. Applicants for a master's degree must have earned a GPA of 3.2 or higher as an undergraduate; applicants for a doctoral degree must have received a master's degree or been accepted into a doctoral program. All applicants must submit a 500-word essay on career goals. Selection is based on that essay, academic excellence, extracurricular activities and leadership, and letters of recommendation.
Financial data The stipend is $2,500 per year.
Duration 1 year; may be renewed.
Number awarded Up to 20 each year.
Deadline April of each year.

[1136]
ILLINOIS NATIONAL GUARD GRANT PROGRAM

Illinois Student Assistance Commission
Attn: Scholarship and Grant Services
1755 Lake Cook Road
Deerfield, IL 60015-5209
(847) 948-8550   Toll Free: (800) 899-ISAC
Fax: (847) 831-8549   TDD: (800) 526-0844
E-mail: isac.studentservices@illinois.gov
Web: www.isac.org

Summary To provide financial assistance to current or former members of the Illinois National Guard who are interested in attending college or graduate school in the state.
Eligibility This program is open to members of the Illinois National Guard who 1) are currently active and have completed at least 1 full year of service; or 2) have been active for at least 5 consecutive years, have had their studies interrupted by being called to federal active duty for at least 6 months, and are within 12 months after their discharge date. Applicants must also be enrolled at an Illinois public 2- or 4-year college or university.
Financial data Recipients are eligible for payment of tuition and some fees for either undergraduate or graduate study at an Illinois state-supported college or university.
Duration This assistance extends for 4 academic years of full-time study (or the equivalent in part-time study) for Guard members with less than 10 years of active duty service. For Guard members with 10 years or more of active duty service, assistance is available for up to the equivalent of 6 academic years of full-time study.
Number awarded Varies each year.
Deadline September of each year for the academic year; February of each year for spring semester, winter quarter, or spring quarter; June of each year for summer term.

[1137]
ILLINOIS VETERAN GRANT PROGRAM

Illinois Student Assistance Commission
Attn: Scholarship and Grant Services
1755 Lake Cook Road
Deerfield, IL 60015-5209
(847) 948-8550   Toll Free: (800) 899-ISAC
Fax: (847) 831-8549   TDD: (800) 526-0844
E-mail: isac.studentservices@illinois.gov
Web: www.isac.org

Summary To provide financial assistance to Illinois veterans who are interested in attending college or graduate school in the state.
Eligibility This program is open to Illinois residents who served in the U.S. armed forces (including members of the Reserves and the Illinois National Guard called to federal active duty) for at least 1 year on active duty and have been honorably discharged. The 1-year service requirement does not apply to veterans who 1) served in a foreign country in a time of hostilities in that country; 2) were medically discharged for service-related reasons; or 3) were discharged prior to August 11, 1967. Illinois residency may be established in 1 of the following ways: 1) currently residing in the state, except those who are serving federal active duty service at the time of enrollment in college or residing with a spouse in continued military service who is currently stationed outside of Illinois; 2) resided in Illinois at the time of entering federal active duty service or within 6 months prior to entering the service or were a student at an Illinois public 2- or 4-year college at the time of entering federal active duty service; or 3) established, or, if on federal active duty service, plan to establish, Illinois residency within 6 months after leaving federal active duty service. Students who cannot establish residency by 1 of those 3 methods may do so if they reside in Illinois at the time of application and at the time of receiving benefits and, at some point after leaving federal active duty service, have been a resident of Illinois for at least 15 consecutive years. Current members of the Reserve Officer Training Corps are not eligible.
Financial data This program pays all tuition and mandatory fees at all Illinois public colleges, universities, and community colleges.
Duration This scholarship may be used for the equivalent of up to 4 years of full-time enrollment at the undergraduate or graduate level, provided the recipient maintains the minimum GPA required by their college or university.

Additional information This is an entitlement program; once eligibility has been established, no further applications are necessary.

Number awarded Varies each year.

Deadline Applications may be submitted at any time.

[1138]
INDIANA PURPLE HEART RECIPIENT VETERAN PROGRAM

Indiana Commission for Higher Education
Attn: Financial Aid and Student Support Services
101 West Ohio Street, Suite 300
Indianapolis, IN 46204-4206
(317) 232-1023   Toll Free: (888) 528-4719 (within IN)
Fax: (317) 232-3260   E-mail: Scholars@che.in.gov
Web: www.in.gov/che/4521.htm

Summary To provide financial assistance to veterans from Indiana who received a Purple Heart and are interested in attending college or graduate school in the state.

Eligibility This program is open to veterans who entered active-duty service from a permanent home address in Indiana, received an honorable discharge, and received the Purple Heart decoration for that active-duty service. Applicants must be interested in working on an undergraduate, graduate, or professional degree at an eligible institution in Indiana.

Financial data Qualified applicants receive a 100% remission of tuition and all mandatory fees for undergraduate, graduate, or professional degrees at eligible postsecondary schools and universities in Indiana. Support is not provided for such fees as room and board.

Duration Up to 124 semester hours of study, provided the recipient maintains satisfactory academic progress. If the veteran initially enlisted on or before June 30, 2011, there is no time limit to use those hours. If the veteran initially enlisted after June 30, 2011, the allotted 124 credit hours must be used within 8 years after the date of initial application.

Number awarded Varies each year.

Deadline Applications must be submitted at least 30 days before the start of the college term.

[1139]
JAMES JOSEPH DAVIS MEMORIAL SCHOLARSHIP

American Society of Safety Professionals
Attn: ASSP Foundation
Scholarship Award Program
520 North Northwest Highway
Park Ridge, IL 60068-2538
(847) 699-2929   Fax: (847) 296-3769
E-mail: asspfoundation@assp.org
Web: foundation.assp.org/scholarships-and-grants

Summary To provide financial assistance to students, especially those who have served in the military, who are working on a degree related to occupational safety.

Eligibility This program is open to students, including international students, who are working full or part time on an undergraduate or graduate degree in occupational safety, health, environment, or a closely-related field. Priority is given to students who have served in the military. Associate degree students must have completed at least 24 semester hours and bachelor's degree students at least 60 semester hours. Membership in the American Society of Safety Professionals (ASSP) is not required, but members receive priority. Applicants must have a GPA of 3.0 or higher as an undergraduate or 3.5 or higher as a graduate student. Along with their application, they must submit 5 short essays of up to 500 words each on the following topics: 1) what drew them to the field of safety and how their education has affected their views of the field; 2) their goals and plans for reaching those; 3) their leadership and volunteer positions within the safety community; 4) the greatest takeaway from their current year in school; and 5) what makes them stand out as an applicant. Selection is based on academic performance, leadership activity in ASSP and the broader safety community, motivations for entering the field, and letters of recommendation.(e.g., industrial or environmental engineering).

Financial data The stipend is $10,000.

Duration 1 year.

Additional information This program is sponsored by Applications International Corporation.

Number awarded 1 each year.

Deadline November of each year.

[1140]
JEWISH WAR VETERANS NATIONAL ACHIEVEMENT PROGRAM

Jewish War Veterans of the U.S.A.
Attn: National Achievement Program
1811 R Street, N.W.
Washington, DC 20009-1659
(202) 265-6280   Fax: (202) 234-5662
E-mail: jwv@jwv.org
Web: www.jwvusafoundation.org

Summary To recognize and reward veterans and current servicemembers who are currently enrolled in college or graduate school and submit outstanding essays on their military experience.

Eligibility This competition is open to veterans and current servicemembers who are enrolled or planning to enroll in an accredited associate, bachelor's, nursing, or graduate degree program. All veterans are eligible, regardless of race, religion, creed, or culture. Applicants must submit an essay of 500 to 750 words on their military experience and how it will help them pursue their academic studies. Selection is based on answering the essay question (50%), logic and coherence of the essay's organization (25%), and description of relevant military experience (25%).

Financial data Awards range from $1,000 to $5,000.

Duration The awards are presented annually.

Additional information This program includes the Robert M. Zweiman Memorial Award, the Sidney Lieppe Memorial Grant, the Charles Kosmutza Memorial Grant, the Max R. and Irene Rubenstein Memorial Grant, and the Leon Brooks Memorial Grant.

Number awarded 6 each year: 2 at $5,000, 1 at $2,500, 1 at $1,500, and 2 at $1,000.

Deadline May of each year.

[1141]
LANCASTER SCHOLARSHIP

VisionCorps Foundation
244 North Queen Street
Lancaster, PA 17603
(717) 291-5951   E-mail: info@visioncorps.net
Web: www.visioncorps.net

Summary To provide financial assistance to Pennsylvania residents who are legally blind veterans and interested in working on a degree at any level at a college in any state.
Eligibility This program is open to veterans who are residents of Pennsylvania and legally blind. Applicants must be attending or planning to attend an institution of higher education at any level in any state. Along with their application, they must submit a brief description of their career goal. Financial need is considered in the selection process. U.S. citizenship is required.
Financial data The stipend is $1,000 per year.
Duration 1 year; may be renewed up to 3 additional years.
Additional information This sponsor was formerly the Susquehanna Foundation for the Blind.
Number awarded 1 or more each year.
Deadline January of each year.

[1142]
LILLIAN CAMPBELL MEDICAL SCHOLARSHIP

VFW Auxiliary-Department of Wisconsin
c/o Donna Butler, Department Scholarship Chair
522 Topaz Lane
Madison, WI 53714
(608) 695-0261　　E-mail: butlerdonna999@yahoo.com
Web: www.wivfwaux.org/department-scholarships.html

Summary To provide financial assistance to students working on a degree in a medical field in Wisconsin who served in the military or are related to a person who did.
Eligibility This program is open to students who have completed at least 1 year of study in Wisconsin in a program in 1) a medical field, including nursing, pharmacy, physician assistant, medical or surgical technology, physical or occupational therapy, dental hygiene, radiology, or other related medical profession; or 2) an emergency medical technician field (EMT), including paramedic studies. Applicants or a member of their immediate family (parent, sibling, child, spouse, or grandparent) must have served in the military. They must have a high school diploma or GED but may be of any age. Along with their application, they must submit a 200-word essay on why they are studying this medical profession. Financial need is considered in the selection process.
Financial data The stipend is $1,000 for students in a medical field or $750 for EMT students.
Duration 1 year.
Number awarded 1 for a student in a medical field and 1 for an EMT student.
Deadline March of each year.

[1143]
LT RUTH CORTES MEMORIAL SCHOLARSHIP

American Academy of Physician Assistants-Veterans Caucus
Attn: Scholarship Program
P.O. Box 362
Ossining, NY 10562
(803) 328-1864　　　　　　　　Fax: (704) 838-8494
E-mail: rmunsee@veteranscaucus.org
Web: www.veteranscaucus.org/scholarships

Summary To provide financial assistance to female veterans who are studying to become physician assistants.
Eligibility This program is open to U.S. citizens who are currently enrolled in a physician assistant program. Applicants must be women who are honorably discharged members of any branch of the uniformed services. Along with their application, they must submit a personal statement about what led them to attend PA school; their background, present, and future intentions; and why they deserve to receive a scholarship. Selection is based on honors and awards received, civic and college honors and awards received, professional memberships and activities, potential for future achievement, and GPA.
Financial data The stipend is $2,000.
Duration 1 year.
Number awarded 1 each year.
Deadline February of each year.

[1144]
LUCILE PARRISH WARD VETERAN'S AWARD

National Federation of Music Clubs
1646 West Smith Valley Road
Greenwood, IN 46142
(317) 882-4003　　　　　　　　Fax: (317) 882-4019
E-mail: info@nfmc-music.org
Web: www.nfmc-music.org

Summary To provide financial assistance to music students whose careers have been delayed or interrupted as a result of their service in the U.S. armed forces.
Eligibility This program is open to undergraduate and graduate students who are majoring in music and whose musical careers were interrupted by service in the armed forces. Veterans who served overseas receive preference. Applicants must be U.S. citizens, but membership in the National Federation of Music Clubs (NFMC) is not required. They must submit a 30-minute performance/audition recording. Selection is based on worthiness, character, background, musical talent, potential ability, and financial need.
Financial data The stipend is $2,250.
Duration 1 year; may be renewed if the recipient maintains a GPA of 3.0 or higher.
Additional information The entry fee is $20.
Number awarded 1 each year.
Deadline April of each year.

[1145]
MAINE VIETNAM VETERANS SCHOLARSHIP FUND

Maine Community Foundation
Attn: Program Director
245 Main Street
Ellsworth, ME 04605
(207) 667-9735　　　　　　　　Toll Free: (877) 700-6800
Fax: (207) 667-0447　　　　　　E-mail: info@mainecf.org
Web: www.mainecf.org

Summary To provide financial assistance for college or graduate school to Vietnam veterans or the dependents of Vietnam or other veterans in Maine.
Eligibility This program is open to residents of Maine who are Vietnam veterans or the descendants of veterans who served in the Vietnam Theater. As a second priority, children of veterans from other time periods are also considered. Graduating high school seniors, nontraditional students, undergraduates, and graduate students are eligible to apply. Selection is based on financial need, extracurricular activities,

work experience, academic achievement, and a personal statement of career goals and how the applicant's educational plans relate to them.
Financial data The stipend is $1,000 per year.
Duration 1 year.
Additional information This program began in 1985. There is a $3 processing fee.
Number awarded 3 to 6 each year.
Deadline April of each year.

[1146]
MARGUERITE MC'ALPIN MEMORIAL SCHOLARSHIP

American Legion Auxiliary
Department of Washington
Attn: Education Chair
3600 Ruddell Road S.E.
P.O. Box 5867
Lacey, WA 98509-5867
(360) 456-5995   Fax: (360) 491-7442
E-mail: secretary@walegion-aux.org
Web: www.walegion-aux.org/EducationScholarships.html

Summary To provide financial assistance to Washington veterans or their descendants who are interested in working on an undergraduate or graduate degree in nursing at a school in any state.
Eligibility This program is open to residents of Washington who are veterans or the children, grandchildren, and great-grandchildren of veterans. Applicants must be interested in studying nursing on the undergraduate or graduate level at a school in any state. Selection is based on a 300-word essay on their desire to study nursing, character, leadership, scholastic history, and financial need.
Financial data The stipend is $1,000.
Duration 1 year.
Number awarded 1 each year.
Deadline February of each year.

[1147]
MARIA C. JACKSON/GENERAL GEORGE A. WHITE SCHOLARSHIP

Oregon Office of Student Access and Completion
Attn: Scholarships
1500 Valley River Drive, Suite 100
Eugene, OR 97401-2146
(541) 687-7400   Toll Free: (800) 452-8807
Fax: (541) 687-7414   TDD: (800) 735-2900
E-mail: osac@hecc.oregon.gov
Web: app.oregonstudentaid.gov/Catalog/Default.aspx

Summary To provide financial assistance to veterans and children of veterans and military personnel in Oregon who are interested in attending college or graduate school in the state.
Eligibility This program is open to residents of Oregon who served, or whose parents are serving or have served, in the U.S. armed forces. Applicants or their parents must have resided in Oregon at the time of enlistment. They must be enrolled or planning to enroll at a college or graduate school in the state. College and university undergraduates must have a GPA of 3.75 or higher, but there is no minimum GPA requirement for graduate students or those attending a technical school. Selection is based on scholastic ability and financial need.

Financial data Stipends for scholarships offered by the Oregon Office of Student Access and Completion (OSAC) range from $1,000 to $10,000 but recently averaged $4,710.
Duration 1 year.
Number awarded Varies each year.
Deadline February of each year.

[1148]
MARINES' MEMORIAL TRIBUTE SCHOLARSHIPS

Marines' Memorial Association
c/o Marines Memorial Club and Hotel
609 Sutter Street
San Francisco, CA 94102
(415) 673-6672, ext. 293   Toll Free: (800) 5-MARINE
Fax: (415) 441-3649
E-mail: scholarship@marineclub.com
Web: www.marinesmemorial.org

Summary To provide financial assistance to military personnel who are transitioning from active duty to civilian or Reserve status and wish to attend college.
Eligibility This program is open to military personnel who have separated from full-time active duty to civilian or Reserve status within the past 3 years. Applicants must be enrolled or planning to enroll full time in an accredited undergraduate or graduate degree program in any field at a college or university. Membership in the sponsoring organization is not required. Along with their application, they must submit an essay of up to 500 words on why they chose their specific path of study, what they hope to accomplish after graduation with their degree, and how their efforts will benefit others in their community. Applicants entering college as freshmen must submit a high school transcript and SAT or ACT scores; continuing college students must submit a college transcript. Selection is based on the essay, academic merit, references, and financial need.
Financial data The stipend ranges from $2,500 to $5,000 per year.
Duration 1 year; recipients may reapply for up to 3 additional years.
Number awarded 8 each year.
Deadline April of each year.

[1149]
MILITARY MBA SCHOLARSHIPS

Military MBA
Attn: Executive Director
P.O. Box 681234
Park City, UT 84068-1234
(435) 649-2190   Fax: (435) 649-2195
E-mail: geisenbarth@militarymba.net
Web: www.militarymba.net

Summary To provide financial assistance to veterans who are interested in working on a master's degree in business administration (M.B.A.) at selected universities.
Eligibility This program is open to U.S. residents who have served in the military and have completed an undergraduate degree. Applicants must be interested in working on an MBA degree at any of 41 universities that are members of this sponsoring organization. Along with their application, they must submit 1) a 300-word essay on their motivations and expectations for going to business school; 2) a 400-word essay on their unique type of leadership; and 3) a 400-word

essay on how their leadership qualities will add value to an MBA program and how they plan to apply themselves upon completion of an M.B.A. degree.
Financial data The stipend is $5,000.
Duration 1 year.
Additional information For a list of member universities, contact the sponsor.
Number awarded 4 each year.
Deadline May of each year.

[1150]
MINNESOTA G.I. BILL PROGRAM
Minnesota Department of Veterans Affairs
Attn: Programs and Services Division
20 West 12th Street, Room 206
St. Paul, MN 55155
(651) 296-2562   Toll Free: (888) LINK-VET
Fax: (651) 296-3954   TDD: (800) 627-3529
E-mail: MNGIBill@state.mn.us
Web: www.mn.gov

Summary To provide financial assistance for college or graduate school in the state to residents of Minnesota who served in the military after September 11, 2001 and the families of deceased or disabled military personnel.
Eligibility This program is open to residents of Minnesota enrolled at colleges and universities in the state as undergraduate or graduate students. Applicants must be 1) a veteran who is serving or has served honorably in a branch of the U.S. armed forces at any time; 2) a non-veteran who has served honorably for a total of 5 years or more cumulatively as a member of the Minnesota National Guard or other active or Reserve component of the U.S. armed forces, and any part of that service occurred on or after September 11, 2001; or 3) a surviving child or spouse of a person who has served in the military at any time and who has died or has a total and permanent disability as a result of that military service. They may be attending college in the state or participating in an apprenticeship or on-the-job (OJT) training program. Financial need is also considered in the selection process.
Financial data The college stipend is $1,000 per semester for full-time study or $500 per semester for part-time study. The maximum award is $3,000 per academic year or $10,000 per lifetime. Apprenticeship and OJT students are eligible for up to $2,000 per fiscal year. Approved employers are eligible to receive $1,000 placement credit payable upon hiring a person under this program and another $1,000 after 12 consecutive months of employment. No more than $3,000 in aggregate benefits under this paragraph may be paid to or on behalf of an individual in one fiscal year, and not more than $9,000 over any period of time.
Duration 1 year; may be renewed, provided the recipient continues to make satisfactory academic progress.
Additional information This program was established by the Minnesota Legislature in 2007.
Number awarded At least 1,000 each year.
Deadline Deadline not specified.

[1151]
MINNESOTA NATIONAL GUARD EXTENDED STATE TUITION REIMBURSEMENT
Minnesota National Guard
Attn: Education Office
600 Cedar Street
St. Paul, MN 5510-2509
(651) 282-4589   Toll Free: (800) 657-3848
Fax: (651) 282-4694
E-mail: ng.mn.mnarng.mbx.assets-education@mail.mil
Web: minnesotanationalguard.ng.mil/education

Summary To provide financial assistance for college or graduate school to former members of the Minnesota National Guard.
Eligibility Eligible for this program are former members of the Minnesota Army or Air National Guard who have satisfactorily completed their service contract or the portions of it involving selective reserve status, of which any part of that service was spent in federal active service or federally-funded state active duty after September 11, 2001. Applicants must be enrolled as undergraduate or graduate students at colleges or universities in Minnesota. Reimbursement is provided for undergraduate courses completed with a grade of "C" or better or for graduate courses completed with a grade of "B" or better. Eligibility extends for 2 years after honorable completion of the National Guard service contract, plus an amount of time equal to the duration of active service. For Guard members who served honorably and were separated or discharged because of a service-connected injury, disease, or illness, eligibility is extended for 8 years beyond the date of separation.
Financial data The maximum reimbursement rate is 100% of the tuition rate at the University of Minnesota Twin Cities campus for undergraduate study or 50% for graduate work, with a maximum benefit of $18,000 per fiscal year for undergraduate course work or $20,000 per fiscal year for graduate course work.
Duration 1 semester, to a maximum of 18 credits per semester; may be renewed until completion of an associate, bachelor's, master's, or doctoral degree or 144 semester credits, whichever comes first.
Number awarded Varies each year.
Deadline Deadline not specified.

[1152]
MONTANA HONORABLY DISCHARGED VETERAN WAIVER
Office of the Commissioner of Higher Education
Attn: Montana University System
State Scholarship Coordinator
560 North Park Avenue, Fourth Floor
P.O. Box 203201
Helena, MT 59620-3201
(406) 449-9168   Toll Free: (800) 537-7508
Fax: (406) 449-9171
E-mail: mtscholarships@montana.edu
Web: www.mus.edu

Summary To provide financial assistance for undergraduate or graduate studies to selected Montana veterans.
Eligibility This program is open to honorably-discharged veterans who served with the U.S. armed forces and who are residents of Montana. Only veterans who at some time quali-

fied for U.S. Department of Veterans Affairs (VA) educational benefits, but who are no longer eligible or have exhausted their benefits, are entitled to this waiver. Veterans who served any time prior to May 8, 1975 are eligible to work on undergraduate or graduate degrees. Veterans whose service began after May 7, 1975 are eligible only to work on their first undergraduate degree. They must have received an Armed Forces Expeditionary Medal for service in Lebanon, Grenada, or Panama; served in a combat theater in the Persian Gulf between August 2, 1990 and April 11, 1991 and received the Southwest Asia Service Medal; were awarded the Kosovo Campaign Medal; or served in a combat theater in Afghanistan or Iraq after September 11, 2001 and received the Global War on Terrorism Expeditionary Medal, the Afghanistan Campaign Medal, or the Iraq Campaign Medal. Financial need must be demonstrated.

Financial data Veterans eligible for this benefit are entitled to attend any unit of the Montana University System without payment of registration or incidental fees.

Duration Students are eligible for continued fee waiver as long as they make reasonable academic progress as full-time students.

Number awarded Varies each year.

Deadline Deadline not specified.

[1153]
MONTGOMERY GI BILL (ACTIVE DUTY)

Department of Veterans Affairs
Attn: Veterans Benefits Administration
810 Vermont Avenue, N.W.
Washington, DC 20420
(202) 418-4343   Toll Free: (888) 442-4551
Web: www.va.gov

Summary To provide financial assistance for college, graduate school, and other types of postsecondary schools to new enlistees in any of the armed forces after they have completed their service obligation.

Eligibility This program is open to veterans who received an honorable discharge and have a high school diploma, a GED, or, in some cases, up to 12 hours of college credit; veterans who already have a bachelor's degree are eligible to work on a master's degree or higher. Applicants must have had their military pay reduced by $100 per month for the first 12 months of service. They must also meet the detailed requirements of 4 special categories; for specifics, contact the Department of Veterans Affairs (VA). Following completion of their service obligation, participants may enroll in colleges or universities for associate, bachelor, or graduate degrees; in courses leading to a certificate or diploma from business, technical, or vocational schools; for apprenticeships or on-the-job training programs; in correspondence courses; in flight training; for preparatory courses necessary for admission to a college or graduate school; for licensing and certification tests approved for veterans; or in state-approved teacher certification programs.

Financial data Stipends depend on the length of service, the type of education or training program, and the special category in which the veteran falls. Recently, basic rates for institutional raining for veterans who completed an enlistment of 3 or more years was $2,050 per month and for those with an enlistment of less than 3 years $1,664 per month. Rates for other types of training were generally lower.

Duration 36 months; active-duty servicemembers must utilize the funds within 10 years of leaving the armed services; Reservists may draw on their funds while still serving.

Additional information Further information is available from local armed forces recruiters. This was the basic VA education program, referred to as Chapter 30, until the passage of the Post-9/11 GI Bill in 2009. Veterans who have remaining benefits available from this program may utilize those or transfer to the new program.

Number awarded Varies each year.

Deadline Deadline not specified.

[1154]
NATIONAL GUARD ASSOCIATION OF NEW HAMPSHIRE SCHOLARSHIPS

National Guard Association of New Hampshire
Attn: Scholarship Committee
P.O. Box 22031
Portsmouth, NH 03802-2031
(603) 227-1597   E-mail: nganhscholarship@gmail.com
Web: www.nganh.org/benefits

Summary To provide financial assistance to members of the National Guard Association of New Hampshire and their dependents who are interested in attending college or graduate school in any state.

Eligibility This program is open to current members of the National Guard Association of New Hampshire (officer, enlisted, or retired), their spouses, and their dependent children. Applicants must be enrolled or planning to enroll full or part time in an associate, bachelor's, graduate, professional, or doctoral degree program at an accredited college or university in any state. Along with their application, they must submit a 1-page essay on a topic that changes annually; recently, they were asked to describe what citizen service means to them.

Financial data The stipend is $1,000.

Duration 1 year.

Number awarded 1 each year.

Deadline April of each year.

[1155]
NATIONAL GUARD ASSOCIATION OF TEXAS SCHOLARSHIP PROGRAM

National Guard Association of Texas
Attn: Education Committee
3706 Crawford Avenue
Austin, TX 78731-6803
(512) 454-7300   Toll Free: (800) 252-NGAT
Fax: (512) 467-6803   E-mail: tbz@ngat.org
Web: www.ngat.org/education.htm

Summary To provide financial assistance to members and dependents of members of the National Guard Association of Texas who are interested in attending college or graduate school in any state.

Eligibility This program is open to annual and life members of the association and their spouses and children (associate members and their dependents are not eligible). Applicants may be high school seniors, undergraduate students, or graduate students, either enrolled or planning to enroll at an institution of higher education in any state. Along with their application, they must submit an essay on their desire to con-

tinue their education. Selection is based on scholarship, citizenship, and leadership.
Financial data Stipends range from $500 to $5,000.
Duration 1 year (nonrenewable).
Additional information This program includes the Len and Jean Tallas Memorial Scholarship, the Texas Capital Area Chapter of the AUSA Scholarship, the Lewis O. King Memorial Scholarship, the Gloria Jenell and Marlin E. Mote Endowed Scholarship, the LTC Gary Parrish Memorial Scholarship, the TXNG Retirees Endowed Scholarship, and 2 scholarships sponsored by USAA Insurance Corporation.
Number awarded Varies each year; recently, 8 were awarded: 1 at $5,000, 1 at $4,000, 1 at $2,000, 1 at $1,250, 3 at $1,000, and 1 at $500.
Deadline February of each year.

[1156]
NAVAL HELICOPTER ASSOCIATION SCHOLARSHIPS

Naval Helicopter Association
Attn: Scholarship Fund
P.O. Box 180578
Coronado, CA 92178-0578
(619) 435-7139   Fax: (619) 435-7354
E-mail: pres@nhascholarshipfund.org
Web: www.nhascholarshipfund.org/about/scholarships

Summary To provide financial assistance for college or graduate school to members of the Naval Helicopter Association (NHA) and their families.
Eligibility This program is open to NHA members and their spouses, children, and grandchildren. Membership in the NHA is open to active-duty and retired U.S. Navy, U.S. Marine Corps, and U.S. Coast Guard helicopter pilots, aircrew, and maintenance professionals. Applicants must be working on or planning to work on an undergraduate or graduate degree in any field. Along with their application, they must submit a personal statement on their academic and career aspirations. Selection is based on that statement, academic proficiency, scholastic achievements and awards, extracurricular activities, employment history, and letters of recommendation. The program includes scholarships 1) reserved for NHA family members; 2) reserved for active-duty personnel; 3) sponsored by private corporations; 4) named as memorials in honor of distinguished individuals; and 5) awarded on a regional basis.
Financial data Stipends are approximately $2,000.
Duration 1 year.
Additional information Corporate sponsors have included FLIR Systems, D.P. Associates, L-3 Communications, CAE, Raytheon Corporation, Lockheed Martin (designated the Sergei Sikorsky Scholarship), and Northrop Grumman. Memorial Scholarships have included the Edward and Veronica Ream Memorial Scholarship, the CDR Mort McCarthy Memorial Scholarship, the Charles Karman Memorial Scholarship, the LT Christian "Horse" Hescock Memorial Scholarship, and the Captain Mark Starr Memorial Scholarship.
Number awarded Varies each year; recently, 17 were awarded: 1 graduate student family member, 3 active-duty graduate students, 1 active-duty undergraduate student, 4 sponsored by corporate donors, 4 memorial scholarships, and 4 regional scholarships.
Deadline January of each year.

[1157]
NBCCF MILITARY SCHOLARSHIPS

National Board for Certified Counselors
Attn: NBCC Foundation
3 Terrace Way
Greensboro, NC 27403
(336) 232-0376   Fax: (336) 232-0010
E-mail: foundation@nbcc.org
Web: nbccf.applicantstack.com/x/detail/a2ei42le608f

Summary To provide financial assistance to current and former military personnel and spouses of servicemembers interested in working on a master's degree in counseling.
Eligibility This program is open to students enrolled full time in an accredited master's degree counseling program. Applicants must be prior or current active-duty U.S. military service personnel or the spouse of a servicemember. Veterans must have received an honorable discharge. Applicants must be able to demonstrate a commitment to apply for the National Certified Counselor (NCC) credential prior to graduation and to provide counseling services to servicemembers and/or veterans for at least 2 years after graduation.
Financial data The stipend is $8,000.
Duration 1 year.
Additional information This program began in 2010.
Number awarded 5 each year.
Deadline January of each year.

[1158]
NBCUNIVERSAL-SVA SCHOLARSHIPS

Student Veterans of America
Attn: Scholarship Committee
1012 14th Street, N.W., Suite 1200
Washington, DC 20005
(202) 223-4710
E-mail: scholarships@studentveterans.org
Web: www.studentveterans.org

Summary To provide financial assistance to veterans who are working on an undergraduate or graduate degree in a field related to the media and entertainment industry.
Eligibility This program is open to veterans who are currently enrolled at an accredited institution of higher education. Applicants must be working on an associate, bachelor's, or graduate degree in film, media, television, journalism, or communications. They must be U.S. citizens or eligible to work in the United States. Along with their application, they must submit essays of 300 to 500 words on 1) their previous leadership experiences during their military service and beyond and how they have carried those experiences forward in the classroom or in other university activities; and 2) why they are interested in NBCUniversal and a career in the entertainment industry. Financial need is not considered in the selection process.
Financial data The stipend is $12,000.
Duration 1 year.
Additional information This program, which began in 2014, is supported by NBCUniversal and administered by Student Veterans of America (SVA).

Number awarded 2 each year.
Deadline November of each year.

[1159]
NEW MEXICO VIETNAM VETERAN SCHOLARSHIPS
New Mexico Department of Veterans' Services
Attn: State Benefits
407 Galisteo Street, Room 134
P.O. Box 2324
Santa Fe, NM 87504-2324
(505) 383-2400   Toll Free: (866) 433-VETS
Fax: (505) 827-6372 E-mail: JosephM.Dorn@state.nm.us
Web: www.nmdvs.org/state-benefits

Summary To provide financial assistance to Vietnam veterans in New Mexico who are interested in working on an undergraduate or master's degree at a public college in the state.

Eligibility This program is open to Vietnam veterans who have been residents of New Mexico for at least 10 years. Applicants must have been honorably discharged and have been awarded the Vietnam Service Medal or the Vietnam Campaign Medal. They must be planning to attend a state-supported college, university, or community college in New Mexico to work on an undergraduate or master's degree. Awards are granted on a first-come, first-served basis.

Financial data The scholarships provide full payment of tuition and purchase of required books at any state-funded postsecondary institution in New Mexico.

Duration 1 year.
Number awarded Varies each year.
Deadline Deadline not specified.

[1160]
NEW MEXICO WARTIME VETERAN SCHOLARSHIP FUND
New Mexico Department of Veterans' Services
Attn: State Benefits
407 Galisteo Street, Room 134
P.O. Box 2324
Santa Fe, NM 87504-2324
(505) 383-2400   Toll Free: (866) 433-VETS
Fax: (505) 827-6372 E-mail: JosephM.Dorn@state.nm.us
Web: www.nmdvs.org/state-benefits

Summary To provide financial assistance to residents of New Mexico who served in the military after 1990 and are interested in working on an undergraduate or master's degree at a public college in the state.

Eligibility This program is open to veterans who have been residents of New Mexico for at least 10 years and have been awarded the Southwest Asia Service Medal, Global War on Terrorism Expeditionary Medal, Iraq Campaign Medal, Afghanistan Campaign Medal, or any other medal issued for service in the U.S. armed forces in support of any U.S. military campaign or armed conflict as defined by Congress or presidential executive order for service after August 1, 1990. Applicants must have exhausted all available federal G.I. education benefits. They must be interested in attending a state-supported college, university, or community college in New Mexico to work on an undergraduate or master's degree. Awards are granted on a first-come, first-served basis.

Financial data The scholarships provide full payment of tuition and purchase of required books at any state-funded postsecondary institution in New Mexico.

Duration 1 year.
Number awarded Varies each year.
Deadline Deadline not specified.

[1161]
NEW YORK VETERANS TUITION AWARDS
New York State Higher Education Services Corporation
Attn: Student Information
99 Washington Avenue
Albany, NY 12255
(518) 473-1574   Toll Free: (888) NYS-HESC
Fax: (518) 473-3749   TDD: (800) 445-5234
E-mail: scholarships@hesc.com
Web: www.hesc.ny.gov

Summary To provide tuition assistance to eligible veterans enrolled in an undergraduate or graduate program in New York.

Eligibility This program is open to veterans who served in the U.S. armed forces in 1) Indochina between February 1, 1961 and May 7, 1975; 2) hostilities that occurred after February 28, 1961 as evidenced by receipt of an Armed Forces Expeditionary Medal, Navy Expeditionary Medal, or Marine Corps Expeditionary Medal; 3) the Persian Gulf on or after August 2, 1990; or 4) Afghanistan on or after September 11, 2001. Applicants must have been discharged from the service under honorable conditions, must be a New York resident, must be a U.S. citizen or eligible noncitizen, must be enrolled full or part time at an undergraduate or graduate degree-granting institution in New York or in an approved vocational training program in the state, must be charged at least $200 tuition per year, and must apply for a New York Tuition Assistance Program (TAP) award.

Financial data For full-time study, the maximum stipend is equivalent to tuition charged to New York residents at the State University of New York (SUNY) or actual tuition charged, whichever is less. For part-time study, the stipend is based on the number of credits certified and the student's actual part-time tuition.

Duration For full-time undergraduate study, up to 8 semesters, or up to 10 semesters for a program requiring 5 years for completion; for full-time graduate study, up to 6 semesters; for full-time vocational programs, up to 4 semesters. Awards for part-time undergraduate study are available for up to 16 semesters, or 20 semesters for a 5-year program; for part-time graduate study, up to 12 semesters; for part-time vocational study, up to 8 semesters.

Additional information If a TAP award is also received, the combined academic year award cannot exceed tuition costs. If it does, the TAP award will be reduced accordingly.

Number awarded Varies each year; recently, 738 veterans received more than $2.7 million from this program.
Deadline April of each year.

[1162]
NGAOK SCHOLARSHIPS

National Guard Association of Oklahoma
c/o Scholarship Foundation
Attn: Rosemary Masters, Scholarship Chair
3501 Military Circle
Oklahoma City, OK 73111
(405) 823-0799   E-mail: ngaok.scholarship@gmail.com
Web: www.ngaok.org/benefits

Summary To provide financial assistance to members of the National Guard Association of Oklahoma (NGAOK) and their dependents who are interested in attending college in any state.

Eligibility This program is open to NGAOK members and their dependent children and spouses who are enrolled or planning to enroll full or part time in an undergraduate or graduate program at a college or university in any state. The primary next of kin of members of the Oklahoma National Guard killed in action after September 11, 2001 are considered life members of NGAOK. Applicants must submit transcripts that include ACT and/or SAT scores; lists of awards and recognitions, community and volunteer services, and extracurricular and sports activities; and a 500-word essay about how they exemplify the traits of selfless service, leadership, character, and their aspirations. Financial need is not considered in the selection process.

Financial data Stipends are $500 or $1,000.
Duration 1 year.
Number awarded 20 to 25 each year.
Deadline January of each year.

[1163]
NJ HIMSS VETERANS AWARD

Healthcare Information and Management Systems
  Society-New Jersey Chapter
c/o Jim Hennessy, Scholarship Committee Chair
e4 Services, LLC
139 West Market Street, Suite C
West Chester, PA 19382
(610) 247-4951   Toll Free: (888) 443-4782
Fax: (888) 521-7874
E-mail: jhennessy@e4-services.com
Web: www.njhimss.org/scholarship

Summary To provide financial assistance to veterans from New Jersey who are working on an undergraduate or graduate degree in a field related to health care information and management.

Eligibility This program is open to veterans who are residents of New Jersey attending college in any state or residents of other states attending college in New Jersey. Applicants must be working on an undergraduate or graduate degree in a field related to health care information and management, such as health care informatics, health care computer science and information systems, health care policy, and quantitative programs in business administration or hospital administration. They must have a GPA of 3.0 or higher. Along with their application, they must submit a 500-word essay on how they will impact the arena of health care informatics and/or health care technology.

Financial data The stipend is $4,000.
Duration 1 year.
Number awarded 1 each year.
Deadline May of each year.

[1164]
OHIO LEGION MEMBER/MILITARY VETERAN SCHOLARSHIP

American Legion
Department of Ohio
60 Big Run Road
P.O. Box 8007
Delaware, OH 43015
(740) 362-7478   Fax: (740) 362-1429
E-mail: legion@ohiolegion.com
Web: www.ohiolegion.com/programs/scholarships

Summary To provide financial assistance to residents of Ohio who are members of the American Legion, veterans, or current military personnel and interested in attending college in any state.

Eligibility This program is open to residents of Ohio who are 1) members of the American Legion; 2) honorably discharged members of the armed forces; or 3) currently on active duty or a member of the National Guard or Reserves. Applicants must be attending or planning to attend colleges, universities, or other approved postsecondary schools in any state as an undergraduate or graduate student. They must have a GPA of 3.5 or higher and an ACT score of at least 25. Along with their application, they must submit a personal statement of 500 to 550 words on their career objectives. Selection is based on academic achievement as measured by course grades, ACT scores, difficulty of curriculum, participation in school and outside activities, and the judging committee's general impression.

Financial data Stipends are normally at least $2,000.
Duration 1 year.
Number awarded 1 each year.
Deadline April of each year.

[1165]
PETER CONNACHER MEMORIAL SCHOLARSHIPS

Oregon Office of Student Access and Completion
Attn: Scholarships
1500 Valley River Drive, Suite 100
Eugene, OR 97401-2146
(541) 687-7400   Toll Free: (800) 452-8807
Fax: (541) 687-7414   TDD: (800) 735-2900
E-mail: osac@hecc.oregon.gov
Web: app.oregonstudentaid.gov/Catalog/Default.aspx

Summary To provide financial assistance for college or graduate school to ex-prisoners of war and their descendants.

Eligibility Applicants must be U.S. citizens who 1) were military or civilian prisoners of war; or 2) are the descendants of ex-prisoners of war. They must be full-time undergraduate or graduate students. A copy of the ex-prisoner of war's discharge papers from the U.S. armed forces must accompany the application. In addition, written proof of POW status must be submitted, along with a statement of the relationship between the applicant and the ex-prisoner of war (father, grandfather, etc.). Selection is based on academic record and financial need. Preference is given to Oregon residents or their dependents.

Financial data Stipends for scholarships offered by the Oregon Office of Student Access and Completion (OSAC) range from $1,000 to $10,000 but recently averaged $4,710.
Duration 1 year; may be renewed for up to 3 additional years for undergraduate students or 2 additional years for graduate students. Renewal is dependent on evidence of continued financial need and satisfactory academic progress.
Additional information This program is administered by the OSAC with funds provided by the Oregon Community Foundation and by the Columbia River Chapter of American Ex-prisoners of War, Inc.
Number awarded Varies each year; recently, 4 were awarded.
Deadline February of each year.

[1166]
POST-9/11 GI BILL
Department of Veterans Affairs
Attn: Veterans Benefits Administration
810 Vermont Avenue, N.W.
Washington, DC 20420
(202) 418-4343   Toll Free: (888) 442-4551
Web: www.va.gov/education/about-gi-bill-benefits/post-9-11

Summary To provide financial assistance to veterans or military personnel who entered service on or after September 11, 2001.
Eligibility This program is open to current and former military personnel who 1) served on active duty for at least 90 aggregate days after September 11, 2001; 2) were discharged with a service-connected disability after 30 days; or 3) received a Purple Heart on or after September 11, 2001 and were discharged after any length of service. Applicants must be planning to enroll in an educational program, including work on an undergraduate or graduate degree, vocational/technical training, on-the-job training, flight training, correspondence training, licensing and national testing programs, entrepreneurship training, and tutorial assistance.
Financial data Participants working on an undergraduate or graduate degree at public institutions in their state receive full payment of tuition and fees. For participants who attend private institutions in most states, tuition and fee reimbursement is capped at $25,162.14 per academic year. Benefits for other types of training programs depend on the amount for which the veteran qualified under prior educational programs. Veterans also receive a monthly housing allowance that is 1) based on the Department of Defense Basic Allowance for Housing (BAH) for an E-5 with dependents (which depends on the location of the school but ranges from approximately $1,000 per month to approximately $2,500 per month); 2) $1,789 per month at schools in foreign countries; or 3) $894.50 per month for online training classes. They also receive an annual book allowance of $1,000 and (for participants who live in a rural county remote from an educational institution) a rural benefit payment of $500 per year.
Duration Most participants receive up to 36 months of entitlement under this program. Benefits are payable for up to 15 years following release from active duty.
Additional information This program, referred to as Chapter 33, began in 2009 as a replacement for previous educational programs for veterans and military personnel (e.g., Montgomery GI Bill, REAP). Current participants in those programs may be able to transfer benefits from those programs to this new plan. To qualify for 100% of Post 9/11-GI Bill benefits, transferees must have at least 36 months of active-duty service. Transferees with less service are entitled to smaller percentages of benefits, ranging down to 40% for those with only 90 days of service.
Number awarded Varies each year; recently, approximately 700,000 veterans received $10.7 billion on benefits through this program.
Deadline Deadline not specified.

[1167]
RAYTHEON SPY-6 SCHOLARSHIPS
Student Veterans of America
Attn: Scholarship Committee
1012 14th Street, N.W., Suite 1200
Washington, DC 20005
(202) 223-4710
E-mail: scholarships@studentveterans.org
Web: www.studentveterans.org

Summary To provide financial assistance to U.S. Navy veterans who are working on an undergraduate or graduate degree in any field.
Eligibility This program is open to U.S. Navy veterans who have been honorably discharged and are currently enrolled full-time at a 4-year college or university as an entering sophomore, junior, senior, or graduate student. Applicants may be working on a degree in any field. Along with their application, they must submit essays on 1) what they hope to accomplish with their degree; and 2) if they served on a Navy ship, an explanation of their experience. Financial need is not considered in the selection process.
Financial data The stipend is $10,000.
Duration 1 year.
Additional information This program, which began in 2013, is supported by Raytheon Company and administered by Student Veterans of America (SVA).
Number awarded 2 each year.
Deadline April of each year.

[1168]
RON PACE MEMORIAL SCHOLARSHIP
American Academy of Physician Assistants
Attn: Physician Assistant Foundation
2318 Mill Road, Suite 1300
Alexandria, VA 22314-6868
(571) 319-4510   E-mail: pafoundation@aapa.org
Web: app.smarterselect.com

Summary To provide financial assistance to student members of the American Academy of Physician Assistants (AAPA) who are veterans from Florida.
Eligibility This program is open to student members of the Florida Academy of Physician Assistants who have completed at least 1 semester of an accredited physician assistant program in Florida. Applicants must be veterans or dependent children of veterans.
Financial data The stipend is $1,000.
Duration 1 year; nonrenewable.
Number awarded 1 each year.
Deadline May of each year.

[1169]
RUARK-WIGHT FAMILY SCHOLARSHIP

Marines' Memorial Association
c/o Marines Memorial Club and Hotel
609 Sutter Street
San Francisco, CA 94102
(415) 673-6672, ext. 293   Toll Free: (800) 5-MARINE
Fax: (415) 441-3649
E-mail: scholarship@marineclub.com
Web: www.marinesmemorial.org/members/scholarships

Summary To provide financial assistance to veterans, military personnel, and their families who are interested in attending college or graduate school to work on a degree in any field.

Eligibility This program is open to students who meet 1 of the following requirements: 1) have served honorably or is currently serving in any branch of the U.S. armed forces; or 2) is the spouse or child of a person who served honorably or is currently serving in any branch of the U.S. armed forces. Applicants must be enrolled as full-time sophomores, juniors, seniors or graduate students working on a degree in any field. They must have a GPA of 2.5 or higher. Membership in the sponsoring organization is not required for student veterans. Along with their application, they must submit an essay of up to 500 words on why they chose their specific path of study, what they hope to accomplish after graduation with their degree, and how their efforts will benefit others in their community. Selection is based on the essay, academic merit, references, and financial need.

Financial data The stipend is $5,000 per year.

Duration 1 year; recipients may reapply for up to 3 additional years.

Number awarded 1 each year.

Deadline April of each year.

[1170]
SENATOR DANIEL K. INOUYE MEMORIAL SCHOLARSHIP

Japanese American Veterans Association
Attn: Chris DeRosa, Scholarship Committee Chair
P.O. Box 341198
Bethesda, MD 20827
E-mail: javascholarship222@gmail.com
Web: www.java.wildapricot.org

Summary To provide financial assistance for college or graduate school to relatives of Japanese American veterans who plan a career in the military or public service.

Eligibility This program is open to students who 1) have completed at least 1 year of an undergraduate program or are currently enrolled in graduate school and are preparing for a career in the military or public service; 2) are currently enrolled in a university or college ROTC program or the U.S. Marine Corps Platoon Leaders Course but are not receiving an ROTC scholarship; or 3) are disabled veterans. Applicants must also be 1) a direct or collateral descendant of a person who served with the 442nd Regimental Combat Team, the 100th Infantry Battalion, Military Intelligence Service, 1399th Engineering Construction Battalion, or other unit associated with those during or after World War II; or 2) a member or child of a member of the Japanese American Veterans Association (JAVA) whose membership extends back at least 1 year. Along with their application, they must submit a 500-word essay on their plan and vision to serve America through public service or the military.

Financial data The stipend is $5,000.

Duration 1 year.

Number awarded 1 each year.

Deadline March of each year.

[1171]
SFC CURTIS MANCINI MEMORIAL SCHOLARSHIPS

Association of the United States Army-Rhode Island Chapter
c/o LTC Robert A. Galvanin, President
31 Canoe River Drive
Mansfield, MA 02048
(508) 339-5301   E-mail: bpje5310@verizon.net
Web: www.riroa.org/ausari/scholarship.htm

Summary To provide financial assistance to members of the Rhode Island Chapter of the Association of the United States Army (AUSA) and their families who are interested in attending college or graduate school in any state.

Eligibility This program is open to members of the AUSA Rhode Island Chapter and their family members (spouses, children, and grandchildren). Applicants must be high school seniors or graduates accepted at an accredited college, university, or vocational/technical school in any state or current undergraduate or graduate students. Along with their application, they must submit a 250-word essay on why they feel their achievements should qualify them for this award. Selection is based on academic and individual achievements; financial need is not considered. Special consideration is given to students or graduates of Lincoln High School in Lincoln, Rhode Island (the alma mater of this program's namesake), especially those preparing for a career in law enforcement or enrolled or planning to enroll in Army ROTC.

Financial data The stipend is $1,000.

Duration 1 year.

Additional information Membership in the AUSA is open to everyone who supports a strong national defense, with special concern for the Army. That includes Regular Army, National Guard, Army Reserve, government civilians, retired soldiers, Wounded Warriors, veterans, concerned citizens and family members.

Number awarded Several each year.

Deadline April of each year.

[1172]
SGT. FREDERICK C. BRACE, JR. MEMORIAL SCHOLARSHIP

American Academy of Physician Assistants-Veterans Caucus
Attn: Scholarship Program
P.O. Box 362
Ossining, NY 10562
(803) 328-1864   Fax: (704) 838-8494
E-mail: rmunsee@veteranscaucus.org
Web: www.veteranscaucus.org/scholarships

Summary To provide financial assistance to Air Force veterans and their dependents who are studying to become physician assistants.

Eligibility This program is open to U.S. citizens who are currently enrolled in a physician assistant program. Applicants must be honorably discharged members of the United

States Air Force or the dependent of an Air Force veteran. Along with their application, they must submit a personal statement about what led them to attend PA school; their background, present, and future intentions; and why they deserve to receive a scholarship. Selection is based on military honors and awards received, civic and college honors and awards received, professional memberships and activities, potential for future achievement, and GPA.
Financial data The stipend is $2,000.
Duration 1 year.
Number awarded 1 each year.
Deadline February of each year.

[1173]
SIGMA CHI MILITARY SERVICE SCHOLARSHIPS
Sigma Chi Foundation
Attn: Scholarship Committee
1714 Hinman Avenue
Evanston, IL 60201
(847) 869-3655, ext. 270   Fax: (847) 869-4906
E-mail: foundation@sigmachi.org
Web: www.sigmachi.org
Summary To provide financial assistance to undergraduate and graduate student members of Sigma Chi who are serving or have served in the military.
Eligibility This program is open to undergraduate and graduate brothers of the fraternity who are currently serving or have served in the military (Army, Navy, Air Force, Marines, Coast Guard, or National Guard). They must have earned a GPA of 2.5 or higher and have completed at least 2 semesters of undergraduate study. ROTC students are not eligible.
Financial data The stipend is $1,000. Funds are to be used for tuition/fees only and are paid directly to the recipient's school.
Duration 1 year.
Number awarded Varies each year; recently, 9 were awarded.
Deadline May of each year.

[1174]
SMSGT. NATHAN L. LIPSCOMB, SR. MEMORIAL SCHOLARSHIP
American Academy of Physician Assistants-Veterans Caucus
Attn: Scholarship Program
P.O. Box 362
Ossining, NY 10562
(803) 328-1864   Fax: (704) 838-8494
E-mail: rmunsee@veteranscaucus.org
Web: www.veteranscaucus.org/scholarships
Summary To provide financial assistance to Air Force veterans and their dependents who are studying to become physician assistants.
Eligibility This program is open to U.S. citizens who are currently enrolled in a physician assistant program. Applicants must be honorably discharged members of the United States Air Force or the dependent of an Air Force veteran. Along with their application, they must submit a personal statement about what led them to attend PA school; their background, present, and future intentions; and why they deserve to receive a scholarship. Selection is based on military honors and awards received, civic and college honors and awards received, professional memberships and activities, potential for future achievement, and GPA.
Financial data The stipend is $2,000.
Duration 1 year.
Number awarded 1 each year.
Deadline February of each year.

[1175]
SOCIETY OF AIR FORCE PHYSICIAN ASSISTANTS MEMORIAL SCHOLARSHIP
American Academy of Physician Assistants-Veterans Caucus
Attn: Scholarship Program
P.O. Box 362
Ossining, NY 10562
(803) 328-1864   Fax: (704) 838-8494
E-mail: rmunsee@veteranscaucus.org
Web: www.veteranscaucus.org/scholarships
Summary To provide financial assistance to Air Force veterans who are studying to become physician assistants.
Eligibility This program is open to U.S. citizens who are currently enrolled in a physician assistant program. Applicants must be honorably discharged members of the United States Air Force. Along with their application, they must submit a personal statement about what led them to attend PA school; their background, present, and future intentions; and why they deserve to receive a scholarship. Selection is based on military honors and awards received, civic and college honors and awards received, professional memberships and activities, potential for future achievement, and GPA.
Financial data The stipend is $2,000.
Duration 1 year.
Number awarded 1 each year.
Deadline February of each year.

[1176]
SOCIETY OF ARMY PHYSICIAN ASSISTANTS MEMORIAL SCHOLARSHIP
American Academy of Physician Assistants-Veterans Caucus
Attn: Scholarship Program
P.O. Box 362
Ossining, NY 10562
(803) 328-1864   Fax: (704) 838-8494
E-mail: rmunsee@veteranscaucus.org
Web: www.veteranscaucus.org/scholarships
Summary To provide financial assistance to Army veterans who are studying to become physician assistants.
Eligibility This program is open to U.S. citizens who are currently enrolled in a physician assistant program. Applicants must be honorably discharged members of the United States Army. Along with their application, they must submit a personal statement about what led them to attend PA school; their background, present, and future intentions; and why they deserve to receive a scholarship. Selection is based on military honors and awards received, civic and college honors and awards received, professional memberships and activities, potential for future achievement, and GPA.
Financial data The stipend is $2,000.
Duration 1 year.

Number awarded 1 each year.
Deadline February of each year.

[1177]
SSGT. ROBERT V. MILNER MEMORIAL SCHOLARSHIP

American Academy of Physician Assistants-Veterans Caucus
Attn: Scholarship Program
P.O. Box 362
Ossining, NY 10562
(803) 328-1864   Fax: (704) 838-8494
E-mail: rmunsee@veteranscaucus.org
Web: www.veteranscaucus.org/scholarships

Summary To provide financial assistance to Air Force veterans and their dependents who are studying to become physician assistants.

Eligibility This program is open to U.S. citizens who are currently enrolled in a physician assistant program. Applicants must be honorably discharged members of the United States Air Force or the dependent of an Air Force veteran. Along with their application, they must submit a personal statement about what led them to attend PA school; their background, present, and future intentions; and why they deserve to receive a scholarship. Selection is based on military honors and awards received, civic and college honors and awards received, professional memberships and activities, potential for future achievement, and GPA.

Financial data The stipend is $2,000.
Duration 1 year.
Number awarded 1 each year.
Deadline February of each year.

[1178]
THE PFC ROGER W. CUMMINS MEMORIAL SCHOLARSHIP

American Academy of Physician Assistants-Veterans Caucus
Attn: Scholarship Program
P.O. Box 362
Ossining, NY 10562
(803) 328-1864   Fax: (704) 838-8494
E-mail: rmunsee@veteranscaucus.org
Web: www.veteranscaucus.org/scholarships

Summary To provide financial assistance to Marine Corps and Navy service members or veterans or family members who are studying to become physician assistants.

Eligibility This program is open to U.S. citizens who are currently enrolled in a physician assistant program. Applicants must be active-duty members of the U.S. Marine Corps or Navy Corpsmen who have served with the Marine Corps, veterans of those services, or their spouses or children. Along with their application, they must submit a personal statement about what led them to attend PA school; their background, present, and future intentions; and why they deserve to receive a scholarship. Selection is based on military honors and awards received, civic and college honors and awards received, professional memberships and activities, potential for future achievement, and GPA.

Financial data The stipend is $2,000.
Duration 1 year.

Number awarded 1 each year.
Deadline February of each year.

[1179]
TILLMAN MILITARY SCHOLARS PROGRAM

Pat Tillman Foundation
222 North Merchandise Mart Plaza, Suite 1212
Chicago, IL 60654
(773) 360-5277
E-mail: scholarships@pattillmanfoundation.org
Web: www.pattillmanfoundation.org/apply-to-be-a-scholar

Summary To provide financial assistance to veterans, active servicemembers, and their spouses who are interested in working on an undergraduate or graduate degree.

Eligibility This program is open to veterans and active servicemembers of all branches of the armed forces from both the pre- and post-September 11 era and their spouses; children are not eligible. Applicants must be enrolled or planning to enroll full time at a 4-year public or private college or university to work on an undergraduate, graduate, or postgraduate degree. Current and former servicemembers must submit 400-word essays on 1) their motivation and decision to serve in the U.S. military and how that decision and experience has changed their life and ambitions; and 2) their educational and career goals, how they will incorporate their military service experience into those goals, and how they intend to continue their service to others and the community. Spouses must submit 400-word essays on 1) their previous service to others and the community; and 2) their educational and career goals, how they will incorporate their service experiences and the impact of their spouse's military service into those goals, and how they intend to continue their service to others and the community. Selection is based on those essays, educational and career ambitions, record of military service, record of personal achievement, demonstration of service to others in the community, desire to continue such service, and leadership potential.

Financial data The stipend depends on the need of the recipient and the availability of funds; recently, stipends averaged approximately $11,000 per year.

Duration 1 year; may be renewed, provided the recipient maintains a GPA of 3.0 or higher, remains enrolled full time, and documents participation in civic action or community service.

Additional information This program began in 2009.
Number awarded Approximately 60 each year. Since the program began, it has awarded more than $15 million to 580 scholars.
Deadline February of each year.

[1180]
TONALAW VETERAN'S SCHOLARSHIP

TonaLaw
152 Islip Avenue, Suite 18
Islip, NY 11751
(631) 780-5355   Toll Free: (844) TONA-LAW
Fax: (631) 780-5685   E-mail: contact@tonalaw.com
Web: www.tonalaw.com/scholarship

Summary To provide financial assistance to veterans who are interested in attending college of law school in any state.

Eligibility This program is open to veterans of all branches of the U.S. armed forces. Applicants must be enrolled at an accredited college or law school in any state or accepted for enrollment to begin within 6 months of application. Along with their application, they must submit an essay of 300 to 600 words on how their military service has made an impact on their life, how it has prepared them for college, and what they plan to do after they complete their education.

Financial data The stipend is $1,000.

Duration 1 year.

Number awarded 2 each year: 1 each semester.

Deadline July of each year for fall semester; November of each year for spring semester.

[1181]
TROOPS-TO-TEACHERS PROGRAM

Defense Activity for Non-Traditional Education Support
Attn: Troops to Teachers
6490 Saufley Field Road
Pensacola, FL 32509-5243
(850) 452-1241   Toll Free: (800) 231-6242
Fax: (850) 452-1096   E-mail: ttt@navy.mil
Web: www.proudtoserveagain.com

Summary To provide a bonus to veterans and military personnel interested in a second career as a public school teacher.

Eligibility This program is open to 1) active-duty military personnel who are retired or currently serving and have an approved date of retirement within 1 year; 2) members of a Reserve component who are retired or currently serving in the Selected Reserve with 6 or more years of credible service and commit to serving an additional 3 years or until eligible for retirement; 3) military personnel with at least 4 years on continuous active duty, will transfer to the Selected Reserve within 3 years, and are willing to commit to at least 3 years in the Selected Reserve or until eligible for retirement; and 4) active-duty or Selected Reserve personnel who separated on or after January 8, 2002 for a service-connected physical disability and who register for this program within 3 years of separation. Applicants must have a baccalaureate or advanced degree, the equivalent of 1 year of college with 6 years of work experience in a vocational or technical field, or meet state requirements for vocational/technical teacher referral. A bonus or stipend is available to applicants who are willing to accept employment as a teacher in 1) an eligible school where the free/reduced cost lunch percentage is 30% or more, at least 13% of students enrolled qualify for assistance under part B of the Individuals with Disabilities Education Act (IDEA), or a Bureau of Indian Affairs funded school; 2) a high needs school where the free/reduced cost lunch percentage is 50% or more for public middle or elementary schools, 40% or more for public high schools, or that qualifies as a rural school.

Financial data A bonus of $10,000 is awarded to recipients who agree to teach for 3 years in an eligible or high needs school. A stipend of $5,000 is awarded to recipients who are enrolled in a program at an accredited institution that will result in licensure as a full time teacher and who agree to teach for 3 years in an eligible or high needs school. All recipients who are not retired or discharged due to service-connected physical disability must commit to serve 3 years in the Reserves or until eligible to retire.

Duration The bonuses are intended as 1-time grants. Stipends are available as long as the recipient remains enrolled.

Additional information This program was established in 1994 by the Department of Defense (DoD). In 2000, program oversight and funding were transferred to the U.S. Department of Education, but DoD continues to operate the program. The No Child Left Behind Act of 2001 provided for continuation of the program.

Number awarded Varies each year; recently, 2,891 applicants were approved for participation in the program.

Deadline Applications may be submitted at any time within 3 years of retirement or separation.

[1182]
TVSHKA (WARRIOR) SCHOLARSHIP

Chahta Foundation
Attn: Scholarship Director
P.O. Box 1849
Durant, OK 74702
(580) 924-8280, ext. 2546
Toll Free: (800) 522-6170, ext. 2546
Fax: (580) 745-9023
E-mail: scholarship@chahtafoundation.com
Web: www.chahtafoundation.com/scholarship/veterans

Summary To provide financial assistance to Choctaw Indians who are serving or have served in the armed services and are planning to attend college or graduate school in any state.

Eligibility This program is open to Choctaw students who are active duty or retired U.S. armed services veterans. Applicants be enrolled or planning to enroll full time in an undergraduate or graduate degree program at a college or university in any state. They must have a GPA of 2.5 or higher. Along with their application, they must submit essays on assigned topics, transcripts, 2 letters of recommendation, a resume, and documentation of financial need.

Financial data The stipend is $3,000.

Duration 1 year.

Additional information This program began in 2016.

Number awarded 1 or more each year.

Deadline March of each year.

[1183]
UNIFIED ARIZONA VETERANS SCHOLARSHIPS

Unified Arizona Veterans, Inc.
Attn: Scholarship Committee
P.O. Box 34338
Phoenix, AZ 85067
E-mail: scholarships@azuav.org
Web: www.azuav.org

Summary To provide financial assistance to veterans and military personnel in Arizona who are interested in attending college in the state.

Eligibility This program is open to residents of Arizona who are 1) honorably discharged veterans; 2) currently on active duty, including service members in good standing with a Reserve or Guard components; or 3) immediate family members of an Arizona veteran killed in action or by an act of terror. Applicants must be enrolled at an institution of higher learning in Arizona and working on a bachelor's or master's degree in any field. Along with their application, they must submit 1) a 1-page essay on why they chose their current academic program and how they plan to use their degree, certificate, or license; 2) letters of recommendation; 3) verifi-

cation of enrollment and Arizona residency; and 4) documentation of financial need.
Financial data Stipends range up to $5,000.
Duration 1 year.
Number awarded 1 or more each year.
Deadline February of each year.

[1184]
UTAH TUITION WAIVER FOR PURPLE HEART RECIPIENTS

Utah Department of Veterans and Military Affairs
Attn: Director
550 Foothill Boulevard, Suite 105
Salt Lake City, UT 84113
(801) 326-2372   Toll Free: (800) 894-9497 (within UT)
Fax: (801) 326-2369   E-mail: veterans@utah.gov
Web: veterans.utah.gov/state-education-benefits

Summary To provide a tuition waiver to veterans in Utah who received a Purple Heart award and are attending a public institution in the state.
Eligibility This program is open to residents of Utah who received a Purple Heart award as a result of military service. Applicants must be working on an undergraduate or master's degree at a public college or university in the state.
Financial data Tuition at the rate for residents of the state is waived for qualified veterans.
Duration Tuition is waived until completion of a bachelor's or master's degree.
Number awarded Varies each year.
Deadline Deadline not specified.

[1185]
VETERANS MAKE GREAT STEM TEACHERS PROGRAM

International Technology and Engineering Educators Association
Attn: Foundation for Technology and Engineering Educators
1914 Association Drive, Suite 201
Reston, VA 20191-1539
(703) 860-2100   Fax: (703) 860-0353
E-mail: iteea@iteea.org
Web: www.iteea.org

Summary To provide financial assistance to veterans who are working on an undergraduate or graduate degree as a technology and engineering teacher.
Eligibility This program is open to veterans of any branch of the military who are enrolled full time as an undergraduate or graduate student at an accredited institution of higher education. Applicants must be preparing for a career as a technology and engineering teacher and have a GPA of 3.0 or higher. They must be members of the International Technology and Engineering Educators Association (ITEEA).
Financial data The stipend is $1,000 for freshmen and sophomores or $3,000 for juniors, seniors, and graduate students. Funds are provided directly to the recipient.
Duration 1 year.
Additional information This program, which began in 2018, is sponsored by CNC Mastercam.

Number awarded 2 each year: 1 to a freshman or sophomore and 1 to a junior, senior, or graduate student.
Deadline November of each year.

[1186]
VICE ADMIRAL ROBERT L. WALTERS SCHOLARSHIP

Surface Navy Association
Attn: Scholarship Coordinator
6564 Loisdale Court, Suite 318
Springfield, VA 22150
(703) 960-6800   Toll Free: (800) NAVY-SNA
Fax: (703) 960-6807   E-mail: navysna@aol.com
Web: www.navysna.org/scholarship/information.html

Summary To provide financial assistance for college or graduate school to members of the Surface Navy Association (SNA) and their dependents.
Eligibility This program is open to SNA members and their children, stepchildren, wards, and spouses. The SNA member must 1) be in the second or subsequent consecutive year of membership; 2) be serving, retired, or honorably discharged; 3) be a Surface Warfare Officer or Enlisted Surface Warfare Specialist; and 4) have served for at least 3 years on a surface ship of the U.S. Navy or Coast Guard (the 3 years need not have been consecutive but must have been served on active duty). Applicants must be enrolled or planning to enroll full time at an accredited undergraduate or graduate institution; the full-time requirement may be waived for spouses. Along with their application, they must submit a 500-word essay about themselves and why they should be selected to receive this scholarship. High school seniors should also include a transcript of high school grades and a copy of ACT or SAT scores. Current college students should also include a transcript of the grades from their most recent 4 semesters of school. Selection is based on academic proficiency, non-scholastic activities, scholastic and non-scholastic awards, character, and financial need.
Financial data The stipend is $2,000 per year.
Duration 4 years, provided the recipient maintains a GPA of 3.0 or higher.
Number awarded Varies each year.
Deadline February of each year.

[1187]
WAPA VETERAN SCHOLARSHIPS

Washington Academy of Physician Assistants
Attn: Veterans Committee
2001 Sixth Avenue, Suite 2700
Seattle, WA 98121
(206) 956-3624   Toll Free: (800) 552-0612, ext. 3006
Fax: (206) 441-5863   E-mail: wapa@wapa.com
Web: www.wapa.com/scholarship-information

Summary To provide financial assistance for college or graduate school to members of the Washington Academy of Physician Assistants (WAPA) who are veterans.
Eligibility This program is open to WAPA members who are veterans working on an undergraduate or graduate degree in a physician assistant program in Washington. Applicants must submit a 1- to 2-page narrative on why they chose the physician assistant profession, their community involvement, their plans for future involvement in WAPA, and how the scholarship will benefit them.

Financial data A stipend is awarded (amount not specified).
Duration 1 year.
Number awarded 1 each year.
Deadline April of each year.

[1188]
WASHINGTON METROPOLITAN AREA NAVY NURSE CORPS ASSOCIATION SCHOLARSHIPS

Washington Metropolitan Area Navy Nurse Corps Association
c/o Susan S. Miller, Scholarship Committee Chair
P.O. Box 571
Arnold, MD 21012
E-mail: Navycapt51@hotmail.com
Web: www.nnca.org/join-nnca-2/local-chapters/wmannca

Summary To provide financial assistance to current and former Navy nurses who live or work in the area served by the Washington Metropolitan Area Navy Nurse Corps Association (WMANNCA) and are interested in working on a graduate nursing degree.
Eligibility This program is open to Navy nurses (active duty, reserve, retired, or former) who plan to continue their studies by working on an advanced graduate degree in nursing. Applicants must live or work in the area served by WMANNCA: Delaware, Maryland, New Jersey, Pennsylvania, Virginia, Washington, D.C., or West Virginia. Along with their application, they must submit a 250-word personal statement on why this degree is important to them, how they will utilize this degree to benefit the Navy or nursing, and how these funds will enable them to achieve their goals.
Financial data The stipend is $1,000.
Duration 1 year.
Number awarded 3 each year.
Deadline March of each year.

[1189]
WELLS FARGO VETERANS SCHOLARSHIP PROGRAM

Scholarship America
Attn: Scholarship Management Services
One Scholarship Way
P.O. Box 297
St. Peter, MN 56082
(507) 931-1682   Toll Free: (844) 402-0357
Fax: (507) 931-9168
E-mail: wellsfargoveterans@scholarshipamerica.org
Web: www.scholarsapply.org/wellsfargoveterans

Summary To provide financial assistance to veterans and the spouses of disabled veterans who are interested in attending college.
Eligibility This program is open to honorably-discharged (no longer drilling) veterans and the spouses of disabled veterans of the U.S. armed forces, including the Reserves and National Guard. Applicants must be enrolled or planning to enroll full time at an accredited 2- or 4-year college, university, or vocational/technical school to work on a bachelor's or master's degree. They must have a GPA of 2.5 or higher and be able to demonstrate financial need. Along with their application, they must submit essays on 1) their military service and career and educational goals and objectives; and 2) any personal or financial challenges that may be barriers to completing postsecondary education. Selection is based on those essays, academic performance, demonstrated leadership, participation in school and community activities, work experience, and financial need.
Financial data The amount of the initial stipend depends on an analysis of the recipient's military education benefits, institutional grants, and other scholarships. If renewed, the stipend increases by $1,000 each year.
Duration 1 year; scholarships may be renewed up to 3 additional years or until completion of a degree, whichever occurs firsts. Renewal depends on the recipient's maintaining satisfactory academic progress and full-time enrollment.
Additional information This trustee for this program is Wells Fargo Bank and the administrator is Scholarship America.
Number awarded Varies each year.
Deadline February of each year.

[1190]
WISCONSIN G.I. BILL TUITION REMISSION PROGRAM

Wisconsin Department of Veterans Affairs
2135 Rimrock Road
P.O. Box 7843
Madison, WI 53707-7843
(608) 266-1311   Toll Free: (800) WIS-VETS
Fax: (608) 267-0403   E-mail: WDVAInfo@dva.state.wi.us
Web: dva.wi.gov

Summary To provide financial assistance for college or graduate school to Wisconsin veterans and their dependents.
Eligibility This program is open to current residents of Wisconsin who 1) were residents of the state when they entered or reentered active duty in the U.S. armed forces; or 2) have moved to the state and have been residents for at least 5 consecutive years after entry or reentry into service. Applicants must have served on active duty for at least 2 continuous years or for at least 90 days during specified wartime periods. Also eligible are 1) qualifying children and unremarried surviving spouses of Wisconsin veterans who died in the line of duty or as the direct result of a service-connected disability; and 2) children and spouses of Wisconsin veterans who have a service-connected disability rated by the U.S. Department of Veterans Affairs as 30% or greater. Children must be between 17 and 25 years of age (regardless of the date of the veteran's death or initial disability rating) and be a Wisconsin resident for tuition purposes. Spouses remain eligible for 10 years following the date of the veteran's death or initial disability rating; they must be Wisconsin residents for tuition purposes, but they may enroll full or part time. Students may attend any institution, center, or school within the University of Wisconsin (UW) System or the Wisconsin Technical College System (WCTS). There are no income limits, delimiting periods following military service during which the benefit must be used, or limits on the level of study (e.g., vocational, undergraduate, professional, or graduate).
Financial data Veterans who qualify as a Wisconsin resident for tuition purposes are eligible for a remission of 100% of standard academic fees and segregated fees at a UW campus or 100% of program and material fees at a WCTS institution. Veterans who qualify as a Wisconsin veteran for purposes of this program but for other reasons fail to meet the definition of a Wisconsin resident for tuition purposes at the

UW system are eligible for a remission of 100% of non-resident fees. Spouses and children of deceased or disabled veterans are entitled to a remission of 100% of tuition and fees at a UW or WCTS institution.

Duration Up to 8 semesters or 128 credits, whichever is greater.

Additional information This program began in 2005 as a replacement for Wisconsin Tuition and Fee Reimbursement Grants.

Number awarded Varies each year.

Deadline Applications must be submitted within 14 days from the office start of the academic term: in October for fall, March for spring, or June for summer.

[1191]
WOMEN MARINES ASSOCIATION SCHOLARSHIP PROGRAM

Women Marines Association
120 State Avenue, Suite 303
Olympia, WA 98501
Toll Free: (888) 525-1943
E-mail: scholarship@womenmarines.org
Web: www.womenmarines.org/scholarships

Summary To provide financial assistance for college or graduate school to students sponsored by members of the Women Marines Association (WMA).

Eligibility Applicants must be sponsored by a WMA member and fall into 1 of the following categories: 1) have served or are serving in the U.S. Marine Corps, regular or Reserve; 2) are a direct descendant by blood or legal adoption or a stepchild of a Marine on active duty or who has served honorably in the U.S. Marine Corps, regular or Reserve; 3) are a sibling or a descendant of a sibling by blood or legal adoption or a stepchild of a Marine on active duty or who has served honorably in the U.S. Marine Corps, regular or Reserve; 4) be a spouse of a Marine; or 5) have completed 2 years in a Marine Corps JROTC program. WMA members may sponsor an unlimited number of applicants per year. High school seniors must submit transcripts (GPA of 3.0 or higher) and SAT or ACT scores. Undergraduate and graduate students must have a GPA of 3.0 or higher. Along with their application, they must submit 1-page statements on 1) the Marine to whom they are related; 2) their community service; and 3) their goals after college.

Financial data Stipends range from $500 to $5,000 per year.

Duration 1 year; may be renewed 1 additional year.

Additional information This program includes the following named scholarships: the WMA Memorial Scholarships, the Lily H. Gridley Memorial Scholarship, the Ethyl and Armin Wiebke Memorial Scholarship, the Maj. Megan McClung Memorial Scholarship, the Agnes Sopcak Memorial Scholarship, the Virginia Guveyan Memorial Scholarship, the LaRue A. Ditmore Music Scholarships, the Fallen Warrior Scholarship, and the Margaret Apel Scholarship. Applicants must know a WMA member to serve as their sponsor; the WMA will not supply listings of the names or addresses of chapters or individual members.

Number awarded Varies each year.

Deadline February of each year.

[1192]
YELLOW RIBBON PROGRAM OF THE POST-9/11 GI BILL

Department of Veterans Affairs
Attn: Veterans Benefits Administration
810 Vermont Avenue, N.W.
Washington, DC 20420
(202) 418-4343   Toll Free: (888) 442-4551
Web: www.va.gov

Summary To provide financial assistance to veterans and their dependents who qualify for the Post-9/11 GI Bill and wish to attend a high cost private or out-of-state public institution.

Eligibility Maximum Post-9/11 GI Bill benefits are available to veterans who 1) served on active duty for at least 36 aggregate months after September 11, 2001; or 2) received a Purple Heart on or after September 11, 2001 and were honorably discharged after any length of service; or 3) received a Fry Scholarship on or after August 1, 2018 and/or are currently receiving that scholarship; or 4) were honorably discharged after 60 days for a service-connected disability and served at least 30 continuous days after September 11, 2001. Military personnel currently on active duty and their spouses may qualify for Post-9/11 GI Bill benefits but are not eligible for the Yellow Ribbon Program. This program is available to veterans who qualify for those benefits at the 100% rate, the children and spouses of those veterans to whom they wish to transfer their benefits, and the children of active-duty personnel who qualify for benefits at the 100% rate to whom they wish to transfer those benefits. Applicants must be working on or planning to work on an undergraduate or graduate degree at a private or out-of-state public institution that charges tuition in excess of the $25,162.14 cap imposed by the Post-9/11 GI Bill and that has agreed with the Department of Veterans Affairs (VA) to participate in this program.

Financial data Colleges and universities that charge more than $25,162.14 per academic year in tuition and fees may agree to waive tuition (up to 50%) for qualifying veterans and dependents. The amount that the college or university waives is matched by VA.

Duration Most participants receive up to 36 months of entitlement under this program. Benefits are payable for up to 15 years following release from active duty.

Number awarded Varies each year.

Deadline Deadline not specified.

Military Personnel

[1193]
ADVANCED CIVIL SCHOOLING PROGRAM
U.S. Army
Human Resources Command
Attn: OPCF ACS Program
1600 Spearhead Division Avenue
Fort Knox, KY 40122-5408
Toll Free: (800) 872-8272
E-mail: usarmy.knox.hrc.mbx.opmd-army-acs@mail.mil
Web: myarmybenefits.us.army.mil

Summary To provide financial assistance to Army officers interested in working on an advanced degree in selected fields.
Eligibility This program is open to Army officers who wish to work on an advanced degree at an approved civilian institution on a full-time basis. Applicants must have a regular Army commission or a commission with Voluntary Indefinite Status (VI) and less than 17 years of active federal service. They must have completed a bachelor's degree with a GPA of 2.5 or higher and must have a GRE score of 153 or higher in verbal reasoning, 144 or higher in quantitative reasoning, and 4.0 or higher in the analytical category; Ph.D. candidates and other designated officers are not required to submit GRE scores. Applicants for management-related degrees must have at least 500 on the GMAT.
Financial data The officer continues to receive regular Army salary and allowances. The fellowship pays tuition up to $14,500 per year, a 1-time payment of $600 for application fees, and a book allotment of $200 per year.
Duration 12 to 22 months, depending on the program.
Additional information Participants in this program incur an additional service obligation of 3 days of service for each day of educational leave. Further information and applications are available from the applicant's assignment officer.
Number awarded Approximately 412 each year.
Deadline September of each year.

[1194]
AFBA NGAUS ACTIVE LIFE MEMBER SCHOLARSHIP
National Guard Association of the United States
Attn: Scholarship
One Massachusetts Avenue, N.W.
Washington, DC 20001
(202) 789-0031   Fax: (202) 682-9358
E-mail: ngaus@ngaus.org
Web: www.ngaus.org

Summary To provide financial assistance to members of the National Guard Association of the United States (NGAUS) and their dependents who are interested in working on an undergraduate or graduate degree.
Eligibility This program is open to active life NGAUS members and their dependents. Applicants must be enrolled or planning to enroll full time at a college or university in any state to work on an undergraduate or graduate degree. Along with their application, they must submit their college acceptance letter, SAT and/or ACT scores, high school or undergraduate transcripts, a publicity photograph, and an essay up to 300 words in length on an experience with the National Guard and how it has shaped their development and goals.
Financial data The stipend is $5,000.
Duration 1 year.
Additional information This program is sponsored by the Armed Forces Benefit Association (AFBA).
Number awarded 2 each year.
Deadline May of each year.

[1195]
AFCEA WAR VETERAN TEACHER CERTIFICATION PROGRAM
Armed Forces Communications and Electronics Association
Attn: AFCEA Educational Foundation
4114 Legato Road, Suite 1000
Fairfax, VA 22033-3342
(703) 631-6147   Toll Free: (800) 336-4583, ext. 6147
Fax: (703) 631-4693   E-mail: edfoundation@afcea.org
Web: www.afcea.org

Summary To provide financial assistance to veterans and military personnel who served in designated Overseas Contingency Operations and are interested in preparing for a career as a STEM teacher.
Eligibility This program is open to active-duty and honorably discharged U.S. military members (including Reservists and National Guard personnel) who served in Operation Enduring Freedom, Operation Iraqi Freedom, Operation New Dawn, Operation Inherent Resolve, or Operation Freedom's Sentinel. Applicants must have earned a bachelor's degree in a field of science and be working on a credential or license for the purpose of teaching STEM in a U.S. K-12 school. They must have a GPA of 3.0 or higher. Their expected date of graduation or certification cannot be in the same year as the award of the scholarship. Selection is based on merit.
Financial data The stipend is $2,500.
Duration 1 year.
Number awarded 1 or more each year.
Deadline November of each year.

[1196]
AIR FORCE CLUB SCHOLARSHIP PROGRAM
Air Force Services Agency
Attn: HQ AFPC/SVOFT
10100 Reunion Place, Suite 501
San Antonio, TX 78216-4138
(210) 395-7351   Toll Free: (800) 443-4834
E-mail: clubs@myairforcelife.com
Web: www.myairforcelife.com/Clubs

Summary To recognize and reward, with academic scholarships, Air Force Club members and their families who submit outstanding essays.
Eligibility This program is open to Air Force Club members and their spouses, children, stepchildren, or grandchildren who have been accepted by or are enrolled at an accredited college or university. Applicants may be traditional (graduating high school seniors) or nontraditional (all other club members). They must submit either 1) an essay of 980 to 1020 words on a topic that changes annually; or 2) a video of 4 minutes 30 seconds to 5 minutes 30 seconds on the same topic. Essays and videos must relate to a topic that changes

annually; recently, students were asked to write about the core values of the U.S. Air Force. Applicants must also include a 1-page summary of their long-term career and life goals and previous accomplishments, including civic, athletic, and academic awards.
Financial data Awards for both traditional and nontraditional applicants are presented as scholarships of $7,000 for first, $5,000 for second, $3,000 for third, $2,000 for fourth, and $1,000 for honorable mention.
Duration The competition is held annually.
Additional information This competition was first held in 1997.
Number awarded 10 each year: 5 for traditional applicants and 5 for nontraditional.
Deadline May of each year.

[1197]
AIR FORCE GRADUATE LAW PROGRAM
U.S. Air Force
Attn: HQ USAF/JAX
1500 West Perimeter Road, Suite 3330
Joint Base Andrews, MD 20762
Toll Free: (800) JAG-USAF
E-mail: airforcejagrecruiting@gmail.com
Web: www.airforce.com

Summary To provide financial assistance to first-year law students who are willing to join Air Force ROTC and serve as Air Force Judge Advocates following completion of their studies.
Eligibility This program is open to students in their first year at an ABA-approved law school that has, or is located near, an AFROTC detachment. Applicants must be in good academic standing and able to meet AFROTC entry standards (U.S. citizenship, weight and medical qualifications, and Air Force Officer Qualification Test minimum score). They must be younger than 40 years of age upon commissioning and entering active duty. Eligible students include veterans, current military personnel, and first-year law students without military experience. Selection is based on academic performance, extracurricular activities, community service, prior military record (if any), work experience, and a recommendation by a staff judge advocate following an interview.
Financial data Participants receive a stipend for 10 months of the year at $400 per month and a salary at pay grade E-5 during summer field training. No other scholarship assistance is available.
Duration 2 years.
Additional information Selectees with no prior military experience attend field training encampment during the summer prior to entering the AFROTC program as contract cadets. Upon completion of their degree, participants are commissioned as inactive second lieutenants in the Air Force Reserves. After passing legal licensing requirements, they enter active duty as first lieutenants in the U.S. Air Force Judge Advocate General's Department. The initial required active-duty service obligation is 4 years.
Number awarded Varies each year.
Deadline January of each year.

[1198]
AIR FORCE HEALTH PROFESSIONS SCHOLARSHIP PROGRAM
U.S. Air Force
Attn: Air Force Personnel Center
Headquarters DP2NP
Physician Education
550 C Street West, Suite 25
Joint Base San Antonio-Randolph, TX 78150
(210) 565-2638   Toll Free: (833) 876-5701
E-mail: AFPC.DP2NP.PhysicianEducation@us.af.mil
Web: www.airforce.com

Summary To provide financial assistance for education in a medical or scientific field to future Air Force medical officers.
Eligibility This program is open to U.S. citizens who are accepted to or already enrolled in a health care professional program. They must be working on a degree that will prepare them for service in Air Force Biomedical Science Corps specialties (pharmacists, optometrists, clinical psychologists, or public health officers), Nurse Corps specialties, Medical Corps, or Dental Corps. Applicants for the Medical Corps must have undergraduate GPAs of at least 3.2 and MCAT scores of 500 or higher with at least 123 in each subsection. Upon acceptance into the program, applicants are commissioned as officers in the U.S. Air Force; after completion of medical school, they must perform at least 3 years of active-duty service in the U.S. Air Force.
Financial data This program pays full tuition at any school of medicine or osteopathy located in the United States or Puerto Rico, and it also covers the cost of fees, books, and other required equipment. In addition, recipients are awarded a stipend of at least $2,300 per month for 10 1/2 months of the year; for the other 1 1/2 months of each year, they perform active-duty service, usually at an Air Force medical facility, and receive the normal pay of a Second Lieutenant.
Duration 1 or 2 years for Biomedical Service Corps specialties, 2 or 3 years for Nurse Corps specialties, 3 or 4 years for Medical Corps or Dental Corps.
Additional information Following receipt of the degree, students serve an internship and residency either in an Air Force hospital (in which case they receive Air Force active-duty pay) or, if not selected for Air Force graduate medical education, in a civilian hospital (where they receive only the regular salary paid by the civilian institution). Only after completion of the residency, in either an Air Force or a civilian hospital, do the students begin the active-duty service obligation. That obligation is equal to the number of years of support received plus 1 year.
Number awarded Approximately 325 each year.
Deadline Deadline not specified.

[1199]
AIR FORCE JUDGE ADVOCATE GENERAL'S DEPARTMENT FUNDED LEGAL EDUCATION PROGRAM
U.S. Air Force
Attn: HQ USAF/JAX
1500 West Perimeter Road, Suite 3330
Joint Base Andrews, MD 20762
Toll Free: (800) JAG-USAF
E-mail: airforcejagrecruiting@gmail.com
Web: www.airforce.com

Summary To provide financial assistance to Air Force officers interested in attending law school.
Eligibility This program is open to commissioned officers in the U.S. Air Force who have at least 2 but no more than 6 years of active-duty military service (including both enlisted and commissioned time) and have graduated from an accredited college or university with a bachelor's degree. Applicants must be currently in the pay grade of O-3 or below. They must submit transcripts from undergraduate (and/or graduate) schools, their LSAT results, and proof of an application or acceptance to an ABA-accredited law school.
Financial data Selectees continue to receive their regular pay and allowances during participation in this program. They also receive payment of tuition (to a maximum of $12,000 per year) and a book allowance.
Duration Until completion of a law degree.
Additional information Selectees are required to perform legal internships each summer they are in law school. Following completion of law school and passage of a bar examination, they enter service as an Air Force judge advocate with an active-duty obligation of 2 years for each year of legal training supported by this program.
Number awarded Varies each year; recently, 8 officers received support from this program.
Deadline February of each year.

[1200]
AIR FORCE ONE-YEAR COLLEGE PROGRAM (OYCP)
U.S. Air Force
Attn: HQ USAF/JAX
1500 West Perimeter Road, Suite 3330
Joint Base Andrews, MD 20762
Toll Free: (800) JAG-USAF
E-mail: airforcejagrecruiting@gmail.com
Web: www.airforce.com

Summary To provide financial assistance to second-year law students who are willing to join Air Force ROTC and serve as Air Force Judge Advocates following completion of their studies.
Eligibility This program is open to students in their second year at an ABA-approved law school that has, or is located near, an AFROTC detachment. Applicants must be in good academic standing and able to meet AFROTC entry standards (U.S. citizenship, weight and medical qualifications, and Air Force Officer Qualification Test minimum score). They must be younger than 40 years of age upon commissioning and entering active duty. Selection is based on academic performance, extracurricular activities, community service, prior military record (if any), work experience, and a recommendation by a staff judge advocate following an interview.
Financial data Participants receive a stipend for 10 months of the year at $400 per month and a salary at pay grade E-5 during summer field training. No other scholarship assistance is available.
Duration 1 year.
Additional information Selectees with no prior military experience attend field training encampment during the summer prior to entering the AFROTC program as contract cadets. Upon completion of their degree, participants are commissioned as inactive second lieutenants in the Air Force Reserves. After passing legal licensing requirements, they enter active duty as first lieutenants in the U.S. Air Force Judge Advocate General's Department. The initial required active-duty service obligation is 4 years.
Number awarded Varies each year.
Deadline January of each year.

[1201]
AIR FORCE RESERVE TUITION ASSISTANCE
U.S. Air Force Reserve
Attn: Air Reserve Recruiting Service
180 Page Road, Building 208
Robins, AFB GA 31098-1815
Toll Free: (800) 257-1212
Web: www.afreserve.com/benefits

Summary To provide financial assistance for college or graduate school to members of the Air Force Reserve.
Eligibility This program is open to Air Force Reserve members interested in working on an undergraduate or graduate degree either through distance learning or on-campus courses from an accredited postsecondary institution. Applicants must be actively participating (for pay and points) and in good standing (not have a UIF, not placed on a control roster, not pending or issued an Article 15, and/or not pending court martial). They must submit a degree plan specifying all classes for which they are seeking assistance. Enlisted students must have retainability that extends beyond the last course approved for assistance or they must extend or re-enlist; commissioned officers must have a mandatory separation date of not less than 48 months of service commitment starting at the end of the last course completed.
Financial data Airmen receive 100% of tuition for undergraduate or graduate study, to a maximum of $250 per semester hour or $4,500 per year.
Duration 1 year; may be renewed.
Number awarded Varies each year.
Deadline Applications may be submitted at any time.

[1202]
AIR FORCE TUITION ASSISTANCE PROGRAM
U.S. Air Force
Attn: Air Force Personnel Center
Headquarters USAF/DPPAT
550 C Street West, Suite 10
Joint Base San Antonio-Randolph, TX 78150-4712
Toll Free: (800) 525-0102　　　　Fax: (210) 565-2328
E-mail: afpc.pa.task@us.af.mil
Web: www.afpc.af.mil

Summary To provide financial assistance for college or graduate school to active-duty Air Force personnel.
Eligibility Eligible to apply for this program are active-duty Air Force personnel who have completed 2 years of their service obligation.
Financial data Air Force personnel chosen for participation in this program continue to receive their regular Air Force pay. The Air Force will pay 100% of the tuition costs in an approved program, to a maximum of $4,500 per year or $250 per semester hour, whichever is less. Funding is available only for tuition, not fees or other associated expenses.
Duration Up to 124 semester hours for a bachelor's degree or up to 42 semester hours for a graduate degree. Undergraduates must complete all courses with a grade of "C" or better; graduate students must complete classes with a grade of "B"

of better. If recipients fail to achieve those grades, they must reimburse the Air Force for all funds received.

Additional information Applications and further information about this program are available from counselors at the education centers on Air Force bases. Most Air Force personnel who receive tuition assistance participate in the Community College of the Air Force; there, participants earn a 2-year associate degree by combining on-the-job technical training or attendance at Air Force schools with enrollment in college courses at a civilian institution during off-duty hours. In addition, each Air Force base offers at least 4 subject areas in which selected Air Force personnel can receive tuition assistance for study leading to a bachelor's degree, and 2 disciplines in which they can pursue graduate study.

Number awarded Varies each year.
Deadline Deadline not specified.

[1203]
ALABAMA NATIONAL GUARD EDUCATIONAL ASSISTANCE PROGRAM

Alabama Commission on Higher Education
Attn: Grants Coordinator
100 North Union Street
P.O. Box 302000
Montgomery, AL 36130-2000
(334) 242-2273   Fax: (334) 242-0268
E-mail: cheryl.newton@ache.alabama.gov
Web: www.ache.edu/StudentAsst.aspx

Summary To provide financial assistance to members of the Alabama National Guard interested in attending college or graduate school in the state.

Eligibility This program is open to Alabama residents who are enrolled in an associate, baccalaureate, master's, or doctoral program at a public college, university, community college, technical college, or junior college in the state; are making satisfactory academic progress as determined by the eligible institution; and are members in good standing of the Alabama National Guard who have completed basic training and advanced individual training. Applicants may be receiving federal veterans benefits, but they must show a cost less aid amount of at least $25.

Financial data Scholarships cover tuition, educational fees, books, and supplies, up to a maximum of $5,406 per semester ($10,812 per year). All Alabama Student Grant program proceeds for which the student is eligible are deducted from this award.

Duration Up to 12 years after the date of the first grant payment to the student through this program.

Number awarded Varies each year; recently, 653 were awarded. Awards are determined on a first-in, first-out basis as long as funds are available.

Deadline July of each year.

[1204]
ALASKA NATIONAL GUARD STATE TUITION REIMBURSEMENT PROGRAM

Alaska National Guard
Attn: Education Services Office
Army Guard Road, Building 49000
P.O. Box 5800
Joint Base Elmendorf-Richardson, AK 99505-5800
(907) 428-6477   Fax: (907) 428-6929
E-mail: maria.j.alvarez10.mil@mail.mil
Web: www.dmva.alaska.gov/FamilyServices/Education

Summary To provide financial assistance to current and former members of the Alaska National Guard who wish to attend a college or university in the state.

Eligibility This program is open to members of the Alaska National Guard (Air and Army) and Naval Militia who have a rating of E-1 through O-5, including warrant officers, and are attending a university program in Alaska. Eligibility extends to members who 1) have satisfactorily completed their service contract and who served honorably in federal active service or federally-funded state active service after September 11, 2001; or 2) have been separated or discharged from the Guard because of a service-connected injury, disease, or disability. First priority is given to undergraduates; if funding is available, students working on a second bachelor's degree or a master's degree may be supported. Non-prior servicemembers must complete Initial Active Duty for Training (IADT); prior servicemembers are eligible immediately.

Financial data Recipients are entitled to reimbursement equivalent to 100% of the cost of tuition and fees at the University of Alaska, to a maximum of $4,500 per fiscal year.

Duration 1 semester; may be renewed for a total of 144 semester credits.

Number awarded Varies each year.

Deadline Applications may be submitted at any time, but they must be received at least 90 days after the last official day of the class or term.

[1205]
ARMY AVIATION ASSOCIATION OF AMERICA SCHOLARSHIPS

Army Aviation Association of America Scholarship Foundation
Attn: AAAA Scholarship Foundation
593 Main Street
Monroe, CT 06468-2806
(203) 268-2450   Fax: (203) 268-5870
E-mail: scholarship@quad-a.org
Web: www.quad-a.org/Scholarship/Scholarship/about.aspx

Summary To provide financial aid for undergraduate or graduate study to members of the Army Aviation Association of America (AAAA) and their relatives.

Eligibility This program is open to current AAAA members and the spouses, children, grandchildren, and unmarried siblings of current or deceased members. Applicants must be enrolled or accepted for enrollment as an undergraduate or graduate student at an accredited college or university. They must include a 300-word essay on their life experiences, work history, and aspirations. Some scholarships are specifically reserved for enlisted, warrant officer, company grade, and Department of the Army civilian members. Selection is based on academic merit and personal achievement.

Financial data Stipends range from $1,000 to $5,000 per year.
Duration Scholarships may be for 1 year, 2 years, or 4 years.
Number awarded Varies each year; recently, $516,000 in scholarships was awarded to 304 students. Since the program began in 1963, the foundation has awarded more than $4 million to more than 4,100 qualified applicants.
Deadline Interested students must submit a pre-qualifying form by March of each year. The final application is due in April.

[1206]
ARMY HEALTH PROFESSIONS SCHOLARSHIP PROGRAM
U.S. Army
Human Resources Command, Health Services Division
Attn: AHRC-OPH-AN
1600 Spearhead Division Avenue
Fort Knox, KY 40122-5408
Toll Free: (800) 872-8272
E-mail: usarmy.knox.hrc.mbx.tagd-pdeei@mail.mil
Web: www.goarmy.com

Summary To provide financial assistance to future Army officers who are interested in preparing for a career in medically-related fields.
Eligibility This program is open to U.S. citizens under 35 years of age. Applicants must be enrolled in or accepted as a full-time student at an accredited professional school located in the United States or Puerto Rico in 1 of the following areas: allopathic or osteopathic medicine, dentistry, counseling/clinical psychology, optometry, veterinary science, or psychiatric nurse practitioner. Upon acceptance into the program, applicants are commissioned as officers in the U.S. Army Reserve; after completion of school, they must perform active-duty service in the U.S. Army Medical Corps, Dental Corps, Medical Service Corps (for clinical psychology and optometry), Nurse Corps, or Veterinary Corps.
Financial data This program pays full tuition at any school or college granting a doctoral or other relevant professional degree located in the United States or Puerto Rico and covers the cost of fees, books, and other required equipment. Recipients are also awarded a stipend of at least $2,300 per month for 10 1/2 months of the year. During the other 1 1/2 months of each year, they perform active-duty service, usually at an Army medical facility, and receive the normal pay of a Second Lieutenant.
Duration 1 to 4 years for the medical program; 1 to 4 years for the dental program; 2 or 3 years for the clinical or counseling psychology program; 2 to 4 years for the optometry program; and 1 to 3 years for the veterinary program.
Additional information Participants incur an active-duty obligation based on existing Department of Defense and Army Directives in effect at the time they sign their contract accepting support through this program. Recently, the obligation has been 1 year for each year of support and a minimum of 2 years for the medical program or 3 years for the dental, clinical or counseling psychology, optometry, or veterinary programs.
Number awarded Varies each year.
Deadline Applications may be submitted at any time.

[1207]
ARMY JUDGE ADVOCATE GENERAL CORPS FUNDED LEGAL EDUCATION PROGRAM
U.S. Army
Attn: Office of the Judge Advocate General
Personnel, Plans and Training Office
2200 Army Pentagon, Room 2B517
Washington, DC 20310
(703) 545-2843   Toll Free: (866) ARMY-JAG
E-mail: usarmy.pentagon.hqda-otjag.mbx.jaro@mail.mil
Web: www.goarmy.com

Summary To provide financial assistance to Army officers interested in obtaining a law degree.
Eligibility This program is open to commissioned active-duty Army officers who have graduated from an accredited college or university with a baccalaureate (or equivalent) degree. Applicants must have completed at least 2 but not more than 6 years of active duty (including warrant officer and enlisted service) and currently hold a rank of O-1 through O-3. They must be interested in attending a regular course of instruction leading to a J.D. or LL.B. degree at an approved civilian law school. U.S. citizenship is required. Selection is based on the "total person concept," including an evaluation of undergraduate and graduate school transcripts, LSAT score, ORB, OERs, SJA interview letter, and statement of motivation to attend law school.
Financial data While participating in this program, officers continue to receive their regular Army salary. The program also covers tuition, fees, and all other educational costs.
Duration 3 years.
Additional information Participants normally are expected to attend a state-supported law school where they qualify for in-state tuition or where military members are granted in-state tuition rates. Following completion of their law degree and admission to the bar, they incur a 2-year active-duty service obligation as an attorney in the Judge Advocate General's Corps (JAGC) for each academic year spent in law school. If they fail to pass the bar examination or are not assigned to the JAGC for any other reason, they are returned to their basic branch of assignment for completion of their service obligation. If they refuse to accept appointment in or assignment to the JAGC, they are returned to their basic branch of assignment for completion of their service obligation; they must also reimburse the government for all costs of their advanced education.
Number awarded Up to 25 each year.
Deadline October of each year.

[1208]
ARMY MEDICAL AND DENTAL SCHOOL STIPEND PROGRAM (MDSSP)
U.S. Army
Human Resources Command, Health Services Division
Attn: AHRC-OPH-AN
1600 Spearhead Division Avenue
Fort Knox, KY 40122-5408
Toll Free: (800) 872-8272
E-mail: usarmy.knox.hrc.mbx.tagd-pdeei@mail.mil
Web: www.goarmy.com

Summary To provide financial assistance to students in designated medically-related fields who are interested in serving in the U.S. Army Reserve after graduation.

Eligibility This program is open to U.S. citizens under 35 years of age. Applicants must be enrolled in or accepted as a full-time student at an accredited professional school located in the United States or Puerto Rico in 1 of the following areas: allopathic or osteopathic medicine, dentistry, psychology (doctoral level only), optometry, or psychiatric nurse practitioner. Upon acceptance into the program, applicants are commissioned as officers in the U.S. Army Reserve; after completion of school, they must train as part of an Army Reserve unit and serve when needed.
Financial data This program pays a stipend of at least $2,300 per month.
Duration Until completion of a degree.
Additional information Participants incur an obligation to serve 1 year in the Selected Reserve for each 6 months of support received, including 12 days of annual training or active duty for training.
Number awarded Varies each year.
Deadline Applications may be submitted at any time.

[1209]
ARMY NATIONAL GUARD FEDERAL TUITION ASSISTANCE
U.S. Army National Guard
Education Support Center
Camp Joseph T. Robinson
Building 5400 Box 46
North Little Rock, AR 72199-9600
Toll Free: (866) 628-5999   Fax: (501) 212-4928
E-mail: esc@ng.army.mil
Web: www.nationalguard.com

Summary To provide financial assistance for college or graduate school to members of the Army National Guard in each state.
Eligibility This program is open to members of the Army National Guard in every state who are interested in attending a college, community college, or university within the state. Applicants must have sufficient time to complete the course before their Expiration Time of Service (ETS) date. They must be interested in working on a high school diploma or equivalent (GED), certificate, associate degree, bachelor's degree, master's degree, or first professional degree, including those in architecture, Certified Public Accountant (C.P.A.), podiatry, dentistry (D.D.S. or D.M.D.), medicine (M.D.), optometry, osteopathic medicine, pharmacy (Pharm.D.), or theology (M.Div. or M.H.L.). Commissioned officers must agree to remain in the Guard for at least 4 years following completion of the course for which assistance is provided, unless they are involuntarily separated from the service.
Financial data Assistance provides up to 100% of tuition (to a maximum of $250 per semester hour or $4,500 per person per fiscal year).
Duration Participants in Officer Candidate School (OCS), Warrant Officer Candidate School (WOCS), and ROTC Simultaneous Membership Program (SMP) may enroll in up to 15 semester hours per year until completion of a baccalaureate degree. Warrant Officers are funded to complete an associate degree.
Additional information Tuition assistance may be used along with federal Pell Grants but not with Montgomery GI Bill benefits. State tuition assistance programs can be used concurrently with this program, but not to exceed 100% of tuition costs.
Number awarded Varies each year; recently, more than 22,000 Guard members received tuition assistance.
Deadline Deadline not specified.

[1210]
ARMY NURSE CORPS ASSOCIATION SCHOLARSHIPS
Army Nurse Corps Association
Attn: Scholarship Program
8000 IH-10 West, Suite 600
San Antonio, TX 78230-3887
(210) 650-3534   Toll Free: (888) 742-9910
E-mail: education@e-anca.org
Web: www.e-anca.org/Scholarships

Summary To provide financial assistance to students who have a connection to the Army and are interested in working on an undergraduate or graduate degree in nursing.
Eligibility This program is open to U.S. citizens attending colleges or universities that have accredited programs offering undergraduate or graduate degrees in nursing. Applicants must be 1) students currently enrolled in an accredited baccalaureate or advanced nursing or nurse anesthesia program who are serving or have served (and received an honorable discharge) in any branch and at any rank of a component of the Active Army, Army National Guard, or Army Reserve; or 2) nursing or anesthesia students whose parent(s), spouse, or child(ren) are serving or have served in a component of the Active Army, Army National Guard, or Army Reserve. Along with their application, they must submit a personal statement on their professional career objectives, reasons for applying for this scholarship, financial need, special considerations, personal and academic interests, and why they are preparing for a nursing career. Students who are receiving any support from any branch of the military, including ROTC scholarships, are not eligible.
Financial data The stipend is $3,000. Funds are sent directly to the recipient's school.
Duration 1 year.
Additional information Although the sponsoring organization is made up of current, retired, and honorably discharged officers of the Army Nurse Corps, it does not have an official affiliation with the Army. Therefore, students who receive these scholarships do not incur any military service obligation.
Number awarded Varies each year.
Deadline March of each year.

[1211]
ARMY RESERVE TUITION ASSISTANCE
U.S. Army Reserve
Attn: Director, USAR Education
ARPC-PS
1 Reserve Way
St. Louis, MO 63132-5200
Toll Free: (800) 452-0201
Web: myarmybenefits.us.army.mil

Summary To provide financial assistance for college or graduate school to specified members of the U.S. Army Reserve (USAR).

Eligibility This program is open to drilling USAR soldiers in good standing. Applicants must be working on their first bachelor's or master's degree and be able to declare an educational goal after completing 15 credit hours. Enlisted members and warrant officers must be able to complete the program under their current term of service or reenlist. Commissioned officers must have at last 4 years of remaining service obligation from the date or course completion.

Financial data Assistance is provided at the rate of $250 per credit hour, to a maximum of $4,500 per fiscal year.

Duration 1 year; may be renewed.

Number awarded Varies each year.

Deadline Applications may be submitted at any time.

[1212]
ARMY SPECIALIZED TRAINING ASSISTANCE PROGRAM (STRAP)

U.S. Army National Guard
Education Support Center
Camp Joseph T. Robinson
Building 5400 Box 46
North Little Rock, AR 72199-9600
Toll Free: (866) 628-5999　　Fax: (501) 212-4928
E-mail: esc@ng.army.mil
Web: www.nationalguard.com

Summary To provide funding for service to members of the United States Army Reserve (USAR) or Army National Guard (ARNG) who are engaged in additional training in designated health care fields that are considered critical for wartime medical needs.

Eligibility This program is open to members of the USAR or ARNG who are 1) medical residents (currently in orthopedic surgery, family practice, emergency medicine, general surgery, obstetrics/gynecology, or internal medicine); 2) dental residents (currently in general dentistry, oral surgery, prosthodontics, or comprehensive dentistry); 3) nursing students working on a master's degree (currently in community health, psychiatric nurse practitioner, or nurse anesthesia; or 4) associate degree or diploma nurses working on a bachelor's degree. Applicants must agree to a service obligation of 1 year for every 6 months of support received.

Financial data This program pays a stipend of at least $2,300 per month.

Duration 1 year; may be renewed.

Additional information During their obligated period of service, participants must attend Extended Combat Training (ECT) at least 12 days each year and complete the Officer Basic Leadership Course (OBLC) within the first year.

Number awarded Varies each year.

Deadline Applications may be submitted at any time.

[1213]
ARMY TUITION ASSISTANCE BENEFITS

U.S. Army
Human Resources Command
AHRC-PDE-EI
Attn: Education Incentives and Counseling Branch
1600 Spearhead Division Avenue
Fort Knox, KY 40122-5408
Toll Free: (800) 872-8272
E-mail: usarmy.knox.hrc.mbx.tagd-pdeei@mail.mil
Web: myarmybenefits.us.army.mil

Summary To provide financial assistance to Army personnel interested in working on an undergraduate or master's degree.

Eligibility This program is open to active-duty Army personnel, including members of the Army National Guard and Army Reserve on active duty, who have completed at least 1 year of service after graduation from AIT, OCS, or BOLC; graduate students must have completed 10 years of service. Applicants must first visit an education counselor to declare an educational goal and establish an educational plan. They may enroll in up to 16 semester hours of academic courses. Support is not provided for a second equivalent degree or for first professional degrees (e.g., Ph.D., M.D., or J.D.).

Financial data Those selected for participation in this program receive their regular Army pay and 100% of tuition at the postsecondary educational institution of their choice, but capped at $4,500 per year or $250 per semester hour, whichever is less. Funding is available only for tuition, not fees or other associated expenses.

Duration Up to 130 semester hours for completion of a bachelor's degree or up to 39 semester hours for completion of a master's degree. Undergraduates must complete all courses with a grade of "C" or better; graduate students must complete classes with a grade of "B" of better. If recipients fail to achieve those grades, they must reimburse the Army for all funds received.

Additional information This program is part of the Army Continuing Education System (ACES). Further information is available from counselors at the education centers at all Army installations with a troop strength of 750 or more. Officers incur a service obligation of 2 years for active duty or 4 years for Reserve and National Guard.

Number awarded Varies each year; recently, this program funded completion of 8,525 degree for active soldiers, 1,359 for Guard soldiers, and 1,469 for Reserve soldiers.

Deadline Deadline not specified.

[1214]
ARMY WOMEN'S FOUNDATION LEGACY SCHOLARSHIPS

Army Women's Foundation
Attn: Scholarship Committee
P.O. Box 5030
Fort Lee, VA 23801-0030
(804) 734-3078　　E-mail: info@awfdn.org
Web: www.awfdn.org/scholarships/general-information

Summary To provide financial assistance for college or graduate school to women who are serving or have served in the Army and their children.

Eligibility This program is open to 1) women who have served or are serving honorably in the U.S. Army, U.S. Army Reserve, or Army National Guard; and 2) children of those women. Applicants must be 1) high school graduates or GED recipients enrolled at a community college or technical certificate program who have a GPA of 2.5 or higher; 2) sophomores or higher at an accredited college or university who have a GPA of 3.0 or higher; or 3) students enrolled in or accepted to a graduate program who have a GPA of 3.0 or higher. Along with their application, they must submit a 2-page essay on why they should be considered for this scholarship; their future plans as related to their program of study; their community service, activities, and work experience; and

how the Army has impacted their life and/or goals. Selection is based on merit, academic potential, community service, and financial need.
Financial data The stipend is $2,500 for college and graduate students or $1,000 for community college and certificate students.
Duration 1 year; recipients may reapply.
Number awarded Varies each year; recently, 21 soldiers and 10 children received these scholarships.
Deadline January of each year.

[1215]
ASMC MEMBERS' CONTINUING EDUCATION GRANTS

American Society of Military Comptrollers
Attn: National Awards Committee
415 North Alfred Street
Alexandria, VA 22314
(703) 549-0360   Toll Free: (800) 462-5637
Fax: (703) 549-3181   E-mail: awards@asmconline.org
Web: asmc.secure-platform.com/a

Summary To provide financial assistance for continuing education to members of the American Society of Military Comptrollers (ASMC).
Eligibility Applicants for this assistance must have been members of the society for at least 2 full years and must have been active in the local chapter at some level (e.g., board member, committee chair or member, volunteer for chapter events), They must be enrolled or planning to enroll at an academic institution in a field of study directly related to military comptrollership, including business administration, economics, public administration, accounting, or finance. Selection is based on individual merit.
Financial data Stipends are $3,000 or $1,500.
Duration 1 year.
Additional information The ASMC is open to all financial management professionals employed by the U.S. Department of Defense or Coast Guard, both civilian and military. The applicant whose service to the society is judged the most exceptional is designated the Dick Vincent Scholarship winner.
Number awarded 11 each year: 1 at $3,000 (the Dick Vincent Scholarship) and 10 at $1,500.
Deadline March of each year.

[1216]
BG BENJAMIN B. TALLEY SCHOLARSHIP

Society of American Military Engineers-Anchorage Post
c/o Thomas Fenoseff
Anchorage School District
Senior Director, Capital Planning and Construction
1301 Labar Street
Anchorage, AK 99515-3517
(907) 348-5223   Fax: (901) 348-5227
E-mail: Fenoseff_Thomas@askd12.org
Web: www.sameanchorage.org/wp/scholarship-information

Summary To provide financial assistance to student members of the Society of American Military Engineers (SAME) from Alaska who are working on a bachelor's or master's degree in designated fields of engineering or the natural sciences.
Eligibility This program is open to members of the Anchorage Post of SAME who are residents of Alaska, attending college in Alaska, an active-duty military member stationed in Alaska, or a dependent of an active-duty military member stationed in Alaska. Applicants must be 1) sophomores, juniors, or seniors majoring in engineering, architecture, construction or project management, natural sciences, physical sciences, applied sciences, or mathematics at an accredited college or university; or 2) students working on a master's degree in those fields. They must have a GPA of 2.5 or higher. U.S. citizenship is required. Along with their application, they must submit an essay of 250 to 500 words on their career goals. Selection is based on that essay, academic achievement, participation in school and community activities, and work/family activities; financial need is not considered.
Financial data Stipends range up to $3,000.
Duration 1 year.
Additional information This program began in 1997.
Number awarded Several each year; at least 1 scholarship is reserved for a master's degree student.
Deadline December of each year.

[1217]
BRAXTON BRAGG CHAPTER AUSA SCHOLARSHIPS

Association of the United States Army-Braxton Bragg Chapter
Attn: Vice President for Scholarship Programs
P.O. Box 70036
Fort Bragg, NC 28307
(910) 396-3755   E-mail: hbraxtonbraggc@nc.rr.com
Web: www.ausa.org/chapters/braxton-bragg-chapter

Summary To provide financial assistance to members of the Braxton Bragg Chapter of the Association of the United States Army (AUSA) in North Carolina and their dependents who are interested in attending college or graduate school in any state.
Eligibility This program is open to chapter members and their families in North Carolina who are working on or planning to work on an undergraduate, graduate, or technical degree at a college or technical school in any state. Applicants must submit a 500-word essay on a topic that changes annually (recently, students were asked to explain how a person makes a difference in our world); letters of recommendation; a list of personal accomplishments; and a transcript that includes their ACT or SAT score. Selection is based on academic achievement (50%), participation in extracurricular activities at school (25%), and participation in community service activities (25%).
Financial data The stipend is $1,000.
Duration 1 year; recipients may reapply.
Additional information Membership in the Braxton Bragg Chapter is open to all Army active, National Guard, and Reserve members in North Carolina, along with Department of the Army civilians, retirees, concerned citizens, and family members.
Number awarded Varies each year; recently, 15 were awarded.
Deadline April of each year.

[1218]
CALIFORNIA MILITARY DEPARTMENT GI BILL AWARD PROGRAM
California State Military Department
Joint Force Headquarters
Attn: Civilian Education Office
CAAD-G1-CE, Box 26
9800 Goethe Road
Sacramento, CA 95826
(916) 854-4446　　　　　　　Fax: (916) 854-3259
E-mail: ng.ca.caarng.list.cn6-eaap-mailbox-access@mail.mil
Web: www.calguard.ca.gov/education

Summary To provide financial assistance to members of services within the California Military Department who are interested in attending college or graduate school in the state.
Eligibility This program is open to residents of California who are active members of the California Army or Air National Guard, the California State Guard, or the California Naval Militia. Applicants must be planning to attend a college, university, or community college in the state to obtain a certificate, degree (associate, bachelor's, master's, or doctoral) or diploma that they do not currently hold. They must agree to remain an active member of the National Guard, State Guard, or Naval Militia for at least 2 years after they complete participation in the program.
Financial data The program pays up to 100% of tuition at branches of the University of California, branches of the California State University system, or community colleges. Graduate students receive an additional stipend of $500 for books and supplies.
Duration 1 year; may be renewed, provided the recipient maintains a GPA of 2.0 or higher.
Additional information This program was formerly named the California National Guard Education Assistance Award Program.
Number awarded Up to 1,000 each year.
Deadline The priority deadline for new applications is April of each year.

[1219]
CALIFORNIA NON-RESIDENT COLLEGE FEE WAIVER PROGRAM FOR MILITARY PERSONNEL AND DEPENDENTS
California Department of Veterans Affairs
Attn: Division of Veterans Services
1227 O Street, Room 101
P.O. Box 942895
Sacramento, CA 94295
(916) 653-2573　　　　　Toll Free: (800) 952-5626
Fax: (916) 653-2563　　　TDD: (800) 324-5966
Web: www.calvet.ca.gov

Summary To waive non-resident fees at public institutions in California for undergraduate or graduate students from other states who are active-duty military personnel, recently-discharged veterans, or dependents of active-duty military personnel.
Eligibility This program is open to residents of states outside California who are 1) veterans of the U.S. armed forces who spent more than 1 year on active duty in California immediately prior to being discharged; 2) members of the U.S. armed forces stationed in California on active duty; or 3) the natural or adopted child, stepchild, or spouse of a member of the U.S. armed forces stationed in California on active duty. Applicants must be attending or planning to attend a community college, branch of the California State University system, or campus of the University of California as an undergraduate or graduate student.
Financial data This program waives non-resident fees of qualifying military personnel, veterans, and families who attend publicly-supported community or state colleges or universities in California.
Duration 1 year; may be renewed until completion of an undergraduate degree or for 1 additional year for military personnel working on a graduate degree; nonrenewable for graduate students who are children or spouses.
Number awarded Varies each year.
Deadline Deadline not specified.

[1220]
CANNON ENDOWMENT SCHOLARSHIP
United Church of Christ
Attn: Associate Director, Grant and Scholarship Administration
700 Prospect Avenue East
Cleveland, OH 44115-1100
(216) 736-2166　　　Toll Free: (866) 822-8224, ext. 2166
Fax: (216) 736-3783　　　E-mail: scholarships@ucc.org
Web: app.smarterselect.com

Summary To provide financial assistance to seminary students who are interested in becoming a military chaplain.
Eligibility This program is open to students at accredited seminaries who are affiliated with the Christian Church (Disciples of Christ), Presbyterian Church (USA), United Church of Christ, or United Methodist Church. Applicants must be planning to become military chaplains. They must have a GPA of 3.0 or higher and be able to demonstrate financial need.
Financial data The stipend is approximately $2,500.
Duration 1 year.
Additional information This program began in 1992.
Number awarded Varies each year; recently, 5 were awarded.
Deadline March of each year.

[1221]
CAPTAIN JODI CALLAHAN MEMORIAL SCHOLARSHIP
Air Force Association
Attn: Scholarships
1501 Lee Highway
Arlington, VA 22209-1198
(703) 247-5800, ext. 4868
Toll Free: (800) 727-3337, ext. 4868
Fax: (703) 247-5853　　　E-mail: scholarships@afa.org
Web: www.app.smarterselect.com

Summary To provide financial assistance for graduate education to Air Force personnel who are members of the Air Force Association.
Eligibility This program is open to active-duty Air Force members and full-time Guard and Reserve personnel (officer or enlisted) who are also members of the association. Applicants must be working on a master's degree in a non-technical field during off-duty time and have a GPA of 3.0 or higher.

Along with their application, they must submit a 600-word essay describing their academic goals and how they expect their degree to enhance their service to the Air Force.
Financial data The stipend is $1,000. Funds may be used for any reasonable expenses related to working on a degree, including tuition, lab fees, and books.
Duration 1 year; nonrenewable.
Number awarded 1 each year.
Deadline April of each year.

[1222]
CAPTAIN MIKI IWATA MEMORIAL SCHOLARSHIP FOR ADVANCED PRACTICE

Florida Navy Nurse Corps Association
c/o Margaret Holder, Scholarship Committee
1033 Inverness Drive
St. Augustine, FL 32092
E-mail: maholder@me.com
Web: www.nnca.org/join-nnca-2/local-chapters/fnnca

Summary To provide financial assistance to advanced practice nursing students in Florida, especially those with ties to the military.
Eligibility This program is open to full- and part-time advanced practice nursing students in Florida. Applicants must have completed at least 1 clinical nursing course and have a current GPA of 3.0 or higher. Along with their application, they must submit an essay, up to 500 words in length, on the reasons they are qualified for the scholarship, how it will benefit them, career goals, and potential for contribution to the profession. Preference is given in the following order to current active-duty and Reserve service members, veterans of military service, family members of current or former military service personnel, civil service employees, and residents of Florida. Financial need is considered in the selection process.
Financial data The stipend is $1,500. Funds are paid directly to the student.
Duration 1 year.
Number awarded 1 each year.
Deadline October of each year.

[1223]
CAPTAIN SEAN P. GRIMES PHYSICIAN ASSISTANT EDUCATIONAL SCHOLARSHIP AWARD

Society of Army Physician Assistants
Attn: Scholarship Committee
P.O. Box 623
Monmouth, IL 61462
(309) 734-5446 Fax: (309) 734-4489
E-mail: orpotter@aol.com
Web: www.sapa.org/scholarships

Summary To provide financial assistance to current and former Army personnel interested in attending a college or university to become a physician assistant.
Eligibility This program is open to Army personnel who are currently on active duty, in the Reserves or National Guard, or veterans with any MOS and in pay grades E-5 through O-4. Applicants must be interested in attending an accredited college or university in order to either 1) gain initial training as a physician assistant; or 2) if already a physician assistant, work on a bachelor's, master's, or doctoral degree. They must have a GPA of 2.5 or higher and be able to demonstrate financial need. Selection is based on academic record, community and professional activities, future goals as a physician assistant, and financial need.
Financial data The stipend is $6,000.
Duration 1 year.
Additional information This program began in 2006.
Number awarded 1 each year.
Deadline January of each year.

[1224]
CHAPLAIN SAMUEL GROVER POWELL SCHOLARSHIP

United Methodist Higher Education Foundation
Attn: Scholarships Administrator
60 Music Square East, Suite 350
P.O. Box 340005
Nashville, TN 37203-0005
(615) 649-3990 Toll Free: (800) 811-8110
Fax: (615) 649-3980
E-mail: umhefscholarships@gbhem.org
Web: www.umhef.org

Summary To provide funding to students interested in preparing for a career as a military chaplain.
Eligibility This program is open to middlers and seniors at accredited theological seminaries who are either involved in the chaplain candidate (seminarian) program or serving in a military Reserve component after having completed an active-duty tour in 1 of the armed forces. Preference is given to students in their senior year who plan to serve in the U.S. Air Force. However, students preparing for chaplaincy in any branch of the military are considered. Applicants must submit a letter that includes a brief personal history and a statement about their decision to choose military chaplaincy as a career, a recent photograph, undergraduate and graduate transcripts, a financial statement, and a report on their ministry in the chaplain candidate (seminarian) program.
Financial data The stipend recently was $2,650. Funds must be used to pay for tuition. Checks are mailed to the recipient's school.
Duration 1 year; recipients may reapply for 1 additional year (but new applicants are given priority each year).
Additional information This program began in 1980. Recipients are expected to serve in the U.S. Military Chaplaincy upon completion of seminary and ordination. If this does not happen (due to factors within the recipient's control), the recipient may be asked to repay the scholarship.
Number awarded 1 or more each year.
Deadline June of each year.

[1225]
CHURCH, STATE AND INDUSTRY FOUNDATION SEMINARY OR GRADUATE SCHOOL GRANT/LOAN

Church, State and Industry Foundation
P.O. Box 438
Polk City, IA 50226
E-mail: info@chaplain-csif.com
Web: www.chaplain-csif.org

Summary To provide forgivable loans to chaplain candidates of the armed forces who are interested in attending a seminary or graduate school.

Eligibility This program is open to members of the Army, Navy, and Air Force (active duty, National Guard, or Reserve) who are "experiencing a Call from God" to serve as qualified clergy (e.g., ministers, priests, imams, rabbis). Applicants must be enrolled or planning to enroll full time at a seminary or graduate school to enroll in a course of study that is required for pre-ordination and/or endorsement. They must have been granted chaplain candidate status and have a GPA of 2.8 or higher.

Financial data Support is provided in the form of a loan of $5,000 per year. If the recipient proceeds to commissioning as a military chaplain, the loan converts to a grant and is forgiven. Otherwise, the loan must be repaid with an interest rate specified at the time of the award.

Duration Up to 3 years. Recipients whose faith requires further study for ordination and endorsement may apply for additional support.

Additional information This program began in 2014.

Number awarded Varies each year.

Deadline January of each year.

[1226]
CIVIL ENGINEER CORPS COLLEGIATE PROGRAM

U.S. Navy
Bureau of Navy Personnel
BUPERS-314E
5720 Integrity Drive
Millington, TN 38055-4630
(901) 874-4034   Toll Free: (866) CEC-NAVY
Fax: (901) 874-2681   E-mail: p4413d@persnet.navy.mil
Web: www.navycs.com/officer/civilengineerofficer.html

Summary To provide financial assistance to undergraduate and graduate students in architecture and engineering who are interested in serving in the Navy's Civil Engineer Corps (CEC) following graduation.

Eligibility This program is open to bachelor's and master's degree students who are U.S. citizens between 19 and 35 years of age. Applicants must be enrolled in an engineering program accredited by the Accreditation Board for Engineering and Technology (ABET) or an architecture program accredited by the National Architectural Accrediting Board (NAAB) and have a GPA of 2.7 or higher overall and 3.0 or higher in science and technical courses. They may be civilians, enlisted personnel of the regular Navy and the Naval Reserve, or enlisted personnel of other branches of the armed services with a conditional release from their respective service. Eligible majors include civil engineering, construction engineering, electrical engineering, environmental engineering, industrial engineering, mechanical engineering, ocean engineering, or architecture. Preference is given to applicants who have engineering or architecture work experience and registration as a Professional Engineer (P.E.) or Engineer-in-Training (EIT). Applicants must also be able to meet the Navy's physical fitness requirements.

Financial data While attending classes, students are assigned to the Naval Reserve and receive the standard pay at E-3 level (approximately $2,042.70 per month) as an undergraduate or E-5 (approximately $2,467.50 per month) as a graduate student.

Duration Up to 24 months.

Additional information While in college, selectees have no uniforms, drills, or military duties. After graduation with a bachelor's or master's degree, they enter the Navy and attend 13 weeks at Officer Candidate School (OCS) in Pensacola, Florida, followed by 15 weeks at Civil Engineer Corps Officers School (CECOS) in Port Hueneme, California. They then serve 4 years in the CEC, rotating among public works, contract management, and the Naval Construction Force (Seabees).

Number awarded Varies each year.

Deadline Deadline not specified.

[1227]
COAST GUARD TUITION ASSISTANCE PROGRAM

U.S. Coast Guard
Attn: Force Readiness Command (FORCECOM)
Tuition Assistance and Grants Division
300 East Main Street, Room 233
Norfolk, VA 23510
(757) 756-5300   E-mail: ETQC-SMB-TAG@uscg.mil
Web: www.forcecom.uscg.mil

Summary To provide financial assistance to members and employees of the Coast Guard who are interested in pursuing additional education during their off-duty hours.

Eligibility This program is open to Coast Guard members on active duty and Reservists on long-term orders greater than 180 days. Applicants must be interested in working on their first associate, bachelor's, or master's degree. Civilian employees with at least 90 days of Coast Guard service are also eligible. Enlisted members must complete the course before their enlistment ends or they retire. Active-duty officers must agree to fulfill a 2-year service obligation following completion of the course; officers of the selected reserve must agree to fulfill a 4-year service obligation following completion of the course. Civilian employees must agree to retain employment with the Coast Guard for 1 month for each completed course credit hour. For military personnel, the command education services officer (ESO) must certify that the course of instruction is Coast Guard mission or career related. The supervisor of civilian employees must certify that the education is career related. All courses must be related to the mission of the Coast Guard or the individual's career or professional development.

Financial data The program reimburses 75% of the cost of tuition, to a maximum of $250 per semester hour (of which the Coast Guard share is $187.50) or $3,000 per fiscal year (of which the Coast Guard share is $2,250). Funding is available only for tuition, not fees or other associated expenses.

Duration Until completion of an associate, bachelor's, or master's degree. Undergraduates must complete all courses with a grade of "C" or better; graduate students must complete classes with a grade of "B" of better. If recipients fail to achieve those grades, they must reimburse the Coast Guard for all funds received.

Number awarded Varies each year; recently, more than 10,000 Coast Guard personnel received tuition assistance worth approximately $14.5 million.

Deadline Applications may be submitted at any time.

[1228]
COL. LOREN J. AND MRS. LAWONA R. SPENCER SCHOLARSHIP

Air Force Association
Attn: Scholarships
1501 Lee Highway
Arlington, VA 22209-1198
(703) 247-5800, ext. 4868
Toll Free: (800) 727-3337, ext. 4868
Fax: (703) 247-5853   E-mail: scholarships@afa.org
Web: www.app.smarterselect.com

Summary To provide financial assistance to Air Force personnel interested in working on a master's degree in a field of management or administration.

Eligibility This program is open to active-duty Air Force members (officer or enlisted), Air Force civilians, and full-time Guard and Reserve personnel. Applicants must be interested in working on a master's degree in a management or administration field in preparation for senior level leadership roles and have a GPA of 3.0 or higher. Along with their application, they must submit a 2-page essay describing their academic goals and how they expect their degree to enhance their service to the Air Force. Selection is based on academic achievement and job performance.

Financial data The stipend is $5,000. Funds are sent directly to the recipient's education office.

Duration 1 year; nonrenewable.

Number awarded Varies each year; recently, 3 were awarded.

Deadline April of each year.

[1229]
COLONEL JERRY W. ROSS SCHOLARSHIP

American Pharmacists Association
Attn: APhA Foundation
2215 Constitution Avenue, N.W.
Washington, DC 20037-2985
(202) 558-2709   Toll Free: (800) 237-APhA
Fax: (202) 638-3793   E-mail: rvaidya@aphanet.org
Web: www.aphafoundation.org

Summary To provide financial assistance for work on a degree in pharmacy to Air Force pharmacy technicians who are members of the Academy of Student Pharmacists of the American Pharmacists Association (APhA-ASP) and their families.

Eligibility This program is open to full-time pharmacy students who are either 1) Air Force pharmacy technicians working on a degree in pharmacy; or 2) family members of an Air Force pharmacist or technician who is enrolled in an accredited college of pharmacy. Applicants must have been actively involved in their school's APhA-ASP chapter. They must have completed at least 1 year in the professional sequence of courses with a GPA of 2.75 or higher. Along with their application, they must submit a 500-word essay that includes 1) how their involvement in APhA-ASP has developed them as a leader; and 2) how they will embrace their calling as a future leader of the profession. Selection is based on the essay (20%), academic performance (10%), pharmacy-related activities (25%), non-pharmacy/community activities (25%), and letters of recommendation (20%).

Financial data The stipend is $1,000.

Duration 1 year; recipients may reapply.

Number awarded 1 each year.

Deadline November of each year.

[1230]
CONNECTICUT TUITION WAIVER FOR VETERANS

Connecticut State Universities and Colleges
61 Woodland Street
Hartford, CT 06105
(860) 723-0013   E-mail: fitzgeralde@ct.edu
Web: www.ct.edu/admission/veterans

Summary To provide financial assistance for college to certain Connecticut veterans and military personnel and their dependents.

Eligibility This program is open to 1) honorably-discharged Connecticut veterans who served at least 90 days during specified periods of wartime; 2) active members of the Connecticut Army or Air National Guard; 3) Connecticut residents who are a dependent child or surviving spouse of a member of the armed forces killed in action on or after September 11, 2001 who was also a Connecticut resident; and 4) Connecticut residents who are a dependent child or surviving spouse of a person officially declared missing in action or a prisoner of war while serving in the armed forces after January 1, 1960. Applicants must be attending or planning to attend a public college or university in the state.

Financial data The program provides a waiver of 100% of tuition for general fund courses at the 4 campuses of Connecticut State University, 50% of tuition for extension and summer courses at campuses of Connecticut State University, 100% of tuition at the 12 Connecticut community colleges, and 50% of fees at Charter Oak State College.

Duration Up to 4 years.

Additional information This is an entitlement program; applications are available at the respective college financial aid offices.

Number awarded Varies each year.

Deadline Deadline not specified.

[1231]
CSM LEONARD MAGLIONE MEMORIAL SCHOLARSHIPS

Association of the United States Army-Rhode Island
  Chapter
c/o LTC Robert A. Galvanin, President
31 Canoe River Drive
Mansfield, MA 02048
(508) 339-5301   E-mail: bpje5310@verizon.net
Web: www.riroa.org/ausari/scholarship.htm

Summary To provide financial assistance to members of the Rhode Island Chapter of the Association of the United States Army (AUSA) and their families who are interested in attending college or graduate school in any state.

Eligibility This program is open to members of the AUSA Rhode Island Chapter and their family members (spouses, children, and grandchildren). Applicants must be high school seniors or graduates accepted at an accredited college, university, or vocational/technical school in any state or current undergraduate or graduate students. Along with their application, they must submit a 250-word essay on why they feel their achievements should qualify them for this award. Selection is based on academic and individual achievements; financial need is not considered. Special consideration is given to students or graduates of LaSalle Academy in Providence (the alma mater of this program's namesake), especially those preparing for a career in the arts or engineering or enrolled or planning to enroll in Army ROTC.

Financial data The stipend is $1,000.

Duration 1 year.

Additional information Membership in the AUSA is open to everyone who supports a strong national defense, with special concern for the Army. That includes Regular Army, National Guard, Army Reserve, government civilians, retired soldiers, Wounded Warriors, veterans, concerned citizens and family members.

Number awarded Several each year.

Deadline April of each year.

[1232]
CSM ROBERT W. ELKEY SCHOLARSHIP

Army Engineer Association
Attn: Director Washington DC Operations
P.O. Box 30260
Alexandria, VA 22310-8260
(703) 428-7084   Fax: (703) 428-6043
E-mail: xd@armyengineer.com
Web: www.armyengineer.com/scholarships

Summary To provide financial assistance for college or graduate school to enlisted members of the Army Engineer Association (AEA).

Eligibility This program is open to AEA members serving in an active, Reserve, or National Guard component Army Engineer unit, school, or organization within the Corps of Engineers of the United States Army. Applicants must be enlisted personnel (PVT, PFC, SPC, CPL, SGT, or SSG). They must be working on or planning to work on an associate, bachelor's, or master's degree at an accredited college or university. Along with their application, they must submit a 1-page essay outlining why they should be selected for an award, including a paragraph on their financial need and their evaluation of their potential for success.

Financial data The stipend is $1,000.

Duration 1 year.

Number awarded 3 each year.

Deadline June of each year.

[1233]
DEDICATED ARMY NATIONAL GUARD (DEDARNG) SCHOLARSHIPS

U.S. Army National Guard
Education Support Center
Camp Joseph T. Robinson
Building 5400 Box 46
North Little Rock, AR 72199-9600
Toll Free: (866) 628-5999   Fax: (501) 212-4928
E-mail: esc@ng.army.mil
Web: www.nationalguard.com/tools/guard-scholarships

Summary To provide financial assistance to college and graduate students who are interested in enrolling in Army ROTC and serving in the Army National Guard following graduation.

Eligibility This program is open to full-time students entering their sophomore or junior year of college with a GPA of 2.5 or higher. Applicants must have a GPA of 2.5 or higher and scores of at least 19 on the ACT or 1000 on the SAT. Graduate students may also be eligible if they have only 2 years remaining for completion of their degree. Students who have been awarded an ROTC campus-based scholarship may apply to convert to this program during their freshman year. Applicants must meet all medical and moral character requirements for enrollment in Army ROTC. They must be willing to enroll in the Simultaneous Membership Program (SMP) of an ROTC unit on their campus; the SMP requires simultaneous membership in Army ROTC and the Army National Guard.

Financial data Participants receive full reimbursement of tuition up to $10,000 per year, a grant of $1,200 per year for books, plus an ROTC stipend for 10 months of the year at $420 per month, and weekend drill pay at the pay grade of a sergeant (approximately $319 per month) while participating in the SMP.

Duration 2 or 3 years.

Additional information After graduation, participants serve 3 to 6 months on active duty in the Officer Basic Course (OBC). Following completion of OBC, they are released from active duty and are obligated to serve 8 years in the Army National Guard.

Number awarded Approximately 600 each year.

Deadline Deadline not specified.

[1234]
DISTRICT OF COLUMBIA NATIONAL GUARD STATE TUITION ASSISTANCE REIMBURSEMENT

District of Columbia National Guard
Attn: Education Services Office
2001 East Capitol Street, S.E.
Washington, DC 20001
(202) 685-9862   Fax: (202) 685-9815
E-mail: sherry.d.mitchell3.mil@mail.mil
Web: dc.ng.mil/Resources/Education/

Summary To provide financial assistance for college or graduate school to current members of the District of Columbia National Guard.

Eligibility This program is open to traditional, technician, and AGR members of the District of Columbia Air and Army National Guard. Applicants must have a high school diploma or equivalency and currently be working on an associate, bachelor's, or master's degree at an accredited postsecondary education institution. In some instances, support may also be available for an M.D., D.O., P.A., or J.D. degree.

Financial data Army National Guard members are eligible for up to $4,500 per year in federal tuition assistance; they may supplement that with up to $2,000 per year in District tuition assistance plus up to $500 for fees. Air National Guard members do not have access to federal tuition assistance, so they may receive up to $6,000 in District tuition assistance. Funds must be used to pay for tuition, fees, and/or books.

Duration 1 semester; recipients may reapply.

Number awarded Varies each year.

Deadline Applications must be submitted between 45 days after the start of the semester and 60 days after the end of the semester.

[1235]
DONALDSON D. FRIZZELL MEMORIAL SCHOLARSHIPS

First Command Educational Foundation
Attn: Scholarship Programs Manager
1 FirstComm Plaza
Fort Worth, TX 76109-4999
(817) 569-2940   Toll Free: (877) 872-8289
Fax: (817) 569-2970   E-mail: scholarships@fcef.com
Web: www.fcef.com/scholarships

Summary To provide financial assistance to students, especially those with ties to the military, entering or attending college or graduate school.

Eligibility This program is open to 1) members of a U.S. uniformed service (active, Guard, Reserve, retired, or non-retired veteran) and their spouses and dependents; 2) clients of First Command Financial Services and their family members; 3) dependent family members of First Command Advisors or field office staff members; or 4) non-contractual ROTC students. Applicants may be traditional students (high school seniors and students already enrolled at a college, university, or accredited trade school) or nontraditional students (those defined by their institution as nontraditional and adult students planning to return to a college, university, or accredited trade school. They must have a GPA of 3.0 or higher and be working on a trade school certification or associate, undergraduate, or graduate degree. Applicants must submit 1-page essays on 1) their active involvement in community service programs; 2) the impact of financial literacy on their future; and 3) why they need this scholarship. Selection is based primarily on the essays, academic merit, and financial need.

Financial data The stipend is $3,000. Funds are disbursed directly to the recipient's college, university, or trade school.

Duration 1 year.

Additional information The sponsoring organization was formerly known as the USPA & IRA Educational Foundation, founded in 1983 to provide scholarships to the children of active, retired, or deceased military personnel.

Number awarded Varies each year; recently, 10 were awarded.

Deadline The online application process begins in February of each year and continues until April or until 2,500 applications have been received.

[1236]
DR. NANCY M. SCHONHER SCHOLARSHIP

Marines' Memorial Association
c/o Marines Memorial Club and Hotel
609 Sutter Street
San Francisco, CA 94102
(415) 673-6672, ext. 293   Toll Free: (800) 5-MARINE
Fax: (415) 441-3649
E-mail: scholarship@marineclub.com
Web: www.marinesmemorial.org

Summary To provide financial assistance to women who have a tie to the military and are interested in working on a degree in a health-related field.

Eligibility This program is open to women who 1) are active-duty service members or reservists in the U.S. armed forces; 2) have separated honorably from the U.S. armed forces within the past 6 years; 3) are a current or former corpsman or medic in any branch of the U.S. armed forces; or 4) are the child or grandchild of an active member of the Marines' Memorial Association. Applicants must be planning to enroll in 1) an advanced medical program with the goal of becoming a nurse, nurse practitioner, physician's assistant, or medical doctor (M.D. or O.D.) from an accredited American college or university; or 2) an accredited paramedic program (must have completed the EMT Basic training program, have taken the National Registry EMT Examination, hold an EMT Certificate, and have at least 6 months' work experience). Membership in the sponsoring organization is not required. Along with their application, they must submit an essay of up to 500 words on why they chose their specific path of study, what they hope to accomplish after graduation with their degree, and how their efforts will benefit others in their community. Selection is based on the essay, academic merit, references, and financial need. Preference is given to Navy Corpsmen.

Financial data The stipend is $5,000.

Duration 1 year.

Additional information Membership in the association is open to veterans of the Marines, Army, Navy, Air Force, or Coast Guard and to personnel currently serving in a branch of the armed forces. This program began in 2017.

Number awarded 1 each year.

Deadline April of each year.

[1237]
EDUCATION FOUNDATION FOR THE COLORADO NATIONAL GUARD GRANTS

National Guard Association of Colorado
Attn: Education Foundation, Inc.
P.O. Box 440889
Aurora, CO 80044-0889
(303) 909-6369   Fax: (720) 535-5925
E-mail: BernieRogoff@comcast.net
Web: www.efcong.org

Summary To provide financial assistance to members of the Colorado National Guard and their families who are interested in attending college or graduate school in any state.

Eligibility This program is open to current and retired members of the Colorado National Guard and their dependent unmarried children and spouses. Applicants must be enrolled or planning to enroll full or part time at a college, university, trade school, business school, or graduate school in any state. Along with their application, they must submit an essay, up to 2 pages in length, on their desire to continue their education, what motivates them, their financial need, their commitment to academic excellence, and their current situation. Selection is based on academic achievement, community involvement, and financial need.

Financial data Stipends are generally at least $1,000 per year.

Duration 1 year; may be renewed.

Number awarded Normally, 15 to 25 of these grants are awarded each semester.

Deadline July of each year for fall semester; January of each year for spring semester.

[1238]
ENLISTED ASSOCIATION OF THE NATIONAL GUARD OF IOWA AUXILIARY SCHOLARSHIP PROGRAM

Enlisted Association of the National Guard of Iowa Auxiliary
c/o Lori Waters, President
1005 Second Street S.W.
Altoona, IA 50009
(515) 490-3202   E-mail: bullriderfan@msn.com
Web: www.eangi.org/auxiliary-scholarship

Summary To provide financial assistance to members of the Enlisted Association of the National Guard of Iowa (EANIG) Auxiliary and their families who are interested in attending college in any state.

Eligibility This program is open to EANGI Auxiliary members and their spouses, dependents, and grandchildren. Applicants must be enrolled, accepted for enrollment, or in the process of applying to a college or vocational/technical school as a full-time undergraduate or graduate student. Along with their application, they must submit a letter describing specific fats about their desire to continue their education and why they need financial assistance. Selection is based on character, leadership, and need.

Financial data The stipend is $1,000.
Duration 1 year; recipients may reapply.
Number awarded 2 each year.
Deadline February of each year.

[1239]
FIRST LIEUTENANT MICHAEL LICALZI MEMORIAL SCHOLARSHIP

Marine Corps Tankers Association
c/o Dan Miller, Scholarship Chair
8212 West Fourth Place
Kennewick, WA 99336
E-mail: dmiller@msn.com
Web: www.usmctankers.org/pageScholarship

Summary To provide financial assistance for college or graduate school to children and grandchildren of members of the Marine Corps Tankers Association and to Marine and Navy personnel currently serving in tank units.

Eligibility This program is open to high school seniors and graduates who are children, grandchildren, or under the guardianship of an active, Reserve, retired, or honorably discharged Marine who served in a tank unit. Marine or Navy Corpsmen currently assigned to tank units are also eligible. Applicants must be enrolled or planning to enroll full time at a college or graduate school. Their parent or grandparent must be a member of the Marine Corps Tankers Association or, if not a member, must join if the application is accepted. Along with their application, they must submit a 500-word essay that explains their reason for seeking this scholarship, their educational goals, and their plans for post-graduation life. Selection is based on that essay, academic record, school activities, leadership potential, and community service.

Financial data The stipend is $3,000.
Duration 1 year.
Number awarded Varies each year; recently, 6 were awarded.
Deadline March of each year.

[1240]
FLEET RESERVE ASSOCIATION GRADUATE SCHOLARSHIPS

Fleet Reserve Association
Attn: FRA Education Foundation
125 North West Street
Alexandria, VA 22314-2754
(703) 683-1400   Toll Free: (800) FRA-1924
Fax: (703) 549-6610   E-mail: scholars@fra.org
Web: www.fra.org

Summary To provide financial assistance for graduate school to members of the Fleet Reserve Association (FRA) and their families.

Eligibility This program is open to members of the FRA and the dependent children, grandchildren, and spouses of living or deceased members. Applicants must be enrolled as full-time graduate students. Along with their application, they must submit an essay on why they want to go to college and what they intend to accomplish with their degree. Selection is based on academic record, financial need, extracurricular activities, leadership skills, and participation in community activities. U.S. citizenship is required.

Financial data The stipend is $5,000 per year.
Duration 1 year; may be renewed.
Additional information Membership in the FRA is open to current and former enlisted members of the Navy, Marine Corps, and Coast Guard. This program, established in 2001, includes the Glenn F. Glezen Scholarship, the Joseph R. Baranski Scholarship, and the Robert W. Nolan Scholarship.
Number awarded At least 3 each year.
Deadline April of each year.

[1241]
FLEET RESERVE ASSOCIATION MEMBER SCHOLARSHIPS

Fleet Reserve Association
Attn: FRA Education Foundation
125 North West Street
Alexandria, VA 22314-2754
(703) 683-1400   Toll Free: (800) FRA-1924
Fax: (703) 549-6610   E-mail: scholars@fra.org
Web: www.fra.org

Summary To provide financial assistance for college or graduate school to members of the Fleet Reserve Association (FRA) and their families.

Eligibility This program is open to members of the FRA and the children, grandchildren, great-grandchildren, and spouses of living or deceased members. Applicants must be enrolled or planning to enroll as full-time undergraduate or graduate students. Along with their application, they must submit transcripts that include (for high school students and college freshmen) SAT and/or ACT scores; a list of school and community activities; at least 2 letters of recommendation; and an essay on why they want to go to college and what they intend to accomplish with their degree. Selection is based on academic record, financial need, extracurricular activities, leadership skills, and participation in community activities. U.S. citizenship is required.

Financial data Stipends range from $1,000 to $5,000.
Duration 1 year; may be renewed.
Additional information Membership in the FRA is open to current and former enlisted members of the Navy, Marine

Corps, and Coast Guard. This program includes awards designated as the MCPO Ken E. Blair Scholarship, the Robert M. Treadwell Annual Scholarship, the Donald Bruce Pringle Family Scholarship, the Tom and Karen Snee Scholarship, the Angelo and Mildred Nunez Scholarships, the Express Scripts Scholarships, the US Family Health Scholarship, and the Navy Department Branch 181 Scholarship.

Number awarded Varies each year; recently, 10 were awarded: 6 at $5,000, 2 at $4,000, 1 at $3,000, and 1 at $2,000.

Deadline April of each year.

[1242]
FLEET RESERVE ASSOCIATION NON-MEMBER SCHOLARSHIPS

Fleet Reserve Association
Attn: FRA Education Foundation
125 North West Street
Alexandria, VA 22314-2754
(703) 683-1400   Toll Free: (800) FRA-1924
Fax: (703) 549-6610   E-mail: scholars@fra.org
Web: www.fra.org

Summary To provide financial assistance for college or graduate school to sea service personnel and their families.

Eligibility This program is open to 1) active-duty, Reserve, honorably-discharged veterans, and retired members of the U.S. Navy, Marine Corps, and Coast Guard; and 2) their spouses, children, grandchildren, and great-grandchildren. Applicants must be enrolled or planning to enroll as full-time undergraduate or graduate students, but neither they nor their family member are required to be members of the sponsoring organization. Along with their application, they must submit transcripts that include (for high school students and college freshmen) SAT and/or ACT scores; a list of school and community activities; at least 2 letters of recommendation; and an essay on why they want to go to college and what they intend to accomplish with their degree. Selection is based on academic record, financial need, extracurricular activities, leadership skills, and participation in community activities. U.S. citizenship is required.

Financial data Stipends range up to $5,000 per year.

Duration 1 year; may be renewed.

Additional information This program includes the GEICO Scholarship and the Rosemary Posekany Memorial Scholarship.

Number awarded Varies each year; recently, 6 were awarded: 5 at $5,000 and 1 at $1,000.

Deadline April of each year.

[1243]
FLORIDA NATIONAL GUARD EDUCATIONAL DOLLARS FOR DUTY (EDD) PROGRAM

Department of Military Affairs
Attn: State Education Program Administrator
82 Marine Street
St. Augustine, FL 32084
(904) 823-0339   Toll Free: (800) 342-6528
E-mail: ng.fl.flarng.list.ngfl-edd-office@mail.mil
Web: fl.ng.mil

Summary To provide financial assistance for college or graduate school to members of the Florida National Guard.

Eligibility This program is open to current members of the Florida National Guard. Applicants must be attending or planning to attend a college or university in Florida to work on an undergraduate or master's degree. College preparatory and vocational/technical programs also qualify. Guard members who already have a master's degree are not eligible.

Financial data The program provides for payment of 100% of tuition and fees at a public college or university or an equivalent amount at a private institution.

Duration 1 year; may be renewed.

Number awarded Varies each year; recently, approximately 765 Florida National Guard members utilized this program.

Deadline Applications may be submitted at any time, but they must be received at least 90 days prior to the start of the class.

[1244]
FLORIDA NAVY NURSE CORPS ASSOCIATION SCHOLARSHIPS

Florida Navy Nurse Corps Association
c/o Margaret Holder, Scholarship Committee
1033 Inverness Drive
St. Augustine, FL 32092
E-mail: maholder@me.com
Web: www.nnca.org/join-nnca-2/local-chapters/fnnca

Summary To provide financial assistance to undergraduate and graduate nursing students, especially residents of Florida with ties to the military.

Eligibility This program is open to students, including registered nursing continuing their studies, who are working on a baccalaureate or graduate degree in nursing. Applicants must have completed at least 1 clinical nursing course and have a GPA of 3.0 or higher. They may be full- or part-time students. Along with their application, they must submit an essay, up to 500 words in length, on the reasons they are qualified for the scholarship, how it will benefit them, career goals, and potential for contribution to the profession. Preference is given in order to current active-duty and Reserve service members, veterans of military service, family members of current or former military service personnel, civil service employees, and residents of Florida. Financial need is considered in the selection process.

Financial data The stipend is $1,500. Funds are paid directly to the student.

Duration 1 year.

Number awarded 2 each year.

Deadline October of each year.

[1245]
FORT WORTH POST SAME SCHOLARSHIP

Society of American Military Engineers-Fort Worth Post
c/o J.B. West, Scholarship Chair
Halff Associates
4000 Fossil Creek Boulevard
Fort Worth, TX 76137
(817) 205-7981   E-mail: warwagon16@gmail.com
Web: www.samefortworth.org/scholarship-application

Summary To provide financial assistance to engineering, architecture, and science college and graduate students, especially those at colleges and universities in Texas.

Eligibility This program is open to U.S. citizens who are currently enrolled in college or graduate school; preference is given to students at colleges and universities in Texas. Applicants must be working full time on a degree in an engineering, architecture, or science-related field. Along with their application, they must submit a 500-word essay that covers why they are preparing for a career in engineering, architecture, or a related science, their understanding of the Society of American Military Engineers (SAME) and how involvement with the organization will help them to achieve their academic and professional aspirations and objectives, and what distinguishes them from other candidates. Selection is based on academic achievement, character, personal merit, and commitment to the field of engineering. Special consideration is given to veterans and students enrolled in ROTC.
Financial data The stipend for the highest-ranked student enrolled in engineering and ROTC is $2,000. Other stipend amounts vary.
Duration 1 year.
Number awarded Varies each year.
Deadline April of each year.

[1246]
GEORGE WASHINGTON CHAPTER AUSA SCHOLARSHIPS
Association of the United States Army-George Washington Chapter
c/o Col (Ret.) William G. Yarborough, Jr., Scholarship Committee
P.O. Box 828
McLean, VA 22101-0828
(703) 748-1717   E-mail: wgyarc@aol.com
Web: www.ausa.org/chapters/george-washington-chapter

Summary To provide financial assistance for undergraduate or graduate study at a school in any state to members of the George Washington Chapter of the Association of the United States Army (AUSA) and their families.
Eligibility This program is open to active members of the AUSA George Washington Chapter and the spouses, children, and grandchildren of active members. Applicants must have a GPA of 2.5 or higher and be working on an undergraduate or graduate degree at a college or university in any state. Along with their application, they must submit a letter describing any family circumstances they believe are relevant and explaining why they deserve the scholarship. Members must also submit a favorable recommendation from their supervisor. Membership in AUSA is open to Army personnel (including Reserves and National Guard) who are either active or retired, ROTC cadets, or civilian employees of the Army.
Financial data Stipends range up to $1,000.
Duration 1 year.
Additional information This program includes the following named awards: the Ed Dauksz Scholarship Award, the Major General Harry Greene STEM Scholarship Award, and the Major General Carl F. McNair Jr. Scholarship Award. The George Washington Chapter serves Washington, D.C.; the Virginia counties of Alexandria, Clarke, Fairfax, Frederick, Loudoun, and Prince William; and the Maryland counties of Calvert, Charles, Montgomery, Prince George's, and St. Mary's.

Number awarded Varies each year; recently, 45 were awarded.
Deadline April of each year.

[1247]
GOOGLE-SVA SCHOLARSHIP
Student Veterans of America
Attn: Scholarship Committee
1012 14th Street, N.W., Suite 1200
Washington, DC 20005
(202) 223-4710
E-mail: scholarships@studentveterans.org
Web: www.studentveterans.org/programs/scholarships

Summary To provide financial assistance to veterans and current military personnel who are working on a bachelor's or graduate degree in a computer-related field.
Eligibility This program is open to sophomores, juniors, seniors, and graduate students at 4-year colleges and universities who are veterans of any branch of service, including Reserves and National Guard, and were honorably discharged or are active-duty military personnel still in good standing with their branch of service. Applicants must be working full time on a degree in computer science, computer engineering, or a closely-related technical field (e.g., software engineering, electrical engineering with a heavy computer science course load, information systems, information technology, applied networking, system administration). Along with their application, they must submit essays of 300 to 500 words each on 1) what sparked their interest in computer science; 2) examples of how they have exhibited leadership; 3) a significant challenge that they believe student veterans in the field of technology face and how they see themselves as being part of the solution(s) to that challenge; and 4) the impact receiving this scholarship would have on their education. Financial need is not considered in the selection process.
Financial data The stipend is $10,000.
Duration 1 year.
Additional information This program is sponsored by Google and administered by Student Veterans of America (SVA).
Number awarded 8 each year.
Deadline November of each year.

[1248]
HENRY J. REILLY SCHOLARSHIPS
Reserve Officers Association of the United States
Attn: Scholarship Program
One Constitution Avenue, N.E.
Washington, DC 20002-5618
(202) 646-7758   Toll Free: (800) 809-9448
E-mail: scholarship@roa.org
Web: www.roa.org/page/Scholarships

Summary To provide financial assistance for college or graduate school to members of the Reserve Officers Association (ROA) and their children or grandchildren.
Eligibility Applicants for this scholarship must be active or associate members of the association or their children or grandchildren (under the age of 26). Children, age 21 or under, of deceased members who were active and paid up at the time of their death are also eligible. Spouses are not eligible, unless they are members of the association. ROTC mem-

bers do not qualify as sponsors. Entering and continuing undergraduates must provide evidence of full-time enrollment at a regionally-accredited 4-year college or university, demonstrate leadership qualities, have earned a GPA of 3.3 or higher in high school and 3.0 or higher in college, have scored at least 1875 on the SAT or 55 on the English/math ACT, and (if appropriate) have registered for the draft. Applicants for a master's degree must have earned a GPA of 3.2 or higher as an undergraduate; applicants for a doctoral degree must have received a master's degree or been accepted into a doctoral program. All applicants must submit a 500-word essay on career goals. Selection is based on that essay, academic excellence, extracurricular activities and leadership, and letters of recommendation.

Financial data The stipend is $2,500 per year.
Duration 1 year; may be renewed.
Number awarded Up to 20 each year.
Deadline April of each year.

[1249]
ILLINOIS NATIONAL GUARD GRANT PROGRAM

Illinois Student Assistance Commission
Attn: Scholarship and Grant Services
1755 Lake Cook Road
Deerfield, IL 60015-5209
(847) 948-8550   Toll Free: (800) 899-ISAC
Fax: (847) 831-8549   TDD: (800) 526-0844
E-mail: isac.studentservices@illinois.gov
Web: www.isac.org

Summary To provide financial assistance to current or former members of the Illinois National Guard who are interested in attending college or graduate school in the state.
Eligibility This program is open to members of the Illinois National Guard who 1) are currently active and have completed at least 1 full year of service; or 2) have been active for at least 5 consecutive years, have had their studies interrupted by being called to federal active duty for at least 6 months, and are within 12 months after their discharge date. Applicants must also be enrolled at an Illinois public 2- or 4-year college or university.
Financial data Recipients are eligible for payment of tuition and some fees for either undergraduate or graduate study at an Illinois state-supported college or university.
Duration This assistance extends for 4 academic years of full-time study (or the equivalent in part-time study) for Guard members with less than 10 years of active duty service. For Guard members with 10 years or more of active duty service, assistance is available for up to the equivalent of 6 academic years of full-time study.
Number awarded Varies each year.
Deadline September of each year for the academic year; February of each year for spring semester, winter quarter, or spring quarter; June of each year for summer term.

[1250]
JEWISH WAR VETERANS NATIONAL ACHIEVEMENT PROGRAM

Jewish War Veterans of the U.S.A.
Attn: National Achievement Program
1811 R Street, N.W.
Washington, DC 20009-1659
(202) 265-6280   Fax: (202) 234-5662
E-mail: jwv@jwv.org
Web: www.jwvusafoundation.org

Summary To recognize and reward veterans and current servicemembers who are currently enrolled in college or graduate school and submit outstanding essays on their military experience.
Eligibility This competition is open to veterans and current servicemembers who are enrolled or planning to enroll in an accredited associate, bachelor's, nursing, or graduate degree program. All veterans are eligible, regardless of race, religion, creed, or culture. Applicants must submit an essay of 500 to 750 words on their military experience and how it will help them pursue their academic studies. Selection is based on answering the essay question (50%), logic and coherence of the essay's organization (25%), and description of relevant military experience (25%).
Financial data Awards range from $1,000 to $5,000.
Duration The awards are presented annually.
Additional information This program includes the Robert M. Zweiman Memorial Award, the Sidney Lieppe Memorial Grant, the Charles Kosmutza Memorial Grant, the Max R. and Irene Rubenstein Memorial Grant, and the Leon Brooks Memorial Grant.
Number awarded 6 each year: 2 at $5,000, 1 at $2,500, 1 at $1,500, and 2 at $1,000.
Deadline May of each year.

[1251]
JOE KING SCHOLARSHIPS

Council of College and Military Educators
c/o Jim Yeonopolus, Scholarship Committee Chair
Central Texas College
P.O. Box 1800
Killeen, TX 76540-1800
(254) 526-1781   Fax: (254) 526-1750
E-mail: jim.yeonopolus@ctcd.edu
Web: www.ccmeonline.org/scholarships

Summary To provide financial assistance to members of the armed services who are interested in working on an undergraduate or master's degree.
Eligibility This program is open to members of the uniformed services currently on active duty. Applicants must be currently enrolled full time at an accredited institution that is a member of the Council of College and Military Educators (CCME) and working on an associate, bachelor's, or master's degree. Undergraduates must have a GPA of 2.5 or higher and graduate students must have a GPA of 3.0 or higher. Along with their application, they must submit an essay of 400 to 750 words on how they would describe military leadership. Financial need is not considered in the selection process.
Financial data The stipend is $1,000. Funds are paid directly to the student.
Duration 1 year; nonrenewable.

Number awarded 5 each year.
Deadline September of each year.

[1252]
JOHN CORNELIUS/MAX ENGLISH MEMORIAL SCHOLARSHIP

Marine Corps Tankers Association
c/o Dan Miller, Scholarship Chair
8212 West Fourth Place
Kennewick, WA 99336
E-mail: dmiller@msn.com
Web: www.usmctankers.org/pageScholarship

Summary To provide financial assistance for college or graduate school to children and grandchildren of members of the Marine Corps Tankers Association and to Marine and Navy personnel currently serving in tank units.

Eligibility This program is open to high school seniors and graduates who are children, grandchildren, or under the guardianship of an active, Reserve, retired, or honorably discharged Marine who served in a tank unit. Marine or Navy Corpsmen currently assigned to tank units are also eligible. Applicants must be enrolled or planning to enroll full time at a college or graduate school. Their parent or grandparent must be a member of the Marine Corps Tankers Association or, if not a member, must join if the application is accepted. Along with their application, they must submit a 500-word essay that explains their reason for seeking this scholarship, their educational goals, and their plans for post-graduation life. Selection is based on that essay, academic record, school activities, leadership potential, and community service.

Financial data The stipend is at least $2,000 per year.
Duration 1 year; recipients may reapply.
Number awarded Varies each year; recently, 4 were awarded.
Deadline March of each year.

[1253]
KENTUCKY NATIONAL GUARD TUITION AWARD PROGRAM

Kentucky Higher Education Assistance Authority
Attn: Student Aid Branch
100 Airport Road
P.O. Box 798
Frankfort, KY 40602-0798
(502) 696-7392   Toll Free: (800) 928-8926, ext. 7392
Fax: (502) 696-7373   TDD: (800) 855-2880
E-mail: studentaid@kheaa.com
Web: www.kheaa.com/website/kheaa/military_ky?main=7

Summary To provide financial assistance for college or graduate school to members of the Kentucky National Guard.

Eligibility This program is open to active enlisted members of the Kentucky National Guard who are interested in working full or part time on an undergraduate or graduate degree. Applicants must have maintained standards of satisfactory membership in the Guard, including passing the most recent physical fitness test, meeting the height-weight standard, meeting attendance standards, having no unsatisfactory performance or absence-without-leave records, and having no other restrictions on their personnel file. Preference is given to applicants working on their first undergraduate degree.

Financial data The program provides payment of full tuition and fees at any state-supported university, community college, or vocational or technical school in Kentucky.
Duration 1 semester; may be renewed.
Number awarded Varies each year.
Deadline March of each year for summer or fall terms; September of each year for spring term.

[1254]
LOUISIANA NATIONAL GUARD STATE TUITION EXEMPTION PROGRAM

Louisiana National Guard
Attn: State Tuition Exemption Manager
Public Affairs Office
6400 St. Claude Avenue
New Orleans, LA 70117
(504) 278-8273   Toll Free: (800) 899-6355
E-mail: leonard.c.acker.civ@mail.mil
Web: www.geauxguard.la.gov/education

Summary To provide financial assistance to members of the Louisiana National Guard who are interested in attending college or graduate school in the state.

Eligibility This program is open to active drilling members of the Louisiana Army National Guard or Air National Guard. Guard members are ineligible if they have been disqualified by their unit commander for any adverse action, have already obtained a bachelor's degree, are placed on academic probation or suspension, test positive on a drug/alcohol test or declare themselves as a self-referral, are separated or transfer to the Inactive National Guard, or have 9 or more AWOLs. Applicants must have been accepted for admission or be enrolled in a Louisiana public institution of higher learning, either part time or full time, to work on an associate, bachelor's, or master's degree.

Financial data Recipients are exempt from all tuition charges at Louisiana state-funded colleges, universities, or community colleges.
Duration The exemption may be claimed for 5 separate academic years or until the receipt of a degree, whichever occurs first.
Additional information The state legislature established this program in 1974.
Number awarded Varies each year.
Deadline Deadline not specified.

[1255]
MAJOR GENERAL GUS HARGETT SCHOLARSHIP

National Guard Association of Tennessee
Attn: Foundation
4332 Kenilwood Drive
Nashville, TN 37204-4401
(615) 833-9100   Toll Free: (888) 642-8448 (within TN)
Fax: (615) 833-9173   E-mail: byron@ngatn.org
Web: www.ngatn.org/scholarships

Summary To provide financial assistance for graduate school to members of the Tennessee National Guard who are also members of the National Guard Association of Tennessee (NGATN).

Eligibility This program is open to active members of the Tennessee Army or Air National Guard who are also annual members of NGATN. Applicants must be working on a master's or doctoral degree at a graduate school in any state.

Along with their application, they must submit transcripts, letters of recommendation, and a letter on their desire to continue their education.
Financial data The stipend is $4,000.
Duration 1 year.
Number awarded 1 each year.
Deadline February of each year.

[1256]
MARINE CORPS FUNDED LAW EDUCATION PROGRAM

U.S. Marine Corps
Manpower and Reserve Affairs
Attn: Graduate Education (MMOA-3)
3280 Russell Road
Quantico, VA 22134-5103
(703) 693-8405   E-mail: Angelissa.Savino@usmc.mil
Web: www.hqmc.marines.mil/sja/flep_elp

Summary To allow selected commissioned Marine Corps officers to earn a law degree by providing financial assistance for full-time study.
Eligibility Eligible to participate in this program are commissioned Marine Corps officers at the rank of captain or below. Applicants must have at least 2 but no more than 6 years of total active service and be able to complete 20 years of active service before their 62nd birthday. They must have graduated from an accredited college or university with a bachelor's degree, have taken the LSAT at their own arrangement and expense, and have been accepted at an accredited law school in the United States.
Financial data Commissioned officers selected to participate in this program receive their regular Marine Corps pay and allowances while attending a college or university on a full-time basis, as well as payment for the cost of tuition (to a maximum of $10,000 per year).
Duration Up to the equivalent of 2 academic years.
Number awarded Varies each year; recently, 2 Marines were selected to participate in this program.
Deadline October of each year.

[1257]
MARINE CORPS SPECIAL EDUCATION PROGRAM

U.S. Marine Corps
Manpower and Reserve Affairs (RAM-3)
Attn: Special Education Program
3280 Russell Road
Quantico, VA 22134-5103
(703) 784-9284   Fax: (703) 784-9844
Web: www.marines.mil

Summary To provide financial assistance to Marine Corps commissioned officers who are interested in earning a graduate degree.
Eligibility Eligible to participate in this program are active-duty Marine Corps commissioned officers at the rank of first lieutenant through major. Applicants must be interested in working on a graduate degree in designated fields at the Naval Postgraduate School in Monterey, California, the Air Force Institute of Technology in Dayton, Ohio, or a civilian institution of their choice. Recently, the program offered a Master of Business Administration degree at the Naval Postgraduate School. Selection is based on career potential, past performance of duty, previous academic record, and availability for assignment.
Financial data The program provides payment of all tuition and required academic fees; travel, dependent transportation, and authorized allowances; up to $100 per academic term for purchase of required textbooks; and a $200 thesis typing fee.
Duration Until completion of a graduate degree.
Additional information Officers must agree not to resign or request retirement while enrolled in the program. They must also agree to remain on active duty, after completion of degree requirements or upon separation from the program for any other reason, for 3 years or, if the enrollment in school is longer than 1 calendar year, for 4 years.
Number awarded Varies each year.
Deadline Deadline dates are announced periodically.

[1258]
MARINE CORPS TUITION ASSISTANCE PROGRAM

U.S. Marine Corps
c/o Naval Education and Training Professional
  Development and Technology Command
Code N814
6490 Saufley Field Road
Pensacola, FL 32509-5241
(850) 452-1001   Toll Free: (877) 838-1659
Fax: (850) 473-6401   E-mail: SFLY_TA.Marine@navy.mil
Web:

Summary To provide financial assistance for undergraduate or graduate study to Marine Corps personnel.
Eligibility Eligible for assistance under this program are active-duty Marines who wish to take college courses for academic credit during off-duty time. Funding is available for vocational/technical, undergraduate, graduate, undergraduate development, independent study, and distance learning programs. Applicants must have completed at least 2 years of service, be eligible for promotion, and have completed designated military training courses. Commissioned officers must agree to remain on active duty for 2 years after the completion of any funded courses. Enlisted Marines must have an end of active duty status (EAS) of at least 60 days beyond the completion date of the course. All students must successfully complete their courses with a satisfactory grade.
Financial data Those selected for participation in this program receive their regular Marine Corps pay and 100% of tuition at the postsecondary educational institution of their choice, but capped at $4,500 per year or $250 per semester hour, whichever is less. Funding is available only for tuition, not fees or other associated expenses.
Duration Until completion of a bachelor's or graduate degree. Undergraduates must complete all courses with a grade of "C" or better; graduate students must complete classes with a grade of "B" of better. If recipients fail to achieve those grades, they must reimburse the Marine Corps for all funds received.
Number awarded Varies each year; in recent years, approximately 20,000 Marines availed themselves of this funding.
Deadline Applications must be submitted within 30 days of the start date of the class.

[1259]
MARINES' MEMORIAL TRIBUTE SCHOLARSHIPS

Marines' Memorial Association
c/o Marines Memorial Club and Hotel
609 Sutter Street
San Francisco, CA 94102
(415) 673-6672, ext. 293   Toll Free: (800) 5-MARINE
Fax: (415) 441-3649
E-mail: scholarship@marineclub.com
Web: www.marinesmemorial.org

Summary To provide financial assistance to military personnel who are transitioning from active duty to civilian or Reserve status and wish to attend college.

Eligibility This program is open to military personnel who have separated from full-time active duty to civilian or Reserve status within the past 3 years. Applicants must be enrolled or planning to enroll full time in an accredited undergraduate or graduate degree program in any field at a college or university. Membership in the sponsoring organization is not required. Along with their application, they must submit an essay of up to 500 words on why they chose their specific path of study, what they hope to accomplish after graduation with their degree, and how their efforts will benefit others in their community. Applicants entering college as freshmen must submit a high school transcript and SAT or ACT scores; continuing college students must submit a college transcript. Selection is based on the essay, academic merit, references, and financial need.

Financial data The stipend ranges from $2,500 to $5,000 per year.

Duration 1 year; recipients may reapply for up to 3 additional years.

Number awarded 8 each year.

Deadline April of each year.

[1260]
MARYLAND NATIONAL GUARD STATE TUITION WAIVER (STW)

Maryland National Guard
Attn: Education Services Office
Fifth Regiment Armory
29th Division Street, Room B-23
Baltimore, MD 21201-2288
(410) 576-1499   Toll Free: (800) 492-2526
Fax: (410) 576-6082
E-mail: mdng_education@md.ngb.army.mil
Web: military.maryland.gov

Summary To waive tuition for members of the Maryland National Guard at colleges and universities in the state.

Eligibility This program is open to members of the Maryland National Guard who wish to attend designated "Partners in Education" institutions in the state. That includes all 5 branches of the University of Maryland, 8 other public colleges and universities, 13 community colleges, 5 private universities, and 4 private career education institutions that have agreed to waive part of the tuition charges for National Guard members. Applicants must have a 2-year obligation remaining from the course start date.

Financial data The amount of the waiver ranges from 25% to 50%. Most 4-year colleges waive 50% of tuition for up to 6 credits per semester.

Duration 1 semester; recipients may reapply.

Additional information Some schools also limit the number of credits for which a Guard member can receive waivers during any semester.

Number awarded Varies each year.

Deadline Deadline not specified.

[1261]
MASSACHUSETTS NATIONAL GUARD TUITION WAIVER PROGRAM

Massachusetts National Guard
Attn: Education Services Officer
2 Randolph Road
Hanscom AFB, MA 01731
(339) 202-3199   Fax: (339) 202-0109
E-mail: ng.ma.maarng.mbx.education-ma@mail.mil
Web: www.massnationalguard.org

Summary To provide financial assistance to members of the Massachusetts National Guard interested in working on an undergraduate or graduate degree at a college in the state.

Eligibility This program is open to actively participating members of the Army or Air National Guard in Massachusetts. Applicants must have less than 9 AWOLs (Absence Without Leave) at all times and must not ETS (Expiration of Term of Service) during the period enrolled. They must be accepted for admission or enrolled at 1 of 28 Massachusetts public colleges, universities, or community colleges and working on an associate, bachelor's, master's, or doctoral degree. The institution must have a vacancy after all tuition-paying students and all students who are enrolled under any scholarship or tuition waiver provisions have enrolled.

Financial data Eligible Guard members are exempt from any tuition payments at colleges or universities operated by the Commonwealth of Massachusetts and funded by the Massachusetts Board of Higher Education.

Duration Up to a total of 130 semester hours.

Additional information Recipients may enroll either part or full time in a Massachusetts state-supported institution. This program is funded through the Massachusetts Board of Higher Education.

Number awarded Varies each year.

Deadline Deadline not specified.

[1262]
MCA CHAPLAIN CANDIDATE SCHOLARSHIPS

Military Chaplains Association of the United States of America
Attn: Executive Director
P.O. Box 7056
Arlington, VA 22207-7056
Fax: (703) 535-5890   E-mail: chaplains@mca-usa.org
Web: www.mca-usa.org/scholarships

Summary To provide financial assistance to seminary students who are serving as chaplain candidates for the U.S. armed forces.

Eligibility This program is open to full-time students in accredited seminaries who are currently approved as and serving as chaplain candidates in the armed forces (Army, Air Force, or Navy). Applicants must be able to demonstrate financial need. Along with their application, they must submit an essay, up to 1,500 words in length on their call and preparation for religious ministry with particular emphasis on 1)

their call to provide pastoral care for military personnel and their families; and 2) their understanding of ministry in a religiously diverse environment (such as the armed forces of the United States).
Financial data The stipend is $2,000.
Duration 1 year.
Additional information This program began in 1992.
Number awarded Several each year. Since the program was established, it has awarded 65 scholarships.
Deadline May of each year.

[1263]
MEDICAL SERVICE CORPS INSERVICE PROCUREMENT PROGRAM (MSC-IPP)
U.S. Navy
Attn: Navy Medicine Professional Development Center
Code O3C HMDT
8955 Wood Road, 16th Floor
Bethesda, MD 20889-5611
(301) 319-4520   Fax: (301) 295-1783
E-mail: beverly.d.kemp.civ@mail.mil
Web: www.navyadvancement.com

Summary To provide funding to Navy and Marine enlisted personnel who wish to earn an undergraduate or graduate degree in selected health care specialties while continuing to receive their regular pay and allowances.
Eligibility This program is open to enlisted personnel who are serving on active duty in any rating in pay grade E-4 through E-9 of the U.S. Navy, U.S. Marine Corps, or the Marine Corps Reserve serving on active duty (including Full Time Support of the Reserve). Applicants must be interested in working on a degree to become commissioned in the following medical specialties: entomology, environmental health, health care administration industrial hygiene, occupational therapy, pharmacy, physician assistant radiation health, or social work. If they plan to work on a graduate degree, they must have scores of at least 300 on the GRE or 525 on the GMAT; if they plan to work on a bachelor's or physician assistant degree, they must have scores of at least 1000 on the SAT (including 460 on the mathematics portion) or 42 on the ACT (21 on the English portion, 21 on the mathematics portion). They must be U.S. citizens who can be commissioned before they reach their 42nd birthday.
Financial data Participants receive payment of tuition, mandatory fees, a book allowance, and full pay and allowances for their enlisted pay grade. They are eligible for advancement while in college.
Duration 24 to 48 months of full-time, year-round study, until completion of a relevant degree.
Additional information Following graduation, participants are commissioned in the Medical Service Corps and attend Officer Indoctrination School. They incur an 8-year military service obligation, including at least 3 years served on active duty.
Number awarded Varies each year; recently, 36 were awarded.
Deadline August of each year.

[1264]
MG LEIF J. SVERDRUP SCHOLARSHIP
Army Engineer Association
Attn: Director Washington DC Operations
P.O. Box 30260
Alexandria, VA 22310-8260
(703) 428-7084   Fax: (703) 428-6043
E-mail: xd@armyengineer.com
Web: www.armyengineer.com/scholarships

Summary To provide financial assistance for college or graduate school to officers who are members of the Army Engineer Association (AEA).
Eligibility This program is open to AEA members serving in an active, Reserve, or National Guard component Army Engineer unit, school, or organization within the Corps of Engineers of the United States Army. Applicants must be commissioned officers (2LT, 1LT, or CPT) or warrant officers (WO1 or WO2). They must be working on or planning to work on an associate, bachelor's, or master's degree at an accredited college or university. Along with their application, they must submit a 1-page essay outlining why they should be selected for an award, including a paragraph on their financial need and their evaluation of their potential for success.
Financial data The stipend is $1,000.
Duration 1 year.
Number awarded 2 each year: 1 to a commissioned officer and 1 to a warrant officer.
Deadline June of each year.

[1265]
MICHIGAN NATIONAL GUARD STATE TUITION ASSISTANCE PROGRAM
Department of Military and Veterans Affairs
Attn: State Operations-Budget Office
3423 North Martin Luther King Boulevard
Lansing, MI 48906
(517) 481-7640   Toll Free: (800) 481-7644
E-mail: MINGSTAP@michigan.gov
Web: ww.michigan.gov

Summary To provide financial assistance to members of the Michigan National Guard who are enrolled at a college in the state.
Eligibility This program is open to all members of the Michigan National Guard who are in good standing with their unit and have completed basic training. Applicants must be enrolled at a college, university, vocational/technical institution, or trade school in the state and working on a certificate, associate degree, bachelor's degree, master's degree, or professional degree.
Financial data Grants provide up to $600 per credit hour or up to $6,000 per year for tuition and fees.
Duration Guard members may receive tuition assistance for up to 144 hours of undergraduate credit or completion of a baccalaureate degree, whichever comes first. If they continue on for a master's or professional degree, they may receive up to 42 credit hours of additional tuition assistance.
Additional information This program began in 2014.
Number awarded Varies each year.
Deadline Applications may be submitted at any time, but they must be received no earlier than 60 calendar days before and no later than 14 calendar days after the course start date.

[1266]
MINNESOTA G.I. BILL PROGRAM

Minnesota Department of Veterans Affairs
Attn: Programs and Services Division
20 West 12th Street, Room 206
St. Paul, MN 55155
(651) 296-2562 Toll Free: (888) LINK-VET
Fax: (651) 296-3954 TDD: (800) 627-3529
E-mail: MNGIBill@state.mn.us
Web: www.mn.gov

Summary To provide financial assistance for college or graduate school in the state to residents of Minnesota who served in the military after September 11, 2001 and the families of deceased or disabled military personnel.

Eligibility This program is open to residents of Minnesota enrolled at colleges and universities in the state as undergraduate or graduate students. Applicants must be 1) a veteran who is serving or has served honorably in a branch of the U.S. armed forces at any time; 2) a non-veteran who has served honorably for a total of 5 years or more cumulatively as a member of the Minnesota National Guard or other active or Reserve component of the U.S. armed forces, and any part of that service occurred on or after September 11, 2001; or 3) a surviving child or spouse of a person who has served in the military at any time and who has died or has a total and permanent disability as a result of that military service. They may be attending college in the state or participating in an apprenticeship or on-the-job (OJT) training program. Financial need is also considered in the selection process.

Financial data The college stipend is $1,000 per semester for full-time study or $500 per semester for part-time study. The maximum award is $3,000 per academic year or $10,000 per lifetime. Apprenticeship and OJT students are eligible for up to $2,000 per fiscal year. Approved employers are eligible to receive $1,000 placement credit payable upon hiring a person under this program and another $1,000 after 12 consecutive months of employment. No more than $3,000 in aggregate benefits under this paragraph may be paid to or on behalf of an individual in one fiscal year, and not more than $9,000 over any period of time.

Duration 1 year; may be renewed, provided the recipient continues to make satisfactory academic progress.

Additional information This program was established by the Minnesota Legislature in 2007.

Number awarded At least 1,000 each year.

Deadline Deadline not specified.

[1267]
MINNESOTA NATIONAL GUARD MEDICAL PROFESSIONAL STUDENT STATE TUITION REIMBURSEMENT PROGRAM

Minnesota National Guard
Attn: Education Office
600 Cedar Street
St. Paul, MN 5510-2509
(651) 282-4589 Toll Free: (800) 657-3848
Fax: (651) 282-4694
E-mail: ng.mn.mnarng.mbx.assets-education@mail.mil
Web: minnesotanationalguard.ng.mil/education

Summary To provide partial tuition reimbursement to medical, dental, and physician assistant students who are interested in serving in the Minnesota National Guard.

Eligibility This program is open to Minnesota Army and Air National Guard members who initially appoint as medical or dental student officers or are already commissioned officers and attain civilian physician assistant master's student status. Applicants must agree to accept a Medical Corps commission in the Guard after graduation.

Financial data This program provides reimbursement of the tuition charged, not to exceed 100% of the tuition costs at the University of Minnesota Twin Cities campus medical or dental schools or a maximum of $26,268 per year. Upon graduation from medical, dental, or physician assistant school, officers must serve 2 years in the Minnesota National Guard for each year that they participated in the program. Failure to fulfill that service obligation will result in recoupment of a prorated portion of the tuition reimbursed.

Duration The program provides funding for up to 144 semester or 208 quarter credits.

Number awarded The number of participants at any given time is limited to 15 Army Guard officers and 4 Air Guard officers.

Deadline Participants must request reimbursement within 60 days of the last official day of the term.

[1268]
MINNESOTA NATIONAL GUARD STATE TUITION REIMBURSEMENT

Minnesota National Guard
Attn: Education Office
600 Cedar Street
St. Paul, MN 5510-2509
(651) 282-4589 Toll Free: (800) 657-3848
Fax: (651) 282-4694
E-mail: ng.mn.mnarng.mbx.assets-education@mail.mil
Web: minnesotanationalguard.ng.mil/education

Summary To provide financial assistance for college or graduate school to current members of the Minnesota National Guard.

Eligibility Eligible for this program are members of the Minnesota Army or Air National Guard who are currently serving in grades E-1 through O-5 (including warrant officers) and are enrolled as undergraduate or graduate students at colleges or universities in Minnesota. Reimbursement is provided only for undergraduate courses completed with a grade of "C" or better or for graduate courses completed with a grade of "B" or better. Applicants must be serving satisfactorily according to National Guard standards.

Financial data The maximum reimbursement rate is 100% of the tuition rate at the University of Minnesota Twin Cities campus for undergraduate study or 50% for graduate work, with a maximum benefit of $18,000 per fiscal year for undergraduate course work or $20,000 per fiscal year for graduate course work.

Duration 1 semester, to a maximum of 18 credits per semester; may be renewed until completion of an associate, bachelor's, master's, or doctoral degree or 144 semester credits, whichever comes first.

Number awarded Varies each year.

Deadline Deadline not specified.

[1269]
MONTGOMERY GI BILL (SELECTED RESERVE)

Department of Veterans Affairs
Attn: Veterans Benefits Administration
810 Vermont Avenue, N.W.
Washington, DC 20420
(202) 418-4343   Toll Free: (888) 442-4551
Web: www.va.gov

Summary To provide financial assistance for college or graduate school to members of the Reserves or National Guard.

Eligibility Eligible to apply are members of the Reserve elements of the Army, Navy, Air Force, Marine Corps, and Coast Guard, as well as the Army National Guard and the Air National Guard. To be eligible, a Reservist must 1) have a 6-year obligation to serve in the Selected Reserves signed after June 30, 1985 (or, if an officer, to agree to serve 6 years in addition to the original obligation); 2) complete Initial Active Duty for Training (IADT); 3) meet the requirements for a high school diploma or equivalent certificate before completing IADT; and 4) remain in good standing in a drilling Selected Reserve unit. Reservists who enlisted after June 30, 1985 can receive benefits for undergraduate degrees, graduate training, or technical courses leading to certificates at colleges and universities. Reservists whose 6-year commitment began after September 30, 1990 may also use these benefits for a certificate or diploma from business, technical, or vocational schools; cooperative training; apprenticeship or on-the-job training; correspondence courses; independent study programs; tutorial assistance; remedial, deficiency, or refresher training; flight training; or state-approved alternative teacher certification programs.

Financial data The current monthly rate is $392 for full-time study, $293 for three-quarter time study, $195 for half-time study, or $98 for less than half-time study. For apprenticeship and on-the-job training, the monthly stipend is $294 for the first 6 months, $215.60 for the second 6 months, and $137.20 for the remainder of the program. Other rates apply for cooperative education, correspondence courses, and flight training.

Duration Up to 36 months for full-time study, 48 months for three-quarter study, 72 months for half-time study, or 144 months for less than half-time study. Benefits end 10 years from the date the Reservist became eligible for the program.

Additional information This program is frequently referred to as Chapter 1606 (formerly Chapter 106).

Number awarded Varies each year.

Deadline Applications may be submitted at any time.

[1270]
NATIONAL CALL TO SERVICE PROGRAM

Department of Veterans Affairs
Attn: Veterans Benefits Administration
810 Vermont Avenue, N.W.
Washington, DC 20420
(202) 418-4343   Toll Free: (844) 698-2311
Web: www.va.gov

Summary To provide educational or other benefits to military personnel who have completed their initial enlistment and agree to additional service in the military.

Eligibility This program is open to military personnel who 1) completed their initial entry training and then continued to serve on active duty for 15 months in an approved military occupational specialty; 2) without a break in service, they served either an additional period of approved active duty or a period of 24 months in active status in the Selected Reserved; and 3) spend the rest of their obligated service on active duty, in the selected reserve, in the individual ready reserve, or in AmeriCorps or another domestic national service program.

Financial data Participants who complete the required service may choose to receive 1) a cash bonus of $5,000; 2) repayment of qualifying student loans up to $18,000; 3) entitlement to the full-time educational allowance established by the Montgomery GI Bill for 3-year enlistees (currently $2,050 per month); or 4) entitlement to 50% of the educational allowance established by the Montgomery GI Bill for less than 3-year enlistees (currently $832 per month).

Duration The cash bonus and loan repayment are 1-time benefits. Educational assistance is provided for up to 12 months at the 3-year enlistee rate or up to 36 months at the less than 3-year enlistee rate.

Additional information This program, which began in 2003, is a Department of Defense program but administered by the Department of Veterans Affairs.

Number awarded Varies each year.

Deadline Applications may be submitted at any time.

[1271]
NATIONAL GUARD ASSOCIATION OF NEW HAMPSHIRE SCHOLARSHIPS

National Guard Association of New Hampshire
Attn: Scholarship Committee
P.O. Box 22031
Portsmouth, NH 03802-2031
(603) 227-1597   E-mail: nganhscholarship@gmail.com
Web: www.nganh.org/benefits

Summary To provide financial assistance to members of the National Guard Association of New Hampshire and their dependents who are interested in attending college or graduate school in any state.

Eligibility This program is open to current members of the National Guard Association of New Hampshire (officer, enlisted, or retired), their spouses, and their dependent children. Applicants must be enrolled or planning to enroll full or part time in an associate, bachelor's, graduate, professional, or doctoral degree program at an accredited college or university in any state. Along with their application, they must submit a 1-page essay on a topic that changes annually; recently, they were asked to describe what citizen service means to them.

Financial data The stipend is $1,000.

Duration 1 year.

Number awarded 1 each year.

Deadline April of each year.

[1272]
NATIONAL GUARD ASSOCIATION OF NEW JERSEY SCHOLARSHIP PROGRAM

National Guard Association of New Jersey
Attn: Scholarship Committee
P.O. Box 266
Wrightstown, NJ 08562
(848) 480-3441   E-mail: scholarship@nganj.org
Web: www.nganj.org/awards-scholarships

Summary To provide financial assistance to members of the National Guard Association of New Jersey (NGANJ) or their dependents who are interested in attending college or graduate school in any state.

Eligibility This program is open to 1) active members of the NGANJ currently enrolled full time at an approved community college, school of nursing, or 4-year college in any state; and 2) the spouses, children, and grandchildren of active, retired, or deceased members entering or attending a 4-year college or university in any state. Applicants must submit transcripts, information on the civic and academic activities in which they have participated, and a list of offices, honors, awards, and special recognitions they have received. Selection is based on academic accomplishment, leadership, and citizenship.

Financial data Stipends up to $1,000 are available.
Duration 1 year; nonrenewable.
Number awarded Varies each year; recently, 5 were awarded.
Deadline February of each year.

[1273]
NATIONAL GUARD ASSOCIATION OF TEXAS SCHOLARSHIP PROGRAM

National Guard Association of Texas
Attn: Education Committee
3706 Crawford Avenue
Austin, TX 78731-6803
(512) 454-7300   Toll Free: (800) 252-NGAT
Fax: (512) 467-6803   E-mail: tbz@ngat.org
Web: www.ngat.org/education.htm

Summary To provide financial assistance to members and dependents of members of the National Guard Association of Texas who are interested in attending college or graduate school in any state.

Eligibility This program is open to annual and life members of the association and their spouses and children (associate members and their dependents are not eligible). Applicants may be high school seniors, undergraduate students, or graduate students, either enrolled or planning to enroll at an institution of higher education in any state. Along with their application, they must submit an essay on their desire to continue their education. Selection is based on scholarship, citizenship, and leadership.

Financial data Stipends range from $500 to $5,000.
Duration 1 year (nonrenewable).
Additional information This program includes the Len and Jean Tallas Memorial Scholarship, the Texas Capital Area Chapter of the AUSA Scholarship, the Lewis O. King Memorial Scholarship, the Gloria Jenell and Marlin E. Mote Endowed Scholarship, the LTC Gary Parrish Memorial Scholarship, the TXNG Retirees Endowed Scholarship, and 2 scholarships sponsored by USAA Insurance Corporation.

Number awarded Varies each year; recently, 8 were awarded: 1 at $5,000, 1 at $4,000, 1 at $2,000, 1 at $1,250, 3 at $1,000, and 1 at $500.
Deadline February of each year.

[1274]
NATIONAL GUARD ASSOCIATION OF VERMONT SCHOLARSHIPS

National Guard Association of Vermont
Attn: Scholarships
P.O. Box 694
Essex Junction, VT 05453
(802) 999-7675   E-mail: ngavtpresident@gmail.com
Web: www.ngavt.org/scholarships

Summary To provide financial assistance to members of the Vermont National Guard (VTNG) or the National Guard Association of Vermont (NGA-VT) and their children or spouses who are interested in attending college or graduate school in any state.

Eligibility This program is open to current members of the VTNG or the NGA-VT, their spouses, and their unmarried children. Applicants must be working, or planning to work, on an associate, undergraduate, technical, or graduate degree as a full-time student at a school in any state. Along with their application, they must submit an essay on their commitment to selfless public service or their plan for pursuing it in the future. Selection is based on academic performance and overall potential for a commitment to selfless public service.

Financial data The stipend is $1,000. Funds are sent directly to the recipient.
Duration 1 year; recipients may reapply.
Additional information This program is sponsored by the New England Federal Credit Union.
Number awarded 4 undergraduate and 1 graduate scholarship are awarded each year.
Deadline January of each year.

[1275]
NATIONAL GUARD OF GEORGIA SCHOLARSHIP FUND FOR GRADUATE STUDENTS

Georgia Guard Insurance Trust
3 Central Plaza, Suite 356
Rome, GA 30161
(770) 739-9651   Toll Free: (800) 229-1053
Fax: (770) 745-0673   E-mail: director@ngaga.org
Web: www.ngaga.org

Summary To provide financial assistance to members of the Georgia National Guard who are interested in attending graduate in any state.

Eligibility This program is open to policyholders with the Georgia Guard Insurance Trust (GGIT) who are members of the National Guard Association of Georgia (NGAGA) or the Enlisted Association of the National Guard of Georgia (EANGGA); spouses, children, and grandchildren of NGAGA and EANGGA members are not eligible. Applicants must be enrolled or planning to enroll as graduate students at a college or university in any state. They must have an undergraduate GPA of 3.0 or higher. Along with their application, they must submit transcripts, a letter with personal specific facts regarding their desire to continue their education, 2 letters of recommendation, a letter of academic reference, and an agreement to retain insurance with the GGIT for at least 2

years following completion of the school year for which the scholarship is awarded. Selection is based on academics, character, and moral and personal traits.
Financial data The stipend is $3,000.
Duration 1 year.
Number awarded 1 or more each year.
Deadline April of each year.

[1276]
NAVAL HELICOPTER ASSOCIATION SCHOLARSHIPS
Naval Helicopter Association
Attn: Scholarship Fund
P.O. Box 180578
Coronado, CA 92178-0578
(619) 435-7139   Fax: (619) 435-7354
E-mail: pres@nhascholarshipfund.org
Web: www.nhascholarshipfund.org/about/scholarships

Summary To provide financial assistance for college or graduate school to members of the Naval Helicopter Association (NHA) and their families.
Eligibility This program is open to NHA members and their spouses, children, and grandchildren. Membership in the NHA is open to active-duty and retired U.S. Navy, U.S. Marine Corps, and U.S. Coast Guard helicopter pilots, aircrew, and maintenance professionals. Applicants must be working on or planning to work on an undergraduate or graduate degree in any field. Along with their application, they must submit a personal statement on their academic and career aspirations. Selection is based on that statement, academic proficiency, scholastic achievements and awards, extracurricular activities, employment history, and letters of recommendation. The program includes scholarships 1) reserved for NHA family members; 2) reserved for active-duty personnel; 3) sponsored by private corporations; 4) named as memorials in honor of distinguished individuals; and 5) awarded on a regional basis.
Financial data Stipends are approximately $2,000.
Duration 1 year.
Additional information Corporate sponsors have included FLIR Systems, D.P. Associates, L-3 Communications, CAE, Raytheon Corporation, Lockheed Martin (designated the Sergei Sikorsky Scholarship), and Northrop Grumman. Memorial Scholarships have included the Edward and Veronica Ream Memorial Scholarship, the CDR Mort McCarthy Memorial Scholarship, the Charles Karman Memorial Scholarship, the LT Christian "Horse" Hescock Memorial Scholarship, and the Captain Mark Starr Memorial Scholarship.
Number awarded Varies each year; recently, 17 were awarded: 1 graduate student family member, 3 active-duty graduate students, 1 active-duty undergraduate student, 4 sponsored by corporate donors, 4 memorial scholarships, and 4 regional scholarships.
Deadline January of each year.

[1277]
NAVY HEALTH PROFESSIONS SCHOLARSHIP PROGRAM
U.S. Navy
Attn: Navy Bureau of Medicine and Surgery
Accessions Department
8955 Wood Road, Suite 13132
Bethesda, MD 20889-5628
(301) 295-1217   Toll Free: (800) USA-NAVY
Fax: (301) 295-1811   E-mail: usn.ohstudent@mail.mil
Web: www.med.navy.mil

Summary To provide financial assistance for education in a medical field to future Navy medical officers.
Eligibility Applicants for this assistance must be U.S. citizens, under 36 years of age, who are enrolled in or accepted at an accredited medical, osteopathic, dental, or optometry school or in their first year of a Ph.D. or Psy.D. program in clinical psychology located in the United States or Puerto Rico. Upon acceptance into the program, applicants are commissioned as officers in the U.S. Navy Medical Corps Reserve; after completion of medical school, they must perform at least 3 years of active-duty service in the U.S. Navy.
Financial data This program pays full tuition at any school of medicine, osteopathy, dentistry, or optometry or a course leading to a doctoral degree as a clinical psychologist located in the United States or Puerto Rico, and covers the cost of fees, books, and required equipment. In addition, recipients are awarded a stipend of at least $2,300 per month for 10 1/2 months of the year; for the other 1 1/2 months of each year, they perform active-duty service, usually at a Navy medical facility, and receive the normal pay of an Ensign.
Duration Assistance under this program continues until the student completes work for a doctorate degree in medicine, osteopathy, dentistry, or optometry or a master's degree as a physician assistant.
Additional information Following receipt of the doctorate degree, recipients serve an internship and residency either in a naval hospital (in which case they receive Navy active-duty pay) or, if not selected for naval graduate medical education, in a civilian hospital (where they receive only the regular salary of the civilian institution). After completion of the residency, the students must begin the active-duty service obligation. That obligation is 1 year for each year of participation in the program, with a minimum service obligation of 3 years.
Number awarded Varies each year.
Deadline August of each year.

[1278]
NAVY LAW EDUCATION PROGRAM
U.S. Navy
Attn: Office of the Judge Advocate General
1322 Patterson Avenue, Suite 300
Washington Navy Yard, DC 20374-5066
(202) 685-5275
Web: www.jag.navy.mil

Summary To provide financial assistance to Navy and Marine Corps officers who are interested in working on a law degree on a full-time basis.
Eligibility This program is open to active-duty Navy and Marine Corps commissioned officers in pay grade O-1 through O-3. Applicants must have served at least 2 but not more than 6 years on active duty and be able to complete 20

years of active service as a commissioned officer before their 55th birthday. They must have a baccalaureate degree from an accredited institution and be interested in working on a degree at an ABA-accredited law school. U.S. citizenship is required.

Financial data This program provides up to $21,500 for payment of mandatory tuition and fees, up to $500 per year for required textbooks, and a 1-time payment of $1,500 for a bar examination review course. Recipients continue to earn full pay and benefits while attending law school.

Duration Participants must complete their law degree within 36 months.

Additional information Following completion of their law degree, participants serve as career judge advocates in the Navy for 2 years for each year of legal training from this program.

Number awarded Up to 25 each year.

Deadline September of each year.

[1279]
NAVY SEAL FOUNDATION SCHOLARSHIPS

Navy Seal Foundation
Attn: Chief Financial Officer
1619 D Street, Building 5326
Virginia Beach, VA 23459
(757) 744-5326   Fax: (757) 363-7491
E-mail: info@navysealfoundation.org
Web: www.navysealfoundation.org

Summary To provide financial assistance for college or graduate school to Naval Special Warfare (NSW) personnel and their families.

Eligibility This program is open to active-duty Navy SEALS, Special Warfare Combatant-craft Crewmen (SWCC), and military personnel assigned to other NSW commands. Their dependent children and spouses are also eligible. Applicants must be entering or continuing full or part-time students working on an associate or bachelor's degree. Active-duty and spouses, but not dependent children, may also work on a graduate degree. Selection is based on GPA, SAT scores, class ranking, extracurricular activities, volunteer community involvement, leadership positions held, military service record, and employment (as appropriate).

Financial data Stipends are $15,000, $7,500, or $5,000 per year.

Duration 1 year; may be renewed.

Number awarded Varies each year; recently, the Navy Seal Foundation awarded 16 scholarships for all of its programs: 3 for 4 years at $15,000 per year to high school seniors and graduates, 3 for 1 year at $7,500 to high school seniors and graduates, 3 for 1 year at $15,000 to current college students, 3 for 1 year at $7,500 to current college students, and 4 for 1 year at $5,000 to spouses.

Deadline February of each year.

[1280]
NAVY TUITION ASSISTANCE PROGRAM

U.S. Navy
Attn: Navy College Virtual Education Center
1155 Nider Boulevard, Building 3510, Room 100
Virginia Beach, VA 23459-2732
(703) 604-5256   Toll Free: (877) 838-1659
E-mail: james.p.johnson@navy.mil
Web: www.navycollege.navy.mil

Summary To provide financial assistance for high school, vocational, undergraduate, or graduate studies to Navy personnel.

Eligibility This program is open to active-duty Navy officers and enlisted personnel with at least 2 years of service, including Naval Reservists on continuous active duty, enlisted Naval Reservists ordered to active duty for 120 days or more, and Naval Reservist officers ordered to active duty for 2 years or more. Applicants must register to take courses at accredited civilian schools during off-duty time. They must be working on their first associate, bachelor's, master's, doctoral, or professional degree. Tuition assistance is provided for courses taken at accredited colleges, universities, vocational/technical schools, private schools, and through independent study/distance learning (but not for flight training).

Financial data Those selected for participation in this program receive their regular Navy pay and 100% of tuition at the postsecondary educational institution of their choice, but capped at $250 per semester hour and 12 semester hours per fiscal year, or a total of $3,000 per fiscal year. Funding is available only for tuition, not fees or other associated expenses.

Duration The lifetime limit is 120 semester hours. Undergraduates must complete all courses with a grade of "C" or better; graduate students must complete classes with a grade of "B" of better. If recipients fail to achieve those grades, they must reimburse the Navy for all funds received.

Additional information Officers must agree to remain on active duty for at least 2 years after completion of courses funded by this program.

Number awarded Varies each year.

Deadline Deadline not specified.

[1281]
NBCCF MILITARY SCHOLARSHIPS

National Board for Certified Counselors
Attn: NBCC Foundation
3 Terrace Way
Greensboro, NC 27403
(336) 232-0376   Fax: (336) 232-0010
E-mail: foundation@nbcc.org
Web: nbccf.applicantstack.com/x/detail/a2ei42le608f

Summary To provide financial assistance to current and former military personnel and spouses of servicemembers interested in working on a master's degree in counseling.

Eligibility This program is open to students enrolled full time in an accredited master's degree counseling program. Applicants must be prior or current active-duty U.S. military service personnel or the spouse of a servicemember. Veterans must have received an honorable discharge. Applicants must be able to demonstrate a commitment to apply for the National Certified Counselor (NCC) credential prior to gradu-

ation and to provide counseling services to servicemembers and/or veterans for at least 2 years after graduation.
Financial data The stipend is $8,000.
Duration 1 year.
Additional information This program began in 2010.
Number awarded 5 each year.
Deadline January of each year.

[1282]
NERA/USAA COLLEGE SCHOLARSHIP PROGRAM
Naval Enlisted Reserve Association
Attn: Scholarship Committee
8116 Arlington Boulevard
Falls Church, VA 22042
(703) 534-1329   Toll Free: (800) 776-9020
Fax: (703) 534-3617   E-mail: members@nera.org
Web: www.nera.org

Summary To provide financial assistance for college to members of the Naval Enlisted Reserve Association (NERA) and their families.
Eligibility This program is open to students enrolled or entering a college or university to work full or part time on an associate degree, vocational or trade school certificate, bachelor's degree, master's degree, or doctoral degree. Applicants or their sponsor must be a member of NERA in good standing. They must have a GPA of 3.0 or higher. Along with their application, they must submit an essay of 500 to 600 words on 1) their aspirations and course of study; and 2) the role of the Reservist in America and the importance of the Reserves to our national defense. In the selection process, priority is given in the following order: 1) currently serving Reserve, active and IRR members of the U.S. armed forces; 2) children and spouses of those currently serving in the U.S. armed forces; and 3) spouses, children, or grandchildren sponsored by any NERA member. Financial need is not considered in the selection process.
Financial data The stipend is $2,000.
Duration 1 year.
Additional information This program is funded in part by USAA Insurance Corporation. Regular membership in NERA is open to enlisted members of the Navy, Marine Corps, and Coast Guard Reserve components, including FTS, IRR, VTU, and retirees; associate membership is open to anyone who wishes to support NERA.
Number awarded 5 each year.
Deadline June of each year.

[1283]
NEVADA NATIONAL GUARD STATE TUITION WAIVER PROGRAM
Nevada National Guard
Attn: Education Services Officer
2460 Fairview Drive
Carson City, NV 89701-6807
(775) 887-7326   Fax: (775) 887-7279
E-mail: NV-TSC@ng.army.mil
Web: nv.ng.mil/Pages/Departments/Education.aspx

Summary To provide financial assistance to Nevada National Guard members who are interested in attending college or graduate school in the state.

Eligibility This program is open to active members of the Nevada National Guard who are interested in attending a public community college, 4-year college, or university in the state. Applicants must be residents of Nevada. Independent study, correspondence courses, and study at the William S. Boyd School of Law, the University of Nevada School of Medicine, and the UNLV School of Dental Medicine are not eligible.
Financial data This program provides a waiver of 100% of tuition at state-supported community colleges, colleges, or universities in Nevada.
Duration 1 year; may be renewed.
Additional information This program was established on a pilot basis in 2003 and became permanent in 2005. Recipients must attain a GPA of at least 2.0 or refund all tuition received.
Number awarded Varies each year.
Deadline Applications must be received at least 3 weeks prior to the start of classes.

[1284]
NEW HAMPSHIRE NATIONAL GUARD TUITION WAIVER PROGRAM
Office of the Adjutant General
Attn: Education Services Officer
1 Minuteman Way
Building 1, Room 125
Concord, NH 03301
(603) 225-1207   Fax: (603) 225-1257
TDD: (800) 735-2964
E-mail: sukari.d.stattonbill.mil@mail.mil
Web: www.nh.ngb.army.mil/members/education

Summary To provide financial assistance to members of the New Hampshire National Guard who are interested in attending college or graduate school in the state.
Eligibility This program is open to active members of the New Hampshire National Guard who have completed advanced individual training or commissioning and have at least a 90% attendance rate at annual training and drill assemblies. Applicants may be working on any type of academic degree at public institutions in New Hampshire. They must apply for financial aid from their school, for the New Hampshire National Guard Scholarship Program, and for federal tuition assistance.
Financial data The program provides full payment of tuition.
Duration 1 year; may be renewed.
Additional information This program began in 1996.
Number awarded Varies each year, depending on availability of space.
Deadline Deadline not specified.

[1285]
NEW JERSEY NATIONAL GUARD TUITION PROGRAM

New Jersey Department of Military and Veterans Affairs
Attn: New Jersey Army National Guard Education
  Services Officer
Second Floor, B204
3650 Saylors Pond Road
Fort Dix, NJ 08640-7600
(609) 562-0975   Toll Free: (888) 859-0352
Fax: (609) 562-0188
E-mail: benjamin.j.stoner.mil@mail.mil
Web: education.njarmyguard.com/njngtp

Summary To provide financial assistance for college or graduate school to New Jersey National Guard members and the surviving spouses and children of deceased members.

Eligibility This program is open to active members of the New Jersey National Guard who have completed Initial Active Duty for Training (IADT). Applicants must be New Jersey residents who have been accepted into a program of undergraduate or graduate study at any of 30 public institutions of higher education in the state. The surviving spouses and children of deceased members of the Guard who had completed IADT and were killed in the performance of their duties while a member of the Guard are also eligible if the school has classroom space available.

Financial data Tuition for up to 16 credits per semester is waived for full-time recipients in state-supported colleges or community colleges in New Jersey.

Duration 1 semester; may be renewed.

Number awarded Varies each year.

Deadline Deadline not specified.

[1286]
NGAOK SCHOLARSHIPS

National Guard Association of Oklahoma
c/o Scholarship Foundation
Attn: Rosemary Masters, Scholarship Chair
3501 Military Circle
Oklahoma City, OK 73111
(405) 823-0799   E-mail: ngaok.scholarship@gmail.com
Web: www.ngaok.org/benefits

Summary To provide financial assistance to members of the National Guard Association of Oklahoma (NGAOK) and their dependents who are interested in attending college in any state.

Eligibility This program is open to NGAOK members and their dependent children and spouses who are enrolled or planning to enroll full or part time in an undergraduate or graduate program at a college or university in any state. The primary next of kin of members of the Oklahoma National Guard killed in action after September 11, 2001 are considered life members of NGAOK. Applicants must submit transcripts that include ACT and/or SAT scores; lists of awards and recognitions, community and volunteer services, and extracurricular and sports activities; and a 500-word essay about how they exemplify the traits of selfless service, leadership, character, and their aspirations. Financial need is not considered in the selection process.

Financial data Stipends are $500 or $1,000.

Duration 1 year.

Number awarded 20 to 25 each year.

Deadline January of each year.

[1287]
NORTH CAROLINA NATIONAL GUARD TUITION ASSISTANCE PROGRAM

North Carolina National Guard
Attn: Education Services Office
1636 Gold Star Drive
Raleigh, NC 27607
(919) 664-6272   Toll Free: (800) 621-4136
Fax: (919) 664-6520
E-mail: ng.nc.ncarng.mbx.education-service-office@mail.
  mil
Web: nc.ng.mil/ESO/Pages/New-Students.aspx

Summary To provide financial assistance to members of the North Carolina National Guard who plan to attend college or graduate school in the state.

Eligibility This program is open to active members of the North Carolina National Guard (officer, warrant officer, or enlisted) who have at least 2 years of enlistment remaining after the end of the academic period for which tuition assistance is provided. Applicants must be enrolled in an eligible business or trade school, private institution, or public college/university in North Carolina. They may be working on a vocational, undergraduate, graduate, or doctoral degree.

Financial data The maximum stipend is currently $4,515 per academic year.

Duration 1 year; may be renewed.

Additional information This program is administered by the North Carolina State Education Assistance Authority.

Number awarded Varies each year; recently, 763 of these grants, with a value of $2,062,815, were awarded.

Deadline Applications must be submitted prior to the start of the term.

[1288]
NORTH DAKOTA NATIONAL GUARD TUITION ASSISTANCE PROGRAM

North Dakota National Guard
Attn: State Tuition Assistance Program
4200 East Divide Avenue
P.O. Box 5511
Bismarck, ND 58506-5511
(701) 333-3008
E-mail: ng.nd.ndarng.list.state-tuition-assistance@mail.
  mil
Web: www.ndguard.nd.gov/education-services

Summary To provide financial assistance to members of the North Dakota National Guard who plan to attend college or graduate school in the state.

Eligibility This program is open to members of the North Dakota National Guard who have a record of satisfactory participation (no more than 9 unexcused absences in the past 12 months) and service remaining after completion of the class for which they are requesting assistance. Applicants must be seeking support for trade or vocational training or work on an associate, baccalaureate, or graduate degree. They must be attending or planning to attend a North Dakota higher education public institution or a participating private institution (currently, Jamestown College, University of Mary in Bismarck, MedCenter One College of Nursing, Rasmussen College, or

Trinity Bible College). Full-time AGR personnel do not qualify for this program. This is an entitlement program, provided all requirements are met.

Financial data Participating colleges and universities waive 25% of tuition for eligible courses (undergraduate only), up to 25% of the tuition at the University of North Dakota. Through this program, the National Guard provides reimbursement of the remaining 75% of tuition for eligible courses (undergraduate and graduate), or up to 75% of the tuition at the University of North Dakota. The program also reimburses 100% of all regular fees, not to exceed 100% of the regular fees charged by the University of North Dakota. State reimbursements are paid directly to the student in the form of a check, based upon the number of credit hours successfully completed.

Duration Benefits are available for up to 144 semester credit hours or the completion of an undergraduate or graduate degree, provided the recipient earns a grade of "C" or higher in each undergraduate course or "B" or higher in each graduate course.

Number awarded Varies each year.

Deadline August of each year for fall; January of each year for spring; June of each year for summer.

[1289]
OHIO LEGION MEMBER/MILITARY VETERAN SCHOLARSHIP

American Legion
Department of Ohio
60 Big Run Road
P.O. Box 8007
Delaware, OH 43015
(740) 362-7478   Fax: (740) 362-1429
E-mail: legion@ohiolegion.com
Web: www.ohiolegion.com/programs/scholarships

Summary To provide financial assistance to residents of Ohio who are members of the American Legion, veterans, or current military personnel and interested in attending college in any state.

Eligibility This program is open to residents of Ohio who are 1) members of the American Legion; 2) honorably discharged members of the armed forces; or 3) currently on active duty or a member of the National Guard or Reserves. Applicants must be attending or planning to attend colleges, universities, or other approved postsecondary schools in any state as an undergraduate or graduate student. They must have a GPA of 3.5 or higher and an ACT score of at least 25. Along with their application, they must submit a personal statement of 500 to 550 words on their career objectives. Selection is based on academic achievement as measured by course grades, ACT scores, difficulty of curriculum, participation in school and outside activities, and the judging committee's general impression.

Financial data Stipends are normally at least $2,000.

Duration 1 year.

Number awarded 1 each year.

Deadline April of each year.

[1290]
PENNSYLVANIA NATIONAL GUARD EDUCATIONAL ASSISTANCE PROGRAM (EAP)

Pennsylvania Higher Education Assistance Agency
Attn: State Grant and Special Programs
1200 North Seventh Street
P.O. Box 8157
Harrisburg, PA 17105-8157
(717) 720-2800   Toll Free: (800) 692-7392
Fax: (717) 720-3786   TDD: (800) 654-5988
E-mail: info@pheaa.org
Web: www.pheaa.org

Summary To provide scholarship/loans for college or graduate school to Pennsylvania National Guard members.

Eligibility This program is open to active members of the Pennsylvania National Guard who are Pennsylvania residents and serving as enlisted personnel, warrant officers, or commissioned officers of any grade. Applicants must accept an obligation to serve in the Pennsylvania National Guard for a period of 6 years from the date of entry into the program. Students who do not possess a baccalaureate degree must be enrolled full or part time in an approved program of education at an approved institution of higher learning in Pennsylvania. Master's degree students are supported on a part-time basis only. Guard members receiving an ROTC scholarship of any type are not eligible.

Financial data Full-time undergraduate students receive the lesser of 100% of tuition plus technology fee at the institution where they are enrolled or the annual tuition rate and technology fee charged to a Pennsylvania resident at a state-owned university. Part-time undergraduates receive the lesser of 100% of the tuition plus technology fee for a part-time course of study at their institution or the per credit tuition rate charged to a Pennsylvania resident at a state-owned university plus the technology fee. Graduate students receive the lesser of 100% of the tuition plus technology fee charged for a part-time course of study at their institution or the per credit tuition rate charged to a Pennsylvania resident at a state-owned university. Recipients who fail to fulfill the service obligation must repay all funds received, plus interest.

Duration Up to 5 years.

Additional information This program, first offered in 1997, is jointly administered by the Pennsylvania Department of Military and Veterans Affairs and the Pennsylvania Higher Education Assistance Agency. Support for summer and graduate school is available only if funding permits.

Number awarded Varies each year; recently, 1,789 members of the Pennsylvania National Guard were enrolled in this program.

Deadline Deadline not specified.

[1291]
POST-9/11 GI BILL

Department of Veterans Affairs
Attn: Veterans Benefits Administration
810 Vermont Avenue, N.W.
Washington, DC 20420
(202) 418-4343   Toll Free: (888) 442-4551
Web: www.va.gov/education/about-gi-bill-benefits/post-9-11

Summary To provide financial assistance to veterans or military personnel who entered service on or after September 11, 2001.

Eligibility This program is open to current and former military personnel who 1) served on active duty for at least 90 aggregate days after September 11, 2001; 2) were discharged with a service-connected disability after 30 days; or 3) received a Purple Heart on or after September 11, 2001 and were discharged after any length of service. Applicants must be planning to enroll in an educational program, including work on an undergraduate or graduate degree, vocational/technical training, on-the-job training, flight training, correspondence training, licensing and national testing programs, entrepreneurship training, and tutorial assistance.

Financial data Participants working on an undergraduate or graduate degree at public institutions in their state receive full payment of tuition and fees. For participants who attend private institutions in most states, tuition and fee reimbursement is capped at $25,162.14 per academic year. Benefits for other types of training programs depend on the amount for which the veteran qualified under prior educational programs. Veterans also receive a monthly housing allowance that is 1) based on the Department of Defense Basic Allowance for Housing (BAH) for an E-5 with dependents (which depends on the location of the school but ranges from approximately $1,000 per month to approximately $2,500 per month); 2) $1,789 per month at schools in foreign countries; or 3) $894.50 per month for online training classes. They also receive an annual book allowance of $1,000 and (for participants who live in a rural county remote from an educational institution) a rural benefit payment of $500 per year.

Duration Most participants receive up to 36 months of entitlement under this program. Benefits are payable for up to 15 years following release from active duty.

Additional information This program, referred to as Chapter 33, began in 2009 as a replacement for previous educational programs for veterans and military personnel (e.g., Montgomery GI Bill, REAP). Current participants in those programs may be able to transfer benefits from those programs to this new plan. To qualify for 100% of Post 9/11-GI Bill benefits, transferees must have at least 36 months of active-duty service. Transferees with less service are entitled to smaller percentages of benefits, ranging down to 40% for those with only 90 days of service.

Number awarded Varies each year; recently, approximately 700,000 veterans received $10.7 billion on benefits through this program.

Deadline Deadline not specified.

[1292]
REAR ADMIRAL SAMUEL ELIOT MORISON SUPPLEMENTAL SCHOLARSHIP

Naval History and Heritage Command
Attn: Senior Historian
Washington Navy Yard
805 Kidder Breese Street, S.E.
Washington Navy Yard, DC 20374-5060
(202) 433-3940   Fax: (202) 433-3593
E-mail: NHHC_Fellowships@navy.mil
Web: www.history.navy.mil

Summary To provide financial assistance to Navy and Marine Corps officers who are working on a graduate degree in a field related to naval history.

Eligibility This program is open to active-duty commissioned officers of the U.S. Navy or U.S. Marine Corps who are working on a graduate degree in history, international relations, or a related field. Applications must be submitted through and endorsed by applicants' commanding officers. Selection is based on the relevance of the chosen area of study to U.S. naval history; demonstrated professional performance with particular emphasis on the officer's specialty; academic ability, including baccalaureate record; career needs of the officer; and potential for professional growth.

Financial data The stipend is $5,000; funds are to be used for expenses related to research, travel, and the purchase of books or other educational materials.

Duration 1 year.

Additional information This program began in 1993.

Number awarded 1 each year.

Deadline April of each year.

[1293]
RHODE ISLAND NATIONAL GUARD STATE TUITION ASSISTANCE PROGRAM

Rhode Island National Guard
Joint Force Headquarters
Attn: Education Office
645 New London Avenue
Cranston, RI 02920-3097
(401) 275-4039   Fax: (401) 275-4014
E-mail: christopher.a.toti.mil@mail.mil
Web: www.vets.ri.gov/includes/benefits/education/stap.php

Summary To provide financial support to members of the National Guard in Rhode Island interested in attending college or graduate school in the state.

Eligibility This program is open to active members of the Rhode Island National Guard in good standing who are currently satisfactorily participating in all unit training assemblies and annual training periods. Applicants must have at least 1 year of service remaining. They must be enrolled in or planning to enroll in an associate, bachelor's, or master's degree program at a public institution in the state.

Financial data Qualified Guard members are exempt from payment of tuition for up to 5 courses per semester.

Duration 1 semester; may be renewed.

Additional information This program began in 1999. The designated institutions are the University of Rhode Island, Rhode Island College, and the Community College of Rhode Island.

Number awarded Varies each year.

Deadline Deadline not specified.

[1294]
ROBERT W. BRUNSMAN MEMORIAL SCHOLARSHIP

International Military Community Executives' Association
Attn: Scholarship Committee
14080 Nacogdoches Road, Suite 329
San Antonio, TX 78247-1944
(940) 463-5145   Fax: (866) 369-2435
E-mail: imcea@imcea.org
Web: www.imcea.org/awards/scholarship-info

Summary To provide financial assistance to members of the International Military Community Executives' Association (IMCEA) who are working in the field of military morale, welfare, and recreation (MWR) and currently enrolled in college or graduate school.

Eligibility This program is open to regular IMCEA members who are currently employed in the field of military MWR. Applicants must be already enrolled at a college or university, either on-campus or online, and taking undergraduate or graduate courses related to MWR. Along with their application, they must submit a 2-page essay comparing other professional organizations with which they have been involved, the value they think IMCEA provides, and how IMCEA can continue to fulfill their professional needs and provide outstanding service in the coming years. Selection is based on that essay, participation in IMCEA activities, and involvement in military MWR services.
Financial data The stipend is $1,000.
Duration 1 year.
Additional information Regular membership in IMCEA is open to Army, Air Force, Navy, Marine Corps, and Coast Guard personnel who provide MWR services at military installations and bases worldwide.
Number awarded 1 each year.
Deadline June of each year.

[1295]
RUARK-WIGHT FAMILY SCHOLARSHIP

Marines' Memorial Association
c/o Marines Memorial Club and Hotel
609 Sutter Street
San Francisco, CA 94102
(415) 673-6672, ext. 293   Toll Free: (800) 5-MARINE
Fax: (415) 441-3649
E-mail: scholarship@marineclub.com
Web: www.marinesmemorial.org/members/scholarships

Summary To provide financial assistance to veterans, military personnel, and their families who are interested in attending college or graduate school to work on a degree in any field.
Eligibility This program is open to students who meet 1 of the following requirements: 1) have served honorably or is currently serving in any branch of the U.S. armed forces; or 2) is the spouse or child of a person who served honorably or is currently serving in any branch of the U.S. armed forces. Applicants must be enrolled as full-time sophomores, juniors, seniors or graduate students working on a degree in any field. They must have a GPA of 2.5 or higher. Membership in the sponsoring organization is not required for student veterans. Along with their application, they must submit an essay of up to 500 words on why they chose their specific path of study, what they hope to accomplish after graduation with their degree, and how their efforts will benefit others in their community. Selection is based on the essay, academic merit, references, and financial need.
Financial data The stipend is $5,000 per year.
Duration 1 year; recipients may reapply for up to 3 additional years.
Number awarded 1 each year.
Deadline April of each year.

[1296]
SCNGF ACADEMIC EXCELLENCE LEADERSHIP SCHOLARSHIPS

National Guard Association of South Carolina
Attn: South Carolina National Guard Foundation
132 Pickens Street
P.O. Box 7606
Columbia, SC 29202
(803) 254-8456   Toll Free: (800) 822-3235
Fax: (803) 254-3869   E-mail: dianne@scngf.org
Web: www.scngf.org/scngfscholarshipapplication

Summary To provide financial assistance to South Carolina National Guard members and their dependents who are interested in attending college or graduate school in any state.
Eligibility This program is open to members of the South Carolina National Guard and dependents of active or retired members. Applicants must be enrolled or planning to enroll full time at a 4-year college or university in any state as an undergraduate student. Guard members, but not dependents, are also eligible to attend graduate school. Applicants must have a GPA of 3.5 or higher and a record of involvement and leadership in school, civic, and/or community activities. Selection is based on excellence in academics and leadership; financial need is not considered.
Financial data The stipend is $1,500 per year. Funds are disbursed directly to the recipient's institution.
Duration 1 year; may be renewed up to 3 additional years.
Number awarded Varies each year; recently, this sponsor awarded a total of 75 scholarships through both of its programs.
Deadline February of each year.

[1297]
SCNGF FINANCIAL NEED/ACADEMIC ACHIEVEMENT SCHOLARSHIPS

National Guard Association of South Carolina
Attn: South Carolina National Guard Foundation
132 Pickens Street
P.O. Box 7606
Columbia, SC 29202
(803) 254-8456   Toll Free: (800) 822-3235
Fax: (803) 254-3869   E-mail: dianne@scngf.org
Web: www.scngf.org/scngfscholarshipapplication

Summary To provide financial assistance to South Carolina National Guard members and their dependents who are interested in attending college or graduate school in any state and can demonstrate financial need.
Eligibility This program is open to members of the South Carolina National Guard and dependents of active or retired members. Applicants must be enrolled or planning to enroll full time at a college or university in any state as an undergraduate student. Guard members, but not dependents, are also eligible to attend graduate school. Applicants must have a GPA of 2.5 or higher and a record of involvement and leadership in school, civic, and/or community activities. High school seniors must also submit SAT and/or ACT scores. Selection is based on excellence in academics and leadership and on financial need.
Financial data The stipend is $1,000 per year. Funds are disbursed directly to the recipient's institution.
Duration 1 year; may be renewed up to 3 additional years.

Number awarded Varies each year; recently, this sponsor awarded a total of 75 scholarships through both of its programs.
Deadline February of each year.

[1298]
SENATOR DANIEL K. INOUYE MEMORIAL SCHOLARSHIP

Japanese American Veterans Association
Attn: Chris DeRosa, Scholarship Committee Chair
P.O. Box 341198
Bethesda, MD 20827
E-mail: javascholarship222@gmail.com
Web: www.java.wildapricot.org

Summary To provide financial assistance for college or graduate school to relatives of Japanese American veterans who plan a career in the military or public service.
Eligibility This program is open to students who 1) have completed at least 1 year of an undergraduate program or are currently enrolled in graduate school and are preparing for a career in the military or public service; 2) are currently enrolled in a university or college ROTC program or the U.S. Marine Corps Platoon Leaders Course but are not receiving an ROTC scholarship; or 3) are disabled veterans. Applicants must also be 1) a direct or collateral descendant of a person who served with the 442nd Regimental Combat Team, the 100th Infantry Battalion, Military Intelligence Service, 1399th Engineering Construction Battalion, or other unit associated with those during or after World War II; or 2) a member or child of a member of the Japanese American Veterans Association (JAVA) whose membership extends back at least 1 year. Along with their application, they must submit a 500-word essay on their plan and vision to serve America through public service or the military.
Financial data The stipend is $5,000.
Duration 1 year.
Number awarded 1 each year.
Deadline March of each year.

[1299]
SFC CURTIS MANCINI MEMORIAL SCHOLARSHIPS

Association of the United States Army-Rhode Island
  Chapter
c/o LTC Robert A. Galvanin, President
31 Canoe River Drive
Mansfield, MA 02048
(508) 339-5301   E-mail: bpje5310@verizon.net
Web: www.riroa.org/ausari/scholarship.htm

Summary To provide financial assistance to members of the Rhode Island Chapter of the Association of the United States Army (AUSA) and their families who are interested in attending college or graduate school in any state.
Eligibility This program is open to members of the AUSA Rhode Island Chapter and their family members (spouses, children, and grandchildren). Applicants must be high school seniors or graduates accepted at an accredited college, university, or vocational/technical school in any state or current undergraduate or graduate students. Along with their application, they must submit a 250-word essay on why they feel their achievements should qualify them for this award. Selection is based on academic and individual achievements; financial need is not considered. Special consideration is given to students or graduates of Lincoln High School in Lincoln, Rhode Island (the alma mater of this program's namesake), especially those preparing for a career in law enforcement or enrolled or planning to enroll in Army ROTC.
Financial data The stipend is $1,000.
Duration 1 year.
Additional information Membership in the AUSA is open to everyone who supports a strong national defense, with special concern for the Army. That includes Regular Army, National Guard, Army Reserve, government civilians, retired soldiers, Wounded Warriors, veterans, concerned citizens and family members.
Number awarded Several each year.
Deadline April of each year.

[1300]
SIGMA CHI MILITARY SERVICE SCHOLARSHIPS

Sigma Chi Foundation
Attn: Scholarship Committee
1714 Hinman Avenue
Evanston, IL 60201
(847) 869-3655, ext. 270   Fax: (847) 869-4906
E-mail: foundation@sigmachi.org
Web: www.sigmachi.org

Summary To provide financial assistance to undergraduate and graduate student members of Sigma Chi who are serving or have served in the military.
Eligibility This program is open to undergraduate and graduate brothers of the fraternity who are currently serving or have served in the military (Army, Navy, Air Force, Marines, Coast Guard, or National Guard). They must have earned a GPA of 2.5 or higher and have completed at least 2 semesters of undergraduate study. ROTC students are not eligible.
Financial data The stipend is $1,000. Funds are to be used for tuition/fees only and are paid directly to the recipient's school.
Duration 1 year.
Number awarded Varies each year; recently, 9 were awarded.
Deadline May of each year.

[1301]
THE PFC ROGER W. CUMMINS MEMORIAL SCHOLARSHIP

American Academy of Physician Assistants-Veterans
  Caucus
Attn: Scholarship Program
P.O. Box 362
Ossining, NY 10562
(803) 328-1864   Fax: (704) 838-8494
E-mail: rmunsee@veteranscaucus.org
Web: www.veteranscaucus.org/scholarships

Summary To provide financial assistance to Marine Corps and Navy service members or veterans or family members who are studying to become physician assistants.
Eligibility This program is open to U.S. citizens who are currently enrolled in a physician assistant program. Applicants must be active-duty members of the U.S. Marine Corps or Navy Corpsmen who have served with the Marine Corps, veterans of those services, or their spouses or children. Along with their application, they must submit a personal statement about what led them to attend PA school; their

background, present, and future intentions; and why they deserve to receive a scholarship. Selection is based on military honors and awards received, civic and college honors and awards received, professional memberships and activities, potential for future achievement, and GPA.

Financial data The stipend is $2,000.
Duration 1 year.
Number awarded 1 each year.
Deadline February of each year.

[1302]
TILLMAN MILITARY SCHOLARS PROGRAM

Pat Tillman Foundation
222 North Merchandise Mart Plaza, Suite 1212
Chicago, IL 60654
(773) 360-5277
E-mail: scholarships@pattillmanfoundation.org
Web: www.pattillmanfoundation.org/apply-to-be-a-scholar

Summary To provide financial assistance to veterans, active servicemembers, and their spouses who are interested in working on an undergraduate or graduate degree.

Eligibility This program is open to veterans and active servicemembers of all branches of the armed forces from both the pre- and post-September 11 era and their spouses; children are not eligible. Applicants must be enrolled or planning to enroll full time at a 4-year public or private college or university to work on an undergraduate, graduate, or postgraduate degree. Current and former servicemembers must submit 400-word essays on 1) their motivation and decision to serve in the U.S. military and how that decision and experience has changed their life and ambitions; and 2) their educational and career goals, how they will incorporate their military service experience into those goals, and how they intend to continue their service to others and the community. Spouses must submit 400-word essays on 1) their previous service to others and the community; and 2) their educational and career goals, how they will incorporate their service experiences and the impact of their spouse's military service into those goals, and how they intend to continue their service to others and the community. Selection is based on those essays, educational and career ambitions, record of military service, record of personal achievement, demonstration of service to others in the community, desire to continue such service, and leadership potential.

Financial data The stipend depends on the need of the recipient and the availability of funds; recently, stipends averaged approximately $11,000 per year.

Duration 1 year; may be renewed, provided the recipient maintains a GPA of 3.0 or higher, remains enrolled full time, and documents participation in civic action or community service.

Additional information This program began in 2009.

Number awarded Approximately 60 each year. Since the program began, it has awarded more than $15 million to 580 scholars.

Deadline February of each year.

[1303]
TROOPS-TO-TEACHERS PROGRAM

Defense Activity for Non-Traditional Education Support
Attn: Troops to Teachers
6490 Saufley Field Road
Pensacola, FL 32509-5243
(850) 452-1241   Toll Free: (800) 231-6242
Fax: (850) 452-1096   E-mail: ttt@navy.mil
Web: www.proudtoserveagain.com

Summary To provide a bonus to veterans and military personnel interested in a second career as a public school teacher.

Eligibility This program is open to 1) active-duty military personnel who are retired or currently serving and have an approved date of retirement within 1 year; 2) members of a Reserve component who are retired or currently serving in the Selected Reserve with 6 or more years of credible service and commit to serving an additional 3 years or until eligible for retirement; 3) military personnel with at least 4 years on continuous active duty, will transfer to the Selected Reserve within 3 years, and are willing to commit to at least 3 years in the Selected Reserve or until eligible for retirement; and 4) active-duty or Selected Reserve personnel who separated on or after January 8, 2002 for a service-connected physical disability and who register for this program within 3 years of separation. Applicants must have a baccalaureate or advanced degree, the equivalent of 1 year of college with 6 years of work experience in a vocational or technical field, or meet state requirements for vocational/technical teacher referral. A bonus or stipend is available to applicants who are willing to accept employment as a teacher in 1) an eligible school where the free/reduced cost lunch percentage is 30% or more, at least 13% of students enrolled qualify for assistance under part B of the Individuals with Disabilities Education Act (IDEA), or a Bureau of Indian Affairs funded school; 2) a high needs school where the free/reduced cost lunch percentage is 50% or more for public middle or elementary schools, 40% or more for public high schools, or that qualifies as a rural school.

Financial data A bonus of $10,000 is awarded to recipients who agree to teach for 3 years in an eligible or high needs school. A stipend of $5,000 is awarded to recipients who are enrolled in a program at an accredited institution that will result in licensure as a full time teacher and who agree to teach for 3 years in an eligible or high needs school. All recipients who are not retired or discharged due to service-connected physical disability must commit to serve 3 years in the Reserves or until eligible to retire.

Duration The bonuses are intended as 1-time grants. Stipends are available as long as the recipient remains enrolled.

Additional information This program was established in 1994 by the Department of Defense (DoD). In 2000, program oversight and funding were transferred to the U.S. Department of Education, but DoD continues to operate the program. The No Child Left Behind Act of 2001 provided for continuation of the program.

Number awarded Varies each year; recently, 2,891 applicants were approved for participation in the program.

Deadline Applications may be submitted at any time within 3 years of retirement or separation.

[1304]
TVSHKA (WARRIOR) SCHOLARSHIP

Chahta Foundation
Attn: Scholarship Director
P.O. Box 1849
Durant, OK 74702
(580) 924-8280, ext. 2546
Toll Free: (800) 522-6170, ext. 2546
Fax: (580) 745-9023
E-mail: scholarship@chahtafoundation.com
Web: www.chahtafoundation.com/scholarship/veterans

Summary To provide financial assistance to Choctaw Indians who are serving or have served in the armed services and are planning to attend college or graduate school in any state.

Eligibility This program is open to Choctaw students who are active duty or retired U.S. armed services veterans. Applicants be enrolled or planning to enroll full time in an undergraduate or graduate degree program at a college or university in any state. They must have a GPA of 2.5 or higher. Along with their application, they must submit essays on assigned topics, transcripts, 2 letters of recommendation, a resume, and documentation of financial need.

Financial data The stipend is $3,000.

Duration 1 year.

Additional information This program began in 2016.

Number awarded 1 or more each year.

Deadline March of each year.

[1305]
UNIFIED ARIZONA VETERANS SCHOLARSHIPS

Unified Arizona Veterans, Inc.
Attn: Scholarship Committee
P.O. Box 34338
Phoenix, AZ 85067
E-mail: scholarships@azuav.org
Web: www.azuav.org

Summary To provide financial assistance to veterans and military personnel in Arizona who are interested in attending college in the state.

Eligibility This program is open to residents of Arizona who are 1) honorably discharged veterans; 2) currently on active duty, including service members in good standing with a Reserve or Guard components; or 3) immediate family members of an Arizona veteran killed in action or by an act of terror. Applicants must be enrolled at an institution of higher learning in Arizona and working on a bachelor's or master's degree in any field. Along with their application, they must submit 1) a 1-page essay on why they chose their current academic program and how they plan to use their degree, certificate, or license; 2) letters of recommendation; 3) verification of enrollment and Arizona residency; and 4) documentation of financial need.

Financial data Stipends range up to $5,000.

Duration 1 year.

Number awarded 1 or more each year.

Deadline February of each year.

[1306]
UTAH NATIONAL GUARD STATE TUITION ASSISTANCE PROGRAM

Utah Army National Guard
Attn: UT-G1-ESO
12953 South Minuteman Drive
P.O. Box 1776
Draper, UT 84020-1776
(801) 432-4354
E-mail: ng.ut.utarng.list.education-office@mail.mil
Web: ut.ng.mil/Resources/Education-Services

Summary To provide tuition assistance to currently-enrolled members of the Utah National Guard.

Eligibility This program is open to Utah residents who are MOS/AFSC qualified members of the Utah National Guard. Applicants must be seeking funding to obtain a 1) high school diploma or GED certification; 2) undergraduate, graduate, vocational, technical, or licensure certificate; 3) associate degree; 4) baccalaureate degree; or 5) master's degree. Support is not provided for doctoral or first professional degrees, such as architecture, certified public accountant, podiatry (D.P.M.), dentistry (D.D.S. or D.M.D.), medicine (M.D.), optometry (O.D.), osteopathic medicine (D.O.), pharmacy (Pharm.D.), law (J.D.), or theology (M.Div. or M.H.L.). Enlisted personnel must have remaining obligation on their existing enlistment contract that will extend to or beyond the last date of course enrollment for these funds. Officers must have at least 4 years of Selected Reserve service remaining from the date of completion of the course for which this funding is provided.

Financial data Support is provided for 100% of the cost of tuition, to a maximum of $250 per hour or a maximum of $6,000 per year combined with federal tuition assistance. Soldiers and airmen majoring in cyber studies or a field of STEM are eligible for up t $7,000 per year.

Duration 1 semester; recipients may renew.

Additional information Recipients of this funding may continue to receive any GI Bill funding to which they are entitled.

Number awarded Varies each year; recently, a total of $750,000 was available for this program.

Deadline Applications must be received at least 3 weeks prior to the course start date. They are processed on a first-come, first-served basis.

[1307]
VICE ADMIRAL ROBERT L. WALTERS SCHOLARSHIP

Surface Navy Association
Attn: Scholarship Coordinator
6564 Loisdale Court, Suite 318
Springfield, VA 22150
(703) 960-6800   Toll Free: (800) NAVY-SNA
Fax: (703) 960-6807   E-mail: navysna@aol.com
Web: www.navysna.org/scholarship/information.html

Summary To provide financial assistance for college or graduate school to members of the Surface Navy Association (SNA) and their dependents.

Eligibility This program is open to SNA members and their children, stepchildren, wards, and spouses. The SNA member must 1) be in the second or subsequent consecutive year of membership; 2) be serving, retired, or honorably discharged; 3) be a Surface Warfare Officer or Enlisted Surface Warfare Specialist; and 4) have served for at least 3 years on a surface ship of the U.S. Navy or Coast Guard (the 3 years need not have been consecutive but must have been served on active duty). Applicants must be enrolled or planning to enroll full time at an accredited undergraduate or graduate institution; the full-time requirement may be waived for spouses. Along with their application, they must submit a 500-word essay about themselves and why they should be selected to receive this scholarship. High school seniors should also include a transcript of high school grades and a copy of ACT or SAT scores. Current college students should also include a transcript of the grades from their most recent 4 semesters of school. Selection is based on academic proficiency, non-scholastic activities, scholastic and non-scholastic awards, character, and financial need.

Financial data The stipend is $2,000 per year.

Duration 4 years, provided the recipient maintains a GPA of 3.0 or higher.

Number awarded Varies each year.

Deadline February of each year.

[1308]
VIRGINIA NATIONAL GUARD TUITION ASSISTANCE PROGRAM

Virginia National Guard
Attn: Educational Services Officer
Fort Pickett, Building 316
Blackstone, VA 23824-6316
(434) 298-6155   Toll Free: (888) 483-2682
Fax: (434) 298-6296 E-mail: vickie.a.kegley2.nfg@mail.mil
Web: vaguard.dodlive.mil/tuitionassistance

Summary To provide financial assistance to members of the Virginia National Guard who are interested in attending college or graduate school in the state.

Eligibility This program is open to active members of the Virginia National Guard who are residents of Virginia and interested in attending college or graduate school in the state. Awards are presented in the following priority order: 1) enlisted personnel who have previously received assistance through this program; 2) officers who need to complete a bachelor's degree in order to be eligible for promotion to captain; 3) warrant officers working on an associate or bachelor's degree; 4) any member working on an undergraduate degree; and 4) any member working on a graduate degree.

Financial data The program provides reimbursement of tuition at approved colleges, universities, and vocational/technical schools in Virginia, to a maximum of $7,000 per year.

Duration 1 semester; may be renewed.

Additional information This program began in 1983. Recipients must remain in the Guard for at least 2 years after being funded.

Number awarded Varies each year.

Deadline June of each year for fall semester; October of each year for spring semester; March of each year for summer session.

[1309]
WASHINGTON METROPOLITAN AREA NAVY NURSE CORPS ASSOCIATION SCHOLARSHIPS

Washington Metropolitan Area Navy Nurse Corps Association
c/o Susan S. Miller, Scholarship Committee Chair
P.O. Box 571
Arnold, MD 21012
E-mail: Navycapt51@hotmail.com
Web: www.nnca.org/join-nnca-2/local-chapters/wmannca

Summary To provide financial assistance to current and former Navy nurses who live or work in the area served by the Washington Metropolitan Area Navy Nurse Corps Association (WMANNCA) and are interested in working on a graduate nursing degree.

Eligibility This program is open to Navy nurses (active duty, reserve, retired, or former) who plan to continue their studies by working on an advanced graduate degree in nursing. Applicants must live or work in the area served by WMANNCA: Delaware, Maryland, New Jersey, Pennsylvania, Virginia, Washington, D.C., or West Virginia. Along with their application, they must submit a 250-word personal statement on why this degree is important to them, how they will utilize this degree to benefit the Navy or nursing, and how these funds will enable them to achieve their goals.

Financial data The stipend is $1,000.

Duration 1 year.

Number awarded 3 each year.

Deadline March of each year.

[1310]
WEST VIRGINIA NATIONAL GUARD EDUCATIONAL ENCOURAGEMENT PROGRAM

Office of the Adjutant General
Attn: Education Services Office
1703 Coonskin Drive
Charleston, WV 25311-1085
(304) 561-6306   Toll Free: (866) 986-4326
Fax: (304) 561-6463   E-mail: valerie.j.lambing.nfg@mail.mil
Web: www.wv.ng.mil/Education

Summary To provide financial assistance to members of the National Guard in West Virginia who are interested in attending college or graduate school in the state.

Eligibility This program is open to active members of the West Virginia National Guard who are residents of West Virginia and interested in attending a public or private college in the state. Applicants must have maintained satisfactory participation in the Guard. They must be interested in working on a vocational, associate, bachelor's, or master's degree. In some instances, support may also be available to Guard members who are interested in working on an M.D., D.O., P.A., or J.D. degree.

Financial data The program provides payment of 100% of the tuition and fees at participating colleges and universities in West Virginia, to a maximum of $7,000 per year.

Duration 1 academic year; may be renewed, provided the recipient maintains a GPA of 2.0 or higher as an undergraduate or 3.0 or higher as a graduate student.

Number awarded Varies each year.
Deadline April of each year for fall, October of each year for spring, or 60 days prior to class start for nontraditional programs and/or cohorts.

[1311]
WISCONSIN NATIONAL GUARD ASSOCIATION PRESIDENT'S SCHOLARSHIP

Wisconsin National Guard Association, Inc.
Attn: Awards, Gifts, and Grants Committee
2400 Wright Street, Room 151
Madison, WI 53704-2572
(608) 242-3114 Fax: (608) 242-3513
E-mail: info@winga.org
Web: www.winga.org/html/members/scholarships.html

Summary To provide financial assistance for graduate study in any state to members of the Wisconsin National Guard Association (WINGA).
Eligibility This program is open to WINGA members who are working on an advanced degree. They must have a GPA of 3.0 or higher and be enrolled at least half time at an accredited college, university, technical college, or trade or business school in any state. Selection is based on academic record, extracurricular activities, community involvement, work experience, and goals.
Financial data The stipend is $1,000. Funds are paid to the recipient's school upon proof of enrollment.
Duration 1 year; nonrenewable.
Additional information This grant was first awarded in 1996.
Number awarded 2 each year.
Deadline June of each year.

[1312]
WISCONSIN NATIONAL GUARD ENLISTED ASSOCIATION COLLEGE GRANT PROGRAM

Wisconsin National Guard Enlisted Association
Attn: Executive Director
2400 Wright Street
Madison, WI 53704-2572
(608) 242-3112 E-mail: WNGEA@yahoo.com
Web: wngea.org/scholarships

Summary To provide financial assistance to members of the Wisconsin National Guard Enlisted Association (WNGEA) and their spouses and children who are interested in attending college or graduate school in any state.
Eligibility This program is open to WNGEA members, the unmarried children and spouses of WNGEA members, and the unmarried children and spouses of deceased WNGEA members. Applicants must be enrolled full or part time at a college, university, graduate school, trade school, or business school in any state. Along with their application, they must submit a letter explaining their desire to continue their education; why financial assistance is needed; awards received, accomplishments, volunteerism, and hours volunteered per week or month; and WNGEA membership and role in the organization. Selection is based on financial need, leadership, and moral character.
Financial data Stipends are $1,000 or $500 per year.
Duration 1 year; recipients may not reapply for 2 years.
Additional information This program includes 1 scholarship sponsored by the USAA Insurance Corporation.

Number awarded Varies each year; recently, 6 were awarded: the Raymond A. Matera Scholarship at $1,000, a grant of $1,000 sponsored by USAA, and 4 others (1 reserved for a graduate student) at $500 each.
Deadline May of each year.

[1313]
WOMEN MARINES ASSOCIATION SCHOLARSHIP PROGRAM

Women Marines Association
120 State Avenue, Suite 303
Olympia, WA 98501
Toll Free: (888) 525-1943
E-mail: scholarship@womenmarines.org
Web: www.womenmarines.org/scholarships

Summary To provide financial assistance for college or graduate school to students sponsored by members of the Women Marines Association (WMA).
Eligibility Applicants must be sponsored by a WMA member and fall into 1 of the following categories: 1) have served or are serving in the U.S. Marine Corps, regular or Reserve; 2) are a direct descendant by blood or legal adoption or a stepchild of a Marine on active duty or who has served honorably in the U.S. Marine Corps, regular or Reserve; 3) are a sibling or a descendant of a sibling by blood or legal adoption or a stepchild of a Marine on active duty or who has served honorably in the U.S. Marine Corps, regular or Reserve; 4) be a spouse of a Marine; or 5) have completed 2 years in a Marine Corps JROTC program. WMA members may sponsor an unlimited number of applicants per year. High school seniors must submit transcripts (GPA of 3.0 or higher) and SAT or ACT scores. Undergraduate and graduate students must have a GPA of 3.0 or higher. Along with their application, they must submit 1-page statements on 1) the Marine to whom they are related; 2) their community service; and 3) their goals after college.
Financial data Stipends range from $500 to $5,000 per year.
Duration 1 year; may be renewed 1 additional year.
Additional information This program includes the following named scholarships: the WMA Memorial Scholarships, the Lily H. Gridley Memorial Scholarship, the Ethyl and Armin Wiebke Memorial Scholarship, the Maj. Megan McClung Memorial Scholarship, the Agnes Sopcak Memorial Scholarship, the Virginia Guveyan Memorial Scholarship, the LaRue A. Ditmore Music Scholarships, the Fallen Warrior Scholarship, and the Margaret Apel Scholarship. Applicants must know a WMA member to serve as their sponsor; the WMA will not supply listings of the names or addresses of chapters or individual members.
Number awarded Varies each year.
Deadline February of each year.

[1314]
WYOMING NATIONAL GUARD EDUCATIONAL ASSISTANCE PLAN

Wyoming National Guard
Attn: Education Services Officer
5410 Bishop Boulevard
Cheyenne, WY 82009
(307) 777-8160　　　　　　　　Fax: (307) 777-8105
E-mail: jenna.chapin@wyo.gov
Web: veteranseducation.wyo.gov/state-tuition-assistance

Summary To provide financial assistance to members of the Wyoming National Guard who are interested in attending college or graduate school in the state.

Eligibility This program is open to members of the Wyoming Army National Guard and the Wyoming Air National Guard who have spent at least 6 years in the Guard or are currently serving under their initial 6-year enlistment period. New enlistees who commit to serving 6 years are also eligible. Applicants may be pursuing, or planning to pursue, a degree at any level at the University of Wyoming, a Wyoming community college, or an approved technical institution in Wyoming.

Financial data The program provides full payment of tuition at eligible institutions.

Duration Guard members may continue to receive these benefits as long as they maintain a GPA of 2.0 or higher, keep up with Guard standards for drill attendance, and remain in good standing with the Guard.

Additional information The Wyoming legislature created this program in 2001. Recipients must agree to serve in the Guard for at least 2 years after they graduate or stop using the plan.

Number awarded Varies each year.

Deadline September of each year.

Family Members

[1315]
100TH INFANTRY BATTALION MEMORIAL SCHOLARSHIP FUND

Hawai'i Community Foundation
Attn: Scholarship Department
827 Fort Street Mall
Honolulu, HI 96813
(808) 566-5570　　　　　　　　Toll Free: (888) 731-3863
Fax: (808) 521-6286
E-mail: scholarships@hcf-hawaii.org
Web: hcf.scholarships.ngwebsolutions.com

Summary To provide financial assistance for college or graduate school to descendants of 100th Infantry Battalion World War II veterans.

Eligibility This program is open to entering and continuing full-time undergraduate and graduate students at 2- and 4-year colleges and universities. Applicants must be a direct descendant of a World War II veteran of the 100th Infantry Battalion (which was comprised of Americans of Japanese descent). They must be able to demonstrate academic achievement (GPA of 3.0 or higher), an active record of extracurricular activities and community service (especially volunteer work connected with the activities of the 100th Infantry Battalion Veterans organization), and a willingness to promote the legacy of the 100th Infantry Battalion of World War II. Along with their application, they must submit personal statements that include 1) 900 words each on their reasons for attending college, why they chose their course of study, and their career goals; and 2) 600 words on how they plan to give back to Hawaii. They must also submit a separate essay on the historical significance of the 100th Infantry Battalion and what the stories of those soldiers have to teach all American citizens. Neither current residency in Hawaii nor financial need is required.

Financial data The amounts of the awards depend on the availability of funds and the need of the recipient. Recently, the average value of the scholarships awarded by the foundation was approximately $2,500.

Duration 1 year.

Additional information This program began in 2006.

Number awarded Varies each year; recently, 2 were awarded.

Deadline February of each year.

[1316]
100TH INFANTRY BATTALION VETERANS STANLEY IZUMIGAWA SCHOLARSHIP FUND

Hawai'i Community Foundation
Attn: Scholarship Department
827 Fort Street Mall
Honolulu, HI 96813
(808) 566-5570　　　　　　　　Toll Free: (888) 731-3863
Fax: (808) 521-6286
E-mail: scholarships@hcf-hawaii.org
Web: hcf.scholarships.ngwebsolutions.com

Summary To provide financial assistance for college or graduate school to descendants of 100th Infantry Battalion World War II veterans.

Eligibility This program is open to entering and continuing full-time undergraduate and graduate students at 2- and 4-year colleges and universities. Applicants must be a direct descendant of a World War II veteran of the 100th Infantry Battalion (which was comprised of Americans of Japanese descent). They must be able to demonstrate academic achievement (GPA of 3.0 or higher), an active record of extracurricular activities and community service, especially volunteer work connected with the activities of the 100th Infantry Battalion Veterans organization, including (but not limited to) educational programs, memorial services, and the anniversary banquet. Along with their application, they must submit a personal statement that includes 1) 900 words each on their reasons for attending college, why they chose their course of study, and their career goals; and 2) 600 words on how they plan to give back to Hawaii. They must also submit a separate essay on the historical significance of the 100th Infantry Battalion and what the stories of those soldiers have to teach all American citizens. Neither current residency in Hawaii nor financial need is required.

Financial data The amounts of the awards depend on the availability of funds and the need of the recipient. Recently, the average value of the scholarships awarded by the foundation was approximately $2,500.

Duration 1 year.
Additional information This program began in 2014.
Number awarded 1 or more each year.
Deadline February of each year.

[1317]
506TH AIRBORNE INFANTRY REGIMENT ASSOCIATION SCHOLARSHIP

506th Airborne Infantry Regiment Association
c/o Alfred May, Scholarship Committee
30 Sweetman Lane
West Milford, NJ 07480-2933
(973) 728-1458   E-mail: alfredmay@aol.com
Web: www.506infantry.org

Summary To provide financial assistance for college or graduate school to former members of the 506th Airborne Infantry Regiment and their families.
Eligibility This program is open to veterans who served with the 506th Airborne Infantry Regiment and their children, grandchildren, spouses, and siblings. Applicants must be entering or attending an undergraduate or graduate program at a college or university in the United States. They must submit a statement describing their personal achievements and career objectives. Selection is based on academic excellence, quality of the institution the applicant has chosen to attend, and financial need.
Financial data The stipend is $1,500 or $1,000.
Duration 1 year; nonrenewable.
Additional information This program includes the Currahee Scholarship Award, the Marcia and John Lally Scholarship Award, the Eugene and Marilyn Overton Scholarship Award, the SPC Edwin Roodhouse Memorial Scholarship Award, the NAVILLUS Award, and the CPT Luke Wullenwaber Memorial Scholarship Award.
Number awarded 3 at $1,500 and 3 at $1,000 each year.
Deadline April of each year.

[1318]
AFBA NGAUS ACTIVE LIFE MEMBER SCHOLARSHIP

National Guard Association of the United States
Attn: Scholarship
One Massachusetts Avenue, N.W.
Washington, DC 20001
(202) 789-0031   Fax: (202) 682-9358
E-mail: ngaus@ngaus.org
Web: www.ngaus.org

Summary To provide financial assistance to members of the National Guard Association of the United States (NGAUS) and their dependents who are interested in working on an undergraduate or graduate degree.
Eligibility This program is open to active life NGAUS members and their dependents. Applicants must be enrolled or planning to enroll full time at a college or university in any state to work on an undergraduate or graduate degree. Along with their application, they must submit their college acceptance letter, SAT and/or ACT scores, high school or undergraduate transcripts, a publicity photograph, and an essay up to 300 words in length on an experience with the National Guard and how it has shaped their development and goals.
Financial data The stipend is $5,000.
Duration 1 year.
Additional information This program is sponsored by the Armed Forces Benefit Association (AFBA).
Number awarded 2 each year.
Deadline May of each year.

[1319]
AHIMA VETERANS SCHOLARSHIP

American Health Information Management Association
Attn: AHIMA Foundation
233 North Michigan Avenue, 21st Floor
Chicago, IL 60601-5809
(312) 233-1131   Fax: (312) 233-1537
E-mail: info@ahimafoundation.org
Web: www.ahimafoundation.org

Summary To provide financial assistance to veterans and spouses of veterans and active-duty service personnel who are interested in working on an undergraduate or graduate degree in health information management (HIM) or health information technology (HIT).
Eligibility This program is open to 1) veterans of the armed forces, including Army, Navy, Air Force, Marine Corps, Coast Guard, Reserves, and National Guard; and 2) spouses and surviving spouses of servicemembers, including active-duty military, retirees, veterans, and wounded warriors. Applicants must be working full time on a degree in HIM or HIT at the associate, bachelor's, post-baccalaureate, master's, or doctoral level. They must have at least 6 credit hours remaining after the date of the award. Along with their application, they must submit an essay of 250 to 400 words on their educational and career ambitions, record of military service, record of personal achievement, community service, desire to serve others and make a positive community impact, and leadership potential. In the selection process, preference is given to 1) physically wounded or disabled veterans; 2) surviving spouses; and 3) those who served in a combat tour of duty.
Financial data Stipends are $1,000 for associate degree students, $1,500 for bachelor's degree or post-baccalaureate certificate students, $2,000 for master's degree students, or $2,500 for doctoral degree students.
Duration 1 year.
Additional information Effective in 2018, this program includes the John Kloss Memorial Veteran Scholarship and other scholarships supported by Nuance Communications and the Walter Reed Society.
Number awarded 4 each year.
Deadline September of each year.

[1320]
AIR FORCE CLUB SCHOLARSHIP PROGRAM

Air Force Services Agency
Attn: HQ AFPC/SVOFT
10100 Reunion Place, Suite 501
San Antonio, TX 78216-4138
(210) 395-7351   Toll Free: (800) 443-4834
E-mail: clubs@myairforcelife.com
Web: www.myairforcelife.com/Clubs

Summary To recognize and reward, with academic scholarships, Air Force Club members and their families who submit outstanding essays.
Eligibility This program is open to Air Force Club members and their spouses, children, stepchildren, or grandchildren

who have been accepted by or are enrolled at an accredited college or university. Applicants may be traditional (graduating high school seniors) or nontraditional (all other club members). They must submit either 1) an essay of 980 to 1020 words on a topic that changes annually; or 2) a video of 4 minutes 30 seconds to 5 minutes 30 seconds on the same topic. Essays and videos must relate to a topic that changes annually; recently, students were asked to write about the core values of the U.S. Air Force. Applicants must also include a 1-page summary of their long-term career and life goals and previous accomplishments, including civic, athletic, and academic awards.
Financial data Awards for both traditional and nontraditional applicants are presented as scholarships of $7,000 for first, $5,000 for second, $3,000 for third, $2,000 for fourth, and $1,000 for honorable mention.
Duration The competition is held annually.
Additional information This competition was first held in 1997.
Number awarded 10 each year: 5 for traditional applicants and 5 for nontraditional.
Deadline May of each year.

[1321]
AL AND WILLAMARY VISTE SCHOLARSHIP PROGRAM

101st Airborne Division Association
32 Screaming Eagle Boulevard
P.O. Box 929
Fort Campbell, KY 42223-0929
(931) 431-0199   Fax: (931) 431-0195
E-mail: 101exec@screamingeagle.org
Web: www.screamingeaglefoundation.org

Summary To provide financial assistance to the spouses, children, and grandchildren of members of the 101st Airborne Division Association who are upper-division or graduate students working on a degree in science.
Eligibility This program is open to college juniors, seniors, and graduate students who maintained a GPA of 3.75 or higher during the preceding school year and whose parent, grandparent, or spouse is (or, if deceased, was) a regular or life (not associate) member of the 101st Airborne Division. Preference is given to students working on a degree in a physical science, medical science, or other scientific research field. Applicants must submit an essay of 500 to 550 words on the importance of the U.S. constitution and their long-term goals, career objectives, community service, hobbies, interests, personal achievements, and how a higher education for them in their chosen field can benefit our nation. Financial need is not considered in the selection process.
Financial data A stipend is awarded (amount not specified).
Duration 1 year; may be renewed.
Number awarded At least 1 each year.
Deadline May of each year.

[1322]
ALABAMA G.I. DEPENDENTS' SCHOLARSHIP PROGRAM

Alabama Department of Veterans Affairs
100 North Union Street, Suite 850
Montgomery, AL 36104
(334) 242-5077   Fax: (334) 242-5102
Web: www.va.alabama.gov/gi_dep_scholarship.aspx

Summary To provide educational benefits to the dependents of disabled, deceased, and other Alabama veterans.
Eligibility This program is open to children, spouses, and unremarried widow(er)s of veterans who are currently rated as 40% or more service-connected disabled or were so rated at time of death, were a former prisoner of war, have been declared missing in action, died as the result of a service-connected disability, or died while on active military duty in the line of duty. The veteran must have been a permanent civilian resident of Alabama for at least 1 year prior to entering active military service and served honorably for at least 90 days during wartime (or less, in case of death or service-connected disability). They must also have been a resident of Alabama for at least 2 years prior to applying, have been discharged within the last 12 months, or filed a resident Alabama income tax return for the past 10 consecutive years. Veterans who were not Alabama residents at the time of entering active military service may also qualify if they have a 100% disability and were permanent residents of Alabama for at least 5 years prior to filing the application for this program or prior to death, if deceased. Children and stepchildren must be under the age of 26, but spouses and widow(er)s may be of any age. Spouses cease to be eligible if they become divorced from the qualifying veteran. Widow(er)s cease to be eligible if they remarry.
Financial data This program provides payment of tuition at public universities in Alabama, to a maximum of $250 per semester hour. Purchase of required textbooks and payment of fees are supported at the rate of $1,000 per semester.
Duration This is an entitlement program for 5 years of full-time undergraduate or graduate study or part-time equivalent for all qualifying children and for spouses and unremarried widow(er)s who veteran spouse is or was rated 100% disabled or meets other qualifying requirements. Spouses and unremarried widow(er)s whose veteran spouse is or was rated between 40% and 90% disabled may attend only 3 standard academic years.
Number awarded Varies each year.
Deadline Applications may be submitted at any time.

[1323]
AMERICAN EDUCATIONAL RESEARCH ASSOCIATION RESEARCH GRANTS PROGRAM

American Educational Research Association
Attn: Grants Program
1430 K Street, N.W., Suite 1200
Washington, DC 20005
(202) 238-3200   Fax: (202) 238-3250
E-mail: grantsprogram@aera.net
Web: www.aera.net

Summary To provide funding to faculty members and other postdoctorates interested in conducting research on educational policy.

Eligibility This program is open to scholars who have completed a doctoral degree in such disciplines as (but not limited to) education, sociology, economics, psychology, demography, statistics, political science, public policy, or psychometrics. Applicants may be U.S. citizens, U.S. permanent residents, or non-U.S. citizens working at a U.S. institution. Underrepresented ethnic and racial minority researchers, women, individuals with disabilities, and veterans are strongly encouraged to apply. Research topics may cover a wide range of policy-related issues, but priority is given to proposals that 1) develop or benefit from advanced statistical or innovative quantitative methods or measures; 2) analyze more than 1 large-scale national or international federally funded data set, or more than one statewide longitudinal data system (SLDS) or incorporate other data enhancements; 3) integrate, link, or blend multiple large-scale data sources; or 4) undertake replication research of major findings or major studies using large-scale, federally supported or enhanced data. Research projects must include the analysis of data from at least 1 of the large-scale, nationally or internationally representative data sets, such as those of the National Science Foundation (NSF), National Center for Education Statistics (NCES), or other federal agencies. Selection is based on the importance of the proposed policy issue, the strength of the methodological model and proposed statistical analysis of the study, and relevant experience or research record.

Financial data Grants up to $20,000 for 1 year or $35,000 for 2 years are available. Funding is linked to the approval of the recipient's progress report and final report. Grantees receive one-third of the total award at the beginning of the grant period, one-third upon acceptance of the progress report, and one-third upon acceptance of the final report.

Duration 1 or 2 years.

Additional information Funding for this program is provided by the NSF. Grantees must submit a brief (3 to 6 pages) progress report midway through the grant period. A final report must be submitted at the end of the grant period.

Number awarded Approximately 15 each year.

Deadline March or September of each year.

[1324]
ARMY AVIATION ASSOCIATION OF AMERICA SCHOLARSHIPS

Army Aviation Association of America Scholarship Foundation
Attn: AAAA Scholarship Foundation
593 Main Street
Monroe, CT 06468-2806
(203) 268-2450   Fax: (203) 268-5870
E-mail: scholarship@quad-a.org
Web: www.quad-a.org/Scholarship/Scholarship/about.aspx

Summary To provide financial aid for undergraduate or graduate study to members of the Army Aviation Association of America (AAAA) and their relatives.

Eligibility This program is open to current AAAA members and the spouses, children, grandchildren, and unmarried siblings of current or deceased members. Applicants must be enrolled or accepted for enrollment as an undergraduate or graduate student at an accredited college or university. They must include a 300-word essay on their life experiences, work history, and aspirations. Some scholarships are specifically reserved for enlisted, warrant officer, company grade, and Department of the Army civilian members. Selection is based on academic merit and personal achievement.

Financial data Stipends range from $1,000 to $5,000 per year.

Duration Scholarships may be for 1 year, 2 years, or 4 years.

Number awarded Varies each year; recently, $516,000 in scholarships was awarded to 304 students. Since the program began in 1963, the foundation has awarded more than $4 million to more than 4,100 qualified applicants.

Deadline Interested students must submit a pre-qualifying form by March of each year. The final application is due in April.

[1325]
ARMY NURSE CORPS ASSOCIATION SCHOLARSHIPS

Army Nurse Corps Association
Attn: Scholarship Program
8000 IH-10 West, Suite 600
San Antonio, TX 78230-3887
(210) 650-3534   Toll Free: (888) 742-9910
E-mail: education@e-anca.org
Web: www.e-anca.org/Scholarships

Summary To provide financial assistance to students who have a connection to the Army and are interested in working on an undergraduate or graduate degree in nursing.

Eligibility This program is open to U.S. citizens attending colleges or universities that have accredited programs offering undergraduate or graduate degrees in nursing. Applicants must be 1) students currently enrolled in an accredited baccalaureate or advanced nursing or nurse anesthesia program who are serving or have served (and received an honorable discharge) in any branch and at any rank of a component of the Active Army, Army National Guard, or Army Reserve; or 2) nursing or anesthesia students whose parent(s), spouse, or child(ren) are serving or have served in a component of the Active Army, Army National Guard, or Army Reserve. Along with their application, they must submit a personal statement on their professional career objectives, reasons for applying for this scholarship, financial need, special considerations, personal and academic interests, and why they are preparing for a nursing career. Students who are receiving any support from any branch of the military, including ROTC scholarships, are not eligible.

Financial data The stipend is $3,000. Funds are sent directly to the recipient's school.

Duration 1 year.

Additional information Although the sponsoring organization is made up of current, retired, and honorably discharged officers of the Army Nurse Corps, it does not have an official affiliation with the Army. Therefore, students who receive these scholarships do not incur any military service obligation.

Number awarded Varies each year.

Deadline March of each year.

[1326]
ARMY WOMEN'S FOUNDATION LEGACY SCHOLARSHIPS

Army Women's Foundation
Attn: Scholarship Committee
P.O. Box 5030
Fort Lee, VA 23801-0030
(804) 734-3078   E-mail: info@awfdn.org
Web: www.awfdn.org/scholarships/general-information

Summary To provide financial assistance for college or graduate school to women who are serving or have served in the Army and their children.

Eligibility This program is open to 1) women who have served or are serving honorably in the U.S. Army, U.S. Army Reserve, or Army National Guard; and 2) children of those women. Applicants must be 1) high school graduates or GED recipients enrolled at a community college or technical certificate program who have a GPA of 2.5 or higher; 2) sophomores or higher at an accredited college or university who have a GPA of 3.0 or higher; or 3) students enrolled in or accepted to a graduate program who have a GPA of 3.0 or higher. Along with their application, they must submit a 2-page essay on why they should be considered for this scholarship; their future plans as related to their program of study; their community service, activities, and work experience; and how the Army has impacted their life and/or goals. Selection is based on merit, academic potential, community service, and financial need.

Financial data The stipend is $2,500 for college and graduate students or $1,000 for community college and certificate students.

Duration 1 year; recipients may reapply.

Number awarded Varies each year; recently, 21 soldiers and 10 children received these scholarships.

Deadline January of each year.

[1327]
BG BENJAMIN B. TALLEY SCHOLARSHIP

Society of American Military Engineers-Anchorage Post
c/o Thomas Fenoseff
Anchorage School District
Senior Director, Capital Planning and Construction
1301 Labar Street
Anchorage, AK 99515-3517
(907) 348-5223   Fax: (901) 348-5227
E-mail: Fenoseff_Thomas@askd12.org
Web: www.sameanchorage.org/wp/scholarship-information

Summary To provide financial assistance to student members of the Society of American Military Engineers (SAME) from Alaska who are working on a bachelor's or master's degree in designated fields of engineering or the natural sciences.

Eligibility This program is open to members of the Anchorage Post of SAME who are residents of Alaska, attending college in Alaska, an active-duty military member stationed in Alaska, or a dependent of an active-duty military member stationed in Alaska. Applicants must be 1) sophomores, juniors, or seniors majoring in engineering, architecture, construction or project management, natural sciences, physical sciences, applied sciences, or mathematics at an accredited college or university; or 2) students working on a master's degree in those fields. They must have a GPA of 2.5 or higher. U.S. citizenship is required. Along with their application, they must submit an essay of 250 to 500 words on their career goals. Selection is based on that essay, academic achievement, participation in school and community activities, and work/family activities; financial need is not considered.

Financial data Stipends range up to $3,000.

Duration 1 year.

Additional information This program began in 1997.

Number awarded Several each year; at least 1 scholarship is reserved for a master's degree student.

Deadline December of each year.

[1328]
BRAXTON BRAGG CHAPTER AUSA SCHOLARSHIPS

Association of the United States Army-Braxton Bragg Chapter
Attn: Vice President for Scholarship Programs
P.O. Box 70036
Fort Bragg, NC 28307
(910) 396-3755   E-mail: hbraxtonbraggc@nc.rr.com
Web: www.ausa.org/chapters/braxton-bragg-chapter

Summary To provide financial assistance to members of the Braxton Bragg Chapter of the Association of the United States Army (AUSA) in North Carolina and their dependents who are interested in attending college or graduate school in any state.

Eligibility This program is open to chapter members and their families in North Carolina who are working on or planning to work on an undergraduate, graduate, or technical degree at a college or technical school in any state. Applicants must submit a 500-word essay on a topic that changes annually (recently, students were asked to explain how a person makes a difference in our world); letters of recommendation; a list of personal accomplishments; and a transcript that includes their ACT or SAT score. Selection is based on academic achievement (50%), participation in extracurricular activities at school (25%), and participation in community service activities (25%).

Financial data The stipend is $1,000.

Duration 1 year; recipients may reapply.

Additional information Membership in the Braxton Bragg Chapter is open to all Army active, National Guard, and Reserve members in North Carolina, along with Department of the Army civilians, retirees, concerned citizens, and family members.

Number awarded Varies each year; recently, 15 were awarded.

Deadline April of each year.

[1329]
BUCKINGHAM MEMORIAL SCHOLARSHIPS

Air Traffic Control Association
Attn: Scholarship Fund
225 Reinekers Lane, Suite 400
Alexandria, VA 22314
(703) 299-2430   Fax: (703) 299-2437
E-mail: info@atca.org
Web: www.atca.org/scholarship

Summary To provide financial assistance for college or graduate school to children of current or former air traffic control specialists.

Eligibility This program is open to U.S. citizens who are the children, natural or adopted, of a person currently or formerly serving as an air traffic control specialist with the U.S. government, with the U.S. military, or in a private facility in the United States. Applicants must be enrolled or planning to enroll at least half time in a baccalaureate or graduate program at an accredited college or university and have at least 30 semester hours to be completed before graduation. Along with their application, they must submit a 500-word essay on how they see your career unfolding, especially how they will blend their career with community service in their adult life. Financial need is considered in the selection process.
Financial data A stipend is awarded; recently, scholarships awarded by this sponsor averaged more than $7,000.
Duration 1 year; may be renewed.
Additional information This program was formerly known as the Children of Air Traffic Control Specialists Scholarship Program.
Number awarded Varies each year; recently, 4 were awarded.
Deadline April of each year.

[1330]
CALIFORNIA NON-RESIDENT COLLEGE FEE WAIVER PROGRAM FOR MILITARY PERSONNEL AND DEPENDENTS

California Department of Veterans Affairs
Attn: Division of Veterans Services
1227 O Street, Room 101
P.O. Box 942895
Sacramento, CA 94295
(916) 653-2573   Toll Free: (800) 952-5626
Fax: (916) 653-2563   TDD: (800) 324-5966
Web: www.calvet.ca.gov

Summary To waive non-resident fees at public institutions in California for undergraduate or graduate students from other states who are active-duty military personnel, recently-discharged veterans, or dependents of active-duty military personnel.
Eligibility This program is open to residents of states outside California who are 1) veterans of the U.S. armed forces who spent more than 1 year on active duty in California immediately prior to being discharged; 2) members of the U.S. armed forces stationed in California on active duty; or 3) the natural or adopted child, stepchild, or spouse of a member of the U.S. armed forces stationed in California on active duty. Applicants must be attending or planning to attend a community college, branch of the California State University system, or campus of the University of California as an undergraduate or graduate student.
Financial data This program waives non-resident fees of qualifying military personnel, veterans, and families who attend publicly-supported community or state colleges or universities in California.
Duration 1 year; may be renewed until completion of an undergraduate degree or for 1 additional year for military personnel working on a graduate degree; nonrenewable for graduate students who are children or spouses.
Number awarded Varies each year.
Deadline Deadline not specified.

[1331]
CAPITOL AREA CHAPTER MOAA COLLEGE SCHOLARSHIP PROGRAM

Military Officers Association of America-Capitol Area Chapter
c/o Major DeLee M. Dankenbring, Treasurer
992 Pennine Ridge Way
Grand Ledge, MI 48837-9809
(517) 614-6090
Web: www.cacmoaa.org/Scholarships.aspx

Summary To provide financial assistance for college or graduate school in any state to residents of Michigan who are disabled veterans, members of the Military Officers Association of America (MOAA) or their children or grandchildren, or children of deceased or disabled servicemembers.
Eligibility This program is open to 1) disabled military servicemembers who entered service after September 11, 2001 and whose home of record is Michigan; 2) members of the national and Capitol Area Chapter of the MOAA and their children and grandchildren; and 3) children of servicemembers who entered the armed forces from Michigan and died or were disabled in the line of duty. Applicants must be enrolled or planning to enroll in a program of college or university study, job training, or graduate school. They must have a GPA of 2.0 or higher. Along with their application they must submit transcripts (that include SAT/ACT scores for high school seniors), a list of honors and awards that includes any ROTC or military training, a 200-word essay on their career goals, and a brief explanation of their financial need.
Financial data The stipend ranges from $1,000 to $1,250 per year.
Duration 1 year; recipients may reapply.
Number awarded Varies each year.
Deadline March of each year.

[1332]
CAPTAIN FREDERICK C. BRACE III MEMORIAL SCHOLARSHIP

American Academy of Physician Assistants-Veterans Caucus
Attn: Scholarship Program
P.O. Box 362
Ossining, NY 10562
(803) 328-1864   Fax: (704) 838-8494
E-mail: rmunsee@veteranscaucus.org
Web: www.veteranscaucus.org/scholarships

Summary To provide financial assistance to Air Force veterans and their dependents who are studying to become physician assistants.
Eligibility This program is open to U.S. citizens who are currently enrolled in a physician assistant program. Applicants must be honorably discharged members of the United States Air Force or the dependent of an Air Force veteran. Along with their application, they must submit a personal statement about what led them to attend PA school; their background, present, and future intentions; and why they deserve to receive a scholarship. Selection is based on military honors and awards received, civic and college honors and awards received, professional memberships and activities, potential for future achievement, and GPA.
Financial data The stipend is $2,000.
Duration 1 year.

Number awarded 1 each year.
Deadline February of each year.

[1333]
CAPTAIN MIKI IWATA MEMORIAL SCHOLARSHIP FOR ADVANCED PRACTICE

Florida Navy Nurse Corps Association
c/o Margaret Holder, Scholarship Committee
1033 Inverness Drive
St. Augustine, FL 32092
E-mail: maholder@me.com
Web: www.nnca.org/join-nnca-2/local-chapters/fnnca

Summary To provide financial assistance to advanced practice nursing students in Florida, especially those with ties to the military.
Eligibility This program is open to full- and part-time advanced practice nursing students in Florida. Applicants must have completed at least 1 clinical nursing course and have a current GPA of 3.0 or higher. Along with their application, they must submit an essay, up to 500 words in length, on the reasons they are qualified for the scholarship, how it will benefit them, career goals, and potential for contribution to the profession. Preference is given in the following order to current active-duty and Reserve service members, veterans of military service, family members of current or former military service personnel, civil service employees, and residents of Florida. Financial need is considered in the selection process.
Financial data The stipend is $1,500. Funds are paid directly to the student.
Duration 1 year.
Number awarded 1 each year.
Deadline October of each year.

[1334]
CHILDREN AND SPOUSES OF INDIANA NATIONAL GUARD PROGRAM

Indiana Commission for Higher Education
Attn: Financial Aid and Student Support Services
101 West Ohio Street, Suite 300
Indianapolis, IN 46204-4206
(317) 232-1023   Toll Free: (888) 528-4719 (within IN)
Fax: (317) 232-3260   E-mail: Scholars@che.in.gov
Web: www.in.gov/che/4523.htm

Summary To provide financial assistance to residents of Indiana who are children or spouses of deceased members of the National Guard and interested in attending college or graduate school in the state.
Eligibility This program is open to residents of Indiana whose father, mother, or spouse was a member of the Indiana National Guard and suffered a service-connected death while serving on state active duty. Applicants must be interested in working on an undergraduate, graduate, or professional degree at an eligible institution in Indiana.
Financial data Qualified applicants receive a 100% remission of tuition and all mandatory fees for undergraduate, graduate, or professional degrees at eligible postsecondary schools and universities in Indiana. Support is not provided for such fees as room and board.
Duration Up to 124 semester hours of study.

Number awarded Varies each year.
Deadline Applications must be submitted at least 30 days before the start of the college term.

[1335]
COL CARL F. BASWELL FALLEN ENGINEER MEMORIAL SCHOLARSHIP

Army Engineer Association
Attn: Director Washington DC Operations
P.O. Box 30260
Alexandria, VA 22310-8260
(703) 428-7084   Fax: (703) 428-6043
E-mail: xd@armyengineer.com
Web: www.armyengineer.com/scholarships

Summary To provide financial assistance for college to children and spouses of U.S. Army Engineers who were killed in Iraq or Afghanistan.
Eligibility This program is open to the children and spouses of U.S. Army Engineers who were killed in combat during Operation Iraqi Freedom or Operation Enduring Freedom. Applicants must be working on or planning to work on an associate, bachelor's, or master's degree at an accredited college or university. Along with their application, they must submit a 1-page essay outlining why they should be selected for an award, including a paragraph on their financial need and their evaluation of their potential for success.
Financial data The stipend is $2,500.
Duration 1 year.
Additional information This program began in 2010.
Number awarded 1 each year.
Deadline June of each year.

[1336]
COLONEL JERRY W. ROSS SCHOLARSHIP

American Pharmacists Association
Attn: APhA Foundation
2215 Constitution Avenue, N.W.
Washington, DC 20037-2985
(202) 558-2709   Toll Free: (800) 237-APhA
Fax: (202) 638-3793   E-mail: rvaidya@aphanet.org
Web: www.aphafoundation.org

Summary To provide financial assistance for work on a degree in pharmacy to Air Force pharmacy technicians who are members of the Academy of Student Pharmacists of the American Pharmacists Association (APhA-ASP) and their families.
Eligibility This program is open to full-time pharmacy students who are either 1) Air Force pharmacy technicians working on a degree in pharmacy; or 2) family members of an Air Force pharmacist or technician who is enrolled in an accredited college of pharmacy. Applicants must have been actively involved in their school's APhA-ASP chapter. They must have completed at least 1 year in the professional sequence of courses with a GPA of 2.75 or higher. Along with their application, they must submit a 500-word essay that includes 1) how their involvement in APhA-ASP has developed them as a leader; and 2) how they will embrace their calling as a future leader of the profession. Selection is based on the essay (20%), academic performance (10%), pharmacy-related activities (25%), non-pharmacy/community activities (25%), and letters of recommendation (20%).
Financial data The stipend is $1,000.

Duration 1 year; recipients may reapply.
Number awarded 1 each year.
Deadline November of each year.

[1337]
CONNECTICUT TUITION WAIVER FOR VETERANS
Connecticut State Universities and Colleges
61 Woodland Street
Hartford, CT 06105
(860) 723-0013   E-mail: fitzgeralde@ct.edu
Web: www.ct.edu/admission/veterans

Summary To provide financial assistance for college to certain Connecticut veterans and military personnel and their dependents.
Eligibility This program is open to 1) honorably-discharged Connecticut veterans who served at least 90 days during specified periods of wartime; 2) active members of the Connecticut Army or Air National Guard; 3) Connecticut residents who are a dependent child or surviving spouse of a member of the armed forces killed in action on or after September 11, 2001 who was also a Connecticut resident; and 4) Connecticut residents who are a dependent child or surviving spouse of a person officially declared missing in action or a prisoner of war while serving in the armed forces after January 1, 1960. Applicants must be attending or planning to attend a public college or university in the state.
Financial data The program provides a waiver of 100% of tuition for general fund courses at the 4 campuses of Connecticut State University, 50% of tuition for extension and summer courses at campuses of Connecticut State University, 100% of tuition at the 12 Connecticut community colleges, and 50% of fees at Charter Oak State College.
Duration Up to 4 years.
Additional information This is an entitlement program; applications are available at the respective college financial aid offices.
Number awarded Varies each year.
Deadline Deadline not specified.

[1338]
CONNIE SETTLES SCHOLARSHIP
American Legion Auxiliary
Department of California
401 Van Ness Avenue, Suite 319
San Francisco, CA 94102-4570
(415) 861-5092   Fax: (415) 861-8365
E-mail: calegionaux@calegionaux.org
Web: www.calegionaux.org/scholarships.htm

Summary To provide financial assistance to members of the American Legion Auxiliary in California who are attending college or graduate school in the state.
Eligibility This program is open to residents of California who are currently working on an undergraduate or graduate degree at a college or university in the state. Applicants must have been members of the American Legion Auxiliary for at least the 2 preceding years and be current members. Each unit of the Auxiliary may nominate only 1 member. Selection is based on transcripts, 2 letters of recommendation, a letter from the applicant about themselves and their goals, and financial need. Support is not provided for programs of study deemed to be nonessential (e.g., sewing classes, aerobics, sculpting).

Financial data The stipend is $5,000. Funds are paid directly to the recipient's college or university.
Duration 1 year.
Number awarded 1 each year.
Deadline Applications must be submitted to Auxiliary units by February of each year.

[1339]
CSM LEONARD MAGLIONE MEMORIAL SCHOLARSHIPS
Association of the United States Army-Rhode Island Chapter
c/o LTC Robert A. Galvanin, President
31 Canoe River Drive
Mansfield, MA 02048
(508) 339-5301   E-mail: bpje5310@verizon.net
Web: www.riroa.org/ausari/scholarship.htm

Summary To provide financial assistance to members of the Rhode Island Chapter of the Association of the United States Army (AUSA) and their families who are interested in attending college or graduate school in any state.
Eligibility This program is open to members of the AUSA Rhode Island Chapter and their family members (spouses, children, and grandchildren). Applicants must be high school seniors or graduates accepted at an accredited college, university, or vocational/technical school in any state or current undergraduate or graduate students. Along with their application, they must submit a 250-word essay on why they feel their achievements should qualify them for this award. Selection is based on academic and individual achievements; financial need is not considered. Special consideration is given to students or graduates of LaSalle Academy in Providence (the alma mater of this program's namesake), especially those preparing for a career in the arts or engineering or enrolled or planning to enroll in Army ROTC.
Financial data The stipend is $1,000.
Duration 1 year.
Additional information Membership in the AUSA is open to everyone who supports a strong national defense, with special concern for the Army. That includes Regular Army, National Guard, Army Reserve, government civilians, retired soldiers, Wounded Warriors, veterans, concerned citizens and family members.
Number awarded Several each year.
Deadline April of each year.

[1340]
DAEDALIAN FOUNDATION DESCENDANTS' SCHOLARSHIP PROGRAM
Order of Daedalians
Attn: Daedalian Foundation
55 Main Circle (Building 676)
P.O. Box 249
Joint Base San Antonio-Randolph, TX 78148-0249
(210) 945-2113   Fax: (210) 945-2112
E-mail: info@daedalians.org
Web: www.daedalians.org/programs/scholarships

Summary To provide financial assistance to descendants of members of the Order of Daedalians who wish to prepare for a career in military aviation or space.
Eligibility This program is open to descendants of members of the order who are working on or planning to work on a

baccalaureate or higher degree. Applicants must be interested in and willing to commit to a career as a commissioned military pilot, flight crew member, astronaut, or commissioned officer in 1 of the armed forces of the United States in a discipline directly supporting aeronautics or astronautics. They must be physically and mentally qualified for flight and/or space; if they intend to pursue a non-flying career as a commissioned officer in a scientific or engineering discipline supporting aviation or space, they must pass a physical examination qualifying for active commissioned duty in the U.S. armed forces. Nominations must be submitted by a local chapter (Flight) of Daedalian. Selection is based on academic achievement and recognition, extracurricular activities, honors, and employment experience. Financial need may be considered if all other factors are equal.

Financial data The stipend is $2,000.

Duration 1 year.

Additional information The Order of Daedalians was founded in 1934 as an organization of the nearly 14,000 aviators who served as military pilots during World War I and are still listed and designated as Founder Members. In the 1950s, the organization expanded eligibility to include 1) on a sponsorship basis, current and former commissioned military pilots from all services; and 2) on a hereditary basis, descendants of Founder Members.

Number awarded Up to 3 each year.

Deadline July of each year.

[1341]
DISABLED AMERICAN VETERANS AUXILIARY NATIONAL EDUCATION SCHOLARSHIP FUND

Disabled American Veterans Auxiliary
Attn: National Education Scholarship Fund
3725 Alexandria Pike
Cold Spring, KY 41076
(859) 441-7300   Toll Free: (877) 426-2838, ext. 4020
Fax: (859) 442-2095   E-mail: dava@davmail.org
Web: auxiliary.dav.org/membership/programs

Summary To provide financial assistance to members of the Disabled American Veterans (DAV) Auxiliary who are interested in attending college or graduate school.

Eligibility This program is open to paid life members of the auxiliary who are attending or planning to attend a college, university, or vocational school as a full- or part-time undergraduate or graduate student. Applicants must be at least seniors in high school, but there is no maximum age limit. Along with their application, they must submit a 500-word essay on their personal or career goals and how their education will help them reach those goals. Selection is based on that essay (35 points), academic information (10 points), DAV membership activities (10 points), participation in DAV activities or projects to benefit veterans or their families (15 points), participation in other extracurricular or volunteer activities (15 points), and financial need (10 points).

Financial data Stipends are $1,500 per year for full-time students or $750 per year for part-time students.

Duration 1 year; may be renewed for up to 4 additional years, provided the recipient maintains a GPA of 2.5 or higher.

Additional information Membership in the DAV Auxiliary is available to extended family members of veterans eligible for membership in Disabled American Veterans (i.e., any man or woman who served in the armed forces during a period of war or under conditions simulating war and was wounded, disabled to any degree, or left with long-term illness as a result of military service and was discharged or retired from military service under honorable conditions). This program was established in September 2010 as a replacement for the educational loan program that the DAV Auxiliary operated from 1931 until August 2010.

Number awarded Varies each year.

Deadline March of each year.

[1342]
DONALDSON D. FRIZZELL MEMORIAL SCHOLARSHIPS

First Command Educational Foundation
Attn: Scholarship Programs Manager
1 FirstComm Plaza
Fort Worth, TX 76109-4999
(817) 569-2940   Toll Free: (877) 872-8289
Fax: (817) 569-2970   E-mail: scholarships@fcef.com
Web: www.fcef.com/scholarships

Summary To provide financial assistance to students, especially those with ties to the military, entering or attending college or graduate school.

Eligibility This program is open to 1) members of a U.S. uniformed service (active, Guard, Reserve, retired, or non-retired veteran) and their spouses and dependents; 2) clients of First Command Financial Services and their family members; 3) dependent family members of First Command Advisors or field office staff members; or 4) non-contractual ROTC students. Applicants may be traditional students (high school seniors and students already enrolled at a college, university, or accredited trade school) or nontraditional students (those defined by their institution as nontraditional and adult students planning to return to a college, university, or accredited trade school). They must have a GPA of 3.0 or higher and be working on a trade school certification or associate, undergraduate, or graduate degree. Applicants must submit 1-page essays on 1) their active involvement in community service programs; 2) the impact of financial literacy on their future; and 3) why they need this scholarship. Selection is based primarily on the essays, academic merit, and financial need.

Financial data The stipend is $3,000. Funds are disbursed directly to the recipient's college, university, or trade school.

Duration 1 year.

Additional information The sponsoring organization was formerly known as the USPA & IRA Educational Foundation, founded in 1983 to provide scholarships to the children of active, retired, or deceased military personnel.

Number awarded Varies each year; recently, 10 were awarded.

Deadline The online application process begins in February of each year and continues until April or until 2,500 applications have been received.

[1343]
DR. NANCY M. SCHONHER SCHOLARSHIP

Marines' Memorial Association
c/o Marines Memorial Club and Hotel
609 Sutter Street
San Francisco, CA 94102
(415) 673-6672, ext. 293   Toll Free: (800) 5-MARINE
Fax: (415) 441-3649
E-mail: scholarship@marineclub.com
Web: www.marinesmemorial.org

Summary To provide financial assistance to women who have a tie to the military and are interested in working on a degree in a health-related field.

Eligibility This program is open to women who 1) are active-duty service members or reservists in the U.S. armed forces; 2) have separated honorably from the U.S. armed forces within the past 6 years; 3) are a current or former corpsman or medic in any branch of the U.S. armed forces; or 4) are the child or grandchild of an active member of the Marines' Memorial Association. Applicants must be planning to enroll in 1) an advanced medical program with the goal of becoming a nurse, nurse practitioner, physician's assistant, or medical doctor (M.D. or O.D.) from an accredited American college or university; or 2) an accredited paramedic program (must have completed the EMT Basic training program, have taken the National Registry EMT Examination, hold an EMT Certificate, and have at least 6 months' work experience). Membership in the sponsoring organization is not required. Along with their application, they must submit an essay of up to 500 words on why they chose their specific path of study, what they hope to accomplish after graduation with their degree, and how their efforts will benefit others in their community. Selection is based on the essay, academic merit, references, and financial need. Preference is given to Navy Corpsmen.

Financial data The stipend is $5,000.
Duration 1 year.
Additional information Membership in the association is open to veterans of the Marines, Army, Navy, Air Force, or Coast Guard and to personnel currently serving in a branch of the armed forces. This program began in 2017.
Number awarded 1 each year.
Deadline April of each year.

[1344]
EASTERN REGION KOREAN WAR VETERAN DESCENDANT SCHOLARSHIPS

Korean American Scholarship Foundation
Eastern Region
1952 Gallows Road, Suite 310
Vienna, VA 22182
(703) 748-5935   Fax: (703) 748-1874
E-mail: erc.scholarship@kasf.org
Web: www.kasf.org/apply-erc

Summary To provide financial assistance to the descendants of the Korean War from any state who are working on an undergraduate or graduate degree in any field at a school in eastern states.

Eligibility This program is open to direct descendants of veterans who served in Korea from June 25, 1950 to January 31, 1955. Applicants may reside in any state, but they must be enrolled as full-time undergraduate or graduate students at a college or university in Delaware, District of Columbia, Kentucky, Maryland, North Carolina, Pennsylvania, Virginia, or West Virginia. They must have a GPA of 3.0 or higher. Selection is based on academic achievement, an essay, extracurricular activities, and recommendations.

Financial data Stipends range from $500 to $5,000.
Duration 1 year.
Additional information This program began in 2013.
Number awarded Varies each year; recently, 3 were awarded.
Deadline June of each year.

[1345]
EDUCATION FOUNDATION FOR THE COLORADO NATIONAL GUARD GRANTS

National Guard Association of Colorado
Attn: Education Foundation, Inc.
P.O. Box 440889
Aurora, CO 80044-0889
(303) 909-6369   Fax: (720) 535-5925
E-mail: BernieRogoff@comcast.net
Web: www.efcong.org

Summary To provide financial assistance to members of the Colorado National Guard and their families who are interested in attending college or graduate school in any state.

Eligibility This program is open to current and retired members of the Colorado National Guard and their dependent unmarried children and spouses. Applicants must be enrolled or planning to enroll full or part time at a college, university, trade school, business school, or graduate school in any state. Along with their application, they must submit an essay, up to 2 pages in length, on their desire to continue their education, what motivates them, their financial need, their commitment to academic excellence, and their current situation. Selection is based on academic achievement, community involvement, and financial need.

Financial data Stipends are generally at least $1,000 per year.
Duration 1 year; may be renewed.
Number awarded Normally, 15 to 25 of these grants are awarded each semester.
Deadline July of each year for fall semester; January of each year for spring semester.

[1346]
EDWARD O. NESHEIM MEMORIAL SCHOLARSHIP

American Legion
Department of North Dakota
405 West Main Street, Suite 4A
P.O. Box 5057
West Fargo, ND 58078
(701) 293-3120   Fax: (701) 293-9951
E-mail: Programs@ndlegion.org
Web: www.ndlegion.org/scholarships

Summary To provide financial assistance to high school seniors in North Dakota who are direct descendants of veterans and interested in attending college in the state to study specified fields.

Eligibility This program is open to seniors graduating from high schools in North Dakota who have a GPA of 2.75 or higher. Applicants must be the children, grandchildren, or great- grandchildren of veterans who served honorably in the

U.S. armed forces. They must be planning to attend a college or university in North Dakota to work on a degree in agriculture, human nutrition, or a medical field (e.g., pre-medicine, physician assistant, dentistry, dental hygiene, pharmacy, chiropractic). Along with their application, they must submit an essay of 500 to 750 words on their educational and career goals, how they plan to accomplish those goals, the part their education will play in attaining those goals, where they plan to attend college and why they chose that institution, and how their secondary education helped prepare them for their choice of college, their life, and their career. Financial need is considered in the selection process.

Financial data The stipend is $1,500 per year.

Duration 1 year; recipients may reapply, provided they have a GPA of 2.5 or higher for the preceding year of college study.

Additional information This program began in 2008.

Number awarded 1 each year.

Deadline March of each year.

[1347]
ENLISTED ASSOCIATION OF THE NATIONAL GUARD OF IOWA AUXILIARY SCHOLARSHIP PROGRAM

Enlisted Association of the National Guard of Iowa Auxiliary
c/o Lori Waters, President
1005 Second Street S.W.
Altoona, IA 50009
(515) 490-3202   E-mail: bullriderfan@msn.com
Web: www.eangi.org/auxiliary-scholarship

Summary To provide financial assistance to members of the Enlisted Association of the National Guard of Iowa (EANGI) Auxiliary and their families who are interested in attending college in any state.

Eligibility This program is open to EANGI Auxiliary members and their spouses, dependents, and grandchildren. Applicants must be enrolled, accepted for enrollment, or in the process of applying to a college or vocational/technical school as a full-time undergraduate or graduate student. Along with their application, they must submit a letter describing specific fats about their desire to continue their education and why they need financial assistance. Selection is based on character, leadership, and need.

Financial data The stipend is $1,000.

Duration 1 year; recipients may reapply.

Number awarded 2 each year.

Deadline February of each year.

[1348]
EXEMPTION FROM TUITION FEES FOR DEPENDENTS OF KENTUCKY VETERANS

Kentucky Department of Veterans Affairs
Attn: Tuition Waiver Coordinator
1111B Louisville Road
Frankfort, KY 40601
(502) 564-9203   Toll Free: (800) 572-6245 (within KY)
Fax: (502) 564-9240   E-mail: kdva.tuitionwaiver@ky.gov
Web: www.veterans.ky.gov

Summary To provide financial assistance for undergraduate or graduate studies to family of deceased Kentucky veterans.

Eligibility This program is open to the children, stepchildren, adopted children, and unremarried widows or widowers of veterans who were residents of Kentucky when they entered military service or joined the Kentucky National Guard. The qualifying veteran must have been killed in action during a wartime period or died as a result of a service-connected disability incurred during a wartime period. Applicants must be attending or planning to attend a state-supported college or university in Kentucky to work on an undergraduate or graduate degree.

Financial data Eligible dependents and survivors are exempt from tuition and matriculation fees at any state-supported institution of higher education in Kentucky.

Duration The exemption continues until completion of an undergraduate or graduate degree. There are no age or time limits.

Number awarded Varies each year.

Deadline Deadline not specified.

[1349]
FIRST LIEUTENANT MICHAEL LICALZI MEMORIAL SCHOLARSHIP

Marine Corps Tankers Association
c/o Dan Miller, Scholarship Chair
8212 West Fourth Place
Kennewick, WA 99336
E-mail: dmiller@msn.com
Web: www.usmctankers.org/pageScholarship

Summary To provide financial assistance for college or graduate school to children and grandchildren of members of the Marine Corps Tankers Association and to Marine and Navy personnel currently serving in tank units.

Eligibility This program is open to high school seniors and graduates who are children, grandchildren, or under the guardianship of an active, Reserve, retired, or honorably discharged Marine who served in a tank unit. Marine or Navy Corpsmen currently assigned to tank units are also eligible. Applicants must be enrolled or planning to enroll full time at a college or graduate school. Their parent or grandparent must be a member of the Marine Corps Tankers Association or, if not a member, must join if the application is accepted. Along with their application, they must submit a 500-word essay that explains their reason for seeking this scholarship, their educational goals, and their plans for post-graduation life. Selection is based on that essay, academic record, school activities, leadership potential, and community service.

Financial data The stipend is $3,000.

Duration 1 year.

Number awarded Varies each year; recently, 6 were awarded.

Deadline March of each year.

[1350]
FLEET RESERVE ASSOCIATION GRADUATE SCHOLARSHIPS

Fleet Reserve Association
Attn: FRA Education Foundation
125 North West Street
Alexandria, VA 22314-2754
(703) 683-1400   Toll Free: (800) FRA-1924
Fax: (703) 549-6610   E-mail: scholars@fra.org
Web: www.fra.org

Summary To provide financial assistance for graduate school to members of the Fleet Reserve Association (FRA) and their families.
Eligibility This program is open to members of the FRA and the dependent children, grandchildren, and spouses of living or deceased members. Applicants must be enrolled as full-time graduate students. Along with their application, they must submit an essay on why they want to go to college and what they intend to accomplish with their degree. Selection is based on academic record, financial need, extracurricular activities, leadership skills, and participation in community activities. U.S. citizenship is required.
Financial data The stipend is $5,000 per year.
Duration 1 year; may be renewed.
Additional information Membership in the FRA is open to current and former enlisted members of the Navy, Marine Corps, and Coast Guard. This program, established in 2001, includes the Glenn F. Glezen Scholarship, the Joseph R. Baranski Scholarship, and the Robert W. Nolan Scholarship.
Number awarded At least 3 each year.
Deadline April of each year.

[1351]
FLEET RESERVE ASSOCIATION MEMBER SCHOLARSHIPS

Fleet Reserve Association
Attn: FRA Education Foundation
125 North West Street
Alexandria, VA 22314-2754
(703) 683-1400   Toll Free: (800) FRA-1924
Fax: (703) 549-6610   E-mail: scholars@fra.org
Web: www.fra.org

Summary To provide financial assistance for college or graduate school to members of the Fleet Reserve Association (FRA) and their families.
Eligibility This program is open to members of the FRA and the children, grandchildren, great-grandchildren, and spouses of living or deceased members. Applicants must be enrolled or planning to enroll as full-time undergraduate or graduate students. Along with their application, they must submit transcripts that include (for high school students and college freshmen) SAT and/or ACT scores; a list of school and community activities; at least 2 letters of recommendation; and an essay on why they want to go to college and what they intend to accomplish with their degree. Selection is based on academic record, financial need, extracurricular activities, leadership skills, and participation in community activities. U.S. citizenship is required.
Financial data Stipends range from $1,000 to $5,000.
Duration 1 year; may be renewed.
Additional information Membership in the FRA is open to current and former enlisted members of the Navy, Marine Corps, and Coast Guard. This program includes awards designated as the MCPO Ken E. Blair Scholarship, the Robert M. Treadwell Annual Scholarship, the Donald Bruce Pringle Family Scholarship, the Tom and Karen Snee Scholarship, the Angelo and Mildred Nunez Scholarships, the Express Scripts Scholarships, the US Family Health Scholarship, and the Navy Department Branch 181 Scholarship.

Number awarded Varies each year; recently, 10 were awarded: 6 at $5,000, 2 at $4,000, 1 at $3,000, and 1 at $2,000.
Deadline April of each year.

[1352]
FLEET RESERVE ASSOCIATION NON-MEMBER SCHOLARSHIPS

Fleet Reserve Association
Attn: FRA Education Foundation
125 North West Street
Alexandria, VA 22314-2754
(703) 683-1400   Toll Free: (800) FRA-1924
Fax: (703) 549-6610   E-mail: scholars@fra.org
Web: www.fra.org

Summary To provide financial assistance for college or graduate school to sea service personnel and their families.
Eligibility This program is open to 1) active-duty, Reserve, honorably-discharged veterans, and retired members of the U.S. Navy, Marine Corps, and Coast Guard; and 2) their spouses, children, grandchildren, and great-grandchildren. Applicants must be enrolled or planning to enroll as full-time undergraduate or graduate students, but neither they nor their family member are required to be members of the sponsoring organization. Along with their application, they must submit transcripts that include (for high school students and college freshmen) SAT and/or ACT scores; a list of school and community activities; at least 2 letters of recommendation; and an essay on why they want to go to college and what they intend to accomplish with their degree. Selection is based on academic record, financial need, extracurricular activities, leadership skills, and participation in community activities. U.S. citizenship is required.
Financial data Stipends range up to $5,000 per year.
Duration 1 year; may be renewed.
Additional information This program includes the GEICO Scholarship and the Rosemary Posekany Memorial Scholarship.
Number awarded Varies each year; recently, 6 were awarded: 5 at $5,000 and 1 at $1,000.
Deadline April of each year.

[1353]
FLORIDA LEGION AUXILIARY MASTER'S PROGRAM GRANT

American Legion Auxiliary
Department of Florida
1912A Lee Road
P.O. Box 547917
Orlando, FL 32854-7917
(407) 293-7411   Toll Free: (866) 710-4192
Fax: (407) 299-0901   E-mail: contact@alafl.org
Web: www.alafl.org/programs/education/scholarships

Summary To provide financial assistance to members of the Florida American Legion Auxiliary who are interested in working on a master's degree in any field at a university in any state.
Eligibility This program is open to residents of Florida who have been members of the American Legion Auxiliary for at least 5 consecutive years. Applicants must be planning to enroll in an accredited master's degree program in any field at a college or university in any state. They must be sponsored

by the local American Legion Auxiliary unit. Selection is based on academic record and financial need.
Financial data The stipend is $2,500 per year. All funds are paid directly to the institution.
Duration 1 year; may be renewed 1 additional year if the recipient needs further financial assistance and has maintained at least a 2.5 GPA.
Number awarded 1 each year.
Deadline January of each year.

[1354]
FLORIDA NAVY NURSE CORPS ASSOCIATION SCHOLARSHIPS

Florida Navy Nurse Corps Association
c/o Margaret Holder, Scholarship Committee
1033 Inverness Drive
St. Augustine, FL 32092
E-mail: maholder@me.com
Web: www.nnca.org/join-nnca-2/local-chapters/fnnca

Summary To provide financial assistance to undergraduate and graduate nursing students, especially residents of Florida with ties to the military.
Eligibility This program is open to students, including registered nursing continuing their studies, who are working on a baccalaureate or graduate degree in nursing. Applicants must have completed at least 1 clinical nursing course and have a GPA of 3.0 or higher. They may be full- or part-time students. Along with their application, they must submit an essay, up to 500 words in length, on the reasons they are qualified for the scholarship, how it will benefit them, career goals, and potential for contribution to the profession. Preference is given in order to current active-duty and Reserve service members, veterans of military service, family members of current or former military service personnel, civil service employees, and residents of Florida. Financial need is considered in the selection process.
Financial data The stipend is $1,500. Funds are paid directly to the student.
Duration 1 year.
Number awarded 2 each year.
Deadline October of each year.

[1355]
FOLDED FLAG FOUNDATION SCHOLARSHIPS AND GRANTS

Folded Flag Foundation
1550 South Pavilion Center Drive
Las Vegas, NV 89135
Toll Free: (844) 204-2856
E-mail: scholarships@foldedflagfoundation.org
Web: www.foldedflagfoundation.org/how-to-apply

Summary To provide financial assistance for education at any level to spouses and children of military and civilian personnel who lost their lives in combat.
Eligibility This program is open to spouses and children of 1) members of the U.S. military who died as a result of hostile action or in an accident related to U.S. combat operations; and 2) employees of the U.S. government who died as a result of hostile action or in an accident related to U.S. combat operations. Applicants may be any age younger than 26. They may apply for 1) a children's education scholarship, which supplies funds for K-12 students to cover private school tuition and fees, tutoring, after-school programs, summer camps, or other related educational expenses; 2) a college or trade/technical school scholarship, to cover tuition and fees, books, computers, living expenses (including child care for students with young children), tutoring, test preparation, and career preparation (e.g., internships, resume writing workshops, interview preparation training). Financial need is considered in the selection process.
Financial data A stipend is provided (amount not specified). Recently, stipends averaged nearly $7,500.
Duration 1 year.
Additional information This program began in 2014.
Number awarded Varies each year; recently, 347 scholarships (167 new and 180 renewal) worth $2.6 million were awarded. Since the program began, it has awarded more than $6 million to more than 400 spouses and children.
Deadline May of each year.

[1356]
GEORGE WASHINGTON CHAPTER AUSA SCHOLARSHIPS

Association of the United States Army-George Washington Chapter
c/o Col (Ret.) William G. Yarborough, Jr., Scholarship Committee
P.O. Box 828
McLean, VA 22101-0828
(703) 748-1717   E-mail: wgyarc@aol.com
Web: www.ausa.org/chapters/george-washington-chapter

Summary To provide financial assistance for undergraduate or graduate study at a school in any state to members of the George Washington Chapter of the Association of the United States Army (AUSA) and their families.
Eligibility This program is open to active members of the AUSA George Washington Chapter and the spouses, children, and grandchildren of active members. Applicants must have a GPA of 2.5 or higher and be working on an undergraduate or graduate degree at a college or university in any state. Along with their application, they must submit a letter describing any family circumstances they believe are relevant and explaining why they deserve the scholarship. Members must also submit a favorable recommendation from their supervisor. Membership in AUSA is open to Army personnel (including Reserves and National Guard) who are either active or retired, ROTC cadets, or civilian employees of the Army.
Financial data Stipends range up to $1,000.
Duration 1 year.
Additional information This program includes the following named awards: the Ed Dauksz Scholarship Award, the Major General Harry Greene STEM Scholarship Award, and the Major General Carl F. McNair Jr. Scholarship Award. The George Washington Chapter serves Washington, D.C.; the Virginia counties of Alexandria, Clarke, Fairfax, Frederick, Loudoun, and Prince William; and the Maryland counties of Calvert, Charles, Montgomery, Prince George's, and St. Mary's.
Number awarded Varies each year; recently, 45 were awarded.
Deadline April of each year.

[1357]
GROGAN MEMORIAL SCHOLARSHIP

American Academy of Physician Assistants-Veterans Caucus
Attn: Scholarship Program
P.O. Box 362
Ossining, NY 10562
(803) 328-1864 Fax: (704) 838-8494
E-mail: rmunsee@veteranscaucus.org
Web: www.veteranscaucus.org/scholarships

Summary To provide financial assistance to veterans and their dependents who are studying to become physician assistants.

Eligibility This program is open to U.S. citizens who are currently enrolled in a physician assistant program. Applicants must be honorably discharged members of any branch of the military or the dependents of those members. Along with their application, they must submit a personal statement about what led them to attend PA school; their background, present, and future intentions; and why they deserve to receive a scholarship. Selection is based on military honors and awards received, civic and college honors and awards received, professional memberships and activities, potential for future achievement, and GPA.

Financial data The stipend is $2,000.
Duration 1 year.
Number awarded 1 each year.
Deadline February of each year.

[1358]
HAZLEWOOD LEGACY ACT (CHILD)

Texas Veterans Commission
1700 North Congress Avenue, Suite 800
P.O. Box 12277
Austin, TX 78711-2277
(512) 463-3168 Toll Free: (800) 252-VETS
Fax: (512) 475-2395 E-mail: hazlewood@tvc.texas.gov
Web: www.tvc.texas.gov/education/hazlewood

Summary To exempt the children of certain Texas veterans from payment of tuition for undergraduate or graduate study at public universities in the state.

Eligibility This program is open to the dependent children under 25 years of age of veterans who are current residents of Texas and were legal residents of the state at the time they entered the U.S. armed forces and served for at least 181 days of active military duty, excluding basic training, during specified periods of wartime. The veteran parent must have received an honorable discharge or separation or a general discharge under honorable conditions. They must have unused hours of exemption from tuition under the Hazlewood Act that they can assign to a dependent child. The dependent children must be enrolled or planning to enroll at a public college or university in Texas and all their other federal veterans' education benefits (not including Pell and SEOG grants) may not exceed the value of this exemption.

Financial data Dependent children who are eligible for this benefit are entitled to free tuition and fees at state-supported colleges and universities in Texas.

Duration The combined exemptions for veteran and child may be claimed up to a cumulative total of 150 credit hours, including undergraduate and graduate study.

Additional information This program was previously administered by the Texas Higher Education Coordinating Board but was transferred to the Texas Veterans Commission in 2013.

Number awarded Varies each year; recently, 16,958 eligible children received $132,471,254 in support at 4-year institutions and 5,727 eligible children received $10,991,860 in support at 2-year colleges.

Deadline Deadline not specified.

[1359]
HENRY J. REILLY SCHOLARSHIPS

Reserve Officers Association of the United States
Attn: Scholarship Program
One Constitution Avenue, N.E.
Washington, DC 20002-5618
(202) 646-7758 Toll Free: (800) 809-9448
E-mail: scholarship@roa.org
Web: www.roa.org/page/Scholarships

Summary To provide financial assistance for college or graduate school to members of the Reserve Officers Association (ROA) and their children or grandchildren.

Eligibility Applicants for this scholarship must be active or associate members of the association or their children or grandchildren (under the age of 26). Children, age 21 or under, of deceased members who were active and paid up at the time of their death are also eligible. Spouses are not eligible, unless they are members of the association. ROTC members do not qualify as sponsors. Entering and continuing undergraduates must provide evidence of full-time enrollment at a regionally-accredited 4-year college or university, demonstrate leadership qualities, have earned a GPA of 3.3 or higher in high school and 3.0 or higher in college, have scored at least 1875 on the SAT or 55 on the English/math ACT, and (if appropriate) have registered for the draft. Applicants for a master's degree must have earned a GPA of 3.2 or higher as an undergraduate; applicants for a doctoral degree must have received a master's degree or been accepted into a doctoral program. All applicants must submit a 500-word essay on career goals. Selection is based on that essay, academic excellence, extracurricular activities and leadership, and letters of recommendation.

Financial data The stipend is $2,500 per year.
Duration 1 year; may be renewed.
Number awarded Up to 20 each year.
Deadline April of each year.

[1360]
H.S. AND ANGELINE LEWIS SCHOLARSHIPS

American Legion Auxiliary
Department of Wisconsin
Attn: Education Chair
2930 American Legion Drive
P.O. Box 140
Portage, WI 53901-0140
(608) 745-0124 Toll Free: (866) 664-3863
Fax: (608) 745-1947
E-mail: deptsec@amlegionauxwi.org
Web: www.amlegionauxwi.org/scholarships

Summary To provide financial assistance to Wisconsin residents who are related to veterans and interested in work-

ing on an undergraduate or graduate degree at a school in any state.
Eligibility This program is open to residents of Wisconsin who are the children, grandchildren, great-grandchildren, wives, or widows of veterans. Students who are members of the Wisconsin American Legion family may live in any state. Applicants must be enrolled or planning to enroll as an undergraduate or graduate students at a college or university in any state. They must have a GPA of 3.5 or higher and be able to demonstrate financial need. Along with their application, they must submit a 300-word essay on "Education—An Investment in the Future."
Financial data The stipend is $1,000.
Duration 1 year; nonrenewable.
Number awarded 6 each year: 1 to a graduate student and 5 to undergraduates.
Deadline March of each year.

[1361]
INDIANA CHILDREN OF DECEASED OR DISABLED VETERANS PROGRAM

Indiana Commission for Higher Education
Attn: Financial Aid and Student Support Services
101 West Ohio Street, Suite 300
Indianapolis, IN 46204-4206
(317) 232-1023   Toll Free: (888) 528-4719 (within IN)
Fax: (317) 232-3260   E-mail: Scholars@che.in.gov
Web: www.in.gov/che/4517.htm

Summary To provide financial assistance to residents of Indiana who are the children of deceased or disabled veterans and interested in attending college in the state.
Eligibility This program is open to residents of Indiana whose parent served in the U.S. armed forces during a war or performed duty equally hazardous that was recognized by the award of a U.S. service or campaign medal, suffered a service-connected death or disability, and received a discharge or separation other than dishonorable. Applicants must be the biological child of the veteran or legally adopted prior to their 24th birthday; stepchildren are not eligible. Parents who enlisted on or before June 30, 2011 must have resided in Indiana for at least 36 consecutive months during their lifetime. Parents who enlisted after June 30, 2011 must have designated Indiana as home of record at the time of enlistment or resided in that state at least 5 years before the child first applies for the benefit.
Financial data If the veterans parent initially enlisted on or before June 30, 2011, the child receives a 100% remission of tuition and all mandatory fees for undergraduate, graduate, or professional degrees at eligible postsecondary schools and universities in Indiana. If the veteran parent initially enlisted after June 30, 2011 and suffered a disability with a rating of 80% or more, the child receives a 100% remission of tuition and all mandatory fees for undergraduate or professional degrees at eligible postsecondary schools and universities in Indiana. If the veteran parent initially enlisted after June 30, 2011 and suffered a disability with a rating less than 80%, the rate of remission for tuition and regularly assessed fees is 20% plus the disability rating. Support is not provided for such fees as room and board.
Duration Up to 124 semester hours of study. If the veteran parent initially enlisted on or before June 30, 2011, there is no time limit to use those hours. If the veteran parent initially enlisted after June 30, 2011, the allotted 124 credit hours must be used within 8 years after the date the child first applied.
Number awarded Varies each year.
Deadline Applications must be submitted at least 30 days before the start of the college term.

[1362]
JAVA FOUNDERS' SCHOLARSHIP

Japanese American Veterans Association
Attn: Chris DeRosa, Scholarship Committee Chair
P.O. Box 341198
Bethesda, MD 20827
E-mail: javascholarship222@gmail.com
Web: www.java.wildapricot.org

Summary To provide financial assistance for college or graduate school to relatives of Japanese American veterans.
Eligibility This program is open to students who have completed at least 2 years of an undergraduate program or are currently enrolled in graduate school. Applicants must be 1) a direct or collateral descendant of a person who served with the 442nd Regimental Combat Team, the 100th Infantry Battalion, Military Intelligence Service, 1399th Engineering Construction Battalion, or other unit associated with those during or after World War II; or 2) a member or child of a member of the Japanese American Veterans Association (JAVA) whose membership extends back at least 1 year. Along with their application, they must submit a 500-word essay on what winning this scholarship will mean to them.
Financial data The stipend is $3,000.
Duration 1 year.
Number awarded 1 each year.
Deadline March of each year.

[1363]
JOHN CORNELIUS/MAX ENGLISH MEMORIAL SCHOLARSHIP

Marine Corps Tankers Association
c/o Dan Miller, Scholarship Chair
8212 West Fourth Place
Kennewick, WA 99336
E-mail: dmiller@msn.com
Web: www.usmctankers.org/pageScholarship

Summary To provide financial assistance for college or graduate school to children and grandchildren of members of the Marine Corps Tankers Association and to Marine and Navy personnel currently serving in tank units.
Eligibility This program is open to high school seniors and graduates who are children, grandchildren, or under the guardianship of an active, Reserve, retired, or honorably discharged Marine who served in a tank unit. Marine or Navy Corpsmen currently assigned to tank units are also eligible. Applicants must be enrolled or planning to enroll full time at a college or graduate school. Their parent or grandparent must be a member of the Marine Corps Tankers Association or, if not a member, must join if the application is accepted. Along with their application, they must submit a 500-word essay that explains their reason for seeking this scholarship, their educational goals, and their plans for post-graduation life. Selection is based on that essay, academic record, school activities, leadership potential, and community service.
Financial data The stipend is at least $2,000 per year.

Duration 1 year; recipients may reapply.
Number awarded Varies each year; recently, 4 were awarded.
Deadline March of each year.

[1364]
KATHERN F. GRUBER SCHOLARSHIPS
Blinded Veterans Association
Attn: Scholarship Coordinator
125 North West Street, Third Floor
Alexandria, VA 22314
(202) 371-8880, ext. 330   Toll Free: (800) 669-7079
Fax: (202) 371-8258   E-mail: bjones@bva.org
Web: www.bva.org

Summary To provide financial assistance for undergraduate or graduate study to immediate family of blinded veterans and servicemembers.
Eligibility This program is open to dependent children, grandchildren, and spouses of blinded veterans and active-duty blinded servicemembers of the U.S. armed forces. The veteran or servicemember must be legally blind; the blindness may be either service-connected or nonservice-connected. Applicants must have been accepted or be currently enrolled as a full-time student in an undergraduate or graduate program at an accredited institution of higher learning. Along with their application, they must submit a 300-word essay on their career goals and aspirations. Financial need is not considered in the selection process.
Financial data The stipend is $2,000; funds are intended to be used to cover the student's expenses, including tuition, other academic fees, books, dormitory fees, and cafeteria fees. Funds are paid directly to the recipient's school.
Duration 1 year; recipients may reapply for up to 3 additional years.
Number awarded 6 each year.
Deadline April of each year.

[1365]
KOREA VETERANS SCHOLARSHIP PROGRAM
Korean War Veterans Association
Attn: American Veterans of Korea Foundation
Scholarship Selection Committee
635 Glover Drive
Lancaster, PA 17601-4110
Web: www.kwva.us/?page=blog

Summary To provide financial assistance to high school seniors and current undergraduate and graduate students who are the descendants of Korean War veterans.
Eligibility This program is open to U.S. citizens who are working full time on an associate, bachelor's, or advanced degree in any discipline. Applicants must be the child, grandchild, or great-grandchild of a veteran who served in Korea and is a regular member of the Korean War Veterans Association. They must have a GPA of 3.5 or higher. Along with their application, they must submit an essay of 300 to 400 words on a topic that changes annually; recently, students were asked to write on the historical lessons learned from the Korean War. Selection is based on scholastic activities, extracurricular activities, community activities, and employment history (including military service).
Financial data The stipend is $2,000 per year.
Duration 1 year; recipients may reapply.

Number awarded Varies each year.
Deadline June of each year.

[1366]
LILLIAN CAMPBELL MEDICAL SCHOLARSHIP
VFW Auxiliary-Department of Wisconsin
c/o Donna Butler, Department Scholarship Chair
522 Topaz Lane
Madison, WI 53714
(608) 695-0261   E-mail: butlerdonna999@yahoo.com
Web: www.wivfwaux.org/department-scholarships.html

Summary To provide financial assistance to students working on a degree in a medical field in Wisconsin who served in the military or are related to a person who did.
Eligibility This program is open to students who have completed at least 1 year of study in Wisconsin in a program in 1) a medical field, including nursing, pharmacy, physician assistant, medical or surgical technology, physical or occupational therapy, dental hygiene, radiology, or other related medical profession; or 2) an emergency medical technician field (EMT), including paramedic studies. Applicants or a member of their immediate family (parent, sibling, child, spouse, or grandparent) must have served in the military. They must have a high school diploma or GED but may be of any age. Along with their application, they must submit a 200-word essay on why they are studying this medical profession. Financial need is considered in the selection process.
Financial data The stipend is $1,000 for students in a medical field or $750 for EMT students.
Duration 1 year.
Number awarded 1 for a student in a medical field and 1 for an EMT student.
Deadline March of each year.

[1367]
LORETTA CORNETT-HUFF SCHOLARSHIPS
Council of College and Military Educators
c/o Jim Yeonopolus, Scholarship Committee Chair
Central Texas College
P.O. Box 1800
Killeen, TX 76540-1800
(254) 526-1781   Fax: (254) 526-1750
E-mail: jim.yeonopolus@ctcd.edu
Web: www.ccmeonline.org/scholarships

Summary To provide financial assistance to spouses of members of the armed services who are interested in working on an undergraduate or master's degree.
Eligibility This program is open to spouses of members of the uniformed services, including active, National Guard, and Reserves. Applicants must be currently enrolled full time at an accredited institution that is a member of the Council of College and Military Educators (CCME) and working on an associate, bachelor's, or master's degree. Undergraduates must have a GPA of 2.5 or higher and graduate students must have a GPA of 3.0 or higher. Along with their application, they must submit an essay of 400 to 750 words on their most meaningful achievements and how those relate to their field of study and their future goals. Financial need is not considered in the selection process.
Financial data The stipend is $1,000.
Duration 1 year.

[1368]
MAINE VETERANS DEPENDENTS EDUCATIONAL BENEFITS

Bureau of Veterans' Services
117 State House Station
Augusta, ME 04333-0117
(207) 430-6035 Toll Free: (800) 345-0116 (within ME)
Fax: (207) 626-4471 E-mail: mainebvs@maine.gov
Web: www.maine.gov

Summary To provide financial assistance for undergraduate or graduate education to dependents of disabled and other Maine veterans.

Eligibility Applicants for these benefits must be children (high school seniors or graduates under 22 years of age), non-divorced spouses, or unremarried widow(er)s of veterans who meet 1 or more of the following requirements: 1) living and determined to have a total permanent disability resulting from a service-connected cause; 2) killed in action; 3) died from a service-connected disability; 4) died while totally and permanently disabled due to a service-connected disability but whose death was not related to the service-connected disability; or 5) a member of the armed forces on active duty who has been listed for more than 90 days as missing in action, captured, forcibly detained, or interned in the line of duty by a foreign government or power. The veteran parent must have been a resident of Maine at the time of entry into service or a resident of Maine for 5 years preceding application for these benefits. Children may be working on a certificate, associate degree, or bachelor's degree. Spouses, widows, and widowers may work on a certificate or an associate, bachelor's, or master's degree.

Financial data Recipients are entitled to free tuition at institutions of higher education supported by the state of Maine.

Duration Recipients are entitled to receive up to 120 credit hours of educational benefits and have 10 years from the date of first entrance to complete their program.

Additional information College preparatory schooling and correspondence courses are not supported under this program.

Number awarded Varies each year.

Deadline Deadline not specified.

[1369]
MAINE VIETNAM VETERANS SCHOLARSHIP FUND

Maine Community Foundation
Attn: Program Director
245 Main Street
Ellsworth, ME 04605
(207) 667-9735 Toll Free: (877) 700-6800
Fax: (207) 667-0447 E-mail: info@mainecf.org
Web: www.mainecf.org

Summary To provide financial assistance for college or graduate school to Vietnam veterans or the dependents of Vietnam or other veterans in Maine.

Eligibility This program is open to residents of Maine who are Vietnam veterans or the descendants of veterans who served in the Vietnam Theater. As a second priority, children of veterans from other time periods are also considered. Graduating high school seniors, nontraditional students, undergraduates, and graduate students are eligible to apply. Selection is based on financial need, extracurricular activities, work experience, academic achievement, and a personal statement of career goals and how the applicant's educational plans relate to them.

Financial data The stipend is $1,000 per year.

Duration 1 year.

Additional information This program began in 1985. There is a $3 processing fee.

Number awarded 3 to 6 each year.

Deadline April of each year.

[1370]
MARGUERITE MC'ALPIN MEMORIAL SCHOLARSHIP

American Legion Auxiliary
Department of Washington
Attn: Education Chair
3600 Ruddell Road S.E.
P.O. Box 5867
Lacey, WA 98509-5867
(360) 456-5995 Fax: (360) 491-7442
E-mail: secretary@walegion-aux.org
Web: www.walegion-aux.org/EducationScholarships.html

Summary To provide financial assistance to Washington veterans or their descendants who are interested in working on an undergraduate or graduate degree in nursing at a school in any state.

Eligibility This program is open to residents of Washington who are veterans or the children, grandchildren, and great-grandchildren of veterans. Applicants must be interested in studying nursing on the undergraduate or graduate level at a school in any state. Selection is based on a 300-word essay on their desire to study nursing, character, leadership, scholastic history, and financial need.

Financial data The stipend is $1,000.

Duration 1 year.

Number awarded 1 each year.

Deadline February of each year.

[1371]
MARIA C. JACKSON/GENERAL GEORGE A. WHITE SCHOLARSHIP

Oregon Office of Student Access and Completion
Attn: Scholarships
1500 Valley River Drive, Suite 100
Eugene, OR 97401-2146
(541) 687-7400 Toll Free: (800) 452-8807
Fax: (541) 687-7414 TDD: (800) 735-2900
E-mail: osac@hecc.oregon.gov
Web: app.oregonstudentaid.gov/Catalog/Default.aspx

Summary To provide financial assistance to veterans and children of veterans and military personnel in Oregon who are interested in attending college or graduate school in the state.

Eligibility This program is open to residents of Oregon who served, or whose parents are serving or have served, in the U.S. armed forces. Applicants or their parents must have resided in Oregon at the time of enlistment. They must be enrolled or planning to enroll at a college or graduate school in the state. College and university undergraduates must have a GPA of 3.75 or higher, but there is no minimum GPA

Number awarded 5 each year.
Deadline September of each year.

requirement for graduate students or those attending a technical school. Selection is based on scholastic ability and financial need.
Financial data Stipends for scholarships offered by the Oregon Office of Student Access and Completion (OSAC) range from $1,000 to $10,000 but recently averaged $4,710.
Duration 1 year.
Number awarded Varies each year.
Deadline February of each year.

[1372]
MARY PAOLOZZI MEMBER'S SCHOLARSHIP
Navy Wives Clubs of America
c/o NSA Mid-South
Attn: Melissa Worthey, National President
P.O. Box 54022
Millington, TN 38054-0022
Toll Free: (866) 511-NWCA
E-mail: nwca@navywivesclubsofamerica.org
Web: www.navywivesclubsofamerica.org/scholarships

Summary To provide financial assistance for undergraduate or graduate study to members of the Navy Wives Clubs of America (NWCA).
Eligibility This program is open to NWCA members who can demonstrate financial need. Applicants must be 1) a high school graduate or senior planning to attend college full time next year; 2) currently enrolled in an undergraduate program and planning to continue as a full-time undergraduate; 3) a college graduate or senior planning to be a full-time graduate student next year; or 4) a high school graduate or GED recipient planning to attend vocational or business school next year. Along with their application, they must submit a brief statement on why they feel they should be awarded this scholarship and any special circumstances (financial or other) they wish to have considered. Financial need is also considered in the selection process.
Financial data Stipends range from $500 to $1,000 each year (depending upon the donations from the NWCA chapters).
Duration 1 year.
Additional information Membership in the NWCA is open to spouses of enlisted personnel serving in the Navy, Marine Corps, Coast Guard, and the active Reserve units of those services; spouses of enlisted personnel who have been honorably discharged, retired, or transferred to the Fleet Reserve on completion of duty; and widows of enlisted personnel in those services.
Number awarded 1 each year.
Deadline March of each year.

[1373]
MIDWESTERN REGION KOREAN WAR VETERAN DESCENDANT SCHOLARSHIPS
Korean American Scholarship Foundation
Midwestern Region
c/o Jane Lee-Kwon, Scholarship Committee Chair
5903 North Campbell Avenue, Apartment 2
Chicago, IL 60659
E-mail: mwrc.scholarship@kasf.org
Web: www.kasf.org/apply-mwrc

Summary To provide financial assistance to the descendants of the Korean War from any state who are working on an undergraduate or graduate degree in any field at a school in eastern states.
Eligibility This program is open to direct descendants of veterans who served in Korea from June 25, 1950 to January 31, 1955. Applicants may reside in any state, but they must be enrolled as full-time undergraduate or graduate students at a college or university in in Illinois, Indiana, Iowa, Michigan, Minnesota, Missouri, North Dakota, Ohio, South Dakota, or Wisconsin. They must have a GPA of 3.0 or higher. Selection is based on academic achievement, extracurricular activities, an essay, and recommendations.
Financial data Stipends range from $500 to $5,000.
Duration 1 year.
Number awarded 1 or more each year.
Deadline June of each year.

[1374]
MIKE AND GAIL DONLEY SPOUSE SCHOLARSHIPS
Air Force Association
Attn: Scholarships
1501 Lee Highway
Arlington, VA 22209-1198
(703) 247-5800, ext. 4868
Toll Free: (800) 727-3337, ext. 4868
Fax: (703) 247-5853   E-mail: scholarships@afa.org
Web: www.app.smarterselect.com

Summary To provide financial assistance for undergraduate or graduate study to spouses of Air Force members.
Eligibility This program is open to spouses of active-duty Air Force, Air National Guard, Air Force Reserve members, or Department of the Air Force civilian employee. Spouses who are themselves military members or in ROTC are not eligible. Applicants must have a GPA of 3.5 or higher in college (or high school if entering college for the first time) and be able to provide proof of acceptance into an accredited undergraduate or graduate degree program. They must submit a 2-page essay on their academic and career goals, the motivation that led them to that decision, and how Air Force and other local community activities in which they are involved will enhance their goals. Selection is based on the essay and 2 letters of recommendation.
Financial data The stipend is $2,500; funds are sent to the recipients' schools to be used for any reasonable cost related to working on a degree.
Duration 1 year; nonrenewable.
Additional information This program began in 1995.
Number awarded Varies each year; recently, 3 were awarded.
Deadline April of each year.

[1375]
MILITARY SPOUSE AND CAREGIVER HONORARY SCHOLARSHIP
Hope for the Warriors
Attn: Scholarship Committee
5518 Port Royal Road
Springfield, VA 22151
(703) 321-0588   Toll Free: (877) 2HOPE4W
Fax: (703) 256-3702
E-mail: scholarships@hopeforthewarriors.org
Web: www.hopeforthewarriors.org

Summary To provide financial assistance for graduate study to spouses and caregivers of deceased and disabled veterans who served after September 11, 2001.
Eligibility This program is open to spouses and caregivers of military personnel who were killed or became disabled as a result of service after September 11, 2001. Applicants must be enrolled or planning to enroll at an accredited college, university, or trade school in any state. They must be working on a graduate or postgraduate degree in any field. Along with their application, they must submit an essay on their academic achievement and personal goals. Financial need is not considered in the selection process.
Financial data The stipend is at least $2,000.
Duration 1 year.
Additional information This program began in 2008.
Number awarded Normally, 2 each year (1 each semester).
Deadline May of each year for fall semester; October of each year for spring semester.

[1376]
MILITARY SPOUSE SCHOLARSHIPS
National Military Family Association, Inc.
Attn: Spouse Scholarship Program
2800 Eisenhower Avenue, Suite 250
Alexandria, VA 22314
(703) 931-NMFA   Toll Free: (800) 260-0218
Fax: (703) 931-4600
E-mail: scholarships@militaryfamily.org
Web: www.scholarships.militaryfamily.org

Summary To provide financial assistance for postsecondary study to spouses of active and retired military personnel.
Eligibility This program is open to students who are 1) spouses of members of the 7 uniformed services who have a valid military ID; 2) married to an active-duty, Reserve, Guard, retired, medically retired, wounded, or fallen service member (must be a service-related wound, illness, injury, or death that took place after September 11, 2001); 3) a dual service military spouse; or 4) a divorced spouse who is receiving 20/20/20 benefits. Applicants must be enrolled or planning to enroll in a program for procurement of professional certification or license in any state. Applicants must be attending or planning to attend an accredited postsecondary institution to work on an undergraduate or graduate degree, professional certification, vocational training, licensure, or other postsecondary training. They may enroll part or full time and on-campus or online. Along with their application, they must submit an essay on a question that changes annually; recently, applicants were asked to write about what they like most about the health care they are receiving as a military family member, what they like the least, and what they would recommend to change it. Selection is based on that essay, community involvement, and academic achievement.
Financial data The stipend is $1,000. Funds are paid directly to the educational institution to be used for tuition, fees, and school room and board. Support is not provided for books, rent, or previous education loans.
Duration 1 year; recipients may reapply.
Additional information This program began in 2004.
Number awarded Varies each year.
Deadline Applications may be submitted at any time.

[1377]
MINNESOTA G.I. BILL PROGRAM
Minnesota Department of Veterans Affairs
Attn: Programs and Services Division
20 West 12th Street, Room 206
St. Paul, MN 55155
(651) 296-2562   Toll Free: (888) LINK-VET
Fax: (651) 296-3954   TDD: (800) 627-3529
E-mail: MNGIBill@state.mn.us
Web: www.mn.gov

Summary To provide financial assistance for college or graduate school in the state to residents of Minnesota who served in the military after September 11, 2001 and the families of deceased or disabled military personnel.
Eligibility This program is open to residents of Minnesota enrolled at colleges and universities in the state as undergraduate or graduate students. Applicants must be 1) a veteran who is serving or has served honorably in a branch of the U.S. armed forces at any time; 2) a non-veteran who has served honorably for a total of 5 years or more cumulatively as a member of the Minnesota National Guard or other active or Reserve component of the U.S. armed forces, and any part of that service occurred on or after September 11, 2001; or 3) a surviving child or spouse of a person who has served in the military at any time and who has died or has a total and permanent disability as a result of that military service. They may be attending college in the state or participating in an apprenticeship or on-the-job (OJT) training program. Financial need is also considered in the selection process.
Financial data The college stipend is $1,000 per semester for full-time study or $500 per semester for part-time study. The maximum award is $3,000 per academic year or $10,000 per lifetime. Apprenticeship and OJT students are eligible for up to $2,000 per fiscal year. Approved employers are eligible to receive $1,000 placement credit payable upon hiring a person under this program and another $1,000 after 12 consecutive months of employment. No more than $3,000 in aggregate benefits under this paragraph may be paid to or on behalf of an individual in one fiscal year, and not more than $9,000 over any period of time.
Duration 1 year; may be renewed, provided the recipient continues to make satisfactory academic progress.
Additional information This program was established by the Minnesota Legislature in 2007.
Number awarded At least 1,000 each year.
Deadline Deadline not specified.

[1378]
MINNESOTA NATIONAL GUARD SURVIVOR ENTITLEMENT TUITION REIMBURSEMENT PROGRAM
Minnesota National Guard
Attn: Education Office
600 Cedar Street
St. Paul, MN 5510-2509
(651) 282-4589   Toll Free: (800) 657-3848
Fax: (651) 282-4694
E-mail: ng.mn.mnarng.mbx.assets-education@mail.mil
Web: minnesotanationalguard.ng.mil/education

Summary To provide financial assistance for college or graduate school to survivors of members of the Minnesota National Guard who were killed on active duty.

Eligibility This program is open to surviving spouses and children of members of the Minnesota Army or Air National Guard who were killed while performing military duty. Dependent children are eligible until their 24th birthday; surviving spouses are eligible regardless of age or remarriage; all survivors remain eligible even if they move out of state and become residents of another state. The Guard member's death must have occurred within the scope of assigned duties while in a federal duty status or on state active service. Applicants must be enrolled as undergraduate or graduate students at colleges or universities in Minnesota. Reimbursement is provided only for undergraduate courses completed with a grade of "C" or better or for graduate courses completed with a grade of "B" or better.

Financial data The maximum reimbursement rate is 100% of the tuition rate at the University of Minnesota Twin Cities campus for undergraduate study or 50% for graduate work, with a maximum benefit of $18,000 per fiscal year for undergraduate course work or $20,000 per fiscal year for graduate course work.

Duration 1 academic term, to a maximum of 18 credits per term; may be renewed for a total of 144 semester credits or 208 quarter credits.

Additional information This program became effective in 1992.

Number awarded Varies each year.

Deadline Participants must request reimbursement within 90 days of the last official day of the term.

[1379]
NATIONAL GUARD ASSOCIATION OF NEW HAMPSHIRE SCHOLARSHIPS

National Guard Association of New Hampshire
Attn: Scholarship Committee
P.O. Box 22031
Portsmouth, NH 03802-2031
(603) 227-1597   E-mail: nganhscholarship@gmail.com
Web: www.nganh.org/benefits

Summary To provide financial assistance to members of the National Guard Association of New Hampshire and their dependents who are interested in attending college or graduate school in any state.

Eligibility This program is open to current members of the National Guard Association of New Hampshire (officer, enlisted, or retired), their spouses, and their dependent children. Applicants must be enrolled or planning to enroll full or part time in an associate, bachelor's, graduate, professional, or doctoral degree program at an accredited college or university in any state. Along with their application, they must submit a 1-page essay on a topic that changes annually; recently, they were asked to describe what citizen service means to them.

Financial data The stipend is $1,000.

Duration 1 year.

Number awarded 1 each year.

Deadline April of each year.

[1380]
NATIONAL GUARD ASSOCIATION OF NEW JERSEY SCHOLARSHIP PROGRAM

National Guard Association of New Jersey
Attn: Scholarship Committee
P.O. Box 266
Wrightstown, NJ 08562
(848) 480-3441   E-mail: scholarship@nganj.org
Web: www.nganj.org/awards-scholarships

Summary To provide financial assistance to members of the National Guard Association of New Jersey (NGANJ) or their dependents who are interested in attending college or graduate school in any state.

Eligibility This program is open to 1) active members of the NGANJ currently enrolled full time at an approved community college, school of nursing, or 4-year college in any state; and 2) the spouses, children, and grandchildren of active, retired, or deceased members entering or attending a 4-year college or university in any state. Applicants must submit transcripts, information on the civic and academic activities in which they have participated, and a list of offices, honors, awards, and special recognitions they have received. Selection is based on academic accomplishment, leadership, and citizenship.

Financial data Stipends up to $1,000 are available.

Duration 1 year; nonrenewable.

Number awarded Varies each year; recently, 5 were awarded.

Deadline February of each year.

[1381]
NATIONAL GUARD ASSOCIATION OF TEXAS SCHOLARSHIP PROGRAM

National Guard Association of Texas
Attn: Education Committee
3706 Crawford Avenue
Austin, TX 78731-6803
(512) 454-7300   Toll Free: (800) 252-NGAT
Fax: (512) 467-6803   E-mail: tbz@ngat.org
Web: www.ngat.org/education.htm

Summary To provide financial assistance to members and dependents of members of the National Guard Association of Texas who are interested in attending college or graduate school in any state.

Eligibility This program is open to annual and life members of the association and their spouses and children (associate members and their dependents are not eligible). Applicants may be high school seniors, undergraduate students, or graduate students, either enrolled or planning to enroll at an institution of higher education in any state. Along with their application, they must submit an essay on their desire to continue their education. Selection is based on scholarship, citizenship, and leadership.

Financial data Stipends range from $500 to $5,000.

Duration 1 year (nonrenewable).

Additional information This program includes the Len and Jean Tallas Memorial Scholarship, the Texas Capital Area Chapter of the AUSA Scholarship, the Lewis O. King Memorial Scholarship, the Gloria Jenell and Marlin E. Mote Endowed Scholarship, the LTC Gary Parrish Memorial Scholarship, the TXNG Retirees Endowed Scholarship, and 2 scholarships sponsored by USAA Insurance Corporation.

Number awarded Varies each year; recently, 8 were awarded: 1 at $5,000, 1 at $4,000, 1 at $2,000, 1 at $1,250, 3 at $1,000, and 1 at $500.
Deadline February of each year.

[1382]
NATIONAL GUARD ASSOCIATION OF VERMONT SCHOLARSHIPS

National Guard Association of Vermont
Attn: Scholarships
P.O. Box 694
Essex Junction, VT 05453
(802) 999-7675 E-mail: ngavtpresident@gmail.com
Web: www.ngavt.org/scholarships

Summary To provide financial assistance to members of the Vermont National Guard (VTNG) or the National Guard Association of Vermont (NGA-VT) and their children or spouses who are interested in attending college or graduate school in any state.
Eligibility This program is open to current members of the VTNG or the NGA-VT, their spouses, and their unmarried children. Applicants must be working, or planning to work, on an associate, undergraduate, technical, or graduate degree as a full-time student at a school in any state. Along with their application, they must submit an essay on their commitment to selfless public service or their plan for pursuing it in the future. Selection is based on academic performance and overall potential for a commitment to selfless public service.
Financial data The stipend is $1,000. Funds are sent directly to the recipient.
Duration 1 year; recipients may reapply.
Additional information This program is sponsored by the New England Federal Credit Union.
Number awarded 4 undergraduate and 1 graduate scholarship are awarded each year.
Deadline January of each year.

[1383]
NAVAL HELICOPTER ASSOCIATION SCHOLARSHIPS

Naval Helicopter Association
Attn: Scholarship Fund
P.O. Box 180578
Coronado, CA 92178-0578
(619) 435-7139 Fax: (619) 435-7354
E-mail: pres@nhascholarshipfund.org
Web: www.nhascholarshipfund.org/about/scholarships

Summary To provide financial assistance for college or graduate school to members of the Naval Helicopter Association (NHA) and their families.
Eligibility This program is open to NHA members and their spouses, children, and grandchildren. Membership in the NHA is open to active-duty and retired U.S. Navy, U.S. Marine Corps, and U.S. Coast Guard helicopter pilots, aircrew, and maintenance professionals. Applicants must be working on or planning to work on an undergraduate or graduate degree in any field. Along with their application, they must submit a personal statement on their academic and career aspirations. Selection is based on that statement, academic proficiency, scholastic achievements and awards, extracurricular activities, employment history, and letters of recommendation. The program includes scholarships 1) reserved for NHA family members; 2) reserved for active-duty personnel; 3) sponsored by private corporations; 4) named as memorials in honor of distinguished individuals; and 5) awarded on a regional basis.
Financial data Stipends are approximately $2,000.
Duration 1 year.
Additional information Corporate sponsors have included FLIR Systems, D.P. Associates, L-3 Communications, CAE, Raytheon Corporation, Lockheed Martin (designated the Sergei Sikorsky Scholarship), and Northrop Grumman. Memorial Scholarships have included the Edward and Veronica Ream Memorial Scholarship, the CDR Mort McCarthy Memorial Scholarship, the Charles Karman Memorial Scholarship, the LT Christian "Horse" Hescock Memorial Scholarship, and the Captain Mark Starr Memorial Scholarship.
Number awarded Varies each year; recently, 17 were awarded: 1 graduate student family member, 3 active-duty graduate students, 1 active-duty undergraduate student, 4 sponsored by corporate donors, 4 memorial scholarships, and 4 regional scholarships.
Deadline January of each year.

[1384]
NAVAL SPECIAL WARFARE DEVELOPMENT GROUP SCHOLARSHIPS

Navy Seal Foundation
Attn: DEVGRU Scholarship Committee
1619 D Street, Building 5326
Virginia Beach, VA 23459
(757) 744-5326 Fax: (757) 363-7491
E-mail: info@navysealfoundation.org
Web: www.navysealfoundation.org

Summary To provide financial assistance for college to the children and spouses of personnel assigned to the Naval Special Warfare Development Group (DEVGRU).
Eligibility This program is open to the dependent children and spouses of former and present Navy SEAL, Special Warfare Combatant-craft Crewmen (SWCC), or Military Direct Support person who are or have been assigned to DEVGRU. Applicants must be enrolled or planning to enroll at a trade school, vocational/technical institute, or undergraduate college. Spouses may also apply for graduate school. Along with their application, they must submit an essay on their plans as related to their educational and career objectives and long-term goals. Selection is based on merit (as measured by GPA, SAT scores, class rank, extracurricular activities, volunteer community involvement, leadership positions held, military service record, and after school employment, as appropriate) and academic potential.
Financial data Stipends are $15,000, $7,500, or $5,000 per year.
Duration 1 year; may be renewed.
Number awarded Varies each year; recently, the Navy Seal Foundation awarded 16 scholarships for all of its programs: 3 for 4 years at $15,000 per year to high school seniors and graduates, 3 for 1 year at $7,500 to high school seniors and graduates, 3 for 1 year at $15,000 to current college students, 3 for 1 year at $7,500 to current college students, and 4 for 1 year at $5,000 to spouses.
Deadline January of each year.

[1385]
NAVY SEAL FOUNDATION SCHOLARSHIPS

Navy Seal Foundation
Attn: Chief Financial Officer
1619 D Street, Building 5326
Virginia Beach, VA 23459
(757) 744-5326   Fax: (757) 363-7491
E-mail: info@navysealfoundation.org
Web: www.navysealfoundation.org

Summary To provide financial assistance for college or graduate school to Naval Special Warfare (NSW) personnel and their families.

Eligibility This program is open to active-duty Navy SEALS, Special Warfare Combatant-craft Crewmen (SWCC), and military personnel assigned to other NSW commands. Their dependent children and spouses are also eligible. Applicants must be entering or continuing full or part-time students working on an associate or bachelor's degree. Active-duty and spouses, but not dependent children, may also work on a graduate degree. Selection is based on GPA, SAT scores, class ranking, extracurricular activities, volunteer community involvement, leadership positions held, military service record, and employment (as appropriate).

Financial data Stipends are $15,000, $7,500, or $5,000 per year.

Duration 1 year; may be renewed.

Number awarded Varies each year; recently, the Navy Seal Foundation awarded 16 scholarships for all of its programs: 3 for 4 years at $15,000 per year to high school seniors and graduates, 3 for 1 year at $7,500 to high school seniors and graduates, 3 for 1 year at $15,000 to current college students, 3 for 1 year at $7,500 to current college students, and 4 for 1 year at $5,000 to spouses.

Deadline February of each year.

[1386]
NAVY WIVES CLUBS OF AMERICA SCHOLARSHIP FOUNDATION DEPENDENT CHILD SCHOLARSHIP

Navy Wives Clubs of America
c/o NSA Mid-South
Attn: Lois Wilber, Scholarship Director
4368 Water Briar Road
P.O. Box 54022
Millington, TN 38054-0022
Toll Free: (866) 511-NWCA
E-mail: nwca@navywivesclubsofamerica.org
Web: www.navywivesclubsofamerica.org/scholarships

Summary To provide financial assistance for college or graduate school to the children of naval personnel.

Eligibility Applicants for these scholarships must be the children (natural born, legally adopted, or stepchildren) of enlisted members of the Navy, Marine Corps, or Coast Guard on active duty, retired with pay, or deceased. Applicants must be attending or planning to attend an accredited college or university as a full-time undergraduate or graduate student. They must have a GPA of 2.5 or higher. Along with their application, they must submit an essay on their career objectives and the reasons they chose those objectives. Selection is based on academic standing, moral character, and financial need. Some scholarships are reserved for students majoring in special education, medical students, and children of members of Navy Wives Clubs of America (NWCA).

Financial data The stipend is $1,500.

Duration 1 year; may be renewed up to 3 additional years.

Additional information Membership in the NWCA is open to spouses of enlisted personnel serving in the Navy, Marine Corps, Coast Guard, and the active Reserve units of those services; spouses of enlisted personnel who have been honorably discharged, retired, or transferred to the Fleet Reserve on completion of duty; and widows of enlisted personnel in those services.

Number awarded 30 each year, including at least 4 to freshmen, 4 to current undergraduates applying for the first time, 2 to medical students, 1 to a student majoring in special education, and 4 to children of NWCA members.

Deadline March of each year.

[1387]
NBCCF MILITARY SCHOLARSHIPS

National Board for Certified Counselors
Attn: NBCC Foundation
3 Terrace Way
Greensboro, NC 27403
(336) 232-0376   Fax: (336) 232-0010
E-mail: foundation@nbcc.org
Web: nbccf.applicantstack.com/x/detail/a2ei42le608f

Summary To provide financial assistance to current and former military personnel and spouses of servicemembers interested in working on a master's degree in counseling.

Eligibility This program is open to students enrolled full time in an accredited master's degree counseling program. Applicants must be prior or current active-duty U.S. military service personnel or the spouse of a servicemember. Veterans must have received an honorable discharge. Applicants must be able to demonstrate a commitment to apply for the National Certified Counselor (NCC) credential prior to graduation and to provide counseling services to servicemembers and/or veterans for at least 2 years after graduation.

Financial data The stipend is $8,000.

Duration 1 year.

Additional information This program began in 2010.

Number awarded 5 each year.

Deadline January of each year.

[1388]
NERA/USAA COLLEGE SCHOLARSHIP PROGRAM

Naval Enlisted Reserve Association
Attn: Scholarship Committee
8116 Arlington Boulevard
Falls Church, VA 22042
(703) 534-1329   Toll Free: (800) 776-9020
Fax: (703) 534-3617   E-mail: members@nera.org
Web: www.nera.org

Summary To provide financial assistance for college to members of the Naval Enlisted Reserve Association (NERA) and their families.

Eligibility This program is open to students enrolled or entering a college or university to work full or part time on an associate degree, vocational or trade school certificate, bachelor's degree, master's degree, or doctoral degree. Applicants or their sponsor must be a member of NERA in good standing. They must have a GPA of 3.0 or higher. Along with their application, they must submit an essay of 500 to 600 words on 1) their aspirations and course of study; and 2) the role of

the Reservist in America and the importance of the Reserves to our national defense. In the selection process, priority is given in the following order: 1) currently serving Reserve, active and IRR members of the U.S. armed forces; 2) children and spouses of those currently serving in the U.S. armed forces; and 3) spouses, children, or grandchildren sponsored by any NERA member. Financial need is not considered in the selection process.
Financial data The stipend is $2,000.
Duration 1 year.
Additional information This program is funded in part by USAA Insurance Corporation. Regular membership in NERA is open to enlisted members of the Navy, Marine Corps, and Coast Guard Reserve components, including FTS, IRR, VTU, and retirees; associate membership is open to anyone who wishes to support NERA.
Number awarded 5 each year.
Deadline June of each year.

[1389]
NEW JERSEY NATIONAL GUARD TUITION PROGRAM

New Jersey Department of Military and Veterans Affairs
Attn: New Jersey Army National Guard Education
  Services Officer
Second Floor, B204
3650 Saylors Pond Road
Fort Dix, NJ 08640-7600
(609) 562-0975   Toll Free: (888) 859-0352
Fax: (609) 562-0188
E-mail: benjamin.j.stoner.mil@mail.mil
Web: education.njarmyguard.com/njngtp

Summary To provide financial assistance for college or graduate school to New Jersey National Guard members and the surviving spouses and children of deceased members.
Eligibility This program is open to active members of the New Jersey National Guard who have completed Initial Active Duty for Training (IADT). Applicants must be New Jersey residents who have been accepted into a program of undergraduate or graduate study at any of 30 public institutions of higher education in the state. The surviving spouses and children of deceased members of the Guard who had completed IADT and were killed in the performance of their duties while a member of the Guard are also eligible if the school has classroom space available.
Financial data Tuition for up to 16 credits per semester is waived for full-time recipients in state-supported colleges or community colleges in New Jersey.
Duration 1 semester; may be renewed.
Number awarded Varies each year.
Deadline Deadline not specified.

[1390]
NEW MEXICO CHILDREN OF DECEASED MILITARY PERSONNEL SCHOLARSHIPS

New Mexico Department of Veterans' Services
Attn: State Benefits
407 Galisteo Street, Room 134
P.O. Box 2324
Santa Fe, NM 87504-2324
(505) 383-2400   Toll Free: (866) 433-VETS
Fax: (505) 827-6372 E-mail: JosephM.Dorn@state.nm.us
Web: www.nmdvs.org/state-benefits

Summary To provide financial assistance for college or graduate school to the children of deceased military personnel in New Mexico.
Eligibility This program is open to the children of military personnel killed in action or as a result of such action during a period of armed conflict. Applicants must be between the ages of 16 and 26 and enrolled in a state-supported school in New Mexico. Selection is based on merit and financial need.
Financial data The scholarships provide full waiver of tuition at state-funded postsecondary schools in New Mexico. A stipend of $150 per semester ($300 per year) provides assistance with books and fees.
Duration 1 year; may be renewed.
Number awarded Varies each year.
Deadline Deadline not specified.

[1391]
NGAOK SCHOLARSHIPS

National Guard Association of Oklahoma
c/o Scholarship Foundation
Attn: Rosemary Masters, Scholarship Chair
3501 Military Circle
Oklahoma City, OK 73111
(405) 823-0799   E-mail: ngaok.scholarship@gmail.com
Web: www.ngaok.org/benefits

Summary To provide financial assistance to members of the National Guard Association of Oklahoma (NGAOK) and their dependents who are interested in attending college in any state.
Eligibility This program is open to NGAOK members and their dependent children and spouses who are enrolled or planning to enroll full or part time in an undergraduate or graduate program at a college or university in any state. The primary next of kin of members of the Oklahoma National Guard killed in action after September 11, 2001 are considered life members of NGAOK. Applicants must submit transcripts that include ACT and/or SAT scores; lists of awards and recognitions, community and volunteer services, and extracurricular and sports activities; and a 500-word essay about how they exemplify the traits of selfless service, leadership, character, and their aspirations. Financial need is not considered in the selection process.
Financial data Stipends are $500 or $1,000.
Duration 1 year.
Number awarded 20 to 25 each year.
Deadline January of each year.

[1392]
NMCCG ENLISTED DEPENDENT SPOUSE SCHOLARSHIP

Navy Wives Clubs of America
c/o NSA Mid-South
Attn: Allison Barnes, National Vice President
8885 Bass Road
P.O. Box 54022
Millington, TN 38054-0022
Toll Free: (866) 511-NWCA
E-mail: nwca@navywivesclubsofamerica.org
Web: www.navywivesclubsofamerica.org/scholarships

Summary To provide financial assistance for undergraduate or graduate study to spouses of naval personnel.
Eligibility This program is open to Navy, Marine Corps, or Coast Guard dependent spouse: active duty, retired, widow, or widower. Applicants must be 1) a high school graduate or senior planning to attend college full time next year; 2) currently enrolled in an undergraduate program and planning to continue as a full-time undergraduate; 3) a college graduate or senior planning to be a full-time graduate student next year; or 4) a high school graduate or GED recipient planning to attend vocational or business school next year. Along with their application, they must submit a brief statement on why they feel they should be awarded this scholarship and any special circumstances (financial or other) they wish to have considered. Financial need is also considered in the selection process.
Financial data The stipends range from $500 to $1,000 each year (depending upon the donations from chapters of the Navy Wives Clubs of America).
Duration 1 year.
Additional information This program includes the Cecilia Clark Scholarship.
Number awarded 2 each year.
Deadline March of each year.

[1393]
NORTHEASTERN REGION KOREAN WAR VETERAN DESCENDANT SCHOLARSHIPS

Korean American Scholarship Foundation
Northeastern Region
Attn: Scholarship Committee Chair
By Design, LLC
463 Seventh Avenue, Suite 200
New York, NY 10018
E-mail: nerc.scholarship@kasf.org
Web: www.kasf.org/apply-nerc

Summary To provide financial assistance to the descendants of the Korean War from any state who are working on an undergraduate or graduate degree in any field at a school in northeastern states.
Eligibility This program is open to direct descendants of veterans who served in Korea from June 25, 1950 to January 31, 1955. Applicants may reside in any state, but they must be enrolled as full-time undergraduate or graduate students at a college or university in Connecticut, Maine, Massachusetts, New Hampshire, New Jersey, New York, Rhode Island, or Vermont. They must have a GPA of 3.0 or higher. Selection is based on academic achievement, an essay, extracurricular activities, and recommendations.
Financial data Stipends range from $500 to $5,000.
Duration 1 year.
Number awarded 1 or more each year.
Deadline June of each year.

[1394]
OHIO LEGION COLLEGE OR UNIVERSITY SCHOLARSHIPS

American Legion
Department of Ohio
60 Big Run Road
P.O. Box 8007
Delaware, OH 43015
(740) 362-7478   Fax: (740) 362-1429
E-mail: legion@ohiolegion.com
Web: www.ohiolegion.com/programs/scholarships

Summary To provide financial assistance to residents of Ohio who are descendants of members of the American Legion and attending college in any state.
Eligibility This program is open to residents of Ohio who are children, grandchildren or great-grandchildren of living or deceased Legionnaires. Applicants must be attending colleges, universities, or other approved postsecondary schools in any state as undergraduate or graduate students. They must have a high school and college GPA of 3.5 or higher and an ACT score of at least 25. Along with their application, they must submit a personal statement of 500 to 550 words on their career objectives. Selection is based on academic achievement as measured by course grades, ACT scores, difficulty of curriculum, participation in school and outside activities, and the judging committee's general impression.
Financial data Stipends are normally at least $2,000.
Duration 1 year.
Number awarded 1 or more each year.
Deadline April of each year.

[1395]
OHIO LEGION SURVIVING SPOUSE OR CHILD SCHOLARSHIPS

American Legion
Department of Ohio
60 Big Run Road
P.O. Box 8007
Delaware, OH 43015
(740) 362-7478   Fax: (740) 362-1429
E-mail: legion@ohiolegion.com
Web: www.ohiolegion.com/programs/scholarships

Summary To provide financial assistance to residents of Ohio who are surviving spouses or children of deceased service members and interested in attending college in any state.
Eligibility This program is open to residents of Ohio who are surviving spouses or children of service members who died on active duty or from injuries received on active duty Applicants must be attending or planning to attend colleges, universities, or other approved postsecondary schools in any state as an undergraduate or graduate student. They must have a GPA of 3.5 or higher and an ACT score of at least 25. Along with their application, they must submit a personal statement of 500 to 550 words on their career objectives. Selection is based on academic achievement as measured by course grades, ACT scores, difficulty of curriculum, partic-

ipation in school and outside activities, and the judging committee's general impression.
Financial data Stipends are normally at least $2,000.
Duration 1 year.
Number awarded 1 or more each year.
Deadline April of each year.

[1396]
PENNSYLVANIA NATIONAL GUARD MILITARY FAMILY EDUCATION PROGRAM (MFEP)

Pennsylvania Higher Education Assistance Agency
Attn: State Grant and Special Programs
1200 North Seventh Street
P.O. Box 8157
Harrisburg, PA 17105-8157
(717) 720-2800 Toll Free: (800) 692-7392
Fax: (717) 720-3786 TDD: (800) 654-5988
E-mail: info@pheaa.org
Web: www.pheaa.org

Summary To provide financial assistance for college or graduate school to dependents of Pennsylvania National Guard members who agree to an additional service commitment.
Eligibility This program is open to children and spouses of members of the Pennsylvania National Guard who have completed an initial service obligation and reenlist for a period of 6 years. Applicants must be enrolled or planning to enroll full or part time in an approved undergraduate or graduate program of education at an approved institution of higher learning in Pennsylvania. Children can use this benefit up to reaching 26 years of age. Spouses can use the benefit up to 6 years after the Guard member's separation from the Guard. The Guard member can assign the entire benefit to 1 dependent or a portion of the benefit to more than 1 dependent.
Financial data Full-time students receive the lesser of 100% of tuition plus technology fee at the institution where they are enrolled or the annual tuition rate and technology fee charged to a Pennsylvania resident at a state-owned university. Part-time students receive the lesser of 100% of the tuition plus technology fee for a part-time course of study at their institution or the per credit tuition rate charged to a Pennsylvania resident at a state-owned university plus the technology fee. The Guard member must honor the service commitment or repay all funds received, plus interest.
Duration Up to 5 years.
Additional information This program, first offered in 2020, is jointly administered by the Pennsylvania Department of Military and Veterans Affairs and the Pennsylvania Higher Education Assistance Agency.
Number awarded Varies each year.
Deadline Deadline not specified.

[1397]
PETER CONNACHER MEMORIAL SCHOLARSHIPS

Oregon Office of Student Access and Completion
Attn: Scholarships
1500 Valley River Drive, Suite 100
Eugene, OR 97401-2146
(541) 687-7400 Toll Free: (800) 452-8807
Fax: (541) 687-7414 TDD: (800) 735-2900
E-mail: osac@hecc.oregon.gov
Web: app.oregonstudentaid.gov/Catalog/Default.aspx

Summary To provide financial assistance for college or graduate school to ex-prisoners of war and their descendants.
Eligibility Applicants must be U.S. citizens who 1) were military or civilian prisoners of war; or 2) are the descendants of ex-prisoners of war. They must be full-time undergraduate or graduate students. A copy of the ex-prisoner of war's discharge papers from the U.S. armed forces must accompany the application. In addition, written proof of POW status must be submitted, along with a statement of the relationship between the applicant and the ex-prisoner of war (father, grandfather, etc.). Selection is based on academic record and financial need. Preference is given to Oregon residents or their dependents.
Financial data Stipends for scholarships offered by the Oregon Office of Student Access and Completion (OSAC) range from $1,000 to $10,000 but recently averaged $4,710.
Duration 1 year; may be renewed for up to 3 additional years for undergraduate students or 2 additional years for graduate students. Renewal is dependent on evidence of continued financial need and satisfactory academic progress.
Additional information This program is administered by the OSAC with funds provided by the Oregon Community Foundation and by the Columbia River Chapter of American Ex-prisoners of War, Inc.
Number awarded Varies each year; recently, 4 were awarded.
Deadline February of each year.

[1398]
PHS COMMISSIONED OFFICERS FOUNDATION DEPENDENT SCHOLARSHIP PROGRAM

Commissioned Officers Association of the U.S. Public Health Service
Attn: PHS Commissioned Officers Foundation for the Advancement of Public Health
8201 Corporate Drive, Suite 200
Landover, MD 20785
(301) 731-9080 Fax: (301) 731-9084
E-mail: scholarship@coausphs.org
Web: www.phscof.org/education/cof-scholarship-program

Summary To provide financial assistance to spouses and descendants of members of the Commissioned Officers Association of the U.S. Public Health Service (COA) who are interested in working on an undergraduate or graduate degree in any of the Public Health Service (PHS) categories.
Eligibility This program is open to high school seniors, undergraduates, and graduate students who are the spouse, child, or grandchild of an active-duty or retired COA member. Applicants must be preparing for a career in a PHS category (e.g., dentist, dietician, engineer, nurse, pharmacist, physician, clinical or rehabilitation therapist, veterinarian). Along with their application, they must submit a 1-page essay on what they intend to accomplish with their degrees and how their area of focus may relate to any of the PHS professional categories.
Financial data The stipend is approximately $1,000.
Duration 1 year.
Number awarded Varies each year; recently, 18 were awarded.
Deadline June of each year.

[1399]
REBECCA POST SIKES MEMORIAL SCHOLARSHIP

Operation Once in a Lifetime
P.O. Box 797052
Dallas, TX 75379
(214) 263-9880
E-mail: contact@operationonceinalifetime.com
Web: www.operationonceinalifetime.com

Summary To provide financial assistance for college to spouses of active duty military members and veterans.

Eligibility This program is open to spouses of active duty military members and veterans who are attending an accredited public or nonprofit independent college. Applicants may be working on an undergraduate or graduate degree. They must have a GPA of 2.0 or higher.

Financial data A stipend is awarded (amount not specified).

Duration 1 year.

Number awarded 1 or more each year.

Deadline Deadline not specified.

[1400]
RED RIVER VALLEY FIGHTER PILOTS ASSOCIATION KINSHIP SCHOLARSHIP GRANT PROGRAM

Red River Valley Association Foundation
Attn: Executive Director
1376 Needham Circle West
York, PA 17404
(717) 505-8529   E-mail: ExecDir@river-rats.org
Web: www.river-rats.org/about-us/scholarship-program.html

Summary To provide financial assistance for college or graduate school to the spouses and children of selected service personnel and members of the Red River Valley Fighter Pilots Association.

Eligibility This program is open to the spouses and children of 1) U.S. aircrew members missing in action (MIA) or killed in action (KIA) in combat situations involving U.S. military forces from August 1964 through the present; 2) U.S. military aircrew members killed in a non-combat aircraft accident in which they were performing aircrew duties; and 3) current members of the association and deceased members who were in good standing at the time of their death. Applicants must be enrolled or planning to enroll full or part time at an accredited college, university, vocational/technical institute, or career school to work on an undergraduate or graduate degree. Selection is based on demonstrated academic achievement, SAT or ACT scores, financial need, and accomplishments in school, church, civic, and social activities.

Financial data The amount awarded varies, depending upon the need of the recipient. Recently, undergraduate stipends have ranged from $500 to $3,500 and averaged $1,725; graduate stipends have ranged from $500 to $2,000 and averaged $1,670. Funds are paid directly to the recipient's institution and are to be used for tuition, fees, books, and room and board for full-time students.

Duration 1 year; may be renewed if the recipient maintains a GPA of 2.0 or higher.

Additional information This program began in 1970, out of concern for the families of aircrews (known as "River Rats") who were killed or missing in action in the Red River Valley of North Vietnam.

Number awarded Varies each year; since this program was established, it has awarded more than 1,130 scholarships worth more than $2,300,000.

Deadline June of each year.

[1401]
RESTORING FAMILY SCHOLARSHIP

Hope for the Warriors
Attn: Scholarship Committee
5518 Port Royal Road
Springfield, VA 22151
(703) 321-0588   Toll Free: (877) 2HOPE4W
Fax: (703) 256-3702
E-mail: scholarships@hopeforthewarriors.org
Web: www.hopeforthewarriors.org

Summary To provide financial assistance for college or graduate school to spouses and caregivers of deceased veterans who served after September 11, 2001.

Eligibility This program is open to spouses and caregivers of military personnel who were killed as a result of service after September 11, 2001. Applicants must be enrolled or planning to enroll at an accredited college, university, or trade school in any state. They must be working on an undergraduate or graduate degree in any field. Along with their application, they must submit an essay on their academic achievement and personal goals. Financial need is not considered in the selection process.

Financial data The stipend is at least $2,000.

Duration 1 year.

Additional information This program began in 2008.

Number awarded Normally, 2 each year (1 each semester).

Deadline May of each year for fall semester; October of each year for spring semester.

[1402]
RESTORING HOPE SCHOLARSHIP

Hope for the Warriors
Attn: Scholarship Committee
5518 Port Royal Road
Springfield, VA 22151
(703) 321-0588   Toll Free: (877) 2HOPE4W
Fax: (703) 256-3702
E-mail: scholarships@hopeforthewarriors.org
Web: www.hopeforthewarriors.org

Summary To provide financial assistance for work on a master's degree in social work to spouses and caregivers of deceased and disabled veterans who served after September 11, 2001.

Eligibility This program is open to spouses and caregivers of military personnel who were killed or became disabled as a result of service after September 11, 2001. Applicants must be enrolled or planning to enroll in a master's degree in social work program at an accredited college, university, or trade school. Along with their application, they must submit an essay on their academic achievement and personal goals. Financial need is not considered in the selection process.

Financial data The stipend is at least $2,000.

Duration 1 year.

Additional information This program began in 2008.

Number awarded Normally, 2 each year (1 each semester).

Deadline May of each year for fall semester; October of each year for spring semester.

[1403]
RON PACE MEMORIAL SCHOLARSHIP

American Academy of Physician Assistants
Attn: Physician Assistant Foundation
2318 Mill Road, Suite 1300
Alexandria, VA 22314-6868
(571) 319-4510   E-mail: pafoundation@aapa.org
Web: app.smarterselect.com

Summary To provide financial assistance to student members of the American Academy of Physician Assistants (AAPA) who are veterans from Florida.

Eligibility This program is open to student members of the Florida Academy of Physician Assistants who have completed at least 1 semester of an accredited physician assistant program in Florida. Applicants must be veterans or dependent children of veterans.

Financial data The stipend is $1,000.

Duration 1 year; nonrenewable.

Number awarded 1 each year.

Deadline May of each year.

[1404]
RUARK-WIGHT FAMILY SCHOLARSHIP

Marines' Memorial Association
c/o Marines Memorial Club and Hotel
609 Sutter Street
San Francisco, CA 94102
(415) 673-6672, ext. 293   Toll Free: (800) 5-MARINE
Fax: (415) 441-3649
E-mail: scholarship@marineclub.com
Web: www.marinesmemorial.org/members/scholarships

Summary To provide financial assistance to veterans, military personnel, and their families who are interested in attending college or graduate school to work on a degree in any field.

Eligibility This program is open to students who meet 1 of the following requirements: 1) have served honorably or is currently serving in any branch of the U.S. armed forces; or 2) is the spouse or child of a person who served honorably or is currently serving in any branch of the U.S. armed forces. Applicants must be enrolled as full-time sophomores, juniors, seniors or graduate students working on a degree in any field. They must have a GPA of 2.5 or higher. Membership in the sponsoring organization is not required for student veterans. Along with their application, they must submit an essay of up to 500 words on why they chose their specific path of study, what they hope to accomplish after graduation with their degree, and how their efforts will benefit others in their community. Selection is based on the essay, academic merit, references, and financial need.

Financial data The stipend is $5,000 per year.

Duration 1 year; recipients may reapply for up to 3 additional years.

Number awarded 1 each year.

Deadline April of each year.

[1405]
SCNGF ACADEMIC EXCELLENCE LEADERSHIP SCHOLARSHIPS

National Guard Association of South Carolina
Attn: South Carolina National Guard Foundation
132 Pickens Street
P.O. Box 7606
Columbia, SC 29202
(803) 254-8456   Toll Free: (800) 822-3235
Fax: (803) 254-3869   E-mail: dianne@scngf.org
Web: www.scngf.org/scngfscholarshipapplication

Summary To provide financial assistance to South Carolina National Guard members and their dependents who are interested in attending college or graduate school in any state.

Eligibility This program is open to members of the South Carolina National Guard and dependents of active or retired members. Applicants must be enrolled or planning to enroll full time at a 4-year college or university in any state as an undergraduate student. Guard members, but not dependents, are also eligible to attend graduate school. Applicants must have a GPA of 3.5 or higher and a record of involvement and leadership in school, civic, and/or community activities. Selection is based on excellence in academics and leadership; financial need is not considered.

Financial data The stipend is $1,500 per year. Funds are disbursed directly to the recipient's institution.

Duration 1 year; may be renewed up to 3 additional years.

Number awarded Varies each year; recently, this sponsor awarded a total of 75 scholarships through both of its programs.

Deadline February of each year.

[1406]
SCNGF FINANCIAL NEED/ACADEMIC ACHIEVEMENT SCHOLARSHIPS

National Guard Association of South Carolina
Attn: South Carolina National Guard Foundation
132 Pickens Street
P.O. Box 7606
Columbia, SC 29202
(803) 254-8456   Toll Free: (800) 822-3235
Fax: (803) 254-3869   E-mail: dianne@scngf.org
Web: www.scngf.org/scngfscholarshipapplication

Summary To provide financial assistance to South Carolina National Guard members and their dependents who are interested in attending college or graduate school in any state and can demonstrate financial need.

Eligibility This program is open to members of the South Carolina National Guard and dependents of active or retired members. Applicants must be enrolled or planning to enroll full time at a college or university in any state as an undergraduate student. Guard members, but not dependents, are also eligible to attend graduate school. Applicants must have a GPA of 2.5 or higher and a record of involvement and leadership in school, civic, and/or community activities. High school seniors must also submit SAT and/or ACT scores. Selection is based on excellence in academics and leadership and on financial need.

Financial data The stipend is $1,000 per year. Funds are disbursed directly to the recipient's institution.

Duration 1 year; may be renewed up to 3 additional years.

Number awarded Varies each year; recently, this sponsor awarded a total of 75 scholarships through both of its programs.
Deadline February of each year.

[1407]
SCREAMING EAGLE SURVIVING CHILDREN'S SCHOLARSHIP

101st Airborne Division Association
32 Screaming Eagle Boulevard
P.O. Box 929
Fort Campbell, KY 42223-0929
(931) 431-0199   Fax: (931) 431-0195
E-mail: 101exec@screamingeagle.org
Web: www.screamingeaglefoundation.org

Summary To provide financial assistance for college or graduate school to the children of soldiers of the 101st Airborne Division and Fort Campbell Units who have been killed or severely wounded since September 11, 2001.
Eligibility This program is open to dependent children of active-duty personnel who were assigned to the 101st Airborne Division or a tenant military organization assigned to Fort Campbell, Kentucky. The parent must have been killed, wounded, or injured while serving in support of the Global War on Terrorism on or after September 11, 2001. Applicants must be high school seniors or graduates up to 22 years of age, enrolled or planning to enroll full time at an accredited 2- or 4-year college, university, graduate program, or vocational/technical school. Along with their application, they must submit a 1-page letter on what this scholarship means to them.
Financial data The stipend is $2,500.
Duration 1 year.
Additional information This program is sponsored by the Screaming Eagle Foundation of the 101st Airborne Division Association in partnership with the Patriot Foundation.
Number awarded Varies each year.
Deadline March of each year.

[1408]
SENATOR DANIEL K. INOUYE MEMORIAL SCHOLARSHIP

Japanese American Veterans Association
Attn: Chris DeRosa, Scholarship Committee Chair
P.O. Box 341198
Bethesda, MD 20827
E-mail: javascholarship222@gmail.com
Web: www.java.wildapricot.org

Summary To provide financial assistance for college or graduate school to relatives of Japanese American veterans who plan a career in the military or public service.
Eligibility This program is open to students who 1) have completed at least 1 year of an undergraduate program or are currently enrolled in graduate school and are preparing for a career in the military or public service; 2) are currently enrolled in a university or college ROTC program or the U.S. Marine Corps Platoon Leaders Course but are not receiving an ROTC scholarship; or 3) are disabled veterans. Applicants must also be 1) a direct or collateral descendant of a person who served with the 442nd Regimental Combat Team, the 100th Infantry Battalion, Military Intelligence Service, 1399th Engineering Construction Battalion, or other unit associated with those during or after World War II; or 2) a member or child of a member of the Japanese American Veterans Association (JAVA) whose membership extends back at least 1 year. Along with their application, they must submit a 500-word essay on their plan and vision to serve America through public service or the military.
Financial data The stipend is $5,000.
Duration 1 year.
Number awarded 1 each year.
Deadline March of each year.

[1409]
SFC CURTIS MANCINI MEMORIAL SCHOLARSHIPS

Association of the United States Army-Rhode Island Chapter
c/o LTC Robert A. Galvanin, President
31 Canoe River Drive
Mansfield, MA 02048
(508) 339-5301   E-mail: bpje5310@verizon.net
Web: www.riroa.org/ausari/scholarship.htm

Summary To provide financial assistance to members of the Rhode Island Chapter of the Association of the United States Army (AUSA) and their families who are interested in attending college or graduate school in any state.
Eligibility This program is open to members of the AUSA Rhode Island Chapter and their family members (spouses, children, and grandchildren). Applicants must be high school seniors or graduates accepted at an accredited college, university, or vocational/technical school in any state or current undergraduate or graduate students. Along with their application, they must submit a 250-word essay on why they feel their achievements should qualify them for this award. Selection is based on academic and individual achievements; financial need is not considered. Special consideration is given to students or graduates of Lincoln High School in Lincoln, Rhode Island (the alma mater of this program's namesake), especially those preparing for a career in law enforcement or enrolled or planning to enroll in Army ROTC.
Financial data The stipend is $1,000.
Duration 1 year.
Additional information Membership in the AUSA is open to everyone who supports a strong national defense, with special concern for the Army. That includes Regular Army, National Guard, Army Reserve, government civilians, retired soldiers, Wounded Warriors, veterans, concerned citizens and family members.
Number awarded Several each year.
Deadline April of each year.

[1410]
SGT. FREDERICK C. BRACE, JR. MEMORIAL SCHOLARSHIP

American Academy of Physician Assistants-Veterans Caucus
Attn: Scholarship Program
P.O. Box 362
Ossining, NY 10562
(803) 328-1864   Fax: (704) 838-8494
E-mail: rmunsee@veteranscaucus.org
Web: www.veteranscaucus.org/scholarships

Summary To provide financial assistance to Air Force veterans and their dependents who are studying to become physician assistants.

Eligibility This program is open to U.S. citizens who are currently enrolled in a physician assistant program. Applicants must be honorably discharged members of the United States Air Force or the dependent of an Air Force veteran. Along with their application, they must submit a personal statement about what led them to attend PA school; their background, present, and future intentions; and why they deserve to receive a scholarship. Selection is based on military honors and awards received, civic and college honors and awards received, professional memberships and activities, potential for future achievement, and GPA.
Financial data The stipend is $2,000.
Duration 1 year.
Number awarded 1 each year.
Deadline February of each year.

[1411]
SMSGT. NATHAN L. LIPSCOMB, SR. MEMORIAL SCHOLARSHIP

American Academy of Physician Assistants-Veterans Caucus
Attn: Scholarship Program
P.O. Box 362
Ossining, NY 10562
(803) 328-1864   Fax: (704) 838-8494
E-mail: rmunsee@veteranscaucus.org
Web: www.veteranscaucus.org/scholarships

Summary To provide financial assistance to Air Force veterans and their dependents who are studying to become physician assistants.
Eligibility This program is open to U.S. citizens who are currently enrolled in a physician assistant program. Applicants must be honorably discharged members of the United States Air Force or the dependent of an Air Force veteran. Along with their application, they must submit a personal statement about what led them to attend PA school; their background, present, and future intentions; and why they deserve to receive a scholarship. Selection is based on military honors and awards received, civic and college honors and awards received, professional memberships and activities, potential for future achievement, and GPA.
Financial data The stipend is $2,000.
Duration 1 year.
Number awarded 1 each year.
Deadline February of each year.

[1412]
SOUTHERN REGION KOREAN WAR VETERAN DESCENDANT SCHOLARSHIPS

Korean American Scholarship Foundation
Southern Region
Attn: Scholarship Committee Chair
P.O. Box 67
Duluth, GA 30097
E-mail: src.scholarship@kasf.org
Web: www.kasf.org/apply-src

Summary To provide financial assistance to the descendants of the Korean War from any state who are working on an undergraduate or graduate degree in any field at a school in southern states.
Eligibility This program is open to direct descendants of veterans who served in Korea from June 25, 1950 to January 31, 1955. Applicants may reside in any state, but they must be enrolled as full-time undergraduate or graduate students at a college or university in Alabama, Florida, Georgia, South Carolina, or Tennessee. They must have a GPA of 3.0 or higher. Selection is based on academic achievement, an essay, extracurricular activities, and recommendations.
Financial data Stipends range from $500 to $5,000.
Duration 1 year.
Number awarded Varies each year; recently, 15 were awarded.
Deadline June of each year.

[1413]
SSGT. ROBERT V. MILNER MEMORIAL SCHOLARSHIP

American Academy of Physician Assistants-Veterans Caucus
Attn: Scholarship Program
P.O. Box 362
Ossining, NY 10562
(803) 328-1864   Fax: (704) 838-8494
E-mail: rmunsee@veteranscaucus.org
Web: www.veteranscaucus.org/scholarships

Summary To provide financial assistance to Air Force veterans and their dependents who are studying to become physician assistants.
Eligibility This program is open to U.S. citizens who are currently enrolled in a physician assistant program. Applicants must be honorably discharged members of the United States Air Force or the dependent of an Air Force veteran. Along with their application, they must submit a personal statement about what led them to attend PA school; their background, present, and future intentions; and why they deserve to receive a scholarship. Selection is based on military honors and awards received, civic and college honors and awards received, professional memberships and activities, potential for future achievement, and GPA.
Financial data The stipend is $2,000.
Duration 1 year.
Number awarded 1 each year.
Deadline February of each year.

[1414]
STANLEY A. DORAN MEMORIAL SCHOLARSHIPS

Fleet Reserve Association
Attn: FRA Education Foundation
125 North West Street
Alexandria, VA 22314-2754
(703) 683-1400   Toll Free: (800) FRA-1924
Fax: (703) 549-6610   E-mail: scholars@fra.org
Web: www.fra.org

Summary To provide financial assistance for college or graduate school to children of members of the Fleet Reserve Association (FRA).
Eligibility This program is open to the dependent children of FRA members who are in good standing (or were at the time of death, if deceased). Applicants must be working on or planning to work full time on an undergraduate or graduate degree. Along with their application, they must submit transcripts that include (for high school students and college freshmen) SAT and/or ACT scores; a list of school and community activities; at least 2 letters of recommendation; and an

essay on why they want to go to college and what they intend to accomplish with their degree. Selection is based on academic record, financial need, extracurricular activities, leadership skills, and participation in community activities. U.S. citizenship is required.

Financial data The stipend is $5,000 per year.

Duration 1 year; may be renewed.

Additional information Membership in the FRA is open to current and former enlisted members of the Navy, Marine Corps, and Coast Guard.

Number awarded 1 each year.

Deadline April of each year.

[1415]
SURVIVORS' AND DEPENDENTS' EDUCATIONAL ASSISTANCE PROGRAM

Department of Veterans Affairs
Attn: Veterans Benefits Administration
810 Vermont Avenue, N.W.
Washington, DC 20420
(202) 418-4343   Toll Free: (844) 698-2311
Web: www.va.gov

Summary To provide financial assistance for undergraduate or graduate study to children and spouses of deceased and disabled veterans, MIAs, and POWs.

Eligibility Eligible for this assistance are spouses and children of 1) veterans who died or are permanently and totally disabled as the result of active service in the armed forces; 2) veterans who died from any cause while rated permanently and totally disabled from a service-connected disability; 3) servicemembers listed as missing in action or captured in the line of duty by a hostile force; 4) servicemembers listed as forcibly detained or interned by a foreign government or power; and 5) servicemembers who are hospitalized or receiving outpatient treatment for a service-connected permanent and total disability and are likely to be discharged for that disability. Children must be between 18 and 26 years of age, although extensions may be granted. Spouses and children over 14 years of age with physical or mental disabilities are also eligible.

Financial data Monthly stipends for study at an academic institution are $1,248 for full time, $986 for three-quarter time, or $724 for half-time. Other rates apply for apprenticeship and on-the-job training, farm cooperative training, and special restorative training.

Duration Benefits are provided for up to 45 months (or the equivalent in part-time training). Some beneficiaries who qualify for more than 1 education program may be eligible for up to 81 months. Spouses must complete their training within 10 years of the date they are first found eligible. For spouses of servicemembers who died on active duty, benefits end 20 years from the date of death.

Additional information Benefits may be used to work on associate, bachelor's, or graduate degrees at colleges and universities, including independent study, cooperative training, and study abroad programs. Courses leading to a certificate or diploma from business, technical, or vocational schools may also be taken. Other eligible programs include apprenticeships, on-the-job training programs, farm cooperative courses, and correspondence courses (for spouses only). Remedial, deficiency, and refresher courses may be approved under certain circumstances.

Number awarded Varies each year.

Deadline Applications may be submitted at any time.

[1416]
TENTH MOUNTAIN DIVISION FOUNDATION SCHOLARSHIP

Tenth Mountain Division Foundation
Attn: Scholarship Fund
133 South Van Gordon Street, Suite 200
Lakewood, CO 80228
(303) 756-8486   Fax: (303) 988-3005
E-mail: tenthmtnfdn@nsp.org
Web: www.10thmountainfoundation.org

Summary To provide financial assistance for college or graduate school to descendants of former members of the 10th Mountain Division.

Eligibility This program is open to the descendants of veterans who served in the 10th Mountain Division during World War II. Applicants must be college juniors, seniors, or graduate students. They must be able to demonstrate financial need and a knowledge of the history of the Division and their ancestor's service in the Division during World War II. If there are more qualifying applicants than available scholarships, selection is based on a lottery.

Financial data The stipend is $5,000 per year.

Duration 1 year; may be renewed 1 additional year.

Number awarded Up to 5 each year.

Deadline April each year.

[1417]
THE PFC ROGER W. CUMMINS MEMORIAL SCHOLARSHIP

American Academy of Physician Assistants-Veterans
  Caucus
Attn: Scholarship Program
P.O. Box 362
Ossining, NY 10562
(803) 328-1864   Fax: (704) 838-8494
E-mail: rmunsee@veteranscaucus.org
Web: www.veteranscaucus.org/scholarships

Summary To provide financial assistance to Marine Corps and Navy service members or veterans or family members who are studying to become physician assistants.

Eligibility This program is open to U.S. citizens who are currently enrolled in a physician assistant program. Applicants must be active-duty members of the U.S. Marine Corps or Navy Corpsmen who have served with the Marine Corps, veterans of those services, or their spouses or children. Along with their application, they must submit a personal statement about what led them to attend PA school; their background, present, and future intentions; and why they deserve to receive a scholarship. Selection is based on military honors and awards received, civic and college honors and awards received, professional memberships and activities, potential for future achievement, and GPA.

Financial data The stipend is $2,000.

Duration 1 year.

Number awarded 1 each year.

Deadline February of each year.

FELLOWSHIPS: FAMILY MEMBERS

[1418]
THOMAS H. MILLER SCHOLARSHIP
Blinded Veterans Association
Attn: Scholarship Coordinator
125 North West Street, Third Floor
Alexandria, VA 22314
(202) 371-8880, ext. 330   Toll Free: (800) 669-7079
Fax: (202) 371-8258   E-mail: bjones@bva.org
Web: www.bva.org

Summary To provide financial assistance for undergraduate or graduate study, especially of music or the fine arts, to immediate family of blinded veterans and servicemembers.
Eligibility This program is open to dependent children, grandchildren, and spouses of blinded veterans and active-duty blinded servicemembers of the U.S. armed forces. The veteran or servicemember must be legally blind; the blindness may be either service-connected or nonservice-connected. Applicants must have been accepted or be currently enrolled as a full-time student in an undergraduate or graduate program at an accredited institution of higher learning. Preference is given to students of music or the fine arts. Along with their application, they must submit a 300-word essay on their career goals and aspirations. Financial need is not considered in the selection process.
Financial data The stipend is $1,000; funds are intended to be used to cover the student's expenses, including tuition, other academic fees, books, dormitory fees, and cafeteria fees. Funds are paid directly to the recipient's school.
Duration 1 year; recipients may reapply for up to 3 additional years.
Number awarded 1 each year.
Deadline April of each year.

[1419]
TILLMAN MILITARY SCHOLARS PROGRAM
Pat Tillman Foundation
222 North Merchandise Mart Plaza, Suite 1212
Chicago, IL 60654
(773) 360-5277
E-mail: scholarships@pattillmanfoundation.org
Web: www.pattillmanfoundation.org/apply-to-be-a-scholar

Summary To provide financial assistance to veterans, active servicemembers, and their spouses who are interested in working on an undergraduate or graduate degree.
Eligibility This program is open to veterans and active servicemembers of all branches of the armed forces from both the pre- and post-September 11 era and their spouses; children are not eligible. Applicants must be enrolled or planning to enroll full time at a 4-year public or private college or university to work on an undergraduate, graduate, or postgraduate degree. Current and former servicemembers must submit 400-word essays on 1) their motivation and decision to serve in the U.S. military and how that decision and experience has changed their life and ambitions; and 2) their educational and career goals, how they will incorporate their military service experience into those goals, and how they intend to continue their service to others and the community. Spouses must submit 400-word essays on 1) their previous service to others and the community; and 2) their educational and career goals, how they will incorporate their service experiences and the impact of their spouse's military service into those goals, and how they intend to continue their service to others and the community. Selection is based on those essays, educational and career ambitions, record of military service, record of personal achievement, demonstration of service to others in the community, desire to continue such service, and leadership potential.
Financial data The stipend depends on the need of the recipient and the availability of funds; recently, stipends averaged approximately $11,000 per year.
Duration 1 year; may be renewed, provided the recipient maintains a GPA of 3.0 or higher, remains enrolled full time, and documents participation in civic action or community service.
Additional information This program began in 2009.
Number awarded Approximately 60 each year. Since the program began, it has awarded more than $15 million to 580 scholars.
Deadline February of each year.

[1420]
TRANSFER OF POST-9/11 GI-BILL BENEFITS TO DEPENDENTS
Department of Veterans Affairs
Attn: Veterans Benefits Administration
810 Vermont Avenue, N.W.
Washington, DC 20420
(202) 418-4343   Toll Free: (888) 442-4551
Web: www.va.gov

Summary To provide financial assistance to dependents of military personnel who qualify for Post-9/11 GI Bill benefits and agree to transfer unused benefits to their spouse or child.
Eligibility This program is open to dependents of current military personnel whose parent or spouse has at least 6 years of service in the armed forces (active duty and/or Selected Reserve) and agrees to serve 4 additional years. The military parent or spouse must agree to transfer unused months of educational benefits to a dependent while still serving on active duty. Dependents must be enrolled or planning to enroll in an educational program, including work on an undergraduate or graduate degree, vocational/technical training, on-the-job training, flight training, correspondence training, licensing and national testing programs, entrepreneurship training, and tutorial assistance.
Financial data Dependents working on an undergraduate or graduate degree at public institutions in their state receive full payment of tuition and fees. For dependents who attend private institutions in most states, tuition and fee reimbursement is capped at $25,162.14 per academic year. Benefits for other types of training programs depend on the amount for which the spouse or parent qualified under prior educational programs. Dependents also receive a monthly housing allowance that is 1) based on the Department of Defense Basic Allowance for Housing (BAH) for an E-5 with dependents (which depends on the location of the school but ranges from approximately $1,000 per month to approximately $2,500 per month); 2) $1,789 per month at schools in foreign countries; or 3) $894.50 per month for online training classes. They also receive an annual book allowance of $1,000 and (for participants who live in a rural county remote from an educational institution) a rural benefit payment of $500 per year.
Duration Military members may transfer all or a portion of their 36 months of entitlement to a dependent. Spouses may start to use the benefit immediately, but children may use the

benefit only after they have completed high school (or equivalency certificate) or reached 18 years of age. They are not subject to the 15-year limit but may not use the benefit after reaching 26 years of age.
Additional information This supplement was added to the Post-9/11 GI Bill program as a result of legislation passed by Congress in 2010.
Number awarded Varies each year.
Deadline Deadline not specified.

[1421]
UNIFIED ARIZONA VETERANS SCHOLARSHIPS
Unified Arizona Veterans, Inc.
Attn: Scholarship Committee
P.O. Box 34338
Phoenix, AZ 85067
E-mail: scholarships@azuav.org
Web: www.azuav.org

Summary To provide financial assistance to veterans and military personnel in Arizona who are interested in attending college in the state.
Eligibility This program is open to residents of Arizona who are 1) honorably discharged veterans; 2) currently on active duty, including service members in good standing with a Reserve or Guard components; or 3) immediate family members of an Arizona veteran killed in action or by an act of terror. Applicants must be enrolled at an institution of higher learning in Arizona and working on a bachelor's or master's degree in any field. Along with their application, they must submit 1) a 1-page essay on why they chose their current academic program and how they plan to use their degree, certificate, or license; 2) letters of recommendation; 3) verification of enrollment and Arizona residency; and 4) documentation of financial need.
Financial data Stipends range up to $5,000.
Duration 1 year.
Number awarded 1 or more each year.
Deadline February of each year.

[1422]
VETERANS UNITED FOUNDATION SCHOLARSHIPS
Veterans United Home Loans
Attn: Veterans United Foundation
1400 Veterans United Drive
Columbia, MO 65203
(573) 445-7999   Toll Free: (800) 884-5560
E-mail: customer_service@vu.com
Web: www.enhancelives.com/scholarships

Summary To provide financial assistance for college or graduate school to surviving children and spouses of deceased or disabled U.S. military veterans.
Eligibility This program is open to surviving spouses and children of deceased servicemembers from a service-related death or of a veteran with a 100% service-connected disability. Applicants must be attending or planning to attend a college or university to work on an associate, bachelor's, graduate, postgraduate, or doctoral degree. Along with their application, they must submit documentation of financial need; a list of community, church, sports, or school involvement or achievements; and an essay on their story, including how losing their spouse or parent has affected them, who they are, where their life has taken them, and what they hope to do with their college education and beyond.
Financial data The stipend ranges up to $20,000.
Duration 1 year; nonrenewable.
Additional information This program began in 2012.
Number awarded Up to 5 each year. Since the program began, it has awarded $200,000 in scholarships to 65 students.
Deadline October of each year. Only the first 250 applications received are accepted.

[1423]
VICE ADMIRAL ROBERT L. WALTERS SCHOLARSHIP
Surface Navy Association
Attn: Scholarship Coordinator
6564 Loisdale Court, Suite 318
Springfield, VA 22150
(703) 960-6800   Toll Free: (800) NAVY-SNA
Fax: (703) 960-6807   E-mail: navysna@aol.com
Web: www.navysna.org/scholarship/information.html

Summary To provide financial assistance for college or graduate school to members of the Surface Navy Association (SNA) and their dependents.
Eligibility This program is open to SNA members and their children, stepchildren, wards, and spouses. The SNA member must 1) be in the second or subsequent consecutive year of membership; 2) be serving, retired, or honorably discharged; 3) be a Surface Warfare Officer or Enlisted Surface Warfare Specialist; and 4) have served for at least 3 years on a surface ship of the U.S. Navy or Coast Guard (the 3 years need not have been consecutive but must have been served on active duty). Applicants must be enrolled or planning to enroll full time at an accredited undergraduate or graduate institution; the full-time requirement may be waived for spouses. Along with their application, they must submit a 500-word essay about themselves and why they should be selected to receive this scholarship. High school seniors should also include a transcript of high school grades and a copy of ACT or SAT scores. Current college students should also include a transcript of the grades from their most recent 4 semesters of school. Selection is based on academic proficiency, non-scholastic activities, scholastic and non-scholastic awards, character, and financial need.
Financial data The stipend is $2,000 per year.
Duration 4 years, provided the recipient maintains a GPA of 3.0 or higher.
Number awarded Varies each year.
Deadline February of each year.

[1424]
VIRGINIA MILITARY SURVIVORS AND DEPENDENTS EDUCATION PROGRAM
Virginia Department of Veterans Services
Attn: VMSDEP Coordinator
101 North 14th Street, 17th Floor
Richmond, VA 23219
(804) 225-2083   Fax: (804) 786-0809
E-mail: vmsdep@dvs.virginia.gov
Web: www.dvs.virginia.gov

Summary To provide educational assistance to the children and spouses of disabled and other Virginia veterans or service personnel.
Eligibility This program is open to residents of Virginia who are the child between 16 and 29 years of age or spouse of a current or former member of the U.S. armed forces. Applicants must be attending or planning to attend a public college or university in Virginia or Eastern Virginia Medical School as an undergraduate or graduate student. For Tier 1 support, applicants must be the child or spouse of a veteran who is rated totally and permanently disabled or at least 90% permanently disabled due to military service. For Tier 2 support, applicants must be the child or spouse of a military service member or veteran who is rated totally and permanently disabled or at least 90% permanently disabled due to direct involvement in covered military combat (includes military operation against terrorism; a peacekeeping mission; a terrorist act; or any armed conflict). The military service member's death or a veteran's total and permanent or at least 90% permanent disability must have been directly caused by the military service member's or veteran's involvement in military operations: 1) against terrorism; 2) on a peacekeeping mission; 3) as a result of a terrorist act; or 4) an armed conflict. The veteran must have been a resident of Virginia at the time of entry into active military service or for at least 5 consecutive years immediately prior to the date of application or death. Surviving spouses must have been residents of Virginia for at least 5 years prior to marrying the veteran or for at least 5 years immediately prior to the date on which the application was submitted.
Financial data Tier 1 support provides a waiver of tuition and all required fees at public institutions of higher education in Virginia. Tier 2 support includes a stipend to offset the costs of room, board, books, and supplies at those institutions; recently, the stipend for full-time study was $1,800 per academic year.
Duration Entitlement extends to a maximum of 36 months (4 years).
Additional information This program was formerly known as the Virginia War Orphans Education Program.
Number awarded Varies each year; recently, funding allowed for a total of 1,000 stipends.
Deadline April of each year for fall; August of each year for spring; December of each year for summer.

[1425]
WELLS FARGO VETERANS SCHOLARSHIP PROGRAM
Scholarship America
Attn: Scholarship Management Services
One Scholarship Way
P.O. Box 297
St. Peter, MN 56082
(507) 931-1682   Toll Free: (844) 402-0357
Fax: (507) 931-9168
E-mail: wellsfargoveterans@scholarshipamerica.org
Web: www.scholarsapply.org/wellsfargoveterans

Summary To provide financial assistance to veterans and the spouses of disabled veterans who are interested in attending college.
Eligibility This program is open to honorably-discharged (no longer drilling) veterans and the spouses of disabled veterans of the U.S. armed forces, including the Reserves and National Guard. Applicants must be enrolled or planning to enroll full time at an accredited 2- or 4-year college, university, or vocational/technical school to work on a bachelor's or master's degree. They must have a GPA of 2.5 or higher and be able to demonstrate financial need. Along with their application, they must submit essays on 1) their military service and career and educational goals and objectives; and 2) any personal or financial challenges that may be barriers to completing postsecondary education. Selection is based on those essays, academic performance, demonstrated leadership, participation in school and community activities, work experience, and financial need.
Financial data The amount of the initial stipend depends on an analysis of the recipient's military education benefits, institutional grants, and other scholarships. If renewed, the stipend increases by $1,000 each year.
Duration 1 year; scholarships may be renewed up to 3 additional years or until completion of a degree, whichever occurs firsts. Renewal depends on the recipient's maintaining satisfactory academic progress and full-time enrollment.
Additional information This trustee for this program is Wells Fargo Bank and the administrator is Scholarship America.
Number awarded Varies each year.
Deadline February of each year.

[1426]
WISCONSIN G.I. BILL TUITION REMISSION PROGRAM
Wisconsin Department of Veterans Affairs
2135 Rimrock Road
P.O. Box 7843
Madison, WI 53707-7843
(608) 266-1311   Toll Free: (800) WIS-VETS
Fax: (608) 267-0403   E-mail: WDVAInfo@dva.state.wi.us
Web: dva.wi.gov

Summary To provide financial assistance for college or graduate school to Wisconsin veterans and their dependents.
Eligibility This program is open to current residents of Wisconsin who 1) were residents of the state when they entered or reentered active duty in the U.S. armed forces; or 2) have moved to the state and have been residents for at least 5 consecutive years after entry or reentry into service. Applicants must have served on active duty for at least 2 continuous years or for at least 90 days during specified wartime periods. Also eligible are 1) qualifying children and unremarried surviving spouses of Wisconsin veterans who died in the line of duty or as the direct result of a service-connected disability; and 2) children and spouses of Wisconsin veterans who have a service-connected disability rated by the U.S. Department of Veterans Affairs as 30% or greater. Children must be between 17 and 25 years of age (regardless of the date of the veteran's death or initial disability rating) and be a Wisconsin resident for tuition purposes. Spouses remain eligible for 10 years following the date of the veteran's death or initial disability rating; they must be Wisconsin residents for tuition purposes, but they may enroll full or part time. Students may attend any institution, center, or school within the University of Wisconsin (UW) System or the Wisconsin Technical College System (WCTS). There are no income limits, delimiting periods following military service during which the benefit must

be used, or limits on the level of study (e.g., vocational, undergraduate, professional, or graduate).
Financial data Veterans who qualify as a Wisconsin resident for tuition purposes are eligible for a remission of 100% of standard academic fees and segregated fees at a UW campus or 100% of program and material fees at a WCTS institution. Veterans who qualify as a Wisconsin veteran for purposes of this program but for other reasons fail to meet the definition of a Wisconsin resident for tuition purposes at the UW system are eligible for a remission of 100% of non-resident fees. Spouses and children of deceased or disabled veterans are entitled to a remission of 100% of tuition and fees at a UW or WCTS institution.
Duration Up to 8 semesters or 128 credits, whichever is greater.
Additional information This program began in 2005 as a replacement for Wisconsin Tuition and Fee Reimbursement Grants.
Number awarded Varies each year.
Deadline Applications must be submitted within 14 days from the office start of the academic term: in October for fall, March for spring, or June for summer.

[1427]
WISCONSIN LEGION AUXILIARY CHILD WELFARE SCHOLARSHIP

American Legion Auxiliary
Department of Wisconsin
Attn: Education Chair
2930 American Legion Drive
P.O. Box 140
Portage, WI 53901-0140
(608) 745-0124   Toll Free: (866) 664-3863
Fax: (608) 745-1947
E-mail: deptsec@amlegionauxwi.org
Web: www.amlegionauxwi.org/scholarships

Summary To provide financial assistance to Wisconsin residents who are related to veterans and interested in working on a graduate degree in special education at a school in any state.
Eligibility This program is open to residents of Wisconsin who are the children, grandchildren, great-grandchildren, wives, or widows of veterans. Students who are also members of the Wisconsin American Legion family may live in any state. Applicants must be attending or entering a college or university in any state to work on a graduate degree in special education; if there are no applicants in the field of special education, students in other fields of education are eligible. They must have a GPA of 3.5 or higher and be able to demonstrate financial need. Along with their application, they must submit a 300-word essay on "Education—An Investment in the Future."
Financial data The stipend is $1,000.
Duration 1 year; nonrenewable.
Number awarded 1 each year.
Deadline March of each year.

[1428]
WISCONSIN NATIONAL GUARD ENLISTED ASSOCIATION COLLEGE GRANT PROGRAM

Wisconsin National Guard Enlisted Association
Attn: Executive Director
2400 Wright Street
Madison, WI 53704-2572
(608) 242-3112   E-mail: WNGEA@yahoo.com
Web: wngea.org/scholarships

Summary To provide financial assistance to members of the Wisconsin National Guard Enlisted Association (WNGEA) and their spouses and children who are interested in attending college or graduate school in any state.
Eligibility This program is open to WNGEA members, the unmarried children and spouses of WNGEA members, and the unmarried children and spouses of deceased WNGEA members. Applicants must be enrolled full or part time at a college, university, graduate school, trade school, or business school in any state. Along with their application, they must submit a letter explaining their desire to continue their education; why financial assistance is needed; awards received, accomplishments, volunteerism, and hours volunteered per week or month; and WNGEA membership and role in the organization. Selection is based on financial need, leadership, and moral character.
Financial data Stipends are $1,000 or $500 per year.
Duration 1 year; recipients may not reapply for 2 years.
Additional information This program includes 1 scholarship sponsored by the USAA Insurance Corporation.
Number awarded Varies each year; recently, 6 were awarded: the Raymond A. Matera Scholarship at $1,000, a grant of $1,000 sponsored by USAA, and 4 others (1 reserved for a graduate student) at $500 each.
Deadline May of each year.

[1429]
WOMEN MARINES ASSOCIATION SCHOLARSHIP PROGRAM

Women Marines Association
120 State Avenue, Suite 303
Olympia, WA 98501
Toll Free: (888) 525-1943
E-mail: scholarship@womenmarines.org
Web: www.womenmarines.org/scholarships

Summary To provide financial assistance for college or graduate school to students sponsored by members of the Women Marines Association (WMA).
Eligibility Applicants must be sponsored by a WMA member and fall into 1 of the following categories: 1) have served or are serving in the U.S. Marine Corps, regular or Reserve; 2) are a direct descendant by blood or legal adoption or a stepchild of a Marine on active duty or who has served honorably in the U.S. Marine Corps, regular or Reserve; 3) are a sibling or a descendant of a sibling by blood or legal adoption or a stepchild of a Marine on active duty or who has served honorably in the U.S. Marine Corps, regular or Reserve; 4) be a spouse of a Marine; or 5) have completed 2 years in a Marine Corps JROTC program. WMA members may sponsor an unlimited number of applicants per year. High school seniors must submit transcripts (GPA of 3.0 or higher) and SAT or ACT scores. Undergraduate and graduate students must have a GPA of 3.0 or higher. Along with their application,

they must submit 1-page statements on 1) the Marine to whom they are related; 2) their community service; and 3) their goals after college.
Financial data Stipends range from $500 to $5,000 per year.
Duration 1 year; may be renewed 1 additional year.
Additional information This program includes the following named scholarships: the WMA Memorial Scholarships, the Lily H. Gridley Memorial Scholarship, the Ethyl and Armin Wiebke Memorial Scholarship, the Maj. Megan McClung Memorial Scholarship, the Agnes Sopcak Memorial Scholarship, the Virginia Guveyan Memorial Scholarship, the LaRue A. Ditmore Music Scholarships, the Fallen Warrior Scholarship, and the Margaret Apel Scholarship. Applicants must know a WMA member to serve as their sponsor; the WMA will not supply listings of the names or addresses of chapters or individual members.
Number awarded Varies each year.
Deadline February of each year.

[1430]
YELLOW RIBBON PROGRAM OF THE POST-9/11 GI BILL

Department of Veterans Affairs
Attn: Veterans Benefits Administration
810 Vermont Avenue, N.W.
Washington, DC 20420
(202) 418-4343   Toll Free: (888) 442-4551
Web: www.va.gov

Summary To provide financial assistance to veterans and their dependents who qualify for the Post-9/11 GI Bill and wish to attend a high cost private or out-of-state public institution.
Eligibility Maximum Post-9/11 GI Bill benefits are available to veterans who 1) served on active duty for at least 36 aggregate months after September 11, 2001; or 2) received a Purple Heart on or after September 11, 2001 and were honorably discharged after any length of service; or 3) received a Fry Scholarship on or after August 1, 2018 and/or are currently receiving that scholarship; or 4) were honorably discharged after 60 days for a service-connected disability and served at least 30 continuous days after September 11, 2001. Military personnel currently on active duty and their spouses may qualify for Post-9/11 GI Bill benefits but are not eligible for the Yellow Ribbon Program. This program is available to veterans who qualify for those benefits at the 100% rate, the children and spouses of those veterans to whom they wish to transfer their benefits, and the children of active-duty personnel who qualify for benefits at the 100% rate to whom they wish to transfer those benefits. Applicants must be working on or planning to work on an undergraduate or graduate degree at a private or out-of-state public institution that charges tuition in excess of the $25,162.14 cap imposed by the Post-9/11 GI Bill and that has agreed with the Department of Veterans Affairs (VA) to participate in this program.
Financial data Colleges and universities that charge more than $25,162.14 per academic year in tuition and fees may agree to waive tuition (up to 50%) for qualifying veterans and dependents. The amount that the college or university waives is matched by VA.
Duration Most participants receive up to 36 months of entitlement under this program. Benefits are payable for up to 15 years following release from active duty.
Number awarded Varies each year.
Deadline Deadline not specified.

Indexes

- *Program Title Index*
- *Sponsoring Organization Index*
- *Residency Index*
- *Tenability Index*
- *Subject Index*
- *Calendar Index*

Program Title Index

If you know the name of a particular funding program and want to find out where it is covered in the directory, use the Program Title Index. Here, program titles are arranged alphabetically, word by word. To assist you in your search, every program is listed by all its known names or abbreviations. In addition, we've used a two-character alphabetical code (within parentheses) to help you determine if the program falls within your scope of interest. The first character (capitalized) in the code identifies program type: S = Scholarships; F = Fellowships; G = Grants-in-Aid. The second character (lower cased) identifies eligible groups: v = Veterans; m = Military Personnel; f = Family Members. Here's how the code works: if a program is followed by (S–v) 241, the program is described in the Scholarships section under Veterans, in entry 241. If the same program title is followed by another entry number—for example, (G–m) 1250—the program is also described in the Grants-in-Aid section, under Military Personnel, in entry 1250. Remember: the numbers cited here refer to program entry numbers, not to page numbers in the book.

100th Infantry Battalion Memorial Scholarship Fund, (S–f) 518, (F–f) 1315
100th Infantry Battalion Veterans Stanley Izumigawa Scholarship Fund, (S–f) 519, (F–f) 1316
10th Mountain Division (Light Infantry) Scholarships, (S–v) 1, (S–m) 222, (S–f) 520
11th Armored Cavalry Veterans of Vietnam and Cambodia Scholarship, (S–f) 521
173rd Airborne Brigade Combat Team Honorary Scholarship, (S–f) 522
1st Lt. Dimitri del Castillo Scholarships, (S–f) 523
3/26 Scholarship Fund, (S–f) 524
327th REG Scholarship. See Chappie Hall Memorial Scholarship Program, entry (S–f) 603
37th Division Veterans Scholarship Grant, (S–v) 2, (S–f) 525
3M "Hire Our Heroes" Scholarships and Tool Grants, (S–v) 3, (S–m) 223, (S–f) 526
43d Infantry Division Veterans Association Scholarships, (S–v) 4, (S–f) 527
506th Airborne Infantry Regiment Association Scholarship, (S–v) 5, (S–f) 528, (F–v) 1093, (F–f) 1317
531 Gray Ghost Squadron Association Scholarship, (S–f) 529
82nd Airborne Division Association Awards, (S–v) 6, (S–f) 530
95th Division Scholarship, (S–f) 531

A

A-7 Corsair Association Scholarship, (S–f) 532
AAPA Veterans Caucus Scholarships, (S–v) 7, (F–v) 1094
Aaron Burgstein Memorial Scholarship. See Colonel Aaron Burgstein Memorial Scholarship, entry (S–f) 623
Abrams Memorial Scholarship. See ProVets Military Scholarships, entries (S–v) 167, (S–f) 962
Ada Mucklestone Memorial Scholarships, (S–f) 533

Adalin Macauley Scholarship. See Wisconsin Legion Auxiliary Merit and Memorial Scholarships, entry (S–f) 1080
Admiral Mike Boorda Loan Program. See Navy-Marine Corps Relief Society Education Assistance, entries (S–m) 412, (S–f) 897
Adrian and Corena Swanier Education Scholarships, (S–f) 534
Adrienne Alix Scholarship, (S–v) 8, (S–f) 535
Advanced Civil Schooling Program, (F–m) 1193
AEA Congressman David L. Hobson STEM Scholarship, (S–m) 224, (S–f) 536
AECP. See U.S. Army Health Care Enlisted Commissioning Program (AECP), entry (S–m) 493
AFAS Merit Scholarships, (S–f) 537
AFBA NGAUS Active Life Member Scholarship, (S–m) 225, (S–f) 538, (F–m) 1194, (F–f) 1318
AFCEA DC STEM Scholarships, (S–f) 539
AFCEA ROTC Scholarships, (S–m) 226
AFCEA War Veteran Teacher Certification Program, (F–v) 1095, (F–m) 1195
AFCEA War Veterans Scholarships, (S–v) 9, (S–m) 227
Afghanistan and Iraq War Veterans Scholarships. See AFCEA War Veterans Scholarships, entries (S–v) 9, (S–m) 227
AFSA Scholarship Program, (S–f) 540
Agnes Sopcak Memorial Scholarship. See Women Marines Association Scholarship Program, entries (S–v) 219, (S–m) 512, (S–f) 1085, (F–v) 1191, (F–m) 1313, (F–f) 1429
AHIMA Veterans Scholarship, (S–v) 10, (S–f) 541, (F–v) 1096, (F–f) 1319
Aileen Webb Tobin Scholarship Program. See Dr. Aileen Webb Tobin Scholarship Program, entry (S–m) 293
Air Force Aid Society Merit Scholarships. See AFAS Merit Scholarships, entry (S–f) 537
Air Force Club Scholarship Program, (S–m) 228, (S–f) 542, (F–m) 1196, (F–f) 1320

| S—Scholarships | F—Fellowships | G—Grants-in-Aid |
| v—Veterans | m—Military Personnel | f—Family Members |

Air Force Graduate Law Program, (F—v) 1097, (F—m) 1197
Air Force Health Professions Scholarship Program, (F—m) 1198
Air Force Judge Advocate General's Department Funded Legal Education Program, (F—m) 1199
Air Force One-Year College Program (OYCP), (F—m) 1200
Air Force Reserve Tuition Assistance, (S—m) 229, (F—m) 1201
Air Force ROTC High School Scholarships, (S—m) 230
Air Force ROTC Nursing Scholarships, (S—m) 231
Air Force Sergeants Association International Auxiliary Education Grants, (S—f) 543
Air Force Sergeants Association Scholarship Program. See AFSA Scholarship Program, entry (S—f) 540
Air Force Tuition Assistance Program, (S—m) 232, (F—m) 1202
Airey Memorial Scholarship. See Chief Master Sergeant of the Air Force Scholarship Program, entry (S—f) 607
Airman Scholarship and Commissioning Program, (S—m) 233
Al and Willamary Viste Scholarship Program, (S—f) 544, (F—f) 1321
Alabama G.I. Dependents' Scholarship Program, (S—f) 545, (F—f) 1322
Alabama National Guard Educational Assistance Program, (S—m) 234, (F—m) 1203
Alan Robert and Veronica Lenox Cotarlu Memorial Scholarship. See Army Scholarship Foundation Scholarships, entry (S—f) 576
Alaska National Guard Enlisted Association Scholarship. See ANGEA Scholarship, entries (S—v) 18, (S—m) 238, (S—f) 566
Alaska National Guard State Tuition Reimbursement Program, (S—v) 11, (S—m) 235, (F—v) 1098, (F—m) 1204
Alaska Sea Services Scholarships, (S—f) 546
Albert Levinson Scholarship. See Navy League Foundation Scholarships, entry (S—f) 892
Albert M. Becker Memorial Military Scholarship, (S—v) 12, (S—m) 236
Albert M. Becker Memorial Youth Scholarship, (S—f) 547
Albert M. Lappin Scholarship, (S—f) 548
Albert T. Kissel Memorial Scholarship. See AAPA Veterans Caucus Scholarships, entries (S—v) 7, (F—v) 1094
Albert T. Marcoux Memorial Scholarship, (S—f) 549
Alberto Rodriquez Memorial Scholarship. See Texas State Council Vietnam Veterans of America Scholarships, entries (S—v) 194, (S—f) 1030
Alexander Kreiglowa Navy and Marine Corps Dependents Education Foundation Scholarship, (S—f) 550
Alexander Memorial Scholarship. See Army Scholarship Foundation Scholarships, entry (S—f) 576
Alice Egan Multi-Year Scholarships. See John and Alice Egan Multi-Year Scholarships, entry (S—m) 348
Alix Scholarship. See Adrienne Alix Scholarship, entries (S—v) 8, (S—f) 535
Allie Mae Oden Memorial Scholarship, (S—f) 551
Allied.com Military Scholarship, (S—v) 13, (S—m) 237, (S—f) 552
Allnatt Memorial Scholarship. See United States Army Warrant Officers Association Scholarship Program, entry (S—f) 1046
Aloha Scholarship, (S—f) 553
Altman Memorial Scholarship. See 82nd Airborne Division Association Awards, entries (S—v) 6, (S—f) 530
Americal Scholarship Program, (S—f) 554
American Academy of Physician Assistants Veteran's Caucus Scholarships. See AAPA Veterans Caucus Scholarships, entries (S—v) 7, (F—v) 1094
American Airlines Veteran's Initiative Scholarship, (S—v) 14

The American College Scholarships, (S—v) 195, (S—f) 1033
American Educational Research Association Research Grants Program, (F—f) 1323
American Health Information Management Association Veterans Scholarship. See AHIMA Veterans Scholarship, entries (S—v) 10, (S—f) 541, (F—v) 1096, (F—f) 1319
American Legion Auxiliary Emergency Fund, (S—f) 555
American Legion Auxiliary Junior Member Loyalty Scholarship, (S—f) 556
American Legion Auxiliary National President's Scholarship. See Children of Warriors National Presidents' Scholarship, entry (S—f) 616
American Legion Auxiliary Scholarship for Non-Traditional Students, (S—v) 15, (S—f) 557
American Legion Auxiliary Spirit of Youth Scholarship for Junior Members. See Spirit of Youth Scholarship Fund, entry (S—f) 1016
American Legion Legacy Scholarships, (S—f) 558
American Patriot Scholarships, (S—f) 559
American Society of Military Comptrollers Members' Continuing Education Grants. See ASMC Members' Continuing Education Grants, entries (S—m) 253, (F—m) 1215
American States Utility Services Scholarship Program, (S—f) 560
American Veterinary Medical Association/American Veterinary Medical Foundation Scholarship for Veterans. See AVMA/AVMF Scholarship for Veterans, entry (F—v) 1106
Americo Bugliani Scholarship. See Japanese American Veterans Association Memorial Scholarships, entry (S—f) 775
AMVETS Generation T Scholarships, (S—v) 16, (S—f) 561
AMVETS JROTC Scholarships, (S—f) 562
AMVETS National Ladies Auxiliary Scholarships, (S—f) 563
AMVETS National Scholarships for High School Seniors, (S—f) 564
AMVETS National Scholarships for Veterans, (S—v) 17, (F—v) 1099
Anchor Scholarships, (S—f) 565
Anderson Scholarship. See Navy League Foundation Scholarships, entry (S—f) 892
Andrew Edmund Topham Memorial Scholarship. See Sergeant Andrew Edmund Topham Memorial Scholarship, entry (S—f) 998
ANGEA Scholarship, (S—v) 18, (S—m) 238, (S—f) 566
Angeline Lewis Scholarships. See H.S. and Angeline Lewis Scholarships, entries (S—f) 747, (F—f) 1360
Angelo and Mildred Nunez Scholarships. See Fleet Reserve Association Member Scholarships, entries (S—v) 62, (S—m) 314, (S—f) 699, (F—v) 1127, (F—m) 1241, (F—f) 1351
Ann E. Clark Foundation Scholarship. See Navy League Foundation Scholarships, entry (S—f) 892
Anne Gannett Veterans Award, (S—v) 19, (F—v) 1100
Annette Hill Scholarship Fund. See Charles W. and Annette Hill Scholarship Fund, entry (S—f) 605
A-OK Student Reward Program. See NEXT Gen Scholars Program, entry (S—f) 913
Apel Scholarship. See Women Marines Association Scholarship Program, entries (S—v) 219, (S—m) 512, (S—f) 1085, (F—v) 1191, (F—m) 1313, (F—f) 1429
Applications International Corporation Impact Scholarships, (S—v) 20, (F—v) 1101
AREA Scholarship Program, (S—f) 567
Arizona VFW Auxiliary Educational Grant, (S—f) 568
Arizona VFW Auxiliary Merit Scholarship, (S—f) 569

S—Scholarships   F—Fellowships   G—Grants-in-Aid
v—Veterans   m—Military Personnel   f—Family Members

PROGRAM TITLE INDEX

Arkansas American Legion Auxiliary Academic Scholarship, (S—f) 570

Arkansas Military Dependents Scholarship Program, (S—f) 571

Arkansas Missing in Action/Killed in Action Dependents Scholarship Program. See Arkansas Military Dependents Scholarship Program, entry (S—f) 571

Arkansas National Guard Tuition Incentive Program. See Arkansas National Guard Tuition Waiver Program, entry (S—m) 239

Arkansas National Guard Tuition Waiver Program, (S—m) 239

Arkansas Service Memorial Scholarships, (S—f) 572

Ark-La-Tex Chapter MOAA Academic Scholarships, (S—f) 573

Armed Forces Benefit Association NGAUS Active Life Member Scholarship. See AFBA NGAUS Active Life Member Scholarship, entries (S—m) 225, (S—f) 538, (F—m) 1194, (F—f) 1318

Armed Forces Communications and Electronics Association ROTC Scholarships. See AFCEA ROTC Scholarships, entry (S—m) 226

Armed Forces Communications and Electronics Association War Veteran Teacher Certification Program. See AFCEA War Veteran Teacher Certification Program, entries (F—v) 1095, (F—m) 1195

Armed Forces Communications and Electronics Association War Veterans Scholarships. See AFCEA War Veterans Scholarships, entries (S—v) 9, (S—m) 227

Armed Forces Tuition Waiver Program of Massachusetts, (S—m) 240

Armin Wiebke Memorial Scholarship. See Women Marines Association Scholarship Program, entries (S—v) 219, (S—m) 512, (S—f) 1085, (F—v) 1191, (F—m) 1313, (F—f) 1429

Army and Air Force Exchange Service Retired Employees Association Scholarships. See AREA Scholarship Program, entry (S—f) 567

Army Aviation Association of America Scholarships, (S—v) 21, (S—m) 241, (S—f) 574, (F—v) 1102, (F—m) 1205, (F—f) 1324

Army Engineer Association Congressman David L. Hobson STEM Scholarship. See AEA Congressman David L. Hobson STEM Scholarship, entries (S—m) 224, (S—f) 536

Army Health Professions Scholarship Program, (F—m) 1206

Army Judge Advocate General Corps Funded Legal Education Program, (F—m) 1207

Army Medical and Dental School Stipend Program (MDSSP), (F—m) 1208

Army Medical Department Enlisted Commissioning Program. See U.S. Army Health Care Enlisted Commissioning Program (AECP), entry (S—m) 493

Army National Guard Federal Tuition Assistance, (S—m) 242, (F—m) 1209

Army Nurse Corps Association Scholarships, (S—v) 22, (S—m) 243, (S—f) 575, (F—v) 1103, (F—m) 1210, (F—f) 1325

Army Reserve Tuition Assistance, (S—m) 244, (F—m) 1211

Army ROTC 4-Year High School Scholarships, (S—m) 245

Army ROTC College Scholarship Program, (S—m) 246

Army ROTC Nurse Program, (S—m) 247

Army Scholarship Foundation Scholarships, (S—f) 576

Army Specialized Training Assistance Program (STRAP), (S—m) 248, (F—m) 1212

Army Tuition Assistance Benefits, (S—m) 249, (F—m) 1213

Army Women's Foundation Legacy Scholarships, (S—v) 23, (S—m) 250, (S—f) 577, (F—v) 1104, (F—m) 1214, (F—f) 1326

Arnold Air Society and Silver Wings Academic Scholarship Program, (S—m) 251

Arnold Air Society and Silver Wings Flying Scholarships, (S—m) 252

Arnold Education Grant Program. See General Henry H. Arnold Education Grant Program, entry (S—f) 718

Arnold Krippendorf Scholarship. See Dolphin Scholarships, entry (S—f) 664

Arnold Nursing Scholarship. See Marcella Arnold Nursing Scholarship, entries (S—v) 108, (S—f) 819

Art and Eleanor Colona Scholarship Grant. See CWOA LT Art and Eleanor Colona Scholarship Grant, entry (S—f) 645

Arthur Robert "Bob" Troutt Memorial Scholarship. See ProVets Military Scholarships, entries (S—v) 167, (S—f) 962

ASMC Members' Continuing Education Grants, (S—m) 253, (F—m) 1215

Association of Aviation Ordnancemen Educational Foundation Scholarships, (S—v) 24, (S—f) 578

Association of Commissioned Officers Scholarships, (S—f) 579

Association of the United States Navy Scholarship Program, (S—m) 254, (S—f) 580

AT&T Veterans Scholarships, (S—v) 25

AT&T War Memorial Scholarship, (S—v) 26, (F—v) 1105

Austal USA STEM Scholarship, (S—f) 581

AVMA/AVMF Scholarship for Veterans, (F—v) 1106

B

Bagley Scholarship. See Marion J. Bagley Scholarship, entry (S—f) 830

Baldassari Memorial Scholarships. See EANGNJ Scholarship Program, entries (S—m) 298, (S—f) 673

Baranski Scholarship. See Fleet Reserve Association Graduate Scholarships, entries (F—v) 1126, (F—m) 1240, (F—f) 1350

Barbara Kranig Scholarship. See Wisconsin Legion Auxiliary Merit and Memorial Scholarships, entry (S—f) 1080

Barger, Sr. Memorial Nursing Scholarships. See Jack E. Barger, Sr. Memorial Nursing Scholarships, entries (S—v) 92, (S—m) 344, (S—f) 774

Barrett Grant. See Dr. Kate Waller Barrett Grant, entry (S—f) 667

Barry Carlson Scholarship. See Nancy and Barry Carlson Scholarship, entry (S—v) 132

Bartel Veteran's Scholarship. See David and Rebecca Bartel Veteran's Scholarship, entries (S—v) 49, (F—v) 1119

Baswell Combat Wounded Engineer Scholarship. See COL Carl F. Baswell Combat Wounded Engineer Scholarship, entries (S—v) 38, (F—v) 1114

Baswell Fallen Engineer Memorial Scholarship. See COL Carl F. Baswell Fallen Engineer Memorial Scholarship, entries (S—f) 621, (F—f) 1335

Beall Scholarship. See Walter Beall Scholarship, entries (S—m) 504, (S—f) 1065

Beardslee Memorial Scholarship Awards. See Colonel Harold M. Beardslee Memorial Scholarship Awards, entry (S—f) 625

Becker Memorial Military Scholarship. See Albert M. Becker Memorial Military Scholarship, entries (S—v) 12, (S—m) 236

Becker Memorial Youth Scholarship. See Albert M. Becker Memorial Youth Scholarship, entry (S—f) 547

Behrend Scholarship. See Wisconsin Legion Auxiliary Merit and Memorial Scholarships, entry (S—f) 1080

Ben Kuroki Scholarship. See Japanese American Veterans Association Memorial Scholarships, entry (S—f) 775

Benjamin B. Talley Scholarship. See BG Benjamin B. Talley Scholarship, entries (S—m) 255, (S—f) 582, (F—m) 1216, (F—f) 1327

S—Scholarships
v—Veterans

F—Fellowships
m—Military Personnel

G—Grants-in-Aid
f—Family Members

Benjamin J. Butler "Century Division" Scholarship Program. *See* MG Benjamin J. Butler "Century Division" Scholarship Program, entries (S—v) 117, (S—m) 377, (S—f) 844

Benn, USMC, Scholarship. *See* Colonel Hazel Benn, USMC, Scholarship, entry (S—f) 626

Benson Elbit Honorary Scholarship. *See* Master Sergeant Neal Benson Elbit Honorary Scholarship, entry (S—f) 839

Bernard Rotberg Memorial Grant. *See* Jewish War Veterans National Youth Achievement Program, entry (S—f) 778

Betty Shima Scholarship. *See* Japanese American Veterans Association Memorial Scholarships, entry (S—f) 775

Beverly Holmes Scholarship. *See* Wyoming National Guard Association Scholarships, entries (S—m) 516, (S—f) 1091

BG Benjamin B. Talley Scholarship, (S—m) 255, (S—f) 582, (F—m) 1216, (F—f) 1327

Bill Creech Scholarship, (S—f) 583

Bill Myers Scholarship. *See* San Antonio Post SAME Scholarships, entry (S—m) 464

Bill Nelson Scholarship. *See* Chappie Hall Memorial Scholarship Program, entry (S—f) 603

Billy Ray Cameron Scholarships. *See* Otis N. Brown/Billy Ray Cameron Scholarships, entry (S—f) 947

Blackburn Memorial Scholarship. *See* Laura Blackburn Memorial Scholarship, entry (S—f) 798

Blackhorse Scholarships, (S—f) 584

Blackmore Scholarship. *See* E.A. Blackmore Scholarship, entry (S—f) 671

Blair Scholarship. *See* Fleet Reserve Association Member Scholarship, entries (S—v) 62, (S—m) 314, (S—f) 699, (F—v) 1127, (F—m) 1241, (F—f) 1351

Blanche Lee Lindsay Memorial Scholarship. *See* John C. and Blanche Lee Lindsay Memorial Scholarship, entry (S—f) 780

Blanton AFBA Family Survivor College Scholarship. *See* General and Mrs. Charles C. Blanton AFBA Family Survivor College Scholarship, entry (S—f) 717

Blottenberger Scholarship. *See* Chappie Hall Memorial Scholarship Program, entry (S—f) 603

Bob Troutt Memorial Scholarship. *See* ProVets Military Scholarships, entries (S—v) 167, (S—f) 962

Boddington Scholarship. *See* William W, Boddington Scholarship, entry (S—f) 1075

Bonner Scholarship. *See* Jewell Hilton Bonner Scholarship, entry (S—f) 777

Bonner Scholarship Award for Medical Excellence. *See* Eileen M. Bonner Scholarship Award for Medical Excellence, entry (S—m) 306

Boorda Loan Program. *See* Navy-Marine Corps Relief Society Education Assistance, entries (S—m) 412, (S—f) 897

Boston Post SAME Scholarships, (S—v) 27, (S—m) 256

Boswell Merit Scholarship Program. *See* General Jim and Pat Boswell Merit Scholarship Program, entry (S—f) 719

Bowden Scholarship. *See* Joan Bowden Scholarship, entry (S—m) 346

Bowfin Memorial Scholarships, (S—f) 585

Bowie Memorial Scholarship. *See* Army Scholarship Foundation Scholarships, entry (S—f) 576

Boyes, Vice Admiral, USN (Ret.) Memorial Scholarship. *See* VADM Jon L. Boyes, Vice Admiral, USN (Ret.) Memorial Scholarship, entry (S—m) 497

Brace III Memorial Scholarship. *See* Captain Frederick C. Brace III Memorial Scholarship, entries (S—v) 35, (S—f) 601, (F—v) 1110, (F—f) 1332

Brace, Jr. Memorial Scholarship. *See* Sgt. Frederick C. Brace, Jr. Memorial Scholarship, entries (S—v) 183, (S—f) 1001, (F—v) 1172, (F—f) 1410

Branch Marine Corps Leadership Scholarships. *See* Frederick C. Branch Marine Corps Leadership Scholarships, entry (S—m) 320

Brand, Jr. Memorial Scholarship. *See* ProVets Military Scholarships, entries (S—v) 167, (S—f) 962

Branstad-Reynolds Scholarship Fund. *See* Children of Fallen Iowa Service Members Scholarship, entry (S—f) 612

Braun Family Scholarship. *See* Richard and Susan Braun Family Scholarship, entry (S—v) 173

Braxton Bragg Chapter AUSA Scholarships, (S—v) 28, (S—m) 257, (S—f) 586, (F—v) 1107, (F—m) 1217, (F—f) 1328

Brigadier General Hubert O. "Hub" Johnson Scholarship. *See* San Antonio Post SAME Scholarships, entry (S—m) 464

Brigadier General John F. Kinney Fellowship, (S—m) 258

Brigadier General Robert L. Denig Foundation Scholarship, (S—m) 259, (S—f) 587

Brigadier General Roscoe C. Cartwright Awards, (S—m) 260

Broaddus DECO Scholarship. *See* T. Nash Broaddus DECO Scholarship, entry (S—f) 1023

Brokaw Scholarship. *See* Navy League Foundation Scholarships, entry (S—f) 892

Brooks Memorial Grant. *See* Jewish War Veterans National Achievement Program, entries (S—v) 94, (S—m) 345, (F—v) 1140, (F—m) 1250

Brown/Billy Ray Cameron Scholarships. *See* Otis N. Brown/Billy Ray Cameron Scholarships, entry (S—f) 947

Brown Memorial Scholarship. *See* Army Scholarship Foundation Scholarships, entry (S—f) 576

Brown Veteran to Teacher Scholarships. *See* Frank N. Brown Veteran to Teacher Scholarships, entry (S—v) 68

Brunsman Memorial Scholarship. *See* Robert W. Brunsman Memorial Scholarship, entries (S—m) 460, (F—m) 1294

Buckingham Memorial Scholarships, (S—f) 588, (F—f) 1329

Bugliani Scholarship. *See* Japanese American Veterans Association Memorial Scholarships, entry (S—f) 775

Burgstein Memorial Scholarship. *See* Colonel Aaron Burgstein Memorial Scholarship, entry (S—f) 623

Butler American Legion Scholarship Fund. *See* Lucian Butler American Legion Scholarship Fund, entry (S—f) 812

Butler "Century Division" Scholarship Program. *See* MG Benjamin J. Butler "Century Division" Scholarship Program, entries (S—v) 117, (S—m) 377, (S—f) 844

C

Caesar Viglienzone Memorial Scholarship, (S—v) 29

Caliendo College Assistance Fund Scholarship. *See* Captain Caliendo College Assistance Fund Scholarship, entry (S—f) 600

California College Fee Waiver Program for Children of Veterans, (S—f) 589

California Enlisted Association of the National Guard of the United States Scholarship Program, (S—m) 261

California Fee Waiver Program for Dependents of Deceased or Disabled National Guard Members, (S—f) 590

California Fee Waiver Program for Dependents of Totally Disabled Veterans, (S—f) 591

California Fee Waiver Program for Recipients of the Medal of Honor and Their Children, (S—v) 30, (S—f) 592

California Legion Auxiliary Educational Assistance General Scholarships, (S—f) 593

California Legion Auxiliary Past Department President's Junior Scholarship, (S—f) 594

California Legion Auxiliary Past Presidents' Parley Nursing Scholarships, (S—v) 31, (S—f) 595

California Legion Auxiliary Scholarships for Continuing and/or Reentry Students, (S—v) 32, (S—m) 262, (S—f) 596

California Military Department GI Bill Award Program, (S—m) 263, (F—m) 1218

California National Guard Education Assistance Award Program. See California Military Department GI Bill Award Program, entries (S—m) 263, (F—m) 1218

California Non-Resident College Fee Waiver Program for Military Personnel and Dependents, (S—v) 33, (S—m) 264, (S—f) 597, (F—v) 1108, (F—m) 1219, (F—f) 1330

Callahan Memorial Scholarship. See Captain Jodi Callahan Memorial Scholarship, entry (F—m) 1221

Cameron Scholarship. See Navy League Foundation Scholarships, entry (S—f) 892

Cameron Scholarships. See Otis N. Brown/Billy Ray Cameron Scholarships, entry (S—f) 947

Campbell Medical Scholarship. See Lillian Campbell Medical Scholarship, entries (S—v) 100, (S—f) 803, (F—v) 1142, (F—f) 1366

Campbell Scholarship. See CAPT Ernest G. "Scotty" Campbell, USN (Ret) and Renee Campbell Scholarship, entry (S—f) 599

Cannon Endowment Scholarship, (F—m) 1220

Capitol Area Chapter MOAA College Scholarship Program, (S—v) 34, (S—f) 598, (F—v) 1109, (F—f) 1331

CAPT Ernest G. "Scotty" Campbell, USN (Ret) and Renee Campbell Scholarship, (S—f) 599

CAPT Winifred Quick Collins, USN (Ret) Scholarship. See Navy League Foundation Scholarships, entry (S—f) 892

Captain Caliendo College Assistance Fund Scholarship, (S—f) 600

Captain Frederick C. Brace III Memorial Scholarship, (S—v) 35, (S—f) 601, (F—v) 1110, (F—f) 1332

Captain Jennifer Shafer Odom Memorial Scholarship. See Army Scholarship Foundation Scholarships, entry (S—f) 576

Captain Jodi Callahan Memorial Scholarship, (F—m) 1221

Captain Mark Starr Memorial Scholarship. See Naval Helicopter Association Scholarships, entries (S—v) 139, (S—m) 407, (S—f) 890, (F—v) 1156, (F—m) 1276, (F—f) 1383

Captain Miki Iwata Memorial Scholarship for Advanced Practice, (F—v) 1111, (F—m) 1222, (F—f) 1333

Captain Sean P. Grimes Physician Assistant Educational Scholarship Award, (S—v) 36, (S—m) 265, (F—v) 1112, (F—m) 1223

Carl F. McNair Jr. Scholarship Award. See George Washington Chapter AUSA Scholarships, entries (S—v) 72, (S—m) 324, (S—f) 724, (F—v) 1131, (F—m) 1246, (F—f) 1356

Carlson Scholarship. See Nancy and Barry Carlson Scholarship, entry (S—v) 132

Carol Anne Abrams Memorial Scholarship. See ProVets Military Scholarships, entries (S—v) 167, (S—f) 962

Carroll H. Payne Memorial Scholarship Endowment, (S—v) 37, (S—m) 266, (S—f) 602

Carruth Scholarship. See San Antonio Post SAME Scholarships, entry (S—m) 464

Cartwright Awards. See Brigadier General Roscoe C. Cartwright Awards, entry (S—m) 260

Casey Scholarship. See John Casey Scholarship, entry (S—f) 781

Catherine and Charles Kratz Scholarships. See Chappie Hall Memorial Scholarship Program, entry (S—f) 603

CDR Mort McCarthy Memorial Scholarship. See Naval Helicopter Association Scholarships, entries (S—v) 139, (S—m) 407, (S—f) 890, (F—v) 1156, (F—m) 1276, (F—f) 1383

Cecilia Clark Scholarship. See NMCCG Enlisted Dependent Spouse Scholarship, entries (S—f) 924, (F—f) 1392

Century Division Scholarship Program. See MG Benjamin J. Butler "Century Division" Scholarship Program, entries (S—v) 117, (S—m) 377, (S—f) 844

Chabraja Scholarship. See Nicholas D. Chabraja Scholarship, entries (S—v) 148, (S—m) 431, (S—f) 923

Chaplain Samuel Grover Powell Scholarship, (F—v) 1113, (F—m) 1224

Chappie Hall Memorial Scholarship Program, (S—f) 603

Charles C. Blanton AFBA Family Survivor College Scholarship. See General and Mrs. Charles C. Blanton AFBA Family Survivor College Scholarship, entry (S—f) 717

Charles J. Wing Family Program Scholarship. See Wyoming National Guard Association Scholarships, entries (S—m) 516, (S—f) 1091

Charles Karman Memorial Scholarship. See Naval Helicopter Association Scholarships, entries (S—v) 139, (S—m) 407, (S—f) 890, (F—v) 1156, (F—m) 1276, (F—f) 1383

Charles Kosmutza Memorial Grant. See Jewish War Veterans National Achievement Program, entries (S—v) 94, (S—m) 345, (F—v) 1140, (F—m) 1250

Charles Kosmutza Scholarship Fund, (S—f) 604

Charles Kratz Scholarships. See Chappie Hall Memorial Scholarship Program, entry (S—f) 603

Charles L. Schmidt Leadership Scholarship. See Colonel Charles L. Schmidt Leadership Scholarship, entry (S—f) 624

Charles W. and Annette Hill Scholarship Fund, (S—f) 605

Charlie Corn Scholarships, (S—f) 606

Chief Master Sergeant of the Air Force Scholarship Program, (S—f) 607

Chief Petty Officer Scholarships, (S—f) 608

Children and Spouses of Indiana National Guard Program, (S—f) 609, (F—f) 1334

Children of Air Traffic Control Specialists Scholarship Program. See Buckingham Memorial Scholarships, entries (S—f) 588, (F—f) 1329

Children of Coast Guard Members Scholarships, (S—f) 610

Children of Fallen Coast Guard Heroes Scholarships, (S—f) 611

Children of Fallen Iowa Service Members Scholarship, (S—f) 612

Children of Fallen Patriots Scholarship, (S—f) 613

Children of Fallen Soldiers Relief Fund College Grants, (S—f) 614

Children of POW/MIA Soldiers of Pennsylvania Grants, (S—f) 615

Children of Warriors National Presidents' Scholarship, (S—f) 616

Chilton Scholarships. See Wilma D. Hoyal/Maxine Chilton Scholarships, entries (S—v) 216, (S—f) 1076

Christian "Horse" Hescock Memorial Scholarship. See Naval Helicopter Association Scholarships, entries (S—v) 139, (S—m) 407, (S—f) 890, (F—v) 1156, (F—m) 1276, (F—f) 1383

Church, State and Industry Foundation Seminary or Graduate School Grant/Loan, (F—m) 1225

Civil Engineer Corps Collegiate Program, (S—m) 267, (F—m) 1226

Civil Engineer Corps Option of the Seaman to Admiral-21 Program, (S—m) 268

Claire Oliphant Memorial Scholarship, (S—f) 617

Clarence L. Huebner Scholarships. See Lieutenant General Clarence L. Huebner Scholarships, entry (S—f) 802

Clark Foundation Scholarship. See Navy League Foundation Scholarships, entry (S—f) 892

S—Scholarships F—Fellowships G—Grants-in-Aid
v—Veterans m—Military Personnel f—Family Members

Clark Scholarship. *See* NMCCG Enlisted Dependent Spouse Scholarship, entries (S—f) 924, (F—f) 1392

Clegg Scholarship. *See* Navy-Marine Corps Relief Society Education Assistance, entries (S—m) 412, (S—f) 897

Cliford Lee Kristal Education Grant. *See* Jewish War Veterans National Youth Achievement Program, entry (S—f) 778

CMSAF Richard D. Kisling Scholarship. *See* Chief Master Sergeant of the Air Force Scholarship Program, entry (S—f) 607

CMSGT Gerald R. Guild Memorial Scholarships, (S—m) 269, (S—f) 618

CMSgt Richard W. Spencer Scholarship. *See* EANGNJ Scholarship Program, entries (S—m) 298, (S—f) 673

Coast Guard Enlisted Dependent Spouse Scholarship. *See* NMCCG Enlisted Dependent Spouse Scholarship, entries (S—f) 924, (F—f) 1392

Coast Guard Exchange Scholarship Program, (S—f) 619

Coast Guard Reserve Families Scholarships, (S—m) 270, (S—f) 620

Coast Guard Tuition Assistance Program, (S—m) 271, (F—m) 1227

COL Carl F. Baswell Combat Wounded Engineer Scholarship, (S—v) 38, (F—v) 1114

COL Carl F. Baswell Fallen Engineer Memorial Scholarship, (S—f) 621, (F—f) 1335

Col. Loren J. and Mrs. Lawona R. Spencer Scholarship, (F—m) 1228

Colbert Scholarship. *See* Pop-A-Smoke Scholarships, entry (S—f) 960

Cold War Veterans Engineering and Science Scholarships, (S—v) 39, (S—m) 272, (S—f) 622

College Student Pre-Commissioning Initiative, (S—m) 273

Collins III Leadership with Honor Scholarships. *See* Richard W. Collins III Leadership with Honor Scholarships, entry (S—m) 459

Collins, USN (Ret) Scholarship. *See* Navy League Foundation Scholarships, entry (S—f) 892

Colona Scholarship Grant. *See* CWOA LT Art and Eleanor Colona Scholarship Grant, entry (S—f) 645

Colonel Aaron Burgstein Memorial Scholarship, (S—f) 623

Colonel Bruce and Mrs. Jeanne Colbert Scholarship. *See* Pop-A-Smoke Scholarships, entry (S—f) 960

Colonel Charles L. Schmidt Leadership Scholarship, (S—f) 624

Colonel Harold M. Beardslee Memorial Scholarship Awards, (S—f) 625

Colonel Hayden W. Wagner Memorial Fund. *See* Society of Daughters of the United States Army Scholarships, entry (S—f) 1006

Colonel Hazel Benn, USMC, Scholarship, (S—f) 626

Colonel Jerry W. Ross Scholarship, (F—m) 1229, (F—f) 1336

Colonel Jimmie Kanaya Scholarship. *See* Japanese American Veterans Association Memorial Scholarships, entry (S—f) 775

Colonel John D. Hedges Memorial Scholarship, (S—m) 274

Colonel Joseph "Ed" Galloway Scholarship. *See* Virginia National Guard Association Scholarship, entries (S—m) 501, (S—f) 1063

Colonel Richard Hallock Scholarships, (S—v) 40, (S—m) 275, (S—f) 627

Colonel Urey Woodson Alexander Memorial Scholarship. *See* Army Scholarship Foundation Scholarships, entry (S—f) 576

Colonel William "Bill" Myers Scholarship. *See* San Antonio Post SAME Scholarships, entry (S—m) 464

Colorado Dependents Tuition Assistance Program, (S—f) 628

Colorado Legion Auxiliary Department President's Scholarship for Junior Auxiliary Members, (S—f) 629

Colorado Legion Auxiliary Department President's Scholarships, (S—f) 630

Colorado Legion Auxiliary Department Scholarship for Non-traditional Students, (S—v) 41, (S—f) 631

Colorado Legion Auxiliary Past President's Parley Health Professional Scholarship, (S—v) 42, (S—f) 632

Colorado National Guard State Tuition Assistance, (S—m) 276

Comai Scholarships. *See* Dennis Comai Scholarships, entry (S—f) 655

Commander William S. Stuhr Scholarships, (S—f) 633

Commissioned Officers' Association Dependent Scholarships, (S—f) 634

Congressman David L. Hobson STEM Scholarship. *See* AEA Congressman David L. Hobson STEM Scholarship, entries (S—m) 224, (S—f) 536

Connacher Memorial Scholarships. *See* Peter Connacher Memorial Scholarships, entries (S—v) 162, (S—f) 956, (F—v) 1165, (F—f) 1397

Connal Scholarship. *See* EANYNG Education Awards, entries (S—m) 302, (S—f) 678

Connecticut Better Business Bureau Military Line Student Ethics Scholarship, (S—f) 635

Connecticut National Guard Educational Assistance Program, (S—m) 277

Connecticut National Guard Foundation Scholarships, (S—m) 278, (S—f) 636

Connecticut Tuition Waiver for Veterans, (S—v) 43, (S—m) 279, (S—f) 637, (F—v) 1115, (F—m) 1230, (F—f) 1337

Connie Liebsack Memorial Scholarship. *See* Department of Nebraska VFW State Scholarships, entries (S—v) 50, (S—f) 656

Connie Settles Scholarship, (S—f) 638, (F—f) 1338

Coon Scholarship. *See* Phillip Coon Scholarship, entry (S—v) 163

Cooper Scholarship. *See* Mary Rowena Cooper Scholarship, entry (S—f) 835

Corena Swanier Education Scholarships. *See* Adrian and Corena Swanier Education Scholarships, entry (S—f) 534

Corn Scholarships. *See* Charlie Corn Scholarships, entry (S—f) 606

Cornelius/Max English Memorial Scholarship. *See* John Cornelius/Max English Memorial Scholarship, entries (S—m) 349, (S—f) 782, (F—m) 1252, (F—f) 1363

Cornett-Huff Scholarships. *See* Loretta Cornett-Huff Scholarships, entries (S—f) 805, (F—f) 1367

Corning Memorial Scholarship. *See* Major General Duane L. "Duke" Corning Memorial Scholarship, entries (S—v) 106, (S—m) 367, (S—f) 815

Corporal Ernesto "Gooie" Gomez Memorial Scholarship. *See* Pop-A-Smoke Scholarships, entry (S—f) 960

Cortes Memorial Scholarship. *See* LT Ruth Cortes Memorial Scholarship, entries (S—v) 103, (F—v) 1143

Corvias Foundation Scholarships for Military Spouses, (S—f) 639

Costello Memorial Scholarship. *See* Army Scholarship Foundation Scholarships, entry (S—f) 576

Cotarlu Memorial Scholarship. *See* Army Scholarship Foundation Scholarships, entry (S—f) 576

Coudret Trust Scholarships, (S—f) 640

Council of College and Military Educators Veterans Scholarships, (S—v) 44, (F—v) 1116

S—Scholarships F—Fellowships G—Grants-in-Aid
v—Veterans m—Military Personnel f—Family Members

Courtney G. Clegg and Mrs. Margaret H. Clegg Scholarship. *See* Navy-Marine Corps Relief Society Education Assistance, entries (S—m) 412, (S—f) 897
CPT James and Ruby Eheman Memorial Scholarship, (S—f) 641
CPT Luke Wullenwaber Memorial Scholarship Award. *See* 506th Airborne Infantry Regiment Association Scholarship, entries (S—v) 5, (S—f) 528, (F—v) 1093, (F—f) 1317
Craig Ivory Memorial Scholarships. *See* AAPA Veterans Caucus Scholarships, entries (S—v) 7, (F—v) 1094
Craig R. McKinley Flight Scholarship. *See* Arnold Air Society and Silver Wings Flying Scholarships, entry (S—m) 252
Creech Scholarship. *See* Bill Creech Scholarship, entry (S—f) 583
Cribbins Scholarship. *See* Joseph P. and Helen T. Cribbins Scholarship, entries (S—v) 96, (S—m) 350, (S—f) 784
Crow Awards. *See* Association of Aviation Ordnancemen Educational Foundation Scholarships, entries (S—v) 24, (S—f) 578
Crow Memorial Scholarship. *See* Chief Petty Officer Scholarships, entry (S—f) 608
CSM Harry and Mary Hensell Scholarship Program, (S—m) 280, (S—f) 642
CSM John H. Humphreys Jr. Memorial Scholarship. *See* EANGNJ Scholarship Program, entries (S—m) 298, (S—f) 673
CSM Leonard Maglione Memorial Scholarships, (S—v) 45, (S—m) 281, (S—f) 643, (F—v) 1117, (F—m) 1231, (F—f) 1339
CSM Robert W. Elkey Scholarship, (S—m) 282, (F—m) 1232
CSM Vincent Baldassari Memorial Scholarships. *See* EANGNJ Scholarship Program, entries (S—m) 298, (S—f) 673
CSM Virgil R. Williams Scholarship Program, (S—m) 283, (S—f) 644
Cummins Memorial Scholarship. *See* The PFC Roger W. Cummins Memorial Scholarship, entries (S—v) 196, (S—m) 487, (S—f) 1034, (F—v) 1178, (F—m) 1301, (F—f) 1417
Currahee Scholarship Award. *See* 506th Airborne Infantry Regiment Association Scholarship, entries (S—v) 5, (S—f) 528, (F—v) 1093, (F—f) 1317
Curtis Mancini Memorial Scholarships. *See* SFC Curtis Mancini Memorial Scholarships, entries (S—v) 182, (S—m) 472, (S—f) 1000, (F—v) 1171, (F—m) 1299, (F—f) 1409
CW04 Mitsugi Kasai Scholarship. *See* Japanese American Veterans Association Memorial Scholarships, entry (S—f) 775
CW4 William C. Singletary Scholarship. *See* Virginia National Guard Association Scholarship, entries (S—m) 501, (S—f) 1063
CWOA LT Art and Eleanor Colona Scholarship Grant, (S—f) 645

D

Daedalian Academic Matching Scholarship Program, (S—m) 284
Daedalian Foundation Descendants' Scholarship Program, (S—f) 646, (F—f) 1340
Dale Spencer Scholarship Fund, (S—v) 46, (S—m) 285
Daniel Drevnick Memorial Fund Scholarships, (S—v) 47, (S—f) 647
Daniel E. Lambert Memorial Scholarship, (S—f) 648
Daniel Geiger Scholarship, (S—f) 649
Daniel K. Inouye Memorial Scholarship. *See* Senator Daniel K. Inouye Memorial Scholarship, entries (S—v) 181, (S—m) 471, (S—f) 997, (F—v) 1170, (F—m) 1298, (F—f) 1408
Darlene Hooley Scholarship for Oregon Veterans, (S—v) 48, (F—v) 1118
Darrell Thibault VFW State Memorial Scholarship. *See* Department of Nebraska VFW State Scholarships, entries (S—v) 50, (S—f) 656
Daughters of the Cincinnati Scholarship Program, (S—f) 650

Dauksz Scholarship Award. *See* George Washington Chapter AUSA Scholarships, entries (S—v) 72, (S—m) 324, (S—f) 724, (F—v) 1131, (F—m) 1246, (F—f) 1356
David and Rebecca Bartel Veteran's Scholarship, (S—v) 49, (F—v) 1119
David Gwinn Memorial Scholarship. *See* AAPA Veterans Caucus Scholarships, entries (S—v) 7, (F—v) 1094
David L. Hobson STEM Scholarship. *See* AEA Congressman David L. Hobson STEM Scholarship, entries (S—m) 224, (S—f) 536
Davis Memorial Scholarship. *See* James Joseph Davis Memorial Scholarship, entries (S—v) 93, (F—v) 1139
Dawn Kilpatrick Memorial AUSA Scholarship. *See* SGM Dawn Kilpatrick Memorial AUSA Scholarship, entry (S—m) 473
DedARNG Scholarships. *See* Dedicated Army National Guard (DedARNG) Scholarships, entries (S—m) 286, (F—m) 1233
Dedicated Army National Guard (DedARNG) Scholarships, (S—m) 286, (F—m) 1233
del Castillo Scholarships. *See* 1st Lt. Dimitri del Castillo Scholarships, entry (S—f) 523
Del Valle Leadership Scholarships. *See* General Pedro Del Valle Leadership Scholarships, entry (S—m) 322
Delaware Educational Benefits for Children of Deceased Veterans and Others, (S—f) 651
Delaware National Guard Education Assistance Program, (S—m) 287
DelGreco, Jr. Scholarship Fund. *See* Sergeant Felix M. DelGreco, Jr. Scholarship Fund, entry (S—f) 999
Della Van Deuren Memorial Scholarships, (S—f) 652
Delta Dental Grants, (S—m) 288, (S—f) 653
Delta Dental Oral Health and Wellness Scholarship, (S—m) 289, (S—f) 654
Denig Foundation Scholarship. *See* Brigadier General Robert L. Denig Foundation Scholarship, entries (S—m) 259, (S—f) 587
Dennis Comai Scholarships, (S—f) 655
Department of Nebraska VFW State Scholarships, (S—v) 50, (S—f) 656
DePuy Memorial Scholarship Program. *See* General William E. DePuy Memorial Scholarship Program, entry (S—f) 722
DFC Society Ward Macauley Scholarships, (S—f) 657
Diane Duscheck Scholarship,. *See* Wisconsin Legion Auxiliary Merit and Memorial Scholarships, entry (S—f) 1080
Diane Lam Minority Woman Veteran Scholarship, (S—v) 51
Dick Vincent Scholarship. *See* ASMC Members' Continuing Education Grants, entries (S—m) 253, (F—m) 1215
Dimitri del Castillo Scholarships. *See* 1st Lt. Dimitri del Castillo Scholarships, entry (S—f) 523
Disabled American Veterans Auxiliary National Education Scholarship Fund, (S—f) 658, (F—f) 1341
Distinguished Flying Cross Society Ward Macauley Scholarships. *See* DFC Society Ward Macauley Scholarships, entry (S—f) 657
District 8 ALR Scholarships, (S—f) 659
District of Columbia National Guard State Tuition Assistance Reimbursement, (S—m) 290, (F—m) 1234
Ditmore Music Scholarships. *See* Women Marines Association Scholarship Program, entries (S—v) 219, (S—m) 512, (S—f) 1085, (F—v) 1191, (F—m) 1313, (F—f) 1429
Division Commander's Hip Pocket Scholarships, (S—m) 291
DKF Veterans Assistance Foundation Scholarships, (S—v) 52, (S—f) 660
DOL1 Scholarship, (S—f) 661
DOL2 Scholarship, (S—f) 662

S—Scholarships F—Fellowships G—Grants-in-Aid
v—Veterans m—Military Personnel f—Family Members

DOL3 Scholarship, (S—f) 663

Dolphin Scholarships, (S—f) 664

Don Carlos Kennedy Memorial Scholarship. See Texas State Council Vietnam Veterans of America Scholarships, entries (S—v) 194, (S—f) 1030

Donald Bruce Pringle Family Scholarship. See Fleet Reserve Association Member Scholarships, entries (S—v) 62, (S—m) 314, (S—f) 699, (F—v) 1127, (F—m) 1241, (F—f) 1351

Donaldson D. Frizzell Memorial Scholarships, (S—v) 53, (S—m) 292, (S—f) 665, (F—v) 1120, (F—m) 1235, (F—f) 1342

Donley Spouse Scholarships. See Mike and Gail Donley Spouse Scholarships, entries (S—f) 849, (F—f) 1374

Donna Jones Moritsugu Memorial Award. See AAPA Veterans Caucus Scholarships, entries (S—v) 7, (F—v) 1094

Doran Memorial Scholarships. See Stanley A. Doran Memorial Scholarships, entries (S—f) 1019, (F—f) 1414

Dorothy Jean Olson Memorial Scholarship. See Roy C. and Dorothy Jean Olson Memorial Scholarship, entry (S—f) 981

Dot Easter Scholarship. See Pop-A-Smoke Scholarships, entry (S—f) 960

Douglas Scholarship for Military Children, (S—f) 666

Dr. Aileen Webb Tobin Scholarship Program, (S—m) 293

Dr. Americo Bugliani Scholarship. See Japanese American Veterans Association Memorial Scholarships, entry (S—f) 775

Dr. Aurelio M. Cacccomo Family Foundation Memorial Scholarship, (S—v) 54, (S—m) 294

Dr. Kate Waller Barrett Grant, (S—f) 667

Dr. Nancy M. Schonher Scholarship, (S—v) 55, (S—m) 295, (S—f) 668, (F—v) 1121, (F—m) 1236, (F—f) 1343

Dr. Philip Shapiro Education Grant. See Leo A. Seigel-Dr. Philip Shapiro Education Grant, entry (S—f) 800

Dr. Sydell Perlmutter Gold Memorial Scholarships, (S—f) 669

Drevnick Memorial Fund Scholarships. See Daniel Drevnick Memorial Fund Scholarships, entries (S—v) 47, (S—f) 647

Duane L. "Duke" Corning Memorial Scholarship. See Major General Duane L. "Duke" Corning Memorial Scholarship, entries (S—v) 106, (S—m) 367, (S—f) 815

Duke Corning Memorial Scholarship. See Major General Duane L. "Duke" Corning Memorial Scholarship, entries (S—v) 106, (S—m) 367, (S—f) 815

Duscheck Scholarship,. See Wisconsin Legion Auxiliary Merit and Memorial Scholarships, entry (S—f) 1080

D.W. Steele Chapter AFA STEM Scholarships, (S—m) 296, (S—f) 670

E

E.A. Blackmore Scholarship, (S—f) 671

EANGMT USAA Scholarships, (S—m) 297, (S—f) 672

EANGNJ Scholarship Program, (S—m) 298, (S—f) 673

EANGTN Scholarship Program, (S—m) 299, (S—f) 674

EANGUS Auxiliary Scholarship Program, (S—f) 675

EANGUS Patriots Scholarships, (S—m) 300, (S—f) 676

EANGUT Scholarships, (S—m) 301, (S—f) 677

EANYNG Education Awards, (S—m) 302, (S—f) 678

EANYNG Memorial Scholarship. See EANYNG Education Awards, entries (S—m) 302, (S—f) 678

EANYNG Patriot Scholarship. See EANYNG Education Awards, entries (S—m) 302, (S—f) 678

Earline Mayberry Scholarship, (S—f) 679

Easter Scholarship. See Pop-A-Smoke Scholarships, entry (S—f) 960

Eastern Region Korean War Veteran Descendant Scholarships, (S—f) 680, (F—f) 1344

Ed Dauksz Scholarship Award. See George Washington Chapter AUSA Scholarships, entries (S—v) 72, (S—m) 324, (S—f) 724, (F—v) 1131, (F—m) 1246, (F—f) 1356

Ed Galloway Scholarship. See Virginia National Guard Association Scholarship, entries (S—m) 501, (S—f) 1063

Ed Scott Memorial Scholarship. See Association of Aviation Ordnancemen Educational Foundation Scholarships, entries (S—v) 24, (S—f) 578

Edgar Jadwin Scholarship. See San Antonio Post SAME Scholarships, entry (S—m) 464

Edith, Louis, and Max S. Millen Memorial Athletic Grant. See Jewish War Veterans National Youth Achievement Program, entry (S—f) 778

Edmund K. Gross Education Scholarship, (S—v) 56, (S—m) 303, (S—f) 681

Education Foundation for the Colorado National Guard Grants, (S—v) 57, (S—m) 304, (S—f) 682, (F—v) 1122, (F—m) 1237, (F—f) 1345

Educational Gratuity of the Pennsylvania Department of Military and Veterans Affairs, (S—f) 683

Edward and Veronica Ream Memorial Scholarship. See Naval Helicopter Association Scholarships, entries (S—v) 139, (S—m) 407, (S—f) 890, (F—v) 1156, (F—m) 1276, (F—f) 1383

Edward Honor Scholarship Award. See LTG Edward Honor Scholarship Award, entry (S—m) 363

Edward O. Nesheim Memorial Scholarship, (S—f) 684, (F—f) 1346

Edwards Memorial Scholarship. See AAPA Veterans Caucus Scholarships, entries (S—v) 7, (F—v) 1094

Edwin J. McGlothin Memorial Scholarship. See Veterans of Foreign Wars Post 81 Trust Fund Scholarship, entry (S—f) 1057

Edwin Roodhouse Memorial Scholarship Award. See 506th Airborne Infantry Regiment Association Scholarship, entries (S—v) 5, (S—f) 528, (F—v) 1093, (F—f) 1317

Egan Multi-Year Scholarships. See John and Alice Egan Multi-Year Scholarships, entry (S—m) 348

Egan ROTC Scholarships, (S—m) 305

Eheman Memorial Scholarship. See CPT James and Ruby Eheman Memorial Scholarship, entry (S—f) 641

Eileen Anderson Scholarship. See Navy League Foundation Scholarships, entry (S—f) 892

Eileen M. Bonner Scholarship Award for Medical Excellence, (S—m) 306

Ekenstam Memorial Scholarship. See G. Ray Ekenstam Memorial Scholarship, entry (S—v) 69

Elary Gromoff, Jr. Military Veteran Scholarship, (S—v) 58, (F—v) 1123

Elbert A. Welsh Education Awards (ROTC). See Major Elbert A. Welsh Education Awards (ROTC), entry (S—m) 366

Eleanor Colona Scholarship Grant. See CWOA LT Art and Eleanor Colona Scholarship Grant, entry (S—f) 645

Eleanor Smith Scholarship. See Wisconsin Legion Auxiliary Merit and Memorial Scholarships, entry (S—f) 1080

Elkey Scholarship. See CSM Robert W. Elkey Scholarship, entries (S—m) 282, (F—m) 1232

Emanuel American Legion Scholarships. See Schneider-Emanuel American Legion Scholarships, entries (S—v) 180, (S—f) 988

Energy Polymer Group Veterans Scholarships. See EPG Veterans Scholarships, entries (S—v) 60, (F—v) 1125

English Memorial Scholarship. See John Cornelius/Max English Memorial Scholarship, entries (S—m) 349, (S—f) 782, (F—m) 1252, (F—f) 1363

PROGRAM TITLE INDEX 443

Enlisted Association National Guard of New Jersey Scholarship Program. *See* EANGNJ Scholarship Program, entries (S—m) 298, (S—f) 673

Enlisted Association of the National Guard of Georgia Scholarships, (S—m) 307, (S—f) 685

Enlisted Association of the National Guard of Iowa Auxiliary Scholarship Program, (S—v) 59, (S—m) 308, (S—f) 686, (F—v) 1124, (F—m) 1238, (F—f) 1347

Enlisted Association of the National Guard of Kansas Scholarships, (S—m) 309, (S—f) 687

Enlisted Association of the National Guard of Montana USAA Scholarships. *See* EANGMT USAA Scholarships, entries (S—m) 297, (S—f) 672

Enlisted Association of the National Guard of Tennessee Scholarship Programs. *See* EANGTN Scholarship Program, entries (S—m) 299, (S—f) 674

Enlisted Association of the National Guard of the United States Auxiliary Scholarship Program. *See* EANGUS Auxiliary Scholarship Program, entry (S—f) 675

Enlisted Association of the National Guard of the United States Patriots Scholarships. *See* EANGUS Patriots Scholarships, entries (S—m) 300, (S—f) 676

Enlisted Association of the National Guard of Utah Scholarships. *See* EANGUT Scholarships, entries (S—m) 301, (S—f) 677

Enlisted Association of the New York National Guard Education Awards. *See* EANYNG Education Awards, entries (S—m) 302, (S—f) 678

Enlisted Association of the New York National Guard Education Memorial Scholarship. *See* EANYNG Education Awards, entries (S—m) 302, (S—f) 678

Enlisted Association of the New York National Guard Education Patriot Scholarship. *See* EANYNG Education Awards, entries (S—m) 302, (S—f) 678

Enlisted National Guard Association of Florida Scholarship Program. *See* NGOA-FL and ENGAF Scholarship Program, entries (S—m) 430, (S—f) 922

EOD Memorial Scholarships. *See* EOD Warrior Foundation Scholarships, entry (S—f) 688

EOD Warrior Foundation Scholarships, (S—f) 688

E.P. Travers Loan Program. *See* Navy-Marine Corps Relief Society Education Assistance, entries (S—m) 412, (S—f) 897

EPG Veterans Scholarships, (S—v) 60, (F—v) 1125

E.R. Smith Memorial Scholarship, (S—f) 689

Ernest and Gisela Hale Scholarships, (S—f) 690

Ernest G. "Scotty" Campbell, USN (Ret) and Renee Campbell Scholarship. *See* CAPT Ernest G. "Scotty" Campbell, USN (Ret) and Renee Campbell Scholarship, entry (S—f) 599

Ernesto "Gooie" Gomez Memorial Scholarship. *See* Pop-A-Smoke Scholarships, entry (S—f) 960

Ernie Wilson Jr. Scholarship, (S—f) 691

Ethyl and Armin Wiebke Memorial Scholarship. *See* Women Marines Association Scholarship Program, entries (S—v) 219, (S—m) 512, (S—f) 1085, (F—v) 1191, (F—m) 1313, (F—f) 1429

Eugene and Marilyn Overton Scholarship Award. *See* 506th Airborne Infantry Regiment Association Scholarship, entries (S—v) 5, (S—f) 528, (F—v) 1093, (F—f) 1317

Eugenia Bradford Roberts Memorial Fund. *See* Society of Daughters of the United States Army Scholarships, entry (S—f) 1006

Evelyn B. Hamilton Health Care Scholarship, (S—v) 61, (S—m) 310, (S—f) 692

Evelyn Oliver Memorial Scholarship. *See* Merrilyn Stock/Evelyn Oliver Memorial Scholarship, entries (S—v) 116, (S—f) 843

Exemption from Tuition Fees for Dependents of Kentucky Veterans, (S—f) 693, (F—f) 1348

Explosive Ordnance Disposal (EOD) Memorial Scholarships. *See* EOD Warrior Foundation Scholarships, entry (S—f) 688

Explosive Ordnance Disposal Option of the Seaman to Admiral-21 Program, (S—m) 311

Express Scripts Scholarships. *See* Fleet Reserve Association Member Scholarships, entries (S—v) 62, (S—m) 314, (S—f) 699, (F—v) 1127, (F—m) 1241, (F—f) 1351

F

Fallen Warrior Scholarship. *See* Women Marines Association Scholarship Program, entries (S—v) 219, (S—m) 512, (S—f) 1085, (F—v) 1191, (F—m) 1313, (F—f) 1429

Feldman Scholarships. *See* Renee Feldman Scholarships, entry (S—f) 971

Felix M. DelGreco, Jr. Scholarship Fund. *See* Sergeant Felix M. DelGreco, Jr. Scholarship Fund, entry (S—f) 999

Ferretti Scholarship. *See* Lt. Col. Romeo and Josephine Bass Ferretti Scholarship, entry (S—f) 809

Fifth Marine Division Association Scholarship, (S—f) 694

First Cavalry Division Association Scholarships, (S—m) 312, (S—f) 695

First Lieutenant Michael LiCalzi Memorial Scholarship, (S—m) 313, (S—f) 696, (F—m) 1239, (F—f) 1349

First Lieutenant Scott McClean Love Memorial Scholarship, (S—f) 697

First Marine Division Association Scholarships, (S—f) 698

Fleet Reserve Association Graduate Scholarships, (F—v) 1126, (F—m) 1240, (F—f) 1350

Fleet Reserve Association Member Scholarships, (S—v) 62, (S—m) 314, (S—f) 699, (F—v) 1127, (F—m) 1241, (F—f) 1351

Fleet Reserve Association Non-Member Scholarships, (S—v) 63, (S—m) 315, (S—f) 700, (F—v) 1128, (F—m) 1242, (F—f) 1352

Florence Lemke Memorial Scholarship in Fine Arts, (S—f) 701

Florida American Legion General Scholarships, (S—f) 702

Florida Legion Auxiliary Department Scholarship, (S—f) 703

Florida Legion Auxiliary Master's Program Grant, (F—f) 1353

Florida Legion Auxiliary Memorial Scholarship, (S—f) 704

Florida National Guard Educational Dollars for Duty (EDD) Program, (S—m) 316, (F—m) 1243

Florida Navy Nurse Corps Association Scholarships, (S—v) 64, (S—m) 317, (S—f) 705, (F—v) 1129, (F—m) 1244, (F—f) 1354

Florida Scholarships for Children and Spouses of Deceased or Disabled Veterans, (S—f) 706

Folded Flag Foundation Scholarships and Grants, (S—f) 707, (F—f) 1355

Folds of Honor Higher Education Scholarships, (S—f) 708

Footwear Warriors Higher Education Scholarships, (S—v) 65

Force Recon Association Scholarships, (S—v) 66, (S—m) 318, (S—f) 709

Ford Scholarships. *See* Lillie Lois Ford Scholarships, entry (S—f) 804

Forester Scholarship. *See* Mark Forester Scholarship, entry (S—f) 832

Foronda Memorial Scholarship. *See* California Legion Auxiliary Scholarships for Continuing and/or Reentry Students, entries (S—v) 32, (S—m) 262, (S—f) 596

Fort Worth Post SAME Scholarship, (S—v) 67, (S—m) 319, (F—v) 1130, (F—m) 1245

Fourth Marine Division Association of WWII Scholarship, (S—f) 710

Francisco Garcia Scholarships, (S—f) 711

S—Scholarships F—Fellowships G—Grants-in-Aid
v—Veterans m—Military Personnel f—Family Members

Frank N. Brown Veteran to Teacher Scholarships, (S—v) 68
Frederick C. Brace III Memorial Scholarship. *See* Captain Frederick C. Brace III Memorial Scholarship, entries (S—v) 35, (S—f) 601, (F—v) 1110, (F—f) 1332
Frederick C. Brace, Jr. Memorial Scholarship. *See* Sgt. Frederick C. Brace, Jr. Memorial Scholarship, entries (S—v) 183, (S—f) 1001, (F—v) 1172, (F—f) 1410
Frederick C. Branch Marine Corps Leadership Scholarships, (S—m) 320
Freedom Alliance Scholarships, (S—f) 712
Freeman Memorial Scholarship. *See* Pete Freeman Memorial Scholarship, entry (S—f) 955
Frizzell Memorial Scholarships. *See* Donaldson D. Frizzell Memorial Scholarships, entries (S—v) 53, (S—m) 292, (S—f) 665, (F—v) 1120, (F—m) 1235, (F—f) 1342
Fry Scholarship. *See* Marine Gunnery Sergeant John David Fry Scholarship, entry (S—f) 828
Fund a Scholar Program, (S—f) 713

G

G. Ray Ekenstam Memorial Scholarship, (S—v) 69
Gail Donley Spouse Scholarships. *See* Mike and Gail Donley Spouse Scholarships, entries (S—f) 849, (F—f) 1374
Galloway Scholarship. *See* Virginia National Guard Association Scholarship, entries (S—m) 501, (S—f) 1063
Gamewardens Association Scholarship, (S—f) 714
Gannett Veterans Award. *See* Anne Gannett Veterans Award, entries (S—v) 19, (F—v) 1100
Garcia Scholarships. *See* Francisco Garcia Scholarships, entry (S—f) 711
Garner Trust Scholarships, (S—f) 715
Gary Parrish Memorial Scholarship. *See* National Guard Association of Texas Scholarship Program, entries (S—v) 138, (S—m) 401, (S—f) 885, (F—v) 1155, (F—m) 1273, (F—f) 1381
Gavenonis Scholarships. *See* Joseph P. Gavenonis Scholarships, entry (S—f) 785
GEICO Scholarship. *See* Fleet Reserve Association Non-Member Scholarships, entries (S—v) 63, (S—m) 315, (S—f) 700, (F—v) 1128, (F—m) 1242, (F—f) 1352
Geiger Scholarship. *See* Daniel Geiger Scholarship, entry (S—f) 649
Gen. Jack N. Merritt Scholarship, (S—v) 70, (S—m) 321, (S—f) 716
General and Mrs. Charles C. Blanton AFBA Family Survivor College Scholarship, (S—f) 717
General Edgar Jadwin Scholarship. *See* San Antonio Post SAME Scholarships, entry (S—m) 464
General George A. White Scholarship. *See* Maria C. Jackson/General George A. White Scholarship, entries (S—v) 110, (S—f) 822, (F—v) 1147, (F—f) 1371
General Henry H. Arnold Education Grant Program, (S—f) 718
General Jerry Wyatt Memorial Scholarship. *See* Margene Mogan Proctor and General Jerry Wyatt Memorial Scholarship, entry (S—f) 820
General Jim and Pat Boswell Merit Scholarship Program, (S—f) 719
General John Paul Ratay Educational Fund Grants, (S—f) 720
General Lawson Memorial Scholarship, (S—f) 721
General Mathew B. Ridgeway Scholarship. *See* 82nd Airborne Division Association Awards, entries (S—v) 6, (S—f) 530
General Pedro Del Valle Leadership Scholarships, (S—m) 322
General (Ret.) Craig R. McKinley Flight Scholarship. *See* Arnold Air Society and Silver Wings Flying Scholarships, entry (S—m) 252

General William E. DePuy Memorial Scholarship Program, (S—f) 722
Genworth Foundation Veterans Scholarships, (S—f) 723
George A. White Scholarship. *See* Maria C. Jackson/General George A. White Scholarship, entries (S—v) 110, (S—f) 822, (F—v) 1147, (F—f) 1371
George L. Patt Scholarship Fund, (S—v) 71, (S—m) 323
George Washington Chapter AUSA Scholarships, (S—v) 72, (S—m) 324, (S—f) 724, (F—v) 1131, (F—m) 1246, (F—f) 1356
Georgia Department American Legion Scholarship, (S—f) 725
Georgia HERO Scholarship Program, (S—m) 325, (S—f) 726
Georgia Legion Auxiliary Past Department Presidents Scholarships, (S—f) 727
Georgia Legion Auxiliary Past President Parley Nursing Scholarship, (S—f) 728
Georgia National Guard Service Cancelable Loan, (S—m) 326
Georgia's Helping Educate Reservists and their Offspring Scholarship Program. *See* Georgia HERO Scholarship Program, entries (S—m) 325, (S—f) 726
Gerald R. Guild Memorial Scholarship. *See* CMSGT Gerald R. Guild Memorial Scholarships, entries (S—m) 269, (S—f) 618
Geraldine K. Morris Award, (S—f) 729
Giehll, IV Memorial Scholarship. *See* Raymond P. Giehll, IV Memorial Scholarship, entry (S—f) 965
Gillen Memorial Scholarship. *See* Isabella M. Gillen Memorial Scholarship, entry (S—f) 773
Gillette Scholarship. *See* Chappie Hall Memorial Scholarship Program, entry (S—f) 603
Gisela Hale Scholarships. *See* Ernest and Gisela Hale Scholarships, entry (S—f) 690
Gladys Ann Smith Greater Los Angeles Women's Council Scholarship. *See* Navy League Foundation Scholarships, entry (S—f) 892
Gladys K. and John K. Simpson Scholarship Fund. *See* Society of Daughters of the United States Army Scholarships, entry (S—f) 1006
Gladys McPartland Scholarships, (S—v) 73, (S—m) 327, (S—f) 730
Glenn F. Glezen Scholarship. *See* Fleet Reserve Association Graduate Scholarships, entries (F—v) 1126, (F—m) 1240, (F—f) 1350
Glezen Scholarship. *See* Fleet Reserve Association Graduate Scholarships, entries (F—v) 1126, (F—m) 1240, (F—f) 1350
Gloria and J. Michael McGrath Scholarship. *See* Navy League Foundation Scholarships, entry (S—f) 892
Gloria Jenell and Marlin E. Mote Endowed Scholarship. *See* National Guard Association of Texas Scholarship Program, entries (S—v) 138, (S—m) 401, (S—f) 885, (F—v) 1155, (F—m) 1273, (F—f) 1381
Gold Memorial Scholarships. *See* Dr. Sydell Perlmutter Gold Memorial Scholarships, entry (S—f) 669
Gold Star Scholarship Programs. *See* Navy-Marine Corps Relief Society Education Assistance, entries (S—m) 412, (S—f) 897
Gomez Memorial Scholarship. *See* Pop-A-Smoke Scholarships, entry (S—f) 960
Gonzales Scholarship. *See* Ruby Gonzales Scholarship, entries (S—v) 178, (S—m) 463, (S—f) 983
Google-SVA Scholarship, (S—v) 74, (S—m) 328, (F—v) 1132, (F—m) 1247
Gooie Gomez Memorial Scholarship. *See* Pop-A-Smoke Scholarships, entry (S—f) 960
Grant Hirabayashi Scholarship. *See* Japanese American Veterans Association Memorial Scholarships, entry (S—f) 775

S—Scholarships F—Fellowships G—Grants-in-Aid
v—Veterans m—Military Personnel f—Family Members

PROGRAM TITLE INDEX

Grant Scholarship Fund. *See* U.S. "Udie" Grant Scholarship Fund, entry (S—f) 1049

Greater Los Angeles Women's Council Scholarship. *See* Navy League Foundation Scholarships, entry (S—f) 892

Green Memorial Scholarship. *See* Army Scholarship Foundation Scholarships, entry (S—f) 576

Green to Gold Non-Scholarship Program, (S—m) 329

Green to Gold Scholarship Program, (S—m) 330

Greene STEM Scholarship Award. *See* George Washington Chapter AUSA Scholarships, entries (S—v) 72, (S—m) 324, (S—f) 724, (F—v) 1131, (F—m) 1246, (F—f) 1356

GRFD Scholarships. *See* Guaranteed Reserve Forces Duty (GRFD) Scholarships, entry (S—m) 331

Gridley Memorial Scholarship. *See* Women Marines Association Scholarship Program, entries (S—v) 219, (S—m) 512, (S—f) 1085, (F—v) 1191, (F—m) 1313, (F—f) 1429

Grimes Physician Assistant Educational Scholarship Award. *See* Captain Sean P. Grimes Physician Assistant Educational Scholarship Award, entries (S—v) 36, (S—m) 265, (F—v) 1112, (F—m) 1223

Grogan Memorial Scholarship, (S—v) 75, (S—f) 731, (F—v) 1133, (F—f) 1357

Gromoff, Jr. Military Veteran Scholarship. *See* Elary Gromoff, Jr. Military Veteran Scholarship, entries (S—v) 58, (F—v) 1123

Gross Education Scholarship. *See* Edmund K. Gross Education Scholarship, entries (S—v) 56, (S—m) 303, (S—f) 681

Grossman VFW State Memorial Scholarship. *See* Department of Nebraska VFW State Scholarships, entries (S—v) 50, (S—f) 656

Gruber Scholarships. *See* Kathern F. Gruber Scholarships, entries (S—f) 789, (F—f) 1364

Guaranteed Reserve Forces Duty (GRFD) Scholarships, (S—m) 331

Guild Memorial Scholarship. *See* CMSGT Gerald R. Guild Memorial Scholarships, entries (S—m) 269, (S—f) 618

Gus Hargett Scholarship. *See* Major General Gus Hargett Scholarship, entry (F—m) 1255

Guveyan Memorial Scholarship. *See* Women Marines Association Scholarship Program, entries (S—v) 219, (S—m) 512, (S—f) 1085, (F—v) 1191, (F—m) 1313, (F—f) 1429

Gwinn Memorial Scholarship. *See* AAPA Veterans Caucus Scholarships, entries (S—v) 7, (F—v) 1094

H

Had Richards UDT-SEAL Memorial Scholarship, (S—f) 732

Haeberle Memorial Scholarship. *See* Rosamond P. Haeberle Memorial Scholarship, entries (S—v) 176, (S—m) 461

Haines Music Scholarship. *See* Marilyn Haines Music Scholarship, entries (S—v) 111, (S—f) 824

Hale Scholarships. *See* Ernest and Gisela Hale Scholarships, entry (S—f) 690

Hall Memorial Scholarship Program. *See* Chappie Hall Memorial Scholarship Program, entry (S—f) 603

Hallock Scholarships. *See* Colonel Richard Hallock Scholarships, entries (S—v) 40, (S—m) 275, (S—f) 627

Hamilton Health Care Scholarship. *See* Evelyn B. Hamilton Health Care Scholarship, entries (S—v) 61, (S—m) 310, (S—f) 692

Hammer Family Scholarships, (S—v) 76

Hargett Scholarship. *See* Major General Gus Hargett Scholarship, entry (F—m) 1255

Harold C. Pierce Jr. Scholarship Program, (S—m) 332, (S—f) 733

Harold M. Beardslee Memorial Scholarship Awards. *See* Colonel Harold M. Beardslee Memorial Scholarship Awards, entry (S—f) 625

Harold Wirth Scholarship. *See* Navy League Foundation Scholarships, entry (S—f) 892

Harper Scholarship. *See* Howard R. Harper Scholarship, entries (S—m) 339, (S—f) 746

Harriet Hass Scholarship. *See* Wisconsin Legion Auxiliary Merit and Memorial Scholarships, entry (S—f) 1080

Harry and Mary Hensell Scholarship Program. *See* CSM Harry and Mary Hensell Scholarship Program, entries (S—m) 280, (S—f) 642

Harry Greene STEM Scholarship Award. *See* George Washington Chapter AUSA Scholarships, entries (S—v) 72, (S—m) 324, (S—f) 724, (F—v) 1131, (F—m) 1246, (F—f) 1356

Hass Scholarship. *See* Wisconsin Legion Auxiliary Merit and Memorial Scholarships, entry (S—f) 1080

Hattie Tedrow Memorial Fund Scholarship, (S—f) 734

Haupt Member's Child Scholarship. *See* Judith Haupt Member's Child Scholarship, entry (S—f) 786

Hawaii Aloha Chapter MOAA Scholarship Fund, (S—m) 333, (S—f) 735

Hayden W. Wagner Memorial Fund. *See* Society of Daughters of the United States Army Scholarships, entry (S—f) 1006

Hazel Benn, USMC, Scholarship. *See* Colonel Hazel Benn, USMC, Scholarship, entry (S—f) 626

Hazlewood Act Exemptions for Veterans, (S—v) 77, (F—v) 1134

Hazlewood Act for Spouse/Child, (S—f) 736

Hazlewood Legacy Act (Child), (S—f) 737, (F—f) 1358

Hedges Memorial Scholarship. *See* Colonel John D. Hedges Memorial Scholarship, entry (S—m) 274

Helen Dyar King Scholarship, (S—v) 78, (S—m) 334, (S—f) 738

Helen Klimek Student Scholarship, (S—f) 739

Helen T. Cribbins Scholarship. *See* Joseph P. and Helen T. Cribbins Scholarship, entries (S—v) 96, (S—m) 350, (S—f) 784

Helping Heroes Grants of Tennessee, (S—v) 79, (S—m) 335

Henry H. Arnold Education Grant Program. *See* General Henry H. Arnold Education Grant Program, entry (S—f) 718

Henry J. Reilly Scholarships, (S—v) 80, (S—m) 336, (S—f) 740, (F—v) 1135, (F—m) 1248, (F—f) 1359

Hensell Scholarship Program. *See* CSM Harry and Mary Hensell Scholarship Program, entries (S—m) 280, (S—f) 642

Herb Altman Memorial Scholarship. *See* 82nd Airborne Division Association Awards, entries (S—v) 6, (S—f) 530

Herb Kelleher Scholarships. *See* Arnold Air Society and Silver Wings Flying Scholarships, entry (S—m) 252

Heroes' Legacy Scholarships, (S—f) 741

Heroes Promise Scholarship of Oklahoma, (S—f) 742

Heroes Tribute Scholarship Program for Children of the Fallen, (S—f) 743

Heroes Tribute Scholarship Program for Children of the Wounded, (S—f) 744

Hescock Memorial Scholarship. *See* Naval Helicopter Association Scholarships, entries (S—v) 139, (S—m) 407, (S—f) 890, (F—v) 1156, (F—m) 1276, (F—f) 1383

High Child Welfare Scholarship Endowment Fund. *See* John A. High Child Welfare Scholarship Endowment Fund, entry (S—f) 779

Hill & Ponton Veterans Scholarships, (S—v) 81

Hill Scholarship Fund. *See* Charles W. and Annette Hill Scholarship Fund, entry (S—f) 605

Hipp Heroes Scholarship. *See* Van Hipp Heroes Scholarship, entries (S—v) 205, (S—m) 498

S—Scholarships F—Fellowships G—Grants-in-Aid
v—Veterans m—Military Personnel f—Family Members

Hirabayashi Scholarship. *See* Japanese American Veterans Association Memorial Scholarships, entry (S—f) 775

Hire Our Heroes Scholarships and Tool Grants. *See* 3M "Hire Our Heroes" Scholarships and Tool Grants, entries (S—v) 3, (S—m) 223, (S—f) 526

Hobson STEM Scholarship. *See* AEA Congressman David L. Hobson STEM Scholarship, entries (S—m) 224, (S—f) 536

Holmes Scholarship. *See* Wyoming National Guard Association Scholarships, entries (S—m) 516, (S—f) 1091

Homegrown by Heroes Scholarships, (S—v) 82, (S—m) 337, (S—f) 745

Honor Scholarship Award. *See* LTG Edward Honor Scholarship Award, entry (S—m) 363

Honorably Discharged Graduate Assistance Program, (S—v) 83, (S—m) 338

Hooks Memorial Scholarship. *See* North Carolina Vietnam Veterans Scholarship Program, entries (S—v) 153, (S—f) 931

Hooley Scholarship for Oregon Veterans. *See* Darlene Hooley Scholarship for Oregon Veterans, entries (S—v) 48, (F—v) 1118

Hopcraft Memorial Scholarship for Veterans. *See* Rick Hopcraft Memorial Scholarship for Veterans, entry (S—v) 174

Horse Hescock Memorial Scholarship. *See* Naval Helicopter Association Scholarships, entries (S—v) 139, (S—m) 407, (S—f) 890, (F—v) 1156, (F—m) 1276, (F—f) 1383

Howard R. Harper Scholarship, (S—m) 339, (S—f) 746

Hoyal/Maxine Chilton Scholarships. *See* Wilma D. Hoyal/Maxine Chilton Scholarships, entries (S—v) 216, (S—f) 1076

H.S. and Angeline Lewis Scholarships, (S—f) 747, (F—f) 1360

Hub Johnson Scholarship. *See* San Antonio Post SAME Scholarships, entry (S—m) 464

Hubert O. "Hub" Johnson Scholarship. *See* San Antonio Post SAME Scholarships, entry (S—m) 464

Huebner Scholarships. *See* Lieutenant General Clarence L. Huebner Scholarships, entry (S—f) 802

Humphreys Jr. Memorial Scholarship. *See* EANGNJ Scholarship Program, entries (S—m) 298, (S—f) 673

I

Ia Drang Scholarship Program, (S—f) 748

Idaho Armed Forces and Public Safety Officer Scholarships, (S—f) 749

Idaho Legion Auxiliary General Studies Non-Traditional Scholarship, (S—v) 84, (S—f) 750

Idaho Legion Auxiliary General Studies Traditional Scholarship, (S—f) 751

Idaho Legion Auxiliary Non-Traditional Nurses Scholarship, (S—v) 85, (S—f) 752

Idaho Legion Auxiliary Traditional Nurses Scholarship, (S—f) 753

Illinois American Legion Auxiliary Past Presidents Parley Nurses Scholarship, (S—v) 86, (S—f) 754

Illinois American Legion Scholarships, (S—f) 755

Illinois American Legion Trade School Scholarships, (S—f) 756

Illinois AMVETS Junior ROTC Scholarships, (S—f) 757

Illinois AMVETS Ladies Auxiliary Memorial Scholarship, (S—f) 758

Illinois AMVETS Service Foundation Scholarships, (S—f) 759

Illinois AMVETS Service Foundation Veterans Scholarships, (S—v) 87

Illinois AMVETS Trade School Scholarships, (S—f) 760

Illinois Children of Veterans Scholarships, (S—f) 761

Illinois Fallen Heroes Scholarship, (S—f) 762

Illinois MIA/POW Scholarship, (S—f) 763

Illinois National Guard Grant Program, (S—v) 88, (S—m) 340, (F—v) 1136, (F—m) 1249

Illinois Scholarships for Junior Members, (S—f) 764

Illinois Veteran Grant Program, (S—v) 89, (F—v) 1137

Imagine America Military Award Program, (S—v) 90, (S—m) 341

Indiana American Legion Family Scholarship, (S—f) 765

Indiana Children of Deceased or Disabled Veterans Program, (S—f) 766, (F—f) 1361

Indiana Children of Former POW/MIA Program, (S—f) 767

Indiana Children of Purple Heart Recipients Program, (S—f) 768

Indiana National Guard Supplemental Grant Program, (S—m) 342

Indiana Purple Heart Recipient Veteran Program, (S—v) 91, (F—v) 1138

Inouye Memorial Scholarship. *See* Senator Daniel K. Inouye Memorial Scholarship, entries (S—v) 181, (S—m) 471, (S—f) 997, (F—v) 1170, (F—m) 1298, (F—f) 1408

Iowa National Guard Educational Assistance Program, (S—m) 343

Iowa National Guard Officers Auxiliary Spouse Scholarship, (S—f) 769

Iowa National Guard Officers Auxiliary Student Scholarship, (S—f) 770

Iowa War Orphan Tuition Assistance, (S—f) 771

Iraq and Afghanistan Service Grants, (S—f) 772

Irene Rubenstein Memorial Grant. *See* Jewish War Veterans National Achievement Program, entries (S—v) 94, (S—m) 345, (F—v) 1140, (F—m) 1250

Irwin Memorial Scholarship Fund. *See* Walter Keith Irwin Memorial Scholarship Fund, entry (S—f) 1066

Isabella M. Gillen Memorial Scholarship, (S—f) 773

Ivory Memorial Scholarships. *See* AAPA Veterans Caucus Scholarships, entries (S—v) 7, (F—v) 1094

Iwata Memorial Scholarship for Advanced Practice. *See* Captain Miki Iwata Memorial Scholarship for Advanced Practice, entries (F—v) 1111, (F—m) 1222, (F—f) 1333

Izumigawa Scholarship Fund. *See* 100th Infantry Battalion Veterans Stanley Izumigawa Scholarship Fund, entries (S—f) 519, (F—f) 1316

J

J. Allan Green Memorial Scholarship. *See* Army Scholarship Foundation Scholarships, entry (S—f) 576

J. Michael McGrath Scholarship. *See* Navy League Foundation Scholarships, entry (S—f) 892

Jack and Eileen Anderson Scholarship. *See* Navy League Foundation Scholarships, entry (S—f) 892

Jack B. Sacks Foundation Scholarship. *See* United States Army Warrant Officers Association Scholarship Program, entry (S—f) 1046

Jack Costello Memorial Scholarship. *See* Army Scholarship Foundation Scholarships, entry (S—f) 576

Jack E. Barger, Sr. Memorial Nursing Scholarships, (S—v) 92, (S—m) 344, (S—f) 774

Jack Murphy Memorial Nurses Training Scholarship. *See* M.D. "Jack" Murphy Memorial Nurses Training Scholarship, entry (S—f) 841

Jack N. Merritt Scholarship. *See* Gen. Jack N. Merritt Scholarship, entries (S—v) 70, (S—m) 321, (S—f) 716

Jackson/General George A. White Scholarship. *See* Maria C. Jackson/General George A. White Scholarship, entries (S—v) 110, (S—f) 822, (F—v) 1147, (F—f) 1371

Jadwin Scholarship. *See* San Antonio Post SAME Scholarships, entry (S—m) 464

James and Ruby Eheman Memorial Scholarship. *See* CPT James and Ruby Eheman Memorial Scholarship, entry (S—f) 641

James Joseph Davis Memorial Scholarship, (S—v) 93, (F—v) 1139

PROGRAM TITLE INDEX

James Ursano Scholarship Fund. *See* MG James Ursano Scholarship Fund, entry (S–f) 845

Jan Pulvermacher-Ryan Scholarship. *See* Wisconsin Legion Auxiliary Merit and Memorial Scholarships, entry (S–f) 1080

Japanese American Veterans Association Founders' Scholarship. *See* JAVA Founders' Scholarship, entries (S–f) 776, (F–f) 1362

Japanese American Veterans Association Memorial Scholarships, (S–f) 775

JAVA Founders' Scholarship, (S–f) 776, (F–f) 1362

Jay Smith Memorial Endowment Scholarship. *See* Lt. Paul (Jay) Smith Memorial Endowment Scholarship, entry (S–m) 361

Jean Tallas Memorial Scholarship. *See* National Guard Association of Texas Scholarship Program, entries (S–v) 138, (S–m) 401, (S–f) 885, (F–v) 1155, (F–m) 1273, (F–f) 1381

Jeanne Colbert Scholarship. *See* Pop-A-Smoke Scholarships, entry (S–f) 960

Jenell and Marlin E. Mote Endowed Scholarship. *See* National Guard Association of Texas Scholarship Program, entries (S–v) 138, (S–m) 401, (S–f) 885, (F–v) 1155, (F–m) 1273, (F–f) 1381

Jennifer Shafer Odom Memorial Scholarship. *See* Army Scholarship Foundation Scholarships, entry (S–f) 576

Jerry W. Ross Scholarship. *See* Colonel Jerry W. Ross Scholarship, entries (F–m) 1229, (F–f) 1336

Jerry Wyatt Memorial Scholarship. *See* Margene Mogan Proctor and General Jerry Wyatt Memorial Scholarship, entry (S–f) 820

Jesse Edwards Memorial Scholarship. *See* AAPA Veterans Caucus Scholarships, entries (S–v) 7, (F–v) 1094

Jewell Hilton Bonner Scholarship, (S–f) 777

Jewish War Veterans National Achievement Program, (S–v) 94, (S–m) 345, (F–v) 1140, (F–m) 1250

Jewish War Veterans National Youth Achievement Program, (S–f) 778

Jim and Pat Boswell Merit Scholarship Program. *See* General Jim and Pat Boswell Merit Scholarship Program, entry (S–f) 719

Jimmie Kanaya Scholarship. *See* Japanese American Veterans Association Memorial Scholarships, entry (S–f) 775

Joan Bowden Scholarship, (S–m) 346

Jodi Callahan Memorial Scholarship. *See* Captain Jodi Callahan Memorial Scholarship, entry (F–m) 1221

Joe Henry Senft Scholarship. *See* USSV CF Scholarship Awards, entry (S–f) 1052

Joe King Scholarships, (S–m) 347, (F–m) 1251

John A. High Child Welfare Scholarship Endowment Fund, (S–f) 779

John Allnatt Memorial Scholarship. *See* United States Army Warrant Officers Association Scholarship Program, entry (S–f) 1046

John and Alice Egan Multi-Year Scholarships, (S–m) 348

John C. and Blanche Lee Lindsay Memorial Scholarship, (S–f) 780

John Casey Scholarship, (S–f) 781

John Cornelius/Max English Memorial Scholarship, (S–m) 349, (S–f) 782, (F–m) 1252, (F–f) 1363

John D. Hedges Memorial Scholarship. *See* Colonel John D. Hedges Memorial Scholarship, entry (S–m) 274

John D. Perrey, Sr. Memorial Scholarship. *See* ProVets Military Scholarships, entries (S–v) 167, (S–f) 962

John David Fry Scholarship. *See* Marine Gunnery Sergeant John David Fry Scholarship, entry (S–f) 828

John F. Kinney Fellowship. *See* Brigadier General John F. Kinney Fellowship, entry (S–m) 258

John F. Kusior Memorial Scholarship. *See* Army Scholarship Foundation Scholarships, entry (S–f) 576

John G. Brokaw Scholarship. *See* Navy League Foundation Scholarships, entry (S–f) 892

John H. Humphreys Jr. Memorial Scholarship. *See* EANGNJ Scholarship Program, entries (S–m) 298, (S–f) 673

John Hill Carruth Scholarship. *See* San Antonio Post SAME Scholarships, entry (S–m) 464

John J. Schiff Scholarship. *See* Navy League Foundation Scholarships, entry (S–f) 892

John K. Simpson Scholarship Fund. *See* Society of Daughters of the United States Army Scholarships, entry (S–f) 1006

John Keys Kentucky Sons of the American Legion Scholarship, (S–v) 95, (S–f) 783

John Kloss Memorial Veteran Scholarship. *See* AHIMA Veterans Scholarship, entries (S–v) 10, (S–f) 541, (F–v) 1096, (F–f) 1319

John Lally Scholarship Award. *See* 506th Airborne Infantry Regiment Association Scholarship, entries (S–v) 5, (S–f) 528, (F–v) 1093, (F–f) 1317

John Paul Ratay Educational Fund Grants. *See* General John Paul Ratay Educational Fund Grants, entry (S–f) 720

John Williams Scholarship. *See* Gamewardens Association Scholarship, entry (S–f) 714

Johnny Mac Soldiers Fund Scholarships. *See* Army Scholarship Foundation Scholarships, entry (S–f) 576

Johnson Scholarship. *See* San Antonio Post SAME Scholarships, entry (S–m) 464

Jon C. Ladda Memorial Foundation Scholarship. *See* Lt. Jon C. Ladda Memorial Foundation Scholarship, entry (S–f) 810

Jon L. Boyes, Vice Admiral, USN (Ret.) Memorial Scholarship. *See* VADM Jon L. Boyes, Vice Admiral, USN (Ret.) Memorial Scholarship, entry (S–m) 497

Joseph A. McAlinden Divers Scholarship. *See* Navy-Marine Corps Relief Society Education Assistance, entries (S–m) 412, (S–f) 897

Joseph "Ed" Galloway Scholarship. *See* Virginia National Guard Association Scholarship, entries (S–m) 501, (S–f) 1063

Joseph Memorial Scholarship. *See* ProVets Military Scholarships, entries (S–v) 167, (S–f) 962

Joseph P. and Helen T. Cribbins Scholarship, (S–v) 96, (S–m) 350, (S–f) 784

Joseph P. Gavenonis Scholarships, (S–f) 785

Joseph P. Joseph Memorial Scholarship. *See* ProVets Military Scholarships, entries (S–v) 167, (S–f) 962

Joseph R. Baranski Scholarship. *See* Fleet Reserve Association Graduate Scholarships, entries (F–v) 1126, (F–m) 1240, (F–f) 1350

Josephine Bass Ferretti Scholarship. *See* Lt. Col. Romeo and Josephine Bass Ferretti Scholarship, entry (S–f) 809

Judith Haupt Member's Child Scholarship, (S–f) 786

K

Kanaya Scholarship. *See* Japanese American Veterans Association Memorial Scholarships, entry (S–f) 775

Kansas Military Service Scholarships, (S–v) 97, (S–m) 351

Kansas National Guard Educational Assistance, (S–m) 352

Kansas ROTC Service Scholarship, (S–m) 353

Kansas Tuition Waiver for Dependents and Spouses of Deceased Military Personnel, (S–f) 787

Kansas VFW Endowment Scholarship, (S–f) 788

S—Scholarships F—Fellowships G—Grants-in-Aid
v—Veterans m—Military Personnel f—Family Members

Kansas Waiver of Tuition and Fees for Prisoners of War, (S—v) 98

Karen Snee Scholarship. *See* Fleet Reserve Association Member Scholarships, entries (S—v) 62, (S—m) 314, (S—f) 699, (F—v) 1127, (F—m) 1241, (F—f) 1351

Karman Memorial Scholarship. *See* Naval Helicopter Association Scholarships, entries (S—v) 139, (S—m) 407, (S—f) 890, (F—v) 1156, (F—m) 1276, (F—f) 1383

Kasai Scholarship. *See* Japanese American Veterans Association Memorial Scholarships, entry (S—f) 775

Kashino Memorial Scholarships. *See* Shiro Kashino Memorial Scholarships, entry (S—f) 1002

Kate Waller Barrett Grant. *See* Dr. Kate Waller Barrett Grant, entry (S—f) 667

Kathern F. Gruber Scholarships, (S—f) 789, (F—f) 1364

Keirn C. Brown Memorial Scholarship. *See* Army Scholarship Foundation Scholarships, entry (S—f) 576

Kelleher Scholarships. *See* Arnold Air Society and Silver Wings Flying Scholarships, entry (S—m) 252

Ken E. Blair Scholarship. *See* Fleet Reserve Association Member Scholarships, entries (S—v) 62, (S—m) 314, (S—f) 699, (F—v) 1127, (F—m) 1241, (F—f) 1351

Kennedy Memorial Scholarship. *See* Texas State Council Vietnam Veterans of America Scholarships, entries (S—v) 194, (S—f) 1030

Kentucky National Guard Tuition Award Program, (S—m) 354, (F—m) 1253

Kentucky Sons of the American Legion Scholarship. *See* John Keys Kentucky Sons of the American Legion Scholarship, entries (S—v) 95, (S—f) 783

Kentucky Veterans Tuition Waiver Program, (S—f) 790

Keys Kentucky Sons of the American Legion Scholarship. *See* John Keys Kentucky Sons of the American Legion Scholarship, entries (S—v) 95, (S—f) 783

Kilpatrick Memorial AUSA Scholarship. *See* SGM Dawn Kilpatrick Memorial AUSA Scholarship, entry (S—m) 473

Kimberly Kay Clark Memorial Scholarship, (S—m) 355

King Memorial Scholarship. *See* National Guard Association of Texas Scholarship Program, entries (S—v) 138, (S—m) 401, (S—f) 885, (F—v) 1155, (F—m) 1273, (F—f) 1381

King Scholarship. *See* Helen Dyar King Scholarship, entries (S—v) 78, (S—m) 334, (S—f) 738

King Scholarships. *See* Joe King Scholarships, entries (S—m) 347, (F—m) 1251

Kinney Fellowship. *See* Brigadier General John F. Kinney Fellowship, entry (S—m) 258

Kisling Scholarship. *See* Chief Master Sergeant of the Air Force Scholarship Program, entry (S—f) 607

Kissel Memorial Scholarship. *See* AAPA Veterans Caucus Scholarships, entries (S—v) 7, (F—v) 1094

Kiyoko Tsuboi Taubkin Legacy Scholarship, (S—f) 791

Klimek Student Scholarship. *See* Helen Klimek Student Scholarship, entry (S—f) 739

Klugow Memorial Scholarships. *See* Marie Klugow Memorial Scholarships, entry (S—f) 823

Knapp Family Scholarship. *See* Chappie Hall Memorial Scholarship Program, entry (S—f) 603

Knoles Scholarships. *See* Mildred R. Knoles Scholarships, entries (S—v) 118, (S—f) 850

Kogutek Scholarship. *See* Past National Commander Michael J. Kogutek Scholarship, entries (S—v) 159, (S—f) 948

Konecny Memorial Endowment Scholarship. *See* M. Alice Konecny Memorial Endowment Scholarship, entry (S—m) 364

Korea Veterans Scholarship Program, (S—f) 792, (F—f) 1365

Korean War Veterans Association Scholarships, (S—f) 793

Korean War Veteran's Children's CC Scholarship, (S—f) 794

Korean War Veteran's Children's Scholarship, (S—f) 795

Kosmutza Memorial Grant. *See* Jewish War Veterans National Achievement Program, entries (S—v) 94, (S—m) 345, (F—v) 1140, (F—m) 1250

Kosmutza Scholarship Fund. *See* Charles Kosmutza Scholarship Fund, entry (S—f) 604

Kranig Scholarship. *See* Wisconsin Legion Auxiliary Merit and Memorial Scholarships, entry (S—f) 1080

Kratz Scholarships. *See* Chappie Hall Memorial Scholarship Program, entry (S—f) 603

Kreiglowa Navy and Marine Corps Dependents Education Foundation Scholarship. *See* Alexander Kreiglowa Navy and Marine Corps Dependents Education Foundation Scholarship, entry (S—f) 550

Kristal Education Grant. *See* Jewish War Veterans National Youth Achievement Program, entry (S—f) 778

Kuroki Scholarship. *See* Japanese American Veterans Association Memorial Scholarships, entry (S—f) 775

Kusior Memorial Scholarship. *See* Army Scholarship Foundation Scholarships, entry (S—f) 576

L

LA FRA National President's Scholarship, (S—f) 796

LA FRA Scholarship, (S—f) 797

Ladda Memorial Foundation Scholarship. *See* Lt. Jon C. Ladda Memorial Foundation Scholarship, entry (S—f) 810

Ladies Auxiliary of the Fleet Reserve Association National President's Scholarship. *See* LA FRA National President's Scholarship, entry (S—f) 796

Ladies Auxiliary of the Fleet Reserve Association Scholarship. *See* LA FRA Scholarship, entry (S—f) 797

Lally Scholarship Award. *See* 506th Airborne Infantry Regiment Association Scholarship, entries (S—v) 5, (S—f) 528, (F—v) 1093, (F—f) 1317

Lam Minority Woman Veteran Scholarship. *See* Diane Lam Minority Woman Veteran Scholarship, entry (S—v) 51

Lambert Memorial Scholarship. *See* Daniel E. Lambert Memorial Scholarship, entry (S—f) 648

Lancaster Scholarship, (S—v) 99, (F—v) 1141

Langkamp Memorial Scholarship. *See* Pauline Langkamp Memorial Scholarship, entry (S—f) 951

Lappin Scholarship. *See* Albert M. Lappin Scholarship, entry (S—f) 548

Larry Martin Small Business Scholarship. *See* San Antonio Post SAME Scholarships, entry (S—m) 464

Larry Strickland Memorial Fund and Scholarship, (S—m) 356

LaRue A. Ditmore Music Scholarships. *See* Women Marines Association Scholarship Program, entries (S—v) 219, (S—m) 512, (S—f) 1085, (F—v) 1191, (F—m) 1313, (F—f) 1429

Latta Scholarship. *See* Chappie Hall Memorial Scholarship Program, entry (S—f) 603

Laura Blackburn Memorial Scholarship, (S—f) 798

Laverne and Phillip Blottenberger Scholarship. *See* Chappie Hall Memorial Scholarship Program, entry (S—f) 603

Lawona R. Spencer Scholarship. *See* Col. Loren J. and Mrs. Lawona R. Spencer Scholarship, entry (F—m) 1228

Lawrence Luterman Memorial Scholarships. *See* New Jersey American Legion Scholarships, entry (S—f) 903

Leach Scholarships. *See* Wesley Hammon Leach Scholarships, entries (S—v) 214, (S—m) 506, (S—f) 1071

Leidos STEM Scholarship, (S—f) 799

S—Scholarships
v—Veterans

F—Fellowships
m—Military Personnel

G—Grants-in-Aid
f—Family Members

PROGRAM TITLE INDEX

Leif J. Sverdrup Scholarship. *See* MG Leif J. Sverdrup Scholarship, entries (S—m) 378, (F—m) 1264

Lemke Memorial Scholarship in Fine Arts. *See* Florence Lemke Memorial Scholarship in Fine Arts, entry (S—f) 701

Len and Jean Tallas Memorial Scholarship. *See* National Guard Association of Texas Scholarship Program, entries (S—v) 138, (S—m) 401, (S—f) 885, (F—v) 1155, (F—m) 1273, (F—f) 1381

Lencioni Family Scholarship. *See* Chappie Hall Memorial Scholarship Program, entry (S—f) 603

Leo A. Seigel-Dr. Philip Shapiro Education Grant, (S—f) 800

Leon Brooks Memorial Grant. *See* Jewish War Veterans National Achievement Program, entries (S—v) 94, (S—m) 345, (F—v) 1140, (F—m) 1250

Leon Van Autreve Scholarships. *See* SMA Leon Van Autreve Scholarships, entries (S—v) 185, (S—m) 476, (S—f) 1004

Leonard Maglione Memorial Scholarships. *See* CSM Leonard Maglione Memorial Scholarships, entries (S—v) 45, (S—m) 281, (S—f) 643, (F—v) 1117, (F—m) 1231, (F—f) 1339

Leonardo DRS Guardian Scholarship, (S—f) 801

Levinson Scholarship. *See* Navy League Foundation Scholarships, entry (S—f) 892

Lewis O. King Memorial Scholarship. *See* National Guard Association of Texas Scholarship Program, entries (S—v) 138, (S—m) 401, (S—f) 885, (F—v) 1155, (F—m) 1273, (F—f) 1381

Lewis Scholarships. *See* H.S. and Angeline Lewis Scholarships, entries (S—f) 747, (F—f) 1360

LiCalzi Memorial Scholarship. *See* First Lieutenant Michael LiCalzi Memorial Scholarship, entries (S—m) 313, (S—f) 696, (F—m) 1239, (F—f) 1349

Liebsack Memorial Scholarship. *See* Department of Nebraska VFW State Scholarships, entries (S—v) 50, (S—f) 656

Lieppe Memorial Grant. *See* Jewish War Veterans National Achievement Program, entries (S—v) 94, (S—m) 345, (F—v) 1140, (F—m) 1250

Lieutenant Colonel Walter R. Bowie Memorial Scholarship. *See* Army Scholarship Foundation Scholarships, entry (S—f) 576

Lieutenant General Clarence L. Huebner Scholarships, (S—f) 802

Lieutenant General Jack Costello Memorial Scholarship. *See* Army Scholarship Foundation Scholarships, entry (S—f) 576

Lieutenant J. Allan Green Memorial Scholarship. *See* Army Scholarship Foundation Scholarships, entry (S—f) 576

Lieutenant Keirn C. Brown Memorial Scholarship. *See* Army Scholarship Foundation Scholarships, entry (S—f) 576

Lillian Campbell Medical Scholarship, (S—v) 100, (S—f) 803, (F—v) 1142, (F—f) 1366

Lillie Lois Ford Scholarships, (S—f) 804

Lily H. Gridley Memorial Scholarship. *See* Women Marines Association Scholarship Program, entries (S—v) 219, (S—m) 512, (S—f) 1085, (F—v) 1191, (F—m) 1313, (F—f) 1429

Lindsay Memorial Scholarship. *See* John C. and Blanche Lee Lindsay Memorial Scholarship, entry (S—f) 780

Lipscomb, Sr. Memorial Scholarship. *See* SMSgt. Nathan L. Lipscomb, Sr. Memorial Scholarship, entries (S—v) 186, (S—f) 1005, (F—v) 1174, (F—f) 1411

Lonnie Stephenson Memorial Scholarship. *See* ProVets Military Scholarships, entries (S—v) 167, (S—f) 962

Lopez Scholarship Program. *See* Tony Lopez Scholarship Program, entries (S—v) 199, (S—m) 489, (S—f) 1038

Loren J. and Mrs. Lawona R. Spencer Scholarship. *See* Col. Loren J. and Mrs. Lawona R. Spencer Scholarship, entry (F—m) 1228

Loretta Cornett-Huff Scholarships, (S—f) 805, (F—f) 1367

Los Angeles Chapter AFCEA Scholarships, (S—m) 357

Louis and Max S. Millen Memorial Athletic Grant. *See* Jewish War Veterans National Youth Achievement Program, entry (S—f) 778

Louis J. Schober Memorial Scholarship, (S—v) 101, (S—m) 358, (S—f) 806

Louisiana National Guard State Tuition Exemption Program, (S—m) 359, (F—m) 1254

Louisiana Title 29 Dependents' Educational Assistance, (S—f) 807

Love Memorial Scholarship. *See* First Lieutenant Scott McClean Love Memorial Scholarship, entry (S—f) 697

Lowenberg Scholarship. *See* NGAW Scholarship Program, entries (S—m) 429, (S—f) 921

Lowe's AMVETS Technology Scholarships, (S—v) 102, (S—m) 360, (S—f) 808

LT Christian "Horse" Hescock Memorial Scholarship. *See* Naval Helicopter Association Scholarships, entries (S—v) 139, (S—m) 407, (S—f) 890, (F—v) 1156, (F—m) 1276, (F—f) 1383

Lt. Col. David Gwinn Memorial Scholarship. *See* AAPA Veterans Caucus Scholarships, entries (S—v) 7, (F—v) 1094

Lt. Col. Romeo and Josephine Bass Ferretti Scholarship, (S—f) 809

Lt. Jon C. Ladda Memorial Foundation Scholarship, (S—f) 810

LT Michael Murphy Memorial Award. *See* Military Order of the Purple Heart Scholarship Program, entries (S—v) 122, (S—f) 856

Lt. Paul (Jay) Smith Memorial Endowment Scholarship, (S—m) 361

LT Ruth Cortes Memorial Scholarship, (S—v) 103, (F—v) 1143

LTC Gary Parrish Memorial Scholarship. *See* National Guard Association of Texas Scholarship Program, entries (S—v) 138, (S—m) 401, (S—f) 885, (F—v) 1155, (F—m) 1273, (F—f) 1381

LTC Michael Warren Memorial Scholarships, (S—m) 362, (S—f) 811

LTG Edward Honor Scholarship Award, (S—m) 363

Lucian Butler American Legion Scholarship Fund, (S—f) 812

Lucile Parrish Ward Veteran's Award, (S—v) 104, (F—v) 1144

Luke Wullenwaber Memorial Scholarship Award. *See* 506th Airborne Infantry Regiment Association Scholarship, entries (S—v) 5, (S—f) 528, (F—v) 1093, (F—f) 1317

Lundell Military Survivors Tuition Waiver. *See* Scott Lundell Military Survivors Tuition Waiver, entry (S—f) 992

Luterman Memorial Scholarships. *See* New Jersey American Legion Scholarships, entry (S—f) 903

M

M. Alice Konecny Memorial Endowment Scholarship, (S—m) 364

Mac Soldiers Fund Scholarships. *See* Army Scholarship Foundation Scholarships, entry (S—f) 576

Macauley Scholarship. *See* Wisconsin Legion Auxiliary Merit and Memorial Scholarships, entry (S—f) 1080

Macauley Scholarships. *See* DFC Society Ward Macauley Scholarships, entry (S—f) 657

Maglione Scholarships. *See* CSM Leonard Maglione Memorial Scholarships, entries (S—v) 45, (S—m) 281, (S—f) 643, (F—v) 1117, (F—m) 1231, (F—f) 1339

Maine National Guard Tuition Assistance, (S—m) 365

Maine Veterans Dependents Educational Benefits, (S—f) 813, (F—f) 1368

Maine Vietnam Veterans Scholarship Fund, (S—v) 105, (S—f) 814, (F—v) 1145, (F—f) 1369

Maj. Megan McClung Memorial Scholarship. *See* Women Marines Association Scholarship Program, entries (S—v) 219, (S—m) 512, (S—f) 1085, (F—v) 1191, (F—m) 1313, (F—f) 1429

S—Scholarships
v—Veterans
F—Fellowships
m—Military Personnel
G—Grants-in-Aid
f—Family Members

Major Elbert A. Welsh Education Awards (ROTC), (S—m) 366
Major General Carl F. McNair Jr. Scholarship Award. *See* George Washington Chapter AUSA Scholarships, entries (S—v) 72, (S—m) 324, (S—f) 724, (F—v) 1131, (F—m) 1246, (F—f) 1356
Major General Duane L. "Duke" Corning Memorial Scholarship, (S—v) 106, (S—m) 367, (S—f) 815
Major General Gus Hargett Scholarship, (F—m) 1255
Major General Harry Greene STEM Scholarship Award. *See* George Washington Chapter AUSA Scholarships, entries (S—v) 72, (S—m) 324, (S—f) 724, (F—v) 1131, (F—m) 1246, (F—f) 1356
Major Muneo "Mike" Okusa Scholarship. *See* Japanese American Veterans Association Memorial Scholarships, entry (S—f) 775
Major Richard L. Ridder Memorial Scholarship, (S—v) 107, (S—m) 368, (S—f) 816
Mancini Memorial Scholarships. *See* SFC Curtis Mancini Memorial Scholarships, entries (S—v) 182, (S—m) 472, (S—f) 1000, (F—v) 1171, (F—m) 1299, (F—f) 1409
Manuela Nehls Re-Entry Scholarships, (S—f) 817
MARC Purple Heart Endowment Scholarship, (S—f) 818
Marcella Arnold Nursing Scholarship, (S—v) 108, (S—f) 819
Marcia and John Lally Scholarship Award. *See* 506th Airborne Infantry Regiment Association Scholarship, entries (S—v) 5, (S—f) 528, (F—v) 1093, (F—f) 1317
Marcoux Memorial Scholarship. *See* Albert T. Marcoux Memorial Scholarship, entry (S—f) 549
Margaret Apel Scholarship. *See* Women Marines Association Scholarship Program, entries (S—v) 219, (S—m) 512, (S—f) 1085, (F—v) 1191, (F—m) 1313, (F—f) 1429
Margaret H. Clegg Scholarship. *See* Navy-Marine Corps Relief Society Education Assistance, entries (S—m) 412, (S—f) 897
Margaret M. Prickett Scholarship Fund. *See* Society of Daughters of the United States Army Scholarships, entry (S—f) 1006
Margene Mogan Proctor and General Jerry Wyatt Memorial Scholarship, (S—f) 820
Marguerite Mc'Alpin Memorial Scholarship, (S—v) 109, (S—f) 821, (F—v) 1146, (F—f) 1370
Maria C. Jackson/General George A. White Scholarship, (S—v) 110, (S—f) 822, (F—v) 1147, (F—f) 1371
Marie Klugow Memorial Scholarships, (S—f) 823
Marilyn Haines Music Scholarship, (S—v) 111, (S—f) 824
Marilyn Overton Scholarship Award. *See* 506th Airborne Infantry Regiment Association Scholarship, entries (S—v) 5, (S—f) 528, (F—v) 1093, (F—f) 1317
Marine Corps/Coast Guard Enlisted Dependent Spouse Scholarship. *See* NMCCG Enlisted Dependent Spouse Scholarship, entries (S—f) 924, (F—f) 1392
Marine Corps Counterintelligence Association Scholarships, (S—f) 825
Marine Corps Funded Law Education Program, (F—m) 1256
Marine Corps League Scholarships, (S—v) 112, (S—f) 826
Marine Corps Scholarships, (S—f) 827
Marine Corps Special Education Program, (F—m) 1257
Marine Corps Tuition Assistance Program, (S—m) 369, (F—m) 1258
Marine Gunnery Sergeant John David Fry Scholarship, (S—f) 828
Marine SSGT Mark Anthony Wojciechowski "Tony Wojo" Scholarship. *See* Remembering Marine SSGT Mark Anthony Wojciechowski "Tony Wojo" Scholarship, entry (S—f) 970
Marines' Memorial Family Scholarships, (S—v) 113, (S—m) 370, (S—f) 829
Marines' Memorial Tribute Scholarships, (S—v) 114, (S—m) 371, (F—v) 1148, (F—m) 1259

Marion J. Bagley Scholarship, (S—f) 830
Maritime Patrol Association Scholarships, (S—f) 831
Mark Anthony Wojciechowski "Tony Wojo" Scholarship. *See* Remembering Marine SSGT Mark Anthony Wojciechowski "Tony Wojo" Scholarship, entry (S—f) 970
Mark Forester Scholarship, (S—f) 832
Mark Starr Memorial Scholarship. *See* Naval Helicopter Association Scholarships, entries (S—v) 139, (S—m) 407, (S—f) 890, (F—v) 1156, (F—m) 1276, (F—f) 1383
Marks Scholarship. *See* Mort Marks Scholarship, entry (S—m) 393
Marlin E. Mote Endowed Scholarship. *See* National Guard Association of Texas Scholarship Program, entries (S—v) 138, (S—m) 401, (S—f) 885, (F—v) 1155, (F—m) 1273, (F—f) 1381
Marshall Scholarship. *See* Mary Barrett Marshall Scholarship, entry (S—f) 833
Martin Small Business Scholarship. *See* San Antonio Post SAME Scholarships, entry (S—m) 464
Mary Barrett Marshall Scholarship, (S—f) 833
Mary Hensell Scholarship Program. *See* CSM Harry and Mary Hensell Scholarship Program, entries (S—m) 280, (S—f) 642
Mary Paolozzi Member's Scholarship, (S—f) 834, (F—f) 1372
Mary Rowena Cooper Scholarship, (S—f) 835
MaryAnn K. Murtha Memorial Scholarship, (S—f) 836
Maryland American Legion General Scholarships, (S—f) 837
Maryland National Guard State Tuition Assistance Reimbursement (STAR), (S—m) 372
Maryland National Guard State Tuition Waiver (STW), (S—m) 373, (F—m) 1260
Maryland Veterans of Afghanistan and Iraq Conflicts Scholarship Program, (S—v) 115, (S—m) 374, (S—f) 838
Massachusetts National Guard Tuition Waiver Program, (S—m) 375, (F—m) 1261
Master Gunnery Sergeant and Mrs. Dot Easter Scholarship. *See* Pop-A-Smoke Scholarships, entry (S—f) 960
Master Sergeant Neal Benson Elbit Honorary Scholarship, (S—f) 839
Matera Scholarship. *See* Wisconsin National Guard Enlisted Association College Grant Program, entries (S—m) 509, (S—f) 1084, (F—m) 1312, (F—f) 1428
Mathew B. Ridgeway Scholarship. *See* 82nd Airborne Division Association Awards, entries (S—v) 6, (S—f) 530
Matsui Scholarship. *See* Japanese American Veterans Association Memorial Scholarships, entry (S—f) 775
Matthews and Swift Educational Trust Scholarships, (S—f) 840
Max English Memorial Scholarship. *See* John Cornelius/Max English Memorial Scholarship, entries (S—m) 349, (S—f) 782, (F—m) 1252, (F—f) 1363
Max R. and Irene Rubenstein Memorial Grant. *See* Jewish War Veterans National Achievement Program, entries (S—v) 94, (S—m) 345, (F—v) 1140, (F—m) 1250
Max S. Millen Memorial Athletic Grant. *See* Jewish War Veterans National Youth Achievement Program, entry (S—f) 778
Maxine Chilton Scholarships. *See* Wilma D. Hoyal/Maxine Chilton Scholarships, entries (S—v) 216, (S—f) 1076
Mayberry Scholarship. *See* Earline Mayberry Scholarship, entry (S—f) 679
MCA Chaplain Candidate Scholarships, (F—m) 1262
McAlinden Divers Scholarship. *See* Navy-Marine Corps Relief Society Education Assistance, entries (S—m) 412, (S—f) 897
Mc'Alpin Memorial Scholarship. *See* Marguerite Mc'Alpin Memorial Scholarship, entries (S—v) 109, (S—f) 821, (F—v) 1146, (F—f) 1370

S—Scholarships   F—Fellowships   G—Grants-in-Aid
v—Veterans   m—Military Personnel   f—Family Members

McCarthy Memorial Scholarship. *See* Naval Helicopter Association Scholarships, entries (S—v) 139, (S—m) 407, (S—f) 890, (F—v) 1156, (F—m) 1276, (F—f) 1383

McClung Memorial Scholarship. *See* Women Marines Association Scholarship Program, entries (S—v) 219, (S—m) 512, (S—f) 1085, (F—v) 1191, (F—m) 1313, (F—f) 1429

McGlothin Memorial Scholarship. *See* Veterans of Foreign Wars Post 81 Trust Fund Scholarship, entry (S—f) 1057

McGrath Scholarship. *See* Navy League Foundation Scholarships, entry (S—f) 892

McKinley Flight Scholarship. *See* Arnold Air Society and Silver Wings Flying Scholarships, entry (S—m) 252

McNair Jr. Scholarship Award. *See* George Washington Chapter AUSA Scholarships, entries (S—v) 72, (S—m) 324, (S—f) 724, (F—v) 1131, (F—m) 1246, (F—f) 1356

McPartland Scholarships. *See* Gladys McPartland Scholarships, entries (S—v) 73, (S—m) 327, (S—f) 730

MCPO Ken E. Blair Scholarship. *See* Fleet Reserve Association Member Scholarships, entries (S—v) 62, (S—m) 314, (S—f) 699, (F—v) 1127, (F—m) 1241, (F—f) 1351

MCPON Thomas Crow Memorial Scholarship. *See* Chief Petty Officer Scholarships, entry (S—f) 608

MCPON Walker Honorary Scholarship. *See* Chief Petty Officer Scholarships, entry (S—f) 608

M.D. "Jack" Murphy Memorial Nurses Training Scholarship, (S—f) 841

MDSSP. *See* Army Medical and Dental School Stipend Program (MDSSP), entry (F—m) 1208

Medical Service Corps Inservice Procurement Program (MSC-IPP), (S—m) 376, (F—m) 1263

Megan McClung Memorial Scholarship. *See* Women Marines Association Scholarship Program, entries (S—v) 219, (S—m) 512, (S—f) 1085, (F—v) 1191, (F—m) 1313, (F—f) 1429

Mel Foronda Memorial Scholarship. *See* California Legion Auxiliary Scholarships for Continuing and/or Reentry Students, entries (S—v) 32, (S—m) 262, (S—f) 596

Memorial Sibling Scholarship, (S—f) 842

Memorial Veteran Scholarship. *See* AHIMA Veterans Scholarship, entries (S—v) 10, (S—f) 541, (F—v) 1096, (F—f) 1319

Merrilyn Stock/Evelyn Oliver Memorial Scholarship, (S—v) 116, (S—f) 843

Merritt Scholarship. *See* Gen. Jack N. Merritt Scholarship, entries (S—v) 70, (S—m) 321, (S—f) 716

MG Benjamin J. Butler "Century Division" Scholarship Program, (S—v) 117, (S—m) 377, (S—f) 844

MG Charles J. Wing Family Program Scholarship. *See* Wyoming National Guard Association Scholarships, entries (S—m) 516, (S—f) 1091

MG James Ursano Scholarship Fund, (S—f) 845

MG Leif J. Sverdrup Scholarship, (S—m) 378, (F—m) 1264

Michael B. Ranger Legacy Scholarships. *See* USARA Michael B. Ranger Legacy Scholarships, entry (S—f) 1051

Michael J. Kogutek Scholarship. *See* Past National Commander Michael J. Kogutek Scholarship, entries (S—v) 159, (S—f) 948

Michael LiCalzi Memorial Scholarship. *See* First Lieutenant Michael LiCalzi Memorial Scholarship, entries (S—m) 313, (S—f) 696, (F—m) 1239, (F—f) 1349

Michael Murphy Memorial Award. *See* Military Order of the Purple Heart Scholarship Program, entries (S—v) 122, (S—f) 856

Michael Warren Memorial Scholarships. *See* LTC Michael Warren Memorial Scholarships, entries (S—m) 362, (S—f) 811

Michigan Chapter NDIA STEM Scholarship Program, (S—f) 846

Michigan Children of Veterans Tuition Grants, (S—f) 847

Michigan National Guard State Tuition Assistance Program, (S—m) 379, (F—m) 1265

Michigan Veterans Trust Fund Tuition Grants. *See* Michigan Children of Veterans Tuition Grants, entry (S—f) 847

Midwest Area Regional Council Purple Heart Endowment Scholarship. *See* MARC Purple Heart Endowment Scholarship, entry (S—f) 818

Midwestern Region Korean War Veteran Descendant Scholarships, (S—f) 848, (F—f) 1373

Mike and Gail Donley Spouse Scholarships, (S—f) 849, (F—f) 1374

Mike Boorda Loan Program. *See* Navy-Marine Corps Relief Society Education Assistance, entries (S—m) 412, (S—f) 897

Mike Hooks Memorial Scholarship. *See* North Carolina Vietnam Veterans Scholarship Program, entries (S—v) 153, (S—f) 931

Mike Okusa Scholarship. *See* Japanese American Veterans Association Memorial Scholarships, entry (S—f) 775

Miki Iwata Memorial Scholarship for Advanced Practice. *See* Captain Miki Iwata Memorial Scholarship for Advanced Practice, entries (F—v) 1111, (F—m) 1222, (F—f) 1333

Mildred Nunez Scholarships. *See* Fleet Reserve Association Member Scholarships, entries (S—v) 62, (S—m) 314, (S—f) 699, (F—v) 1127, (F—m) 1241, (F—f) 1351

Mildred R. Knoles Scholarships, (S—v) 118, (S—f) 850

Military Benefit Association Scholarships, (S—v) 119, (S—m) 380, (S—f) 851

Military Chaplains Association Chaplain Candidate Scholarships. *See* MCA Chaplain Candidate Scholarships, entry (F—m) 1262

Military College Scholarship, (S—v) 120, (S—m) 381, (S—f) 852

Military Commanders' Scholarship Fund, (S—f) 853

Military Family Support Trust Scholarships, (S—f) 854

Military Intelligence Corps Association Scholarships, (S—v) 121, (S—m) 382, (S—f) 855

Military MBA Scholarships, (F—v) 1149

Military Order of the Purple Heart Scholarship Program, (S—v) 122, (S—f) 856

Military Scholarship Essay Contest, (S—v) 123, (S—m) 383, (S—f) 857

Military Spouse and Caregiver Honorary Scholarship, (F—f) 1375

Military Spouse and Caregiver New Beginnings Scholarship, (S—f) 858

Military Spouse Career Advancement Accounts (MyCAA) Program, (S—f) 859

Military Spouse Scholarships, (S—f) 860, (F—f) 1376

Military Spouses of Newport Dependent Child Scholarship. *See* MSoN Dependent Child Scholarship, entry (S—f) 874

Military Spouses of Newport Freshman Scholarship. *See* MSoN Freshman Scholarship, entry (S—f) 875

Military Spouses of Newport Spouse Scholarships. *See* MSoN Spouse Scholarships, entry (S—f) 876

Military Veteran Automotive Technician Scholarship, (S—v) 124

Millen Memorial Athletic Grant. *See* Jewish War Veterans National Youth Achievement Program, entry (S—f) 778

Miller Scholarship. *See* Thomas H. Miller Scholarship, entries (S—f) 1036, (F—f) 1418

Milner Memorial Scholarship. *See* SSgt. Robert V. Milner Memorial Scholarship, entries (S—v) 192, (S—f) 1018, (F—v) 1177, (F—f) 1413

Minnesota G.I. Bill Program, (S—v) 125, (S—m) 384, (S—f) 861, (F—v) 1150, (F—m) 1266, (F—f) 1377

Minnesota Legion Auxiliary Department Scholarships, (S—f) 862

Minnesota Legion Auxiliary Past Presidents Parley Health Care Scholarship, (S—f) 863

S—Scholarships
v—Veterans

F—Fellowships
m—Military Personnel

G—Grants-in-Aid
f—Family Members

Minnesota National Guard Enlisted Association Auxiliary Minuteman Scholarships, (S—v) 126, (S—m) 385, (S—f) 864

Minnesota National Guard Extended State Tuition Reimbursement, (S—v) 127, (F—v) 1151

Minnesota National Guard Medical Professional Student State Tuition Reimbursement Program, (F—m) 1267

Minnesota National Guard State Tuition Reimbursement, (S—m) 386, (F—m) 1268

Minnesota National Guard Survivor Entitlement Tuition Reimbursement Program, (S—f) 865, (F—f) 1378

Minority Serving Institution Scholarship Program, (S—m) 387

Mississippi Educational Assistance for MIA/POW Dependents, (S—f) 866

Mississippi National Guard NCO Association Scholarships, (S—f) 867

Mississippi National Guard State Educational Assistance Program, (S—m) 388

Missouri American Legion Commander's Scholarships, (S—v) 128

Missouri National Guard Association Scholarships, (S—m) 389, (S—f) 868

Missouri National Guard State Tuition Assistance Program, (S—m) 390

Missouri Past National Presidents' Scholarship, (S—f) 869

Missouri Patriot Guard Riders Scholarship, (S—f) 870

Missouri State Society Daughters of the Revolution Veterans Scholarship. *See* MSSDAR Veterans Scholarship, entry (S—v) 131

Missouri Wartime Veteran's Survivor Grant Program, (S—f) 871

Mitsugi Kasai Scholarship. *See* Japanese American Veterans Association Memorial Scholarships, entry (S—f) 775

Montana Honorably Discharged Veteran Waiver, (S—v) 129, (F—v) 1152

Montana National Guard Scholarships, (S—m) 391

Montana War Orphans Waiver, (S—f) 872

Montgomery GI Bill (Active Duty), (S—v) 130, (F—v) 1153

Montgomery GI Bill (Selected Reserve), (S—m) 392, (F—m) 1269

Morison Supplemental Scholarship. *See* Rear Admiral Samuel Eliot Morison Supplemental Scholarship, entry (F—m) 1292

Moritsugu Memorial Scholarship. *See* AAPA Veterans Caucus Scholarships, entries (S—v) 7, (F—v) 1094

Morphine 1 2 Memorial Scholarship. *See* Pop-A-Smoke Scholarships, entry (S—f) 960

Morris Award. *See* Geraldine K. Morris Award, entry (S—f) 729

Morrow Scholarship. *See* Fourth Marine Division Association of WWII Scholarship, entry (S—f) 710

Mort Marks Scholarship, (S—m) 393

Mort McCarthy Memorial Scholarship. *See* Naval Helicopter Association Scholarships, entries (S—v) 139, (S—m) 407, (S—f) 890, (F—v) 1156, (F—m) 1276, (F—f) 1383

Mote Endowed Scholarship. *See* National Guard Association of Texas Scholarship Program, entries (S—v) 138, (S—m) 401, (S—f) 885, (F—v) 1155, (F—m) 1273, (F—f) 1381

Mrs. Beverly Holmes Scholarship. *See* Wyoming National Guard Association Scholarships, entries (S—m) 516, (S—f) 1091

Mrs. Charles C. Blanton AFBA Family Survivor College Scholarship. *See* General and Mrs. Charles C. Blanton AFBA Family Survivor College Scholarship, entry (S—f) 717

Mrs. Dot Easter Scholarship. *See* Pop-A-Smoke Scholarships, entry (S—f) 960

Mrs. Lawona R. Spencer Scholarship. *See* Col. Loren J. and Mrs. Lawona R. Spencer Scholarship, entry (F—m) 1228

Mrs. Margaret H. Clegg Scholarship. *See* Navy-Marine Corps Relief Society Education Assistance, entries (S—m) 412, (S—f) 897

Mrs. Patty Shinseki Spouse Scholarship Program, (S—f) 873

MSoN Dependent Child Scholarship, (S—f) 874

MSoN Freshman Scholarship, (S—f) 875

MSoN Spouse Scholarships, (S—f) 876

MSSDAR Veterans Scholarship, (S—v) 131

Mucklestone Memorial Scholarships. *See* Ada Mucklestone Memorial Scholarships, entry (S—f) 533

Muneo "Mike" Okusa Scholarship. *See* Japanese American Veterans Association Memorial Scholarships, entry (S—f) 775

Murphy Memorial Award. *See* Military Order of the Purple Heart Scholarship Program, entries (S—v) 122, (S—f) 856

Murphy Memorial Nurses Training Scholarship. *See* M.D. "Jack" Murphy Memorial Nurses Training Scholarship, entry (S—f) 841

Murtha Memorial Scholarship. *See* MaryAnn K. Murtha Memorial Scholarship, entry (S—f) 836

MyCAA Program. *See* Military Spouse Career Advancement Accounts (MyCAA) Program, entry (S—f) 859

Myers Scholarship. *See* San Antonio Post SAME Scholarships, entry (S—m) 464

N

Nakamoto Scholarship. *See* Japanese American Veterans Association Memorial Scholarships, entry (S—f) 775

Nancy and Barry Carlson Scholarship, (S—v) 132

Nancy M. Schonher Scholarship. *See* Dr. Nancy M. Schonher Scholarship, entries (S—v) 55, (S—m) 295, (S—f) 668, (F—v) 1121, (F—m) 1236, (F—f) 1343

Nannie Norfleet Educational Scholarship, (S—f) 877

Nathan Grossman VFW State Memorial Scholarship. *See* Department of Nebraska VFW State Scholarships, entries (S—v) 50, (S—f) 656

Nathan L. Lipscomb, Sr. Memorial Scholarship. *See* SMSgt. Nathan L. Lipscomb, Sr. Memorial Scholarship, entries (S—v) 186, (S—f) 1005, (F—v) 1174, (F—f) 1411

National 4th Infantry (IVY) Division Association Annual Educational Scholarship, (S—v) 133, (S—f) 878

National Board for Certified Counselors Foundation Military Scholarships. *See* NBCCF Military Scholarships, entries (F—v) 1157, (F—m) 1281, (F—f) 1387

National Call to Service Program, (S—m) 394, (F—m) 1270

National Guard Association of California Scholarships, (S—v) 134, (S—m) 395, (S—f) 879

National Guard Association of Colorado Scholarship Program. *See* Education Foundation for the Colorado National Guard Grants, entries (S—v) 57, (S—m) 304, (S—f) 682, (F—v) 1122, (F—m) 1237, (F—f) 1345

National Guard Association of Florida and Enlisted National Guard Association of Florida Scholarship Program. *See* NGOA-FL and ENGAF Scholarship Program, entries (S—m) 430, (S—f) 922

National Guard Association of Indiana Member Educational Grants. *See* NGAI Member Educational Grants, entries (S—v) 145, (S—m) 423, (S—f) 914

National Guard Association of Maryland Scholarships, (S—v) 135, (S—m) 396, (S—f) 880

National Guard Association of Massachusetts Scholarships. *See* NGAMA Scholarship Program, entries (S—m) 424, (S—f) 915

National Guard Association of Michigan Educational Grants, (S—m) 397

S—Scholarships F—Fellowships G—Grants-in-Aid
v—Veterans m—Military Personnel f—Family Members

National Guard Association of Minnesota Scholarships, (S—v) 136, (S—m) 398, (S—f) 881

National Guard Association of New Hampshire Scholarships, (S—v) 137, (S—m) 399, (S—f) 882, (F—v) 1154, (F—m) 1271, (F—f) 1379

National Guard Association of New Jersey Scholarship Program, (S—m) 400, (S—f) 883, (F—m) 1272, (F—f) 1380

National Guard Association of Oklahoma Scholarships. *See* NGAOK Scholarships, entries (S—v) 146, (S—m) 425, (S—f) 916, (F—v) 1162, (F—m) 1286, (F—f) 1391

National Guard Association of Rhode Island Scholarship Program. *See* NGARI Scholarship Program, entries (S—v) 147, (S—m) 426, (S—f) 917

National Guard Association of South Carolina Auxiliary College Scholarship Grant, (S—f) 884

National Guard Association of Tennessee Foundation Dependent Scholarships. *See* NGATN Foundation Dependent Scholarships, entry (S—f) 918

National Guard Association of Tennessee Foundation Legacy Scholarship. *See* NGATN Foundation Legacy Scholarship, entries (S—m) 427, (S—f) 919

National Guard Association of Texas Scholarship Program, (S—v) 138, (S—m) 401, (S—f) 885, (F—v) 1155, (F—m) 1273, (F—f) 1381

National Guard Association of the United States Active Life Member Scholarship. *See* AFBA NGAUS Active Life Member Scholarship, entries (S—m) 225, (S—f) 538, (F—m) 1194, (F—f) 1318

National Guard Association of Utah "Minuteman" Scholarships. *See* NGAUT "Minuteman" Scholarships, entries (S—m) 428, (S—f) 920

National Guard Association of Vermont Scholarships, (S—m) 402, (S—f) 886, (F—m) 1274, (F—f) 1382

National Guard Association of Washington Scholarship Program. *See* NGAW Scholarship Program, entries (S—m) 429, (S—f) 921

National Guard of Georgia Scholarship Fund for Colleges or Universities, (S—m) 403, (S—f) 887

National Guard of Georgia Scholarship Fund for Graduate Students, (F—m) 1275

National Guard of Georgia Scholarship Fund for Vocational or Business Schools, (S—m) 404, (S—f) 888

National Guard Tuition Waiver Program of Oklahoma, (S—m) 405

Naval Cryptologic Veterans Association Scholarships, (S—f) 889

Naval Enlisted Reserve Association/USAA College Scholarship Program. *See* NERA/USAA College Scholarship Program, entries (S—m) 418, (S—f) 900, (F—m) 1282, (F—f) 1388

Naval Flight Officer Option of the Seaman to Admiral-21 Program, (S—m) 406

Naval Helicopter Association Scholarships, (S—v) 139, (S—m) 407, (S—f) 890, (F—v) 1156, (F—m) 1276, (F—f) 1383

Naval Special Warfare Development Group Scholarships, (S—f) 891, (F—f) 1384

NAVILLUS Award. *See* 506th Airborne Infantry Regiment Association Scholarship, entries (S—v) 5, (S—f) 528, (F—v) 1093, (F—f) 1317

Navy Department Branch 181 Scholarship. *See* Fleet Reserve Association Member Scholarships, entries (S—v) 62, (S—m) 314, (S—f) 699, (F—v) 1127, (F—m) 1241, (F—f) 1351

Navy Health Professions Scholarship Program, (F—m) 1277

Navy Law Education Program, (F—m) 1278

Navy League Foundation Scholarships, (S—f) 892

Navy/Marine Corps/Coast Guard Enlisted Dependent Spouse Scholarship. *See* NMCCG Enlisted Dependent Spouse Scholarship, entries (S—f) 924, (F—f) 1392

Navy Nurse Candidate Program, (S—m) 408

Navy Nurse Corps NROTC Scholarship Program, (S—m) 409

Navy Seal Foundation Scholarships, (S—m) 410, (S—f) 893, (F—m) 1279, (F—f) 1385

Navy SEAL LT Michael Murphy Memorial Award. *See* Military Order of the Purple Heart Scholarship Program, entries (S—v) 122, (S—f) 856

Navy Supply Corps Foundation Memorial Scholarships, (S—f) 894

Navy Supply Corps Foundation Scholarships, (S—f) 895

Navy Tuition Assistance Program, (S—m) 411, (F—m) 1280

Navy Wives Clubs of America Scholarship Foundation Dependent Child Scholarship, (S—f) 896, (F—f) 1386

Navy-Marine Corps Relief Society Education Assistance, (S—m) 412, (S—f) 897

Navy-Marine Corps ROTC 2- and 3-Year Scholarships, (S—m) 413

Navy-Marine Corps ROTC College Program, (S—m) 414

Navy-Marine Corps ROTC National Scholarships, (S—m) 415

NBCCF Military Scholarships, (F—v) 1157, (F—m) 1281, (F—f) 1387

NBCUniversal-SVA Scholarships, (S—v) 140, (F—v) 1158

ND Dependent Tuition Waiver, (S—f) 898

Neal Benson Elbit Honorary Scholarship. *See* Master Sergeant Neal Benson Elbit Honorary Scholarship, entry (S—f) 839

Nebraska National Guard State Tuition Assistance Program, (S—m) 416

Nebraska Reservist Tuition Credit, (S—m) 417

Nebraska Waiver of Tuition for Veterans' Dependents, (S—f) 899

Nehls Re-Entry Scholarships. *See* Manuela Nehls Re-Entry Scholarships, entry (S—f) 817

Nelson Scholarship. *See* Chappie Hall Memorial Scholarship Program, entry (S—f) 603

NERA/USAA College Scholarship Program, (S—m) 418, (S—f) 900, (F—m) 1282, (F—f) 1388

Nesheim Memorial Scholarship. *See* Edward O. Nesheim Memorial Scholarship, entries (S—f) 684, (F—f) 1346

Nevada National Guard State Tuition Waiver Program, (S—m) 419, (F—m) 1283

New Hampshire Chapter MOAA Scholarship Loan Program, (S—f) 901

New Hampshire Higher Education Scholarships for Orphans of Veterans, (S—f) 902

New Hampshire National Guard Tuition Waiver Program, (S—m) 420, (F—m) 1284

New Jersey American Legion Scholarships, (S—f) 903

New Jersey Bankers Education Foundation Scholarships, (S—f) 904

New Jersey Healthcare Information and Management Systems Society Veterans Award. *See* NJ HIMSS Veterans Award, entries (S—v) 149, (F—v) 1163

New Jersey Legion Auxiliary Past Presidents' Parley Nursing Grant, (S—f) 905

New Jersey National Guard Tuition Program, (S—m) 421, (S—f) 906, (F—m) 1285, (F—f) 1389

New Jersey POW/MIA Tuition Benefit Program, (S—f) 907

New Mexico Children of Deceased Military Personnel Scholarships, (S—f) 908, (F—f) 1390

New Mexico Vietnam Veteran Scholarships, (S—v) 141, (F—v) 1159

New Mexico Wartime Veteran Scholarship Fund, (S—v) 142, (F—v) 1160

S—Scholarships F—Fellowships G—Grants-in-Aid
v—Veterans m—Military Personnel f—Family Members

New York Legion Auxiliary Department Scholarship, (S—f) 909
New York Legion Auxiliary District Scholarships, (S—f) 910
New York Legion Auxiliary Past Presidents Parley Student Scholarship in Medical Field, (S—f) 911
New York MERIT Scholarships. *See* New York Military Enhanced Recognition Incentive and Tribute (MERIT) Scholarships, entries (S—v) 143, (S—f) 912
New York Military Enhanced Recognition Incentive and Tribute (MERIT) Scholarships, (S—v) 143, (S—f) 912
New York Recruitment Incentive and Retention Program, (S—m) 422
New York State Military Service Recognition Scholarships. *See* New York Military Enhanced Recognition Incentive and Tribute (MERIT) Scholarships, entries (S—v) 143, (S—f) 912
New York Veterans Tuition Awards, (S—v) 144, (F—v) 1161
NEXT Gen Scholars Program, (S—f) 913
NGAI Member Educational Grants, (S—v) 145, (S—m) 423, (S—f) 914
NGAMA Scholarship Program, (S—m) 424, (S—f) 915
NGAOK Scholarships, (S—v) 146, (S—m) 425, (S—f) 916, (F—v) 1162, (F—m) 1286, (F—f) 1391
NGARI Scholarship Program, (S—v) 147, (S—m) 426, (S—f) 917
NGATN Foundation Dependent Scholarships, (S—f) 918
NGATN Foundation Legacy Scholarship, (S—m) 427, (S—f) 919
NGAUS Active Life Member Scholarship. *See* AFBA NGAUS Active Life Member Scholarship, entries (S—m) 225, (S—f) 538, (F—m) 1194, (F—f) 1318
NGAUT "Minuteman" Scholarships, (S—m) 428, (S—f) 920
NGAW Scholarship Program, (S—m) 429, (S—f) 921
NGOA-FL and ENGAF Scholarship Program, (S—m) 430, (S—f) 922
Nicholas D. Chabraja Scholarship, (S—v) 148, (S—m) 431, (S—f) 923
Nisei Veterans Committee/Women's Auxiliary Club Scholarship. *See* NVC/WAC Scholarship, entry (S—f) 937
NJ HIMSS Veterans Award, (S—v) 149, (F—v) 1163
NMCCG Enlisted Dependent Spouse Scholarship, (S—f) 924, (F—f) 1392
No Angel Left Behind Scholarship, (S—f) 925
No Greater Sacrifice Scholarship, (S—f) 926
Nolan Scholarship. *See* Fleet Reserve Association Graduate Scholarships, entries (F—v) 1126, (F—m) 1240, (F—f) 1350
Norfleet Educational Scholarship. *See* Nannie Norfleet Educational Scholarship, entry (S—f) 877
North Carolina National Guard Association Academic Excellence and Leadership Scholarships, (S—v) 150, (S—m) 432, (S—f) 927
North Carolina National Guard Association Citizenship Scholarships, (S—v) 151, (S—m) 433, (S—f) 928
North Carolina National Guard Association Scholarships, (S—v) 152, (S—m) 434, (S—f) 929
North Carolina National Guard Tuition Assistance Program, (S—m) 435, (F—m) 1287
North Carolina Scholarships for Children of War Veterans, (S—f) 930
North Carolina Vietnam Veterans Scholarship Program, (S—v) 153, (S—f) 931
North Dakota Dependent Tuition Waiver. *See* ND Dependent Tuition Waiver, entry (S—f) 898
North Dakota Dollars for Scholars Military Scholarships, (S—f) 932
North Dakota National Guard Enlisted Association Scholarships, (S—m) 436, (S—f) 933

North Dakota National Guard Tuition Assistance Program, (S—m) 437, (F—m) 1288
North Dakota Tuition and Fee Waivers, (S—m) 438, (S—f) 934
NorthAmerican.com Military Scholarship, (S—v) 154, (S—m) 439, (S—f) 935
Northeastern Region Korean War Veteran Descendant Scholarships, (S—f) 936, (F—f) 1393
Northern New Jersey Chapter ROTC Scholarships, (S—m) 440
Northrop Rice Foundation Veteran Scholarship, (S—v) 155
Nuance Communications Scholarship. *See* AHIMA Veterans Scholarship, entries (S—v) 10, (S—f) 541, (F—v) 1096, (F—f) 1319
Nuclear Propulsion Officer Candidate (NUPOC) Program, (S—m) 441
Nuclear (Submarine and Surface) Option of the Seaman to Admiral-21 Program, (S—m) 442
Nunez Scholarships. *See* Fleet Reserve Association Member Scholarships, entries (S—v) 62, (S—m) 314, (S—f) 699, (F—v) 1127, (F—m) 1241, (F—f) 1351
NUPOC Program. *See* Nuclear Propulsion Officer Candidate (NUPOC) Program, entry (S—m) 441
Nurse Corps Option of the Seaman to Admiral-21 Program, (S—m) 443
Nuske Memorial Scholarships. *See* Richard T. Nuske Memorial Scholarships, entry (S—f) 976
NVC/WAC Scholarship, (S—f) 937

O

O'Connell Memorial Veterans Rehabilitation Scholarship. *See* William P. O'Connell Memorial Veterans Rehabilitation Scholarship, entry (S—f) 1074
Oden Memorial Scholarship. *See* Allie Mae Oden Memorial Scholarship, entry (S—f) 551
Odom Memorial Scholarship. *See* Army Scholarship Foundation Scholarships, entry (S—f) 576
Ohio AMVETS Service Foundation Scholarships, (S—v) 156, (S—f) 938
Ohio Legion Auxiliary Department President's Scholarship, (S—v) 157, (S—f) 939
Ohio Legion College or University Scholarships, (S—f) 940, (F—f) 1394
Ohio Legion High School Scholarships, (S—f) 941
Ohio Legion Member/Military Veteran Scholarship, (S—v) 158, (S—m) 444, (F—v) 1164, (F—m) 1289
Ohio Legion Surviving Spouse or Child Scholarships, (S—f) 942, (F—f) 1395
Ohio National Guard Association Leadership Grants. *See* ONGA Leadership Grants, entries (S—m) 446, (S—f) 945
Ohio National Guard Scholarship Program, (S—m) 445
Ohio Safety Officers College Memorial Fund, (S—f) 943
Ohio War Orphan and Severely Disabled Veterans' Children Scholarship, (S—f) 944
Oklahoma Tuition Waiver for Prisoners of War, Persons Missing in Action, and Dependents. *See* Heroes Promise Scholarship of Oklahoma, entry (S—f) 742
Okusa Scholarship. *See* Japanese American Veterans Association Memorial Scholarships, entry (S—f) 775
Oliphant Memorial Scholarship. *See* Claire Oliphant Memorial Scholarship, entry (S—f) 617
Oliver Memorial Scholarship. *See* Merrilyn Stock/Evelyn Oliver Memorial Scholarship, entries (S—v) 116, (S—f) 843
Olson Memorial Scholarship. *See* Roy C. and Dorothy Jean Olson Memorial Scholarship, entry (S—f) 981

S—Scholarships   F—Fellowships   G—Grants-in-Aid
v—Veterans   m—Military Personnel   f—Family Members

PROGRAM TITLE INDEX

ONGA Leadership Grants, (S—m) 446, (S—f) 945

Oregon National Guard Association Scholarships, (S—m) 447, (S—f) 946

Orville Shirey Scholarship. See Japanese American Veterans Association Memorial Scholarships, entry (S—f) 775

Otis N. Brown/Billy Ray Cameron Scholarships, (S—f) 947

Overton Scholarship Award. See 506th Airborne Infantry Regiment Association Scholarship, entries (S—v) 5, (S—f) 528, (F—v) 1093, (F—f) 1317

P

Pace Memorial Scholarship. See Ron Pace Memorial Scholarship, entries (S—v) 175, (S—f) 979, (F—v) 1168, (F—f) 1403

Paolozzi Member's Scholarship. See Mary Paolozzi Member's Scholarship, entries (S—f) 834, (F—f) 1372

Paralyzed Veterans of America Educational Scholarship Program. See PVA Educational Scholarship Program, entries (S—v) 168, (S—f) 963

Parrish Memorial Scholarship. See National Guard Association of Texas Scholarship Program, entries (S—v) 138, (S—m) 401, (S—f) 885, (F—v) 1155, (F—m) 1273, (F—f) 1381

Past National Commander Michael J. Kogutek Scholarship, (S—v) 159, (S—f) 948

Past President Herb Altman Memorial Scholarship. See 82nd Airborne Division Association Awards, entries (S—v) 6, (S—f) 530

Past State Commanders Scholarship. See Department of Nebraska VFW State Scholarships, entries (S—v) 50, (S—f) 656

Pat Boswell Merit Scholarship Program. See General Jim and Pat Boswell Merit Scholarship Program, entry (S—f) 719

Patriot Education Fund Scholarships, (S—v) 160, (S—f) 949

Patriot Scholarship of the University Interscholastic League, (S—f) 950

Patt Scholarship Fund. See George L. Patt Scholarship Fund, entries (S—v) 71, (S—m) 323

Patty Shinseki Spouse Scholarship Program. See Mrs. Patty Shinseki Spouse Scholarship Program, entry (S—f) 873

Paul (Jay) Smith Memorial Endowment Scholarship. See Lt. Paul (Jay) Smith Memorial Endowment Scholarship, entry (S—m) 361

Paul W. Airey Memorial Scholarship. See Chief Master Sergeant of the Air Force Scholarship Program, entry (S—f) 607

Pauline Langkamp Memorial Scholarship, (S—f) 951

Payne Memorial Scholarship Endowment. See Carroll H. Payne Memorial Scholarship Endowment, entries (S—v) 37, (S—m) 266, (S—f) 602

Pearl Behrend Scholarship. See Wisconsin Legion Auxiliary Merit and Memorial Scholarships, entry (S—f) 1080

Pedro Del Valle Leadership Scholarships. See General Pedro Del Valle Leadership Scholarships, entry (S—m) 322

Pedro Memorial Scholarship. See Richard M. Pedro Memorial Scholarship, entry (S—f) 975

Pennsylvania National Guard Educational Assistance Program (EAP), (S—m) 448, (F—m) 1290

Pennsylvania National Guard Military Family Education Program (MFEP), (S—f) 952, (F—f) 1396

Pennsylvania National Guard Scholarship Fund, (S—m) 449, (S—f) 953

Pennsylvania Postsecondary Educational Gratuity Program, (S—f) 954

Pentagon Federal Credit Union Scholarship. See United States Army Warrant Officers Association Scholarship Program, entry (S—f) 1046

Perot Family Scholarship. See Army Scholarship Foundation Scholarships, entry (S—f) 576

Perrey, Sr. Memorial Scholarship. See ProVets Military Scholarships, entries (S—v) 167, (S—f) 962

Personal Money Service Scholarship for Veterans, (S—v) 161, (S—m) 450

Pete Freeman Memorial Scholarship, (S—f) 955

Peter Connacher Memorial Scholarships, (S—v) 162, (S—f) 956, (F—v) 1165, (F—f) 1397

The PFC Roger W. Cummins Memorial Scholarship, (S—v) 196, (S—m) 487, (S—f) 1034, (F—v) 1178, (F—m) 1301, (F—f) 1417

Philip Shapiro Education Grant. See Leo A. Seigel-Dr. Philip Shapiro Education Grant, entry (S—f) 800

Phillip Blottenberger Scholarship. See Chappie Hall Memorial Scholarship Program, entry (S—f) 603

Phillip Coon Scholarship, (S—v) 163

Phillips Scholarship. See Department of Nebraska VFW State Scholarships, entries (S—v) 50, (S—f) 656

PHS Commissioned Officers Foundation Dependent Scholarship Program, (S—f) 957, (F—f) 1398

Pierce Jr. Scholarship Program. See Harold C. Pierce Jr. Scholarship Program, entries (S—m) 332, (S—f) 733

Pilot Option of the Seaman to Admiral-21 Program, (S—m) 451

Piscataqua Post SAME Scholarships, (S—v) 164, (S—m) 452, (S—f) 958

Planning Systems Incorporated Science and Engineering Scholarship, (S—f) 959

Pop-A-Smoke Scholarships, (S—f) 960

Portland Post Society of American Military Engineers Scholarship, (S—v) 165, (S—m) 453

Posekany Memorial Scholarship. See Fleet Reserve Association Non-Member Scholarships, entries (S—v) 63, (S—m) 315, (S—f) 700, (F—v) 1128, (F—m) 1242, (F—f) 1352

Post-9/11 GI Bill, (S—v) 166, (S—m) 454, (F—v) 1166, (F—m) 1291

Powell Scholarship. See Chaplain Samuel Grover Powell Scholarship, entries (F—v) 1113, (F—m) 1224

Prairie Minuteman Scholarship, (S—f) 961

Pratt Scholarships. See Chappie Hall Memorial Scholarship Program, entry (S—f) 603

Prickett Scholarship Fund. See Society of Daughters of the United States Army Scholarships, entry (S—f) 1006

Pringle Family Scholarship. See Fleet Reserve Association Member Scholarships, entries (S—v) 62, (S—m) 314, (S—f) 699, (F—v) 1127, (F—m) 1241, (F—f) 1351

Proctor and General Jerry Wyatt Memorial Scholarship. See Margene Mogan Proctor and General Jerry Wyatt Memorial Scholarship, entry (S—f) 820

Professional Officer Course Early Release Program, (S—m) 455

ProVets Military Scholarships, (S—v) 167, (S—f) 962

Pulvermacher-Ryan Scholarship. See Wisconsin Legion Auxiliary Merit and Memorial Scholarships, entry (S—f) 1080

PVA Educational Scholarship Program, (S—v) 168, (S—f) 963

R

RADM Courtney G. Clegg and Mrs. Margaret H. Clegg Scholarship. See Navy-Marine Corps Relief Society Education Assistance, entries (S—m) 412, (S—f) 897

Ranger Battalions Association of WWII Scholarships. See Ranger Memorial Scholarships, entries (S—v) 169, (S—m) 456, (S—f) 964

S—Scholarships F—Fellowships G—Grants-in-Aid
v—Veterans m—Military Personnel f—Family Members

PROGRAM TITLE INDEX

Ranger Grant Hirabayashi Scholarship. *See* Japanese American Veterans Association Memorial Scholarships, entry (S—f) 775

Ranger Legacy Scholarships. *See* USARA Michael B. Ranger Legacy Scholarships, entry (S—f) 1051

Ranger Memorial Scholarships, (S—v) 169, (S—m) 456, (S—f) 964

RAO Freedom Scholarship. *See* United States Army Warrant Officers Association Scholarship Program, entry (S—f) 1046

Ratay Educational Fund Grants. *See* General John Paul Ratay Educational Fund Grants, entry (S—f) 720

Raymond A. Matera Scholarship. *See* Wisconsin National Guard Enlisted Association College Grant Program, entries (S—m) 509, (S—f) 1084, (F—m) 1312, (F—f) 1428

Raymond P. Giehll, IV Memorial Scholarship, (S—f) 965

Raymond T. Wellington, Jr. Memorial Scholarship, (S—f) 966

Raytheon SPY-6 Scholarships, (S—v) 170, (F—v) 1167

Raytheon-Zumwalt Endowed Scholarship, (S—f) 967

Ream Memorial Scholarship. *See* Naval Helicopter Association Scholarships, entries (S—v) 139, (S—m) 407, (S—f) 890, (F—v) 1156, (F—m) 1276, (F—f) 1383

Rear Admiral Samuel Eliot Morison Supplemental Scholarship, (F—m) 1292

Rebecca Bartel Veteran's Scholarship. *See* David and Rebecca Bartel Veteran's Scholarship, entries (S—v) 49, (F—v) 1119

Rebecca Post Sikes Memorial Scholarship, (S—f) 968, (F—f) 1399

Recycling Research Foundation Veterans Scholarship Program, (S—v) 171, (S—m) 457

Red River Valley Fighter Pilots Association Kinship Scholarship Grant Program, (S—f) 969, (F—f) 1400

Reed Society Scholarship. *See* AHIMA Veterans Scholarship, entries (S—v) 10, (S—f) 541, (F—v) 1096, (F—f) 1319

Rees Scholarship Foundation Veterans Program, (S—v) 172

Reilly Scholarships. *See* Henry J. Reilly Scholarships, entries (S—v) 80, (S—m) 336, (S—f) 740, (F—v) 1135, (F—m) 1248, (F—f) 1359

Remembering Marine SSGT Mark Anthony Wojciechowski "Tony Wojo" Scholarship, (S—f) 970

Renee Campbell Scholarship. *See* CAPT Ernest G. "Scotty" Campbell, USN (Ret) and Renee Campbell Scholarship, entry (S—f) 599

Renee Feldman Scholarships, (S—f) 971

REOC Charitable Fund Scholarship, (S—f) 972

Restoring Family Scholarship, (S—f) 973, (F—f) 1401

Restoring Hope Scholarship, (F—f) 1402

Restoring Self Scholarship, (S—f) 974

The Retired Enlisted Association Memorial Foundation Scholarships. *See* TREA Memorial Foundation Scholarships, entry (S—f) 1040

The Retired Enlisted Association National Auxiliary Scholarships. *See* TREA National Auxiliary Scholarships, entry (S—f) 1041

Rhode Island National Guard State Tuition Assistance Program, (S—m) 458, (F—m) 1293

Richard and Susan Braun Family Scholarship, (S—v) 173

Richard D. Kisling Scholarship. *See* Chief Master Sergeant of the Air Force Scholarship Program, entry (S—f) 607

Richard Hallock Scholarships. *See* Colonel Richard Hallock Scholarships, entries (S—v) 40, (S—m) 275, (S—f) 627

Richard L. Ridder Memorial Scholarship. *See* Major Richard L. Ridder Memorial Scholarship, entries (S—v) 107, (S—m) 368, (S—f) 816

Richard M. Pedro Memorial Scholarship, (S—f) 975

Richard T. Nuske Memorial Scholarships, (S—f) 976

Richard W. Collins III Leadership with Honor Scholarships, (S—m) 459

Richard W. Spencer Scholarship. *See* EANGNJ Scholarship Program, entries (S—m) 298, (S—f) 673

Richards UDT-SEAL Memorial Scholarship. *See* Had Richards UDT-SEAL Memorial Scholarship, entry (S—f) 732

Rick Hopcraft Memorial Scholarship for Veterans, (S—v) 174

Ridder Memorial Scholarship. *See* Major Richard L. Ridder Memorial Scholarship, entries (S—v) 107, (S—m) 368, (S—f) 816

Ridgeway Scholarship. *See* 82nd Airborne Division Association Awards, entries (S—v) 6, (S—f) 530

RIVDIV 534/551 Scholarship. *See* Gamewardens Association Scholarship, entry (S—f) 714

Robert Dale Spencer Memorial Scholarship. *See* Texas State Council Vietnam Veterans of America Scholarships, entries (S—v) 194, (S—f) 1030

Robert H. Connal Scholarship. *See* EANYNG Education Awards, entries (S—m) 302, (S—f) 678

Robert L. Crow Awards. *See* Association of Aviation Ordnancemen Educational Foundation Scholarships, entries (S—v) 24, (S—f) 578

Robert L. Denig Foundation Scholarship. *See* Brigadier General Robert L. Denig Foundation Scholarship, entries (S—m) 259, (S—f) 587

Robert L. Walters Scholarship. *See* Vice Admiral Robert L. Walters Scholarship, entries (S—v) 210, (S—m) 500, (S—f) 1060, (F—v) 1186, (F—m) 1307, (F—f) 1423

Robert M. Treadwell Annual Scholarship. *See* Fleet Reserve Association Member Scholarships, entries (S—v) 62, (S—m) 314, (S—f) 699, (F—v) 1127, (F—m) 1241, (F—f) 1351

Robert M. Zweiman Memorial Award. *See* Jewish War Veterans National Achievement Program, entries (S—v) 94, (S—m) 345, (F—v) 1140, (F—m) 1250

Robert Nakamoto Scholarship. *See* Japanese American Veterans Association Memorial Scholarships, entry (S—f) 775

Robert V. Milner Memorial Scholarship. *See* SSgt. Robert V. Milner Memorial Scholarship, entries (S—v) 192, (S—f) 1018, (F—v) 1177, (F—f) 1413

Robert W. Brunsman Memorial Scholarship, (S—m) 460, (F—m) 1294

Robert W. Elkey Scholarship. *See* CSM Robert W. Elkey Scholarship, entries (S—m) 282, (F—m) 1232

Robert W. Nolan Scholarship. *See* Fleet Reserve Association Graduate Scholarships, entries (F—v) 1126, (F—m) 1240, (F—f) 1350

Roberts Memorial Fund. *See* Society of Daughters of the United States Army Scholarships, entry (S—f) 1006

Rockwell Collins Navy League Scholarship, (S—f) 977

Rodriquez Memorial Scholarship. *See* Texas State Council Vietnam Veterans of America Scholarships, entries (S—v) 194, (S—f) 1030

Roger W. Cummins Memorial Scholarship. *See* The PFC Roger W. Cummins Memorial Scholarship, entries (S—v) 196, (S—m) 487, (S—f) 1034, (F—v) 1178, (F—m) 1301, (F—f) 1417

Rolls-Royce STEM Scholarship, (S—f) 978

Romeo and Josephine Bass Ferretti Scholarship. *See* Lt. Col. Romeo and Josephine Bass Ferretti Scholarship, entry (S—f) 809

Ron Gillette Scholarship. *See* Chappie Hall Memorial Scholarship Program, entry (S—f) 603

Ron Pace Memorial Scholarship, (S—v) 175, (S—f) 979, (F—v) 1168, (F—f) 1403

Roodhouse Memorial Scholarship Award. *See* 506th Airborne Infantry Regiment Association Scholarship, entries (S—v) 5, (S—f) 528, (F—v) 1093, (F—f) 1317

S—Scholarships   F—Fellowships   G—Grants-in-Aid
v—Veterans   m—Military Personnel   f—Family Members

PROGRAM TITLE INDEX

Rosamond P. Haeberle Memorial Scholarship, (S–v) 176, (S–m) 461

Roscoe C. Cartwright Awards. *See* Brigadier General Roscoe C. Cartwright Awards, entry (S–m) 260

Rose Memorial Scholarship. *See* Sam Rose Memorial Scholarship, entry (S–f) 985

Rosedale Post 346 Scholarship Fund, (S–f) 980

Rosemary Posekany Memorial Scholarship. *See* Fleet Reserve Association Non-Member Scholarships, entries (S–v) 63, (S–m) 315, (S–f) 700, (F–v) 1128, (F–m) 1242, (F–f) 1352

Ross Scholarship. *See* Colonel Jerry W. Ross Scholarship, entries (F–m) 1229, (F–f) 1336

Rotberg Memorial Grant. *See* Jewish War Veterans National Youth Achievement Program, entry (S–f) 778

Roy C. and Dorothy Jean Olson Memorial Scholarship, (S–f) 981

Ruark-Wight Family Scholarship, (S–v) 177, (S–m) 462, (S–f) 982, (F–v) 1169, (F–m) 1295, (F–f) 1404

Rubenstein Memorial Grant. *See* Jewish War Veterans National Achievement Program, entries (S–v) 94, (S–m) 345, (F–v) 1140, (F–m) 1250

Ruby Eheman Memorial Scholarship. *See* CPT James and Ruby Eheman Memorial Scholarship, entry (S–f) 641

Ruby Gonzales Scholarship, (S–v) 178, (S–m) 463, (S–f) 983

Russell Scholarship. *See* San Antonio Post SAME Scholarships, entry (S–m) 464

Ruth Cortes Memorial Scholarship. *See* LT Ruth Cortes Memorial Scholarship, entries (S–v) 103, (F–v) 1143

S

Sacks Foundation Scholarship. *See* United States Army Warrant Officers Association Scholarship Program, entry (S–f) 1046

Sad Sacks Nursing Scholarship, (S–f) 984

Sam Rose Memorial Scholarship, (S–f) 985

Samsung American Legion Scholarships, (S–f) 986

Samuel Eliot Morison Supplemental Scholarship. *See* Rear Admiral Samuel Eliot Morison Supplemental Scholarship, entry (F–m) 1292

Samuel Grover Powell Scholarship. *See* Chaplain Samuel Grover Powell Scholarship, entries (F–v) 1113, (F–m) 1224

San Antonio Post SAME Scholarships, (S–m) 464

SAPA Annual Scholarship Awards, (S–v) 179, (S–m) 465, (S–f) 987

Schiff Scholarship. *See* Navy League Foundation Scholarships, entry (S–f) 892

Schmidt Leadership Scholarship. *See* Colonel Charles L. Schmidt Leadership Scholarship, entry (S–f) 624

Schneider-Emanuel American Legion Scholarships, (S–v) 180, (S–f) 988

Schober Memorial Scholarship. *See* Louis J. Schober Memorial Scholarship, entries (S–v) 101, (S–m) 358, (S–f) 806

Scholarships for Military Children, (S–f) 989

Scholarships for Outstanding Airmen to ROTC (SOAR), (S–m) 466

Schonher Scholarship. *See* Dr. Nancy M. Schonher Scholarship, entries (S–v) 55, (S–m) 295, (S–f) 668, (F–v) 1121, (F–m) 1236, (F–f) 1343

SCNGF Academic Excellence Leadership Scholarships, (S–m) 467, (S–f) 990, (F–m) 1296, (F–f) 1405

SCNGF Financial Need/Academic Achievement Scholarships, (S–m) 468, (S–f) 991, (F–m) 1297, (F–f) 1406

Scott Lundell Military Survivors Tuition Waiver, (S–f) 992

Scott McClean Love Memorial Scholarship. *See* First Lieutenant Scott McClean Love Memorial Scholarship, entry (S–f) 697

Scott Memorial Scholarship. *See* Association of Aviation Ordnancemen Educational Foundation Scholarships, entries (S–v) 24, (S–f) 578

Scotty Campbell, USN (Ret) and Renee Campbell Scholarship. *See* CAPT Ernest G. "Scotty" Campbell, USN (Ret) and Renee Campbell Scholarship, entry (S–f) 599

Screaming Eagle Surviving Children's Scholarship, (S–f) 993, (F–f) 1407

SDNGEA Auxiliary Scholarships, (S–m) 469, (S–f) 994

Seabee Memorial Scholarship Association Program, (S–f) 995

Seabee Wounded in Action Scholarship, (S–f) 996

Seaman to Admiral-21 Core Program, (S–m) 470

Sean P. Grimes Physician Assistant Educational Scholarship Award. *See* Captain Sean P. Grimes Physician Assistant Educational Scholarship Award, entries (S–v) 36, (S–m) 265, (F–v) 1112, (F–m) 1223

Seigel-Dr. Philip Shapiro Education Grant. *See* Leo A. Seigel-Dr. Philip Shapiro Education Grant, entry (S–f) 800

Senator Daniel K. Inouye Memorial Scholarship, (S–v) 181, (S–m) 471, (S–f) 997, (F–v) 1170, (F–m) 1298, (F–f) 1408

Senft Scholarship. *See* USSV CF Scholarship Awards, entry (S–f) 1052

Sergeant Andrew Edmund Topham Memorial Scholarship, (S–f) 998

Sergeant Felix M. DelGreco, Jr. Scholarship Fund, (S–f) 999

Sergei Sikorsky Scholarship. *See* Naval Helicopter Association Scholarships, entries (S–v) 139, (S–m) 407, (S–f) 890, (F–v) 1156, (F–m) 1276, (F–f) 1383

Settles Scholarship. *See* Connie Settles Scholarship, entries (S–f) 638, (F–f) 1338

SFC Curtis Mancini Memorial Scholarships, (S–v) 182, (S–m) 472, (S–f) 1000, (F–v) 1171, (F–m) 1299, (F–f) 1409

SGM Dawn Kilpatrick Memorial AUSA Scholarship, (S–m) 473

Sgt. Frederick C. Brace, Jr. Memorial Scholarship, (S–v) 183, (S–f) 1001, (F–v) 1172, (F–f) 1410

Sgt. Lonnie Stephenson Memorial Scholarship. *See* ProVets Military Scholarships, entries (S–v) 167, (S–f) 962

Shapiro Education Grant. *See* Leo A. Seigel-Dr. Philip Shapiro Education Grant, entry (S–f) 800

Shima Scholarship. *See* Japanese American Veterans Association Memorial Scholarships, entry (S–f) 775

Shinseki Spouse Scholarship Program. *See* Mrs. Patty Shinseki Spouse Scholarship Program, entry (S–f) 873

Shirey Scholarship. *See* Japanese American Veterans Association Memorial Scholarships, entry (S–f) 775

Shiro Kashino Memorial Scholarships, (S–f) 1002

Siblings of Combat Related Suicide Loss Scholarship, (S–f) 1003

Sidney Lieppe Memorial Grant. *See* Jewish War Veterans National Achievement Program, entries (S–v) 94, (S–m) 345, (F–v) 1140, (F–m) 1250

Sigma Chi Military Service Scholarships, (S–v) 184, (S–m) 474, (F–v) 1173, (F–m) 1300

Sikes Memorial Scholarship. *See* Rebecca Post Sikes Memorial Scholarship, entries (S–f) 968, (F–f) 1399

Sikorsky Scholarship. *See* Naval Helicopter Association Scholarships, entries (S–v) 139, (S–m) 407, (S–f) 890, (F–v) 1156, (F–m) 1276, (F–f) 1383

Simpson Scholarship Fund. *See* Society of Daughters of the United States Army Scholarships, entry (S–f) 1006

Simultaneous Membership Program (SMP), (S–m) 475

Singletary Scholarship. *See* Virginia National Guard Association Scholarship, entries (S–m) 501, (S–f) 1063

S—Scholarships   F—Fellowships   G—Grants-in-Aid
v—Veterans   m—Military Personnel   f—Family Members

PROGRAM TITLE INDEX

SMA Leon Van Autreve Scholarships, (S—v) 185, (S—m) 476, (S—f) 1004

Smith Greater Los Angeles Women's Council Scholarship. *See* Navy League Foundation Scholarships, entry (S—f) 892

Smith Memorial Endowment Scholarship. *See* Lt. Paul (Jay) Smith Memorial Endowment Scholarship, entry (S—m) 361

Smith Scholarship. *See* Wisconsin Legion Auxiliary Merit and Memorial Scholarships, entry (S—f) 1080

SMP. *See* Simultaneous Membership Program (SMP), entry (S—m) 475

SMSgt. Nathan L. Lipscomb, Sr. Memorial Scholarship, (S—v) 186, (S—f) 1005, (F—v) 1174, (F—f) 1411

Snee Scholarship. *See* Fleet Reserve Association Member Scholarships, entries (S—v) 62, (S—m) 314, (S—f) 699, (F—v) 1127, (F—m) 1241, (F—f) 1351

Society of Air Force Physician Assistants Memorial Scholarship, (S—v) 187, (F—v) 1175

Society of Army Physician Assistants Annual Scholarship Awards. *See* SAPA Annual Scholarship Awards, entries (S—v) 179, (S—m) 465, (S—f) 987

Society of Army Physician Assistants Memorial Scholarship, (S—v) 188, (F—v) 1176

Society of Daughters of the United States Army Scholarships, (S—f) 1006

Society of the 3rd Infantry Division Scholarships, (S—f) 1007

Sons and Daughters, Pearl Harbor Survivors Scholarships, (S—f) 1008

Sons of Union Veterans of the Civil War Scholarships, (S—f) 1009

Sopcak Memorial Scholarship. *See* Women Marines Association Scholarship Program, entries (S—v) 219, (S—m) 512, (S—f) 1085, (F—v) 1191, (F—m) 1313, (F—f) 1429

South Carolina National Guard College Assistance Program, (S—m) 477

South Carolina National Guard Foundation Academic Excellence Leadership Scholarships. *See* SCNGF Academic Excellence Leadership Scholarships, entries (S—m) 467, (S—f) 990, (F—m) 1296, (F—f) 1405

South Carolina National Guard Foundation Financial Need/Academic Achievement Scholarships. *See* SCNGF Financial Need/Academic Achievement Scholarships, entries (S—m) 468, (S—f) 991, (F—m) 1297, (F—f) 1406

South Carolina National Guard Student Loan Repayment Program. *See* South Carolina National Guard College Assistance Program, entry (S—m) 477

South Carolina Tuition Assistance for Certain War Veterans Children, (S—f) 1010

South Dakota American Legion Educational Scholarship, (S—v) 189, (S—f) 1011

South Dakota National Guard Enlisted Association Auxiliary Scholarships. *See* SDNGEA Auxiliary Scholarships, entries (S—m) 469, (S—f) 994

South Dakota USAA Scholarship, (S—m) 478, (S—f) 1012

Southern Region Korean War Veteran Descendant Scholarships, (S—f) 1013, (F—f) 1412

SPC Edwin Roodhouse Memorial Scholarship Award. *See* 506th Airborne Infantry Regiment Association Scholarship, entries (S—v) 5, (S—f) 528, (F—v) 1093, (F—f) 1317

Special Duty Officer (Information Professional) Option of the Seaman to Admiral-21 Program, (S—m) 479

Special Operations Warrior Foundation Scholarships, (S—f) 1014

Special Ops Survivors Education and Career Advancement Grants, (S—f) 1015

Special Warfare Option of the Seaman to Admiral-21 Program, (S—m) 480

Spencer Memorial Scholarship. *See* Texas State Council Vietnam Veterans of America Scholarships, entries (S—v) 194, (S—f) 1030

Spencer Scholarship. *See* EANGNJ Scholarship Program, entries (S—m) 298, (S—f) 673, (F—m) 1228

Spencer Scholarship Fund. *See* Dale Spencer Scholarship Fund, entries (S—v) 46, (S—m) 285

Spirit of Youth Scholarship Fund, (S—f) 1016

Sports Clips Help a Hero Scholarships, (S—v) 190, (S—m) 481

SR Education Group Military Scholarships, (S—v) 191, (S—m) 482, (S—f) 1017

SSGT Craig Ivory Memorial Scholarships. *See* AAPA Veterans Caucus Scholarships, entries (S—v) 7, (F—v) 1094

SSgt. Robert V. Milner Memorial Scholarship, (S—v) 192, (S—f) 1018, (F—v) 1177, (F—f) 1413

Staff Sergeant John F. Kusior Memorial Scholarship. *See* Army Scholarship Foundation Scholarships, entry (S—f) 576

Stanley A. Doran Memorial Scholarships, (S—f) 1019, (F—f) 1414

Stanley Izumigawa Scholarship Fund. *See* 100th Infantry Battalion Veterans Stanley Izumigawa Scholarship Fund, entries (S—f) 519, (F—f) 1316

Starr Memorial Scholarship. *See* Naval Helicopter Association Scholarships, entries (S—v) 139, (S—m) 407, (S—f) 890, (F—v) 1156, (F—m) 1276, (F—f) 1383

State Tuition Assistance Program of the Texas National Guard, (S—m) 483

Steele Chapter AFA Open Scholarships. *See* D.W. Steele Chapter AFA STEM Scholarships, entries (S—m) 296, (S—f) 670

Stephenson Memorial Scholarship. *See* ProVets Military Scholarships, entries (S—v) 167, (S—f) 962

Stock/Evelyn Oliver Memorial Scholarship. *See* Merrilyn Stock/Evelyn Oliver Memorial Scholarship, entries (S—v) 116, (S—f) 843

STRAP. *See* Army Specialized Training Assistance Program (STRAP), entries (S—m) 248, (F—m) 1212

Strickland Memorial Fund and Scholarship. *See* Larry Strickland Memorial Fund and Scholarship, entry (S—m) 356

Stuhr Scholarships. *See* Commander William S. Stuhr Scholarships, entry (S—f) 633

Stutz Memorial Scholarship. *See* New Jersey American Legion Scholarships, entry (S—f) 903

Subic Bay-Cubi Point Scholarship, (S—f) 1020

Surface Warfare Officer Option of the Seaman to Admiral-21 Program, (S—m) 484

SURFLANT Scholarship Foundation Award. *See* Anchor Scholarships, entry (S—f) 565

Surviving Dependents of Montana National Guard Member Waiver, (S—f) 1021

Survivors' and Dependents' Educational Assistance Program, (S—f) 1022, (F—f) 1415

Susan Braun Family Scholarship. *See* Richard and Susan Braun Family Scholarship, entry (S—v) 173

Sverdrup Scholarship. *See* MG Leif J. Sverdrup Scholarship, entries (S—m) 378, (F—m) 1264

Swanier Education Scholarships. *See* Adrian and Corena Swanier Education Scholarships, entry (S—f) 534

Swift Educational Trust Scholarships. *See* Matthews and Swift Educational Trust Scholarships, entry (S—f) 840

Sydell Perlmutter Gold Memorial Scholarships. *See* Dr. Sydell Perlmutter Gold Memorial Scholarships, entry (S—f) 669

S—Scholarships
v—Veterans

F—Fellowships
m—Military Personnel

G—Grants-in-Aid
f—Family Members

PROGRAM TITLE INDEX

T

T. Nash Broaddus DECO Scholarship, (S—f) 1023

Tailhook Educational Foundation Scholarships, (S—v) 193, (S—m) 485, (S—f) 1024

Tallas Memorial Scholarship. *See* National Guard Association of Texas Scholarship Program, entries (S—v) 138, (S—m) 401, (S—f) 885, (F—v) 1155, (F—m) 1273, (F—f) 1381

Talley Scholarship. *See* BG Benjamin B. Talley Scholarship, entries (S—m) 255, (S—f) 582, (F—m) 1216, (F—f) 1327

Taubkin Legacy Scholarship. *See* Kiyoko Tsuboi Taubkin Legacy Scholarship, entry (S—f) 791

Tedrow Memorial Fund Scholarship. *See* Hattie Tedrow Memorial Fund Scholarship, entry (S—f) 734

Tennessee Boys State Samsung Scholarship, (S—f) 1025

Tenth Mountain Division Foundation Community College/Professional Program Scholarship, (S—f) 1026

Tenth Mountain Division Foundation Scholarship, (S—f) 1027, (F—f) 1416

Teru and Victor Matsui Scholarship. *See* Japanese American Veterans Association Memorial Scholarships, entry (S—f) 775

Texas American Legion Auxiliary Past President's Parley Scholarships, (S—f) 1028

Texas Armed Services Scholarship Program, (S—m) 486

Texas Capital Area Chapter of the AUSA Scholarship. *See* National Guard Association of Texas Scholarship Program, entries (S—v) 138, (S—m) 401, (S—f) 885, (F—v) 1155, (F—m) 1273, (F—f) 1381

Texas Children of U.S. Military Who Are Missing in Action or Prisoners of War Exemption Program, (S—f) 1029

Texas National Guard Retirees Endowed Scholarship. *See* National Guard Association of Texas Scholarship Program, entries (S—v) 138, (S—m) 401, (S—f) 885, (F—v) 1155, (F—m) 1273, (F—f) 1381

Texas State Council Vietnam Veterans of America Scholarships, (S—v) 194, (S—f) 1030

ThanksUSA Scholarships, (S—f) 1031

That Others May Live Foundation Scholarships, (S—f) 1032

Thibault VFW State Memorial Scholarship. *See* Department of Nebraska VFW State Scholarships, entries (S—v) 50, (S—f) 656

Third Marine Division Association Memorial Scholarship Fund, (S—f) 1035

Thomas Crow Memorial Scholarship. *See* Chief Petty Officer Scholarships, entry (S—f) 608

Thomas H. Miller Scholarship, (S—f) 1036, (F—f) 1418

Thomas Russell Scholarship. *See* San Antonio Post SAME Scholarships, entry (S—m) 464

Thomas W. Morrow Scholarship. *See* Fourth Marine Division Association of WWII Scholarship, entry (S—f) 710

Tillman Military Scholars Program, (S—v) 197, (S—m) 488, (S—f) 1037, (F—v) 1179, (F—m) 1302, (F—f) 1419

Tobin Scholarship Program. *See* Dr. Aileen Webb Tobin Scholarship Program, entry (S—m) 293

Tom and Karen Snee Scholarship. *See* Fleet Reserve Association Member Scholarships, entries (S—v) 62, (S—m) 314, (S—f) 699, (F—v) 1127, (F—m) 1241, (F—f) 1351

TonaLaw Veteran's Scholarship, (S—v) 198, (F—v) 1180

Tony Lopez Scholarship Program, (S—v) 199, (S—m) 489, (S—f) 1038

Tony Wojo Scholarship. *See* Remembering Marine SSGT Mark Anthony Wojciechowski "Tony Wojo" Scholarship, entry (S—f) 970

Topham Memorial Scholarship. *See* Sergeant Andrew Edmund Topham Memorial Scholarship, entry (S—f) 998

Transfer of Post-9/11 GI-Bill Benefits to Dependents, (S—f) 1039, (F—f) 1420

Travers Loan Program. *See* Navy-Marine Corps Relief Society Education Assistance, entries (S—m) 412, (S—f) 897

TREA Memorial Foundation Scholarships, (S—f) 1040

TREA National Auxiliary Scholarships, (S—f) 1041

Treadwell Annual Scholarship. *See* Fleet Reserve Association Member Scholarships, entries (S—v) 62, (S—m) 314, (S—f) 699, (F—v) 1127, (F—m) 1241, (F—f) 1351

Troops-to-Teachers Program, (F—v) 1181, (F—m) 1303

Troutt Memorial Scholarship. *See* ProVets Military Scholarships, entries (S—v) 167, (S—f) 962

Tuition Waiver for Disabled Children of Kentucky Veterans, (S—f) 1042

Tvshka (Warrior) Scholarship, (S—v) 200, (S—m) 490, (F—v) 1182, (F—m) 1304

TXNG Retirees Endowed Scholarship. *See* National Guard Association of Texas Scholarship Program, entries (S—v) 138, (S—m) 401, (S—f) 885, (F—v) 1155, (F—m) 1273, (F—f) 1381

U

Udie Grant Scholarship Fund. *See* U.S. "Udie" Grant Scholarship Fund, entry (S—f) 1049

UDT-SEAL Scholarship, (S—f) 1043

Unified Arizona Veterans Scholarships, (S—v) 201, (S—m) 491, (S—f) 1044, (F—v) 1183, (F—m) 1305, (F—f) 1421

Unilever Rewards of Caring Scholarship Contest, (S—f) 1045

United Airlines Veteran Scholarship, (S—v) 202

United Armed Forces Association Scholarship. *See* Navy League Foundation Scholarships, entry (S—f) 892

United States Army Warrant Officers Association Scholarship Program, (S—f) 1046

United States Field Artillery Association Scholarships, (S—m) 492, (S—f) 1047

United States Marine Corps Combat Correspondents Association Scholarship. *See* Brigadier General Robert L. Denig Foundation Scholarship, entries (S—m) 259, (S—f) 587

United States Submarine Veterans Charitable Foundation Scholarship Awards. *See* USSV CF Scholarship Awards, entry (S—f) 1052

Urey Woodson Alexander Memorial Scholarship. *See* Army Scholarship Foundation Scholarships, entry (S—f) 576

Ursano Scholarship Fund. *See* MG James Ursano Scholarship Fund, entry (S—f) 845

U.S. Army Health Care Enlisted Commissioning Program (AECP), (S—m) 493

U.S. Army Ranger Association Michael B. Ranger Legacy Scholarships. *See* USARA Michael B. Ranger Legacy Scholarships, entry (S—f) 1051

US Family Health Scholarship. *See* Fleet Reserve Association Member Scholarships, entries (S—v) 62, (S—m) 314, (S—f) 699, (F—v) 1127, (F—m) 1241, (F—f) 1351

U.S. Mountain Ranger Association Scholarships, (S—f) 1048

U.S. Submarine Veterans of World War II Scholarship. *See* Dolphin Scholarships, entry (S—f) 664

U.S. "Udie" Grant Scholarship Fund, (S—f) 1049

USAA/EANGKY Scholarship, (S—m) 494, (S—f) 1050

USARA Michael B. Ranger Legacy Scholarships, (S—f) 1051

USMCCCA Scholarship. *See* Brigadier General Robert L. Denig Foundation Scholarship, entries (S—m) 259, (S—f) 587

USSV CF Scholarship Awards, (S—f) 1052

S—Scholarships
v—Veterans

F—Fellowships
m—Military Personnel

G—Grants-in-Aid
f—Family Members

PROGRAM TITLE INDEX

Utah National Guard State Tuition Assistance Program, (S—m) 495, (F—m) 1306

Utah National Guard State Tuition Waiver, (S—m) 496

Utah Tuition Waiver for Purple Heart Recipients, (S—v) 203, (F—v) 1184

Utah Veteran Tuition Gap Program, (S—v) 204

V

VADM Jon L. Boyes, Vice Admiral, USN (Ret.) Memorial Scholarship, (S—m) 497

Van Autreve Scholarships. See SMA Leon Van Autreve Scholarships, entries (S—v) 185, (S—m) 476, (S—f) 1004

Van Deuren Memorial Scholarships. See Della Van Deuren Memorial Scholarships, entry (S—f) 652

Van Hipp Heroes Scholarship, (S—v) 205, (S—m) 498

VAW/VRC Memorial Scholarships, (S—f) 1053

VAW/VRC Merit Scholarships, (S—f) 1054

Vermont Armed Services Scholarship, (S—f) 1055

Vermont National Guard Enlisted Association Scholarships. See VTNGEA Scholarships, entries (S—m) 503, (S—f) 1064

Vermont National Guard Tuition Benefit Program, (S—m) 499

Veronica Lenox Cotarlu Memorial Scholarship. See Army Scholarship Foundation Scholarships, entry (S—f) 576

Veronica Ream Memorial Scholarship. See Naval Helicopter Association Scholarships, entries (S—v) 139, (S—m) 407, (S—f) 890, (F—v) 1156, (F—m) 1276, (F—f) 1383

Veterans in Plumbing, Heating, Cooling and Electrical Scholarship, (S—v) 206

Veterans Make Great STEM Teachers Program, (S—v) 207, (F—v) 1185

Veterans of Foreign Wars of Mexican Ancestry Scholarship Program, (S—f) 1056

Veterans of Foreign Wars Post 81 Trust Fund Scholarship, (S—f) 1057

Veterans Pursuing a Career in Law Scholarship, (S—v) 208

Veterans Tuition Waiver Program of Massachusetts, (S—v) 209

Veterans United Foundation Scholarships, (S—f) 1058, (F—f) 1422

VFW Auxiliary Continuing Education Scholarships, (S—f) 1059

Vice Admiral E.P. Travers Loan Program. See Navy-Marine Corps Relief Society Education Assistance, entries (S—m) 412, (S—f) 897

Vice Admiral Robert L. Walters Scholarship, (S—v) 210, (S—m) 500, (S—f) 1060, (F—v) 1186, (F—m) 1307, (F—f) 1423

Vicki Lianne Moritsugu Memorial Scholarship. See AAPA Veterans Caucus Scholarships, entries (S—v) 7, (F—v) 1094

Victor Matsui Scholarship. See Japanese American Veterans Association Memorial Scholarships, entry (S—f) 775

Viglienzone Memorial Scholarship. See Caesar Viglienzone Memorial Scholarship, entry (S—v) 29

VII Corps Desert Storm Veterans Association Scholarship, (S—v) 211, (S—f) 1061

Vincent Baldassari Memorial Scholarships. See EANGNJ Scholarship Program, entries (S—m) 298, (S—f) 673

Vincent Scholarship. See ASMC Members' Continuing Education Grants, entries (S—m) 253, (F—m) 1215

Virgil R. Williams Scholarship Program. See CSM Virgil R. Williams Scholarship Program, entries (S—m) 283, (S—f) 644

Virginia Guveyan Memorial Scholarship. See Women Marines Association Scholarship Program, entries (S—v) 219, (S—m) 512, (S—f) 1085, (F—v) 1191, (F—m) 1313, (F—f) 1429

Virginia Military Survivors and Dependents Education Program, (S—f) 1062, (F—f) 1424

Virginia National Guard Association Scholarship, (S—m) 501, (S—f) 1063

Virginia National Guard Tuition Assistance Program, (S—m) 502, (F—m) 1308

Virginia War Orphans Education Program. See Virginia Military Survivors and Dependents Education Program, entries (S—f) 1062, (F—f) 1424

Viste Scholarship Program. See Al and Willamary Viste Scholarship Program, entries (S—f) 544, (F—f) 1321

VTNGEA Scholarships, (S—m) 503, (S—f) 1064

W

Wagner Memorial Fund. See Society of Daughters of the United States Army Scholarships, entry (S—f) 1006

Walker Honorary Scholarship. See Chief Petty Officer Scholarships, entry (S—f) 608

Walter Beall Scholarship, (S—m) 504, (S—f) 1065

Walter Keith Irwin Memorial Scholarship Fund, (S—f) 1066

Walter R. Bowie Memorial Scholarship. See Army Scholarship Foundation Scholarships, entry (S—f) 576

Walter Reed Society Scholarship. See AHIMA Veterans Scholarship, entries (S—v) 10, (S—f) 541, (F—v) 1096, (F—f) 1319

Walters Scholarship. See Vice Admiral Robert L. Walters Scholarship, entries (S—v) 210, (S—m) 500, (S—f) 1060, (F—v) 1186, (F—m) 1307, (F—f) 1423

WAPA Veteran Scholarships, (S—v) 212, (F—v) 1187

Ward Macauley Scholarships. See DFC Society Ward Macauley Scholarships, entry (S—f) 657

Ward Veteran's Award. See Lucile Parrish Ward Veteran's Award, entries (S—v) 104, (F—v) 1144

Warren Memorial Scholarships. See LTC Michael Warren Memorial Scholarships, entries (S—m) 362, (S—f) 811

Warren-Ragan Junior Scholarship Fund, (S—f) 1067

Warrior's Legacy Scholarship Fund, (S—f) 1068

Washington Legion Children and Youth Scholarships, (S—f) 1069

Washington Metropolitan Area Navy Nurse Corps Association Scholarships, (F—v) 1188, (F—m) 1309

Washington National Guard Conditional Scholarship Program. See Washington National Guard Postsecondary Education Grant, entry (S—m) 505

Washington National Guard Postsecondary Education Grant, (S—m) 505

Washington State Academy of Physician Assistants Veteran Scholarships. See WAPA Veteran Scholarships, entries (S—v) 212, (F—v) 1187

Wellington, Jr. Memorial Scholarship. See Raymond T. Wellington, Jr. Memorial Scholarship, entry (S—f) 966

Wells Fargo Veterans Scholarship Program, (S—v) 213, (S—f) 1070, (F—v) 1189, (F—f) 1425

Welsh Education Awards (ROTC). See Major Elbert A. Welsh Education Awards (ROTC), entry (S—m) 366

Wesley C. Cameron Scholarship. See Navy League Foundation Scholarships, entry (S—f) 892

Wesley Hammon Leach Scholarships, (S—v) 214, (S—m) 506, (S—f) 1071

West Virginia National Guard Educational Encouragement Program, (S—m) 507, (F—m) 1310

West Virginia Sons of the American Legion Scholarship, (S—f) 1072

West Virginia State War Orphans Educational Program, (S—f) 1073

S—Scholarships
v—Veterans

F—Fellowships
m—Military Personnel

G—Grants-in-Aid
f—Family Members

West Virginia Veteran's Reeducation Scholarship Program, (S—v) 215

White Scholarship. *See* Maria C. Jackson/General George A. White Scholarship, entries (S—v) 110, (S—f) 822, (F—v) 1147, (F—f) 1371

Wiebke Memorial Scholarship. *See* Women Marines Association Scholarship Program, entries (S—v) 219, (S—m) 512, (S—f) 1085, (F—v) 1191, (F—m) 1313, (F—f) 1429

Willamary Viste Scholarship Program. *See* Al and Willamary Viste Scholarship Program, entries (S—f) 544, (F—f) 1321

William "Bill" Myers Scholarship. *See* San Antonio Post SAME Scholarships, entry (S—m) 464

William C. Singletary Scholarship. *See* Virginia National Guard Association Scholarship, entries (S—m) 501, (S—f) 1063

William E. Brand, Jr. Memorial Scholarship. *See* ProVets Military Scholarships, entries (S—v) 167, (S—f) 962

William E. DePuy Memorial Scholarship Program. *See* General William E. DePuy Memorial Scholarship Program, entry (S—f) 722

William Latta Scholarship. *See* Chappie Hall Memorial Scholarship Program, entry (S—f) 603

William P. O'Connell Memorial Veterans Rehabilitation Scholarship, (S—f) 1074

William S. Stuhr Scholarships. *See* Commander William S. Stuhr Scholarships, entry (S—f) 633

William W, Boddington Scholarship, (S—f) 1075

Williams Scholarship. *See* Gamewardens Association Scholarship, entry (S—f) 714

Williams Scholarship Program. *See* CSM Virgil R. Williams Scholarship Program, entries (S—m) 283, (S—f) 644

Wilma D. Hoyal/Maxine Chilton Scholarships, (S—v) 216, (S—f) 1076

Wilson Jr. Scholarship. *See* Ernie Wilson Jr. Scholarship, entry (S—f) 691

Wing Family Program Scholarship. *See* Wyoming National Guard Association Scholarships, entries (S—m) 516, (S—f) 1091

Wings Over America Scholarships, (S—f) 1077

Winifred Quick Collins, USN (Ret) Scholarship. *See* Navy League Foundation Scholarships, entry (S—f) 892

Wirth Scholarship. *See* Navy League Foundation Scholarships, entry (S—f) 892

Wisconsin G.I. Bill Tuition Remission Program, (S—v) 217, (S—f) 1078, (F—v) 1190, (F—f) 1426

Wisconsin Legion Auxiliary Child Welfare Scholarship, (F—f) 1427

Wisconsin Legion Auxiliary Department President's Scholarship, (S—f) 1079

Wisconsin Legion Auxiliary Merit and Memorial Scholarships, (S—f) 1080

Wisconsin Legion Auxiliary Past Presidents Parley Health Career Scholarships, (S—f) 1081

Wisconsin Legion Auxiliary Past Presidents Parley Registered Nurse Scholarships, (S—f) 1082

Wisconsin National Guard Association Education Grant, (S—m) 508, (S—f) 1083

Wisconsin National Guard Association President's Scholarship, (F—m) 1311

Wisconsin National Guard Enlisted Association College Grant Program, (S—m) 509, (S—f) 1084, (F—m) 1312, (F—f) 1428

Wisconsin National Guard Tuition Grant, (S—m) 510

Wisconsin Tuition and Fee Reimbursement Grants. *See* Wisconsin G.I. Bill Tuition Remission Program, entries (S—v) 217, (S—f) 1078, (F—v) 1190, (F—f) 1426

Wives of the U.S. Submarine Veterans of World War II Scholarship. *See* Dolphin Scholarships, entry (S—f) 664

WMA Memorial Scholarships. *See* Women Marines Association Scholarship Program, entries (S—v) 219, (S—m) 512, (S—f) 1085, (F—v) 1191, (F—m) 1313, (F—f) 1429

Wojciechowski "Tony Wojo" Scholarship. *See* Remembering Marine SSGT Mark Anthony Wojciechowski "Tony Wojo" Scholarship, entry (S—f) 970

Women in Defense Palmetto Chapter Horizons Scholarship, (S—v) 218, (S—m) 511

Women Marines Association Scholarship Program, (S—v) 219, (S—m) 512, (S—f) 1085, (F—v) 1191, (F—m) 1313, (F—f) 1429

Women Military Aviators Dream of Flight Scholarship, (S—v) 220, (S—m) 513

Women's Army Corps Veterans' Association Scholarship, (S—f) 1086

Women's Auxiliary Club Scholarship. *See* NVC/WAC Scholarship, entry (S—f) 937

Women's Overseas Service League Scholarships for Women, (S—m) 514

Women's Scuba Association Dive Training Grant, (S—m) 515

Worchid Scholarship, (S—f) 1087

World War II Illinois Descendants Scholarship, (S—f) 1088

Wullenwaber Memorial Scholarship Award. *See* 506th Airborne Infantry Regiment Association Scholarship, entries (S—v) 5, (S—f) 528, (F—v) 1093, (F—f) 1317

Wyatt Memorial Scholarship. *See* Margene Mogan Proctor and General Jerry Wyatt Memorial Scholarship, entry (S—f) 820

Wyoming Army National Guard Combined Club Scholarship. *See* Wyoming National Guard Association Scholarships, entries (S—m) 516, (S—f) 1091

Wyoming Elks Association Angels Scholarship, (S—f) 1089

Wyoming Legion Auxiliary Past President's Parley Field of Health Care Scholarships, (S—f) 1090

Wyoming National Guard Association Scholarships, (S—m) 516, (S—f) 1091

Wyoming National Guard Educational Assistance Plan, (S—m) 517, (F—m) 1314

Wyoming USAA Insurance Company Scholarship. *See* Wyoming National Guard Association Scholarships, entries (S—m) 516, (S—f) 1091

Y

Yellow Ribbon Program of the Post-9/11 GI Bill, (S—v) 221, (S—f) 1092, (F—v) 1192, (F—f) 1430

YNC John Williams Scholarship. *See* Gamewardens Association Scholarship, entry (S—f) 714

Z

Zweiman Memorial Award. *See* Jewish War Veterans National Achievement Program, entries (S—v) 94, (S—m) 345, (F—v) 1140, (F—m) 1250

Sponsoring Organization Index

The Sponsoring Organization Index makes it easy to identify agencies that offer financial aid to veterans, military personnel, or members of their families. In this index, sponsoring organizations are listed alphabetically, word by word. In addition, we've used a two-character alphabetical code (within parentheses) to help you identify which programs sponsored by these organizations fall within your scope of interest. The first character (capitalized) in the code identifies program type: S = Scholarships; F = Fellowships; G = Grants-in-Aid. The second character (lower cased) identifies eligible groups: v = Veterans; m = Military Personnel; f = Family Members. For example, if the name of a sponsoring organization is followed by (S–v) 241, a program sponsored by that organization is described in the Scholarship section under Veterans, in entry 241. If that sponsoring organization's name is followed by another entry number—for example, (G–m) 1250—the same or a different program sponsored by that organization is described in the Grants-in-Aid section, under Military Personnel, in entry 1250. Remember: the numbers cited here refer to program entry numbers, not to page numbers in the book.

101st Airborne Division Association, (S–f) 544, 603, 993, (F–f) 1321, 1407
11th Armored Cavalry Veterans of Vietnam and Cambodia, (S–f) 521, 624
173rd Airborne Brigade, (S–f) 522
28th Infantry Division Association, (S–m) 449, (S–f) 953
37th Division Veterans Association, (S–v) 2, (S–f) 525
3M Company, (S–v) 3, (S–m) 223, (S–f) 526
3rd Battalion 26th Marines (Vietnam), (S–f) 524
43d Infantry Division Veterans Association, (S–v) 4, (S–f) 527
506th Airborne Infantry Regiment Association, (S–v) 5, (S–f) 528, (F–v) 1093, (F–f) 1317
531 Gray Ghost Squadron Association, (S–f) 529
7th Infantry Regiment Association, (S–f) 719
82nd Airborne Division Association, (S–v) 6, (S–f) 530

A

A Million Thanks, Inc., (S–f) 713
A-7 Corsair Association, (S–f) 532
AgHeritage Farm Credit Services, (S–v) 82, (S–m) 337, (S–f) 745
Air Force Aid Society, (S–f) 537, 718
Air Force Association, (S–m) 252, 288, (S–f) 623, 653, 669, 780, 809, 849, (F–m) 1221, 1228, (F–f) 1374
Air Force Association. Donald W. Steele, Sr. Chapter, (S–m) 296, (S–f) 670
Air Force Association. Rocky Mounhtain Region, (S–f) 711
Air Force Sergeants Association, (S–f) 540, 543, 607
Air Force Services Agency, (S–m) 228, (S–f) 542, (F–m) 1196, (F–f) 1320
Air Traffic Control Association, (S–f) 588, (F–f) 1329
Airlift Tanker Association, (S–m) 251-252
Airmen Memorial Foundation, (S–f) 607

Airpower Foundation, (S–m) 252
Alabama Commission on Higher Education, (S–m) 234, (F–m) 1203
Alabama Department of Veterans Affairs, (S–f) 545, (F–f) 1322
Alaska National Guard, (S–v) 11, (S–m) 235, (F–v) 1098, (F–m) 1204
Alaska National Guard Enlisted Association, (S–v) 18, (S–m) 238, (S–f) 566
The Aleut Corporation, (S–v) 58, (F–v) 1123
Allied Van Lines, (S–v) 13, (S–m) 237, (S–f) 552
Alpha Tau Omega, (S–m) 258
Americal Division Veterans Association, (S–f) 554
American Academy of Physician Assistants, (S–v) 175, (S–f) 979, (F–v) 1168, (F–f) 1403
American Academy of Physician Assistants. Veterans Caucus, (S–v) 7, 35, 75, 103, 183, 186-188, 192, 196, (S–m) 487, (S–f) 601, 731, 1001, 1005, 1018, 1034, (F–v) 1094, 1110, 1133, 1143, 1172, 1174-1178, (F–m) 1301, (F–f) 1332, 1357, 1410-1411, 1413, 1417
American Airlines, (S–v) 14
The American College of Financial Services, (S–v) 195, (S–f) 1033
American Educational Research Association, (F–f) 1323
American Ex-prisoners of War, Inc. Columbia River Chapter, (S–v) 162, (S–f) 956, (F–v) 1165, (F–f) 1397
American GI Forum Colorado State Women, (S–f) 817
American Health Information Management Association, (S–v) 10, (S–f) 541, (F–v) 1096, (F–f) 1319
American Legion. Alaska Auxiliary, (S–v) 116, (S–f) 843
American Legion. Americanism and Children & Youth Division, (S–f) 558, 986
American Legion. Arizona Auxiliary, (S–v) 216, (S–f) 1076
American Legion. Arkansas Auxiliary, (S–f) 570

S—Scholarships
v—Veterans

F—Fellowships
m—Military Personnel

G—Grants-in-Aid
f—Family Members

SPONSORING ORGANIZATION INDEX

American Legion. Arkansas Department, (S—f) 640, 715
American Legion Auxiliary, (S—v) 15, (S—f) 555-557, 616, 986, 1016
American Legion. California Auxiliary, (S—v) 31-32, (S—m) 262, (S—f) 593-596, 638, (F—f) 1338
American Legion. Colorado Auxiliary, (S—v) 41-42, (S—f) 629-632
American Legion. Erie County, (S—v) 159, (S—f) 948
American Legion. Florida Auxiliary, (S—f) 703-704, (F—f) 1353
American Legion. Florida Department, (S—f) 702
American Legion. Georgia Auxiliary, (S—f) 727-728
American Legion. Georgia Department, (S—f) 725
American Legion. Idaho Auxiliary, (S—v) 84-85, (S—f) 750-753
American Legion. Illinois Auxiliary, (S—v) 86, 118, (S—f) 533, 754, 764, 850
American Legion. Illinois Department, (S—f) 755-756
American Legion. Indiana Department, (S—f) 765
American Legion. Kansas Department, (S—f) 548, 605, 980
American Legion. Kentucky Auxiliary, (S—f) 798, 833
American Legion. Maine Department, (S—f) 648
American Legion. Maryland Department, (S—f) 837
American Legion. Minnesota Auxiliary, (S—f) 862-863
American Legion. Missouri Department, (S—v) 128, (S—f) 804, 841
American Legion. Montana Auxiliary, (S—f) 553
American Legion. New Hampshire Auxiliary, (S—v) 8, (S—f) 535, 830
American Legion. New Hampshire Department, (S—f) 549, 779
American Legion. New Jersey Auxiliary, (S—f) 617, 905
American Legion. New Jersey Department, (S—f) 781, 903
American Legion. New York Auxiliary, (S—f) 739, 836, 909-911, 966
American Legion. New York Department, (S—f) 975
American Legion. North Carolina Auxiliary, (S—f) 877, 1067
American Legion. North Dakota Department, (S—f) 684, 734, (F—f) 1346
American Legion. Ohio Auxiliary, (S—v) 157, (S—f) 939
American Legion. Ohio Department, (S—v) 158, (S—m) 444, (S—f) 940-942, (F—v) 1164, (F—m) 1289, (F—f) 1394-1395
American Legion. Pennsylvania Department, (S—f) 785
American Legion. South Dakota Department, (S—v) 189, (S—f) 1011
American Legion. Tennessee Department, (S—f) 1025
American Legion. Texas Auxiliary, (S—f) 1028
American Legion. Virginia Auxiliary, (S—f) 667
American Legion. Virginia Department, (S—f) 812
American Legion. Washington Auxiliary, (S—v) 109, (S—f) 701, 821, (F—v) 1146, (F—f) 1370
American Legion. Washington Department, (S—f) 1069
American Legion. Wisconsin Auxiliary, (S—f) 652, 747, 1079-1082, (F—f) 1360, 1427
American Legion. Wisconsin Department, (S—v) 180, (S—f) 988
American Legion. Wyoming Auxiliary, (S—f) 1090
American Legion. Wyoming Department, (S—f) 671
American Logistics Association. New York Chapter, (S—f) 853
American Pharmacists Association, (F—m) 1229, (F—f) 1336
American Society of Military Comptrollers, (S—m) 253, (F—m) 1215
American Society of Safety Professionals, (S—v) 20, 93, (F—v) 1101, 1139
American States Utility Services, Inc., (S—f) 560
American Veterinary Medical Association, (F—v) 1106

American Welding Society, (S—v) 132
AMVETS. Department of Illinois, (S—v) 87, (S—f) 757-760, 984, 1087
AMVETS. Department of Ohio, (S—v) 156, (S—f) 938
AMVETS National Headquarters, (S—v) 16-17, 54, 102, (S—m) 294, 360, (S—f) 561-562, 564, 808, (F—v) 1099
AMVETS National Ladies Auxiliary, (S—f) 563
Anchor Scholarship Foundation, (S—f) 565, 581, 799, 967, 978, 1023
Andromeda Systems Incorporated, (S—f) 955
Applications International Corporation, (S—v) 20, 93, (F—v) 1101, 1139
Arizona Community Foundation, (S—v) 46, 78, (S—m) 285, 334, (S—f) 738, 1066
Arkansas Agriculture Department, (S—v) 82, (S—m) 337, (S—f) 745
Arkansas Community Foundation, (S—v) 26, (S—f) 572, (F—v) 1105
Arkansas Department of Higher Education, (S—f) 571
Arkansas National Guard, (S—m) 239
Armed Forces Benefit Association, (S—m) 225, 283, (S—f) 538, 644, 717, (F—m) 1194, (F—f) 1318
Armed Forces Communications and Electronics Association, (S—v) 9, (S—m) 226-227, 346, 393, 497, (F—v) 1095, (F—m) 1195
Armed Forces Communications and Electronics Association. Los Angeles Chapter, (S—m) 357
Armed Forces Communications and Electronics Association. Montgomery Chapter, (S—m) 346, 393
Armed Forces Communications and Electronics Association. Northern Virginia Chapter, (S—v) 9, (S—m) 227
Armed Forces Communications and Electronics Association. Washington D.C. Chapter, (S—f) 539
Army and Air Force Exchange Service, (S—f) 567, 1045
Army Aviation Association of America Scholarship Foundation, (S—v) 21, (S—m) 241, (S—f) 574, (F—v) 1102, (F—m) 1205, (F—f) 1324
Army Emergency Relief, (S—f) 845, 873
Army Engineer Association, (S—v) 38, (S—m) 224, 282, 378, (S—f) 536, 621, 625, (F—v) 1114, (F—m) 1232, 1264, (F—f) 1335
Army Engineer Spouses' Club, (S—f) 729
Army Nurse Corps Association, (S—v) 22, (S—m) 243, (S—f) 575, (F—v) 1103, (F—m) 1210, (F—f) 1325
Army Scholarship Foundation, (S—f) 522, 576, 641, 697, 839, 998
Army Unit Scholarship Fund, (S—f) 690
Army Women's Foundation, (S—v) 23, (S—m) 250, (S—f) 577, (F—v) 1104, (F—m) 1214, (F—f) 1326
Arnold Air Society-Silver Wings, (S—m) 251-252
Association of Aviation Ordnancemen, (S—v) 24, (S—f) 578
Association of the Century, Inc., (S—v) 117, (S—m) 377, (S—f) 844
Association of the United States Army, (S—v) 70, 96, 148, 185, (S—m) 289, 321, 350, 356, 431, 473, 476, (S—f) 654, 716, 784, 923, 1004
Association of the United States Army. Braxton Bragg Chapter, (S—v) 28, (S—m) 257, (S—f) 586, (F—v) 1107, (F—m) 1217, (F—f) 1328
Association of the United States Army. George Washington Chapter, (S—v) 72, (S—m) 324, (S—f) 724, (F—v) 1131, (F—m) 1246, (F—f) 1356
Association of the United States Army. Rhode Island Chapter, (S—v) 45, 182, (S—m) 281, 472, (S—f) 643, 1000, (F—v) 1117, 1171, (F—m) 1231, 1299, (F—f) 1339, 1409

S—Scholarships F—Fellowships G—Grants-in-Aid
v—Veterans m—Military Personnel f—Family Members

SPONSORING ORGANIZATION INDEX

Association of the United States Army. Texas Capital Area Chapter, (S—v) 138, (S—m) 401, (S—f) 885, (F—v) 1155, (F—m) 1273, (F—f) 1381
Association of the United States Navy, (S—m) 254, (S—f) 580
AT&T, (S—v) 26, (F—v) 1105
AT&T Veterans, (S—v) 25
Austal USA, (S—f) 581
Aviation Boatswain's Mates Association, (S—f) 773

B

BAE Systems, (S—f) 576
Bell Helicopter, (S—f) 576
Better Business Bureau Serving Connecticut, (S—f) 635
Blackhorse Association, (S—f) 584
Blinded Veterans Association, (S—f) 789, 1036, (F—f) 1364, 1418
Blinded Veterans Association Auxiliary, (S—f) 971
Boeing Company, (S—m) 252, (S—f) 1077

C

CAE Inc., (S—v) 139, (S—m) 407, (S—f) 890, (F—v) 1156, (F—m) 1276, (F—f) 1383
California Department of Veterans Affairs, (S—v) 30, 33, (S—m) 264, (S—f) 589-592, 597, (F—v) 1108, (F—m) 1219, (F—f) 1330
California Enlisted Association of the National Guard of the United States, (S—m) 261
California State Military Department, (S—m) 263, (F—m) 1218
Central Indiana Community Foundation, (S—v) 107, (S—m) 368, (S—f) 816
Chahta Foundation, (S—v) 200, (S—m) 490, (F—v) 1182, (F—m) 1304
Chief Petty Officer Scholarship Fund, (S—f) 608
Chief Warrant and Warrant Officers Association, USCG, (S—f) 645
Children of Fallen Patriots Foundation, (S—f) 613
Children of Fallen Soldiers Relief Fund, (S—f) 614
Church, State and Industry Foundation, (F—m) 1225
Cincinnati Scholarship Foundation, (S—f) 970
Clifford H. "Ted" Rees, Jr. Scholarship Foundation, (S—v) 172
CNC Mastercam, (S—v) 207, (F—v) 1185
Coast Guard Exchange, (S—f) 619
Coast Guard Foundation, (S—m) 270, (S—f) 610-611, 620
Collision Repair Education Foundation, (S—v) 3, (S—m) 223, (S—f) 526
Colorado Commission on Higher Education, (S—f) 628
Colorado. Department of Military and Veterans Affairs, (S—m) 276
Combat Control Association, (S—f) 832
Commander William S. Stuhr Scholarship Fund, (S—f) 633
Commissioned Officers Association of the U.S. Public Health Service, (S—f) 957, (F—f) 1398
Community Foundation for the Land of Lincoln, (S—f) 1088
Community Foundation of Greater Des Moines, (S—f) 612
Community Foundation of Louisville, (S—v) 117, (S—m) 377, (S—f) 844
Connecticut Community Foundation, (S—f) 999
Connecticut National Guard, (S—m) 277
Connecticut National Guard Foundation, Inc., (S—m) 278, (S—f) 636, 999
Connecticut State Universities and Colleges, (S—v) 43, (S—m) 279, (S—f) 637, (F—v) 1115, (F—m) 1230, (F—f) 1337
Corvias Foundation, (S—f) 639
Council of College and Military Educators, (S—v) 44, (S—m) 347, (S—f) 805, (F—v) 1116, (F—m) 1251, (F—f) 1367
CPS Products, (S—v) 124

D

Daniel Drevnick Memorial Fund, (S—v) 47, (S—f) 647
Daughters of the American Revolution. Michigan State Society, (S—v) 176, (S—m) 461
Daughters of the American Revolution. Missouri State Society, (S—v) 131
Daughters of the Cincinnati, (S—f) 650
Defense Activity for Non-Traditional Education Support, (F—v) 1181, (F—m) 1303
Delaware Department of Education, (S—f) 651
Delaware National Guard, (S—m) 287
Delta Dental, (S—m) 288-289, (S—f) 653-654
Disabled American Veterans Auxiliary, (S—f) 658, (F—f) 1341
Disabled American Veterans. Department of New Jersey, (S—f) 604
Distinguished Flying Cross Society, (S—f) 657
District 8 American Legion Riders, (S—f) 659
District of Columbia National Guard, (S—m) 290, (F—m) 1234
DKF Veterans Assistance Foundation, (S—v) 52, (S—f) 660
Dolphin Scholarship Foundation, (S—f) 664
D.P. Associates Inc., (S—v) 139, (S—m) 407, (S—f) 890, (F—v) 1156, (F—m) 1276, (F—f) 1383
DRS Technologies, Inc., (S—f) 801

E

EducationDynamics, LLC, (S—v) 123, (S—m) 383, (S—f) 857
Elbit Systems of America, LLC, (S—f) 839
Energy Polymer Group, (S—v) 60, (F—v) 1125
The Enlisted Association, (S—f) 1040-1041
Enlisted Association National Guard of Arizona, (S—m) 269, 280, (S—f) 618, 642
Enlisted Association National Guard of Kansas, (S—m) 309, (S—f) 687
Enlisted Association National Guard of Kentucky, (S—m) 494, (S—f) 1050
Enlisted Association National Guard of New Jersey, (S—m) 298, (S—f) 673
Enlisted Association of the National Guard of Georgia, (S—m) 307, (S—f) 685
Enlisted Association of the National Guard of Iowa, (S—m) 339, (S—f) 746
Enlisted Association of the National Guard of Iowa Auxiliary, (S—v) 59, (S—m) 308, (S—f) 686, (F—v) 1124, (F—m) 1238, (F—f) 1347
Enlisted Association of the National Guard of Montana, (S—m) 297, (S—f) 672
Enlisted Association of the National Guard of Tennessee, (S—m) 299, (S—f) 674
Enlisted Association of the National Guard of the United States, (S—m) 283, 300, (S—f) 644, 675-676
Enlisted Association of the National Guard of Utah, (S—m) 301, (S—f) 677
Enlisted Association of the National Guard of West Virginia, (S—m) 332, (S—f) 733
Enlisted Association of the New York National Guard, Inc., (S—m) 302, (S—f) 678
Enlisted National Guard Association of Florida, (S—m) 430, (S—f) 922
EOD Warrior Foundation, (S—f) 688
Epsilon Sigma Alpha International, (S—f) 818

S—Scholarships F—Fellowships G—Grants-in-Aid
v—Veterans m—Military Personnel f—Family Members

F

Farm Credit Midsouth, (S—v) 82, (S—m) 337, (S—f) 745
Farm Credit of Western Arkansas, (S—v) 82, (S—m) 337, (S—f) 745
Federal Resources Supply Company, (S—f) 1068
Fifth Marine Division Association Scholarship Fund, (S—f) 694
First Cavalry Division Association, (S—m) 312, (S—f) 695, 748
First Command Educational Foundation, (S—v) 37, 53, 195, (S—m) 266, 292, 361, 364, (S—f) 602, 665, 1033, 1077, (F—v) 1120, (F—m) 1235, (F—f) 1342
First Marine Division Association, (S—f) 698
Fisher House Foundation, (S—f) 741, 989
Fleet Reserve Association, (S—v) 62-63, (S—m) 314-315, (S—f) 626, 699-700, 1019, (F—v) 1126-1128, (F—m) 1240-1242, (F—f) 1350-1352, 1414
Fleet Reserve Association. Past Regional Presidents Club, (S—m) 504, (S—f) 1065
FLIR Systems, (S—v) 139, (S—m) 407, (S—f) 890, (F—v) 1156, (F—m) 1276, (F—f) 1383
Florida Department of Education, (S—v) 83, (S—m) 338, (S—f) 706
Florida. Department of Military Affairs, (S—m) 316, (F—m) 1243
Florida Navy Nurse Corps Association, (S—v) 64, (S—m) 317, (S—f) 705, (F—v) 1111, 1129, (F—m) 1222, 1244, (F—f) 1333, 1354
Fluor Corporation, (S—f) 576
Folded Flag Foundation, (S—f) 707, (F—f) 1355
Folds of Honor, (S—f) 708
Force Recon Association, (S—v) 66, (S—m) 318, (S—f) 709
Foundation for the Carolinas, (S—f) 666
Fourth Marine Division Association of WWII, (S—f) 710
Freedom Alliance, (S—f) 712
Friedl Richardson Trial Lawyers, (S—v) 208

G

Gamewardens Association, Vietnam to Present, (S—f) 714
GEICO Insurance, (S—f) 607
General Dynamics, (S—f) 576
Genworth Foundation, (S—f) 723
George and Vicki Muellner Foundation, (S—m) 251
Georgia Guard Insurance Trust, (S—m) 403-404, (S—f) 887-888, (F—m) 1275
Georgia Student Finance Commission, (S—m) 325-326, (S—f) 726
Google Inc., (S—v) 74, (S—m) 328, (F—v) 1132, (F—m) 1247
Great Aspirations Scholarship Program, Inc., (S—f) 723
Green Beret Foundation, (S—f) 661-663

H

Hawai'i Community Foundation, (S—f) 518-519, 585, 794-795, (F—f) 1315-1316
Healthcare Information and Management Systems Society. New Jersey Chapter, (S—v) 149, (F—v) 1163
Hill & Ponton, P.A., (S—v) 81
Hope for the Warriors, (S—f) 858, 973-974, (F—f) 1375, 1401-1402

I

Idaho State Board of Education, (S—f) 749
Illinois Association of Realtors, (S—v) 71, (S—m) 323
Illinois Department of Veterans' Affairs, (S—f) 763
Illinois. Office of the Illinois State Treasurer, (S—f) 762
Illinois Student Assistance Commission, (S—v) 88-89, (S—m) 340, (F—v) 1136-1137, (F—m) 1249
Imagine America Foundation, (S—v) 90, (S—m) 341
Indiana Commission for Higher Education, (S—v) 91, (S—m) 342, (S—f) 609, 766-768, (F—v) 1138, (F—f) 1334, 1361
Institute of Electrical and Electronics Engineers. Power and Energy Society, (S—v) 69
Institute of Scrap Recycling Industries, (S—v) 171, (S—m) 457
International Military Community Executives' Association, (S—m) 460, (S—f) 981, (F—m) 1294
International Technology and Engineering Educators Association, (S—v) 207, (F—v) 1185
Iowa Department of Veterans Affairs, (S—f) 612, 771
Iowa National Guard, (S—m) 343
Iowa National Guard Officers Auxiliary, (S—f) 721, 769-770

J

Japanese American Veterans Association, (S—v) 181, (S—m) 471, (S—f) 775-776, 791, 997, (F—v) 1170, (F—m) 1298, (F—f) 1362, 1408
Jewish War Veterans of the U.S.A., (S—v) 94, (S—m) 345, (S—f) 778, (F—v) 1140, (F—m) 1250
Jewish War Veterans of the U.S.A. New Jersey Chapter, (S—f) 800
Jolley Associates, (S—m) 503, (S—f) 1064
Jolly Green Association, (S—f) 1032

K

Kansas Army National Guard, (S—m) 353
Kansas Board of Regents, (S—v) 97-98, (S—m) 351-352, (S—f) 787
KBR, (S—f) 576
Kentucky Department of Veterans Affairs, (S—f) 693, 790, 1042, (F—f) 1348
Kentucky Higher Education Assistance Authority, (S—m) 354, (F—m) 1253
Ketia4Kidz Foundation, (S—f) 534
Knights of Columbus, (S—f) 840
Korean American Scholarship Foundation. Eastern Region, (S—f) 680, (F—f) 1344
Korean American Scholarship Foundation. Midwestern Region, (S—f) 848, (F—f) 1373
Korean American Scholarship Foundation. Northeastern Region, (S—f) 936, (F—f) 1393
Korean American Scholarship Foundation. Southern Region, (S—f) 1013, (F—f) 1412
Korean War Veterans Association, (S—f) 792-793, (F—f) 1365

L

L-3 Communications, (S—v) 139, (S—m) 407, (S—f) 890, (F—v) 1156, (F—m) 1276, (F—f) 1383
Ladies Auxiliary of the Fleet Reserve Association, (S—f) 551, 796-797, 985
Leidos, (S—f) 799
Lockheed Martin Corporation, (S—v) 139, (S—m) 252, 407, (S—f) 890, 955, 1054, 1077, (F—v) 1156, (F—m) 1276, (F—f) 1383
Louisiana Department of Veterans Affairs, (S—f) 807
Louisiana National Guard, (S—m) 359, (F—m) 1254
Louisiana National Guard Enlisted Association, (S—v) 199, (S—m) 489, (S—f) 1038
Louisiana National Guard Enlisted Association Auxiliary, (S—v) 178, (S—m) 463, (S—f) 983
Low VA Rates, (S—v) 120, (S—m) 381, (S—f) 852
Lowe's, (S—v) 16, 102, (S—m) 360, (S—f) 561, 808
Lt. Jon C. Ladda Memorial Foundation, (S—f) 810

S—Scholarships F—Fellowships G—Grants-in-Aid
v—Veterans m—Military Personnel f—Family Members

M

Maine. Bureau of Veterans' Services, (S—m) 365, (S—f) 813, (F—f) 1368

Maine Community Foundation, (S—v) 105, (S—f) 814, (F—v) 1145, (F—f) 1369

Marine Corps Aviation Association. Donald E. Davis Squadron, (S—f) 955

Marine Corps Counterintelligence Association, (S—f) 825

Marine Corps League, (S—v) 112, (S—f) 826

Marine Corps Scholarship Foundation, Inc., (S—f) 743-744, 827

Marine Corps Tankers Association, (S—m) 313, 349, (S—f) 696, 782, (F—m) 1239, 1252, (F—f) 1349, 1363

Marines' Memorial Association, (S—v) 29, 39-40, 55-56, 61, 76, 113-114, 173, 177, 214, (S—m) 272, 275, 295, 303, 310, 370-371, 462, 506, (S—f) 622, 627, 668, 681, 692, 829, 982, 1071, (F—v) 1121, 1148, 1169, (F—m) 1236, 1259, 1295, (F—f) 1343, 1404

Maritime Patrol Association, (S—f) 831

The Marlee Foundation, (S—f) 690

Maryland Higher Education Commission, (S—v) 115, (S—m) 374, 459, (S—f) 838

Maryland National Guard, (S—m) 372-373, (F—m) 1260

Massachusetts Board of Higher Education, (S—m) 375, (F—m) 1261

Massachusetts National Guard, (S—m) 375, (F—m) 1261

Massachusetts Office of Student Financial Assistance, (S—v) 209, (S—m) 240

The Matthew Freeman Project, (S—f) 842, 1003

McGough Construction Company, LLC, (S—v) 136, (S—m) 398, (S—f) 881

Merrill Lynch, (S—f) 1054

Michigan. Department of Military and Veterans Affairs, (S—m) 379, (F—m) 1265

Michigan Department of Treasury, (S—f) 847

Military Benefit Association, (S—v) 119, (S—m) 380, (S—f) 851

Military Chaplains Association of the United States of America, (F—m) 1262

Military Family Support Trust, (S—f) 854

Military Intelligence Corps Association, (S—v) 121, (S—m) 382, (S—f) 855

Military MBA, (F—v) 1149

Military Officers Association of America, (S—f) 559, 720

Military Officers Association of America. Ark-La-Tex Chapter, (S—f) 573

Military Officers Association of America. Capitol Area Chapter, (S—v) 34, (S—f) 598, (F—v) 1109, (F—f) 1331

Military Officers Association of America. Hawaii Aloha Chapter, (S—m) 333, (S—f) 735

Military Officers Association of America. New Hampshire Chapter, (S—f) 901

Military Officers Association of America. Northern New Jersey Chapter, (S—m) 440

Military Order of the Purple Heart, (S—v) 122, (S—f) 856

Military Spouses of Newport, (S—f) 874-876

Minnesota Department of Veterans Affairs, (S—v) 125, (S—m) 384, (S—f) 861, (F—v) 1150, (F—m) 1266, (F—f) 1377

Minnesota National Guard, (S—v) 127, (S—m) 386, (S—f) 865, (F—v) 1151, (F—m) 1267-1268, (F—f) 1378

Minnesota National Guard Enlisted Association Auxiliary, (S—v) 126, (S—m) 385, (S—f) 864

Mississippi Military Department, (S—m) 388

Mississippi National Guard NCO Association, (S—f) 867

Mississippi State Veterans Affairs Board, (S—f) 866

Missouri Department of Higher Education and Workforce Development, (S—f) 871

Missouri National Guard Association, (S—m) 389, (S—f) 868

Missouri. Office of the Adjutant General, (S—m) 390

Missouri Patriot Guard Riders, (S—f) 870

Montana National Guard, (S—m) 391

Montana. Office of the Commissioner of Higher Education, (S—v) 129, (S—f) 872, 1021, (F—v) 1152

Muscogee (Creek) Nation of Oklahoma, (S—v) 163

N

National 4th Infantry (IVY) Division Association, (S—v) 133, (S—f) 689, 878

National Board for Certified Counselors, (F—v) 1157, (F—m) 1281, (F—f) 1387

National Defense Industrial Association. Michigan Chapter, (S—f) 846

National Federation of Music Clubs, (S—v) 19, 104, (F—v) 1100, 1144

National Guard Association of Arizona, (S—m) 362, (S—f) 811

National Guard Association of California, (S—v) 134, (S—m) 395, (S—f) 879

National Guard Association of Colorado, (S—v) 57, (S—m) 304, (S—f) 682, (F—v) 1122, (F—m) 1237, (F—f) 1345

National Guard Association of Florida, (S—m) 430, (S—f) 922

National Guard Association of Illinois, (S—f) 961

National Guard Association of Indiana, (S—v) 145, (S—m) 423, (S—f) 914

National Guard Association of Maryland, (S—v) 135, (S—m) 396, (S—f) 880

National Guard Association of Massachusetts, (S—m) 424, (S—f) 915

National Guard Association of Michigan, (S—m) 397

National Guard Association of Minnesota, (S—v) 136, (S—m) 398, (S—f) 881

National Guard Association of New Hampshire, (S—v) 137, (S—m) 399, (S—f) 882, (F—v) 1154, (F—m) 1271, (F—f) 1379

National Guard Association of New Jersey, (S—m) 400, (S—f) 883, (F—m) 1272, (F—f) 1380

National Guard Association of Oklahoma, (S—v) 146, (S—m) 425, (S—f) 916, (F—v) 1162, (F—m) 1286, (F—f) 1391

National Guard Association of Rhode Island, (S—v) 147, (S—m) 426, (S—f) 917

National Guard Association of South Carolina, (S—m) 467-468, (S—f) 990-991, (F—m) 1296-1297, (F—f) 1405-1406

National Guard Association of South Carolina Auxiliary, (S—f) 884

National Guard Association of South Dakota, (S—v) 106, (S—m) 367, (S—f) 815

National Guard Association of Tennessee, (S—m) 299, 427, (S—f) 674, 918-919, (F—m) 1255

National Guard Association of Tennessee Auxiliary, (S—f) 820

National Guard Association of Texas, (S—v) 138, (S—m) 401, (S—f) 885, (F—v) 1155, (F—m) 1273, (F—f) 1381

National Guard Association of the United States, (S—m) 225, (S—f) 538, (F—m) 1194, (F—f) 1318

National Guard Association of Utah, (S—m) 428, (S—f) 920

National Guard Association of Vermont, (S—m) 402, (S—f) 886, (F—m) 1274, (F—f) 1382

National Guard Association of Washington, (S—m) 429, (S—f) 921

National Guard Educational Foundation, (S—v) 205, (S—m) 498, (S—f) 801

S—Scholarships　　　F—Fellowships　　　G—Grants-in-Aid
v—Veterans　　　m—Military Personnel　　　f—Family Members

SPONSORING ORGANIZATION INDEX

National Military Family Association, Inc., (S—f) 639, 860, (F—f) 1376
National Ranger Memorial Foundation, (S—v) 169, (S—m) 456, (S—f) 964
National Science Foundation, (F—f) 1323
Naval Cryptologic Veterans Association, (S—f) 889
Naval Enlisted Reserve Association, (S—m) 418, (S—f) 900, (F—m) 1282, (F—f) 1388
Naval Helicopter Association, (S—v) 139, (S—m) 407, (S—f) 890, (F—v) 1156, (F—m) 1276, (F—f) 1383
Navy Federal Credit Union, (S—f) 1077
Navy League of the United States, (S—f) 546, 599, 777, 892, 959, 977, 1020
Navy League of the United States. San Diego Council, (S—f) 550
Navy Seal Foundation, (S—m) 410, (S—f) 732, 891, 893, 1043, (F—m) 1279, (F—f) 1384-1385
Navy Seal Museum Foundation, (S—f) 690
Navy Supply Corps Foundation, (S—f) 894-895
Navy Wives Clubs of America, (S—f) 786, 834, 896, 924, 951, (F—f) 1372, 1386, 1392
Navy-Marine Corps Relief Society, (S—m) 412, (S—f) 897
NBCUniversal, (S—v) 140, (F—v) 1158
Nebraska. Department of Veterans' Affairs, (S—m) 417, (S—f) 899
Nebraska Military Department, (S—m) 416
Nevada National Guard, (S—m) 419, (F—m) 1283
New England Federal Credit Union, (S—m) 402, (S—f) 886, (F—m) 1274, (F—f) 1382
New Hampshire Department of Education, (S—f) 902
New Hampshire. Office of the Adjutant General, (S—m) 420, (F—m) 1284
New Jersey Bankers Association, (S—f) 904
New Jersey Department of Military and Veterans Affairs, (S—m) 421, (S—f) 906-907, (F—m) 1285, (F—f) 1389
New Mexico Department of Veterans' Services, (S—v) 141-142, (S—f) 908, (F—v) 1159-1160, (F—f) 1390
New York American Legion Press Association, (S—v) 12, (S—m) 236, (S—f) 547
New York State Division of Military and Naval Affairs, (S—m) 422
New York State Higher Education Services Corporation, (S—v) 143-144, (S—f) 912, (F—v) 1161
Nexstar Legacy Foundation, (S—v) 206
Nisei Veterans Committee, (S—f) 937, 1002
No Angel Left Behind, (S—f) 925
No Greater Sacrifice, (S—f) 926
NOAA Officers' Family Association, (S—f) 579
North American Van Lines, (S—v) 154, (S—m) 439, (S—f) 935
North Carolina Department of Military and Veterans Affairs, (S—f) 930
North Carolina National Guard, (S—m) 435, (F—m) 1287
North Carolina National Guard Association, (S—v) 150-152, (S—m) 432-434, (S—f) 927-929
North Carolina State Education Assistance Authority, (S—m) 435, (F—m) 1287
North Carolina Vietnam Veterans, Inc., (S—v) 153, (S—f) 931
North Dakota Department of Veterans Affairs, (S—f) 898
North Dakota Dollars for Scholars, (S—f) 932
North Dakota National Guard, (S—m) 437, (F—m) 1288
North Dakota National Guard Enlisted Association, (S—m) 436, (S—f) 933
North Dakota University System, (S—m) 438, (S—f) 934
Northern New York Community Foundation, Inc., (S—v) 1, (S—m) 222, (S—f) 520

Northrop Grumman Corporation, (S—v) 139, (S—m) 407, (S—f) 576, 890, 1054, (F—v) 1156, (F—m) 1276, (F—f) 1383
Northrop Rice Foundation, (S—v) 155, 202
Nuance Communications, (S—v) 10, (S—f) 541, (F—v) 1096, (F—f) 1319
Nursing Foundation of Pennsylvania, (S—v) 92, (S—m) 344, (S—f) 774

O

Ohio. Adjutant General's Department, (S—m) 445
Ohio Department of Higher Education, (S—f) 943-944
Ohio National Guard Association, (S—m) 446, (S—f) 945
Oklahoma City Community Foundation, (S—m) 355, (S—f) 531
Oklahoma State Regents for Higher Education, (S—m) 405, (S—f) 742
Operation Once in a Lifetime, (S—f) 968, (F—f) 1399
Orange County Community Foundation, (S—v) 174
Order of Daedalians, (S—m) 274, 284, 305, 348, (S—f) 646, (F—f) 1340
Oregon Community Foundation, (S—v) 48, 162, (S—f) 956, (F—v) 1118, 1165, (F—f) 1397
Oregon National Guard Association, (S—m) 447, (S—f) 946
Oregon Office of Student Access and Completion, (S—v) 110, 162, 165, (S—m) 453, (S—f) 822, 956, (F—v) 1147, 1165, (F—f) 1371, 1397

P

Pacific Fleet Submarine Memorial Association, (S—f) 585
Paralyzed Veterans of America, (S—v) 168, (S—f) 963
Pat Tillman Foundation, (S—v) 197, (S—m) 488, (S—f) 1037, (F—v) 1179, (F—m) 1302, (F—f) 1419
Patriot Education Fund, (S—v) 160, (S—f) 949
Patriot Foundation, (S—f) 993, (F—f) 1407
Pennsylvania. Department of Military and Veterans Affairs, (S—m) 448, (S—f) 683, 952, (F—m) 1290, (F—f) 1396
Pennsylvania Higher Education Assistance Agency, (S—m) 448, (S—f) 615, 952, 954, (F—m) 1290, (F—f) 1396
Pennsylvania National Guard Associations, (S—m) 449, (S—f) 953
Personal Money Service, (S—v) 161, (S—m) 450
PHS Commissioned Officers Foundation for the Advancement of Public Health, (S—f) 634
ProNet International Gifts and Scholarships, Inc., (S—v) 167, (S—f) 962

R

Ranger Battalions Association of WWII, (S—v) 169, (S—m) 456, (S—f) 964
Raytheon Corporation, (S—v) 139, 170, (S—m) 407, (S—f) 576, 890, 967, (F—v) 1156, 1167, (F—m) 1276, (F—f) 1383
Red River Valley Association Foundation, (S—f) 969, (F—f) 1400
Reserve Officers Association of the United States, (S—v) 80, (S—m) 306, 336, (S—f) 740, (F—v) 1135, (F—m) 1248, (F—f) 1359
Rhode Island National Guard, (S—m) 458, (F—m) 1293
Robbins-Giola LLC, (S—f) 955
The ROCKS, Inc., (S—m) 260, 363
Rockwell Collins, Inc., (S—f) 977
Rolls-Royce Marine North America Inc., (S—f) 978

S

Samsung Electronics Company, Ltd., (S—f) 986
San Antonio Area Foundation, (S—f) 972

S—Scholarships F—Fellowships G—Grants-in-Aid
v—Veterans m—Military Personnel f—Family Members

Scholarship America, (S—v) 65, 119, 213, (S—m) 380, (S—f) 560, 851, 853, 1031, 1070, (F—v) 1189, (F—f) 1425
Seabee Memorial Scholarship Association, (S—f) 995-996
Second Indianhead Division Association, (S—f) 583
SECU Foundation, (S—v) 152, (S—m) 434, (S—f) 929
Sigma Chi Foundation, (S—v) 184, (S—m) 474, (F—v) 1173, (F—m) 1300
Society of American Military Engineers. Anchorage Post, (S—m) 255, (S—f) 582, (F—m) 1216, (F—f) 1327
Society of American Military Engineers. Boston Post, (S—v) 27, (S—m) 256
Society of American Military Engineers. Detroit Post, (S—m) 366
Society of American Military Engineers. Fort Worth Post, (S—v) 67, (S—m) 319, (F—v) 1130, (F—m) 1245
Society of American Military Engineers. Guam Post, (S—f) 606
Society of American Military Engineers. Piscataqua Post, (S—v) 164, (S—m) 452, (S—f) 958
Society of American Military Engineers. Portland Post, (S—v) 165, (S—m) 453
Society of American Military Engineers. San Antonio Post, (S—m) 464
Society of American Military Engineers-Louisiana Post, (S—v) 101, (S—m) 358, (S—f) 806
Society of Army Physician Assistants, (S—v) 36, 179, (S—m) 265, 465, (S—f) 987, (F—v) 1112, (F—m) 1223
Society of Daughters of the United States Army, (S—f) 1006
Society of Exploration Geophysicists, (S—v) 49, (F—v) 1119
Society of the 3rd Infantry Division, (S—f) 1007
Society of the First Infantry Division, (S—f) 722, 802
Sons and Daughters, Pearl Harbor Survivors, Inc., (S—f) 1008
Sons of the American Legion. Indiana Detachment, (S—f) 965
Sons of the American Legion. Kansas Detachment, (S—f) 1049
Sons of the American Legion. Kentucky Detachment, (S—v) 95, (S—f) 783
Sons of the American Legion. New Jersey Detachment, (S—f) 691
Sons of the American Legion. New York Detachment, (S—f) 1074
Sons of the American Legion. Vermont Detachment, (S—f) 655
Sons of the American Legion. West Virginia Detachment, (S—f) 1072
Sons of Union Veterans of the Civil War, (S—f) 1009
South Carolina Commission on Higher Education, (S—m) 477
South Carolina Division of Veterans' Affairs, (S—f) 1010
South Carolina. Office of the Adjutant General, (S—m) 477
South Dakota National Guard Enlisted Association, (S—v) 106, (S—m) 367, 478, (S—f) 815, 1012
South Dakota National Guard Enlisted Association Auxiliary, (S—m) 469, (S—f) 994
Southwest Airlines, (S—m) 252
Special Operations Warrior Foundation, (S—f) 1014
Special Ops Survivors, (S—f) 1015
Sports Clips, Inc., (S—v) 190, (S—m) 481
SR Education Group, (S—v) 191, (S—m) 482, (S—f) 1017
Student Veterans of America, (S—v) 74, 140, 170, (S—m) 328, (F—v) 1132, 1158, 1167, (F—m) 1247
Surface Navy Association, (S—v) 210, (S—m) 500, (S—f) 1060, (F—v) 1186, (F—m) 1307, (F—f) 1423

T

Tailhook Educational Foundation, (S—v) 193, (S—m) 485, (S—f) 1024
Tennessee Student Assistance Corporation, (S—v) 79, (S—m) 335

Tenth Mountain Division Foundation, (S—f) 1026-1027, 1075, (F—f) 1416
Texas Higher Education Coordinating Board, (S—m) 486, (S—f) 1029
Texas Military Department, (S—m) 483
Texas Veterans Commission, (S—v) 77, (S—f) 736-737, (F—v) 1134, (F—f) 1358
ThanksUSA, (S—f) 1031
That Others May Live Foundation, (S—f) 1032
Third Marine Division Association, Inc., (S—f) 1035
TonaLaw, (S—v) 198, (F—v) 1180
Trimble, (S—m) 224, (S—f) 536
Two Ten Footwear Foundation, (S—v) 65

U

Unified Arizona Veterans, Inc., (S—v) 201, (S—m) 491, (S—f) 1044, (F—v) 1183, (F—m) 1305, (F—f) 1421
Unilever Corporation, (S—f) 1045
United Airlines, (S—v) 202
United Church of Christ, (F—m) 1220
United Methodist Higher Education Foundation, (F—v) 1113, (F—m) 1224
United States Army Warrant Officers Association, (S—f) 1046
United States Field Artillery Association, (S—m) 492, (S—f) 1047
United States Marine Corps Combat Correspondents Association, (S—v) 73, (S—m) 259, 327, (S—f) 587, 730
United States Submarine Veterans, Inc., (S—f) 1052
University Interscholastic League, (S—f) 950
University of Illinois at Urbana-Champaign. Office of Student Financial Aid, (S—f) 761
University of the Aftermarket Foundation, (S—v) 124
U.S. Air Force, (S—m) 232, (F—m) 1198, 1202
U.S. Air Force. Judge Advocate General's Department, (F—m) 1199
U.S. Air Force Reserve, (S—m) 229, (F—m) 1201
U.S. Air Force. Reserve Officers' Training Corps, (S—m) 230-231, 233, 455, 466, (F—v) 1097, (F—m) 1197, 1200
U.S. Army. Human Resources Command, (S—m) 249, (F—m) 1193, 1206, 1208, 1213
U.S. Army. Judge Advocate General's Corps, (F—m) 1207
U.S. Army. National Guard, (S—m) 242, 248, 286, 331, (F—m) 1209, 1212, 1233
U.S. Army Ordnance Corps Association, (S—m) 293
U.S. Army Ranger Association, (S—f) 523, 1051
U.S. Army. Recruiting Command, (S—m) 493
U.S. Army Reserve, (S—m) 244, (F—m) 1211
U.S. Army. Reserve Officers' Training Corps, (S—m) 245-247, 291, 329-330, 475
U.S. Coast Guard, (S—m) 271, 273, (F—m) 1227
U.S. Coast Guard Chief Petty Officers Association, (S—f) 600
U.S. Defense Commissary Agency, (S—f) 989
U.S. Department of Defense, (S—m) 394, (S—f) 859, (F—v) 1181, (F—m) 1270, 1303
U.S. Department of Education, (F—v) 1181, (F—m) 1303
U.S. Department of Education. Office of Postsecondary Education, (S—f) 772
U.S. Department of Veterans Affairs, (S—v) 130, 166, 221, (S—m) 392, 394, 454, (S—f) 828, 1022, 1039, 1092, (F—v) 1153, 1166, 1192, (F—m) 1269-1270, 1291, (F—f) 1415, 1420, 1430
U.S. Marine Corps, (S—m) 369, (F—m) 1256-1258
U.S. Mountain Ranger Association, (S—f) 1048

S—Scholarships F—Fellowships G—Grants-in-Aid
v—Veterans m—Military Personnel f—Family Members

SPONSORING ORGANIZATION INDEX

U.S. Navy. Bureau of Medicine and Surgery, (S—m) 408, (F—m) 1277
U.S. Navy. Civil Engineer Corps, (S—m) 267, (F—m) 1226
U.S. Navy. Naval History and Heritage Command, (F—m) 1292
U.S. Navy. Naval Service Training Command, (S—m) 268, 311, 406, 442-443, 451, 470, 479-480, 484
U.S. Navy. Naval Service Training Command Officer Development, (S—m) 320, 322, 387, 409, 413-415
U.S. Navy. Navy College Virtual Education Center, (S—m) 411, (F—m) 1280
U.S. Navy. Navy Exchange Service Command, (S—f) 913
U.S. Navy. Navy Medicine Professional Development Center, (S—m) 376, (F—m) 1263
U.S. Navy. Navy Personnel Command, (S—m) 441
U.S. Navy. Office of the Judge Advocate General, (F—m) 1278
U.S. Submarine Veterans of World War II, (S—f) 664
USAA Insurance Corporation, (S—v) 126, 138, 152, 185, (S—m) 252, 270, 280, 283, 297-299, 301-302, 307, 309, 385, 389, 401, 418, 429, 434, 449, 476, 478, 494, 503, 509, 516, (S—f) 576, 620, 642, 644, 672-675, 677-678, 685, 687, 864, 868, 885, 900, 921, 929, 953, 961, 1004, 1012, 1050, 1064, 1077, 1084, 1091, (F—v) 1155, (F—m) 1273, 1282, 1312, (F—f) 1381, 1388, 1428
USMC/Combat Helicopter & Tiltrotor Association, (S—f) 960
Utah Army National Guard, (S—m) 495-496, (F—m) 1306
Utah Department of Veterans and Military Affairs, (S—v) 203-204, (S—f) 992, (F—v) 1184

V

VAW/VRC Officers' Spouses' Association, (S—f) 1053-1054
Vermont National Guard Enlisted Association, (S—m) 503, (S—f) 1064
Vermont Student Assistance Corporation, (S—m) 499, (S—f) 1055
Veterans of Foreign Wars of the United States, (S—v) 190, (S—m) 481
Veterans of Foreign Wars of the United States. Department of Kansas, (S—f) 788
Veterans of Foreign Wars of the United States. Department of Nebraska, (S—v) 50, 111, (S—f) 656, 824
Veterans of Foreign Wars of the United States. Department of North Carolina, (S—f) 947
Veterans of Foreign Wars of the United States. Department of Oregon, (S—f) 1057
Veterans of Foreign Wars of the United States. Department of Pennsylvania, (S—v) 92, (S—m) 344, (S—f) 649, 774
Veterans of Foreign Wars of the United States. Department of Wisconsin, (S—v) 68
Veterans of Foreign Wars of the United States of Mexican Ancestry, (S—f) 1056
Veterans United Home Loans, (S—f) 1058, (F—f) 1422
VFW Auxiliary, (S—f) 1059
VFW Auxiliary. Department of Arizona, (S—f) 568-569
VFW Auxiliary. Department of California, (S—f) 823
VFW Auxiliary. Department of Minnesota, (S—v) 108, (S—f) 819
VFW Auxiliary. Department of Missouri, (S—f) 869
VFW Auxiliary. Department of North Carolina, (S—f) 679
VFW Auxiliary. Department of Wisconsin, (S—v) 100, (S—f) 803, (F—v) 1142, (F—f) 1366
Vietnam Veterans of America. Texas State Council, (S—v) 194, (S—f) 1030
Vietnam Veterans of America. Wisconsin State Council, (S—f) 976
VII Corps Desert Storm Veterans Association, (S—v) 211, (S—f) 1061

Virginia Department of Veterans Services, (S—f) 1062, (F—f) 1424
Virginia National Guard, (S—m) 502, (F—m) 1308
Virginia National Guard Association, (S—m) 501, (S—f) 1063
VisionCorps Foundation, (S—v) 99, (F—v) 1141

W

Walter Beall Scholarship Foundation, (S—m) 504, (S—f) 1065
Walter Reed Society, (S—v) 10, (S—f) 541, (F—v) 1096, (F—f) 1319
Washington Academy of Physician Assistants, (S—v) 212, (F—v) 1187
Washington Metropolitan Area Navy Nurse Corps Association, (F—v) 1188, (F—m) 1309
Washington State Business and Professional Women's Foundation, (S—v) 51
Washington Student Achievement Council, (S—m) 505
Wells Fargo Bank, (S—v) 213, (S—f) 1070, (F—v) 1189, (F—f) 1425
West Virginia Department of Veteran's Assistance, (S—v) 215, (S—f) 1073
West Virginia. Office of the Adjutant General, (S—m) 507, (F—m) 1310
Wings Over America Scholarship Foundation, (S—f) 532, 831, 1054, 1077
Winston-Salem Foundation, (S—f) 835
Wisconsin Department of Military Affairs, (S—m) 510
Wisconsin Department of Veterans Affairs, (S—v) 217, (S—f) 1078, (F—v) 1190, (F—f) 1426
Wisconsin National Guard Association, Inc., (S—m) 508, (S—f) 1083, (F—m) 1311
Wisconsin National Guard Enlisted Association, (S—m) 509, (S—f) 1084, (F—m) 1312, (F—f) 1428
Women Divers Hall of Fame, (S—m) 515
Women in Aviation International, (S—v) 14, 220, (S—m) 513
Women in Defense. Palmetto Chapter, (S—v) 218, (S—m) 511
Women Marines Association, (S—v) 219, (S—m) 512, (S—f) 1085, (F—v) 1191, (F—m) 1313, (F—f) 1429
Women Military Aviators, Inc., (S—v) 220, (S—m) 513
Women's Army Corps Veterans' Association, (S—f) 1086
Women's Overseas Service League, (S—m) 514
Wyoming Elks Association, (S—f) 1089
Wyoming National Guard, (S—m) 517, (F—m) 1314
Wyoming National Guard Association, (S—m) 516, (S—f) 1091

S—Scholarships F—Fellowships G—Grants-in-Aid
v—Veterans m—Military Personnel f—Family Members

Residency Index

Some programs listed in this book are restricted to residents of a particular state or region. Others are open to applicants wherever they may live. The Residency Index will help you pinpoint programs available only to residents in your area as well as programs that have no residency restrictions at all (these are listed under the term "United States"). To use this index, look up the geographic areas that apply to you (always check the listings under "United States"), jot down the entry numbers listed after the program types and recipient groups that apply to you, and use those numbers to find the program descriptions in the directory. To help you in your search, we've provided some "see also" references in the index entries. Remember: the numbers cited here refer to program entry numbers, not to page numbers in the book.

A

Alabama
  Scholarships: **Military Personnel,** 234; **Family Members,** 545, 581
  Fellowships: **Military Personnel,** 1203; **Family Members,** 1322
  See also United States

Alaska
  Scholarships: **Veterans,** 11, 18, 116; **Military Personnel,** 235, 238, 255; **Family Members,** 546, 566, 582, 843
  Fellowships: **Veterans,** 1098; **Military Personnel,** 1204, 1216; **Family Members,** 1327
  See also United States

Alexandria, Virginia
  Scholarships: **Veterans,** 72; **Military Personnel,** 324; **Family Members,** 539, 724
  Fellowships: **Veterans,** 1131; **Military Personnel,** 1246; **Family Members,** 1356
  See also Virginia

Arizona
  Scholarships: **Veterans,** 46, 78, 201, 216; **Military Personnel,** 269, 280, 285, 334, 362, 491; **Family Members,** 568-569, 618, 642, 738, 811, 1044, 1066, 1076
  Fellowships: **Veterans,** 1183; **Military Personnel,** 1305; **Family Members,** 1421
  See also United States

Arkansas
  Scholarships: **Veterans,** 26, 82; **Military Personnel,** 239, 337; **Family Members,** 570-572, 640, 715, 745
  Fellowships: **Veterans,** 1105
  See also United States

Arlington County, Virginia
  Scholarships: **Family Members,** 539
  See also Virginia

C

California
  Scholarships: **Veterans,** 30-32, 52, 134, 174; **Military Personnel,** 261-263, 395; **Family Members,** 550, 589-596, 638, 660, 823, 879, 1056
  Fellowships: **Military Personnel,** 1218; **Family Members,** 1338
  See also United States

Calvert County, Maryland
  Scholarships: **Veterans,** 72; **Military Personnel,** 324; **Family Members,** 724
  Fellowships: **Veterans,** 1131; **Military Personnel,** 1246; **Family Members,** 1356
  See also Maryland

Campbellsville, Kentucky. See Kentucky

Canada
  Scholarships: **Veterans,** 206
  See also Foreign countries

Charles County, Maryland
  Scholarships: **Veterans,** 72; **Military Personnel,** 324; **Family Members,** 539, 724
  Fellowships: **Veterans,** 1131; **Military Personnel,** 1246; **Family Members,** 1356
  See also Maryland

Chatham County, North Carolina
  Scholarships: **Veterans,** 153; **Family Members,** 931
  See also North Carolina

Clarke County, Virginia
  Scholarships: **Veterans,** 72; **Military Personnel,** 324; **Family Members,** 724
  Fellowships: **Veterans,** 1131; **Military Personnel,** 1246; **Family Members,** 1356
  See also Virginia

Colorado
  Scholarships: **Veterans,** 41-42, 57; **Military Personnel,** 276, 304; **Family Members,** 628-632, 682, 711, 817
  Fellowships: **Veterans,** 1122; **Military Personnel,** 1237; **Family Members,** 1345
  See also United States

Columbia, South Carolina
    Scholarships: **Family Members,** 560
    See also South Carolina
Connecticut
    Scholarships: **Veterans,** 43; **Military Personnel,** 277-279;
        Family Members, 635-637, 999
    Fellowships: **Veterans,** 1115; **Military Personnel,** 1230;
        Family Members, 1337
    See also New England states; United States
Cumberland County, North Carolina
    Scholarships: **Family Members,** 560
    See also North Carolina

D

Delaware
    Scholarships: **Military Personnel,** 287; **Family Members,**
        651
    Fellowships: **Veterans,** 1188; **Military Personnel,** 1309
    See also United States
District of Columbia. *See* Washington, D.C.
Durham County, North Carolina
    Scholarships: **Veterans,** 153; **Family Members,** 931
    See also North Carolina

E

El Paso, Texas
    Scholarships: **Family Members,** 560
    See also Texas

F

Fairfax County, Virginia
    Scholarships: **Veterans,** 72; **Military Personnel,** 324; **Family
        Members,** 539, 724
    Fellowships: **Veterans,** 1131; **Military Personnel,** 1246;
        Family Members, 1356
    See also Virginia
Fairfax, Virginia
    Scholarships: **Family Members,** 539
    See also Virginia
Falls Church, Virginia
    Scholarships: **Family Members,** 539
    See also Virginia
Florida
    Scholarships: **Veterans,** 64, 83, 175; **Military Personnel,**
        316-317, 338, 430; **Family Members,** 702-706, 922, 979
    Fellowships: **Veterans,** 1111, 1129, 1168; **Military Personnel,**
        1222, 1243-1244; **Family Members,** 1333, 1353-1354, 1403
    See also United States
Foreign countries
    Scholarships: **Veterans,** 20, 93; **Family Members,** 840, 1045
    Fellowships: **Veterans,** 1101, 1139; **Family Members,** 1323
Fort Eustis, Virginia
    Scholarships: **Family Members,** 560
    See also Virginia
Fort Lee, Virginia
    Scholarships: **Family Members,** 560
    See also Virginia
Fort Story, Virginia
    Scholarships: **Family Members,** 560
    See also Virginia
Franklin County, North Carolina
    Scholarships: **Veterans,** 153; **Family Members,** 931
    See also North Carolina

Frederick County, Maryland
    Scholarships: **Family Members,** 539
    See also Maryland
Frederick County, Virginia
    Scholarships: **Veterans,** 72; **Military Personnel,** 324; **Family
        Members,** 724
    Fellowships: **Veterans,** 1131; **Military Personnel,** 1246;
        Family Members, 1356
    See also Virginia

G

Geary County, Kansas
    Scholarships: **Family Members,** 560
    See also Kansas
Georgia
    Scholarships: **Military Personnel,** 307, 325-326, 403-404;
        Family Members, 685, 725-728, 887-888
    Fellowships: **Military Personnel,** 1275
    See also United States
Granville County, North Carolina
    Scholarships: **Veterans,** 153; **Family Members,** 931
    See also North Carolina
Guam
    Scholarships: **Veterans,** 205; **Military Personnel,** 498;
        Family Members, 606, 801
    See also Pacific Islands

H

Harnett County, North Carolina
    Scholarships: **Veterans,** 153; **Family Members,** 560, 931
    See also North Carolina
Hawaii
    Scholarships: **Military Personnel,** 333; **Family Members,**
        585, 735
    See also Pacific Islands; United States
Hoke County, North Carolina
    Scholarships: **Family Members,** 560
    See also North Carolina

I

Idaho
    Scholarships: **Veterans,** 84-85; **Family Members,** 749-753
    See also United States
Illinois
    Scholarships: **Veterans,** 71, 86-89, 118; **Military Personnel,**
        323, 340; **Family Members,** 533, 754-764, 850, 961, 984,
        1087-1088
    Fellowships: **Veterans,** 1136-1137; **Military Personnel,** 1249
    See also United States
Indiana
    Scholarships: **Veterans,** 91, 107, 145; **Military Personnel,**
        342, 368, 423; **Family Members,** 609, 765-768, 816, 914,
        965
    Fellowships: **Veterans,** 1138; **Family Members,** 1334, 1361
    See also United States
Iowa
    Scholarships: **Veterans,** 47, 59; **Military Personnel,** 308, 339,
        343; **Family Members,** 612, 647, 686, 721, 746, 769-771
    Fellowships: **Veterans,** 1124; **Military Personnel,** 1238;
        Family Members, 1347
    See also United States

J

Johnston County, North Carolina
Scholarships: **Veterans,** 153; **Family Members,** 931
See also North Carolina

K

Kansas
Scholarships: **Veterans,** 97-98; **Military Personnel,** 309, 351-353; **Family Members,** 548, 605, 687, 787-788, 980, 1049
See also United States

Kentucky
Scholarships: **Veterans,** 95; **Military Personnel,** 354, 494; **Family Members,** 693, 783, 790, 798, 833, 1042, 1050
Fellowships: **Military Personnel,** 1253; **Family Members,** 1348
See also United States

L

Lincoln, Rhode Island
Scholarships: **Veterans,** 182; **Military Personnel,** 472; **Family Members,** 1000
Fellowships: **Veterans,** 1171; **Military Personnel,** 1299; **Family Members,** 1409
See also Rhode Island

Loudoun County, Virginia
Scholarships: **Veterans,** 72; **Military Personnel,** 324; **Family Members,** 539, 724
Fellowships: **Veterans,** 1131; **Military Personnel,** 1246; **Family Members,** 1356
See also Virginia

Louisiana
Scholarships: **Veterans,** 101, 178, 199; **Military Personnel,** 358-359, 463, 489; **Family Members,** 806-807, 983, 1038
Fellowships: **Military Personnel,** 1254
See also United States

M

Maine
Scholarships: **Veterans,** 105, 164; **Military Personnel,** 365, 452; **Family Members,** 648, 813-814, 958
Fellowships: **Veterans,** 1145; **Family Members,** 1368-1369
See also New England states; United States

Manassas Park, Virginia
Scholarships: **Family Members,** 539
See also Virginia

Manassas, Virginia
Scholarships: **Family Members,** 539
See also Virginia

Maryland
Scholarships: **Veterans,** 115, 135; **Military Personnel,** 372-374, 396, 459; **Family Members,** 837-838, 880
Fellowships: **Veterans,** 1188; **Military Personnel,** 1260, 1309
See also United States

Maryland, southern
Scholarships: **Military Personnel,** 296; **Family Members,** 560, 581, 670
See also Maryland

Massachusetts
Scholarships: **Veterans,** 164, 209; **Military Personnel,** 240, 375, 424, 452; **Family Members,** 915, 958
Fellowships: **Military Personnel,** 1261
See also New England states; United States

Michigan
Scholarships: **Veterans,** 34, 176; **Military Personnel,** 379, 397, 461; **Family Members,** 598, 846-847
Fellowships: **Veterans,** 1109; **Military Personnel,** 1265; **Family Members,** 1331
See also United States

Minnesota
Scholarships: **Veterans,** 47, 108, 125-127, 136; **Military Personnel,** 384-386, 398; **Family Members,** 647, 819, 861-865, 881
Fellowships: **Veterans,** 1150-1151; **Military Personnel,** 1266, 1268; **Family Members,** 1377-1378
See also United States

Mississippi
Scholarships: **Military Personnel,** 388; **Family Members,** 866-867
See also United States

Missouri
Scholarships: **Veterans,** 128, 131; **Military Personnel,** 389-390; **Family Members,** 804, 841, 868-871
See also United States

Montana
Scholarships: **Veterans,** 129; **Military Personnel,** 297, 391; **Family Members,** 553, 672, 872, 1021
Fellowships: **Veterans,** 1152
See also United States

Montgomery County, Maryland
Scholarships: **Veterans,** 72; **Military Personnel,** 324; **Family Members,** 539, 724
Fellowships: **Veterans,** 1131; **Military Personnel,** 1246; **Family Members,** 1356
See also Maryland

Moore County, North Carolina
Scholarships: **Family Members,** 560
See also North Carolina

N

Nash County, North Carolina
Scholarships: **Veterans,** 153; **Family Members,** 931
See also North Carolina

Nebraska
Scholarships: **Veterans,** 50, 111; **Military Personnel,** 416-417; **Family Members,** 656, 824, 899
See also United States

Nevada
Scholarships: **Military Personnel,** 419
Fellowships: **Military Personnel,** 1283
See also United States

New England states
Scholarships: **Veterans,** 27; **Military Personnel,** 256
See also United States

New Hampshire
Scholarships: **Veterans,** 8, 137, 164; **Military Personnel,** 399, 420, 452; **Family Members,** 535, 549, 779, 830, 882, 901-902, 958
Fellowships: **Veterans,** 1154; **Military Personnel,** 1271, 1284; **Family Members,** 1379
See also New England states; United States

New Jersey
Scholarships: **Veterans,** 149; **Military Personnel,** 298, 400, 421, 440; **Family Members,** 604, 617, 673, 691, 781, 800, 883, 903-907
Fellowships: **Veterans,** 1163, 1188; **Military Personnel,** 1272, 1285, 1309; **Family Members,** 1380, 1389
See also United States

New Mexico
  Scholarships: **Veterans,** 141-142; **Family Members,** 908
  Fellowships: **Veterans,** 1159-1160; **Family Members,** 1390
  See also United States
New York
  Scholarships: **Veterans,** 12, 143-144, 159; **Military Personnel,** 236, 302, 422; **Family Members,** 547, 678, 739, 836, 909-912, 948, 966, 975, 1074
  Fellowships: **Veterans,** 1161
  See also United States
North Carolina
  Scholarships: **Veterans,** 28, 150-153; **Military Personnel,** 257, 432-435; **Family Members,** 586, 679, 877, 927-931, 947, 1067
  Fellowships: **Veterans,** 1107; **Military Personnel,** 1217, 1287; **Family Members,** 1328
  See also United States
North Dakota
  Scholarships: **Military Personnel,** 436-438; **Family Members,** 659, 684, 734, 898, 932-934
  Fellowships: **Military Personnel,** 1288; **Family Members,** 1346
  See also United States

O

Ohio
  Scholarships: **Veterans,** 156-158; **Military Personnel,** 444-446; **Family Members,** 938-945
  Fellowships: **Veterans,** 1164; **Military Personnel,** 1289; **Family Members,** 1394-1395
  See also United States
Okaloosa County, Florida
  Scholarships: **Family Members,** 560
  See also Florida
Oklahoma
  Scholarships: **Veterans,** 146; **Military Personnel,** 405, 425; **Family Members,** 742, 916
  Fellowships: **Veterans,** 1162; **Military Personnel,** 1286; **Family Members,** 1391
  See also United States
Oregon
  Scholarships: **Veterans,** 48, 110, 162, 165; **Military Personnel,** 447, 453; **Family Members,** 822, 946, 956, 1057
  Fellowships: **Veterans,** 1118, 1147, 1165; **Family Members,** 1371, 1397
  See also United States

P

Pacific Islands
  Scholarships: **Family Members,** 606
  See also Foreign countries
Pennsylvania
  Scholarships: **Veterans,** 92, 99; **Military Personnel,** 344, 448-449; **Family Members,** 615, 649, 683, 774, 785, 952-954
  Fellowships: **Veterans,** 1141, 1188; **Military Personnel,** 1290, 1309; **Family Members,** 1396
  See also United States
Prince George's County, Maryland
  Scholarships: **Veterans,** 72; **Military Personnel,** 324; **Family Members,** 539, 724
  Fellowships: **Veterans,** 1131; **Military Personnel,** 1246; **Family Members,** 1356
  See also Maryland

Prince William County, Virginia
  Scholarships: **Veterans,** 72; **Military Personnel,** 324; **Family Members,** 539, 724
  Fellowships: **Veterans,** 1131; **Military Personnel,** 1246; **Family Members,** 1356
  See also Virginia
Providence, Rhode Island
  Scholarships: **Veterans,** 45; **Military Personnel,** 281; **Family Members,** 643
  Fellowships: **Veterans,** 1117; **Military Personnel,** 1231; **Family Members,** 1339
  See also Rhode Island
Puerto Rico
  Scholarships: **Veterans,** 205; **Military Personnel,** 498; **Family Members,** 801
  Fellowships: **Military Personnel,** 1206, 1277

R

Rhode Island
  Scholarships: **Veterans,** 45, 147, 182; **Military Personnel,** 281, 426, 458, 472; **Family Members,** 643, 874-876, 917, 1000
  Fellowships: **Veterans,** 1117, 1171; **Military Personnel,** 1231, 1293, 1299; **Family Members,** 1339, 1409
  See also New England states; United States
Riley County, Kansas
  Scholarships: **Family Members,** 560
  See also Kansas

S

St. Mary's County, Maryland
  Scholarships: **Veterans,** 72; **Military Personnel,** 324; **Family Members,** 724
  Fellowships: **Veterans,** 1131; **Military Personnel,** 1246; **Family Members,** 1356
  See also Maryland
San Diego County, California
  Scholarships: **Family Members,** 581
  See also California
South Carolina
  Scholarships: **Military Personnel,** 467-468, 477; **Family Members,** 884, 990-991, 1010
  Fellowships: **Military Personnel,** 1296-1297; **Family Members,** 1405-1406
  See also United States
South Dakota
  Scholarships: **Veterans,** 106, 189; **Military Personnel,** 367, 469, 478; **Family Members,** 815, 994, 1011-1012
  See also United States

T

Tennessee
  Scholarships: **Veterans,** 79; **Military Personnel,** 299, 335, 427; **Family Members,** 674, 820, 918-919, 1025
  Fellowships: **Military Personnel,** 1255
  See also United States
Texas
  Scholarships: **Veterans,** 77, 138, 194; **Military Personnel,** 401, 483, 486; **Family Members,** 736-737, 885, 950, 1028-1030
  Fellowships: **Veterans,** 1134, 1155; **Military Personnel,** 1273; **Family Members,** 1358, 1381
  See also United States

U

United States
Scholarships: **Veterans,** 1-7, 9-10, 13-17, 19-25, 29, 33, 35-40, 44, 49, 51, 53-56, 58, 60-63, 65-70, 73-76, 80-81, 90, 93-94, 96, 102-104, 112-114, 117, 119-124, 130, 132-133, 139-140, 148, 154-155, 160-163, 166-173, 177, 179, 181, 183-188, 190-193, 195-198, 200, 202, 205-208, 210-211, 213-214, 218-221; **Military Personnel,** 222-233, 237, 241-254, 258-260, 264-268, 270-275, 282-284, 286, 288-289, 291-295, 300, 303, 305-306, 310-315, 318-322, 327-331, 336, 341, 345-350, 355-357, 360-361, 363-364, 366, 369-371, 376-378, 380-383, 387, 392-394, 406-415, 418, 431, 439, 441-443, 450-451, 454-457, 460, 462, 464-466, 470-471, 473-476, 479-482, 484-485, 487-488, 490, 492-493, 497-498, 500, 504, 506, 511-515; **Family Members,** 518-532, 534, 536-538, 540-544, 551-552, 554-559, 561-565, 567, 573-580, 583-584, 587-588, 594, 597, 599-603, 607-608, 610-611, 613-614, 616, 619-627, 633-634, 639, 641, 644-646, 650, 653-654, 657-658, 661-666, 668-669, 675-676, 680-681, 688-690, 692, 694-700, 707-710, 712-714, 716-720, 722, 729-732, 740-741, 743-744, 748, 772-773, 775-778, 780, 782, 784, 786, 789, 791-797, 799, 801-802, 805, 808-810, 818, 825-829, 831-832, 834-835, 839-840, 842, 844-845, 848-849, 851-860, 873, 878, 889-897, 900, 913, 923-926, 935-937, 949, 951, 955-957, 959-960, 962-964, 967-974, 977-978, 981-982, 985-987, 989, 993, 995-998, 1001-1009, 1013-1020, 1022-1024, 1026-1027, 1031-1037, 1039-1041, 1043, 1045-1048, 1051-1054, 1058-1061, 1065, 1068, 1070-1071, 1075, 1077, 1085-1086, 1092
Fellowships: **Veterans,** 1093-1097, 1099-1104, 1106, 1108, 1110, 1112-1114, 1116, 1119-1121, 1123, 1125-1128, 1130, 1132-1133, 1135, 1139-1140, 1143-1144, 1148-1149, 1153, 1156-1158, 1165-1167, 1169-1170, 1172-1182, 1185-1186, 1189, 1191-1192; **Military Personnel,** 1193-1202, 1205-1215, 1219-1221, 1223-1229, 1232-1233, 1235-1236, 1239-1242, 1245, 1247-1248, 1250-1252, 1256-1259, 1262-1264, 1267, 1269-1270, 1276-1282, 1291-1292, 1294-1295, 1298, 1300-1304, 1307, 1313; **Family Members,** 1315-1321, 1323-1326, 1329-1330, 1332, 1335-1336, 1340-1344, 1349-1352, 1355, 1357, 1359, 1362-1365, 1367, 1372-1376, 1383-1388, 1392-1393, 1397-1402, 1404, 1407-1408, 1410-1420, 1422-1423, 1425, 1429-1430

Utah
Scholarships: **Veterans,** 203-204; **Military Personnel,** 301, 428, 495-496; **Family Members,** 677, 920, 992
Fellowships: **Veterans,** 1184; **Military Personnel,** 1306
See also United States

V

Vermont
Scholarships: **Military Personnel,** 402, 499, 503; **Family Members,** 655, 886, 1055, 1064
Fellowships: **Military Personnel,** 1274; **Family Members,** 1382
See also New England states; United States

Virgin Islands
Scholarships: **Veterans,** 205; **Military Personnel,** 498; **Family Members,** 801

Virginia
Scholarships: **Military Personnel,** 501-502; **Family Members,** 667, 723, 812, 1062-1063
Fellowships: **Veterans,** 1188; **Military Personnel,** 1308-1309; **Family Members,** 1424
See also United States

Virginia, northern
Scholarships: **Military Personnel,** 296; **Family Members,** 560, 581, 670
See also Virginia

W

Wake County, North Carolina
Scholarships: **Veterans,** 153; **Family Members,** 931
See also North Carolina

Washington
Scholarships: **Veterans,** 109, 212; **Military Personnel,** 429, 505; **Family Members,** 701, 821, 921, 1069
Fellowships: **Veterans,** 1146, 1187; **Family Members,** 1370
See also United States

Washington, D.C.
Scholarships: **Veterans,** 72; **Military Personnel,** 290, 296, 324; **Family Members,** 539, 560, 581, 670, 724
Fellowships: **Veterans,** 1131, 1188; **Military Personnel,** 1234, 1246, 1309; **Family Members,** 1356
See also United States

West Virginia
Scholarships: **Veterans,** 215; **Military Personnel,** 332, 507; **Family Members,** 733, 1072-1073
Fellowships: **Veterans,** 1188; **Military Personnel,** 1309-1310
See also United States

Wisconsin
Scholarships: **Veterans,** 47, 100, 180, 217; **Military Personnel,** 508-510; **Family Members,** 647, 652, 747, 803, 976, 988, 1078-1084
Fellowships: **Veterans,** 1142, 1190; **Military Personnel,** 1311-1312; **Family Members,** 1360, 1366, 1426-1428
See also United States

Wyoming
Scholarships: **Military Personnel,** 516-517; **Family Members,** 671, 1089-1091
Fellowships: **Military Personnel,** 1314
See also United States

Tenability Index

Some programs listed in this book can be used only in specific cities, counties, states, or regions. Others may be used anywhere in the United States (or even abroad). The Tenability Index will help you locate funding that is restricted to a specific area as well as funding that has no tenability restrictions (these are listed under the term "United States"). To use this index, look up the geographic areas where you'd like to go (always check the listings under "United States"), jot down the entry numbers listed after the program types and recipient groups that apply to you, and use those numbers to find the program descriptions in the directory. To help you in your search, we've provided some "see also" references in the index entries. Remember: the numbers cited here refer to program entry numbers, not to page numbers in the book.

A

Alabama
   Scholarships: **Military Personnel,** 234, 346, 393; **Family Members,** 545, 1013
   Fellowships: **Military Personnel,** 1203; **Family Members,** 1322, 1412
   See also United States

Alaska
   Scholarships: **Veterans,** 11; **Military Personnel,** 235, 255, 274; **Family Members,** 582
   Fellowships: **Veterans,** 1098; **Military Personnel,** 1204, 1216; **Family Members,** 1327
   See also United States

Albuquerque, New Mexico
   Scholarships: **Military Personnel,** 322, 387, 442
   See also New Mexico

Ames, Iowa
   Scholarships: **Military Personnel,** 442
   See also Iowa

Arizona
   Scholarships: **Veterans,** 46, 201, 216; **Military Personnel,** 285, 362, 491; **Family Members,** 811, 1044, 1066, 1076
   Fellowships: **Veterans,** 1183; **Military Personnel,** 1305; **Family Members,** 1421
   See also United States

Arkansas
   Scholarships: **Veterans,** 26; **Military Personnel,** 239, 274; **Family Members,** 571-572, 715
   Fellowships: **Veterans,** 1105
   See also United States

Atlanta, Georgia
   Scholarships: **Military Personnel,** 320, 387
   See also Georgia

Auburn, Alabama
   Scholarships: **Military Personnel,** 442
   See also Alabama

Austin, Texas
   Scholarships: **Military Personnel,** 320, 387, 442
   See also Texas

B

Baton Rouge, Louisiana
   Scholarships: **Military Personnel,** 320, 387, 442
   See also Louisiana

C

California
   Scholarships: **Veterans,** 30-33; **Military Personnel,** 261-264; **Family Members,** 589-597, 638
   Fellowships: **Veterans,** 1108; **Military Personnel,** 1218-1219; **Family Members,** 1330, 1338
   See also United States

Campbellsville, Kentucky. See Kentucky

Canada
   Scholarships: **Veterans,** 206
   See also Foreign countries

Champaign, Illinois
   Scholarships: **Military Personnel,** 442
   See also Illinois

Charleston, South Carolina
   Scholarships: **Military Personnel,** 442
   See also South Carolina

Chicago, Illinois
   Scholarships: **Military Personnel,** 387
   See also Illinois

Colorado
   Scholarships: **Veterans,** 41-42; **Military Personnel,** 276; **Family Members,** 628-632
   See also United States

Columbia, Missouri
   Scholarships: **Military Personnel,** 442
   See also Missouri

Columbia, South Carolina
   Scholarships: **Military Personnel,** 320, 387, 442
   See also South Carolina

Connecticut
> Scholarships: **Veterans,** 43; **Military Personnel,** 277, 279; **Family Members,** 637, 936
> Fellowships: **Veterans,** 1115; **Military Personnel,** 1230; **Family Members,** 1337, 1393
> See also United States

Corvallis, Oregon
> Scholarships: **Military Personnel,** 442
> See also Oregon

D

Dayton, Ohio
> Fellowships: **Military Personnel,** 1257
> See also Ohio

Delaware
> Scholarships: **Military Personnel,** 287; **Family Members,** 651, 680
> Fellowships: **Veterans,** 1188; **Military Personnel,** 1309; **Family Members,** 1344
> See also United States

District of Columbia. See Washington, D.C.

F

Florida
> Scholarships: **Veterans,** 83, 175; **Military Personnel,** 316, 338, 430; **Family Members,** 703, 706, 922, 979, 1013
> Fellowships: **Veterans,** 1168; **Military Personnel,** 1243; **Family Members,** 1403, 1412
> See also United States

Florida, northwestern
> Scholarships: **Military Personnel,** 346, 393
> See also Florida

Foreign countries
> Scholarships: **Military Personnel,** 394; **Family Members,** 762, 840, 1022, 1045
> Fellowships: **Military Personnel,** 1270; **Family Members,** 1415

Fullerton, California
> Scholarships: **Veterans,** 174
> See also California

G

Georgia
> Scholarships: **Military Personnel,** 325-326, 346, 393; **Family Members,** 726, 1013
> Fellowships: **Family Members,** 1412
> See also United States

Guam
> Scholarships: **Veterans,** 205; **Military Personnel,** 498; **Family Members,** 606, 801
> See also Pacific Islands; United States territories

H

Hampton, Virginia
> Scholarships: **Military Personnel,** 320, 387
> See also Virginia

Houston, Texas
> Scholarships: **Military Personnel,** 320, 387
> See also Texas

I

Idaho
> Scholarships: **Family Members,** 749
> See also United States

Illinois
> Scholarships: **Veterans,** 71, 87-89; **Military Personnel,** 323, 340; **Family Members,** 760-761, 763, 848, 984
> Fellowships: **Veterans,** 1136-1137; **Military Personnel,** 1249; **Family Members,** 1373
> See also United States

Indiana
> Scholarships: **Veterans,** 91; **Military Personnel,** 342; **Family Members,** 609, 765-768, 848, 965
> Fellowships: **Veterans,** 1138; **Family Members,** 1334, 1361, 1373
> See also United States

Iowa
> Scholarships: **Veterans,** 47; **Military Personnel,** 343; **Family Members,** 612, 647, 771, 848
> Fellowships: **Family Members,** 1373
> See also United States

Irvine, California
> Scholarships: **Veterans,** 174
> See also California

K

Kansas
> Scholarships: **Veterans,** 97-98; **Military Personnel,** 351-353; **Family Members,** 548, 605, 787, 1049
> See also United States

Kentucky
> Scholarships: **Military Personnel,** 354; **Family Members,** 680, 693, 790, 833, 1042
> Fellowships: **Military Personnel,** 1253; **Family Members,** 1344, 1348
> See also United States

L

Lawrence, Kansas
> Scholarships: **Military Personnel,** 442
> See also Kansas

Los Angeles, California
> Scholarships: **Veterans,** 174
> See also California

Los Angeles County, California
> Scholarships: **Military Personnel,** 357
> See also California

Louisiana
> Scholarships: **Veterans,** 101; **Military Personnel,** 358-359; **Family Members,** 806-807
> Fellowships: **Military Personnel,** 1254
> See also United States

M

Madison, Wisconsin
> Scholarships: **Military Personnel,** 442
> See also Wisconsin

Maine
> Scholarships: **Military Personnel,** 365; **Family Members,** 813, 936
> Fellowships: **Family Members,** 1368, 1393
> See also United States

Malibu, California
    Scholarships: **Veterans,** 174
    See also California
Maryland
    Scholarships: **Veterans,** 115; **Military Personnel,** 373-374, 459; **Family Members,** 680, 838
    Fellowships: **Veterans,** 1188; **Military Personnel,** 1260, 1309; **Family Members,** 1344
    See also United States
Massachusetts
    Scholarships: **Veterans,** 209; **Military Personnel,** 240, 375; **Family Members,** 936
    Fellowships: **Military Personnel,** 1261; **Family Members,** 1393
    See also United States
Michigan
    Scholarships: **Veterans,** 176; **Military Personnel,** 366, 379, 461; **Family Members,** 846-848
    Fellowships: **Military Personnel,** 1265; **Family Members,** 1373
    See also United States
Minnesota
    Scholarships: **Veterans,** 47, 108, 125, 127; **Military Personnel,** 384, 386, 510; **Family Members,** 647, 819, 848, 861-863, 865
    Fellowships: **Veterans,** 1150-1151; **Military Personnel,** 1266, 1268; **Family Members,** 1373, 1377-1378
    See also United States
Mississippi
    Scholarships: **Military Personnel,** 346, 388, 393; **Family Members,** 866
    See also United States
Missouri
    Scholarships: **Veterans,** 128, 131; **Military Personnel,** 390; **Family Members,** 848, 870-871
    Fellowships: **Family Members,** 1373
    See also United States
Montana
    Scholarships: **Veterans,** 129; **Military Personnel,** 391; **Family Members,** 872, 1021
    Fellowships: **Veterans,** 1152
    See also United States
Monterey, California
    Fellowships: **Military Personnel,** 1257
    See also California
Moscow, Idaho
    Scholarships: **Military Personnel,** 442
    See also Idaho

N

Nashville, Tennessee
    Scholarships: **Military Personnel,** 320, 387
    See also Tennessee
Nebraska
    Scholarships: **Veterans,** 50, 111; **Military Personnel,** 416-417; **Family Members,** 656, 824, 899
    See also United States
Nevada
    Scholarships: **Military Personnel,** 419
    Fellowships: **Military Personnel,** 1283
    See also United States

New Hampshire
    Scholarships: **Military Personnel,** 420; **Family Members,** 902, 936
    Fellowships: **Military Personnel,** 1284; **Family Members,** 1393
    See also United States
New Jersey
    Scholarships: **Veterans,** 149; **Military Personnel,** 421, 440; **Family Members,** 906-907, 936
    Fellowships: **Veterans,** 1163, 1188; **Military Personnel,** 1285, 1309; **Family Members,** 1389, 1393
    See also United States
New Mexico
    Scholarships: **Veterans,** 141-142; **Family Members,** 908
    Fellowships: **Veterans,** 1159-1160; **Family Members,** 1390
    See also United States
New Orleans, Louisiana
    Scholarships: **Military Personnel,** 320, 387
    See also Louisiana
New York
    Scholarships: **Veterans,** 143-144; **Military Personnel,** 422; **Family Members,** 912, 936
    Fellowships: **Veterans,** 1161; **Family Members,** 1393
    See also United States
New York, New York
    Scholarships: **Military Personnel,** 442
    See also New York
Norfolk, Virginia
    Scholarships: **Military Personnel,** 320, 387, 442
    See also Virginia
North Carolina
    Scholarships: **Military Personnel,** 435; **Family Members,** 679-680, 930, 947
    Fellowships: **Military Personnel,** 1287; **Family Members,** 1344
    See also United States
North Dakota
    Scholarships: **Military Personnel,** 436-438; **Family Members,** 684, 848, 898, 932-934
    Fellowships: **Military Personnel,** 1288; **Family Members,** 1346, 1373
    See also United States

O

Ohio
    Scholarships: **Military Personnel,** 445; **Family Members,** 848, 943-944
    Fellowships: **Family Members,** 1373
    See also United States
Oklahoma
    Scholarships: **Military Personnel,** 405; **Family Members,** 742
    See also United States
Orange, California
    Scholarships: **Veterans,** 174
    See also California
Orange County, California
    Scholarships: **Veterans,** 174
    See also California
Oregon
    Scholarships: **Veterans,** 48, 110, 165; **Military Personnel,** 453; **Family Members,** 822
    Fellowships: **Veterans,** 1118, 1147; **Family Members,** 1371
    See also United States

P

Pacific Islands
Scholarships: **Family Members,** 606
See also Foreign countries

Pennsylvania
Scholarships: **Veterans,** 92; **Military Personnel,** 344, 448; **Family Members,** 615, 680, 683, 774, 785, 952, 954
Fellowships: **Veterans,** 1188; **Military Personnel,** 1290, 1309; **Family Members,** 1344, 1396
See also United States

Prairie View, Texas
Scholarships: **Military Personnel,** 320, 387
See also Texas

Puerto Rico
Scholarships: **Veterans,** 205; **Military Personnel,** 498; **Family Members,** 801
Fellowships: **Military Personnel,** 1206, 1277
See also United States territories

R

Raleigh, North Carolina
Scholarships: **Military Personnel,** 442
See also North Carolina

Rhode Island
Scholarships: **Military Personnel,** 458; **Family Members,** 936
Fellowships: **Military Personnel,** 1293; **Family Members,** 1393
See also United States

S

Salt Lake City, Utah
Scholarships: **Military Personnel,** 442
See also Utah

San Diego, California
Scholarships: **Veterans,** 174; **Military Personnel,** 322
See also California

San Marcos, California
Scholarships: **Military Personnel,** 322
See also California

Savannah, Georgia
Scholarships: **Military Personnel,** 320, 387
See also Georgia

Seattle, Washington
Scholarships: **Military Personnel,** 442
See also Washington

South Carolina
Scholarships: **Veterans,** 218; **Military Personnel,** 477, 511; **Family Members,** 1010, 1013
Fellowships: **Family Members,** 1412
See also United States

South Dakota
Scholarships: **Veterans,** 189; **Family Members,** 848, 1011
Fellowships: **Family Members,** 1373
See also United States

T

Tallahassee, Florida
Scholarships: **Military Personnel,** 320, 387
See also Florida

Tennessee
Scholarships: **Veterans,** 79; **Military Personnel,** 274, 335; **Family Members,** 820, 1013, 1025
Fellowships: **Family Members,** 1412
See also United States

Texas
Scholarships: **Veterans,** 67, 77, 194; **Military Personnel,** 274, 319, 464, 483, 486; **Family Members,** 736-737, 950, 1028-1030
Fellowships: **Veterans,** 1130, 1134; **Military Personnel,** 1245; **Family Members,** 1358
See also United States

Throggs Neck, New York
Scholarships: **Military Personnel,** 442
See also New York

Toledo, Ohio
Scholarships: **Military Personnel,** 366
See also Ohio

Tucson, Arizona
Scholarships: **Military Personnel,** 387, 442
See also Arizona

Tuskegee, Alabama
Scholarships: **Military Personnel,** 320, 387
See also Alabama

U

United States
Scholarships: **Veterans,** 1-10, 12-25, 27-29, 34-40, 44-45, 49, 51-66, 68-70, 72-76, 78, 80-82, 84-86, 90, 93-96, 99, 101-107, 109, 112-114, 116-124, 126, 130, 132-140, 145-164, 166-173, 177-188, 190-193, 195-200, 202, 205-208, 210-211, 213-214, 219-221; **Military Personnel,** 222-233, 236-238, 241-260, 265-273, 275, 278, 280-284, 286, 288-300, 302-315, 317-318, 321, 324, 327-334, 336-337, 339, 341, 345, 347-350, 355-356, 358, 360-361, 363-365, 367-372, 376-378, 380-383, 385, 389, 392, 394-404, 406-415, 418, 423-428, 431-434, 439, 441, 443-444, 446-447, 449-452, 454-457, 460, 462-463, 465-476, 478-482, 484-485, 487-490, 492-494, 497-498, 500-501, 503-504, 506, 508-509, 512-516; **Family Members,** 518-544, 546-547, 549-570, 573-588, 598-608, 610-611, 613-627, 633-636, 639-646, 648-655, 657-676, 678, 681-682, 685-692, 694-700, 702, 704-705, 707-714, 716-725, 727-735, 738-741, 743-748, 750-759, 762, 764, 769-770, 772-773, 775-784, 786, 788-789, 791-802, 804-806, 808-810, 812-818, 821, 823, 825-832, 834-837, 839-845, 849-860, 864, 867-869, 873-897, 900-901, 903-905, 909-911, 913-920, 923-929, 931, 935, 937-942, 945-946, 948-949, 951, 953, 955-964, 966-975, 977-978, 980-983, 985-991, 993-1009, 1012, 1014-1020, 1022-1024, 1026-1027, 1031-1041, 1043, 1045-1048, 1050-1054, 1056-1061, 1063-1065, 1067-1068, 1070-1071, 1074-1075, 1077, 1079-1092
Fellowships: **Veterans,** 1093-1097, 1099-1104, 1106-1107, 1109-1114, 1116-1117, 1119-1129, 1131-1133, 1135, 1139-1141, 1143-1146, 1148-1149, 1153-1158, 1162-1167, 1169-1182, 1185-1186, 1189, 1191-1192; **Military Personnel,** 1193-1202, 1205-1217, 1220-1229, 1231-1242, 1244, 1246-1248, 1250-1252, 1255-1259, 1262-1264, 1267, 1269-1282, 1286, 1289, 1291-1292, 1294-1304, 1307, 1311-1313; **Family Members,** 1315-1321, 1323-1329, 1331-1333, 1335-1336, 1339-1343, 1345, 1347, 1349-1357, 1359-1360, 1362-1365, 1367-1370, 1372, 1374-1376, 1379-1388, 1391-1392, 1394-1395, 1397-1402, 1404-1411, 1413-1420, 1422-1423, 1425, 1427-1430

United States territories
Scholarships: **Family Members,** 794-795

University Park, Pennsylvania
   Scholarships: **Military Personnel,** 442
   See also Pennsylvania
Utah
   Scholarships: **Veterans,** 203-204; **Military Personnel,** 301, 495-496; **Family Members,** 677, 992
   Fellowships: **Veterans,** 1184; **Military Personnel,** 1306
   See also United States

V

Vermont
   Scholarships: **Military Personnel,** 499; **Family Members,** 936, 1055
   Fellowships: **Family Members,** 1393
   See also United States
Virgin Islands
   Scholarships: **Veterans,** 205; **Military Personnel,** 498; **Family Members,** 801
   See also United States territories
Virginia
   Scholarships: **Military Personnel,** 502; **Family Members,** 680, 1062
   Fellowships: **Veterans,** 1188; **Military Personnel,** 1308-1309; **Family Members,** 1344, 1424
   See also United States

W

Washington
   Scholarships: **Veterans,** 212; **Military Personnel,** 429, 505; **Family Members,** 701, 921, 1069
   Fellowships: **Veterans,** 1187
   See also United States
Washington, D.C.
   Scholarships: **Military Personnel,** 320, 387; **Family Members,** 680
   Fellowships: **Veterans,** 1188; **Military Personnel,** 1309; **Family Members,** 1344
   See also United States
West Lafayette, Indiana
   Scholarships: **Military Personnel,** 442
   See also Indiana
West Virginia
   Scholarships: **Veterans,** 215; **Military Personnel,** 507; **Family Members,** 680, 1072-1073
   Fellowships: **Veterans,** 1188; **Military Personnel,** 1309-1310; **Family Members,** 1344
   See also United States
Wisconsin
   Scholarships: **Veterans,** 47, 68, 100, 217; **Military Personnel,** 510; **Family Members,** 647, 803, 848, 976, 1078
   Fellowships: **Veterans,** 1142, 1190; **Family Members,** 1366, 1373, 1426
   See also United States
Wyoming
   Scholarships: **Military Personnel,** 517
   Fellowships: **Military Personnel,** 1314
   See also United States

Subject Index

There are more than 250 different subject areas indexed in this directory. Use the Subject Index when you want to identify the subject focus of available funding programs. To help you pinpoint your search, we've also included hundreds of "see" and "see also" references. In addition to looking for terms that represent your specific subject interest, be sure to check the "General programs" entry; hundreds of programs are listed there that can be used to support study, research, or other activities in *any* subject area (although the programs may be restricted in other ways). Remember: the numbers cited in this index refer to program entry numbers, not to page numbers in the book.

A

Accounting
    Scholarships: **Military Personnel,** 253
    Fellowships: **Military Personnel,** 1215
    See also Finance; General programs
Actuarial sciences
    Scholarships: **Veterans,** 167; **Family Members,** 962
    See also General programs; Statistics
Administration. *See* Business administration; Management; Public administration
Aeronautical engineering. *See* Engineering, aeronautical
Aeronautics
    Scholarships: **Family Members,** 646
    Fellowships: **Family Members,** 1340
    See also Aviation; Engineering, aeronautical; General programs; Physical sciences
Aerospace engineering. *See* Engineering, aerospace
Aerospace sciences. *See* Space sciences
Agriculture and agricultural sciences
    Scholarships: **Veterans,** 82; **Military Personnel,** 337; **Family Members,** 684, 745
    Fellowships: **Family Members,** 1346
    See also Biological sciences; General programs
Air conditioning industry. *See* Cooling industry
American history. *See* History, American
Anesthetic nurses and nursing. *See* Nurses and nursing, anesthesiology
Aquatic sciences. *See* Oceanography
Arabic language. *See* Language, Arabic
Architectural engineering. *See* Engineering, architectural
Architecture
    Scholarships: **Veterans,** 27, 67; **Military Personnel,** 230, 255-256, 267-268, 319, 366, 464; **Family Members,** 582, 606, 701
    Fellowships: **Veterans,** 1130; **Military Personnel,** 1216, 1226, 1245; **Family Members,** 1327
    See also Fine arts; General programs

Arithmetic. *See* Mathematics
Armed services. *See* Military affairs
Art
    Scholarships: **Family Members,** 701
    See also Fine arts; General programs; names of specific art forms
Astronautics
    Scholarships: **Family Members,** 646
    Fellowships: **Family Members,** 1340
    See also General programs; Space sciences
Attorneys. *See* Law, general
Automation. *See* Computer sciences; Technology
Automotive repair
    Scholarships: **Veterans,** 3; **Military Personnel,** 223; **Family Members,** 526
    See also General programs
Automotive technology
    Scholarships: **Veterans,** 124
    See also General programs
Aviation
    Scholarships: **Veterans,** 14, 155, 202, 220; **Military Personnel,** 252, 274, 284, 305, 348, 504, 513; **Family Members,** 646, 1065-1066
    Fellowships: **Family Members,** 1340
    See also General programs; Space sciences

B

Ballet. *See* Dance
Biological sciences
    Scholarships: **Family Members,** 560
    See also General programs; Sciences; names of specific biological sciences
Biomedical engineering. *See* Engineering, biomedical
Biomedical sciences
    Scholarships: **Family Members,** 634
    See also Biological sciences; General programs; Medical sciences
Biometrics
    Scholarships: **Veterans,** 9; **Military Personnel,** 226-227, 346, 393
    See also Biological sciences; Statistics

SUBJECT INDEX

Building trades
　Scholarships: **Veterans,** 16; **Family Members,** 561
　See also Construction industry; General programs
Business administration
　Scholarships: **Veterans,** 149; **Military Personnel,** 253, 460; **Family Members,** 560, 605, 723
　Fellowships: **Veterans,** 1149, 1163; **Military Personnel,** 1215, 1228, 1294
　See also General programs; Management

C

Cantonese language. See Language, Cantonese
Chemical engineering. See Engineering, chemical
Chemistry
　Scholarships: **Military Personnel,** 230, 311, 441, 480, 484; **Family Members,** 539, 560
　See also Engineering, chemical; General programs; Physical sciences
Chinese language. See Language, Chinese
Chiropractic
　Scholarships: **Family Members,** 684
　Fellowships: **Family Members,** 1346
　See also General programs; Medical sciences
City and regional planning. See Urban and regional planning
Civil engineering. See Engineering, civil
Commerce. See Business administration
Communications
　Scholarships: **Veterans,** 12, 140; **Military Personnel,** 236, 259; **Family Members,** 547, 587
　Fellowships: **Veterans,** 1158
　See also General programs
Computer engineering. See Engineering, computer
Computer sciences
　Scholarships: **Veterans,** 9, 74, 102, 149; **Military Personnel,** 226-227, 230, 311, 328, 346, 357, 360, 393, 479-480, 484; **Family Members,** 539, 808
　Fellowships: **Veterans,** 1132, 1163; **Military Personnel,** 1247
　See also General programs; Mathematics; Technology
Computers. See Computer sciences
Conservation. See Environmental sciences
Construction. See Building trades
Construction engineering. See Engineering, construction
Construction industry
　Scholarships: **Veterans,** 16, 27; **Military Personnel,** 256, 464; **Family Members,** 561
　See also General programs
Cooling industry
　Scholarships: **Veterans,** 172, 206
　See also General programs
Counseling
　Fellowships: **Veterans,** 1157; **Military Personnel,** 1281; **Family Members,** 1387
　See also General programs; Psychology
Counter-intelligence service. See Intelligence service
Criminal justice
　Scholarships: **Veterans,** 47, 182; **Military Personnel,** 472; **Family Members,** 647, 1000
　Fellowships: **Veterans,** 1171; **Military Personnel,** 1299; **Family Members,** 1409
　See also General programs; Law, general

Critical care nurses and nursing. See Nurses and nursing, critical care
Cyber security
　Scholarships: **Family Members,** 539
　See also Computer sciences

D

Dance
　Scholarships: **Family Members,** 701
　See also General programs
Data entry. See Computer sciences
Defense. See Military affairs
Demography. See Population studies
Dental assisting
　Scholarships: **Military Personnel,** 288-289; **Family Members,** 653-654, 863
　See also General programs; Health and health care
Dental hygiene
　Scholarships: **Veterans,** 100; **Military Personnel,** 288-289; **Family Members,** 653-654, 684, 803, 863
　Fellowships: **Veterans,** 1142; **Family Members,** 1346, 1366
　See also General programs; Health and health care
Dentistry
　Scholarships: **Military Personnel,** 248, 288-289; **Family Members,** 634, 653-654, 684, 957
　Fellowships: **Military Personnel,** 1198, 1206, 1208, 1212, 1267, 1277; **Family Members,** 1346, 1398
　See also General programs; Health and health care; Medical sciences
Diesel technology
　Scholarships: **Veterans,** 124
　See also Automotive technology
Dietetics
　Scholarships: **Military Personnel,** 306
　See also Nutrition
Divinity. See Religion and religious activities
Documentaries. See Filmmaking

E

Earth sciences
　Scholarships: **Veterans,** 49
　Fellowships: **Veterans,** 1119
　See also General programs; Natural sciences; names of specific earth sciences
Ecology. See Environmental sciences
Economic planning. See Economics
Economics
　Scholarships: **Military Personnel,** 253; **Family Members,** 925
　Fellowships: **Military Personnel,** 1215; **Family Members,** 1323
　See also General programs
Education
　Scholarships: **Veterans,** 56, 68; **Military Personnel,** 303; **Family Members,** 681, 925
　Fellowships: **Family Members,** 1323
　See also General programs; names of specific types and levels of education
Education, elementary
　Fellowships: **Veterans,** 1181; **Military Personnel,** 1303
　See also Education; General programs

SUBJECT INDEX

Education, science and mathematics
    Fellowships: **Veterans,** 1095; **Military Personnel,** 1195; **Family Members,** 1323
    See also Education; General programs; Sciences

Education, secondary
    Fellowships: **Veterans,** 1181; **Military Personnel,** 1303
    See also Education; General programs

Education, special
    Scholarships: **Veterans,** 216; **Family Members,** 896, 1076
    Fellowships: **Family Members,** 1386, 1427
    See also Education; General programs

Education, technology
    Scholarships: **Veterans,** 207
    Fellowships: **Veterans,** 1185
    See also Education; General programs; Technology

Electrical engineering. *See* Engineering, electrical

Electricity. *See* Utilities

Electronic engineering. *See* Engineering, electronic

Electronics
    Scholarships: **Family Members,** 539
    See also Engineering, electronic; General programs; Physics

Elementary education. *See* Education, elementary

Emergency medical technology
    Scholarships: **Veterans,** 55, 100; **Military Personnel,** 295; **Family Members,** 668, 803
    Fellowships: **Veterans,** 1121, 1142; **Military Personnel,** 1236; **Family Members,** 1343, 1366
    See also General programs; Health and health care

Energy
    Scholarships: **Veterans,** 60
    Fellowships: **Veterans,** 1125
    See also Environmental sciences; General programs

Engineering, aeronautical
    Scholarships: **Veterans,** 165; **Military Personnel,** 230, 453, 504; **Family Members,** 1065
    See also Aeronautics; Engineering, general; General programs

Engineering, aerospace
    Scholarships: **Military Personnel,** 230; **Family Members,** 539, 711
    See also Engineering, general; General programs; Space sciences

Engineering, architectural
    Scholarships: **Military Personnel,** 230
    See also Architecture; Engineering, general; General programs

Engineering, biomedical
    Scholarships: **Veterans,** 165; **Military Personnel,** 453; **Family Members,** 957
    Fellowships: **Family Members,** 1398
    See also Biomedical sciences; Engineering, general; General programs

Engineering, chemical
    Scholarships: **Veterans,** 60, 165; **Military Personnel,** 453; **Family Members,** 539
    Fellowships: **Veterans,** 1125
    See also Chemistry; Engineering, general; General programs

Engineering, civil
    Scholarships: **Veterans,** 27, 165; **Military Personnel,** 230, 256, 267-268, 453
    Fellowships: **Military Personnel,** 1226
    See also Engineering, general; General programs

Engineering, computer
    Scholarships: **Veterans,** 9, 74; **Military Personnel,** 226-227, 230, 328, 346, 393; **Family Members,** 539
    Fellowships: **Veterans,** 1132; **Military Personnel,** 1247
    See also Computer sciences; Engineering, general; Engineering, software; General programs

Engineering, construction
    Scholarships: **Veterans,** 27; **Military Personnel,** 256, 267
    Fellowships: **Military Personnel,** 1226
    See also Engineering, general; General programs

Engineering, electrical
    Scholarships: **Veterans,** 9, 69, 74, 165; **Military Personnel,** 226-227, 230, 267-268, 328, 346, 393, 453, 497; **Family Members,** 539
    Fellowships: **Veterans,** 1132; **Military Personnel,** 1226, 1247
    See also Engineering, general; General programs

Engineering, electronic
    Scholarships: **Veterans,** 9; **Military Personnel,** 226-227, 346, 393, 479
    See also Electronics; Engineering, general; General programs

Engineering, environmental
    Scholarships: **Veterans,** 27; **Military Personnel,** 230, 256, 267; **Family Members,** 560
    Fellowships: **Military Personnel,** 1226
    See also Engineering, general; Environmental sciences; General programs

Engineering, general
    Scholarships: **Veterans,** 39, 45, 67, 76, 96, 101, 148, 164, 218; **Military Personnel,** 224, 255, 268, 272, 281-282, 296, 311, 319, 350, 357-358, 366, 378, 431, 441, 452, 464, 480, 484, 504, 511; **Family Members,** 536, 581-582, 599, 605-606, 622, 634, 641, 643, 669-670, 723, 780, 784, 799, 806, 809, 839, 846, 923, 925, 958-959, 967, 977-978, 1023, 1065
    Fellowships: **Veterans,** 1117, 1130; **Military Personnel,** 1216, 1231-1232, 1245, 1264; **Family Members,** 1327, 1339
    See also General programs; Physical sciences; names of specific types of engineering

Engineering, industrial
    Scholarships: **Military Personnel,** 267
    Fellowships: **Military Personnel,** 1226
    See also Engineering, general; General programs

Engineering, mechanical
    Scholarships: **Veterans,** 165; **Military Personnel,** 230, 267-268, 453
    Fellowships: **Military Personnel,** 1226
    See also Engineering, general; General programs

Engineering, nuclear
    Scholarships: **Military Personnel,** 230
    See also Engineering, general; General programs; Nuclear science

Engineering, ocean
    Scholarships: **Military Personnel,** 267-268
    Fellowships: **Military Personnel,** 1226
    See also Engineering, general; General programs; Oceanography

Engineering, software
    Scholarships: **Veterans,** 74; **Military Personnel,** 328, 479
    Fellowships: **Veterans,** 1132; **Military Personnel,** 1247
    See also Computer sciences; Engineering, computer; Engineering, general; General programs

Engineering, systems
    Scholarships: **Family Members,** 539
    See also Engineering, general; General programs

SUBJECT INDEX

Entertainment industry
  Scholarships: **Veterans,** 140
  Fellowships: **Veterans,** 1158
  See also General programs
Entomology
  Scholarships: **Military Personnel,** 376
  Fellowships: **Military Personnel,** 1263
  See also General programs
Environmental engineering. *See* Engineering, environmental
Environmental health
  Scholarships: **Veterans,** 20, 93; **Military Personnel,** 376; **Family Members,** 634
  Fellowships: **Veterans,** 1101, 1139; **Military Personnel,** 1263
  See also General programs; Public health
Environmental sciences
  Scholarships: **Veterans,** 49; **Family Members,** 560
  Fellowships: **Veterans,** 1119
  See also General programs; Sciences
Ethics
  Scholarships: **Veterans,** 167; **Family Members,** 962
  See also General programs
Eye doctors. *See* Optometry

F

Farming. *See* Agriculture and agricultural sciences
Farsi language. *See* Language, Farsi
Filmmaking
  Scholarships: **Veterans,** 140
  Fellowships: **Veterans,** 1158
  See also General programs; Television
Finance
  Scholarships: **Veterans,** 195; **Military Personnel,** 253; **Family Members,** 925, 1033
  Fellowships: **Military Personnel,** 1215
  See also Accounting; Economics; General programs
Fine arts
  Scholarships: **Veterans,** 45; **Military Personnel,** 281; **Family Members,** 643, 697, 701, 1036
  Fellowships: **Veterans,** 1117; **Military Personnel,** 1231; **Family Members,** 1339, 1418
  See also General programs; names of specific fine arts
Flight science. *See* Aviation
Flying. *See* Aviation
Food. *See* Nutrition
Foreign affairs. *See* International relations

G

General programs
  Scholarships: **Veterans,** 1-2, 4-6, 8, 11, 15, 17-18, 21, 23-26, 28-30, 32-34, 37-38, 40-41, 43-46, 48, 50-54, 57-59, 62-63, 65-66, 70, 72-73, 77-81, 83-84, 87-91, 94-95, 97-99, 105-107, 110-123, 125-131, 133-139, 141-147, 150-153, 156-163, 166, 168-171, 173, 176-180, 182, 184-185, 189-191, 193-194, 197-201, 203-205, 209-211, 213-215, 217, 219, 221; **Military Personnel,** 222, 225, 228-230, 232-235, 238-242, 244-246, 249-251, 254, 257-258, 260-264, 266, 269-271, 273, 275-281, 283, 285-287, 290-294, 297-302, 304, 307-309, 312-316, 318, 320-322, 324-327, 329-336, 338-343, 345, 347, 349, 351-356, 359, 361-363, 365, 367-375, 377, 379-392, 394-407, 410-430, 432-438, 440, 444-451, 454-459, 461-463, 465-470, 472-478, 481-483, 485-486, 488-492, 494-496, 498-503, 505-510, 512, 514, 516-517; **Family Members,** 518-525, 527-535, 537-538, 540, 542-543, 545-546, 548-551, 554-559, 562-574, 576-580, 583-586, 588-594, 596-598, 600, 602-605, 607-621, 623-631, 633, 635-640, 642-645, 648-652, 655-667, 671-680, 682-683, 685-691, 693-696, 698-700, 702-704, 706-710, 712-722, 724-727, 730, 732-744, 746-751, 755-773, 775-783, 785-798, 800-802, 804-805, 807, 810-818, 820, 822-838, 840, 842-845, 847-862, 864-904, 906-910, 912-922, 924, 926-934, 936-956, 960-961, 963-966, 968-976, 980-983, 985-996, 998-1000, 1002-1004, 1006-1017, 1019-1022, 1024-1027, 1029-1032, 1035, 1037-1064, 1067-1075, 1077-1080, 1083-1089, 1091-1092
  Fellowships: **Veterans,** 1093, 1098-1099, 1102, 1104-1105, 1107-1109, 1114-1118, 1120, 1122-1124, 1126-1128, 1131, 1134-1138, 1140-1141, 1145, 1147-1148, 1150-1156, 1159-1162, 1164-1167, 1169, 1171, 1173, 1179-1180, 1182-1184, 1186, 1189-1192; **Military Personnel,** 1193-1194, 1196, 1201-1205, 1209, 1211, 1213-1214, 1217-1219, 1221, 1227, 1230-1231, 1233-1235, 1237-1243, 1246, 1248-1255, 1257-1261, 1265-1266, 1268-1276, 1279-1280, 1282-1291, 1293, 1295-1297, 1299-1300, 1302, 1304-1308, 1310-1314; **Family Members,** 1315-1318, 1320, 1322, 1324, 1326, 1328-1331, 1334-1335, 1337-1339, 1341-1342, 1344-1345, 1347-1353, 1355-1356, 1358-1365, 1367-1369, 1371-1386, 1388-1397, 1399-1401, 1404-1407, 1409, 1412, 1414-1416, 1419-1426, 1428-1430
Geology
  Scholarships: **Veterans,** 49
  Fellowships: **Veterans,** 1119
  See also Earth sciences; General programs; Physical sciences
Geophysics
  Scholarships: **Veterans,** 49
  Fellowships: **Veterans,** 1119
  See also General programs; Meteorology; Oceanography; Physics
Geosciences. *See* Earth sciences
Geospatial information technology
  Scholarships: **Veterans,** 9; **Military Personnel,** 226-227, 346, 393
  See also General programs
Government. *See* Political science and politics; Public administration
Grade school. *See* Education, elementary
Graphic design
  Scholarships: **Veterans,** 12; **Military Personnel,** 236; **Family Members,** 547
  See also General programs
Guidance. *See* Counseling
Gynecology
  Scholarships: **Military Personnel,** 248
  Fellowships: **Military Personnel,** 1212
  See also General programs; Medical sciences; Obstetrics

H

Health and health care
  Scholarships: **Veterans,** 20, 42, 61, 93; **Military Personnel,** 288-289, 310; **Family Members,** 632, 634, 653-654, 692, 1081
  Fellowships: **Veterans,** 1101, 1139
  See also General programs; Medical sciences
Health and health care, administration
  Scholarships: **Veterans,** 10, 149; **Military Personnel,** 376; **Family Members,** 541
  Fellowships: **Veterans,** 1096, 1163; **Military Personnel,** 1263; **Family Members,** 1319
  See also Business administration; General programs; Health and health care

Health and health care, informatics
    Scholarships: **Veterans,** 10, 149; **Family Members,** 541
    Fellowships: **Veterans,** 1096, 1163; **Family Members,** 1319
    See also General programs; Health and health care
Health information. *See* Health and health care, informatics
Health information administration. *See* Health and health care, informatics
Heating industry
    Scholarships: **Veterans,** 172, 206
    See also Building trades; General programs
High schools. *See* Education, secondary
History
    Scholarships: **Family Members,** 1066
    See also General programs; names of specific types of history
History, American
    Scholarships: **Veterans,** 12; **Military Personnel,** 236; **Family Members,** 547
    Fellowships: **Military Personnel,** 1292
    See also General programs; History
History, military
    Fellowships: **Military Personnel,** 1292
    See also History; Military affairs; Military science
Hospitals. *See* Health and health care

I

Indonesian language. *See* Language, Indonesian
Industrial engineering. *See* Engineering, industrial
Industrial hygiene
    Scholarships: **Military Personnel,** 376
    Fellowships: **Military Personnel,** 1263
    See also General programs; Health and health care; Safety studies
Information systems
    Scholarships: **Veterans,** 74, 149; **Military Personnel,** 328; **Family Members,** 539
    Fellowships: **Veterans,** 1132, 1163; **Military Personnel,** 1247
    See also Business administration; General programs
Information technology
    Scholarships: **Veterans,** 9, 74; **Military Personnel,** 226-227, 328, 346, 393, 479
    Fellowships: **Veterans,** 1132; **Military Personnel,** 1247
    See also Computer sciences; General programs
Insurance. *See* Actuarial sciences
Intelligence service
    Scholarships: **Veterans,** 9; **Military Personnel,** 226-227, 346, 393, 479
    See also General programs; International relations; Military affairs
International affairs. *See* International relations
International relations
    Fellowships: **Military Personnel,** 1292
    See also General programs; Political science and politics

J

Japanese language. *See* Language, Japanese
Journalism
    Scholarships: **Veterans,** 12, 140; **Military Personnel,** 236; **Family Members,** 547
    Fellowships: **Veterans,** 1158
    See also Communications; General programs; names of specific types of journalism

Jurisprudence. *See* Law, general

K

Korean language. *See* Language, Korean

L

Language, Arabic
    Scholarships: **Military Personnel,** 230
    See also General programs
Language, Cantonese
    Scholarships: **Military Personnel,** 230
    See also General programs; Language, Chinese
Language, Chinese
    Scholarships: **Military Personnel,** 230
    See also General programs
Language, Farsi
    Scholarships: **Military Personnel,** 230
    See also General programs
Language, Indonesian
    Scholarships: **Military Personnel,** 230
    See also General programs
Language, Japanese
    Scholarships: **Military Personnel,** 230
    See also General programs
Language, Korean
    Scholarships: **Military Personnel,** 230
    See also General programs
Language, Mandarin
    Scholarships: **Military Personnel,** 230
    See also General programs; Language, Chinese
Language, Pashto
    Scholarships: **Military Personnel,** 230
    See also General programs
Language, Punjabi
    Scholarships: **Military Personnel,** 230
    See also General programs
Language, Russian
    Scholarships: **Military Personnel,** 230
    See also General programs
Language, Somali
    Scholarships: **Military Personnel,** 230
    See also General programs
Language, Turkish
    Scholarships: **Military Personnel,** 230
    See also General programs
Language, Turkmen
    Scholarships: **Military Personnel,** 230
    See also General programs
Law enforcement. *See* Criminal justice
Law, general
    Scholarships: **Veterans,** 198, 208
    Fellowships: **Veterans,** 1097, 1180; **Military Personnel,** 1197, 1199-1200, 1207, 1256, 1278
    See also Criminal justice; General programs; names of legal specialties
Lawyers. *See* Law, general
Legal studies and services. *See* Law, general
Life insurance. *See* Actuarial sciences
Life sciences. *See* Biological sciences
Literature
    Scholarships: **Family Members,** 701
    See also General programs; names of specific types of literature

Logistics
    Scholarships: **Veterans,** 13, 154; **Military Personnel,** 237, 439; **Family Members,** 552, 935
    See also Business administration; General programs

M

Magazines. *See* Journalism; Literature

Management
    Scholarships: **Family Members,** 560
    Fellowships: **Military Personnel,** 1228
    See also General programs

Management, construction
    Scholarships: **Military Personnel,** 255, 366, 464; **Family Members,** 582
    Fellowships: **Military Personnel,** 1216; **Family Members,** 1327
    See also Construction industry; General programs; Management

Mandarin language. *See* Language, Mandarin

Mass communications. *See* Communications

Mathematics
    Scholarships: **Veterans,** 9, 39, 76, 96, 148, 218; **Military Personnel,** 224, 226-227, 230, 255, 272, 296, 311, 346, 350, 357, 393, 431, 441, 480, 484, 511; **Family Members,** 536, 539, 560, 581-582, 599, 622, 641, 669-670, 723, 780, 784, 799, 809, 839, 846, 923, 967, 977-978
    Fellowships: **Military Personnel,** 1216; **Family Members,** 1327
    See also Computer sciences; General programs; Physical sciences; Statistics

Mechanical engineering. *See* Engineering, mechanical

Media. *See* Communications

Medical sciences
    Scholarships: **Veterans,** 55, 214; **Military Personnel,** 248, 295, 306, 506; **Family Members,** 544, 560, 634, 668, 684, 896, 911, 957, 1028, 1071
    Fellowships: **Veterans,** 1121; **Military Personnel,** 1198, 1206, 1208, 1212, 1236, 1267, 1277; **Family Members,** 1321, 1343, 1346, 1386, 1398
    See also General programs; Health and health care; Sciences; names of medical specialties; names of specific diseases

Medical technology
    Scholarships: **Veterans,** 100; **Military Personnel,** 306; **Family Members,** 803, 863
    Fellowships: **Veterans,** 1142; **Family Members,** 1366
    See also General programs; Medical sciences; Technology

Mental health nurses and nursing. *See* Nurses and nursing, psychiatry and mental health

Meteorology
    Scholarships: **Military Personnel,** 230
    See also General programs

Microcomputers. *See* Computer sciences

Microscopy. *See* Medical technology

Military affairs
    Fellowships: **Military Personnel,** 1292
    See also General programs; Military science

Military history. *See* History, military

Military law
    Fellowships: **Veterans,** 1097; **Military Personnel,** 1197, 1199-1200, 1207
    See also General programs; Law, general

Military science
    Scholarships: **Veterans,** 181; **Military Personnel,** 471; **Family Members,** 997
    Fellowships: **Veterans,** 1170; **Military Personnel,** 1298; **Family Members,** 1408
    See also General programs; Military affairs

Missionary work. *See* Religion and religious activities

Music
    Scholarships: **Veterans,** 19, 104, 219; **Military Personnel,** 512; **Family Members,** 701, 1036, 1085
    Fellowships: **Veterans,** 1100, 1144, 1191; **Military Personnel,** 1313; **Family Members,** 1418, 1429
    See also Fine arts; General programs

N

Natural sciences
    Scholarships: **Military Personnel,** 255, 357; **Family Members,** 582
    Fellowships: **Military Personnel,** 1216; **Family Members,** 1327
    See also General programs; Sciences; names of specific sciences

Naval science
    Scholarships: **Military Personnel,** 320, 322, 387, 413-415
    See also General programs; Military science

Newspapers. *See* Journalism; Newsroom management

Newsroom management
    Scholarships: **Veterans,** 12; **Military Personnel,** 236; **Family Members,** 547
    See also General programs

Nuclear engineering. *See* Engineering, nuclear

Nuclear science
    Scholarships: **Military Personnel,** 230, 442
    See also General programs; Physical sciences

Nurses and nursing, anesthesiology
    Scholarships: **Veterans,** 22; **Military Personnel,** 243, 248; **Family Members,** 575
    Fellowships: **Veterans,** 1103; **Military Personnel,** 1210, 1212; **Family Members,** 1325
    See also General programs; Nurses and nursing, general

Nurses and nursing, critical care
    Scholarships: **Military Personnel,** 248
    Fellowships: **Military Personnel,** 1212
    See also General programs; Nurses and nursing, general

Nurses and nursing, general
    Scholarships: **Veterans,** 22, 31, 55, 64, 85-86, 92, 100, 108-109, 214; **Military Personnel,** 231, 243, 247-248, 288-289, 295, 306, 317, 344, 364, 408-409, 443, 493, 506; **Family Members,** 553, 575, 595, 634, 653-654, 668, 705, 728-729, 752-754, 774, 803, 819, 821, 823, 841, 863, 905, 957, 984, 1071, 1082, 1090
    Fellowships: **Veterans,** 1103, 1111, 1121, 1129, 1142, 1146, 1188; **Military Personnel,** 1198, 1210, 1212, 1222, 1236, 1244, 1309; **Family Members,** 1325, 1333, 1343, 1354, 1366, 1370, 1398
    See also General programs; Health and health care; Medical sciences; names of specific nursing specialties

Nurses and nursing, psychiatry and mental health
    Fellowships: **Military Personnel,** 1206, 1208
    See also General programs; Nurses and nursing, general

Nutrition
    Scholarships: **Military Personnel,** 306; **Family Members,** 634, 684, 863
    Fellowships: **Family Members,** 1346
    See also General programs; Medical sciences

SUBJECT INDEX

O

Obstetrics
Scholarships: **Military Personnel,** 248
Fellowships: **Military Personnel,** 1212
See also General programs; Gynecology; Medical sciences

Occupational safety
Scholarships: **Veterans,** 20, 93
Fellowships: **Veterans,** 1101, 1139
See also General programs; Health and health care

Occupational therapy
Scholarships: **Veterans,** 100; **Military Personnel,** 306, 376; **Family Members,** 803, 1090
Fellowships: **Veterans,** 1142; **Military Personnel,** 1263; **Family Members,** 1366
See also Counseling; General programs

Ocean engineering. See Engineering, ocean

Oceanography
Scholarships: **Military Personnel,** 311, 480, 484, 515
See also General programs

Opera. See Music

Operations research
Scholarships: **Veterans,** 9; **Military Personnel,** 226-227, 230, 311, 346, 393, 480, 484
See also General programs; Mathematics; Sciences

Optometry
Scholarships: **Family Members,** 1090
Fellowships: **Military Personnel,** 1198, 1206, 1208, 1277
See also General programs; Medical sciences

Orthopedics
Scholarships: **Military Personnel,** 248
Fellowships: **Military Personnel,** 1212
See also General programs; Medical sciences

Osteopathy
Scholarships: **Veterans,** 55; **Military Personnel,** 295; **Family Members,** 668
Fellowships: **Veterans,** 1121; **Military Personnel,** 1206, 1208, 1236, 1277; **Family Members,** 1343
See also General programs; Medical sciences

P

Painting
Scholarships: **Family Members,** 701
See also Art; General programs

Pashto language. See Language, Pashto

Pharmaceutical sciences
Scholarships: **Veterans,** 100; **Military Personnel,** 376; **Family Members,** 634, 803, 957, 1090
Fellowships: **Veterans,** 1142; **Military Personnel,** 1198, 1229, 1263; **Family Members,** 1336, 1366, 1398
See also General programs; Medical sciences

Photography
Scholarships: **Family Members,** 701
See also Fine arts; General programs

Photojournalism
Scholarships: **Veterans,** 12; **Military Personnel,** 236; **Family Members,** 547
See also General programs; Journalism; Photography

Physical sciences
Scholarships: **Veterans,** 164; **Military Personnel,** 255, 311, 452, 464, 480, 484; **Family Members,** 544, 582, 958
Fellowships: **Military Personnel,** 1216; **Family Members,** 1321, 1327
See also General programs; Sciences; names of specific physical sciences

Physical therapy
Scholarships: **Veterans,** 100; **Military Personnel,** 306; **Family Members,** 803, 863, 1090
Fellowships: **Veterans,** 1142; **Family Members,** 1366
See also General programs; Health and health care; Rehabilitation

Physician assistant
Scholarships: **Veterans,** 7, 35-36, 55, 75, 100, 103, 175, 183, 186-188, 192, 196, 212; **Military Personnel,** 265, 295, 306, 376, 487; **Family Members,** 601, 668, 684, 731, 803, 979, 1001, 1005, 1018, 1034
Fellowships: **Veterans,** 1094, 1110, 1112, 1121, 1133, 1142-1143, 1168, 1172, 1174-1178, 1187; **Military Personnel,** 1223, 1236, 1263, 1267, 1301; **Family Members,** 1332, 1343, 1346, 1357, 1366, 1403, 1410-1411, 1413, 1417
See also General programs; Health and health care; Medical sciences

Physics
Scholarships: **Veterans,** 9, 49; **Military Personnel,** 226-227, 230, 311, 346, 393, 441, 480, 484; **Family Members,** 539
Fellowships: **Veterans,** 1119
See also General programs; Mathematics; Physical sciences

Plumbing industry
Scholarships: **Veterans,** 206
See also Building trades; General programs

Police science. See Criminal justice

Political science and politics
Scholarships: **Veterans,** 12, 216; **Military Personnel,** 236; **Family Members,** 547, 1076
Fellowships: **Family Members,** 1323
See also General programs; Public administration

Polymer science
Scholarships: **Veterans,** 60
Fellowships: **Veterans,** 1125
See also Chemistry; General programs

Population studies
Fellowships: **Family Members,** 1323
See also General programs

Presidents, U.S.. See History, American

Press. See Journalism

Print journalism. See Journalism

Prints. See Art

Psychiatric nurses and nursing. See Nurses and nursing, psychiatry and mental health

Psychology
Fellowships: **Military Personnel,** 1198, 1206, 1208, 1277; **Family Members,** 1323
See also Counseling; General programs

Public administration
Scholarships: **Veterans,** 216; **Military Personnel,** 253; **Family Members,** 1076
Fellowships: **Military Personnel,** 1215, 1228; **Family Members,** 1323
See also General programs; Management; Political science and politics

Public affairs. See Public administration

Public health
Fellowships: **Military Personnel,** 1198
See also General programs; Health and health care

Public policy. See Public administration

Public relations
Scholarships: **Veterans,** 12; **Military Personnel,** 236; **Family Members,** 547
See also General programs

Public sector. *See* Public administration
Public service
> Scholarships: **Veterans,** 181; **Military Personnel,** 471, 514; **Family Members,** 997
> Fellowships: **Veterans,** 1170; **Military Personnel,** 1298; **Family Members,** 1408
> *See also* General programs; Public administration

Public utilities. *See* Utilities
Publicity. *See* Public relations

R

Radiology
> Scholarships: **Veterans,** 100; **Military Personnel,** 376; **Family Members,** 803
> Fellowships: **Veterans,** 1142; **Military Personnel,** 1263; **Family Members,** 1366
> *See also* General programs; Medical sciences

Real estate
> Scholarships: **Veterans,** 71, 174; **Military Personnel,** 323
> *See also* General programs

Refrigeration industry. *See* Cooling industry
Regional planning. *See* Urban and regional planning
Rehabilitation
> Scholarships: **Family Members,** 634, 957
> Fellowships: **Family Members,** 1398
> *See also* General programs; Health and health care; names of specific types of therapy

Religion and religious activities
> Fellowships: **Veterans,** 1113; **Military Personnel,** 1220, 1224-1225, 1262
> *See also* General programs

Respiratory therapy
> Scholarships: **Military Personnel,** 306; **Family Members,** 1090
> *See also* General programs; Health and health care

Robotics
> Scholarships: **Veterans,** 9; **Military Personnel,** 226-227, 346, 393
> *See also* General programs; Technology

Russian language. *See* Language, Russian

S

Safety studies
> Scholarships: **Veterans,** 20, 93
> Fellowships: **Veterans,** 1101, 1139
> *See also* Engineering, general; General programs

Schools. *See* Education
Science education. *See* Education, science and mathematics
Sciences
> Scholarships: **Veterans,** 39, 67, 76, 96, 148, 218; **Military Personnel,** 224, 272, 296, 319, 350, 357, 431, 511; **Family Members,** 536, 544, 581, 599, 605, 622, 641, 669-670, 723, 780, 784, 799, 809, 839, 846, 923, 925, 959, 967, 977-978
> Fellowships: **Veterans,** 1130; **Military Personnel,** 1245; **Family Members,** 1321
> *See also* General programs; names of specific sciences

Sculpture
> Scholarships: **Family Members,** 701
> *See also* Fine arts; General programs

Secondary education. *See* Education, secondary
Secret service. *See* Intelligence service
Social work
> Scholarships: **Military Personnel,** 376
> Fellowships: **Military Personnel,** 1263; **Family Members,** 1402
> *See also* General programs

Sociology
> Fellowships: **Family Members,** 1323
> *See also* General programs

Somali language. *See* Language, Somali
Songs. *See* Music
Space sciences
> Scholarships: **Family Members,** 711
> *See also* General programs; Physical sciences

Special education. *See* Education, special
Speech therapy
> Scholarships: **Family Members,** 1090
> *See also* General programs; Health and health care

Spying. *See* Intelligence service
Statistics
> Scholarships: **Veterans,** 9; **Military Personnel,** 226-227, 346, 393
> Fellowships: **Family Members,** 1323
> *See also* General programs; Mathematics

Supply chain management. *See* Logistics
Surgery
> Scholarships: **Veterans,** 100; **Military Personnel,** 248; **Family Members,** 803
> Fellowships: **Veterans,** 1142; **Military Personnel,** 1212; **Family Members,** 1366
> *See also* General programs; Medical sciences

Systems engineering. *See* Engineering, systems

T

Teaching. *See* Education
Technology
> Scholarships: **Veterans,** 39, 96, 148, 218; **Military Personnel,** 224, 272, 296, 350, 431, 442, 511; **Family Members,** 536, 560, 581, 622, 641, 669-670, 723, 780, 784, 799, 809, 839, 846, 923, 967, 978
> *See also* Computer sciences; General programs; Sciences

Television
> Scholarships: **Veterans,** 140
> Fellowships: **Veterans,** 1158
> *See also* Communications; Filmmaking; General programs

Theater. *See* Entertainment industry
Theology. *See* Religion and religious activities
Turkish language. *See* Language, Turkish
Turkmen language. *See* Language, Turkmen
TV. *See* Television

U

Unrestricted programs. *See* General programs
Urban and regional planning
> Scholarships: **Military Personnel,** 464
> *See also* General programs

Utilities
> Scholarships: **Veterans,** 206
> *See also* Energy; General programs

V

Veteran law. *See* Military law

Veterans. *See* Military affairs

Veterinary sciences
　Scholarships: **Family Members,** 634, 957
　Fellowships: **Veterans,** 1106; **Military Personnel,** 1206; **Family Members,** 1398
　See also General programs; Sciences

Video. *See* Filmmaking; Television

W

Welding
　Scholarships: **Veterans,** 132
　See also Building trades; General programs

World literature. *See* Literature

Calendar Index

Since most financial aid programs have specific deadline dates, some may have already closed by the time you begin to look for funding. You can use the Calendar Index to identify which programs are still open. To do that, go to the recipient category and program type that applies to you, think about when you'll be able to complete your application forms, go to the appropriate months, jot down the entry numbers listed there, and use those numbers to find the program descriptions in the directory. Keep in mind that the numbers cited here refer to program entry numbers, not to page numbers in the book.

Veterans

Scholarships:
January: 23, 36, 57, 79, 99, 122, 131, 139, 146, 150-152, 155, 176, 179, 202
February: 3, 7, 15, 27, 35, 41, 49, 59-60, 75, 87-88, 103, 107, 109-110, 115-116, 119, 123, 132, 138, 150-152, 162, 165, 178, 180, 183, 186-188, 192-194, 196-197, 201, 210, 213, 219
March: 1, 8, 18, 21-22, 26, 31-32, 34, 48, 50, 65, 71, 82, 92, 100, 106, 108, 111, 118, 124, 126, 135, 145, 153, 156-157, 160, 164, 174, 181, 200, 217
April: 2, 5, 9, 12, 16-17, 19, 28-29, 39-40, 42, 45, 53-56, 61-63, 67, 72, 76, 79-81, 84-86, 97, 101, 104-105, 113-114, 128, 137, 143-144, 158-159, 170, 173, 177, 182, 190, 199, 212, 214
May: 4, 46, 68, 73, 78, 94, 121, 134, 147, 149, 163, 169, 171-172, 175, 184, 216
June: 24, 38, 51, 58, 66, 69-70, 88, 96, 117, 133, 136, 148, 164, 168, 185, 205, 217
July: 16, 25, 57, 102, 112, 198, 206, 208
August: 79, 120
September: 10, 13, 88, 108, 154, 172, 204
October: 6, 44, 64, 81, 217
November: 9, 14, 20, 74, 93, 140, 190, 198, 207, 218, 220
December: 120, 161, 163, 189, 191, 211
Any time: 11, 83, 89, 95, 215
Deadline not specified: 30, 33, 37, 43, 47, 52, 77, 90-91, 98, 125, 127, 129-130, 141-142, 166-167, 195, 203, 209, 221

Fellowships:
January: 1097, 1104, 1112, 1122, 1141, 1156-1157, 1162
February: 1094, 1110, 1119, 1124-1125, 1133, 1136, 1143, 1146-1147, 1155, 1165, 1172, 1174-1179, 1183, 1186, 1189, 1191
March: 1102-1103, 1105, 1109, 1118, 1142, 1170, 1182, 1188, 1190
April: 1093, 1099-1100, 1107, 1117, 1120-1121, 1126-1128, 1130-1131, 1135, 1144-1145, 1148, 1154, 1161, 1164, 1167, 1169, 1171, 1187
May: 1106, 1140, 1149, 1163, 1168, 1173
June: 1113-1114, 1123, 1136, 1190
July: 1122, 1180
September: 1096, 1136
October: 1111, 1116, 1129, 1190
November: 1095, 1101, 1132, 1139, 1158, 1180, 1185
Any time: 1098, 1137, 1181
Deadline not specified: 1108, 1115, 1134, 1138, 1150-1153, 1159-1160, 1166, 1184, 1192

Military Personnel

Scholarships:
January: 230, 245, 250, 265, 273, 287, 304, 320, 322, 335, 352-353, 366, 402, 405, 407, 425, 428, 432-434, 437, 445, 461, 465, 483
February: 223-224, 256, 308, 339-340, 368, 374, 380, 383, 400-401, 410, 424, 427, 432-434, 453, 463, 467-468, 485, 487-488, 491, 500, 512, 514
March: 222, 238, 241, 243, 253, 258, 262, 287, 291, 297, 299, 313, 323, 329, 337, 342, 344, 349, 354, 357, 362, 367, 385, 389, 396, 416, 423, 445, 447, 452, 469, 471, 478, 490, 502, 504
April: 226-227, 236, 240, 257, 263, 269, 272, 275-276, 278, 280-281, 288, 292, 294-295, 303, 307, 309-310, 314-315, 319, 324, 335-336, 346, 351, 358, 370-371, 393, 399, 403-404, 444, 462, 472, 481, 489, 492, 494, 496-497, 506-507, 516
May: 225, 228, 254, 259, 283, 285, 296, 300, 327, 334, 345, 382, 395, 412, 426, 429-430, 456-457, 474, 509
June: 231, 268, 282, 287, 289, 293, 298, 306, 311, 318, 321, 325, 332, 340, 343, 350, 355-356, 377-378, 397-398, 405-406, 416, 418, 431, 437, 442-443, 445, 449, 451-452, 460, 470, 473, 476, 479-480, 484, 493, 498, 502, 508
July: 234, 261, 276, 284, 301-302, 304, 312, 348, 360, 459, 503
August: 270, 335, 352, 376, 381, 405, 422, 437, 483, 486

September: 237, 273, 287, 329, 340, 347, 354, 416, 439, 483, 501, 517

October: 233, 252, 317, 445, 455, 464, 466, 502, 507, 515

November: 227, 247, 251, 276, 284, 328, 330, 343, 397, 436, 446, 481, 483, 511, 513

December: 246, 255, 260, 274, 305, 363, 381, 387, 409, 413-416, 422, 450, 482

Any time: 229, 235, 239, 244, 248, 271, 290, 316, 338, 379, 392, 394, 499, 510

Deadline not specified: 232, 242, 249, 264, 266-267, 277, 279, 286, 326, 331, 333, 341, 359, 361, 364-365, 369, 372-373, 375, 384, 386, 388, 390-391, 408, 411, 417, 419-421, 435, 438, 440-441, 448, 454, 458, 475, 477, 495, 505

Fellowships:

January: 1197, 1200, 1214, 1223, 1225, 1237, 1274, 1276, 1281, 1286, 1288

February: 1199, 1238, 1249, 1255, 1272-1273, 1279, 1296-1297, 1301-1302, 1305, 1307, 1313

March: 1205, 1210, 1215, 1220, 1239, 1252-1253, 1298, 1304, 1308-1309

April: 1217-1218, 1221, 1228, 1231, 1235-1236, 1240-1242, 1245-1246, 1248, 1259, 1271, 1275, 1289, 1292, 1295, 1299, 1310

May: 1194, 1196, 1250, 1262, 1300, 1312

June: 1224, 1232, 1249, 1264, 1282, 1288, 1294, 1308, 1311

July: 1203, 1237

August: 1263, 1277, 1288

September: 1193, 1249, 1251, 1253, 1278, 1314

October: 1207, 1222, 1244, 1256, 1308, 1310

November: 1195, 1229, 1247

December: 1216

Any time: 1201, 1204, 1206, 1208, 1211-1212, 1227, 1234, 1243, 1265, 1269-1270, 1303

Deadline not specified: 1198, 1202, 1209, 1213, 1219, 1226, 1230, 1233, 1254, 1257-1258, 1260-1261, 1266-1268, 1280, 1283-1285, 1287, 1290-1291, 1293, 1306

Family Members

Scholarships:

January: 532, 577, 606, 682, 703-704, 721, 769-770, 788, 818, 831, 842, 854, 856, 867, 884, 886, 890-891, 916, 920, 927-929, 937, 987, 1002-1003, 1053-1054, 1073, 1077, 1086

February: 518-519, 524, 526, 529, 536, 546, 548, 556-557, 559, 565, 581, 599, 601, 605, 616-617, 619, 629-631, 633, 638, 666, 679, 686, 688, 694, 701-702, 710, 720, 729, 731-732, 739, 741, 743-744, 746, 757-760, 777, 781, 794-795, 799, 812, 816, 821-822, 827, 836, 838, 840, 843, 851, 853, 857, 883, 885, 892-895, 903, 905, 907, 909-911, 915, 918-919, 927-930, 947, 956, 959, 966-967, 972, 976-978, 980, 983-984, 988-991, 1001, 1005, 1016, 1018, 1020, 1023-1024, 1030, 1034, 1037, 1043-1044, 1049, 1057, 1059-1060, 1070, 1085, 1087-1088

March: 520, 533, 535, 537, 540, 543, 553, 560, 566-569, 572, 574-575, 584-585, 593-596, 598, 600, 607-608, 610, 640, 649-650, 652, 656, 658, 664, 667, 672, 674, 684, 696, 706, 708, 713, 715, 723, 745, 747, 755-756, 764-765, 774-776, 782, 786, 791, 798, 803, 810-811, 815, 819, 824, 830, 833-834, 845-846, 850, 862-864, 868, 870, 877, 880, 896, 914, 924, 931-932, 938-939, 946, 949, 951, 954, 958, 993-994, 997, 999, 1006, 1009, 1012, 1048, 1056, 1065-1067, 1069, 1078-1082

April: 522-523, 525, 528, 531, 539, 547, 549-551, 554, 558, 561-562, 564, 573, 576, 579, 586, 588, 614-615, 618, 622-623, 625-627, 632, 636, 641-643, 648, 653, 655, 659, 665, 668-669, 681, 685, 687, 691-692, 697, 699-700, 711, 718-719, 724, 734, 740, 750-754, 779-780, 789, 793, 796-797, 804, 806, 809, 814, 817, 823, 829, 837, 839, 841, 849, 869, 874-876, 882, 887-888, 912, 926, 940-942, 948, 970-971, 982, 985, 995-996, 998, 1000, 1019, 1026-1028, 1031-1032, 1036, 1038, 1040, 1045-1047, 1050-1051, 1062, 1071, 1074-1075, 1091

May: 521, 527, 538, 542, 544, 570-571, 580, 583, 587, 603-604, 624, 644-645, 670-671, 676, 690, 707, 727-728, 730, 738, 773, 778, 785, 800, 802, 855, 858, 879, 897, 901, 917, 921-922, 930, 944, 950, 961, 964-965, 973-974, 979, 1007-1008, 1035, 1041, 1052, 1068, 1072, 1076, 1084, 1089-1090

June: 563, 578, 621, 654, 657, 661-663, 673, 675, 680, 689, 709, 716, 725-726, 733, 772, 784, 792, 801, 825, 844, 848, 878, 881, 889, 900, 904, 923, 936, 953, 957-958, 963, 969, 975, 981, 1004, 1013, 1015, 1078, 1083

July: 561, 615, 634-635, 646, 677-678, 682, 695, 712, 714, 748, 762, 808, 820, 826, 832, 835, 925, 1064

August: 620, 852, 902, 1062, 1073

September: 541, 552, 805, 819, 907, 935, 960, 1063

October: 530, 614, 705, 713, 858, 973-974, 1058, 1078

November: 930, 933, 945

December: 582, 612, 761, 852, 925, 1011, 1017, 1061-1062

Any time: 545, 555, 611, 613, 639, 651, 749, 783, 827, 859-860, 873, 1014, 1022, 1055

Deadline not specified: 534, 589-592, 597, 602, 609, 628, 637, 647, 660, 683, 693, 698, 717, 722, 735-737, 742, 763, 766-768, 771, 787, 790, 807, 813, 828, 847, 861, 865-866, 871-872, 898-899, 906, 908, 913, 934, 943, 952, 955, 962, 968, 986, 992, 1010, 1021, 1025, 1029, 1033, 1039, 1042, 1092

Fellowships:

January: 1326, 1345, 1353, 1382-1384, 1387, 1391

February: 1315-1316, 1332, 1338, 1347, 1357, 1370-1371, 1380-1381, 1385, 1397, 1405-1406, 1410-1411, 1413, 1417, 1419, 1421, 1423, 1425, 1429

March: 1323-1325, 1331, 1341, 1346, 1349, 1360, 1362-1363, 1366, 1372, 1386, 1392, 1407-1408, 1426-1427

April: 1317, 1328-1329, 1339, 1342-1343, 1350-1352, 1356, 1359, 1364, 1369, 1374, 1379, 1394-1395, 1404, 1409, 1414, 1416, 1418, 1424

May: 1318, 1320-1321, 1355, 1375, 1401-1403, 1428

June: 1335, 1344, 1365, 1373, 1388, 1393, 1398, 1400, 1412, 1426

July: 1340, 1345

August: 1424

September: 1319, 1323, 1367

October: 1333, 1354, 1375, 1401-1402, 1422, 1426

November: 1336

December: 1327, 1424

Any time: 1322, 1376, 1415

Deadline not specified: 1330, 1334, 1337, 1348, 1358, 1361, 1368, 1377-1378, 1389-1390, 1396, 1399, 1420, 1430

Made in the USA
Las Vegas, NV
26 January 2021